船舶能效和营运碳强度国际公约及国内法规汇编 （第二版）

Compilation of International Conventions & Domestic Laws and Regulations on Ship Energy Efficiency and Operational Carbon Intensity （Second Edition）

上海海事局　**编译**

上海浦江教育出版社

图书在版编目（CIP）数据

船舶能效和营运碳强度国际公约及国内法规汇编 =
Compilation of International Conventions &
Domestic Laws and Regulations on Ship Energy
Efficiency and Operational Carbon Intensity：英汉
对照 / 上海海事局编译 . -- 2 版 . -- 上海：上海浦江
教育出版社有限公司，2024.12. -- ISBN 978 - 7 - 81121
- 936 - 4

I. D816；D922.690.9

中国国家版本馆 CIP 数据核字第 2024QF1650 号

CHUANBO NENGXIAO HE YINGYUN TANQIANGDU GUOJI GONGYUE JI
GUONEI FAGUI HUIBIAN（DI-ER BAN）

船舶能效和营运碳强度国际公约及国内法规汇编（第二版）

上海浦江教育出版社出版发行

社址：上海海港大道 1550 号上海海事大学校内　　邮政编码：201306
电话：（021）38284910（12）（发行）　　38284923（总编室）　　38284910（传真）
E-mail：cbs@shmtu.edu.cn　　URL：http://www.pujiangpress.com
上海商务联西印刷有限公司印装
幅面尺寸：185 mm × 260 mm　　印张：55　　字数：1441 千字
2025 年 3 月第 1 版　　2025 年 3 月第 1 次印刷
策划编辑：于 杰　　责任编辑：张丽媛　　封面设计：赵宏义
定价：128.00 元

序

根据《国际海事组织第四次温室气体研究报告》，航运业作为全球贸易的重要支柱，其产生的温室气体排放量约占全球人为温室气体排放量的2.89%，到2050年，此类排放量可能占2008年排放量的90%至130%，航运业碳减排对于实现《巴黎协定》的目标至关重要。在《联合国气候变化框架公约》（UNFCCC）下，国际海事组织（IMO）正积极采取措施推动航运业温室气体减排。

2018年4月，IMO通过了《国际海事组织船舶温室气体减排初步战略》，并设定了短、中、长期减排措施作为实施路径。2023年7月，IMO海洋环境保护委员会（MEPC）第80届会议审议通过了《2023年国际海事组织船舶温室气体减排战略》，进一步提高了国际航运业减排目标：与2008年相比，国际航运温室气体排放量到2030年至少减少20%，到2040年至少减少70%，到2050年前后实现净零排放。目前，包含船舶能耗数据收集（DCS）、船舶能效指数（EEDI/EEXI）、年度营运碳强度（CII）评级和船舶能效管理计划（SEEMP）等一系列航运碳减排短期措施在全球船队中得到全面履行，国际航行船舶正不断从技术和营运两方面提升能效。在温室气体减排短期措施实施的过程中，中期措施也在同步推进，并将于2027年生效，届时国际航运业为实现净零排放目标的新规则体系将全面形成。

2021年以来，为推动实现碳达峰碳中和目标，我国陆续发布了重点领域和行业碳达峰实施方案以及一系列支撑保障措施，构建起碳达峰碳中和"1+N"政策体系。航运业是中国经济社会发展的重要战略性基础产业，2021年交通运输部印发了《绿色交通"十四五"发展规划》，明确了绿色低碳作为交通领域的发展目标，并提出"推广应用新能源，构建低碳交通运输体系"的主要任务。交通运输部海事局2022年发布了《船舶能耗数据和碳强度管理办法》，系统地规定了我国船舶能耗数据和碳强度管理要求，并授权上海海事局具体负责中国籍国际航行船舶碳强度管理有关实施工作。为全面履行国际公约，积极落实我国"双碳"战略，经交通运输部党组批准，上海海事局船舶能效管理中心于2023年12月正式成立。

为做好我国船舶能耗数据收集和碳强度管理工作，在交通运输部海事局指导下，上海海事局组织编译了船舶能效和营运碳强度相关的国际公约、导则、通函和国内法律法规及标准等文件。本书将为我国航运企业更好地履行国际公约要求，提升船舶能效提供指导，同时可作为海事管理机构、船舶（船员）、专业技术人员，以及其他相关工作人员的参考和指南，也可为各船员培训机构、航海类院校培训提供教学参考。

上海海事局

二〇二四年十二月

编译说明

　　《船舶能效和营运碳强度国际公约及国内法规汇编（第二版）》在第一版的基础上，更新了国际海事组织（IMO）制定的《国际防止船舶造成污染公约》附则 VI "防止船舶造成空气污染规则"和海洋环境保护委员会（MEPC）为实施国际航运碳强度规则而通过的相关导则、通函，以及国内相关法律法规及标准等。

　　本书共分上下两篇：上篇为船舶能效和营运碳强度管理相关的国际公约、导则和通函（中英文对照）；下篇为国内相关法律法规及标准等文件。

　　本书旨在为各船东、船舶管理公司、航海院校、海事管理机构、船舶（船员）、专业技术人员，以及其他有关人员开展船舶能效和营运碳强度管理相关工作提供技术参考。

　　本书在交通运输部海事局指导下，由上海海事局组织编译，编委会组成如下：

主 任 委 员：谢群威

副主任委员：孙大斌　曹　杰　白宇明　王汝岩

委　　　员：张春昌　张　炜　徐　旻　杨伟华　杨智慧

　　　　　　王仲儒　周传贺　郑旭然　谢　昕

编 译 人 员：梁葱葱　陈亚楠　秦怡雯　张璐珩　邵　磊

　　　　　　刘　斌　张云峰　薛树业　程　迈　王雨茜

　　　　　　钟　娟　邝献文　李秋月

　　本书在编译过程中，上海海事大学、大连海事大学以及业内相关专家、学者对此项工作给予了大力支持，在此表示衷心感谢。需要说明的是，本书编译的相关文件截至 2024 年 12 月。由于时间仓促，书中难免有疏漏和错误，敬请读者批评指正。

二〇二四年十二月

目录

上篇　国际公约及相关导则、通函

国际公约

船舶能效管理计划（SEEMP）相关

船舶燃油消耗数据相关

营运碳强度指数（CII）相关

EEDI/EEXI 相关

船用燃料相关

下篇　国内法律法规及标准等文件

上篇
国际公约及相关导则、通函

国际公约

RESOLUTION MEPC.377(80)
(adopted on 7 July 2023)

2023 IMO STRATEGY ON REDUCTION OF GHG EMISSIONS FROM SHIPS

THE MARINE ENVIRONMENT PROTECTION COMMITTEE,

RECALLING Article 38(e) of the Convention on the International Maritime Organization concerning the functions of the Marine Environment Protection Committee (the Committee) to consider and take appropriate action with respect to any other matters falling within the scope of the Organization which would contribute to the prevention and control of marine pollution from ships,

ACKNOWLEDGING that work to address greenhouse gas (GHG) emissions from ships has been undertaken by the Organization continuously since the adoption of Conference resolution 8 on *CO_2 emissions from ships* in September 1997, in particular, through the adoption of global mandatory technical and operational energy efficiency measures for ships under MARPOL Annex VI,

ACKNOWLEDGING ALSO the decisions of the Assembly at its thirtieth and thirty-second sessions in December 2017 and December 2021, respectively, that approved for the Organization a strategic direction to "Respond to climate change",

RECALLING that the Committee at its seventy-second session (MEPC 72) in April 2018 adopted, by resolution MEPC.304(72), the *Initial IMO Strategy on Reduction of GHG Emissions from Ships* (Initial IMO GHG Strategy),

NOTING that the Initial IMO GHG Strategy foresees that a revised IMO GHG Strategy should be adopted in 2023,

RECALLING the United Nations 2030 Agenda for Sustainable Development,

RECALLING ALSO the Paris Agreement adopted at the UN Climate Change Conference (COP 21), which identifies the long-term goal to hold the increase in the global average temperature to well below 2°C above pre-industrial levels and to pursue efforts to limit the temperature increase to 1.5°C above pre-industrial levels, recognizing that this would significantly reduce the risks and impacts of climate change, as was also reaffirmed in the Glasgow Climate Pact at COP 26 and in the Sharm el-Sheikh Implementation Plan at COP 27,

RECALLING FURTHER IMO Assembly resolution A.998(25) on the need to develop capacity-building for the development and implementation of new instruments and amendments to existing instruments,

RECALLING that the Maritime Safety Committee at its 107th session decided to initiate work on the "Development of a safety regulatory framework to support the reduction of GHG emissions from ships using new technologies and alternative fuels",

HAVING CONSIDERED, at its eightieth session, the draft 2023 IMO strategy on reduction of GHG emissions from ships,

第 MEPC.377（80）号决议
（2023 年 7 月 7 日通过）

2023 年国际海事组织船舶温室气体减排战略

海上环境保护委员会，

忆及《国际海事组织公约》关于海上环境保护委员会（本委员会）审议在本组织范围内的有助于防止和控制船舶造成海洋污染的任何其他事宜，并就此采取适当行动的职能的第 38（e）条，

认识到自 1997 年 9 月通过关于船舶二氧化碳排放的第 8 号大会决议以来，本组织一直在持续地开展解决船舶温室气体（GHG）排放的工作，特别是在《防污公约》附则Ⅵ下通过了针对船舶的全球强制性技术和营运能效措施，

还认识到 2017 年 12 月和 2021 年 12 月大会在其第 30 和 32 届会议上的决定，批准了本组织"应对气候变化"的战略方向，

忆及 2018 年 4 月本委员会在其第 72 届会议（MEPC72）上以第 MPEC.304（72）号决议通过了《国际海事组织船舶温室气体减排初步战略》（《海事组织温室气体初步战略》），

注意到《海事组织温室气体初步战略》预期应于 2023 年通过经修订的《海事组织温室气体战略》，

忆及联合国《2030 年可持续发展议程》，

还忆及联合国气候变化大会（COP 21）通过的《巴黎协定》，其中确定了把全球平均气温升幅控制在工业化前水平以上低于 2 ℃之内的长期目标，并努力将气温升幅限制在工业化前水平以上 1.5 ℃之内，同时认识到这将大大减少气候变化的风险和影响，COP 26 通过的《格拉斯哥气候公约》和 COP 27 通过的《沙姆沙伊赫实施计划》中也重申了这一点，

进一步忆及海事组织关于《制定和执行新文书和现有文书的修正案的能力建设需要》的第 A.998（25）号大会决议，

忆及海上安全委员会在其第 107 届会议上决定启动关于"制定安全法规框架以支持使用新技术和替代燃料减少船舶温室气体排放"的工作，

在其第 80 届会议上，**审议了**《2023 年国际海事组织船舶温室气体减排战略》草案，

1   ADOPTS the *2023 IMO Strategy on Reduction of GHG Emissions from Ships* (2023 IMO GHG Strategy) as set out in the annex to the present resolution;

2   ACKNOWLEDGES the challenges that developing countries, in particular least developed countries (LDCs) and small island developing States (SIDS), may face in the implementation of the 2023 IMO GHG Strategy;

3   ALSO ACKNOWLEDGES the importance of addressing the human element, including the impact on seafarers and other maritime professionals, in the safe implementation of the 2023 IMO GHG Strategy;

4   INVITES the Secretary-General to make adequate provisions in the Integrated Technical Cooperation Programme (ITCP), the IMO GHG TC-Trust Fund and any other means of support related to follow-up actions to the 2023 IMO GHG Strategy that may be further decided by the Committee and undertaken by developing countries, in particular LDCs and SIDS;

5   AGREES to keep the 2023 IMO GHG Strategy under review with a view to the adoption of a revised IMO GHG Strategy in 2028;

6   ALSO AGREES that the 2023 IMO GHG Strategy revokes the 2018 Initial IMO GHG Strategy, as from this date.

1　**通过**《2023 年国际海事组织船舶温室气体减排战略》（《2023 年海事组织温室气体战略》），载于本决议附件；

2　**认识到**发展中国家，特别是最不发达国家（LDCs）和小岛屿发展中国家（SIDS）在执行《2023 年海事组织温室气体战略》方面可能面临的挑战；

3　**还认识到**在安全实施《2023 年海事组织温室气体战略》中解决人的因素，包括解决对海员和其他海事专业人员的影响的重要性；

4　**提请**秘书长在综合技术合作方案（ITCP）、海事组织温室气体技术合作信托基金以及本委员会可能进一步做出决定并由发展中国家，特别是最不发达国家和小岛屿发展中国家采取的与《2023 年海事组织温室气体战略》后续行动有关的任何其他支持手段中做出充分安排；

5　**同意**对《2023 年海事组织温室气体战略》保持审查，以期于 2028 年通过经修订的《海事组织温室气体战略》；

6　**还同意**，自即日起，由《2023 年海事组织温室气体战略》废止《2018 年海事组织温室气体初步战略》。

ANNEX

2023 IMO STRATEGY ON REDUCTION OF GHG EMISSIONS FROM SHIPS

Contents

附件

2023 年国际海事组织船舶温室气体减排战略

目录

1 INTRODUCTION

1.1   The International Maritime Organization (IMO or the Organization) is the United Nations specialized agency responsible for safe, secure and efficient shipping and the prevention of pollution from ships.

1.2   The *2023 IMO Strategy on Reduction of GHG Emissions from Ships* (the 2023 IMO GHG Strategy) represents the continuation of work by IMO as the appropriate international body to address greenhouse gas (GHG) emissions from international shipping. This work includes Assembly resolution A.963(23) on *IMO policies and practices related to the reduction of greenhouse gas emissions from ships*, adopted on 5 December 2003, urging the Marine Environment Protection Committee (MEPC or the Committee) to identify and develop the mechanisms needed to achieve the limitation or reduction of GHG emissions from international shipping.

1.3   In response to the Assembly's request, work to address GHG emissions from ships has been undertaken by the Organization, as summarized in appendix 1.

1.4   The *Initial IMO Strategy on Reduction of GHG Emissions from Ships* (resolution MEPC.304(72)) was the first milestone set out in the *Road map for developing a comprehensive IMO strategy on reduction of GHG emissions from ships* (the Road Map) approved at MEPC 70. The Road Map identified that a revised strategy was to be adopted in 2023.

1.5   The adoption of the 2023 IMO GHG Strategy is the latest milestone set out in the Road Map. The 2023 IMO GHG Strategy also sustains the momentum and represents the continuation of work by IMO as the appropriate international body to address GHG emissions from international shipping.

Context

1.6   The 2023 IMO GHG Strategy falls within a broader context that includes:

    .1   other existing instruments related to the law of the sea, including UNCLOS, and to climate change, including the UNFCCC and its related legal instruments, including the Paris Agreement;

    2   the leading role of the Organization in the development, adoption and assistance in implementation of environmental regulations applicable to international shipping;

    .3   the decision of the thirty-second session of the Assembly (A 32) in December 2021 that adopted for the Organization a strategic direction entitled "Respond to climate change"; and

    .4   the United Nations 2030 Agenda for Sustainable Development.

Emissions and emission scenarios

1.7   The Third IMO GHG Study 2014 estimated that GHG emissions from international shipping in 2012 accounted for some 2.2% of anthropogenic CO_2 emissions and that such emissions could grow by between 50% and 250% by 2050.

1 引言

1.1 国际海事组织（IMO 或本组织）是负责安全、保安和高效航运以及防止船舶造成污染的联合国专门机构。

1.2 《2023 年国际海事组织船舶温室气体减排战略》（《2023 年海事组织温室气体战略》）代表了海事组织作为处理国际航运温室气体（GHG）排放的适当国际机构所开展工作的延续。这项工作包括 2003 年 12 月 5 日通过的关于《国际海事组织减少船舶温室气体排放的政策和做法》的第 A.963（23）号大会决议，其中敦请海上环境保护委员会（MEPC 或本委员会）确定和制定必要的机制，以限制或减少国际航运温室气体排放。

1.3 应大会的要求，本组织已开展了附录 1 中概述的解决船舶温室气体排放的工作。

1.4 《国际海事组织船舶温室气体减排初步战略》（第 MEPC.304（72）号决议）是第 70 届环保会批准的《制定国际海事组织船舶温室气体减排综合战略的路线图》（路线图）中列出的第一个里程碑。该路线图明确将于 2023 年通过一项经修订的战略。

1.5 《2023 年海事组织温室气体战略》的通过是路线图中列出的最新里程碑。《2023 年海事组织温室气体战略》还保持了这一势头，并代表了海事组织作为处理国际航运温室气体排放的适当国际机构所开展的工作的延续。

背景

1.6 《2023 年国际海事组织温室气体战略》具有更广泛的背景，其中包括：

.1 与海洋法有关的其他现有文书，包括《联合国海洋法公约》，以及与气候变化有关的其他现有文书，包括《联合国气候变化框架公约》及其相关法律文书，包括《巴黎协定》；

.2 本组织在制定、通过和协助实施适用于国际航运的环境规则方面的领导作用；

.3 2021 年 12 月大会第 32 届会议（A32）的决定，为本组织通过了题为"应对气候变化"的战略方向；和

.4 联合国《2030 年可持续发展议程》。

排放和排放情景

1.7 2014 年第三次国际海事组织温室气体研究估算，2012 年国际航运温室气体排放量约占人为二氧化碳排放量的 2.2%，到 2050 年，此类排放量可能增长 50% 至 250%。

1.8   The Fourth IMO GHG Study 2020 estimated that GHG emissions from shipping in 2018 accounted for some 2.89% of global anthropogenic GHG emissions and that such emissions could represent between 90% and 130% of 2008 emissions by 2050.

1.9   Future annual IMO emission and carbon intensity estimates using the available data from the IMO Ship Fuel Oil Consumption Database (IMO DCS) and other relevant sources would help reduce the uncertainties associated with these emission estimates and scenarios.

Objectives of the 2023 IMO GHG Strategy

1.10   The 2023 IMO GHG Strategy is aimed at:

   .1   enhancing IMO's contribution to global efforts by addressing GHG emissions from international shipping. International efforts in addressing GHG emissions include the Paris Agreement and its goals and the United Nations 2030 Agenda for Sustainable Development and its SDG 13: *"Take urgent action to combat climate change and its impacts"*;

   .2   identifying actions to be implemented by the international shipping sector, as appropriate, while addressing impacts on States and recognizing the critical role of international shipping in supporting the continued development of global trade and maritime transport services; and

   .3   identifying actions and measures, as appropriate, to help achieve the above objectives, including incentives for research and development and monitoring of GHG emissions from international shipping.

2   VISION

IMO remains committed to reducing GHG emissions from international shipping and, as a matter of urgency, aims to phase them out as soon as possible, while promoting, in the context of this Strategy, a just and equitable transition.

3   LEVELS OF AMBITION, INDICATIVE CHECKPOINTS, AND GUIDING PRINCIPLES

Levels of ambition

3.1   Subject to amendment depending on reviews to be conducted by the Organization in accordance with section 7, the 2023 IMO GHG Strategy identifies levels of ambition for the international shipping sector noting that technological innovation and the global introduction and availability of zero or near-zero GHG emission technologies, fuels and/or energy sources for international shipping will be integral to achieving the overall level of ambition.

3.2   The levels of ambition and indicative checkpoints should take into account the well-to-wake GHG emissions of marine fuels as addressed in the *Guidelines on life cycle GHG intensity of marine fuels* (LCA guidelines) developed by the Organization[1] with the overall objective of reducing GHG emissions within the boundaries of the energy system of international shipping and preventing a shift of emissions to other sectors.

---

[1]   Resolution MEPC.376(80)

1.8 2020 年第四次国际海事组织温室气体研究估算，2018 年航运的温室气体排放量约占全球人为温室气体排放量的 2.89%，到 2050 年，此类排放量可能会达到 2008 年排放量的 90% 至 130%。

1.9 未来年度海事组织排放量和碳强度估算将使用海事组织船舶燃油消耗数据库（IMO DCS）和其他相关来源的可用数据，这将有助于减少与这些排放估算和情景相关的不确定性。

《2023 年海事组织温室气体战略》的目标

1.10 《2023 年海事组织温室气体战略》旨在：

.1 通过解决国际航运的温室气体排放，加强海事组织对全球努力的贡献。国际社会在应对温室气体排放方面的努力包括《巴黎协定》及其目标以及联合国《2030 年可持续发展议程》及其可持续发展目标 13："采取紧急行动应对气候变化及其影响"；

.2 确定国际航运部门应酌情采取的行动，同时处理对各国的影响，并认识到国际航运在支持全球贸易和海运服务持续发展方面的关键作用；和

.3 酌情确定有助于实现上述目标的行动和措施，包括鼓励研发以及监测国际航运温室气体排放。

2 愿景

海事组织一直致力于减少国际航运的温室气体排放，并将其作为当务之急，力求尽快逐步消除这些排放，同时在本战略的范围内促进公正和公平的过渡。

3 目标水平、指示性核查点和指导原则

目标水平

3.1 《2023 年海事组织温室气体战略》确定了国际航运部门的目标水平（须依照本组织按第 7 节所做的审查进行修正），同时指出技术创新和全球引进并为国际航运提供零或接近零温室气体排放技术、燃料和 / 或能源对于实现总体目标水平而言是不可或缺的。

3.2 目标水平和指示性核查点应考虑到本组织制定的《船用燃料生命周期温室气体强度导则》（LCA 导则）[1] 中所述的船用燃料从开采到使用的温室气体排放，其总体目标是减少国际航运能源系统边界范围内的温室气体排放，并防止将排放转移到其他部门。

---

[1] 第 MEPC.376（80）号决议。

3.3 Levels of ambition directing the 2023 IMO GHG Strategy are as follows:

>.1 ***carbon intensity of the ship to decline through further improvement of the energy efficiency for new ships***
>
>to review with the aim of strengthening the energy efficiency design requirements for ships;
>
>.2 ***carbon intensity of international shipping to decline***
>
>to reduce CO_2 emissions per transport work, as an average across international shipping, by at least 40% by 2030, compared to 2008;
>
>.3 ***uptake of zero or near-zero GHG emission technologies, fuels and/or energy sources to increase***
>
>uptake of zero or near-zero GHG emission technologies, fuels and/or energy sources to represent at least 5%, striving for 10%, of the energy used by international shipping by 2030; and
>
>.4 ***GHG emissions from international shipping to reach net zero***
>
>to peak GHG emissions from international shipping as soon as possible and to reach net-zero GHG emissions by or around, i.e. close to, 2050, taking into account different national circumstances, whilst pursuing efforts towards phasing them out as called for in the Vision consistent with the long-term temperature goal set out in Article 2 of the Paris Agreement.

Indicative checkpoints

3.4 Indicative checkpoints to reach net-zero GHG emissions from international shipping:

>.1 to reduce the total annual GHG emissions from international shipping by at least 20%, striving for 30%, by 2030, compared to 2008; and
>
>.2 to reduce the total annual GHG emissions from international shipping by at least 70%, striving for 80%, by 2040, compared to 2008.

Guiding principles

3.5 The principles guiding the 2023 IMO GHG Strategy include:

>.1 the need to be cognizant of the principles enshrined in instruments already developed, such as:
>
>>.1 the principle of non-discrimination and the principle of no more favourable treatment, enshrined in MARPOL and other IMO conventions; and
>>
>>.2 the principle of common but differentiated responsibilities and respective capabilities, in the light of different national circumstances, enshrined in UNFCCC, its Kyoto Protocol and the Paris Agreement;

3.3 指导《2023 年海事组织温室气体战略》的目标水平如下：

.1 通过进一步提高新船的能效，降低船舶的碳强度

以加强船舶能效设计要求为目的进行审查；

.2 国际航运碳强度下降

到 2030 年，国际航运平均每运输工作的二氧化碳排放量与 2008 年相比至少减少 40%；

.3 增加采用零或接近零温室气体排放技术、燃料和 / 或能源

到 2030 年，零或接近零温室气体排放技术、燃料和 / 或能源的采用至少占国际航运所用能源的 5%，力争达到 10%；和

.4 国际航运的温室气体排放达到净零

考虑到不同的国情，尽快达到国际航运温室气体排放峰值并于 2050 年或其前后达到温室气体净零排放，同时按照"愿景"的要求，努力逐步消除温室气体排放，并与《巴黎协定》第二条规定的长期气温目标保持一致。

指示性核查点

3.4 实现国际航运温室气体净零排放的指示性检查点：

.1 与 2008 年相比，到 2030 年，国际航运每年的温室气体排放总量至少减少 20%，力争减少 30%；和

.2 与 2008 年相比，到 2040 年，国际航运每年的温室气体排放总量至少减少 70%，力争减少 80%。

指导原则

3.5 《2023 年海事组织温室气体战略》的指导原则包括：

.1 需要认识到已经制定的文书中铭刻的原则，例如：

.1 《防污公约》和海事组织其他公约中铭刻的不歧视原则和不给予更优惠待遇原则；和

.2 《联合国气候变化框架公约》及其《京都议定书》以及《巴黎协定》中铭刻的依据不同国情的共同但有区别的责任和各自能力原则；

.2   the requirement for all ships to give full and complete effect, regardless of flag, to implementing mandatory measures to ensure the effective implementation of this Strategy;

.3   the need to consider the impacts of measures on States, including developing countries, in particular on LDCs and SIDS, and their specific emerging needs, as recognized in the Revised Strategic Plan for the Organization (resolution A.1149(32)); and

.4   the need for evidence-based decision-making balanced with the precautionary approach as set out in resolution MEPC.67(37).

4   CANDIDATE SHORT-, MID- AND LONG-TERM GHG REDUCTION MEASURES WITH POSSIBLE TIMELINES AND THEIR IMPACTS ON STATES

Timelines

4.1   Candidate measures set out in this 2023 IMO GHG Strategy should be consistent with the following timelines:

.1   short-term GHG reduction measures are the measures finalized and agreed by the Committee between 2018 and 2023, as included in appendix 1;

.2   the basket of mid-term GHG reduction measures should be finalized and agreed by the Committee by 2025. Dates of entry into force and when the measure(s) can effectively start to reduce GHG emissions could be defined for the basket or for each measure individually;

.3   other candidate mid-term GHG reduction measures could be finalized and agreed by the Committee between 2023 and 2030. Dates of entry into force and when the measure can effectively start to reduce GHG emissions would be defined for each measure individually; and

.4   possible long-term measures could be measures finalized and agreed by the Committee beyond 2030, to be developed as part of the 2028 review of the IMO GHG Strategy.

4.2   The list of candidate measures is non-exhaustive and is without prejudice to measures the Organization may further consider and adopt.

Short-term GHG reduction measures

4.3   In accordance with regulations 25.3 and 28.11 of MARPOL Annex VI, a review of the mandatory goal-based technical and operational measures to reduce carbon intensity of international shipping (the "short-term GHG reduction measures") shall be completed by 1 January 2026.

4.4   The Committee may decide to initiate a review of the other short-term measure(s) as included in appendix 1.

Basket of candidate mid-term GHG reduction measures

4.5   In accordance with the timelines set out in this Strategy and the Work Plan, a basket of candidate measure(s), delivering on the reduction targets, should be developed and finalized comprised of both:

.2 要求所有船舶，不论其船旗，全面执行强制性措施，以确保本战略的有效实施；

.3 正如经修订的《本组织战略规划》（第 A.1149（32）号决议）所确认的那样，需要考虑各项措施对各国，包括发展中国家，特别是最不发达国家和小岛屿发展中国家的影响，及其具体的新兴需求；和

.4 需要做出循证决策，并与第 MEPC.67（37）号决议规定的预防办法取得平衡。

4 备选的短期、中期和长期温室气体减排措施，其预期时限以及对各国的影响

时限

4.1 《2023 年海事组织温室气体战略》中列出的备选措施应符合以下时限：

.1 短期温室气体减排措施是指本委员会在 2018 至 2023 年期间最终确定并商定的措施，载于附录 1；

.2 到 2025 年，本委员会应最终确定并商定一篮子中期温室气体减排措施；可以为一篮子措施或为每项措施单独确定生效日期以及措施何时能够有效地开始减少温室气体排放；

.3 本委员会可在 2023 至 2030 年间最终确定并商定其他备选中期温室气体减排措施；可以为每项措施单独确定生效日期以及措施何时能够有效地开始减少温室气体排放；和

.4 可能的长期措施可作为《海事组织温室气体战略》2028 年审查工作的一部分，由本委员会在 2030 年之后最终确定并商定。

4.2 备选措施清单并非详尽无遗，并不妨碍本组织可能进一步审议和通过的措施。

短期温室气体减排措施

4.3 根据《防污公约》附则 Ⅵ 第 25.3 和 28.11 条，须于 2026 年 1 月 1 日前完成对减少国际航运碳强度的强制性目标型技术和营运措施（"短期温室气体减排措施"）的审查。

4.4 本委员会可决定启动对附录 1 中所列其他短期措施的审查。

一篮子备选中期温室气体减排措施

4.5 根据本战略中规定的时限和工作计划，应制定并最终确定实现减排目标的一篮子备选措施，其中同时包括：

.1   a technical element, namely a goal-based marine fuel standard regulating the phased reduction of the marine fuel's GHG intensity; and

.2   an economic element, on the basis of a maritime GHG emissions pricing mechanism.

The candidate economic elements will be assessed observing specific criteria to be considered in the comprehensive impact assessment, with a view to facilitating the finalization of the basket of measures.

The mid-term GHG reduction measures should effectively promote the energy transition of shipping and provide the world fleet with a needed incentive while contributing to a level playing field and a just and equitable transition.

4.6   In accordance with Phase III of the Work Plan, the measure(s) in the basket should be developed and adopted, along with the assessments of impacts on States.

4.7   The development of the basket of candidate mid-term GHG reduction measures should take into account the well-to-wake GHG emissions of marine fuels as addressed in the LCA guidelines developed by the Organization with the overall objective of reducing GHG emissions within the boundaries of the energy system of international shipping and preventing a shift of emissions to other sectors.

Synergies with existing measures

4.8   In addition, the potential synergies with other existing measures such as the Carbon Intensity Indicator (CII) will be considered, in particular regarding incentives for energy efficiency and for the adoption of better operational practices in the shipping value chain or other technologies to reduce emissions from ships.

Other candidate mid-term GHG reduction measures

4.9   In addition to the basket of candidate mid-term GHG reduction measures, the Organization should continue to develop other mid-term GHG reduction measures to reduce GHG emissions from ships. All the following candidate mid-term measures represent possible mid-term further action by the Organization on matters related to the reduction of GHG emissions from ships:

Informed policymaking:

.1   the Secretariat to undertake annual IMO GHG emission and carbon intensity estimates using the available data from the IMO DCS and other relevant sources; and other studies to inform policy decisions;

.2   development of a feedback mechanism to enable lessons learned on implementation of measures to be collated and shared through a possible information exchange on best practice;

Supporting global availability and uptake of zero or near-zero GHG emission technologies, fuels and/or energy sources:

.3   further development of the LCA guidelines;

.1 技术要素，即目标型船用燃料标准，对分阶段减少船用燃料温室气体强度进行规范；和

.2 经济要素，以海运温室气体排放定价机制为基础。

将根据综合影响评估中应考虑的具体标准对备选经济要素进行评估，以便最终确定一篮子措施。

中期温室气体减排措施应有效地促进航运的能源转型，并为世界船队提供必要的激励，同时促进公平的竞争环境以及公正和公平的转型。

4.6 根据工作计划第Ⅲ阶段，应制定和通过一篮子措施，同时评估对各国的影响。

4.7 在制定一篮子备选中期温室气体减排措施时，应考虑到本组织制定的《LCA 导则》中所述的船用燃料从开采到使用的温室气体排放，其总体目标是减少国际航运能源系统边界范围内的温室气体排放，并防止将排放转移到其他部门。

与现有措施的协同作用

4.8 此外，还将考虑与诸如碳强度指标（CII）等其他现有措施的潜在协同作用，特别是在能效激励措施和在航运价值链中采用更佳操作做法或减少船舶排放的其他技术方面。

其他备选中期温室气体减排措施

4.9 除了一篮子备选中期温室气体减排措施外，本组织应继续制定其他中期温室气体减排措施，以减少船舶温室气体排放。以下所有备选中期措施都是本组织在减少船舶温室气体排放相关事项上可能采取的进一步中期行动：

知情决策：

.1 秘书处使用 IMO DCS 和其他相关来源提供的数据，进行年度海事组织温室气体排放和碳强度估算；以及其他研究为政策决定提供信息；

.2 建立一个反馈机制，以便通过可能的最佳做法的信息交流以梳理和分享在措施执行方面汲取的经验教训；

支持全球获得和采用零或接近零温室气体排放技术、燃料和／或能源：

.3 进一步制定《LCA 导则》；

.4 undertake a regulatory assessment of safety aspects associated with reducing GHG emissions in accordance with this Strategy and develop a road map to support the safe delivery of the Strategy;

.5 consider and analyse measures to address emissions of methane and nitrous oxide and further enhance measures to address emissions of volatile organic compounds;

.6 incentives for first movers to develop and take up new technologies; and

.7 consider and analyse measures to both encourage port developments and activities globally to facilitate reduction of GHG emissions from shipping, including provision of ship and shoreside/onshore power supply from renewable sources, and infrastructure to support supply of zero or near-zero GHG emission fuels and/or energy sources, and to further optimize the logistic chain and its planning, including ports.

Impacts on States

4.10   The impacts on States of a measure/combination of measures should be assessed and taken into account as appropriate before adoption of the measure(s) in accordance with the *Revised procedure for assessing impacts on States of candidate measures.*[2] Particular attention should be paid to the needs of developing countries, in particular LDCs and SIDS.

4.11   The Committee should consider the comprehensive impact assessment in order to inform further consideration of the proposed measure(s), and take action as appropriate.

4.12   When assessing impacts on States, the impact of (a) measure(s) should be considered, as appropriate, inter alia, in the following terms:

.1 geographic remoteness of and connectivity to main markets;
.2 cargo value and type;
.3 transport dependency;
.4 transport costs;
.5 food security;
.6 disaster response;
.7 cost-effectiveness; and
.8 socio-economic progress and development.

4.13   Once the comprehensive impact assessment is completed, and disproportionately negative impacts assessed and addressed, as appropriate, the measure(s) may be considered for adoption.

4.14   Once a measure is adopted and enacted, the Committee should keep its implementation and impacts under review, upon request by Member States, so that any necessary adjustments may be made.

5   BARRIERS AND SUPPORTIVE ACTIONS, CAPACITY-BUILDING AND TECHNICAL COOPERATION, AND R&D

5.1   The Committee recognizes that developing countries, in particular LDCs and SIDS, have special needs with regard to capacity-building and technical cooperation.

---

[2]   MEPC.1/Circ.885/Rev.1

.4　根据本战略，对与温室气体减排相关的安全问题进行监管评估，并制定路线图，以支持本战略的安全实施；

.5　审议和分析解决甲烷和一氧化二氮排放的措施，并进一步加强解决挥发性有机化合物排放的措施；

.6　鼓励先行者开发和采用新技术；和

.7　审议和分析鼓励全球港口发展和活动的措施，以促进航运温室气体减排，包括提供船舶和岸上 / 陆上可再生能源供电，同时支持供应零或接近零温室气体排放燃料和 / 或能源的基础设施，并进一步优化物流链及其规划，包括港口。

对各国的影响

4.10　在采取措施之前，应根据《经修订的备选措施对国家的影响的评估程序》[2]，评估并酌情考虑一项 / 一组措施对国家的影响。应特别关注发展中国家，特别是最不发达国家和小岛屿发展中国家的需求。

4.11　本委员会应审议综合影响评估，以便为进一步审议建议的措施提供信息，并酌情采取行动。

4.12　在评估对国家的影响时，尤其应酌情从以下方面考虑措施的影响：

.1　地理位置偏远程度及与主要市场的连通情况；
.2　货物价值和类型；
.3　运输依赖性；
.4　运输成本；
.5　粮食安全；
.6　灾害响应；
.7　成本效益；和
.8　社会经济进步和发展。

4.13　一旦完成综合影响评估，且酌情评估并处理不成比例的负面影响后，即可考虑通过措施。

4.14　一旦通过并颁布一项措施，本委员会应按照会员国的请求，对其实施和影响保持审查，以便进行任何必要的调整。

5　障碍和支助行动、能力建设和技术合作以及研发

5.1　本委员会认识到，发展中国家，特别是最不发达国家和小岛屿发展中国家，在能力建设和技术合作方面有着特殊需求。

---

[2]　第 MEPC.1/Circ.885/Rev.1 号通函。

5.2   The Committee recognizes the challenges that some delegations of developing countries, in particular LDCs and SIDS, may face in participating in the work of the Organization, in particular on GHG-related matters. In this regard, the Organization should periodically assess the provision of financial resources through the Voluntary Multi-Donor Trust Fund established by the Organization for the purpose of assisting developing countries, in particular LDCs and SIDS, in attending the meetings of MEPC and the Intersessional Working Group on Reduction of GHG Emissions (ISWG-GHG).

5.3   When developing candidate mid- and long-term GHG reduction measures, due account should be taken to ensure a just and equitable transition that leaves no country behind, including supportive measures.

5.4   The Committee acknowledges that developing and making globally available zero and near-zero GHG emission technologies, fuels and/or energy sources, and developing the necessary associated port infrastructure could be specific barriers to the implementation of possible measures.

5.5   The Committee recognizes the need for a broad approach to regulating safety of ships using zero or near-zero GHG emission technologies, fuels and/or energy sources, including addressing the human element, to ensure the safe implementation of this Strategy.

5.6   Recognizing the impact this Strategy will have on seafarers and other maritime professionals, the Organization is further requested to assess its instruments, guidance and training standards to help ensure a just transition for seafarers and other maritime workforce that leaves no one behind.

Continue and enhance partnerships, technical cooperation, capacity-building activities and technology cooperation

5.7   The Committee could assist the efforts to promote zero and near-zero GHG emission technologies, fuels and/or energy sources by facilitating public-private partnerships and information exchange.

5.8   The Committee should continue to provide mechanisms for facilitating information sharing, technology transfer, capacity-building and technical cooperation, taking into account resolution MEPC.229(65) on *Promotion of technical co-operation and transfer of technology relating to the improvement of energy efficiency of ships*.

5.9   The Committee recognizes that the decarbonization of shipping should be possible for all IMO Member States and may create new opportunities also for developing countries, including LDCs and SIDS, to take part in the value chain of the production and distribution of zero and near-zero GHG emission technologies, fuels and/or energy sources for international shipping.

5.10   The Organization should assess periodically the provision of financial and technological resources and capacity-building to implement the Revised Strategy through the Integrated Technical Cooperation Programme (ITCP), the IMO GHG TC-Trust Fund and other initiatives, including both IMO and Member States-sponsored programmes, as listed in appendix 2.

5.11   In addition, the Organization may:

        .1   develop a seafarers' training and skills programme to support the reduction of GHG emissions from ships;

5.2 本委员会认识到，一些发展中国家，特别是最不发达国家和小岛屿发展中国家的代表团在参与本组织的工作，特别是与温室气体有关的工作方面可能面临挑战。在此方面，本组织应通过其设立的自愿性多方捐助者信托基金定期评估财政资源的提供情况，以协助发展中国家，特别是最不发达国家和小岛屿发展中国家出席环保会会议和船舶温室气体减排会间工作组（ISWG–GHG）会议。

5.3 在制定备选的中期和长期温室气体减排措施时，应适当考虑确保公正和公平的转型，包括支持性措施，不让任何国家掉队。

5.4 本委员会认识到，开发和在全球范围内提供零和接近零温室气体排放技术、燃料和 / 或能源，以及建设必要的相关港口基础设施，可能会对实施潜在的措施构成具体障碍。

5.5 本委员会认识到，有必要对使用零或接近零温室气体排放技术、燃料和 / 或能源的船舶的安全采取广泛的管理方式，包括解决人的因素，以确保本战略的安全实施。

5.6 认识到本战略将对海员和其他海事专业人员产生的影响，进一步要求本组织评估其文书、指南和培训标准，以帮助确保海员和其他海事劳动力的公正转型，不让任何人掉队。

继续并加强伙伴关系、技术合作、能力建设活动和科技合作

5.7 本委员会可通过促进公共 – 私营伙伴关系和信息交流，协助努力推广零和接近零温室气体排放技术、燃料和 / 或能源。

5.8 本委员会应继续提供促进信息共享、技术转让、能力建设和技术合作的机制，同时考虑到关于《促进有关改进船舶能效的技术合作和技术转让》的第 MEPC.229（65）号决议。

5.9 本委员会认识到，航运脱碳应能为所有海事组织会员国实现，并可能为发展中国家，包括最不发达国家和小岛屿发展中国家创造新的机会，使其参与到生产和分销用于国际航运的零和近零温室气体排放技术、燃料和 / 或能源的价值链中来。

5.10 本组织应通过综合技术合作方案（ITCP）、海事组织温室气体技术合作信托基金和其他举措，包括附录 2 中所列的海事组织和会员国赞助的方案，对为实施经修订的战略而提供的财政和技术资源以及能力建设情况进行定期评估。

5.11 此外，本组织可以：

.1 制定海员培训和技能方案，以支持减少船舶温室气体排放；

.2　initiate R&D activities and pilots addressing marine propulsion, zero or near-zero GHG emission technologies, fuels and/or energy sources to further enhance the energy efficiency of ships and supporting the global availability and uptake of low-carbon and zero-carbon fuels and technologies;

.3　support, including through partnerships and provision of financial and technological resources, enhanced technical cooperation, capacity-building activities and technology cooperation, the implementation of the existing short-term GHG reduction measures; and

.4　initiate efforts to explore renewable fuel production opportunities to be made available to international shipping, notably in developing countries, including LDCs and SIDS.

6　FOLLOW-UP ACTIONS

6.1　A programme of follow-up actions for the 2023 IMO GHG Strategy should be developed.

6.2　The key stages towards the adoption of a 2028 IMO GHG Strategy are as follows:

Target dates	Milestones		
	Comprehensive impact assessment of the basket of candidate mid-term measures	Development of candidate mid-term measures	Other milestones
MEPC 80 (Summer 2023)	Initiation of CIA	Initiate Phase III of the Work Plan on the development of mid-term measures	
MEPC 81 (Spring 2024)	Interim report	Finalization of basket of measures	
MEPC 82 (Autumn 2024)	Finalized report		
MEPC 83 (Spring 2025)		Approval of measures	Review of the short-term measure to be completed by 1 January 2026
Extraordinary one or two-day MEPC (six months after MEPC 83 in Autumn 2025)		Adoption of measures	
MEPC 84 (Spring 2026)			
MEPC 85 (Autumn 2026)			
16 months after adoption (2027)		Entry into force of measures	

.2 启动船用推进系统、零或接近零温室气体排放技术、燃料和 / 或能源的研发活动和试点，以进一步提高船舶能效，并支持全球提供和采用低碳和零碳燃料和技术；

.3 通过包括伙伴关系与提供财政和技术资源，加强技术合作，能力建设活动和科技合作在内的手段支持实施现有的短期温室气体减排措施；和

.4 开始努力探索可再生燃料生产机会，以便向国际航运提供，在发展中国家，包括最不发达国家和小岛屿发展中国家尤其如此。

6 后续行动

6.1 应制定《2023 年海事组织温室气体战略》的后续行动方案。

6.2 通过《2028 年海事组织温室气体战略》的关键阶段如下：

目标日期	里程碑		
	一篮子备选中期措施的综合影响评估	制定备选中期措施	其他里程碑
第 80 届环保会（2023 年夏季）	启动综合影响评估	启动制定中期措施的工作计划的第Ⅲ阶段	
第 81 届环保会（2024 年春季）	中期报告	最终确定一篮子措施	
第 82 届环保会（2024 年秋季）	最终报告		
第 83 届环保会（2025 年春季）		批准措施	2026 年 1 月 1 日前完成短期措施审查
为期一天或两天的特别环保会会议（2025 年秋季，第 83 届环保会 6 个月后）		通过措施	
第 84 届环保会（2026 年春季）			
第 85 届环保会（2026 年秋季）			
通过后 16 个月（2027 年）		措施生效	

Target dates	Milestones		
	Comprehensive impact assessment of the basket of candidate mid-term measures	Development of candidate mid-term measures	Other milestones
MEPC 86 (Summer 2027)			Initiate the review of the 2023 IMO GHG Strategy
MEPC 87 (Spring 2028)			
MEPC 88 (Autumn 2028)			Finalization of the review of the 2023 IMO GHG Strategy with a view to adoption of the 2028 IMO GHG Strategy

6.3   The Marginal Abatement Cost Curve (MACC) for each measure, as appropriate, should be ascertained and updated, and then evaluated on a regular basis.

7   PERIODIC REVIEW OF THE STRATEGY

7.1   The IMO GHG Strategy should be subject to a five-yearly review with the first review due in 2028.

7.2   The Committee should undertake the review including defining the scope of the review and its terms of reference.

7.3   The reviews of the levels of ambition should take into account updated emission estimates, emission reduction options and availability for international shipping, and the reports of the Intergovernmental Panel on Climate Change (IPCC), and future IMO GHG inventories and studies, as relevant, to assess progress towards reaching net-zero GHG emissions of international shipping. The reviews should also take into account available data on the impact on States of any measure(s) applied, including information provided by the States or by international organizations or institutions, so that any necessary adjustments may be made as provided for in the *Revised procedure for assessing impacts on States of candidate measures* (MEPC.1/Circ.885/Rev.1).

目标日期	里程碑		
	一篮子备选中期措施的综合影响评估	制定备选中期措施	其他里程碑
第86届环保会（2027年夏季）			启动对《2023年海事组织温室气体战略》的审查
第87届环保会（2028年春季）			
第88届环保会（2028年秋季）			最终完成对《2023年海事组织温室气体战略》的审查，以通过《2028年海事组织温室气体战略》

6.3 应酌情确定和更新每项措施的边际减排成本曲线（MACC），然后定期进行评估。

7 对战略的定期审查

7.1 《海事组织温室气体战略》应进行五年一次的审查，第一次审查将于2028年进行。

7.2 本委员会应进行审查，包括界定审查的范围及其职责范围。

7.3 对目标水平的审查应考虑到最新的排放估算、减排备选方案和对国际航运的可用性，以及政府间气候变化专门委员会（IPCC）的报告，并酌情考虑到海事组织今后的温室气体清单和研究，以评估国际航运实现温室气体净零排放的进展情况。审查还应考虑到所采取的任何措施对各国影响的现有数据，包括各国或国际组织或机构提供的信息，以便按照《经修订的备选措施对国家的影响的评估程序》（第MEPC.1/Circ.885/Rev.1号通函）的规定做出任何必要的调整。

APPENDIX 1

OVERVIEW OF PREVIOUS WORK UNDERTAKEN BY THE ORGANIZATION TO ADDRESS GHG EMISSIONS FROM SHIPS

An overview of IMO work undertaken to address GHG emissions from ships is provided below:

.1 MEPC 62 (July 2011) adopted resolution MEPC.203(62) on *Inclusion of regulations on energy efficiency for ships in MARPOL Annex VI* introducing mandatory technical (EEDI) and operational (SEEMP) measures for the energy efficiency of ships;

.2 MEPC 65 (May 2013) adopted resolution MEPC.229(65) on *Promotion of technical co-operation and transfer of technology relating to the improvement of energy efficiency of ships*, to provide technical assistance to Member States to enable cooperation in the transfer of energy efficient technologies, in particular to developing countries;

.3 MEPC 67 (October 2014) approved the Third IMO GHG Study 2014, estimating that GHG emissions from international shipping in 2012 accounted for some 2.2% of anthropogenic CO_2 emissions and that such emissions could grow by between 50% and 250% by 2050;

.4 MEPC 70 (October 2016) adopted, by resolution MEPC.278(70), amendments to MARPOL Annex VI to introduce the data collection system for fuel oil consumption of ships, containing mandatory requirements for ships to record and report their fuel oil consumption, and also adopted the *Road map for developing a comprehensive IMO strategy on reduction of GHG emissions from ships* (the Road Map). Ships of 5,000 gross tonnage and above (representing approximately 85% of the total GHG emissions from international shipping) are required to collect consumption data for each type of fuel oil they use, as well as other, additional, specified data including proxies for "transport work";

.5 MEPC 72 (April 2018) adopted, by resolution MEPC.304(72), the *Initial IMO Strategy on Reduction of GHG Emissions from Ships*, setting out a vision which confirmed IMO's commitment to reducing GHG emissions from international shipping and to phasing them out as soon as possible, and agreed to keep the Initial Strategy under review, with a view to adoption of a Revised Strategy in 2023;

.6 MEPC 73 (October 2018) approved the *Programme of follow-up actions of the Initial IMO Strategy*, intended to be used as a planning tool in meeting the timelines identified in the Initial IMO Strategy;

.7 MEPC 74 (May 2019) approved MEPC.1/Circ.885 on *Procedure for assessing the impacts on States of candidate measures*; adopted resolution MEPC.323(74) on *Inviting Member States to encourage voluntary cooperation between the port and shipping sectors to contribute to reducing GHG emissions from ships,* as revised by MEPC 79 by resolution MEPC.366(79); and agreed to establish a voluntary multi-donor trust fund ("GHG TC-Trust Fund"), to provide a dedicated source of financial support for technical cooperation and capacity development activities to support the implementation of the Initial IMO Strategy on Reduction of GHG Emissions from Ships;

附录 1

本组织之前为解决船舶温室气体排放问题所开展的工作的概述

下文概述了海事组织为解决船舶温室气体排放所开展的工作：

.1 第 62 届环保会（2011 年 7 月）通过了关于《在〈防污公约〉附则Ⅵ中纳入船舶能效规则》的第 MEPC.203（62）号决议，引入了船舶能效的强制性技术措施（能效设计指数）和营运措施（船舶能效管理计划）；

.2 第 65 届环保会（2013 年 5 月）通过了关于《促进有关改进船舶能效的技术合作和技术转让》的第 MEPC.229（65）号决议，以向会员国，特别是向发展中国家提供技术援助，促进在能效技术转让方面的合作；

.3 第 67 届环保会（2014 年 10 月）批准了 2014 年第三次国际海事组织温室气体研究，该研究估算 2012 年国际航运温室气体排放量约占人为二氧化碳排放量的 2.2%，到 2050 年，此类排放量可能增长 50% 至 250%。

.4 第 70 届环保会（2016 年 10 月）以第 MEPC.278（70）号决议通过了《防污公约》附则Ⅵ的修正案，引入了船舶燃油消耗数据收集系统，其中包含船舶记录并报告其燃油消耗的强制性要求，并通过了《制定国际海事组织船舶温室气体减排综合战略的路线图》（路线图）。要求 5 000 总吨及以上船舶（约占国际航运温室气体排放总量的 85%）收集其使用的每种燃油的消耗数据，以及其他额外的具体数据，包括"运输工作"的替代数据；

.5 第 72 届环保会（2018 年 4 月）以第 MEPC.304（72）号决议通过了《国际海事组织船舶温室气体减排初步战略》，确立了一个愿景，确认了海事组织承诺减少国际航运温室气体排放且尽快逐步消除排放，同时同意对《初步战略》保持审查，以期于 2023 年通过经修订的战略；

.6 第 73 届环保会（2018 年 10 月）批准了《海事组织船舶温室气体减排初步战略的后续行动方案》，旨在将其用作满足《海事组织初步战略》所确定时限的规划工具；

.7 第 74 届环保会（2019 年 5 月）批准了关于《备选措施对国家的影响的评估程序》的第 MEPC.1/Circ.885 号通函；通过了关于《邀请会员国鼓励港口与航运部门之间自愿合作以减少船舶温室气体排放》的第 MEPC.323（74）号决议（经第 79 届环保会以第 MEPC.366（79）号决议修订）；并同意设立一个自愿性多方捐助者信托基金（"温室气体技术合作信托基金"），为技术合作和能力建设活动提供专项资金支持，以支持实施《国际海事组织船舶温室气体减排初步战略》；

.8 MEPC 75 (November 2020) adopted resolution MEPC.327(75) on *Encouraging Member States to develop and submit voluntary National Action Plans to address GHG emissions from ships,* as revised by MEPC 79 by resolution MEPC.367(79); approved the Fourth IMO GHG Study 2020; and adopted, by resolution MEPC.324(75), amendments to MARPOL Annex VI advancing and strengthening EEDI Phase 3 requirements for several ship types;

.9 MEPC 76 (June 2021) adopted, by resolution MEPC. 328(76), amendments to MARPOL Annex VI introducing the short-term GHG reduction measure containing a technical Energy Efficiency Existing Ship Index (EEXI), an operational Carbon Intensity Indicator (CII) and an enhanced Ship Energy Efficiency Management Plan (SEEMP); adopted a series of seven technical guidelines supporting the EEXI and CII frameworks; approved a *Work plan to progress development of mid- and long-term GHG reduction measures in line with the Initial IMO Strategy on Reduction of GHG Emissions from Ships and its Programme of follow-up actions*;

.10 MEPC 77 (November 2021) agreed to initiate the revision of the *Initial IMO Strategy on Reduction of GHG Emissions from Ships*, recognizing the need to strengthen the ambition during the revision process; and adopted resolution MEPC.342(77) on *Protecting the Arctic from shipping Black Carbon emissions* recognizing that Black Carbon was a potent short-lived contributor to climate warming; and

.11 MEPC 78 (June 2022) adopted a series of 10 technical guidelines to support the implementation of the short-term GHG reduction measure;

.12 Council 128 (November 2022) endorsed the finalized terms of reference of a Voluntary Multi-Donor Trust Fund to Facilitate the Participation of Developing Countries, Especially Small Island Developing States (SIDS) and Least Developed Countries (LDCs) in IMO GHG Meetings, and agreed to review the terms of reference, based on the experience of the first full year of operations of the Fund, no later than at the 130th session of the Council;

.13 MEPC 79 (December 2022) adopted amendments to MARPOL Annex VI to revise the data collection system for fuel oil consumption for the implementation of the EEXI and the CII framework, approved a *Revised procedure for assessing the impacts on States of candidate measures* (MEPC.1/Circ.885/Rev.1) and adopted resolutions MEPC.366(79) and MEPC.367(79) on *Invitation to Member States to encourage voluntary cooperation between the port and the shipping sectors to contribute to reducing GHG emissions from ships* and *Encouragement of Member States to develop and submit voluntary National Action Plans (NAPs) to address GHG emissions from ships*, respectively; and

.14 MEPC 80 (July 2023) adopted resolution MEPC.376(80) on *Guidelines on life cycle GHG intensity of marine fuels* (LCA guidelines); initiated the comprehensive impact assessment of the basket of candidate mid-term measures; and adopted resolution MEPC.377(80) on *2023 IMO Strategy on Reduction of GHG Emissions from Ships* (2023 IMO GHG Strategy).

.8 第 75 届环保会（2020 年 11 月）通过了关于《鼓励会员国制定和提交解决船舶温室气体排放问题的自愿性国家行动计划》的第 MEPC.327（75）号决议（经第 79 届环保会以第 MEPC.367（79）号决议修订）；批准了 2020 年第四次国际海事组织温室气体研究；并以第 MEPC.324（75）号决议通过了《防污公约》附则 Ⅵ 的修正案，提高并加强了对若干船型的能效设计指数第 3 阶段要求；

.9 第 76 届环保会（2021 年 6 月）以第 MEPC328（76）号决议通过了《防污公约》附则 Ⅵ 的修正案，引入了短期温室气体减排措施，包括技术性现有船舶能效指数（EEXI）、营运碳强度指标（CII）和增强的船舶能效管理计划（SEEMP）；通过了支持 EEXI 和 CII 框架的 7 项系列技术导则；批准了按照《国际海事组织船舶温室气体减排初步战略》及其后续行动方案推进制定中长期温室气体减排措施的工作计划；

.10 第 77 届环保会（2021 年 11 月）同意启动对《国际海事组织船舶温室气体减排初步战略》的修订，同时认识到在修订过程中需要加强目标水平；并通过了关于《保护北极免受航运黑碳排放造成的影响》的第 MEPC.342（77）号决议，同时认识到黑碳是导致气候变暖的有力短期因素；

.11 第 78 届环保会（2022 年 6 月）通过了支持实施短期温室气体减排措施的 10 项系列技术导则；

.12 第 128 届理事会（2022 年 11 月）核准了为促进发展中国家，特别是小岛屿发展中国家和最不发达国家参加海事组织温室气体会议而设立的自愿性多方捐助者信托基金的最终职责范围，并同意在理事会第 130 届会议之前，根据该基金第一个整年的运作经验，对该职责范围进行审查；

.13 第 79 届环保会（2022 年 12 月）通过了《防污公约》附则 Ⅵ 的修正案，以修订用于实施 EEXI 和 CII 框架的燃油消耗数据收集系统，批准了《经修订的备选措施对国家的影响的评估程序》（第 MEPC.1/Circ.885/Rev.1 号通函），并分别通过了关于《邀请会员国鼓励港口与航运部门之间自愿合作以减少船舶温室气体排放》的第 MEPC.366（79）号决议和关于《鼓励会员国制定和提交解决船舶温室气体排放问题的自愿性国家行动计划（NAPs）》的第 MEPC.367（79）号决议；和

.14 第 80 届环保会（2023 年 7 月）通过了关于《船用燃料生命周期温室气体强度导则》（LCA 导则）的第 MEPC.376（80）号决议；启动了一篮子备选中期措施的综合影响评估；并通过了关于《2023 年国际海事组织船舶温室气体减排战略》（《2023 年海事组织温室气体战略》）的第 MEPC.377（80）号决议。

APPENDIX 2

OVERVIEW OF RELEVANT INITIATIVES BY THE ORGANIZATION SUPPORTING THE REDUCTION OF GHG EMISSIONS FROM SHIPS

An overview of relevant IMO initiatives supporting the reduction of GHG emissions from ships is provided below:

.1 The **Integrated Technical Cooperation Programme (ITCP)** is designed to assist Governments which lack the technical knowledge and resources that are needed to operate a shipping industry safely and efficiently. Support for IMO's GHG-related activities under the ITCP is a clear priority for the Organization. For 2022-2023, a dedicated global programme "Reducing atmospheric emissions from ships and in ports and effective implementation of MARPOL Annex VI and the Initial IMO GHG Strategy" was designed to assist Member States with the implementation of the Initial IMO Strategy, thereby increasing energy efficiency measures for ships, as well as reducing atmospheric pollution from ships, including when in ports.

.2 MEPC 74 (May 2019) agreed to establish a **voluntary multi-donor trust fund ("GHG TC-Trust Fund")**, to provide a dedicated source of financial support for technical cooperation and capacity development activities to support the implementation of the *Initial IMO Strategy on Reduction of GHG Emissions from Ships* (MEPC 74/18/Add.1, annex 17). The resources of the Trust Fund include voluntary contributions from IMO Member States, UN agencies, international organizations and other entities who have expressed support for the Initial IMO Strategy.

.3 With support from the European Union, the **Global Maritime Technologies Cooperation Centres (MTCC) Network (GMN)** project (approximately $11 million, 2016-2022) established five MTCCs in China (MTCC Asia), Fiji (MTCC Pacific), Kenya (MTCC Africa), Panama (MTCC Latin America) and Trinidad and Tobago (MTCC Caribbean). Plans are now being finalized for a GMN Phase II project for the five MTCCs to continue their work to support maritime decarbonization in the respective regions and to be linked to other IMO projects and initiatives. Phase II is to pay particular attention to the delivery of smaller scale (for example, ships retrofitting) pilot demonstration projects, with a focus on the needs of developing countries, in particular LDCs and SIDS.

.4 With support from Norway, the **Green Voyage 2050** project (approximately $7.1 million, 2019-2023) is currently supporting countries to undertake assessments of maritime emissions in the national context, develop policy frameworks and National Action Plans (NAPs) to address GHG emissions from ships, and draft legislation to implement MARPOL Annex VI into national law. Partnering countries are also supported in identifying and implementing of low- and zero-carbon pilot projects on board ships and in ports. Phase 1 of the project is expected to terminate in December 2023 and a new phase envisioned to ensure that efforts can be further continued both in relation to scaled-up pilot projects and NAP development.

.5 The **GHG-SMART Programme** (Sustainable Maritime Transport Training Programme to Support the Implementation of the GHG Strategy) project ($2.5 million, 2020-2025), funded by the Republic of Korea, is a training

附录 2

本组织支持减少船舶温室气体排放的相关举措的概述

下文概述了海事组织支持减少船舶温室气体排放的相关举措：

.1 **综合技术合作方案（ITCP）**旨在协助缺乏安全有效地经营航运业所需的技术知识和资源的政府。支持海事组织在 ITCP 下开展的温室气体相关活动是本组织一项明确的优先事项。2022 至 2023 年，"减少船舶和港口空气排放以及有效执行《防污公约》附则Ⅵ和《海事组织船舶温室气体减排初步战略》"的专门全球方案旨在协助会员国执行《海事组织初步战略》，从而增加船舶能效措施，减少船舶造成的空气污染，包括在港口时造成的空气污染。

.2 第 74 届环保会（2019 年 5 月）同意设立一个**自愿性多方捐助者信托基金（"温室气体技术合作信托基金"）**，为技术合作和能力建设活动提供专项资金支持，以支持实施《国际海事组织船舶温室气体减排初步战略》（第 MEPC 74/18/Add.1 号文件，附件 17）；信托基金的资源包括海事组织会员国、联合国机构、国际组织和表示支持《海事组织初步战略》的其他实体的自愿捐款。

.3 在欧盟的支持下，**全球海事技术合作中心（MTCC）网络（GMN）项目**（约 1 100 万美元，2016—2022 年）在中国（MTCC 亚洲）、斐济（MTCC 太平洋）、肯尼亚（MTCC 非洲）、巴拿马（MTCC 拉丁美洲）与特立尼达和多巴哥（MTCC 加勒比）建立了五个海事技术合作中心。目前正在最终确定 GMN 项目第二阶段的计划，以支持五个海事技术合作中心继续进行各自区域的海上脱碳工作，并与海事组织的其他项目和倡议相互关联。第二阶段将特别注意实施规模较小的试点示范项目（例如船舶改装），重点关注发展中国家，特别是最不发达国家和小岛屿发展中国家的需求。

.4 在挪威的支持下，2050 **绿色航行项目（Green Voyage 2050）**（约 710 万美元，2019—2023 年）目前正在支持各国在国家范围内进行海上排放评估，制定政策框架和国家行动计划（NAPs）以解决船舶温室气体排放问题，并起草立法将《防污公约》附则Ⅵ纳入国内法。还支持伙伴国在船上和港口确定和实施低碳与零碳试点项目。该项目的第一阶段预计将于 2023 年 12 月结束，设想的新阶段将确保进一步推进扩大试点项目和制定国家行动计划的工作。

.5 由韩国资助的**支持实施温室气体战略的可持续海运培训方案（GHG-SMART）项目**（250 万美元，2020—2025 年）是一项旨在通过发展最不发达国家和小岛屿发展中国家的能力以支持实施《国际海事组织船舶温室气体减排初步战略》的培训

programme to support the implementation of the *Initial IMO Strategy on Reduction of GHG Emissions from Ships* by developing capacity in LDCs and SIDS. This is a series of annual training programmes consisting of comprehensive training online, followed by individual training plans, and a practical training and study visit, combined with an opportunity for two trainees (one female and one male) to further benefit from a World Maritime University (WMU) scholarship.

.6   The **GloFouling Partnerships** project (approximately $7 million, 2018-2025) is part of the wider efforts by IMO, in collaboration with UNDP and GEF, to improve biofouling management and protect marine ecosystems from the negative effects of invasive aquatic species. By supporting the implementation of the IMO *2011 Guidelines for the control and management of ships' biofouling to minimize the transfer of invasive aquatic species*, this project also contributes to the reduction of GHG emissions from ships. The project has developed and published in 2022 a study entitled *Analysing the Impact of Marine Biofouling on the Energy Efficiency of Ships and the GHG Abatement Potential of Biofouling Management Measures*.

.7   The **TEST Biofouling** (Transfer of Environmentally Sound Technologies) project ($4 million, 2022-2025), funded by Norway, aims to assist developing countries to build their knowledge on control and management of biofouling and showcase effective approaches to biofouling management and the mitigation of environmental risks associated with the transfer of invasive aquatic species through biofouling by means of demonstration projects at both regional and country levels. The project focuses on testing novel technologies and new sustainable methods of biofouling management, which, in line with the above study, indirectly contributes to reducing GHG emissions.

.8   The **IMO CARES** (Coordinated Actions to Reduce Emissions from Shipping) Foundation Project, project (approximately $1.5 million, 2022-2024), funded by Saudi Arabia, started its implementation phase in early 2023, with the ultimate objective to help link the global North and global South for the identification and trial of ready for market technology solutions, technology transfer, technology diffusion and uptake activities, pilot demonstration projects and green financing initiatives. This project will assist the maritime sector in developing countries in their transition towards a low-carbon future with key involvement of the MTCCs at a regional level.

.9   The Future Fuels and Technology for Low- and Zero-carbon Shipping Project (**FFT project**) (approximately $1.2 million, 2022-2024) is a partnership project between the Republic of Korea and IMO, designed to support GHG reduction from international shipping by providing technical analysis to the Organization in support of policy discussions held in the Marine Environment Protection Committee (MEPC).

.10   The **IMO-UNEP-Norway Innovation Forum** (approximately $650,000, 2020-2023) identified as championing innovation to accelerate the transition of the marine sector towards a zero- and low-emission future. Its aim is to promote innovation by providing a global platform to exchange best practices and fill necessary gaps by gathering ideas and latest developments from all competent international policy makers.

方案。该项目包含一系列年度培训方案，包括在线综合培训、个人培训计划，以及实际培训和考察访问，两名学员（一名女性和一名男性）还有机会获得世界海事大学（WMU）奖学金资助。

.6 **全球防污底伙伴关系项目**（约 700 万美元，2018—2025 年）是海事组织与联合国开发计划署和全球环境基金合作开展得更广泛工作的一部分，旨在改善生物污垢管理并保护海洋生态系统免受入侵水生物种的负面影响。通过支持实施海事组织《2011 年控制和管理船舶生物污垢以最大程度减少入侵水生物种转移的导则》，该项目还有助于减少船舶温室气体排放。该项目于 2022 年撰写并出版了一份题为《分析海洋生物污垢对船舶能效影响以及生物污垢管理措施温室气体减排潜力》的研究报告。

.7 由挪威资助的**生物污垢无害环境技术转让（TEST Biofouling）项目**（400 万美元，2022—2025 年）旨在协助发展中国家积累关于控制和管理生物污垢的知识，并通过在地区级和国家级的示范项目，展示生物污垢管理和减少入侵水生物种通过生物污垢转移有关的环境风险的有效方法。该项目侧重于测试新颖技术和新的可持续生物污垢管理方法，与上述研究一致，该项目有助于间接减少温室气体排放。

.8 由沙特阿拉伯资助的**海事组织减少航运排放协调行动（IMO CARES）基金会项目**（约 150 万美元，2022—2024 年）于 2023 年初进入实施阶段，其最终目标是促进全球北方和全球南方的联系，以确定和试验可用于市场的技术解决方案、技术转让、技术传播和采纳活动、试点示范项目和绿色融资举措。该项目将协助发展中国家的海事部门向低碳未来过渡，并由区域一级海事技术合作中心重点参与。

.9 **低碳和零碳航运未来燃料和技术项目（FFT 项目）**（约 120 万美元，2022—2024 年）是韩国和海事组织之间的一个合作项目，旨在通过向本组织提供技术分析支持国际航运温室气体减排，以支持海上环境保护委员会（MEPC）开展政策讨论。

.10 **国际海事组织－联合国环境规划署－挪威创新论坛**（约 65 万美元，2020—2023 年）确定支持创新，以加速海事部门向零和低排放未来过渡。其目的是通过提供一个全球平台以促进创新，交流最佳做法，并通过收集所有相关国际决策者的想法和最新做法以填补必要的空白。

The second Innovation Forum was held in a hybrid format on 28 and 29 September 2022 and was linked to the IMO World Maritime Day (WMD) theme 2022 "New Technologies for Greener Shipping". It was attended by a total of 1,900 in-person and virtual participants.

The 2023 session will be held in conjunction with WMD, under the theme "MARPOL at 50 — Our commitment goes on", celebrating the fiftieth anniversary of the MARPOL Convention, continuing to support the global South and the green transition of the maritime sector into a sustainable future.

.11 The IMO-EBRD-World Bank co-led **Financing Sustainable Maritime Transport (FIN-SMART) Roundtable** initiative has been providing a platform among Member State representatives, international financial institutions, representatives of private banks and other key maritime stakeholders to identify maritime decarbonization investment risks, opportunities and potential financial solutions and innovative financial instruments to address financing needs and investment opportunities in developing countries, in particular LDCs and SIDS.

The third FIN-SMART roundtable in June 2023, through concrete examples of maritime decarbonization projects resulting in investment or having the potential to become bankable projects in developing countries, aims to highlight concrete success factors and the role of the various actors in achieving investment in maritime decarbonization. It also showcases to the financial community the investment opportunity in more concrete terms, as developing countries may have large unused sustainable resources (for example, wind or solar energy) that could be used for the production of green fuels that the maritime industry requires to accelerate decarbonization.

.12 The **NextGEN** (Green and Efficient Navigation) portal, which was launched by IMO and the Maritime and Port Authority of Singapore (MPA) in September 2021, is an online platform to support information sharing and collaboration on decarbonization initiatives and projects in the field of maritime, presenting an opportunity to provide an online platform of collaboration across the maritime value chain. The next phase of the NextGEN initiative was launched in 2022 as the NextGEN Connect Project, the new phase of which supports a pilot route-based action in the Asia-Pacific region to reduce emissions from international shipping.

***

第二届创新论坛于 2022 年 9 月 28 和 29 日以混合会议方式举行，并与国际海事组织 2022 年世界海事日（WMD）主题"运用新技术，助力航运更绿色"相关联。共计 1 900 名与会者亲自到会和以虚拟方式出席了活动。

2023 年会议将与主题为"《防污公约》五十周年——我们的承诺一如既往"的世界海事日同期举办，以庆祝《防污公约》五十周年纪念日，继续支持全球南方和海事部门向可持续未来的绿色转型。

.11   国际海事组织 – 欧洲复兴开发银行 – 世界银行共同主导的**可持续海运融资（FIN-SMART）圆桌会议**倡议为会员国代表、国际金融机构、私营银行代表和其他主要海事利益攸关方提供了一个平台，以明确海事脱碳投资风险与机遇，以及可能的财务解决方案和创新的金融工具，从而解决发展中国家，特别是最不发达国家和小岛屿国家的融资需求和投资机会。

2023 年 6 月举行的第三次 FIN-SMART 圆桌会议，通过发展中国家获得投资或拥有可融资潜力的海上脱碳项目的具体案例以突出具体的成功因素以及各参与方在实现海上脱碳投资方面的作用。它还以更加具体的方式向金融界展示了投资机会，因为发展中国家可能拥有大量未使用的可持续资源（例如风能或太阳能），可用于生产海运业加速脱碳所需的绿色燃料。

.12   由国际海事组织与新加坡海事及港务管理局（MPA）于 2021 年 9 月推出的**绿色和高效航行（NextGEN）**门户网站是一个旨在支持海事领域脱碳倡议和项目的信息共享与合作的在线平台，为整个海事价值链提供在线合作平台。NextGEN 倡议的第二阶段于 2022 年启动，称为 NextGEN Connect 项目，其在新阶段支持亚太地区基于航线的试点行动，以减少国际航运的排放。

***

MARPOL ANNEX VI

REGULATIONS FOR THE PREVENTION OF AIR POLLUTION FROM SHIPS

Chapter 1　General

Regulation 1 Application

The provisions of this Annex shall apply to all ships, except where expressly provided otherwise.

Regulation 2 Definitions

1   For the purpose of this Annex:

.1   **Annex** means Annex VI to the International Convention for the Prevention of Pollution from Ships, 1973 (MARPOL), as modified by the Protocol of 1978 relating thereto, and as modified by the Protocol of 1997, as amended by the Organization, provided that such amendments are adopted and brought into force in accordance with the provisions of article 16 of the present Convention.

.2   **A similar stage of construction** means the stage at which:

.1   construction identifiable with a specific ship begins; and

.2   assembly of that ship has commenced comprising at least 50 tonnes or one per cent of the estimated mass of all structural material, whichever is less.

.3   **Anniversary date** means the day and the month of each year that will correspond to the date of expiry of the International Air Pollution Prevention Certificate.

.4   **Audit** means a systematic, independent and documented process for obtaining audit evidence and evaluating it objectively to determine the extent to which audit criteria are fulfilled.

.5   **Audit Scheme** means the IMO Member State Audit Scheme established by the Organization and taking into account the guidelines developed by the Organization.*

.6   **Audit Standard** means the Code for Implementation.

.7   **Auxiliary control device** means a system, function or control strategy installed on a marine diesel engine that is used to protect the engine and/or its ancillary equipment against operating conditions that could result in damage or failure, or that is used to facilitate the starting of the engine. An auxiliary control device may also be a strategy or measure that has been satisfactorily demonstrated not to be a defeat device.

.8   **Code for Implementation** means the IMO Instruments Implementation Code (III Code) adopted by the Organization by resolution A.1070(28).

.9   **Continuous feeding** is defined as the process whereby waste is fed into a combustion chamber without human assistance while the incinerator is in normal operating conditions with the combustion chamber operative temperature between 850°C and 1,200°C.

.10   **Defeat device** means a device that measures, senses or responds to operating variables (e.g. engine speed, temperature, intake pressure or any other parameter) for the purpose of activating, modulating, delaying or deactivating the operation of any component or the function of the emission control system such that the effectiveness of the emission control system is reduced under conditions encountered during normal operation, unless the use of such a device is substantially included in the applied emission certification test procedures.

.11   **Electronic Record Book** means a device or system, approved by the Administration, used to electronically record the required entries for discharges, transfers and other operations as required under this Annex in lieu of a hard copy record book. **

---

* Refer to Framework and procedures for the IMO Member State Audit Scheme (resolution A.1067(28)).
** Refer to Guidelines for the use of electronic record books under MARPOL (resolution MEPC.312(74)).

《防污公约》附则 VI

防止船舶造成空气污染规则

第 1 章 总 则

第 1 条 适用范围

除另有明文规定外，本附则的规定应适用于所有船舶。

第 2 条 定义

1 就本附则而言：

.1 **附则**系指经《1997 年议定书修订的并经 1978 年议定书修订的 1973 年国际防止船舶造成污染公约》（《防污公约》）的附则 VI，该附则可由本组织修订，但这些修正案应按本公约第 16 条的规定予以通过并生效。

.2 **类似建造阶段**系指在该阶段：

　　.1 可辨认出某一具体船舶的建造开始；和

　　.2 船舶业已开始的装配量至少为 50 吨，或为全部结构材料估算重量的 1%，取较小者。

.3 **周年日**系指每年与《国际防止空气污染证书》期满之日对应的该月该日。

.4 **审核**系指为确定满足审核标准的程度而进行的获取审核证据并客观的对其进行评价的一个系统的、独立的且有文件记录的过程。

.5 **审核机制**系指本组织建立的、考虑到本组织制订的各项导则的国际海事组织会员国审核机制。*

.6 **审核标准**系指《文书实施规则》。

.7 **辅助控制装置**系指船用柴油机上安装的用于保护柴油机和/或其辅助设备不受可导致其损坏或故障的操作条件的影响或有助于柴油机起动的系统、功能或控制策略。辅助控制装置也可以是业已证明为非抑制装置的策略或措施。

.8 **文书实施规则**系指本组织以第 A.1070（28）号决议通过的《国际海事组织文书实施规则》（《文书实施规则》）。

.9 **连续进料**系指当焚烧炉在正常操作条件下，燃烧室工作温度在 850 ℃和 1 200 ℃之间时，无须人工辅助将废物送入燃烧室的过程。

.10 **减效装置**是指一种测量、感应或响应操作变量（例如发动机转速、温度、进气压力或任何其他参数）的装置，激活、调整、延迟或停用排放控制系统的任何部件或功能的操作，从而在正常操作遇到的工况下降低排放控制系统的有效性，但在适用的基本使用该装置的排放认证测试程序者除外。

.11 **电子记录簿**系指经主管机关批准的、用于以电子方式记录本附则要求的排放、驳运和其他操作所要求的记录以代替纸质记录簿的设备或系统。**

---

* 参见《关于国际海事组织成员国审核计划的程序和框架》（第 A.1067（28）号决议）。

** 参见《防污公约下的电子记录簿使用导则》（第 MEPC.312（74）号决议）。

.12 **Emission** means any release of substances, subject to control by this Annex, from ships into the atmosphere or sea.

.13 **Emission control area** means an area where the adoption of special mandatory measures for emissions from ships is required to prevent, reduce and control air pollution from NOx or SOx and particulate matter or all three types of emissions and their attendant adverse impacts on human health and the environment. Emission control areas shall include those listed in, or designated under, regulations 13 and 14 of this Annex.

.14 **Fuel oil** means any fuel delivered to and intended for use on board a ship.

.15 **Gross tonnage** means the gross tonnage calculated in accordance with the tonnage measurement regulations contained in Annex I to the International Convention on Tonnage Measurements of Ships, 1969, or any successor Convention.

.16 **In-use sample** means a sample of fuel oil in use on a ship.

.17 **Installations** in relation to regulation 12 of this Annex means the installation of systems, equipment, including portable fire-extinguishing units, insulation, or other material on a ship, but excludes the repair or recharge of previously installed systems, equipment, insulation or other material, or the recharge of portable fire-extinguishing units.

.18 **Installed** means a marine diesel engine that is or is intended to befitted on a ship, including a portable auxiliary marine diesel engine, only if its fuelling, cooling or exhaust system is an integral part of the ship. A fuelling system is considered integral to the ship only if it is permanently affixed to the ship. This definition includes a marine diesel engine that is used to supplement or augment the installed power capacity of the ship and is intended to be an integral part of the ship.

.19 **Irrational emission control strategy** means any strategy or measure that, when the ship is operated under normal conditions of use, reduces the effectiveness of an emission control system to a level below that expected on the applicable emission test procedures.

.20 **Low-flashpoint fuel** means gaseous or liquid fuel oil having a flashpoint lower than otherwise permitted under paragraph 2.1.1 of regulation 4 of chapter II-2 of the International Convention for the Safety of Life at Sea (SOLAS), 1974, as amended.

.21 **Marine diesel engine** means any reciprocating internal combustion engine operating on liquid or dual fuel, to which regulation 13 of this Annex applies, including booster/compound systems if applied. In addition, a gas-fuelled engine installed on a ship constructed on or after 1 March 2016 or a gas-fuelled additional or non-identical replacement engine installed on or after that date is also considered as a marine diesel engine.

.22 **MARPOL delivered sample** means the sample of fuel oil delivered in accordance with regulation 18.8.1 of this Annex.

.23 **NOx Technical Code** means the Technical Code on Control of Emission of Nitrogen Oxides from Marine Diesel Engines adopted by resolution 2 of the 1997 MARPOL Conference, as amended by the Organization, provided that such amendments are adopted and brought into force in accordance with the provisions of article 16 of the present Convention.

.24 **Onboard sample** means a sample of fuel oil intended to be used or carried for use on board that ship.

.25 **Ozone-depleting substances** means controlled substances defined in paragraph (4) of article 1 of the Montreal Protocol on Substances that Deplete the Ozone Layer, 1987, listed in Annexes A, B, C or E to the said Protocol in force at the time of application or interpretation of this Annex.

Ozone-depleting substances that may be found on board ship include, but are not limited to:

Halon 1211   Bromochlorodifluoromethane

Halon 1301   Bromotrifluoromethane

.12 **排放**系指从船舶上向大气或海洋释放受本附则控制的任何物质。

.13 **排放控制区**系指要求对船舶排放采取特殊强制措施以防止、减少和控制氮氧化物或硫氧化物和颗粒物质或所有三种排放类型造成大气污染以及随之对人类健康和环境造成不利影响的区域。排放控制区域应包括本附则第 13 和 14 条所列或所指定的区域。

.14 **燃油**系指交付给船上并在船上使用的任何燃料。

.15 **总吨位**系指按《1969 年国际船舶吨位丈量公约》附则 I 或其他替代公约所述的吨位丈量规定计算的总吨位。

.16 **在用样品**系指船舶使用中的燃油样品。

.17 **装置**系指与本附则第 12 条有关的在船上安装的系统、设备，包括手提式灭火器、绝缘体或其他材料，但不包括对以前安装的系统、设备、绝缘体或其他材料的修理或重新充注，或者对手提灭火器的重新充注。

.18 **安装**系指安装或拟安装上船的船用柴油机，包括便携式辅助船用柴油发动机，仅当其供油、冷却或排气系统是船舶的组成部分。供油系统只有在永久固定在船上时才可视为船舶的构成部分。该定义包括用于补充或增强船舶已装功率容量并拟成为船舶组成部分的船用柴油机。

.19 **不合理排放控制策略**系指当船舶在正常使用条件下营运时，将排放控制系统的有效性降至低于适用的排放试验程序所预期的水平的任何策略或措施。

.20 **低闪点燃料**系指其闪点低于经修正的《1974 年国际海上人命安全公约》（《安全公约》）第 II –2 章第 4 条第 2.1.1 款允许的气体或液体燃油。

.21 **船用柴油机**系指本附则第 13 条所适用的以液体或双燃料运行的任何往复式内燃机，包括增压 / 复合系统（如适用）。此外，2016 年 3 月 1 日或以后建造的船舶上安装的气体燃料发动机，或在该日期或以后安装的新增气体燃料发动机或非完全相同的替代气体燃料发动机也视为船用柴油机。

.22 **《防污公约》交付的样品**系指按本附则第 18.8.1 条交付的燃油样品。

.23 **《氮氧化物技术规则》**系指 1997 年防污公约缔约国大会第 2 号决议通过的《船用柴油机氮氧化物排放控制技术规则》；该规则可经本组织修正，但这些修正案应按照本公约第 16 条的规定予以通过并生效。

.24 **船上样品**系指旨在船上使用或载运供船上使用的燃油样品。

.25 **消耗臭氧物质**系指在应用或解释本附则时有效的《1987 年消耗臭氧层物质蒙特利尔议定书》第 1（4）条中定义的并在该议定书附则 A、B、C 或 E 中所列的受控制物质。

　　在船上可能存在的消耗臭氧物质包括但不限于下列各项：

　　　　Halon 1211　溴氯二氟甲烷

　　　　Halon 1301　溴三氟甲烷

Halon 2402   1,2-Dibromo-1,1,2,2-tetrafluoroethane (also known as Halon 114B2)
CFC-11   Trichlorofluoromethane
CFC-12   Dichlorodifluoromethane
CFC-113   1,1,2-Trichloro-1,2,2-trifluoroethane
CFC-114   1,2-Dichloro-1,1,2,2-tetrafluoroethane
CFC-115   Chloropentafluoroethane

.26 **Shipboard incineration** means the incineration of wastes or other matter on board a ship, if such wastes or other matter were generated during the normal operation of that ship.

.27 **Shipboard incinerator** means a shipboard facility designed for the primary purpose of incineration.

.28 **Ships constructed** means ships the keels of which are laid or that are at a similar stage of construction.

.29 **Sludge oil** means sludge from the fuel oil or lubricating oil separators, waste lubricating oil from main or auxiliary machinery, or waste oil from bilge water separators, oil filtering equipment or drip trays.

.30 **Sulphur content of fuel oil** means the concentration of sulphur in a fuel oil, measured in % m/m as tested in accordance with a standard acceptable to the Organization. *

.31 **Tanker in relation to regulation 15 of this Annex** means an oil tanker as defined in regulation 1 of Annex I to the present Convention or a chemical tanker as defined in regulation 1 of Annex II to the present Convention.

.32 **Unmanned non-self-propelled (UNSP) barge** means a barge that:
    .1   is not propelled by mechanical means;
    .2   has no system, equipment and/or machinery fitted that may generate emissions regulated by this Annex; and
    .3   has neither persons nor living animals on board.

.33 **Gas fuel** means a fuel oil with a vapour pressure exceeding 0.28 MPa absolute at a temperature of 37.8°C.**

2   For the purpose of chapter 4:

.1   **A ship delivered on or after 1 September 2019** means a ship:
    .1   for which the building contract is placed on or after 1 September 2015; or
    .2   in the absence of a building contract, the keel of which is laid, or which is at a similar stage of construction, on or after 1 March 2016; or
    .3   the delivery of which is on or after 1 September 2019.

.2   **Attained annual operational CII** is the operational carbon intensity indicator value achieved by an individual ship in accordance with regulations 26 and 28 of this Annex.

.3   **Attained EEDI** is the EEDI value achieved by an individual ship in accordance with regulation 22 of this Annex.

.4   **Attained EEXI** is the EEXI value achieved by an individual ship in accordance with regulation 23 of this Annex.

.5   **Bulk carrier** means a ship which is intended primarily to carry dry cargo in bulk, including such types as ore carriers as defined in regulation 1 of chapter XII of the International Convention for the Safety of Life at Sea (SOLAS), 1974, (as amended) but excluding combination carriers.

.6   **Calendar year** means the period from 1 January until 31 December inclusive.

.7   **Combination carrier** means a ship designed to load 100% deadweight with both liquid and dry cargo in bulk.

.8   **Company** means the owner of the ship or any other organization or person such as the manager, or the bareboat charterer, who has assumed the responsibility for operation of the ship from the owner of the ship and who on assuming such responsibility has agreed to take over all the duties and responsibilities imposed by the International Management Code for the Safe Operation of Ships and for Pollution Prevention, as amended.

---

* Refer to ISO 8754:2003 Petroleum products – Determination of sulphur content – Energy –dispersive X-ray fluorescence spectrometry.

**Refer to paragraph 2.2.18 of the International Code of Safety for Ships using Gases or other Low-flashpoint Fuels (IGF Code).

Halon 2402	1, 2- 二溴化物 –1, 1, 2, 2- 四氟乙烷（亦称作 Halon 114B2 ）
CFC–11	三氯氟甲烷
CFC–12	二氯二氟甲烷
CFC–113	1,1, 2- 三氯 –1, 2, 2- 三氟乙烷
CFC–114	1, 2- 二氯 –1, 1, 2, 2- 四氟乙烷
CFC–115	氯五氟乙烷

.26 **船上焚烧**系指将船舶正常作业时产生的废物或其他物质在船上进行焚烧。

.27 **船上焚烧炉**系指以焚烧为主要目的而设计的船上设备。

.28 **建造的船舶**系指已安放龙骨或处于类似建造阶段的船舶。

.29 **污油**系指来自燃油或润滑油分离器的油泥，主机或辅机的废弃润滑油，或舱底水分离器、滤油设备或滴油盘的废油。

.30 **燃油的硫含量**系指按照本组织接受的标准进行试验测出的燃油中的硫浓度，以质量百分比（％ m/m）为单位。*

.31 **与本附则第 15 条有关的液货船**系指在本公约附则 I 第 1 条中定义的油船或附则 II 第 1 条中定义的化学品船。

.32 **无人非自航（UNSP）驳船**系指一驳船：

　　.1 不是通过机械方式推进的；

　　.2 没有安装可能产生受本附则约束的排放的系统、设备和 / 或机器；和

　　.3 船上无人员或活体动物。

.33 **气体燃料**是指在温度为 37.8 ℃时，蒸汽压力绝对值超过 0.28 MPa 的燃料**。

2　就第 4 章而言：

　.1 **2019 年 9 月 1 日或以后交付的船舶**系指：

　　.1 2015 年 9 月 1 日或以后签订建造合同；或

　　.2 如无建造合同，2016 年 3 月 1 日或以后安放龙骨或处于类似建造阶段；或

　　.3 2019 年 9 月 1 日或以后交付的船舶。

　.2 **达到的年度营运碳强度指标（CII）**系指根据本附则第 26 和 28 条，单艘船舶所达到的营运碳强度指标值。

　.3 **达到的能效设计指数（EEDI）**系指根据本附则第 22 条，单艘船舶所达到的能效设计指数值。

　.4 **现有船舶达到的能效指数（EEXI）**系指根据本附则第 23 条，单艘船舶所达到的现有船舶能效指数值。

　.5 **散货船**系指经修正的《1974 年国际海上人命安全公约》第XII章第 1 条中定义的主要用于运输散装干货的船舶，包括矿砂船等船型，但不包括兼用船。

　.6 **日历年**系指从 1 月 1 日至 12 月 31 日的时间段。

　.7 **兼用船**系指设计上既能散装液货也能散装干货达到 100% 载重量的船舶。

　.8 **公司**系指船舶所有人或任何其他组织或个人，如船舶管理人或光船承租人自船舶所有人处接管船舶营运责任，并同意承担经修正的《国际船舶安全营运和防止污染管理规则》规定的所有责任和义务。

---

* 　参见 ISO 8754：2003 石油产品 – 硫含量的测定 – 能量 – 色散 X 射线荧光光谱法。

** 　参见《国际使用气体或其他低闪点燃料的船舶安全规则》（《IGF 规则》）第 2.2.18 段。

.9   **Containership** means a ship designed exclusively for the carriage of containers in holds and on deck.

.10   **Conventional propulsion** means a method of propulsion where a main reciprocating internal combustion engine(s) is the prime mover and coupled to a propulsion shaft either directly or through a gear box.

.11   **Cruise passenger ship** means a passenger ship not having a cargo deck, designed exclusively for commercial transportation of passengers in overnight accommodations on a sea voyage.

.12   **Distance travelled** means distance travelled over ground.

.13   **Existing ship** means a ship which is not a new ship.

.14   **Gas carrier** means a cargo ship, other than an LNG carrier as defined in paragraph 2.16 of this regulation, constructed or adapted and used for the carriage in bulk of any liquefied gas.

.15   **General cargo ship** means a ship with a multi-deck or single deck hull designed primarily for the carriage of general cargo. This definition excludes specialized dry cargo ships, which are not included in the calculation of reference lines for general cargo ships, namely livestock carrier, barge carrier, heavy load carrier, yacht carrier, nuclear fuel carrier.

SEE INTERPRETATION 1

.16   **LNG carrier** means a cargo ship constructed or adapted and used for the carriage in bulk of liquefied natural gas (LNG).

.17   **Major conversion** means a conversion of a ship:

    .1   which substantially alters the dimensions, carrying capacity or engine power of the ship; or

    .2   which changes the type of the ship; or

    .3   the intent of which in the opinion of the Administration is substantially to prolong the life of the ship; or

    .4   which otherwise so alters the ship that, if it were a new ship, it would become subject to relevant provisions of the present Convention not applicable to it as an existing ship; or

    .5   which substantially alters the energy efficiency of the ship and includes any modifications that could cause the ship to exceed the applicable required EEDI as set out in regulation 24 of this Annex or the applicable required EEXI as set out in regulation 25 of this Annex.

SEE INTERPRETATION 2

.18   **New ship** means a ship:

    .1   for which the building contract is placed on or after 1 January 2013; or

    .2   in the absence of a building contract, the keel of which is laid or which is at a similar stage of construction on or after 1 July 2013; or

    .3   the delivery of which is on or after 1 July 2015.

SEE INTERPRETATION 3

.19   **Non-conventional propulsion** means a method of propulsion, other than conventional propulsion, including diesel-electric propulsion, turbine propulsion, and hybrid propulsion systems.

.20   **Passenger ship** means a ship which carries more than 12 passengers.

.21   **Polar Code** means the International Code for Ships Operating in Polar Waters, consisting of an introduction, parts I-A and II-A and parts I-B and II-B, as adopted by resolutions MSC.385(94) and MEPC.264(68), as may be amended, provided that:

    .1   amendments to the environment-related provisions of the introduction and chapter 1 of part II-A of the Polar Code are adopted, brought into force and take effect in accordance with the provisions of article 16 of the present Convention concerning the amendment procedures applicable to an appendix to an annex; and

    .2   amendments to part II-B of the Polar Code are adopted by the Marine Environment Protection Committee in accordance with its Rules of Procedure.

.9 **集装箱船**系指专门设计用于在货舱内和甲板上载运集装箱的船舶。

.10 **常规推进**系指主要以往复式内燃机为原动机并且直接或通过齿轮箱连接推进轴的推进方式。

.11 **豪华邮轮**系指无货物甲板且专门设计用于对海上航行中过夜住宿乘客进行商业运输的客船。

.12 **航行距离**系指对地的航行距离。

.13 **现有船舶**系指非新船的船舶。

.14 **气体运输船**系指除本条第2.16款所定义的液化天然气运输船外的、经建造或改建用于散装运输任何液化气体的货船。

.15 **杂货船**系指设有多层甲板或单层甲板结构，主要用于载运杂货的船舶。该定义排除了在计算杂货船基准线时未包括的专用干货船，即活牲畜运输船、载驳船、重大件货物运输船、游艇运输船、核燃料运输船。

见统一解释1

.16 **液化天然气运输船**系指经建造或改建用于散装运输液化天然气（LNG）的货船。

.17 **重大改建**系指对船舶所做的改建：

.1 实质上改变了船舶的尺度、载运能力或发动机功率；或

.2 改变了船舶的类型；或

.3 根据主管机关的判断，这种改建的目的实际上是为了要延长船舶的使用年限；或

.4 这种改建使得船舶如同是一艘新船，该船应遵守本公约中不适用于现有船舶的有关规定；或

.5 实质上改变了船舶的能效并且包括能使该船超出本附则第24条适用的要求的能效设计指数

（EEDI）或本附则第25条适用的现有船舶要求的能效指数（EEXI）的任何改装。

见统一解释2

.18 **新船**系指：

.1 2013年1月1日或以后签订建造合同；或

.2 如无建造合同，2013年7月1日或以后安放龙骨或处于类似建造阶段；或

.3 2015年7月1日或以后交付的船舶。

见统一解释3

.19 **非常规推进**系指除常规推进以外的推进方式，包括柴油—电力推进、涡轮推进以及混合推进系统。

.20 **客船**系指载客超过12人的船舶。

.21 **《极地规则》**系指《国际极地水域营运船舶规则》，由引言、第Ⅰ-A和Ⅱ-A部分以及第Ⅰ-B和Ⅱ-B部分组成，该规则由第MSC.385（94）和MEPC.264（68）号决议通过并可经修正，但：

.1 《极地规则》引言中与环境相关的规定和第Ⅱ-A部分第1章的修正案应按本公约第16条适用于附则附录修正程序的规定予以通过、生效和实施：和

.2 《极地规则》第Ⅱ-B部分的修正案由海上环境保护委员会按其议事规则予以通过。

.22 **Refrigerated cargo carrier** means a ship designed exclusively for the carriage of refrigerated cargoes in holds.

SEE INTERPRETATION 4

.23 **Required annual operational CII** is the target value of attained annual operational CII in accordance with regulations 26 and 28 of this Annex for the specific ship type and size.

.24 **Required EEDI** is the maximum value of attained EEDI that is allowed by regulation 24 of this Annex for the specific ship type and size.

.25 **Required EEXI** is the maximum value of attained EEXI that is allowed by regulation 25 of this Annex for the specific ship type and size.

.26 **Ro-ro cargo ship** means a ship designed for the carriage of roll-on-roll-off cargo transportation units.

.27 **Ro-ro cargo ship (vehicle carrier)** means a multi-deck roll-on-roll-off cargo ship designed for the carriage of empty cars and trucks.

.28 **Ro-ro passenger ship** means a passenger ship with roll-on-roll-off cargo spaces.

.29 **Tanker** means an oil tanker as defined in regulation 1 of Annex I of the present Convention or a chemical tanker or an NLS tanker as defined in regulation 1 of Annex II to the present Convention.

Regulation 3 Exceptions and exemptions

General

1 Regulations of this Annex shall not apply to:

.1 any emission necessary for the purpose of securing the safety of a ship or saving life at sea; or

.2 any emission resulting from damage to a ship or its equipment:

.1 provided that all reasonable precautions have been taken after the occurrence of the damage or discovery of the emission for the purpose of preventing or minimizing the emission; and

.2 except if the owner or the master acted either with intent to cause damage, or recklessly and with knowledge that damage would probably result.

Trials for ship emission reduction and control technology research

2 The Administration of a Party may, in cooperation with other Administrations as appropriate, issue an exemption from specific provisions of this Annex for a ship to conduct trials for the development of ship emission reduction and control technologies and engine design programmes. Such an exemption shall only be provided if the applications of specific provisions of the Annex or the revised NOx Technical Code 2008 could impede research into the development of such technologies or programmes. A permit issued under this regulation shall not exempt a ship from the reporting requirement under regulation 27 and shall not alter the type and scope of data required to be reported under regulation 27. A permit for such an exemption shall only be provided to the minimum number of ships necessary and be subject to the following provisions:

.1 for marine diesel engines with a per cylinder displacement up to 30 L, the duration of the sea trial shall not exceed 18 months. If additional time is required, a permitting Administration or Administrations may permit a renewal for one additional 18-month period; or

.2 for marine diesel engines with a per cylinder displacement at or above 30 L, the duration of the ship trial shall not exceed five years and shall require a progress review by the permitting Administration or Administrations at each intermediate survey. A permit may be withdrawn based on this review if the testing has not adhered to the conditions of the permit or if it is determined that the technology or programme is not likely to produce effective results in the reduction and control of ship emissions. If the reviewing Administration or Administrations determine that additional time is required to conduct a test of a particular technology or programme, a permit may be renewed for an additional time period not to exceed five years.

.22 **冷藏货船**系指专门设计在货舱内载运冷藏货物的船舶。

见统一解释 4

.23 **要求的年度营运碳强度指标（CII）**系指按本附则第 26 和 28 条对特定船型和尺度的所达到的年度营运碳强度指标的目标值。

.24 **要求的能效设计指数（EEDI）**系指本附则第 24 条对特定船型和尺度所允许的所达到的能效设计指数的最大值。

.25 **现有船舶要求的能效指数（EEXI）**系指本附则第 25 条对特定船型和尺度所允许的所达到的能效指数的最大值。

.26 **滚装货船**系指设计用于载运滚装货物运输单元的船舶。

.27 **滚装货船（车辆运输船）**系指具有多层甲板的设计用于载运空载小汽车和卡车的滚装货船。

.28 **滚装客船**系指具有滚装货物处所的客船。

.29 **液货船**系指在本公约附则 I 第 1 条中定义的油船或本公约附则 II 第 1 条中定义的化学品船或有毒物质液货船。

第 3 条 例外和免除

一般规定

1 本附则的规定不适用于：

　.1 任何为保障船舶安全或救助海上人命所必需的排放；或

　.2 任何因船舶或其设备遭到损坏的排放：

　　.1 但应在发生损坏或发现排放后，已采取了一切合理的预防措施防止排放或使排放减至最低程度；和

　　.2 如果船东或船长是故意造成损坏，或明知损坏可能发生而又草率行事者不在此例。

为减少和控制船舶排放技术研究进行的试航

2 缔约国主管机关可在适当情况下与其他主管机关合作，对为开发减少和控制船舶排放技术及发动机设计程序而进行试航的船舶，签发对本附则具体规定的免除证书。只有当适用本附则或经修订的《2008 年氮氧化物技术规则》中的具体规定会妨碍此类技术或程序的研发时，才能给予此种免除。在本条下签发的许可不得免除船舶在第 27 条下的报告要求，也不得改变第 27 条要求报告的数据类型和范围。应尽可能减少免除，仅向有必要免除的船舶签发免除证书，同时应满足下列规定：

　.1 对于单缸排量低于 30 L 的船用柴油机，海上试航时间不应超过 18 个月。如需更长时间，给予免除的一个或多个主管机关可对免除证书进行换新，增加 18 个月的免除期限；或

　.2 对于单缸排量为 30 L 或以上的船用柴油机，船舶试航时间不得超过五年，并需要给予免除的一个或多个主管机关在每次中间检验时进行进度审核。如试验未能遵守免除条件或确定该技术或程序在减少和控制船舶排放方面产生有效结果的可能性不大，则可根据该审核撤销免除证书。如审核的一个或多个主管机关确定进行某项技术或程序的试验需要更长时间，则可对免除证书进行换新，增加不超过五年的期限。

Emissions from seabed mineral activities

3.1 Emissions directly arising from the exploration, exploitation and associated offshore processing of seabed mineral resources are, consistent with article 2(3)(b)(ii) of the present Convention, exempt from the provisions of this Annex. Such emissions include the following:

.1 emissions resulting from the incineration of substances that are solely and directly the result of exploration, exploitation and associated offshore processing of seabed mineral resources, including but not limited to the flaring of hydrocarbons and the burning of cuttings, muds, and/or stimulation fluids during well completion and testing operations, and flaring arising from upset conditions;

.2 the release of gases and volatile compounds entrained in drilling fluids and cuttings;

.3 emissions associated solely and directly with the treatment, handling or storage of seabed minerals; and

.4 emissions from marine diesel engines that are solely dedicated to the exploration, exploitation and associated offshore processing of seabed mineral resources.

3.2 The requirements of regulation 18 of this Annex shall not apply to the use of hydrocarbons that are produced and subsequently used on site as fuel, when approved by the Administration.

Unmanned non-self-propelled barges

4 The Administration may exempt an unmanned non-self-propelled (UNSP) barge* from the requirements of regulations 5.1 and 6.1 of this Annex by means of an International Air Pollution Prevention Exemption Certificate for Unmanned Non-self-propelled (UNSP) Barges, for a period not exceeding five years provided that the barge has undergone a survey to confirm that conditions referred to in regulations 2.1.32.1 to 2.1.32.3 of this Annex are met.

Regulation 4 Equivalents

1 The Administration of a Party may allow any fitting, material, appliance or apparatus to befitted in a ship or other procedures, alternative fuel oils, or compliance methods used as an alternative to those required by this Annex if such fitting, material, appliance or apparatus or other procedures, alternative fuel oils, or compliance methods are at least as effective in terms of emissions reductions as those required by this Annex, including any of the standards set forth in regulations 13 and 14.

2 The Administration of a Party that allows a fitting, material, appliance or apparatus or other procedures, alternative fuel oils, or compliance methods used as an alternative to those required by this Annex shall communicate to the Organization for circulation to the Parties particulars thereof, for their information and appropriate action, if any.

3 The Administration of a Party should take into account any relevant guidelines developed by the Organization** pertaining to the equivalents provided for in this regulation.

4 The Administration of a Party that allows the use of an equivalent as set forth in paragraph 1 of this regulationshall endeavour not to impair or damage its environment, human health, property or resources or those of other States.

---

* Refer to Guidelines for exemption of unmanned non-self-propelled (UNSP) barges from certain survey and certification requirements under the MARPOL Convention (MEPC.1/Circ.892).
** Refer to the 2021 Guidelines for exhaust gas cleaning systems (resolution MEPC.340(77)).

海底采矿活动产生的排放

3.1 按本公约第 2（3）（b）（ii）条规定，对由海底矿藏资源的勘探、开发和相关近海加工直接产生的排放免除本附则的规定。此类排放包括：

　　.1 仅焚烧直接由海底矿藏资源的勘探、开发和相关近海加工产生的物质而造成的排放，包括但不限于在完井和试验作业期间烃类物质的明火燃烧和掘出物、泥浆和/或井涌液体的燃烧，以及意外情况引起的明火燃烧；

　　.2 钻井液体和掘出物夹带的气体和挥发性化合物的释放；

　　.3 只与海底矿藏的加工、处理或贮存直接相关的排放；和

　　.4 仅用于海底矿藏资源的勘探、开发和相关近海加工的柴油机的排放。

3.2 经主管机关认可，本附则第 18 条的要求不适用于在现场生产并在现场用作燃料的烃类物质的使用。

无人非自航驳船

4 无人非自航（UNSP）驳船经过检验确认满足本附则第 2.1.32.1 至 2.1.32.3 条的条件，主管机关可以通过《无人非自航（UNSP）驳船国际防止空气污染免除证书》，免除其本附则第 5.1 和 6.1 条的要求 *，免除期限不得超过 5 年。

第 4 条　等效

1 缔约国主管机关可允许在船上安装任何装置、材料、设备或器具，或允许使用其他程序、替代燃油、或符合方法，以代替本附则所要求者，条件是这种装置、材料、设备或器具或其他程序、替代燃油、或符合方法与本附则，包括第 13 和 14 条所述的任何标准，对减排方面的要求至少同等有效。

2 允许以某种装置、材料、设备或器具或其他程序、替代燃油、或符合方法代替本附则所要求者的缔约国主管机关应将其详细资料送交本组织，以便转发各缔约国，供其参考和采取适当行动（如有）。

3 缔约国主管机关应考虑到本组织针对本条等效规定制定的任何相关导则。**

4 允许使用本条第 1 款所述等效者的缔约国主管机关应致力于不损害或不破坏本国和其他国家的环境、人类健康、财产或资源。

---

* 参见《防污公约下免除无人非自航（UNSP）驳船检验和发证要求导则》（第 MEPC.1/Circle.892 号通函）。

** 参见《2021 年废气滤清系统导则》（第 MEPC.340（77）号决议）。

Chapter 2 Survey, certification and means of control

Regulation 5 Surveys

1　Every ship of 400 gross tonnage and above and every fixed and floating drilling rig or other platform shall, to ensure compliance with the requirements of chapter 3 of this Annex, be subject to the surveys specified below:

.1　An initial survey before the ship is put into service or before the certificate required under regulation 6 of this Annex is issued for the first time. This survey shall be such as to ensure that the equipment, systems, fittings, arrangements and material fully comply with the applicable requirements of chapter 3 of this Annex;

.2　A renewal survey at intervals specified by the Administration, but not exceeding five years, except where regulation 9.2, 9.5, 9.6 or 9.7 of this Annex is applicable. The renewal survey shall be such as to ensure that the equipment, systems, fittings, arrangements and material fully comply with applicable requirements of chapter 3 of this Annex;

.3　An intermediate survey within three months before or after the second anniversary date or within three months before or after the third anniversary date of the certificate which shall take the place of one of the annual surveys specified in paragraph 1.4 of this regulation. The intermediate survey shall be such as to ensure that the equipment and arrangements fully comply with the applicable requirements of chapter 3 of this Annex and are in good working order. Such intermediate surveys shall be endorsed on the IAPP Certificate issued under regulation 6 or 7 of this Annex;

.4　An annual survey within three months before or after each anniversary date of the certificate, including a general inspection of the equipment, systems, fittings, arrangements and material referred to in paragraph 1.1 of this regulation to ensure that they have been maintained in accordance with paragraph 5 of this regulation and that they remain satisfactory for the service for which the ship is intended. Such annual surveys shall be endorsed on the IAPP Certificate issued under regulation 6 or 7 of this Annex; and

.5　An additional survey either general or partial, according to the circumstances, shall be made whenever any important repairs or renewals are made as prescribed in paragraph 5 of this regulation or after a repair resulting from investigations prescribed in paragraph 6 of this regulation. The survey shall be such as to ensure that the necessary repairs or renewals have been effectively made, that the material and workmanship of such repairs or renewals are in all respects satisfactory and that the ship complies in all respects with the requirements of chapter 3 of this Annex.

2　In the case of ships of less than 400 gross tonnage, the Administration may establish appropriate measures in order to ensure that the applicable provisions of chapter 3 of this Annex are complied with.

3　Surveys of ships as regards the enforcement of the provisions of this Annex shall be carried out by officers of the Administration.

.1　The Administration may, however, entrust the surveys either to surveyors nominated for the purpose or to organizations recognized by it. Such organizations shall comply with the guidelines adopted by the Organization; *

.2　The survey of marine diesel engines and equipment for compliance with regulation 13 of this Annex shall be conducted in accordance with the revised NOx Technical Code 2008.

---

* Refer to the Code for Recognized Organizations (RO Code) (resolution MEPC. 237(65), as may be amended). Refer also to Survey Guidelines under the Harmonized System of Survey and Certification (HSSC), 2021 (resolution A. 1156(32)).

第2章 检验、发证和监督手段

第5条 检验

1 为确保符合本附则第 3 章的要求，凡 400 总吨及以上的船舶以及固定和移动钻井平台和其他平台，应接受下列检验：

.1 初次检验，在船舶投入营运前或首次签发本附则第 6 条所要求的证书之前进行。该检验应确保其设备、系统、配件、装置和材料完全符合本附则第 3 章的适用要求；

.2 换证检验，按主管机关规定的间隔期限进行，但不得超过五年，但本附则第 9.2、9.5、9.6 或 9.7 条适用者除外。换证检验应确保其设备、系统、配件、装置和材料完全符合本附则第 3 章的适用要求；

.3 中间检验，在证书的第二个周年日之前或之后三个月内，或第三个周年日之前或之后三个月内进行，并取代本条第 1.4 项规定的其中一次年度检验。中间检验应确保设备及其装置完全符合本附则第 3 章的适用要求，并处于良好的工作状态。该中间检验应在按本附则第 6 或 7 条所签发的《国际防止空气污染证书》上予以签注；

.4 年度检验，在证书的每个周年日之前或之后三个月内进行，包括对本条第 1.1 项所述的设备、系统、配件、装置及材料的总体检查，以确保其已按本条第 5 款的规定进行保养并继续满足船舶预定的营运要求。该年度检验应在按本附则第 6 或 7 条所签发的《国际防止空气污染证书》上予以签注；和

.5 附加检验，在按本条第 5 款规定的任何重大修理或换新后，或在按本条第 6 款规定的调查结果进行修理后，应根据情况进行全面或部分检验。该检验应确保已有效地进行了必要的修理或换新，确保这种修理或换新所用的材料和工艺在各方面均合格而且该船在各方面均符合本附则第 3 章的要求。

2 对小于 400 总吨的船舶，主管机关可制定适当措施确保其符合本附则第 3 章的适用规定。

3 为执行本附则规定而对船舶进行的检验，应由主管机关的官员进行。

.1 但主管机关可将这些检验委托给为此目的而指定的验船师或由其认可的组织。这些组织应符合本组织通过的导则；[*]

.2 对船用柴油机和设备进行是否符合本附则第 13 条规定的检验应根据经修订的《2008 年氮氧化物技术规则》；

---

[*] 参见《认可组织规则》（RO 规则）（第 MEPC.237（65）号决议，可经修订）。另参见《2021 年检验与发证协调系统（HSSC）检验导则》（第 A.1156（32）号决议）。

.3 When a nominated surveyor or recognized organization determines that the condition of the equipment does not correspond substantially with the particulars of the certificate, it shall ensure that corrective action is taken and shall in due course notify the Administration. If such corrective action is not taken, the certificate shall be withdrawn by the Administration. If the ship is in a port of another Party, the appropriate authorities of the port State shall also be notified immediately. When an officer of the Administration, a nominated surveyor or recognized organization has notified the appropriate authorities of the port State, the Government of the port State concerned shall give such officer, surveyor or organization any necessary assistance to carry out their obligations under this regulation; and

.4 In every case, the Administration concerned shall fully guarantee the completeness and efficiency of the survey and shall undertake to ensure the necessary arrangements to satisfy this obligation.

4 Ships to which chapter 4 of this Annex applies shall also be subject to the surveys specified below, taking into account the guidelines adopted by the Organization: *

.1 An initial survey carried out before a new ship is put in service and before the International Energy Efficiency Certificate is issued. The survey shall verify that the ship's attained EEDI is in accordance with the requirements in chapter 4 of this Annex, and that the SEEMP required by regulation 26 of this Annex is on board;

.2 A general or partial survey, according to the circumstances, carried out after a major conversion of a new ship to which this regulation applies. The survey shall ensure that the attained EEDI is recalculated as necessary and meets the requirement of regulation 24 of this Annex, with the reduction factor applicable to the ship type and size of the converted ship in the phase corresponding to the date of contract or keel laying or delivery determined for the original ship in accordance with regulation 2.2.18 of this Annex;

.3 In cases where the major conversion of a new or existing ship is so extensive that the ship is regarded by the Administration as a newly constructed ship, the Administration shall determine the necessity of an initial survey on attained EEDI. Such a survey, if determined necessary, shall ensure that the attained EEDI is calculated and meets the requirement of regulation 24 of this Annex, with the reduction factor applicable corresponding to the ship type and size of the converted ship at the date of the contract of the conversion, or in the absence of a contract, the commencement date of the conversion. The survey shall also verify that the SEEMP required by regulation 26 of this Annex is on board and, for a ship to which regulation 27 applies, has been revised appropriately to reflect a major conversion in those cases where the major conversion affects data collection methodology and/or reporting processes;

.4 For existing ships, the verification of the requirement to have a SEEMP on board according to regulation 26 of this Annex shall take place at the first intermediate or renewal survey identified in paragraph 1 of this regulation, whichever is the first, on or after 1 January 2013;

SEE INTERPRETATION 5

.5 The Administration shall ensure that for each ship to which regulation 27 applies, the SEEMP complies with regulation 26.2 of this Annex. This shall be done prior to collecting data under regulation 27 of this Annex in order to ensure the methodology and processes are in place prior to the beginning of the ship's first reporting period. Confirmation of compliance shall be provided to and retained on board the ship;

SEE INTERPRETATION 6

---

* Refer to the 2014 Guidelines on Survey and Certification of the Energy Efficiency Design Index (resolution MEPC. 254(67), as amended by resolutions MEPC. 261(68) and MEPC. 309(73): consolidated text in MEPC.1/Circ.855/Rev.2, as may be further amended; and the 2022 Guidelines on survey and certification of the attained Energy Efficiency Existing Ship Index (EEXI) (resolution MEPC. 351(78)).

.3 经指定验船师或被认可组织在确定设备的状况在实质上与证书所载内容不符时，应确保采取纠正措施并及时通知主管机关。如未能采取此种纠正措施，主管机关应撤销证书。如该船是在另一缔约国的港口内，则还应立即通知该港口国的有关当局。当主管机关的官员、经指定验船师或被认可组织通知该港口国的有关当局后，有关的港口国政府应向该官员、验船师或组织提供履行本条规定的义务所必要的帮助；和

.4 在所有情况下，主管机关均应保证检验的完整性和有效性，确保为履行这一义务作出必要的安排。

4 适用本附则第 4 章的船舶还应进行下列规定的检验，并考虑到本组织通过的导则[*]：

.1 初次检验，在新船投入营运之前和签发《国际船舶能效证书》之前进行。检验应验证船舶达到的能效设计指数符合本附则第 4 章的要求，并且船上保存第 26 条要求的《船舶能效管理计划》；

.2 在适用本条的新船发生重大改建后，根据情况进行的全面或部分检验。检验应保证，必要时重新计算达到的能效设计指数并满足本附则第 24 条的要求，其折减系数为按本附则第 2.2.18 条确定原始船舶的签订合同日期或安放龙骨日期或交船日期所对应的那个阶段中适用于该改建船舶的船型和尺寸的折减系数；

.3 如新船或现有船舶重大改建的范围大至被主管机关视为新建船舶，主管机关应确定对达到的能效设计指数进行初次检验的必要性。如确定必要，该检验应确保计算达到的能效设计指数并满足本附则第 24 条的要求，其折减系数应与签订改建合同之日，或无合同情况下改建开始之日该改建船舶的船型和尺度相符。该检验还应验证船上保存本附则第 26 条要求的《船舶能效管理计划》，且适用第 27 条的船舶，在重大改建影响到数据收集方法和 / 或报告程序情况时做出适当修订；

.4 对现有船舶，对根据本附则第 26 条在船上保存船舶能效管理计划要求的验证应在 2013 年 1 月 1 日或以后，在本条第 1 款所述的首次中间或换证检验时进行，取早者；

见统一解释 5

.5 主管机关应确保适用第 27 条的每艘船舶，其《船舶能效管理计划》符合本附则第 26.2 条。本要求应在按照本附则第 27 条收集数据之前完成，以确保船舶首次报告期开始前方法和程序已就绪。应向船舶提供符合声明并保存在船上；

见统一解释 6

---

[*] 参见《2014 年能效设计指数检验和发证导则》（第 MEPC.254（67）号决议，经第 MEPC.261（88）号决议和第 MEPC.309（73）号决议修订）：综合文本见第 MEPC.1/Circle.855/Rev.2 号通函，后可经修订；及《2022 年现有船舶达到的能效指数（EEXI）检验和发证导则》（第 MEPC.351（78）号决议）。

.6 The Administration shall ensure that, for each ship to which regulation 28 applies, the SEEMP complies with regulation 26.3.1 of this Annex. This shall be done prior to 1 January 2023. Confirmation of compliance shall be provided to and retained on board, the ship;

.7 The verification that the ship's attained EEXI is in accordance with the requirements in regulations 23 and 25 of this Annex shall take place at the first annual, intermediate or renewal survey identified in paragraph 1 of this regulation or the initial survey identified in paragraphs 4.1 and 4.3 of this regulation, whichever is the first, on or after 1 January 2023; and

.8 Notwithstanding paragraph 4.7 of this regulation, a general or partial survey, according to the circumstances, carried out after a major conversion of a ship to which regulation 23 of this Annex applies. The survey shall ensure that the attained EEXI is recalculated as necessary and meets the requirement of regulation 25 of this Annex.

5 The equipment shall be maintained to conform with the provisions of this Annex and no changes shall be made in the equipment, systems, fittings, arrangements or material covered by the survey, without the express approval of the Administration. The direct replacement of such equipment and fittings with equipment and fittings that conform with the provisions of this Annex is permitted.

6 Whenever an accident occurs to a ship or a defect is discovered that substantially affects the efficiency or completeness of its equipment covered by this Annex, the master or owner of the ship shall report at the earliest opportunity to the Administration, a nominated surveyor or recognized organization responsible for issuing the relevant certificate.

Regulation 6 Issue or endorsement of Certificates and Statements of Compliance related to fuel oil consumption reporting and operational carbon intensity rating

International Air Pollution Prevention Certificate

1 An International Air Pollution Prevention (IAPP) Certificate shall be issued, after an initial or renewal survey in accordance with the provisions of regulation 5 of this Annex, to:

.1 any ship of 400 gross tonnage and above engaged in voyages to ports or offshore terminals under the jurisdiction of other Parties; and

.2 platforms and drilling rigs engaged in voyages to waters under the sovereignty or jurisdiction of other Parties.

2 A ship constructed before the date this Annex enters into force for that particular ship's Administration, shall be issued with an IAPP Certificate in accordance with paragraph 1 of this regulation no later than the first scheduled dry-docking after the date of such entry into force, but in no case later than three years after this date.

3 Such certificate shall be issued or endorsed either by the Administration or by any person or organization duly authorized by it. In every case, the Administration assumes full responsibility for the certificate.

International Energy Efficiency Certificate

4 An International Energy Efficiency Certificate for the ship shall be issued after a survey in accordance with the provisions of regulation 5.4 of this Annex to any ship of 400 gross tonnage and above before that ship may engage in voyages to ports or offshore terminals under the jurisdiction of other Parties.

SEE INTERPRETATION 5

5 The certificate shall be issued or endorsed either by the Administration or any organization duly authorized by it*. In every case, the Administration assumes full responsibility for the certificate.

* Refer to the Code for Recognized Organizations (RO Code) (resolution MEPC. 237(65), as may be amended).

.6 主管机关应在 2023 年 1 月 1 日之前，确保适用第 28 条的每艘船舶，其《船舶能效管理计划》符合本附则第 26.3.1 条，并向船舶提供符合声明并保存在船上；

.7 验证现有船舶达到的能效指数是否符合本附则第 23 和 25 条的要求，应在 2023 年 1 月 1 日或之后，按本条第 1 款所述的首次年度、中间或换证检验或本条第 4.1 和 4.3 款所述的初次检验时进行，取早者；和

.8 尽管有本条第 4.7 款的规定，在对适用本附则第 23 条的船舶进行重大改建后，应根据具体情况进行全面或部分检验。检验应确保必要时重新计算现有船舶达到的能效指数，并满足本附则第 25 条的要求。

5 设备应保持符合本附则的各项规定，未经主管机关的专门批准，经过检验的设备、系统、配件、布置或材料不得有任何变动。但允许以符合本附则规定的设备和配件直接替换此类设备和附件。

6 当船舶发生事故或发现缺陷，对本附则所涉及的设备的有效性或完整性产生重大影响时，该船的船长或船舶所有人应尽早向负责签发有关证书的主管机关、经指定验船师或被认可组织报告。

第 6 条　证书和有关《燃油消耗报告和营运碳强度评级符合声明》的签发或签注

国际防止空气污染证书

1 在按本附则第 5 条规定进行了初次或换证检验后，应为下列船舶签发《国际防止空气污染证书》（IAPP）：

.1 驶往其他缔约国管辖范围的港口或近海装卸站的所有 400 总吨及以上的船舶；和

.2 驶往其他缔约国主权或管辖海域的平台和钻井平台。

2 对某一特定船舶，如建造于本附则对其主管机关生效日之前，应按照本条第 1 款，在不迟于生效之日后的第一次计划干坞检修时签发《国际防止空气污染证书》，但在任何情况下不得迟于该生效日后三年。

3 该证书应由主管机关或经其正式授权的任何个人或组织签发或签注。在任何情况下，主管机关对证书负有全部责任。

国际能效证书

4 对任何可能驶往其他缔约国管辖范围的港口或近海装卸站的 400 总吨及以上的船舶，在按本附则第 5.4 条规定进行了检验后，应在其开航前为其签发《国际能效证书》。

见统一解释 5

---

5 该证书应由主管机关或经其正式授权的任何组织 * 签发或签注。在任何情况下，主管机关对证书负有全部责任。

---

* 参见《认可组织规则》（RO 规则）（第 MEPC.237（65）号决议，可经修订）。

Statement of Compliance related to fuel oil consumption reporting and operational carbon intensity rating

6   Upon receipt of reported data pursuant to regulation 27.3 of this Annex and attained annual operational CII pursuant to regulation 28.2 of this Annex, the Administration or any organization duly authorized by it shall:

.1   determine whether the data has been reported in accordance with regulation 27 of this Annex;

.2   verify that the attained annual operational CII reported is based on the data submitted in accordance with regulation 27 of this Annex;

.3   based on the verified attained annual operational CII, determine the operational carbon intensity rating of the ship in accordance with regulation 28.6 of this Annex; and

.4   issue a Statement of Compliance related to fuel oil consumption reporting and operational carbon intensity rating to the ship no later than five months from the beginning of the calendar year, upon determination and verification pursuant to regulations 6.6.1 to 6.6.3 of this Annex. In every case, the Administration assumes full responsibility for this Statement of Compliance.

7   Upon receipt of reported data pursuant to regulations 27.4, 27.5 or 27.6 of this Annex, the Administration or any organization duly authorized by it* shall promptly determine whether the data has been reported in accordance with regulation 27 and, if so, issue a Statement of Compliance to the ship. In every case, the Administration assumes full responsibility for this Statement of Compliance.

8   Notwithstanding paragraph 6 of this regulation, a ship rated as D for three consecutive years or rated as E in accordance with regulation 28 of this Annex shall not be issued a Statement of Compliance unless a plan of corrective actions is duly developed and reflected in the SEEMP and verified by the Administration or any organization duly authorized by it in accordance with regulations 28.7 and 28.8 of this Annex.

Regulation 7 Issue of a Certificate by another Party

1   A Party may, at the request of the Administration, cause a ship to be surveyed and, if satisfied that the provisions of this Annex are complied with, shall issue or authorize the issue of an IAPP Certificate or an International Energy Efficiency Certificate to the ship, and where appropriate, endorse or authorize the endorsement of such certificates on the ship, in accordance with this Annex.

2   A copy of the certificate and a copy of the survey report shall be transmitted as soon as possible to the requesting Administration.

3   A certificate so issued shall contain a statement to the effect that it has been issued at the request of the Administration and it shall have the same force and receive the same recognition as a certificate issued under regulation 6 of this Annex.

4   No IAPP Certificate, International Energy Efficiency Certificate or UNSP Exemption Certificate shall be issued to a ship which is entitled to fly the flag of a State which is not a Party.

Regulation 8 Form of Certificates and Statements of Compliance related to fuel oil consumption reporting and operational carbon intensity rating

International Air Pollution Prevention Certificate

1   The IAPP Certificate shall be drawn up in a form corresponding to the model given in appendix I to this Annex and shall be at least in English, French or Spanish. If an official language of the issuing country is also used, this shall prevail in case of a dispute or discrepancy.

SEE INTERPRETATION 7

---

* Refer to the Code for Recognized Organizations (RO Code) (resolution MEPC. 237(65), as may be amended).

燃油消耗报告和营运碳强度评级符合声明

6 在收到按照本附则第 27.3 条报告的数据，以及按照本附则第 28.2 条提交的达到的年度营运碳强度指标时，主管机关或经其正式授权的任一组织应：

    .1 确定数据是否按照本附则第 27 条报告；

    .2 验证其报告的达到的年度营运碳强度指标系基于根据本附则第 27 条提交的数据；

    .3 依据经验证的达到的年度营运碳强度指标，按照本附则第 28.6 条确定船舶的营运碳强度评级；和

    .4 在按照本附则第 6.6.1 至 6.6.3 条进行确认并验证后，自日历年开始后不晚于五个月内，为船舶签发《燃油消耗报告和营运碳强度评级符合声明》。在任何情况下，主管机关对符合声明负有全部责任。

7 在收到按照本附则第 27.4、27.5 或 27.6 条报告的数据时，主管机关或经其正式授权的任一组织[*]应立即确认数据是否按照本附则第 27 条报告，如是，为船舶签发符合声明。在任何情况下，主管机关对符合声明负有全部责任。

8 尽管有本条第 6 款的规定，不得向按照本附则第 28 条连续三年被评为 D 级或被评为 E 级的船舶签发符合声明，除非已适当制定纠正行动并反映在《船舶能效管理计划》中，并由主管机关或经其正式授权的任一组织按照本附则第 28.7 和 28.8 条进行了验证。

第 7 条　由另一缔约国签发证书

1 应主管机关的请求，一缔约国可对船舶进行检验，如果认为其符合本附则的规定，应为该船签发或授权签发《国际防止空气污染证书》或《国际能效证书》，并在适用时，按照本附则为该船签注或授权签注证书。

2 证书和检验报告副本各一份应尽快送交提出请求的主管机关。

3 所发证书应声明，该证书系根据主管机关的请求签发，并应与按本附则第 6 条规定所签发的证书具有同等效力和得到同样的承认。

4 对于悬挂非缔约国国旗的船舶，不得向其签发《国际防止空气污染证书》、《国际能效证书》或《无人非自航驳船免除证书》。

第 8 条　证书和《燃油消耗报告和营运碳强度评级符合声明》格式

国际防止空气污染证书

1 《国际防止空气污染证书》应按与本附则附录 I 所示范本相一致的格式，并应至少以英文、法文或西班牙文写成。如同时使用发证国的官方语言，则在有争议或分歧时，应以该国官方语言文本为准。

见统一解释 7

---

[*] 参见《认可组织规则》（RO 规则）（第 MEPC.237（65）号决议，可经修订）。

International Energy Efficiency Certificate

2   The International Energy Efficiency Certificate shall be drawn up in a form corresponding to the model given in appendix VIII to this Annex and shall be at least in English, French or Spanish. If an official language of the issuing Party is also used, this shall prevail in case of a dispute or discrepancy.

Statement of Compliance related to fuel oil consumption reporting and operational carbon intensity rating

3   The Statement of Compliance pursuant to regulations 6.6 and 6.7 of this Annex shall be drawn up in a form corresponding to the model given in appendix X to this Annex and shall be at least in English, French or Spanish. If an official language of the issuing Party is also used, this shall prevail in case of a dispute or discrepancy.

SEE INTERPRETATION 8

International Air Pollution Prevention Exemption Certificate for Unmanned Non-self-propelled Barges

4   In accordance with regulation 3.4 of this Annex, the International Air Pollution Prevention Exemption Certificate for Unmanned Non-self-propelled Barges shall be drawn up in the form corresponding to the model given in appendix XI to this Annex and shall be at least in English, French or Spanish. If an official language of the issuing country is also used, this shall prevail in the event of a dispute or discrepancy.

Regulation 9 Duration and validity of Certificates and Statements of Compliance related to fuel oil consumption reporting and operational carbon intensity rating

International Air Pollution Prevention Certificate

1   An IAPP Certificate shall be issued for a period specified by the Administration, which shall not exceed five years.

2   Notwithstanding the requirements of paragraph 1 of this regulation:

.1   when the renewal survey is completed within three months before the expiry date of the existing certificate, the new certificate shall be valid from the date of completion of the renewal survey to a date not exceeding five years from the date of expiry of the existing certificate;

.2   when the renewal survey is completed after the expiry date of the existing certificate, the new certificate shall be valid from the date of completion of the renewal survey to a date not exceeding five years from the date of expiry of the existing certificate; and

.3   when the renewal survey is completed more than three months before the expiry date of the existing certificate, the new certificate shall be valid from the date of completion of the renewal survey to a date not exceeding five years from the date of completion of the renewal survey.

3   If a certificate is issued for a period of less than five years, the Administration may extend the validity of the certificate beyond the expiry date to the maximum period specified in paragraph 1 of this regulation, provided that the surveys referred to in regulations 5.1.3 and 5.1.4 of this Annex applicable when a certificate is issued for a period of five years are carried out as appropriate.

4   If a renewal survey has been completed and a new certificate cannot be issued or placed on board the ship before the expiry date of the existing certificate, the person or organization authorized by the Administration may endorse the existing certificate and such a certificate shall be accepted as valid for a further period that shall not exceed five months from the expiry date.

5   If a ship, at the time when a certificate expires, is not in a port in which it is to be surveyed, the Administration may extend the period of validity of the certificate, but this extension shall be granted only for the purpose of allowing the ship to complete its voyage to the port in which it is to be surveyed, and then only in cases where it appears proper and reasonable to do so. No certificate shall be extended for a period longer than three months, and a ship to which an extension is granted shall not, on its arrival in the port in which it is to be surveyed, be entitled by virtue of such extension to leave that port without having a new certificate. When the renewal survey is completed, the new certificate shall be valid to a date not exceeding five years from the date of expiry of the existing certificate before the extension was granted.

国际能效证书

2 《国际能效证书》应按与本附则附录Ⅷ所示范本相一致的格式，并应至少以英文、法文或西班牙文写成。如同时使用发证国的官方语言，则在有争议或分歧时，应以该国官方语言文本为准。

燃油消耗报告和营运碳强度评级符合声明

3 按照本附则第6.6和6.7条的符合声明应按与本附则附录Ⅹ所示范本相一致的格式，并应至少以英文、法文或西班牙文写成。如同时使用发证国的官方语言，则在有争议或分歧时，应以该国官方语言文本为准。

见统一解释8

无人非自航驳船国际防止空气污染免除证书

4 按照本附则第3.4条，《无人非自航驳船国际防止空气污染免除证书》应按与本附则附录Ⅺ所示范本相一致的格式，并应至少以英文、法文或西班牙文写成。如同时使用发证国的官方语言，则在有争议或分歧时，应以该国官方语言文本为准。

第9条 证书和《燃油消耗报告和营运碳强度评级符合声明》的有效期和有效性

国际防止空气污染证书

1 《国际防止空气污染证书》的有效期限由主管机关规定，但不得超过五年。

2 尽管有本条第1款的要求：

 .1 如果换证检验在现有证书期满之日前三个月内完成，则新证书应从换证检验完成之日起，至现有证书期满之日后不超过五年的日期内有效；

 .2 如果换证检验在现有证书期满之日后完成，则新证书应从换证检验完成之日起，至现有证书期满之日后不超过五年的日期内有效；和

 .3 如果换证检验早于现有证书期满之日前三个月以上完成，则新证书应从换证检验完成之日起，至不超过五年的日期内有效。

3 如果所发证书的有效期限短于五年，主管机关可将证书有效期自期满日延长至本条第1款规定的最长期限，条件是在签发五年期的证书时进行了本附则第5.1.3和5.1.4条所述的相应检验。

4 如果换证检验已完成，而新证书在现有证书期满之日前不能签发或不能存放在船上，经主管机关授权的人员或组织可在现有证书上签注，签注后的证书自期满日起不超过五个月的期限内应视为继续有效。

5 如果证书期满时船舶不在应进行检验的港口，主管机关可展延该证书的有效期，但此项展期仅以能使该船完成其驶抵应进行检验的港口的航次为限，并且仅在正当和合理的情况下才能采取此种方法。证书的展期不得超过三个月。获得展期的船舶在抵达应进行检验的港口后，不得因有此项展期而在没有获得新证书的情况下驶离该港口。换证检验完成后，新证书的有效期应自现有证书展期前的期满日起不超过五年。

6　A certificate issued to a ship engaged on short voyages that has not been extended under the foregoing provisions of this regulation may be extended by the Administration for a period of grace of up to one month from the date of expiry stated on it. When the renewal survey is completed, the new certificate shall be valid to a date not exceeding five years from the date of expiry of the existing certificate before the extension was granted.

7　In special circumstances, as determined by the Administration, a new certificate need not be dated from the date of expiry of the existing certificate as required by paragraph 2.1, 5 or 6 of this regulation. In these special circumstances, the new certificate shall be valid to a date not exceeding five years from the date of completion of the renewal survey.

8　If an annual or intermediate survey is completed before the period specified in regulation 5 of this Annex, then:

.1　the anniversary date shown on the certificate shall be amended by endorsement to a date that shall not be more than three months later than the date on which the survey was completed;

.2　the subsequent annual or intermediate survey required by regulation 5 of this Annex shall be completed at the intervals prescribed by that regulation using the new anniversary date; and

.3　the expiry date may remain unchanged, provided one or more annual or intermediate surveys, as appropriate, are carried out so that the maximum intervals between the surveys prescribed by regulation 5 of this Annex are not exceeded.

9　A certificate issued under regulation 6 or 7 of this Annex shall cease to be valid in any of the following cases:

.1　if the relevant surveys are not completed within the periods specified under regulation 5.1 of this Annex;

.2　if the certificate is not endorsed in accordance with regulation 5.1.3 or 5.1.4 of this Annex; and

.3　upon transfer of the ship to the flag of another State. A new certificate shall only be issued when the Government issuing the new certificate is fully satisfied that the ship is in compliance with the requirements of regulation 5.4 of this Annex. In the case of a transfer between Parties, if requested within three months after the transfer has taken place, the Government of the Party whose flag the ship was formerly entitled to fly shall, as soon as possible, transmit to the Administration copies of the certificate carried by the ship before the transfer and, if available, copies of the relevant survey reports.

International Energy Efficiency Certificate

10　The International Energy Efficiency Certificate shall be valid throughout the life of the ship subject to the provisions of paragraph 11 below.

11　An International Energy Efficiency Certificate issued under this Annex shall cease to be valid in any of the following cases:

.1　if the ship is withdrawn from service or if a new certificate is issued following major conversion of the ship; or

.2　upon transfer of the ship to the flag of another State. A new certificate shall only be issued when the Government issuing the new certificate is fully satisfied that the ship is in compliance with the requirements of chapter 4 of this Annex. In the case of a transfer between Parties, if requested within three months after the transfer has taken place, the Government of the Party whose flag the ship was formerly entitled to fly shall, as soon as possible, transmit to the Administration copies of the certificate carried by the ship before the transfer and, if available, copies of the relevant survey reports; or

.3　if the ship's equipment, systems, fittings, arrangements, or material covered by the survey were changed without the express approval of the Administration, as provided for in regulation 5.5 of this Annex, unless regulation 3 of this Annex applies.

6 发给短程航行船舶的证书未按本条前述之规定展期时，主管机关可给予自该证书所示的期满之日起至多一个月的宽限期。换证检验完成后，新证书的有效期应自现有证书展期前的期满日起不超过五年。

7 在特殊情况下（由主管机关确定），新证书无须按本条第 2.1、5 或 6 款的要求从现有证书的期满之日起计算日期。在此特殊情况下，新证书的有效期应自换证检验完成之日起不超过五年。

8 如年度检验或中间检验在本附则第 5 条规定的期限前完成，则：

 .1 证书上所示的周年日应予以签注修正，修正后的周年日不得超过检验完成之日起三个月；

 .2 本附则第 5 条要求的其后的年度检验或中间检验应使用新的周年日按该条规定的间隔期完成；和

 .3 如进行一次或多次相应的年度检验或中间检验，以使本附则第 5 条规定的最大检验间隔期不被超过，则该期满日可保持不变。

9 按本附则第 6 或 7 条签发的证书，在下列任一情况下应不再有效：

 .1 如果相关检验未在本附则第 5.1 条规定的期限内完成；

 .2 如果证书未按本附则第 5.1.3 或 5.1.4 条予以签注；和

 .3 船舶变更船旗国。只有当换发新证书的政府认为该船符合本附则第 5.4 条的要求时，才签发新的证书。如果变更船旗系在缔约国之间进行，则在变更后的三个月内，前船旗国政府接到请求后，尽快将变更船旗前该船所携证书的副本以及相关的检验报告副本（如有）送交该船新的主管机关。

国际能效证书

10 除下述第 11 款的规定外，《国际能效证书》应在船舶整个寿命期间内有效。

11 按本附则签发的《国际能效证书》在下列任一情况下应不再有效：

 .1 如果船舶退出营运或船舶经重大改建后对其签发新证书；或

 .2 船舶变更船旗国。只有在换发新证书的政府确认该船符合本附则第 4 章的要求时，才签发新的证书。如果变更船旗系在缔约国之间进行，则在变更后的三个月内，前船旗国政府接到请求后，应尽快将变更船旗前该船所携证书的副本以及相关的检验报告副本（如有）送交该船新的主管机关；或

 .3 经过检验的船舶设备、系统、配件、布置或材料的改变未按照本附则第 5.5 条的规定经主管机关的专门批准，适用木附则第 3 条者除外。

Statement of Compliance related to fuel oil consumption reporting and operational carbon intensity rating

12   The Statement of Compliance issued pursuant to regulation 6.6 of this Annex shall be valid for the calendar year in which it is issued and for the first five months of the following calendar year. The Statement of Compliance issued pursuant to regulation 6.7 of this Annex shall be valid for the calendar year in which it is issued, for the following calendar year, and for the first five months of the subsequent calendar year. All Statements of Compliance shall be kept on board for at least five years.

Regulation 10 Port State control on operational requirements

1   A ship, when in a port or an offshore terminal under the jurisdiction of another Party, is subject to inspection by officers duly authorized by such Party concerning operational requirements under this Annex,* where there are clear grounds for believing that the master or crew are not familiar with essential shipboard procedures relating to the prevention of air pollution from ships.

2   In the circumstances given in paragraph 1 of this regulation, the Party shall take steps to ensure that the ship shall not sail until the situation has been brought to order in accordance with the requirements of this Annex.

3   Procedures relating to the port State control prescribed in article 5 of the present Convention shall apply to this regulation.

4   Nothing in this regulation shall be construed to limit the rights and obligations of a Party carrying out control over operational requirements specifically provided for in the present Convention.

5   In relation to chapter 4 of this Annex, any port State inspection may verify, when appropriate, that there is a valid Statement of Compliance related to fuel oil consumption reporting and operational carbon intensity rating, an International Energy Efficiency Certificate and a Ship Energy Efficiency Management Plan on board, in accordance with article 5 of the present Convention.

6   Notwithstanding the requirements in paragraph 5 of this regulation, any port State inspection may inspect whether the Ship Energy Efficiency Management Plan is duly implemented by the ship in accordance with regulation 28 of this Annex.

Regulation 11 Detection of violations and enforcement

1   Parties shall cooperate in the detection of violations and the enforcement of the provisions of this Annex, using all appropriate and practicable measures of detection and environmental monitoring, and adequate procedures for reporting and accumulation of evidence.

2   A ship to which this Annex applies may, in any port or offshore terminal of a Party, be subject to inspection by officers appointed or authorized by that Party for the purpose of verifying whether the ship has emitted any of the substances covered by this Annex in violation of the provision of this Annex. If an inspection indicates a violation of this Annex, a report shall be forwarded to the Administration for any appropriate action.

3   Any Party shall furnish to the Administration evidence, if any, that the ship has emitted any of the substances covered by this Annex in violation of the provisions of this Annex. If it is practicable to do so, the competent authority of the former Party shall notify the master of the ship of the alleged violation.

4   Upon receiving such evidence, the Administration shall investigate the matter and may request the other Party to furnish further or better evidence of the alleged contravention. If the Administration is satisfied that sufficient evidence is available to enable proceedings to be brought in respect of the alleged violation, it shall cause such proceedings to betaken in accordance with its law as soon as possible. The Administration shall promptly inform the Party that has reported the alleged violation, as well as the Organization, of the action taken.

---

* Refer to the Procedures for port State control, 2021 (resolution A.1155(32)). Refer also to the 2019 Guidelines for port State control under MARPOL Annex VI Chapter 3 (resolution MEPC. 321(74)).

燃油消耗报告和营运碳强度评级符合声明

12　按照本附则第6.6条签发的符合声明应在其签发日历年和下一日历年的前五个月有效。按照本附则第6.7条签发的符合声明应在其签发日历年和下一日历年以及随后日历年的前五个月有效。所有符合声明应至少在船上保存五年。

第10条　关于操作性要求的港口国监督

1　当船舶停靠在另一缔约国所管辖的港口或近海装卸站时，如有明显理由确信该船船长或船员不熟悉船上主要的防止船舶造成空气污染程序，该船应接受该缔约国正式授权的官员按照本附则进行的有关操作性要求的检查。*

2　在本条第1款所述的情况下，该缔约国应采取措施，确保该船在按本附则的要求调整至正常状态前，不得开航。

3　本公约第5条规定的港口国监督程序应适用于本条。

4　本条的任何内容均不得解释为限制缔约国在本公约明确规定的操作要求方面进行监督的权利和义务。

5　与本附则第4章有关的任何港口国检查可按照本公约第5条核实（如适用）船上是否备有有效的《燃油消耗报告和营运碳强度评级符合声明》、《国际能效证书》和《船舶能效管理计划》。

6　尽管有本条第5款的要求，港口国检查可以检查船舶是否按照本附则第28条适当地实施了《船舶能效管理计划》。

第11条　对违规事件的侦查和执法

1　各缔约国应使用一切适当和可行的侦查和环境监测措施、合适的报告和证据收集程序，在查明违规事件和执行本附则规定方面进行合作。

2　适用本附则的船舶，在某一缔约国的任何港口或近海装卸站均可受到由该缔约国指定或授权的官员的检查，以核实该船是否违反本附则的规定而排放了本附则所包括的任何物质。如检查表明有违反本附则的事件，应向主管机关提交一份报告以便采取适当行动。

3　任何缔约国应向该主管机关提供其船舶违反本附则规定已排放本附则所包括的任何物质的证据（如有）。如可行，该缔约国的主管当局应将所指称违规事件通知该船船长。

4　在收到此类证据后，被通知的主管机关应对此事进行调查，并可要求其他缔约国对所指称违规提供进一步的或更完善的证据。如果该主管机关确信有充分的证据可对所指称违规事件提起诉讼，应尽快按照法律规定启动诉讼程序。该主管机关应将所采取的行动立即通知报告所指称违规事件的缔约国，以及本组织。

---

*　参见《2021年港口国监督程序》（第A.1155（32）号决议）。另参见《防污公约附则 VI 第3章下的港口国监督导则》（第MEPC.321（74）号决议）。

5   A Party may also inspect a ship to which this Annex applies when it enters the ports or offshore terminals under its jurisdiction, if a request for an investigation is received from any Party together with sufficient evidence that the ship has emitted any of the substances covered by the Annex in any place in violation of this Annex. The report of such investigation shall be sent to the Party requesting it and to the Administration so that the appropriate action may be taken under the present Convention.

6   The international law concerning the prevention, reduction and control of pollution of the marine environment from ships, including that law relating to enforcement and safeguards, in force at the time of application or interpretation of this Annex, applies, mutatis mutandis, to the rules and standards set forth in this Annex.

Chapter 3 Requirements for control of emissions from ships

Regulation 12 Ozone-depleting substances

1   This regulation does not apply to permanently sealed equipment where there are no refrigerant charging connections or potentially removable components containing ozone-depleting substances.

2   Subject to the provisions of regulation 3.1, any deliberate emissions of ozone-depleting substances shall be prohibited. Deliberate emissions include emissions occurring in the course of maintaining, servicing, repairing or disposing of systems or equipment, except that deliberate emissions do not include minimal releases associated with the recapture or recycling of an ozone-depleting substance. Emissions arising from leaks of an ozone-depleting substance, whether or not the leaks are deliberate, may be regulated by Parties.

3.1 Installations that contain ozone-depleting substances, other than hydrochlorofluorocarbons, shall be prohibited:

　.1   on ships constructed on or after 19 May 2005; or

　.2   in the case of ships constructed before 19 May 2005 which have a contractual delivery date of the equipment to the ship on or after 19 May 2005 or, in the absence of a contractual delivery date, the actual delivery of the equipment to the ship on or after 19 May 2005.

3.2 Installations that contain hydrochlorofluorocarbons shall be prohibited:

　.1   on ships constructed on or after 1 January 2020; or

　.2   in the case of ships constructed before 1 January 2020 which have a contractual delivery date of the equipment to the ship on or after 1 January 2020 or, in the absence of a contractual delivery date, the actual delivery of the equipment to the ship on or after 1 January 2020.

4   The substances referred to in this regulation, and equipment containing such substances, shall be delivered to appropriate reception facilities when removed from ships.

5   Each ship subject to regulation 6.1 shall maintain a list of equipment containing ozone-depleting substances.*

6   Each ship subject to regulation 6.1 that has rechargeable systems that contain ozone-depleting substances shall maintain an ozone-depleting substances record book. This record book may form part of an existing logbook or electronic record book as approved by the Administration. An electronic recording system referred to in regulation 12.6, as adopted by resolution MEPC.176(58), shall be considered an electronic record book, provided the electronic recording system is approved by the Administration on or before the first IAPP Certificate renewal survey carried out on or after 1 October 2020, but not later than 1 October 2025, taking into account the guidelines developed by the Organization. **

* See appendix I, Supplement to International Air Pollution Prevention Certificate (IAPP Certificate), section 2.1.
** Refer to Guidelines for the use of electronic record books under MARPOL (resolution MEPC. 312(74)).

5 如果收到任何缔约国的调查请求，连同船舶违反本附则规定在任何地方已排放本附则所包括的任何物质的充分证据，则缔约国也可对适用本附则的船舶在其进入该缔约国管辖的港口或近海装卸站时进行检查。这种调查报告应送交提出请求的缔约国以及主管机关，以便根据本公约规定采取适当的行动。

6 在适用或解释本附则时正在实施的关于防止、减少和控制船舶造成海洋环境污染的国际法，包括有关实施和保护的法律，在细节上作必要的修正后均适用于本附则所述的规范和标准。

第 3 章　船舶排放控制要求

第 12 条　消耗臭氧物质

1 本条不适用于无制冷剂充注接头的永久密封设备或无可拆卸的含有消耗臭氧物质部件的永久密封设备。

2 在第 3.1 条规定的前提下，应禁止消耗臭氧物质的任何故意排放。故意排放包括在系统或设备的维护、检修、修理或处置过程中发生的排放，但故意排放不包括与消耗臭氧物质的回收或循环使用产生的微量释放。由消耗臭氧物质泄漏引起的排放，无论此泄漏是否属于故意，由各缔约国进行管理。

3.1 在下列情形里，应禁止使用含消耗臭氧物质（氢化氯氟烃除外）的装置：

　　.1 在 2005 年 5 月 19 日或以后建造的船舶；或

　　.2 对于 2005 年 5 月 19 日以前建造的船舶，设备交付船上的合同日期为 2005 年 5 月 19 日或以后，或者无合同交付日期，设备交付船上的实际日期为 2005 年 5 月 19 日或以后。

3.2 在下列情形里，应禁止使用含氢化氯氟烃的装置：

　　.1 在 2020 年 1 月 1 日或以后建造的船舶；或

　　.2 对于 2020 年 1 月 1 日以前建造的船舶，设备交付船上的合同日期为 2020 年 1 月 1 日或以后，或者无合同交付日期，设备交付船上的实际日期为 2020 年 1 月 1 日或以后。

4 本条所述的物质以及含有此类物质的设备，当其从船上拆解后，应送到合适的接收设施中。

5 受第 6.1 条约束的每艘船舶应保存一份含消耗臭氧物质的设备清单。*

6 适用第 6.1 条的设有含消耗臭氧物质的可重新充注系统的每艘船舶应保存一份《消耗臭氧物质记录簿》。经主管机关批准，该记录簿可以是现有航海日志或电子记录簿的一部分。经第 MEPC.176（58）号决议通过的第 12.6 条中所述的电子记录系统，如经主管机关虑及本组织制定的导则于 2020 年 10 月 1 日或之后，但不迟于 2025 年 10 月 1 日进行初次《国际防止空气污染证书》换证检验之日或之前予以批准，则须视为电子记录簿。**

---

* 见附录Ⅰ，国际防止大气污染证书（IAPP 证书）的附页第 2.1 节。

** 参见《防污公约下的电子记录簿使用导则》（第 MEPC.312（74）号决议）。

7   Entries in the ozone-depleting substances record book shall be recorded in terms of mass (kg) of substance and shall be completed without delay on each occasion, in respect of the following:

.1   recharge, full or partial, of equipment containing ozone-depleting substances;

.2   repair or maintenance of equipment containing ozone-depleting substances;

.3   discharge of ozone-depleting substances to the atmosphere:

.3.1   deliberate; and

.3.2   non-deliberate;

.4   discharge of ozone-depleting substances to land-based reception facilities; and

.5   supply of ozone-depleting substances to the ship.

Regulation 13 Nitrogen oxides (NOx)

Application

1.1 This regulation shall apply to:

.1   each marine diesel engine with a power output of more than 130 kW installed on a ship; and

.2   each marine diesel engine with a power output of more than 130 kW that undergoes a major conversion on or after 1 January 2000 except when demonstrated to the satisfaction of the Administration that such engine is an identical replacement to the engine that it is replacing and is otherwise not covered under paragraph 1.1.1 of this regulation.

SEE INTERPRETATION 9

1.2 This regulation does not apply to:

.1   a marine diesel engine intended to be used solely for emergencies or solely to power any device or equipment intended to be used solely for emergencies on the ship on which it is installed, or a marine diesel engine installed in lifeboats intended to be used solely for emergencies; and

.2   a marine diesel engine installed on a ship solely engaged in voyages within waters subject to the sovereignty or jurisdiction of the State the flag of which the ship is entitled to fly, provided that such engine is subject to an alternative NOx control measure established by the Administration.

1.3 Notwithstanding the provisions of paragraph 1.1 of this regulation, the Administration may provide an exclusion from the application of this regulation for any marine diesel engine that is installed on a ship constructed, or for any marine diesel engine that undergoes a major conversion, before 19 May 2005, provided that the ship on which the engine is installed is solely engaged in voyages to ports or offshore terminals within the State the flag of which the ship is entitled to fly.

Major conversion

2.1 For the purpose of this regulation, major conversion means a modification on or after 1 January 2000 of a marine diesel engine that has not already been certified to the standards set forth in paragraph 3, 4 or 5.1.1 of this regulation where:

.1   the engine is replaced by a marine diesel engine or an additional marine diesel engine is installed, or

.2   any substantial modification, as defined in the revised NOx Technical Code 2008, is made to the engine, or

.3   the maximum continuous rating of the engine is increased by more than 10% compared to the maximum continuous rating of the original certification of the engine.

7 消耗臭氧物质记录簿中的物质应按其质量单位（kg）记录，且在任何情况下都应及时记入下列内容：

.1 含消耗臭氧物质的设备的全部或部分重新充注；

.2 含消耗臭氧物质的设备的修理或维护；

.3 向大气排放消耗臭氧物质：

.3.1 故意排放；和

.3.2 非故意排放；

.4 向岸基接收设施排放消耗臭氧物质；和

.5 向船舶供应消耗臭氧物质。

第13条　氮氧化物（NOx）

适用范围

1.1 本条应适用于：

.1 安装在船上的输出功率超过 130 kW 的船用柴油机；和

.2 2000 年 1 月 1 日或以后经重大改装的、输出功率超过 130 kW 的船用柴油机，但能证明并使主管机关认为，该柴油机与其将替代的柴油机完全相同，且不受本条第 1.1.1 款规定者除外。

见统一解释 9

1.2 本条不适用于：

.1 仅用于应急情况使用的、或仅为其所安装船上的仅在应急情况下使用的任何装置或设备提供动力的船用柴油机，或安装在救生艇上的仅在应急情况下使用的船用柴油机；和

.2 安装在仅航行于悬挂其国旗的该国主权或管辖范围水域内的船舶上的船用柴油机，但此类柴油机应受到由该主管机关制定的氮氧化物控制替代方法的管理。

1.3 尽管有本条第 1.1 款的规定，对于 2005 年 5 月 19 日以前建造的船舶上安装的任何船用柴油机或 2005 年 5 月 19 日以前经重大改装的任何船用柴油机，如安装该柴油机的船舶仅在其船旗国的港口或近海装卸站间航行，主管机关可对其免除本条要求。

重大改装

2.1 就本条而言，"重大改装"系指 2000 年 1 月 1 日或以后对尚未按本条第 3、4 或 5.1.1 款所述标准认证的船用柴油机的改变，即：

.1 柴油机由其他船用柴油机代替或新增安装柴油机，或

.2 对柴油机进行了经修订的《2008 年氮氧化物技术规则》中定义的任何实质性改变，或

.3 与柴油机初始证书上的最大持续额定功率相比，柴油机的最大持续额定功率增加超过 10%。

2.2 For a major conversion involving the replacement of a marine diesel engine with a non-identical marine diesel engine, or the installation of an additional marine diesel engine, the standards in this regulation at the time of the replacement or addition of the engine shall apply. For the purpo se of this regulation, the installation of a marine diesel engine replacing a steam system shall be considered a replacement engine. In the case of replacement engines only, if it is not possible for such a replacement engine to meet the standards set forth in paragraph 5.1.1 of this regulation (Tier III, as applicable), then that replacement engine shall meet the standards set forth in paragraph 4 of this regulation (Tier II), taking into account the guidelines developed by the Organization*. The Adminis-tration shall notify the Organization in those instances where a Tier II rather than a Tier III replacement engine has been installed on or after 1 August 2025 in accordance with the provisions of this paragraph.

SEE INTERPRETATION 9 AND 10

2.3 A marine diesel engine referred to in paragraph 2.1.2 or 2.1.3 of this regulation shall meet the following standards:

.1 for ships constructed prior to 1 January 2000, the standards set forth in paragraph 3 of this regulationshall apply; and

.2 for ships constructed on or after 1 January 2000, the standards in force at the time the ship was constructed shall apply.

Tier I**

3 Subject to regulation 3 of this Annex, the operation of a marine diesel engine that is installed on a ship constructed on or after 1 January 2000 and prior to 1 January 2011 is prohibited, except when the emission of nitrogen oxides (calculated as the total weighted emission of NO_2) from the engine is within the following limits, where n = rated engine speed (crankshaft revolutions per minute):

.1 17.0 g/kWh when n is less than 130 rpm;

.2 $45 \cdot n^{(-0.2)}$ g/kWh when n is 130 or more but less than 2,000 rpm; and

.3 9.8 g/kWh when n is 2,000 rpm or more.

Tier II

4 Subject to regulation 3 of this Annex, the operation of a marine diesel engine that is installed on a ship constructed on or after 1 January 2011 is prohibited, except when the emission of nitrogen oxides (calculated as the total weighted emission of NO_2) from the engine is within the following limits, where n = rated engine speed (crankshaft revolutions per minute):

.1 14.4 g/kWh when n is less than 130 rpm;

.2 $44 \cdot n^{(-0.23)}$ g/kWh when n is 130 or more but less than 2,000 rpm;

.3 7.7 g/kWh when n is 2,000 rpm or more.

Tier III

5.1 Subject to regulation 3 of this Annex, in an emission control area designated for Tier III NOx control under paragraph 6 of this regulation (NOx Tier III emission control area), the operation of a marine diesel engine that is installed on a ship is prohibited:

.1 except when the emission of nitrogen oxides (calculated as the total weighted emission of NO_2) from the engine is within the following limits, where n = rated engine speed (crankshaft revolutions per minute):

.1 3.4 g/kWh when n is less than 130 rpm;

.2 $9 \cdot n^{(-0.2)}$ g/kWh when n is 130 or more but less than 2,000 rpm;

.3 2.0 g/kWh when n is 2,000 rpm or more;

when:

* Refer to the 2024 Guidelines as required by regulation 13.2.2 of MARPOL Annex VI in respect of non-identical replacement engines not required to meet the Tier III limit (resolution MEPC. 386(81)).

** Refer to Guidelines for the application of the NOx Technical Code relative to certification and amendments of Tier I engines (MEPC.1/Circ.679).

2.2　如重大改装涉及船用柴油机被非完全相同的柴油机替代，或涉及新增安装柴油机，则在替代或新增柴油机时适用本条标准应。就本条而言，安装取代蒸汽系统的船用柴油机应视为替代柴油机。仅对替代柴油机而言，如其不能符合本条 5.1.1 所述标准（Ⅲ级，如适用），则该替代柴油机应符合本条第 4 段所述标准（Ⅱ级），并考虑本组织制定的导则。* 如果在 2025 年 8 月 1 日或之后按照本段的规定安装了 Ⅱ 级而不是 Ⅲ 级替代柴油机，主管机关应通知本组织。

见统一解释 9 和 10

2.3　本条第 2.1.2 或 2.1.3 款所述的船用柴油机应符合下列标准：

　　.1　于 2000 年 1 月 1 日以前建造的船舶，本条第 3 款所述标准应适用；和

　　.2　于 2000 年 1 月 1 日或以后建造的船舶，其建造时执行的标准应适用。

第Ⅰ级 **

3　在满足本附则第 3 条规定的前提下，对 2000 年 1 月 1 日或以后至 2011 年 1 月 1 日以前建造的船上安装的船用柴油机，除非其氮氧化物排放量（按二氧化氮加权排放总量计算）在下列极限值内，其中 n 为发动机额定转速（每分钟曲轴转速），否则应禁止使用：

　　.1　17.0 g/kWh，当 n 小于 130 rpm；

　　.2　$45 \cdot n^{(-0.2)}$ g/kWh，当 n 等于或大于 130 rpm，但小于 2 000 rpm；

　　.3　9.8 g/kWh，当 n 等于或大于 2 000 rpm。

第Ⅱ级

4　在满足本附则第 3 条规定的前提下，对 2011 年 1 月 1 日或以后建造的船上安装的船用柴油机，除非其 氮氧化物排放量（按二氧化氮加权排放总量计算）在下列极限值内，其中 n 为发动机额定转速（每分钟曲轴转速），否则应禁止使用：

　　.1　14.4 g/kWh，当 n 小于 130 rpm；

　　.2　$44 \cdot n^{(-0.23)}$ g/kWh，当 n 等于或大于 130 rpm，但小于 2 000 rpm；

　　.3　7.7 g/kWh，当 n 等于或大于 2 000 rpm。

第Ⅲ级

5.1　在满足本附则第 3 条规定的前提下，在根据本条第 6 款指定的第Ⅲ级氮氧化物排放控制区（氮氧化物第Ⅲ级排放控制区）内，对船上安装的柴油机：

　　.1　除非该柴油机氮氧化物排放量（按二氧化氮加权排放总量计算）在下列极限值内，其中 n 为发动机额定转速（每分钟曲轴转速），否则应禁止使用：

　　　　.1　3.4 g/kWh，当 n 小于 130 rpm；

　　　　.2　$9 \cdot n^{(-0.2)}$ g/kWh，当 n 等于或大于 130 rpm，但小于 2 000 rpm；

　　　　.3　2.0 g/kWh，当 n 等于或大于 2 000 rpm；

　　若：

---

*　参见《2024 年 MARPOL 附则Ⅵ第 13.2.2 条关于不要求满足Ⅲ级限值的非完全相同替代柴油机导则》（第 MEPC.386(81) 号决议）。

**　参见《应用 NOx 技术规则对第Ⅰ级柴油机发证和修改导则》（第 MEPC.1/Circ.679 号通函）。

.2 that ship is constructed on or after:
  .1 1 January 2016 and is operating in the North American Emission Control Area or the United States Caribbean Sea Emission Control Area;
  .2 1 January 2021 and is operating in the Baltic Sea Emission Control Area or the North Sea Emission Control Area;
.3 that ship is operating in a NOx Tier III emission control area other than an emission control area described in paragraph 5.1.2 of this regulation, and is constructed on or after the date of adoption of such an emission control area, or a later date as may be specified in the amendment designating the NOx Tier III emission control area, whichever is later.

5.2 The standards set forth in paragraph 5.1.1 of this regulationshall not apply to:
  .1 a marine diesel engine installed on a ship with a length (L), as defined in regulation 1.19 of Annex I to the present Convention, of less than 24 metres when it has been specifically designed, and is used solely, for recreational purposes; or
  .2 a marine diesel engine installed on a ship with a combined nameplate diesel engine propulsion power of less than 750 kW if it is demonstrated, to the satisfaction of the Administration, that the ship cannot comply with the standards set forth in paragraph 5.1.1 of this regulation because of design or construction limitations of the ship; or
  .3 a marine diesel engine installed on a ship constructed prior to 1 January 2021 of less than 500 gross tonnage, with a length (L), as defined in regulation 1.19 of Annex I to the present Convention, of 24 metres or over when it has been specifically designed, and is used solely, for recreational purposes.

5.3 The tier and on/off status of marine diesel engines installed on board a ship to which paragraph 5.1 of this regulation applies which are certified to both Tier II and Tier III or which are certified to Tier II only shall be recorded in such logbook or electronic record book* as prescribed by the Administration at entry into and exit from a NOx Tier III emission control area, or when the on/off status changes within such an area, together with the date, time and position of the ship.

SEE INTERPRETATION 11

5.4 Emissions of nitrogen oxides from a marine diesel engine subject to paragraph 5.1 of this regulation that occur immediately following building and sea trials of a newly constructed ship, or before and following converting, repairing, and/or maintaining the ship, or maintenance or repair of a Tier II engine or a dual fuel engine when the ship is required to not have gas fuel or gas cargo on board due to safety requirements, for which activities take place in a shipyard or other repair facility located in a NOx Tier III emission control area, are temporarily exempted provided the following conditions are met:
  .1 the engine meets the Tier II NOx limits; and
  .2 the ship sails directly to or from the shipyard or other repair facility, does not load or unload cargo during the duration of the exemption, and follows any additional specific routeing requirements indicated by the port State in which the shipyard or other repair facility is located, if applicable.

5.5 The exemption described in paragraph 5.4 of this regulation applies only for the following period:
  .1 for a newly constructed ship, the period beginning at the time the ship is delivered from the shipyard, including sea trials, and ending at the time the ship directly exits the NOx Tier III emission control area(s) or, with regard to a ship fitted with a dual fuel engine, the ship directly exits the NOx Tier III emission control area(s) or proceeds directly to the nearest gas fuel bunkering facility appropriate to the ship located in the NOx Tier III emission control area(s);
  .2 for a ship with a Tier II engine undergoing conversion, maintenance or repair, the period beginning at the time the ship enters the NOx Tier III emission control area(s) and proceeds directly to the shipyard or other repair facility, and ending at the time the ship is released from the shipyard or other repair facility and directly exits the NOx Tier III emission control area(s) after performing sea trials, if applicable; or

* Refer to Guidelines for the use of electronic record books under MARPOL (resolution MEPC.312(74)).

.2 船舶建造于:

    .1 2016 年 1 月 1 日或以后,并在北美排放控制区或美国加勒比海排放控制区内营运;

    .2 2021 年 1 月 1 日或以后,并在波罗的海排放控制区或北海排放控制区内营运;

.3 船舶在氮氧化物第Ⅲ级排放控制区(除本条第 5.1.2 款所述的排放控制区)内营运,并且在该排放控制区通过日期或以后建造,或在指定第Ⅲ级氮氧化物排放控制区的修正案中规定的日期或以后建造,以较晚者为准。

5.2 本条第 5.1.1 款所述标准不适用于:

.1 船长(L)(如本公约附则Ⅰ第 1.19 条所界定)小于 24 m,经特殊设计并仅用于娱乐目的之船舶上安装的船用柴油机;或

.2 船上安装的、其铭牌显示柴油机推进功率之和小于 750 kW 的船用柴油机,如证明,并使主管机关确信,该船因设计或构造限制而不能符合本条第 5.1.1 款所述标准;或

.3 船长(L)(如本公约附则Ⅰ第 1.19 条所界定)大于或等于 24 m,经特殊设计并仅用于娱乐目的,在 2021 年 1 月 1 日以前建造的,且小于 500 总吨的船舶上安装的船用柴油机。

5.3 适用本条第 5.1 款并按第Ⅱ和Ⅲ级发证或仅按第Ⅱ级发证的船舶,其船上安装的船用柴油发动机的级别和开/闭状态应在进入和离开氮氧化物第Ⅲ级排放控制区时,或在此类区域中改变开/闭状态时,连同日期、时间和船位,记录于主管机关所规定的航海日志或电子记录簿[*]中。

见统一解释 11

5.4 适用本条第 5.1 款的船用柴油机,在新建船舶的建造和海试后紧跟发生的,或船舶改装、维修和保养前后,或第Ⅱ级发动机或双燃料发动机在位于第Ⅲ级排放控制区的船坞或修船厂维护或修理时因安全要求船上不装载气体燃料或气体货物时,如满足下列条件,可予以临时免除:

.1 该发动机满足第Ⅱ级氮氧化物排放限值;和

.2 免除期间,船舶直接驶往或驶离船坞或修船厂且不装载或卸载货物,且遵守船坞或修船厂所在港口国指定的任何额外的特定航线要求(如适用)。

5.5 本条第 5.4 款所述免除仅适用于下列时间段:

.1 对新建船舶,该时间段始于从船厂交付船舶之时,包括海试,结束于船舶直接离开氮氧化物第Ⅲ级排放控制区,或对装有双燃料发动机的船舶,直接离开氮氧化物第Ⅲ级排放控制区或直接驶进最近的氮氧化物第Ⅲ级排放控制区内适于船舶的气体燃料加油站;

.2 对装有第Ⅱ级发动机的船舶进行改建、保养或维修时,该时间段始于船舶进入氮氧化物第Ⅲ级排放控制区并直接驶进船坞或修船厂之时,并结束于船舶海试后驶离船坞或修船厂,直接离开氮氧化物第Ⅲ级排放控制区(如适用);或

---

[*] 参见《防污公约下的电子记录簿使用导则》(第 MEPC.312(74)号决议)。

.3 for a ship with a dual fuel engine undergoing conversion, maintenance or repair, when the ship is required to not have gas fuel or gas cargo on board due to safety requirements, the period beginning at the time the ship enters the NOx Tier III emission control area(s) or when it is degassed in the NOx Tier III emission control area(s) and proceeds directly to the shipyard or other repair facility, and ending at the time when the ship is released from the shipyard or other repair facility and directly exits the NOx Tier III emission control area(s) or proceeds directly to the nearest gas fuel bunkering facility appropriate to the ship located in the NOx Tier III emission control area(s).

Emission control area

6 For the purposes of this regulation, a NOx Tier III emission control area shall be any sea area, including any port area, designated by the Organization in accordance with the criteria and procedures set forth in appendix III to this Annex. The NOx Tier III emission control areas are:

.1 the North American Emission Control Area, which means the area described by the coordinates provided in appendix VII to this Annex;

.2 the United States Caribbean Sea Emission Control Area, which means the area described by the coordinates provided in appendix VII to this Annex;

.3 the Baltic Sea area as defined in regulation 1.11.2 of Annex I of the present Convention; and

.4 the North Sea area as defined in regulation 1.14.6 of Annex V of the present Convention.

Marine diesel engines installed on a ship constructed prior to 1 January 2000

7.1 Notwithstanding paragraph 1.1.1 of this regulation, a marine diesel engine with a power output of more than 5,000 kW and a per cylinder displacement at or above 90 L installed on a ship constructed on or after 1 January 1990 but prior to 1 January 2000 shall comply with the emission limits set forth in paragraph 7.4 of this regulation, provided that an approved method* for that engine has been certified by an Administration of a Party and notification of such certification has been submitted to the Organization by the certifying Administration.** Compliance with this paragraphshall be demonstrated through one of the following:

.1 installation of the certified approved method, as confirmed by a survey using the verification procedure specified in the approved method file, including appropriate notation on the ship's IAPP Certificate of the presence of the approved method; or

.2 certification of the engine confirming that it operates within the limits set forth in paragraph 3, 4, or 5.1.1 of this regulation and an appropriate notation of the engine certification on the ship's IAPP Certificate.

7.2 Paragraph 7.1 of this regulation shall apply no later than the first renewal survey that occurs 12 months or more after deposit of the notification in paragraph 7.1. If a shipowner of a ship on which an approved method is to be installed can demonstrate to the satisfaction of the Administration that the approved method was not commercially available despite best efforts to obtain it, then that approved method shall be installed on the ship no later than the next annual survey of that ship that falls after the approved method is commercially available.

7.3 With regard to a marine diesel engine with a power output of more than 5,000 kW and a per cylinder displacement at or above 90 L installed on a ship constructed on or after 1 January 1990, but prior to 1 January 2000, the IAPP Certificate shall, for a marine diesel engine to which paragraph 7.1 of this regulation applies, indicate one of the following:

.1 an approved method has been applied pursuant to paragraph 7.1.1 of this regulation;

.2 the engine has been certified pursuant to paragraph 7.1.2 of this regulation;

.3 an approved method is not yet commercially available as described in paragraph 7.2 of this regulation; or

.4 an approved method is not applicable.

* Refer to the 2014 Guidelines on the approved method process (resolution MEPC. 243(66)).

** Refer to the 2014 Guidelines in respect of the information to be submitted by an Administration to the Organization covering the certification of an approved method as required under regulation 13.7.1 of MARPOL Annex VI (resolution MEPC. 242(66)).

.3 对装有双燃料发动机的船舶进行改建、保养和维修时，当船舶因安全要求船上不装载气体燃料或气体货物时，该时间段始于船舶进入氮氧化物第Ⅲ级排放控制区或当其在氮氧化物第Ⅲ级排放控制区脱气并直接驶进船坞或修船厂之时，并结束于船舶驶离船坞或修船厂并直接离开氮氧化物第Ⅲ级排放控制区或直接驶进最近的氮氧化物第Ⅲ级排放控制区内适于船舶的气体燃料加油站。

排放控制区

6 就本条而言，氮氧化物第Ⅲ级排放控制区系指本组织按照本附则附录Ⅲ所列标准和程序而指定的海域，包括港口区域。氮氧化物第Ⅲ级排放控制区有：

.1 本附则附录Ⅶ中坐标所划定的北美排放控制区；

.2 本附则附录Ⅶ中坐标所划定的美国加勒比海排放控制区；

.3 本公约附则Ⅰ第1.11.2条中定义的波罗的海排放控制区；和

.4 本公约附则Ⅴ第1.14.6条中定义的北海排放控制区。

2000年1月1日以前建造的船舶上安装的船用柴油机

7.1 尽管有本条第1.1.1款的规定，在1990年1月1日或以后但在2000年1月1日以前建造的船舶上安装的、输出功率超过5 000 kW且单缸排量在90 L或以上的船用柴油机应符合本条第7.4款所述的排放限值，除非该柴油机的经认可方法[*]已经缔约国主管机关的认证，且发证主管机关已将此认证的信息通知本组织[**]。应通过以下方法之一证明符合性：

.1 安装获认证的认可方法，且通过使用经认可方法文件中规定的验证程序检验证实，在船舶《国际防止大气污染证书》中就该经认可方法做出适当注释；或

.2 发动机认证证明其在符合本条第3、4或5.1.1款中所述的限值范围内运转，且在船舶的《国际防止大气污染证书》中就该发动机认证做出适当注释。

7.2 本条第7.1款应不迟于自该段所述的通知交存之后12个月或以后进行的首次换证检验时适用。如应安装经认可方法的该船船舶所有人能够证明，并使主管机关认为，尽管已尽最大努力但市场没有供应该经认可方法，则应在市场供应该经认可方法后的下一个年度检验前在船上安装该方法。

7.3 对于在1990年1月1日或以后但在2000年1月1日以前建造的船舶上安装的输出功率超过5 000 kW、单缸排量在90 L或以上的船用柴油机，对于适用本条第7.1款的船用柴油机，其《国际防止空气污染证书》应按下列情况之一予以标明：

.1 已按照本条第7.1.1款应用经认可的方法；

.2 已按照本条第7.1.2款对发动机予以认证；

.3 按照本条第7.2款所述，尚无可商业获得的经认可方法；或

.4 经认可的方法不适用。

---

[*] 参见《2014年认可方法程序导则》（第MEPC.243（66）号决议）。

[**] 参见《2014年主管机关根据防污公约附则Ⅵ第13.7.1条将认可方法相关信息提交至IMO导则》（第MEPC.242（66）号决议）。

7.4 Subject to regulation 3 of this Annex, the operation of a marine diesel engine described in paragraph 7.1 of this regulation is prohibited, except when the emission of nitrogen oxides (calculated as the total weighted emission of NO_2) from the engine is within the following limits, where n = rated engine speed (crankshaft revolutions per minute):

.1 17.0 g/kWh when n is less than 130 rpm;

.2 $45 \cdot n^{(-0.2)}$ g/kWh when n is 130 or more but less than 2,000 rpm; and

.3 9.8 g/kWh when n is 2,000 rpm or more.

7.5 Certification of an approved method shall be in accordance with chapter 7 of the revised NOx Technical Code 2008 and shall include verification:

.1 by the designer of the base marine diesel engine to which the approved method applies that the calculated effect of the approved method will not decrease engine rating by more than 1.0%, increase fuel consumption by more than 2.0% as measured according to the appropriate test cycle set forth in the revised NOx Technical Code 2008, or adversely affect engine durability or reliability; and

.2 that the cost of the approved method is not excessive, which is determined by a comparison of the amount of NOx reduced by the approved method to achieve the standard set forth in paragraph 7.4 of this regulation and the cost of purchasing and installing such approved method. *

Certification

8 The revised NOx Technical Code 2008 shall be applied in the certification, testing and measurement procedures for the standards set forth in this regulation.

9 The procedures for determining NOx emissions set out in the revised NOx Technical Code 2008 are intended to be representative of the normal operation of the engine. Defeat devices and irrational emission control strategies undermine this intention and shall not be allowed. This regulationshall not prevent the use of auxiliary control devices that are used to protect the engine and/or its ancillary equipment against operating conditions that could result in damage or failure or that are used to facilitate the starting of the engine.

Regulation 14 Sulphur oxides (SOx) and particulate matter

General requirements

1 The sulphur content of fuel oil used or carried for use on board a shipshall not exceed 0.50% m/m.

SEE INTERPRETATION 12

2 The worldwide average sulphur content of residual fuel oil supplied for use on board ships shall be monitored taking into account the guidelines developed by the Organization. **

Requirements within emission control areas

3 For the purpose of this regulation, an emission control area shall be any sea area, including any port area, designated by the Organization in accordance with the criteria and procedures set forth in appendix III to this Annex. The emission control areas under this regulation are:

.1 the Baltic Sea area as defined in regulation 1.11.2 of Annex I of the present Convention;

.2 the North Sea area as defined in regulation 1.14.6 of Annex V of the present Convention;

---

* The cost of an approved method shall not exceed 375 Special Drawing Rights/ metric tonne NOx calculated in accordance with the cost-effectiveness (Ce) formula below: Refer to Definitions for the cost-effectiveness formula in regulation 13.7.5 of the revised MARPOL Annex VI (MEPC.1/Circ.678).

** Refer to the 2020 Guidelines for monitoring the worldwide average sulphur content of fuel oils supplied for use on board ships (resolution MEPC. 326(75)).

7.4 在满足本附则第 3 条的前提下，禁止使用本条第 7.1 款所述的船用柴油机，除非其氮氧化物排放量（按二氧化氮加权排放总量计算）在下列极限值内，其中 n 为发动机额定转速（每分钟曲轴转速）：

.1 17.0 g/kWh，当 n 小于 130 rpm；

.2 $45 \cdot n^{(-0.2)}$ g/kWh，当 n 等于或大于 130 rpm，但小于 2 000 rpm；和

.3 9.8 g/kWh，当 n 等于或大于 2 000 rpm。

7.5 应按经修订的《2008 年氮氧化物技术规则》第 7 章对经认可方法进行认证，并应包括如下验证：

.1 由适用经认可方法的基准船用柴油机的设计方验证：根据经修订的《2008 年氮氧化物技术规则》中相应的试验循环进行的测量表明，由经认可方法算出的影响不会降低柴油机额定功率的 1.0% 以上、不会增加燃油消耗量的 2.0% 以上，或不会对柴油机的寿命或可靠性造成不利影响；和

.2 经认可方法的成本不会过高，该成本通过比较为达到本条第 7.4 款所述标准而使用经认可方法减少的氮氧化物量以及购买和安装该经认可方法的费用予以确定。[*]

发证

8 本条所述标准的发证、试验和测量程序应适用经修订的《2008 年氮氧化物技术规则》。

9 经修订的《2008 年氮氧化物技术规则》所述的确定氮氧化物的排放程序拟作为柴油机正常运转的典型情况。减效装置和不合理排放控制策略会有悖于这一目的，因而不得允许。本条不得妨碍辅助控制装置的使用，这些控制装置用于保护柴油机和 / 或其辅助设备不受可导致其损坏或故障的操作条件的影响或有助于柴油机的启动。

第 14 条 硫氧化物（SO_x）和颗粒物质

一般要求

1 船上使用的或载运用于使用的燃油的硫含量不得超过 0.50% m/m。

见统一解释 12

---

2 应考虑到本组织制定的导则[**]，对世界范围内供船上使用的燃油的平均硫含量作监测。

排放控制区内的要求

3 就本条而言，排放控制区系指本组织按本附则附录Ⅲ中所列标准和程序而指定的海域，包括港口区域。本条中的排放控制区有：

.1 本公约附则Ⅰ第 1.11.2 条中定义的波罗的海排放控制区；

.2 本公约附则Ⅴ第 1.14.6 条中定义的北海排放控制区；

---

[*] 根据下列成本效益（Ce）公式计算，认可方法的成本不应超过 375 特别提款权 / 吨氮氧化物：参见《关于防污公约附则Ⅵ第 13.7.5 条中成本效益公式的定义》（MEPC.1/Circ.678）。

[**] 参见《2020 年世界范围内船用燃油硫含量监测导则》（第 MEPC.326（75）号决议）。

.3 the North American Emission Control Area, which means the area described by the coordinates provided in appendix VII to this Annex;

.4 the United States Caribbean Sea Emission Control Area, which means the area described by the coordinates provided in appendix VII to this Annex; and

.5 the Mediterranean Sea Emission Control Area, which means the are a described by the coordinates provided in appendix VII to this annex.

4 While a ship is operating within an emission control area, the sulphur content of fuel oil used on board that shipshall not exceed 0.10% m/m.

5 The sulphur content of fuel oil referred to in paragraph 1 and paragraph 4 of this regulation shall be documented by its supplier as required by regulation 18 of this Annex.

6 Those ships using separate fuel oils to comply with paragraph 4 of this regulation and entering or leaving an emission control area set forth in paragraph 3 of this regulation shall carry a written procedure showing how the fuel oil changeover is to be done, allowing sufficient time for the fuel oil service system to be fully flushed of all fuel oils exceeding the applicable sulphur content specified in paragraph 4 of this regulation prior to entry into an emission control area. The volume of low sulphur fuel oils in each tank as well as the date, time and position of the ship when any fuel oil changeover operation is completed prior to the entry into an emission control area or commenced after exit from such an area shall be recorded in such logbook or electronic record book* as prescribed by the Administration.

7 During the first 12 months immediately following entry into force of an amendment designating a specific emission control area under paragraph 3 of this regulation, ships operating in that emission control area are exempt from the requirements in paragraphs 4 and 6 of this regulation and from the requirements of paragraph 5 of this regulation insofar as they relate to paragraph 4 of this regulation.

In-use and onboard fuel oil sampling and testing

8 If the competent authority of a Party requires the in-use or onboard sample to be analysed, it shall be done in accordance with the verification procedure set forth in appendix VI to this Annex to determine whether the fuel oil being used or carried for use on board meets the requirements in paragraph 1 or paragraph 4 of this regulation. The in-use sample shall be drawn taking into account the guidelines developed by the Organization.** The onboard sample shall be drawn taking into account the guidelines developed by the Organization. ***

9 The sample shall be sealed by the representative of the competent authority with a unique means of identification installed in the presence of the ship's representative. The ship shall be given the option of retaining a duplicate sample.

In-use fuel oil sampling point

10 For each ship subject to regulations 5 and 6 of this Annex, sampling point(s) shall be fitted or designated for the purpose of taking representative samples of the fuel oil being used on board the ship taking into account the guidelines developed by the Organization.**

11 For a ship constructed before 1 April 2022, the sampling point(s) referred to in paragraph 10 shall befitted or designated not later than the first renewal survey as identified in regulation 5.1.2 of this Annex on or after 1 April 2023.

12 The requirements of paragraphs 10 and 11 above are not applicable to a fuel oil service system used for a low-flashpoint fuel or a gas fuel.

* Refer to Guidelines for the use of electronic record books under MARPOL (resolution MEPC. 312(74)).
** Refer to the 2019 Guidelines for on board sampling for the verification of the sulphur content of the fuel oil used on board ships (MEPC.1/Circ.864/Rev.1).
*** Refer to the 2020 Guidelines for on board sampling of fuel oil intended to be used or carried for use on board a ship (MEPC.1/Circ.889).

.3 本附则附录Ⅶ中坐标所划定的北美排放控制区；

.4 本附则附录Ⅶ中坐标所划定的美国加勒比海排放控制区；和

.5 本附则附录Ⅶ中坐标所划定的地中海排放控制区。

4 当船舶在排放控制区内营运时，船上使用的燃油硫含量不得超过 0.10%m/m。

5 本条第 1 和 4 款中所述的燃油硫含量应由供应商按本附则第 18 条的要求提供证明文件。

6 使用不同燃油以符合本条第 4 款规定进入或离开本条第 3 款所述排放控制区域的船舶，应携有一份书面程序表明燃油转换如何完成，在其进入排放控制区域之前规定足够的时间对供油系统进行全面冲洗，以去除硫含量超过本条第 4 款所规定的适用硫含量的所有燃油。在燃油转换作业进入排放控制区域以前完成或离开该区域后开始时，应将每一燃油舱中的低硫燃油的体积以及日期、时间及船位记录在主管机关规定的航海日志或电子记录簿*中。

7 在按照本条第 3 款指定某一排放控制区的修正案生效后的前 12 个月内，对在该排放控制区营运的船舶可免除本条第 4 款和第 6 款的要求以及本条第 5 款中与本条第 4 款相关的要求。

在用和船上燃油取样和试验

8 如一缔约国的主管当局要求对在用或船上样品进行分析，则应按本附则附录Ⅵ中规定的验证程序进行，以确定正在使用或载运用于使用的燃油是否符合本条第 1 或 4 款中的要求。在用样品的取样应考虑到本组织制定的导则**。船上样品的取样应考虑到本组织制定的导则。***

9 样品应由主管机关的代表在船方代表在场的情况下，使用唯一的识别标志进行密封。应向船舶提供保留样品的平行样的选择。

在用燃油取样点

10 对于适用本附则第 5 和 6 条的船舶，应虑及到本组织制定的导则**，应设置或指定为采集船上正在使用的燃油的代表性样品的取样点。

11 对于 2022 年 4 月 1 日以前建造的船舶，不得迟于 2023 年 4 月 1 日或之后的本附则第 5.1.2 条中所述的首次换证检验，设置或指定第 10 款所指的取样点。

12 以上第 10 和第 11 段的要求不适用于低闪点燃料或气体燃料的燃油系统。

---

* 参见《防污公约下的电子记录簿使用导则》（第 MEPC.312（74）号决议）。

** 参见《2019 年船上燃油取样以核验船上使用的燃油硫含量导则》（第 MEPC.1/Circ.864/Rev.1 号通函）。

*** 参见《2020 年船上使用或载运的船用燃油取样导则》（第 MEPC.1/Circ.889 号通函）。

13 The competent authority of a Party shall, as appropriate, utilize the sampling point(s) which is(are) fitted or designated for the purpose of taking representative sample(s) of the fuel oil being used on board in order to verify that the fuel oil complies with this regulation. Taking fuel oil samples by the competent authority of the Party shall be performed as expeditiously as possible without causing the ship to be unduly delayed.

Regulation 15 Volatile organic compounds (VOCs)

1 If the emissions of volatile organic compounds (VOCs) from a tanker are to be regulated in a port or ports or a terminal or terminals under the jurisdiction of a Party, they shall be regulated in accordance with the provisions of this regulation.

2 A Party regulating tankers for VOC emissions shall submit a notification to the Organization.* This notificationshall include information on the size of tankers to be controlled, the cargoes requiring vapour emission control systems and the effective date of such control. The notification shall be submitted at least six months before the effective date.

3 A Party that designates ports or terminals at which VOC emissions from tankers are to be regulated shall ensure that vapour emission control systems, approved by that Party taking into account the safety standards for such systems developed by the Organization, are provided in any designated port and terminal and are operated safely and in a manner so as to avoid undue delay to a ship.

4 The Organization shall circulate a list of the ports and terminals designated by Parties to other Parties and Member States of the Organization for their information.

5 A tanker to which paragraph 1 of this regulation applies shall be provided with a vapour emission collection system approved by the Administration taking into account the safety standards for such systems developed by the Organization,** and shall use this system during the loading of relevant cargoes. A port or terminal that has installed vapour emission control systems in accordance with this regulation may accept tankers that are not fitted with vapour collection systems for a period of three years after the effective date identified in paragraph 2 of this regulation.

6 A tanker carrying crude oil shall have on board and implement a VOC management plan approved by the Administration. Such a planshall be prepared taking into account the guidelines developed by the Organization.*** The planshall be specific to each ship and shall at least:

.1 provide written procedures for minimizing VOC emissions during the loading, sea passage and discharge of cargo;

.2 give consideration to the additional VOC generated by crude oil washing;

.3 identify a person responsible for implementing the plan; and

.4 for ships on international voyages, be written in the working language of the master and officers and, if the working language of the master and officers is not English, French or Spanish, include a translation into one of these languages.

SEE INTERPRETATION 13

7 This regulationshall also apply to gas carriers only if the types of loading and containment systems allow safe retention of non-methane VOCs on board or their safe return ashore. ****

SEE INTERPRETATION 13

* Refer to Notification to the Organization on ports or terminals where volatile organic compounds (VOCs) emissions are to be regulated (MEPC.1/Circ.509).
** Refer to Standards for vapour emission control systems (MSC/Circ.585).
*** Refer to Guidelines for the development of a VOC management plan (resolution MEPC. 185(59)). Refer also to Technical information on systems and operation to assist development of VOC management plans (MEPC.1/Circ.680), and Technical information on a vapour pressure control system to facilitate the development and update of VOC management plans (MEPC.1/Circ.719).
**** Refer to the International Code for the construction and equipment of ships carrying liquefied gases in bulk.

13　缔约国主管机关应酌情使用为采集船上正在使用的燃油的代表性样品而设置或指定的取样点，以验证燃油符合本规定。缔约国主管机关应尽可能迅速地采集燃油样品，而不对船舶造成不当延误。

第 15 条　挥发性有机化合物（VOCs）

1　如在缔约国管辖的港口或装卸站对液货船产生的挥发性有机化合物（VOCs）排放进行管控，应按照本条规定进行。

2　对液货船挥发性有机化合物排放进行控制的缔约国应向本组织提交一份通知书[*]。该通知书应包括所需控制的液货船的尺度、需要蒸气释放控制系统的货物种类以及该规定的生效日期等信息。该通知书应至少在生效日期之前六个月提交。

3　在指定港口或装卸站对液货船的挥发性有机化合物排放进行控制的缔约国，应保证在其指定的港口和装卸站配备经该缔约国根据本组织制定的蒸气排放控制系统安全标准认可的蒸汽排放控制系统，并确保该系统的安全操作和防止对船舶造成不当延误。

4　本组织应将由缔约国指定的港口和装卸站清单散发给其他缔约国和本组织的成员国。

5　本条第 1 款适用的液货船应配备由主管机关根据本组织制定的蒸汽排放收集系统安全标准[**]认可的蒸汽排放收集系统，并应在这些货物装载过程中使用该系统。根据本条要求安装了蒸汽排放控制系统的港口或装卸站可以接纳在本条第 2 款确定的生效日期之后的三年内没有安装蒸汽收集系统的液货船。

6　载运原油的液货船应在船上备有并实施经主管机关认可的《挥发性有计划物管理计划》[***]。该计划应根据本组织制定的导则编写。该计划应根据每船情况制定，并至少应：

　.1　为装载、海上航行和卸货时将挥发性有机化合物排放降至最低提供书面程序；

　.2　考虑到原油洗舱产生的额外挥发性有机化合物；

　.3　指定负责实施该计划的人员；和

　.4　对于国际航行船舶，用船长和高级船员的工作语言编写，如船长和高级船员的工作语言既非英语、法语，也非西班牙语，则应包括其中一种语言的译文。

见统一解释 13

7　对气体运输船而言，只有其装载和围护系统的类型使得非甲烷的挥发性有机化合物安全保存在船上或安全回输到岸上时才适用本条[****]。

见统一解释 13

Regulation 16 Shipboard incineration

1   Except as provided in paragraph 4 of this regulation, shipboard incineration shall be allowed only in a shipboard incinerator.

2   Shipboard incineration of the following substances shall be prohibited:
.1   residues of cargoes subject to Annex I, II or III or related contaminated packing materials;
.2   polychlorinated biphenyls (PCBs);
.3   garbage, as defined by Annex V, containing more than traces of heavy metals;
.4   refined petroleum products containing halogen compounds;
.5   sewage sludge and sludge oil neither of which is generated on board the ship; and
.6   exhaust gas cleaning system residues.

3   Shipboard incineration of polyvinyl chlorides (PVCs) shall be prohibited, except in shipboard incinerators for which IMO Type Approval Certificates* have been issued.

4   Shipboard incineration of sewage sludge and sludge oil generated during normal operation of a ship may also take place in the main or auxiliary power plant or boilers, but in those cases, shall not take place inside ports, harbours or estuaries.

5   Nothing in this regulation either:
.1   affects the incineration at sea prohibitions of the Convention on the Prevention of Marine Pollution by Dumping of Wastes and Other Matter, 1972, as amended, and the 1996 Protocol thereto, or other requirements thereof, or
.2   precludes the development, installation and operation of alternative design shipboard thermal waste treatment devices that meet or exceed the requirements of this regulation.

6.1   Except as provided in paragraph 6.2 of this regulation, each incinerator on a ship constructed on or after 1 January 2000 or incinerator that is installed on board a ship on or after 1 January 2000 shall meet the requirements contained in appendix IV to this Annex. Each incinerator subject to this paragraph shall be approved by the Administration taking into account the standard specification for shipboard incinerators developed by the Organization**; or

6.2   The Administration may allow exclusion from the application of paragraph 6.1 of this regulation to any incinerator installed on board a ship before 19 May 2005, provided that the ship is solely engaged in voyages within waters subject to the sovereignty or jurisdiction of the State the flag of which the ship is entitled to fly.

7   Incinerators installed in accordance with the requirements of paragraph 6.1 of this regulationshall be provided with a manufacturer's operating manual, which is to be retained with the unit and which shall specify how to operate the incinerator within the limits described in paragraph 2 of appendix IV of this Annex.

8   Personnel responsible for the operation of an incinerator installed in accordance with the requirements of paragraph 6.1 of this regulation shall be trained to implement the guidance provided in the manufacturer's operating manual as required by paragraph 7 of this regulation.

9   For incinerators installed in accordance with the requirements of paragraph 6.1 of this regulation the combustion chamber gas outlet temperature shall be monitored at all times the unit is in operation. Where that incinerator is of the continuous-feed type, waste shall not be fed into the unit when the combustion chamber gas outlet temperature is below 850°C. Where that incinerator is of the batch-loaded type, the unitshall be designed so that the combustion chamber gas outlet temperature shall reach 600°C within five minutes after start-up and will thereafter stabilize at a temperature not less than 850°C.

SEE INTERPRETATION 14

* Type Approval Certificates issued in accordance with Revised guidelines for the implementation of Annex V of MARPOL 73/78 (resolution MEPC.59(33), as amended by resolution MEPC.92(45)), or Standard specification for shipboard incinerators (resolution MEPC.76(40), as amended by resolution MEPC.93(45)),or the 2014 Standard specification for shipboard incinerators (resolution MEPC.244(60)).

** Refer to the 2014 Standard specification for shipboard incinerators (resolution MEPC.244(60)), or Standard specification for shipboard incinerators (resolution MEPC.76(40), as amended by resolution MEPC.93(45)),and Type approval of shipboard incinerators (MEPC.1/Circ.793).

第 16 条　船上焚烧

1　除本条第 4 款规定者外，船上焚烧应只允许在船上焚烧炉中进行。

2　应禁止下列物质在船上焚烧：

　　.1　附则 Ⅰ、Ⅱ 或 Ⅲ 规定的货物残余物或有关的被污损的包装材料；

　　.2　多氯联苯（PCBs）；

　　.3　附则 Ⅴ 定义的含有超过痕量重金属的垃圾；

　　.4　含有卤素化合物的精炼石油产品；

　　.5　并非在船上产生的污泥和油渣；和

　　.6　废气清洗系统的残余物。

3　应禁止在船上焚烧聚氯乙烯（PVCs），但在已颁发"国际海事组织型式认可证书"[*]的船上焚烧炉内焚烧除外。

4　在船舶正常营运过程中产生的污泥和污油也可在主、辅发电机或锅炉内焚烧，但不得在码头、港口和河口内进行。

5　本条规定：

　　.1　不影响经修正的《1972 年防止倾倒废弃物及其他物质污染海洋公约》及其 1996 年议定书的禁令或其他要求，或

　　.2　不排除符合或超过本条要求的船上废弃物热处理装置替代设计的开发、安装和使用。

6.1　除本条第 6.2 款规定者外，2000 年 1 月 1 日或以后建造的船舶上的焚烧炉或 2000 年 1 月 1 日或以后安装在船上的焚烧炉均应符合本附则附录Ⅳ的要求。符合本段要求的焚烧炉应经主管机关根据本组织制定的船上焚烧炉标准技术条件[**]予以认可。

6.2　对于仅航行于有权悬挂其国旗的该国主权或管辖的水域内的船舶，主管机关可以允许对 2005 年 5 月 19 日以前安装上船的焚烧炉免除本条第 6.1 款的适用要求。

7　本条第 6.1 款要求安装的焚烧炉应持有一份制造商的操作手册。该手册应随焚烧炉装置存放，并应说明如何在本附则附录Ⅳ第 2 款所述的限制内操作焚烧炉。

8　应对按本条第 6.1 款要求安装的焚烧炉操作的人员进行培训，使其能执行本条第 7 款所要求的制造商操作手册中规定的指导。

9　对于按本条第 6.1 款要求安装的焚烧炉，在该炉运行的任何时候均应对燃烧室气体出口温度进行监测。如焚烧炉为连续进料型，在燃烧室气体出口温度低于 850 ℃时不得将废弃物送入该焚烧炉。如焚烧炉为分批装料型，该装置应设计成其燃烧室气体出口的温度在启动后 5 分钟内达 600 ℃且随后稳定在不低于 850 ℃的温度上。

见统一解释 14

---

[*]　根据《修订的防污公约附则 Ⅴ 实施指南》（第 MEPC.59（33）号决议，经第 MEPC.92（45）号决议修订）签发的型式认可证书，或《船上焚烧炉标准技术条件》（第 MEPC.76（40）号决议，经第 MEPC.93（45）号决议修订），或《2014 年船上焚烧炉标准技术条件》（第 MEPC.244（60）号决议）。

[**]　参见《2014 年船上焚烧炉标准技术条件》（第 MEPC.244（60）号决议），或《船上焚烧炉标准技术条件》（第 MEPC.76（40）号决议，经第 MEPC.93（45）号决议修订）和《船上焚烧炉的型式认可》（第 MEPC.1/Circ.793 号通函）。

Regulation 17 Reception facilities

1   Each Party undertakes to ensure the provision of facilities adequate to meet the:

.1   needs of ships using its repair ports for the reception of ozone-depleting substances and equipment containing such substances when removed from ships;

.2   needs of ships using its ports, terminals or repair ports for the reception of exhaust gas cleaning residues from an exhaust gas cleaning system;
without causing undue delay to ships, and

.3   needs in ship-breaking facilities for the reception of ozone-depleting substances and equipment containing such substances when removed from ships.

"2   The following States may satisfy the requirements in paragraph 1 of this regulation through regional arrangements when, because of those States' unique circumstances, such arrangements are the only practical means to satisfy these requirements:

.1   small island developing States; and

.2   States the coastline of which borders on Arctic waters, provided that regional arrangements shall cover only ports within Arctic waters of those States.

Parties participating in a regional arrangement shall develop a Regional Reception Facilities Plan, taking into account the guidelines developed by the Organization.*

The Government of each Party paricipating in the arrangement shall consult with the Organization, for circulation to the Parties of the present Convention,on:

.1   how the Regional Reception Facities Plan takes into account the guldelines developed by the Organization;*

.2   particulars of the identified Regional Ships Waste Reception Centres taking into account the guidelines developed by the Organization*; and

.3   particulars of those ports with only limited facilties."

3   If a particular port or terminal of a Party is, taking into account the guidelines to be developed by the Organization, remotely located from, or lacking in, the industrial infrastructure necessary to manage and process those substances referred to in paragraph 1 of this regulation and therefore cannot accept such substances, then the Party shall inform the Organization of any such port or terminal so that this information may be circulated to all Parties and Member States of the Organization for their information and any appropriate action. Each Party that has provided the Organization with such information shall also notify the Organization of its ports and terminals where reception facilities are available to manage and process such substances.

4   Each Party shall notify the Organization for circulation to the Members of the Organization of all cases where the facilities provided under this regulation are unavailable or alleged to be inadequate.

---

* Refer to the 2012 Guidelines for the development of a regional reception facilities plan (resolution MEPC.221(63)).
** Refer to the 2011 Guidelines for reception facilities under MARPOL Annex VI (resolution MEPC. 199(62)).

第 17 条　接收设施

1　各缔约国应保证提供足够的设施以满足：

.1　船舶使用其修理港时接收从船上卸下的消耗臭氧物质和含有这些物质的设备的需要；

.2　船舶使用其港口、装卸站或修理港时接收废气清洗系统产生的废气清洗残余物的需要；而不对船舶造成不当延误，和

.3　在拆船厂中用以接收从船上卸下的消耗臭氧物质和含有这些物质的设备的需要。

"2　以下国家如由于其独特情况而只有区域安排系满足本条第 1 款要求的唯一实际可行手段，可通过区域安排满足这些要求：

.1　小岛屿发展中国家；和

.2　其海岸线与北极水域接壤的国家，但是区域安排须仅涵盖这些国家在北极水域内的港口。

参加区域安排的缔约国须制定区域接收设施计划，并考虑到本组织制定的导则。*

参加此等安排的各缔约国政府须与本组织协商，以向本公约的缔约国通告：

.1　区域接收设施计划如何考虑到本组织制定的导则*；

.2　考虑到本组织制定的导则*，所确定的区域船舶废物接收中心的细节；和

.3　仅具备有限设施的港口的细节。"

3　考虑到本组织将要制定的导则，如缔约国的港口或装卸站远离或缺乏管理和处理本条第 1 款所述物质所必需的工业基础设施，因而不能接收这些物质，则该缔约国应将所有此类港口或装卸站通知本组织，以使该信息可转发给所有缔约国和本组织各成员国，供其参考和采取任何相应的行动。已向本组织提供此类信息的各缔约国应同时将其可提供管理和处理这些物质的接收设施的港口和装卸站通知本组织。

4　各缔约国应将不具备本条规定的设施或被指认设施不足的一切情况通知本组织，以便转发本组织各成员国。

---

* 　参见《2012 年制定接收设施区域计划导则》（第 MEPC.221（63）号决议）。

** 　参见《2011 年防污公约附则Ⅵ下的接收设施导则》（第 MEPC.199（62）号决议）。

Regulation 18 Fuel oil availability and quality

Fuel oil availability

1   Each Party shall take all reasonable steps to promote the availability of fuel oils that comply with this Annex and inform the Organization of the availability of compliant fuel oils in its ports and terminals.

2.1 If a ship is found by a Party not to be in compliance with the standards for compliant fuel oils set forth in this Annex, the competent authority of the Party is entitled to require the ship to:

.1   present a record of the actions taken to attempt to achieve compliance; and

.2   provide evidence that it attempted to purchase compliant fuel oil in accordance with its voyage plan and, if it was not made available where planned, that attempts were made to locate alternative sources for such fuel oil and that despite best efforts to obtain compliant fuel oil, no such fuel oil was made available for purchase.

2.2 The ship should not be required to deviate from its intended voyage or to delay unduly the voyage in order to achieve compliance.

2.3 If a ship provides the information set forth in paragraph 2.1 of this regulation, a Party shall take into account all relevant circumstances and the evidence presented to determine the appropriate action to take, including not taking control measures.

2.4 A ship shall notify its Administration and the competent authority of the relevant port of destination when it cannot purchase compliant fuel oil.

2.5 A Party shall notify the Organization when a ship has presented evidence of the nonavailability of compliant fuel oil.

Fuel oil quality

3   Fuel oil delivered to and used on board a ship to which this Annex applies shall meet the following requirements:

.1   except as provided in paragraph 3.2 of this regulation:

.1   the fuel oil shall be blends of hydrocarbons derived from petroleum refining. This shall not preclude the incorporation of small amounts of additives intended to improve some aspects of performance;

.2   the fuel oil shall be free from inorganic acid; and

.3   the fuel oil shall not include any added substance or chemical waste that:

.1   jeopardizes the safety of ships or adversely affects the performance of the machinery, or

.2   is harmful to personnel, or

.3   contributes overall to additional air pollution.

.2   fuel oil derived by methods other than petroleum refining shall not:

.1   exceed the applicable sulphur content set forth in regulation 14 of this Annex;

.2   cause an engine to exceed the applicable NOx emission limit set forth in paragraphs 3, 4, 5.1.1 and 7.4 of regulation 13;

.3   contain inorganic acid; or

.4   .1   jeopardize the safety of ships or adversely affect the performance of the machinery, or

.2   be harmful to personnel, or

.3   contribute overall to additional air pollution.

SEE INTERPRETATION 15

---

4   This regulation does not apply to coal in its solid form or nuclear fuels. Paragraphs 5.1, 8.1 and 8.2 of this regulation do not apply to a low-flashpoint fuel or a gas fuel.

第18条 燃油可获得性和质量

燃油可获得性

1 各缔约国应采取一切合理措施促进符合本附则规定的燃油的供应，并将其能够提供合格燃油的港口和装卸站通知本组织。

2.1 如缔约国发现船舶不符合本附则规定的合格燃油的标准，该缔约国主管机关有权要求船舶：

 .1 提交为达到符合标准而采取行动的记录；和

 .2 提供其根据航次计划购买合格燃油的证据，以及如不能按原计划购得，已努力寻找该燃油的替代资源，并且尽管为获得合格燃油尽了最大努力，仍不能购得该燃油的证据。

2.2 不应要求船舶为符合标准而偏离其拟定的航程或不当延误航期。

2.3 如船舶提供了本条第2.1款规定的信息，缔约国应考虑到所有相关情况和所提供的证据，以确定采取相应行动，包括不采取监督措施。

2.4 未能购得合格燃油的船舶应通知其主管机关和相关目的港的主管机关。

2.5 如船舶已提供未能购得合格燃油的证据，缔约国应通知本组织。燃油质量

3 交付至本附则适用的船舶并在船舶上使用的燃油应符合下列要求：

 .1 除本条第3.2款规定之外：

   .1 燃油应为从石油炼制产生的烃的混合物，但不得排除加入少量用于改善某些方面性能的添加剂；

   .2 燃油应不含无机酸；和

   .3 燃油不得含有具有下列危害的添加的物质或化学杂质：

     .1 危害船舶安全或对机械性能有不利影响，或

     .2 对人员有害，或

     .3 总体上增加空气污染。

 .2 以石油炼制之外的方法得到的燃油不得：

   .1 超过本附则第14条中规定的适用硫含量；

   .2 导致发动机超过本附则第13条第3、4、5.1.1和7.4款中规定的适用氮氧化物排放极限值；

   .3 含有无机酸；或

   .4 .1 危害船舶安全或对机械性能有不利影响，或

     .2 对人员有害，或

     .3 总体上增加空气污染。

见统一解释15

---

4 本条不适用于固态煤或核燃料。本条第5.1、8.1和8.2段不适用于低闪点燃料或气体燃料。

5.1 For each ship subject to regulations 5 and 6 of this Annex, details of fuel oil delivered to and used on board that ship shall be recorded by means of a bunker delivery note that shall contain at least the information specifed in appendixV to this Annex.

5.2 For each ship subject to regulations 5 and 6 of this Annex, details of low-flashpoint fuel or gas fuel delivered to and used on board that ship shall be recorded by means of a bunker delivery note that shall include at least the information specified in items 1 to 6 of appendix V to this Annex, the density as determined by a test method appropriate to the fuel type together with the associated temperature and a declaration signed and certified by the fuel oil supplier's representative that the fuel oil is in conformity with paragraph 3 of this regulation. In addition the sulphur content of a low-flashpoint fuel or a gas fuel delivered to a ship specifically for use on board that ship shall be documented on the bunker delivery note by the suppler in terms of either the actual value as determined by a test method appropriate to the fuel type or, with the agreement of the appropriate authority at the port of supply, a statement that the sulphur content, When tested by such a method, is less than 0.001% m/m.

SEE INTERPRETATION 16

---

6 The bunker delivery note shall be kept on board the ship in such a place as to be readily available for inspection at all reasonable times. It shall be retained for a period of three years after the fuel oil has been delivered on board.

SEE INTERPRETATION 16

7.1 The competent authority of a Party may inspect the bunker delivery notes on board any ship to which this Annex applies while the ship is in itsport or offshore terminal, may make a copy of each delivery note, and may require the master or person in charge of the ship to certify that each copy is a true copy of such bunker delivery note. The competent authority may also verify the contents of each note through consultations with the port where the note was issued.

7.2 The inspection of the bunker delivery notes and the taking of certified copies by the competent authority under paragraph 7.1 of this regulation shall be performed as expeditiously as possible without causing the ship to be unduly delayed.

8.1 The bunker delivery noteshall be accompanied by a representative sample of the fuel oil delivered taking into account the guidelines developed by the Organization.* The sample is to be sealed and signed by the supplier's representative and the master or officer in charge of the bunker operation on completion of bunkering operations and retained under the ship's control until the fuel oil is substantially consumed, but in any case for a period of not less than 12 months from the time of delivery.

---

* Refer to the 2009 Guidelines for the sampling of fuel oil for determination of compliance with the revised MARPOL Annex VI (resolution MEPC. 182(59)).

5.1 对适用本附则第 5 条和第 6 条的船舶，应以燃油交付单的方式对交付并在船上使用的燃油的详细情况加以记录，该交付单应至少包含本附则附录 V 中规定的信息。

5.2 对适用本附则第 5 条和第 6 条的船舶，应以燃油交付单的方式对交付并在船上使用的低闪点燃料或气体燃料的详细情况加以记录，该交付单应至少包含本附则附录 V 第 1 至 6 项规定的信息，以适合该燃料类型的测试方法所确定的密度，连同有关的温度，以及由燃油供应商代表签署并证明该燃油符合本条第 3 段的声明。此外，供应商应在燃油交付单上记录交付给船舶的专门用于船上使用的低闪点燃料或气体燃料的硫含量，记录方式为通过适用于燃料类型的测试方法确定的实际值，或在供应港相关主管机关同意的情况下，说明通过该方法测试时硫含量小于 0.001 %m/m。

见统一解释 16

---

6 燃料交付单应存放在船上，在任何合理时间随时可供检查，并应在燃油交付船上之后保存三年。

见统一解释 16

7.1 缔约国的主管机关可检查停靠本国港口或近海装卸站的适用本附则的船舶的燃料交付单，并可复制每份交付单，也可要求船长或船舶负责人员证明该副本是该燃料交付单的真实副本。主管机关还可通过与出具该交付单的港口核实每份交付单的内容。

7.2 主管机关根据第 7.1 款的规定对燃料交付单的检查和制作核正无误的副本应尽速进行，并且不对船舶造成不当延误。

8.1 燃料交付单应按本组织制定的导则附有一份所交付燃油的代表样品 *。该样品应由供应商代表和船长或负责加油作业的高级船员在完成加油作业后铅封并签字，并应由船方保存直到燃油被基本消耗掉，但无论如何其保存期自加油日期算起应不少于 12 个月。

---

* 参见《为确定符合防污公约附则 Ⅵ 要求的燃油取样指南》（第 MEPC.182（59）号决议）。

8.2 If a Party requires the representative sample to be analysed, it shall be done in accordance with the verification procedure set forth in appendix VI to this Annex to determine whether the fuel oil meets the requirements of this Annex.

9 Parties undertake to ensure that appropriate authorities designated by them:

.1 maintain a register of local suppliers of fuel oil;

.2 require local suppliers to provide the bunker delivery note and, if applicable, the MARPOL delivered sample as required by this regulation, certified by the fuel oil supplier that the fuel oil meets the requirements of regulations 14 and 18 of this Annex;

.3 require local suppliers to retain a copy of the bunker delivery note for at least three years for inspection and verification by the port State as necessary;

.4 take action as appropriate against fuel oil suppliers that have been found to deliver fuel oil that does not comply with that stated on the bunker delivery note;

.5 inform the Administration of any ship receiving fuel oil found to be non-compliant with the requirements of regulation 14 or 18 of this Annex; and

.6 inform the Organization for circulation to Parties and Member States of the Organization of all cases where fuel oil suppliers have failed to meet the requirements specified in regulations 14 or 18 of this Annex.

10 In connection with port State inspections carried out by Parties, the Parties further undertake to:

.1 inform the Party or non-Party under whose jurisdiction a bunker delivery note was issued of cases of delivery of non-compliant fuel oil, giving all relevant information; and

.2 ensure that remedial action as appropriate is taken to bring non-compliant fuel oil discovered into compliance.

11 For every ship of 400 gross tonnage and above on scheduled services with frequent and regular port calls, an Administration may decide after application and consultation with affected States that compliance with paragraph 6 of this regulation may be documented in an alternative manner that gives similar certainty of compliance with regulations 14 and 18 of this Annex.

8.2 如一缔约国要求对代表性样品进行分析，则应按本附则附录Ⅵ中规定的验证程序进行，以确定燃油是否符合本附则的要求。

9 缔约国应保证其指定的主管机关：

.1 保持一份当地燃油供应商的登记表；

.2 要求当地供应商提供本条要求的燃油交付单和（如适用）MARPOL 交付样品，并由燃油供应商书面证明该燃油符合本附则第 14 和 18 条的要求；

.3 要求当地供应商保存一份燃料交付单的副本至少三年以供港口国必要时检查和核实；

.4 对所供燃油与燃料交付单所述内容不符的燃油供应商采取适当措施；

.5 将任何船舶发现收到不符合本附则第 14 或 18 条要求燃油的情况通知其主管机关；和

.6 将燃油供应商没能按本附则第 14 或 18 条规定的所有情况通知本组织，以转发各缔约国和本组织各成员国。

10 关于由缔约国进行的港口国检查，缔约国进一步承诺：

.1 通知缔约国或非缔约国在其管辖下出具的燃料交付单中交付不合格燃油的情况，并提供所有相关资料；和

.2 确保采取适当的补救措施，使被发现的不合格的燃油符合要求。

11 对 400 总吨及以上从事定期营运并频繁和定期停靠港口的船舶，主管机关在向相关各国申请和协商后可决定，对本条第 6 款的符合性可通过一种替代方法予以证明，该方法类似证明对本附则第 14 和 18 条的符合性。

2024 REVISED MARPOL ANNEX VI chapter 4—REGULATIONS ON THE CARBON INTENSITY OF INTERNATIONAL SHIPPING（RESOLUTION MEPC.385（81））

Regulation 19 Application

1   This chaptershall apply to all ships of 400 gross tonnage and above.

2   The provisions of this chaptershall not apply to:

  .1   ships solely engaged in voyages within waters subject to the sovereignty or jurisdiction of the State the flag of which the ship is entitled to fly. However, each Party should ensure, by the adoption of appropriate measures, that such ships are constructed and act in a manner consistent with the requirements of chapter 4 of this Annex, so far as is reasonable and practicable.

  .2   ships not propelled by mechanical means, and platforms including FPSOs and FSUs and drilling rigs, regardless of their propulsion.

3   Regulations 22, 23, 24 and 25 of this Annex shall not apply to ships which have non-conventional propulsion, except that regulations 22 and 24 shall apply to cruise passenger ships having non-conventional propulsion and LNG carriers having conventional or non-conventional propulsion, delivered on or after 1 September 2019, as defined in regulation 2.2.1, and regulations 23 and 25 shall apply to cruise passenger ships having non-conventional propulsion and LNG carriers having conventional or non-conventional propulsion. Regulations 22, 23, 24, 25 and 28 shall not apply to category A ships as defined in the Polar Code.

4   Notwithstanding the provisions of paragraph 1 of this regulation, the Administration may waive the requirement for a ship of 400 gross tonnage and above to comply with regulations 22 and 24 of this Annex.

5   The provision of paragraph 4 of this regulationshall not apply to ships of 400 gross tonnage and above:

  .1   for which the building contract is placed on or after 1 January 2017; or

  .2   in the absence of a building contract, the keel of which is laid or which is at a similar stage of construction on or after 1 July 2017; or

  .3   the delivery of which is on or after 1 July 2019; or

  .4   in cases of a major conversion of a new or existing ship, as defined in regulation 2.2.17 of this Annex, on or after 1 January 2017, and in which regulations 5.4.2 and 5.4.3 of this Annex apply.

6   The Administration of a Party to the present Convention which allows the application of paragraph 4, or suspends, withdraws or declines the application of that paragraph, to a ship entitled to fly its flag shall forthwith communicate to the Organization for circulation to the Parties to the present Protocol particulars thereof, for their information.

Regulation 20 Goal

The goal of this chapter is to reduce the carbon intensity of international shipping, working towards the levels of ambition set out in the Initial IMO Strategy on reduction of GHG emissions from ships.*

Regulation 21 Functional requirements

In order to achieve the goal set out in regulation 20 of this Annex, a ship to which this chapter applies shall comply, as applicable, with the following functional requirements to reduce its carbon intensity:

  .1   the technical carbon intensity requirements in accordance with regulations 22, 23, 24 and 25 of this Annex; and

  .2   the operational carbon intensity requirements in accordance with regulations 26, 27 and 28 of this Annex.

---

* Refer to Initial IMO Strategy on reduction of GHG emissions from ships (resolution MEPC.304(72)).

2024 年经修订的 MARPOL 公约附则 VI 第四章——国际航运碳强度规则（第 MEPC.385(81) 号决议）

第 19 条　适用范围

1　本章应适用于 400 总吨及以上的所有船舶。

2　本章规定不适用于：

　.1　仅航行于船舶有权悬挂其国旗的国家主权或管辖范围水域内的船舶。但是，各缔约国应通过采取相应措施确保此类船舶的建造和营运在合理和可行的范围内按本附则第 4 章的规定进行。

　.2　非机动船，以及包括浮式生产、储存和卸载设施（FPSO）、浮式储存装置（FSU）和钻井装置等平台，不论其推进方式如何。

3　本附则第 22、23、24 和 25 条不适用于非常规推进的船舶，但第 22 和 24 条应适用于第 2.2.1 条界定的、2019 年 9 月 1 日或以后交付的非常规推进的豪华邮轮和常规推进或非常规推进的液化天然气运输船，且第 23 和 25 条应适用于非常规推进的豪华邮轮和常规推进或非常规推进的液化天然气运输船。第 22、23、24、25 和 28 条不适用于《极地规则》中界定的 A 类船舶。

4　尽管有本条第 1 款的规定，主管机关可对 400 总吨及以上的船舶免除适用本附则第 22 条和 24 条的要求。

5　本条第 4 款的规定不适用于下述情况的 400 总吨及以上的船舶：

　.1　在 2017 年 1 月 1 日或以后签订建造合同；或

　.2　无建造合同，在 2017 年 7 月 1 日或以后安放龙骨或处于类似建造阶段；或

　.3　在 2019 年 7 月 1 日或以后交船；或

　.4　新船或现有船舶在 2017 年 1 月 1 日或以后进行本附则第 2.2.17 条定义的重大改建，且适用本附则第 5.4.2 和 5.4.3 条。

6　允许有权悬挂其国旗的船舶适用本条第 4 款，或推迟、撤销或拒绝适用该款的本公约缔约国的主管机关，应将其详细信息立即送交本组织，由本组织将该信息转发给本议定书各缔约国，供其参考。

第 20 条　目标

本章的目标是减少国际航运碳强度，以努力实现《国际海事组织船舶温室气体减排初步战略》* 中设定的目标减排水平。

第 21 条　功能要求

为了实现本附则第 20 条中规定的目标，本章适用的船舶应符合以下功能要求（如适用），以降低其碳强度：

　.1　按照本附则第 22、23、24 和 25 条的碳强度技术要求；和

　.2　按照本附则第 26、27 和 28 条的营运碳强度要求。

---

*　参见《IMO 船舶温室气体减排初步战略》（第 MEPC.304（72）号决议）。

Regulation 22 Attained Energy Efficiency Design Index (attained EEDI)

1   The attained EEDI shall be calculated for:

.1   each new ship;

.2   each new ship which has undergone a major conversion; and

.3   each new or existing ship which has undergone a major conversion that is so extensive that the ship is regarded by the Administration as a newly constructed ship which falls into one or more of the categories in regulations 2.2.5, 2.2.7, 2.2.9, 2.2.11, 2.2.14 to 2.2.16, 2.2.20, 2.2.22, and 2.2.26 to 2.2.29 of this Annex. The attained EEDI shall be specific to each ship and shall indicate the estimated performance of the ship in terms of energy efficiency, and be accompanied by the EEDI technical file that contains the information necessary for the calculation of the attained EEDI and that shows the process of calculation. The attained EEDI shall be verified, based on the EEDI technical file, either by the Administration or by any organization duly authorized by it.*

2   The attained EEDI shall be calculated taking into account the guidelines developed by the Organization.***

3   For each ship subject to regulation 24 of this Annex, the Administration or any organization duly authorized by it* shall report to the Organization the required and attained EEDI values and relevant information, taking into account the guidelines developed by the Organization**, via electronic communication:

.1   within seven months of completing the survey required under regulation 5.4 of this Annex; or

.2   within seven months following 1 April 2022 for a ship delivered prior to 1 April 2022.

SEE INTERPRETATION 17

Regulation 23 Attained Energy Efficiency Existing Ship Index (attained EEXI)

1   The attained EEXI shall be calculated for:

.1   each ship; and

.2   each ship which has undergone a major conversion

which falls into one or more of the categories in regulations 2.2.5, 2.2.7, 2.2.9, 2.2.11, 2.2.14 to 2.2.16, 2.2.22, and 2.2.26 to 2.2.29 of this Annex. The attained EEXI shall be specific to each ship and shall indicate the estimated performance of the ship in terms of energy efficiency, and be accompanied by the EEXI technical file which contains the information necessary for the calculation of the attained EEXI and which shows the process of the calculation. The attained EEXI shall be verified, based on the EEXI technical file, either by the Administration or by any organization duly authorized by it.*

2   The attained EEXI shall be calculated taking into account the guidelines developed by the Organization. ***

3   Notwithstanding paragraph 1 of this regulation, for each ship to which regulation 22 of this Annex applies, the attained EEDI verified by the Administration or by any organization duly authorized by it in accordance with regulation 22.1 of this Annex may be taken as the attained EEXI if the value of the attained EEDI is equal to or less than that of the required EEXI as required by regulation 25 of this Annex. In this case, the attained EEXI shall be verified based on the EEDI technical file.

---

* Refer to the Code for Recognized Organizations (RO Code) (resolution MEPC. 237(65), as may be amended).

** Refer to the 2018 Guidelines on the method of calculation of the attained Energy Efficiency Design Index (EEDI) for new ships (resolution MEPC. 308(73), as amended by resolutions MEPC.322(74) and MEPC.332(76)).

*** Refer to the 2022 Guidelines on the method of calculation of the attained Energy Efficiency Existing Ship Index (EEXI) (resolution MEPC.350(78)).

第 22 条　达到的能效设计指数（达到的 EEDI）

1　应为下列船舶计算达到的能效设计指数：

.1　每艘新船；

.2　每艘经过重大改建的新船；和

.3　每艘经过重大改建、且因改建范围大至被主管机关视为新造船舶的新船或现有船舶属于本附则第 2.2.5、2.2.7、2.2.9、2.2.11、2.2.14 至 2.2.16、2.2.20、2.2.22 及 2.2.26 至 2.2.29 条中一类或多类船型者。达到的能效设计指数应依据每一船舶的具体情况，并应表示出船舶在能效方面的预估性能，并附有用于计算达到的能效设计指数所需必要信息的能效设计指数技术案卷，并说明计算过程。达到的能效设计指数应经主管机关或经其正式授权的组织 * 根据能效设计指数技术案卷进行验证。

2　计算达到的能效设计指数应考虑到本组织制定的导则。***

3　对适用本附则第 24 条的船舶，主管机关或经其正式授权的组织 * 应考虑到本组织制定的导则 ** 通过电子通信方式，向本组织报告要求的和到达的能效设计指数值和相关信息：

.1　在完成本附则第 5.4 条要求的检验后七个月内；或

.2　对于 2022 年 4 月 1 日以前交付的船舶，在 2022 年 4 月 1 日之后的七个月内。

见统一解释 17

第 23 条　现有船舶达到的能效指数（达到的 EEXI）

1　应为下列船舶计算现有船舶达到的能效指数：

.1　每艘船舶；和

.2　经过重大改建的每艘船舶

属于本附则第 2.2.5、2.2.7、2.2.9、2.2.11、2.2.14 至 2.2.16、2.2.22 及 2.2.26 至 2.2.29 条中一类或多类船型者。现有船舶达到的能效指数应依据每一船舶的具体情况，并应表明船舶在能效方面的预估性能，并附有用于计算现有船舶达到的能效指数所需必要信息的现有船舶能效指数技术案卷，并说明计算过程。现有船舶达到的能效指数应经主管机关或经其正式授权的组织 * 根据现有船舶能效指数技术案卷进行验证。

2　计算现有船舶达到的能效指数应考虑到本组织制定的导则。***

3　尽管有本条第 1 款的要求，对适用本附则第 22 条的船舶，主管机关或经其正式授权的组织按照本附则第 22.1 条验证的达到的能效设计指数可作为现有船舶能达到的能效指数，只要达到的能效设计指数值等于或小于本附则第 25 条规定的现有船舶要求的能效指数。在这种情况下，现有船舶达到的能效指数应根据能效设计指数技术案卷进行验证。

---

*　参见《认可组织规则》（RO 规则）（第 MEPC.237（65）号决议，可经修订）。

**　参见《2018 年新船达到的能效设计指数（EEDI）计算方法导则》（第 MEPC.308（73）号决议，经第 MEPC.322（74）号决议和第 MEPC.332（76）号决议修订）。

***　参见《2022 年现有船舶达到的能效指数（EEXI）计算导则》（第 MEPC.350（78）号决议）。

Regulation 24 Required EEDI

1   For each:

.1   new ship,

.2   new ship which has undergone a major conversion, and

.3   new or existing ship which has undergone a major conversion that is so extensive that the ship is regarded by the Administration as a newly constructed ship which falls into one of the categories in regulations 2.2.5, 2.2.7, 2.2.9, 2.2.11, 2.2.14 to 2.2.16, 2.2.22, and 2.2.26 to 2.2.29 and to which this chapter is applicable, the attained EEDI shall be as follows:

$$\text{Attained EEDI} \leqslant \text{Required EEDI} = \left(1 - \frac{X}{100}\right) \cdot \text{Reference line value}$$

where X is the reduction factor specified in table 1 for the required EEDI compared to the EEDI reference line.

2   For each new and existing ship that has undergone a major conversion which is so extensive that the ship is regarded by the Administration as a newly constructed ship, the attained EEDI shall be calculated and meet the requirement of paragraph 1 of this regulation with the reduction factor applicable corresponding to the ship type and size of the converted ship at the date of the contract of the conversion, or in the absence of a contract, the commencement date of the conversion.

Table 1 Reduction factors (in percentage) for the EEDI relative to the EEDI reference line

Ship Type	Size	Phase 0 1 Jan 2013 -31 Dec 2014	Phase 1 1 Jan 2015 -31 Dec 2019	Phase 2 1 Jan 2020 -31 Mar 2022	Phase 2 1 Jan 2020 -31 Dec 2024	Phase 3 1 Apr 2022 and onwards	Phase 3 1 Jan 2025 and onwards
Bulk carrier	20,000 DWT and above	0	10		20		30
	10,000 and above but less than 20,000 DWT	n/a	0-10*		0-20*		0-30*
Gas carrier	15,000 DWT and above	0	10	20		30	
	10,000 and above but less than 15,000 DWT	0	10		20		30
	2,000 and above but less than 10,000 DWT	n/a	0-10*		0-20*		0-30*
Tanker	20,000 DWT and above	0	10		20		30
	4,000 and above but less than 20,000 DWT	n/a	0-10*		0-20*		0-30*
Container ship	200,000 DWT and above	0	10	20		50	
	120,000 and above but less than 200,000 DWT	0	10	20		45	
	80,000 and above but less than 120,000 DWT	0	10	20		40	
	40,000 and above but less than 80,000 DWT	0	10	20		35	
	15,000 and above but less than 40,000 DWT	0	10	20		30	
	10,000 and above but less than 15,000 DWT	n/a	0-10*	0-20*		15-30*	
General Cargo ships	15,000 DWT and above	0	10		15		30
	3,000 and above but less than 15,000 DWT	n/a	0-10*	0-15*		0-30*	

第24条 要求的能效设计指数

1 对每艘：

.1 新船，

.2 经过重大改建的新船，和

.3 经过重大改建、且因改建范围过大而被主管机关视为新造船舶的新船或现有船舶属于本附则第 2.2.5、2.2.7、2.2.9、2.2.11、2.2.14 至 2.2.16、2.2.22 及 2.2.26 至 2.2.29 条中一类或多类船型者且适用于本章者，其达到的能效设计指数应为：

$$达到的能效设计指数 \leq 要求的能效设计指数 = \left(1 - \frac{X}{100}\right) 参考线值$$

式中，X 为表1所规定的相对于能效设计指数参考线的要求的能效设计指数的折减系数。

2 对于经过重大改建且因改建范围大至被主管机关视为新造船舶的新船或现有船舶，应计算达到的能效设计指数并应符合本条第 1 款的要求，其折减系数应与签订改建合同之日，或无合同情况下改建开始之日该改建船舶的船型和尺寸相符合。

表1 相对于能效设计指数参考线的能效设计指数值的折减系数（百分比）

船舶类型	尺度	第0阶段 2013年1月1日—2014年12月31日	第1阶段 2015年1月1日—2019年12月31日	第2阶段 2020年1月1日—2022年3月31日	第2阶段 2020年1月1日—2024年12月31日	第3阶段 2022年4月1日及以后	第3阶段 2025年1月1日及以后
散货船	20 000 载重吨及以上	0	10		20		30
	10 000 载重吨及以上，20 000 载重吨以下	n/a	0~10*		0~20*		0~30*
气体运输船	15 000 载重吨及以上	0	10	20		30	
	10 000 载重吨及以上，15 000 载重吨以下	0	10		20		30
	2 000 载重吨及以上，10 000 载重吨以下	n/a	0~10*		0~20*		0~30*
液货船	20 000 载重吨及以上	0	10		20		30
	4 000 载重吨及以上，20 000 载重吨以下	n/a	0~10*		0~20*		0~30*
集装箱船	200 000 载重吨及以上	0	10	20		50	
	120 000 载重吨及以上，200 000 载重吨以下	0	10	20		45	
	80 000 载重吨及以上，120 000 载重吨以下	0	10	20		40	
	40 000 载重吨及以上，80 000 载重吨以下	0	10	20		35	
	15 000 载重吨及以上，40 000 载重吨以下	0	10	20		30	
	10 000 载重吨及以上，15 000 载重吨以下	n/a	0~10*	0~20*		15~30*	
杂货船	15 000 载重吨及以上	0	10		15		30
	3 000 载重吨及以上，15 000 载重吨以下	n/a	0~10*	0~15*		0~30*	

Ship Type	Size	Phase 0 1 Jan 2013 -31 Dec 2014	Phase 1 1 Jan 2015 -31 Dec 2019	Phase 2 1 Jan 2020 -31 Mar 2022	Phase 2 1 Jan 2020 -31 Dec 2024	Phase 3 1 Apr 2022 and onwards	Phase 3 1 Jan 2025 and onwards
Refrigerated cargo carrier	5,000 DWT and above	0	10		15		30
	3,000 and above but less than 5,000 DWT	n/a	0-10*		0-15*		0-30*
Combination carrier	20,000 DWT and above	0	10		20		30
	4,000 and above but less than 20,000 DWT	n/a	0-10*		0-20*		0-30*
LNG carrier***	10,000 DWT and above	n/a	10**	20		30	
Ro-ro cargo ship (vehicle carrier)***	10,000 DWT and above	n/a	5**		15		30
Ro-ro cargo ship***	2,000 DWT and above	n/a	5**		20		30
	1,000 and above but less than 2,000 DWT	n/a	0-5*,**		0-20*		0-30*
Ro-ro passenger ship***	1,000 DWT and above	n/a	5**		20		30
	250 and above but less than 1,000 DWT	n/a	0-5*,**		0-20*		0-30*
Cruise passenger ship***having non-conventional propulsion	85,000 DWT and above	n/a	5**	20		30	
	25,000 and above but less than 85,000 GT	n/a	0-5*,**	0-20*		0-30*	

*   Reduction factor to be linearly interpolated between the two values dependent upon vessel size. The lower value of the reduction factor is to be applied to the smaller ship size.

**   Phase 1 commences for those ships on 1 September 2015.

***   Reduction factor applies to those ships delivered on or after 1 September 2019, as defined in paragraph 2.1 of regulation 2.

Note: n/a means that no required EEDI applies.

3   The reference line values shall be calculated as follows:

$$\text{Reference line values} = a \cdot b^{-c}$$

where a, b and c are the parameters given in Table 2.

船舶类型	尺度	第0阶段 2013年1月1日—2014年12月31日	第1阶段 2015年1月1日—2019年12月31日	第2阶段 2020年1月1日—2022年3月31日	第2阶段 2020年1月1日—2024年12月31日	第3阶段 2022年4月1日及以后	第3阶段 2025年1月1日及以后
冷藏货船	5 000 载重吨及以上	0	10		15		30
	3 000 载重吨及以上，5 000 载重吨以下	n/a	0~10*		0~15*		0~30*
兼用船	20 000 载重吨及以上	0	10		20		30
	4 000 载重吨及以上，20 000 载重吨以下	n/a	0~10*		0~20*		0~30*
液化天然气运输船***	10 000 载重吨及以上	n/a	10**	20		30	
滚装货船（车辆运输船）***	10 000 载重吨及以上	n/a	5**	15		30	
滚装货船***	2 000 载重吨及以上	n/a	5**	20		30	
	1 000 载重吨及以上，2 000 载重吨以下	n/a	0~5*,**	0~20*		0~30*	
滚装客船***	1 000 载重吨及以上	n/a	5**	20		30	
	250 载重吨及以上，1 000 载重吨以下	n/a	0~5*,**	0~20*		0~30*	
采用非常规推进的豪华邮轮***	85 000 总吨及以上	n/a	5**	20		30	
	25 000 总吨及以上，85 000 总吨以下	n/a	0~5*,**	0~20*		0~30*	

表中： * 表示折减系数根据船舶吨位在这两个值之间取线性插值。小的折减系数应用于小吨位的船舶。

    ** 对此类船舶，第1阶段于2015年9月1日开始。

    *** 折减系数适用于第2条2.1款所界定的，2019年9月1日或以后交付的船舶。注：n/a系指没有适用的要求的能效设计指数。

3 参考线值应按照以下方法计算：

$$参考线值 = a \cdot b^{-c}$$

式中 a、b 和 c 分别为表2所列参数。

Table 2 Parameters for determination of reference values for the different ship types

Ship type defined in regulation 2	a	b	c
2.2.5 Bulk carrier	961.79	DWT of the ship where DWT≤279,000 279,000 where DWT > 279,000	0.477
2.2.7 Combination carrier	1,219.00	DWT of the ship	0.488
2.2.9 Container ship	174.22	DWT of the ship	0.201
2.2.11 Cruise passenger ship having non-conventional propulsion	170.84	GT of the ship	0.214
2.2.14 Gas carrier	1,120.00	DWT of the ship	0.456
2.2.15 General cargo ship	107.48	DWT of the ship	0.216
2.2.16 LNG carrier	2,253.7	DWT of the ship	0.474
2.2.22 Refrigerated cargo carrier	227.01	DWT of the ship	0.244
2.2.26 Ro-ro cargo ship	1,405.15	DWT of the ship	0.498
	1,686.17*	DWT of the ship where DWT≤17,000* 17,000 where DWT>17,000*	
2.2.27 Ro-ro cargo ship (vehicle carrier)	$(DWT/GT)^{0.7} \cdot 780.36$ where DWT/GT<0.3 1,812.63 where DWT/GT≥0.3	DWT of the ship	0.471
2.2.28 Ro-ro passenger ship	752.16	DWT of the ship	0.381
	902.59*	DWT of the ship where DWT≤10,000* 10,000 where DWT>10,000*	
2.2.29 Tanker	1,218.80	DWT of the ship	0.488

*   to be used from phase 2 and thereafter.

4   If the design of a ship allows it to fall into more than one of the ship type definitions specified in table 2, the required EEDI for the ship shall be the most stringent (the lowest) required EEDI.

5   For each ship to which this regulation applies, the installed propulsion power shall not be less than the propulsion power needed to maintain the manoeuvrability of the ship under adverse conditions as defined in the guidelines to be developed by the Organization. *

6   At the beginning of phase 1 and at the midpoint of phase 2, the Organization shall review the status of technological developments and, if proven necessary, amend the time periods, the EEDI reference line parameters for relevant ship types and reduction rates set out in this regulation.

* Refer to Guidelines for determining minimum propulsion power to maintain the maneuverability of ships in adverse conditions (MEPC.1/Circ.850/Rev.3).

表 2　用于确定不同船型参考线值的参数

第 2 条所定义的船型	a	b	c
2.2.5 散货船	961.79	船舶载重吨（如该船载重吨 ≤ 279 000） 279 000（如该船载重吨 >279 000）	0.477
2.2.7 兼用船	1 219.00	船舶载重吨	0.488
2.2.9 集装箱船	174.22	船舶载重吨	0.201
2.2.11 采用非常规推进的豪华邮轮	170.84	船舶总吨	0.214
2.2.14 气体运输船	1 120.00	船舶载重吨	0.456
2.2.15 杂货船	107.48	船舶载重吨	0.216
2.2.16 液化天然气运输船	2 253.7	船舶载重吨	0.474
2.2.22 冷藏货船	227.01	船舶载重吨	0.244
2.2.26 滚装货船	1 405.15	船舶载重吨	0.498
	1 686.17*	船舶载重吨（如该船载重吨 ≤ 17 000）* 17 000（如该船载重吨 >17 000）*	
2.2.27 滚装货船（车辆运输船）	$(DWT/GT)^{0.7} \cdot 780.36$（如载重吨 / 总吨 <0.3）1 812.63（如载重吨 / 总吨 ≥ 0.3）	船舶载重吨	0.471
2.2.28 滚装客船	752.16	船舶载重吨	0.381
	902.59*	船舶载重吨（如该船载重吨 ≤ 10 000）* 10 000（如该船载重吨 >10 000）*	
2.2.29 液货船	1 218.80	船舶载重吨	0.488

* 第 2 阶段及之后开始使用。

4　如船舶的设计允许其属于表 2 中规定的一类以上船型的定义，则该船要求的能效设计指数应为最严格的要求值（最低值）。

5　对本条适用的每艘船舶，所安装的推进动力应不小于在本组织将要制定的导则 * 中定义的恶劣工况下保持船舶操纵性所需要的推进动力。

6　在第 1 阶段开始和第 2 阶段中间，本组织应对技术发展状况进行复审，并且，如证明有必要，修正本条所列的时间段、相关船型的能效设计指数参考线参数和折减系数。

* 参见《确定船舶在恶劣工况下保持船舶操纵性能所需最小推进动力导则》（第 MEPC.1/Circ.850/Rev.3 号通函）。

Regulation 25 Required EEXI

1   For:

.1   each ship; and

.2   each ship which has undergone a major conversion

which falls into one of the categories in regulations 2.2.5, 2.2.7, 2.2.9, 2.2.11, 2.2.14 to 2.2.16, 2.2.22, and 2.2.26 to 2.2.29 and to which this chapter is applicable, the attained EEXI shall be as follows:

$$\text{Attained EEXI} \leqslant \text{Required EEXI} = \left(1-\frac{Y}{100}\right) \cdot \text{EEDI reference line value}$$

Where Y is the reduction factor specified in Table 3 for the required EEXI compared to the EEDI reference line.

Table 3 Reduction factors (in percentage) for the EEXI relative to the EEDI reference line

Ship type	Size	Reduction factor
Bulk carrier	200,000 DWT and above	15
	20,000 and above but less than 200,000 DWT	20
	10,000 and above but less than 20,000 DWT	0-20*
Gas carrier	15,000 DWT and above	30
	10,000 and above but less than 15,000 DWT	20
	2,000 and above but less than 10,000 DWT	0-20*
Tanker	200,000 DWT and above	15
	20,000 and above but less than 200,000 DWT	20
	4,000 and above but less than 20,000 DWT	0-20*
Container ship	200,000 DWT and above	50
	120,000 and above but less than 200,000 DWT	45
	80,000 and above but less than 120,000 DWT	35
	40,000 and above but less than 80,000 DWT	30
	15,000 and above but less than 40,000 DWT	20
	10,000 and above but less than 15,000 DWT	0-20*
General cargo ship	15,000 DWT and above	30
	3,000 and above but less than 15,000 DWT	0-30*
Refrigerated cargo carrier	5,000 DWT and above	15
	3,000 and above but less than 5,000 DWT	0-15*
Combination carrier	20,000 DWT and above	20
	4,000 and above but less than 20,000 DWT	0-20*
LNG carrier	10,000 DWT and above	30
Ro-ro cargo ship (vehicle carrier)	10,000 DWT and above	15
Ro-ro cargo ship	2,000 DWT and above	5
	1,000 and above but less than 2,000 DWT	0-5*
Ro-ro passenger ship	1,000 DWT and above	5
	250 and above but less than 1,000 DWT	0-5*
Cruise passenger ship having non-conventional propulsion	85,000 GT and above	30
	25,000 and above but less than 85,000 GT	0-30*

*   Reduction factor to be linearly interpolated between the two values dependent upon ship size. The lower value of the reduction factor is to be applied to the smaller ship size.

第25条 现有船舶要求的能效指数

1 对每艘：

.1 船舶；和

.2 经过重大改建的每艘船舶

属本附则第 2.2.5、2.2.7、2.2.9、2.2.11、2.2.14 至 2.2.16、2.2.22 和 2.2.26 至 2.2.29 条中定义的类型之一且适用于本章者，其现有船舶达到的能效指数应为：

$$现有船舶达到的能效指数 \leq 现有船舶要求的能效指数 = \left(1 - \frac{Y}{100}\right) 能效设计指数参考线值$$

式中，Y 为表 3 中所规定的相对于能效设计指数参考线的现有船舶要求的能效指数的折减系数。

表 3 相对于能效设计指数参考线的现有船舶能效指数的折减系数（百分比）

船舶类型	尺度	折减系数
散货船	200 000 载重吨及以上	15
	20 000 载重吨及以上，200 000 载重吨以下	20
	10 000 载重吨及以上，20 000 载重吨以下	0~20*
气体运输船	15 000 载重吨及以上	30
	10 000 载重吨及以上，15 000 载重吨以下	20
	2 000 载重吨及以上，10 000 载重吨以下	0~20*
液货船	200 000 载重吨及以上	15
	20 000 载重吨及以上，200 000 载重吨以下	20
	4 000 载重吨及以上，20 000 载重吨以下	0~20*
集装箱船	200 000 载重吨及以上	50
	120 000 载重吨及以上，200 000 载重吨以下	45
	80 000 载重吨及以上，120 000 载重吨以下	35
	40 000 载重吨及以上，80 000 载重吨以下	30
	15 000 载重吨及以上，40 000 载重吨以下	20
	10 000 载重吨及以上，15 000 载重吨以下	0~20*
杂货船	15 000 载重吨及以上	30
	3 000 载重吨及以上，15 000 载重吨以下	0~30*
冷藏货船	5 000 载重吨及以上	15
	3 000 载重吨及以上，5 000 载重吨以下	0~15*
兼用船	20 000 载重吨及以上	20
	4 000 载重吨及以上，20 000 载重吨以下	0~20*
液化天然气运输船	10 000 载重吨及以上	30
滚装货船（车辆运输船）	10 000 载重吨及以上	15
滚装货船	2 000 载重吨及以上	5
	1 000 载重吨及以上，2 000 载重吨以下	0~5*
滚装客船	1 000 载重吨及以上	5
	250 载重吨及以上，1 000 载重吨以下	0~5*
采用非常规推进的豪华邮轮	85 000 总吨及以上	30
	25 000 总吨及以上，85 000 总吨以下	0~30*

* 根据船舶尺度折减系数在两个值之间取线性插值。较低的折减系数适用于较小的船舶尺度。

2   The EEDI reference line values shall be calculated in accordance with regulations 24.3 and 24.4 of this Annex. For ro-ro cargo ships and ro-ro passenger ships, the reference line value to be used from phase 2 and thereafter under regulation 24.3 of this Annex shall be referred to.

3   A review shall be completed by 1 January 2026 by the Organization to assess the effectiveness of this regulation taking into account any guidelines developed by the Organization. If, based on the review, the Parties decide to adopt amendments to this regulation, such amendments shall be adopted and brought into force in accordance with the provisions of article 16 of the present Convention.

Regulation 26 Ship Energy Efficiency Management Plan (SEEMP)

1   Each ship shall keep on board a ship specific Ship Energy Efficiency Management Plan (SEEMP). This may form part of the ship's Safety Management System (SMS). The SEEMP shall be developed and reviewed, taking into account the guidelines adopted by the Organization.*

2   In the case of a ship of 5,000 gross tonnage and above, the SEEMP shall include a description of the methodology that will be used to collect the data required by regulation 27.1 of this Annex and the processes that will be used to report the data to the ship's Administration.

3   In the case of a ship of 5,000 gross tonnage and above, which falls into one or more of the categories in regulations 2.2.5, 2.2.7, 2.2.9, 2.2.11, 2.2.14 to 2.2.16, 2.2.22, and 2.2.26 to 2.2.29 of this Annex:

.1   On or before 1 January 2023 the SEEMP shall include:

   .1   a description of the methodology that will be used to calculate the ship's attained annual operational CII required by regulation 28 of this Annex and the processes that will be used to report this value to the ship's Administration;

   .2   the required annual operational CII, as specified in regulation 28 of this Annex, for the next three years;

   .3   an implementation plan documenting how the required annual operational CII will be achieved during the next three years; and

   .4   a procedure for self-evaluation and improvement.

SEE INTERPRETATION 18

.2   For a ship rated as D for three consecutive years or rated as E in accordance with regulation 28 of this Annex, the SEEMP shall be reviewed in accordance with regulation 28.8 of this Annex to include a plan of corrective actions to achieve the required annual operational CII.

.3   The SEEMP shall be subject to verification and company audits taking into account the guidelines to be developed by the Organization. **

Regulation 27 Collection and reporting of ship fuel oil consumption data

1   From calendar year 2019, each ship of 5,000 gross tonnage and above shall collect the data specified in appendix IX to this Annex, for that and each subsequent calendar year or portion thereof, as appropriate according to the methodology included in the SEEMP.

SEE INTERPRETATION 19

---

2   Except as provided for in paragraphs 4, 5 and 6 of this regulation, at the end of each calendar year, the ship shall aggregate the data collected in that calendar year or portion thereof, as appropriate.

3   Except as provided for in paragraphs 4, 5 and 6 of this regulation, within three months after the end of each calendar year, the ship shall report to its Administration or any organization duly authorized by it,*** the aggregated value for each datum specified in appendix IX to this Annex, via electronic communication and using a standardized format to be developed by the Organization. *

---

* Refer to the 2024 Guidelines for the Development of a Ship Energy Efficiency Management Plan (SEEMP) (resolution MEPC. 395(82)).

** Refer to Guidelines for the verification and company audits by the Administration of part III of the Ship Energy Efficiency Management Plan (SEEMP) (resolution MEPC. 347(78)).

*** Refer to the Code for Recognized Organizations (RO Code) (resolution MEPC. 237(65), as may be amended).

2　应按照本附则第24.3和24.4条计算能效设计指数参考线值。对于滚装货船和滚装客船，从第2阶段开始使用参考线值，此后应参照本附则第24.3条。

3　本组织应在2026年1月1日之前完成对本条有效性的复审，并考虑到本组织制定的导则。如果基于复审的结果，缔约国决定通过对本条的修正案，则此修正案应按照本公约第16条的规定予以通过并生效。

第 26 条　船舶能效管理计划（SEEMP）

1　每艘船舶应在船上持有一份适用本船的《船舶能效管理计划》（SEEMP）。该计划可作为船舶安全管理体系（SMS）的一部分。制定和复审船舶能效管理计划应考虑到本组织通过的导则。[*]

2　对于5 000总吨及以上的船舶，其《船舶能效管理计划》应包括对将用于收集本附则第27.1条要求的数据的方法的说明和将用于向船舶主管机关报告数据的程序的说明。

3　对于5 000总吨及以上的船舶，且属本附则第2.2.5、2.2.7、2.2.9、2.2.11、2.2.14至2.2.16、2.2.22和2.2.26至2.2.29条中一类或多类船型者：

　.1　2023年1月1日或以前，其《船舶能效管理计划》应包含：

　　.1　对将用于计算本附则第28条要求的船舶达到的年度营运碳强度指标的方法的说明和将用于向船舶主管机关报告该值的程序的说明；

　　.2　本附则第28条规定的未来三年要求的年度营运碳强度指标；

　　.3　记录未来三年如何达到要求的年度营运碳强度指标的实施计划；和

　　.4　自评估和改进程序。

见统一解释18

　.2　对于按照本附则第28条连续三年被评为D级或被评为E级的船舶，应按照本附则第28.8条对《船舶能效管理计划》进行复审，并制定整改行动计划，以达到要求的年度营运碳强度指标。

　.3　应对《船舶能效管理计划》进行验证和公司审核，并考虑到本组织制定的导则[**]。

第 27 条　收集和报告船舶燃油消耗数据

1　从2019日历年开始，凡5 000总吨及以上的船舶应按照《船舶能效管理计划》中的方法，在该日历年和下一一日历年或部分时间段内（适用时）收集本附则附录Ⅸ要求的数据。

见统一解释19

2　除本条第4、5和6款规定者外，每一日历年年末，船舶应汇总在该日历年内或部分时间段内所收集的数据。

3　除本条第4、5和6款规定者外，每一日历年年末后的三个月内，船舶应通过电子通信方式并使用本组织制定的标准格式[*]，向主管机关或经其正式授权的组织[***]，报告本附则附录Ⅸ规定的各项数据的汇总值。

---

[*]　参见《2024年制定船舶能效管理计划（SEEMP）导则》（第MEPC.395（82）号决议）。

[**]　参见《主管机关对船舶和公司审核船舶能效管理计划（SEEMP）第Ⅲ部分导则》（（第MEPC.347（78）号决议）。

[***]　参见《认可组织规则》（RO规则）（第MEPC.237（65）号决议，可经修订）。

4 In the event of the transfer of a ship from one Administration to another, the ship shall on the day of completion of the transfer or as close as practical thereto report to the losing Administration or any organization duly authorized by it, the aggregated data for the period of the calendar year corresponding to that Administration, as specified in appendix IX to this Annex and, upon prior request of that Administration, the disaggregated data.

5 In the event of a change from one company to another, the ship shall on the day of completion of the change or as close as practical thereto report to its Administration or any organization duly authorized by it,* the aggregated data for the portion of the calendar year corresponding to the company, as specified in appendix IX to this Annex and, upon request of its Administration, the disaggregated data.

6 In the event of change from one Administration to another and from one company to another concurrently, paragraph 4 of this regulation shall apply.

7 The data shall be verified according to procedures established by the Administration, taking into account the guidelines developed by the Organization.**

8 Except as provided for in paragraphs 4, 5 and 6 of this regulation, the disaggregated data that underlies the reported data noted in appendix IX to this Annex for the previous calendar year shall be readily accessible for a period of not less than 12 months from the end of that calendar year and be made available to the Administration upon request.

SEE INTERPRETATION 20

---

9 The Administration shall ensure that the reported data noted in appendix IX to this Annex by its registered ships of 5,000 gross tonnage and above are transferred to the IMO Ship Fuel Oil Consumption Database via electronic communication and using a standardized format to be developed by the Organization*** not later than one month after issuing the Statements of Compliance of these ships.

10 On the basis of the reported data submitted to the IMO Ship Fuel Oil Consumption Database, the Secretary-General of the Organization shall produce an annual report to the Marine Environment Protection Committee summarizing the data collected, the status of missing data, and such other relevant information as may be requested by the Committee.

11 The Secretary-General of the Organization shall grant the Administration of a ship to which regulation 28 of this Annex applies access to all the reported data for all the preceding calendar year in the IMO Ship Fuel Oil Consumption Database for that ship.

12 Tho Socrotary-General of the Organization shall maintain an anonymized database such that identification of a specific ship will not be possible. Parties shall have access to the anonymized data strictly for their analysis and consideration.

13 The IMO Ship Fuel Oil Consumption Database shall be undertaken and managed by the Secretary-General of the Organization, pursuant to guidelines to be developed by the Organization. ****

14 On an ad hoc basis, the Secretary-General of the Organization may share data with analytical consultancies and research entities, under strict confidentiality rules.

15 The Secretary-General of the Organization, on the request of a company, shall grant access to the fuel oil consumption reports of the company's owned ship(s) in a non-anonymized form to the general public.

---

* Refer to the Code for Recognized Organizations (RO Code) (resolution MEPC.237(65), as may be amended).
** Refer to the 2022 Guidelines for Administration verification of ship fuel oil consumption data and operational carbon intensity (resolution MEPC. 348(78)).
*** Refer to the 2024 Guidelines for the development of a Ship Energy Efficiency Management Plan (SEEMP) (resolution MEPC. 395(82)).
**** Refer to the 2022 Guidelines for the development and management of the IMO Ship Fuel Oil Consumption Database (resolution MEPC. 349(78)).

4　如船舶变更主管机关，应按照本附则附录Ⅸ的规定，在变更完成之日或尽实际可能接近的日期向原主管机关或经其正式授权的组织 * 报告该日历年中与该主管机关相应时期的汇总数据，以及该主管机关的事先要求下未汇总的数据。

5　如船舶变更公司，应按照本附则附录Ⅸ的规定，在变更完成之日或尽实际可能接近的日期向其主管机关或经其正式授权的组织 * 报告该日历年中与该公司相应部分时间段内的汇总数据，以及该主管机关要求的未汇总的数据。

6　如船舶同时变更主管机关和公司，则应适用本条第 4 款。

7　应按照主管机关确定的程序对数据进行验证，并考虑到本组织制定的导则 **。

8　除本条第 4、5 和 6 款规定外，本附则附录Ⅸ中所指的上一日历年报告数据的未汇总数据应自该日历年末至少 12 个月内随时可用，并在要求时，向主管机关提供。

见统一解释 20

9　主管机关应确保，其 5 000 总吨及以上的登记船舶所报告的本附则附录Ⅸ中所指的数据，在不晚于签发了这些船舶的符合声明后的一个月内，通过电子通信并使用本组织制定的标准格式 ***，转交至国际海事组织船舶燃油消耗数据库。

10　根据提交给国际海事组织船舶燃油消耗数据库的报告数据，本组织秘书长应向海上环境保护委员会提交一份年度报告，总结所收集到的数据、缺失数据的情况以及委员会可能要求的此类其他相关信息。

11　本组织秘书长应授权适用本附则第 28 条的船舶的主管机关访问该船舶在国际海事组织船舶燃油消耗量数据库中所有上一日历年的全部报告数据。

12　本组织秘书长应维护一个无法识别特定船舶的匿名数据库，缔约国有权访问匿名数据，仅限于分析和研究。

13　本组织秘书长应按照本组织制定的导则负责管理国际海事组织燃油消耗数据库。****

14　本组织秘书长可根据严格的保密规则，临时与分析咨询机构和研究实体共享数据。

15　本组织秘书长应某公司的请求，允许以非匿名形式查阅该公司所属船舶的燃油消耗报告。

Regulation 28 Operational carbon intensity

Attained annual operational carbon intensity indicator (attained annual operational CII)

1 After the end of calendar year 2023 and after the end of each following calendar year, each ship of 5,000 gross tonnage and above which falls into one or more of the categories in regulations 2.2.5, 2.2.7, 2.2.9, 2.2.11, 2.2.14 to 2.2.16, 2.2.22, and 2.2.26 to 2.2.29 of this Annex shall calculate the attained annual operational CII over a 12-month period from 1 January to 31 December for the preceding calendar year, using the data collected in accordance with regulation 27 of this Annex, taking into account the guidelines to be developed by the Organization.*

2 Within three months after the end of each calendar year, the ship shall report to its Administration, or any organization duly authorized by it,** the attained annual operational CII via electronic communication and using a standardized format to be developed by the Organization.***

3 Notwithstanding 1 and 2 of this regulation, in the event of any transfer of a ship addressed in regulations 27.4, 27.5 or 27.6 completed after 1 January 2023, a ship shall, after the end of the calendar year in which the transfer takes place, calculate and report the attained annual operational CII for the full 12-month period from 1 January to 31 December in the calendar year during which the transfer took place, in accordance with regulations 28.1 and 28.2, for verification in accordance with regulation 6.6 of this Annex, taking into account guidelines to be developed by the Organization.*** Nothing in this regulation relieves any ship of its reporting obligations under regulation 27 or this regulation of this Annex.

Required annual operational carbon intensity indicator (required annual operational CII)

4 For each ship of 5,000 gross tonnage and above which falls into one or more of the categories in regulations 2.2.5, 2.2.7, 2.2.9, 2.2.11, 2.2.14 to 2.2.16, 2.2.22, and 2.2.26 to 2.2.29 of this Annex, the required annual operational CII shall be determined as follows:

$$\text{Required annual operational CII} = \left(1 - \frac{Z}{100}\right) \cdot \text{CII}_R$$

where,

Z is the annual reduction factor to ensure continuous improvement of the ship's operational carbon intensity within a specific rating level; and

CII_R is the reference value.

5 The annual reduction factor Z**** and the reference value CII_R shall be the values defined taking into account the guidelines to be developed by the Organization.*****

---

* Refer to the 2022 Guidelines on operational carbon intensity indicators and the calculation methods (CII guidelines, G1) (resolution MEPC. 352(78)), and the 2022 Interim guidelines on correction factors and voyage adjustments for CII calculations (CII guidelines, G5) (resolution MEPC. 355(78)).

** Refer to the Code for Recognized Organizations (RO Code) (resolution MEPC. 237(65), as may be amended).

*** Refer to the 2024 Guidelines for the development of a Ship Energy Efficiency Management Plan (SEEMP) (resolution MEPC. 395(82)).

**** The annual reduction factor is specific to each category of ship. This factor is defined to increase progressively to meet the objectives of the 2023 IMO Strategy on reduction of GHG emissions from ships (resolution MEPC.377(80)).

***** Refer to the 2021 Guidelines on the operational carbon intensity reduction factors relative to reference lines (CII reduction factor guidelines, G3) (resolution MEPC. 338(76)) and 2022 Guidelines on the reference lines for use with operational carbon intensity indicators (CII reference lines guidelines, G2) (resolution MEPC. 353(78)).

第 28 条　营运碳强度

达到的年度营运碳强度指标（达到的年度营运 CII）

1 2023 年日历年年末后且以后每一日历年年末，凡 5 000 总吨及以上、属于本附则第 2.2.5、2.2.7、2.2.9、2.2.11、2.2.14 至 2.2.16、2.2.22 和 2.2.26 至 2.2.29 条中一类或多类船型的船舶，应使用按照本附则第 27 条所收集的数据，虑及本组织制定的导则[*]，计算前一日历年从 1 月 1 日至 12 月 31 日的 12 个月内达到的年度营运碳强度指标。

2 每一日历年年末之后的三个月内，船舶应通过电子通信方式并使用本组织制定的标准格式[**]，向主管机关或经其正式授权的组织[***]报告达到的年度营运碳强度指标。

3 尽管有本条第 1 和 2 款的规定，如第 27.4、27.5 或 27.6 条中所述的船舶变更在 2023 年 1 月 1 日之后完成的，船舶应在发生变更的日历年年末之后，按照第 28.1 和 28.2 条，计算和报告变更发生的日历年从 1 月 1 日至 12 月 31 日的 12 个月内完整的达到的年度营运碳强度指标，虑及本组织制定的导则[**]，按本附则第 6.6 条进行验证。本条中的任何规定均不得免除任何船舶按照本附则第 27 条或本条报告的义务。

要求的年度营运碳强度指标（要求的年度营运 CII）

4 凡 5 000 总吨及以上、属于本附则第 2.2.5、2.2.7、2.2.9、2.2.11、2.2.14 至 2.2.16、2.2.22 和 2.2.26 至 2.2.29 条中一类或多类船型的船舶，其要求的年度营运碳强度指标应为：

$$\text{要求的年度营运碳强度指标} = \left(1 - \frac{Z}{100}\right) \cdot CII_R$$

式中：

Z 为年度折减系数，以确保在特定评级水平中持续地改进船舶营运碳强度；和

CII_R 为参考值。

5 年度折减系数 Z[****]和参考值 CII_R 应为虑及到本组织制定的导则[*****]所界定的值。

[*]　参见《2022 年营运碳强度指标及计算方法导则》（CII 导则，G1）（第 MEPC.352（78）号决议）和《2022 年 CII 计算中的校正系数和航程调整临时导则》（CII 导则，G5）（第 MEPC.355（78）号决议）。

[**]　参见《认可组织规则》（RO 规则）（第 MEPC.237（65）号决议，可经修订）。

[***]　参见《2024 年制定船舶能效管理计划（SEEMP）导则》（第 MEPC.395（82）号决议）。

[****]　年度折减系数由船型来确定。这一系数将会逐年递增以满足《2023 国际海事组织船舶温室气体减排初步战略》（第 MEPC.377（80）号决议）的目标。

[*****]　参见《2021 年相对于参考线的营运碳强度折减系数导则》（CII 折减系数导则，G3）（第 MEPC.338（76）号决议）和《2022 年营运碳强度指标参考线导则》（CII 参考线导则，G2）（第 MEPC.353（78）号决议）。

Operational carbon intensity rating

6 The attained annual operational CII shall be documented and verified against the required annual operational CII to determine operational carbon intensity rating A, B, C, D or E, indicating a major superior, minor superior, moderate, minor inferior, or inferior performance level, either by the Administration or by any organization duly authorized by it,* taking into account the guidelines developed by the Organization.** The middle point of rating level C shall be the value equivalent to the required annual operational CII set out in paragraph 4 of this regulation.

Corrective actions and incentives

7 A ship rated as D for three consecutive years or rated as E shall develop a plan of corrective actions to achieve the required annual operational CII.

SEE INTERPRETATION 21

8 The SEEMP shall be reviewed to include the plan of corrective actions accordingly, taking into account the guidelines to be developed by the Organization.*** The revised SEEMP shall be submitted to the Administration or any organization duly authorized by it* for verification, preferably together with, but in no case later than 1 month after reporting the attained annual operational CII in accordance with paragraph 2 of this regulation.

9 A ship rated as D for three consecutive years or rated as E shall duly undertake the planned corrective actions in accordance with the revised SEEMP.

SEE INTERPRETATION 21

10 Administrations, port authorities and other stakeholders as appropriate, are encouraged to provide incentives to ships rated as A or B.

Review

11 A review shall be completed by 1 January 2026 by the Organization to assess:
.1 the effectiveness of this regulation in reducing the carbon intensity of international shipping;
.2 the need for reinforced corrective actions or other means of remedy, including possible additional EEXI requirements;
.3 the need for enhancement of the enforcement mechanism;
.4 the need for enhancement of the data collection system; and
.5 the revision of the Z factor and CII_R values.

If based on the review the Parties decide to adopt amendments to this regulation, such amendments shall be adopted and brought into force in accordance with the provisions of article 16 of the present Convention.

Regulation 29 Promotion of technical cooperation and transfer of technology relating to the improvement of energy efficiency of ships****

1 Administrations shall, in cooperation with the Organization and other international bodies, promote and provide support, as appropriate, directly or through the Organization to States that request technical assistance, especially developing States.

2 The Administration of a Party shall cooperate actively with other Parties, subject to its national laws, regulations and policies, to promote the development and transfer of technology and exchange of information to States which request technical assistance, particularly developing States, in respect of the implementation of measures to fulfil the requirements of chapter 4 of this Annex, in particular regulations 19.4 to 19.6.

---

* Refer to the Code for Recognized Organizations (RO Code) (resolution MEPC. 237(65), as may be amended).
** Refer to the 2024 Guidelines on the operational carbon intensity rating of ships (CII rating guidelines, G4) (resolution MEPC. 354(78)).
*** Refer to the 2024 Guidelines for the development of a Ship Energy Efficiency Management Plan (SEEMP) (resolution MEPC. 395(82)).
**** Refer to Promotion of technical cooperation and transfer of technology relating to the improvement of energy efficiency of ships (resolution MEPC. 229(65)), and the Model agreement between governments on technological cooperation for the implementation of the regulations in chapter 4 of MARPOL Annex VI (MEPC.1/Circ.861).

营运碳强度评级

6 应记录达到的年度运营碳强度指标，并对照要求的年度营运碳强度指标进行验证，由主管机关或经其正式授权的组织*，虑及本组织制定的导则**，确定营运碳强度评级 A、B、C、D 或 E，以表明优秀、良好、普通、稍差或不合格绩效水平。评级水平 C 的中间点的值应等于本条第 4 款中规定的要求的年度营运碳强度指标。

纠正行动和激励措施

7 连续三年被评为 D 级或被评为 E 级的船舶，应制定整改行动计划，以达到要求的年度营运碳强度指标。

见统一解释 21

---

8 应对船舶能效管理计划进行复审并制定整改行动计划，同时虑及本组织制定的导则***。经修订的船舶能效管理计划，最好与按照本条第 2 款报告的达到的年度营运碳强度指标共同（无论如何不得晚于报告达到的年度营运碳强度指标后的一个月）提交至主管机关或经其正式授权的组织*以供验证。

9 连续三年被评为 D 级或被评为 E 级的船舶，应按照修订后的《船舶能效管理计划》，按计划采取适当的纠正行动。

见统一解释 21

---

10 鼓励各主管机关、港口当局和其他利益相关方酌情为被评为 A 和 B 级的船舶提供激励措施。

复审

11 本组织应在 2026 年 1 月 1 日之前完成复审，以评估：

   .1 本条在减少国际航运碳强度方面的有效性；

   .2 加强纠正行动或其他补救方式的必要性，包括可能通过额外的现有船舶能效指数要求；

   .3 加强执行机制的必要性；

   .4 加强数据收集系统的必要性；和

   .5 修订 Z 系数和 CIIR 值。

如果基于复审的结果，缔约国决定通过对本条的修正案，则此修正案应按照本公约第 16 条的规定予以通过并生效。

第 29 条 促进改进船舶能效的技术合作和技术转让****

1 主管机关应与本组织和其他国际机构合作，直接或通过本组织，为请求技术援助的国家，特别是发展中国家，酌情促进和提供支持。

2 缔约国主管机关应与其他缔约国积极合作，根据其国内法律、法规和政策，促进向请求技术援助的国家，特别是发展中国家就有关满足本附则第 4 章，特别是第 19.4 至 19.6 条要求的实施措施方面的技术开发、转让和信息交流。

---

* 参见《认可组织规则》（RO 规则）（第 MEPC.237（65）号决议，可经修订）。

** 参见《2022 年船舶营运碳强度评级导则》（CII 评级导则，G4）（第 MEPC.354（78）号决议）。

*** 参见《2024 年制定船舶能效管理计划（SEEMP）导则》（第 MEPC.395（82）号决议）。

**** 参见《促进提高船舶能效有关的技术合作和技术转让》（第 MEPC.229（65）号决议）和《为实施防污公约附则Ⅵ第 4 章的政府间技术合作协议范本》（第 MEPC.1/Circ.861 号通函）。

Chapter 5 Verification of compliance with the provisions of this Annex

Regulation 30 Application

Parties shall use the provisions of the Code for Implementation in the execution of their obligations and responsibilities contained in this Annex.

Regulation 31 Verification of compliance

1   Every Party shall be subject to periodic audits by the Organization in accordance with the audit standard to verify compliance with and implementation of this Annex.

2   The Secretary-General of the Organization shall have responsibility for administering the Audit Scheme, based on the guidelines developed by the Organization. *

3   Every Party shall have responsibility for facilitating the conduct of the audit and implementation of a programme of actions to address the findings, based on the guidelines developed by the Organization.*

4   The audits of all Parties shall be:

   .1   based on an overall schedule developed by the Secretary-General of the Organization, taking into account the guidelines developed by the Organization;* and

   .2   conducted at periodic intervals, taking into account the guidelines developed by the Organization.*

---

* Refer to Framework and procedures for the IMO Member State Audit Scheme (resolution A. 1067(28)).

第 5 章　本附则各项规定的符合性验证

第 30 条　适用范围

各缔约国在按本附则履行其责任和义务时，应根据《文书实施规则》的规定。

第 31 条　符合性验证

1　每一缔约国均应接受本组织按审核标准进行的定期审核，以验证其是否符合并实施了本附则的要求。

2　本组织秘书长应基于本组织制定的导则[*]，负责对审核机制实施管理。

3　每一缔约国均应基于本组织通过的导则[*]，负责为开展审核提供便利并实施针对审核发现问题的行动计划。

4　对所有缔约国的审核均应：

　　.1　基于本组织秘书长制定的总体计划，并虑及本组织制定的导则[*]；和

　　.2　定期进行，并虑及本组织制定的导则[*]。

---

[*]　参见《IMO 成员国审核机制框架和程序》（第 A.1067（28）号决议）。

Appendices to Annex VI

Appendix I Form of International Air Pollution Prevention (IAPP) Certificate (Regulation 8)

INTERNATIONAL AIR POLLUTION PREVENTION CERTIFICATE

Issued under the provisions of the Protocol of 1997, as amended, to amend the International Convention for the Prevention of Pollution from Ships, 1973, as modified by the Protocol of 1978 related thereto (hereinafter referred to as "the Convention") under the authority of the Government of:

....

(full designation of the country)

by...

(full designation of the competent person or organization authorized under the provisions of the Convention)

Particulars of ship*

Name of ship ....

Distinctive number or letters ....

IMO Number** ....

Port of registry ....

Gross tonnage ....

THIS IS TO CERTIFY:

1 That the ship has been surveyed in accordance with regulation 5 of Annex VI of the Convention; and

2 That the survey shows that the equipment, systems, fittings, arrangements and materials fully comply with the applicable requirements of Annex VI of the Convention.This Certificate is valid until (dd/mm/yyyy)*** ....

subject to surveys in accordance with regulation 5 of Annex VI of the Convention. Completion date of the survey on which this Certificate is based (dd/mm/yyyy) ....

Issued at ....

(place of issue of Certificate)

Date (dd/mm/yyyy) ....

(date of issue)   (signature of duly authorized official issuing the Certificate)

(seal or stamp of the authority, as appropriate)

* Alternatively, the particulars of the ship may be placed horizontally in boxes.
** In accordance with the IMO ship identification number scheme (resolution A. 1117(30)).
*** Insert the date of expiry as specified by the Administration in accordance with regulation 9.1 of Annex VI of the Convention. The day and the month of this date correspond to the anniversary date as defined in regulation 2.1.3 of Annex VI of the Convention, unless amended in accordance with regulation 9.8 of Annex VI of the Convention.

国际防止大气污染证书

本证书系根据经修正的《经 1978 年议定书修订的〈1973 年国际防止船舶造成污染公约〉的 1997 年议定书》（以下简称本公约）的规定，

经＿＿＿＿＿＿＿＿＿＿＿＿＿＿＿＿＿＿＿＿＿＿＿＿＿国政府授权，

（国家全称）

由＿＿＿＿＿＿＿＿＿＿＿＿＿＿＿＿＿＿＿＿＿＿＿签发。

（按本公约规定授权的适任组织或个人全称）

船舶概况 *

船名＿＿＿＿＿＿＿＿＿＿＿＿＿＿＿＿＿＿＿＿＿＿＿＿＿＿＿

船舶编号或呼号＿＿＿＿＿＿＿＿＿＿＿＿＿＿＿＿＿＿＿＿＿＿＿

IMO 编号 **＿＿＿＿＿＿＿＿＿＿＿＿＿＿＿＿＿＿＿＿＿＿＿

船籍港＿＿＿＿＿＿＿＿＿＿＿＿＿＿＿＿＿＿＿＿＿＿＿＿＿＿＿

总吨位＿＿＿＿＿＿＿＿＿＿＿＿＿＿＿＿＿＿＿＿＿＿＿＿＿＿＿

兹证明：

1 本船已按公约附则VI第 5 条要求进行了检验；以及

2 检验查明设备、系统、附件、布置和材料完全符合公约附则VI的适用要求。根据本公约附则VI第 5 条的检验，本证书的有效期至（日 / 月 / 年）***＿＿＿＿＿＿＿＿＿，

本证书基于的检验完成日期（日 / 月 / 年）＿＿＿＿＿＿＿＿＿＿＿＿

签发于＿＿＿＿＿＿＿＿＿＿＿＿＿＿＿＿＿＿＿＿＿＿＿＿＿＿＿

（发证地点）

日期（日 / 月 / 年）：＿＿＿＿＿＿＿＿＿

（发证日期）　　　　　　　　　　　　　　　　（经授权发证的官员签字）

（主管机关盖章或钢印）

---

* 船舶概况可在表格中横向排列。

** 根据《IMO 船舶编号机制》（第 A.1117（30）号决议）。

*** 填入由主管机关按本公约附则VI第 9.1 条规定的失效日期。除非按本公约附则VI第 9.8 条另行修订，否则该日期的月、日与公约附则VI第 2.1.3 条定义的周年日相同。

ENDORSEMENT FOR ANNUAL AND INTERMEDIATE SURVEYS

THIS IS TO CERTIFY that, at a survey required by regulation 5 of Annex VI of the Convention, the ship was found to comply with the relevant provisions of that Annex:

Annual survey

Signed ....
(signature of duly authorized official)

Place ....
Date (dd/mm/yyyy) ....
(seal or stamp of the authority, as appropriate)

Annual/Intermediate* survey

Signed ....
(signature of duly authorized official)

Place ....
Date (dd/mm/yyyy) ....
(seal or stamp of the authority, as appropriate)

Annual/Intermediate* survey

Signed ....
(signature of duly authorized official)

Place ....
Date (dd/mm/yyyy) ....
(seal or stamp of the authority, as appropriate)

Annual survey

Signed ....
(signature of duly authorized official)

Place ....
Date (dd/mm/yyyy) ....
(seal or stamp of the authority, as appropriate)

ANNUAL/INTERMEDIATE SURVEY IN ACCORDANCE WITH REGULATION 9.8.3

THIS IS TO CERTIFY that, at an annual/intermediate* survey in accordance with regulation 9.8.3 of Annex VI of the Convention, the ship was found to comply with the relevant provisions of that Annex:

Signed. ....
(signature of duly authorized official)

Place ....
Date (dd/mm/yyyy) ....
(seal or stamp of the authority, as appropriate)

ENDORSEMENT TO EXTEND THE CERTIFICATE IF VALID FOR LESS THAN 5 YEARS WHERE REGULATION 9.3 APPLIES

The ship complies with the relevant provisions of the Convention, and this Certificate shall, in accordance with regulation 9.3 of Annex VI of the Convention, be accepted as valid until (dd/mm/yyyy) .

Signed. ....
(signature of duly authorized official)

Place ....
Date (dd/mm/yyyy) ....
(seal or stamp of the authority, as appropriate)

* Delete as appropriate.

年度／期间检验的签注

兹证明业已按公约附则Ⅵ第 5 条的要求进行了检验，查明该船符合公约的有关规定：

年度检验：

签字： _____

（经正式授权的官员签字）

地点： _____

日期（日／月／年）： _____

（主管机关盖章或钢印）

年度／中间*检验：

签字： _____

（经正式授权的官员签字）

地点： _____

日期（日／月／年）： _____

（主管机关盖章或钢印）

年度／中间*检验：

签字： _____

（经正式授权的官员签字）

地点： _____

日期（日／月／年）： _____

（主管机关盖章或钢印）

年度检验：

签字： _____

（经正式授权的官员签字）

地点： _____

日期（日／月／年）： _____

（主管机关盖章或钢印）

按第 9.8.3 条进行的年度／中间检验

兹证明业已按公约附则Ⅵ第 9.8.3 条的要求进行了年度／中间检验*，查明该船符合公约的有关规定：

签字： _____

（经授权的官员签字）

地点： _____

日期（日／月／年）： _____

（主管机关盖章或钢印）

在适用第 9.3 条情况下，有效期少于 5 年的证书展期签注

该船符合本附则的有关规定，本证书根据公约附则Ⅵ第 9.3 条应视为有效，有效期限至（日／月／年）

_____止。

签字： _____

（经授权的官员签字）

地点： _____

日期（日／月／年）： _____

（主管机关盖章或钢印）

---

*　不适用者删除。

ENDORSEMENT WHERE THE RENEWAL SURVEY HAS BEEN COMPLETED AND REGULATION 9.4 APPLIES

The ship complies with the relevant provisions of the Annex, and this Certificate shall, in accordance with regulation 9.4 of Annex VI of the Convention, be accepted as valid until (dd/mm/yyyy) ....

Signed. ....
(signature of duly authorized official)

Place ....

Date (dd/mm/yyyy) ....

(seal or stamp of the authority, as appropriate)

ENDORSEMENT TO EXTEND THE VALIDITY OF THE CERTIFICATE UNTIL REACHING THE PORT OF SURVEY OR FOR A PERIOD OF GRACE WHERE REGULATION 9.5 OR 9.6 APPLIES

This Certificate shall, in accordance with regulation 9.5 or 9.6* of Annex VI of the Convention, be accepted as valid until (dd/mm/yyyy)..

Signed. ....
(signature of duly authorized official)

Place ....

Date (dd/mm/yyyy) ....

(seal or stamp of the authority, as appropriate)

ENDORSEMENT FOR ADVANCEMENT OF ANNIVERSARY DATE WHERE REGULATION 9.8 APPLIES

In accordance with regulation 9.8 of Annex VI of the Convention, the new anniversary date is (dd/mm/yyyy)

....

Signed. ....
(signature of duly authorized official)

Place ....

Date (dd/mm/yyyy) ....

(seal or stamp of the authority, as appropriate)

In accordance with regulation 9.8 of Annex VI of the Convention, the new anniversary date is (dd/mm/yyyy)

....

Signed. ....
(signature of duly authorized official)

Place ....

Date (dd/mm/yyyy) ....

(seal or stamp of the authority, as appropriate)

* Delete as appropriate.

在已完成换证检验并适用第 9.4 条情况下的签注

该船符合本附则的有关规定，本证书根据公约附则Ⅵ第 9.4 条应视为有效，有效期限至（日 / 月 / 年）

_____ 止。

签字：_____

（经授权的官员签字）

地点：_____

日期（日 / 月 / 年）：_____

（主管机关盖章或钢印）

在适用第 9.5 或 9.6 条情况下，将证书有效期展期至
驶抵进行检验的港口或给予宽限期的签注

本证书根据公约附则Ⅵ第 9.5 或 9.6 条 * 应视为有效，有效期限至（日 / 月 / 年）_____

_____ 止。

签字：_____

（经授权的官员签字）

地点：_____

日期（日 / 月 / 年）：_____

（主管机关盖章或钢印）

在适用第 9.8 条情况下，周年日提前的签注

根据本公约附则Ⅵ第 9.8 条，新的周年日为（年 / 月 / 日）：

签字：_____

（经授权的官员签字）

地点：_____

日期（日 / 月 / 年）：_____

（主管机关盖章或钢印）

根据公约附则Ⅵ第 9.8 条，新的周年日为（年 / 月 / 日）：

签字：_____

（经授权的官员签字）

地点：_____

日期（日 / 月 / 年）：_____

（主管机关盖章或钢印）

---

* 不适用者删除。

SUPPLEMENT TO INTERNATIONAL AIR POLLUTION PREVENTION CERTIFICATE (IAPP CERTIFICATE)

RECORD OF CONSTRUCTION AND EQUIPMENT

Notes:

1 This Record shall be permanently attached to the IAPP Certificate. The IAPP Certificate shall be available on board the ship at all times.

2 The Record shall be at least in English, French or Spanish. If an official language of the issuing country is also used, this shall prevail in case of a dispute or discrepancy.

3 Entries in boxes shall be made by inserting either a cross (x) for the answer "yes" and "applicable" or a (–) for the answers "no" and "not applicable" as appropriate.

4 Unless otherwise stated, regulations mentioned in this Record refer to regulations of Annex VI of the Convention and resolutions or circulars refer to those adopted by the International Maritime Organization.

1 Particulars of ship

1.1 Name of ship ....

1.2 IMO Number ....

1.3 Date on which keel was laid or ship was at a similar stage of construction (dd/mm/yyyy) ....

1.4 Length (L) * metres...

2 Control of emissions from ships

2.1 Ozone-depleting substances (regulation 12)

2.1.1 The following fire-extinguishing systems, other systems and equipment containing ozone-depleting substances, other than hydrochlorofluorocarbons (HCFCs), installed before 19 May 2005 may continue in service:

System or equipment	Location on board	Substance

2.1.2 The following systems containing HCFCs installed before 1 January 2020 may continue in service:

System or equipment	Location on board	Substance

2.2 Nitrogen oxides (NOx) (regulation 13)

2.2.1 The following marine diesel engines installed on this ship are in accordance with the requirements of regulation 13, as indicated:

* Completed only in respect of ships constructed on or after 1 January 2016 that are specially designed, and used solely for recreational purposes and to which, in accordance with regulation 13.5.2.1 or regulation 13.5.2.3, the NOx emission limit as given by regulation 13.5.1.1 will not apply.

国际防止大气污染证书（IAPP 证书）的附页
结构和设备记录

> 注：
> 1 本记录应永久附于 IAPP 证书之后。IAPP 证书应随时保存在船上。
> 2 记录应至少使用英文、法文或西班牙文的其中一种语言。如还使用发证国的官方语言，则在发生争执或不一致时，应以该官方语言为准。
> 3 在方格内应填入 (×) 表示"是"和"适用"；或填入（—）表示"否"和"不适用"。
> 4 除非另有说明，本记录中所提及的条款系指本公约附则 VI 的条款，及决议或通函系指由国际海事组织通过的决议或通函。

1 船舶概况

1.1 船名_____

1.2 IMO 编号_____

1.3 船舶安放龙骨或处于类似建造阶段的日期_____

1.4 船长（L）*米_____

2 船舶排放的控制

2.1 消耗臭氧物质（第 12 条）

2.1.1 下列于 2005 年 5 月 19 日前安装的含有消耗臭氧物质，但不含氢化氟烃（HCFCs）的灭火系统、其他系统和设备可以继续使用：

系统或设备	船上位置	物质

2.1.2 下列在 2020 年 1 月 1 日以前安装的含有含氢氟氯烃（HCFCs）的系统可以继续使用：

系统或设备	船上位置	物质

2.2 氮氧化物（NOx）（第 13 条）

2.2.1 下列船上安装的船用柴油机符合第 13 条所示要求：

---

* 仅用于 2016 年 1 月 1 日或以后建造的经特殊设计并仅用于娱乐目的，根据第 13.5.2.1 或第 13.5.2.3 条不适用于第 13.5.1.1 条规定的氮氧化物排放极限的船舶填写。

Applicable regulation of MARPOL Annex VI (NTC=NOx Technical Code 2008) (AM=Approved Method)			Engine #1	Engine #2	Engine #3	Engine #4	Engine #5
1	Manufacturer and model						
2	Serial number						
3	Use (applicable application cycle(s)-NTC 3.2						
4	Rated power (kW) (NTC 1.3.11)						
5	Rated speed (rpm) (NTC 1.3.12)						
6	Identical engine installed≥1/1/2000 exempted by 13.1.1.2						
7	Identical engine installation date (dd/mm/yyyy) as per 13.1.1.2						
8a	Major Conversion (dd/mm/yyyy)	13.2.1.1 & 13.2.2					
8b		13.2.1.2 & 13.2.3					
8c		13.2.1.3 & 13.2.3					
9a	Tier I	13.4					
9b		13.2.2					
9c		13.2.3.1					
9d		13.2.3.2					
9e		13.7.1.2					
10a	Tier II	13.4					
10b		13.2.2					
10c		13.2.2(Tier III not possible)					
10d		13.2.3.2					
10e		13.5.2 (Exemptions)					
10f		13.7.1.2					
11a	NOx Tier III (ECA-NOx only)	13.5.1.1					
11b		13.2.2					
11c		13.2.3.2					
11d		13.7.1.2					
12	AM*	installed					
13		not commercially available at this survey					
14		not applicable					

* Refer to the 2014 Guidelines on the approved method process (resolution MEPC.243(66)).

防污公约附则Ⅵ适用的规定 （NTC=2008 年氮氧化物计数规则） （AM= 经认可的方法）			发动机 #1	发动机 #2	发动机 #3	发动机 #4	发动机 #5
1	制造商和型号						
2	序列号						
3	使用（适用的应用循环 –NTC 3.2）						
4	额定功率（kW）（NTC 1.3.11）						
5	额定转速（rpm）（NTC 1.3.12）						
6	第 13.1.1.2 条所免除的 2000 年 1 月 1 日或之后安装的完全相同的柴油机						
7	按照第 13.1.1.2 条，完全相同柴油机的安全日期（日 / 月 / 年）						
8a	重大改装 （日 / 月 / 年）	13.2.1.1 & 13.2.2					
8b		13.2.1.2 & 13.2.3					
8c		13.2.1.3 & 13.2.3					
9a	Ⅰ 级	13.4					
9b		13.2.2					
9c		13.2.3.1					
9d		13.2.3.2					
9e		13.7.1.2					
10a	Ⅱ 级	13.4					
10b		13.2.2					
10c		13.2.2（不符合Ⅲ级）					
10d		13.2.3.2					
10e		13.5.2（免除）					
10f		13.7.1.2					
11a	Ⅲ 级（仅氮氧化物排放控制区）	13.5.1.1					
11b		13.2.2					
11c		13.2.3.2					
11d		13.7.1.2					
12	AM*	已安装					
13		本次检验时无可购者					
14		不适用					

* 参见《2014 年认可方法程序指南》（第 MEPC.243（66）号决议）。

2.3   Sulphur oxides (SOx) and particulate matter (regulation 14)

2.3.1 When the ship operates outside of an emission control area specified in regulation 14.3, the ship uses:

.1   fuel oil with a sulphur content as documented by bunker delivery notes that does not exceed the limit value of 0.50% m/m, and/or .... □

.2   an equivalent arrangement approved in accordance with regulation 4.1 as listed in paragraph 2.6 that is at least as effective in terms of SOx emission reductions as compared to using a fuel oil with a sulphur content limit value of 0.50% m/m .... □

2.3.2 When the ship operates inside an emission control area specified in regulation 14.3, the ship uses:

.1   fuel oil with a sulphur content as documented by bunker delivery notes that does not exceed the limit value of 0.10% m/m, and/or .... □

.2   an equivalent arrangement approved in accordance with regulation 4.1 as listed in paragraph 2.6 that is at least as effective in terms of SOx emission reductions as compared to using a fuel oil with a sulphur content limit value of 0.10% m/m .... □

2.3.3 For a ship without an equivalent arrangement approved in accordance with regulation 4.1 as listed in paragraph 2.6, the sulphur content of fuel oil carried for use on board the ship shall not exceed 0.50% m/m as documented by bunker delivery notes .... □

2.3.4 The ship is fitted with designated sampling points(s) in accordance with regulation 14.10 or 14.11 .... □

2.3.5 In accordance with regulation 14.12 the requirement for fitting or designating sampling point(s) in accordance with regulation 14.10 or 14.11 is not applicable for a fuel oil service system used for a low-flashpoint fuel or a gas fuel
.... □

2.4   Volatile organic compounds (VOCs) (regulation 15)

2.4.1 The tanker has a vapour collection system installed and approved in accordance with MSC/Circ.585 .... □

2.4.2.1 For a tanker carrying crude oil, there is an approved VOC management plan.......................... □

2.4.2.2 VOC management plan approval reference: .... □

2.5   Shipboard incineration (regulation 16)

The ship has an incinerator:

.1   installed on or after 1 January 2000 that complies with:

    .1   resolution MEPC.76(40), as amended* .... □
    .2   resolution MEPC.244(66) .... □

.2   installed before 1 January 2000 that complies with:

    .1   resolution MEPC.59(33)** .... □
    .2   resolution MEPC.76(40)* .... □

2.6   Equivalents (regulation 4)

The ship has been allowed to use the following fitting, material, appliance or apparatus to be fitted in a ship or other procedures, alternative fuel oils, or compliance methods used as an alternative to that required by this Annex:

System or equipment	Location on board	Substance

* As amended by MEPC.93(45).

** As amended by MEPC.92(45).

2.3 硫氧化物（SOx）和颗粒物质（第 14 条）

2.3.1 当船舶在第 14.3 条规定的排放控制区外营运时，该船使用：

　　.1 燃油交付单记录的硫含量不超过 0.50% m/m 限值的燃油，和 / 或 _____ □

　　.2 第 2.6 段中所列的按第 4.1 条经认可的等效布置，该等效布置在硫氧化物减排方面至少与使用硫含量为 0.50% m/m 限值的燃油同等有效 _____ □

2.3.2 当船舶在第 14.3 条规定的排放控制区内营运时，该船使用：

　　.1 燃油交付单记录的硫含量不超过 0.10% m/m 限值的燃油，和 / 或 _____ □

　　.2 第 2.6 段中所列的按第 4.1 条经认可的等效安排，该等效安排在硫氧化物减排方面至少与使用硫含量为 0.10% m/m 限值的燃油同等有效 _____ □

2.3.3 未使用第 2.6 段中所列的按第 4.1 条经认可的等效安排的船舶，船上载运供使用的燃油的硫含量不得超过 0.50% m/m（燃油交付单记录） _____ □

2.3.4 该船按 14.10 或 14.11 条设置有指定的取样点 _____ □

2.3.5 按照第 14.12 条，第 14.10 或 14.11 条安装或指定采样点的要求不适用于低闪点燃料或气体燃料的燃油日用系统 _____ □

2.4 挥发性有机化合物（VOCs）（第 15 条）

2.4.1 本液货船备有一套按照 MSC/Circ.585 号通函安装和认可的蒸汽收集系统 _____ □

2.4.2.1 对于装载原油的液货船，备有认可的《挥发性有机化合物管理计划》 _____ □

2.4.2.2 《挥发性有机化合物管理计划》的批准参考： _____ □

2.5 船上焚烧（第 16 条）

本船装有 1 台焚烧炉：

　　.1 2000 年 1 月 1 日或以后安装的，符合

　　　　.1 经修正的 MEPC.76（40）号决议 * _____ □

　　　　.2 第 MEPC.246（66）号决议 _____ □

　　.2 2000 年 1 月 1 日前安装的，符合：

　　　　.1 MEPC.59（33）号决议 ** _____ □

　　　　.2 MEPC.76（40）号决议 * _____ □

2.6 等效（第 4 条）

已允许该船舶使用下列在船上安装的装置、材料、设备或仪器，或其他程序、替代燃油或符合方法，以代替本附则的要求：

系统或设备	等效使用	批准索引

---

* 由 MEPC.93（45）决议修正。

** 由 MEPC.92（45）决议修正。

THIS IS TO CERTIFY that this Record is correct in all respects.

Issued at ....

(place of issue of the Record)

Date (dd/mm/yyyy) ....

....

(date of issue)   (signature of duly authorized official issuing the Record)

(seal or stamp of the authority, as appropriate)

兹证明本记录在各方面均正确无误。

签发于 _____

（记录签发地点）

日期(日 / 月 / 年): _____

....

（签发日期）   （正式授权签发本记录的官员签字）

（主管机关盖章或钢印）

Appendix II Test cycles and weighting factors (Regulation 13)

The following test cycles and weighting factors shall be applied for verification of compliance of marine diesel engines with the applicable NOx limit in accordance with regulation 13 of this Annex using the test procedure and calculation method as specified in the revised NOx Technical Code 2008.

.1 For constant-speed marine engines for ship main propulsion, including diesel-electric drive, test cycle E2 shall be applied;

.2 For controllable-pitch propeller sets test cycle E2 shall be applied;

.3 For propeller-law-operated main and propeller-law-operated auxiliary engines the test cycle E3 shall be applied;

.4 For constant-speed auxiliary engines test cycle D2 shall be applied; and

.5 For variable-speed, variable-load auxiliary engines, not included above, test cycle C1 shall be applied.

Test cycle for constant-speed main propulsion application
(including diesel-electric drive and all controllable-pitch propeller installations)

Test cycle type E2	Speed	100%	100%	100%	100%
	Power	100%	75%	50%	25%
	Weighting factor	0.2	0.5	0.15	0.15

Test cycle for propeller-law-operated main and propeller-law-operated auxiliary engine application

Test cycle type E3	Speed	100%	91%	80%	63%
	Power	100%	75%	50%	25%
	Weighting factor	0.2	0.5	0.15	0.15

Test cycle for constant-speed auxiliary engine application

Test cycle type D2	Speed	100%	100%	100%	100%	100%
	Power	100%	75%	50%	25%	10%
	Weighting factor	0.05	0.25	0.3	0.3	0.1

Test cycle for variable-speed and variable-load auxiliary engine application

Test cycle type C1	Speed	Rated							Idle
	Power	100%	75%	50%	10%	100%	75%	50%	0%
	Weighting factor	0.15	0.15	0.15	0.1	0.1	0.1	0.1	0.15

In the case of an engine to be certified in accordance with paragraph 5.1.1 of regulation 13, the specific emission at each individual mode point shall not exceed the applicable NOx emission limit value by more than 50% except as follows:

.1 The 10% mode point in the D2 test cycle.

.2 The 10% mode point in the C1 test cycle.

.3 The idle mode point in the C1 test cycle.

附录 II 试验循环和加权因数（第 13 条）

在采用经修订的《2008 年 NOx 技术规则》中规定的试验程序和计算方法核实船用柴油机是否符合本附则第 13 条规定的氮氧化物限值时，应使用下列试验循环和加权因数。

.1 对于作为船舶主推进装置的定转速船用发动机，包括柴油电力驱动应采用试验循环 E2；

.2 对于可调螺距螺旋桨装置应采用试验循环 E2；

.3 对于按螺旋桨特性运转的主辅发动机应采用试验循环 E3；

.4 对于定转速速辅发动机应采用试验循环 D2；以及

.5 对于除上述发动机以外的变速、变载辅发动机应采用试验循环 C1。

定转速主推进机应用的试验循环
（包括柴油电力驱动或可调螺距螺旋桨装置）

试验循环类型 E2	转速	100%	100%	100%	100%
	功率	100%	75%	50%	25%
	加权因数	0.2	0.5	0.15	0.15

按螺旋桨特性运转的主辅发动机应用的试验循环

试验循环类型 E3	转速	100%	91%	80%	63%
	功率	100%	75%	50%	25%
	加权因数	0.2	0.5	0.15	0.15

定转速辅发动机应用的试验循环

试验循环类型 D2	转速	100%	100%	100%	100%	100%
	功率	100%	75%	50%	25%	10%
	加权因数	0.05	0.25	0.3	0.3	0.1

变速和变载辅发动机应用的试验循环

试验循环类型 C1	转速	额定				过渡			空转
	扭转	100%	75%	50%	10%	100%	75%	50%	0%
	加权因数	0.15	0.15	0.15	0.1	0.1	0.1	0.1	0.15

证明符合第 13 条的第 5.1.1 段规定的发动机，在每个模式的具体排放不应超过适用的氮氧化物排放限值的 50%，下列除外：

.1 试验循环 D2 中 10% 模式点。

.2 试验循环 C1 中 10% 模式点。

.3 试验循环 C1 中空转模式点。

Appendix III Criteria and procedures for designation of emission control areas (Regulation 13.6 and regulation 14.3)

1 Objectives

1.1 The purpose of this appendix is to provide the criteria and procedures to Parties for the formulation and submission of proposals for the designation of emission control areas and to set forth the factors to be considered in the assessment of such proposals by the Organization.

1.2 Emissions of NOx, SOx and particulate matter from ocean-going ships contribute to ambient concentrations of air pollution in cities and coastal areas around the world. Adverse public health and environmental effects associated with air pollution include premature mortality, cardiopulmonary disease, lung cancer, chronic respiratory ailments, acidification and eutrophication.

1.3 An emission control area should be considered for adoption by the Organization if supported by a demonstrated need to prevent, reduce and control emissions of NOx or SOx and particulate matter or all three types of emissions (hereinafter emissions) from ships.

2 Process for the designation of emission control areas

2.1 A proposal to the Organization for designation of an emission control area for NOx or SOx and particulate matter or all three types of emissions may be submitted only by Parties. Where two or more Parties have a common interest in a particular area, they should formulate a coordinated proposal.

2.2 A proposal to designate a given area as an emission control area should be submitted to the Organization in accordance with the rules and procedures established by the Organization.

3 Criteria for designation of an emission control area

3.1 The proposal shall include:

   .1 a clear delineation of the proposed area of application, along with a reference chart on which the area is marked;

   .2 the type or types of emission(s) that is or are being proposed for control (i.e., NOx or SOx and particulate matter or all three types of emissions);

   .3 a description of the human populations and environmental areas at risk from the impacts of ship emissions;

   .4 an assessment that emissions from ships operating in the proposed area of application are contributing to ambient concentrations of air pollution or to adverse environmental impacts. Such assessment shall include a description of the impacts of the relevant emissions on human health and the environment, such as adverse impacts to terrestrial and aquatic ecosystems, areas of natural productivity, critical habitats, water quality, human health, and areas of cultural and scientific significance, if applicable. The sources of relevant data including methodologies used shall be identified;

   .5 relevant information, pertaining to the meteorological conditions in the proposed area of application, to the human populations and environmental areas at risk, in particular prevailing wind patterns, or to topographical, geological, oceanographic, morphological or other conditions that contribute to ambient concentrations of air pollution or adverse environmental impacts;

   .6 the nature of the ship traffic in the proposed emission control area, including the patterns and density of such traffic;

   .7 a description of the control measures taken by the proposing Party or Parties addressing landbased sources of NOx, SOx and particulate matter emissions affecting the human populations and environmental areas at risk that are in place and operating concurrent with the consideration of measures to be adopted in relation to provisions of regulations 13 and 14 of Annex VI; and

附录Ⅲ 指定排放控制区的标准和程序（第 13.6 条和第 14.3 条）

1 目的

1.1 本附录目的是向各缔约国提供制定和提交指定排放控制区域建议的标准和程序，并提出本组织评估此类建议时应考虑的因素。

1.2 远洋船舶排放的 NOx、SOx 和颗粒物质导致世界各城市和沿海地区空气污染物浓度的升高。大气污染对公众健康和环境产生的危害包括：过早死亡、心肺病、肺癌、慢性呼吸道疾病、酸化和富营养化。

1.3 如证实有必要防止、减少和控制船舶排放硫氧化物和颗粒物质或氮氧化物或所有 3 类物质的排放（以下称为排放），本组织应考虑通过一个排放控制区。

2 指定排放控制区的程序

2.1 指定氮氧化物或硫氧化物和颗粒物质或所有 3 类物质排放控制区域的建议，只能由缔约国向本组织提交。如果两个或以上缔约国对某一特定的区域有共同的利益，他们应起草一份经过协调的建议。

2.2 应根据本组织制定的规则和程序向本组织提交指定一个特定区域作为排放控制区建议的提案。

3 指定排放控制区的标准

3.1 建议应包括：

.1 一份所建议的适用区域的明确描述，连同一份标有该区域位置的参照海图；

.2 所建议控制的一种或多种类物质（即：硫氧化物和颗粒物质或氮氧化物或所有 3 类物质）；

.3 一份受到船舶排放威胁的人口和环境区域的说明；

.4 一份对在所建议的适用区域内航行的船舶排放造成大气污染环境浓度的增加或对环境造成不利影响的评估。该评估应包括相关排放对人类健康和环境影响的说明，如对陆地生态和水生生态系统、自然生产力区域、重要栖息地、水质、人类健康以及具有重要文化科学价值区域（如有）的不利影响。并应标明有关资料，包括所用的方法的来源；

.5 在所建议的适用区域与受威胁人口和环境区域有关的气象条件的相关资料，特别是盛行风型，或有关地形学、地质学、海洋学、形态学资料，或其他可能导致空气污染物浓度升高或对环境造成不利影响的条件的相关资料；

.6 所建议的排放控制区内船舶交通状况，包括这种交通流和密度；

.7 一份由一个或多个提案国针对影响受威胁人口和环境区域的硫氧化物、氮氧化物和颗粒物质岸基排放源已经采取的控制措施的说明，该措施与根据附则Ⅵ第 13 和 14 条规定考虑拟采取的有关措施的运作相协调并予以说明；以及

.8 the relative costs of reducing emissions from ships when compared with land-based controls, and the economic impacts on shipping engaged in international trade.

3.2 The geographical limits of an emission control area will be based on the relevant criteria outlined above, including emissions and deposition from ships navigating in the proposed area, traffic patterns and density, and wind conditions.

4 Procedures for the assessment and adoption of emission control areas by the Organization

4.1 The Organization shall consider each proposal submitted to it by a Party or Parties.

4.2 In assessing the proposal, the Organization shall take into account the criteria that are to be included in each proposal for adoption as set forth in section 3 above.

4.3 An emission control area shall be designated by means of an amendment to this Annex, considered, adopted and brought into force in accordance with article 16 of the present Convention.

5 Operation of emission control areas

5.1 Parties that have ships navigating in the area are encouraged to bring to the Organization any concerns regarding the operation of the area.

.8 与岸基控制相比，减少船舶排放的相对费用，和对从事国际贸易船舶的经济影响。

3.2 排放控制区的地理界限将根据上述所列的有关标准，包括来自航行于所建议的区域内的船舶排放和沉积量，交通流和密度以及风况予以确定。

4 本组织评估并通过排放控制区域的程序

4.1 本组织应审议由一个或多个缔约国提交的每份建议。

4.2 在评估建议时，本组织应考虑每份建议提案中应包括的上述第3节中所述的标准。

4.3 排放控制区应以本附则修正案的形式指定，并根据本公约第16条规定予以审议、通过和生效。

5 排放控制区的管理

5.1 鼓励拥有航行于这些区域的船舶的缔约国向本组织提供任何有关该区域管理的情况。

Appendix IV Type approval and operating limits for shipboard incinerators (Regulation 16)

1   Shipboard incinerators described in regulation 16.6.1 shall possess an IMO Type Approval Certificate for each incinerator. In order to obtain such certificate, the incinerator shall be designed and built to an approved standard as described in regulation 16.6.1. Each model shall be subject to a specified type approval test operation at the factory or an approved test facility, and under the responsibility of the Administration, using the following standard fuel/waste specification for the type approval test for determining whether the incinerator operates within the limits specified in paragraph 2 of this appendix:

Sludge oil consisting of: 75% sludge oil from heavy fuel oil (HFO);

                              5% waste lubricating oil; and

                              20% emulsified water.

Solid waste consisting of: 50% food waste;

                              50% rubbish containing;

                                  approx. 30% paper,

                                  approx. 40% cardboard,

                                  approx. 10% rags,

                                  approx. 20% plastic

                              The mixture will have up to 50% moisture and 7% incombustible solids.

2   Incinerators described in regulation 16.6.1 shall operate within the following limits:

O_2 in combustion chamber: 6–12%

CO in flue gas maximum average: 200 mg/MJ

Soot number maximum average: Bacharach 3 or Ringelman 1 (20% opacity) (a higher soot number is acceptable only during very short periods such as starting up)

Unburned components in ash residues: Maximum 10% by weight

Combustion chamber flue gas outlet temperature range: 850–1,200°C

附录 IV 船上焚烧炉的型式认可和操作限制
（第 16 条）

1 第 16.6.1 条所述船上焚烧炉都应有 IMO 型式认可证书。为获取该证书，焚烧炉应按照第 16.6.1 条所述的认可标准进行设计和建造。每一型号均应在制造厂或经认可的测试机构接受规定的型式认可试验，并由主管机关负责，在型式认可试验中使用下列标准燃料/废物，以确定焚烧炉的运转是否在本附录第 2 段所规定的限值之内。

污油成分为：　　　　　　　　75% 重质燃油的污油；

　　　　　　　　　　　　　　5% 废润滑油；以及

　　　　　　　　　　　　　　20% 乳化水。

固体废弃物成分为：　　　　　50% 食品废弃物；

　　　　　　　　　　　　　　50% 垃圾包括；

　　　　　　　　　　　　　　　　约 30% 纸

　　　　　　　　　　　　　　　　约 40% 硬纸板

　　　　　　　　　　　　　　　　约 10% 破布

　　　　　　　　　　　　　　　　约 20% 塑料

　　　　　　　　　　　　　　混合物的含水率可达 50% 且不可燃固体可达 7%。

2 第 16.6.1 条所述的焚烧炉应在下列限值内运转：

　　燃烧室中的氧气：　　　　　6%~12%

　　烟气中一氧化碳的最大平均值：

　　　　200 mg/MJ

烟灰数的最大平均值：Bacharach 3 或 Ringelman 1（20% 浑浊度）

　　　　　　　　　　　（只有在非常短的时间内如起动时，才能接受更高的灰数）

灰渣中的未燃烧组分：最大 10%，按重量计

燃烧室烟气出口的温度范围：

　　　　850 ℃ ~1 200 ℃

Appendix V Information to be included in the bunker delivery note (Regulation 18.5)

1 Name and IMO Number of receiving ship
2 Port
3 Date of commencement of delivery
4 Name, address and telephone number of marine fuel oil supplier
5 Product name(s)
6 Quantity in metric tonnes
7 Density at 15°C (kg/m^3) *
8 Sulphur content** (% m/m) **
9 The flashpoint (°C) specified in accordance with standards acceptable to the Organization***, or a statement that the flashpoint has been measured at or above 70°C***
10 A declaration signed and certified by the fuel oil supplier's representative that the fuel oil supplied is in conformity with regulation 18.3 of this Annex and that the sulphur content of the fuel oil supplied does not exceed:
   ☐ the limit value given by regulation 14.1 of this Annex;
   ☐ the limit value given by regulation 14.4 of this Annex; or
   ☐ the purchaser's specified limit value of _____ (% m/m), as completed by the fuel oil supplier's representative and on the basis of the purchaser's notification that the fuel oil is intended to be used:
      .1 in combination with an equivalent means of compliance in accordance with regulation 4 of this Annex; or
      .2 is subject to a relevant exemption for a ship to conduct trials for sulphur oxides emission reduction and control technology research in accordance with regulation 3.2 of this Annex.

The declaration shall be completed by the fuel oil supplier's representative by marking the applicable box(es) with a cross (x).

---

* Fuel oil shall be tested in accordance with ISO 3675:1998 or ISO 12185:1996.
** Fuel oil shall be tested in accordance with ISO 8754:2003.
*** ISO 2719:2016, Determination of flashpoint – Pensky-Martens closed cup method, Procedure A (for Distillate Fuels) or Procedure B (for Residual Fuels).

附录 V 燃油交付单中包括的信息（第 18.5 条）

1　接受燃油的船舶名称和 IMO 编号

2　港口

3　交付开始日期

4　船用燃油供应商名称、地址和电话号码

5　产品名称

6　数量（吨）

7　15 ℃时的密度（kg/m³）[*]

8　硫含量[**]（% m/m）[**]

9　按本组织可接受的标准[***]规定的闪点 (℃)，或已在 70 ℃或以上测得的闪点的声明[***]；

10　由燃油供应商代表签署并核证的申明，其所提供的燃油符合本规则第 18.3 条规定以及所供燃油含硫量不超过：

　　□　本附则第 14 规定的极限值；

　　□　本附则第 14.4 条规定的极限值；或

　　□　买方指定的极限值_____ (% m/m)，由燃油供应商代表完成，并根据买方的通知准备燃油：

　　　　.1　以按照本附则第 4 条等效符合方式一并使用；或

　　　　.2　其使用符合本附则第 3.2 条对船舶进行减少和控制硫氧化物排放技术研究试验的相关免除。该申明应由燃油供应商代表通过用 "X" 标记适用的方格来填写。

---

[*]　燃油应按 ISO 3675:1998 或 ISO 12185:1996 进行试验。

[**]　燃油应按 ISO 8754:2003 进行试验。

[***]　ISO 2719:2016．闪点测定－平斯克·马丁斯闭杯法，程序 A（馏分油）或程序 B（渣油）。

Appendix VI Verification procedures for a MARPOL Annex VI fuel oil sample (regulation 18.8.2 or regulation 14.8)

The following relevant verification procedure shall be used to determine whether the fuel oil delivered to, in use or carried for use on board a ship has met the applicable sulphur limit of regulation 14 of this Annex.

This appendix refers to the following representative MARPOL Annex VI fuel oil samples:

Part 1 – sample of fuel oil delivered* in accordance with regulation 18.8.1, hereafter referred to as the "MARPOL delivered sample" as defined in regulation 2.1.22.

Part 2 – sample of fuel oil in use,** intended to be used or carried for use on board in accordance with regulation 14.8, hereafter referred to as the "in-use sample"*** as defined in regulation 2.1.16 and "onboard sample" as defined in regulation 2.1.24.

Part 1 MARPOL delivered sample

1 General Requirements

1.1 The representative sample of the fuel oil, which is required by regulation 18.8.1 (the MARPOL delivered sample), shall be used to verify the sulphur content of the fuel oil delivered to a ship.

1.2 A Party, through its competent authority, shall manage the verification procedure.

1.3 A laboratory undertaking the sulphur testing procedure given in this appendix shall have valid accreditation**** in respect of the test method to be used.

2 Verification Procedure Part 1

2.1 The MARPOL delivered sampleshall be conveyed by the competent authority to the laboratory.

2.2 The laboratory shall:

    .1 record the details of the seal number and the sample label on the test record;

    .2 record the condition of the seal of the sample as received on the test record; and

    .3 reject any sample where the seal has been broken prior to receipt and record that rejection on the test record.

2.3 If the seal of the sample as received has not been broken, the laboratory shall proceed with the verification procedure and shall:

    .1 unseal the sample;

    .2 ensure that the sample is thoroughly homogenized;

    .3 draw two subsamples from the sample; and

    .4 reseal the sample and record the new reseal details on the test record.

---

* Samples taken in accordance with the 2009 Guidelines for the sampling of fuel oil for determination of compliance with the revised MARPOL Annex VI (resolution MEPC. 182(59)).

** Samples taken in accordance with the 2019 Guidelines for on board sampling for the verification of the sulphur content of the fuel oil used on board ships (MEPC.1/Circ.864/Rev.1).

*** Refer to the 2020 Guidelines for on board sampling of fuel oil intended to be used or carried for use on board a ship (MEPC.1/Circ.889).

**** The laboratory is to be accredited to ISO/IEC 17025: 2017 or an equivalent standard for the performance of the given sulphur content test ISO 8754: 2003.

附录Ⅵ　《防污公约》附则Ⅵ燃油样品验证程序（第18.8.2条或14.8条）

应使用下列程序判定船上交付、船上使用或载运用于船上使用的燃油是否符合本附则第14条适用的硫含量限值。

本附录涉及以下《防污公约》附则Ⅵ的代表性燃油样品：

第1部分——按照第18.8.1条交付的燃油样品[*]，以下称为第2.1.22条定义的"《防污公约》交付的样品。"

第2部分——按照第14.8条旨在船上使用或载运用于船上使用的燃油样品[**]，以下称为第2.1.16条定义的"在用样品"[***]和第2.1.24条定义的"船上样品"。

第1部分　《防污公约》交付的样品

1　一般要求

1.1　应使用第18.8.1条要求的代表性燃油样品（《防污公约》交付的样品）验证供应上船的燃油硫含量。

1.2　缔约国应通过其主管机关管理验证程序。

1.3　负责本附录所述硫试验程序的实验室应就其使用的试验方法获得有效认证[****]。

2　验证程序第1部分

2.1　《防污公约》交付的样品应由主管机关送交实验室。

2.2　实验室应：

　　.1　将密封号和样品标签的详细信息记入试验记录；

　　.2　将收到的样品的封印状况记入试验记录；和

　　.3　拒绝收到的任何封印受损的样品，并将拒收记入试验记录。

2.3　如所收到样品的封印未受损，实验室应继续验证程序并应：

　　.1　开封样品；

　　.2　确保样品完全均匀；

　　.3　从样品中提取两份子样品；和

　　.4　重新密封样品，并在试验记录中记入新的重新密封的详细信息。

---

[*]　根据《2009年燃油取样以确定经修订的防污公约符合性导则》采集的样品（第MEPC.182（59）号决议）。

[**]　参见《2019年船上燃油取样以核验船上使用的燃油硫含量导则》（第MEPC.1/Circ.864/Rev.1号通函）。

[***]　参见《2020年船上使用或载运的船用燃油取样导则》（第MEPC.1/Circ.889号通函）。

[****]　按照ISO 8754:2003进行燃油硫含量测试的实验室应按照ISO/IEC 17025:2017或等效标准认证。

2.4 The two subsamples shall be tested in succession, in accordance with the specified test method referred to in regulation 2.1.30 of this Annex. For the purposes of this Part 1 verification procedure, the results of the test analysis shall be referred to as '1A' and '1B':

.1 results 1A and 1B shall be recorded on the test record in accordance with the requirements of the test method; and

.2 if the results of 1A and 1B are within the repeatability (r)* of the test method, the results shall be considered valid; or

.3 if the results 1A and 1B are not within the repeatability (r) of the test method, both results shall be rejected and two new subsamples shall be taken by the laboratory and tested. The sample bottle shall be resealed in accordance with paragraph 2.3.4 after the new subsamples have been taken;

.4 in the case of two failures to achieve repeatability between 1A and 1B, the cause of that failureshall be investigated by the laboratory and resolved before further testing of the sample is undertaken. On resolution of that repeatability issue, two new subsamples shall betaken in accordance with paragraph 2.3. The sampleshall be resealed in accordance with paragraph 2.3.4 after the new subsamples have been taken.

2.5 If the test results of 1A and 1B are valid, an average of these two results shall be calculated. The average valueshall be referred to as 'X' and shall be recorded on the test record:

.1 if the result X is equal to or less than the applicable limit required by regulation 14, the fuel oil shall be considered to have met the requirement; or

.2 if the result X is greater than the applicable limit required by regulation 14, the fuel oil shall be considered to have not met the requirement.

Table 1 Summary of Part 1 MARPOL delivered sample procedure

On the basis of the test method referred to in regulation 2.1.30 of this Annex		
Applicable limit % m/m: V	Result 2.5.1: X ≤ V	Result 2.5.2: X > V
0.10	Met the requiremen	Not met the requirement
0.50		
	Result X reported to 2 decimal places	

2.6 The final results obtained from this verification procedure shall be evaluated by the competent authority.

2.7 The laboratory shall provide a copy of the test record to the competent authority managing the verification procedure.

Part 2 In-use and onboard samples

3   General Requirements

3.1 The in-use or onboard sample, as appropriate, shall be used to verify the Sulphur content of the fuel oil as represented by that sample of fuel oil at the point of sampling.

3.2 A Party, through its competent authority, shall manage the verification procedure.

3.3 A laboratory undertaking the sulphur testing procedure given in this appendix shall have valid accreditation** in respect of the test method to be used.

4   Verification Procedure Part 2

4.1 The in-use or onboard sampleshall be conveyed by the competent authority to the laboratory.

---

* Repeatability (r) calculation in accordance with ISO 4259: 2017-2 and as defined in the test method used.
** The laboratory is to be accredited to ISO/IEC 17025: 2017 or an equivalent standard for the performance of the given sulphur content test ISO 8754: 2003.

2.4 应按照本附则第 2.1.30 条中所述的具体的试验方法对两份子样品依次进行测试。就本验证程序第 1 部分而言，该测试分析结果应称为'1A'和'1B'：

.1 结果'1A'和'1B'应按照试验方法的要求记入试验记录；和

.2 如结果'1A'和'1B'在试验方法的可重复性（r）*内，则结果应被视为有效；或

.3 如结果'1A'和'1B'不在试验方法的可重复性（r）内，则应放弃两个结果，实验室应提取两份新子样品进行试验。提取了新子样品后，应按照第 2.3.4 项重新密封样品瓶。

.4 如果两次未能达到'1A'和'1B'之间的可重复性，则在进行进一步样品试验之前，应由实验室调查导致失败的原因并予以解决。在解决了该可重复性问题后，应按照第 2.3 项提取两份新子样品。提取了新子样品后，应按照第 2.3.4 项重新密封样品。

2.5 如试验结果'1A'和'1B'有效，则应计算这两个结果的平均值。平均值应称为'X'，并应记入试验记录：

.1 如结果'X'等于或低于第 14 条要求的适用限值，则燃油应被视为符合要求；或

.2 如结果'X'高于第 14 条要求的适用限值，则燃油应被视为不符合要求。

表 1 《防污公约》交付的样品程序第 1 部分总结

基于本附则第 2.1.30 条中所述的试验方法		
适用的限值 % m/m：V	结果 2.5.1:X ≤ V	结果 2.5.2:X>V
0.10	符合要求	不符合要求
0.50		
结果'X'报告到小数点后两位		

2.6 从该验证程序获得的最终结果应由主管机关进行评估。

2.7 实验室应将试验记录的副本提供给管理验证程序的主管机关。

第 2 部分 在用和船上燃油样品

3 一般要求

3.1 在用或船上燃油样品应酌情用于验证在取样点以该燃油样品为代表的燃油的硫含量。

3.2 缔约国应通过其主管机关管理验证程序。

3.3 负责本附录所述硫试验程序的实验室应就其使用的试验方法获得有效认证**。

4 验证程序第 2 部分

4.1 在用或船上样品应由主管机关送交实验室。

---

* 可重复性（r）的计算根据 ISO 4256:2017–2 所用试验方法的规定。

** 按照 ISO 8754:2003 进行燃油硫含量测试的实验室应按照 ISO/IEC 17025:2017 或等效标准认证。

4.2 The laboratory shall:

  .1   record the details of the seal number and the sample label on the test record;

  .2   record the condition of the seal of the sample as received on the test record; and

  .3   reject any sample where the seal has been broken prior to receipt and record that rejection on the test record.

4.3 If the seal of the sample as received has not been broken, the laboratory shall proceed with the verification procedure and shall:

  .1   unseal the sample;

  .2   ensure that the sample is thoroughly homogenized;

  .3   draw two subsamples from the sample; and

  .4   reseal the sample and record the new reseal details on the test record.

4.4 The two subsamples shall be tested in succession, in accordance with the specified test method referred to in regulation 2.1.30 of this Annex. For the purposes of this Part 2 verification procedure, the results obtained shall be referred to as '2A' and '2B':

  .1   results 2A and 2B shall be recorded on the test record in accordance with the requirements of the test method; and

  .2   if the results of 2A and 2B are within the repeatability (r)* of the test method, the results shall be considered valid; or

  .3   if the results of 2A and 2B are not within the repeatability (r) of the test method, both results shall be rejected and two new subsamples shall be taken by the laboratory and tested. The sample bottle shall be resealed in accordance with paragraph 4.3.4 after the new subsamples have been taken; and

  .4   in the case of two failures to achieve repeatability between 2A and 2B, the cause of that failureshall be investigated by the laboratory and resolved before further testing of the sample is undertaken. On resolution of that repeatability issue, two new subsamples shall betaken in accordance with paragraph 4.3. The sampleshall be resealed in accordance with paragraph 4.3.4 after the new subsamples have been taken.

4.5 If the test results of 2A and 2B are valid, an average of these two results shall be calculated. That average valueshall be referred to as 'Z' and shall be recorded on the test record:

  .1   if Z is equal to or less than the applicable limit required by regulation 14, the sulphur content of the fuel oil as represented by the tested sample shall be considered to have met the requirement;

  .2   if Z is greater than the applicable limit required by regulation 14 but less than or equal to that applicable limit + 0.59R (where R is the reproducibility of the test method), ** the sulphur content of the fuel oil as represented by the tested sample shall be considered to have met the requirement; or

  .3   if Z is greater than the applicable limit required by regulation 14 + 0.59R, the sulphur content of the fuel oil as represented by the tested sample shall be considered to have not met the requirement.

Table 2 Summary of in-use or onboard sample procedure

On the basis of the test method referred to in regulation 2.1.30 of this Annex				
Applicable limit % m/m: V	Test margin value: W	Result 4.5.1: $Z \leq V$	Result 4.5.2: $V < Z \leq W$	Result 4.5.3: $Z > W$
0.10	0.11	Met the requiremen	Met the requiremen	Met the requiremen
0.50	0.53			
		Result Z reported to 2 decimal places		

4.6 The final results obtained from this verification procedure shall be evaluated by the competent authority.

4.7 The laboratory shall provide a copy of the test record to the competent authority managing the verification procedure.

* Repeatability (r) calculation in accordance with ISO 4259: 2017-2 and as defined in the test method used.

** Reproducibility (R) calculation in accordance with ISO 4259: 2017-2 and as defined in the test method used.

4.2 实验室应：

.1 将密封号和样品标签的详细信息记入试验记录；

.2 将收到的样品的封印状况记入试验记录；和

.3 拒绝收到的任何封印受损的样品，并将拒收记入试验记录。

4.3 如所收到样品的封印未受损，实验室应继续验证程序并应：

.1 开封样品；

.2 确保样品完全均匀；

.3 从样品中提取两份子样品；和

.4 重新密封样品，并在试验记录中记入新的重新密封的详细信息。

4.4 应按照本附则第 2.1.30 条中所述的具体的试验方法对两份子样品依次进行测试。就本验证程序第 2 部分而言，该测试分析结果应称为'2A'和'2B'：

.1 结果'2A'和'2B'应按照试验方法的要求记入试验记录；和

.2 如结果'2A'和'2B'在试验方法的可重复性（r）[*]内，则结果应被视为有效；或

.3 如结果'2A'和'2B'不在试验方法的可重复性（r）内，则应放弃两个结果，实验室应提取两份新子样品进行试验。提取了新小样后，应按照第 4.3.4 项重新密封样品瓶；和

.4 如果两次未能达到'2A'和'2B'之间的可重复性，则在进行进一步样品试验之前，应由实验室调查导致失败的原因并予以解决。在解决了该可重复性问题后，应按照第 4.3 项提取两份新子样品。提取了新子样品后，应按照第 4.3.4 项重新密封样品。

4.5 如试验结果'2A'和'2B'有效，则应计算这两个结果的平均值。平均值应称为'Z'，并应记入试验记录：

.1 如结果'Z'等于或低于第 14 条要求的适用限值，则由经试验样品代表的燃油应被视为符合要求；

.2 如结果'Z'高于第 14 条要求的适用限值，但是低于或等于适用的限值 +0.59R（R 是试验方法的复现性）[**]，则由试验样品代表的燃油应被视为符合要求；或

.3 如结果'Z'高于第 14 条要求的适用限值 +0.59R，则由经试验样品代表的燃油应被视为不符合要求。

表 2　在用或船上样品程序总结

基于本附则第 2.1.30 条中所述的试验方法				
适用的限值 % m/m：V	试验边际值：W	结果 4.5.1：$Z \leq V$	结果 4.5.2：$V < Z \leq W$	结果 4.5.3：$Z > W$
0.10	0.11	符合要求	符合要求	不符合要求
0.50	0.53			
		结果'Z'报告到小数点后两位		

4.6 从该验证程序获得的最终结果应由主管机关进行评估。

4.7 实验室应将试验记录的副本提供给管理验证程序的主管机关。

---

[*] 可重复性（r）的计算根据 ISO 4256.2017-2 所用试验方法的规定。

[**] 复现性（R）的计算根据 ISO 4256:2017-2 所用试验方法的规定。

Appendix VII Emission control areas (Regulation 13.6 and Regulation 14.3)

1 The boundaries of emission control areas designated under regulations 13.6 and 14.3, other than the Baltic Sea and the North Sea areas, are set forth in this appendix.

2 The North American area comprises:

.1 the sea area located off the Pacific coasts of the United States and Canada, enclosed by geodesic lines connecting the following coordinates:

Point	Latitude	Longtitude
1	32°32'.10 N	117°06'.11 W
2	32°32'.04 N	117°07'.29 W
3	32°31'.39 N	117°14'.20 W
4	32°33'.13 N	117°15'.50 W
5	32°34'.21 N	117°22'.01 W
6	32°35'.23 N	117°27'.53 W
7	32°37'.38 N	117°49'.34 W
8	31°07'.59 N	118°36'.21 W
9	30°33'.25 N	121°47'.29 W
10	31°46'.11 N	123°17'.22 W
11	32°21'.58 N	123°50'.44 W
12	32°56'.39 N	124°11'.47 W
13	33°40'.12 N	124°27'.15 W
14	34°31'.28 N	125°16'.52 W
15	35°14'.38 N	125°43'.23 W
16	35°43'.60 N	126°18'.53 W
17	36°16'.25 N	126°45'.30 W
18	37°01'.35 N	127°07'.18 W
19	37°45'.39 N	127°38'.02 W
20	38°25'.08 N	127°52'.60 W
21	39°25'.05 N	128°31'.23 W
22	40°18'.47 N	128°45'.46 W
23	41°13'.39 N	128°40'.22 W
24	42°12'.49 N	129°00'.38 W
25	42°47'.34 N	129°05'.42 W
26	43°26'.22 N	129°01'.26 W
27	44°24'.43 N	128°41'.23 W
28	45°30'.43 N	128°40'.02 W
29	46°11'.01 N	128°49'.01 W
30	46°33'.55 N	129°04'.29 W

附录Ⅶ 排放控制区（第13.6条和第14.3条）

1 在13.6和14.3条下指定的排放控制区，除了波罗的海和北海地区，排放控制区域的边界在本附录中提出。

2 北美区域包括：

.1 美国和加拿大太平洋沿岸外的海区，由连接下述坐标的曲线围成：

点	纬度	经度
1	32°32′.10 N	117°06′.11 W
2	32°32′.04 N	117°07′.29 W
3	32°31′.39 N	117°14′.20 W
4	32°33′.13 N	117°15′.50 W
5	32°34′.21 N	117°22′.01 W
6	32°35′.23 N	117°27′.53 W
7	32°37′.38 N	117°49′.34 W
8	31°07′.59 N	118°36′.21 W
9	30°33′.25 N	121°47′.29 W
10	31°46′.11 N	123°17′.22 W
11	32°21′.58 N	123°50′.44 W
12	32°56′.39 N	124°11′.47 W
13	33°40′.12 N	124°27′.15 W
14	34°31′.28 N	125°16′.52 W
15	35°14′.38 N	125°43′.23 W
16	35°43′.60 N	126°18′.53 W
17	36°16′.25 N	126°45′.30 W
18	37°01′.35 N	127°07′.18 W
19	37°45′.39 N	127°38′.02 W
20	38°25′.08 N	127°52′.60 W
21	39°25′.05 N	128°31′.23 W
22	40°18′.47 N	128°45′.46 W
23	41°13′.39 N	128°40′.22 W
24	42°12′.49 N	129°00′.38 W
25	42°47′.34 N	129°05′.42 W
26	43°26′.22 N	129°01′.26 W
27	44°24′.43 N	128°41′.23 W
28	45°30′.43 N	128°40′.02 W
29	46°11′.01 N	128°49′.01 W
30	46°33′.55 N	129°04′.29 W

Point	Latitude	Longtitude
31	47°39'.55 N	131°15'.41 W
32	48°32'.32 N	132°41'.00 W
33	48°57'.47 N	133°14'.47 W
34	49°22'.39 N	134°15'.51 W
35	50°01'.52 N	135°19'.01 W
36	51°03'.18 N	136°45'.45 W
37	51°54'.04 N	137°41'.54 W
38	52°45'.12 N	138°20'.14 W
39	53°29'.20 N	138°40'.36 W
40	53°40'.39 N	138°48'.53 W
41	54°13'.45 N	139°32'.38 W
42	54°39'.25 N	139°56'.19 W
43	55°20'.18 N	140°55'.45 W
44	56°07'.12 N	141°36'.18 W
45	56°28'.32 N	142°17'.19 W
46	56°37'.19 N	142°48'.57 W
47	58°51'.04 N	153°15'.03 W

.2 the sea areas located off the Atlantic coasts of the United States, Canada, and France (Saint-Pierre-et-Miquelon) and the Gulf of Mexico coast of the United States enclosed by geodesic lines connecting the following coordinates:

Point	Latitude	Longtitude
1	60°00'.00 N	64°09'.36 W
2	60°00'.00 N	56°43'.00 W
3	58°54'.01 N	55°38'.05 W
4	57°50'.52 N	55°03'.47 W
5	57°35'.13 N	54°00'.59 W
6	57°14'.20 N	53°07'.58 W
7	56°48'.09 N	52°23'.29 W
8	56°18'.13 N	51°49'.42 W
9	54°23'.21 N	50°17'.44 W
10	53°44'.54 N	50°07'.17 W
11	53°04'.59 N	50°10'.05 W
12	52°20'.06 N	49°57'.09 W
13	51°34'.20 N	48°52'.45 W
14	50°40'.15 N	48°16'.04 W
15	50°02'.28 N	48°07'.03 W

点	纬度	经度
31	47°39′.55 N	131°15′.41 W
32	48°32′.32 N	132°41′.00 W
33	48°57′.47 N	133°14′.47 W
34	49°22′.39 N	134°15′.51 W
35	50°01′.52 N	135°19′.01 W
36	51°03′.18 N	136°45′.45 W
37	51°54′.04 N	137°41′.54 W
38	52°45′.12 N	138°20′.14 W
39	53°29′.20 N	138°40′.36 W
40	53°40′.39 N	138°48′.53 W
41	54°13′.45 N	139°32′.38 W
42	54°39′.25 N	139°56′.19 W
43	55°20′.18 N	140°55′.45 W
44	56°07′.12 N	141°36′.18 W
45	56°28′.32 N	142°17′.19 W
46	56°37′.19 N	142°48′.57 W
47	58°51′.04 N	153°15′.03 W

.2 美国、加拿大和法国（圣皮埃尔密克隆）大西洋沿岸外的海区以及美国墨西哥湾，由连接下述坐标的曲线围成：

点	纬度	经度
1	60°00′.00 N	64°09′.36 W
2	60°00′.00 N	56°43′.00 W
3	58°54′.01 N	55°38′.05 W
4	57°50′.52 N	55°03′.47 W
5	57°35′.13 N	54°00′.59 W
6	57°14′.20 N	53°07′.58 W
7	56°48′.09 N	52°23′.29 W
8	56°18′.13 N	51°49′.42 W
9	54°23′.21 N	50°17′.44 W
10	53°44′.54 N	50°07′.17 W
11	53°04′.59 N	50°10′.05 W
12	52°20′.06 N	49°57′.09 W
13	51°34′.20 N	48°52′.45 W
14	50°40′.15 N	48°16′.04 W
15	50°02′.28 N	48°07′.03 W

Point	Latitude	Longtitude
16	49°24′.03 N	48°09′.35 W
17	48°39′.22 N	47°55′.17 W
18	47°24′.25 N	47°46′.56 W
19	46°35′.12 N	48°00′.54 W
20	45°19′.45 N	48°43′.28 W
21	44°43′.38 N	49°16′.50 W
22	44°16′.38 N	49°51′.23 W
23	43°53′.15 N	50°34′.01 W
24	43°36′.06 N	51°20′.41 W
25	43°23′.59 N	52°17′.22 W
26	43°19′.50 N	53°20′.13 W
27	43°21′.14 N	54°09′.20 W
28	43°29′.41 N	55°07′.41 W
29	42°40′.12 N	55°31′.44 W
30	41°58′.19 N	56°09′.34 W
31	41°20′.21 N	57°05′.13 W
32	40°55′.34 N	58°02′.55 W
33	40°41′.38 N	59°05′.18 W
34	40°38′.33 N	60°12′.20 W
35	40°45′.46 N	61°14′.03 W
36	41°04′.52 N	62°17′.49 W
37	40°36′.55 N	63°10′.49 W
38	40°17′.32 N	64°08′.37 W
39	40°07′.46 N	64°59′.31 W
40	40°05′.44 N	65°53′.07 W
41	39°58′.05 N	65°59′.51 W
42	39°28′.24 N	66°21′.14 W
43	39°01′.54 N	66°48′.33 W
44	38°39′.16 N	67°20′.59 W
45	38°19′.20 N	68°02′.01 W
46	38°05′.29 N	68°46′.55 W
47	37°58′.14 N	69°34′.07 W
48	37°57′.47 N	70°24′.09 W
49	37°52′.46 N	70°37′.50 W
50	37°18′.37 N	71°08′.33 W
51	36°32′.25 N	71°33′.59 W

点	纬度	经度
16	49°24′.03 N	48°09′.35 W
17	48°39′.22 N	47°55′.17 W
18	47°24′.25 N	47°46′.56 W
19	46°35′.12 N	48°00′.54 W
20	45°19′.45 N	48°43′.28 W
21	44°43′.38 N	49°16′.50 W
22	44°16′.38 N	49°51′.23 W
23	43°53′.15 N	50°34′.01 W
24	43°36′.06 N	51°20′.41 W
25	43°23′.59 N	52°17′.22 W
26	43°19′.50 N	53°20′.13 W
27	43°21′.14 N	54°09′.20 W
28	43°29′.41 N	55°07′.41 W
29	42°40′.12 N	55°31′.44 W
30	41°58′.19 N	56°09′.34 W
31	41°20′.21 N	57°05′.13 W
32	40°55′.34 N	58°02′.55 W
33	40°41′.38 N	59°05′.18 W
34	40°38′.33 N	60°12′.20 W
35	40°45′.46 N	61°14′.03 W
36	41°04′.52 N	62°17′.49 W
37	40°36′.55 N	63°10′.49 W
38	40°17′.32 N	64°08′.37 W
39	40°07′.46 N	64°59′.31 W
40	40°05′.44 N	65°53′.07 W
41	39°58′.05 N	65°59′.51 W
42	39°28′.24 N	66°21′.14 W
43	39°01′.54 N	66°48′.33 W
44	38°39′.16 N	67°20′.59 W
45	38°19′.20 N	68°02′.01 W
46	38°05′.29 N	68°46′.55 W
47	37°58′.14 N	69°34′.07 W
48	37°57′.47 N	70°24′.09 W
49	37°52′.46 N	70°37′.50 W
50	37°18′.37 N	71°08′.33 W
51	36°32′.25 N	71°33′.59 W

Point	Latitude	Longtitude
52	35°34'.58 N	71°26'.02 W
53	34°33'.10 N	71°37'.04 W
54	33°54'.49 N	71°52'.35 W
55	33°19'.23 N	72°17'.12 W
56	32°45'.31 N	72°54'.05 W
57	31°55'.13 N	74°12'.02 W
58	31°27'.14 N	75°15'.20 W
59	31°03'.16 N	75°51'.18 W
60	30°45'.42 N	76°31'.38 W
61	30°12'.48 N	77°18'.29 W
62	29°25'.17 N	76°56'.42 W
63	28°36'.59 N	76°47'.60 W
64	28°17'.13 N	76°40'.10 W
65	28°17'.12 N	79°11'.23 W
66	27°52'.56 N	79°28'.35 W
67	27°26'.01 N	79°31'.38 W
68	27°16'.13 N	79°34'.18 W
69	27°11'.54 N	79°34'.56 W
70	27°05'.59 N	79°35'.19 W
71	27°00'.28 N	79°35'.17 W
72	26°55'.16 N	79°34'.39 W
73	26°53'.58 N	79°34'.27 W
74	26°45'.46 N	79°32'.41 W
75	26°44'.30 N	79°32'.23 W
76	26°43'.40 N	79°32'.20 W
77	26°41'.12 N	79°32'.01 W
78	26°38'.13 N	79°31'.32 W
79	26°36'.30 N	79°31'.06 W
80	26°35'.21 N	79°30'.50 W
81	26°34'.51 N	79°30'.46 W
82	26°34'.11 N	79°30'.38 W
83	26°31'.12 N	79°30'.15 W
84	26°29'.05 N	79°29'.53 W
85	26°25'.31 N	79°29'.58 W
86	26°23'.29 N	79°29'.55 W
87	26°23'.21 N	79°29'.54 W

点	纬度	经度
52	35°34′.58 N	71°26′.02 W
53	34°33′.10 N	71°37′.04 W
54	33°54′.49 N	71°52′.35 W
55	33°19′.23 N	72°17′.12 W
56	32°45′.31 N	72°54′.05 W
57	31°55′.13 N	74°12′.02 W
58	31°27′.14 N	75°15′.20 W
59	31°03′.16 N	75°51′.18 W
60	30°45′.42 N	76°31′.38 W
61	30°12′.48 N	77°18′.29 W
62	29°25′.17 N	76°56′.42 W
63	28°36′.59 N	76°47′.60 W
64	28°17′.13 N	76°40′.10 W
65	28°17′.12 N	79°11′.23 W
66	27°52′.56 N	79°28′.35 W
67	27°26′.01 N	79°31′.38 W
68	27°16′.13 N	79°34′.18 W
69	27°11′.54 N	79°34′.56 W
70	27°05′.59 N	79°35′.19 W
71	27°00′.28 N	79°35′.17 W
72	26°55′.16 N	79°34′.39 W
73	26°53′.58 N	79°34′.27 W
74	26°45′.46 N	79°32′.41 W
75	26°44′.30 N	79°32′.23 W
76	26°43′.40 N	79°32′.20 W
77	26°41′.12 N	79°32′.01 W
78	26°38′.13 N	79°31′.32 W
79	26°36′.30 N	79°31′.06 W
80	26°35′.21 N	79°30′.50 W
81	26°34′.51 N	79°30′.46 W
82	26°34′.11 N	79°30′.38 W
83	26°31′.12 N	79°30′.15 W
84	26°29′.05 N	79°29′.53 W
85	26°25′.31 N	79°29′.58 W
86	26°23′.29 N	79°29′.55 W
87	26°23′.21 N	79°29′.54 W

Point	Latitude	Longtitude
88	26°18'.57 N	79°31'.55 W
89	26°15'.26 N	79°33'.17 W
90	26°15'.13 N	79°33'.23 W
91	26°08'.09 N	79°35'.53 W
92	26°07'.47 N	79°36'.09 W
93	26°06'.59 N	79°36'.35 W
94	26°02'.52 N	79°38'.22 W
95	25°59'.30 N	79°40'.03 W
96	25°59'.16 N	79°40'.08 W
97	25°57'.48 N	79°40'.38 W
98	25°56'.18 N	79°41'.06 W
99	25°54'.04 N	79°41'.38 W
100	25°53'.24 N	79°41'.46 W
101	25°51'.54 N	79°41'.59 W
102	25°49'.33 N	79°42'.16 W
103	25°48'.24 N	79°42'.23 W
104	25°48'.20 N	79°42'.24 W
105	25°46'.26 N	79°42'.44 W
106	25°46'.16 N	79°42'.45 W
107	25°43'.40 N	79°42'.59 W
108	25°42'.31 N	79°42'.48 W
109	25°40'.37 N	79°42'.27 W
110	25°37'.24 N	79°42'.27 W
111	25°37'.08 N	79°42'.27 W
112	25°31'.03 N	79°42'.12 W
113	25°27'.59 N	79°42'.11 W
114	25°24'.04 N	79°42'.12 W
115	25°22'.21 N	79°42'.20 W
116	25°21'.29 N	79°42'.08 W
117	25°16'.52 N	79°41'.24 W
118	25°15'.57 N	79°41'.31 W
119	25°10'.39 N	79°41'.31 W
120	25°09'.51 N	79°41'.36 W
121	25°09'.03 N	79°41'.45 W
122	25°03'.55 N	79°42'.29 W
123	25°02'.60 N	79°42'.56 W

点	纬度	经度
88	26°18′.57 N	79°31′.55 W
89	26°15′.26 N	79°33′.17 W
90	26°15′.13 N	79°33′.23 W
91	26°08′.09 N	79°35′.53 W
92	26°07′.47 N	79°36′.09 W
93	26°06′.59 N	79°36′.35 W
94	26°02′.52 N	79°38′.22 W
95	25°59′.30 N	79°40′.03 W
96	25°59′.16 N	79°40′.08 W
97	25°57′.48 N	79°40′.38 W
98	25°56′.18 N	79°41′.06 W
99	25°54′.04 N	79°41′.38 W
100	25°53′.24 N	79°41′.46 W
101	25°51′.54 N	79°41′.59 W
102	25°49′.33 N	79°42′.16 W
103	25°48′.24 N	79°42′.23 W
104	25°48′.20 N	79°42′.24 W
105	25°46′.26 N	79°42′.44 W
106	25°46′.16 N	79°42′.45 W
107	25°43′.40 N	79°42′.59 W
108	25°42′.31 N	79°42′.48 W
109	25°40′.37 N	79°42′.27 W
110	25°37′.24 N	79°42′.27 W
111	25°37′.08 N	79°42′.27 W
112	25°31′.03 N	79°42′.12 W
113	25°27′.59 N	79°42′.11 W
114	25°24′.04 N	79°42′.12 W
115	25°22′.21 N	79°42′.20 W
116	25°21′.29 N	79°42′.08 W
117	25°16′.52 N	79°41′.24 W
118	25°15′.57 N	79°41′.31 W
119	25°10′.39 N	79°41′.31 W
120	25°09′.51 N	79°41′.36 W
121	25°09′.03 N	79°41′.45 W
122	25°03′.55 N	79°42′.29 W
123	25°02′.60 N	79°42′.56 W

Point	Latitude	Longtitude
124	25°00'.30 N	79°44'.05 W
125	24°59'.03 N	79°44'.48 W
126	24°55'.28 N	79°45'.57 W
127	24°44'.18 N	79°49'.24 W
128	24°43'.04 N	79°49'.38 W
129	24°42'.36 N	79°50'.50 W
130	24°41'.47 N	79°52'.57 W
131	24°38'.32 N	79°59'.58 W
132	24°36'.27 N	80°03'.51 W
133	24°33'.18 N	80°12'.43 W
134	24°33'.05 N	80°13'.21 W
135	24°32'.13 N	80°15'.16 W
136	24°31'.27 N	80°16'.55 W
137	24°30'.57 N	80°17'.47 W
138	24°30'.14 N	80°19'.21 W
139	24°30'.06 N	80°19'.44 W
140	24°29'.38 N	80°21'.05 W
141	24°28'.18 N	80°24'.35 W
142	24°28'.06 N	80°25'.10 W
143	24°27'.23 N	80°27'.20 W
144	24°26'.30 N	80°29'.30 W
145	24°25'.07 N	80°32'.22 W
146	24°23'.30 N	80°36'.09 W
147	24°22'.33 N	80°38'.56 W
148	24°22'.07 N	80°39'.51 W
149	24°19'.31 N	80°45'.21 W
150	24°19'.16 N	80°45'.47 W
151	24°18'.38 N	80°46'.49 W
152	24°18'.35 N	80°46'.54 W
153	24°09'.51 N	80°59'.47 W
154	24°09'.48 N	80°59'.51 W
155	24°08'.58 N	81°01'.07 W
156	24°08'.30 N	81°01'.51 W
157	24°08'.26 N	81°01'.57 W
158	24°07'.28 N	81°03'.06 W
159	24°02'.20 N	81°09'.05 W

点	纬度	经度
124	25°00′.30 N	79°44′.05 W
125	24°59′.03 N	79°44′.48 W
126	24°55′.28 N	79°45′.57 W
127	24°44′.18 N	79°49′.24 W
128	24°43′.04 N	79°49′.38 W
129	24°42′.36 N	79°50′.50 W
130	24°41′.47 N	79°52′.57 W
131	24°38′.32 N	79°59′.58 W
132	24°36′.27 N	80°03′.51 W
133	24°33′.18 N	80°12′.43 W
134	24°33′.05 N	80°13′.21 W
135	24°32′.13 N	80°15′.16 W
136	24°31′.27 N	80°16′.55 W
137	24°30′.57 N	80°17′.47 W
138	24°30′.14 N	80°19′.21 W
139	24°30′.06 N	80°19′.44 W
140	24°29′.38 N	80°21′.05 W
141	24°28′.18 N	80°24′.35 W
142	24°28′.06 N	80°25′.10 W
143	24°27′.23 N	80°27′.20 W
144	24°26′.30 N	80°29′.30 W
145	24°25′.07 N	80°32′.22 W
146	24°23′.30 N	80°36′.09 W
147	24°22′.33 N	80°38′.56 W
148	24°22′.07 N	80°39′.51 W
149	24°19′.31 N	80°45′.21 W
150	24°19′.16 N	80°45′.47 W
151	24°18′.38 N	80°46′.49 W
152	24°18′.35 N	80°46′.54 W
153	24°09′.51 N	80°59′.47 W
154	24°09′.48 N	80°59′.51 W
155	24°08′.58 N	81°01′.07 W
156	24°08′.30 N	81°01′.51 W
157	24°08′.26 N	81°01′.57 W
158	24°07′.28 N	81°03′.06 W
159	24°02′.20 N	81°09′.05 W

Point	Latitude	Longtitude
160	23°59'.60 N	81°11'.16 W
161	23°55'.32 N	81°12'.55 W
162	23°53'.52 N	81°19'.43 W
163	23°50'.52 N	81°29'.59 W
164	23°50'.02 N	81°39'.59 W
165	23°49'.05 N	81°49'.59 W
166	23°49'.05 N	82°00'.11 W
167	23°49'.42 N	82°09'.59 W
168	23°51'.14 N	82°24'.59 W
169	23°51'.14 N	82°39'.59 W
170	23°49'.42 N	82°48'.53 W
171	23°49'.32 N	82°51'.11 W
172	23°49'.24 N	82°59'.59 W
173	23°49'.52 N	83°14'.59 W
174	23°51'.22 N	83°25'.49 W
175	23°52'.27 N	83°33'.01 W
176	23°54'.04 N	83°41'.35 W
177	23°55'.47 N	83°48'.11 W
178	23°58'.38 N	83°59'.59 W
179	24°09'.37 N	84°29'.27 W
180	24°13'.20 N	84°38'.39 W
181	24°16'.41 N	84°46'.07 W
182	24°23'.30 N	84°59'.59 W
183	24°26'.37 N	85°06'.19 W
184	24°38'.57 N	85°31'.54 W
185	24°44'.17 N	85°43'.11 W
186	24°53'.57 N	85°59'.59 W
187	25°10'.44 N	86°30'.07 W
188	25°43'.15 N	86°21'.14 W
189	26°13'.13 N	86°06'.45 W
190	26°27'.22 N	86°13'.15 W
191	26°33'.46 N	86°37'.07 W
192	26°01'.24 N	87°29'.35 W
193	25°42'.25 N	88°33'.00 W
194	25°46'.54 N	90°29'.41 W
195	25°44'.39 N	90°47'.05 W

点	纬度	经度
160	23°59′.60 N	81°11′.16 W
161	23°55′.32 N	81°12′.55 W
162	23°53′.52 N	81°19′.43 W
163	23°50′.52 N	81°29′.59 W
164	23°50′.02 N	81°39′.59 W
165	23°49′.05 N	81°49′.59 W
166	23°49′.05 N	82°00′.11 W
167	23°49′.42 N	82°09′.59 W
168	23°51′.14 N	82°24′.59 W
169	23°51′.14 N	82°39′.59 W
170	23°49′.42 N	82°48′.53 W
171	23°49′.32 N	82°51′.11 W
172	23°49′.24 N	82°59′.59 W
173	23°49′.52 N	83°14′.59 W
174	23°51′.22 N	83°25′.49 W
175	23°52′.27 N	83°33′.01 W
176	23°54′.04 N	83°41′.35 W
177	23°55′.47 N	83°48′.11 W
178	23°58′.38 N	83°59′.59 W
179	24°09′.37 N	84°29′.27 W
180	24°13′.20 N	84°38′.39 W
181	24°16′.41 N	84°46′.07 W
182	24°23′.30 N	84°59′.59 W
183	24°26′.37 N	85°06′.19 W
184	24°38′.57 N	85°31′.54 W
185	24°44′.17 N	85°43′.11 W
186	24°53′.57 N	85°59′.59 W
187	25°10′.44 N	86°30′.07 W
188	25°43′.15 N	86°21′.14 W
189	26°13′.13 N	86°06′.45 W
190	26°27′.22 N	86°13′.15 W
191	26°33′.46 N	86°37′.07 W
192	26°01′.24 N	87°29′.35 W
193	25°42′.25 N	88°33′.00 W
194	25°46′.54 N	90°29′.41 W
195	25°44′.39 N	90°47′.05 W

Point	Latitude	Longtitude
196	25°51'.43 N	91°52'.50 W
197	26°17'.44 N	93°03'.59 W
198	25°59'.55 N	93°33'.52 W
199	26°00'.32 N	95°39'.27 W
200	26°00'.33 N	96°48'.30 W
201	25°58'.32 N	96°55'.28 W
202	25°58'.15 N	96°58'.41 W
203	25°57'.58 N	97°01'.54 W
204	25°57'.41 N	97°05'.08 W
205	25°57'.24 N	97°08'.21 W
206	25°57'.24 N	97°08'.47 W

.3 the sea area located off the coasts of the Hawaiian Islands of Hawai'i, Maui, Oahu, Moloka'i, Ni'ihau, Kaua'i, Lana'i, and Kaho'olawe, enclosed by geodesic lines connecting the following coordinates:

Point	Latitude	Longtitude
1	22°32'.54 N	153°00'.33 W
2	23°06'.05 N	153°28'.36 W
3	23°32'.11 N	154°02'.12 W
4	23°51'.47 N	154°36'.48 W
5	24°21'.49 N	155°51'.13 W
6	24°41'.47 N	156°27'.27 W
7	24°57'.33 N	157°22'.17 W
8	25°13'.41 N	157°54'.13 W
9	25°25'.31 N	158°30'.36 W
10	25°31'.19 N	159°09'.47 W
11	25°30'.31 N	159°54'.21 W
12	25°21'.53 N	160°39'.53 W
13	25°00'.06 N	161°38'.33 W
14	24°40'.49 N	162°13'.13 W
15	24°15'.53 N	162°43'.08 W
16	23°40'.50 N	163°13'.00 W
17	23°03'.20 N	163°32'.58 W
18	22°20'.09 N	163°44'.41 W
19	21°36'.45 N	163°46'.03 W
20	20°55'.26 N	163°37'.44 W
21	20°13'.34 N	163°19'.13 W

点	纬度	经度
196	25°51′.43 N	91°52′.50 W
197	26°17′.44 N	93°03′.59 W
198	25°59′.55 N	93°33′.52 W
199	26°00′.32 N	95°39′.27 W
200	26°00′.33 N	96°48′.30 W
201	25°58′.32 N	96°55′.28 W
202	25°58′.15 N	96°58′.41 W
203	25°57′.58 N	97°01′.54 W
204	25°57′.41 N	97°05′.08 W
205	25°57′.24 N	97°08′.21 W
206	25°57′.24 N	97°08′.47 W

.3 夏威夷岛、毛伊岛、瓦胡岛、莫洛凯岛、尼豪岛、考艾岛、拉奈岛、卡霍奥拉维岛等夏威夷岛屿沿岸外的海区，由连接下述坐标的曲线围成：

点	纬度	经度
1	22°32′.54 N	153°00′.33 W
2	23°06′.05 N	153°28′.36 W
3	23°32′.11 N	154°02′.12 W
4	23°51′.47 N	154°36′.48 W
5	24°21′.49 N	155°51′.13 W
6	24°41′.47 N	156°27′.27 W
7	24°57′.33 N	157°22′.17 W
8	25°13′.41 N	157°54′.13 W
9	25°25′.31 N	158°30′.36 W
10	25°31′.19 N	159°09′.47 W
11	25°30′.31 N	159°54′.21 W
12	25°21′.53 N	160°39′.53 W
13	25°00′.06 N	161°38′.33 W
14	24°40′.49 N	162°13′.13 W
15	24°15′.53 N	162°43′.08 W
16	23°40′.50 N	163°13′.00 W
17	23°03′.20 N	163°32′.58 W
18	22°20′.09 N	163°44′.41 W
19	21°36′.45 N	163°46′.03 W
20	20°55′.26 N	163°37′.44 W
21	20°13′.34 N	163°19′.13 W

Point	Latitude	Longtitude
22	19°39'. 03 N	162°53'. 48 W
23	19°09'. 43 N	162°20'. 35 W
24	18°39'. 16 N	161°19'. 14 W
25	18°30'. 31 N	160°38'. 30 W
26	18°29'. 31 N	159°56'. 17 W
27	18°10'. 41 N	159°14'. 08 W
28	17°31'. 17 N	158°56'. 55 W
29	16°54'. 06 N	158°30'. 29 W
30	16°25'. 49 N	157° 59'. 25 W
31	15°59'. 57 N	157°17'. 35 W
32	15°40'. 37 N	156°21'. 06 W
33	15°37'. 36 N	155°22'. 16 W
34	15°43'. 46 N	154°46'. 37 W
35	15°55'. 32 N	154°13'. 05 W
36	16°46'.27 N	152°49'. 11 W
37	17°33'. 42 N	152°00'. 32 W
38	18°30'. 16 N	151 30'. 24 W
39	19°02'. 47 N	151°22'. 17 W
40	19°34'. 46 N	151°19'. 47 W
41	20°07'. 42 N	151°22'. 58 W
42	20°38'. 43 N	151°31'. 36 W
43	21°29'. 09 N	151° 59'. 50 W
44	22°06'. 58 N	152°31'. 25 W
45	22°32'. 54 N	153°00'. 33 W

点	纬度	经度
22	19°39′.03 N	162°53′.48 W
23	19°09′.43 N	162°20′.35 W
24	18°39′.16 N	161°19′.14 W
25	18°30′.31 N	160°38′.30 W
26	18°29′.31 N	159°56′.17 W
27	18°10′.41 N	159°14′.08 W
28	17°31′.17 N	158°56′.55 W
29	16°54′.06 N	158°30′.29 W
30	16°25′.49 N	157°59′.25 W
31	15°59′.57 N	157°17′.35 W
32	15°40′.37 N	156°21′.06 W
33	15°37′.36 N	155°22′.16 W
34	15°43′.46 N	154°46′.37 W
35	15°55′.32 N	154°13′.05 W
36	16°46′.27 N	152°49′.11 W
37	17°33′.42 N	152°00′.32 W
38	18°30′.16 N	151 30′.24 W
39	19°02′.47 N	151°22′.17 W
40	19°34′.46 N	151°19′.47 W
41	20°07′.42 N	151°22′.58 W
42	20°38′.43 N	151°31′.36 W
43	21°29′.09 N	151°59′.50 W
44	22°06′.58 N	152°31′.25 W
45	22°32′.54 N	153°00′.33 W

3   The United States Caribbean Sea area includes:

.1   the sea area located off the Atlantic and Caribbean coasts of the Commonwealth of Puerto Rico and the United States Virgin Islands, enclosed by geodesic lines connecting the following coordinates:

Point	Latitude	Longtitude
1	17°18'.37 N	67°32'.14 W
2	19°11'.14 N	67°26'.45 W
3	19°30'.28 N	65°16'.48 W
4	19°12'.25 N	65°06'.08 W
5	18°45'.13 N	65°00'.22 W
6	18°41'.14 N	64°59'.33 W
7	18°29'.22 N	64°53'.51 W
8	18°27'.35 N	64°53'.22 W
9	18°25'.21 N	64°52'.39 W
10	18°24'.30 N	64°52'.19 W
11	18°23'.51 N	64°51'.50 W
12	18°23'.42 N	64°51'.23 W
13	18°23'.36 N	64°50'.17 W
14	18°23'. 48 N	64°49'. 41 W
15	18°24'. 11 N	64°49'. 00 W
16	18°24'. 28 N	64°47'. 57 W
17	18°24'. 18 N	64°47'. 01 W
18	18°23'. 13 N	64°46'. 37 W
19	18°22'. 37 N	64°45'. 20 W
20	18°22'. 39 N	64°44'. 42 W
21	18°22'. 42 N	64°44'. 36 W
22	18°22'. 37 N	64°44'. 24 W
23	18°22'. 39 N	64°43'. 42 W
24	18°22'. 30 N	64°43'. 36 W
25	18°22'. 25 N	64°42'. 58 W
26	18°22'. 26 N	64°42'. 28 W
27	18°22'. 15 N	64°42'. 03 W
28	18°22'. 22 N	64°38'. 23 W
29	18°21'. 57 N	64°40'. 60 W
30	18°21'. 51 N	64°40'. 15 W
31	18°21'. 22 N	64° 38'. 16 W
32	18°20'. 39 N	64° 38'. 33 W
33	18°19'. 15 N	64° 38'. 14 W

3 美国加勒比海区域包括：

.1 位于波多黎各自由邦和美属维京群岛大西洋和加勒比海岸附近由测地线连接的下列坐标范围内的海域：

点	纬度	经度
1	17°18′.37 N	67°32′.14 W
2	19°11′.14 N	67°26′.45 W
3	19°30′.28 N	65°16′.48 W
4	19°12′.25 N	65°06′.08 W
5	18°45′.13 N	65°00′.22 W
6	18°41′.14 N	64°59′.33 W
7	18°29′.22 N	64°53′.51 W
8	18°27′.35 N	64°53′.22 W
9	18°25′.21 N	64°52′.39 W
10	18°24′.30 N	64°52′.19 W
11	18°23′.51 N	64°51′.50 W
12	18°23′.42 N	64°51′.23 W
13	18°23′.36 N	64°50′.17 W
14	18°23′.48 N	64°49′.41 W
15	18°24′.11 N	64°49′.00 W
16	18°24′.28 N	64°47′.57 W
17	18°24′.18 N	64°47′.01 W
18	18°23′.13 N	64°46′.37 W
19	18°22′.37 N	64°45′.20 W
20	18°22′.39 N	64°44′.42 W
21	18°22′.42 N	64°44′.36 W
22	18°22′.37 N	64°44′.24 W
23	18°22′.39 N	64°43′.42 W
24	18°22′.30 N	64°43′.36 W
25	18°22′.25 N	64°42′.58 W
26	18°22′.26 N	64°42′.28 W
27	18°22′.15 N	64°42′.03 W
28	18°22′.22 N	64°38′.23 W
29	18°21′.57 N	64°40′.60 W
30	18°21′.51 N	64°40′.15 W
31	18°21′.22 N	64°38′.16 W
32	18°20′.39 N	64°38′.33 W
33	18°19′.15 N	64°38′.14 W

Point	Latitude	Longtitude
34	18°19'. 07 N	64° 38'. 16 W
35	18°17'. 23 N	64° 39'. 38 W
36	18°16'. 43 N	64° 39'. 41 W
37	18°11'. 33 N	64° 38'. 58 W
38	18°03'. 02 N	64° 38'. 03 W
39	18°02'. 56 N	64° 29'. 35 W
40	18°02'. 51 N	64° 27'. 02 W
41	18°02'. 30 N	64° 21'. 08 W
42	18 02'. 31 N	64° 20'. 08 W
43	18°02 03 N	64° 15'. 57 W
44	18°00 12 N	64° 02'. 29 W
45	17°59 58 N	64° 01'. 04 W
46	17°58 47 N	63° 57'. 01 W
47	17°57 51 N	63° 53'. 54 W
48	17° 56 38 N	63° 53'. 21 W
49	17 °39 40 N	63° 54'. 53 W
50	17 °37 08 N	63° 55'. 10 W
51	17 °30 21 N	63° 55'. 56 W
52	17° 11 36 N	63° 57'. 57 W
53	17° 04 60 N	63° 58'. 41 W
54	16° 59 49 N	63° 59'. 18 W
55	17° 18 37 N	67° 32'. 14 W

4   In respect of the application of regulation 14.4, the Mediterranean Sea Emission Control Area for Sulphur Oxides and Particulate Matter includes all waters bounded by the coasts of Europe, Africa and Asia, and is described by the following coordinates:

.1   the western entrance to the Straits of Gibraltar, defined as a line joining the extremities of Cape Trafalgar, Spain (36°11'.00 N, 6°02'.00 W) and Cape Spartel, Morocco (35°48'.00 N, 5° 55'.00 W);

.2   the Strait of Canakkale, defined as a line joining Mehmetcik Burnu (40°03'N, 26°11'E) and Kumkale Burnu (40°01'.00 N, 26°12'.00 E); and

.3   the northern entrance to the Suez Canal excluding the area enclosed by geodesic lines connecting points 1-4 with the following coordinates:

Point	Latitude	Longtitude
1	31°29'.00 N	32°16'.00 E
2	31°29'.00 N	32°28'.48 E
3	31°14'.00 N	32°32'.62 E
4	31°14'.00 N	32°16'.00 E

点	纬度	经度
34	18°19′.07 N	64°38′.16 W
35	18°17′.23 N	64°39′.38 W
36	18°16′.43 N	64°39′.41 W
37	18°11′.33 N	64°38′.58 W
38	18°03′.02 N	64°38′.03 W
39	18°02′.56 N	64°29′.35 W
40	18°02′.51 N	64°27′.02 W
41	18°02′.30 N	64°21′.08 W
42	18 02′.31 N	64°20′.08 W
43	18°02 03 N	64°15′.57 W
44	18°00 12 N	64°02′.29 W
45	17°59 58 N	64°01′.04 W
46	17°58 47 N	63°57′.01 W
47	17°57 51 N	63°53′.54 W
48	17°56 38 N	63°53′.21 W
49	17°39 40 N	63°54′.53 W
50	17°37 08 N	63°55′.10 W
51	17°30 21 N	63°55′.56 W
52	17°11 36 N	63°57′.57 W
53	17°04 60 N	63°58′.41 W
54	16°59 49 N	63°59′.18 W
55	17°18 37 N	67°32′.14 W

4 就适用第 14.4 条而言，地中海硫氧化物和颗粒物质排放控制区包括以欧洲、非洲和亚洲海岸为边界的全部水域并以下列坐标所划定：

.1 直布罗陀海峡西面入口，由连接西班牙特拉法加角（36°11'.00N，6°02'.00W）和摩洛哥斯巴泰尔角（35°48'.00N，5°55'.00W）两端的线所界定；

.2 卡纳卡莱海峡，由连接 Mehmetcik Burnu（40°03'N，26°11'E）和 Kumkale Burnu（40°01'.00N，26°12'.00 E）的线所界定；和

.3 苏伊士运河北面入口，不包括由测地线连接点 1 至 4 的下列坐标包围的区域：

点	纬度	经度
1	31°29′.00 N	32°16′.00 E
2	31°29′.00 N	32°28′.48 E
3	31°14′.00 N	32°32′.62 E
4	31°14′.00 N	32°16′.00 E

Appendix VIII Form of International Energy Efficiency (IEE) Certificate (Regulation 8.2)

INTERNATIONAL ENERGY EFFICIENCY CERTIFICATE

Issued under the provisions of the Protocol of 1997, as amended, to amend the International Convention for the Prevention of Pollution by Ships, 1973, as modified by the Protocol of 1978 related thereto (hereinafter referred to as "the Convention") under the authority of the Government of:

(full designation of the Party)

by. ....

(full designation of the competent person or organization
authorized under the provisions of the Convention)

Particulars of ship∗

Name of ship ....

Distinctive number or letters ....

IMO Number∗∗ ....

Port of registry ....

Gross tonnage ....

THIS IS TO CERTIFY:

1   That the ship has been surveyed in accordance with regulation 5.4 of Annex VI of the Convention; and

2   That the survey shows that the ship complies with the applicable requirements in regulations 22, 23, 24, 25 and 26.

Completion date of survey on which this Certificate is based .... (dd/mm/yyyy)

Issued at ....

(place of issue of Certificate)

Date (dd/mm/yyyy) ....

(date of issue)   (signature of duly authorized official
issuing the Certificate)

(seal or stamp of the authority, as appropriate)

∗ Alternatively, the particulars of the ship may be placed horizontally in boxes.

∗∗ In accordance with the IMO ship identification number scheme(resolution A.1117(30)).

附录Ⅷ 国际能效（IEE）证书的格式
（第8.2条）

国际能效证书

本证书系根据经修正的《经1978年议定书修订的〈1973年国际防止船舶造成污染公约〉的1997年议定书》（以下简称本公约）的规定，

经＿＿＿＿＿＿＿＿＿＿＿＿＿＿＿＿＿＿＿＿＿＿＿＿＿＿＿国政府授权
（国家全称）

由＿＿＿＿＿＿＿＿＿＿＿＿＿＿＿＿＿＿＿＿＿＿＿＿＿签发，
（按本公约规定正式授权的组织或个人全称）

船舶概况 *

船名＿＿＿＿＿＿＿＿＿＿＿＿＿＿＿＿＿＿＿＿＿＿＿＿＿＿＿＿＿

船舶编号或呼号＿＿＿＿＿＿＿＿＿＿＿＿＿＿＿＿＿＿＿＿＿＿＿＿

IMO 编号 **＿＿＿＿＿＿＿＿＿＿＿＿＿＿＿＿＿＿＿＿＿＿＿＿＿＿

船籍港＿＿＿＿＿＿＿＿＿＿＿＿＿＿＿＿＿＿＿＿＿＿＿＿＿＿＿＿＿

总吨位＿＿＿＿＿＿＿＿＿＿＿＿＿＿＿＿＿＿＿＿＿＿＿＿＿＿＿＿＿

兹证明：

1. 该船已按本公约附则 VI 第 5.4 条的规定进行了检验；和

2. 检验表明，该船符合第 22、23、24、25 和 26 条的适用要求。

本证书基于的检验完成日期：＿＿＿＿＿＿＿＿＿＿＿＿＿（日 / 月 / 年）

签发于＿＿＿＿＿＿＿＿＿＿＿＿＿＿＿＿＿＿＿＿＿＿＿＿＿＿＿＿＿
（证书签发地点）

（日 / 月 / 年）＿＿＿＿＿＿＿＿＿＿＿＿＿＿＿   ＿＿＿＿＿＿＿＿＿＿＿＿＿＿＿＿＿
（签发日期）　　　　　　　　　　　（经正式授权的发证官员签字）

（主管机关盖章或钢印）

＊　船舶概况也可在表格中横向排列。

＊＊　根据《IMO 船舶编号机制》（第 A.1117（30）号决议）。

Supplement to the International Energy Efficiency Certificate
(IEE Certificate)

RECORD OF CONSTRUCTION RELATING TO ENERGY EFFICIENCY

> Notes:
> 1 This Record shall be permanently attached to the IEE Certificate. The IEE Certificate shall be available on board the ship at all times.
> 2 The Record shall be at least in English, French or Spanish. If an official language of the issuing Party is also used, this shall prevail in case of a dispute or discrepancy.
> 3 Entries in boxes shall be made by inserting either: a cross (x) for the answers "yes" and "applicable"; or a dash (-) for the answers "no" and "not applicable", as appropriate.
> 4 Unless otherwise stated, regulations mentioned in this Record refer to regulations in Annex VI of the Convention, and resolutions or circulars refer to those adopted by the International Maritime Organization.

1 Particulars of ship

1.1 Name of ship ....

1.2 IMO number ....

1.3 Date of building contract ....

1.3 Date of building contract ....

1.4 Date of major conversion (if applicable) ....

1.5 Gross tonnage ....

1.6 Deadweight ....

1.7 Type of ship* ....

2 Propulsion system

2.1 Diesel propulsion .... ☐

2.2 Diesel-electric propulsion .... ☐

2.3 Turbine propulsion .... ☐

2.4 Hybrid propulsion .... ☐

2.5 Propulsion system other than any of the above................................ ☐

3 Attained Energy Efficiency Design Index (EEDI)

3.1 The attained EEDI in accordance with regulation 22.1 is calculated based on the information contained in the EEDI technical file, which also shows the process of calculating the attained EEDI .... ☐

The Attained EEDI is: .... grams CO_2/tonne-nautical mile

3.2 The Attained EEDI is not calculated as:

3.2.1 the ship is exempt under regulation 22.1 as it is not a new ship as defined in regulation 2.2.18 . ☐

3.2.2 the type of propulsion system is exempt in accordance with regulation 19.3 .... ☐

3.2.3 the requirement of regulation 22 is waived by the ship's Administration in accordance with regulation 19.4 .... ☐

3.2.4 the type of ship is exempt in accordance with regulation 22.1 .... ☐

---

* Insert ship type in accordance with definitions specified in regulation 2.2. Ships falling into more than one of the ship types defined in regulation 2.2 should be considered as being the ship type with the most stringent (the lowest) required EEDI. If the ship does not fall into the ship types defined in regulation 2.2, insert "Ship other than ship types defined in regulation 2.2" .

国际能效证书（IEE 证书）的附页

能效相关的结构记录

> 备注：
> 1 本记录应永久地附于 IEE 证书之后，IEE 证书应保存在船上随时可查。
> 2 记录应至少使用英文、法文或西班牙文的其中一种语言。如同时使用发证国的官方语言，则在 发生争执或不一致时，应以该官方语言为准。
> 3 在方格内应填入 (×) 表示"是"和"适用"；或填入（–）表示"不"和"不适用"。
> 4 除非另有说明，本记录中所提及的规定系指本公约附则Ⅵ的规定，决议或通函系指由国际海事 组织通过的决议或通函。

1 船舶概况

1.1 船名_____

1.2 IMO 编号_____

1.3 签订建造合同日期_____

1.4 重大改建日期（如适用）_____

1.5 总吨_____

1.6 载重吨_____

1.7 船型 *_____

2 推进系统

2.1 柴油机推进_____☐

2.2 柴油电力推进_____☐

2.3 汽轮机推进_____☐

2.4 混合推进_____☐

2.5 上述推进以外的推进系统_____☐

3 达到的能效设计指数（Attained EEDI）

3.1 按 EEDI 技术文件中包含的信息，包括给出的 Attained EEDI 的计算过程计算第 22.1 条要求的 Attained EEDI_____☐

Attained EEDI 是：................. CO_2 克 / 吨 – 海里

3.2 当有下列情况时，无须计算 Attained EEDI：

3.2.1 船舶不属于第 2.2.18 条定义的新船，根据第 22.1 条规定免除要求_____☐

3.2.2 根据第 19.3 条免除的推进系统的类型_____☐

3.2.3 根据第 19.4 条规定船舶主管机关对其免除第 22 条要求_____☐

3.2.4 根据第 22.1 条规定免除的船型_____☐

---

* 根据第 2.2 条定义的船型填写。如果船舶属于第 2.2 条定义中的一种以上船型，应考虑适用最严格的（最小的）要求的能效 设计指数。如果船舶未包括在第 2.2 条定义内，填写"第 2 条定义以外的船舶"。

4 Required EEDI

4.1 Required EEDI is: ....grams CO_2/tonne-nautical mile

4.2 The required EEDI is not applicable as:

4.2.1 the ship is exempt under regulation 24.1 as it is not a new ship as defined in regulation 2.2.18 . ☐

4.2.2 the type of propulsion system is exempt in accordance with regulation 19.3 .... ☐

4.2.3 the requirement of regulation 24 is waived by the ship's Administration in accordance with regulation 19.4 .... ☐

4.2.4 the type of ship is exempt in accordance with regulation 24.1 .... ☐

4.2.5 the ship's capacity is below the minimum capacity threshold in table 1 of regulation 24.2 .... ☐

5 Attained Energy Efficiency Existing Ship Index (EEXI)

5.1 The attained EEXI in accordance with regulation 23.1 is calculated taking into account the guidelines* developed by the Organization .... ☐

The attained EEXI is:_____grams-CO_2/tonne-nautical mile

5.2 The attained EEXI is not calculated, as:

5.2.1 the type of propulsion system is exempt in accordance with regulation 19.3 .... ☐

5.2.2 the type of ship is exempt in accordance with regulation 23.1 .... ☐

6 Required EEXI

6.1 The required EEXI is:.................. grams-CO_2/tonne-nautical mile in accordance with regulation 25

6.2 The required EEXI is not applicable, as:

6.2.1 the type of propulsion system is exempt in accordance with regulation 19.3 .... ☐

6.2.2 the type of ship is exempt in accordance with regulation 25.1 .... ☐

6.2.3 the ship's capacity is below the minimum capacity threshold in table 3 of regulation 25.1 .... ☐

7 Ship Energy Efficiency Management Plan

7.1 The ship is provided with a Ship Energy Efficiency Management Plan (SEEMP) in compliance with regulation 26... ☐

8 EEDI technical file

8.1 The IEE Certificate is accompanied by the EEDI technical file in compliance with regulation 22.1 .... ☐

8.1.1 The EEDI technical file identification/verification number .... ☐

8.1.2 The EEDI technical file verification date .... ☐

9 EEXI technical file

9.1 The IEE Certificate is accompanied by the EEXI technical file in compliance with regulation 23.1 .... ☐

9.1.1 The EEXI technical file identification/verification number .... ☐

9.1.2 The EEXI technical file verification date .... ☐

9.2 The IEE Certificate is not accompanied by the EEXI technical file as the attained EEDI is used as an alternative to the attained EEXI .... ☐

---

* Refer to the 2022 Guidelines on the method of calculation of the attained Energy Efficiency Existing Ships Index (EEXI) (resolution MEPC. 350(78)).

4 要求的能效设计指数（Required EEDI）

4.1 Required EEDI 是：_____CO$_2$ 克 / 吨 – 海里

4.2 当有下列情况时，Required EEDI 不适用：

4.2.1 船舶不属于第 2.2.18 条的定义新船，根据第 24.1 条规定免除要求_____ ☐

4.2.2 根据第 19.3 条免除的推进系统的类型_____ ☐

4.2.3 根据第 19.4 条规定船舶主管机关对其免除第 24 条要求_____ ☐

4.2.4 根据第 24.1 条规定免除的船型_____ ☐

4.2.5 船舶载运能力低于第 24.2 条中表 1 规定的最小载运能力阈值_____ ☐

5 现有船舶达到的能效指数（EEXI）

5.1 考虑到本组织制定的导则[*]，计算第 23.1 条要求的现有船舶达到的能效指数
_____ ☐

现有船舶达到的能效指数为：_____克 –CO$_2$/ 吨 – 海里

5.2 在下列情况下，不计算现有船舶达到的能效指数：

5.2.1 按照第 19.3 条免除的推进系统类型_____ ☐

5.2.2 按照第 23.1 条免除的船型_____ ☐

6 现有船舶要求的能效指数

6.1 按照第 25 条，现有船舶要求的能效指数为：_____克 –CO$_2$/ 吨 – 海里

6.2 在下列情况下，现有船舶要求的能效指数不适用，因其：

6.2.1 按照第 19.3 条免除的推进系统类型_____ ☐

6.2.2 按照第 25.1 条免除的船型_____ ☐

6.2.3 船舶载运能力低于第 25.1 条中表 3 规定的最小载运能力阈值_____ ☐

7 船舶能效管理计划

7.1 根据第 26 条的规定船舶应持有《船舶能效管理计划》（SEEMP）_____ ☐

8 能效设计指数技术案卷

8.1 根据第 22.1 条的规定，IEE 证书应有 EEDI 技术案卷做附件_____ ☐

8.2 EEDI 技术案卷识别/验证码_____ ☐

8.3 EEDI 技术案卷认证日期_____ ☐

9 现有船舶能效指数技术案卷

9.1 按照第 23.1 条"国际能效证书"附有现有船舶能效指数技术案卷_____ ☐

9.1.1 现有船舶能效指数技术案卷识别 / 验证号_____ ☐

9.1.2 现有船舶能效指数技术案卷认证日期_____ ☐

9.2 因使用达到的能效设计指数替代现有船舶达到的能效指数，"国际能效证书"未附有
现有船舶能效指数技术案卷_____ ☐

---

[*] 参见《2022 年现有船舶达到的能效指数（EEXI）计算导则》（第 MEPC.350（78）号决议）。

THIS IS TO CERTIFY that this Record is correct in all respects.

Issued at ....
(place of issue of the Record)

Date (dd/mm/yyyy) ....

(date of issue)
(signature of duly authorized official

issuing the Record)

(seal or stamp of the authority, as appropriate)

兹证明本记录在各方面均正确无误。

签发于＿＿＿＿＿＿＿＿＿＿＿＿＿＿＿＿＿＿＿＿＿＿＿＿＿＿＿＿＿＿＿＿

（本记录的签发地点）

（日 / 月 / 年）：＿＿＿＿＿＿＿＿＿　　　　＿＿＿＿＿＿＿＿＿＿＿＿＿＿

（签发时间）　　　　　　　（正式授权签发本记录的官员签字）

（主管当局盖章或钢印）

Appendix IX   Information to be submitted to the IMO Ship Fuel Oil Consumption Database (regulation 27)

Identity of the ship

IMO Number ....

Period of calendar year for which the data is submitted

      Start date (dd/mm/yy) ....

      End date (dd/mm/yy) ....

Technical characteristics of the ship

Year of delivery ....

Ship type, as defined in regulation 2.2 of this Annex or other (to be stated) ....

Gross tonnage[1] (GT) ....

Net tonnage (NT)[2] ....

Deadweight tonnage (DWT)[3] ....

Power output (rated power)[4] of main and auxiliary reciprocating internal combustion engines over 130 kW (to be stated in kW) ....

Attained EEXI[5] (if applicable) ....

Attained EEXI[6] (if applicable) ....

Ice class[7] ....

Fuel oil consumption data

Total fuel oil consumption by fuel oil type[5] in metric tonnes and methods used for collecting fuel oil consumption aa ....

Total fuel oil consumption by fuel oil type[5] per consumer type in metric tonnes and methods used for collecting fuel oil consumption data:

      Main Engine(s) ....

      Auxiliary Engine(s)/Generator(s) ....

      Oil-fired Boiler(s) ....

      Others (specify) ....

Fuel oil consumption while the ship is not under way by fuel oil type[5] per consumer type in metric tonnes and methods used for collecting fuel oil consumption data:

      Main Engine(s) ....

      Auxiliary Engine(s)/Generator(s) ....

      Oil-fired Boiler(s) ....

      Others (specify) ....

Total distance tavelled (nm)...

---

[1] Gross tonnage should be calculated in accordance with the International Convention on Tonnage Measurement of Ships, 1969.

[2] Net tonnage should be calculated in accordance with the International Convention on Tonnage Measurement of Ships, 1969. If not applicable, note "N/A".

[3] DWT means the difference in tonnes between the displacement of a ship in water of relative density of 1,025 kg/m^3 at the summer load draught and the lightweight of the ship. The summer load draught should be taken as the maximum summer draught as certifed in the stability booklet approved by the Administration or an orgarization authorized by it. If not applicable, note "N/A".

[4] Rated power means the maximum continuous rated power as specifed on the nameplate of the engine.

[5] Refer to the 2022 *Guidelines on the method of calculation of the attained Energy Efficiency Design Index (EEDI) for new ships* (resolution MEPC.364(79)).

[6] Refer to the 2022 *Guidelines on the method of calculation of the attained Energy Efficiency Existing Ship Index (EEXI)* (resolution MEPC.350(78)).

[7] Ice class should be consistent with the definition set out in the International Code for Ships Operating in Polar Waters (Polar Code) (resolutions MEPC 264(68) and MSC .385(94)). If not applicable, note "N/A".

附录IX 提交给国际海事组织船舶燃油消耗数据库的信息（第27条）

船舶识别号

IMO 编号..

每日历年数据提交的起止时间

    开始日期（日/月/年）....................................

    结束日期（日/月/年）....................................

船舶技术参数

交付年份..

按本附则第 2.2 条定义的船型或其他（请列明）...................

总吨位（GT）[1]..

净吨位（NT）[2]..

载重吨（DWT）[3]..

主机和大于 130 kW 的副往复式内燃机的输出功率（额定功率[4]）（以 kW 标明）...........

达到的能效设计指数[5]（如适用）

现有船舶达到的能效指数[6]（如适用）..........................

冰级[7]

燃油消耗数据

按燃油类型[5]划分的燃油消耗总量（吨），以及收集燃油消耗数据的方法：..........

每种耗能类型按燃油种类[5]划分的燃油总消耗量（吨），以及收集燃油消耗数据的方法：

    主机（组）...

    副机（组）/发电机（组）..............................

    燃油锅炉（组）.....................................

    其他（具体说明）...................................

船舶在非航行状态下，每种耗能类型按燃油种类[5]划分的燃油总消耗量（吨），以及收集燃油消耗数据的方法：

    主机（组）...

    副机（组）/发电机（组）..............................

    燃油锅炉（组）.....................................

    其他（具体说明）...................................

总航行距离（nm）..

---

[1] 总吨应按《1969 年国际船舶吨位丈量公约》计算。

[2] 净吨应按《1969 年国际船舶吨位丈量公约》计算。如不适用，注明"N/A"。

[3] DWT 系指船舶在密度为 $1\,025\ kg/m^3$ 的海水中，夏季载重吃水的排水量与该船空船重量之差，以吨计。夏季载重吃水应取主管机关或经其授权的组织批准的稳性手册中核准的最大夏季吃水。如不适用，注明"N/A"。

[4] 额定功率系指发动机铭牌上标明的最大持续额定功率。

[5] 参见《2022 年新船达到的能效设计指数 (EEDI) 计算方法导则》（第 MEPC.364(79) 号决议）。

[6] 参见《2022 年现有船达到的能效指数 (EEXI) 计算方法导则》（第 MEPC.350(78) 号决议）。

[7] 冰级应与《国际极地水域营运船舶规则 (极地规则)》（第 MEPC.264(68) 号决议和第 MSC.385(94) 号决议）中的定义一致。如不适用，注明"N/A"。

Laden distance travelled (nm) (on a voluntary basis)...

Hours under way ....

Total amount of onshore power supplied (kWh) ....

For ships to which regulation 28 of MARPOL Annex VI applies.....................................

Total transport work ....

Applicable CII[8]:   ☐ AER ☐ cgDIST

Required annual operational CII[9] ....

Attained annual operational CII before any correction[10] ....

Attained annual operational CII[11] ....

Installation of Innovative technology[12], if applicable: ☐ A ☐ B-1 ☐ B-2 ☐ C-1 ☐ C-2

Operational carbon intensity rating[13]:   ☐ A   ☐ B ☐ C ☐ D ☐ E

CII for trial purpose (on voluntary basis)[14]:

    ☐ EEPI (gCO$_2$/t/nm)...

    ☐ cbDIST (gCO$_2$/berth/nm)..

    ☐ clDIST (gCO$_2$/m/nm) ....

    ☐ EEOI (gCO$_2$/t/nm)[15] ....

***

---

[8] Refer to the *2022 Guidelines on operational carbon intensity indicators and the calculation methods (CII guidelines, G1)* (resolution MEPC.352(78)).

[9] Refer to the *2022 Guidelines on the reference lines for use with operational carbon intensity indicators (CII reference lines guidelines, G2) (resolution MEPC.353(78))* and *2021 Guidelines on the operational carbon intensity reduction factors relative to reference lines (CII reduction factors guidelines, G3)* (resolution MEPC.338(76)).

[10] As calculated in accordance with the *2022 Guidelines on operational carbon intensity indicators and the calculation methods (CII guidelines, G1) (resolution MEPC 352(78))* before any correction using *Interim guidelines on correction factors and voyage adjustments for CII calculations(G5)* (resolution MEPC.355(78)).

[11] As calculated in accordance with the *2022 Guidelines on operational carbon intensity indicators and the calculation methods (CII guidelines, G1) (resolution MEPC.352(78))* and having been corrected taking into account *Interim guidelines on correction factors and voyage adjustments for CII calculations (G5)* (resolution MEPC.355(78)).

[12] Refer to the *2021 Guidance on treatment of innovative energy efficiency technologies for calculation and verification of the attained EEDI and EEXI* (MEPC.1/Circ.896).

[13] Refer to the *2022 Guidelines on the operational carbon intensity rating of ships (CII rating guidelines, G4)* (resolution MEPC.354(78))

[14] Refer to the *2022 Guidelines on operational carbon intensity indicators and the calculation methods (CII guidelines, G1)* (resolution MEPC.352(78)).

[15] Refer to the *Guidelines for voluntary use of the ship energy efficiency operational indicator (EEOI)* (MEPC.1/Circ.684).

载货航行距离（nm）（自愿）...

航行小时数...

岸电供应总量（kWh）...

对于适用 MARPOL 附则Ⅵ第 28 条的船舶：

总运输工作量...

适用的 CII[8]：□ AER　□ cgDIST

要求的年度营运 CII[9]..

修正前达到的年度营运 CII[10]...

达到的年度营运 CII[11]..

安装的创新技术 [12]（如适用）：□ A □ B–1 □ B–2 □ C–1 □ C–2

营运碳强度等级 [13]：□ A □ B □ C □ D □ E

用于试验目的的 CII（基于自愿）[14]：

　　□ EEPI（gCO$_2$/t/nm）..

　　□ cbDIST（gCO$_2$/ berth/nm）...

　　□ clDIST（gCO$_2$/m/nm）..

　　□ EEOI（gCO$_2$/t/nm）[15]...

***

8　参见《2022 年营运碳强度指标和计算方法导则》（CII 导则，G1）（第 MEPC.352(78) 号决议）。

9　参见《2022 年营运碳强度指标基线导则》（CII 基线导则，G2）（第 MPEC.353(78) 号决议）和《2021 年相对于基线的营运碳强度折减率导则》（CII 折减率导则，G3）（第 MPEC.338(76) 号决议）。

10　在按《2022 年 CII 计算的修正系数和航次调整临时导则》(G5)（第 MEPC.355(78) 号决议）修正前，按《2022 年营运碳强度指标和计算方法导则（CII 导则，G1）（第 MEPC.352(78) 号决议）计算。

11　按《2022 年营运碳强度指标和计算方法导则(CII 导则，G1)(第 MEPC.352(78) 号决议）计算，并已按《2022 年 CII 计算的修正系数和航次调整临时导则》(G5)（第 MEPC.355(78) 号决议）修正。

12　参见《2021 年关于计算和验证达到的 EEDI 和 EEXI 的创新能效技术处理导则》(MEPC.1/Circ.896)。

13　参见《2022 年船舶营运碳强度评级导则》(CII 评级导则，G4)（第 MPEC.354(78) 号决议）。

14　参见《2022 年营运碳强度指标和计算方法导则》（CII 导则，G1）（第 MEPC.352(78) 号决议）。

15　参见《船舶能效营运指数 (EEOI) 自愿使用导则》（第 MEPC.1/Circ.684 号通函）。

Appendix X Form of Statement of Compliance – Fuel Oil Consumption Reporting and Operational Carbon Intensity rating (regulation 8.3)

STATEMENT OF COMPLIANCE – FUEL OIL CONSUMPTION REPORTING AND OPERATIONAL CARBON INTENSITY RATING

Issued under the provisions of the Protocol of 1997, as amended, to amend the International Convention for the Prevention of Pollution from Ships, 1973, as modified by the Protocol of 1978 relating thereto (hereinafter referred to as "the Convention") under the authority of the Government

of...

(full designation of the country)

by...

(full designation of the competent person or organization authorized under the provisions of the Convention)

Particulars of ship*

Name of ship ....

Distinctive number or letters ....

IMO Number** ....

Port of registry ....

Gross tonnage ....

Deadweight...

Type of ship ....

THIS IS TO DECLARE THAT:

1   the ship has submitted to this Administration the data required by regulation 27 of Annex VI to the Convention, covering ship operations from (dd/mm/yyyy) to (dd/mm/yyyy);

2   the data was collected and reported in accordance with the methodology and processes set out in the ship's SEEMP that was in effect over the period from (dd/mm/yyyy) to (dd/mm/yyyy);

3   the attained annual operational CII of the ship from (dd/mm/yyyy) through (dd/mm/yyyy) was: _____ pursuant to regulations 28.1 and 28.2 of Annex VI of the Convention, for ships to which regulation 28 applies;

4   the annual operational carbon intensity of the ship in this period is rated as ☐ A ☐ B ☐ C ☐ D ☐ E in accordance with regulation 28 of Annex VI to the Convention, for a ship to which regulation 28 applies; and

5   a corrective action plan has been developed and included in the SEEMP (for a ship to which regulation 28 applies, rated as D for three consecutive years or rated as E)*** .

This Statement of Compliance is valid until (dd/mm/yyyy) ....

Issued at: ....

(place of issue of Statement)

Date(dd/mm/yyyy) ....

(date of issue)   (signature of duly authorized official issuing the Statement)

(seal or stamp of the authority, as appropriate)

---

* Alternatively, the particulars of the ship may be placed horizontally in boxes.

** In accordance with the IMO Ship identification number scheme (resolution A.1117(30)).

** In the event of any transfer of a ship addressed in regulations 27.4, 27.5 or 27.6, these sections should be completed consistent with regulation 28.3 of MARPOL Annex VI.

附录X 符合声明格式—燃油消耗报告和营运碳强度评级（第8.3条）

符合声明 — 燃油消耗报告和营运碳强度评级

根据经修正的《经1978年议定书修订的〈1973年国际防止船舶造成污染公约〉的1997年议定书》（以下简称本公约）的规定，

经＿＿＿＿＿＿＿＿＿＿＿＿＿＿＿＿＿＿＿＿＿＿＿＿＿＿＿＿＿政府授权，

（国家全称）

由＿＿＿＿＿＿＿＿＿＿＿＿＿＿＿＿＿＿＿＿＿＿＿＿＿＿＿＿签发。

（按本公约规定正式授权的组织或个人全称）

船舶资料*
船名＿＿＿＿＿＿＿＿＿＿＿＿＿＿＿＿＿＿＿＿＿＿＿＿＿＿＿＿＿＿＿＿＿
船舶编号或呼号＿＿＿＿＿＿＿＿＿＿＿＿＿＿＿＿＿＿＿＿＿＿＿＿＿＿＿
IMO编号**＿＿＿＿＿＿＿＿＿＿＿＿＿＿＿＿＿＿＿＿＿＿＿＿＿＿＿＿＿＿
船籍港＿＿＿＿＿＿＿＿＿＿＿＿＿＿＿＿＿＿＿＿＿＿＿＿＿＿＿＿＿＿＿＿
总吨位＿＿＿＿＿＿＿＿＿＿＿＿＿＿＿＿＿＿＿＿＿＿＿＿＿＿＿＿＿＿＿＿
载重吨＿＿＿＿＿＿＿＿＿＿＿＿＿＿＿＿＿＿＿＿＿＿＿＿＿＿＿＿＿＿＿＿
船型＿＿＿＿＿＿＿＿＿＿＿＿＿＿＿＿＿＿＿＿＿＿＿＿＿＿＿＿＿＿＿＿＿
兹证明：

1. 该船已向主管机关提交了涉及该船自（日/月/年）至（日/月/年）营运的本公约附则VI第27条要求的数据；和

2. 数据系该船自（日/月/年）至（日/月/年）期间，按照《船舶能效管理计划》中所列方法和程序收集和报告；

3. 按照公约附则VI第28.1和28.2条，对于适用第28条的船舶，该船自（日/月/年）到（日/月/年）期间
   达到的年度营运碳强度指标为：＿＿＿＿＿＿＿＿＿＿；

4. 按照公约附则VI第28条，对于适用第28条的船舶，在此期间，该船的营运碳强度评级为：
   □ A   □ B   □ C   □ D   □ E；和

5. 对于适用第28条的船舶，连续三年被评为D级或被评为E级的船舶，已制定纠正行动计划并包含在《船舶能效管理计划》中***。

符合声明有效期至（日/月/年）＿＿＿＿＿＿＿＿＿＿＿＿＿＿＿＿＿＿＿＿
签发于：＿＿＿＿＿＿＿＿＿＿＿＿＿＿＿＿＿＿＿＿＿＿＿＿＿＿＿＿＿＿

（声明签发地点）

日期（日/月/年）＿＿＿＿＿＿＿＿＿＿＿   ＿＿＿＿＿＿＿＿＿＿＿＿＿

（签发日期）   （经正式授权的发证官员签字）

（主管当局盖章或钢印）

* 船舶概况也可在表格中横向排列。
** 根据《IMO船舶编号机制》（第A.1117（30）号决议）。
*** 如船舶发生第27.4、27.5和27.6条所述的变更，本节应完全符合防污公约附则VI第28.3条。

Appendix XI Form of Exemption Certificate for UNSP Barges (regulation 8.4)

INTERNATIONAL AIR POLLUTION PREVENTION EXEMPTION CERTIFICATE FOR UNMANNED NON-SELF-PROPELLED (UNSP) BARGES

Issued under the provisions of the Protocol of 1997, as amended, to amend the International Convention for the Prevention of Pollution from Ships, 1973, as modified by the Protocol of 1978 relating thereto (hereinafter referred to as "the Convention") under the authority of the Government of:

....
(full designation of the country)

by..
(full designation of the competent person or organization authorized under the provisions of the Convention)

Particulars of ship*

Name of ship ....

Distinctive number or letters ....

IMO Number** ....

Port of registry ....

Gross tonnage ....

THIS IS TO CERTIFY THAT:

1   the UNSP barge has been surveyed in accordance with regulation 3.4 of Annex VI to the Convention;

2   the survey shows that the UNSP barge:

    .1   is not propelled by mechanical means;

    .2   has no system, equipment and/or machinery fitted that may generate emissions controlled by Annex VI to the Convention; and

    .3   has neither persons nor living animals on board; and

3   the UNSP barge is exempted, under regulation 3.4 of Annex VI to the Convention from the certification and related survey requirements of regulations 5.1 and 6.1 of Annex VI to the Convention.

This Certificate is valid until (dd/mm/yyyy) ....
subject to the exemption conditions being maintained.

Completion date of the survey on which this Certificate is based (dd/mm/yyyy)

Issued at: ....
(place of issue of certificate)

Date(dd/mm/yyyy) ....
(date of issue)   (signature of duly authorized official
                                                              issuing the certificate)

* Alternatively, the particulars of the ship may be placed horizontally in boxes.

** In accordance with the IMO Ship identification number scheme (resolution A.1117(30)).

附附录 XI 无人非自航驳船免除证书格式（第 8.4 条）

无人非自航驳船国际防止空气污染免除证书

根据经修正的《经 1978 年议定书修订的〈1973 年国际防止船舶造成污染公约〉的 1997 年议定书》（以下简称本公约）的规定，

经＿＿＿＿＿＿＿＿＿＿＿＿＿＿＿＿＿＿＿＿＿＿＿＿＿＿＿＿＿＿政府授权，

（国家全称）

由＿＿＿＿＿＿＿＿＿＿＿＿＿＿＿＿＿＿＿＿＿＿＿＿＿＿＿＿＿签发。

（按本公约规定正式授权的组织或个人全称）

船舶概况 *

船名＿＿＿＿＿＿＿＿＿＿＿＿＿＿＿＿＿＿＿＿＿＿＿＿＿＿＿＿＿＿＿

船舶编号或呼号＿＿＿＿＿＿＿＿＿＿＿＿＿＿＿＿＿＿＿＿＿＿＿＿＿

IMO 编号 **＿＿＿＿＿＿＿＿＿＿＿＿＿＿＿＿＿＿＿＿＿＿＿＿＿＿＿

船籍港＿＿＿＿＿＿＿＿＿＿＿＿＿＿＿＿＿＿＿＿＿＿＿＿＿＿＿＿＿＿

总吨位＿＿＿＿＿＿＿＿＿＿＿＿＿＿＿＿＿＿＿＿＿＿＿＿＿＿＿＿＿＿

兹证明：

1 该无人非自航驳船已按公约附则 VI 第 3.4 条的规定进行了检验；

2 检验表明该无人非自航驳船：

   .1 不是通过机械方式推进的；

   .2 没有安装可能产生适用公约附则的排放的系统、设备和 / 或机械；和

   .3 船上无人员或活体动物；和

3 按公约附则 VI 第 3.4 条，免除该无人非自航驳船的公约附则 VI 第 5.1 和 6.1 条的发证和相关检验要求。

本证书有效期至（日 / 月 / 年）＿＿＿＿＿＿＿＿＿＿＿＿＿＿＿＿＿＿＿

应一直满足免除的条件。

本证书所依据的检验的完成日期＿＿＿＿＿＿＿＿＿＿＿＿＿＿＿＿＿＿＿

签发于：＿＿＿＿＿＿＿＿＿＿＿＿＿＿＿＿＿＿＿＿＿＿＿＿＿＿＿＿＿

（证书签发地点）

日期（年 / 月 / 日）＿＿＿＿＿＿＿＿＿＿＿　　＿＿＿＿＿＿＿＿＿＿＿＿＿

（签发日期）　　　　　　（经正式授权的发证官员签字）

（主管当局盖章或钢印）

---

* 船舶概况也可在表格中横向排列。

** 根据《IMO 船舶编号机制》（第 A.1117（30）号决议）。

UNIFIED INTERPRETATIONS TO MARPOL ANNEX VI

1   The Marine Environment Protection Committee, at its eighty-first session (17 to 22 March 2024), approved unified interpretations to regulations 2.2.15 and 2.2.18 of MARPOL Annex VI, in order to provide clarity concerning:

.1   the definition of "heavy load carrier" within the definition of "general cargo ship"; and

.2   the applicable dates for the different ship types for the calculation of the required EEDI under each EEDI Phase.

2   The consolidated text of all existing unified interpretations to MARPOL Annex VI, listed in numerical order of interpreted regulations in MARPOL Annex VI, is set out in the annex.

3   Member Governments are invited to apply the annexed unified interpretations to MARPOL Annex VI, as appropriate, and bring them to the attention of all Parties concerned.

4   This circular revokes MEPC.1/Circ.795/Rev.8.

***

MEPC.1/Circ.795/Rev.9 通函
（2024 年 4 月 29 日）

《防污公约》附则Ⅵ的统一解释

1　海上环境保护委员会在其第 81 届会议（2024 年 3 月 17 日至 22 日）上批准了 MARPOL 附则Ⅵ第 2.2.15 和 2.2.18 条的统一解释，以澄清：

　　.1　"杂货船"定义中"重货运输船"的定义；和

　　.2　每个 EEDI 阶段不同船型计算 Required EEDI 的适用日期。

2　MARPOL 附则Ⅵ所有现有统一解释的综合文本，按所解释的 MARPOL 附则Ⅵ各条的数字顺序列出，载于附件。

3　请各成员国政府视具体情况应用附件中的《MARPOL 附则Ⅵ的统一解释》，并使所有相关方注意到附件中的统一解释。

4　本通函替代 MEPC.1/Circ.795/Rev.8 通函。

＊＊＊

ANNEX

UNIFIED INTERPRETATIONS TO MARPOL ANNEX VI

1   Definition of "heavy load carrier"

Regulation 2
Definitions

Regulation 2.2.15 reads as follows:

> "*General cargo ship* means a ship with a multi-deck or single deck hull designed primarily for the carriage of general cargo. This definition excludes specialized dry cargo ships, which are not included in the calculation of reference lines for general cargo ships, namely livestock carrier, barge carrier, heavy load carrier, yacht carrier, nuclear fuel carrier."

Interpretation:

1.1   The following are considered as a "heavy load carrier":

.1   heavy load deck carriers[1];

.2   semi-submersible project cargo carriers;

.3   semi-submersible heavy load deck carriers (including dock lift ships);

.4   heavy lift multi-purpose ships (see paragraph 1.2 below);

.5   premium project carriers (see paragraph 1.2 below); and

.6   project cargo carriers (see paragraph 1.3 below).

1.2   Heavy lift multi-purpose ships and premium project carriers should fulfil the adapted criterion of "ships engaged in lifting operations" contained in regulation 2.3 of the International Code on Intact Stability, 2008 (2008 IS Code), as amended by resolution MSC.443(99), and comply as follows:

$$SWL \times Outreach \geq 0.67 \times Displacement \times (D - T) / B$$

where:

SWL = maximum safe working load of crane of one single crane;

Outreach = outreach from turning axis of crane;

Displacement = displacement of vessel at draft T;

T = freeboard draft;

---

[1]   Ships, which do not feature a cargo hold and carry project cargo on a flat deck; not fitted with cargo coamings/chutes/tippers.

附件
MARPOL 附则Ⅵ的统一解释

1 "重货运输船"定义

第 2 条 定义

第 2.2.15 条原文如下：

"**杂货船**系指设有多层甲板或单层甲板主要用于载运杂货的船舶。该定义不包括专用干货船，其不属于杂货船基线计算范围，即牲畜运输船、载驳母船、重货运输船、游艇运输船和核燃料运输船。"

解释：

1.1 下列船舶被视为"重货运输船"：

.1 重货甲板运输船[1]；

.2 半潜式工程货物运输船；

.3 半潜式重货甲板运输船（包括载驳船）；

.4 多用途重吊船（见下文第 1.2 段）；

.5 高端工程运输船（见下文第 1.2 段）；

.6 工程货物运输船（见下文第 1.3 段）。

1.2 多用途重吊船和高端工程运输船应符合经 MSC.443（99）决议修订的《2008 年国际完整稳定规则》（2008 年 IS 规则）第 2.3 条所载的"从事起重作业的船舶"的适用标准，并符合以下规定：

$$SWL \times Outreach \geq 0.67 \times Displacement \times （D\text{-}T）/B$$

式中：

SWL= 单台起重机最大安全工作载荷，单位：吨

Outreach= 从起重机转动轴伸出吊臂的长度，单位：米

Displacement= 吃水 T 时船舶的排水量

T= 干舷吃水，单位：米

---

[1] 没有货舱并在平甲板上载运项目货物的船舶；未设有货物围板／斜槽／倾卸斗。

B = moulded breadth of the vessel measured amidships at draft T;

D = depth for freeboard.

1.3   For project cargo carriers with or without cargo gear, the Administration may base its decision on a design and operation-specific application compiled by the owner/company.

2   Major conversion

Regulation 2
Definitions

Regulation 2.2.17 reads as follows:

"*Major conversion* means in relation to chapter 4 of this Annex a conversion of a ship:

.1   which substantially alters the dimensions, carrying capacity or engine power of the ship; or

.2   which changes the type of the ship; or

.3   the intent of which in the opinion of the Administration is substantially to prolong the life of the ship; or

.4   which otherwise so alters the ship that, if it were a new ship, it would become subject to relevant provisions of the present Convention not applicable to it as an existing ship; or

.5   which substantially alters the energy efficiency of the ship and includes any modifications that could cause the ship to exceed the applicable required EEDI as set out in regulation 24 of this Annex or the applicable required EEXI as set out in regulation 25 of this Annex."

Interpretation:

2.1   For regulation 2.2.17.1, any substantial change in hull dimensions and/or capacity (e.g. change of length between perpendiculars (L_{PP}) or change of assigned freeboard) should be considered a major conversion. Any substantial increase of total engine power for propulsion (e.g. 5% or more) should be considered a major conversion. In any case, it is the Administration's authority to evaluate and decide whether an alteration should be considered a major conversion, consistent with chapter 4.

> **Note:**   Notwithstanding paragraph 2.1, assuming no alteration to the ship structure, both decrease of assigned freeboard and temporary increase of assigned freeboard due to the limitation of deadweight or draft at calling port should not be construed as a major conversion. However, an increase of assigned freeboard, except a temporary increase, should be construed as a major conversion.

2.2   Notwithstanding paragraph 2.1, for regulation 2.2.17.5, the effect on Attained EEDI as a result of any change of ships' parameters, particularly any increase in total engine power for propulsion, should be investigated. In any case, it is the Administration's authority to evaluate and decide whether an alteration should be considered a major conversion, consistent with chapter 4.

$B=$ 干舷吃水处船中位置的型宽，单位：米

$D=$ 干舷深度，单位：米

1.3 对于设有或未设货物装卸设备的工程货物运输船，主管机关可根据船东 / 公司编制的安排和特定操作申请作出决定。

2 重大改建

第 2 条 定义

第 2.2.17 条原文如下：

"**重大改建**系指与本附则第 4 章有关的对船舶所作的下述改建：

.1 实质上改变了该船的尺度、装载容量或发动机功率；或

.2 改变了该船的类型；或

.3 根据主管机关的意见，目的在于实质上是为了延长该船的使用年限；或

.4 这种改建如使该船成为一艘新船，应遵守本公约中不适用于其作为现有船舶的有关规定；或

.5 实质上改变了该船的能效，并且包括任何能使该船超出本附则第 24 条所述适用 Required EEDI 或本附则第 25 条所述适用 Required EEXI 的改装。"

解释：

2.1 对于第 2.2.17.1 条，对船体的尺度和 / 或容量的任何实质性改变（例如，垂线间长（L_{pp}）的改变或核定干舷的改变）应被视为重大改建。用于推进的发动机总功率的任何实质性增大（例如，5% 或以上）应被视为重大改建。在任何情况下，主管机关有权评估并决定改装是否应被视为与第 4 章相符的重大改建。

注：尽管有上述 2.1 的解释，假定没有进行对船舶结构的改装，由于所停靠港口对载重吨或吃水的限制而对核定干舷的减少和暂时增加不应理解为重大改建。但是，对核定干舷的增加，除暂时增加外，应理解为重大改建。

2.2 尽管有上述 2.1 的解释，对于第 2.2.17.5 条，对船舶参数的任何改变尤其是用于推进的发动机总功率的任何增大而导致的对 Attained EEDI 的影响应进行调查。在任何情况下，主管机关有权评估并决定改装是否应被视为与第 4 章相符的重大改建。

2.3   A company may, at any time, voluntarily request re-certification of the EEDI, with IEE Certificate reissuance, on the basis of any new improvements to the ships' efficiency that are not considered to be major conversions.

2.4   In regulation 2.2.17.4, the terms "new ship" and "existing ship" should be understood as they are used in MARPOL Annex I, regulation 1.9.1.4, rather than as the defined terms in regulations 2.2.13 and 2.2.18.

2.5   The term "a ship" referred to in regulation 5.4.2 is interpreted as "new ship".

3   Definition of "new ship" for calculation of the required EEDI

Regulation 2
Definitions

Regulation 2.2.18 reads as follows:

"*New ship* means a ship:

.1   for which the building contract is placed on or after 1 January 2013; or

.2   in the absence of a building contract, the keel of which is laid or which is at a similar stage of construction on or after 1 July 2013; or

.3   the delivery of which is on or after 1 July 2015."

Interpretation:

3.1   For the application of the definition "new ship" as specified in regulation 2.2.18 to each Phase specified in table 1 of regulation 24, it should be interpreted as follows:

.1   the date specified in regulation 2.2.18.1 should be replaced with the start date of each Phase;

.2   the date specified in regulation 2.2.18.2 should be replaced with the date six months after the start date and end date of each Phase; and

.3   the date specified in regulation 2.2.18.3 should, for Phases 1, 2 and 3, be replaced with the date 48 months after the start date and end date of each Phase.

3.2   With the above interpretations, the required EEDI of each phase is applied to the following new ship to which chapter 4 is applicable:

.1   the required EEDI of Phase 0 is applied to the following new ship which falls into one of the categories defined in regulations 2.2.5, 2.2.7, 2.2.9, 2.2.14, 2.2.15, 2.2.22 and 2.2.29:

.1   the building contract of which is placed in Phase 0, and the delivery is before 1 January 2019; or

.2   the building contract of which is placed before Phase 0, and the delivery is on or after 1 July 2015 and before 1 January 2019; or

in the absence of a building contract:

2.3 在任何时候，公司可基于未被视为重大改建的任何船舶能效新改进自愿要求重新认证 EEDI 并重新签发 IEE 证书。

2.4 在第 2.2.17.4 条中，术语"新船"和"现有船舶"应理解为其在 MARPOL 附则 I 第 1.9.1.4 条中所使用的含义，而不是第 2.2.13 和 2.2.18 条中所定义的术语。

2.5 第 5.4.2 条中所述的术语"船舶"解释为"新船"。

3 用于计算 Required EEDI 的"新船"的定义

第 2 条 定义

第 2.2.18 条原文如下：

"新船系指：

.1 2013 年 1 月 1 日或以后签订建造合同；或

.2 无建造合同，2013 年 7 月 1 日或以后安放龙骨或处于类似建造阶段；或

.3 2015 年 7 月 1 日或以后交付的船舶。"

解释：

3.1 对于第 2.2.18 条规定的"新船"定义在第 24 条表 1 规定的每一阶段中的应用，应作如下解释：

.1 应将第 2.2.18.1 条规定的日期替换为每一阶段的起始日期；

.2 应将第 2.2.18.2 条规定的日期替换为每一阶段起始之日和结束之日起 6 个月后的日期；和

.3 对于 Phase 1、2 和 3，应将第 2.2.18.3 条规定的日期替换为每一阶段起始之日和结束之日起 48 个月后的日期。

3.2 结合上述解释，每一阶段的 Required EEDI 适用于属于第 4 章适用的下列新船：

.1 Phase 0 的 Required EEDI 适用于属于第 2.2.5、2.2.7、2.2.9、2.2.14、2.2.15、2.2.22 和 2.2.29 条定义的类别之一的下列新船：

.1 在 Phase 0 期间签订建造合同，并在 2019 年 1 月 1 日以前交付；或

.2 在 Phase 0 以前签订建造合同，并在 2015 年 7 月 1 日或以后且在 2019 年 1 月 1 日以前交付；或

当无建造合同时，

186

.3   the keel of which is laid or which is at a similar stage of construction on or after 1 July 2013 and before 1 July 2015, and the delivery is before 1 January 2019; or

.4   the keel of which is laid or which is at a similar stage of construction before 1 July 2013, and the delivery is on or after 1 July 2015 and before 1 January 2019;

.2   the required EEDI of Phase 1 is applied to the following new ship which falls into one of the categories defined in regulations 2.2.5, 2.2.7, 2.2.9, 2.2.11, 2.2.14, 2.2.15, 2.2.16, 2.2.22, 2.2.26, 2.2.27, 2.2.28 and 2.2.29:

    .1   for ship types where Phase 1 commences on 1 January 2015:

        .1   the building contract of which is placed in Phase 1, and the delivery is before 1 January 2024; or

        .2   the building contract of which is placed before Phase 1, and the delivery is on or after 1 January 2019 and before 1 January 2024; or

        in the absence of a building contract:

        .3   the keel of which is laid or which is at a similar stage of construction on or after 1 July 2015 and before 1 July 2020, and the delivery is before 1 January 2024; or

        .4   the keel of which is laid or which is at a similar stage of construction before 1 July 2015, and the delivery is on or after 1 January 2019 and before 1 January 2024;

    .2   for ship types where Phase 1 commences on 1 September 2015:

        .1   the building contract of which is placed in Phase 1, and the delivery is before 1 January 2024; or

        .2   the building contract of which is placed before Phase 1, and the delivery is on or after 1 September 2019 and before 1 January 2024; or

        in the absence of a building contract:

        .3   the keel of which is laid or which is at a similar stage of construction on or after 1 March 2016 and before 1 July 2020, and the delivery is before 1 January 2024; or

        .4   the keel of which is laid or which is at a similar stage of construction before 1 March 2016, and the delivery is on or after 1 September 2019 and before 1 January 2024;

.3   the required EEDI of Phase 2 is applied to the following new ship which falls into one of the categories defined in regulations 2.2.5, 2.2.7, 2.2.9, 2.2.11, 2.2.14, 2.2.15, 2.2.16, 2.2.22, 2.2.26, 2.2.27, 2.2.28, and 2.2.29:

    .1   for ship types where Phase 2 ends on 31 March 2022:

.3 在 2013 年 7 月 1 日或以后并在 2015 年 7 月 1 日以前安放龙骨或处于类似建造阶段，并在 2019 年 1 月 1 日以前交付；或

.4 在 2013 年 7 月 1 日以前安放龙骨或处于类似建造阶段，并在 2015 年 7 月 1 日或以后且在 2019 年 1 月 1 日以前交付。

.2 Phase 1 的 Required EEDI 适用于属于第 2.2.5、2.2.7、2.2.9、2.2.11、2.2.14、2.2.15、2.2.16、2.2.22、2.2.26、2.2.27、2.2.28 和 2.2.29 条定义的类别之一的下列新船：

.1 Phase 1 开始于 2015 年 1 月 1 日的船型：

.1 在 Phase 1 期间签订建造合同，并在 2024 年 1 月 1 日以前交付；或

.2 在 Phase 1 以前签订建造合同，并在 2019 年 1 月 1 日或以后且在 2024 年 1 月 1 日以前交付；或

当无建造合同时，

.3 在 2015 年 7 月 1 日或以后并在 2020 年 7 月 1 日以前安放龙骨或处于类似建造阶段，并在 2024 年 1 月 1 日以前交付；或

.4 在 2015 年 7 月 1 日或以后安放龙骨或处于类似建造阶段，并在 2019 年 1 月 1 日或以后且在 2024 年 1 月 1 日以前交付。

.2 Phase 1 开始于 2015 年 9 月 1 日的船型：

.1 在 Phase 1 期间签订建造合同，并在 2024 年 1 月 1 日以前交付；或

.2 在 Phase 1 以前签订建造合同，并在 2019 年 9 月 1 日或以后且在 2024 年 1 月 1 日以前交付；或

当无建造合同时，

.3 在 2016 年 3 月 1 日或以后并在 2020 年 7 月 1 日以前安放龙骨或处于类似建造阶段，并在 2024 年 1 月 1 日以前交付；或

.4 在 2016 年 3 月 1 日以前安放龙骨或处于类似建造阶段，并在 2019 年 9 月 1 日或以后且在 2024 年 1 月 1 日以前交付。

.3 Phase 2 的 Required EEDI 适用于属于第 2.2.5、2.2.7、2.2.9、2.2.11、2.2.14、2.2.15、2.2.16、2.2.22、2.2.26、2.2.27、2.2.28 和 2.2.29 条定义的类别之一的下列新船：

.1 Phase 2 结束于 2022 年 3 月 31 日时的船舶类型：

.1   the building contract of which is placed in Phase 2, and the delivery is before 1 April 2026; or

.2   the building contract of which is placed before Phase 2, and the delivery is on or after 1 January 2024 and before 1 April 2026; or

in the absence of a building contract:

.3   the keel of which is laid or which is at a similar stage of construction on or after 1 July 2020 and before 1 October 2022, and the delivery is before 1 April 2026; or

.4   the keel of which is laid or which is at a similar stage of construction before 1 July 2020, and the delivery is on or after 1 January 2024 and before 1 April 2026;

.2   for ship types where Phase 2 ends on 31 December 2024:

.1   the building contract of which is placed in Phase 2, and the delivery is before 1 January 2029; or

.2   the building contract of which is placed before Phase 2, and the delivery is on or after 1 January 2024 and before 1 January 2029; or

in the absence of a building contract:

.3   the keel of which is laid or which is at a similar stage of construction on or after 1 July 2020 and before 1 July 2025, and the delivery is before 1 January 2029; or

.4   the keel of which is laid or which is at a similar stage of construction before 1 July 2020, and the delivery is on or after 1 January 2024 and before 1 January 2029;

.4   the required EEDI of Phase 3 is applied to the following new ship which falls into one of the categories defined in regulations 2.2.5, 2.2.7, 2.2.9, 2.2.11, 2.2.14, 2.2.15, 2.2.16, 2.2.22, 2.2.26, 2.2.27, 2.2.28 and 2.2.29:

.1   for ship types where Phase 3 commences with 1 April 2022 and onwards:

.1   the building contract of which is placed in Phase 3; or

.2   the building contract of which is placed before Phase 3, and the delivery is on or after 1 April 2026; or

in the absence of a building contract:

.3   the keel of which is laid or which is at a similar stage of construction on or after 1 October 2022; or

.1 在 Phase 2 期间签订建造合同，并在 2026 年 4 月 1 日以前交付；或

.2 在 Phase 2 以前签订建造合同，并在 2024 年 1 月 1 日或以后且在 2026 年 4 月 1 日以前交付；或

当无建造合同时，

.3 在 2020 年 7 月 1 日或以后并在 2022 年 10 月 1 日以前安放龙骨或处于类似建造阶段，并在 2026 年 4 月 1 日以前交付；或

.4 在 2020 年 7 月 1 日以前安放龙骨或处于类似建造阶段，并在 2024 年 1 月 1 日或以后且在 2026 年 4 月 1 日以前交付；

.2 Phase 2 结束于 2024 年 12 月 31 日时的船舶类型：

.1 在 Phase 2 期间签订建造合同，并在 2029 年 1 月 1 日以前交付；或

.2 在 Phase 2 以前签订建造合同，并在 2024 年 1 月 1 日或以后且在 2029 年 1 月 1 日以前交付；或

当无建造合同时，

.3 在 2020 年 7 月 1 日或以后并在 2025 年 7 月 1 日以前安放龙骨或处于类似建造阶段，并在 2029 年 1 月 1 日以前交付；或

.4 在 2020 年 7 月 1 日以前安放龙骨或处于类似建造阶段，并在 2024 年 1 月 1 日或以后且在 2029 年 1 月 1 日以前交付；

.4 Phase 3 的 Required EEDI 适用于属于第 2.2.5、2.2.7、2.2.9、2.2.11、2.2.14、2.2.15、2.2.16、2.2.22、2.2.26、2.2.27、2.2.28 和 2.2.29 条定义的类别之一的下列新船：

.1 Phase 3 开始于 2022 年 4 月 1 日及以后的船舶类型：

.1 在 Phase 3 期间签订建造合同；或

.2 在 Phase 3 以前签订建造合同，并在 2026 年 4 月 1 日或以后交付；或

当无建造合同时，

.3 在 2022 年 10 月 1 日或以后安放龙骨或处于类似建造阶段；或

.4   the keel of which is laid or which is at a similar stage of construction before 1 October 2022 and the delivery of which is on or after 1 April 2026;

  .2   for ship types where Phase 3 commences with 1 January 2025 and onwards:

    .1   the building contract of which is placed in Phase 3; or

    .2   the building contract of which is placed before Phase 3, and the delivery is on or after 1 January 2029; or

in the absence of a building contract:

    .3   the keel of which is laid or which is at a similar stage of construction on or after 1 July 2025; or

    .4   the keel of which is laid or which is at a similar stage of construction before 1 July 2025 and the delivery of which is on or after 1 January 2029.

4   Ships dedicated to the carriage of fruit juice in refrigerated cargo tanks

Regulation 2
Definitions

Regulation 2.2.22 reads as follows:

"*Refrigerated cargo carrier* means a ship designed exclusively for the carriage of refrigerated cargoes in holds."

Interpretation:

Ships dedicated to the carriage of fruit juice in refrigerated cargo tanks should be categorized as refrigerated cargo carriers.

5   Timing for existing ships to have a SEEMP on board

Regulation 5
Surveys

Regulation 5.4.4 reads as follows:

"For existing ships, the verification of the requirement to have a SEEMP on board according to regulation 26 of this Annex shall take place at the first intermediate or renewal survey identified in paragraph 1 of this regulation, whichever is the first, on or after 1 January 2013."

Regulation 6
Issue or endorsement of Certificates and Statements of Compliance related to fuel oil consumption reporting and operational carbon intensity rating

Regulation 6.4 reads as follows:

.4 在 2022 年 10 月 1 日以前安放龙骨或处于类似建造阶段，并在 2026 年 4 月 1 日或以后交付；

.2 Phase 3 开始于 2025 年 1 月 1 日及以后的船舶类型：

.1 在 Phase 3 期间签订建造合同；或

.2 在 Phase 3 以前签订建造合同，并在 2029 年 1 月 1 日或以后交付；或当无建造合同时，

.3 2025 年 7 月 1 日或以后安放龙骨或处于类似建造阶段；或

.4 在 2025 年 7 月 1 日以前安放龙骨或处于类似建造阶段，并在 2029 年 1 月 1 日或以后交付。

4 专门用于在冷藏货舱内载运果汁的船舶

第 2 条 定义

第 2.2.22 条原文如下：

"**冷藏货船**系指专门设计用于在货舱内载运冷藏货物的船舶。"

解释：

专门用于在冷藏货舱内载运果汁的船舶应被归类为冷藏货船。

5 现有船舶船上保存 SEEMP 的时间

第 5 条 检验

第 5.4.4 条原文如下：

"对现有船舶，对根据本附则第 26 条船上保存 SEEMP 要求的验证应在 2013 年 1 月 1 日或以后的由本条 1 所述的首次中间或换证检验时（取先者）进行。"

第 6 条 证书和关于燃油消耗报告和营运碳强度评级的符合声明的签发或签署

第 6.4 条原文如下：

"An International Energy Efficiency Certificate for the ship shall be issued after a survey in accordance with the provisions of regulation 5.4 of this Annex to any ship of 400 gross tonnage and above before that ship may engage in voyages to ports or offshore terminals under the jurisdiction of other Parties."

Regulation 26
Ship Energy Efficiency Management Plan (SEEMP)

Regulation 26.1 reads as follows:

"Each ship shall keep on board a ship specific Ship Energy Efficiency Management Plan (SEEMP). This may form part of the ship's Safety Management System (SMS)."

Interpretation:

5.1   The International Energy Efficiency Certificate (IEEC) should be issued for both new and existing ships to which chapter 4 applies. Ships which are not required to keep a SEEMP on board are not required to be issued with an IEEC.

5.2   The SEEMP required by regulation 26.1 is not required to be placed on board an existing ship to which this regulation applies until the verification survey specified in regulation 5.4.4 is carried out.

5.3   For existing ships, a SEEMP required in accordance with regulation 26 should be verified on board according to regulation 5.4.4, and an IEEC should be issued, not later than the first intermediate or renewal survey, in accordance with chapter 2, whichever is earlier, on or after 1 January 2013, i.e. a survey connected to an intermediate/renewal survey of the IAPP Certificate.

5.4   The intermediate or renewal survey referenced in paragraph 5.3 relates solely to the timing of the verification of the SEEMP on board, i.e. these IAPP Certificate survey windows will also become the IEEC initial survey date for existing ships. The SEEMP is, however, a survey item solely under chapter 4 and is not a survey item relating to IAPP Certificate surveys.

5.5   In the event that the SEEMP is not available on board during the first intermediate/renewal survey of the IAPP Certificate on or after 1 January 2013, the RO should seek the advice of the Administration concerning the issuance of an IEEC and be guided accordingly. However, the validity of the IAPP Certificate is not impacted by the lack of a SEEMP as the SEEMP is a survey item solely under chapter 4 and not under the IAPP Certificate surveys.

5.6   With respect to ships required to keep on board a SEEMP, such ships exclude platforms (including FPSOs and FSUs) and drilling rigs, regardless of their propulsion, and any other ship without means of propulsion.

5.7   The SEEMP should be written in a working language or languages understood by ships' personnel.

6   Confirmation of compliance for new ships
Regulation 5
Surveys

Regulation 5.4.5 reads as follows:

"对任何驶往其他缔约国管辖范围的港口或近海装卸站的 400 总吨及以上的船舶，在按本附则第 5.4 条规定进行了检验后，应在其开航前为其签发《国际能效证书》。"

第 26 条　船舶能效管理计划（SEEMP）

第 26.1 条原文如下：

"每艘船舶应在船上保存一份具体的船舶能效管理计划（SEEMP）。该计划可为船舶安全管理体系（SMS）的一部分。"

解释：

5.1　应对第 4 章适用的新船和现有船舶都签发《国际能效证书》（IEEC）。不要求在船上保存 SEEMP 的船舶无须签发 IEEC。

5.2　在进行第 5.4.4 条规定的验证检验以前，不要求第 26.1 条所适用的现有船舶上保存该条所要求的 SEEMP。

5.3　对于现有船舶，应不迟于 2013 年 1 月 1 日或以后进行的第 2 章所述的首次中间或换证检验（取先者）（即与 IAPP 证书的中间／换证检验相结合的检验），根据第 5.4.4 条在船上对第 26 条所要求的 SEEMP 进行验证，并签发 IEEC。

5.4　5.3 所述的中间或换证检验只与船上 SEEMP 的验证时间有关，即这些 IAPP 证书的检验窗口期还将成为现有船舶 IEEC 的初次检验日期。但是，SEEMP 只是第 4 章要求的一个检验项目，而不是与 IAPP 证书检验相关的检验项目。

5.5　如在 2013 年 1 月 1 日或以后进行的 IAPP 证书首次中间／换证检验期间船上无法提供 SEEMP，RO 应向主管机关征求关于 IEEC 签发的意见并据此行事。但是，缺少 SEEMP 并不影响 IAPP 证书的有效性，因为 SEEMP 只是第 4 章要求的一个检验项目，而不是 IAPP 证书检验要求的检验项目。

5.6　关于要求船上保存 SEEMP 的船舶，不包括平台（包括 FPSO 和 FSU）和钻井装置，不论其采用何种推进方式，以及任何其他无推进装置的船舶。

5.7　SEEMP 应用工作语言或船上人员通晓的语言编写。

6　新船符合性的确认书

第 5 条　检验

第 5.4.5 条原文如下：

"The Administration shall ensure that for each ship to which regulation 27 applies, the SEEMP complies with regulation 26.2 of this Annex. This shall be done prior to collecting data under regulation 27 of this Annex in order to ensure the methodology and processes are in place prior to the beginning of the ship's first reporting period. Confirmation of compliance shall be provided to and retained on board the ship."

Regulation 26
Ship Energy Efficiency Management Plan (SEEMP)

Regulation 26.2 reads as follows:

"In the case of a ship of 5,000 gross tonnage and above, the SEEMP shall include a description of the methodology that will be used to collect the data required by regulation 27.1 of this Annex and the processes that will be used to report the data to the ship's Administration."

Interpretation:

Ships should keep on board both a SEEMP that is in compliance with regulation 26.2 and confirmation of compliance as required by regulation 5.4.5.

7   Section 2.3 of the supplement to the IAPP Certificate

Regulation 8
Form of Certificates and Statements of Compliance related to fuel oil consumption reporting and operational carbon intensity rating

Regulation 8.1 reads as follows:

"The International Air Pollution Prevention Certificate shall be drawn up in a form corresponding to the model given in appendix I to this Annex and shall be at least in English, French or Spanish. If an official language of the issuing country is also used, this shall prevail in case of a dispute or discrepancy."

Appendix I
Form of International Air Pollution Prevention (IAPP) Certificate (Regulation 8)

Section 2.3 of the supplement to the International Air Pollution Prevention Certificate reads as follows:

"2.3   Sulphur oxides (SO_x) and particulate matter (regulation 14).

2.3.1   When the ship operates outside of an emission control area specified in regulation 14.3, the ship uses:

.1   fuel oil with a sulphur content as documented by bunker delivery notes that does not exceed the limit value of 0.50% m/m, and/or
....□

.2   an equivalent arrangement approved in accordance with regulation 4.1 as listed in paragraph 2.6 that is at least as effective in terms of SO_x emission reductions as compared to using a fuel oil with a sulphur content limit value of 0.50% m/m
....□

"主管机关应确保第 27 条适用的每艘船舶的 SEEMP 符合本附则的第 26.2 条。本要求应在按本附则第 27 条收集数据前完成，以确保在船舶的第一个报告周期开始前方法和程序已就绪。应向船舶提供合规性确认并保存在船上。"

第 26 条　船舶能效管理计划（SEEMP）

第 26.2 条原文如下：

"对于 5 000 总吨及以上的船舶，SEEMP 应包括对用于收集本附则第 27.1 条规定的数据方法和用于向船舶主管机关报告这些数据的过程的描述。"

解释：

船舶应在船上保留符合第 26.2 条的 SEEMP 和第 5.4.5 条要求的符合性确认书。

7　IAPP 证书附件的 2.3

第 8 条　证书和关于燃油消耗报告和营运碳强度评级的符合声明格式

第 8.1 条原文如下：

"《国际防止空气污染证书》应按与本附则附录 I 所示样本相一致的格式编写，并应至少使用英文、法文或西班牙文的其中一种语言。如同时使用发证国的官方语言，则在有争议或分歧时，应以该国官方语言为准。"

附录 I　《国际防止空气污染（IAPP）证书》格式（第 8 条）

《国际防止空气污染证书》附件的 2.3 为：

"2.3　硫氧化物（SOx）和颗粒物（第 14 条）

2.3.1　当船舶在第 14.3 条规定的排放控制区域外营运时，该船使用：

　　.1　硫含量不超过 0.50% m/m 限值的燃油（燃油交付单记录），和 / 或：　……□

　　.2　2.6 列出的按第 4.1 条认可的等效布置，该等效布置在 SOx 减排方面至少与使用硫含量为 0.50%m/m 限值的燃油一样有效：　………………………□

2.3.2   When the ship operates inside an emission control area specified in regulation 14.3, the ship uses:

.1   fuel oil with a sulphur content as documented by bunker delivery notes that does not exceed the limit value of 0.10% m/m, and/or

....☐

.2   an equivalent arrangement approved in accordance with regulation 4.1 as listed in paragraph 2.6 that is at least as effective in terms of SO$_x$ emission reductions as compared to using a fuel oil with a sulphur content limit value of 0.10% m/m

....☐

2.3.3   For a ship without an equivalent arrangement approved in accordance with regulation 4.1 as listed in paragraph 2.6, the sulphur content of fuel oil carried for use on board the ship shall not exceed 0.50% m/m as documented by bunker delivery notes

....☐"

Interpretation:

Section 2.3 of the Supplement ("as documented by bunker delivery notes") allows for an "x" to be entered in advance of the dates indicated in all of the relevant check boxes recognizing that the bunker delivery notes, required to be retained on board for a minimum period of three years, provide the subsequent means to check that a ship is actually operating in a manner consistent with the intent as given in section 2.3.

8   Inclusion of the annual operational CII and rating in the Statement of Compliance

Regulation 8
Form of Certificates and Statements of Compliance related to fuel oil consumption reporting and operational carbon intensity rating

Regulation 8.3 reads as follows:

"The Statement of Compliance pursuant to regulations 6.6 and 6.7 of this Annex shall be drawn up in a form corresponding to the model given in appendix X to this Annex and shall be at least in English, French or Spanish. If an official language of the issuing Party is also used, this shall prevail in case of a dispute or discrepancy."

Interpretation:

The Statement of Compliance form given in appendix X of MARPOL Annex VI has been updated to include the attained annual operational CII and the rating for ships to which regulation 28 applies. The new form should be used from the entry into force date (1 November 2022); however, the new parts for the attained CII and rating will not be populated until 2024 when the relevant values are available.

2.3.2 当船舶在第 14.3 条规定的排放控制区域内营运时，该船使用：

    .1 硫含量不超过 0.10%m/m 限值的燃油（燃油交付单记录），和 / 或：………□

    .2 2.6 列出的按第 4.1 条认可的等效布置，该等效布置在 SO_x 减排方面至少与使用硫含量为 0.10%m/m 限值的燃油一样有效：……………………………□

2.3.3 对于没有 2.6 列出的按第 4.1 条认可的等效布置的船舶，载运供船上使用的燃油硫含量不得超过 0.50% m/m（燃油交付单记录）……………………………………□"

解释：

5.1 附录 2.3 节（"燃油交付单记录"）允许在标明的日期以前在所有相关的核查框内打"×"，被要求在船上留存至少 3 年的燃油交付单为船舶的实际营运方式与 2.3 节所述的目的相一致提供了后续核查方法。

8 在符合声明中增加年度营运 CII 和评级

第 8 条 证书和关于燃油消耗报告和营运碳强度评级的符合声明格式

第 8.3 条原文如下：

"根据本附则第 6.6 和 6.7 条签发的符合声明应按与本附则附录 X 所示样本相一致的格式编写，并应至少使用英文、法文或西班牙文的其中一种语言。如同时使用发证国的官方语言，则在有争议或分歧时，应以该国官方语言为准。"

解释：

MARPOL 附则Ⅵ附录 X 中的符合声明格式已经过更新，对适用于第 28 条的船舶纳入了达到的年度营运 CII 和评级。新的格式应自生效日期（2022 年 11 月 1 日）起使用，但有关达到的 CII 和评级的新部分要到 2024 年相关值具备时才能填入。

9   Identical replacement engines

Regulation 13
Nitrogen oxides (NOₓ)

Regulation 13.1.1.2 reads as follows:

> "Each marine diesel engine with a power output of more than 130 kW that undergoes a major conversion on or after 1 January 2000 except when demonstrated to the satisfaction of the Administration that such engine is an identical replacement to the engine that it is replacing and is otherwise not covered under paragraph 1.1.1 of this regulation."

Regulation 13.2.2 reads as follows:

> "For a major conversion involving the replacement of a marine diesel engine with a non-identical marine diesel engine or the installation of an additional marine diesel engine, the standards in this regulation at the time of the replacement or addition of the engine shall apply."

Interpretation:

9.1   In regulation 13.1.1.2, the term "identical" (and hence, by application of the converse, in regulation 13.2.2 the term "non-identical") as applied to engines under regulation 13 should be taken as:

9.2   An "identical engine" is, as compared to the engine being replaced,[2] an engine which is of the same:

    .1   design and model;

    .2   rated power;

    .3   rated speed;

    .4   use;

    .5   number of cylinders; and

    .6   fuel system type (including, if applicable, injection control software):

---

[2]   In those instances where the replaced engine will not be available to be directly compared with the replacing engine at the time of updating the Supplement to the IAPP Certificate reflecting that engine change, it is to be ensured that the necessary records in respect of the replaced engine are available in order that it can be confirmed that the replacing engine represents "an identical engine".

9 完全相同替代的柴油机

第 13 条　氮氧化物（NOₓ）

第 13.1.1.2 条原文如下：

"每台 2000 年 1 月 1 日后以后经重大改装的、输出功率超过 130 kW 的船用柴油机，但能证明并使主管机关确信该柴油机与其将替代的柴油机完全相同，且不受本条 1.1.1 规定者除外。"

第 13.2.2 条原文如下：　"如重大改装涉及船用柴油机被非完全相同的柴油机替代，或涉及新增安装柴油机，则在替代或新增柴油机时执行的本条标准应适用。"

解释：

9.1　对第 13 条规定的柴油机而言，第 13.1.1.2 条中的"完全相同的"一词（由此而在 13.2.2 条中用了反义词"非完全相同的"）应理解为：

9.2　与被替代的柴油机 [2] 相比，"完全相同的柴油机"系指具有下列共同点的柴油机：

　.1　设计和型号；

　.2　额定功率；

　.3　额定转速；

　.4　用途；

　.5　气缸数；和

　.6　燃料系统类型（包括喷射控制软件，如适用）：

---

[2]　如在更新 IAPP 证书附件以反映柴油机更换的时候，被替代的柴油机不能直接与替代的柴油机进行比较，则应保证取得被替代柴油机方面的必要记录以确认替代的柴油机为"一台完全相同的柴油机"。

.1   for engines without EIAPP certification, have the same NO_x critical components and settings;[3] or

.2   for engines with EIAPP certification, belonging to the same Engine Group/Engine Family.

10   Time of replacement of an engine

Regulation 13
Nitrogen oxides (NO$_x$)

Regulation 13.2.2 reads as follows:

"For a major conversion involving the replacement of a marine diesel engine with a non-identical marine diesel engine, or the installation of an additional marine diesel engine, the standards in this regulation at the time of the replacement or addition of the engine shall apply."

Interpretation:

10.1   The term "time of the replacement or addition" of the engine in regulation 13.2.2 should be taken as the date of:

.1   the contractual delivery date of the engine to the ship;[4] or

.2   in the absence of a contractual delivery date, the actual delivery date of the engine to the ship,[3] provided that the date is confirmed by a delivery receipt; or

.3   in the event the engine is fitted on board and tested for its intended purpose on or after six months from the date specified in sub-paragraphs of regulation 13.5.1.2, as appropriate, the actual date that the engine is tested on board for its intended purpose applies in determining the standards in this regulation in force at the time of the replacement or addition of the engine.

10.2   Entry of the date in paragraph 10.1 above, provided the conditions associated with those dates apply, should be made in item 8.a "Major conversion – According to regulations 13.2.1.1 and 13.2.2" of the Supplement of IAPP Certificate.

---

[3]   For engines without EIAPP Certification there will not be the defining NO_x critical component markings or setting values as usually given in the approved Technical File. Consequently, in these instances, the assessment of "... same NO_x critical components and settings ..." shall be established on the basis that the following components and settings are the same:

Fuel system:

.1   fuel pump model and injection timing; and

.2   injection nozzle model.

Charge air:

.1   configuration and, if applicable, turbocharger model and auxiliary blower specification; and

.2   cooling medium (seawater/freshwater).

[4]   The engine is to be fitted on board and tested for its intended purpose within six months after the date specified in sub-paragraphs of regulation 13.5.1.2, as appropriate.

.1 对于没有 EIAPP 证书的柴油机，具有相同的 NO_x 关键部件和设定值[3]；或

.2 对于具有 EIAPP 证书的柴油机，属于同一柴油机组 / 族。

10 柴油机的替代时间

第 13 条 氮氧化物（NO_x）

第 13.2.2 条原文如下：

"如重大改装涉及船用柴油机被非完全相同的柴油机替代，或涉及新增安装柴油机，则在替代或新增柴油机时执行的本条标准应适用。"

解释：

10.1 第 13.2.2 条中的术语"替代或新增柴油机时"应理解为如下日期：

.1 合同规定的柴油机交货上船日期[4]；或

.2 如无合同规定的交货日期，则取经交货回单确认的柴油机实际交货上船日期[3]；或

.3 如柴油机于自第 13.5.1.2 条中规定的日期起 6 个月或以后安装上船并对其预定用途进行试验，则在确定替代或新增柴油机时适用的本条标准时，取柴油机按其预定用途进行船上试验的实际日期。

10.2 如上述 7.1 规定的日期相关条件适用，则适用的日期应记入 IAPP 证书附件中第 8.a 条"重大改装——按第 13.2.1.1 和 13.2.2 条规定"。

---

[3] 对于没有 EIAPP 证书的柴油机，则一般无法确定如批准的技术案卷中规定的 NO_x 关键部件标志或设定值。这种情况下，应以下列部件和设定值相同为基础，进行"NO_x 关键部件和设定值相同"的评估。
燃料系统：
.1 燃料泵型号和喷射时间；和
.2 喷嘴型号。
增压空气：
.1 配置、涡轮增压机型号和辅助鼓风机规格（如适用）；和
.2 冷却介质（海水 / 淡水）。
[4] 柴油机应于第 13.5.1.2 条的分段内所规定的日期之后 6 个月内安装上船并对其预定用途进行试验。

10.3   If the engine is not tested within six months after the date specified in the sub-paragraphs of regulation 13.5.1.2, as appropriate due to unforeseen circumstances beyond the control of the shipowner, then the provisions of "unforeseen delay in delivery" may be considered by the Administration in a manner similar to UI4 of MARPOL Annex I.

11   Engine change-over/on-off recording requirements

Regulation 13
Nitrogen oxides (NOₓ)

Regulation 13.5.3 reads as follows:

> "The tier and on/off status of marine diesel engines installed on board a ship to which paragraph 5.1 of this regulation applies which are certified to both Tier II and Tier III or which are certified to Tier II only shall be recorded in such logbook or electronic record book as prescribed by the Administration at entry into and exit from a NOₓ Tier III emission control area, or when the on/off status changes within such an area, together with the date, time and position of the ship."

Interpretation:

For the application of this regulation:

.1   "marine diesel engines installed on board a ship to which paragraph 5.1 of this regulation applies" includes additional or replaced engines;[5] installed on or after the relevant emission control area takes effect;

.2   "certified to Tier II only" means a Tier II engine that is installed on board a ship which is constructed on or after the emission control area where the ship is operating takes effect;

.3   Tier II engines stipulated under the Tier II requirement of regulation 13.4, i.e. Tier II engines installed on board a ship constructed before the entry into force of the emission control area where the ship is operating, are not considered to be a "Tier II only" engine in the context of record keeping. Such exclusion is extended to Tier II engines replaced after the entry into force of the relevant emission control areas on board ships of this category, if the replacement engines meet resolution MEPC.230(65);

.4   if an engine installed on a ship constructed before the entry into force of the emission control area where the ship is operating has undergone a major conversion as described in regulation 13.2.1, those engines are to be Tier III engines; thus the above interpretation in .1 above applies; and

.5   recording is required for the Tier II engine operation in a NECA under the exemption according to regulation 13.5.4.

---

[5]   Additional or replaced engine: refer to section 10.1 above.

10.3　由于船东无法控制的意外情况，柴油机未能在第 13.5.1.2 条中规定的日期后 6 个月内进行试验，则主管机关可考虑按 MARPOL 附则 I UI4 "交货的意外延迟" 的规定进行类似处理。

11　发动机转换／开关记录要求

第 13 条　氮氧化物（NO_x）

第 13.5.3 条原文如下：

"对于核准为 II 和 III 级或仅核准为 II 级、本条 5.1 适用的船上安装的船用柴油机，在进入和离开本条 6 指定的排放控制区时或在此区域内开／关状态改变时，应将等级和开／关状态连同日期、时间和船舶位置记录在主管机关规定的航海日志中。"

解释：

关于本条的应用：

.1　"本条 5.1 适用的船上安装的船用柴油机" 包括相关排放控制区生效时或生效后安装的新增或替代柴油机[5]；

.2　"仅核准为 II 级" 系指船舶作业所在的排放控制区生效时或生效后建造的船上安装的 II 级发动机；

.3　就记录保持而言，按 13.4 条中 II 级要求规定的 II 级发动机，即：船舶作业所在的排放控制区生效之前建造的船上安装的 II 级发动机，不视为 "仅核准为 II 级" 的发动机。这一排除扩展至相关排放控制区生效后此类船上替代的 II 级柴油机（如该替代柴油机满足 MEPC.230（65）决议的规定）；

.4　如果船舶作业所在的排放控制区生效之前建造的船上安装的 II 级发动机进行了第 13.2.1 条所述的重大改装，则该柴油机应为 III 级发动机，从而上述 .1 中的解释适用；和

.5　在按第 13.5.4 条免除的 NECA 区内运行的 II 级发动机要求进行记录。

---

[5]　新增或替代发动机：参见上述第 10.1 节。

12   Application of sulphur limit to emergency equipment

Regulation 14
Sulphur oxides (SO$_x$) and particulate matter

Regulation 14.1 reads as follows:

> "The sulphur content of fuel oil used or carried for use on board a ship shall not exceed 0.50% m/m."

Interpretation:

Regulation 14.1 of MARPOL Annex VI for the prohibition on the carriage of non-compliant fuel oil should be applied to the fuel oil of emergency equipment.

13   VOC management plan

Regulation 15
Volatile organic compounds (VOCs)

Regulations 15.6 and 15.7 read as follows:

> "6   A tanker carrying crude oil shall have on board and implement a VOC management plan approved by the Administration. Such a plan shall be prepared taking into account the guidelines developed by the Organization. The plan shall be specific to each ship and shall at least:
>
> .1   provide written procedures for minimizing VOC emissions during the loading, sea passage and discharge of cargo;
>
> .2   give consideration to the additional VOC generated by crude oil washing;
>
> .3   identify a person responsible for implementing the plan; and
>
> .4   for ships on international voyages, be written in the working language of the master and officers and, if the working language of the master and officers is not English, French or Spanish, include a translation into one of these languages.
>
> 7   This regulation shall also apply to gas carriers only if the types of loading and containment systems allow safe retention of non-methane VOCs on board or their safe return ashore.[6] "

Interpretation:

The requirement for a VOC management plan applies only to a tanker carrying crude oil.

---

[6]   Resolution MSC.30(61) on *International Code for the Construction and Equipment of Ships Carrying Liquefied Gases in Bulk.*

12 对应急设备适用硫含量限值

第 14 条 硫氧化物（SO$_x$）和颗粒物质

第 14.1 条原文如下：

"船上使用的或为使用而载运的燃油的硫含量不应超过 0.50% m/m。"

解释：

MARPOL 附则Ⅵ第 14.1 条禁止携带不合规燃油应适用于应急设备的燃油。

13 VOC 管理计划

第 15 条 挥发性有机化合物（VOC）

第 15.6 和 15.7 条原文如下：

"6 载运原油的液货船应备有并实施经主管机关认可的 VOC 管理计划。该计划应根据本组织制定的指南编写。该计划应具体到各船并至少应：

　　.1 为装载、海上航行和卸货时的 VOC 排放减至最低限度提供书面程序；

　　.2 考虑到原油洗舱产生的额外 VOC；

　　.3 指定负责实施该计划的人员；和

　　.4 对于国际航行船舶，用船长和高级船员的工作语言编写，如船长和高级船员的工作语言既非英语、法语，也非西班牙语，则应包括其中一种语言的译文。

7 对气体运输船而言，只有其装载和围护系统的类型使得非甲烷 VOC 安全保存在船上或安全回输到岸上时才适合本条[6]。"

解释：

VOC 管理计划的要求仅适用于载运原油的液货船。

---

[6] MSC.30（61）决议《国际散装运输液化气体船舶构造和设备规则》。

14   Continuous-feed type shipboard incinerators

Regulation 16
Shipboard incineration

Regulation 16.9 reads as follows:

> "For incinerators installed in accordance with the requirements of paragraph 6.1 of this regulation the combustion chamber gas outlet temperature shall be monitored at all times the unit is in operation. Where that incinerator is of the continuous-feed type, waste shall not be fed into the unit when the combustion chamber gas outlet temperature is below 850°C. Where that incinerator is of the batch-loaded type, the unit shall be designed so that the combustion chamber gas outlet temperature shall reach 600°C within five minutes after start-up and will thereafter stabilize at a temperature not less than 850°C."

Interpretation:

14.1   For the application of this regulation, the term "waste shall not be fed into the unit" should be interpreted as follows:

> For continuous-feed incinerators solid waste shall not be fed into the unit when the combustion chamber flue gas outlet temperature is below 850°C. Sludge oil generated during normal operation of a ship should not be regarded as waste in connection with this regulation, and can be fed into the unit when the required preheat temperature of 650°C in the combustion chamber is achieved.

14.2   For the application of this regulation, the term "the unit shall be designed so that the combustion chamber gas outlet temperature shall reach 600°C within five minutes after start-up" should be interpreted as follows:

> Batch loaded incinerators should be designed so that the temperature in the actual combustion space where the solid waste is combusted should reach 600°C within five minutes after start-up.

15   Application of regulation 18.3 for biofuel and synthetic fuel

Regulation 18
Fuel oil availability and quality

Regulation 18.3 reads as follows:

> "Fuel oil for combustion purposes delivered to and used on board ships to which this Annex applies shall meet the following requirements."

Interpretation:

15.1   A fuel oil which is a blend of not more than 30% by volume of biofuel or synthetic fuel should meet the requirements of regulation 18.3.1 of MARPOL Annex VI. A fuel oil which is a blend of more than 30% by volume of biofuel or synthetic fuel should meet the requirements of regulation 18.3.2 of MARPOL Annex VI. For the purposes of this interpretation, a biofuel is a fuel oil which is derived from biomass and hence includes, but is not limited to, processed used cooking oils, fatty-acid-methyl-esters (FAME) or fatty-acid-ethyl-esters (FAEE), straight vegetable oils (SVO), hydrotreated vegetable oils (HVO), glycerol or other biomass to liquid (BTL) type products. For the purposes of this interpretation, a synthetic fuel is a fuel oil from

14 连续进料型船上焚烧炉

第 16 条　船上焚烧

第 16.9 条原文如下：

"对于按本条 6.1 要求安装的焚烧炉，在该炉进行操作的任何时候均应对燃烧室气体出口温度进行监测。如焚烧炉为连续进料型，在燃烧室气体出口温度低于 850 ℃时废弃物不应送入该焚烧炉。如焚烧炉为分批装料型，该炉应设计成其燃烧室气体出口的温度在起动后 5 min 内达 600 ℃且随后稳定在不低于 850 ℃。"

解释：

14.1　对于本条的应用，对术语"废弃物不应送入该焚烧炉"应作如下解释：对于连续进料型焚烧炉，在燃烧室烟气出口的温度低于 850 ℃时，固体废弃物不应送入该焚烧炉。本条中船舶正常营运期间产生的油渣不应视为废弃物，当燃烧室达到所需预热温度 650 ℃，可以送入该焚烧炉。

14.2　对于本条的应用，对术语"该炉应设计成其燃烧室气体出口的温度在起动后 5 min 内达 600 ℃"应作如下解释：

分批装料型焚烧炉应设计成燃烧固体废弃物实际燃烧处所的温度在起动后 5 min 内达 600 ℃。

15　第 18.3 条关于生物燃料和合成燃料的应用

第 18 条　燃油的提供和质量

第 18.3 条原文如下：

"交付并作为本附则适用的船上燃烧用的燃油应符合下列要求。"

解释

15.1　混合不超过 30%（按体积计）生物燃料或合成燃料的燃油应符合 MARPOL 附则Ⅵ第 18.3.1 条的要求。混合 30%（按体积计）以上生物燃料或合成燃料的燃油应符合 MARPOL 附则Ⅵ第 18.3.2 条的要求。就本解释而言，生物燃料系指从生物质产生的燃油，因此包括但不限于加工过的废弃食用油、脂肪酸甲酯（FAME）或脂肪酸乙酯（FAEE）、纯植油（SVO）、加氢处理植物油（HVO）、甘油或其他生物质转化为液体（BTL）类型的产品。就本解释而言，合成燃料系指来自合成或可再生资源的燃油，其组成与石油馏分燃料相似。燃油交付单上

synthetic or renewable sources similar in composition to petroleum distillate fuels. The Product Name, as entered onto the bunker delivery note, should be of sufficient detail to identify whether, and to what extent, a biofuel or a synthetic fuel is blended into the product as supplied.

Regulation 18.3.2.2 reads as follows:

> "fuel oil for combustion purposes derived by methods other than petroleum refining shall not cause an engine to exceed the applicable NO_x emission limit set forth in paragraphs 3, 4, 5.1.1 and 7.4 of regulation 13."

Interpretation:

15.2   A marine diesel engine certified in accordance with the requirements of regulation 13 of MARPOL Annex VI, which can operate on a biofuel or a synthetic fuel or blends containing these fuels without changes to its NO_x critical components or settings/operating values outside those as given by that engine's approved Technical File, should be permitted to use such a fuel oil without having to undertake the assessment as given by regulation 18.3.2.2 of MARPOL Annex VI. For the purposes of this interpretation, parent engine emissions tests undertaken on DM or RM grade fuels to the ISO 8217:2005 standard, as required by paragraph 5.3.2 of the NO_x Technical Code, should be valid for all DM or RM grade fuels used in operation, or that the engine may be designed for, or capable of operation on, including those meeting ISO 8217 standards superseding ISO 8217:2005.

15.3   Where fuel oils are derived from methods other than petroleum refining, or fuel oil which is a blend of more than 30% by volume of biofuel or synthetic fuel and does not fall under 15.2 of this unified interpretation, or other fuels required to undertake the assessment as given by regulation 18.3.2.2 of MARPOL Annex VI and for which have not been specifically certified in accordance with the regulation 13 limits at test bed for that specific fuel and Engine Group/Family, the following is interpreted as an acceptable route to demonstrate compliance with regulation 18.3.2.2:

> The ship's IAPP Certificate may continue to be issued where the overall NO_x emissions performance has been verified to not cause the specified engine to exceed the applicable NO_x emissions limit when burning said fuels using the onboard simplified measurement method in accordance with 6.3 of the NO_x Technical Code 2008, or the direct measurement and monitoring method in accordance with 6.4 of the NO_x Technical Code 2008, or by reference to relevant test-bed testing. For the purposes of this interpretation and demonstration of compliance with regulation 18.3.2.2 of MARPOL Annex VI, and as applicable to possible deviations when undertaking measurements on board, an allowance of 10% of the applicable limit may be accepted.

16   Applicability of the requirements for a bunker delivery note (BDN)

Regulation 18
Fuel oil availability and quality

Regulation 18.5 reads as follows:

> "For each ship subject to regulations 5 and 6 of this Annex, details of fuel oil for combustion purposes delivered to and used on board shall be recorded by means of a bunker delivery note that shall contain at least the information specified in appendix V to this Annex."

填写的产品名称应足够详细，以识别是否以及以何种程度将生物燃料或合成燃料混合到所提供的产品中。

第 18.3.2.2 条原文如下：

"以石油精炼之外的方法得到的用于燃烧的燃油应不导致发动机超过本附则第 13 条 3、4、5.1.1 和 7.4 中规定的适用 NO_x 排放极限。"

解释

15.2　按 MARPOL 附则Ⅵ第 13 条要求核准的船用柴油机，如使用生物燃料或合成燃料或含有这些燃料的混合物运行对 NO_x 关键部件或设置／操作值的更改没有超出该发动机批准的技术案卷所述值，应允许该发动机使用此类燃油，而无须按 MARPOL 附则Ⅵ第 18.3.2.2 条进行评估。就本解释而言，根据 NO_x 技术规则第 5.3.2 段的要求，使用 ISO8217：2005 标准 DM 或 RM 级燃料进行的母型机排放测试，应对运行中所有使用的 DM 或 RM 级燃料有效，或者发动机可设计为或能够使用包括满足 ISO 8217 标准（替代 ISO 8217：2005）的燃料运行。

15.3　如以石油精炼之外的方法得到燃油，或燃油混合 30%（按体积计）以上生物燃料或合成燃料且不属于本统一解释的第 1.2 段，或需要按 MARPOL 附则Ⅵ第 18.3.2.2 条要求进行评估且未按第 13 条限值在试验台针对该特定燃料和发动机组／族予以专门核准的其他燃料，以下解释为证明符合第 18.3.2.2 条的可接受途径：

如按《2008 年 NO_x 技术规则》的第 6.3 条使用船上简化测量方法、或按《2008 年 NO_x 技术规则》的第 6.4 条使用直接测量和监测方法、或通过参考相关试验台测试，燃烧所述燃料时，已验证整体 NO_x 排放性能不会导致指定发动机超过适用的 NO_x 排放限值，可继续签发船舶的 IAPP 证书。就本解释和证明符合 MARPOL 附则Ⅵ第 18.3.2.2 条而言，对在船上进行测量时可能出现的偏差，可接受适用限值 10% 的容许偏差。

16　燃油交付单（BDN）要求适用性

第 18 条　燃油的提供和质量

第 18.5 条原文如下：

"对受本附则第 5 条和第 6 条约束的每一艘船舶，应以燃油交付单的方式对交付并作为船上燃烧用的燃油的细节加以记录，该交付单应至少包含本附则附录 V 中规定的资料。"

Regulation 18.6 reads as follows:

> "The bunker delivery note shall be kept on board the ship in such a place as to be readily available for inspection at all reasonable times. It shall be retained for a period of three years after the fuel oil has been delivered on board."

Interpretation:

16.1   For the application of these regulations, they should be interpreted as being applicable to all ships of 400 gross tonnage or above and, at the Administration's discretion, to ships of less than 400 gross tonnage.

16.2   The bunker delivery note (BDN) required by regulation 18.5 is acceptable in either hard copy or electronic format provided it contains at least the information specified in appendix V to MARPOL Annex VI and is retained and made available on board in accordance with regulation 18.6. In addition, an electronic BDN should be protected from edits, modifications or revisions and authentication be possible by a verification method such as a tracking number, watermark, date and time stamp, QR code, GPS coordinates or other verification methods.

17   Requirements for reporting attained EEDI and relevant information

Regulation 22
Attained Energy Efficiency Design Index (attained EEDI)

Regulation 22.3 reads as follows:

> "For each ship subject to regulation 24 of this Annex, the Administration or any organization duly authorized by it shall report to the Organization the required and attained EEDI values and relevant information, taking into account the guidelines developed by the Organization, via electronic communication:
>
> > .1   within seven months of completing the survey required under regulation 5.4 of this Annex; or
> >
> > .2   within seven months following 1 April 2022 for a ship delivered prior to 1 April 2022."

Interpretation:

17.1   For new ships that have completed the initial survey required in regulation 5.4.1 of MARPOL Annex VI on or after 1 April 2022, the EEDI data and relevant information shall be submitted within seven months after the completion date of the initial survey (in accordance with regulation 22.3.1).

17.2   For new ships that have completed the initial survey required in regulation 5.4.1 of MARPOL Annex VI prior to 1 April 2022:

> .1   if they have not undergone a major conversion specified in regulation 5.4.2 or 5.4.3, the EEDI data and relevant information shall be submitted within seven months after 1 April 2022 (in accordance with regulation 22.3.2);
>
> .2   if they have undergone a major conversion specified in regulation 5.4.2 or 5.4.3 on or after 1 April 2022, the EEDI data and relevant information of

第 18.6 条原文如下：

"燃油交付单在船上的存放位置应易于在任何合理时间随时可供检查，并应在燃油交付船上之后保存三年。"

解释：

16.1 对于本条的应用，应解释为适用于所有 400 总吨或以上的船舶，对于 400 总吨以下的船舶，由主管机关自行决定。

16.2 第 18.5 条要求的燃油交付单（BDN）可以是硬拷贝或电子格式，但应至少包括 MARPOL 附则 VI 附录 V 规定的信息，并按第 18.6 条在船上保存和供检查。此外，电子燃油交付单应受保护以防止被编辑、修改或修订，并可通过跟踪号、水印、日期和时间戳、二维码、GPS 坐标或其他验证方法予以认证。

17 Attained EEDI 和相关信息的报告要求

第 22 条 达到的能效设计指数（Attained EEDI）

第 22.3 条原文如下：

"对本附则第 24 条适用的每艘船舶，主管机关或其正式授权的任何组织应基于本组织制定的指南通过电子通信向本组织报告其 Required EEDI 和 Attained EEDI 值及相关信息：

.1 在本附则第 5.4 条要求的检验完成的 7 个月内；或

.2 对 2022 年 4 月 1 日以前交船的船舶，在 2022 年 4 月 1 日以后的 7 个月内。"

解释：

17.1 对于在 2022 年 4 月 1 日或以后完成 MARPOL 附则 VI 第 5.4.1 条所要求的初次检验的新船，应在初次检验完成之日以后 7 个月内提交 EEDI 数据和相关信息（按第 22.3.1 条）。

17.2 对于在 2022 年 4 月 1 日以前完成 MARPOL 附则 VI 第 5.4.1 条规定的初次检验的新船：

.1 如果没有经历第 5.4.2 或 5.4.3 条规定的重大改建，则应在 2022 年 4 月 1 日以后 7 个月内提交 EEDI 数据和相关信息（按第 22.3.2 条）；

.2 如果在 2022 年 4 月 1 日或以后经历了第 5.4.2 或 5.4.3 条规定的重大改建，则应在第 5.4.2 条要求的全面或部分检验或第 5.4.3 条要求的初次检验完成之日后 7

the major conversion shall be submitted within seven months after the completion date of general or partial survey required in regulation 5.4.2 or the initial survey required in regulation 5.4.3 (in accordance with regulation 22.3.1); and

.3 if they have completed a major conversion specified in regulation 5.4.2 or 5.4.3 prior to 1 April 2022, the EEDI data and relevant information of the major conversion shall be submitted within seven months after 1 April 2022 (in accordance with regulation 22.3.2).

17.3 For existing ships that have completed the initial survey required in regulation 5.4.3 of MARPOL Annex VI on or after 1 April 2022, the EEDI data and relevant information shall be submitted within seven months after the completion date of the initial survey (in accordance with regulation 22.3.1).

17.4 For existing ships that have completed the initial survey required in regulation 5.4.3 of MARPOL Annex VI prior to 1 April 2022, the EEDI data and relevant information shall be submitted within seven months after 1 April 2022 (in accordance with regulation 22.3.2).

17.5 For ships for which up-to-date EEDI data has already been reported to the Organization prior to 1 April 2022, the reporting of EEDI data and information shall not be required on or after 1 April 2022.

18 Ship Energy Efficiency Management Plan (SEEMP) Part III

Regulation 26
Ship Energy Efficiency Management Plan (SEEMP)

Regulation 26.3.1 reads as follows:

"In the case of a ship of 5,000 gross tonnage and above, which falls into one or more of the categories in regulations 2.2.5, 2.2.7, 2.2.9, 2.2.11, 2.2.14 to 2.2.16, 2.2.22, and 2.2.26 to 2.2.29 of this Annex:

.1 On or before 1 January 2023 the SEEMP shall include:

.1 a description of the methodology that will be used to calculate the ship's attained annual operational CII required by regulation 28 of this Annex and the processes that will be used to report this value to the ship's Administration;

.2 the required annual operational CII, as specified in regulation 28 of this Annex, for the next three years;

.3 an implementation plan documenting how the required annual operational CII will be achieved during the next three years; and

.4 a procedure for self-evaluation and improvement."

个月内提交 EEDI 数据和重大改建相关信息（按第 22.3.1 条）；和

.3 如果在 2022 年 4 月 1 日以前完成了第 5.4.2 或 5.4.3 条中规定的重大改建，则应在 2022 年 4 月 1 日以后 7 个月内提交 EEDI 数据和重大改建相关信息（按第 22.3.2 条）。

17.3 对于在 2022 年 4 月 1 日或以后完成 MARPOL 附则Ⅵ第 5.4.3 条所要求的初次检验的现有船，应在初次检验完成之日后 7 个月内提交 EEDI 数据和相关信息（按第 22.3.1 条）。

17.4 对于在 2022 年 4 月 1 日以前完成 MARPOL 附则Ⅵ第 5.4.3 条所要求的初次检验的现有船，应在 2022 年 4 月 1 日以后 7 个月内提交 EEDI 数据和相关信息（按第 22.3.2 条）。

17.5 对于在 2022 年 4 月 1 日以前已经向本组织报告了最新 EEDI 数据的船舶，在 2022 年 4 月 1 日或以后不应要求报告 EEDI 数据和信息。

18 船舶能效管理计划（SEEMP）第Ⅲ部分

第 26 条 船舶能效管理计划（SEEMP）

第 26.3.1 条原文如下：

"对于 5 000 总吨及以上且属于本附则第 2.2.5、2.2.7、2.2.9、2.2.11、2.2.14 至 2.2.16、2.2.22 和 2.2.26 至 2.2.29 条规定的一种或多种类别的船舶：

.1 在 2023 年 1 月 1 日或以前，SEEMP 应包括：

.1 对用于计算本附则第 28 条要求的船舶达到的年度营运 CII 的方法和用于向船舶主管机关报告该值的过程的描述；

.2 未来三年的要求的年度营运 CII（按本附则第 28 条规定）；

.3 记录如何在未来三年达到要求的年度营运 CII 的实施计划；和

.4 自我评估和改进程序。"

Interpretation:

18.1   A ship delivered after 1 January 2023 should comply with regulation 26.3.1 of MARPOL Annex VI at delivery. If delivered on 1 October or later, the following year will then be the first year of the three-year implementation plan and an inferior rating given, in accordance with regulation 28.6 of MARPOL Annex VI, for the remainder of the calendar year of delivery needs not to be counted in for the determination of whether the ship should develop a Corrective Action Plan required by regulation 26.3.2 of MARPOL Annex VI. Nothing in this interpretation relieves any ship of its reporting obligations under regulations 27 and 28 of MARPOL Annex VI.

18.2   A ship changing company, or changing from one Administration to another and from one company to another concurrently, after 1 January 2023 should comply with regulation 26.3.1 at change of company and a new SEEMP III will be required. The year of change should be the first year of the next three-year implementation plan.

18.3   In order to document how the required annual operational CII will be achieved during the next three years, the SEEMP Part III should be a rolling three-year plan, YYYY (first year of implementation plan), YYYY+1 and YYYY+2.

18.4   In the case of updating the SEEMP Part III on the elements in regulation 26.3.1 of MARPOL Annex VI, the original three-year plan may remain.

19   Boil-off gas consumed on board ships

Regulation 2
Definitions

Regulation 2.1.14 reads as follows:

> "*Fuel oil* means any fuel delivered to and intended for combustion purposes for propulsion or operation on board a ship, including gas, distillate and residual fuels."

Regulation 27
Collection and reporting of ship fuel oil consumption data

Regulation 27.1 reads as follows:

> "From calendar year 2019, each ship of 5,000 gross tonnage and above shall collect the data specified in appendix IX to this Annex, for that and each subsequent calendar year or portion thereof, as appropriate, according to the methodology included in the SEEMP."

Appendix IX
Information to be submitted to the IMO Ship Fuel Oil Consumption Database

Appendix IX reads as follows:

> "Fuel oil consumption, by fuel oil type in metric tonnes and methods used for collecting fuel oil consumption data".

解释：

18.1   2023 年 1 月 1 日以后交付的船舶在交付时应符合 MARPOL 附则Ⅵ第 26.3.1 条的规定。如果在 10 月 1 日或以后交付，那么下一年将是三年实施计划的第一年，在确定船舶是否应制定 MARPOL 附则Ⅵ第 26.3.2 条要求的整改行动计划时，交付日历年的剩余时间内按 MARPOL 附则Ⅵ第 28.6 条给予的不合格评级无须计入。本解释不免除任何船舶在 MARPOL 附则Ⅵ第 27 条和第 28 条规定下的报告义务。

18.2   在 2023 年 1 月 1 日以后，船舶变更公司，或从一个主管机关变更到另一个主管机关并同时从一个公司变更到另一个公司，在变更公司时应符合第 26.3.1 条，并要求新的 SEEMP Ⅲ。变更年应为下一个三年实施计划的第一年。

18.3   为了记录如何在未来三年达到要求的年度营运 CII，SEEMP 第Ⅲ部分应该是一个滚动的三年计划，YYYY（实施计划的第一年）、YYYY+1 和 YYYY+2。

18.4   在更新 SEEMP 第Ⅲ部分有关就 MARPOL 附则Ⅵ第 26.3.1 条的要素时，原三年计划可以保持不变。

19   船上消耗的蒸发气体

第 2 条   定义

第 2.1.14 条原文如下：

"燃油系指为了船舶推进或运转而交付船上的用于燃烧的任何燃料，包括气体燃料、馏分燃油和残余燃油。"

第 27 条   收集和报告船舶燃油消耗数据

第 27.1 条原文如下：

"从日历年 2019 年开始，每艘 5 000 总吨及以上的船舶应酌情按 SEEMP 所述方法在该日历年和其后每一日历年或日历年中的月份收集本附则附录Ⅸ规定的数据。"

附录Ⅸ   应向 IMO 船舶燃油消耗数据库提交的信息

附录Ⅸ原文如下：

"燃油消耗，按燃油类型以吨计，以及用于收集燃油消耗数据的方法"

Interpretation:

For Data relating to boil-off gas (BOG) consumed on board the ship for propulsion or operation (e.g. BOG used for propulsion, operational needs such as in a boiler, or burnt in a gas combustion unit (GCU) for cargo tank pressure control or other operational purposes) is required to be collected and reported as fuel as part of the Ship Fuel Oil Consumption Data Collection System.

20 Access to the disaggregated data

Regulation 27
Collection and reporting of ship fuel oil consumption data

Regulation 27.8 reads as follows:

> "Except as provided for in paragraphs 4, 5 and 6 of this regulation, the disaggregated data that underlies the reported data noted in appendix IX to this Annex for the previous calendar year shall be readily accessible for a period of not less than 12 months from the end of that calendar year and be made available to the Administration upon request."

Interpretation:

The disaggregated data is not required to be kept on board the ship provided that the disaggregated data can be made available by the Company.

21 Plan of corrective actions to achieve the required annual operational CII

Regulation 28
Operational carbon intensity

Regulation 28.7 reads as follows:

> "A ship rated as D for three consecutive years or rated as E shall develop a plan of corrective actions to achieve the required annual operational CII."

Regulation 28.9 reads as follows:

> "A ship rated as D for three consecutive years or rated as E shall duly undertake the planned corrective actions in accordance with the revised SEEMP."

Interpretation:

In case an inferior rating is given for data collected in calendar year YYYY, the revised SEEMP, including the plan of corrective actions, should be verified in year YYYY+1, and it should be developed to achieve the required annual operational CII for data collected in the calendar year YYYY+2.

解释：

对船上消耗的用于船舶推进或运转的蒸发气体（BOG）（用于满足推进、运转所需的蒸发气体，如在锅炉内，或为货舱压力控制或其他运转目的在气体燃烧装置（GCU）内燃烧的蒸发气体）相关数据，需作为燃料进行收集和报告，作为船舶燃油消耗量数据收集系统的一部分。

20　获取分解数据

第 27 条　船舶燃油消耗数据的收集和报告

第 27.8 条原文如下：

"除本条 4、5 和 6 规定外，对于上一个日历年的本附则附录Ⅸ规定的报告数据的未合计数据，应从该日历年结束开始的至少 12 个月内随时可获得，并可应要求提供给主管机关。"

解释：

如果公司能够提供分解数据，则不需要将分解数据保存在船上。

21　为达到要求的年度营运 CII 的整改行动计划

第 28 条　营运碳强度

第 28.7 条原文如下：

"被评为 E 级或连续三年被评为 D 级的船舶应制定整改行动计划以达到要求的年度营运 CII。"

第 28.9 条原文如下：

"被评为 E 级或连续三年被评为 D 级的船舶应按修订后的 SEEMP 合理实施既定的纠正行动。"

解释：

如果对 YYYY 日历年收集的数据给出不合格评级，应在 YYYY+1 年对修订后的 SEEMP（包括整改行动计划）进行验证，该计划应基于使 YYYY+2 日历年收集的数据达到要求的年度运营 CII 制定。

船舶能效管理计划（SEEMP）相关

RESOLUTION MEPC.395(82)
(adopted on 4 October 2024)

2024 GUIDELINES FOR THE DEVELOPMENT OF
A SHIP ENERGY EFFICIENCY MANAGEMENT PLAN (SEEMP)

THE MARINE ENVIRONMENT PROTECTION COMMITTEE,

RECALLING Article 38(a) of the Convention on the International Maritime Organization concering the functions of the Marine Environment Protection Committee conferred upon it by international conventions for the prevention and control of marine pollution from ships,

NOTING that regulation 26 of MARPOL Annex VI requires each ship to keep on board a Ship Energy Efficiency Management Plan (SEEMP), to be developed and reviewed, taking into account the guidelines adopted by the Organization,

RECALLING that, at its seventy-eighth session, it adopted, by resolution MEPC.346(78), the *2022 Guidelines for the development of a Ship Energy Efficiency Management Plan (SEEMP)*,

RECALLING ALSO that, at its eighty-first session, it adopted, by resolution MEPC. 388(81), amendments to the *2022 Guidelines for the development of a Ship Energy Efficiency Management Plan (SEEMP)*,

HAVING CONSIDERED, at its eighty-second session, draft amendments to the *2022 Guidelines for the development of a Ship Energy Efficiency Management Plan (SEEMP), as amended,*

1   ADOPTS the *2024 Guidelines for the development of a Ship Energy Efficiency Management Plan (SEEMP),* as set out in the annex to the present resolution;

2   REQUESTS the Parties to MARPOL Annex VI and other Member Goverments to bring the annexed Guidelines to the attention of masters, seafarers, shipowners, ship operators and any other interested parties;

3   REVOKES the *2022 Guidelines for the development of a Ship Energy Efficiency Management Plan (SEEMP)* adopted by resolution MEPC.346(78).

第 MEPC.395（82）号决议
（2024 年 10 月 4 日通过）

2024 年船舶能效管理计划（SEEMP）编制导则

海上环境保护委员会，

忆及《国际海事组织公约》关于防止和控制船舶造成海洋污染国际公约赋予海上环境保护委员会职能的第 38（a）条，

注意到 MARPOL 附则 Ⅵ 第 26 条要求，每艘船舶应在船上备有一份船舶能效管理计划（SEEMP）。制定和审查船舶能效管理计划须考虑到本组织通过的导则，

忆及在其第 78 届会议上，委员会通过了《2022 年船舶能效管理计划（SEEMP）编制导则》（第 MEPC.346（78）号决议），

在其第 81 届会议上，**审议了**《2022 年船舶能效管理计划（SEEMP）编制导则》的建议修正案（第 MEPC.388（81）号决议），

考虑到在其第 82 届会议上，**审议了**《2022 年船舶能效管理计划（SEEMP）编制导则》修订草案，

1　**通过**《2024 年船舶能效管理计划（SEEMP）编制导则》修正案，其文本载于本决议附件；

2　**要求**《防污公约》附则 Ⅵ 各缔约国和其他成员国政府将所附修正案提请船长、海员、船东、船舶经营人和任何其他有关各方注意；

3　**撤销** MEPC.346(78)号决议通过的《2022 年船舶能效管理计划(SEEMP)编制导则》。

2024 GUIDELINES FOR THE DEVELOPMENT OF
A SHIP ENERGY EFFICIENCY MANAGEMENT PLAN (SEEMP)

CONTENTS

2024 年船舶能效管理计划（SEEMP）编制导则

目录

附录 4——主管机关数据收集系统和营运碳强度标准数据报告格式

附录 5——计算自愿试用碳强度指标参数的标准数据报告格式

1   INTRODUCTION

1.1   The *Guidelines for the development of a Ship Energy Efficiency Management Plan* have been developed to assist with the preparation of the Ship Energy Efficiency Management Plan (SEEMP) required by regulation 26 of MARPOL Annex VI.

1.2   Taken together, the aims of the SEEMP should assist the international shipping sector to achieve the goal of Chapter 4 of MARPOL Annex VI set out in regulation 20, which is reducing the carbon intensity of international shipping. The aims of the SEEMP are threefold:

1.2.1   To encourage companies to incorporate actions to improve the energy efficiency and carbon intensity of their ships and ship management practices.

1.2.2   To specify the methodology the ship should use to collect the data required by regulation 27.1 of MARPOL AnnexVI and the processes that should be used to report the data to the ship's Administration or any organization duly authorized by it.

1.2.3   To specify the methodology the ship should use to calculate the attained annual operational carbon intensity indicator (CII) as required by regulation 28.1 of MARPOL Annex VI and the processes that should be used to report the data to the ship's Administration or any organization duly authorized by it.

1.3   There are three parts to a SEEMP:

1.3.1   Guidance for Part I of the SEEMP required by regulation 26.1 of MARPOL Annex VI, is addressed in sections 3, 4, and 5 of these Guidelines. The purpose of this part is to provide an approach to monitor ship and fleet efficiency performance over time and describe ways to improve the ship's energy efficiency performance and carbon intensity. Part I of the SEEMP applies to any ship of 400 GT and above.

1.3.2   Guidance for part II of the SEEMP required by regulation 26.2 of MARPOL Annex VI, is addressed in sections 6, 7, and 8 of these Guidelines. The purpose of this part is to provide a description of the methodologies that should be used to collect the data required pursuant to regulation 27 of MARPOL Annex VI and the processes that the ship should use to report the data to the ship's Administration or any organization duly authorized by it. Part II of the SEEMP applies to any ship of 5,000 GT and above.

1.3.3   Guidance for part III of the SEEMP required by regulations 26.3 and 28.8 of MARPOL Annex VI is addressed in sections 9, 10, 11, 12, 13, 14 and 15 of these Guidelines. The purpose of this part is to provide:

> .1   a description of the methodology that should be used to calculate the ship's attained annual operational CII required by regulation 28 of MARPOL Annex VI;
>
> .2   the processes that should be used to report this value to the ship's Administration or any organization duly authorized by it;
>
> .3   the required annual operational CII for the next three years;
>
> .4   an implementation plan documenting how the required annual operational CII should be achieved during the next three years;
>
> .5   a procedure for self-evaluation and improvement; and

1 引言

1.1 制定《船舶能效管理计划制定导则》旨在帮助编制《防污公约》附则Ⅵ第26条要求的船舶能效管理计划（SEEMP）。

1.2 总而言之，SEEMP 的目标应协助国际航运界实现《防污公约》附则Ⅵ第4章第20条规定的目标，即降低国际航运的碳强度。SEEMP 的目标有三个：

1.2.1 鼓励公司采取行动，改善其船舶的能效，碳强度以及船舶管理实践。

1.2.2 规定船舶应用于收集按《防污公约》附则Ⅵ第27.1条要求的数据的方法和船舶应用于向船舶主管机关或经其正式授权的任一组织报告数据的流程。

1.2.3 规定船舶应使用的计算《防污公约》附则Ⅵ第28.1条要求达到的年度营运碳强度指标（CII）的方法和船舶应用于向船舶主管机关或经其正式授权的任一组织报告数据的流程。

1.3 SEEMP 由三部分构成：

1.3.1 本导则第3、4和5节涉及《防污公约》附则Ⅵ第26.1条要求的 SEEMP 第Ⅰ部分的指南。该部分的目的是提供监测船舶和船队在一段时间内能效的方法，并描述改善船舶能效性能和碳强度的方式。SEEMP 第Ⅰ部分适用于400 GT 及以上的任何船舶。

1.3.2 本导则第6、7和8节涉及《防污公约》附则Ⅵ第26.2条要求的 SEEMP 第Ⅱ部分的指南。该部分的目的是提供用于收集按《防污公约》附则Ⅵ第27条要求的数据方法和船舶用于向船舶主管机关或经其正式授权的任一组织报告数据的流程说明。SEEMP 第Ⅱ部分适用于5 000 GT 及以上的任何船舶。

1.3.3 本导则第9、10、11、12、13、14和15节涉及《防污公约》附则Ⅵ第26.3和28.8条要求的 SEEMP 第Ⅲ部分的指南。该部分指南旨在提供：

.1 应使用的计算《防污公约》附则Ⅵ第28条要求达到的年度营运碳强度指标（CII）的方法描述；

.2 应用于向船舶主管机关或经其正式授权的任一组织报告数据的流程；

.3 未来三年的要求的年度营运 CII；

.4 记录在未来三年内应如何实现要求的年度营运 CII 的实施计划；

.5 自我评估和改进程序；和

.6   for ships rated as D for three consecutive years or rated as E, a plan of corrective actions to achieve the required annual operational CII.

1.4   Part III of the SEEMP applies to any ship of 5,000 GT and above which falls into one or more of the categories in regulations 2.2.5, 2.2.7, 2.2.9, 2.2.11, 2.2.14 to 2.2.16, 2.2.22, and 2.2.26 to 2.2.29 of MARPOL Annex VI.

1.5   Sample forms of the various sections of the SEEMP are presented in appendices 1, 2, and 3 for illustrative purposes. A standardized data-reporting format for the data collection system and operational carbon intensity is presented in appendix 4. A standardized data reporting format for the trial carbon intensity indicators on voluntary basis is presented in appendix 5.

2   DEFINITIONS

2.1   For the purpose of these Guidelines, the definitions in MARPOL Annex VI apply.

2.2   "Ship fuel oil consumption data" means the data required to be collected on an annual basis and reported as specified in appendix IX to MARPOL Annex VI.

2.3   "Safety management system" means a structured and documented system enabling company personnel to implement effectively the company safety and environmental protection policy, as defined in paragraph 1.1 of International Safety Management Code.

2.4   "Carbon Intensity Indicator" means a performance indicator by which it is possible to measure the carbon intensity of the ship, as defined in the guidelines developed by the Organization,[1] taking into account data listed for reporting in appendix IX to MARPOL Annex VI.

2.5   *Consumer type* means a type of engine or set of engines, boiler, fuel cell or others used for the same purpose.

PART I OF THE SEEMP: SHIP MANAGEMENT PLAN TO IMPROVE ENERGY EFFICIENCY

3   GENERAL

3.1   Regulation 26.1 of MARPOL Annex VI requires each ship of 400 gross tonnage and above, subject to chapter 4 to keep on board a ship-specific Ship Energy Efficiency Management Plan (SEEMP).

3.2   The purpose of part I of the SEEMP is to establish a mechanism for a company and/or a ship to improve the energy efficiency and reduce the carbon intensity of a ship's operation. Preferably, this aspect of the ship-specific SEEMP is linked to a broader corporate energy management policy for the company that owns, operates or controls the ship, recognizing that no two shipping companies are the same, and that ships operate under a wide range of different conditions.

3.3   Many companies will already have an environmental management system (EMS) in place under ISO 14001 which contains procedures for selecting the best measures for particular ships and then setting objectives for the measurement of relevant parameters, along with relevant control and feedback features. Monitoring of operational environmental efficiency should therefore be treated as an integral element of broader company management systems.

---

[1]   Refer to the *2021 Guidelines on operational carbon intensity indicators and the calculation methods (CII guidelines, G1)* (Resolution MEPC.336(76)) and the *2022 Guidelines on correction factors and voyage adjustments for CII calculations (G5)* (Resolution MEPC.355(78)).

.6 对于连续三年被评为 D 级或被评为 E 级的船舶，为达到要求的年度营运 CII 的整改行动计划。

1.4 SEEMP 第Ⅲ部分适用于 5 000 GT 及以上且属于《防污公约》附则Ⅵ第 2.2.5、2.2.7、2.2.9、2.2.11、2.2.14 至 2.2.16、2.2.22 以及 2.2.26 至 2.2.29 条中的一个或多个类别的任何船舶。

1.5 附录 1、2 和 3 提供了用作示范作用的 SEEMP 各节的格式样本。附录 4 提供了用于数据收集系统和营运碳强度的标准数据报告格式。附录 5 提供了用于自愿试用碳强度指标的标准数据报告格式。

2 定义

2.1 就本导则而言，《防污公约》附则Ⅵ中的定义适用。

2.2 "船舶燃油消耗数据"系指按《防污公约》附则Ⅵ附录Ⅸ规定要求每年收集和报告的数据。

2.3 "安全管理体系"系指《国际安全管理规则》的第 1.1 款中定义的能使公司人员有效实施公司的安全及环境保护政策的结构化和文件化的体系。

2.4 "碳强度指标"系指性能指标，由此可测量本组织制定的导则[1]中定义的碳强度，并考虑到《防污公约》附则Ⅵ附录Ⅸ中用于报告列出的数据。

2.5 燃油消耗设备类型系指一种类型的发动机或一组发动机、锅炉、燃料电池或具有相同用途的其他设备。

SEEMP 第Ⅰ部分：提高能效的船舶管理计划

3 总则

3.1 《防污公约》附则Ⅵ第 26.1 条要求，受第 4 章约束的每艘 400 总吨及以上船舶应在船上保存一份针对船舶具体的船舶能效管理计划（SEEMP）。

3.2 SEEMP 第Ⅰ部分的目的是为公司和 / 或船舶建立提高船舶营运能效和降低碳强度的机制。认识到没有两个航运公司是一样的且船舶在各种不同条件下营运，船舶具体的 SEEMP 的这个方面最好与拥有、经营或控制船舶的公司的更广泛的能源管理政策关联起来。

3.3 许多公司已根据 ISO 14001 具有适当的环境管理系统（EMS），其包含为特定船舶选择最好的方法然后设定目标测量相关参数的程序，以及相关控制和反馈功能。因此，作为环保效能的监测应视作更广泛的公司管理系统的组成项。

---

[1] 参见《2021 年营运碳强度指标和计算方法导则》（CII 导则，G1）（第 MEPC.336（76）号决议）和《2022 年 CII 计算的修止系数和航次调整临时导则》（G5）（第 MEPC.355（78）号决议）。

3.4 In addition, many companies already develop, implement and maintain a safety management system. In such case, part I of SEEMP may form part of the ship's safety management system.

3.5 This section provides guidance for the development of part I of SEEMP that should be adjusted to the characteristics and needs of individual companies and ships. Part I of the SEEMP is intended to be a management tool to assist a company in managing the ongoing environmental performance of its ships and, as such, it is recommended that a company develop procedures for implementing the plan in a manner which limits any onboard administrative burden to the minimum necessary.

3.6 Part I of the SEEMP should be developed as a ship-specific plan by the company, and should reflect efforts to improve the energy efficiency and reduce carbon intensity of a ship through four steps: planning, implementation, monitoring, and self-evaluation and improvement. These components play a critical role in the continuous cycle to improve ship energy efficiency management and reduce its carbon intensity. With each iteration of the cycle, some elements of part I will necessarily change while others may remain as before.

3.7 At all times safety considerations should be paramount. The trade a ship is engaged in may determine the feasibility of the energy efficiency and carbon intensity reduction measures under consideration. For example, ships that perform services at sea (pipe laying, seismic survey, OSVs, dredgers, etc.) may choose different methods of improving energy efficiency when compared to conventional cargo carriers. The nature of operations and influence of prevailing weather conditions, tides and currents combined with the necessity of maintaining safe operations may require adjustment of general procedures to maintain the efficiency of the operation, for example the ships which are dynamically positioned. The length of a voyage and the need to avoid high risk areas may also be important parameters as well as trade specific safety considerations.

4 FRAMEWORK AND STRUCTURE OF PART I OF THE SEEMP

4.1 Planning

4.1.1 Planning is the most crucial stage of part I of theSEEMP, in that it primarily determines both the current status of ship energy usage and carbon intensity and the expected improvement of ship energy efficiency and reduction of carbon intensity. Therefore, it is encouraged to devote sufficient time to planning so that the most appropriate, effective and implementable plan can be developed.

Ship-specific measures

4.1.2 Recognizing that there are a variety of options to improve energy efficiency and reduce carbon intensity (e.g. speed optimization, confirming berth availability and arrival time with port of destination, weather routeing, hull maintenance, retrofitting of energy efficiency devices, and use of alternative fuels), the best package of measures for a ship to improve energy efficiency and reduce carbon intensity depends to a great extent upon ship type, cargoes, routes and other factors that should be identified in the first place. These measures should be listed as a package of measures to be implemented, thus providing the overview of the actions to be taken for that ship.

4.1.3 During the planning process, therefore, it is important to determine and understand the ship's current status of energy usage. Part I of the SEEMP should identify energy-saving and carbon intensity reducing measures that already have been undertaken, and should determine how effective these measures are in terms of improving energy efficiency and

3.4 此外，许多公司已制定、实施和保持安全管理体系。在此情况下，SEEMP 第 I 部分可构成船舶安全管理体系的一部分。

3.5 本章节为 SEEMP 第 I 部分的编制提供指南，其应根据各个公司和船舶的特性和需要进行调整。第 I 部分旨在成为一个管理工具以帮助公司管理船舶的现有环保行为，因此建议公司以将船上的行政负担降至所需最低限度的方式制定执行计划的程序。

3.6 SEEMP 第 I 部分应作为船舶具体计划由公司编制并应体现力图通过 4 个步骤提高船舶能效和降低碳强度：计划、执行、监测、自我评估和改进。这些组成部分在提高船舶能效管理和降低碳强度的连续周期中起到重要作用。随着这些步骤的每次循环，第 I 部分的某些因素有必要改变，而其他则可保持不变。

3.7 安全应一直是首要考虑项。船舶从事的贸易可决定所考虑的能效和降低碳强度措施的可行性。例如，在海上进行服务（管道铺设、地震勘测、近海供应船、挖泥船等）的船舶可选择与常规货物运输船不同的能效改进方法。营运的性质和主导天气情况、潮汐和波浪的影响结合保持安全营运的必要性可能要求调整总体程序以保持营运的效率，例如，动力定位船舶。如同贸易特定安全考虑，航程的长度和避免高风险区域的必要性也可能是重要的参数。

4　SEEMP 第 I 部分的框架和结构

4.1　计划

4.1.1 计划是 SEEMP 第 I 部分最关键的阶段，主要由其确定船舶能源使用和碳强度的当前状况以及船舶能效的预期提高和碳强度的降低。因此，鼓励用足够的时间进行计划以编制最合适、有效和可实施的计划。

船舶特定措施

4.1.2 认识到有许多提高能效和降低碳强度的选项（例如航速优化，与目的港确认泊位可用性和到达时间，气象航线划定，船体保养，能效装置改装，和使用替代燃料），船舶提高能效和降低碳强度的最佳系列措施在很大程度上取决于船型、货物、航线和应首先确定的其他因素。这些措施应作为所要执行的系列措施列出，从而提供该船应采取行动的大致情况。

4.1.3 因此在计划过程期间，重要的是确定和理解船舶现状和能源使用情况。SEEMP 第 I 部分应指出已采取的节能和降低碳强度措施，并应确定这些措施对于提高能效和降低碳强度如何有效。第 I 部分还应指出能采取什么措施来进一步提高船舶能效和降低碳强度。

reducing carbon intensity. Part I also should identify what measures can be adopted to further improve the energy efficiency and reduce the carbon intensity of the ship. It should be noted, however, that not all measures can be applied to all ships, or even to the same ship under different operating conditions and that some of them are mutually exclusive. Ideally, initial measures could yield energy (and cost) saving results that then can be reinvested in more difficult or expensive efficiency upgrades identified by part I.

4.1.4   Guidance on best practices for fuel-efficient operation of ships, set out in chapter 5, can be used to facilitate this part of the planning phase. Also, in the planning process, particular consideration should be given to minimize any onboard administrative burden.

Company-specific measures

4.1.5   The improvement of energy efficiency and reduction of carbon intensity of ship operation does not necessarily depend on single ship management only. Rather, it may depend on many stakeholders including ship repair yards, shipowners, operators, charterers, cargo owners, fuel suppliers, ports and traffic management services. For example, "just in time" - as explained in paragraph 5.2.4 - requires good early communication among operators, ports and traffic management services. The better the coordination among such stakeholders, the more improvement can be expected. In most cases, such coordination or total management is better made by a company rather than by a ship. In this sense, it is recommended that a company should also establish an energy efficiency and carbon intensity management plan to improve the performance of its fleet (should it not have one in place already) and make necessary coordination among stakeholders.

Human resource development

4.1.6   For effective and steady implementation of the adopted measures, raising awareness of and providing necessary training for personnel both onshore and on board are an important element. Such human resource development is encouraged and should be considered as an important component of planning as well as a critical element of implementation.

Goal setting

4.1.7   The last part of planning is goal setting.

.1   For ships also subject to regulation 28 of MARPOL Annex VI, the goal setting should be consistent with the continuous CII improvements set out by that regulation, and should include the relevant information (see paragraph 9.7). These ships are also encouraged to consider setting ship-specific goals in addition to the applicable CII requirements that strive for additional energy efficiency improvements and carbon intensity reductions.

.2   For ships or companies not subject to regulation 28, there are no requirements to define a goal and to communicate it to the public, or to be a subject to external inspection, surveys, or audits with respect to the SEEMP. Nevertheless, a meaningful goal should be defined to serve as a signal on a company's commitment to improve the energy efficiency and carbon intensity of the ship. The goal can be set using different indicators, including the annual fuel consumption, Annual Efficiency Ratio (AER), cgDIST, Energy

但是，应注意到所有措施并非对所有船舶，甚至并非对处于不同营运条件下的同一船舶都适用，且它们中的一些是互相排斥的。理想的状况是，最初的措施所带来的节能（和节约成本）的效果能转用于第 I 部分确定的更困难或昂贵的能效升级。

4.1.4 可使用第 5 章中的实现船舶营运燃油效率的最佳操作指南，以便利计划阶段的这一部分。同样，在计划过程中，应特别考虑将船上的行政负担降至最低。

公司特定措施

4.1.5 船舶营运能效的提高和碳强度的降低不一定只取决于单船管理，而是取决于许多利益相关方，包括船舶修理厂、船东、船舶经营者，租船方、货主、燃料供方、港口和交通管理服务机构。例如，第 5.2.4 段中所述的"及时"要求船舶经营者、港口和交通管理服务机构之间良好的早期沟通。此类利益相关方协调地越好，可预期的改进越多。在大多数情况下，最好由公司而不是船舶进行这种协调或整体管理。在这种意义上，建议公司也制订能效和碳强度管理计划以提高其船队的表现（如尚未有此计划）并在利益相关方之间进行必要的协调。

人力资源开发

4.1.6 为了有效和稳定地执行所采取的措施，增强岸上和船上人员的意识并向其提供必要的培训是一个重要因素。此类人力资源开发应予以鼓励并应视作计划重要的组成部分及实施的关键因素。

设定目标

4.1.7 计划的最后部分是设定目标。

　　.1　对于还受《防污公约》附则Ⅵ第 28 条约束的船舶，目标设定应与该条规定的持续 CII 改进相一致，并应包括相关信息（见第 9.7 段）。除了适用的 CII 要求外，还鼓励这些船舶考虑设定船舶特定目标，从而争取额外的能效提高和碳强度降低。

　　.2　对于不受第 28 条约束的船舶或公司，没有要求其明确并公布目标，或接受与 SEEMP 相关的外部检查、检验或审核。但是，应设定有意义的目标，作为公司承诺提高船舶能效和降低碳强度的信号。可使用不同的指标来设定目标，包括

Efficiency Operational Indicator (EEOI) or other carbon intensity indicators (CIIs).[2] In all cases, the goal should be measurable and easy to understand.

4.2   Implementation

Establishment of implementation system

4.2.1   After a ship and a company identify the energy efficiency and carbon intensity measures to be implemented, it is essential to establish a system for their implementation. This is done by developing the procedures for energy management, defining tasks associated with those procedures, and assigning those tasks to responsible personnel. The implementation system should include procedures to ensure execution of measures and specify defined levels of authority and lines of communication. Also, it should include procedures for internal audits and management review, where relevant. In sum, part I of the SEEMP should describe how each measure should be implemented and who the responsible person or persons are. The implementation period (start and end dates) of each selected measure should be indicated. The development of such an implementation system can be considered as a part of planning, and therefore may be completed at the planning stage.

Implementation and record-keeping

4.2.2   The planned measures should be carried out in accordance with the predetermined implementation system. Record-keeping for the implementation of each measure is beneficial for self-evaluation at a later stage and should be encouraged. If any identified measure cannot be implemented for any reason, the reason or reasons should be recorded for internal use. It is recommended that events and operational conditions outside the control of the ship's crew (for example, waiting for berths, extended port dwell times, operation in severe adverse weather) which may affect the ships rating be documented.

4.3   Monitoring

Monitoring tools

4.3.1   The energy efficiency of a ship should be monitored quantitatively. This should be done by an established method, preferably by an international standard. In many cases, the monitoring tool should target the goal indicator set out in paragraph 4.1.7 (e.g. AER, cgDIST, EEOI, or other CIIs as agreed by the Organization). If a quantitative goal is not defined for a ship, a quantitative performance indicator developed by the Organization (e.g. AER, EEOI, CII) or another internationally established tool should be selected. A ship subject to regulation 28 is likely to use the CII as its monitoring tool.

4.3.2   If used, these CIIs should be calculated in accordance with the guidelines developed by the Organization,[3] adjusted, as necessary, to a specific ship and trade.

4.3.3   Ships subject to regulation 28 may use other measurement tools in addition to the CII, if convenient and/or beneficial for a ship or a company. In the case where other monitoring

---

[2]   Refer to the *2022 Guidelines on operational carbon intensity indicators and the calculation methods (CII guidelines, G1)* (Resolution MEPC.352(78)) and the *2022 Interim guidelines on correction factors and voyage adjustments for CII calculations (G5)* (Resolution MEPC.355(78)).

[3]   Refer to the *Guidelines for voluntary use of the ship energy efficiency operational indicator (EEOI)* (MEPC.1/Circ.684) and the *2022 Guidelines on operational carbon intensity indicators and the calculation methods (CII guidelines, G1)* (Resolution MEPC.352(78)) and the *2022 Interim guidelines on correction factors and voyage adjustments for CII calculations (G5)* (Resolution MEPC.355(78)).

年度燃料消耗、年度效率比（AER）、cgDIST、能效营运指数（EEOI）或其他碳强度指标（CII）[2]。在所有情况下，目标应可测量且易理解。

4.2 执行

建立实施体系

4.2.1 在船舶和公司确定要实施的能效和碳强度措施后，需要建立实施体系，可通过制定能源管理程序。还应包括内审和管理评审的程序，如相关。总而言之，SEEMP 第 I 部分应描述每个措施应如何执行以及由谁负责。应说明每个所选措施的执行期限（开始和结束日期）。该执行体系的制订可视作计划的一部分，因此可在计划阶段完成。

执行和保存记录

4.2.2 应按照预先确定的执行体系实行计划的措施。保存每个措施的执行记录有助于在下一阶段进行自我评估并应予以鼓励。如果确定的措施由于任何原因不能执行，该原因应予以记录供内部使用。建议记录不受船员控制、可能影响船舶评级的事件和操作条件（例如，等待泊位、延长港口停留时间、恶劣天气下的操作）。

4.3 监测

监测工具

4.3.1 船舶能效应定量监测。这应通过确定的方法进行，最好按照国际标准。在许多情况下，监测工具应针对第 4.1.7 段中规定的目标指标（例如，AER、cgDIST、EEOI 或本组织同意的其他 CIIs）。如果没有为船舶定义一个量化目标，应选择本组织制定的定量绩效指标（例如，AER、EEOI、CII）或其他国际公认的工具。受第 28 条约束的船舶可能会使用 CII 作为其监测工具。

4.3.2 如使用 CII 作为监测工具，应按照本组织制定的导则[3]进行计算，并在必要时根据特定船舶和贸易进行调整。

4.3.3 除 CII 外，如果便于和 / 或有益于船舶或公司，受第 28 条约束的船舶可使用其他测

---

[2] 参见《2022 年营运碳强度指标和计算方法导则》（CII 导则，G1）（第 MEPC.352（78）号决议）和《2022 年 CII 计算的修正系数和航次调整临时导则》（G5）（第 MEPC.355（78）号决议）。

[3] 参见《船舶能效营运指数（EEOI）自愿使用导则》（MEPC.1/Circ.684）和《2022 年营运碳强度指标和计算方法 导则》（CII 导则，G1）（第 MEPC.352（78）号决议）和《2022 年 CII 计算的修正系数和航次调整临时导则》（G5）（第 MEPC.355（78）号决议）。

tools are used, the reason for the use of the tool and the method of monitoring should be clarified at the planning stage.

4.3.4   It is highly advised to conduct monitoring at regular intervals for checking consistency of data and verification assistance. The ship's fuel oil consumption should be monitored using daily reporting, such as noon reports, or higher frequency data.

Establishment of monitoring system

4.3.5   It should be noted that whatever measurement tools are used, continuous and consistent and reliable data collection is the foundation of monitoring. To allow for meaningful and consistent monitoring, a monitoring system, including the procedures for collecting data and the assignment of responsible personnel, should be developed. The development of such a system can be considered as a part of planning, and therefore should be completed at the planning stage.

4.3.6   It should be noted that, in order to avoid unnecessary administrative burdens on ships' staff, monitoring should be carried out as much as possible by shore staff when the data can be automatically transferred, utilizing data obtained from existing required records such as the official and engineering logbooks and oil record books. Additional data could be obtained as appropriate.

Search and rescue

4.3.7   When a ship diverts from its scheduled passage to engage in search and rescue operations, and for which emissions are excluded pursuant to regulation 3, it is recommended that data obtained during such operations is not used in ship energy efficiency monitoring, and that such data should be recorded separately.

4.4   Self-evaluation and improvement

4.4.1   Self-evaluation and improvement is the final phase of the management cycle. This phase should produce meaningful feedback for the coming first stage, i e planning stage of the next improvement cycle.

4.4.2   The purpose of self-evaluation is to:

.1   evaluate the effectiveness of the planned measures and their implementation;

.2   deepen the understanding of the overall characteristics of the ship's operation such as what types of measures can or cannot function effectively, and how and/or why;

.3   comprehend the trend of the efficiency improvement of that ship; and

.4   develop the improved management plan for the next cycle through identification of further opportunities for improving energy efficiency and reducing carbon intensity.

4.4.3   For this process, procedures for self-evaluation of the ship energy efficiency management plan should be developed. Furthermore, self-evaluation should be implemented periodically by using data collected through monitoring. In addition, it is recommended that time be invested in identifying the cause and effect of the performance during the evaluated

量工具。如果使用其他监测工具，可在计划阶段确定使用该工具的原因和监测方法。

4.3.4 强烈建议定期进行监测，以检查数据的一致性和验证协助。应使用每日报告（例如中午报告或更高频率的数据）监测船舶的燃油消耗量。

建立监测系统

4.3.5 应注意到不管使用什么测量工具，连续一贯和可靠的数据收集是监测的基础。为能进行有意义且一致的监测，应开发监测系统（包括收集数据和指派相关责任人员的程序）。这种系统的开发可视作计划的一部分，因此应在计划阶段完成。

4.3.6 应注意到为了避免对船上员工造成不必要的行政负担，当可自动传输数据时，应尽可能由岸上员工使用从要求的现有记录（例如航行日志和轮机日志及油类记录簿等）获得的数据进行监测。可视具体情况获得附加数据。

搜救

4.3.7 当船舶偏离其预定航线进行搜救作业时，并根据（MARPOL 附则Ⅵ）第 3 条，此类排放不包括在内，建议搜救作业期间获得的数据不在船舶能效监测中使用，其可分开记录。

4.4 自我评估和改进

4.4.1 自我评估和改进是管理周期的最后阶段。该阶段应为接下来的第 1 阶段（即下一个改进周期的计划阶段）提供有意义的反馈。

4.4.2 自我评估的目的是：

.1 评估计划的措施的有效性及其执行情况；

.2 深化对船舶营运的整体特性的理解，诸如何种类型的措施能 / 不能有效运行，以及如何和 / 或为什么不能有效运行；

.3 了解该船能效改进的趋势；和

.4 通过识别提高能效和降低碳强度的进一步机会，编制下一周期改进的管理计划。

4.4.3 对于此过程，应制定船舶能效管理自我评估的程序。此外，应通过使用监测收集到的数据定期进行自我评估。另外，建议在评估期间花时间确定能效水平的因果，从而在修

period so lessons learned can be taken into account when revising and improving the next stage of the ship's energy efficiency management plan.

5   GUIDANCE ON BEST PRACTICES FOR FUEL-EFFICIENT OPERATION OF SHIPS

5.1   The search for energy efficiency and carbon intensity improvement across the entire transport chain takes responsibility beyond what can be delivered by the company alone. A list of all the possible stakeholders in the efficiency of a single voyage is long: obvious parties are designers, shipyards and engine manufacturers for the characteristics of the ship; and charterers, fuel suppliers, ports and vessel traffic management services, etc. for the specific voyage. All parties involved should consider the inclusion of efficiency measures in their operations both individually and collectively.

5.2   Fuel-efficient operations

Improved voyage planning

5.2.1   The optimum route and improved efficiency can be achieved through the careful planning and execution of voyages. Thorough voyage planning needs time, but a number of software tools are available to assist in voyage planning.

5.2.2   The *Guidelines for voyage planning*, adopted by resolution A.893(21), provide essential guidance for the ship's crew and voyage planners.

Weather routeing

5.2.3   Weather routeing has a high potential for efficiency savings on specific routes. It is commercially available for all types of ship and for many trade areas.

Just in time

5.2.4   Good early communication with the next port should be an aim in order to give maximum notice of berth availability and facilitate the use of optimum speed where port operational procedures support this approach.

5.2.5   Optimized port operation could involve a change in procedures involving different ship handling arrangements in ports. Port authorities should be encouraged to maximize efficiency and minimize delay.

Speed optimization

5.2.6   Speed optimization can produce significant savings. However, optimum speed means the speed at which the fuel used per tonne mile is at a minimum level for that voyage. It does not mean minimum speed; in fact, sailing at less than optimum speed will consume more fuel rather than less. Reference should be made to the engine manufacturer's power/consumption curve and the ship's propeller curve. Possible adverse consequences of slow speed operation may include increased vibration and problems with soot deposits in combustion chambers and exhaust systems. These possible consequences should be taken into account. For LNG carriers speed optimization means, quite often, a higher speed at the start of laden passages to control tanks pressure and at the end of ballast passages to use the operational LNG quantity needed for cargo tank cooling in propulsion instead of wasting in GCU or condenser steam dump. Charterers are generally aware of the improved efficiency of this speed pattern.

订和完善船舶能效管理计划的下一阶段时考虑获得的经验。

5 船舶节能营运的最佳操作指南

5.1 整个运输链中的寻求能效和碳强度改善承担的责任超过了公司所能单独行使的职责范围。在单个航次的能效方面，所有可能的利益攸关方很多，对于船舶特征，明显的相关方为设计者、船厂和发动机制造商，对于特定航次，明显的相关方为租船方、燃料供应方、港口和船舶交通管理服务机构等。所有相关方应各自或共同考虑在其营运中纳入能效措施。

5.2 提高燃油效率的营运

改进的航次计划

5.2.1 最佳航线和改进的能效可通过仔细地计划和执行航次来实现。考虑周全的航次计划需要时间，但是，可使用许多软件工具进行航次计划。

5.2.2 以第 A.893（21）号决议通过的《航次计划导则》为船员和航次计划者提供了极为重要的指导。

气象航线划定

5.2.3 气象航线划定对特定航线上的节能有很大潜力。这对于所有类型船舶和许多贸易区域都能以付费方式得到。

及时

5.2.4 应将与下一港口良好的早期沟通设为目标，以便在港口作业程序支持这一做法时，最大限度告知泊位的可用性并便于使用最佳航速。

5.2.5 最佳港口作业会涉及包括港口不同船舶装卸装置的程序变化。应鼓励港口当局最大限度提高效率并将船期延误减至最低。

航速优化

5.2.6 航速优化有显著节能收益。但是，最佳航速意味着在该航速下，航行时每吨海里使用的燃料最少。最佳航速并不是指最小航速；实际上，以小于最佳航速的速度航行会消耗更多的燃料而不是更少的燃料。应参照发动机制造商的功率／燃油消耗曲线和船舶螺旋桨曲线。低速运行可能的负面后果可包括振动增加以及燃烧室和排气系统的积炭问题。这些可能的后果应予以考虑。对于 LNG 运输船的航速优化，通常意味着在满载开始时提高速度以控制液舱压力，并在压载结束时使用液货舱冷却所需 LNG 量进行推进，而不是浪费在 GCU 或冷凝器蒸汽排放。租船方普遍意识到这种速度模式的效率提高。

5.2.7   As part of the speed optimization process, due account may need to be taken of the need to coordinate arrival times with the availability of loading/discharge berths, etc. The number of ships engaged in a particular trade route may need to be taken into account when considering speed optimization.

5.2.8   A gradual increase in speed when leaving a port or estuary whilst keeping the engine load within certain limits may help to reduce fuel consumption.

5.2.9   It is recognized that under many charter parties the speed of the ships is determined by the charterer and not the operator. Efforts should be made when agreeing charter party terms to encourage the ship to operate at optimum speed in order to maximize energy efficiency.

Optimized shaft power

5.2.10   Operation at constant shaft RPM can be more efficient than continuously adjusting speed through engine power. The use of automated engine management systems to control speed rather than relying on human intervention may be beneficial.

5.2.11   When optimizing shaft power, due attention should be given to overall power system efficiency. For example, in some cases reducing load or shaft speed below the minimum necessary to operate energy recovery systems and shaft generators may increase overall emissions.

5.3   Optimized ship handling

Optimum trim

5.3.1   Most ships are designed to carry a designated amount of cargo at a certain speed for a certain fuel consumption. This implies the specification of set trim conditions. Loaded or unloaded, trim has a significant influence on the resistance of the ship through the water and optimizing trim can deliver significant fuel savings. For any given draft there is a trim condition that gives minimum resistance. In some ships, it is possible to assess optimum trim conditions for fuel efficiency continuously throughout the voyage. Design or safety factors may preclude full use of trim optimization.

Optimum ballast

5.3.2   Ballast should be adjusted taking into consideration the requirements to meet optimum trim and steering conditions and optimum ballast conditions achieved through good cargo planning.

5.3.3   When determining the optimum ballast conditions, the limits, conditions and ballast management arrangements set out in the ship's Ballast Water Management Plan are to be observed for that ship.

5.3.4   Ballast conditions have a significant impact on steering conditions and autopilot settings, and it needs to be noted that less ballast water does not necessarily mean improved energy efficiency.

Optimum propeller and propeller inflow considerations

5.3.5   Selection of the propeller is normally determined at the design and construction stage of a ship's life but new developments in propeller design have made it possible for retrofitting of later designs to deliver greater fuel economy. Whilst it is certainly for consideration, the

5.2.7 作为航速优化过程的一部分，需要适当考虑协调到达时间和装卸泊位可用性的必要性。考虑航速优化时，可能需要考虑从事某些贸易航线的船舶数量。

5.2.8 离开港口或河口时航速的逐渐增加并将发动机载荷保持在一定限度内可有助于减少燃料消耗。

5.2.9 认识到根据许多租船合同，航速是由租船方而不是船舶经营者确定的。在达成租船合同时应尽力鼓励船舶以最佳航速营运以使能效最大。

最佳轴功率

5.2.10 以恒定的轴每分钟转速（RPM）营运较之通过发动机功率连续调整航速的营运效率更高。使用发动机自动管理系统控制航速而不是依赖人为介入可能是有益的。

5.2.11 在优化轴功率时，应适当注意整个动力系统的效率。例如，在某些情况下，如将负载或轴速降低到运行能量回收系统和轴带发电机所需的最低值以下，可能会增加总排放量。

5.3 最佳船舶操纵

最佳纵倾

5.3.1 大多数船舶设计成以一定的航速和一定的燃油消耗量载运指定数量的货物。这意味着对所设各个纵倾状态作出规定。不管是装货还是卸货，纵倾对船舶对水移动的阻力有很大影响，优化纵倾能节省很多燃料。对于任何给定的吃水，都有一个纵倾状态实现最小的阻力。在一些船舶中，评定整个航程期间燃油效率的最佳纵倾状态是可能的。设计或安全因素会阻碍充分使用纵倾最优化。

最佳压载

5.3.2 调整压载时，应考虑到满足通过良好的货物计划达到最佳纵倾和操舵状态以及最佳压载状态的要求。

5.3.3 确定最佳压载状态时，船舶应遵循其压载水管理计划中规定的限制、条件和压载管理安排。

5.3.4 压载状态对操舵状态和自动操舵仪的设定有很大影响，需要注意较少的压载水并不意味着能效提高。

螺旋桨优化和螺旋桨进水因素

5.3.5 螺旋桨的选择通常在船舶设计和建造阶段确定，但螺旋桨设计的新发展已使翻新设

propeller is but one part of the propulsion train and a change of propeller in isolation may have no effect on efficiency and may even increase fuel consumption.

5.3.6   Improvements to the water inflow to the propeller using arrangements such as fins and/or nozzles could increase propulsive efficiency power and hence reduce fuel consumption.

Optimum use of rudder and heading control systems (autopilots)

5.3.7   There have been large improvements in automated heading and steering control systems technology. Whilst originally developed to make the bridge team more effective, modern autopilots can achieve much more. An integrated Navigation and Command System can achieve significant fuel savings by simply reducing the distance sailed "off track". The principle is simple: better course control through less frequent and smaller corrections will minimize losses due to rudder resistance. Retrofitting of a more efficient autopilot to existing ships could be considered.

5.3.8   During approaches to ports and pilot stations the autopilot cannot always be used efficiently as the rudder has to respond quickly to given commands. Furthermore, at certain stages of the voyage it may have to be deactivated or very carefully adjusted, i.e. during heavy weather and approaches to ports.

5.3.9   Consideration may be given to the retrofitting of improved rudder blade design (e.g. "twist-flow" rudder).

Hull maintenance

5.3.10   Docking intervals should be integrated with the company's ongoing assessment of ship performance. Hull resistance can be optimized by new technology-coating systems, possibly in combination with cleaning intervals. Regular in-water inspection of the condition of the hull is recommended.

5.3.11   Propeller cleaning and polishing or even appropriate coating may significantly increase fuel efficiency. The need for ships to maintain efficiency through in-water hull cleaning should be recognized and facilitated by port States.

5.3.12   Consideration may be given to the possibility of timely full removal and replacement of underwater paint systems to avoid the increased hull roughness caused by repeated spot blasting and repairs over multiple dockings.

5.3.13   Generally, the smoother the hull, the better the fuel efficiency.

Propulsion system

5.3.14   Marine diesel engines have a very high thermal efficiency (~50%). This excellent performance is only exceeded by fuel cell technology with an average thermal efficiency of 60%. This is due to the systematic minimization of heat and mechanical loss. In particular, the new breed of electronic controlled engines can provide efficiency gains. However, specific training for relevant staff may need to be considered to maximize the benefits.

计以更节约燃料成为可能。虽然这无疑是仅供考虑，但螺旋桨只是推进序列的一部分，单独改变螺旋桨可能对效率没有影响并可能增加燃油消耗量。

5.3.6 使用一些装置（例如鳍和／或喷嘴）改善螺旋桨进水会增加有效推进功率并减少燃料消耗。

舵和航向控制系统（自动操舵仪）的最佳使用

5.3.7 自动航向和操舵控制系统技术已有很大改进。虽然最初是用来使驾驶台团队更有效率，但现代自动操舵仪能实现更多功能。综合航行和指挥系统单凭减少"偏离轨道"航行距离就能节省大量的燃料。原理很简单：通过较少和较小的修正进行较好的航向控制可将由于舵阻力造成的损失降至最低。可考虑在现有船舶上改装更有效的自动操舵仪。

5.3.8 在接近港口和领航站期间，由于舵必须对收到的命令快速做出反应，自动操舵仪不能总是高效使用。而且在航行的某个阶段，自动操舵仪可能不得不停用或非常仔细地予以调整，即恶劣天气和临近港口时。

5.3.9 可考虑安装改进的舵叶设计（例如"扭流"舵）。

船体保养

5.3.10 进坞周期应与船舶经营者对船舶性能进行的评估结合在一起。船体阻力可通过新技术—涂层系统进行优化，可能与清洁周期结合在一起。建议对船体状况进行定期的水下检查。

5.3.11 螺旋桨的清洁和抛光或甚至适当的涂层会大大提高燃料能效。港口国应认识到船舶通过水下船体清洁保持能效的必要性并为此提供便利。

5.3.12 可考虑及时完全去除和更换水下油漆系统的可能性以避免重复的点喷砂和多次进坞修理引起的船体粗糙度增加。

5.3.13 一般来说，船体越平滑，燃料效率越好。

推进系统

5.3.14 船用柴油机具有很高的热效率（~50%）。这一出色性能仅次于平均热效率达到60%的燃料电池技术。这是由于系统地将热量和机械损失降至最低。特别是，新式的电子控制发动机能提高效率。但是，可能需要考虑相关员工的特殊培训以将效益最大化。

Propulsion system maintenance

5.3.15 Maintenance in accordance with manufacturers' instructions in the company's planned maintenance schedule will also maintain efficiency. The use of engine condition monitoring can be a useful tool to maintain high efficiency.

5.3.16 Additional means to improve engine efficiency might include use of fuel additives, adjustment of cylinder lubrication oil consumption, valve improvements, torque analysis, and automated engine monitoring systems.

5.4   Waste heat recovery

5.4.1   Waste heat recovery systems use thermal heat losses from the exhaust gas for either electricity generation, heating or additional propulsion with a shaft power take in.

5.4.2   It may not be possible to retrofit such systems into existing ships. However, they may be a beneficial option for new ships. Shipbuilders should be encouraged to incorporate new technology into their designs.

5.5   Improved fleet management

5.5.1   Better utilization of fleet capacity can often be achieved by improvements in fleet planning. For example, it may be possible to avoid or reduce long ballast voyages through improved fleet planning. There is opportunity here for charterers to promote efficiency. This can be closely related to the concept of "just in time" arrivals.

5.5.2   Efficiency, reliability and maintenance-oriented data sharing within a company can be used to promote best practice among ships within a company and should be actively encouraged.

5.6   Improved cargo handling

Cargo handling is in most cases under the control of the port or terminal operators and optimum solutions matched to ship and port or terminal requirements should be explored. However, in cases where ships use their own cargo handling equipment (e.g. cargo cranes, self-unloading booms, cargo pumps (tankers)), procedures should be in place to efficiently utilize the energy produced from any additional generators required to operate the equipment.

5.7   Energy management

5.7.1   A review of electrical services on board can reveal the potential for unexpected efficiency gains. However, care should be taken to avoid the creation of new safety hazards when turning off electrical services (e.g. lighting). Thermal insulation is an obvious means of saving energy. Also see comment below on shore power.

5.7.2   Optimization of reefer container stowage locations may be beneficial in reducing the effect of heat transfer from compressor units. This might be combined as appropriate with cargo tank heating, ventilation, etc. The use of water-cooled reefer plant with lower energy consumption might also be considered.

5.8   Fuel type

The use of emerging alternative fuels may be considered as a CO_2 reduction method, but availability will often determine the applicability.

推进系统保养

5.3.15　在公司计划保养日程表中按照制造商的说明书进行的保养也应保持效率。发动机状态监测的使用是一个保持高效的有用工具。

5.3.16　提高发动机能效的附加方法可包括：使用燃料添加剂、调整汽缸润滑油消耗、阀改进、扭矩分析和发动机自动监测系统。

5.4　废热回收

5.4.1　废热回收系统使用来自废气的热损耗进行发电、加热或用轴马达进行附加推进。

5.4.2　可能无法在现有船舶中改装这类系统。但是，这对于新船来说是一个有益的选择。应鼓励船厂在其设计中纳入新技术。

5.5　改进的船队管理

5.5.1　可通过更好地利用船队载运能力实现改进船队计划。例如，有可能通过改进的船队计划避免或减少长压载航程。租船方有机会提高效率。这能与"及时"到达的概念紧密联系起来。

5.5.2　公司内部分享的效率、可靠性和维护数据可用于促进公司船舶之间的最佳实践并应积极鼓励。

5.6　改进的货物装卸

在大多数情况下，货物装卸由港口或码头运营商控制，应探索与船舶和港口或码头要求相适应的最佳解决方案。但是，如果船舶使用自己的货物装卸设备（例如，货物起重机、自动卸货臂、货泵（液货船）），应制定程序以有效利用运行设备所需的任何额外发电机产生的能量。

5.7　能源管理

5.7.1　检查船上供电能发现意想不到的增效潜力。但是，应注意在关闭供电（例如照明）时避免产生新的安全危险。隔热是一种显而易见的节能方式。也参见下列关于岸电的意见。

5.7.2　冷藏集装箱积载位置的最优化对减少压缩机组的传热影响有益。这可视具体情况与货柜加热、通风等结合在一起，也可考虑使用能耗较低的水冷却冷藏装置。

5.8　燃料类型

新出现的替代燃料的使用可视作减少 CO_2 的方法，但可获得性通常决定适用性。

5.9   Other measures

5.9.1   Development of computer software for the calculation of current fuel consumption, for the establishment of an emissions "footprint," to optimize operations, and the establishment of goals for improvement and tracking of progress may be considered.

5.9.2   Renewable energy sources, such as solar (or photovoltaic) cell technology, have improved enormously in recent years and should be considered for onboard application.

5.9.3   In some ports shore power maybe available for some ships but this is generally aimed at improving air quality in the port area. If the shore-based power source is carbon efficient, there may be a net efficiency benefit. Ships may consider using onshore power if available.

5.9.4   Even wind-assisted propulsion may be worthy of consideration. Various systems are available for retrofit, including Flettner rotors, wing sails and aerofoil kites.

5.9.5   Efforts could be made to source fuel of improved quality in order to minimize the amount of fuel required to provide a given power output.

5.10   Compatibility of measures

5.10.1   These Guidelines indicate a wide variety of possibilities for energy efficiency improvements for the existing fleet. While there are many options available, they are not necessarily cumulative, are often area and trade dependent and likely to require the agreement and support of a number of different stakeholders if they are to be utilized most effectively.

Age and operational service life of a ship

5.10.2   All measures identified in this document as applied to part I of the SEEMP are potentially cost-effective in case of high oil prices. The financial feasibility of a specific energy efficiency enhancement can be evaluated by various means. One way would be to estimate the return on investment (ROI) time. However, while measures with lower ROI may have the lowest cost, this does not guarantee the best results in energy efficiency performance improvement. Clearly, this equation is heavily influenced by the remaining service life of a ship and the cost of fuel.

Trade and sailing area

5.10.3   The feasibility of many of the measures described in this guidance will be dependent on the trade and sailing area of the ship. Sometimes ships will change their trade areas as a result of a change in chartering requirements, but this cannot be taken as a general assumption. For example, certain types of wind-enhanced power sources might not be feasible for short sea shipping as these ships generally sail in areas with high traffic densities or in restricted waterways. Air draft limitations may also affect the feasibility of wind assistance technology and certain other emission reduction measures. Another aspect is that the world's oceans and seas each have characteristic conditions and so ships designed for specific routes and trades may not obtain the same energy efficiency benefits by adopting the same measures or combination of measures as other ships that operate in different areas. It is also likely that some measures will have a greater or lesser effect in different sailing areas.

5.10.4   The trade a ship is engaged in may also determine the feasibility of the efficiency measures under consideration. For example, ships that perform services at sea (pipe laying, seismic survey, OSVs, dredgers, etc.) may choose different methods of improving energy efficiency when compared to conventional cargo carriers. The length of voyage may also be an important parameter as may trade specific safety considerations. The pathway to the most efficient combination of measures will be unique to each vessel within each shipping company.

5.9 其他措施

5.9.1 可考虑开发用于计算燃料消耗量、确定排放"足迹"、优化作业以及制定改进目标和跟踪进程的计算机软件。

5.9.2 可再生的能源，例如风、太阳能（或光电）电池技术，已在近年来大大改进，应考虑将其应用于船上。

5.9.3 在一些港口，船舶可使用岸电，但这通常旨在提高港口区域的空气质量。如果岸基电源是具有碳效的，可能有净效益。船舶可考虑使用岸上供电（如可用）。

5.9.4 甚至风力助航也可能值得考虑。有多种系统可供改装，包括弗莱特纳转子、翼帆和翼型风帆。

5.9.5 可尽力寻求质量更高的燃料来源，以将提供给定的功率输出所需的燃料数量降至最低。

5.10 措施的兼容性

5.10.1 本导则指出现有船队能效提高的许多可能性。选项虽然很多，但并非有累加效应，而是通常视区域和贸易而定，如要将其以最有效的方式采用，可能要求许多不同利益相关方的同意和支持。

船龄和船舶营运服务年限

5.10.2 本文件中确定的适用于SEEMP第Ⅰ部分的所有措施，在高油价的情况下都具有潜在的成本效益。可以通过多种方式评估特定能效提升的经济可行性。一种方法是估计投资回报（ROI）时间。然而，虽然投资回报率较低的措施可能成本最低，但这并不能保证能效性能提高的最佳结果。很明显，是否具有成本效益优势在很大程度上受到船舶剩余服务年限和燃料费用的影响。

贸易和航行区域

5.10.3 本导则中许多措施的可行性取决于船舶的贸易和航行区域。有时，船舶会由于租船要求的改变而改变其贸易区域，但这不能作为一般的假定。例如利用某些类型风力增强的能源可能对于短途航运不可行，因为这些船舶通常在高交通密度区域或受到限制的航道中航行。气流限制也可能影响风力辅助技术和某些其他减排措施的可行性。另一个方面是世界各处的海洋各有特定的条件，所以以为特定航线和贸易设计的船舶不可能通过采取相同的措施或措施组合获得与在不同区域营运的其他船舶相同的能效收益。一些措施还可能会在不同航行区域中有或多或少的影响。

5.10.4 船舶从事的贸易可决定所考虑的能效措施的可行性。例如，与常规货物运输船相比，在海上进行服务（管路铺设、地震勘测、近海供应船、挖泥船等）的船舶可选择不同的方法提高能效。如同贸易特定安全考虑，航程的长度也是一个重要的参数。节能措施达到最有效组合的途径对每一航运公司内的每艘船舶都将是独特的。

5.10.5   Environmental conditions and the nature of cargo carried also varies between regions. For example, some routes may carry greater volumes of goods requiring careful temperature conditioning, or some transit regions may be subject to frequent severe adverse weather conditions. This may lead to an increase of emissions of ships serving those routes and regions.

PART II OF THE SEEMP: SHIP FUEL OIL CONSUMPTION DATA COLLECTION PLAN

6   GENERAL

6.1   Regulation 26.2 of MARPOL Annex VI specifies that, "in the case of a ship of 5,000 gross tonnage and above, the SEEMP shall include a description of the methodology that will be used to collect the data required by regulation 27.1 of this Annex and the processes that will be used to report the data to the ship's Administration". Part II of the SEEMP, the Ship Fuel Oil Consumption Data Collection Plan (hereinafter referred to as "Data Collection Plan") contains such methodology and processes.

6.2   With respect to Part II of the SEEMP, these Guidelines provide guidance for developing a ship-specific method to collect, aggregate and report ship data with regard to annual fuel oil consumption, distance travelled, hours under way and other data required by regulation 27 of MARPOL Annex VI to be reported to the Administration.

6.3   Pursuant to regulation 5.4.5 of MARPOL Annex VI, the Administration should ensure that each covered ship's SEEMP complies with regulation 26.2 of MARPOL Annex VI prior to collecting any data.

7   GUIDANCE ON METHODOLOGY FOR COLLECTING DATA ON FUEL OIL CONSUMPTION, DISTANCE TRAVELLED AND HOURS UNDER WAY AND OTHER ITEMS

Total annual fuel oil[1] consumption

7.1   Fuel oil consumption should include all the fuel oil consumed on board including but not limited to the fuel oil consumed by the main engines, auxiliary engines, gas turbines, boilers and inert gas generator, for each type of fuel oil consumed, regardless of whether a ship is under way or not. Methods for collecting data on annual fuel oil consumption in metric tonnes include (in no particular order):

       .1   method using bunker delivery notes (BDNs):

       This method determines the annual total amount of fuel oil used based on BDNs, which are required for fuel oil for combustion purposes delivered to and used on board a ship in accordance with regulation 18 of MARPOL Annex VI; BDNs are required to be retained on board for three years after the fuel oil has been delivered. The Data Collection Plan should set out how the ship will operationalize the summation of BDN information and conduct tank readings. The main components of this approach are as follows:

---

[1]   Regulation 2.1.14 of MARPOL Annex VI defines "fuel oil" as any fuel delivered to and intended for combustion purposes for propulsion or operation on board a ship, including gas, distillate and residual fuels.

5.10.5 环境条件和所载货物的性质也因地区而异。例如，某些航线可能会运送需要仔细调节温度的大量货物，或者某些运输地区可能会经常遇到恶劣的不利天气条件。这可能导致服务于这些航线和地区的船舶排放量增加。

SEEMP 第 Ⅱ 部分：船舶燃油消耗数据收集计划

6 总则

6.1 《防污公约》附则Ⅵ第 26.2 条规定"对于 5 000 总吨及以上的船舶，其船舶能效管理计划须包括对将用于收集本附则第 27.1 条要求的数据的方法的说明和将用于向船舶主管机关报告数据的程序的说明。"SEEMP 第 Ⅱ 部分，船舶燃油消耗数据收集计划（以下称"数据收集计划"）包含此方法和流程。

6.2 关于 SEEMP 第 Ⅱ 部分，本导则为制定因船而异的方法提供指导，以收集、整合和报告关于每年燃油消耗、航行距离和在航时长的船舶数据和《防污公约》附则Ⅵ第 27 条要求向主管机关报告的其他数据。

6.3 按《防污公约》附则Ⅵ第 5.4.5 条规定，主管机关应确保在收集任何数据前每艘船舶的 SEEMP 符合《防污公约》附则Ⅵ第 26.2 条的规定。

7 燃油消耗、航行距离和在航时长及其他的数据收集方法指南

年度燃油 [1] 总消耗

7.1 燃油消耗应包括船上消耗的所有燃油，包括但不限于主机、辅机、燃气轮机、锅炉和惰性气体发生器消耗的燃油，针对消耗的每种类型的燃油，而不论船舶航行与否。收集每年燃油消耗（以吨为单位）的方法包括（排名不分先后）：

　　.1 使用燃油装舱单（BDNs）的方法：

　　　　本方法在 BDNs 的基础上，确定按《防污公约》附则Ⅵ第 18 条要求为燃烧目的交付至船上并使用的燃油的年度使用总量；要求燃油交付后船上保留 BDNs 三年。数据收集计划应规定船舶如何实施 BDN 信息的汇总和读取舱柜数据。本方法的主要内容如下：

---

[1] 《MARPOL》附则Ⅵ第 2.1.14 条将"燃油"定义为人为船舶推进或运转而向船上供给的燃料，包括气体、蒸馏和残余燃油。

.1   annual fuel oil consumption would be the total mass of fuel oil used on board the vessel as reflected in the BDNs. In this method, the BDN fuel oil quantities would be used to determine the annual total mass of fuel oil consumption, plus the amount of fuel oil left over from the last calendar year period and less the amount of fuel oil carried over to the next calendar year period;

.2   to determine the difference between the amount of remaining tank oil before and after the period, the tank reading should be carried out at the beginning and the end of the period;

.3   in the case of a voyage that extends across the data reporting period, the tank reading should occur by tank monitoring at the ports of departure and arrival of the voyage and by statistical methods, such as rolling average using voyage days;

.4   fuel oil tank readings should be carried out by appropriate methods such as automated systems, soundings and dip tapes. The method for tank readings should be specified in the Data Collection Plan;

.5   the amount of any fuel oil offloaded should be subtracted from the fuel oil consumption of that reporting period. This amount should be based on the records of the ship's oil record book; and

.6   any supplemental data used for closing identified difference in bunker quantity should be supported with documentary evidence;

.2   method using flow meters:

This method determines the annual total amount of fuel oil consumption by measuring fuel oil flows on board by using flow meters. In case of the breakdown of flow meters, manual tank readings or other alternative methods will be conducted instead. The Data Collection Plan should set out information about the ship's flow meters and how the data will be collected and summarized, as well as how necessary tank readings should be conducted, as follows:

.1   annual fuel oil consumption may be the sum of daily fuel oil consumption data of all relevant fuel oil consuming processes on board measured by flow meters;

.2   the flow meters applied to monitoring should be located so as to measure all fuel oil consumption on board. The flow meters and their link to specific fuel oil consumers should be described in the Data Collection Plan;

.3   note that it should not be necessary to correct this fuel oil measurement method for sludge if the flow meter is installed after the daily tank as sludge will be removed from the fuel oil prior to the daily tank;

.1 年度燃油消耗量为如 BDNs 中反映的船上使用的燃油总量。这种方法通过对 BDN 燃油量加总，加上上一日历年报告期的盘存燃油量，减去结转到下一日历年报告期的燃油消耗量，来最终确定燃油消耗总量。

.2 为确定报告期前后剩余舱柜油量的差值，应在报告期开始和结束时分别读取舱柜数据；

.3 如航程横跨数据报告周期，应在出发港和航行到达时通过舱柜监测和统计法，诸如使用航行天数得到滚动平均值以获取舱柜数据；

.4 应通过适当的方法获取燃油舱柜数据，如自动化系统、量油尺和液位计。应在数据收集计划中规定获取舱柜数据的方法；

.5 任何被卸掉的燃油量应从报告周期的燃油消耗量中减去。此燃油量应以船舶油类记录簿的记录为基础；和

.6 用于结算已确定的燃油舱油量差异的任何补充数据均应提供书面证明；

.2 使用流量计的方法：

本方法使用流量计测量船上燃油流量确定年度燃油消耗总量。如流量计故障，应进行人工获取舱柜数据或其他替代方法来替代。数据收集计划应说明船舶流量计的信息和如何收集与汇总数据，以及如何获取必要的舱柜数据：

.1 年度燃油消耗量可以为流量计测量的船上所有相关燃油消耗过程的日燃油消耗量数据的总和；

.2 用于监测的流量计应布置为可测量船上所有的燃油消耗。应在数据收集计划中描述流量计及其与特定燃油消耗装置的连接；

.3 注意如流量计安装在日用柜后，那么此种燃油监测方法不需要考虑油渣的校正问题，因为燃油在进入日用柜前已将油渣去除；

.4 the flow meters applied to monitoring fuel oil flow should be identified in the Data Collection Plan. Any consumer not monitored with a flow meter should be clearly identified, and an alternative fuel oil consumption measurement method should be included; and

.5 calibration of the flow meters should be specified. Calibration and maintenance records should be available on board;

.3 method using bunker fuel oil tank monitoring on board:

.1 to determine the annual fuel oil consumption, the amount of daily fuel oil consumption data measured by tank readings which are carried out by appropriate methods such as automated systems, soundings and dip tapes will be aggregated. The tank readings will normally occur daily when the ship is at sea and each time the ship is bunkering or de-bunkering; and

.2 the summary of monitoring data containing records of measured fuel oil consumption should be available on board;

.4 method using LNG cargo tank monitoring on board:

LNG ships use the Custody Transfer Monitoring System (CTMS) to monitor/record the cargo volumes inside the tanks. When calculating the consumption:

.1 the LNG liquid volume consumed is converted to mass using the methane density of 422 kg/m³. This is because LNG is transported at methane boiling point, while other heavier hydrocarbons have a higher boiling point and remain at liquid state; and

.2 nitrogen mass content is subtracted for each laden voyage from LNG consumption as it does not contribute to CO_2 emissions;

.5 method using cargo tank monitoring on board for ships using cargo other than LNG as a fuel:

.1 to determine the annual fuel oil consumption, the amount of daily fuel oil consumption data measured by tank readings which are carried out by appropriate methods to the cargo used as a fuel. The method for tank readings should be specified in the SEEMP Data Collection Plan; and

.2 the tank readings will normally occur daily when the ship is at sea and each time the ship is loading or discharging cargo; and the summary of monitoring data containing records of measured fuel oil consumption should be available on board.

.4 应在数据收集计划中确定应用于监测燃油流的流量计。应清楚识别任何无流量计监测的消耗装置，并应包含替代的燃油消耗量测量方法；和

.5 应规定流量计的校准。船上应能提供校准和维修记录；

.3 使用船上燃油舱柜监测的方法：

.1 使用适当的方法如自动化系统、量油尺、液位计等对船舶燃油舱柜存油进行测量，获得燃油日消耗量，再进行加总，得到年度燃油耗量。一般当船舶在日常航行和每次装卸燃料时测量舱柜数据；

.2 船上应提供监测数据的汇总，包括测量燃油消耗量的记录；

.4 用船上 LNG 液货舱监测的方法：

LNG 船使用贸易交接计量系统（CTMS）监控/记录液舱内的货物量。计算消耗时：

.1 使用 422 kg/m³ 的甲烷密度将消耗的 LNG 液体体积转换为质量。这是因为液化天然气在甲烷沸点下运输，而其他较重的碳氢化合物具有更高的沸点并保持液态；和

.2 从 LNG 消耗中减去每次载货航次的氮质量含量，因为它不会导致 CO_2 排放；

.5 对于使用 LNG 以外的货物为燃料的船舶，使用船上液货舱监测的方法：

.1 为确定年度燃油消耗量，通过适当的方法对用作燃料的货物进行液舱读数以测得每日燃油消耗量数据。应在 SEEMP 数据收集计划中规定液舱读数的方法；和

.2 当船舶在海上时以及每次船舶装卸货物时，通常每天都会读取液舱读数；船上应提供监测数据的汇总，包括测量燃油消耗量的记录。

7.2   Any corrections, e.g. density, temperature, nitrogen content for LNG, if applied, should be documented.[2]

Fuel oil consumption per consumer type

7.3   For the collection of fuel oil consumption per consumer type (main engines, auxiliaries, boilers and others), the methods can include:

.1   method using flow meters:

This method determines the annual fuel oil consumption by measuring fuel oil flows on board by using flow meters. In case of the breakdown of flow meters, manual tank readings or other alternative methods will be conducted instead. The Data Collection Plan should set out information about the ship's flow meters and how the data will be collected and summarized, as well as how necessary tank readings should be conducted, as follows:

.1   annual fuel oil consumption may be the sum of daily fuel oil consumption data of each consumer type on board measured by flow meters;

.2   the flow meters applied to monitoring should be located so as to measure all fuel oil consumption for each consumer type;

.3   note that it should not be necessary to correct this fuel oil measurement method for sludge if the flow meter is installed after the daily tank as sludge will be removed from the fuel oil prior to the daily tank;

.4   the flow meters applied to monitoring fuel oil flow and their link to specific fuel consumer types should be identified in the Data Collection Plan. Any individual consumer of a consumer type not monitored with a flow meter should be clearly identified, and an alternative fuel oil consumption measurement method should be included; and

.5   calibration of the flow meters should be specified. Calibration and maintenance records should be available on board;

.2   method using bunker fuel oil tank monitoring on board:

.1   to determine the annual fuel oil consumption of each consumer type, the amount of daily fuel oil consumption data measured by tank readings which are carried out by appropriate methods such as automated systems, soundings and dip tapes will be aggregated. The tank readings will normally occur daily when the ship is at sea and each time the ship is bunkering or de-bunkering; and

.2   the summary of monitoring data containing records of measured fuel oil consumption should be available on board;

[2]   For example, ISO 8217 provides a method for liquid fuel.

7.2 如果采用任何修正，如密度、温度、LNG 氮含量，应予以记录。[2]

按照燃油消耗设备类型分类的燃油消耗

7.3 收集按照燃油消耗设备类型（主机、辅机、锅炉和其他）分类的燃油消耗的方法包括：

.1 使用流量计的方法：

本方法使用流量计测量船上燃油流量确定年度燃油消耗量。如流量计故障，应进行人工获取舱柜数据或其他替代方法来替代。数据收集计划应如下说明船舶流量计的信息和如何收集与汇总数据，以及如何获取必要的舱柜数据：

.1 年度燃油消耗量可以为流量计测量的船上每种燃油消耗设备类型的日燃油消耗量数据的总和；

.2 用于监测的流量计应布置为可测量每种燃油消耗设备类型的所有燃油消耗；

.3 注意如流量计安装在日用柜后，那么此种燃油监测方法不需要考虑油渣的校正问题，因为燃油在进入日用柜前已将油渣去除；

.4 应在数据收集计划中确定应用于监测燃油流的流量计及其与特定燃油消耗设备类型的连接。应清楚识别任何无流量计监测的燃油消耗设备类型的单独消耗装置，并应包含替代的燃油消耗量测量方法；和

.5 应规定流量计的校准。船上应能提供校准和维修记录；

.2 使用船上燃油舱柜监测的方法：

.1 使用适当的方法如自动化系统、量油尺、液位计等对船舶燃油舱柜存油进行测量，获得燃油日消耗量，再进行加总，确定每种燃油消耗设备类型的年度燃油消耗量。一般当船舶在日常航行和每次装卸燃料时测量舱柜数据；和

.2 船上应提供监测数据的汇总，包括测量燃油消耗量的记录；

---

[2] 例如，ISO 8217 提供了液体燃料的方法。

7.4   If there is a consumer type whose fuel oil consumption cannot be determined directly according to one of the methods indicated in paragraphs 7.3.1 and 7.3.2, the annual fuel oil consumption of that consumer type should be determined according to one of the following methods. The method used to determine the annual fuel oil consumption of each consumer type should be described in detail in the Data Collection Plan. Note that each consumer type may use a different method to measure fuel oil consumption.

.1   method using subtraction:

If the fuel consumption for only one of the consumer types is not available, the fuel consumption of this consumer type may be derived by subtracting the fuel consumption of the other consumer types from the total annual fuel oil consumption measured in paragraph 7.1; and

.2   method using estimated fuel oil consumption:

In cases where none of the above methods in paragraphs 7.3.1, 7.3.2 and 7.4.1 can be applied, an alternative method that is to the satisfaction of the Administration or any organization recognized by it may be used to estimate the annual fuel oil consumption of the consumer type, based for example on manufacturer data or actual historic fuel consumption for a specified period.

Conversion factor C_F

7.5   If fuel oils are used that do not fall into one of the categories as described in the *2022 Guidelines on the method of calculation of the attained Energy Efficiency Design Index (EEDI) for new ships* (resolution MEPC.364(79)), and have no C_F-factor assigned (e.g. some "hybrid fuel oils"), the fuel oil supplier should provide a C_F-factor for the respective product supported by documentary evidence.

Distance travelled

7.6   Appendix IX of MARPOL Annex VI specifies that distance travelled should be submitted to the Administration and:

.1   distance travelled over ground in nautical miles should be recorded in the logbook in accordance with SOLAS regulation V/28.1;[3]

.2   the distance travelled while the ship is under way under its own propulsion should be included in the aggregated data of distance travelled for the calendar year; and

.3   other methods to measure distance travelled accepted by the Administration may be applied. In any case, the method applied should be described in detail in the Data Collection Plan.

7.7   Laden distance should be calculated as the distance sailed when the ship is loaded.

---

[3]   Distance travelled measured using satellite data is distance travelled over the ground.

7.4 如果无法按照第 7.3.1 和 7.3.2 段规定的其中一种方法直接确定某种燃油消耗设备类型的燃油消耗，该燃油消耗设备类型的年度燃油消耗应按照以下其中一种方法确定。数据收集计划应详细说明确定每种燃油消耗设备类型的年度燃油消耗使用的方法。注意每种燃油消耗设备类型可能使用不同的方法来测量燃油消耗。

    .1 使用减法的方法：

        如果仅有一种燃油消耗设备类型的燃油消耗无法获取，可通过将按照第 7.1 段测量的年度燃油总消耗减去其他燃油消耗设备类型的燃油消耗而得出；和

    .2 使用估算燃油消耗的方法：

        如果上述第 7.3.1、7.3.2 和 7.4.1 段中的方法都不适用，可使用使主管机关或经主管机关认可的任何组织满意的一种替代方法来估算某种燃油消耗设备类型的年度燃油消耗，例如可根据在规定时期内的生产商数据或历史实际燃油消耗予以估算。

转换系数 C_F

7.5 如使用的燃油不属于经修正的《2022 年新船达到的能效设计指数（EEDI）计算方法导则》（第 MEPC.364（79）号决议）规定的类型且无指定 C_F 系数（如一些"混合燃油"），燃油供应商应为相关产品提供 C_F 系数并辅以证明文件。

航行距离

7.6 《防污公约》附则 VI 附录 IX 规定应向主管机关提交航行距离和：

    .1 按 SOLAS 第 V/28.1 条规定应在航海日志中记录对地航行距离，以海里计；[3]

    .2 船舶靠自身推进航行的距离应包括在本日历年度航行距离的累计数据中；和

    .3 可使用其他主管机关认可的方法测量航行距离。在任何情况下，使用的方法应在数据收集计划中予以详细说明。

7.7 满载距离应按船舶装载货物情况下的航行距离进行计算。

---

[3] 使用卫星数据测量的航行距离为对地航行距离。

Hours underway

7.8   Appendix IX of MARPOL Annex VI specifies that hours underway should be submitted to the Administration. Hours under way should be an aggregated duration while the ship is underway under its own propulsion.

Data quality

7.9   The Data Collection Plan should include data quality control measures which should be incorporated into the existing safety management system. Additional measures to be considered could include:

    .1   the procedure for identification of data gaps and correction thereof; and

    .2   the procedure to address data gaps if monitoring data is missing, for example, flow meter malfunctions.

Total amount of onshore power supplied

7.10   Total amount of onshore power supplied should be calculated as the sum of amount of onshore power supplied in kWh. The amount of onshore power supplied should be recorded based on relevant document by power supplier. The document should be stored. This information as shown on the bill from the port or electricity provider could be included in the electronic record.

Total transport work

7.11   Total transport work is the annual sum of each voyage's transport work which is distance sailed multiplied by cargo carried during a voyage. Relevant transport work metrics per ship types are provided in Table 1 below.

Table 1: Transport work to be reported per ship type

Ship type	Transport work metric
bulk carriers, tankers, combination carriers, gas carriers, LNG carriers, general cargo ships, ro-ro cargo ships (vehicle carriers), ro-ro cargo ships	$\sum_V (\text{cargo\_mass}_V \times \text{distance}_V)$
containerships	$\sum_V ((\text{cargo\_mass}_V + \text{container\_mass}_V) \times \text{distance}_V))$ and $\sum_V (\text{No\_of\_TEU}_V \times \text{distance}_V)$
cruise passenger ships	$\sum_V (\text{No\_of\_passengers}_V \times \text{distance}_V)$
ro-ro passenger ships	$\sum_V (\text{No\_of\_passengers}_V \times \text{distance}_V)$ and $\sum_V (\text{cargo\_mass}_V \times \text{distance}_V)$

A standardized data reporting format

7.12   Regulation 27.3 of MARPOL Annex VI states that the data specified in appendix IX of the Annex are to be communicated electronically using a standardized form

在航时长

7.8 《防污公约》附则Ⅵ附录Ⅸ规定应向主管机关提交在航时长。在航时长应为船舶靠自身推进航行的累计持续时间。

数据质量

7.9 数据收集计划应包括数据质量控制措施，应纳入现有的船舶安全管理系统中。其他要考虑的措施可包括：

.1 数据误差识别及其修正程序；和

.2 当监测数据丢失时解决数据误差的程序，如流量计发生故障。

岸电供应总量

7.10 岸电供应总量应按岸电供应量（单位 kWh）的总数进行计算。应按照电力供应商的相关文件对岸电供应量进行记录。记录文件应予以保存。港口或电力供应商出具的账单上显示的信息可被纳入电子记录。

总运输功

7.11 总运输功系指每个航程运输工作的年度总和，通过将每次航程的航行距离乘以装载的货物而得到。以下表 1 规定了针对不同船型的相关运输功测量标准。

表 1　按不同船型报告的运输功

船型	运输工作测量标准
散货船、液货船、兼装船、气体运输船、LNG 船、杂货船、滚装货船（车辆运输船）、滚装船	$\sum_v$（货物质量$_v$ × 距离$_v$）
集装箱船	$\sum_v$（（货物质量$_v$+ 集装箱质量$_v$）× 距离$_v$）和 $\sum_v$（标准集装箱数量$_v$ × 距离$_v$）
豪华邮轮	$\sum_v$（乘客数量$_v$ × 距离$_v$）
客滚船	$\sum_v$（乘客数量$_v$ × 距离$_v$）和 $\sum_v$（货物质量$_v$ × 距离$_v$）

标准数据报告格式

7.12 《防污公约》附则Ⅵ第 27.3 条载明该附则附录Ⅸ规定的数据应通过电子通信并使用

Administration in the standardized format shown in appendix 4.

8 DIRECT CO$_2$ EMISSIONS MEASUREMENT

8.1   Direct CO$_2$ emission measurement is not required by regulation 27 of MARPOL Annex VI.

8.2   Direct CO$_2$ emissions measurement, if used, should be carried out as follows:

   .1   this method is based on the determination of CO$_2$ emission flows in exhaust gas stacks by multiplying the CO$_2$ concentration of the exhaust gas with the exhaust gas flow. In case of the absence or/and breakdown of direct CO$_2$ emissions measurement equipment, manual tank readings will be conducted instead;

   .2   the direct CO$_2$ emissions measurement equipment applied to monitoring is located so as to measure all CO$_2$ emissions from the ship. The locations of all equipment applied are described in the monitoring plan; and

   .3   calibration of the CO$_2$ emissions measurement equipment should be specified. Calibration and maintenance records should be available on board.

PART III OF THE SEEMP: SHIP OPERATIONAL CARBON INTENSITY PLAN

9 GENERAL

9.1   Regulation 26.3.1 of MARPOL Annex VI specifies that, for certain categories of ships of 5,000 GT and above, on or before 1 January 2023, the SEEMP shall include:

   .1   a description of the methodology that will be used to calculate the ship's attained annual operational CII required by regulation 28 of MARPOL Annex VI and the processes that will be used to report this value to the ship's Administration;

   .2   the required annual operational CIIs, as specified in regulation 28 of MARPOL Annex VI, for the next three years;

   .3   an implementation plan documenting how the required annual operational CIIs will be achieved during the next three years; and

   .4   a procedure for self-evaluation and improvement.

9.2   Sections 9 to 15 of these Guidelines provide guidance for ships to which regulation 26.3 of MARPOL Annex VI applies for the following purposes:

   .1   to assist them in developing part III of the ship's SEEMP, including guidance on developing a ship-specific method to collect necessary data;

   .2   to describe the methodology that will be used to calculate the ship's attained annual operational CII value and report this to the ship's Administration;

本组织制定的标准格式。应以附录 4 所示的标准格式向主管机关报告收集的数据。

8 CO_2 排放直接测量方法

8.1 MARPOL 附则Ⅵ第 27 条不要求进行 CO_2 排放直接测量。

8.2 如使用 CO_2 排放直接测量的方法，应按以下方式进行：

.1 这种方法基于将废气中 CO_2 浓度乘以废气流量来确定排气管中的 CO_2 排放量；在没有 CO_2 排放直接测量设备，或 / 和测量设备故障的情况下，应使用人工燃油舱测量来替代；

.2 用于监测的 CO_2 排放直接测量设备应处于能测量船舶所有 CO_2 排放的位置。监测计划应说明所有使用设备的位置；和

.3 CO_2 排放测量设备的校准应予说明。校准和保养记录应保留在船。

SEEMP 第Ⅲ部分：船舶营运碳强度计划

9 总则

9.1 《防污公约》附则Ⅵ第 26.3.1 条规定，对于 5 000 GT 及以上特定船型的船舶，在 2023 年 1 月 1 日或之前，其 SEEMP 须包含：

.1 用于计算本附则第 28 条要求船舶达到的年度营运碳强度指标（以下简称 CII）的方法以及向船舶主管机关报告该值的程序说明；

.2 本附则Ⅵ第 28 条规定的未来三年要求的年度营运 CII；

.3 记录如何达到未来三年要求的年度营运 CII 的实施计划；和

.4 自我评估和改进程序

9.2 本导则第 9 至 15 节对《防污公约》附则Ⅵ第 26.3 条适用的船舶提供指南，从而：

.1 帮助其制定船舶 SEEMP 第Ⅲ部分，包括关于制定收集必要数据的船舶具体方法的指南；

.2 说明用于计算船舶达到的年度营运 CII 值和向船舶主管机关报告该值的方法；

.3   to determine the ship's required annual operational CII for the next three years;

.4   to develop and apply an implementation plan documenting how the required annual operational CIIs will be achieved during the next three years;

.5   to define a procedure for self-evaluation and improvement; and

.6   to develop corrective actions, as applicable.

9.3   The required annual operational CII is to be calculated in accordance with regulation 28 and taking into account the guidelines developed by the Organization.[7]

9.4   In addition, pursuant to regulation 28 of MARPOL Annex VI, part III of the SEEMP is further to include calculation methodologies and a plan of corrective actions for ships that are rated D for three consecutive years or rated as E.

9.5   The ship's attained annual operational carbon intensity is to be calculated taking into account the guidelines developed by the Organization.[8]

9.6   Ships of 5,000 gross tonnage and above that are subject to regulations 26.3 and 28 of MARPOL Annex VI are strongly encouraged to review part I of their SEEMP to revise it as needed to reflect the actions taken to achieve the ship's CII requirements.

9.7   The goal setting, as referred to in paragraph 4.1.7 in part I, should be consistent with the requirements of regulation 28 of MARPOL Annex VI and should include the ship's required annual operational CII for the next three years following the updating of the SEEMP.

9.8   In addition, while ships subject to regulation 28 of MARPOL Annex VI may relay on the CII requirements when defining goals under part I of the SEEMP, they are encouraged to consider setting additional ship-specific goals that go beyond the applicable CII requirements and strive for energy efficiency improvements and carbon intensity reductions beyond such requirements.

9.9   Ships subject to regulation 28 of MARPOL Annex VI may consider voluntarily using one or more of the trial CIIs (EEPI, cbDIST,clDIST or EEOI), where applicable, for the purpose of providing supporting data for decision-making to support the review clause set out in regulation 28.11 of MARPOL Annex VI. A standardized data reporting format for the parameters to calculate the trial carbon intensity indicators on a voluntary basis is presented in appendix 5. A description of the methodology that should be used to calculate the trial CII should be included in the SEEMP.

9.10   Part III of the ship's SEEMP should be updated in case of voluntary modifications or necessary corrective actions are involved (every three years).

---

[7]   Refer to the *2022 Guidelines on the reference lines for use with operational carbon intensity indicators (CII reference lines guidelines, G2)* (Resolution MEPC.353(78) and the *2021 Guidelines on the operational carbon intensity reduction factors relative to reference lines (CII reduction factors guidelines, G3)* (Resolution MEPC.338(76).

[8]   Refer to the *2022 Guidelines on operational carbon intensity indicators and calculation methods (CII Guidelines, G1)* (Resolution MEPC.352(78)) and the *2022 Interim guidelines on correction factors and voyage adjustments for CII calculations (G5)* (Resolution MEPC.355(78)).

.3 确定未来三年船舶要求的年度营运 CII；

.4 制定和应用记录如何在未来三年达到要求的年度营运 CII 的实施计划；

.5 规定自我评估和改进的程序；和

.6 制定整改行动，如适用。

9.3 按第 28 条并考虑本组织制定的导则 [7] 计算要求的年度营运 CII。

9.4 此外，根据《防污公约》附则 VI 第 28 条，对于连续三年被评为 D 级或被评为 E 级的船舶，SEEMP 第 III 部分应进一步包括计算方法和整改行动计划。

9.5 应考虑本组织制定的导则 [8] 计算船舶达到的年度营运碳强度。

9.6 强烈鼓励受《防污公约》附则 VI 第 26.3 和 28 条约束的 5 000 总吨及以上船舶审核其 SEEMP 第 I 部分，以根据需要对其进行修订，以反映为达到船舶 CII 要求所采取的行动。

9.7 第 I 部分第 4.1.7 段提及的目标设定应符合《防污公约》附则 VI 第 28 条的要求，并应包括在 SEEMP 更新后未来三年船舶要求的年度营运 CII。

9.8 此外，虽然受《防污公约》附则 VI 第 28 条约束的船舶在根据 SEEMP 第 I 部分定义目标时可能会依据 CII 要求，但鼓励他们考虑设定超出适用 CII 要求的额外船舶具体目标，并努力实现超出这些要求的能效提高和碳强度降低。

9.9 受《防污公约》附则 VI 第 28 条约束的船舶可考虑自愿使用一种或多种试用 CIIs（EEPI、cbDIST、clDIST 或 EEOI），如适用，为决策提供支持数据以支持《防污公约》附则 VI 第 28.11 条中的审查规定。附录 5 介绍了用于计算自愿试用碳强度指标的参数的标准化数据报告格式。SEEMP 应包含用于计算试用 CII 的方法说明。

9.10 如果涉及自愿修改或必要的纠正行动（每三年），应更新船舶 SEEMP 第 III 部分。

---

[7] 参见《2022 年营运碳强度指标基线导则》（CII 基线导则，G2）（第 MEPC.353（78）号决议）和《2021 年相对于基线的营运碳强度折减因素导则》（CII 折减率导则，G3）（第 MEPC.338（76）号决议）。

[8] 参见《2022 年营运碳强度指标和计算方法导则》（CII 导则，G1）（第 MEPC.352（78）号决议）和《2022 年 CII 计算的修正系数和航次调整临时导则》（G5）（第 MEPC.355（78）号决议）。

10 ATTAINED ANNUAL OPERATIONAL CII CALCULATION METHODOLOGY; DATA COLLECTION PLAN AND DATA QUALITY

10.1   Taking into account the guidelines developed by the Organization,[9] part III of the SEEMP provides detailed information on how the ship's attained annual operational CII should be calculated. Regulation 28 of MARPOL Annex VI states that the attained annual operational CII shall be calculated, using the data collected in accordance with regulation 27 (Fuel Oil Data Collection System).

10.2   In describing the calculation methodology, part III of the SEEMP should include a detailed description of the data required for the calculation of the attained annual operational CII. The data collection should follow the relevant methodology and requirements on the Fuel Oil Data Collection System pursuant to regulation 27 of MARPOL AnnexVI (see part II of these Guidelines).

10.3   In case of transfer of the ship from one company to another according to regulation 27.5 or 27.6 of MARPOL Annex VI, all relevant data necessary for the calculation of the attained annual operational CII should be submitted by the former company to the receiving company within one month after the date of transfer. The data should have been verified by the Administration or any organization duly authorized by it according to regulation 6.7 of MARPOL Annex VI before they are transferred to the receiving company. The format of the transfer should be consistent with appendix 4 and such that the receiving company can use it in the calculations of the attained annual operational CII for the whole year in which the transfer takes place.

10.4   In case the former company does not transfer the required data, the Administration may make relevant data submitted to the IMO Fuel Oil Consumption Database available to the receiving company. In case of a transfer of both company and Administration concurrently, the incoming Administration may make a request to the Organization for access to the data according to regulation 27.11. If no such data is available, the attained annual operational CII can be calculated and verified using the available data covering a period of the preceding calendar year as long as practically possible.

10.5   In case of transfer of a ship from one Administration to another according to regulation 27.4 of MARPOL Annex VI the data needed for calculating the annual attained CII is already in the possession of the relevant company and no further exchange of data is needed.

11 REQUIRED ANNUAL OPERATIONAL CII FOR NEXT THREE YEARS

11.1   Part III of the SEEMP describes the required annual operational CII values for the ship for each of the next three years, calculated in accordance with regulation 28 of MARPOL Annex VI and taking into account the guidelines developed by the Organization,[10] as the basis for those calculations.

---

[9]   Refer to the *2022 Guidelines on operational carbon intensity indicators and calculation methods (CII Guidelines, G1)* (Resolution MEPC.352(78)) and the *2022 Interim guidelines on correction factors and voyage adjustments for CII calculations (G5)* (Resolution MEPC.355(78)).

[10]   Refer to the *2022 Guidelines on the reference lines for use with operational carbon intensity indicators (CII reference lines guidelines, G2)* (Resolution MEPC.353(78)) and the *2021 Guidelines on the operational carbon intensity reduction factors relative to reference lines (CII reduction factors guidelines, G3)* (Resolution MEPC.338(76)).

10 达到的年度营运 CII 计算方法；数据收集计划和数据质量

10.1　考虑到本组织制定的导则[9]，SEEMP 第Ⅲ部分提供关于如何计算船舶达到的年度营运 CII 的详细信息。《防污公约》附则Ⅵ第 28 条规定，应使用按第 27 条（燃油数据收集系统）收集的数据计算达到的年度营运 CII。

10.2　在说明计算方法时，SEEMP 第Ⅲ部分应包括对计算达到的年度营运 CII 所需数据的详细描述。数据收集应遵循符合《防污公约》附则Ⅵ第 27 条的燃油数据收集系统的相关方法和要求（参见本导则第Ⅱ部分）。

10.3　如果根据《防污公约》附则Ⅵ第 27.5 或 27.6 条将船舶从一家公司变更至另一家公司，转出公司应在转出日后一个月内将计算达到的年度营运 CII 所需的所有相关数据提交给转入公司。在变更至转入公司前，数据应已由主管机关或经其正式授权的任一组织按《防污公约》附则Ⅵ第 6.7 条进行验证。变更的格式应与附录 4 一致，以便转入公司可以将其用于计算变更发生的全年达到的年度营运 CII。

10.4　如果转出公司未传输所需数据，主管机关可将提交至 IMO 燃油消耗数据库的相关数据提供给转入公司。如果同时变更公司和主管机关，转入主管机关可根据第 27.11 条向本组织提出要求以查阅数据。如果没有此类数据，可尽实际可行使用涵盖上一日历年时期的可用数据计算和验证达到的年度营运 CII。

10.5　当按《防污公约》附则Ⅵ第 27.4 条船舶从一个主管机关变更至另一个主管机关时，相关公司已有计算年度达到的 CII 所需的数据，无须进一步交换数据。

11 未来三年的要求的年度营运 CII

11.1　SEEMP 第Ⅲ部分描述了船舶在未来三年每年要求的年度营运 CII 值，根据《防污公约》附则Ⅵ第 28 条计算并考虑到本组织制定的导则[10]，作为这些计算的基础。

---

[9]　参见《2022 年营运碳强度指标和计算方法导则》（CII 导则，G1）（第 MEPC.352（78）号决议）和《2022 年 CII 计算的修正系数和航次调整临时导则》（G5）（第 MEPC.355（78）号决议）。

[10]　参见《2022 年营运碳强度指标基线导则》（CII 基线导则，G2）（第 MEPC.353（78）号决议）和《2021 年相对于基线的营运碳强度折减因素导则》（CII 折减率导则，G3）（第 MEPC.338（76）号决议）。

12 THREE-YEAR IMPLEMENTATION PLAN

12.1   The three-year implementation plan describes the measures the ship plans to take to continue to achieve the required annual operational CII over the next three-year period. These may include, but are not limited to, measures as outlined in section 5 of these Guidelines.

12.2   The three-year implementation plan is ship-specific.

12.3   The three-year implementation plan should be SMART (Specific, Measurable, Achievable, Realistic, and Time-bound) to the extent envisaged and feasible. It should include:

> .1   a list of measures that improve the energy efficiency and reduce the carbon intensity of the ship, with time and method of implementation necessary for achieving the required operational CII;
>
> .2   a description of how, when the listed measures are implemented, the required operational CII will be achieved, taking into consideration the combined effect of the measures on operational carbon intensity;
>
> .3   the company personnel responsible for the three-year implementation plan, and for monitoring and recording performance throughout the year for the reviewing of the effectiveness of the three-year implementation plan; and
>
> .4   identification of possible impediments to the effectiveness of the measures for improving the energy efficiency and reducing the carbon intensity of the ship, including possible contingency measures put in place to overcome these impediments.

12.4   The three-year implementation plan should be monitored and adjusted when necessary, and the data to be monitored, identified.

13 PROCESS FOR SELF-EVALUATION AND IMPROVEMENT (IN ADDITION TO SECTION 4.4. OF THESE GUIDELINES)

13.1   The purpose of self-evaluation is to evaluate the effectiveness of the planned measures and their implementation, to deepen the understanding of the overall characteristics of the ship's operation, such as what types of measures can function effectively, and how or why, to comprehend the trend of the efficiency improvement of that ship, to understand trends in the ship's utilization in terms of cargo carried and areas of operation, and to develop an improved action plan for the next cycle. This evaluation should produce meaningful feedback based on experience in the previous period, to enhance performance in the next period.

13.2   Procedures for self-evaluation of the ship's energy usage and carbon intensity should be developed and included in this section of the SEEMP. Self-evaluation should be carried out periodically based on data collected through monitoring. It is recommended that the cause and effect of the ship's performance in the evaluated period be identified in order to identify measures for improving performance during the next period.

13.3   The process of self-evaluation and improvement could consist of the following elements:

> .1   regular internal shipboard and company audits to verify implementation and the effectiveness of the system;

12 三年实施计划

12.1 三年实施计划描述了为了在未来三年内继续实现要求的年度营运 CII 船舶计划采取的措施。这些可能包括但不限于本导则第 5 节中概述的措施。

12.2 三年实施计划是船舶特定的。

12.3 三年实施计划应在设想和可行的范围内实现 SMART（明确的、可衡量的、可完成的、现实的、有时限的）。应包括：

　.1　为实现要求的营运 CII 所需的提高船舶能效和降低碳强度的措施清单，包括实施时间和方法；

　.2　描述在实施所列措施时，将如何实现要求的营运 CII，并考虑到这些措施对营运碳强度的综合影响；

　.3　负责三年实施计划的公司人员，对全年绩效进行监测和记录，以审查三年实施计划的有效性；和

　.4　确定提高船舶能效和降低碳强度措施的有效性的可能障碍，包括为克服这些障碍而采取的可能应急措施。

12.4 必要时应监测和调整三年实施计划，并监测和确定数据。

13 自我评估和改进程序（补充本导则第 4.4 节）

13.1 自我评估的目的是：评估计划的措施的有效性及其执行情况；深化对船舶营运的整体特性的理解，诸如何种类型的措施能 / 不能有效运行，以及如何和 / 或为什么不能有效运行；了解该船能效改进的趋势；理解关于所载货物和营运区域的船舶使用的趋势；编制下一周期改进的行动计划。评估应根据前期的经验提供有意义的反馈，以提升下一阶段的实施效果。

13.2 应制定船舶能源使用和碳强度自我评估的程序，并将其纳入 SEEMP 的此节中。应通过使用监测收集到的数据定期进行自我评估。建议在评估期间确定船舶表现的因果，从而识别下个时期改善表现的措施。

13.3 自我评估和改进程序应包括以下要素：

　.1　定期进行船上和公司内部审核，以验证体系的实施情况和有效性；

.2 improvement, i.e. implementing preventive or modifying measures (responsible personnel within the company should evaluate such audit reports and implement corrective actions including preventive or modifying measures); and

.3 periodical review of the SEEMP and associated documents, to update the SEEMP in a manner which minimizes any administrative and unnecessary burdens on company's personnel and ship's staff.

13.4 The content of the self-evaluation and improvement could include the following elements:

.1 criteria for evaluation, including elements to evaluate, such as quality of monitoring, record-keeping, effectiveness of implemented measures (including cause and effect) and achievement of the goal;

.2 the evaluation of the effectiveness of the different measures taken, in terms of energy efficiency and carbon intensity;

.3 which measures contribute the most and how much, which measures do not contribute and are therefore not efficient, which ship and/or company-specific elements adversely affect the CII and how these could be improved;

.4 timeline for starting the review process ahead of the end of the compliance period and for implementation of new measures in the subsequent year;

.5 measures identified to address deficiencies and discrepancies including correction of data gaps and system weaknesses, new measures to improve implementation (e.g. training) as well as new carbon intensity improvement measures as needed;

.6 where relevant, actions that will be taken to bring the ship into better CII ratings including estimated quantification of the additional expected reduction in carbon intensity;

.7 where applicable, if a plan of corrective actions is required, the plan should include items listed under 15.4.5 to bring the ship out of inferior performance; and

.8 where relevant, identification of critical factors that contributed to missing the CII target.

14   REVIEW AND UPDATE OF PART III OF THE SEEMP

14.1   Regulation 26.1 of MARPOL Annex VI provides: "Each ship shall keep on board a ship-specific Ship Energy Efficiency Management Plan (SEEMP). This may form part of the ship's safety management system. The SEEMP shall be developed and reviewed, taking into account guidelines adopted by the Organization". Regulation 26.3.2 of MARPOL Annex VI provides: "For ships rated as D for three consecutive years or rated as E, in accordance with regulation 28 of this Annex, the SEEMP shall be reviewed in accordance with regulation 28.8 of this Annex to include a plan of corrective actions to achieve the required annual operational CII".

.2 改进,即实施预防或修改措施(公司负责人员应评估此审核报告并实施纠正措施,包括预防或修改措施); 和

.3 定期审核 SEEMP 和相关文件,更新 SEEMP 的方式应最大程度减少对公司人员和船舶人员造成的任何行政上和不必要的负担。

13.4 自我评估和改进的内容可包括以下要素:

.1 评估标准,包括评估要素,例如监测质量、记录保存、实施措施的有效性(包括因果关系)和目标的实现;

.2 评估所采取的关于能效和碳强度措施的有效性;

.3 哪些措施贡献最大,贡献了多少,哪些措施没有贡献,因此效率不高,哪些船舶和 / 或公司具体元素对 CII 产生不利影响,以及如何改进;

.4 在履约期结束前开始审查进程和在下一年实施新措施的时间表;

.5 为解决缺陷和差异而确定的措施,包括纠正数据偏差和系统缺陷、改进实施的新措施(如培训)以及根据需要采取新的碳强度改进措施;

.6 如相关,为使船舶获得更好的 CII 评级而采取的行动,包括对额外预期碳强度降低的估计量化;

.7 如适用,如果需要制定整改行动计划,该计划应包括第 15.4.5 段中列出的项目,以使船舶摆脱表现不佳; 和

.8 如相关,确定导致未实现 CII 目标的关键因素。

14 SEEMP 第 III 部分的审查和更新

14.1 《防污公约》附则 VI 第 26.1 条规定“每艘船舶须在船上保存一份具体的船舶能效管理计划(SEEMP)。该计划可作为船舶安全管理体系(SMS)的一部分。制定和审查船舶能效管理计划须考虑到本组织通过的导则。”《防污公约》附则 VI 第 26.3.2 条规定“对于按照本附则第 28 条连续三年被评为 D 级或被评为 E 级的船舶,须对船舶能效管理计划进行审查以包括整改行动计划,以按照本附则第 28.8 条实现要求的年度营运碳强度指标。”

14.2   The company should ensure that the SEEMP is reviewed and updated when necessary, as per paragraph 9.10.

14.3   The SEEMP should include a log for when it has been reviewed and updated and identify which parts have been changed.

15   PLAN OF CORRECTIVE ACTIONS

15.1   A plan of corrective actions is not required to be included in the SEEMP unless a ship has been rated D for three consecutive years or E for one year.

15.2   For a ship that is required to develop a plan of corrective actions in accordance with regulation 28.7 of MARPOL Annex VI, a revised SEEMP including the corrective actions for CII reduction shall be submitted to the Administration or any organization duly authorized by it for verification in accordance regulation 28.8 of MARPOL Annex VI. The revised SEEMP should be submitted together with, but in no case later than one month after reporting the attained annual operational CII in accordance with regulation 28.2.

15.3   Regulation 28.9 of MARPOL Annex VI further provides that "A ship rated as D for three consecutive years or rated as E shall duly undertake the planned corrective actions in accordance with the revised SEEMP."

15.4   Developing the plan of corrective actions

15.4.1   The purpose of the plan of corrective actions is to set out what actions a ship that was rated D for three consecutive years or E for one year should take to achieve at least a C rating for the calendar year following the adoption of the plan of corrective actions and ultimately the required annual operational CII.

15.4.2   The plan of corrective actions is ship-specific.

15.4.3   Many of the approaches described in section 5 of these guidelines or any other suitable measure may be applied to a ship to improve its fuel efficiency and thus its CII rating.

15.4.4   The plan for corrective action should describe the actions that the ship plans to take, the timeline in which those actions will be applied, and the expected impact their application will have on the ship's CII rating. It should be demonstrated how the corrective actions will contribute to achieving the required annual operational CII, so as to ascertain the effectiveness of the corrective actions. Experience gained from previously taken corrective actions and their degree of effectiveness should be taken into account when selecting the proper corrective actions.

15.4.5   The plan of corrective actions should be SMART (Specific, Measurable, Achievable, Realistic, and Time-bound). It should include:

> .1   an analysis of the cause of the inferior CII rating;
>
> .2   an analysis of the performance of implemented measures;
>
> .3   a list of additional measures and revised measures to be added to the implementation plan with time and method of implementation necessary for achieving the required operational CII;

14.2 公司应确保必要时按第 9.10 段对 SEEMP 进行审查和更新。

14.3 SEEMP 应包括何时进行审查和更新并标识哪些部分已更改的日志。

15 整改行动计划

15.1 除非船舶连续三年被评为 D 级或一年被评为 E 级的船舶，SEEMP 中无须包括整改行动计划。

15.2 对于要求按《防污公约》附则Ⅵ第 28.7 条制定整改行动计划的船舶，应按《防污公约》附则Ⅵ第 28.8 条将包括降低 CII 的纠正行动的经修订的 SEEMP 提交至主管机关或经经其正式授权的任一组织进行验证。经修订的 SEEMP 应在不迟于按第 28.2 条报告达到的年度营运 CII 后的一个月与达到的年度营运 CII 一起提交。

15.3 《防污公约》附则Ⅵ第 28.9 条进一步规定"连续三年被评为 D 级或被评为 E 级的船舶，须按照经修订的船舶能效管理计划，适当采取计划的纠正行动。"

15.4 制定整改行动计划

15.4.1 整改行动计划的目的是规定连续三年被评为 D 级或一年被评为 E 级的船舶应采取的行动，从而在采取整改行动计划后的日历年至少达到 C 级，并最终达到要求的年度营运 CII。

15.4.2 整改行动计划是船舶特定的。

15.4.3 本导则第 5 节中描述的许多方法或任何其他合适的措施可应用于船舶以提高其燃油效率，从而提高其 CII 等级。

15.4.4 整改行动计划应说明船舶计划采取的措施、应用这些措施的时间线以及应用这些措施对船舶 CII 等级的预期影响。应证明整改行动如何有助于达到要求的年度营运 CII，从而确定整改行动的有效性。在选择适当的整改行动时，应考虑从以前采取的整改行动中获得的经验及其有效性程度。

15.4.5 整改行动计划应在设想和可行的范围内实现 SMART（明确的、可衡量的、可完成的、现实的、有时限的）。应包括：

    .1 CII 等级低的原因分析；

    .2 分析已实施措施的绩效；

    .3 为达到要求的营运 CII 所必需的在实施计划中增加的附加措施和修订措施清单，以及实施时间和实施方法；

.4   designation of a company person to be responsible for the added and revised measures in the implementation plan, monitoring and recording performance throughout and reviewing of the effectiveness of the corrective actions; and

.5   identification of possible impediments to the effectiveness of the measures for improving the energy efficiency and reducing the carbon intensity of the ship, including possible additional contingency measures put in place to overcome and how these impediments will be overcome.

15.4.6   The implementation of the plan of corrective actions should be monitored and adjusted when necessary. Additional measures should be taken to strengthen corrective actions in case of insufficient intermediate results.

15.4.7   The company should ensure that it is in a position to perform the actions set out in the plan of corrective actions and confirm that it is able to do so when submitting its updated SEEMP.

.4   指定公司人员负责实施计划中增加和修订的措施，全程监控和记录绩效，审核纠正行动的有效性；和

.5   确定提高船舶能效和降低碳强度的措施有效性的可能障碍，包括为克服这些障碍而采取的可能的附加应急措施，以及如何克服这些障碍。

15.4.6   必要时应对整改行动计划的实施进行监控和调整。在中间结果不足的情况下，应采取额外措施加强纠正行动。

15.4.7   公司应确保能够执行整改行动计划中规定的行动，并在提交更新的 SEEMP 时确认其能够做到。

SAMPLE FORM OF SHIP MANAGEMENT PLAN TO IMPROVE ENERGY EFFICIENCY (PART I OF THE SEEMP)

Name of ship:		Gross tonnage:	
Ship type:		Capacity:	
IMO number:			

Date of development:		Developed by:	
Implementation period:	From: Until:	Implemented by:	
Planned date of next evaluation:			

Review and update log

Date/timeline	Updated parts	Developed by	Implemented by

1   MEASURES

Energy efficiency measures	Implementation (including the starting date)	Responsible personnel

2   MONITORING

Description of monitoring tools

3   GOAL

Measurable goals

4   EVALUATION

Procedures of evaluation

附录1
提高能效的船舶管理计划格式样本
（SEEMP 第 I 部分）

船名：		总吨位：	
船型：		载运能力：	
IMO 编号：			

编制日期：		编制者：	
执行时间：	自： 至：	执行者：	
计划的下一次评估日期：			

审查和更新日志

日期 / 时间线	更新部分	编制者	执行者

1 措施

能效措施	执行（包括开始日期）	负责人员

2 监测

监测工具的说明。

3 目标

可测量的目标。

4 评估

评估程序。

**SAMPLE FORM OF SHIP FUEL OIL CONSUMPTION DATA COLLECTION PLAN
(PART II OF THE SEEMP)**

1 Review and update log

Date/timeline	Updated parts	Developed by	Implemented by

2 Ship particulars

Name of ship	
IMO number	
Company	
Flag	
Year of delivery	
Ship type	
Gross tonnage	
NT	
DWT	
Attained EEDI (if applicable)	
Attained EEXI (if applicable)	
Ice class	

3 Record of revision of Fuel Oil Consumption Data Collection Plan

Date of revision	Revised provision

4 Ship engines and other fuel oil consumers and fuel oil types used

	Engines or other fuel oil consumer type	Power	Fuel oil types
1	Type/model of main engine	(kW)	
2	Type/model of auxiliary engine	(kW)	
3	Boiler	(...)	
4	Inert gas generator	(...)	
5	Others (Specify)	(...)	

船舶燃油消耗数据收集计划格式样本
（SEEMP 第 II 部分）

1 审查和更新日志

日期 / 时间线	更新的部分	编制者	执行者

2 船舶资料

船名	
IMO 编号	
公司	
船旗	
交船年份	
船型	
总吨位	
净吨位	
载重吨	
达到的 EEDI（如适用）	
达到的 EEXI（如适用）	
冰级	

3 燃油消耗数据收集计划修改记录

修改日期	修改条款

4 船舶发动机和其他燃油消耗设备及使用的燃油类型

	发动机或其他燃料消耗设备	功率	燃油类型
1	主机类型 / 型号	（kW）	
2	副机类型 / 型号	（kW）	
3	锅炉	（…）	
4	惰性气体发生器	（…）	
5	其他（具体说明）	（…）	

5   Emission factor

C_F is a non-dimensional conversion factor between fuel oil consumption and CO_2 emission in the *2018 Guidelines on the method of calculation of the attained Energy Efficiency Design Index (EEDI) for new ships* (resolution MEPC.308(73)), as amended. The annual total amount of CO_2 is calculated by multiplying annual fuel oil consumption and C_F for the type of fuel.

Fuel oil type	C_F (t-CO_2 / t-Fuel)
Diesel/Gas oil (e.g. ISO 8217 grades DMX through DMB)	3.206
Light fuel oil (LFO) (e.g. ISO 8217 grades RMA through RMD)	3.151
Heavy fuel oil (HFO) (e.g. ISO 8217 grades RME through RMK)	3.114
Liquefied petroleum gas (LPG) (Propane)	3.000
Liquefied petroleum gas (LPG) (Butane)	3.030
Liquefied natural gas (LNG)	2.750
Methanol	1.375
Ethanol	1.913
Other (.........)	

6   Method to measure fuel oil consumption

The applied methods for measurement for each consumer type of this ship are given below. The description explains the procedure for measuring data and calculating annual values, measurement equipment involved, etc.

Engines or other fuel oil consumer type	Method	Description
Type/model of main engine		
Type/model of auxiliary engine		
Boiler		
Others (Specify)		

7   Method to measure distance travelled including laden distance

Description

8   Method to measure hours underway

Description

9   Processes that will be used to report the data to the Administration

Description

10   Data quality

Description

5 排放系数

C_F 是经修正的《2018 年新船达到的能效设计指数（EEDI）计算方法导则》（第 MEPC.308（73）号决议）中燃油消耗量和二氧化碳排放量之间的无因次转换系数。用年度燃油消耗量乘以燃料类型的 C_F 计算得出二氧化碳的年度总量。

燃油类型	C_F （t-CO_2/t- 燃料）
柴 / 汽油（如 ISO 8217 DMX 级至 DMB 级）	3.206
轻燃油（LFO）（如 ISO 8217 RMA 级至 RMD 级）	3.151
重燃油（HFO）（如 ISO 8217 RME 级至 RMK 级）	3.114
液化石油气（LPG）（丙烷）	3.000
液化石油气（LPG）（丁烷）	3.030
液化天然气（LNG）	2.750
甲醇	1.375
乙醇	1.913
其他（……）	

6 测量燃油消耗的方法

以下给出了本船每种耗能类型适用的监测方法。描述一栏中说明了数据测量和年度值计算程序、相关测量设备等。

发动机或其他燃料消耗设备	方法	说明
主机类型 / 型号		
副机类型 / 型号		
锅炉		
其他（具体说明）		

7 测量航行距离的方法，包括载货距离

说明

8 测量在航时长的方法

说明

9 用于向主管机关报告数据的程序

说明

10 数据质量

说明

APPENDIX 3

SAMPLE FORM OF SHIP OPERATIONAL CARBON INTENSITY PLAN
(PART III OF THE SEEMP)

1 Review and update log

Date/timeline	Updated parts	Developed by	Implemented by
<1st time>			
<2nd time>			
Etc.			

2 Required CII over the next three years, attained CII and rating over three consecutive years

Name of the ship		IMO number	
Company		Year of delivery	
Flag		Ship type	
Gross tonnage		DWT	
Applicable CII		☐ AER ; ☐ cgDIST	

Year	Required annual operational CII	Attained annual operational CII (before any correction)	Attained annual operational CII	Operational carbon intensity rating (A, B, C, D or E):
<year -1>				
<year -2>				
<year -3>				

	Required annual operational CII
<year>:	
<year + 1>	
<year + 2>	

3 Calculation methodology of the ship's attained annual CII, including required data and how to obtain these data as far as not addressed in part II

Description

4 Three-year implementation plan

Description

船舶营运碳强度计划格式样本
（SEEMP 第Ⅲ部分）

1 审查和更新日志

日期 / 时间线	更新的部分	编制者	执行者
＜第 1 次＞			
＜第 2 次＞			
等			

2 未来三年要求的 CII，连续三年达到的 CII 和等级

船名		IMO 编号		
公司		交船年份		
船旗		船型		
总吨位		载重吨		
适用的 CII			□ AER；□ cgDIST	
年份	要求的年度营运 CII	达到的年度营运 CII（在任何修正之前）	达到的年度营运 CII	营运碳强度等级（A，B，C，D 或 E）：
＜年份 –1＞				
＜年份 –2＞				
＜年份 –3＞				
	要求的年度营运 CII			
＜年份＞：				
＜年份 +1＞				
＜年份 +2＞				

3 船舶达到的年度 CII 的计算方法，包括要求的数据和如何获取这些数据（如第Ⅱ部分未涉及）

说明

4 三年实施计划

说明

Company personnel to be responsible for the three-year implementation plan, monitoring and recording performance

List of measures to be considered and implemented

Measure	Impact on CII	Time and method of implementation and responsible personnel			Impediments and contingency measures	
		Milestone	Due	Responsible	Impediment	Contingencies
		Milestone	Due	Responsible	Impediment	Contingencies
		Milestone	Due	Responsible	Impediment	Contingencies
		Milestone	Due	Responsible	Impediments	Contingencies

Calculation showing the combined effect of the measures and that the required operational CII will be achieved

Year	Required annual operational CII	Targeted operational annual CII	Targeted rating
<year>:			
<year + 1>			
<year + 2>			

5 Self-evaluation and improvement

Description

6 Plan of corrective actions (if applicable)

Analysis of causes for inferior CII rating

Cause	Analysis of effect	Actions

负责三年实施计划，监控和记录绩效的公司人员

考虑和实施的措施清单

措施	对 CII 的影响	实施时间、方法和责任人员			障碍和应急措施	
		重要事项	预期时间	负责人	障碍	应急措施
		重要事项	预期时间	负责人	障碍	应急措施
		重要事项	预期时间	负责人	障碍	应急措施
		重要事项	预期时间	负责人	障碍	应急措施

显示措施的组合影响以及将达到要求的营运 CII 的计算

年份	要求的年度营运 CII	营运年度 CII 目标	等级目标
< 年份 >:			
< 年份 +1>			
< 年份 +2>			

5　自我评估和改进

说明

6　整改行动计划（如适用）

说明

CII 等级差的原因分析

原因	影响分析	行动

Analysis of measures in the implementation plan

Measure	Analysis of effect	Actions

List of additional measures and revised measures to be added to the implementation plan

Measure	Impact on CII	Time and method of implementation and responsible personnel			Impediments and contingency measures	
		Milestone	Due	Responsible	Impediments	Contingencies

实施计划中的措施分析

措施	影响分析	行动

在实施计划中增加的附加措施和修订措施清单

措施	对 CII 的影响	实施时间、方法和责任人员			障碍和应急措施	
		重要事项	预期时间	负责人	障碍	应急措施

APPENDIX 4

STANDARDIZED DATA-REPORTING FORMAT FOR THE DATA-COLLECTION SYSTEM AND OPERATIONAL CARBON INTENSITY TO THE ADMINISTRATION

Identity of the ship

Name of the ship	
Company	
Flag	
IMO number	
Period of the calendar year for which the data is submitted	
Start date for DCS (dd/mm/yy)	
End date for DCS (dd/mm/yy)	

Technical characteristics of the ship

Year of delivery		
Ship type, as defined in regulation 2.2 of MARPOL Annex VI or other (to be stated)		
Gross tonnage (GT)		
Net tonnage (NT)		
Deadweight tonnage (DWT)		
Power output (rated power) over 130 (kW)	Main Engine(s)	
	Auxiliary Engine(s)	
Attained EEDI (if applicable)		
Attained EEXI (if applicable)		
Ice class (if applicable)		

Fuel oil[1] consumption data

Total fuel oil consumption data		
Fuel oil type	Quantity in metric tonnes (t)	Method(s) used for collecting fuel oil consumption data (BDN / Flow meters / bunker FO tank monitoring / LNG cargo tank monitoring / Cargo tank monitoring other than LNG)
Diesel/Gas Oil (C_F: 3.206)		
LFO (C_F: 3.151)		
HFO (C_F: 3.114)		
LPG (Propane) (C_F::3.000)		
LPG (Butane) (C_F: 3.030)		
Ethane (C_F: 2.927)		
LNG (C_F: 2.750)		

---

[1]   Regulation 2.1.14 of MARPOL Annex VI defines "fuel oil" as any fuel delivered to and intended for combustion purposes for propulsion or operation on board a ship, including gas, distillate and residual fuels.

附录 4
提交主管机关的数据收集机制和营运碳强度数据报告的标准表格

船舶信息

船名		
公司		
船旗		
IMO 编号		
提交数据的日历年期间		
数据收集系统的开始日期（年 / 月 / 日）		
数据收集系统的截止日期（年 / 月 / 日）		

船舶技术信息

交付年份		
船舶类型，参照 MARPOL 附则Ⅵ第 2.2 或其他（需说明）		
总吨（GT）		
净吨（NT）		
载重吨（DWT）		
输出功率（额定功率）超过 130（kW）	主机	
	副机	
达到的 EEDI（如适用）		
达到的 EEXI（如适用）		
冰级（如适用）		

燃料[1] 消耗数据

燃料消耗总量		
燃料种类	消耗量（吨）	测量燃料消耗使用的方法：燃油加油单（BDNs）累加法 / 流量计法 / 使用船上燃油舱柜监测方法 / 使用船上 LNG 货舱监测方法 / 对使用 LNG 以外的货物作为燃料的船舶使用船上监测的方法
重柴油 / 轻柴油（C_F: 3.206）		
轻质燃料油（C_F: 3.151）		
重质燃料油（C_F: 3.114）		
液化石油气（丙烷）（C_F: 3.000）		
液化石油气（丁烷）（C_F: 3.030）		
乙烷（C_F: 2.927）		
液化天然气（C_F: 2.750）		

---

[1] MARPOL 附则Ⅵ第 2.1.14 条将"燃油"定义为"为船舶推进或运转而向船上供给用于燃烧的任何燃料，包括气体、蒸馏和残余燃料。"

Total fuel oil consumption data		
Methanol (CF: 1.375)		
Ethanol (CF: 1.913)		
Other (........) (Cf: ....)		

Total fuel oil consumption data per consumer type			
Fuel oil type	Consumer type	Quantity in metric tonnes (t)	Method used for collecting fuel oil consumption data (Flow meters / bunker FO tank monitoring / subtraction / estimated)
Diesel/Gas Oil (CF: 3.206)	Main engines(s)		
	Auxiliary engine(s)/Generator(s)		
	Fired Boiler(s)		
	Others (specify)		
LFO (CF: 3.151)	Main engines(s)		
	Auxiliary engine(s)/Generator(s)		
	Fired Boiler(s)		
	Others (specify)		
HFO (CF: 3.114)	Main engines(s)		
	Auxiliary engine(s)/Generator(s)		
	Fired Boiler(s)		
	Others (specify)		
LPG (Propane) (CF: 3.000)	Main engines(s)		
	Auxiliary engine(s)/Generator(s)		
	Fired Boiler(s)		
	Others (specify)		
LPG (Butane) (CF: 3.030)	Main engines(s)		
	Auxiliary engine(s)/Generator(s)		
	Fired Boiler (s)		
	Others (specify)		
Ethano (CF: 2.927)	Main engines (s)		
	Auxiliary engine(s)/Generator(s)		
	Fired Boiler (s)		
	Others (specify)		
LNG (CF: 2.750)	Main engines(s)		
	Auxiliary engine(s)/Generator(s)		
	Fired Boiler(s)		
	Others (specify)		
Methanol (CF: 1.375)	Main engines(s)		
	Auxiliary engine(s)/Generator(s)		
	Fired Boiler(s)		
	Others (specify)		
Ethanol (CF: 1.913)	Main engines(s)		
	Auxiliary engine(s)/Generator(s)		
	Fired Boiler(s)		
	Others (specify)		
Other(........) (Cf: ....)	Main engines(s)		
	Auxiliary engine(s)/Generator(s)		
	Fired Boiler (s)		
	Others (specify)		

燃料消耗总量		
甲醇（C_F: 1.375）		
乙醇（C_F: 1.913）		
其他（C_F: ……）		

每种耗能设备燃料消耗量			
燃料种类	耗能设备	消耗量（吨）	测量燃料消耗使用的方法：使用流量计法 / 使用船上燃油舱柜监测的方法 / 使用减法 / 使用估算燃油消耗量的方法
重柴油 / 轻柴油 （C_F: 3.206）	主机		
	副机 / 发电机		
	锅炉		
	其他		
轻质燃料油 （C_F: 3.151）	主机		
	副机 / 发电机		
	锅炉		
	其他		
重质燃料油 HFO（C_F: 3.114）	主机		
	副机 / 发电机		
	锅炉		
	其他		
液化石油气（丙烷） LPG（C_F: 3.000）	主机		
	副机 / 发电机		
	锅炉		
	其他		
液化石油气（丁烷） LPG（C_F: 3.030）	主机		
	副机 / 发电机		
	锅炉		
	其他		
乙烷 （C_F: 2.927）	主机		
	副机 / 发电机		
	锅炉		
	其他		
液化天然气 LNG（C_F: 2.750）	主机		
	副机 / 发电机		
	锅炉		
	其他		
甲醇（C_F: 1.375）	主机		
	副机 / 发电机		
	锅炉		
	其他		
乙醇 （C_F: 1.913）	主机		
	副机 / 发电机		
	锅炉		
	其他		
其他（……） Other（C_F: ……）	主机		
	副机 / 发电机		
	锅炉		
	其他		

Fuel oil consumption data while the ship is not under way, per consumer type			
Fuel oil type	Consumer type	Quantity in metric tonnes (t)	Method used for collecting fuel oil consumption data
Diesel/Gas Oil (CF: 3.206)	Main engines(s)		
	Auxiliary engine(s)/Generator(s)		
	Fired Boiler(s)		
	Others (specify)		
LFO (CF: 3.151)	Main engines(s)		
	Auxiliary engine(s)/Generator(s)		
	Fired Boiler(s)		
	Others (specify)		
HFO (CF: 3.114)	Main engines(s)		
	Auxiliary engines		
	Fired Boiler(s)		
	Others (specify)		
LPG (Propane) (CF: 3.000)	Main engines(s)		
	Auxiliary engine(s)/Generator(s)		
	Fired Boiler(s)		
	Others (specify)		
LPG (Butane) (CF: 3.030)	Main engines(s)		
	Auxiliary engine(s)/Generator(s)		
	Fired Boiler(s)		
	Others (specify)		
Ethane (CF: 2.927)	Main engines(s)		
	Auxiliary engine(s)/Generator(s)		
	Fired Boiler(s)		
	Others (specify)		
LNG (CF: 2.750)	Main engines(s)		
	Auxiliary engine(s)/Generator(s)		
	Fired Boiler(s)		
	Others (specify)		
Methanol (CF: 1.375)	Main engines(s)		
	Auxiliary engine(s)/Generator(s)		
	Fired Boiler (s)		
	Others (specify)		
Ethanol (CF: 1.913)	Main engines (s)		
	Auxiliary engine(s)/Generator(s)		
	Fired Boiler(s)		
	Others (specify)		
Other (.......) (Cf: ....)	Main engines(s)		
	Auxiliary engine(s)/Generator(s)		
	Fired Boiler(s)		
	Others (specify)		

Total distance travelled (nm)	
Laden distance travelled (nm) (on a voluntary basis)	
Hours under way (h)	
Total amount of onshore power supplied (kWh)	

非在航时船舶每种耗能设备燃料消耗量			
燃料种类	耗能设备	消耗量（吨）	测量燃料消耗使用的方法
重柴油 / 轻柴油 （C_F: 3.206）	主机		
	副机 / 发电机		
	锅炉		
	其他		
轻质燃料油 LFO（C_F: 3.151）	主机		
	副机 / 发电机		
	锅炉		
	其他		
重质燃料油 HFO（C_F: 3.114）	主机		
	副机 / 发电机		
	锅炉		
	其他		
液化石油气（丙烷） LPG（C_F: 3.000）	主机		
	副机 / 发电机		
	锅炉		
	其他		
液化石油气（丁烷） LPG（C_F: 3.030）	主机		
	副机 / 发电机		
	锅炉		
	其他		
乙烷 （C_F: 2.927）	主机		
	副机 / 发电机		
	锅炉		
	其他		
液化天然气 LNG（C_F: 2.750）	主机		
	副机 / 发电机		
	锅炉		
	其他		
甲醇 （C_F: 1.375）	主机		
	副机 / 发电机		
	锅炉		
	其他		
乙醇 （C_F: 1.913）	主机		
	副机 / 发电机		
	锅炉		
	其他		
其他（……） （C_F: ……）	主机		
	副机 / 发电机		
	锅炉		
	其他		

总航行距离（nm）	
载货航行距离（nm）（自愿）	
在航时长（h）	
岸电消耗量（kWh）	

For ships to which regulation 28 of MARPOL Annex VI applies:

Total transport work	
Applicable CII	□AER ; □cgDIST
Required annual operational CII	
Start date for annual CII (dd/mm/yy)[2]	
End date for annual CII (dd/mm/yy)[2]	
Attained annual operational CII before any correction (AER in g CO_2/dwt.nm or cgDIST in g CO_2/gt.nm)	
Attained annual operational CII (AER in g CO_2/dwt.nm or cgDIST in g CO_2/gt.nm)	
Installation of innovative technology, if applicable (refer to MEPC.1/Circ.896)	□A ; □B-1 ; □B-2 ; □C-1 ; □C-2
Operational carbon intensity rating	□A ; □B ; □C ; □D ; □E
CII for trial purpose (none, one or more on voluntary basis)	□EEPI ; □cbDIST ; □clDIST ; □EEOI
EEPI (gCO_2/dwt.nm)	
cbDIST (gCO_2/berth.nm)	
clDIST (gCO_2/m.nm)	
EEOI (gCO_2/t.nm or others)	

[2]   In the event of any transfer of a ship addressed in regulations 27.4, 27.5 or 27.6, these dates should be completed consistent with regulation 28.3 of MARPOL Annex VI (i.e. full 12-month period from 1 January to 31 December in the calendar year during which the transfer took place).

对于适用 MARPOL 公约附则Ⅵ第 28 条的船舶：

总运输工作量	
适用的 CII	☐ AER;　☐ cgDIST
要求的年度营运 CII	
年度营运 CII 的开始日期（日 / 月 / 年）[2]	
年度营运 CII 的截止日期（日 / 月 / 年）	
达到的年度营运 CII（修正前）	
达到的年度营运 CII	
安装的创新技术（如适应）	☐ A; ☐ B–1; ☐ B–2; ☐ C–1; ☐ C–2;
年度营运碳强度评级	☐ A; ☐ B; ☐ C; ☐ D; ☐ E;
试验用的 CII	☐ EEPI ; ☐ cbDIST; ☐ clDIST; ☐ EEOI;
EEPI（gCO_2/dwt.nm）	
cbDIST（gCO_2/berth.nm）	
clDIST（gCO_2/m.nm）	
EEOI（gCO_2/t.nm or others）	

[2] 如船舶发生第 27.4、27.5 或 27.6 条所述的变更，这些数据应按照 MARPOL 附则Ⅵ第 28.3 条的规定完成（即：变更发生年份自 1 月 1 日至 12 月 31 日整 12 个月周期）。

APPENDIX 5

STANDARDIZED DATA REPORTING FORMAT FOR THE PARAMETERS TO CALCULATE THE TRIAL CARBON INTENSITY INDICATORS ON VOLUNTARY BASIS*

Attained annual EEOI	
Metric of Cargo Mass Carried or Work Done in EEOI calculation (gCO_2/t.nm or others)*****	
Transport work*****	
Attained annual EEPI (gCO_2/dwt.nm)	
Laden distance travelled (n.m)	
Attained annual clDIST (gCO_2/m.nm) ****	
Length of lanes (metre) ****	
Attained annual cbDIST(gCO_2/berth.nm) ***	
Available lower berths***	
End date for trial CII (dd/mm/yy)**	
Start date for trial CII (dd/mm/yy)**	
IMO number**	
End date for DCS (dd/mm/yy)**	
Start date for DCS (dd/mm/yy)**	

*   For reporting a trial CII, the data should be reported as applicable taking into account the information already provided in appendix 4.
**   Consistent with appendix 4.
***   Only applicable to cruise passenger ships.
****   Only applicable to ro-ro ships.
*****   As defined in section 3 of *Guidelines for voluntary use of the ship energy efficiency operational indicator (EEOI)* circulated by MEPC.1/Circ.684. The distance travelled shall be determined from berth of the port of departure to berth of the port of arrival and shall be expressed in nautical miles.

***

附录 5
计算自愿试用碳强度指标的参数的标准数据报告格式 *

达到的年度船舶能效营运指数（EEOI）	
在 EEOI 计算中所载运的货物质量或所做的工作的度量（gCO_2/t.nm 或其他）*****	
运输功 *****	
达到的年度能效性能指标（EEPI）（$g\,CO_2$/dwt.nm）	
载货航行距离（n.m）	
滚装船达到的年度 clDIST（gCO_2/m.nm）****	
车道长度（米）****	
邮轮达到的年度 cbDIST（gCO_2/berth.nm）***	
可用下铺数量 ***	
试用 CII 的截止日期（日 / 月 / 年）**	
试用 CII 的开始日期（日 / 月 / 年）**	
IMO 编号 **	
DCS 的截止日期（日 / 月 / 年）**	
DCS 的开始日期（日 / 月 / 年）**	

---

*　报告试用 CII 时，应在考虑附录 4 中已经提供的信息的情况下报告适用的数据。

**　与附录 4 一致。

***　只适用于邮轮。

****　只适用于滚装船。

*****　如第 MEPC.1/Circ.684 号通函关于《船舶能效营运指数（EEOI）自愿使用导则》第 3 节中的定义，航行距离应从出发港泊位至到达港泊位确定，以海里表示。

RESOLUTION MEPC.347(78)
(adopted on 10 June 2022)

GUIDELINES FOR THE VERIFICATION AND COMPANY AUDITS BY THE ADMINISTRATION OF PART III OF THE SHIP ENERGY EFFICIENCY MANAGEMENT PLAN (SEEMP)

THE MARINE ENVIRONMENT PROTECTION COMMITTEE,

RECALLING Article 38(a) of the Convention on the International Maritime Organization concerning the functions of the Marine Environment Protection Committee (the Committee) conferred upon it by international conventions for the prevention and control of marine pollution from ships,

NOTING that the Committee adopted, at its seventy-sixth session, by resolution MEPC.328(76), the *2021 Revised MARPOL Annex VI* which will enter into force on 1 November 2022,

NOTING IN PARTICULAR that the *2021 Revised MARPOL Annex VI* (MARPOL Annex VI) contains amendments concerning mandatory goal-based technical and operational measures to reduce carbon intensity of international shipping,

NOTING FURTHER that regulation 26 of MARPOL Annex VI requires each ship to keep on board a Ship Energy Efficiency Management Plan (SEEMP), to be developed and reviewed, taking into account the guidelines adopted by the Organization,

RECOGNIZING that the aforementioned amendments to MARPOL Annex VI require relevant guidelines for uniform and effective implementation of the regulations and to provide sufficient lead time for industry to prepare,

HAVING CONSIDERED, at its seventy-eighth session, draft *Guidelines for the verification and company audits by the Administration of part III of the Ship Energy Efficiency Management Plan (SEEMP)*,

1   ADOPTS the *Guidelines for the verification and company audits by the Administration of part III of the Ship Energy Efficiency Management Plan (SEEMP)*, as set out in the annex to the present resolution;

2   INVITES Administrations to take the annexed Guidelines into account when developing and enacting national laws which give force to and implement requirements set forth in regulation 26 of MARPOL Annex VI;

3   REQUESTS the Parties to MARPOL Annex VI and other Member Governments to bring the annexed Guidelines to the attention of masters, seafarers, shipowners, ship operators and any other interested parties;

4   AGREES to keep the Guidelines under review in light of experience gained with their implementation, also taking into consideration that, in accordance with regulations 25.3 and 28.11 of MARPOL Annex VI, a review of the technical and operational measures to reduce carbon intensity of international shipping shall be completed by 1 January 2026.

第 MEPC.347（78）号决议
（2022 年 6 月 10 日通过）

主管机关对船舶能效管理计划（SEEMP）第Ⅲ部分验证和公司审核导则

海上环境保护委员会，

忆及《国际海事组织公约》第 38（a）条关于防止和控制船舶造成海洋污染国际公约赋予海上环境保护委员会（本委员会）的职能，

注意到委员会在其第 76 届会议上以 MEPC.328（76）号决议通过了将于 2022 年 11 月 1 日生效的 2021 年经修订的 MARPOL 附则Ⅵ，

特别注意到 2021 年经修订的 MARPOL 附则Ⅵ包含关于基于目标的强制性技术和营运措施以减少国际航运碳强度的修正案，

进一步注意到 MARPOL 附则Ⅵ第 26 条要求每艘船都备有一份船舶能效管理计划（SEEMP），同时考虑到本组织制定的导则制定和审查该计划，

认识到上述 MARPOL 附则Ⅵ的修正案需要有相关导则，以便于统一和有效实施各条规定，并为业界提供充足的准备时间，

在其第 78 届会议上**审议了**《主管机关对船舶能效管理计划（SEEMP）第Ⅲ部分验证和公司审核导则》草案，

1 **通过**载于本决议附件的《主管机关对船舶能效管理计划（SEEMP）第Ⅲ部分验证和公司审核导则》；

2 **提请**主管机关在制定和颁布本国法律，以执行和实施 MARPOL 附则Ⅵ第 26 条要求时，考虑到附件中的导则；

3 **要求** MARPOL 附则Ⅵ的各缔约方和其他成员国政府提请船长、船员、船东、船舶经营者以及任何其他利益相关方注意到附件中的导则；

4 **同意**根据实施过程中取得的经验不断审查该导则，同时考虑到根据 MARPOL 附则Ⅵ第 25.3 条和 28.11 条，对减少国际航运碳强度的技术和营运措施的审查应于 2026 年 1 月 1 日前完成。

ANNEX

GUIDELINES FOR THE VERIFICATION AND COMPANY AUDITS BY THE ADMINISTRATION OF PART III OF THE SHIP ENERGY EFFICIENCY MANAGEMENT PLAN (SEEMP)

CONTENTS

附件
主管机关对船舶能效管理计划（SEEMP）第Ⅲ部分验证和公司审核导则

目录

1 INTRODUCTION

1.1 The *Guidelines for the verification and company audits by the Administration of part III of the Ship Energy Efficiency Management Plan (SEEMP)* have been developed to assist Administrations with carrying out the verifications and company audits required by regulation 26.3.3 of MARPOL Annex VI.

1.2 The aim of these Guidelines is to:

.1 provide guidance to Administrations to effectively and efficiently carry out verifications of, and company audits related to, the Ship Energy Efficiency Management Plan (SEEMP) to ensure compliance with regulation 26.3 and with regulation 28 of MARPOL Annex VI; and

.2 ensure that the SEEMP includes the relevant elements in accordance with regulation 26.3 of MARPOL Annex VI, as applicable, and that the SEEMP is reliable, while minimizing the costs and associated burdens to the ship and the Administration.

1.3 The verification of and the company audits related to the SEEMP may be carried out by the Administration or an organization recognized by it.[1]

1.4 It should be noted that the Organization has adopted separate *2022 Guidelines for Administration verification of ship fuel oil consumption data and operational carbon intensity* (resolution MEPC.348(78), adopted 10 June 2022).

2 DEFINITIONS

For the purpose of these Guidelines, the definitions in MARPOL Annex VI apply.

3 RESPONSIBILITIES

3.1 The responsibilities of Administrations and ships are set out in MARPOL Annex VI. These Guidelines do not change those responsibilities or create any new obligations.

3.2 An Administration may authorize an organization to carry out verifications of, and company audits related to, the SEEMP, and issue the Confirmation of Compliance, submit the data to the Organization and perform other actions authorized by the Administration. In every case, the Administration assumes full responsibility for all tasks conducted by the Administration, or any organization duly authorized by it (hereinafter referred to as "the Administration").

3.3 Verification of, and company audits related to, the SEEMP do not relieve the company, management, those undertaking delegated SEEMP tasks, officers or seafarers of their obligations as to compliance with those requirements in regulation 28 of MARPOL Annex VI.

3.4 The company is responsible for:

.1 informing relevant personnel and those undertaking the delegated SEEMP tasks about the content of the SEEMP;

---

[1] Refer to the *Code for Recognized Organizations (RO Code)*, as adopted by the Organization by resolution MEPC.237(65), as may be amended by the Organization.

1 引言

1.1 制定主管机关对船舶能效管理计划第Ⅲ部分验证和公司审核导则，用以协助主管机关执行 MARPOL 附则Ⅵ第 26.3.3 条规定的验证和公司审核。

1.2 本导则旨在：

    .1 向主管机关提供指导，以有效和高效地开展与船舶能效管理计划（SEEMP）相关的验证和公司审核，确保符合 MARPOL 附则Ⅵ第 26.3 条和第 28 条的规定；和

    .2 确保船舶能效管理计划（SEEMP）包括符合 MARPOL 附则Ⅵ第 26.3 条要求的相关要素（如适用），以及 SEEMP 的可靠性，同时最大限度地降低船舶和主管机关成本和相关负担。

1.3 与 SEEMP 相关的验证和公司审核可由主管机关或其认可的组织进行。[1]

1.4 应该注意的是，本组织已通过单独的《船舶燃料消耗数据和营运碳强度主管机关验证导则》（MEPC.348（78）号决议，2022 年 6 月 10 日通过）。

2 定义

就本导则而言，MARPOL 附则Ⅵ中的定义适用。

3 职责

3.1 MARPOL 附则Ⅵ规定了主管机关和船舶的职责。本导则不会改变这些职责或产生任何新的义务。

3.2 主管机关可授权某组织进行与 SEEMP 相关的验证和公司审核，并签发符合性确认书，同时向本组织提交数据以及执行主管机关授权的其他行动。在任何情况下，主管机关对其或其正式授权的任何组织（以下简称"主管机关"）采取的行动承担全部责任。

3.3 与 SEEMP 相关的验证和公司审核并不免除公司、管理层、承担 SEEMP 委派任务的人员、工作人员或船员遵守 MARPOL 附则Ⅵ第 28 条规定的义务。

3.4 公司负责：
    .1 将 SEEMP 的内容通知相关人员和承担 SEEMP 委派任务的人员；

---

[1] 参见可能经本组织修正的、本组织以第 MEPC.237（65）号决议通过的《被认可组织规则》。

.2 appointing responsible members of staff to accompany the verifier; and

.3 providing access and evidential materials as requested by the verifier.

4 VERIFICATION OF THE SEEMP AND DOCUMENTATION

4.1 To facilitate the verification, the Administration should indicate what documentation, if any, the company should submit along with its SEEMP.

5 INITIAL, PERIODICAL, ADDITIONAL VERIFICATIONS AND COMPANY AUDITS

5.1 The verification and audit process for the SEEMP according to regulation 26.3.3 of MARPOL Annex VI should normally involve the following:

.1 initial verification;

.2 periodical verifications;

.3 additional verifications; and

.4 company audits.

5.2 The initial, periodical, additional verifications and company audits should be based on documentary evidence.

Initial verification (regulation 5.4.6 of MARPOL Annex VI)

5.3 The Administration should perform an initial verification to ensure that for each ship to which regulation 26.3 of MARPOL Annex VI applies, the SEEMP complies with regulation 26.3.1 of MARPOL Annex VI. In accordance with regulation 5.4.6 of MARPOL Annex VI, this process must be done prior to 1 January 2023 for existing ships or before a new ship is put in service.

5.4 On satisfactory assessment of the SEEMP part III, the Administration can issue the Confirmation of Compliance (sample format in the annex to this document).

Periodical verification (regulation 5.4.6 of MARPOL Annex VI)

5.5 If any of the elements in regulation 26.3.1 is updated, and in any case every three years, the Administration should perform a periodical verification to ensure the SEEMP complies with regulation 26.3.1 of MARPOL Annex VI in accordance with regulation 5.4.6 of MARPOL Annex VI.

5.6 On satisfactory assessment of SEEMP part III, the Administration should issue the Confirmation of Compliance (sample format in the annex to this document).

Additional verifications (regulation 6.8 of MARPOL Annex VI)

5.7 The Administration should, in the case of a ship rated as D for three consecutive years or a ship rated as E, perform an additional verification to ensure that a plan of corrective actions has been established in accordance with regulations 28.7 and 28.8.

5.8 On satisfactory verification of the plan of corrective actions, the Administration can issue the Statement of Compliance according to regulation 6.8.

2. 指派负责人员陪同验证人员；和

3. 按照验证人员的要求提供访问权限和证据材料。

4 SEEMP 和文件的验证

4.1 为便于验证，主管机关应指明公司应连同其 SEEMP 提交哪些文件（如有）。

5 初次、定期、附加验证和公司审核

5.1 根据 MARPOL 附则Ⅵ第 26.3.3 条，对 SEEMP 的验证和审核过程通常应包括以下内容：

1. 初次验证；

2. 定期验证；

3. 附加验证；和

4. 公司审核

5.2 初次、定期、附加验证以及公司审核应以书面证明为基础。

初次验证（MARPOL 附则Ⅵ第 5.4.6 条）

5.3 主管机关应进行初次验证，以确保适用 MARPOL 附则Ⅵ第 26.3 条的每艘船舶的 SEEMP 符合 MARPOL 附则Ⅵ第 26.1 条的规定。根据 MARPOL 附则Ⅵ第 5.4.6 条，现有船舶或新船投入使用之前必须在 2023 年 1 月 1 日之前完成初次验证。

5.4 如果对 SEEMP 第Ⅲ部分的评估通过后，主管机关可以签发符合性确认书（Confirmation of Compliance，COC）（样本格式见本文件附录）。

定期验证（MARPOL 附则Ⅵ第 5.4.6 条）

5.5 如果第 26.3.1 条中的任何内容更新，且每三年必须更新一次，主管机关应根据 MARPOL 第 5.4.6 条进行定期验证，确保 SEEMP 符合 MARPOL 附则Ⅵ第 26.3.1 条规定。

5.6 对 SEEMP 第Ⅲ部分的评估满意后，主管机关可以签发符合性确认书（样本格式见本文件附录）。

附加验证（MARPOL 附则Ⅵ第 6.8 条）

5.7 对于连续三年被评为 D 级或被评为 E 级的船舶，主管机关应进行附加验证，以确保已按照第 28.7 条和 28.8 条制定了整改行动计划。

5.8 如果对整改行动计划的验证满意后，主管机关可根据第 6.8 条签发符合声明（Statement of Compliance，SOC）。

Company audits

5.9   The Administration should, in accordance with regulation 26.3.3, perform periodical company audits to:

     .1   verify that the SEEMP for which the Confirmation of Compliance has previously been issued complies with regulation 26.3.1 and, in the case of non-compliance, require remedial action;

     .2   confirm that the ship is being operated in accordance with SEEMP part III, regardless of its rating;

     .3   verify the progress made in the (corrective) actions to be taken in the execution of the three-year implementation plan and the plan of corrective actions;

     .4   verify self-assessment and improvement of actions taken; and

     .5   verify the assignment of responsibilities related to the implementation and monitoring of measures.

5.10   The periodical company audits may include annual audits of the company (company audits) and verifications on board the ship (shipboard audits).

5.11   These additional shipboard verifications and company audits, if undertaken, should be six months after the issuance of the Statement of Compliance at the latest.

6   ELEMENTS OF VERIFICATION

6.1   Verification could consist of, but not be limited to, the following elements:

     .1   verification of the method of calculations of the CII and that there is a proper description of the method to report ship data to the Administration;

     .2   assessment of the effectiveness (of the combination) of measures, so that when implemented the ship will with reasonable assurance achieve the required annual operational CII, including the goal as set in accordance with paragraph 4.1.7 and 9.7 of the SEEMP Guidelines; and

     .3   robustness of the three-year implementation plan and, where applicable, the plan of corrective actions, including whether realistic timelines for implementation of actions have been included.

7   COMBINATION WITH ISM AUDITS

7.1   Verification of implementation aspects of the SEEMP on board (monitoring, self-evaluation and improvements, etc.) could be combined with the ISM audits.

7.2   The verifications may be carried out in accordance with guidelines on implementation of the ISM Code referred to in Chapter 15 of the ISM Code.

公司审核

5.9 主管机关应根据第 26.3.3 条定期进行公司审核，以：

1. 验证先前已签发符合性确认书的 SEEMP 符合第 26.3.1 条的规定，如果不符合规定，要求采取补救措施；

2. 确认船舶正在按照 SEEMP 第Ⅲ部分操作，无论其评级如何；

3. 验证在执行三年实施计划和整改行动计划中要采取的（整改）行动的进展；

4. 验证自我评估和所采取的改进措施；和

5. 验证与实施和监测相关的职责分工。

5.10 定期公司审核可包括公司年度审核（公司审核）和船上验证（船上审核）。

5.11 如果进行这些附加的船上验证和公司审核，最迟应在签发符合声明（SOC）6 个月内进行。

6 验证要素

6.1 验证可以包括但不限于以下要素：

1. 验证 CII 的计算方法，以及向主管机关报告船舶数据方法的适当描述；

2. 评估（组合）措施的有效性，以便在实施时船舶合理确保达到年度营运 CII，包括根据 SEEMP 导则第 4.1.7 和 9.7 条设定的目标；和

3. 三年实施计划，以及整改行动计划（如适用）的稳健性，包括是否已包含实施行动的可实现的时间表。

7 与 ISM 审核相结合

7.1 船上 SEEMP 实施方面的验证（监测、自我评估和改进等）可以与 ISM 审核相结合。

7.2 验证可按照 ISM 规则第 15 章所指的 ISM 规则实施指南进行。

ANNEX

SAMPLE FORMAT FOR CONFIRMATION OF COMPLIANCE

CONFIRMATION OF COMPLIANCE – SEEMP PART III

Issued under the provisions of the Protocol of 1997, as amended, to amend the International Convention for the Prevention of Pollution from Ships, 1973, as modified by the Protocol of 1978 related thereto (hereinafter referred to as "the Convention") under the authority of the Government of:

. . . .

(full designation of the Country)

by . . . .

(full designation of the competent person or organization authorized under the provisions of the Convention)

Particulars of ship*

      Name of ship . . . .

      Distinctive number or letters. . . . .

      IMO number[†]. . . . .

      Port of registry . . . .

      Gross tonnage. . . . .

      SEEMP part III date of revision, as applicable . . . .

THIS IS TO CONFIRM:

Taking into account the *2024 Guidelines for the development of a Ship Energy Efficiency Management Plan (SEEMP)* adopted by resolution MEPC.395(82), the ship's SEEMP has been developed and complies with regulation 26.3.1 of Annex VI of the Convention.

Issued at: . . . .

(place of issue of the Confirmation)

Date (dd/mm/yyyy) . . . .
        (date of issue)   *(signature of duly authorized official issuing the Confirmation)*

(seal or stamp of the authority, as appropriate)

---

*   Alternatively, the particulars of the ship may be placed horizontally in boxes.

†   In accordance with the IMO Ship Identification Number Scheme, adopted by the Organization by resolution A.1117(30).

***

附录—符合性确认书格式样本

符合性确认书样本格式—SEEMP 第Ⅲ部分

根据经修正的《经 1978 年议定书修订的 1973 年国际防止船舶造成污染公约 1997 年议定书》（以下称"公约"）的规定，经

....

（国家全称）政府授权，

由 ....

（按公约规定经授权的主管人员或组织全称）签发

船舶资料[*]

     船名 ....

     船舶编号或呼号 ....

     IMO 编号[†] ....

     船籍港 ....

     总吨 ....

     SEEMP 第Ⅲ部分修订日期（如适用）...........................

兹证明：

考虑到 MEPC.395（82）决议通过的《2024 年船舶能效管理（SEEMP）编制导则》，船舶的 SEEMP 已经制定，并符合"公约"附则Ⅵ第 26.3.1 条的规定。

签发于：..

（确认书的签发地）

日期（日／月／年）...........................   ....

（签发日期）   （经正式授权的发证官员签字）

（主管机关的盖章或钢印（视情况而定））

* 船舶资料也可在表格中横向排列。

† 按照本组织第 A.1117（30）号决议通过的《国际海事组织船舶识别号计划》。

***

—— 船舶燃油消耗数据相关 ——

2022 GUIDELINES FOR ADMINISTRATION VERIFICATION OF SHIP FUEL OIL CONSUMPTION DATA AND OPERATIONAL CARBON INTENSITY (RESOLUTION MEPC.348(78), AS AMENDED BY RESOLUTION MEPC.389(81))

THE MARINE ENVIRONMENT PROTECTION COMMITTEE,

RECALLING Article 38(a) of the Convention on the International Maritime Organization concerning the functions of the Marine Environment Protection Committee conferred upon it by international conventions for the prevention and control of marine pollution from ships,

NOTING that regulation 27.7 of MARPOL Annex VI requires that ship fuel oil consumption data be verified according to procedures established by the Administration, taking into account guidelines developed by the Organization,

NOTING ALSO that regulation 28.6 of MARPOL Annex VI specifies that the attained annual operational CII shall be documented and verified against the required annual operational CII to determine operational carbon intensity rating, taking into account the guidelines developed by the Organization,

NOTING FURTHER that, at its seventy-eighth session, it adopted, by resolution MEPC.348(78), the *2022 Guidelines for Administration verification of ship fuel oil consumption data and operational carbon intensity*,

HAVING CONSIDERED, at its eighty-first session, proposed amendments to the *2022 Guidelines for Administration verification of ship fuel oil consumption data and operational carbon intensity*,

1   ADOPTS amendments to the *2022 Guidelines for Administration verification of ship fuel oil consumption data and operational carbon intensity*, as set out in the annex to the present resolution;

2   REQUESTS the Parties to MARPOL Annex VI and other Member Governments to bring the annexed amendments to the attention of masters, seafarers, shipowners, ship operators and any other interested parties.

环保会 MEPC.389（81）号决议
（2024 年 3 月 22 日通过）

2022 年船舶燃油消耗数据和营运碳强度主管机关验证导则
（经第 MEPC.389（81）号决议修正的第 MEPC.348（78）号决议）

海上环境保护委员会，

忆及《国际海事组织公约》关于防止和控制船舶造成海洋污染国际公约赋予海上环境保护委员会（本委员会）职能的第 38（a）条，

注意到 MARPOL 附则Ⅵ第 27.7 条要求，船舶燃油消耗数据应按主管机关制定的程序予以验证，并考虑本组织制定的导则，

还注意到 MARPOL 附则Ⅵ第 28.6 条规定，应记录达到的年度营运 CII，并结合本组织制定的导则对照要求的年度营运 CII 对其进行验证，以确定其营运碳强度等级，

进一步注意到本委员会在其第 78 届会议上以 MEPC.348（78）决议通过的《2022 年船舶燃油消耗数据和营运碳强度主管机关验证导则》，

在其第 81 届会议上，**审议了**《2022 年船舶燃油消耗数据和营运碳强度主管机关验证导则》提出的修正案，

1 通过《2022 年船舶燃油消耗数据和营运碳强度主管机关验证导则》的修正案，其文本载于本决议附件；

2 要求 MARPOL 附则Ⅵ的各缔约国和其他成员国政府使船长、海员、船东、船舶经营者和任何其他相关方注意到附件中的导则。

AMENDMENTS TO THE 2022 GUIDELINES FOR ADMINISTRATION VERIFICATION OF SHIP FUEL OIL CONSUMPTION DATA AND OPERATIONAL CARBON INTENSITY (RESOLUTION MEPC.348(78))

1 INTRODUCTION

1.1 Regulation 27 of MARPOL Annex VI establishes the IMO Ship Fuel Oil Consumption Database, to be administered by the Organization, to which each Administrations will submit relevant data for their registered ships of 5,000 gross tonnage (GT) and above. Regulation 27.7 specifies that "the data shall be verified according to procedures established by the Administration, taking into account guidelines developed by the Organization".

1.2 Regulation 28 of MARPOL Annex VI establishes the operational carbon intensity rating mechanism. Regulation 28.6 specifies that the attained annual operational CII shall be documented and verified against the required annual operational CII to determine operational carbon intensity rating A, B, C, D or E, either by the Administration or by any organization duly authorized by it, taking into account the guidelines developed by the Organization.

1.3 This document contains the Guidelines referred to in regulations 27.7 and 28.6 and is intended to assist Administrations in developing their own verification programme.

1.4 A verification procedure should ensure the reliability of the collected data and the correctness of the attained annual operational CII, while minimizing the costs and associated burdens to the ship and the Administration.

2 DEFINITIONS

For the purpose of these Guidelines, the definitions in MARPOL Annex VI apply.

3 RESPONSIBILITIES

3.1 The responsibilities of Administrations and ships are set out in MARPOL Annex VI. These Guidelines do not change those or create any new obligations.

3.2 Under the data collection system for fuel oil consumption and the operational carbon intensity rating of ships, as specified in MARPOL Annex VI, an Administration may authorize an organization[1] to receive the data from a ship, verify the data for compliance with the requirements, verify the attained annual operational CII against the required annual operational CII, determine the operational carbon intensity rating, issue the Statement of Compliance, and submit the data to the Organization. In every case, the Administration assumes full responsibility for all tasks conducted by the Administration or any organization duly authorized by it (hereinafter referred to as "the Administration").

4 VERIFICATION OF THE REPORTED DATA

4.1 To facilitate data verification, the Administration should indicate what additional documentation a ship should submit along with its annual data report. Specification of this

---

[1] Refer to the *Guidelines for the authorization of organizations acting on behalf of the Administration*, adopted by the Organization by resolution A.739(18), as amended by resolution MSC.208(81), and the *Specifications on the survey and certification functions of recognized organizations acting on behalf of the Administration*, adopted by the Organization by resolution A.789(19), as may be amended by the Organization.

附件

《2022 年船舶燃油消耗数据和营运碳强度主管机关验证导则》
（第 MEPC.348（78）号决议）修正案

1 引言

1.1 《防污公约》附则Ⅵ第 27 条建立了 IMO 船舶燃油消耗数据库，该库将由本组织管理，每个主管机关将向该库提交其 5 000 总吨（GT）及以上的登记船舶的相关数据。第 27.7 条规定"须按照主管机关确定的程序对数据进行验证，并考虑本组织制定的导则"。

1.2 《防污公约》附则Ⅵ第 28 条建立了营运碳强度评级机制。第 28.6 条规定，须记录达到的年度运营碳强度指标，并对照要求的年度营运碳强度指标进行验证，以由主管机关或经其正式授权的任一组织，考虑到本组织制定的导则，确定营运碳强度评级 A、B、C、D 或 E。

1.3 本文件包含第 27.7 和 28.6 条所提及的导则，旨在协助主管机关制定其验证计划。

1.4 验证程序应确保所收集数据的可靠性和达到的年度营运 CII 的正确性，同时把对船舶和主管机关的成本和相关负担降至最低。

2 定义

就本导则而言，《防污公约》附则Ⅵ中的定义适用。

3 责任

3.1 《防污公约》附则Ⅵ规定了主管机关和船舶的责任。本导则不改变这些责任或增加任何新的义务。

3.2 根据《防污公约》附则Ⅵ规定的船舶燃油消耗数据收集系统和营运碳强度评级，主管机关可授权一个组织[1]接收来自船舶的数据，验证数据是否符合要求，对照要求的年度营运 CII 验证达到的年度营运 CII，确定营运碳强度等级，签发符合声明，并向本组织提交数据。在任何情况下，主管机关对其或经其正式授权的任何组织（以下称"主管机关"）执行的所有任务承担全部责任。

4 对报告数据的验证

4.1 为了便利数据验证，主管机关应说明船舶应随其年度数据报告一并提交的附加文件。

---

[1] 参见本组织以第 A.739（18）号决议通过并经第 MSC.208（81）号决议修正的《授权代表主管机关行事的组织的导则》和本组织以第 A.789（19）号决议通过并可能由本组织修正的《被认可组织代表主管机关执行检验和发证的细则》。

documentation can be done on a ship basis, as part of the assessment of the Data Collection Plan,[2] or it may be done as a general policy statement or through such other policy instruments as the Administration deems appropriate. Additional documentation to facilitate data verification may include the following, as well as other documentation that the Administration deems relevant:

.1   a copy of the verified ship's Data Collection Plan (SEEMP Part II);

.2   summaries of bunker delivery notes (BDNs), in sufficient detail to show that all fuel oil consumed by the ship is accounted for (see sample form of BDN summary set out in appendix 1);

.3   summaries of disaggregated data of fuel oil consumption, distance travelled and hours under way, in a format specified by the Administration (see sample form of data summary set out in appendix 2);

.4   information to demonstrate that the ship followed the Data Collection Plan set out in its SEEMP, including information on data gaps and how they were filled as well as how the event that caused the data gap was resolved;

.5   copies of documents containing information on the amount of fuel oil and consumption, distance travelled, hours under way for the ship's voyages and the other data during the reporting period (e.g. the ship's official logbook, oil record book, BDNs, arrival/noon/departure reports, and from auto-log data files);

.6   supported by documentary evidence, copies of the fuel oil mass to CO_2 mass conversion factor provided by fuel supplier in case the type of fuel is not covered by the guidelines developed by the Organization.[3]

4.2   In addition to the documentation described in paragraph 4.1, the Administration may request a ship to submit such documentation needed to perform a comprehensive review of a ship's annual fuel oil consumption, distance travelled, and hours under way. The Administration may request that this documentation be submitted by all ships or a subset of the ships under its jurisdiction. This documentation may be used by the Administration to verify whether the ship followed the methodology specified in its Data Collection Plan, with a view to confirming:

.1   consistency of reported data and calculated values, including with previous reporting periods (if applicable), through recalculating the annual reported values using the underlying data, etc.;

.2   completeness of data (e.g. perform substantive testing based on reconciliation, recalculations, and document cross-check, for example with official logbook and/or arrival/noon/departure reports, auto-log report files; recalculate total quantities of fuel oil used, distance travelled and hours under way); and

.3   reliability and accuracy of the data (e.g. test that the data quality procedures as described in the Data Collection Plan have been properly implemented, carry out site visits (typically to the company's offices rather than to the ship) to test the systems, processes and the control activities) through

---

[2]   Refer to the *2022 Guidelines for the development of a Ship Energy Efficiency Management Plan (SEEMP)*, adopted by resolution MEPC.346(78).

[3]   Refer to the *2018 Guidelines on the method of calculation of the attained Energy Efficiency Design Index (EEDI) for new ships* (resolution MEPC.308(73)), as may be amended.

此类文件的规定可以是作为数据收集计划[2]评估的一部分，根据具体船舶提出，或可以作为一般政策声明或通过主管机关认为合适的其他政策文件。便利数据验证的附加文件可包括下列文件，以及主管机关认为相关的其他文件：

.1 经验证的船舶数据收集计划（SEEMP 第 Ⅱ 部分）的副本；

.2 燃料交付单（BDN）汇总，提供足够的细节表明已计入船舶消耗的所有燃油（参见附录 1 的 BDN 汇总样表）；

.3 燃油消耗、航行距离和在航时长的未合计数据汇总，使用主管机关规定的格式（参见附录 2 的数据汇总样表）；

.4 证明船舶遵循其 SEEMP 中规定的数据收集计划的资料，包括数据缺口和如何填补缺口的资料以及如何解决造成数据缺口的事件；

.5 包含报告期间船舶航行的燃油消耗量、距离、小时数信息和其他数据的文件副本（例如船舶官方船舶日志、油类记录簿、BDN、到港 / 中午 / 离港报告、和来自自动日志数据文件等）；和

.6 经文件证据支持，对于本组织制定的导则[3]未涵盖的燃料类型，燃料供应方提供的燃油质量至 CO_2 质量的转换因数。

4.2 除第 4.1 段所述的文件外，主管机关可要求船舶提交全面审核船舶年度燃油消耗、航行距离和在航时长所需的文件。主管机关可要求其管辖范围内的全部船舶或其中一部分船舶提交此类文件。主管机关可使用此类文件以验证船舶是否遵循其数据收集计划中规定的方法，旨在确认：

.1 通过使用基础数据重新计算年度报告值等，报告数据和计算值的一致性，包括与上一报告期相比（如适用）；

.2 数据的完整性（例如，基于核对、重新计算、和文件交叉比对（例如与官方船舶日志和/或到港 / 中午 / 离港报告，自动日志报告文件；重新计算所使用的燃油总量，航行距离和航行时间）进行实质性测试）；和

.3 数据的可靠性和准确性（例如，正确实施测试数据收集计划中描述的数据质量程序，进行实地视察（通常去公司的办公室而非船舶）以测试各类系统、程序和控制活动），通过证实燃油消耗数据和航行距离和在航时长、比较报告的燃油消耗

2　参见以第 MEPC.346（78）号决议通过的《2022 年船舶能效管理计划（SEEMP）制定导则》。
3　参见可能经修正的《2018 年新船达到的能效设计指数（EEDI）计算方法导则》（第 MEPC.308（73）号决议）。

corroborating fuel oil consumption data with distance travelled and hours under way, comparing reported fuel oil consumption with that which is expected for the ship size, operational profile, and technical characteristics, and/or comparing reported fuel oil consumption total fuel bunkered, etc.

4.3   For a ship which has undergone a transfer addressed in regulations 27.4, 27.5 or 27.6 of MARPOL Annex VI, the losing Administration needs to verify the data before the transfer.

5   VERIFICATION OF THE ATTAINED ANNUAL OPERATIONAL CII AND DETERMINATION OF THE CII RATING

5.1   To facilitate the verification of the attained annual operational CII, the Administration should indicate what additional documentation a ship should submit along with its annual data report. Additional documentation to facilitate the verification may include the following, as well as other documentation that the Administration deems relevant:

.1   a copy of the verified ship's Operational Carbon Intensity Plan (SEEMP part III);

.2   documents (IEE certificate, Stability Booklet or International Tonnage Certificate) evidencing the capacity parameter of the ship in the metric relevant for the calculation of its operational carbon intensity (deadweight or gross tonnage);

.3   aggregated data of fuel oil consumption and distance travelled covering the entire calendar year to calculate the attained annual operational CII (AER or cgDIST) (see sample form of data summary set out in appendix 2);

.4   the aggregated values of the parameters and associated calculation methods to determine the annual metric value of the trial CIIs on voluntary basis, if any (see sample form of data summary set out in appendix 2 – Add.1);

.5   supported by documentary evidence, the correction factors and voyage adjustments[4] applied in the attained annual operational CII calculation, if any, during the reporting period (see sample form of data summary set out in appendix 2; and

.6   statements of compliance for previous two calendar years where applicable.

5.2   The attained annual operational CII should be verified using the data over a 12-month period from 1 January to 31 December for the preceding calendar year, by the Administration. In cases where the calculation of the attained annual operational CII is not possible due to the unavailability of some data, such as where a new ship is delivered after 1 January in the preceding year, the attained annual operational CII should be verified using the available data covering the corresponding period of the preceding calendar year.

5.3   In case of a ship with multiple load line certificates or with a load line certificate containing multiple load lines, the highest deadweight value should be used to calculate and verify the required and attained annual operational CII.

---

[4]   Refer to the *2022 Interim guidelines on correction factors and voyage adjustments for CII calculations* (G5), adopted by resolution MEPC.355(78).

与船舶尺寸、营运概要和技术特点所预期的燃油消耗，和／或比较报告的燃油消耗与总加油量等。

4.3 对已进行《防污公约》附则Ⅵ第 27.4、27.5 或 27.6 条所述变更的船舶，转出的主管机关需在变更前验证数据。

5 验证达到的年度营运 CII 和确定 CII 评级

5.1 为了便利对达到的年度营运 CII 进行验证，主管机关应说明船舶应随其年度数据报告一并提交的附加文件。便利验证的附加文件可包括下列文件，以及主管机关认为相关的其他文件：

.1 经验证的船舶营运碳强度计划（SEEMP 第Ⅲ部分）的副本；

.2 与计算营运碳强度相关，以证明船舶的载货量（载重吨或总吨）参数的文件（IEE 证书、稳性手册或国际吨位证书）；

.3 为计算达到的年度营运 CII（AER 或 cgDIST），涵盖整个日历年的燃油消耗和航行距离的汇总数据（见附录 2 中列出的数据汇总样表）；

.4 为确定自愿试用 CII 指标的参数和相关计算方法的汇总值，如有（见附录 2——补充文件 1 中列出的数据汇总样表）；

.5 经文件证据支持，在报告期间计算达到的年度营运 CII 应用的修正系数和航次调整[4]（如有）（见附录 2 中列出的数据汇总样表）；和

.6 先前两个日历年的符合声明（如适用）。

5.2 主管机关应使用上一日历年 1 月 1 日至 12 月 31 日 12 个月期间的数据来验证达到的年度营运 CII。如果由于某些数据不可用而无法计算达到的年度营运 CII，例如在上一年 1 月 1 日之后交付的新船，应使用涵盖上一日历年的相应时期的可用数据验证达到的年度营运 CII。

5.3 对于具有多份载重线证书或一份载重线证书包含多条载重线的船舶，应使用最高载重吨值计算和验证要求和达到的年度营运 CII。

5.4 对于在年内永久改变载重吨（DWT）和／或总吨位（GT）的船舶，SEEMP 或整改行

---

[4] 参见《2022 年 CII 计算的修正系数和航次调整临时导则》（G5）（第 MEPC.355（78）号决议）。

5.4   For a ship which permanently changes its deadweight (DWT) and/or its gross tonnage (GT) during the year, which the SEEMP or a corrective action plan identifies as being undertaken to improve the ship's operational carbon intensity performance:

.1   the required annual operational CII should always be calculated and verified using the original DWT or GT value before conversion; however, the attained CII which is used to assess compliance should be calculated and verified using the new DWT or GT value after conversion; and

.2   for the year when the conversion is made, the attained annual operational CII should be calculated and verified for the entire calendar year on the average DWT or GT value weighted on distance travelled before and after conversion.

5.5   Except for those specified in 5.4, for a ship which is regarded by the Administration as a newly constructed ship as per regulation 5.4.3 of MARPOL Annex VI due to major conversion, including extensive changes of carrying capacity and/or ship type during the year, the required and attained annual operational CII should be calculated and verified as per a newly constructed ship for the period after conversion. For the year when the major conversion is made, the data for partial year before conversion should still be reported for verification but will not be included in the calculation and verification of the attained annual operational CII.

5.6   For a ship which has undergone a transfer addressed in regulations 27.4, 27.5 or 27.6 of MARPOL Annex VI, the losing Administration neither needs to verify the attained annual operational CII nor to determine the annual CII rating of the ship for partial year. The attained annual operational CII should be verified by the receiving Administration using the data over an entire calendar year. In such cases, the aggregated data necessary to calculate the attained annual operational CII before transfer, which should have already been verified by the losing Administration, can be directly used by the receiving Administration without further verification (see sample form set out in appendix 3 and appendix 3 – Add.1).

5.7   The administration should determine the operational carbon intensity rating for the ship, taking into account the guidelines developed by the Organization.[5] The attained and required annual operational CII, as well as the rating boundaries, should be all given with three decimal places. If the attained annual operational CII happens to land on a rating boundary, the ship should be rated as the better of the two ratings.

5.8   The trial CIIs (e.g. EEPI, cbDIST, clDIST or EEOI),[6] if voluntarily calculated and reported, should be verified by the Administration following the same procedure as for the attained annual operational CII (AER or cgDIST). The Administration does not need to assign a rating to a ship based on trial CIIs.

6   ISSUE OF A STATEMENT OF COMPLIANCE

6.1   In accordance with regulation 6.6 of MARPOL Annex VI, upon receipt of reported data pursuant to regulation 27 of MARPOL Annex VI and attained annual operational CII pursuant to regulation 28 of MARPOL Annex VI and satisfactory completion of the verification, the Statement of Compliance should be issued by the Administration.

---

[5]   Refer to the *2022 Guidelines on the operational carbon intensity rating of ships (CII Rating Guidelines, G4)* adopted by resolution MEPC.354(78).

[6]   Refer to the *2022 Guidelines on operational carbon intensity indicators and the calculation methods (CII Guidelines, G1)* adopted by resolution MEPC.352(78).

动计划确定为提高船舶营运碳强度性能：

.1 应始终使用改变前的原 DWT 或 GT 值计算和验证要求的年度营运 CII，但应使用改变后的新 DWT 或 GT 值计算和验证达到的年度营运 CII；和

.2 对于改建的当年，应根据改建前后航行距离加权的平均 DWT 或 GT 值计算和验证整个日历年达到的年度营运 CII。

5.5 除第 5.4 段中的规定外，对于因重大改建，包括载运能力和 / 或船型在年内发生较大变化而被主管机关按《防污公约》附则Ⅵ第 5.4.3 条视为新建船舶的船舶，应按改建后的新建船舶计算和验证要求和达到的年度营运 CII。重大改建当年，仍应报告改建前的部分数据进行验证，但不计入达到的年度营运 CII 的计算和验证。

5.6 对已进行《防污公约》附则Ⅵ第 27.4、27.5 或 27.6 条所述变更的船舶，转出主管机关不必验证达到的年度营运 CII，也不必确定部分年份的船舶年度 CII 等级。应由转入主管机关使用整个日历年的数据验证达到的年度营运 CII。在此情况下，转出主管机关应已验证转移前的计算达到的年度营运 CII 所需的汇总数据，转入主管机关可直接使用该数据而无须进一步验证（见附录 3 和附录 3——补充文件 1 中列出的样表）。

5.7 主管机关应考虑本组织制定的导则[5]，确定船舶的营运碳强度评级。达到和要求的年度营运 CII 以及评级界限均应保留三位小数。如果达到的年度营运 CII 恰好落在一个等级边界上，则该船应被评定为两个等级中较好的一个。

5.8 如自愿计算和报告 CII 试用指标（例如 EEPI、cbDIST、clDIST 或 EEOI）[6]，应由主管机关按照与达到的年度营运 CII（AER 或 cgDIST）相同的程序进行验证。主管机关无须根据 CII 试用指标对船舶进行评级。

6 签发符合声明

6.1 根据《防污公约》附则Ⅵ第 6.6 条，收到按《防污公约》附则Ⅵ第 27 条报告的数据和按《防污公约》附则Ⅵ第 28 条规定的达到的年度营运 CII 后，并满意地完成验证，主管机关应签发符合声明。

---

[5] 参见以第 MPEC.354（78）号决议通过的《2022 年船舶营运碳强度评级导则》（CII 评级导则，G4）。

[6] 参见以第 MEPC.352（78）号决议通过的《2022 年营运碳强度指标和计算方法导则》（CII 导则，G1）。

6.2   Notwithstanding paragraph 6.1, the Administration should consider whether a corrective action plan is required according to regulation 6.8 of MARPOL Annex VI. In the case of a corrective actions plan being required but not submitted together with the attained annual operational CII, the administration should inform the company in a timely manner that a revised SEEMP including a plan of corrective actions, must be submitted for verification no later than one month after reporting the attained annual operational CII. The Statement of Compliance should not be issued in such a case unless a corrective action plan is duly developed and reflected in the SEEMP and verified by the Administration, taking into account the guidelines developed by the Organization.[7]

6.3   Should any material discrepancy be identified by the Administration in the reported data and/or the calculation of required/attained annual operational CII, it should be communicated to the company on a timely basis for clarification or correction. A discrepancy is considered material if the discrepancy or aggregation of discrepancies could influence the reported total by more than ±5%. The Statement of Compliance should not be issued in such a case unless the material discrepancy is clarified or corrected.

---

[7]   Refer to the *Guidelines for the verification and company audits by the Administration of part III of the Ship Energy Efficiency Management Plan (SEEMP)* adopted by resolution MEPC.347(78).

6.2　尽管有第 6.1 段的规定，主管机关应考虑是否需要根据《防污公约》附则Ⅵ第 6.8 条制定整改行动计划。如果需要整改行动计划但未与达到的年度营运 CII 一起提交，主管机关应及时通知公司，必须不迟于报告达到的年度营运 CII 后一个月提交经修订的 SEEMP（包括整改行动计划）以供验证。在这种情况下，除非考虑到本组织制定的导则 [7]，适当制定并在 SEEMP 中体现整改行动计划且经主管机关验证，否则不应签发符合声明。

6.3　如果主管机关在报告的数据和 / 或要求的 / 达到的年度营运 CII 的计算中发现任何实质差异，应及时通知公司以进行澄清或更正。如果差异或差异的汇总可能对报告总数的影响超过 ±5%，则差异被视为实质。在这种情况下，除非实质差异得到澄清或更正，否则不应签发符合声明。

[7]　参见以第 MEPC.347（78）号决议通过的《船舶能效管理计划（SEEMP）第Ⅲ部分主管机关验证和公司审核导则》。

APPENDIX 1

SAMPLE OF THE BDN SUMMARIES

Date of Operations (dd/mm/yyyy)	Fuel Oil Type/Mass(MT)									Descriptions
	DO/GO	LFO	HFO	LPG(P)	LPG(B)	LNG	Methanol	Ethanol	Others(CF)	
① BDN										
09/01/2023										
02/05/2023			150							
08/07/2023										
09/10/2023										
10/12/2023			300							
①Annual Supply Amount	0	0	450	0	0	0	0	0	0	
② Correction for the tank oil remainings										
01/01/2023			400							
31/12/2023			200							
②Correction for the tank oil remaining	0	0	200	0	0	0	0	0	0	The difference in the amount of the remaining tank oil at the beginning/end of the data collection period.
③ Other corrections										
30/03/2023										
15/09/2023										
31/12/2023										
③Annual other corrections	0	0	0	0	0	0	0	0	0	
Annual Fuel Consumption										
Annual Fuel Consumption (①+②+③)	0	0	650	0	0	0	0	0	0	

Explanatory remarks;
If bunker supply/correction data have been recorded in a Company's electronic reporting system,the data is acceptable to be submitted in the existing format instead of submitting the data by this format.

附录 1

BDN 汇总样表

操作时间 （年/月/日）	燃油类型/重量（MT）									描述
	DO/GO	LFO	HFO	LPG（P）	LPG（B）	LNG	甲醇	乙醇	其他（CF）	
① BDN										
09/01/2023										
02/05/2023			150							
08/07/2023										
09/10/2023										
10/12/2023			300							
①年供应量	0	0	450	0	0	0	0	0	0	
②液舱燃油余量更正										
01/01/2023			400							
31/12/2023			200							
②液舱燃油余量更正	0	0	200	0	0	0			0	剩余液舱燃油量在数据收集期开始/结束的差值
③其他更正										
30/03/2023										
15/09/2023										
31/12/2023										
③年其他更正	0	0	0	0	0	0	0	0	0	
年燃油消耗										
年燃油消耗（①+②+③）	0	0	650	0	0	0	0	0	0	

备注：

如果燃油供应/更正数据已被记录于公司的电子报告系统内，可接受以现有格式而非此格式提交数据。

SAMPLE OF THE COLLECTED DATA SUMMARIES

Date and time from (dd/mm/yyyy; hh:mm UTC)	* Date and time to (dd/mm/yyyy; hh:mm UTC)	Distance travelled (nm)	Hours under way (hh:mm) **	Cargo carried (metric tons)	Cargo carried (TEU)	Cargo carried (Passenger)	(voluntary basis) Laden voyage (Y/N)	***exceptional conditions Specified in regulation 3.1 of MARPOL Annex VI (Y/N)	***Sailing in ice condition (Y/N)	***STS Operation (Y/N) …….	Fuel consumption (metric tons) Main engine(s)			
											HFO****	LFO	MGO	etc.
01/01/2023 00:00	01/01/2023 13:20	150	13:20	1,500			Y	N	N	N				
……	……	……	……	…….				…….	…….	…….				
31/12/2023 00:00	31/12/2023 24:00	290	24:00	1,500			Y	N	N	N				
Annual Total														

(continued from the table above)

Fuel consumption (metric tons)																							
Auxiliary engine(s)				Boiler(s)				Others (Specify)				***mass to be deducted from the total											
												consumed for production of electrical power($FC_{electrical}$)				consumed by oil-fired boiler for cargo heating/discharge on tankers (FC_{boiler})				consumed by stand-alone engine driven cargo pumps during discharge operations on tankers(FC_{others})			
HFO	LFO	MGO	etc.	HFO	LFO	MGO	etc.	HFO	LFO	MGO	etc.	HFO	LFO	MGO	etc.	HFO	LFO	MGO	etc.	HFO	LFO	MGO	etc.

* In the case of daily underlying data, this column would be left blank.

** Hours under way should be equal to the time between the start and end date and time. In case the segment is not under way, it should be left blank.

*** Refer to the *2022 Interim guidelines on correction factors and voyage adjustments for CII calculations (G5)*, adopted by resolution MEPC.355(78). Supporting documentation may be additionally submitted to facilitate the verification when necessary, such as Baplie files where the number of in-use reefer containers on board are recorded. Note that voyages in different sailing or operational conditions should be recorded in separate rows so that the correction factors and voyage adjustments can be duly calculated and verified.

**** Refer to fuel types specified in the *2022 Guidelines on the method of calculation of the attained Energy Efficiency Design Index (EEDI) for new ships* (resolution MEPC.364(79), as may be amended)

Explanatory remarks: If bunker supply/correction data have been recorded in a company's electronic reporting system, the data is acceptable to be submitted in the existing format instead of submitting the data by this format.

***

收集数据总结表

起始日期和时间（日/月/年 小时：分钟 UTC）	结束日期和时间（日/月/年 小时：分钟 UTC）	航行距离（海里）**	航行小时数（小时：分钟）**	运载的货物（吨）	运载的货物（TEU）	运载的货物/乘客（自愿报告）满载航行（是/否）	MARPOL附则VI第3.1条规定的例外情况***（是/否）	冰况下航行***（是/否）	STS操作***（是/否）	燃料消耗（吨）主机 HFO****	LFO	MGO	等等
01/01/2023 00：00	01/01/2023 13：20	150	13：20	1 500		是	否	否	否				
......	......	......	......			......	......	......	......				
31/12/2023 00：00	31/12/2023 24：00	290	24：00	1 500		是	否	否	否				
年总量													

（续上表）

燃料消耗（吨）辅机 HFO	LFO	MGO	等等	锅炉 HFO	LFO	MGO	等等	其他（请注明） HFO	LFO	MGO	等等	发电消耗（$FC_{electrical}$） HFO	LFO	MGO	等等	液货船用于货物加热/卸货的燃油锅炉消耗（FC_{boiler}） HFO	LFO	MGO	等等	液货船卸货作业期间由独立的发动机驱动的货泵消耗（FC_{others}） HFO	LFO	MGO	等等

*** 从总数减去的质量

备注：

* 对于每日基本数据，本栏无须填写。

** 航行小时数应等于起始和结束日期和时间之间的时间。如果船舶未航行，本栏无须填写。

*** 参见 MEPC.355（78）决议通过的《2022 年 CII 计算和航次调整临时导则（G5）》。必要时可额外提交支持文件以方便验证，例如记录船上使用冷藏集装箱数量的船图文件。注意到不同航行或操作条件下的航程应分行记录，以便及时计算和验证修正系数和航次调整。

**** 参见《2022 年新造船能效设计指数（EEDI）计算方法导则》（可能经修订的 MEPC.364（79）决议）规定的燃料类型。

备注：

如果燃料供应/修正数据已被记录于公司的电子报告系统内，可接受以现有格式而非此格式提交数据。

APPENDIX 2 – ADD.1

SAMPLE OF THE COLLECTED DATA SUMMARIES TO CALCULATE TRIAL CII ON A VOLUNTARY BASIS

The following aggregated data should be additionally included in the table in appendix 2, if one or more trial CII metrics have been applied on a voluntary basis:

Date from (dd/mm/yyyy)	*Date to (dd/mm/yyyy)	Laden distance travelled (n.m)	****Transport work (metric of transport work)
01/01/2023			
02/01/2023			
03/01/2023			
31/12/2023			
Annual total			

* In the case of daily underlying data, this column would be left blank.
**** As defined in section 3 of the *Guidelines for voluntary use of the ship energy efficiency operational indicator (EEOI)* circulated by MEPC.1/Circ.684.

Explanatory remarks: If bunker supply/correction data have been recorded in a Company's electronic reporting system, the data is acceptable to be submitted in the existing format instead of submitting the data by this format.

附录 2—补充文件 1

计算自愿试用 CII 的收集数据数据总结样表

如自愿应用一个或多个试用 CII 指标，附录 2 的表格应额外包括以下汇总数据：

起始日期（日／月／年）	*结束日期（日／月／年）	满载航行距离（海里）	****运输功（运输功的度量）
01/01/2023			
02/01/2023			
03/01/2023			
31/12/2023			
年总量			

* 对于每日基本数据，本栏无须填写。

**** 《船舶能效营运指数（EEOI）自愿使用导则》（MEPC.1/Circ.684）第 3 节定义。

备注：如果燃料供应／修正数据已被记录于公司的电子报告系统内，可接受以现有格式而非此格式式提交数据。

SAMPLE OF THE AGGREGATED DATA BEFORE A TRANSFER OF FLAG/COMPANY ADDRESSED IN REGULATIONS 27.4, 27.5 OR 27.6 OF MARPOL ANNEX VI

Date of transfer (dd/mm/yyyy)	Type of transfer (flag/company/both)	Reporting period		Distance (n.m) Travelled		Hours under way (hh:mm)	Fuel consumption (metric tons)		
		Date from (dd/mm/yyyy)	Date to (dd/mm/yyyy)	Total distance travelled	*distance to be deducted from CII calculation		total mass ***DO/GO ...	*mass to be deducted from the total DO/GO ...	**mass consumed in STS operations DO/GO ...
12/05/2023	Flag	01/01/2023	11/05/2023						
15/06/2023	Company	12/05/2023	14/06/2023						
02/11/2023	Both	15/06/2023	01/11/2023						
....									

* Refer to the aggregated mass of fuel consumption to calculate FC_{voyage}, $FC_{electrical}$, FC_{boiler} and FC_{others} in the 2022 Interim guidelines on correction factors and voyage adjustments for CII calculations (G5), (resolution MEPC.355(78)).
** Refer to the aggregated mass of fuel consumption to calculate $AF_{Tanker,STS}$ in the 2022 Interim guidelines on correction factors and voyage adjustments for CII calculations (G5), (resolution MEPC.355(78)).
*** Refer to fuel types specified in 2018 Guidelines on the method of calculation of the attained Energy Efficiency Design Index (EEDI) for new ships (resolution MEPC.308(73), as may be amended).

APPENDIX 3 – ADD.1

SAMPLE OF THE AGGREGATED DATA BEFORE A TRANSFER OF FLAG/COMPANY ADDRESSED IN REGULATIONS 27.4, 27.5 OR 27.6 OF MARPOL ANNEX VI TO CALCULATE TRIAL CII METRICS ON A VOLUNTARY BASIS

The following aggregated data may be additionally included in the table in appendix 3, if one or more trial CII metrics have been applied on a voluntary basis:

Date of transfer (dd/mm/yyyy)	Type of transfer (flag/company/both)	Reporting period		Laden distance travelled (n.m)	****Transport work (metric of transport work)
		Date from (dd/mm/yyyy)	Date to (dd/mm/yyyy)		
12/05/2023	Flag	01/01/2023	11/05/2023		
15/06/2023	Company	12/05/2023	14/06/2023		
02/11/2023	Both	15/06/2023	01/11/2023		
....					

**** As defined in section 3 of Guidelines for voluntary use of the ship energy efficiency operational indicator (EEOI) circulated by MEPC.1/Circ.684.

***

附录 3

《防污公约》附则VI第 27.4、27.5 或 27.6 条所述的变更船旗/公司之前的汇总数据样表

变更日期（日/月/年）	变更类型（船旗/公司/两者都是）	报告时期		航行距离（海里）		在航时长（时：分）	燃料消耗（吨）					
		起始日期（日/月/年）	结束日期（日/月/年）	总航行距离	*从CII计算扣除的距离		总质量		*从总数减去的质量		**STS 操作消耗的质量	
							***柴油/汽油	...	柴油/汽油	...	柴油/汽油	...
12/05/2023	船旗	01/01/2023	11/05/2023									
15/06/2023	公司	12/05/2023	14/06/2023									
02/11/2023	两者都是	15/06/2023	01/11/2023									
……												

* 参见《2022 年 CII 计算的修正系数和航次调整临时导则》（G5）中用于计算 FCvoyage、FCelectrical、FCboiler 和 FCothers 的燃料消耗总质量。

** 参见《2022 年 CII 计算的修正系数和航次调整临时导则》（G5）中用于计算 AFtanker、STS 的燃料消耗总质量。

*** 参见《2018 年新船达到的能效设计指数（EEDI）计算方法导则》（可经修正的第 MEPC.308（73）号决议）规定的燃料类型。

附录 3—补充文件 1

《防污公约》附则VI第 27.4、27.5 或 27.6 条所述的变更船旗/公司之前的计算自愿试用 CII 指标的汇总数据样表

如自愿应用一个或多个试用 CII 指标，附录 3 的表格应额外包括以下汇总数据：

变更日期（日/月/年）	变更类型（船旗/公司/两者都是）	报告时期		满载航行距离（海里）	****运输功(运输功的度量)
		起始日期（日/月/年）	结束日期（日/月/年）		
12/05/2023	船旗	01/01/2023	11/05/2023		
15/06/2023	公司	12/05/2023	14/06/2023		
02/11/2023	两者都是	15/06/2023	01/11/2023		
……					

**** 《船舶能效营运指数（EEOI）自愿使用导则》（MEPC.1/Circ.684）第 3 节定义。

***

RESOLUTION MEPC.349(78)
(adopted on 10 June 2022)

**2022 GUIDELINES FOR THE DEVELOPMENT AND MANAGEMENT OF THE IMO SHIP
FUEL OIL CONSUMPTION DATABASE**

THE MARINE ENVIRONMENT PROTECTION COMMITTEE,

RECALLING Article 38(a) of the Convention on the International Maritime Organization concerning the functions of the Marine Environment Protection Committee (the Committee) conferred upon it by international conventions for the prevention and control of marine pollution from ships,

NOTING that the Committee, at its seventy-sixth session, adopted, by resolution MEPC.328(76), the *2021 Revised MARPOL Annex VI*, which will enter into force on 1 November 2022,

NOTING IN PARTICULAR that the *2021 Revised MARPOL Annex VI* (MARPOL Annex VI) contains amendments concerning mandatory goal-based technical and operational measures to reduce carbon intensity of international shipping,

NOTING ALSO that regulation 27.12 of MARPOL Annex VI specifies that the Secretary-General of the Organization shall maintain an anonymized database such that identification of a specific ship will not be possible,

NOTING FURTHER that regulation 27.13 of MARPOL Annex VI requires that the IMO Ship Fuel Oil Consumption Database be undertaken and managed by the Secretary-General of the Organization, pursuant to guidelines developed by the Organization,

RECOGNIZING that the aforementioned amendments to MARPOL Annex VI require relevant guidelines for uniform and effective implementation of the regulations and to provide sufficient lead time for industry to prepare,

NOTING that the Committee, at its seventy-first session, adopted, by resolution MEPC.293(71), the *2017 Guidelines the development and management of the IMO Ship Fuel Oil Consumption Database,*

HAVING CONSIDERED, at its seventy-eighth session, draft *2022 Guidelines for the development and management of the IMO Ship Fuel Oil Consumption Database,*

1   ADOPTS the *2022 Guidelines for the development and management of the IMO Ship Fuel Oil Consumption Database*, as set out in the annex to the present resolution;

2   INVITES Administrations to take the annexed Guidelines into account when developing and enacting national laws which give force to and implement requirements set forth in regulation 27 of MARPOL Annex VI;

第 MEPC.349（78）号决议
（2022 年 6 月 10 日通过）

2022 年国际海事组织船舶燃油消耗数据库开发与管理导则

海上环境保护委员会，

忆及《国际海事组织公约》第 38（a）条关于防止和控制船舶造成海洋污染国际公约赋予海上环境保护委员会的职能，

注意到委员会在其第 76 届会议上以 MEPC.328（76）号决议通过了 2021 年经修订的 MARPOL 附则 VI，将于 2022 年 11 月 1 日生效，

特别注意到 2021 年经修订的 MARPOL 附则 VI 包含关于基于目标的强制性技术和营运措施以减少国际航运碳强度的修正案，

还注意到 MARPOL 附则 VI 第 27.12 条明确了本组织秘书长须维护一个无法识别特定船舶的匿名数据库，

进一步注意到 MARPOL 附则 VI 第 27.13 条要求国际海事组织船舶燃油消耗数据库应由本组织秘书长依据本组织制定的导则进行负责和管理，

认识到 MARPOL 附则 VI 的上述修正案需要相关的导则，以统一和有效实施各条规定，并为业界提供足够的准备时间，

注意到委员会在其第 71 届会议上，以第 MEPC.293（71）号决议通过了《2017 年国际海事组织船舶燃油消耗数据库开发与管理导则》，

考虑到在其第 78 届会议上，审议了《2022 年国际海事组织船舶燃油消耗数据库开发与管理导则》草案，

1　**通过**《2022 年国际海事组织船舶燃油消耗数据库开发与管理导则》，其文本载于本决议附件；

2　**提请**主管机关在制定和颁布本国法律，以执行和实施 MARPOL 附则 VI 第 27 条要求时，考虑到附件中的导则；

3   REQUESTS the Parties to MARPOL Annex VI and other Member Governments to bring the annexed Guidelines to the attention of masters, seafarers, shipowners, ship operators and any other interested parties;

4   AGREES to keep the Guidelines under review in light of experience gained with their implementation, also taking into consideration that in accordance with regulations 25.3 and 28.11 of MARPOL Annex VI a review of the technical and operational measures to reduce carbon intensity of international shipping shall be completed by 1 January 2026;

5   REVOKES the *2017 Guidelines the development and management of the IMO Ship Fuel Oil Consumption Database* adopted by resolution MEPC.293(71).

3　**要求** MARPOL 附则Ⅵ的各缔约方和其他成员国政府提请船长、船员、船东、船舶经营者以及任何其他利益相关方注意到附件中的导则；

4　**同意**根据本导则实施中获得的经验，并考虑到根据 MARPOL 附则Ⅵ第 25.3 条和28.11 条应在 2026 年 1 月 1 日之前完成对减少国际航运碳强度的技术和营运措施的审查，对本导则保持审查；和

5　**撤销**以第 MEPC.293（71）号决议通过的《2017 年国际海事组织船舶燃油消耗数据库开发与管理导则》。

2022 GUIDELINES FOR THE DEVELOPMENT AND MANAGEMENT OF THE IMO SHIP FUEL OIL CONSUMPTION DATABASE

1   INTRODUCTION

1.1   These Guidelines provide guidance on the development and management of the IMO Ship Fuel Oil Consumption Database (hereafter "the database"), and describe methods that will be used to anonymize ship data for use by Parties, in accordance with regulation 27 of MARPOL Annex VI, and to ensure the completeness of the database.

1.2   In general, the purpose of the database is to provide data for establishing annual CO_2 emissions from ships and support consideration of further measures for reducing carbon intensity of international shipping.

1.3   With regard to data confidentiality, regulation 27.12 stipulates that "The Secretary-General of the Organization shall maintain an anonymized database such that identification of a specific ship will not be possible. Parties shall have access to the anonymized data strictly for their analysis and consideration." These Guidelines balance data anonymization with the usability of data for analysis by the Parties and Organization.

1.4   Regulation 27.13 states that "The IMO Ship Fuel Oil Consumption Database shall be undertaken and managed by the Secretary-General of the Organization, pursuant to guidelines to be developed by the Organization." With regard to the establishment of the database and for data visualization, it will be developed as a module within the Global Integrated Shipping Information System (GISIS) platform and associated web application, as necessary, with the integrated IMO Web Accounts framework utilized to manage secure access to the module.

2   DEFINITIONS

For the purpose of these Guidelines, the definitions in MARPOL Annex VI apply.

3   DATA ANONYMIZATION

Pursuant to regulation 27.12 of MARPOL Annex VI, the data are to be anonymized such that identification of a specific ship will not be possible. For the purpose of the anonymization of the fuel oil consumption data, the following should apply for the database:

.1   the IMO number and ship flag should not be shown;

.2   gross tonnage (GT), net tonnage (NT), deadweight tonnage (DWT) and power output (rated power) should be rounded to two significant digits, for example, a ship tonnage of 167,430 GT should be shown as 170,000 GT;

.3   attained EEDI and attained EEXI should be rounded to two decimal places;

.4   required annual operational CII (AER or cgDIST), attained annual operational CII (AER or cgDIST), attained annual operational CII (AER or cgDIST) before any correction and operational carbon intensity indicators for trial purpose on voluntary basis (e.g. EEPI, cbDIST, clDIST and EEOI)[1] should be rounded to one decimal place;

---

[1]   Refer to *2022 Guidelines on operational carbon intensity indicators and the calculation methods (CII guidelines, G1)* (resolution MEPC.352(78)).

附件

2022 年国际海事组织船舶燃油消耗数据库开发与管理导则

1 引言

1.1 本导则为国际海事组织船舶燃油消耗数据库（以下简称"数据库"）开发与管理提供指导，并根据 MARPOL 附则Ⅵ第 27 条的规定描述缔约方使用船舶数据时确保数据匿名性的方法，并确保数据库的完整性。

1.2 总体而言，数据库旨在为确定船舶的年度二氧化碳排放量提供数据，支持降低国际航运碳强度的进一步措施的审议。

1.3 关于数据保密性，第 27.12 条规定"本组织秘书长须保持数据的匿名性，以确保无法识别某一特定船舶。缔约方须能够获得严格匿名后的数据以便进行分析和参考。"本导则平衡了数据的匿名性和供缔约方与本组织分析的可用性。

1.4 第 27.13 条规定"国际海事组织船舶燃油消耗数据库须根据本组织制定的导则，由本组织秘书长负责和管理。"关于数据库的建立和数据可视化，将视需要在全球综合航运信息系统（GISIS）平台和相关的网络应用程序内作为一个模块开发，使用 IMO 综合网站账户管理模块的安全访问。

2 定义

就本导则而言，MARPOL 附则Ⅵ中的定义适用。

3 数据匿名

根据 MARPOL 附则Ⅵ第 27.12 条，数据应当被匿名以致无法识别某一特定船舶。为了对燃油消耗数据进行匿名，数据库应当适用以下要求：

.1 IMO 编号和船旗不应显示；

.2 总吨（GT），净吨（NT），载重吨（DWT），输出功率（额定功率）应当四舍五入至 2 位有效数字，例如，一艘吨位为 167 430 GT 的船舶应当显示为 170 000 GT；

.3 达到的 EEDI 和 EEXI 应当四舍五入到小数点后两位；

.4 要求的年度营运 CII（AER 或 cgDIST），达到的年度营运 CII（AER 或 cgDIST），修正前的达到的年度营运 CII（AER 或 cgDIST），和自愿基础上试用碳强度指数（如：EEPI，cbDIST，clDIST 和 EEOI）[1]，应当四舍五入到小数点后一位；

---

[1] 参见《2022 年营运碳强度指标和计算方法导则》（CII 导则，G1）（（MEPC.352（78）号决议）。

.5   the annual data of fuel oil consumption, distance travelled and hours under way should be provided in full without modification;

.6   ship types other than those defined in regulation 2 should be shown as "others"; and

.7   ice class should be shown as "Yes" or "No".

4   DATA SUBMISSION AND ACCESS

4.1   An Administration should be able to log in to the online database to submit its data via an online form. The data input into the database should be checked by the database system to ensure that the data are being submitted in the standardized format and be cross-referenced with the data from the Ship Particulars module of GISIS.

4.2   The Administration should designate a contact person for the purposes of the database who is responsible for communication with the Secretariat if any matter arises with regard to the submission of data by the respective Administration.

4.3   To encourage the consistent submission of data and improve the usability of the database, automatic notifications and reminders concerning data submission, modification and database update could be incorporated as features in the database.

4.4   An Administration will have access to non-anonymized data of ships flying its flag. Furthermore, the Administration of a ship, to which regulation 28 of MARPOL Annex VI applies, will have access to all reported data for the preceding calendar year for that ship regardless of flag history.

4.5   An Administration should be able to log in to the online database to download the anonymized dataset.

5   MEASURES TO ENSURE THE COMPLETENESS OF THE DATABASE

In accordance with the requirements of regulation 27.10 of MARPOL Annex VI concerning reporting of the status of missing data, the Secretary-General should:

.1   at the beginning of each calendar year, produce a list of ships falling under the scope of regulation 27 by cross-referencing with the data from the Ship Particulars module of GISIS;

.2   send the aforementioned list of ships to the Administration for reference, in order to receive feedback in case of any discrepancies;

.3   check the completeness of the database by comparing the list produced under .1 with the reported data;

.4   remind Administrations which have failed to submit the data in the required form;

.5   report the status of missing data to the Committee on an annual basis; and

.6   request non-reporting Administrations to submit the data of all their registered ships falling under the scope of regulation 27.

.5 年度燃油消耗、航行距离和航行时间应当不经修改完整提供；

.6 第 2 条定义之外的其他船型应当显示为"其他"；和

.7 冰级应当显示为"是"或"否"。

4 数据提交和获取

4.1 主管机关应当能够登录在线数据库在线提交数据。输入数据库的数据应当由数据库系统进行核查以保证数据以标准表格进行提交，并且与 GISIS 船舶资料模块中的数据进行交叉对照。

4.2 主管机关应当指定一名数据库联络人员，负责与秘书处就该主管机关数据提交出现的任何问题进行沟通。

4.3 为鼓励数据提交的一致性并提升数据库的可使用性，关于数据提交、修改和数据库更新的自动通知和提醒可以纳入数据库功能。

4.4 主管机关将能够获取悬挂其船旗的船舶的非匿名数据。此外，无论其历史船旗如何，主管机关都有权获取适用 MARPOL 附则 VI 第 28 条的船舶先前日历年的所有报告数据。

4.5 主管机关应当能够登录在线数据库下载匿名数据集。

5 保障数据库完整性的措施

根据 MARPOL 附则 VI 第 27.10 条关于报送缺失数据情况的要求，秘书长应当：

.1 在每个日历年年初，通过与 GISIS 船舶资料模块中的数据进行交叉对照，列出符合第 27 条规定范围的船舶清单；

.2 将上述船舶清单发送给主管机关以供参考，以在出现任何不一致的情况时接收反馈；

.3 通过比对根据第 1 款列出的清单和报告的数据，核查数据库的完整性；

.4 提醒未按照要求格式提交数据的主管机关；

.5 每年向委员会报告缺失数据的情况；并

.6 要求未进行报告的主管机关提交其符合第 27 条规定范围的所有登记船舶的数据。

6 ANNUAL REPORT TO THE MARINE ENVIRONMENT PROTECTION COMMITTEE

Regulation 27.10 states that "the Secretary-General of the Organization shall produce an annual report to the Marine Environment Protection Committee summarizing the data collected, the status of missing data, and such other relevant information as may be requested by the Committee." At a minimum, each annual report should include the following and also any other information as requested by the Committee:

.1   an aggregated annual amount of each type of fuel oil consumed by all ships of 5,000 GT and above engaged on international voyages;

.2   the aggregated annual amount of each type of fuel oil consumed, distance travelled and hours under way for ships of 5,000 GT and above engaged on international voyages, by ship type and size category as defined in MARPOL Annex VI,[2] including the "other" category for ships not defined in MARPOL Annex VI regulation 2;

.3   the number of ships of 5,000 GT and above engaged on international voyages reported to the database, by ship type and size category as defined in MARPOL Annex VI, including the "other" category for ships not defined in MARPOL Annex VI regulation 2;

.4   the number of ships of 5,000 GT and above engaged on international voyages registered with the Party of Annex VI for which data was not received, by ship type and size category as defined in MARPOL Annex VI, including the "other" category for ships not defined in MARPOL Annex VI regulation 2; and

.5   the annual development in operational carbon intensity of the ship types and international shipping, as well as the uncertainties in the data and results, using both demand-based measurement and supply-based measurement, as stated in paragraph 1 5 of the *2021 Guidelines on the operational carbon intensity reduction factors relative to reference lines (CII reduction factors guidelines, G3).*

***

---

[2]   In order to facilitate year-over-year comparison, the Secretariat may also consider using ship type and size categories as used in the Fourth IMO GHG Study 2020, as appropriate.

6　向海上环境保护委员会年度报告

第 27.10 条规定"本组织秘书长须向海上环境保护委员会提交一份年度报告，总结收集的数据、数据缺失情况，以及委员会要求的其他相关信息"。每份年度报告应当至少包括以下内容以及委员会要求的其他任何信息：

.1　所有 5 000 GT 及以上的国际航行船舶每年消耗的各种燃油总数；

.2　5 000 GT 及以上的国际航行船舶每年消耗的各种燃油，航行距离和航行时间的总数，根据 MARPOL 附则 VI 定义的船型和船舶大小进行分类，包括 MARPOL 附则 VI 第 2 行未定义的"其他"船舶类型[2]；

.3　向数据库进行报告的 5 000 GT 及以上的国际航行船舶总数，根据 MARPOL 附则 VI 定义的船型和船舶大小进行分类，包括 MARPOL 附则 VI 第 2 行未定义的"其他"船舶类型；

.4　未收到数据的附则 VI 缔约方登记下 5 000 GT 及以上的国际航行船舶总数，根据 MARPOL 附则 VI 定义的船型和船舶大小进行分类，包括 MARPOL 附则 VI 第 2 行未定义的"其他"船舶类型；以及

.5　《2021 年相对于基线的营运碳强度折减系数导则》（CII 折减系数导则，G3）第 1.5 段中指出，使用基于需求和基于供给的测量来分析船舶和国际航运营运碳强度的年度发展，以及数据和结果中的不确定性。

***

---

[2]　为便于逐年比较，秘书处还可酌情考虑按照国际海事组织 2020 年第四次温室气体研究中使用的船舶类型和船舶大小进行分类。

—— 营运碳强度指数（CII）相关 ——

RESOLUTION MEPC.352(78)
(adopted on 10 June 2022)

2022 GUIDELINES ON OPERATIONAL CARBON INTENSITY INDICATORS AND THE CALCULATION METHODS (CII GUIDELINES, G1)

THE MARINE ENVIRONMENT PROTECTION COMMITTEE,

RECALLING Article 38(a) of the Convention on the International Maritime Organization concerning the functions of the Marine Environment Protection Committee, the Committee, conferred upon it by international conventions for the prevention and control of marine pollution from ships,

NOTING that the Committee adopted, at its seventy-sixth session, by resolution MEPC.328(76), the *2021 Revised MARPOL Annex VI*, which will enter into force on 1 November 2022,

NOTING IN PARTICULAR that the *2021 Revised MARPOL Annex VI* (MARPOL Annex VI) contains amendments concerning mandatory goal-based technical and operational measures to reduce carbon intensity of international shipping,

NOTING FURTHER that regulation 28.1 of MARPOL Annex VI requires ships to which this regulation apply to calculate the attained annual operational CII taking into account the guidelines developed by the Organization,

RECOGNIZING that the aforementioned amendments to MARPOL Annex VI require relevant guidelines for uniform and effective implementation of the regulations and to provide sufficient lead time for industry to prepare,

NOTING that the Committee, at its seventy-sixth session, adopted, by resolution MEPC.336(76), the *2021 Guidelines on operational carbon intensity indicators and the calculation methods (CII Guidelines, G1)*,

HAVING CONSIDERED, at its seventy-eighth session, the draft *2022 Guidelines on operational carbon intensity indicators and the calculation methods (CII Guidelines, G1)*,

1   ADOPTS the *2022 Guidelines on operational carbon intensity indicators and the calculation methods (CII Guidelines, G1)*, as set out in the annex to the present resolution;

2   INVITES Administrations to take the annexed Guidelines into account when developing and enacting national laws which give force to and implement requirements set forth in regulation 28.1 of MARPOL Annex VI;

3   REQUESTS the Parties to MARPOL Annex VI and other Member Governments to bring the annexed Guidelines to the attention of masters, seafarers, shipowners, ship operators and any other interested parties;

4   AGREES to keep the Guidelines under review in light of experience gained with their implementation, also taking into consideration that in accordance with regulation 28.11 of

第 MEPC.352（78）号决议
（2022 年 6 月 10 日通过）

2022 年营运碳强度指标和计算方法导则（CII 导则，G1）

海上环境保护委员会，

忆及《国际海事组织公约》第 38（a）条关于防止和控制船舶造成海洋污染国际公约赋予海上环境保护委员会的职能，

注意到委员会在其第 76 届会议上以 MEPC.328（76）号决议通过了将于 2022 年 11 月 1 日生效的 2021 年经修订的 MARPOL 附则 Ⅵ，

特别注意到 2021 年经修订的 MARPOL 附则 Ⅵ包含关于基于目标的强制性技术和营运措施以减少国际航运碳强度的修正案，

进一步注意到 MARPOL 附则 Ⅵ第 28.1 条要求对本条适用的船舶计算达到的年度营运碳强度指标（以下简称 CII），并考虑到本组织制定的导则，

认识到上述 MARPOL 附则 Ⅵ的修正案需要有相关导则，以便于统一和有效实施各条规定，并为业界提供充足的准备时间，

注意到委员会在其第 76 届会议上，以第 MEPC.336（76）号决议通过了《2021 年营运碳强度指标和计算方法导则（CII 导则，G1）》，

在其第 78 届会议上，**审议了**《2022 年营运碳强度指标和计算方法导则（CII 导则，G1）》草案，

1 **通过**《2022 年营运碳强度指标和计算方法导则（CII 导则，G1）》，其文本载于本决议附件；

2 **提请**主管机关在制定和颁布本国法律，以执行和实施 MARPOL 附则 Ⅵ第 28.1 条要求时，考虑到附件中的导则；

3 **要求** MARPOL 附则 Ⅵ的各缔约方和其他成员国政府提请船长、船员、船东、船舶经营者以及任何其他利益相关方注意到附件中的导则；

4 **同意**根据本导则实施中获得的经验，并考虑到根据 MARPOL 附则 Ⅵ第 28.11 条

MARPOL Annex VI a review of the operational measure to reduce carbon intensity of international shipping shall be completed by 1 January 2026,

5   REVOKES the *2021 Guidelines on operational carbon intensity indicators and the calculation methods (CII Guidelines, G1)* adopted by resolution MEPC.336(76).

须在 2026 年 1 月 1 日之前完成对减少国际航运碳强度的营运措施的审查，对本导则保持审查；

5　**撤销**以第 MEPC.336（76）号决议通过的《2021 年营运碳强度指标和计算方法导则（CII 导则，G1）》。

ANNEX

2022 GUIDELINES ON OPERATIONAL CARBON INTENSITY INDICATORS AND THE CALCULATION METHODS (CII GUIDELINES, G1)

1 Introduction

1.1 In the *Initial IMO Strategy on Reduction of GHG Emissions from Ships* (Resolution MEPC.304(72)), the level of ambition on carbon intensity of international shipping is quantified by the CO_2 emissions per transport work, as an average across international shipping.

1.2 These Guidelines address the calculation methods and the applicability of the operational carbon intensity indicator (CII) for individual ships to which chapter 4 of MARPOL Annex VI, as amended, applies.

2 Definitions

2.1 *MARPOL* means the International Convention for the Prevention of Pollution from Ships, 1973, as modified by the Protocols of 1978 and 1997 relating thereto, as amended.

2.2 *IMO DCS* means the data collection system for fuel oil consumption of ships referred to in regulation 27 and related provisions of MARPOL Annex VI.

2.3 For the purpose of these Guidelines, the definitions in MARPOL Annex VI, as amended, apply.

2.4 The metrics indicating the average CO_2 emissions per transport work of a ship are generally referred to as operational carbon intensity indicator (CII) in these Guidelines.

.1 A specific CII calculated based on the actual or estimated mass or volume of the shipment carried on board a ship is generally referred to as *demand-based CII*; and

.2 A specific CII, in which calculation the capacity of a ship is taken as proxy of the actual mass or volume of the shipment carried on board, is generally referred to as *supply-based CII*.

2.5 The supply-based CII which uses DWT as the capacity is referred to as *AER*, and the supply-based CII which uses GT as the capacity is referred to as *cgDIST*.

3 Application

3.1 For all ships to which regulation 28 of MARPOL Annex VI applies, the operational carbon intensity indicators defined in section 4 should be applied.

3.2 The operational carbon intensity indicators defined in section 5 are encouraged to be additionally used by ships, where applicable, for trial purposes.

附件
2022 年营运碳强度指标和计算方法导则（CII 导则，G1）

1 引言

1.1 在《国际海事组织船舶温室气体减排初步战略》（第 MEPC.304（72）号决议）中，国际航运碳强度目标水平通过国际航运每运输功的平均 CO_2 排放来进行量化。

1.2 本导则规定了经修正的 MARPOL 附则 VI 第 4 章适用的单艘船舶的营运碳强度指标（CII）的计算方法和适用范围。

2 定义

2.1 MARPOL 系指经修正的《经 1978 年和 1997 年议定书修订的 1973 年国际防止船舶造成污染公约》。

2.2 IMO DCS 系指 MARPOL 附则 VI 第 27 条和 MARPOL 附则 VI 相关规定中所述的船舶燃油消耗数据收集系统。

2.3 就本导则而言，经修正的 MARPOL 附则 VI 中的定义适用。

2.4 在本导则中，指示船舶每运输功的平均 CO_2 排放的度量一般指的是营运碳强度指标（CII）。

 .1 基于船载货物实际或估算的质量或容积计算的特定 CII 一般称为基于需求的 CII；和

 .2 将船舶载运能力作为船舶实际载货质量或体积计算的特定 CII 一般称为基于供给的 CII。

2.5 使用 DWT 作为载运能力计算基于供给的 CII 称为 AER；使用 GT 作为载运能力计算基于供给的 CII 称为 cgDIST。

3 适用范围

3.1 对于 MARPOL 附则 VI 第 28 条适用的所有船舶，应适用第 4 节中定义的营运碳强度指标。

3.2 出于试用的目的，鼓励船舶在适用时额外使用第 5 节中定义的营运碳强度指标。

4   **Operational carbon intensity indicator (CII) of individual ships for use in implementing regulation 28 of MARPOL Annex VI**

In its most simple form, the attained annual operational CII of individual ships is calculated as the ratio of the total mass of CO_2 (*M*) emitted to the total transport work (*W*) undertaken in a given calendar year, as follows:

$$attained\ CII_{ship} = \frac{M}{W}$$

4.1   Mass of CO₂ emissions (M)

The total mass of CO_2 is the sum of CO_2 emissions (in grams) from all the fuel oil consumed on board a ship in a given calendar year, as follows:

$$M = FC_j \times C_{Fj} \tag{2}$$

where:

- *j* is the fuel oil type;

- FC_j is the total mass (in grams) of consumed fuel oil of type *j* in the calendar year, as reported under IMO DCS; and

- C_{Fj} represents the fuel oil mass to CO_2 mass conversion factor for fuel oil type

  j, in line with those specified in the *2018 Guidelines on the method of calculation of the attained Energy Efficiency Design Index (EEDI) for new ships (resolution MEPC.308(73))*, as may be further amended. In case the type of the fuel oil is not covered by the guidelines, the conversion factor should be obtained from the fuel oil supplier supported by documentary evidence.

4.2   Transport work (W)

In the absence of the data on actual transport work, the supply-based transport work (W_s) can be taken as a proxy, which is defined as the product of a ship's capacity and the distance travelled in a given calendar year, as follows:

$$W_s = C \times D_t \tag{3}$$

where:

- *C* represents the ship's capacity:

  - For bulk carriers, tankers, container ships, gas carriers, LNG carriers, general cargo ships, refrigerated cargo carrier and combination carriers, deadweight tonnage (DWT)[1] should be used as Capacity;

  - For cruise passenger ships, ro-ro cargo ships (vehicle carriers), ro-ro cargo

---

[1]   Deadweight tonnage (DWT) means the difference in tonnes between the displacement of a ship in water of relative density of 1,025 kg/m3 at the summer load draught and the lightweight of the ship. The summer load draught should be taken as the maximum summer draught as certified in the stability booklet approved by the Administration or any organization recognized by it.

4 实施 MARPOL 附则Ⅵ第 28 条时使用的单艘船舶营运碳强度指标（CII）

简单而言，单艘船舶达到的年度营运 CII 是按某一给定日历年内所排放的 CO_2 总质量（M）与所承担的总运输功（W）之比来计算的，如下式所示：

$$attained\ CII_{ship} = \frac{M}{W}$$

4.1 CO_2 排放质量（M）

CO_2 总质量是指某一给定日历年内船上消耗的所有燃油产生的 CO_2 排放质量总和（单位为克），如下式所示：

$$M = FC_j \times C_{Fj} \qquad (2)$$

式中：

- j 为燃油类型；

- FC_j 为 IMODCS 中所报告的，日历年内消耗的 j 型燃油的总质量（单位克）；和

- C_{Fj} 为 j 型燃油的燃油质量与 CO_2 质量的转换系数，与《2018 年新船达到的能效设计指数（EEDI）计算方法导则》（第 MEPC.308（73）号决议）（可能会进一步修订）中的规定一致。对于导则中未包括的燃油类型，则应从燃油供应商处获得有文件证明的转换系数。

4.2 运输功（W）

在没有实际运输功数据的情况下，可取基于供给的运输功（W_S），定义为船舶的载运能力与给定日历年内航行距离的乘积，如下式所示：

$$W_S = C \times D_t \qquad (3)$$

式中：
- C 为船舶的载运能力：
  —— 对于散货船、液货船、集装箱船、气体运输船、LNG 运输船、杂货船、冷藏货船和兼用船，应使用载重吨（DWT）[1] 作为载运能力；
  —— 对于邮轮、滚装货船（车辆运输船）、滚装货船、滚装客船，应使用

---

[1] 载重吨（DWT）指船舶在相对密度为 1 025 kg/m³ 的水中，在夏季载重吃水的排水量与和空船重量之间的吨数差。夏季载重吃水应取主管机关或经其认可组织批准的稳性手册中核准的最大夏季吃水。

ships and ro-ro passenger ships, gross tonnage (GT)[2] should be used as Capacity; and

· D_t represents the total distance travelled (in nautical miles), as reported under IMO DCS.

5   Operational carbon intensity indicator (CII) of individual ships for trial purpose

The following metrics are encouraged to be used for trial purposes, where applicable:

.1   Energy Efficiency Performance Indicator (EEPI)

$$EEPI = \frac{M}{C \times D_l}$$

.2   cbDIST

$$cbDIST = \frac{M}{ALB \times D_t}$$

.3   clDIST

$$clDIST = \frac{M}{Lanemeter \times D_t}$$

.4   EEOI, as defined in MEPC.1/Circ.684 on *Guidelines for voluntary use of the ship energy efficiency operational indicator (EEOI)*.

In the formulas above:

- the mass of CO_2 (*M*), the ship's capacity (*C*) and the total distance travelled (D_t) are identical with those used to calculate the attained CII of individual ships, as specified in section 4.1 and 4.2;

- D_l means the laden distance travelled (in nautical miles) when the ship is loaded;

- *ALB* means the number of available lower berths of a cruise passenger ship; and

- *Lanemeter* means the length (in metres) of the lanes of a ro-ro ship.

***

---

2   Gross tonnage (GT) should be calculated in accordance with the International Convention on Tonnage Measurement of Ships, 1969.

总吨（GT）^{2} 作为载运能力；和

- D_t 为 IMODCS 中报告的总航行距离（单位为海里）。

5 基于试用的单艘船舶营运碳强度指标（CII）

出于试用目的，鼓励在适用时采用下列度量方式：

.1 能效性能指标（EEPI）

$$EEPI = \frac{M}{C \times D_l}$$

.2 cbDIST

$$cbDIST = \frac{M}{ALB \times D_t}$$

.3 clDIST

$$clDIST = \frac{M}{Lanemeter \times D_t}$$

.4 EEOI，见第 MEPC.1/Circ.684 号通函关于《船舶能效营运指数（EEOI）自愿使用导则》中的定义。

在上述公式中：

- CO_2 的质量（M）、船舶载运能力（C）和总航行距离（D_t）与用于计算单艘船舶达到的 CII 一致，见第 4.1 和 4.2 节中的规定；

- D_l 系指船舶装载时的装载航行距离（单位为海里）；

- ALB 系指邮轮的可用下铺数量；和

- $Lanemeter$ 系指滚装船车道的长度（单位为米）。

***

---

^{2} 总吨（GT）应按《1969 年国际船舶吨位丈量公约》进行计算。

RESOLUTION MEPC.353(78)
(adopted on 10 June 2022)

2022 GUIDELINES ON THE REFERENCE LINES FOR USE WITH OPERATIONAL CARBON INTENSITY INDICATORS (CII REFERENCE LINES GUIDELINES, G2)

THE MARINE ENVIRONMENT PROTECTION COMMITTEE,

RECALLING Article 38(a) of the Convention on the International Maritime Organization concerning the functions of the Marine Environment Protection Committee (the Committee) conferred upon it by international conventions for the prevention and control of marine pollution from ships,

NOTING that the Committee adopted, at its seventy-sixth session, by resolution MEPC.328(76), the *2021 Revised MARPOL Annex VI*, which will enter into force on 1 November 2022,

NOTING IN PARTICULAR that the *2021 Revised MARPOL Annex VI* (MARPOL Annex VI) contains amendments concerning mandatory goal-based technical and operational measures to reduce carbon intensity of international shipping,

NOTING FURTHER that regulation 28.4 of MARPOL Annex VI requires reference lines to be established for each ship type to which regulation 28 is applicable,

NOTING that the Committee, at its seventy-sixth session, adopted, by resolution MEPC.337(76), *2021 Guidelines on the reference lines for use with operational carbon intensity indicators (CII Reference Lines Guidelines, G2)*

HAVING CONSIDERED, at its seventy-eighth session, the draft *2022 Guidelines on the reference lines for use with operational carbon intensity indicators (CII reference lines guidelines, G2)*,

1   ADOPTS the *2022 Guidelines on the reference lines for use with operational carbon intensity indicators (CII reference lines guidelines, G2)*, as set out in the annex to the present resolution;

2   INVITES Administrations to take the annexed Guidelines into account when developing and enacting national laws which give force to and implement requirements set forth in regulation 28.4 of MARPOL Annex VI;

3   REQUESTS the Parties to MARPOL Annex VI and other Member Governments to bring the annexed Guidelines to the attention of masters, seafarers, shipowners, ship operators and any other interested parties;

4   AGREES to keep the Guidelines under review in light of experience gained with their implementation, also taking into consideration that in accordance with regulation 28.11 of MARPOL Annex VI a review of the operational measures to reduce carbon intensity of international shipping shall be completed by 1 January 2026;

第 MEPC.353（78）号决议
（2022 年 6 月 10 日通过）

2022 年营运碳强度指标基线导则
（CII 基线导则，G2）

海上环境保护委员会，

忆及《国际海事组织公约》第 38（a）条关于防止和控制船舶造成海洋污染国际公约赋予海上环境保护委员会的职能，

注意到委员会在其第 76 届会议上以 MEPC.328（76）号决议通过了将于 2022 年 11 月 1 日生效的 2021 年经修订的 MARPOL 附则Ⅵ，

特别注意到 2021 年经修订的 MARPOL 附则Ⅵ包含关于基于目标的强制性技术和营运措施以减少国际航运碳强度的修正案，

进一步注意到 MARPOL 附则Ⅵ第 28.4 条要求为适用第 28 条的每一种船型设立基线，

注意到委员会在其第 76 届会议上，以第 MEPC.337（76）号决议通过了《2021 年营运碳强度指标基线导则（CII 基线导则，G2）》，

在其第 78 届会议上，**审议了**《2022 年营运碳强度指标基线导则（CII 基线导则，G2）》草案，

1　**通过**《2022 年营运碳强度指标基线导则（CII 基线导则，G2）》，其文本载于本决议附件；

2　**提请**主管机关在制定和颁布本国法律，以执行和实施 MARPOL 附则Ⅵ第 28.4 条要求时，考虑附件中的导则；

3　**要求** MARPOL 附则Ⅵ的各缔约方和其他成员国政府提请船长、船员、船东、船舶经营者以及任何其他利益相关方注意到附件中的导则；

4　**同意**根据本导则实施中获得的经验，并考虑到根据 MARPOL 附则Ⅵ第 28.11 条须在 2026 年 1 月 1 日之前完成对减少国际航运碳强度的营运措施的审查，对本导则保持审查；

5   REVOKES the *2021 Guidelines on the reference lines for use with operational carbon intensity indicators (CII Reference Lines Guidelines, G2).*

5　撤销《2021 年营运碳强度指标基线导则（CII 基线导则，G2）》。

ANNEX

2022 GUIDELINES ON THE REFERENCE LINES FOR USE WITH OPERATIONAL CARBON INTENSITY INDICATORS (CII REFERENCE LINES GUIDELINES, G2)

1   Introduction

1.1   These Guidelines provide the methods to calculate the reference lines for use with operational carbon intensity indicators, and the ship type specific carbon intensity reference lines as referred to in regulation 28 of MARPOL Annex VI.

1.2   One reference line is developed for each ship type to which regulation 28 of MARPOL Annex VI applies, based on the specific indicators stipulated in *2022 Guidelines on operational carbon intensity indicators and the calculation methods* (G1) developed by the Organization, ensuring that only data from comparable ships are included in the calculation of each reference line.

2   Definition

2.1   *MARPOL* means the International Convention for the Prevention of Pollution from Ships, 1973, as modified by the Protocols of 1978 and 1997 relating thereto, as amended.

2.2   *IMO DCS* means the data collection system for fuel oil consumption of ships referred to in regulation 27 and related provisions of MARPOL Annex VI.

2.3   For the purpose of these Guidelines, the definitions in MARPOL Annex VI, as amended, apply.

2.4   An operational carbon intensity indicator (CII) reference line is defined as a curve representing the median attained operational carbon intensity performance, as a function of Capacity, of a defined group of ships in year of 2019.

3   Method to develop the CII reference lines

3.1   Given the limited data available for the year of 2008, the operational carbon intensity performance of ship types in year 2019 is taken as the reference.

3.2   For a defined group of ships, the reference line is formulated as follows:

$$CII_{ref} = aCapacity^{-c} \qquad (1)$$

where CII_{ref} is the reference value of year 2019, $Capacity$ is identical with the one defined in the specific carbon intensity indicator (CII) for a ship type, as shown in Table. 1; a and c are parameters estimated through median regression fits, taking the attained CII and the Capacity of individual ships collected through IMO DCS in year 2019 as the sample.

4   Ship type specific operational carbon intensity reference lines

The parameters for determining the ship type specific reference lines, for use in Eq.(1), are specified as follows:

附件

2022 年营运碳强度指标基线导则
（CII 基线导则，G2）

1 引言

1.1 本导则提供了用于计算营运碳强度指标基线的方法，以及 MARPOL 附则Ⅵ第 28 条所述的船型特定碳强度基线。

1.2 基于本组织制定的《2022 年营运碳强度指标和计算方法导则（G1）》中规定的特定指标，为适用 MARPOL 附则Ⅵ第 28 条的每种船型制定一条基线，确保每条基线的计算中仅包含来自可比船舶的数据。

2 定义

2.1 MARPOL 系指经修正的《经 1978 年和 1997 年议定书修订的 1973 年国际防止船舶造成污染公约》。

2.2 IMO DCS 系指 MARPOL 附则Ⅵ第 27 条和 MARPOL 附则Ⅵ相关规定中所述的船舶燃油消耗数据收集系统。

2.3 就本导则而言，经修正的 MARPOL 附则Ⅵ中的定义适用。

2.4 营运碳强度指标（CII）基线的定义为一条代表了一组规定的船舶在 2019 年达到的营运碳强度性能中值的曲线，是以载运能力为自变量的函数。

3 制定 CII 基线的方法

3.1 鉴于 2008 年的数据有限，以 2019 年船型营运碳强度性能为基准。

3.2 对于规定的一组船舶，基线的公式如下：

$$CII_{ref}=aCapacity^{-c} \tag{1}$$

式中：CII_{ref} 系指 2019 年的基准值，$Capacity$（载运能力）与某一船型特定碳强度指标（CII）规定的值相同，见表 1；a 和 c 系指通过中位数回归拟合所估算的参数，以 2019 年通过 IMO DCS 收集的单艘船舶的达到的 CII 和 Capacity 为样本。

4 船型特定营运碳强度基线

用于公式（1）中确定船型特定基线的参数规定如下：

Table 1: Parameters for determining the 2019 ship type specific reference lines

Ship type		Capacity	a	c
Bulk carrier	279,000 DWT and above	279,000	4745	0.622
	less than 279,000 DWT	DWT	4745	0.622
Gas carrier	65,000 and above	DWT	14405E7	2.071
	less than 65,000 DWT	DWT	8104	0.639
Tanker		DWT	5247	0.610
Container ship		DWT	1984	0.489
General cargo ship	20,000 DWT and above	DWT	31948	0.792
	less than 20,000 DWT	DWT	588	0.3885
Refrigerated cargo carrier		DWT	4600	0.557
Combination carrier		DWT	5119	0.622
LNG carrier	100,000 DWT and above	DWT	9.827	0.000
	65,000 DWT and above, but less than 100,000 DWT	DWT	14479E10	2.673
	less than 65,000 DWT	65,000	14779E10	2.673
Ro-ro cargo ship (vehicle carrier)	57,700 GT and above	57,700	3627	0.590
	30,000 GT and above, but less than 57,700 GT	GT	3627	0.590
	Less than 30,000 GT	GT	330	0.329
Ro-ro cargo ship		GT	1967	0.485
Ro-ro passenger ship	Ro-ro passenger ship	GT	2023	0.460
	High-speed craft designed to SOLAS chapter X	GT	4196	0.460
Cruise passenger ship		GT	930	0.383

***

表 1　确定 2019 年船型特定基线的参数

船型		载运能力	a	c
散货船	279 000 DWT 及以上	279 000	4 745	0.622
	小于 279 000 DWT	DWT	4 745	0.622
气体运输船	65 000 DWT 及以上	DWT	14 405E7	2.071
	小于 65 000 DWT	DWT	8 104	0.639
液货船		DWT	5 247	0.610
集装箱船		DWT	1 984	0.489
杂货船	20 000 DWT 及以上	DWT	31 948	0.792
	小于 20 000 DWT	DWT	588	0.388 5
冷藏货船		DWT	4 600	0.557
兼用船		DWT	5 119	0.622
LNG 运输船	100 000 DWT 及以上	DWT	9.827	0.000
	65 000 DWT 及以上，但小于 100 000 DWT	DWT	14 479E10	2.673
	小于 65 000 DWT	65 000	14 779E10	2.673
滚装货船 （车辆运输船）	57 700 GT 及以上	57 700	3 627	0.590
	30 000 GT 及以上，但小于 57 700 GT	GT	3 627	0.590
	小于 30 000 GT	GT	330	0.329
滚装货船		GT	1 967	0.485
滚装客船	滚装客船	GT	2 023	0.460
	适用 SOLAS 第 X 章的高速船	GT	4 196	0.460
邮轮		GT	930	0.383

***

RESOLUTION MEPC.338(76)
(adopted on 17 June 2021)

2021 GUIDELINES ON THE OPERATIONAL CARBON INTENSITY REDUCTION FACTORS RELATIVE TO REFERENCE LINES (CII REDUCTION FACTORS GUIDELINES, G3)

THE MARINE ENVIRONMENT PROTECTION COMMITTEE,

RECALLING Article 38(a) of the Convention on the International Maritime Organization concerning the functions of the Marine Environment Protection Committee conferred upon it by international conventions for the prevention and control of marine pollution from ships,

NOTING that it adopted, by resolution MEPC.328(76), the 2021 revised MARPOL Annex VI, which is expected to enter into force on 1 November 2022 upon its deemed acceptance on 1 May 2022,

NOTING IN PARTICULAR that the 2021 revised MARPOL Annex VI contains amendments concerning mandatory goal-based technical and operational measures to reduce carbon intensity of international shipping,

NOTING FURTHER that regulation 28.4 of MARPOL Annex VI requires reduction factors to be established for each ship type to which regulation 28 is applicable,

HAVING CONSIDERED, at its seventy-sixth session, draft *2021 Guidelines on the operational carbon intensity reduction factors relative to reference lines (CII reduction factors guidelines, G3)*,

1   ADOPTS the *2021 Guidelines on the operational carbon intensity reduction factors relative to reference lines (CII reduction factors guidelines, G3)*, as set out in the annex to the present resolution;

2   INVITES Administrations to take the annexed Guidelines into account when developing and enacting national laws which give force to and implement requirements set forth in regulation 28.4 of MARPOL Annex VI;

3   REQUESTS the Parties to MARPOL Annex VI and other Member Governments to bring the annexed Guidelines to the attention of masters, seafarers, shipowners, ship operators and any other interested parties;

4   AGREES to keep the Guidelines under review in light of experience gained with their implementation and in light of the review of CII regulations to be completed by the Organization by 1 January 2026 as identified in regulation 28.11 of MARPOL Annex VI, and that annual reduction rates for the period 2027-2030 will be further strengthened and developed taking into account that review.

第 MEPC.338（76）号决议
（2021 年 6 月 17 日通过）

2021 年相对于基线的营运碳强度折减系数导则
（CII 折减系数导则，G3）

海上环境保护委员会，

忆及《国际海事组织公约》第 38（a）条关于防止和控制船舶造成海洋污染国际公约赋予海上环境保护委员会的职能，

注意到以第 MEPC.328（76）号决议通过的 2021 年经修订的 MARPOL 附则Ⅵ，在 2022 年 5 月 1 日被视为获得接受后，预计将于 2022 年 11 月 1 日生效，

特别注意到 2021 年经修订的 MARPOL 附则Ⅵ包含关于基于目标的强制性技术和营运措施以减少国际航运碳强度的修正案，

进一步注意到 MARPOL 附则Ⅵ第 28.4 条要求为适用第 28 条的每一种船型确定折减系数，

在其第 76 届会议上，**审议了**《2021 年相对于基线的营运碳强度折减系数导则》（CII 折减系数导则，G3）草案，

1   **通过**《2021 年相对于基线的营运碳强度折减系数导则（CII 折减系数导则，G3）》，其文本载于本决议附件；

2   **提请**主管机关在制定和颁布本国法律，以执行和实施 MARPOL 附则Ⅵ第 28.4 条要求时，考虑到附件中的导则；

3   **要求** MARPOL 附则Ⅵ的各缔约方和其他成员国政府提请船长、船员、船东、船舶经营者以及任何其他利益相关方注意到附件中的导则；

4   **同意**根据本导则实施中获得的经验，并根据 MARPOL 附则Ⅵ第 28.11 条中确定的本组织将在 2026 年 1 月 1 日之前完成的对 CII 各条规则的审查情况，对本导则保持审查。考虑到该审查，将进一步制定和加强 2027—2030 年期间的年折减率。

ANNEX

2021 GUIDELINES ON THE OPERATIONAL CARBON INTENSITY REDUCTION FACTORS RELATIVE TO REFERENCE LINES (CII REDUCTION FACTORS GUIDELINES, G3)

1 Introduction

1.1 These Guidelines provide the methods to determine the annual operational carbon intensity reduction factors and their concrete values from year 2023 to 2030, as referred to in regulation 28 of MARPOL Annex VI.

1.2 The annual operational carbon intensity reduction factors apply to each ship type to which regulation 28 of MARPOL Annex VI applies, in a transparent and robust manner, based on the specific carbon intensity indicators stipulated in the *2021 Guidelines on operational carbon intensity indicators and the calculation methods (G1)* (resolution MEPC.336(76)) and the reference lines developed in the *2021 Guidelines on the reference lines for use with operational carbon intensity indicators (G2)*(resolution MEPC.337(76)).

1.3 The reduction factors have been set at the levels to ensure that, in combination with other relevant requirements of MARPOL Annex VI, the reduction in CO_2 emissions per transport work by at least 40% by 2030, compared to 2008, can be achieved as an average across international shipping.

1.4 Section 5 of these Guidelines provides background information on rational ranges of reduction factors of ship types in year 2030 using demand-based measurement and supply-based measurement.

1.5 The Organization should continue to monitor development in annual carbon intensity improvement using both demand-based measurement and supply-based measurement in parallel to the annual analysis of the fuel consumption data reported to the IMO DCS.

2 Definitions

2.1 *MARPOL* means the International Convention for the Prevention of Pollution from Ships, 1973, as modified by the Protocols of 1978 and 1997 relating thereto, as amended.

2.2 *IMO DCS* means the data collection system for fuel oil consumption of ships referred to in regulation 27 and related provisions of MARPOL Annex VI.

2.3 For the purpose of these Guidelines, the definitions in MARPOL Annex VI, as amended, apply.

2.4 The annual operational carbon intensity reduction factor, generally denoted as "Z" in regulation 28 of MARPOL Annex VI, is a positive value, stipulating the percentage points of the required annual operational carbon intensity indicator of a ship for a given year lower than the reference value.

附件

2021 年相对于基线的营运碳强度折减系数导则
（CII 折减系数导则，G3）

1 引言

1.1 本导则规定了确定 MARPOL 附则Ⅵ第 28 条所提到的年度营运碳强度折减系数及其从 2023—2030 年具体值的方法。

1.2 基于《2021 年营运碳强度指标和计算方法导则（G1）》（第 MEPC.336（76）号决议）规定的具体碳强度指数和《2021 年营运碳强度指标基线导则（G2）》（第 MEPC.337（76）号决议）制定的基线，年度营运碳强度折减系数以透明和稳健的方式适用于 MARPOL 附则Ⅵ第 28 条适用的每一种船型。

1.3 结合 MARPOL 附则Ⅵ的其他相关要求，设定的折减系数是为了确保国际航运能实现平均每运输功在 2030 年的 CO_2 排放相对 2008 年减少至少 40%。

1.4 根据基于需求的测量和基于供给的测量，本导则第 5 节提供了 2030 年船型折减系数合理范围的背景资料。

1.5 本组织应采用基于需求的测量和基于供给的测量，以及报告至 IMO DCS 的年度燃油消耗数据分析，继续监测年度碳强度改善的发展情况。

2 定义

2.1 MARPOL 系指经修正的《经 1978 年和 1997 年议定书修订的 1973 年国际防止船舶造成污染公约》。

2.2 IMO DCS 系指 MARPOL 附则Ⅵ第 27 条和 MARPOL 附则Ⅵ相关规定中所述的船舶燃油消耗数据收集系统。

2.3 就本导则而言，经修正的 MARPOL 附则Ⅵ中的定义适用。

2.4 年度营运碳强度折减系数，在 MARPOL 附则Ⅵ第 28 条通常用 "Z" 表示，是一个正值，规定了指定年份所要求的船舶年度营运碳强度指标低于基准值的百分点。

3 Method to determine the annual reduction factor of ship types

3.1 Operational carbon intensity of international shipping

Given significant heterogeneity across ship types, the attained annual operational CII of international shipping as a whole is calculated as the ratio of the aggregated mass (in grams) of CO_2 ($aggregated\ M$) emitted to the aggregated mass (in tonne·nmiles) of transport work ($aggregated\ W$) undertaken by all individual ships of representative ship types in a given calendar year, as follows:

$$attained\ CII_{shipping} = aggregated\ M\ /\ aggregated\ W \qquad (1)$$

In the absence of the data on actual annual transport work of individual ships, the aggregated transport work obtained from other reliable sources, such as UNCTAD, can be taken as approximation. The representative ship types refer to bulk carriers, gas carriers, tankers, container ships, general cargo ships, refrigerated cargo carrier and LNG carriers, as per the *Fourth IMO GHG Study 2020.*

3.2 The achieved carbon intensity reduction in international shipping

For a given year y, the achieved carbon intensity reduction in international shipping relative to the reference year y_{ref}, denoted as $R_{shipping,y}$, can be calculated as follows:

$$R_{shipping,y} = 100\% \times (attained\ CII_{shipping,y} - attained\ CII_{shipping,y_{ref}})\ /\ attained\ CII_{shipping,y_{ref}} \qquad (2)$$

where the $attained\ CII_{shipping,y}$ and $attained\ CII_{shipping,y_{ref}}$ represents the attained annual operational carbon intensity of international shipping in year y and in the reference year y_{ref}, as defined in Eq.(1).

The achieved carbon intensity reduction in international shipping can be alternatively calculated on the carbon intensity performance of ship types. Since CII metrics for different ship types may not be identical, the weighted average of the carbon intensity reduction achieved by ship types can be applied, as follows:

$$R_{shipping,y} = \sum_{type} f_{type,y} R_{type,y} \qquad (3)$$

In Eq(3),

- $type$ represents the ship type;

- $f_{type,y}$ is the weight, which is equal to the proportion of CO_2 emitted by the ship type to the total CO_2 emissions of international shipping in year y; and

- $R_{type,y}$ represents the carbon intensity reduction achieved by the ship type in year y, calculated as $R_{type,y} = 100\% \times (attained\ CII_{type,y} - attained\ CII_{type,y_{ref}})\ /\ attained\ CII_{type,y_{ref}}$, where the $attained\ CII_{type,y}$ and $attained\ CII_{type,ref}$ represents the attained annual operational carbon intensity of the ship type in year y and in the reference year y_{ref}, as defined in Eq.(4), as follows:

$$attained\ CII_{type} = \sum_{ship} M_{ship,t}\ /\ \sum_{ship} W_{ship,t} \qquad (4)$$

3 确定船型年度折减系数的方法

3.1 国际航运的营运碳强度

鉴于船型之间的显著异质性，国际航运达到的年度营运 CII 作为一个整体，为指定日历年代表性船型的所有单艘船舶排放的 CO_2 的总质量（*aggregated M*，以 g 为单位）与承担的运输功的总量（*aggregated W*，以 t·n mile 为单位）之比，计算如下：

$$attained\ CII_{shipping} = aggregated\ M\ /\ aggregated\ W \qquad (1)$$

在没有单艘船舶实际年度运输功数据的情况下，从其他可靠来源获得的总运输功（如 UNCTAD）可视为近似值。根据《2020 年第四次国际海事组织温室气体研究》，代表性船型指散货船、气体运输船、液货船、集装箱船、杂货船、冷藏货船和 LNG 运输船。

3.2 国际航运中实现的碳强度折减

对于指定年份 y，相对基准年 y_{ref} 的国际航运中实现的碳强度折减，用 $R_{shipping, y}$ 表示，可计算如下：

$$R_{shipping, y} = 100\% \times (attained\ CII_{shipping, y} - attained\ CII_{shipping, y_{ref}}) / attained\ CII_{shipping, y_{ref}} \qquad (2)$$

式中，*attained CII*$_{shipping, y}$ 和 *attained CII*$_{shipping, y_{ref}}$ 分别代表国际航运在年份 y 和基准年 y_{ref} 达到的年度营运碳强度，如式（1）所定义。

或者，国际航运实现的碳强度折减可通过船型的碳强度表现计算。由于不同船型的 CII 度量可能不是完全相同，可采用船型实现的碳强度折减的加权平均，如下所示：

$$R_{shipping, y} = \sum_{type} f_{type, y} R_{type, y} \qquad (3)$$

在式（3）中，

- *type* 代表船型；

- $f_{type, y}$ 是权重，等于在年份 y 该船型排放的 CO_2 在全球航运总 CO_2 排放的占比；和

- $R_{type, y}$ 代表在年份 y 该船型实现的碳强度折减，计算方法为 $R_{type, y} = 100\% \times ($ *attained CII*$_{type, y}$ – *attained CII*$_{type, y_{ref}}) / attained\ CII_{type, y_{ref}}$，式中 *attained CII*$_{type, y}$ 和 *attained CII*$_{type, y_{ref}}$ 代表在年份 y 和基准年 y_{ref} 该船型达到的年度营运碳强度，如式（4）所定义，如下所示：

$$attained\ CII_{type} = \sum_{ship} M_{ship, t} / \sum_{ship} W_{ship, t} \qquad (4)$$

where:

$M_{ship,t}$ and $W_{ship,t}$ represents the total mass of CO_2 emitted from and the total transport work undertaken by a ship of this type in a given calendar year, as stipulated in the *Guidelines on operational carbon intensity indicators and the calculation methods (G1)*.

4 The reduction factors for the required annual operational CII of ship types

4.1 In accordance with regulation 28 of MARPOL Annex VI, the required annual operational CII for a ship is calculated as follows:

$$\text{Required annual operational } CII = (1 - Z/100) \times CII_R$$

where CII_R is the reference value in year 2019 as defined in the *Guidelines on the reference lines for use with operational carbon intensity indicators (G2)*, Z is a general reference to the reduction factors for the required annual operational CII of ship types from year 2023 to 2030, as specified in table 1.

Table 1: Reduction factor (Z%) for the CII relative to the 2019 reference line

Year	Reduction factor relative to 2019
2023	5%*
2024	7%
2025	9%
2026	11%
2027	- **
2028	- **
2029	- **
2030	- **

Note:

* Z factors of 1%, 2% and 3% are set for the years of 2020 to 2022, similar as business as usual until entry into force of the measure.

** Z factors for the years of 2027 to 2030 to be further strengthened and developed taking into account the review of the short-term measure.

式中：$M_{ship,t}$ 和 $W_{ship,t}$ 分别代表在给定日历年该船型单艘船舶排放的 CO_2 的总重量与承担的运输功总量，如《2021 年营运碳强度指标和计算方法导则（G1）》所规定的。

4 对船型要求的年度营运 CII 折减系数

4.1 按照 MARPOL 附则Ⅵ第 28 条，对船舶要求的年度营运 CII 折减系数计算如下：

$$\text{Required annual operational } CII= \left(1-\frac{Z}{100}\right) \times CII_R$$

式中：CII_R 是 2019 年的基准值，定义见《2021 年营运碳强度基线导则（G2）》，Z 是 2023—2030 年对各船型要求的年度营运 CII 折减系数的一般参考，详见表 1。

表 1　CII 相对于 2019 年基线的折减系数（$Z\%$）

年份	相对于 2019 年的折减系数
2023	5%*
2024	7%
2025	9%
2026	11%
2027	—**
2028	—**
2029	—**
2030	—**
注：*2020—2022 年 $Z\%$ 系数设为 1%、2% 和 3%，在措施生效以前与往常相似。 **2027—2030 年 $Z\%$ 系数将在考虑到对短期措施的审查后，予以进一步加强和制定。	

5 Background information on rational ranges of reduction factors of ship types in year 2030

5.1   In the *Initial IMO Strategy on Reduction of GHG Emissions from Ships* (Resolution MEPC.304(72)), the levels of ambition on carbon intensity of international shipping have been set taking year 2008 as reference. The carbon intensity of international shipping in year 2008, as well as the improvement through 2012 to 2018, has been estimated in the *Fourth IMO GHG Study 2020*. However, since the scope and data collection methods applied in the *Fourth IMO GHG Study 2020* were inconsistent with those under IMO DCS, the results derived from the two sources cannot be compared directly.

5.2   To ensure the comparability of the attained carbon intensity of international shipping through year 2023 to 2030 with the reference line, the following methods are applied to calculate the equivalent carbon intensity target in year 2030 ($eR_{shipping,2030}$), taking year 2019 as reference, i.e. how much additional improvement is needed by 2030 from the 2019 performance level.

5.3   The achieved carbon intensity reduction of international shipping in year 2019 relative to year 2008 ($R_{shipping,2019}$) can be estimated as the sum of the achieved carbon intensity reduction of international shipping in year 2018 relative to year 2008 ($R_{shipping,2018}$) as given by the *Fourth IMO GHG Study 2020* and the estimated average annual improvement during 2012 and 2018 ($\overline{r}_{shipping}$), as follows:

$$R_{shipping,2019} = R_{shipping,2018} + \overline{r}_{shipping} \quad (5)$$

5.4   The following provides the calculations using demand-based measurement and supply-based measurement.

5.4.1   Demand-based measurement of 2030 target

As estimated by the *Fourth IMO GHG Study 2020*, the attained CII of international shipping (on aggregated demand-based metric) has reduced by **31.8%** ($R_{shipping,2018}=31.8\%$) compared to 2008, with an estimated average annual improvement at **1.5** percentage points ($\overline{r}_{shipping}=1.5\%$). In accordance with Eq.(5), the carbon intensity reduction achieved in year 2019 is estimated as **33.3%** ($R_{shipping,2019}=33.3\%$).

5.4.2   Supply-based measurement of 2030 target

As estimated by the *Fourth IMO GHG Study 2020*, the attained CII of international shipping (on aggregated supply-based metric) has reduced by **22.0%** ($R_{shipping,2018}=22.0\%$) compared to 2008, with an estimated average annual improvement at **1.6** percentage points ($\overline{r}_{shipping}=1.6\%$). In accordance with Eq.(5), the carbon intensity reduction achieved in year 2019 relative to 2008 is estimated as **23.6%** ($R_{shipping,2019}=23.6\%$).

5.5   Given the achieved carbon intensity reduction of international shipping in year 2019 relative to year 2008, the carbon intensity reduction target of international shipping in year 2030 can be converted to the equivalent target ($eR_{shipping,2030}$) relative to year 2019, as follows:

$$eR_{shipping,2030} = \frac{40\% - R_{shipping,2019}}{1 - R_{shipping,2019}} \quad (6)$$

5　2030 年船型折减系数合理范围的背景资料

5.1　在《国际海事组织船舶温室气体减排初步战略》（第 MEPC.304（72）号决议）中，已设立国际航运碳强度减排目标水平，将 2008 年设为基准。2008 年国际航运碳强度，以及 2012—2018 年的改进，已在《2020 年第四次国际海事组织温室气体研究》中进行估算。但是，由于《2020 年第四次国际海事组织温室气体研究》应用的范围和数据收集方法与 IMO DCS 中的不一致，两处来源得到的数据无法直接进行比较。

5.2　为确保 2023—2030 年国际航运达到的碳强度能与基线比较，采用了下列方法计算 2030 年的等效碳强度目标（$eR_{shipping,2030}$），以 2019 年为基准，即 2030 年在 2019 年的表现水平上需要额外提高多少。

5.3　2019 年国际航运相对于 2008 年实现的碳强度折减（$R_{shipping,2019}$）可估算为 2018 年国际航运相对于 2008 年实现的碳强度折减（$R_{shipping,2018}$）（见《2020 年第四次国际海事组织温室气体研究》）与估算的 2012 至 2018 年的平均年度改善值（$\overline{r}_{shipping}$）之和，如下所示：

$$R_{shipping,2019}=R_{shipping,2018}+\overline{r}_{shipping} \qquad (5)$$

5.4　下文给出了使用基于需求的测算和基于供给的测算的计算

5.4.1　基于需求的 2019 年（译者注：原文为 2030 年）目标测算

正如《2020 年第四次国际海事组织温室气体研究》估算的，与 2008 年相比国际航运达到的 CII（按总基于需求的度量）已减少 **31.8%**（$R_{shipping,2018}$=31.8%），估算的平均年度改善水平在 1.5 个百分点（$\overline{r}_{shipping}$=1.5%）。根据式（5），2019 年实现的碳强度折减估算为 **33.3%**（$R_{shipping,2018}$=33.3%）。

5.4.2　基于供给的 2019 年（译者注：原文为 2030 年）目标测算

正如《2020 年第四次国际海事组织温室气体研究》估算的，与 2008 年相比国际航运达到的 CII（按总基于供给的度量）已减少 **22.0%**（$R_{shipping,2018}$=22%），估算的平均年改善率在 **1.6** 个百分点（$\overline{r}_{shipping}$=1.6%）。根据式（5），2019 年实现的碳强度折减估算为 **23.6%**（$R_{shipping,2018}$=23.6%）。

5.5　鉴于国际航运 2019 年相对于 2008 年实现的碳强度折减，国际航运 2030 年碳强度折减目标可转换为相对于 2019 年的等效目标（$eR_{shipping,2030}$），如下所示：

$$eR_{shipping,2030}=\frac{40\%-R_{shipping,2019}}{1-R_{shipping,2019}} \qquad (6)$$

5.5.1 Demand-based measurement of 2030 target

In accordance with Eq.(6), the equivalent reduction factor of international shipping in year 2030 relative to year 2019 ($eR_{shipping,2030}$) would be at least **10.0%** measured in aggregated demand-based CII metric, i.e. at least additional **10.0%** improvement from the 2019 level is needed by 2030.

5.5.2 Supply-based measurement of 2030 target

In accordance with Eq.(6), the equivalent reduction factor of international shipping in 2030 relative to year 2019 ($eR_{shipping,2030}$) would be at least **21.5%**, measured in aggregated supply-based CII metric, i.e. at least additional **21.5%** improvement from the 2019 level is needed by 2030.

***

5.5.1 基于需求的 2030 年目标测算

根据式（6），国际航运 2030 年相对于 2019 年的等效折减系数（$eR_{shipping,\,2030}$）按总基于需求的 CII 测量将至少为 **10.0%**，即 2030 年在 2019 年水平上需要至少额外改进 **10.0%**。

5.5.2 基于供给的 2030 年目标测算

根据式（6），国际航运 2030 年相对于 2019 年的等效折减系数（$eR_{shipping,\,2030}$）按总基于供给的 CII 测量将至少为 **21.5%**，即 2030 年在 2019 年水平上需要至少额外改进 **21.5%**。

***

RESOLUTION MEPC.354(78)
(adopted on 10 June 2022)

2022 GUIDELINES ON THE OPERATIONAL CARBON INTENSITY
RATING OF SHIPS (CII RATING GUIDELINES, G4)

THE MARINE ENVIRONMENT PROTECTION COMMITTEE,

RECALLING Article 38(a) of the Convention on the International Maritime Organization concerning the functions of the Marine Environment Protection Committee (the Committee) conferred upon it by international conventions for the prevention and control of marine pollution from ships,

NOTING that the Committee adopted, by resolution MEPC.328(76), the *2021 Revised MARPOL Annex VI*, which will enter into force on 1 November 2022,

NOTING IN PARTICULAR that the *2021 Revised MARPOL Annex VI* (MARPOL Annex VI) contains amendments concerning mandatory goal-based technical and operational measures to reduce carbon intensity of international shipping,

NOTING FURTHER that regulation 28.6 of MARPOL Annex VI requires ships to which this regulation apply to determine operational carbon intensity rating taking into account guidelines developed by the Organization,

RECOGNIZING that the aforementioned amendments to MARPOL Annex VI require relevant guidelines for uniform and effective implementation of the regulations and to provide sufficient lead time for industry to prepare,

NOTING that, at its seventy-sixth session, the Committee adopted, by resolution MEPC.339(76) the *2021 Guidelines on the operational carbon intensity rating of ships (CII rating guidelines, G4)*,

HAVING CONSIDERED, at its seventy-eighth session, draft *2022 Guidelines on the operational carbon intensity rating of ships (CII rating guidelines, G4)*,

1   ADOPTS the *2022 Guidelines on the operational carbon intensity rating of ships (CII rating guidelines, G4)*, as set out in the annex to the present resolution;

2   INVITES Administrations to take the annexed Guidelines into account when developing and enacting national laws which give force to and implement requirements set forth in regulation 28.6 of MARPOL Annex VI;

3   REQUESTS the Parties to MARPOL Annex VI and other Member Governments to bring the annexed Guidelines to the attention of masters, seafarers, shipowners, ship operators and any other interested parties;

4   AGREES to keep the Guidelines under review in light of experience gained with their implementation, of additional data collected and analysed, also taking into consideration that

第 MEPC.354（78）号决议
（2022 年 6 月 10 日通过）

2022 年船舶营运碳强度评级导则（CII 评级导则，G4）

海上环境保护委员会，

忆及《国际海事组织公约》第 38（a）条关于防止和控制船舶造成海洋污染国际公约赋予海上环境保护委员会的职能，

注意到委员会在其第 76 届会议上以 MEPC.328（76）号决议通过了将于 2022 年 11 月 1 日生效的 2021 年经修订的 MARPOL 附则Ⅵ，

特别注意到 2021 年经修订的 MARPOL 附则Ⅵ包含关于基于目标的强制性技术和营运措施以减少国际航运碳强度的修正案，

进一步注意到 MARPOL 附则Ⅵ第 28.6 条要求为本条适用的船舶确定营运碳强度等级，并考虑到本组织制定的导则，

认识到上述 MARPOL 附则Ⅵ的修正案需要有相关导则，以便于统一和有效实施各条规定，并为业界提供充足的准备时间，

注意到委员会在其第 76 届会议上，以第 MEPC.339（76）号决议通过了《2021 年船舶营运碳强度评级导则（CII 评级导则，G4）》，

在其第 78 届会议上，**审议了**《2022 年船舶营运碳强度评级导则（CII 评级导则，G4）》草案，

1 **通过**《2022 年船舶营运碳强度评级导则（CII 评级导则，G4》），其文本载于本决议附件；

2 **提请**主管机关在制定和颁布本国法律，以执行和实施 MARPOL 附则Ⅵ第 28.6 条要求时，考虑附件中的导则；

3 **要求** MARPOL 附则Ⅵ的各缔约方和其他成员国政府提请船长、船员、船东、船舶经营者以及任何其他利益相关方注意到附件中的导则；

in accordance with regulation 28.11 of MARPOL Annex VI a review of the operational measure to reduce carbon intensity of international shipping shall be completed by 1 January 2026;

5   REVOKES the *2021 Guidelines on the operational carbon intensity rating of ships (CII rating guidelines, G4)*, adopted by resolution MEPC.339(76).

4　**同意**根据本导则实施中获得的经验、收集和分析的额外数据，并考虑到根据 MARPOL 附则Ⅵ第 28.11 条须在 2026 年 1 月 1 日之前完成对减少国际航运碳强度的营运措施的审查，对本导则保持审查。

5　**撤销**以第 MEPC.339（76）号决议通过的《2021 年船舶营运碳强度评级导则（CII 评级导则，G4）》。

2022 GUIDELINES ON THE OPERATIONAL CARBON INTENSITY RATING OF SHIPS (CII RATING GUIDELINES, G4)

1 Introduction

1.1 These Guidelines provide the methods to assign operational energy efficiency performance ratings to ships, as referred to in regulation 28 of MARPOL Annex VI. On this basis, the boundaries for determining a ship's annual operational carbon intensity performance from year 2023 to 2030 are also provided.

2 Definitions

2.1 *MARPOL* means the International Convention for the Prevention of Pollution from Ships, 1973, as modified by the Protocols of 1978 and 1997 relating thereto, as amended.

2.2 *IMO DCS* means the data collection system for fuel oil consumption of ships referred to in regulation 27 and related provisions of MARPOL Annex VI.

2.3 For the purpose of these Guidelines, the definitions in MARPOL Annex VI, as amended, apply.

2.4 *Operational carbon intensity rating* means to assign a ranking label from among the five grades (A, B, C, D and E) to the ship based on the attained annual operational carbon intensity indicator, indicating a major superior, minor superior, moderate, minor inferior, or inferior performance level.

3 Framework of the operational energy efficiency performance rating

3.1 An operational energy efficiency performance rating should be assigned annually to each ship to which regulation 28 of MARPOL Annex VI applies, in a transparent and robust manner, based on the deviation of the attained annual operational carbon intensity indicator (CII) of a ship from the required value.

3.2 To facilitate the rating assignment, for each year from 2023 to 2030, four boundaries are defined for the five-grade rating mechanism, namely superior boundary, lower boundary, upper boundary, and inferior boundary. Thus, a rating can be assigned through comparing the attained annual operational CII of a ship with the boundary values.

3.3 The boundaries are set based on the distribution of CIIs of individual ships in year 2019. The appropriate rating boundaries are expected to generate the following results: the middle 30% of individual ships across the fleet segment, in terms of the attained annual operational CIIs, are to be assigned rating C, while the upper 20% and further upper 15% of individuals are to be assigned rating D and E respectively, and the lower 20% and further lower 15% of the individuals are to be assigned rating B and A, respectively, as illustrated in figure 1.

附件

2022 年船舶营运碳强度评级导则（CII 评级导则，G4）

1 引言

1.1 本导则规定了 MARPOL 附则Ⅵ第 28 条所提及的评定船舶营运能效性能等级的方法。在此基础上，还规定了确定 2023—2030 年船舶年度营运碳强度性能的边界。

2 定义

2.1 MARPOL 系指经修正的《经 1978 年和 1997 年议定书修订的 1973 年国际防止船舶造成污染公约》。

2.2 IMO DCS 系指 MARPOL 附则Ⅵ中的第 27 条和相关规定所述的船舶燃油消耗数据收集系统。

2.3 就本导则而言，经修正的 MARPOL 附则Ⅵ中的定义适用。

2.4 营运碳强度评级系指基于达到的年度营运碳强度指标从 5 个等级（A、B、C、D 和 E）评定船舶，表示优秀、良好、普通、稍差或不合格的性能水平。

3 营运能效性能评级框架

3.1 对 MARPOL 附则Ⅵ第 28 条适用的每艘船舶应基于船舶达到的年度营运碳强度指标（CII）与要求的值的偏差以透明和稳健的方式每年评定营运能效性能等级。

3.2 为方便评级，对 2023—2030 年的每一年，为五级评定机制设定了四个边界，即优秀边界、良好边界、合格边界和不合格边界。这样，通过将船舶达到的年度营运 CII 与边界值进行比较可评定等级。

3.3 边界是基于 2019 年单艘船舶 CII 的分布设定的。适当的评级边界预计产生如下结果：就达到的年度营运 CII 而言，整个船队中间 30% 的单艘船舶应被评为 C 级，高 20% 和再高 15% 的单艘船舶相应分别被评为 D 级和 E 级，低 20% 和再低 15% 的单艘船舶相应分别被评为 B 级和 A 级，如图 1 所示。

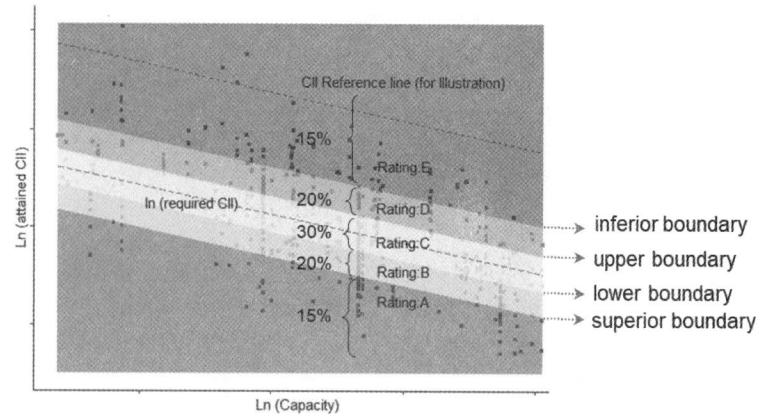

Figure 1: Operational energy efficiency performance rating scale

3.4 Given the incremental operational carbon intensity reduction factors over time, the boundaries for defining performance ratings should be synchronized accordingly, although the relative distance between the boundaries should not change. The rating of a ship would be determined by the attained CII and the predetermined rating boundaries, rather than the attained CII of other ships. Note that the distribution of ship individual ratings in a specific year may not be always identical with the scenario in 2019, where for example 20% may achieve A, 30% may achieve B, 40% may achieve C, 8% may achieve D and 2% may achieve E in a given year.

4 Method to determine the rating boundaries

4.1 The boundaries can be determined by the required annual operational CII in conjunction with the vectors, indicating the direction and distance they deviate from the required value (denoted as dd vectors for easy reference), as illustrated in figure 2.

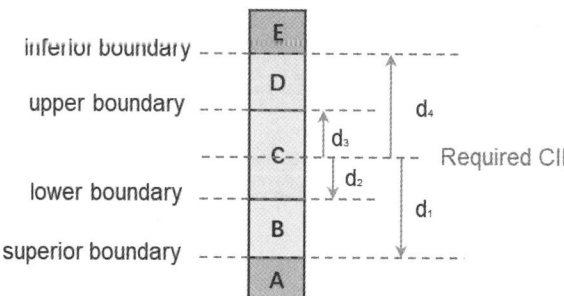

Figure 2: dd vectors and rating bands

4.2 Statistically, the dd vectors depend on the distribution of the attained annual operational CII of ships of the type concerned, which can be estimated through a quantile regression, taking data collected through DCS in year 2019 as the sample.

4.3 The quantile regression model for a specific ship type can be developed as follows:

$$\ln(attained\ CII) = \delta^{(p)} - c\ln(Capacity) + \varepsilon^{(p)}, \quad p = \{0.15, 0.35, 0.50, 0.65, 0.85\} \ (1)$$

where *Capacity* is identical with the one used in the operation carbon intensity indicator as specified in the Guidelines on operational carbon intensity indicators and the calculation

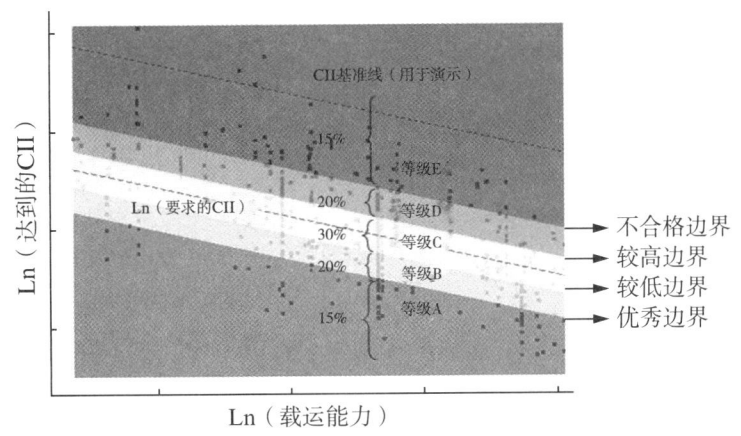

图 1：营运能效性能评级表

3.4 考虑到随时间递增的营运碳强度折减因素，定义性能等级的边界应相应地同步，但边界之间的相对距离不应改变。一艘船舶的评级是由达到的 CII 和预设的等级边界决定的，而不是其他船舶达到的 CII 决定的。注意，在特定年份船舶单个评级的分布情况可能并不总是与 2019 年的情况完全相同，比如，在给定年份中，20% 可以达到 A，30% 可以达到 B，40% 可以达到 C，8% 可以达到 D，2% 可以达到 E。

4 确定等级边界的方法

4.1 边界可由要求的年度营运 CII 与向量结合确定，向量表示其偏离的方向和偏离要求值的距离（表示为 dd 向量以便于参考），如图 2 所示。

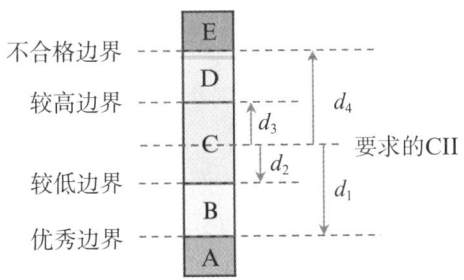

图 2：dd 向量和等级带状分布图

4.2 统计上，dd 向量取决于相关船型船舶达到的年度营运 CII 的分布，可以通过分位数回归估算（以 2019 年通过 DCS 收集的数据为样本）。

4.3 指定船型的分位数回归模型可推导如下：

$$\ln(attainedCII) = \delta^{(p)} - c\ln(Capacity) + \varepsilon^{(p)}, \; p=\{0.15, 0.35, 0.50, 0.65, 0.85\} \quad （1）$$

式中：$Capacity$ 与《2022 年营运碳强度指标和计算方法导则（G1）》中规定的营运

methods (G1); p is the typical quantile, meaning the proportion of observations with a lower value is $p\%$; $\delta^{(p)}$ is the constant term, and $\varepsilon^{(p)}$ is the error term.

4.4   The quantile regression lines in logarithm form are illustrated in Fig.3.

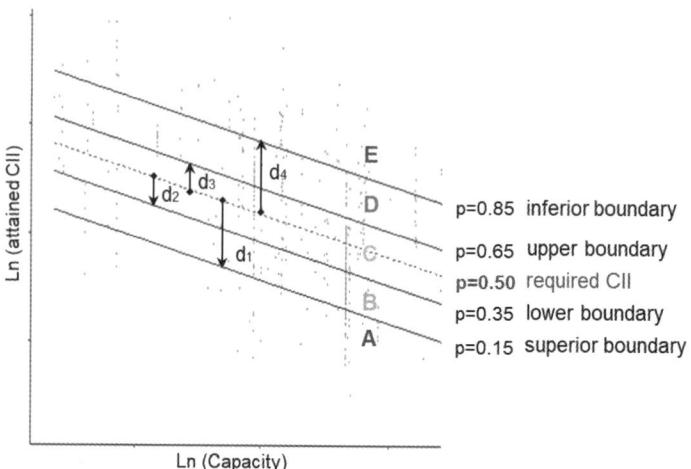

Figure 3: Quantile regression lines in logarithm form

4.5   Then, the dd vectors can be calculated based on the estimates of the intercept ($\hat{\delta}^{(p)}$), in accordance with Eq.(2), as follows:

$$\left.\begin{array}{l} d_1 = \hat{\delta}^{(0.15)} - \hat{\delta}^{(0.50)} \\ d_2 = \hat{\delta}^{(0.35)} - \hat{\delta}^{(0.50)} \\ d_3 = \hat{\delta}^{(0.65)} - \hat{\delta}^{(0.50)} \\ d_4 = \hat{\delta}^{(0.85)} - \hat{\delta}^{(0.50)} \end{array}\right\} \qquad (2)$$

4.6   Through an exponential transformation of each dd vector, the four boundaries fitted in the original data form can be derived based on the required annual operational carbon intensity indicator ($required\ CII$), as follows:

$$\left.\begin{array}{l} \text{superior boundary} = \exp(d_1) \cdot required\ CII \\ \text{lower boundary} = \exp(d_2) \cdot required\ CII \\ \text{upper boundary} = \exp(d_3) \cdot required\ CII \\ \text{inferior boundary} = \exp(d_4) \cdot required\ CII \end{array}\right\} \qquad (3)$$

Rating boundaries of ship types

The estimated dd vectors after exponential transformation for determining the rating boundaries of ship types are as follows:

碳强度指标所使用的载运能力完全相同；p 为典型分位数，表示观测值较低部分为 $p\%$；$\delta^{(p)}$ 为常数项，为误差项。

4.4　对数形式的分位数回归线如图 3 所示。

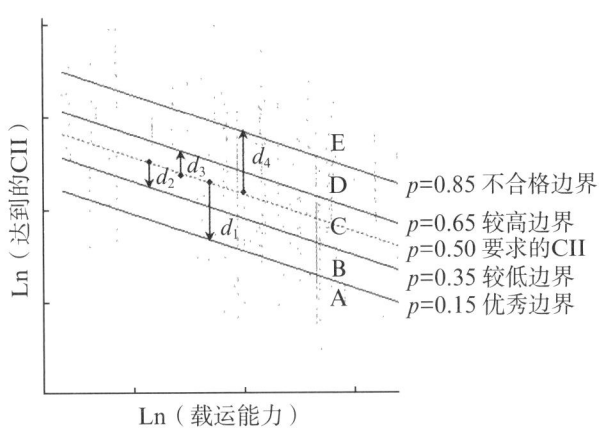

图 3：对数形式的分位数回归线

4.5　然后基于截距 $\hat{\delta}^{(p)}$ 的估算，根据式（2）计算 dd 向量，如下所示：

$$
\left.\begin{aligned}
d_1 &= \hat{\delta}^{(0.15)} - \hat{\delta}^{(0.50)} \\
d_2 &= \hat{\delta}^{(0.35)} - \hat{\delta}^{(0.50)} \\
d_3 &= \hat{\delta}^{(0.65)} - \hat{\delta}^{(0.50)} \\
d_4 &= \hat{\delta}^{(0.85)} - \hat{\delta}^{(0.50)}
\end{aligned}\right\}
\tag{2}
$$

4.6　通过对每个 dd 向量进行指数变换，根据要求的年度营运碳强度指标（required CII），可以得到原始数据形式拟合的四个边界，如下所示：

$$
\left.\begin{aligned}
\text{superior boundary} &= \exp(d_1) \cdot required\ CII \\
\text{lower boundary} &= \exp(d_2) \cdot required\ CII \\
\text{upper boundary} &= \exp(d_3) \cdot required\ CII \\
\text{inferior boundary} &= \exp(d_4) \cdot required\ CII
\end{aligned}\right\}
\tag{3}
$$

船型等级边界

为确定船型等级边界，指数变换后估算的 dd 向量如下：

Table 1: *dd* vectors for determining the rating boundaries of ship types

Ship type		Capacity in CII calculation	*dd* vectors (after exponential transformation)			
			exp(d1)	exp(d2)	exp(d3)	exp(d4)
Bulk carrier		DWT	0.86	0.94	1.06	1.18
Gas carrier	65,000 DWT and above	DWT	0.81	0.91	1.12	1.44
	less than 65,000 DWT	DWT	0.85	0.95	1.06	1.25
Tanker		DWT	0.82	0.93	1.08	1.28
Container ship		DWT	0.83	0.94	1.07	1.19
General cargo ship		DWT	0.83	0.94	1.06	1.19
Refrigerated cargo carrier		DWT	0.78	0.91	1.07	1.20
Combination carrier		DWT	0.87	0.96	1.06	1.14
LNG carrier	100,000 DWT and above	DWT	0.89	0.98	1.06	1.13
	less than 100,000 DWT		0.78	0.92	1.10	1.37
Ro-ro cargo ship (vehicle carrier)		GT	0.86	0.94	1.06	1.16
Ro-ro cargo ship		GT	0.76	0.89	1.08	1.27
Ro-ro passenger ship		GT	0.76	0.92	1.14	1.30
Cruise passenger ship		GT	0.87	0.95	1.06	1.16

By comparing the attained annual operational CII of a specific ship with the four boundaries, a rating can then be assigned. For example, given the required CII of a bulk carrier in a specific year as 10 gCO_2/(dwt.nmile), then the superior boundary, lower boundary, upper boundary, and inferior boundary is 8.6, 9.4, 10.6 and 11.8 gCO_2/(dwt.nmile). If the attained CII is 9 gCO_2/(dwt.nmile), the ship would be rated as "B".

***

表 1 用于确定船型等级边界的 dd 向量

船型		CII 计算中的载运能力指数（d_1）	dd 向量（指数变换后）			
			指数（d_1）	指数（d_2）	指数（d_3）	指数（d_4）
散货船		DWT	0.86	0.94	1.06	1.18
气体运输船	65 000 载重吨及以上	DWT	0.81	0.91	1.12	1.44
	小于 65 000 载重吨	DWT	0.85	0.95	1.06	1.25
液货船		DWT	0.82	0.93	1.08	1.28
集装箱船		DWT	0.83	0.94	1.07	1.19
杂货船		DWT	0.83	0.94	1.06	1.19
冷藏货船		DWT	0.78	0.91	1.07	1.20
兼用船		DWT	0.87	0.96	1.06	1.14
LNG 运输船	100 000 载重吨及以上	DWT	0.89	0.98	1.06	1.13
	小于 100 000 载重吨		0.78	0.92	1.10	1.37
滚装货船（车辆运输船）		GT	0.86	0.94	1.06	1.16
滚装货船		GT	0.76	0.89	1.08	1.27
滚装客船		GT	0.76	0.92	1.14	1.30
邮轮		GT	0.87	0.95	1.06	1.16

通过将特定船舶达到的年度营运 CII 与四个边界进行比较，可以评定等级。例如，给定某一年散货船要求的 CII 为 10 gCO_2/（载重吨·海里），则优秀边界、良好边界、合格边界和不合格边界分别为 8.6、9.4、10.6 和 11.8 gCO_2/（载重吨·海里）。如果达到的 CII 是 9 gCO_2/（载重吨·海里），则该船被评级为"B"。

***

RESOLUTION MEPC.355(78)
(adopted on 10 June 2022)

2022 INTERIM GUIDELINES ON CORRECTION FACTORS AND VOYAGE ADJUSTMENTS FOR CII CALCULATIONS (CII GUIDELINES, G5)

THE MARINE ENVIRONMENT PROTECTION COMMITTEE,

RECALLING Article 38(a) of the Convention on the International Maritime Organization concerning the functions of the Marine Environment Protection Committee (the Committee) conferred upon it by international conventions for the prevention and control of marine pollution from ships,

NOTING that the Committee, at its seventy-sixth session, adopted, by resolution MEPC.328(76), the *2021 Revised MARPOL Annex VI,* which will enter into force on 1 November 2022,

NOTING IN PARTICULAR that the *2021 Revised MARPOL Annex VI* (MARPOL Annex VI) contains amendments concerning mandatory goal-based technical and operational measures to reduce carbon intensity of international shipping,

NOTING ALSO that regulation 28.1 of MARPOL Annex VI requires ships to which this regulation apply to calculate the attained annual operational carbon intensity indicator (CII) taking into account the guidelines developed by the Organization,

NOTING FURTHER that the in adopting resolution MEPC.336(76) on the *2021 Guidelines on operational carbon intensity indicators and the calculation methods (CII Guidelines, G1)*, the Committee agreed to consider substantiated proposals for CII correction factors for certain ship types, operational profiles and/or voyages with a view to enhancing, as appropriate, the CII Guidelines (G1), before entry into force of the aforementioned amendments to MARPOL Annex VI,

RECOGNIZING that the aforementioned amendments to MARPOL Annex VI require relevant guidelines for uniform and effective implementation of the regulations and to provide sufficient lead time for industry to prepare,

HAVING CONSIDERED, at its seventy-eighth session, the draft *2022 Interim Guidelines on correction factors and voyage adjustments for CII calculations (CII Guidelines, G5)*,

1   ADOPTS the *2022 Interim Guidelines on correction factors and voyage adjustments for CII calculations (CII Guidelines, G5)*, as set out in the annex to the present resolution;

2   INVITES Administrations to take the annexed Guidelines into account when developing and enacting national laws which give force to and implement requirements set forth in regulation 28.1 of MARPOL Annex VI;

3   REQUESTS the Parties to MARPOL Annex VI and other Member Governments to bring the annexed Guidelines to the attention of masters, seafarers, shipowners, ship operators and any other interested parties;

第 MEPC.355（78）号决议
（2022 年 6 月 10 日通过）

2022 年 CII 计算的修正系数和航程调整临时导则（CII 导则，G5）

海上环境保护委员会，

忆及《国际海事组织公约》第 38（a）条关于防止和控制船舶造成海洋污染国际公约赋予海上环境保护委员会（委员会）的职能，

注意到委员会在其第 76 届会议上以 MEPC.328（76）号决议通过了将于 2022 年 11 月 1 日生效的 2021 年经修订的 MARPOL 附则Ⅵ，

特别注意到 2021 年经修订的 MARPOL 附则Ⅵ包含关于基于目标的强制性技术和营运措施以减少国际航运碳强度的修正案，

还注意到 MARPOL 附则Ⅵ第 28.1 条要求本条适用的船舶计算达到的年度营运碳强度指标，并考虑到本组织制定的导则，

进一步注意到委员会在通过第 MEPC.336（76）号决议《2021 年营运碳强度指标和计算方法导则（CII 导则，G1）》时，同意审议关于某些船型、营运信息和 / 或航程的 CII 修正系数的实质性建议，以期在 MARPOL 附件 VI 的上述修正案生效之前，酌情加强 CII 导则（G1），

认识到上述 MARPOL 附则Ⅵ的修正案需要有相关导则，以便于统一和有效实施各条规定，并为业界提供充足的准备时间，

在其第 78 届会议上，审议了《2022 年 CII 计算的修正系数和航程调整临时导则（CII 导则，G5）》，

1 通过《2022 年 CII 计算的修正系数和航程调整临时导则（CII 导则，G5）》，其文本载于本决议附件；

2 提请主管机关在制定和颁布本国法律，以执行和实施 MARPOL 附则Ⅵ第 28.1 条要求时，考虑附件中的导则；

3 要求 MARPOL 附则Ⅵ的各缔约方和其他成员国政府请船长、船员、船东、船舶经营者以及任何其他利益相关方注意到附件中的导则；

4   AGREES to keep the Guidelines under review in light of experience gained with their implementation, also taking into consideration that in accordance with regulation 28.11 of MARPOL Annex VI a review of the operational measure to reduce carbon intensity of international shipping shall be completed by 1 January 2026.

4　**同意**根据本导则实施中获得的经验，并考虑到根据 MARPOL 附则Ⅵ第 28.11 条应在 2026 年 1 月 1 日之前完成对减少国际航运碳强度的营运措施的审查，对本导则保持审查。

ANNEX

2022 INTERIM GUIDELINES ON CORRECTION FACTORS AND VOYAGE ADJUSTMENTS FOR CII CALCULATIONS (CII GUIDELINES, G5)

CONTENTS

2022 年 CII 计算的修正系数和航程调整临时导则（CII 导则，G5）

目录

1   Introduction

1.1   These Guidelines address the corrections factors and voyage adjustments which may be applied to the calculation of the attained annual operational carbon intensity indicator (CII$_{ship}$) of regulation 28 of MARPOL Annex VI, and as defined by the *2022 Guidelines on operational carbon intensity indicators and the calculation methods (CII Guidelines, G1)* (resolution MEPC.352 (78)). It should be noted that the use of correction factors and voyage adjustments should in no way undermine the goal of reducing the carbon intensity of international shipping as set out in regulation 20 of MARPOL Annex VI.

2   Definitions

For the purpose of these Guidelines, the definitions in regulation 2 of MARPOL Annex VI, as amended, apply. In addition and for the scope of these guidelines, the following definitions apply.

2.1   *MARPOL* means the International Convention for the Prevention of Pollution from Ships, 1973, as modified by the Protocols of 1978 and 1997 relating thereto, as amended.

2.2   *IMO DCS* means the IMO Ship Fuel Oil Consumption Database referred to in regulation 27 and related provisions of MARPOL Annex VI.

2.3   A *voyage period* is a period of time where the ship meets the criteria to apply a voyage adjustment in these Guidelines.

2.4   A *voyage adjustment* deducts relevant fuel consumption, as well as the associated distance travelled from the calculation of attained CII for a defined period subject to certain threshold conditions being met.

2.5   A *correction factor* means a factor in the numerator or denominator of the CII formula which adjusts the calculation of the attained CII.

2.6   A *refrigerated container* is an intermodal shipping container that is refrigerated (including chilled and frozen containers) or heated for the transportation of temperature-sensitive cargo, which will receive its power from the ship's power supply.

2.7   *Ice edge* is defined by paragraph 4.4. of the WMO Sea-Ice Nomenclature, March 2014 as the demarcation at any given time between the open sea and sea ice of any kind, whether fast or drifting.

2.8   A tanker should be considered in *Ship-to-Ship (STS)* operation when operating in accordance with regulation 41.2 of MARPOL Annex I and applying the best practices in accordance with the OCIMF Ship to Ship Transfer Guide for Petroleum, Chemical and Liquefied Gases. For the purpose of these guidelines, a tanker is engaged in an STS voyage if a voyage between cargo loading and cargo discharging locations, or a voyage between cargo discharging and cargo loading locations does not exceed 600 nautical miles and the time for each of these voyages (which does not include port or discharge time) is limited to 72 hours.

2.9   A *shuttle tanker* is a tanker which is equipped with dynamic positioning and specialized cargo handling equipment making it capable of loading crude oil at offshore installations.

1 引言

1.1 本导则提出可适用于 MARPOL 附则Ⅵ第 28 条规定且由《2022 年营运碳强度指标和计算方法导则（CII 导则，G1）》（第 MEPC.352（78）号决议）所定义的计算达到的年度营运碳强度指标（CIIship）的修正系数和航程调整。需要注意的是，使用修正系数和航程调整不应削弱 MARPOL 附则Ⅵ中第 20 条规定的降低国际航运碳强度的目标。

2 定义

就本导则而言，经修正的 MARPOL 附则Ⅵ第 2 条中的定义适用。此外，本导则还适用于下列定义。

2.1 *MARPOL* 是指经修正的《经 1978 年和 1997 年议定书修订的 1973 年国际防止船舶造成污染公约》。

2.2 *IMO DCS* 是指 MARPOL 附则Ⅵ第 27 条和 MARPOL 附则Ⅵ相关规定中所述的船舶燃油消耗数据收集系统。

2.3 *航程期间* 是指船舶满足本导则适用航程调整条件的时间段。

2.4 *航程调整* 是指在满足某些阈值条件的规定期限内，从达到的 CII 的计算中扣除有关的燃油消耗以及相关的航行距离。

2.5 *修正系数* 是指 CII 公式中分子或分母的一个因子，用来对计算达到的 CII 进行修正。

2.6 *冷藏集装箱* 是为运输温度敏感货物而冷藏（包括冷藏和冷冻集装箱）或加热的多式联运集装箱，其电力来自船上的电源。

2.7 *冰缘* 根据 2014 年 3 月《世界气象组织海冰命名法》第 4.4 段定义，指在任何给定的时间，公海和任何类型的海冰（固定冰或浮冰）之间的分界线。

2.8 当液货船按照 MARPOL 附则 I 第 41.2 条的规定作业，并根据石油公司国际海事论坛(Oil Companies International Marine Forum，OCIMF)《石油、化学品和液化气体船对船过驳指南》进行最佳操作，可作为船对船（Ship-to-Ship，STS）作业。就本导则而言，如果一液货船的装货和卸货地点之间的航程，或卸货和装货地点之间的航程不超过 600 海里，且每次航程的时间（不包括港口或卸货时间）不超过 72 小时，则属于船对船作业。

2.9 *穿梭油轮* 是一种配有动力定位和专用货物装卸设备，使其能够在海上设施装载原油的油轮。

2.10　A *self-unloading bulk carrier* is a bulk carrier with an onboard cargo handling system that is utilized to discharge dry bulk cargo via a boom conveyor or shipboard cargo pipeline equipment.

3　Application

3.1　For all ships to which regulation 28 of MARPOL Annex VI applies, the operational carbon intensity formula defined in section 4 should be applied when using voyage adjustments or correction factors.

3.2　Rating of ships according to the *2022 Guidelines on the operational carbon intensity rating of ships (CII Rating Guidelines G4)* (resolution MEPC.354(78)) should be carried out using the corrected attained annual operational CII.

3.3　Corrections factors for electrical related fuel consumption $FC_{electrical}$, boiler consumption FC_{boiler}, and other related fuel consumption FC_{others} should not be used for periods where voyage adjustments apply.

4　Attained annual operational CII (CII$_{Ship}$) formula for voyage adjustments and correction factors

Use of voyage adjustments and correction factors require changes to be made to the overall attained annual operational CII (CII$_{Ship}$) formula as follows:

$$\frac{\sum_j C_{Fj} \cdot \left\{ FC_j - \left(FC_{voyage,j} + TF_j + (0.75 - 0.03y_i) \cdot \left(FC_{electrical,j} + FC_{boiler,j} + FC_{others,j} \right) \right) \right\}}{f_i \cdot f_m \cdot f_c \cdot f_{iVSE} \cdot Capacity \cdot (D_t - D_x)}$$

Where:

- j is the fuel type;

- C_{F_j} represents the fuel mass to CO_2 mass conversion factor for fuel type j, in line with those specified in the *2018 Guidelines on the method of calculation of the attained EEDI for new ships* (resolution MEPC.308(73) as amended by resolutions MEPC.322(74) and MEPC.332(76)), as may be further amended);

- FC_j is the total mass of consumed fuel of type j in the calendar year, as reported under IMO DCS, converted to grams;

- $FC_{voyage,j}$ is the mass (in grams) of fuel of type j, consumed in voyage periods during the calendar year which may be deducted according to paragraph 4.1 of these Guidelines;

- $TF_j = (1 - AF_{Tanker}) \cdot FC_{S,j}$ represents the quantity of fuel j removed for STS or shuttle tanker operation, where $FC_{S,j} = FC_j$ for shuttle tankers and $FC_{S,j}$ is the total quantity of fuel j used on STS voyages for STS ships. If $TF_j > 0$ then $FC_{electrical,j} = FC_{boiler,j} = FC_{others,j} = 0$;

- AF_{Tanker} represents the correction factor to be applied to shuttle tankers or STS voyages according to paragraph 4.2 of these Guidelines;

- y_i is a consecutive numbering system starting at $y_{2023} = 0$, $y_{2024} = 1$, $y_{2025} = 2$,

2.10 自卸散货船是一种配有船上货物装卸系统的散货船，该系统通过臂架式输送机或船上货物管道设备来卸干散货。

3 适用

3.1 对于适用 MARPOL 附则 Ⅵ 第 28 条的所有船舶，在使用航程调整或修正系数时，应适用第 4 条中定义的营运碳强度公式。

3.2 根据《2022 年船舶营运碳强度评级导则（CII 评级导则，G4）》（MEPC.354（78）号决议）对船舶进行评级，应使用修正后的达到的年度营运 CII。

3.3 适用航程调整时，不应使用用电相关的燃料消耗 $FC_{electrical}$、锅炉的燃料消耗 FC_{boiler} 以及其他相关燃料消耗 FC_{others} 等修正系数。

4 使用航程调整和修正系数计算达到的年度营运 CII（CII$_{ship}$）公式

使用航程调整和修正系数，须对达到的年度营运 CII（CII$_{ship}$）公式整体进行修改，如下所示：

$$\frac{\sum_j C_{Fj} \cdot \left\{ FC_j - \left(FC_{voyage,j} + TF_j + (0.75 - 0.03y_i) \cdot \left(FC_{electrical,j} + FC_{boiler,j} + FC_{others,j} \right) \right) \right\}}{f_i \cdot f_m \cdot f_c \cdot f_{iVSE} \cdot Capacity \cdot (D_t - D_x)}$$

式中：

- j 为燃料类型；

- C_{Fj} 为燃料 j 的质量与 CO_2 质量的转换系数，与《2018 年新船达到的能效设计指数（EEDI）计算方法导则》（经 MEPC.332（76）和 MEPC.322（74）号决议修订的 MEPC.308（73）号决议，可能进一步修订）中的规定一致；

- FC_j 为向 IMO DCS 报告的日历年内消耗的燃料 j 的总质量，单位换算为克；

- $FC_{voyage,j}$ 为日历年内根据本导则第 4.1 段可被扣除的航程期间消耗的燃料 j 的总质量，单位为克；

- $TF_j = (1 - AF_{Tanker}) \cdot FC_{S,j}$ 为从 STS 或穿梭油轮作业扣除的燃料 j 的质量，其中，对于穿梭油轮 $FC_{S,j} = FC_j$，对于 STS 船舶，$FC_{S,j}$ 为在 STS 航程中使用的燃料 j 的总质量。如果 $TF_j > 0$，则 $FC_{electrical,j} = FC_{boiler,j} = FC_{others,j} = 0$。

- AF_{Tanker} 为根据本导则第 4.2 段适用于穿梭油轮或 STS 航程的修正系数；

- y_i 是一个连续的编号系数，从 $y_{2023} = 0$ 开始、$y_{2024} = 1$、$y_{2025} = 2$，以此类推；

etc;

- $FC_{electrical,j}$ is the mass (in grams) of fuel type j, consumed for production of electrical power which is allowed to be deducted according to paragraph 4.3 of these Guidelines;

- $FC_{boiler,j}$ is the mass (in grams) of fuel type j, consumed by the boiler which may be deducted according to paragraph 4.4 of these Guidelines;

- $FC_{others,j}$ is the mass (in grams) of fuel type j, consumed by other related fuel consumption devices according to paragraph 4.5 of these Guidelines;

- f_i is the capacity correction factor for ice-classed ships as specified in the *2018 Guidelines on the method of calculation of the attained EEDI for new ships* (resolution MEPC.308(73) as amended by resolutions MEPC.322(74) and MEPC.332(76), as may be further amended);

- f_m is the factor for ice-classed ships having IA Super and IA as specified in the *2018 Guidelines on the method of calculation of the attained EEDI for new ships* (resolution MEPC.308(73) as amended by resolutions MEPC.322(74) and MEPC.332(76), as may be further amended);

- f_c represents the cubic capacity correction factors for chemical tankers as specified in paragraph 2.2.12 of the *2018 Guidelines on the method of calculation of the attained EEDI for new ships* (resolution MEPC.308(73) as amended by resolutions MEPC.322(74) and MEPC.332(76), as may be further amended);

- $f_{i,VSE}$ represents the correction factor for ship-specific voluntary structural enhancement as specified in paragraph 2.2.11.2 of the *2018 Guidelines on the method of calculation of the attained EEDI for new ships* (resolution MEPC.308(73) as amended by resolutions MEPC.322(74) and MEPC.332(76), as may be further amended), to be applied only to self-unloading bulk carriers;

- *Capacity* is deadweight or gross tonnes as defined for each specific ship type in the *2022 Guidelines on the reference lines for use with operational carbon intensity indicators (CII Reference lines Guidelines, G2)* (resolution MEPC.353(78));

- D_t represents the total distance travelled (in nautical miles), as reported under IMO DCS; and

- D_x represents distance travelled (in nautical miles) for voyage periods which may be deducted from CII calculation according to paragraph 4.1 of these Guidelines.

In case the above voyage exclusion or correction factors are applied, the ship should still report total fuel oil consumption (t) of each type of fuel, total hours under way (h) and total distance travelled (nm) to the Administration pursuant to regulation 27 of MARPOL Annex VI.

All relevant data should be recorded in the ship's logbook. Each parameter, if used, should also be reported to the Administration.

- $FC_{electrical, j}$ 为根据本导则第 4.3 段可被扣除的发电所消耗的燃料 j 的质量，单位为克；

- $FC_{boiler, j}$ 为根据本导则第 4.4 段可被扣除的锅炉消耗的燃料 j 的质量，单位为克；

- $FC_{others, j}$ 为根据本导则第 4.5 段的其他相关燃料消耗装置所消耗的燃料 j 的质量，单位为克；

- f_i 是《2018 年新船达到的能效设计指数（EEDI）计算方法导则》（经 MEPC.332（76）和 MEPC.322（74）号决议修订的 MEPC.308（73）号决议，可能进一步修订）中规定的冰级船舶的载运能力修正系数；

- f_m 是《2018 年新船达到的能效设计指数（EEDI）计算方法导则》（经 MEPC.332（76）和 MEPC.322（74）号决议修订的 MEPC.308（73）号决议，可能进一步修订）中规定的具有 1A Super 和 1A 级的冰级船舶的系数；

- f_c 是《2018 年新船达到的能效设计指数（EEDI）计算方法导则》（经 MEPC.332（76）和 MEPC.322（74）号决议修订的 MEPC.308（73）号决议，可能进一步修订）2.2.12 段中规定的化学品船的舱容量修正系数；

- $f_{i, vse}$ 是《2018 年新船达到的能效设计指数（EEDI）计算方法导则》（经 MEPC.332（76）号决议和 MEPC.322（74）号决议修订的 MEPC.308（73）号决议，可能进一步修订）2.2.11.2 段中规定的船舶特定自愿结构增强的修正系数，仅适用于自卸散货船；

- $Capacity$ 为《2022 年营运碳强度指标基线导则（CII 基线导则，G2）》（第 MEPC.353（78）号决议）中对每种特定船型定义的载重吨或总吨；

- D_t 为向 IMO DCS 报告的总航行距离，单位为海里；和

- D_x 为根据本导则第 4.1 段可从 CII 计算中扣除的航程期间的航行距离，单位为海里。

在适用于上述航程调整或修正系数的情况下，船舶仍应按照 MARPOL 附则Ⅵ第 27 条的规定，向主管机关报告每种燃料的总燃料消耗量（t）、总的航行小时数（h）和总的航行距离（n mile）。

所有相关数据都应记录在船舶日志中。若使用相关参数，也应向主管机关报告。

4.1 $FC_{voyage,j}$ for voyage adjustment

The parameter $FC_{voyage,j}$ is the total mass (in grams) of fuel of type j, consumed in voyage periods during the calendar year which may be deducted from the calculation of the attained CII in case the ship encounters one of the following situations:

.1   scenarios specified in regulation 3.1 of MARPOL Annex VI, which may endanger safe navigation of a ship; and

.2   sailing in ice conditions, which means sailing of an ice-classed ship in a sea area within the ice edge.

In cases where $FC_{voyage,j}$ is used:

- any associated distance travelled must also be deducted using D_x otherwise ships will benefit from distance travelled without any associated CO_2 emission.

- the ship should report data for the deductions associated with voyage adjustments to the Administration in accordance with appendix 2 of these guidelines.

4.2 AF_{Tanker} for corrections to shuttle tankers or STS voyages on tankers

Tankers engaged in STS voyages as defined above in paragraph 2.8 may apply the correction factor $AF_{Tanker,STS}$ to all fuel consumption relating to STS voyages, including cargo transfer at offshore location, voyage, cargo discharge and waiting periods at anchor or drifting during which the ship reports being part of an STS operation and voyage. The STS operation includes fuel consumption in port where the transferred cargo is discharged after such a voyage.

The correction is calculated as:

$$AF_{Tanker,STS} = 6.1742 \times DWT^{-0.246}$$

Where $AF_{Tanker,STS}$ is applied, $FC_{electrical}$, FC_{boiler} and FC_{others} should not be used.

Shuttle tankers equipped with dynamic positioning as defined above in paragraph 2.9 may apply the correction factor $AF_{Tanker,Shuttle}$ to total fuel consumption:

The correction factor is calculated as:

$$AF_{Tanker,Shuttle} = 5.6805 \; x \; DWT^{-0.208}$$

Where $AF_{Tanker,Shuttle}$ is applied, $FC_{electrical}$, FC_{boiler}, FC_{others} and $AF_{Tanker,STS}$ should not be used.

4.3 $FC_{electrical,j}$ for corrections relating to electrical power

The parameter $FC_{electrical,j}$ is the mass (in grams) of fuel of type j, consumed for production of electrical power during the calendar year which may be deducted from the calculation of the attained CII for the following purposes:

.1   Electrical consumption of refrigerated containers (on all ships where they are carried) using the calculation methodology specified in part A of appendix 1.

4.1 航程调整 $FC_{voyage, j}$

参数 $FC_{voyage, j}$ 为在日历年内当船舶遇到下列情况之一时，可从达到的 CII 的计算中扣除的航程期间消耗的燃料 j 的总质量（单位为克）：

.1 MARPOL 附则 Ⅵ 第 3.1 条规定的可能危及船舶航行安全的情况；和

.2 在冰区航行，即冰级船舶在冰缘内的海域航行。

在使用 $FC_{voyage, j}$ 的情况下：

- 相关的航行距离也必须使用 D_x 予以扣除，否则船舶将受益于没有任何 CO_2 排放的航行距离。

- 船舶应按照本导则附录 2 的规定向主管机关报告与航程调整有关的扣除数据。

4.2 穿梭油轮或液货船 STS 航程的修正 AF_{Tanker}

从事上文 2.8 段定义的 STS 航程的液货船可将修正系数 $AF_{Tanker, STS}$ 适用于与 STS 航程有关的所有燃料消耗，包括属于 STS 作业和航程中船舶报告的海上货物过驳、航行、卸货以及锚泊或漂航的等待时间等。STS 作业包括该航程后在港口卸下过驳货物的燃料消耗。

修正系数计算如下：

$$AF_{Tanker, STS} = 6.174\,2 \times DWT^{-0.246}$$

如果使用了 $AF_{Tanker, STS}$，则不应再使用 $FC_{electrical}$、FC_{bolier} 和 FC_{others}。

配备有上述第 2.9 段定义的动力定位的穿梭油轮可以将修正系数 $AF_{Tanker, Shuttle}$ 适用于总的燃料消耗。

修正系数计算如下：

$$AF_{Tanker, Shuttle} = 5.680\,5 \times DWT^{-0.208}$$

如果使用了 $AF_{Tanker, Shuttle}$，则不应再使用 $FC_{electrical}$、FC_{bolier}、FC_{others}、$AF_{Tanker, STS}$。

4.3 电力相关的修正 $FC_{electrical, j}$

参数 $FC_{electrical, j}$ 是在日历年内可从达到的 CII 计算中扣除的，用于以下用途的发电所消耗的燃料 j 的质量（单位为克）：

.1 按附录 1A 部分所列明的计算方法计算（所有装运冷藏集装箱船舶上的）冷藏集装箱的用电消耗。

.2   Electrical consumption of cargo cooling/reliquefaction systems on gas carriers and LNG Carriers.

.3   Electrical consumption of discharge pumps on tankers.

4.4 $FC_{Boiler,j}$ for corrections relating to boiler fuel consumption

The parameter $FC_{Boiler,j}$ is the mass (in grams) of fuel of type j, consumed by the oil-fired boiler during the calendar year which may be deducted from the calculation of the attained CII, for the purposes of cargo heating and cargo discharge on tankers. The calculation methodology for $FC_{Boiler,j}$ is specified in part B of appendix 1.

4.5 $FC_{others,j}$ for corrections relating to other related fuel consumption devices

The parameter $FC_{others,j}$ is the mass (in grams) of fuel of type j, consumed by standalone engine driven cargo pumps during discharge operations on tankers which may be deducted from the calculation of the attained CII.

4.6   EEDI and EEXI Correction factors

The EEDI correction factors as defined above in paragraph 4 may be applied, provided they are included in the ship's EEDI Technical File or EEXI Technical file.

.2 气体运输船和液化天然气运输船货物冷却/再液化系统的用电消耗。

.3 液货船卸货泵的用电消耗。

4.4 锅炉燃料消耗相关的修正 $FC_{Boiler,\,j}$

参数 $FC_{Boiler,\,j}$ 是在日历年内可从达到的 CII 计算中扣除的液货船上燃油锅炉用于货物加热和卸货消耗的燃料 j 的质量（单位为克）。$FC_{Boiler,\,j}$ 的计算方法见附录 1 的 B 部分。

4.5 其他相关燃料消耗设备的修正 $FC_{others,\,j}$

参数 $FC_{others,\,j}$ 是可从达到的 CII 计算中扣除的由独立发动机驱动的货泵在液货船卸货作业期间消耗的燃料 j 的质量（单位为克）。

4.6 EEDI 和 EEXI 修正系数

如果 EEDI 修正系数包含在船舶的 EEDI 技术文件或 EEXI 技术文件中，则可适用上文第 4 段中定义的 EEDI 修正系数。

APPENDIX 1

CORRECTION FACTORS FOR USE IN CII CALCULATION

Part A. FC_{Electrical} for Corrections relating to electrical power

1   Refrigerated containers

For ships carrying refrigerated containers, the correction factor FC_{Electrical} may be applied as follows:

.1   For ships that have the ability to monitor reefer electrical consumption, the ship may calculate reefer container kWh consumption as follows:

$$FC_{electrical\_reefer,j} = Reefer\ kWh \times SFOC$$

where:

- $FC_{electrical\_reefer,j}$ (Reefer fuel oil consumption) represents the estimated fuel consumption attributed to in-use refrigerated containers carried.

- $Reefer\ kWh$ is measured on the ship by the kWh meter counter on the ship.

- $SFOC$ represents the specific fuel consumption in g/kWh as a weighted average of the engines used to provide the electrical power, as per the EEDI/EEXI Technical File or the NO$_x$ Technical File. In the case of ships without a Technical File, a default value of 175 g/kWh for 2 stroke engines and 200 g/kWh for 4 stroke engines may be applied. In the case of waste heat recovery systems as defined under Category C1 in MEPC.1/Circ.896 the SFOC to be used will be at the discretion of the Administration.

Alternatives such as derivation of fuel consumption or kWh from auto-logged data may be used subject to approval by the Administration. Note that ship reefer kWh consumption should not include consumption during voyage adjustment periods.

.2   For ships that do not have the ability to monitor reefer electrical consumption, the ship may calculate reefer kWh consumption as follows:

$$FC_{electrical\_reefer,j} = Cx \cdot 24 \cdot SFOC_{avg} \cdot \left(Reefer\_days_{sea} + \sum Reefer\_days_{port} \right)$$

where:

- Cx represents a default reefer consumption of 2.75 kW/h.

- $Reefer\_days_{sea}$ represents the number of in-use reefer-days over the declared period and may be derived using the number of reefer containers as recorded in the BAPLIE file multiplied by the number of days at sea.

- $SFOC_{avg}$ represents the specific fuel consumption in g/kWh as a weighted average of the engines used to provide the electrical power, as per the EEDI/EEXI Technical File or NO$_x$ Technical File. In the case of ships without a Technical File, a default value of 175 g/kWh for 2 stroke engines and 200 g/kWh for 4 stroke

附录 1   用于 CII 计算的修正系数

A. 电力相关的修正系数 $FC_{electrical}$

1   冷藏集装箱

对于装运冷藏集装箱的船舶，修正系数 $FC_{electrical}$ 可应用如下：

.1   对于有能力监测冷藏集装箱用电量的船舶，可按下式计算冷藏集装箱的千瓦时消耗：

$$FC_{electrical\_reefer,\ j} = Reefer\ \text{kWh} \times SOFC$$

式中：

- $FC_{electrical\_reefer,\ j}$（冷藏集装箱的燃油消耗量）表示估算的因载运在用冷藏集装箱而导致的燃料消耗量。

- $Reefer\ \text{kWh}$ 是由船上千瓦时计量表测量得到的。

- SFOC 为根据 EEDI/EEXI 技术文件或 NO_x 技术文件，用于提供电力的发动机的以 g/kWh 为单位的加权平均的燃料消耗率。对于没有技术文件的船舶，二冲程发动机可采用默认值 175 g/kWh，四冲程发动机可采用默认值 200 g/kWh。对于 MEPC.1/Circ.896 中 C1 类别下定义的废热回收系统，使用的 SFOC 将由主管机关酌情决定。

经主管部门批准，可使用替代方法，如从自动记录数据中推导出燃料消耗或千瓦时。应注意，船舶冷藏集装箱千瓦时消耗不应包括航程调整期间的消耗。

.2   对于没有能力监测冷藏集装箱耗电量的船舶，可按下式计算冷藏集装箱的千瓦时消耗：

$$FC_{electrical\_reefer,j} = Cx \cdot 24 \cdot SFOC_{avg} \cdot \left(Reefer\_days_{sea} + \sum Reefer\_days_{port} \right)$$

式中：

- C_x 为默认的冷藏集装箱消耗，取 2.75 kW/h。

- $Reefer\_days_{sea}$ 为报告期内在用的冷藏集装箱 – 天的数量，可通过船图（BAPLIE）文件中记录的冷藏集装箱数量乘以海上天数得到。

- $SFOC_{avg}$ 为根据 EEDI/EEXI 技术文件或 NO_x 技术文件，用于提供电力的发动机的以 g/kWh 为单位的加权平均的燃料消耗率。对于没有技术文件的船舶，

engines may be applied. In the case of waste heat recovery systems as defined under Category C1 in MEPC.1/Circ.896 the SFOC to be used will be at the discretion of the Administration.

In ports where shore-power is not used, the number of in-use reefers at port should be calculated as:

$$Reefer\_days_{port} = \frac{No_c\ Arrival + No_c\ Departure}{2} \times Days_{port}$$

where:

- $Days_{port}$ represents number of days in port.

- $Reefer\_days_{port}$ represents the number of in-use reefer days while at port.[*]

- $No_c\ Arrival$ represents number of reefer containers on arrival.

- $No_c\ Departure$ represents number of reefer containers at departure.

In all cases, the actual number of in-use reefers carried is documented in the BAPLIE file.

Note that ship reefer kWh consumption should not include consumption during voyage adjustment periods.

---

[*] The number of reefers on board while in port should be calculated to equal the number of reefers at arrival and at departure as calculated above. Same calculation applies for Reefer days $_{sea}$ in port.

二冲程发动机可采用默认值 175 g/kWh，四冲程发动机可采用默认值 200 g/kWh。对于 MEPC.1/Circ.896 中 C1 类别下定义的废热回收系统，使用的 SFOC 将由主管机关酌情决定。

在不使用岸电的港口，在港在用的冷藏集装箱的数量应按如下公式计算：

$$Reefer\_days_{port} = \frac{No_c\, Arrival + No_c\, Departure}{2} \times Days_{port}$$

式中：

- $Days_{port}$ 为在港天数；

- $Reefer\_days_{port}$ 为在港时使用的冷藏集装箱数量 [*]；

- $No_c\, Arrival$ 为抵港时冷藏集装箱的数量；

- $No_c\, Departure$ 为离港时冷藏集装箱的数量。

在所有情况下，载运的在用冷藏集装箱实际数量记录在船图（BAPLIE）文件中。

应注意，船舶冷藏集装箱千瓦时消耗不应包括航程调整期间的消耗。

---

[*] 在港口时船上的冷藏箱数量应计算为与上述计算的到港和离港时的冷藏集装箱数量相等。同样计算适用于在港口时的 Reefer–days$_{sea}$。

2   Cargo cooling systems on gas carriers and LNG carriers

For gas carriers and LNG carriers with electrical cargo cooling systems or reliquefaction plants, the correction factor FC$_{electrical}$ may be applied as follows:

.1   Gas carriers and LNG carriers may calculate cargo cooling kWh consumption as follows:

$$FC_{electrical\_cooling,j} = Cooling\ kWh \times SFOC$$

where:

- $FC_{electrical\_cooling,j}$ (cargo cooling fuel oil consumption) represents the estimated fuel consumption attributed to cooling of gas cargoes.

- $Cooling\ kWh$ is measured on the ship by the kWh meter counter on the ship.

- $SFOC$ represents the specific fuel consumption in g/kWh associated with the relevant source of electrical power as per the EEDI/EEXI Technical File or NO$_x$ Technical File. In the case of ships without a Technical File, a default value of 175 g/kWh for 2 stroke engines and 200 g/kWh for 4 stroke engines may be applied. In the case of waste heat recovery systems as defined under Category C1 in MEPC.1/Circ.896 the SFOC to be used will be at the discretion of the Administration.

Alternatives such as derivation of fuel consumption or kWh from auto-logged data may be used subject to approval by the Administration. Note that cargo cooling kWh consumption should not include consumption during voyage adjustment periods.

3   Electric cargo discharge pumps on tankers

For tankers with directly or indirectly electrically powered discharge pumps, the correction factor FC$_{electrical}$ may be applied as follows:

.1   Tankers may calculate cargo discharge kWh consumption as follows:

$$FC_{electrical\_discharge,j} = discharge\ kWh \times SFOC$$

where:

- $FC_{electrical\_discharge,j}$ (cargo discharge fuel oil consumption) represents the estimated fuel consumption attributed to use of cargo discharge pumps.

- $Discharge\ kWh$ is measured on the ship by the kWh meter counter on the ship.

- $SFOC$ represents the specific fuel oil consumption in g/kWh associated with the relevant source of electrical power as per the EEDI/EEXI Technical File or NO$_x$ Technical File. In the case of ships without a Technical File, a default value of 175 g/kWh for 2 stroke engines and 200 g/kWh for 4 stroke engines may be applied. In the case of waste heat recovery systems as defined under Category C1 in MEPC.1/Circ.896 the SFOC to be used will be at the discretion of the Administration.

2 气体运输船和液化天然气运输船上的货物冷却系统

对于配有电力货物冷却系统或再液化装置的气体运输船和液化天然气运输船，修正系数 $FC_{electrical}$ 可应用如下：

.1 气体运输船和液化天然气运输船可按下式计算货物冷却千瓦时消耗：

$$FC_{electrical\_cooling,\,j}=Cooling\ \text{kWh} \times SFOC$$

式中：

- $FC_{electrical\_cooling,\,j}$（货物冷却的燃油消耗量）表示估算的用于冷却气体货物的燃料消耗量。

- $Cooling$ kWh 由船上千瓦时计量表测量得到。

- SFOC 为根据 EEDI/EEXI 技术文件或 NO_x 技术文件，与相关电源相联系的以 g/kWh 为单位的燃料消耗率。对于没有技术文件的船舶，二冲程发动机可采用默认值 175 g/kWh，四冲程发动机可采用默认值 200 g/kWh。对于 MEPC.1/Circ.896 中 C1 类别下定义的废热回收系统，使用的 SFOC 将由主管机关酌情决定。

经主管部门批准，可使用替代方法，如从自动记录数据中推导出燃料消耗或千瓦时。应注意，货物冷却千瓦时消耗不应包括航程调整期间的消耗。

3 液货船的电动卸货泵

对于液货船直接或间接使用电力驱动的卸货泵，修正系数可应用如下：

.1 液货船可按下式计算卸货千瓦时消耗：

$$FC_{electrical\_discharge,\,j}=discharge\ \text{kWh} \times SFOC$$

式中：

- $FC_{electrical\_discharge,\,j}$（卸货燃料消耗）表示估算的因使用卸货泵而导致的燃料消耗量。

- $discharge$ kWh 由船上千瓦时计量表测量得到。

- SFOC 为根据 EEDI/EEXI 技术文件或 NOx 技术文件，与相关电源相联系的以 g/kWh 为单位的燃料消耗率。对于没有技术文件的船舶，二冲程发动机可采用默认值 175 g/kWh，四冲程发动机可采用默认值 200 g/kWh。对于 MEPC.1/Circ.896 中 C1 类别下定义的废热回收系统，使用的 SFOC 将由主管机关酌情决定。

Alternatives such as derivation of actual fuel consumption from auto-logged data may be used subject to approval by the Administration. Note that cargo cooling kWh consumption should not include consumption during voyage adjustment periods.

Part B. FC$_{Boiler}$ and FC$_{Others}$ for corrections relating to cargo heating and discharge on tankers

1   FC$_{Boiler}$ for cargo heating and discharge pumps on tankers

For tankers with fuel fired boilers used for cargo heating or steam driven cargo pumps, the following correction factor may be applied for the period that the cargo heating or discharge pumps are in operation:

.1   In the case of boilers used for cargo heating, the amount of fuel used by the boiler (FC_{Boiler}) should be measured by accepted means, e.g. tank soundings, flow meters.

.2   For tankers which use steam driven cargo pumps, the amount of fuel used by the boiler (FC_{Boiler}) should be measured by accepted means, e.g. tank soundings, flow meters.

Some amount of fuel consumed by the boiler during cargo heating or discharge operations may be attributed to other purposes, e.g. calorifiers. It is not necessary to split these out from reporting.

Note that boiler consumption should not include consumption during voyage adjustment periods.

2   FC$_{Others}$ for discharge pumps on tankers

For tankers with discharge pumps powered by their own generator, the amount of fuel used for the period that the discharge pumps are in operation (FC_{Others}) should be measured by accepted means, e.g. tank soundings, flow meters.

Note that fuel deducted under FC$_{Others}$ should not include consumption during voyage adjustment periods.

经主管部门批准，可使用替代方法，如从自动记录数据中推导出燃料消耗或千瓦时。应注意，液货船卸货千瓦时消耗（译者注：英文原文为 cargo cooling kWh consumption）不应包括航程调整期间的消耗。

B. 液货船货物加热和卸货相关的修正 FC_{Boiler} 和 FC_{Others}

1　用于液货船货物加热和卸货泵的 FC_{Boiler}

对于配有燃油锅炉用于货物加热或蒸汽驱动（卸）货泵的液货船，下列修正系数可应用于货物加热或卸货泵运行期间：

.1　对于用于货物加热的锅炉，锅炉所使用的燃料总量（ FC_{Bolier} ）应该用可接受的方法进行测量，例如舱位测量、流量计。

.2　对于使用蒸汽驱动（卸）货泵的液货船，锅炉所使用的燃料总量（ FC_{Boiler} ）应该用可接受的方法进行测量，例如舱位测量、流量计。

在货物加热或卸货作业期间，锅炉消耗的部分燃料可能用于其他目的，例如加热器。没有必要将这些从报告中分离出来。

应注意，锅炉消耗不应包括航程调整期间的消耗。

2　用于液货船卸货泵的 FC_{Others}

对于配有独立发电机驱动卸货泵的液货船，在卸货泵运行期间的燃料消耗量应采用可接受的方法进行测量，例如舱柜测量、流量计。

应注意，在 FC_{Others} 项下扣除的燃料不应包括航程调整期间的消耗。

APPENDIX 2

GUIDANCE ON REPORTING OF FUEL OIL CONSUMPTION AND DISTANCE TRAVELLED
FOR VOYAGE PERIODS WHERE THE SHIP MEETS THE CRITERIA TO APPLY ANY
VOYAGE ADJUSTMENT

In this appendix guidance is given for reporting and verification of fuel oil consumption and distance travelled concerning voyage adjustments when a scenario specified in regulation 3.1 of MARPOL Annex VI applies, which may endanger safe navigation of a ship, or when sailing in ice conditions.

1   Fuel oil consumption for voyage periods should include all the fuel oil consumed on board including but not limited to the fuel oil consumed by the main engines, auxiliary engines, gas turbines, boilers and inert gas generator, for each type of fuel oil consumed, regardless of whether a ship is under way or not. Methods for collecting data on fuel oil consumption in metric tonnes include the method using flow meters or method using bunker fuel oil tank monitoring on board as described in paragraphs 7.1.2 and 7.1.3 of the *2022 Guidelines for the development of a Ship Energy Efficiency Management Plan (SEEMP Guidelines)* (resolution MEPC.346(78)) correspondingly.

2   The distance travelled over ground in nautical miles for voyage periods should be recorded in the logbook in accordance with SOLAS regulation V/28.1 and submitted to the Administration.

3   At the end of the voyage, if the ship has encountered ice conditions during its voyage, when the ship was under way sailing between the ice edges or between the ice edge and the port, or when a scenario specified in regulation 3.1 of MARPOL Annex VI applies:

        .1   the fuel oil consumed measured in accordance with 7.1.2 or 7.1.3 of the SEEMP Guidelines for the voyage period should not be included in the calculations for the annual average attained CII index value;

        .2   if the voyage period is excluded from calculations of the attained CII index value when a scenario specified in regulation 3.1 of MARPOL Annex VI applies, the distance travelled should be clearly marked in the SEEMP monitoring plan, the ship's logbook should include data entries for the voyage period with date, time and position of the ship, when a scenario specified in regulation 3.1 of MARPOL Annex VI started to apply and ceased to apply, and data should be added to the data reporting format;

        .3   if the voyage period is excluded from calculations of the attained CII index value due to sailing in ice conditions, the distance travelled should be clearly marked in the SEEMP monitoring plan, the ship's logbook should include data entries for the voyage period with date, time and position of the ship when the ship encountered ice conditions and left ice conditions, and data should be added to the data reporting format.

4   The summary of monitoring data containing records of measured fuel oil consumption and distance travelled for voyage periods should be available on board. Ice charts related to the voyage periods should also be available if the ship has sailed in ice conditions.

附录 2

关于船舶满足任何航程调整标准的航程期间燃油消耗量和航行距离报告的指南

当适用 MARPOL 附则Ⅵ规则第 3.1 条规定的可能危及船舶航行安全的情况时或在冰区航行时，本附录就有关航程调整的燃油消耗和航行距离的报告和验证提供指南。

1　无论船舶是否在航，航程期间的燃油消耗量应包含船上所有的燃油消耗，包括但不限于主机、副机、燃气轮机、锅炉和惰性气体发生器消耗的每种类型的燃油。按《2022 年船舶能效管理计划编制导则》（SEEMP 导则）（MEPC.346（78）号决议）第 7.1.2 和 7.1.3 段所述，收集以吨为单位的燃油消耗数据的方法包括使用流量计的方法或使用船上燃油舱监测的方法。

2　航行期间的对地航行距离（以海里为单位）应记录在船舶日志中（根据《国际海上人命安全公约》（SOLAS）第 V/28.1 条的规定），并提交给主管机关。

3　在航行结束时，如果船舶在航行中遇到冰区（当船舶在冰缘之间或冰缘与港口之间航行时），或 MARPOL 附则Ⅵ第 3.1 条规定的情形适用时：

.1　根据 SEEMP 导则 7.1.2 或 7.1.3 测量的在航程期间的燃油消耗不应包括在计算年度平均达到的 CII 指数值中。

.2　如果在 MARPOL 附则Ⅵ第 3.1 条规定的情况适用时，该航次不计入达到的 CII 计算中，航行距离应在 SEEMP 监测计划中明确标记，船舶日志上应当包含该航程期间的数据项，这些数据项包括 MARPOL 附则Ⅵ第 3.1 条规定的情况开始适用和停止适用的日期、时间和船舶位置，以及应添加到数据报告格式中的数据。

.2　若由于冰区航行，从计算达到的 CII 指数值内扣除该航程期间，航行距离应在 SEEMP 监测计划中明确标记，船舶日志上应当包含该航程期间的数据项，这些数据项包括船舶遇到冰区和离开冰区的日期、时间和船舶位置，以及应添加到数据报告格式中的数据。

4　船上应备有监测数据汇总表，其中包括航程期间测量的燃油消耗量和航行距离的记录。如果船舶在冰区航行，还应备有与航程期间相关的冰区图。

Figure 1: An example of an ice chart of the Baltic Sea area

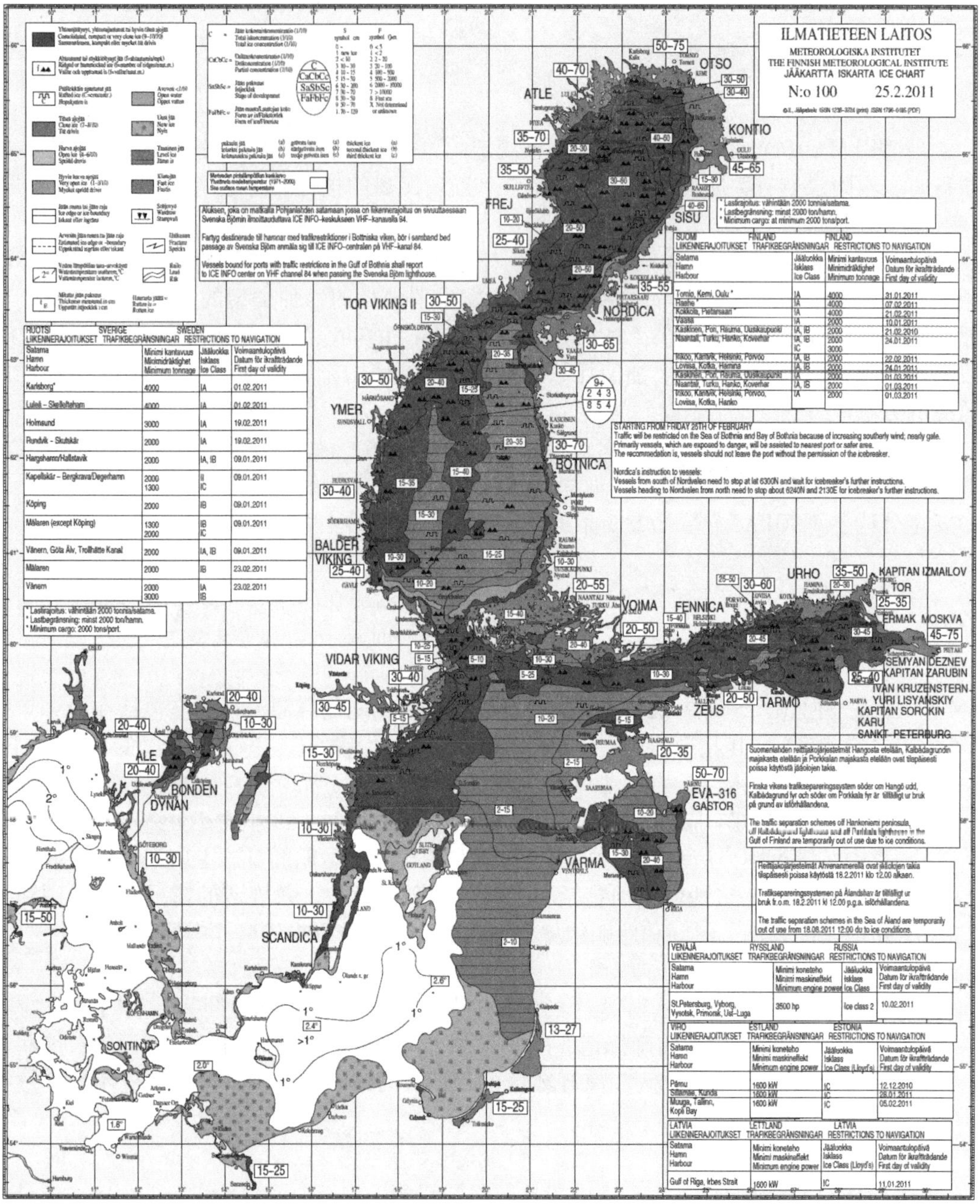

图 1 波罗的海地区冰区图示例

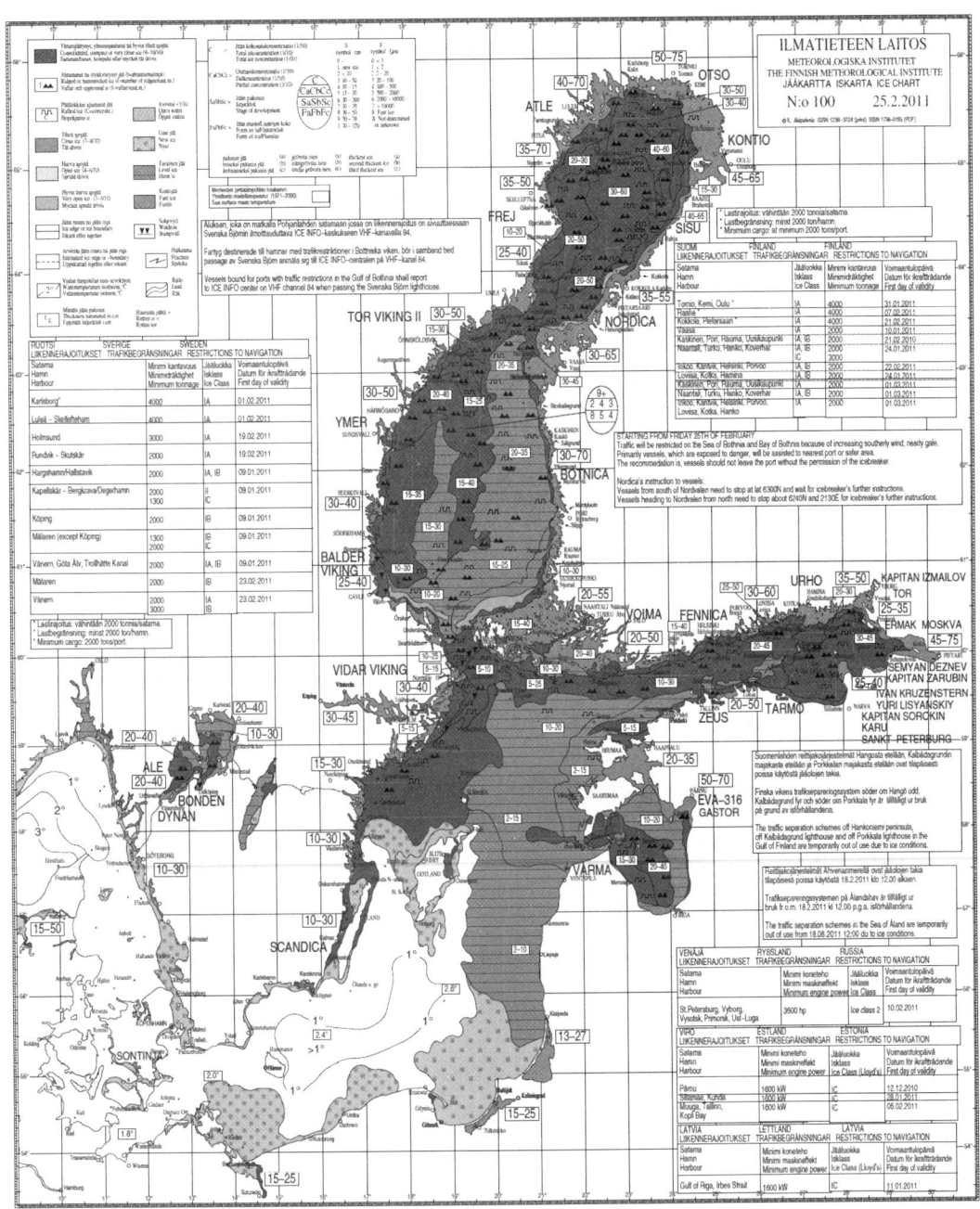

***

GUIDELINES FOR VOLUNTARY USE OF THE SHIP ENERGY EFFICIENCY OPERATIONAL INDICATOR (EEOI)

1   The Marine Environment Protection Committee, at its fifty-ninth session (13 to 17 July 2009), agreed to circulate the Guidelines for voluntary use of the Ship Energy Efficiency Operational Indicator (EEOI) as set out in the annex.

2   Member Governments are invited to bring the Guidelines to the attention of all parties concerned and recommend them to use the Guidelines on a voluntary basis.

3   Member Governments and observer organizations are also invited to provide information on the outcome and experiences in applying the Guidelines to future sessions of the Committee.

***

MEPC.1/Circ.684

2009 年 8 月 17 日

船舶能效营运指数（EEOI）自愿使用导则

1   海上环境保护委员会在其第 59 届会议（2009 年 7 月 13 日至 17 日）上，同意分发载于附件中的《船舶能效营运指数（EEOI）自愿使用导则》。

2   提请各成员国政府使所有相关方注意到本导则，并建议其自愿使用本导则。

3   还提请各成员国政府和观察员组织向本委员会的未来几届会议提供应用本导则的结果和经验。

***

ANNEX

GUIDELINES FOR VOLUNTARY USE OF THE SHIP ENERGY EFFICIENCY OPERATIONAL INDICATOR (EEOI)

1   The Conference of Parties to the International Convention for the Prevention of Pollution from Ships, 1973, as modified by the Protocol of 1978 relating thereto, held from 15 to 26 September 1997 in conjunction with the Marine Environment Protection Committee's fortieth session, adopted Conference resolution 8, on CO_2 emissions from ships.

2   IMO Assembly resolution A.963(23) on IMO policies and practices related to the reduction of greenhouse gas emissions from ships urged the Marine Environment Protection Committee (MEPC) to identify and develop the mechanism or mechanisms needed to achieve the limitation or reduction of Greenhouse Gas (GHG) emissions from international shipping and, in doing so, to give priority to the establishment of a GHG baseline; and the development of a methodology to describe the GHG efficiency of a ship in terms of GHG emission indicator for that ship.

3   As urged by the Assembly, MEPC 53 approved Interim Guidelines for Voluntary Ship CO_2 Emission Index for Use in Trials.

4   These Guidelines can be used to establish a consistent approach for voluntary use of an EEOI, which will assist shipowners, ship operators and parties concerned in the evaluation of the performance of their fleet with regard to CO_2 emissions. As the amount of CO_2 emitted from a ship is directly related to the consumption of bunker fuel oil, the EEOI can also provide useful information on a ship's performance with regard to fuel efficiency.

5   These Guidelines may be updated periodically, to take account of:

- Operational experiences from use of the indicator for different ship types, as reported to MEPC by industry organizations and Administrations; and

- Any other relevant developments.

6   Industry organizations and interested Administrations are invited to promote the use of the attached Guidelines or equivalent approaches and their incorporation in company and ship environmental management plans. In addition, they are invited to report their experience in applying the EEOI concept back to MEPC.

7   In addition to these Guidelines, due account should be taken of the pertinent clauses within the ISM Code in voluntary basis along with reference to relevant industry guidance on the management and reduction of CO_2 emissions.

* * *

附件

船舶能效营运指数（EEOI）自愿使用导则

1 自 1997 年 9 月 15 日至 26 日召开的经 1978 年议定书修订的 1973 年国际防止船舶造成污染公约缔约方大会连同海上环境保护委员会第 40 届会议通过关于船舶 CO_2 排放的大会决议 8。

2 IMO 大会第 A.963（23）号决议"IMO 关于船舶温室气体减排的政策和实施"敦促海上环境保护委员会（MEPC）认同并开发实现限制或减少国际航运温室气体（GHG）排放所需的机制并优先建立 GHG 基准线；并就船舶的 GHG 排放指数方面制定方法来描述船舶的 GHG 效率。

3 经大会敦促，MEPC 第 53 届会议批准了《船舶 CO_2 排放指数自愿试用临时导则》。

4 本导则可用于建立一致的方式自愿使用 EEOI，这将协助船东、船舶经营者和相关方评估其船队关于 CO_2 排放的性能。由于船舶的 CO_2 排放量与燃油舱的燃油消耗量直接相关，EEOI 也可提供关于燃油效能的船舶性能的有用信息。

5 本导则可定期更新，以考虑：

– 从使用不同船舶类型的指数获得的操作经验，由行业组织和主管机关向 MEPC 报告；和

– 任何其他相关发展。

6 提请行业组织和相关主管机关促进所附的导则或等效方法的使用，并纳入公司和船舶环境管理计划。此外，提请其向 MEPC 反馈其应用 EEOI 概念的经验。

7 除本导则外，还应基于自愿的原则适当考虑 ISM 规则中的相关条款，并参照关于管理和减少 CO_2 排放的相关行业导则。

***

ANNEX

GUIDELINES FOR VOLUNTARY USE OF THE SHIP ENERGY EFFICIENCY OPERATIONAL INDICATOR (EEOI)

Contents

附件

船舶能效营运指数（EEOI）自愿使用导则

目录

1　INTRODUCTION

In 1997 IMO adopted a resolution on CO_2 emissions from ships[1].

IMO Assembly further adopted resolution A.963(23) on IMO policies and practices related to the reduction of greenhouse gas emissions from ships, which requests the MEPC to develop a greenhouse gas emission index for ships, and guidelines for use of that index.

This document constitutes the Guidelines for the use of an Energy Efficiency Operational Indicator (EEOI) for ships. It sets out:

- what the objectives of the IMO CO_2 emissions indicator are;

- how a ship's CO_2 performance should be measured; and

- how the index could be used to promote low-emission shipping, in order to help limit the impact of shipping on global climate change.

2　OBJECTIVES

The objective of these Guidelines is to provide the users with assistance in the process of establishing a mechanism to achieve the limitation or reduction of greenhouse gas emissions from ships in operation.

These Guidelines present the concept of an indicator for the energy efficiency of a ship in operation, as an expression of efficiency expressed in the form of CO_2 emitted per unit of transport work. The Guidelines are intended to provide an example of a calculation method which could be used as an objective, performance-based approach to monitoring the efficiency of a ship's operation.

These Guidelines are recommendatory in nature and present a possible use of an operational indicator. However, shipowners, ship operators and parties concerned are invited to implement either these Guidelines or an equivalent method in their environmental management systems and consider adoption of the principles herein when developing plans for performance monitoring.

3　DEFINITIONS

3.1　Indicator definition

In its most simple form *the Energy Efficiency Operational Indicator* is defined as the ratio of mass of CO_2 (M) emitted per unit of transport work:

$$\text{Indicator} = M_{CO_2}/(\text{transport work})$$

For more details of indicator calculation, see 3.2 to 3.4 and Appendix 1.

---

[1]　Resolution 8 of the 1997 International Conference of Parties to MARPOL 73/78.

1 引言

IMO 于 1997 年通过关于船舶 CO_2 排放的决议[1]。

IMO 大会进一步通过大会第 A.963（23）号决议 "IMO 关于船舶温室气体减排的政策和实施"，要求 MEPC 制定船舶温室气体排放指数以及该指数的使用导则。

本文件构成船舶能效营运指数（EEOI）使用导则。它规定：

— IMO CO_2 排放指数的目的是什么；

— 应如何测量船舶的 CO_2 性能；和

— 如何使用指数促进低排放航运以帮助限制航运对全球气候变化的影响。

2 目标

本导则的目的是帮助使用者建立机制以实现限制或减少营运船舶温室气体排放。

本导则提出营运船舶能效指数的概念，以单位运输功排放的 CO_2 的形式表示效率。本导则旨在举例说明一种计算方法，该方法可作为一种客观、基于性能的方法，用于监测船舶的营运效率。

本导则实际上是值得推荐的，其提出一种可能使用的营运指数。但是，提请船东、船舶经营者和相关方在其环境管理系统中执行本导则或等效方法，并在制定性能监测计划时考虑采用本导则的原则。

3 定义

3.1 指数定义

以最简单的形式，能效营运指数定义为船舶单位运输功所排放的 CO_2 质量：

$$Indicator = M_{CO_2} / (\text{transport work})$$

指数计算的更多详情参见 3.2 至 3.4 和附录 1。

---

[1] 1997 年国际 MARPOL 73/78 缔约大会决议 8。

3.2 Fuel consumption

Fuel consumption, FC, is defined as all fuel consumed at sea and in port or for a voyage or period in question, e.g., a day, by main and auxiliary engines including boilers and incinerators.

3.3 Distance sailed

Distance sailed means the actual distance sailed in nautical miles (deck log-book data) for the voyage or period in question.

3.4 Ship and cargo types

The Guidelines are applicable for all ships performing transport work.

.1   Ships:

- dry cargo carriers
- tankers
- gas tankers
- containerships
- ro-ro cargo ships
- general cargo ships
- passenger ships including ro-ro passenger ships

.2   Cargo:

Cargo includes but not limited to:
all gas, liquid and solid bulk cargo, general cargo, containerized cargo (including the return of empty units), break bulk, heavy lifts, frozen and chilled goods, timber and forest products, cargo carried on freight vehicles, cars and freight vehicles on ro-ro ferries and passengers (for passenger and ro-ro passenger ships)

3.5 Cargo Mass Carried or Work Done

In general, cargo mass carries or work done is expressed as follows:

.1   for dry cargo carriers, liquid tankers, gas tankers, ro-ro cargo ships and general cargo ships, metric tonnes (*t*) of the cargo carried should be used;

.2   for containerships carrying solely containers, number of containers (TEU) or metric tons (*t*) of the total mass of cargo and containers should be used;

.3   for ships carrying a combination of containers and other cargoes, a TEU mass of 10 t could be applied for loaded TEUs and 2 t for empty TEUs; and

.4   for passenger ships, including ro-ro passenger ships, number of passengers or gross tonnes of the ship should be used;

In some particular cases, work done can be expressed as follows:

.5   for car ferries and car carriers, number of car units or occupied lane metres;

3.2 燃料消耗量

燃料消耗量 FC 定义为在海上、在港或在所考虑的航次或时间段消耗的所有燃料量，例如 1 天，由主机和副机（包括锅炉和焚烧炉）所消耗的所有燃料量。

3.3 航行距离

航行距离 是指在所考虑的航次或时间段的以海里为单位的实际航行距离（甲板航海日志数据）。

3.4 船舶和货物类型

本导则适用于所有进行运输作业的船舶。

.1 船舶：

- 干货船

- 液货船

- 气体运输船

- 集装箱船

- 滚装货船

- 杂货船

- 客船，包括滚装客船

.2 货物：

货物包括但不限于：

所有气体、液体和固体散装货物，杂货，集装箱货物（包括空箱的返回），件杂货，重件，冷冻和冷藏货物，木材和林产品，货车上所载货物，滚装渡轮上的汽车和货车，以及乘客（客船和滚装客船）。

3.5 载运的货物质量或所做的功

一般来说，载运的货物质量或所做的功表述如下：

.1 对于干货船、液货船、气体运输船、滚装货船和杂货船，应使用所载货物质量（t）；

.2 对于仅装运集装箱的集装箱船，应使用集装箱数量（TEU）或货物和集装箱总质量（t）；

.3 对于载运集装箱和其他货物的船舶，每一载货 TEU 按 10 t 计算，空的 TEU 按 2t 计算；和

.4 对于客船（包括滚装客船），应使用乘客数量或船舶总吨；在某些特定情况下，所做的功表述如下：

.5 对于汽车渡船或车辆运输船，车辆单元数量或占用的车道长度；

.6   for containerships, number of TEUs (empty or full); and

.7   for railway and ro-ro vessels, number of railway cars and freight vehicles, or occupied lane metres.

For vessels such as, for example, certain ro-ro vessels, which carry a mixture of passengers in cars, foot passengers and freight, operators may wish to consider some form of weighted average based on the relative significance of these trades for their particular service or the use of other parameters or indicators as appropriate.

3.6   Voyage

Voyage generally means the period between a departure from a port to the departure from the next port. Alternative definitions of a voyage could also be acceptable.

4   ESTABLISHING AN ENERGY EFFICIENCY OPERATIONAL INDICATOR (EEOI)

The EEOI should be a representative value of the energy efficiency of the ship operation over a consistent period which represents the overall trading pattern of the vessel. Guidance on a basic calculation procedure for a generic EEOI is provided in the Appendix.

In order to establish the EEOI, the following main steps will generally be needed:

.1   define the period for which the EEOI is calculated[*];

.2   define data sources for data collection;

.3   collect data;

.4   convert data to appropriate format; and

.5   calculate EEOI.

[*]   Ballast voyages, as well as voyages which are not used for transport of cargo, such as voyage for docking service, should also be included. Voyages for the purpose of securing the safety of a ship or saving life at sea should be excluded.

5   GENERAL DATA RECORDING AND DOCUMENTATION PROCEDURES

Ideally, the data recording method used should be uniform so that information can be easily collated and analysed to facilitate the extraction of the required information. The collection of data from ships should include the distance travelled, the quantity and type of fuel used, and all fuel information that may affect the amount of carbon dioxide emitted. For example, fuel information is provided on the bunker delivery notes that are required under regulation 18 of MARPOL Annex VI.

If the example formula given in the Appendix is used, then the unit used for distance travelled and quantity of fuel should be expressed in nautical miles and metric tonnes. The work done can be expressed using units appropriate for the ship type in paragraph 3.5.

.6 对于集装箱船，TEU（空或满）的数量；和

.7 对于铁路及滚装船，铁路车辆和货车数量，或占用的车道长度。

对于混合载运包括车上乘客、行人和货物的船舶（例如某些滚装船），经营者可能希望考虑基于其特定业务的相对重要性的某些形式的加权平均值或使用其他适当的参数或指数。

3.6 航次

*航次*通常是指从一个港口出发至从下一个港口出发的时间段。也可接受航次的替代定义。

4 建立能效营运指数（EEOI）

EEOI 应为船舶在一段持续时间内具有代表性的营运能效值，代表船舶整体交易模式。附录提供了通用 EEOI 的基本计算程序导则。

为了建立 EEOI，通常需要下列主要步骤：

.1 规定计算 EEOI 的时间段[*]；

.2 规定数据收集的数据源；

.3 收集数据；

.4 将数据转换成适当的格式；和

.5 计算 EEOI。

[*] 还应包括压载航次，以及未用于载运货物的航次，例如进坞航次。应排除为保护船舶安全或救助海上人命的航次。

5 数据记录和报告程序

理想情况下，所使用的数据记录方法应该是统一的，这样易于整理和分析信息，以便于提取所需信息。船舶数据的收集应包括航行距离、所使用的燃料数量和类型，以及可能影响二氧化碳排放量的所有燃料信息。例如，在 MARPOL 附则六第 18 条要求的燃油交付单上提供燃料信息。

如果使用附录中给出的示例公式，则用于航行距离和燃料数量的单位应分别以海里和吨表示。所做的功可以使用第 3.5 段中适于船舶类型的单位来表示。

It is important that sufficient information is collected on the ship with regard to fuel type and quantity, distance travelled and cargo type so that a realistic assessment can be generated.

The distance travelled should be calculated by actual distance travelled, as contained in the ship's log-book.

Amount and type of fuel used (bunker delivery notes) and distance travelled (according to the ship's log-book) could be documented by the ship based either on the example described in the Appendix or on an equivalent company procedure.

6 MONITORING AND VERIFICATION

6.1 General

Documented procedures to monitor and measure, on a regular basis, should be developed and maintained. Elements to be considered when establishing procedures for monitoring could include:

- identification of operations/activities with impact on the performance;

- identification of data sources and measurements that are necessary, and specification of the format;

- identification of frequency and personnel performing measurements; and

- maintenance of quality control procedures for verification procedures.

The results of this type of self-assessment could be reviewed and used as indicators of the System's success and reliability, as well as identifying those areas in need of corrective action or improvement.

It is important that the source of figures established are properly recorded, the basis on which figures have been calculated and any decisions on difficult or grey areas of data. This will provide assistance on areas for improvement and be helpful for any later analysis.

In order to avoid unnecessary administrative burdens on ships' staff, it is recommended that monitoring of an EEOI should be carried out by shore staff, utilizing data obtained from existing required records such as the official and engineering log-books and oil record books, etc. The necessary data could be obtained during internal audits under the ISM Code, routine visits by superintendents, etc.

6.2 Rolling average indicator

As a ship energy efficiency management tool, the rolling average indicator, when used, should be calculated by use of a methodology whereby the minimum period of time or a number of voyages that is statistically relevant is used as appropriate. "Statistically relevant" means that the period set as standard for each individual ship should remain constant and be wide enough so the accumulated data mass reflects a reasonable mean value for operation of the ship in question over the selected period.

船上收集足够的关于燃料类型和数量、航行距离和货物类型的信息是重要的，这样就可进行实际可行的评估。

航行距离应根据船舶航海日志中包含的实际航行距离进行计算。

所使用的燃料数量和类型（燃油交付单）和航行距离（按照船舶航海日志）可由船舶基于附录中的示例或等效公司程序以文件形式记录。

6 监测和验证

6.1 通则

应制定和保持定期用文件记录的监测和测量程序。建立监测程序时应考虑的事项可包括：

* 判定营运 / 活动对性能的影响；

* 判定必需的数据源和测量，以及格式的详细说明；

* 判定频率和人员进行的测量；和

* 为验证程序保持质量控制程序。

这类自我评定的结果可加以审查并用作系统成功和可靠性的指数，并判定需要采取纠正措施或改进的方面。

重要的是，应正确记录所建立的数据来源、计算数据的依据以及关于数据困难或灰色区域的任何决定。这会帮助需要改进的方面，并有助于以后的任何分析。

为了避免对船舶职员造成不必要的行政负担，建议应由岸上人员使用从现有的要求的记录（例如航海日志、轮机日志和油类记录簿等）获得的数据，对 EEOI 进行监测。必需的数据可在 ISM 规则的内部审核、主管定期访问等期间获得。

6.2 滚动平均指数

作为一种船舶能效管理工具，在使用滚动平均指数时，应使用最周期或酌情使用与统计相关的许多航次的方法进行计算。"与统计相关"是指为每艘船舶设定的作为标准的周期应保持不变，且应足够长，这样积累的数据量才能反映出在所选时间段内所计算船舶在营运中的一个合理平均值。

7   USE OF GUIDELINES

Methodology and use of EEOI, as described in these Guidelines, provide an example of a transparent and recognized approach for assessment of the GHG efficiency of a ship with respect to CO_2 emissions. The Guidelines are considered to be suitable for implementation within a company environmental management system.

Implementation of the EEOI in an established environmental management system should be performed in line with the implementation of any other chosen indicator and follow the main elements of the recognized standards (planning, implementation and operation, checking and corrective action, management review).

When using the EEOI as a performance indicator, the indicator could provide a basis for consideration of both current performance and trends over time.

One approach could be to set internal performance criteria and targets based on the EEOI data.

* * *

7 导则的使用

如本导则所述，EEOI 的方法和使用为评估船舶 CO_2 排放的温室气体效率提供了一个透明和公认的方法示例。本导则被视作适合在公司环境管理系统内执行。

在已建立的环境管理体系中，EEOI 的实施应与任何其他选定指标的实施相一致，并遵循公认标准的主要要素（计划、实施和操作、检查和纠正措施、管理评审）。

当使用 EEOI 作为性能指标时，该指标可为审议当前性能和长期趋势提供依据。

一种方法是根据 EEOI 数据制定内部性能标准和目标。

**

APPENDIX

CALCULATION OF ENERGY EFFICIENCY OPERATIONAL INDICATOR (EEOI) BASED ON OPERATIONAL DATA

1   General

The objective of the Appendix is to provide guidance on calculation of the Energy Efficiency Operational Indicator (EEOI) based on data from the operation of the ship.

2   Data sources

Primary data sources selected could be the ship's log-book (bridge log-book, engine log-book, deck log-book and other official records).

3   Fuel mass to CO_2 mass conversion factors (C_F)

C_F is a non-dimensional conversion factor between fuel consumption measured in g and CO_2 emission also measured in g based on carbon content. The value of C_F is as follows:

Type of fuel	Reference	Carbon content	C_F (t-CO_2/t-Fuel)
1. Diesel/Gas Oil	ISO 8217 Grades DMX through DMC	0.875	3.206000
2. Light Fuel Oil (LFO)	ISO 8217 Grades RMA through RMD	0.86	3.151040
3. Heavy Fuel Oil (HFO)	ISO 8217 Grades RME through RMK	0.85	3.114400
4. Liquified Petroleum Gas (LPG)	Propane	0.819	3.000000
	Butane	0.827	3.030000
5. Liquified Natural Gas (LNG)		0.75	2.750000

4   Calculation of EEOI

The basic expression for EEOI for a voyage is defined as:

$$\text{EEOI} = \frac{\sum_j FC_j \times C_{Fj}}{m_{cargo} \times D} \qquad \text{Equation 1}$$

Where average of the indicator for a period or for a number of voyages is obtained, the Indicator is calculated as:

$$\text{Average EEOI} = \frac{\sum_i \sum_j (FC_{ij} \times C_{Fj})}{\sum_i (m_{cargo,i} \times D_i)} \qquad \text{Equation 2}$$

附录

基于营运数据的能效营运指标（EEOI）的计算

1 通则

本附录的目的是为基于船舶营运数据计算能效营运指数（EEOI）提供指导。

2 数据源

所选的主要数据源可为船舶航海日志(驾驶台日志、轮机日志、甲板日志和其他正式记录)。

3 燃料质量到 CO_2 质量转换系数（C_F）

C_F 是测量的燃油消耗量（单位为 g）和测量的基于碳含量 CO_2 排放量（单位为 g）之间的无量纲转换系数。C_F 值如下：

燃料类型	参照等级	碳含量	C_F（t-CO$_2$/t-Fuel）
1. 柴油 / 汽油	ISO8217DMX 级 –DMC 级	0.875	3.206 000
2. 轻燃油（LFO）	ISO8217RMA 级 –RMD 级	0.86	3.151 040
3. 重燃油（HFO）	ISO8217RME 级 –RMK 级	0.85	3.114 400
4. 液化石油气（LPG）	丙烷	0.819	3.000 000
	丁烷	0.827	3.030 000
5. 液化天然气（LNG）		0.75	2.750 000

4 EEOI 的计算

一个航次 EEOI 的基本表达式定义为：

$$EEOI = \frac{\sum\limits_{j} FC_j \times C_{Fj}}{m_{cargo} \times D} \tag{1}$$

如获得某段时间或多个航次的指数平均值，指数计算为：

$$Average\ EEOI = \frac{\sum\limits_{i}\sum\limits_{j}(FC_{ij} \times C_{Fj})}{\sum\limits_{i}(m_{cargo,i} \times D_i)} \tag{2}$$

Where:

- j is the fuel type;
- i is the voyage number;
- FC_{ij} is the mass of consumed fuel j at voyage i;
- C_{Fj} is the fuel mass to CO_2 mass conversion factor for fuel j;
- m_{cargo} is cargo carried (tonnes) or work done (number of TEU or passengers) or gross tonnes for passenger ships; and
- D is the distance in nautical miles corresponding to the cargo carried or work done.

The unit of EEOI depends on the measurement of cargo carried or work done, e.g., tonnes CO_2/(tonnes • nautical miles), tonnes CO_2/(TEU • nautical miles), tonnes CO_2/(person • nautical miles), etc.

It should be noted that Equation 2 does not give a simple average of EEOI among number of voyage i.

5   Rolling average

Rolling average, when used, can be calculated in a suitable time period, for example one year closest to the end of a voyage for that period, or number of voyages, for example six or ten voyages, which are agreed as statistically relevant to the initial averaging period. The Rolling Average EEOI is then calculated for this period or number of voyages by Equation 2 above.

6   Data

For a voyage or period, e.g., a day, data on fuel consumption/cargo carried and distance sailed in a continuous sailing pattern could be collected as shown in the reporting sheet below.

式中：

- j 是燃料类型；

- i 是航次数；

- FC_{ij} 是在航次 i 消耗的燃料 j 的质量；

- C_{Fj} 是燃料 j 的燃料质量到 CO_2 质量的转换系数；

- m_{cargo} 是指所载货物（吨）或所作的功（TEU 或乘客数量）或客船总吨数；和

- D 是与所载货物或所作的功相对应的距离，单位为海里。

EEOI 的单位取决于所载货物或所作的功的测量，例如吨 CO_2/（吨·海里）、吨 CO_2/（标准箱·海里）、吨 CO_2/（人·海里）等。

应注意的是，式（2）并不是给出 i 个航次的 EEOI 的简单平均值。

5 滚动平均

滚动平均值（如使用），可在一个适当的时间段内计算，例如在该时间段内距离航次结束最近的一年，或在统计上与初始平均期相关的航次数（例如 6 个或 10 个航次）。然后根据上述式（2）计算该时期或航次数的滚动平均 EEOI。

6 数据

对于一个航次或一段时间，例如 1 天，可以收集连续航行模式下的燃料消耗/所载货物和航行距离的数据，如下列报告表所示。

CO₂ Indicator reporting sheet

NAME AND TYPE OF SHIP						
Voyage or day (i)	Fuel consumption (FC) at sea and in port in tonnes				Voyage or time period data	
	Fuel type ( )	Fuel type ( )	Fuel type ( )		Cargo (m) (tonnes or units)	Distance (D) (NM)
1						
2						
3						

NOTE: For voyages with $m_{cargo}=0$, it is still necessary to include the fuel used during this voyage in the summation above the line.

7   Conversion from g/tonne-mile to g/tonne-km

The CO_2 indicator may be converted from g/tonne-mile to g/tonne-km by multiplication by 0.54.

8   Example:

A simple example including one ballast voyage, for illustration purpose only, is provided below. The example illustrates the application of the formula based on the data reporting sheet.

NAME AND TYPE OF SHIP						
Voyage or day (i)	Fuel consumption (FC) at sea and in port in tonnes				Voyage or time period data	
	Fuel type (HFO)	Fuel type (LFO)	Fuel type ( )		Cargo (m) (tonnes or units)	Distance (D) (NM)
1	20	5			25,000	300
2	20	5			0	300
3	50	10			25,000	750
	10	3			15,000	150

$$EEOI = \frac{100 \times 3.114 + 23 \times 3.151}{(25,000 \times 300) + (0 \times 300) + (25,000 \times 750) + (15,000 \times 150)} = 13.47 \times 10^{-6}$$

unit: tonnes CO_2/(tons • nautical miles)

CO_2 指数报告表

航次或天（i）	海上和港口燃料消耗量（FC）（t）				航次或时间段数据	
	燃料类型（ ）	燃料类型（ ）	燃料类型（ ）		货物（m）（t 或单位）	距离（D）（n mile）
1						
2						
3						

注：对于 $m_{cargo}=0$ 的航次，仍需要将该航次使用的燃料包含在线上的总和（即式（2）的分子）中。

7 从克/吨英里到克/吨公里的转换

CO_2 指数可通过乘以 0.54 从 g/t– 英里转换为 g/t–km。

8 示例

下面提供一个包括一个压载航次的简单例子（仅供说明）。该示例说明了基于数据报告表的公式的应用。

航次或天（i）	海上和港口燃料消耗（FC）（t）				航次或时间段数据	
	燃料类型（HFO）	燃料类型（LFO）	燃料类型（ ）		货物（m）（t 或单位）	距离（D）（n mile）
1	20	5			25 000	300
2	20	5			0	300
3	50	10			25 000	750
	10	3			15 000	150

$$EEOI = \frac{100 \times 3.114 + 23 \times 3.151}{(25\,000 \times 300) + (0 \times 300) + (25\,000 \times 750) + (15\,000 \times 150)} = 13.47 \times 10^{-6}$$

单位：吨 CO_2/（t·n mile）

—— EEDI/EEXI 相关 ——

RESOLUTION MEPC.364(79)

2022 GUIDELINES ON THE METHOD OF CALCULATION OF THE ATTAINED ENERGY EFFICIENCY DESIGN INDEX (EEDI) FOR NEW SHIPS

THE MARINE ENVIRONMENT PROTECTION COMMITTEE,

RECALLING article 38(a) of the Convention on the International Maritime Organization concerning the functions of the Marine Environment Protection Committee (the Committee) conferred upon it by international conventions for the prevention and control of marine pollution from ships,

NOTING that regulation 22 (Attained Energy Efficiency Design Index (attained EEDI)) of MARPOL Annex VI, as amended, requires that the EEDI shall be calculated taking into account the guidelines developed by the Organization,

NOTING ALSO that the Committee adopted, at its seventy-third session, *2018 Guidelines on the method of calculation of the attained Energy Efficiency Design Index (EEDI) for new ships* (resolution MEPC.308(73)),

NOTING FURTHER that, at its seventy-fourth and seventy-sixth sessions, it adopted, by resolutions MEPC.322(74) and MEPC.332(76), respectively, amendments to the *2018 Guidelines on the method of calculation of the attained Energy Efficiency Design Index (EEDI) for new ships*,

HAVING NOTED, at its seventy-ninth session, the need to further amend the *2018 Guidelines on the method of calculation of the attained Energy Efficiency Design Index (EEDI) for new ships* (resolution MEPC.308(73), as amended),

1   ADOPTS the *2022 Guidelines on the method of calculation of the attained Energy Efficiency Design Index (EEDI) for new ships*, as set out in the annex to the present resolution;

2   INVITES Administrations to implement the 2022 EEDI Calculation Guidelines when developing and enacting national laws which give force to, and implement provisions set forth in regulation 22 of MARPOL Annex VI, as amended;

3   REQUESTS the Parties to MARPOL Annex VI and other Member Governments to bring the amendments to the attention of shipowners, ship operators, shipbuilders, ship designers and any other interested parties;

4   AGREES to keep these Guidelines, as amended, under review, in light of experience gained with their implementation;

5   AGREES that these Guidelines supersede the *2018 Guidelines on the method of calculation of the attained Energy Efficiency Design Index (EEDI) for new ships* (resolution MEPC.308(73), as amended by resolutions MEPC.322(74) and MEPC.332(76)).

第 MEPC.364（79）号决议
（2022 年 12 月 16 日通过）

2022 年新造船达到的能效设计指数（EEDI）计算方法导则

海上环境保护委员会，

忆及《国际海事组织公约》关于防止和控制船舶造成海洋污染国际公约赋予海上环境保护委员会职能的第 38（a）条，

注意到经修正的《防污公约》附则 Ⅵ 第 22 条（达到的能效设计指数（达到的 EEDI））要求在计算能效设计指数时应考虑到本组织制定的导则，

还注意到本委员会在其第 73 届会议上通过的《2018 年新造船达到的能效设计指数（EEDI）计算方法导则》（第 MEPC.308（73）号决议），

进一步注意到其在第 74 和 76 届会议上分别以第 MEPC.322（74）和 MEPC.332（76）号决议通过的《2018 年新造船达到的能效设计指数（EEDI）计算方法导则》的修正案，

在其第 79 届会议上，注意到有必要进一步修正《2018 年新造船达到的能效设计指数（EEDI）计算方法导则》（经修正的第 MEPC.308（73）号决议），

1　**通过**《2022 年新造船达到的能效设计指数（EEDI）计算方法导则》，其文本载于本决议附件；

2　**提请**各主管机关在制定和颁布本国法律，以执行和实施经修正的《防污公约》附则 Ⅵ 第 22 条要求时，施行《2022 年 EEDI 计算导则》；

3　**要求**《防污公约》附则 Ⅵ 各缔约国和其他会员国政府提请船东、船舶经营者、船厂、船舶设计方以及任何其他攸关方注意到本修正案；

4　**同意**根据实施中获得的经验对经修正的本导则保持审查；

5　**同意**本导则替代《2018 年新造船达到的能效设计指数（EEDI）计算方法导则》（经第 MEPC.322（74）和 MEPC.332（76）号决议修正的第 MEPC.308（73）号决议）。

ANNEX

2022 GUIDELINES ON THE METHOD OF CALCULATION OF THE ATTAINED ENERGY EFFICIENCY DESIGN INDEX (EEDI) FOR NEW SHIPS

CONTENTS

附件

2022 年新造船达到的能效设计指数（EEDI）计算方法导则

目录

1 Definitions

1.1 MARPOL means the International Convention for the Prevention of Pollution from Ships, 1973, as modified by the Protocols of 1978 and 1997 relating thereto, as amended.

1.2 For the purpose of these Guidelines, the definitions in chapter 4 of MARPOL Annex VI, as amended, apply.

2 Energy Efficiency Design Index (EEDI)

2.1 EEDI formula

The attained new ship Energy Efficiency Design Index (EEDI) is a measure of ships' energy efficiency (g/t·nm) and calculated by the following formula:

$$\frac{\left(\prod\limits_{j=1}^{n}f_j\right)\left(\sum\limits_{i=1}^{nME}P_{ME(i)}\cdot C_{FME(i)}\cdot SFC_{ME(i)}\right)+\left(P_{AE}\cdot C_{FAE}\cdot SFC_{AE}*\right)+\left(\left(\prod\limits_{j=1}^{n}f_j\cdot\sum\limits_{i=1}^{nPTI}P_{PTI(i)}-\sum\limits_{i=1}^{neff}f_{eff(i)}\cdot P_{AEeff(i)}\right)C_{FAE}\cdot SFC_{AE}\right)-\left(\sum\limits_{i=1}^{neff}f_{eff(i)}\cdot P_{eff(i)}\cdot C_{FME}\cdot SFC_{ME}**\right)}{f_i\cdot f_c\cdot f_l\cdot Capacity\cdot f_w\cdot V_{ref}\cdot f_m}$$

*   If part of the Normal Maximum Sea Load is provided by shaft generators, SFC_{ME} and C_{FME} may – for that part of the power – be used instead of SFC_{AE} and C_{FAE}

**   In case of $P_{PTI(i)} > 0$, the average weighted value of ($SFC_{ME}\cdot C_{FME}$) and ($SFC_{AE}\cdot C_{FAE}$) to be used for calculation of P_{eff}

> **Note:**   This formula may not be applicable to a ship having diesel electric propulsion, turbine propulsion or hybrid propulsion system, except for cruise passenger ships and LNG carriers.

2.2 Parameters

For the calculation of EEDI by the formula in paragraph 2.1, the following parameters apply.

2.2.1 C_F ; Conversion factor between fuel consumption and CO_2 emission

C_F is a non-dimensional conversion factor between fuel consumption measured in g and CO_2 emission also measured in g based on carbon content. The subscripts $ME(i)$ and $AE(i)$ refer to the main and auxiliary engine(s) respectively. C_F corresponds to the fuel used when determining SFC listed in the applicable test report included in a Technical File as defined in paragraph 1.3.15 of the NO_x Technical Code ("test report included in a NO_x Technical File" hereafter). The value of C_F is as follows:

Type of fuel	Reference	Lower calorific value (kJ/kg)	Carbon content	C_F (t-CO_2/t-Fuel)
1 Diesel/Gas Oil	ISO 8217 Grades DMX through DMB	42,700	0.8744	3.206
2 Light Fuel Oil (LFO)	ISO 8217 Grades RMA through RMD	41,200	0.8594	3.151
3 Heavy Fuel Oil (HFO)	ISO 8217 Grades RME through RMK	40,200	0.8493	3.114
4 Liquefied Petroleum Gas (LPG)	Propane	46,300	0.8182	3.000
	Butane	45,700	0.8264	3.030
5 Ethane		46,400	0.7989	2.927

1 定义

1.1 《防污公约》系指经修正的《经 1978 年和 1997 年议定书修订的 1973 年国际防止船舶造成污染公约》。

1.2 就本导则而言，经修正的《防污公约》附则Ⅵ第 4 章中的定义适用。

2 能效设计指数（EEDI）

2.1 EEDI 公式

达到的新船能效设计指数（EEDI）是衡量船舶能效（g/t·nm）的一个指标，通过下列公式计算：

$$\dfrac{\left(\prod_{j=1}^{n}f_j\right)\left(\sum_{i=1}^{nME}P_{ME(i)}\cdot C_{FME(i)}\cdot SFC_{ME(i)}\right)+\left(P_{AE}\cdot C_{FAE}\cdot SFC_{AE}*\right)+\left(\left(\prod_{j=1}^{n}f_j\cdot\sum_{i=1}^{nPTI}P_{PTI(i)}-\sum_{i=1}^{neff}f_{eff(i)}\cdot P_{AEeff(i)}\right)C_{FAE}\cdot SFC_{AE}\right)-\left(\sum_{i=1}^{neff}f_{eff(i)}\cdot P_{eff(i)}\cdot C_{FME}\cdot SFC_{ME}**\right)}{f_i\cdot f_c\cdot f_l\cdot Capacity\cdot f_w\cdot V_{ref}\cdot f_m}$$

* 如果正常最大海上负荷部分由轴带发电机提供，对于那部分功率，可使用 SFC_{ME} 和 C_{FME} 取代 SFC_{AE} 和 C_{FAE}。

** 如果 $P_{PTI(i)}>0$，（$SFC_{ME}\cdot C_{FME}$）和（$SFC_{AE}\cdot C_{FAE}$）的平均加权值应用于计算 P_{eff}。

注：本公式可能不适用于具有柴油—电力推进、涡轮推进或混合推进系统的船舶，但豪华邮轮和 LNG 运输船除外。

2.2 参数

使用第 2.1 段中的公式计算 EEDI 时，下列参数适用。

2.2.1 C_F；燃油消耗量和 CO_2 排放量之间的转换系数

C_F 系指无量纲转换系数，其基于含碳量将燃油消耗量（单位 g）转换为 CO_2 排放量（单位也为 g）。下标 $ME(i)$ 和 $AE(i)$ 分别代表主机和辅机。C_F 对应于在确定《NO_x 技术规则》第 1.3.15 段中定义的技术案卷中包括的适用试验报告（以下简称 NO_x 技术案卷中包括的试验报告）中所列的 SFC 时所使用的燃料。C_F 值如下：

燃料类型	参照	低热值（kJ/kg）	碳含量	C_F(t–CO_2/t– 燃油)
1 柴油 / 汽油	ISO 8217 DMX 级至 DMB 级	42 700	0.874 4	3.206
2 轻燃油（LFO）	ISO 8217 RMA 级至 RMD 级	41 200	0.859 4	3.151
3 重燃油（HFO）	ISO 8217 RME 级至 RMK 级	40 200	0.849 3	3.114
4 液化石油气（LPG）	丙烷	46 300	0.818 2	3.000
	丁烷	45 700	0.826 4	3.030
5 乙烷		46 400	0.798 9	2.927

Type of fuel	Reference	Lower calorific value (kJ/kg)	Carbon content	C_F (t-CO$_2$/t-Fuel)
6 Liquefied Natural Gas (LNG)		48,000	0.7500	2.750
7 Methanol		19,900	0.3750	1.375
8 Ethanol		26,800	0.5217	1.913

In the case of a ship equipped with a dual-fuel main or auxiliary engine, the C_F factor for gas fuel and the C_F factor for fuel oil should apply and be multiplied with the specific fuel oil consumption of each fuel at the relevant EEDI load point. Meanwhile, it should be identified whether gas fuel is regarded as the "primary fuel" in accordance with the formula below:

$$f_{DFgas} = \frac{\sum\limits_{i=1}^{ntotal} P_{total(i)}}{\sum\limits_{i=1}^{ngasfuel} P_{gasfuel(i)}} \times \frac{V_{gas} \times \rho_{gas} \times LCV_{gas} \times K_{gas}}{\left(\sum\limits_{i=1}^{nLiquid} V_{liquid(i)} \times \rho_{liquid(i)} \times LCV_{liquid(i)} \times K_{liquid(i)} \right) + V_{gas} \times \rho_{gas} \times LCV_{gas} \times K_{gas}}$$

$f_{DFliquid} = 1 - f_{DFgas}$

where,

f_{DFgas} is the fuel availability ratio of gas fuel corrected for the power ratio of gas engines to total engines; f_{DFgas} should not be greater than 1;

V_{gas} is the total net gas fuel capacity on board in m^3. If other arrangements, like exchangeable (specialized) LNG tank-containers and/or arrangements allowing frequent gas refuelling are used, the capacity of the whole LNG fuelling system should be used for V_{gas}. The boil-off rate (BOR) of gas cargo tanks can be calculated and included in V_{gas} if it is connected to the fuel gas supply system (FGSS);

V_{liquid} is the total net liquid fuel capacity on board in m^3 of liquid fuel tanks permanently connected to the ship's fuel system. If one fuel tank is disconnected by permanent sealing valves, V_{liquid} of the fuel tank can be ignored;

ρ_{gas} is the density of gas fuel in kg/m^3;

ρ_{liquid} is the density of each liquid fuel in kg/m^3;

LCV_{gas} is the low calorific value of gas fuel in kJ/kg;

LCV_{liquid} is the low calorific value of liquid fuel in kJ/kg;

K_{gas} is the filling rate for gas fuel tanks;

K_{liquid} is the filling rate for liquid fuel tanks;

P_{total} is the total installed engine power, P_{ME} and P_{AE} in kW;

$P_{gasfuel}$ is the dual-fuel engine installed power, P_{ME} and P_{AE} in kW;

> .1 If the total gas fuel capacity is at least 50% of the fuel capacity dedicated to the dual-fuel engines , namely $f_{DFgas} \geq 0.5$, then gas fuel is regarded as the "Primary fuel," and $f_{DFgas} = 1$ and $f_{DFliquid} = 0$ for each dual-fuel engine.

燃料类型	参照	低热值（kJ/kg）	碳含量	CF（t–CO$_2$/t– 燃油）
6 液化天然气（LNG）		48 000	0.750 0	2.750
7 甲醇		19 900	0.375 0	1.375
8 乙醇		26 800	0.521 7	1.913

如船舶设有双燃料主机或辅机，针对气体燃料的 C_F 系数和针对燃油的 C_F 系数应适用，并应在相关的 EEDI 负荷点乘上每一燃料的单位燃油消耗量。同时，应按下式确定气体燃料是否应被视为"主要燃料"：

$$f_{DFgas} = \frac{\sum_{i=1}^{ntotal} P_{total(i)}}{\sum_{i=1}^{ngasfuel} P_{gasfuel(i)}} \times \frac{V_{gas} \times \rho_{gas} \times LCV_{gas} \times K_{gas}}{\left(\sum_{i=1}^{nLiquid} V_{liquid(i)} \times \rho_{liquid(i)} \times LCV_{liquid(i)} \times K_{liquid(i)}\right) + V_{gas} \times \rho_{gas} \times LCV_{gas} \times K_{gas}}$$

$$f_{DFliquid} = 1 - f_{DFgas}$$

式中：

f_{DFgas} 系指为燃气发动机与总发动机的功率比修正的气体燃料的燃料可获得性，f_{DFgas} 应不大于 1；

V_{gas} 系指船上总净气体燃料容积，m^3。如使用其他布置，例如可更换（专用）LNG 罐和 / 或允许频繁重新注入燃气的布置，V_{gas} 应使用整个 LNG 注入系统的容积。如果气体货物舱与燃气供应系统（FGSS）相连，可计算气体货物舱的蒸发率（BOR），并将其计入 V_{gas}；

V_{liquid} 系指船上与船舶燃料系统固定连接的液体燃料舱的总净液体燃料容积，m^3。如果一个燃料舱通过固定密封阀断开连接，可忽略该燃料舱的 V_{liquid}；

ρ_{gas} 系指气体燃料的密度，kg/m^3；

ρ_{liquid} 系指每种液体燃料的密度，kg/m^3；

LCV_{gas} 系指气体燃料的低热值，kJ/kg；

LCV_{liquid} 系指液体燃料的低热值，kJ/kg；

K_{gas} 系指气体燃料舱的充装率；

K_{liquid} 系指液体燃料舱的充装率；

P_{total} 系指发动机总安装功率，P_{ME} 和 P_{AE}，kW；

$P_{gasfuel}$ 系指双燃料发动机的安装功率，P_{ME} 和 P_{AE}，kW；

.1 如果总气体燃料容积至少是双燃料发动机专用燃料容积的 50%，即 $f_{DFgas} \geqslant 0.5$，则视气体燃料为"主要燃料"，并且对于每个双燃料发动机 $f_{DFgas}=1$，$f_{DFliquid}=0$。

.2　　　　If f_{DFgas} < 0.5, gas fuel is not regarded as the "primary fuel." The C_F and SFC in the EEDI calculation for each dual-fuel engine (both main and auxiliary engines) should be calculated as the weighted average of C_F and SFC for liquid and gas mode, according to f_{DFgas} and $f_{DFliquid}$, such as the original item of $P_{ME(i)} \cdot C_{FME(i)} \cdot SFC_{ME(i)}$ in the EEDI calculation is to be replaced by the formula below.

$$P_{ME(i)} \cdot \left(f_{DFgas(i)} \cdot \left(C_{FME \text{ pilot fuel}(i)} \cdot SFC_{ME \text{ pilot fuel}(i)} + C_{FME \text{ gas}(i)} \cdot SFC_{ME \text{ gas}(i)}\right) + f_{DFliquid(i)} \cdot C_{FME \text{ liquid}(i)} \cdot SFC_{ME \text{ liquid}(i)}\right)$$

2.2.2　V_{ref} ; Ship speed

V_{ref} is the ship speed, measured in nautical miles per hour (knot), on deep water in the condition corresponding to the *capacity* as defined in paragraphs 2.2.3.1 and 2.2.3.3 (in the case of passenger ships and cruise passenger ships, this condition should be summer load draught as provided in paragraph 2.2.4) at the shaft power of the engine(s) as defined in paragraph 2.2.5 and assuming the weather is calm with no wind and no waves.

2.2.3　*Capacity*

Capacity is defined as follows.

2.2.3.1　For bulk carriers, tankers, gas carriers, LNG carriers, ro-ro cargo ships (vehicle carriers), ro-ro cargo ships, ro-ro passenger ships, general cargo ships, refrigerated cargo carrier and combination carriers, deadweight should be used as *capacity*.

2.2.3.2　For passenger ships and cruise passenger ships, gross tonnage in accordance with the International Convention of Tonnage Measurement of Ships 1969, annex I, regulation 3, should be used as *capacity*.

2.2.3.3　For containerships, 70% of the deadweight (DWT) should be used as *capacity*. EEDI values for containerships are calculated as follows:

.1　　　　attained EEDI is calculated in accordance with the EEDI formula using 70% deadweight for *capacity*;

.2　　　　estimated index value in the Guidelines for calculation of the reference line is calculated using 70% deadweight as:

$$Estimated \ Index \ Value = 3.1144 \cdot \frac{190 \cdot \sum_{i=1}^{NME} P_{MEi} + 215 \cdot P_{AE}}{70\% \text{DWT} \cdot V_{ref}}$$

.3　　　　parameters a and c for containerships in table 2 of regulation 24 of MARPOL Annex VI are determined by plotting the estimated index value against 100% deadweight, i.e. a = 174.22 and c = 0.201 were determined;

.4　　　　required EEDI for a new containership is calculated using 100% deadweight as:

Required EEDI = (1-X/100) $\cdot$ a $\cdot$ 100% deadweight $^{-c}$

where X is the reduction factor (in percentage) in accordance with table 1 in regulation 24 of MARPOL Annex VI relating to the applicable phase and size of new containership.

.2 如果 $f_{DFgas}<0.5$，则气体燃料不是"主要燃料"。对于每个双燃料发动机（主机和辅机）EEDI 计算中的 C_F 和 SFC 应根据 f_{DFgas} 和 $f_{DFliquid}$ 作为液体和气体模式 C_F 和 SFC 的加权平均数计算，例如 EEDI 计算中的 $P_{ME(i)} \cdot C_{FME(i)} \cdot SFC_{ME(i)}$ 应由下式替代。

$$P_{ME(i)} \cdot (f_{DFgas(i)} \cdot (C_{FME\ pilot\ fuel(i)} \cdot SFC_{ME\ pilot\ fuel(i)} + C_{FME\ gas(i)} \cdot SFC_{ME\ gas(i)}) + f_{DFliquid(i)} \cdot C_{FME\ liquid(i)} \cdot SFC_{ME\ liquid(i)})$$

2.2.2　V_{ref}；航速

V_{ref} 系指船舶航速，单位为海里/小时（节）。该船速是在假定无风无浪的平静气象条件下，在第 2.2.5 段中定义的发动机的轴功率以及第 2.2.3.1 和 2.2.3.3 段中定义的载运能力所对应工况（对于客船和豪华邮轮，该工况应为第 2.2.4 段中所述的夏季载重吃水）下在深水中的航速。

2.2.3　载运能力

载运能力定义为：

2.2.3.1　对于散货船、液货船、气体运输船、LNG 运输船、滚装货船（车辆运输船）、滚装货船、客滚船、杂货船、冷藏货物运输船和兼用船，载重吨应用作载运能力。

2.2.3.2　对于客船和豪华邮轮，《1969 年国际吨位丈量公约》附则 I 第 3 条所述总吨应用作载运能力。

2.2.3.3　对于集装箱船，载重吨（DWT）的 70% 应用作载运能力。集装箱船的 EEDI 值计算如下：

.1　达到的 EEDI 按照 EEDI 公式计算，将 70% 的载重吨用作载运能力进行计算。

.2　本导则中用于计算基准线的估计指数值使用 70% 的载重吨计算如下：

$$Estimated\ Index\ Value = 3.1144 \cdot \frac{190 \cdot \sum_{i=1}^{NME} P_{MEi} + 215 \cdot P_{AE}}{70\%DWT \cdot V_{ref}}$$

.3　《防污公约》附则 Ⅵ 第 24 条的表 2 中对集装箱船的参数 a 和 c 通过按 100% 载重吨标出估计指数值来确定，即确定 a=174.22 和 c=0.201。

.4　新集装箱船的要求的 EEDI 使用 100% 载重吨计算如下：
要求的 EEDI=（1–X/100）· a · 100% 载重吨 $^{-c}$

式中 X 是按《防污公约》附则 Ⅵ 第 24 条表 1 中有关新集装箱船适用阶段和尺度确定的折减系数（百分比）。

2.2.4　*Deadweight*

Deadweight means the difference in tonnes between the displacement of a ship in water of relative density of 1,025 kg/m^3 at the summer load draught and the lightweight of the ship. The summer load draught should be taken as the maximum summer draught as certified in the stability booklet approved by the Administration or an organization recognized by it.

2.2.5　*P ;* Power of main and auxiliary engines

P is the power of the main and auxiliary engines, measured in kW. The subscripts $ME(i)$ and $AE(i)$ refer to the main and auxiliary engine(s), respectively. The summation on *i* is for all engines with the number of engines (nME) (see diagram in appendix 1).

2.2.5.1　$P_{ME(i)}$; Power of main engines

$P_{ME(i)}$ is 75% of the rated installed power (MCR[1]) for each main engine (*i*).

For LNG carriers having diesel electric propulsion system, $P_{ME(i)}$ should be calculated by the following formula:

$$P_{ME(i)} = 0.83 \times \frac{MPP_{Motor(i)}}{\eta_{(i)}}$$

Where:

$MPP_{Motor(i)}$ is the rated output of motor specified in the certified document.

$\eta_{(i)}$ is to be taken as the product of electrical efficiency of generator, transformer, converter and motor, taking into consideration the weighted average as necessary.

The electrical efficiency, $\eta_{(i)}$, should be taken as 91.3% for the purpose of calculating attained EEDI. Alternatively, if the value more than 91.3% is to be applied, the $\eta_{(i)}$ should be obtained by measurement and verified by method approved by the verifier.

For LNG carriers having steam turbine propulsion systems, $P_{ME(i)}$ is 83% of the rated installed power ($MCR_{SteamTurbine}$) for each steam turbine$_{(i)}$.

The influence of additional shaft power take off or shaft power take in is defined in the following paragraphs.

2.2.5.2　$P_{PTO(i)}$; Shaft generator

Where shaft generators are installed, $P_{PTO(i)}$ is 75% of the rated electrical output power of each shaft generator. In the case of shaft generators installed with a steam turbine, $P_{PTO(i)}$ is 83% of the rated electrical output power and the factor of 0.75 should be replaced by 0.83.

For calculating the effect of shaft generators, two options are available:

---

[1]　　The value of MCR specified on the EIAPP certificate should be used for calculation. If the main engines are not required to have an EIAPP certificate, the MCR on the nameplate should be used.

2.2.4 载重吨

载重吨系指在比重为 1 025 kg/m³ 的水中夏季载重吃水时的船舶排水量与船舶空船重量之间的吨位差。夏季载重吃水应取由主管机关或经主管机关认可的组织批准的稳性手册核定的最大夏季吃水。

2.2.5 P；主机和辅机的功率

P 系指主机和辅机的功率（单位 kW）。下标 $ME(i)$ 和 $AE(i)$ 分别代表主机和辅机。i 的总和代表发动机数量（nME）（见附录 1 中的图表。）

2.2.5.1 $P_{ME(i)}$；主机功率

$P_{ME(i)}$ 系指每台主机（i）的额定装机功率（MCR[1]）的 75%。

对于具有柴油电力推进系统的 LNG 运输船，应按下式计算 $P_{ME(i)}$：

$$P_{ME(i)} = 0.83 \times \frac{MPP_{Motor(i)}}{\eta_{(i)}}$$

式中：

$MPP_{Motor(i)}$ 系指核准文件中规定的马达额定输出功率。

$\eta(i)$ 应取发电机、变压器、变换器和马达的电效率的乘积，且如必要，考虑进行加权平均。

为计算达到的 EEDI，电效率 $\eta(i)$ 应取 91.3%。如果拟采用的值大于 91.3%，则应 $\eta(i)$ 通过测量获得，并应采用验证方批准的方法进行验证。

对于设有蒸汽涡轮推进系统的 LNG 运输船，$P_{ME(i)}$ 为每一蒸汽涡轮 (i) 额定安装功率（$MCR_{SteamTurbine}$）的 83%。

附加轴功率增减的影响在下列段落中予以规定。

2.2.5.2 $P_{PTO(i)}$；轴带发电机

如果安装轴带发电机，$P_{PTO(i)}$ 为每个轴带发电机额定电输出功率的 75%。如果该轴带发电机安装于蒸汽涡轮上，$P_{PTO(i)}$ 为额定电输出功率的 83%，且系数 0.75 应变更为 0.83。

对于轴带发电机影响计算，有 2 种选择：

---

[1] 应将 EIAPP 证书上规定的 MCR 值用于计算。如果不要求主机具有 EIAPP 证书，应使用铭牌上的 MCR。

Option 1:

The maximum allowable $P_{PTO(i)}$ deduction should be no more than $P_{AE}/0.75$ with P_{AE} as defined in paragraph 2.2.5.6. For this case, $\Sigma\, P_{ME(i)}$ is calculated as:

$$\sum_{i=1}^{nME} PME_{(i)}=0.75\times\sum MCR_{ME(i)}-0.75\times\sum P_{PTO(i)}. \quad with \sum P_{PTO(i)} \leq \frac{P_{AE}}{0.75}$$

or

Option 2:

Where an engine is installed with a higher rated power output than that which the propulsion system is limited to by verified technical means, then the value of $\Sigma\, P_{ME(i)}$ is 75% of that limited power for determining the reference speed, V_{ref} and for EEDI calculation. The following figure gives guidance for determination of $\Sigma\, P_{ME(i)}$:

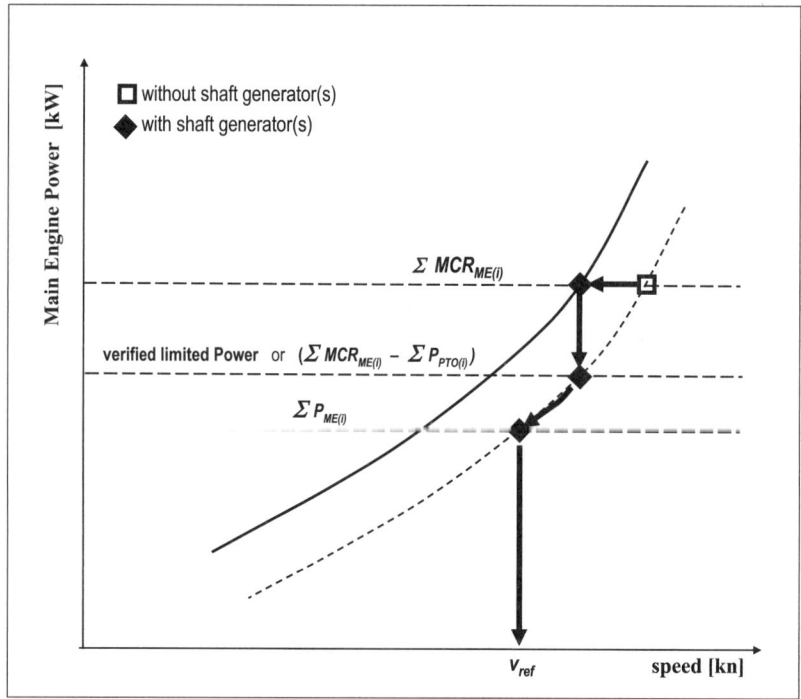

2.2.5.3 $P_{PTI(i)}$; Shaft motor

Where shaft motors are installed, $P_{PTI(i)}$ is 75% of the rated power consumption of each shaft motor divided by the weighted average efficiency of the generator(s), as follows:

$$\sum P_{PTI(i)} = \frac{\sum\left(0.75 \cdot P_{SM,\max(i)}\right)}{\eta_{\overline{Gen}}}$$

Where:

$P_{SM,\max(i)}$ is the rated power consumption of each shaft motor

$\eta_{\overline{Gen}}$ is the weighted average efficiency of the generator(s)

选择 1：

最大允许 $P_{PTO(i)}$ 减额应不大于 $P_{AE}/0.75$，P_{AE} 如 2.2.5.6 中定义。在此情况下，$\Sigma P_{ME(i)}$ 按下列公式计算：

$$\sum_{i=1}^{nME} PME_{(i)} = 0.75 \times \sum MCR_{ME(i)} - 0.75 \times \sum P_{PTO(i)}. \quad with \sum P_{PTO(i)} \leqslant \frac{P_{AE}}{0.75}$$

或

选择 2：

如果安装的发动机额定输出功率大于推进系统通过经验证的技术方法限定的功率，则 $\Sigma P_{ME(i)}$ 值为用于确定基准航速 V_{ref} 和 EEDI 计算的限定功率的 75%。下图为 $\Sigma P_{ME(i)}$ 的确定提供指导：

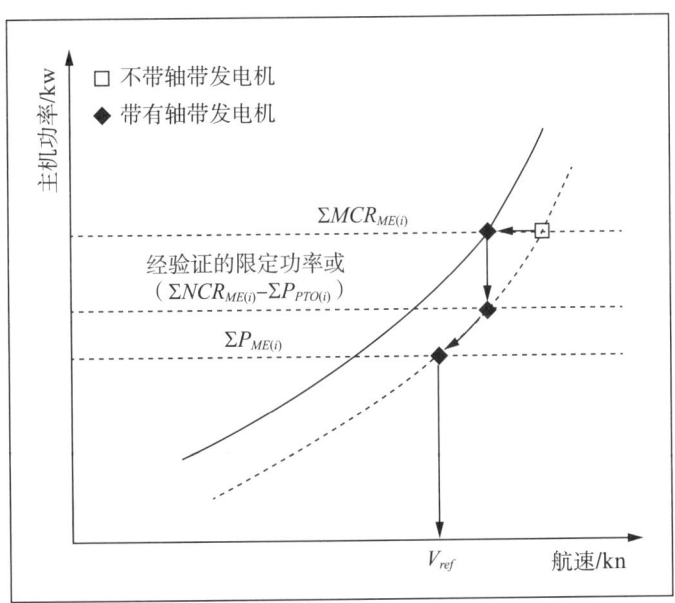

2.2.5.3 $P_{PTI(i)}$；轴马达

如果设有轴马达，$P_{PTI(i)}$ 系指每台轴马达的额定功率消耗的 75% 除以发电机的加权平均效率，如下所示：

$$\sum P_{PTI(i)} = \frac{\sum \left(0.75 \cdot P_{SM,\max(i)} \right)}{\eta_{\overline{Gen}}}$$

式中：
$P_{SM,max(i)}$ 系指每台轴马达的额定功率消耗
$\eta_{\overline{Gen}}$ 系指发电机的加权平均效率

Where shaft motors are installed with a steam turbine, $P_{PTI(i)}$ is 83% of the rated power consumption and the factor of 0.75 should be replaced to 0.83.

The propulsion power at which V_{ref} is measured, is:

$$\sum P_{ME(i)} + \sum P_{PTI(i),Shaft}$$

Where:

$$\sum P_{PTI(i),Shaft} = \sum \left(0.75 \cdot P_{SM,max(i)} \cdot \eta_{PTI(i)}\right)$$

$\eta_{PTI(i)}$ is the efficiency of each shaft motor installed

Where the total propulsion power as defined above is higher than 75% of the power the propulsion system is limited to by verified technical means, then 75% of the limited power is to be used as the total propulsion power for determining the reference speed, V_{ref} and for EEDI calculation.

In the case of combined PTI/PTO, the normal operational mode at sea will determine which of these is to be used in the calculation.

Note: The shaft motor's chain efficiency may be taken into consideration to account for the energy losses in the equipment from the switchboard to the shaft motor, if the chain efficiency of the shaft motor is given in a verified document.

2.2.5.4 $P_{eff(i)}$; Innovative mechanical energy-efficient technology for main engine

$P_{eff(i)}$ is the output of the innovative mechanical energy-efficient technology for propulsion at 75% main engine power.

Mechanical recovered waste energy directly coupled to shafts need not be measured, since the effect of the technology is directly reflected in the V_{ref}.

In the case of a ship equipped with a number of engines, the C_F and SFC should be the power-weighted average of all the main engines.

In the case of a ship equipped with dual-fuel engine(s), the C_F and SFC should be calculated in accordance with paragraphs 2.2.1 and 2.2.7.

2.2.5.5 P_{AEeff} ; Innovative mechanical energy-efficient technology for auxiliary engine

$P_{AEeff(i)}$ is the auxiliary power reduction due to innovative electrical energy-efficient technology measured at $P_{ME(i)}$.

2.2.5.6 P_{AE} ; Auxiliary engine power

P_{AE} is the required auxiliary engine power to supply normal maximum sea load including necessary power for propulsion machinery/systems and accommodation, e.g. main engine pumps, navigational systems and equipment and living on board, but excluding the power not for propulsion machinery/systems, e.g. thrusters, cargo pumps, cargo gear, ballast pumps, maintaining cargo, e.g. reefers and cargo hold fans, in the condition where the ship engaged in voyage at the speed (V_{ref}) under the condition as mentioned in paragraph 2.2.2.

如果轴马达安装于蒸汽涡轮上，$P_{PTI(i)}$ 为额定输出功率的 83%，且系数 0.75 应变更为 0.83。

测量 V_{ref} 时的推进功率为：

$$\sum P_{ME(i)} + \sum P_{PTI(i),Shaft}$$

式中：

$$\sum P_{PTI(i),Shaft} = \sum \left(0.75 \cdot P_{SM,\max(i)} \cdot \eta_{PTI(i)}\right)$$

$\eta_{PTI(i)}$ 系指安装的每台轴马达的效率

如果上述定义的总推进功率大于推进系统通过经验证的技术方法限定的功率的 75%，则应用所限定功率的 75% 作为总推进功率用于确定基准航速 V_{ref} 和 EEDI 计算。

如果兼用 PTI/PTO，应根据船舶在海上的常规营运模式来确定在计算中使用其中哪个参数。

注： 如果在经验证的文件中给出轴马达系统链效率，可考虑用轴马达系统链效率来代表从配电板至轴马达的设备能量损失。

2.2.5.4　$P_{eff(i)}$；主机创新机械能效技术

$P_{eff(i)}$ 系指在主机功率的 75% 状态下用于推进的创新机械能效技术的输出。

无须测量直接与轴相连的机械回收废能，因为 V_{ref} 直接体现该技术的影响。

如船舶装有若干发动机，C_F 和 SFC 应为所有主机的功率加权平均值。

如船舶装有双燃料发动机，应按第 2.2.1 和 2.2.7 段计算 C_F 和 SFC。

2.2.5.5　P_{AEeff}；辅机创新机械能效技术

$P_{AEeff(i)}$ 系指在 $P_{ME(i)}$ 状态下测得的因采用创新的电能效技术而减少的辅机功率。

2.2.5.6　P_{AE}；辅机功率

P_{AE} 系指船舶在第 2.2.2 段所述工况下以 V_{ref} 航速航行时所要求的提供正常最大海况下的辅机功率，包括推进机械／系统和船上生活（例如主机泵、导航系统和设备及船上起居）所需的功率，但不包括不用于推进机械／系统（例如推力器、货泵、起货设备、压载泵、货物维护用的冰箱和货舱风机等）的功率。

2.2.5.6.1 For ships whose total propulsion power ($\sum MCR_{ME(i)} + \dfrac{\sum P_{PTI(i)}}{0.75}$) is 10,000 kW or above, P_{AE} is defined as:

$$P_{AE\,(\Sigma MCR_{ME}(i) \geq 10,000\,kW)} = \left(0.025 \times \left(\sum_{i=1}^{nME} MCR_{ME(i)} + \frac{\sum_{i=1}^{nPTI} P_{PTI(i)}}{0.75} \right) \right) + 250$$

2.2.5.6.2 For ships whose total propulsion power ($\sum MCR_{ME(i)} + \dfrac{\sum P_{PTI(i)}}{0.75}$) is below 10,000 kW, P_{AE} is defined as:

$$P_{AE\,(\Sigma MCR_{ME}(i) < 10,000\,kW)} = \left(0.05 \times \left(\sum_{i=1}^{nME} MCR_{ME(i)} + \frac{\sum_{i=1}^{nPTI} P_{PTI(i)}}{0.75} \right) \right)$$

2.2.5.6.3 For LNG carriers with a reliquefaction system or compressor(s), designed to be used in normal operation and essential for maintaining the LNG cargo tank pressure below the maximum allowable relief valve setting of a cargo tank in normal operation, the following terms should be added to above P_{AE} formula in accordance with 2.2.5.6.3.1, 2.2.5.6.3.2 or 2.2.5.6.3.3 as below:

.1   For ships having reliquefaction system:

$$+ CargoTankCapacity_{LNG} \times BOR \times COP_{reliquefy} \times R_{reliquefy}$$

Where:

$CargoTankCapacity_{LNG}$ is the LNG Cargo Tank Capacity in m³.

BOR is the design rate of boil-off gas of entire ship per day, which is specified in the specification of the building contract.

$COP_{reliquefy}$ is the coefficient of design power performance for reliquefying boil-off gas per unit volume, as follows:

$$COP_{reliquefy} = \frac{425\,(kg/m^3) \times 511\,(kJ/kg)}{24\,(h) \times 3\,600\,(sec) \times COP_{cooling}}$$

$COP_{cooling}$ is the coefficient of design performance of reliquefaction and 0.166 should be used. Another value calculated by the manufacturer and verified by the Administration or an organization recognized by the Administration may be used.

2.2.5.6.1 对于总推进功率（$\sum MCR_{ME(i)} + \dfrac{\sum P_{PTI(i)}}{0.75}$）为 10 000 kW 或以上的船舶，$P_{AE}$ 定义为

$$P_{AE\,\left(\Sigma MCR_{ME(i)} \geq 10,000\,kW\right)} = \left(0.025 \times \left(\sum_{i=1}^{nME} MCR_{ME(i)} + \frac{\displaystyle\sum_{i=1}^{nPTI} P_{PTI(i)}}{0.75} \right) \right) + 250$$

2.2.5.6.2 对于总推进功率（$\sum MCR_{ME(i)} + \dfrac{\sum P_{PTI(i)}}{0.75}$）小于 10 000 kW 的船舶，$P_{AE}$ 定义为

$$P_{AE\,\left(\Sigma MCR_{ME(i)} < 10,000\,kW\right)} = \left(0.05 \times \left(\sum_{i=1}^{nME} MCR_{ME(i)} + \frac{\displaystyle\sum_{i=1}^{nPTI} P_{PTI(i)}}{0.75} \right) \right)$$

2.2.5.6.3 对于具有再液化系统或压缩机的 LNG 运输船，该再液化系统或压缩机设计用于正常营运，并对保持 LNG 货舱压力低于正常营运时液货舱释放阀最大调定压力至关重要，则应按下列第 2.2.5.6.3.1、2.2.5.6.3.2 或 2.2.5.6.3.3 段对上述 P_{AE} 公式添加以下参数：

.1 对于具有再液化系统的船舶：

$$+CargoTankCapacity_{LNG} \times BOR \times COP_{reliquefy} \times R_{reliquefy}$$

式中：

$CargoTankCapacity_{LNG}$ 系指 LNG 货舱舱容，单位为 m^3；

BOR 系指每天整船蒸发气体的设计蒸发率，见建造合同中规格书的规定；

$COP_{reliquefy}$ 系指再液化每单位容积蒸发气体的设计功率性能系数，如下所示：

$$COP_{reliquefy} = \frac{425(kg/m^3) \times 511(kJ/kg)}{24(h) \times 3\,600(sec) \times COP_{cooling}}$$

$COP_{cooling}$ 系指再液化设计性能系数，应取 0.166，也可使用由制造商计算并经主管机关或经主管机关认可的组织验证的其他值；

$R_{reliquefy}$ is the ratio of boil-off gas (BOG) to be reliquefied to entire BOG, calculated as follows:

$$R_{reliquefy} = \frac{BOG_{reliquefy}}{BOG_{total}}$$

.2 For LNG carriers with direct diesel driven propulsion system or diesel electric propulsion system, having compressor(s) which are used for supplying high-pressured gas derived from boil-off gas to the installed engines (typically intended for 2-stroke dual-fuel engines):

$$+ COP_{comp} \times \sum_{i=1}^{nME} SFC_{ME(i),gasmode} \times \frac{P_{ME(i)}}{1000}$$

Where:

COP_{comp} is the design power performance of compressor and 0.33 (kWh/kg) should be used. Another value calculated by the manufacturer and verified by the Administration or an organization recognized by the Administration may be used.

.3 For LNG carriers with direct diesel driven propulsion system or diesel electric propulsion system, having compressor(s) which are used for supplying low-pressured gas derived from boil-off gas to the installed engines (typically intended for 4-stroke dual-fuel engines):

$$+ 0.02 \times \sum_{i=1}^{nME} P_{ME(i)}{}^2$$

2.2.5.6.4 For LNG carriers having diesel electric propulsion system, $MPP_{Motor(i)}$ should be used instead of $MCR_{ME(i)}$ for P_{AE} calculation.

2.2.5.6.5 For LNG carriers having a steam turbine propulsion system and whose electric power is primarily supplied by turbine generator closely integrated into the steam and feed water systems, P_{AE} may be treated as 0(zero) instead of taking into account electric load in calculating $SFC_{SteamTurbine}$.

2.2.5.7 Use of electric power table

For ships where the P_{AE} value calculated by paragraphs 2.2.5.6.1 to 2.2.5.6.3 is significantly different from the total power used at normal seagoing, e.g. in cases of passenger ships (see NOTE under the formula of EEDI), the P_{AE} value should be estimated by the consumed electric power (excluding propulsion) in conditions when the ship is engaged in a voyage at reference speed (V_{ref}) as given in the electric power table,[3] divided by the average efficiency of the generator(s) weighted by power (see appendix 2).

---

[2]   With regard to the factor of 0.02, it is assumed that the additional energy needed to compress BOG for supplying to a 4-stroke dual fuel engine is approximately equal to 2% of P_{ME}, compared to the energy needed to compress BOG for supplying to a steam turbine.

[3]   The electric power table should be examined and validated by the verifier. Where ambient conditions affect any electrical load in the power table, such as that for heating ventilation and air conditioning systems, the contractual ambient conditions leading to the maximum design electrical load of the installed system for the ship in general should apply.

$R_{reliquefy}$ 系指拟再液化的蒸发气体（BOG）与所有蒸发气体之比，按下式计算：

$$R_{reliquefy} = \frac{BOG_{reliquefy}}{BOG_{total}}$$

    .2   对于有直接柴油驱动推进系统或柴油电力推进系统的 LNG 运输船，该船具有一个或多个压缩机，用于向安装的发动机输送蒸发气体所产生的高压气体（通常用于 2 冲程双燃料发动机）：

$$+ COP_{comp} \times \sum_{i=1}^{nME} SFC_{ME(i),gasmode} \times \frac{P_{ME(i)}}{1\,000}$$

式中：

COP_{comp} 系指压缩机的设计功率性能，应取 0.33（kWh/kg）。也可使用由制造商计算并经主管机关或经主管机关认可的组织验证的其他值。

    .3   对于具有直接柴油驱动推进系统或柴油电力推进系统的 LNG 运输船，该船具有一个或多个压缩机，用于向安装的发动机输送蒸发气体所产生的低压气体（通常用于 4 冲程双燃料发动机）：

$$+ 0.02 \times \sum_{i=1}^{nME} P_{ME(i)}{}^2$$

2.2.5.6.4   对于具有柴油电力推进系统的 LNG 运输船，计算 P_{AE} 时应采用 $MPP_{Motor(i)}$ 替代 $M_{CRME(i)}$。

2.2.5.6.5   对于具有蒸汽涡轮推进系统的 LNG 运输船，其电力主要由与蒸汽和给水系统紧密相连的涡轮发电机供应，P_{AE} 可取 0（零），在计算 $SFC_{SteamTurbine}$ 时无须计及电力负荷。

2.2.5.7　电功率表的使用

    如果船舶（例如客船）按第 2.2.5.6.1 至 2.2.5.6.3 段计算所得的 P_{AE} 值与正常航行时所使用的总功率相差很大（参见 EEDI 公式下的注），P_{AE} 值应通过船舶以电力负荷表[3] 中给出的基准航速（V_{ref}）航行时所消耗的电功率（不包括推进功率）除以功率加权的发电机平均效率进行估算（参见附录 2）。

---

[2] 0.02 这一系数是假定：与压缩蒸发气体以供给蒸汽涡轮所需的能量相比，压缩蒸发气体以供给 4 冲程双燃料发动机所需的额外能量约等于 2%P_{ME}。

[3] 电力负荷表应经验证方检查和认证。如果环境条件影响电力负荷表中的任何电力负荷（如：供暖通风和空调系统），一般应使用合同中规定的导致船上安装系统的最大设计电力负荷的环境条件。

2.2.6　Consistency of parameters V_{ref}, *Capacity* and *P*

V_{ref}, *Capacity* and *P* should be consistent with each other. As for LNG carries having diesel electric or steam turbine propulsion systems, V_{ref} is the relevant speed at 83% of MPP_{Motor} or $MCR_{SteamTubine}$ respectively.

2.2.7　*SFC;* Certified specific fuel consumption

SFC is the certified specific fuel consumption, measured in g/kWh, of the engines or steam turbines.

2.2.7.1　*SFC* for main and auxiliary engines

The subscripts $_{ME(i)}$ and $_{AE(i)}$ refer to the main and auxiliary engine(s), respectively. For engines certified to the E2 or E3 test cycles of the NO_x Technical Code 2008, the engine specific fuel consumption ($SFC_{ME(i)}$) is that recorded in the test report included in a NO_x Technical File for the engine(s) at 75% of MCR power of its torque rating. For engines certified to the D2 or C1 test cycles of the NO_x Technical Code 2008, the engine specific fuel consumption ($SFC_{AE(i)}$) is that recorded on the test report included in a NO_x Technical File at the engine(s) 50% of MCR power or torque rating. If gas fuel is used as primary fuel in accordance with paragraph 4.2.3 of the *Guidelines on survey and certification of the Energy Efficiency Design Index (EEDI)*, *SFC* in gas mode should be used. Where installed engines have no approved NO_x Technical File tested in gas mode, the *SFC* of gas mode should be submitted by the manufacturer and confirmed by the verifier.

The *SFC* should be corrected to the value corresponding to the ISO standard reference conditions using the standard lower calorific value of the fuel oil (42,700kJ/kg), referring to ISO 15550:2002 and ISO 3046-1:2002.

For ships where the P_{AE} value calculated by paragraphs 2.2.5.6.1 to 2.2.5.6.3 is significantly different from the total power used at normal seagoing, e.g. conventional passenger ships, the specific fuel consumption (SFC_{AE}) of the auxiliary generators is that recorded in the test report included in a NO_x Technical File for the engine(s) at 75% of MCR power of its torque rating.

SFC_{AE} is the power-weighted average among $SFC_{AE(i)}$ of the respective engines *i*.

For those engines which do not have a test report included in a NO_x Technical File because their power is below 130 kW, the *SFC* specified by the manufacturer and endorsed by a competent authority should be used.

At the design stage, in case of unavailability of test report in the NO_x file, the *SFC* specified by the manufacturer and endorsed by a competent authority should be used.

For LNG driven engines of which *SFC* is measured in kJ/kWh, the *SFC* value should be corrected to g/kWh using the standard lower calorific value of the LNG (48,000 kJ/kg), referring to the 2006 IPCC Guidelines.

Reference lower calorific values of additional fuels are given in the table in paragraph 2.2.1 of these Guidelines. The reference lower calorific value corresponding to the conversion factor of the respective fuel should be used for calculation.

2.2.6 参数 V_{ref}、载运能力和 P 的一致

V_{ref}、载运能力和 P 应相互一致。对于具有柴油电力或蒸汽涡轮推进系统的 LNG 运输船，V_{ref} 系指分别在 $83\%MPP_{Motor}$ 或 $MCR_{SteamTurbine}$ 时的对应速度。

2.2.7 SFC；经核定的单位燃油消耗量

SFC 系指发动机或蒸汽涡轮经核定的单位燃油消耗量（单位 g/kWh）。

2.2.7.1 主机和辅机的 SFC

下标 $_{ME(i)}$ 和 $_{AE(i)}$ 分别表示主机和辅机。对于按照《2008 年 NOx 技术规则》的 E2 或 E3 试验循环发证的发动机，发动机的单位燃油消耗量（$SFC_{ME(i)}$）是记录在 NO$_x$ 技术案卷包括的试验报告中的处于发动机 75% 的 MCR 功率或其额定扭矩时的燃油消耗量。对于按照《2008 年 NO$_x$ 技术规则》的 D2 或 C1 试验循环发证的发动机，发动机的单位燃油消耗量（$SFC_{AE(i)}$）是记录在 NOx 技术案卷包括的试验报告中的处于发动机 50% 的 MCR 功率或额定扭矩时的燃油消耗量。如果按《能效设计指数（EEDI）检验和发证导则》第 4.2.3 段所述使用气体燃料作为主要燃料，应使用气体模式下的 SFC。如安装的一个或多个发动机无经批准的按气体模式试验的 NO$_x$ 技术案卷，则气体模式下的 SFC 应由制造商提交并经验证方确认。

应使用燃油的标准低热值（42 700 kJ/kg）将 SFC 修正至 ISO 标准基准条件对应的值，参见 ISO 15550:2002 和 ISO 3046−1:2002。

如果船舶（例如常规客船）按第 2.2.5.6.1 至 2.2.5.6.3 段计算所得的 P_{AE} 值与正常航行时使用的总功率相差很大，辅助发电机的单位燃油消耗量（SFC_{AE}）是记录在 NO$_x$ 技术案卷包括的试验报告中的处于发动机的 75% 的 MCR 功率或其额定扭矩时的燃油消耗量。

SFC_{AE} 是每台发动机 i 的 $SFC_{AE(i)}$ 的功率加权平均值。

对于那些由于功率小于 130 kW 而不具有 NO$_x$ 技术案卷包括的试验报告的发动机，应使用由发动机制造商规定并经主管当局认可的 SFC 值。

在设计阶段，如无法获得 NO$_x$ 技术案卷包括的试验报告，应使用由发动机制造商规定并经主管当局认可的 SFC 值。

对于 SFC 的测量单位为 kJ/kWh 的 LNG 发动机，应使用 LNG 的标准低热值（48 000 kJ/kg）将其修正为单位为 g/kWh 的 SFC 值，参见 2006 年 IPCC 导则。

本导则第 2.2.1 段的表格中给出附加燃料的参考低热值。在计算中应使用与每种燃料转换系数相对应的参考低热值。

2.2.7.2 *SFC* for steam turbines (*SFC$_{SteamTurbine}$*)

The *SFC$_{SteamTurbine}$* should be calculated by the manufacturer and verified by the Administration or an organization recognized by the Administration as follows:

$$SFC_{SteamTurbine} = \frac{FuelConsumption}{\sum\limits_{i=1}^{nME} P_{ME(i)}}$$

Where:

.1   *Fuel consumption* is fuel consumption of boiler per hour (g/h). For ships whose electric power is primarily supplied by turbine generator closely integrated into the steam and feed water systems, not only P_{ME} but also *electric loads* corresponding to paragraph 2.2.5.6 should be taken into account.

.2   The *SFC* should be corrected to the value of LNG using the standard lower calorific value of the LNG (48,000 kJ/kg) at SNAME Condition (condition standard; air temperature 24°C, inlet temperature of fan 38°C, seawater temperature 24°C).

.3   In this correction, the difference of the boiler efficiency based on lower calorific value between test fuel and LNG should be taken into account.

2.2.8 f_j ; Ship-specific design elements

f_j is a correction factor to account for ship-specific design elements:

2.2.8.1   Power correction factor for ice-classed ships

The power correction factor, f_j, for ice-classed ships should be taken as the greater value of f_{j0} and $f_{j,min}$ as tabulated in table 1 but not greater than $f_{i,max} = 1.0$.

For further information on approximate correspondence between ice classes, see HELCOM Recommendation 25/7.[4]

Table 1: Correction factor for power f_j for ice-classed ships

Ship type	f_{j0}	$f_{j,min}$ depending on the ice class			
		IA Super	IA	IB	IC
Tanker	$\dfrac{17.444 \cdot DWT^{0.5766}}{\sum_{i=1}^{nME} MCR_{ME(i)}}$	$0.2488 \cdot DWT^{0.0903}$	$0.4541 \cdot DWT^{0.0524}$	$0.7783 \cdot DWT^{0.0145}$	$0.8741 \cdot DWT^{0.0079}$
Bulk carrier	$\dfrac{17.207 \cdot DWT^{0.5705}}{\sum_{i=1}^{nME} MCR_{ME(i)}}$	$0.2515 \cdot DWT^{0.0851}$	$0.3918 \cdot DWT^{0.0556}$	$0.8075 \cdot DWT^{0.0071}$	$0.8573 \cdot DWT^{0.0087}$
General cargo ship	$\dfrac{1.974 \cdot DWT^{0.7987}}{\sum_{i=1}^{nME} MCR_{ME(i)}}$	$0.1381 \cdot DWT^{0.1435}$	$0.1574 \cdot DWT^{0.144}$	$0.3256 \cdot DWT^{0.0922}$	$0.4966 \cdot DWT^{0.0583}$
Refrigerated cargo ship	$\dfrac{5.598 \cdot DWT^{0.696}}{\sum_{i=1}^{nME} MCR_{ME(i)}}$	$0.5254 \cdot DWT^{0.0357}$	$0.6325 \cdot DWT^{0.0278}$	$0.7670 \cdot DWT^{0.0159}$	$0.8918 \cdot DWT^{0.0079}$

---

[4]   HELCOM Recommendation 25/7 may be found at http://www.helcom.fi

2.2.7.2 对于蒸汽涡轮的 SFC（$SFC_{SteamTurbine}$）

$SFC_{SteamTurbine}$ 应由制造商计算并经主管机关或经主管机关认可的组织验证，如下所示：

$$SFC_{SteamTurbine} = \frac{FuelConsumption}{\sum_{i=1}^{nME} P_{ME(i)}}$$

式中：

.1 燃油消耗量系指每小时锅炉的燃油消耗量（g/h）。对于电力供应主要来自于与蒸汽和给水系统紧密相连的涡轮发电机的船舶，不仅应计及 P_{ME}，还应计及第 2.2.5.6 段所述的电力负荷。

.2 应使用 SNAME 工况（工况标准：气温 24 ℃、风机进风温度 38 ℃、海水温度 24 ℃）下的 LNG 标准低热值（48 000kJ/kg）将 SFC 值修正为 LNG 的 SFC 值。

.3 修正时应考虑到基于试验燃料低热值和基于 LNG 低热值的锅炉效率的差别。

2.2.8 f_j；船舶特定设计要素

f_j 系指用于补偿船舶特定设计要素的修正系数。

2.2.8.1 冰区加强船舶的功率修正系数

冰区加强船舶的功率修正系数 f_j 应取表 1 中的 f_{j0} 和 $f_{j,\,min}$ 的较大值，但不大于 $f_{j,\,max}=1.0$。关于冰级之间近似对应的更多信息，参见 HELCOM 建议书 25/7. [4]

表 1　冰区加强船舶功率修正系数 f_j

船舶类型	f_{j0}	基于冰级的 $f_{j,\,min}$			
		IA Super	IA	IB	IC
液货船	$\dfrac{17.444 \cdot DWT^{0.576\,6}}{\sum_{i=1}^{nME} MCR_{ME(i)}}$	$0.248\,8 \cdot DWT^{0.090\,3}$	$0.454\,1 \cdot DWT^{0.052\,4}$	$0.778\,3 \cdot DWT^{0.014\,5}$	$0.874\,1 \cdot DWT^{0.007\,9}$
散货船	$\dfrac{17.207 \cdot DWT^{0.570\,5}}{\sum_{i=1}^{nME} MCR_{ME(i)}}$	$0.251\,5 \cdot DWT^{0.085\,1}$	$0.391\,8 \cdot DWT^{0.055\,6}$	$0.807\,5 \cdot DWT^{0.007\,1}$	$0.857\,3 \cdot DWT^{0.008\,7}$
杂货船	$\dfrac{1.974 \cdot DWT^{0.798\,7}}{\sum_{i=1}^{nME} MCR_{ME(i)}}$	$0.138\,1 \cdot DWT^{0.143\,5}$	$0.157\,4 \cdot DWT^{0.144}$	$0.325\,6 \cdot DWT^{0.092\,2}$	$0.496\,6 \cdot DWT^{0.058\,3}$
冷藏货船	$\dfrac{5.598 \cdot DWT^{0.696}}{\sum_{i=1}^{nME} MCR_{ME(i)}}$	$0.525\,4 \cdot DWT^{0.035\,7}$	$0.632\,5 \cdot DWT^{0.027\,8}$	$0.767\,0 \cdot DWT^{0.015\,9}$	$0.891\,8 \cdot DWT^{0.007\,9}$

---

[4]　HELCOM 建议书 25/7 可参见 http：//www.helcom.fi。

Alternatively, if an ice-class ship is designed and constructed based on an open water ship with the same shape and size of hull with EEDI certification, the power correction factor, f_j, for ice-classed ships can be calculated by using propulsion power of the new ice-class ship required by ice-class regulations, $P_{ice\ class}$, and the existing open water ship, P_{ow}, as follows:

$$f_j = \frac{P_{ow}}{P_{ice\ class}}$$

In this case, V_{ref} should be measured at the shaft power of the engine(s) installed on the existing open water ship as defined in paragraph 2.2.5.

2.2.8.2 Power correction factor for shuttle tankers with propulsion redundancy

The power correction factor f_j, for shuttle tankers with propulsion redundancy should be $f_j = 0.77$. This correction factors applies to shuttle tankers with propulsion redundancy between 80,000 and 160,000 dwt. Shuttle tankers with propulsion redundancy are tankers used for loading crude oil from offshore installations equipped with dual-engine and twin-propellers need to meet the requirements for dynamic positioning and redundancy propulsion class notation.

2.2.8.3 Correction factor for ro-ro cargo and ro-ro passenger ships (f_{jRoRo})

For ro-ro cargo and ro-ro passenger ships f_{jRoRo} is calculated as follows:

$$f_{jRoRo} = \frac{1}{F_{n_L}^{\alpha} \cdot \left(\frac{L_{pp}}{B_s}\right)^{\beta} \cdot \left(\frac{B_s}{d_s}\right)^{\gamma} \cdot \left(\frac{L_{pp}}{\nabla^{1/3}}\right)^{\delta}} \qquad ; \quad \text{If } f_{jRoRo} > 1 \text{ then } f_j = 1$$

where the Froude number, F_{n_L}, is defined as:

$$F_{n_L} = \frac{0.514\ 4 \cdot V_{ref}}{\sqrt{L_{pp} \cdot g}}$$

and the exponents α, β, γ and δ are defined as follows:

Ship type	Exponent:			
	α	β	γ	δ
Ro-ro cargo ship	2.00	0.50	0.75	1.00
Ro-ro passenger ship	2.50	0.75	0.75	1.00

作为替代，如果冰区加强船舶基于开敞水域船舶（与其船体形状和尺寸相同，且经 EEDI 认证）进行设计和建造，可用冰级规则要求的新冰区加强船舶的推进功率 $P_{ice\ class}$ 和现有开敞水域船舶的推进功率 P_{ow} 来计算冰区加强船舶的功率修正系数 f_j，如下所示：

$$f_j = \frac{P_{ow}}{P_{ice\ class}}$$

在这种情况下，应在现有开敞水域船舶上安装的发动机的轴功率（见第 2.2.5 段中的定义）下测量 V_{ref}。

2.2.8.2 具有推进冗余的穿梭运输油船的功率修正系数

对于具有推进冗余的穿梭运输油船的功率修正系数 f_j，f_j=0.77。该修正系数适用于在 80 000 和 160 000 载重吨之间的具有推进冗余的穿梭运输油船。具有推进冗余的穿梭运输油船系指为满足动力定位和冗余推进附加标志的要求而设有双发动机和双螺旋桨、用于从海上设施装载原油的液货船。

2.2.8.3 滚装货船和滚装客船（f_{jRoRo}）修正系数

对于滚装货船和滚装客船，f_{jRoRo} 按下式计算：

$$f_{jRoRo} = \frac{1}{F_{n_L}^{\alpha} \cdot \left(\frac{L_{pp}}{B_s}\right)^{\beta} \cdot \left(\frac{B_s}{d_s}\right)^{\gamma} \cdot \left(\frac{L_{pp}}{\nabla^{1/3}}\right)^{\delta}} \qquad ;\quad \text{If } f_{jRoRo} > 1 \text{ then } f_j = 1$$

式中弗劳德数 F_{nL} 定义为：

$$F_{n_L} = \frac{0.514\ 4 \cdot V_{ref}}{\sqrt{L_{pp} \cdot g}}$$

而指数 α、β、γ 和 δ 定义如下：

船型	指数			
	α	β	γ	δ
滚装货船	2.00	0.50	0.75	1.00
滚装客船	2.50	0.75	0.75	1.00

2.2.8.4 Correction factor for general cargo ships

The factor f_j for general cargo ships is calculated as follows:

$$f_j = \frac{0.174}{Fn_\nabla^{2.3} \cdot C_b^{0.3}} \qquad ; \qquad \text{If } f_j > 1 \text{ then } f_j = 1$$

Where

$$Fn_\nabla = \frac{0.5144 \cdot V_{ref}}{\sqrt{g \cdot \nabla^{\frac{1}{3}}}} \qquad ; \qquad \text{If } Fn_\nabla > 0.6 \text{ then } Fn_\nabla = 0.6$$

and

$$C_b = \frac{\nabla}{L_{pp} \cdot B_s \cdot d_s}$$

2.2.8.5 Correction factor for other ship types

For other ship types, f_j should be taken as 1.0.

2.2.9 f_w ; Factor for speed reduction at sea

f_w is a non-dimensional coefficient indicating the decrease of speed in representative sea conditions of wave height, wave frequency and wind speed (e.g. Beaufort Scale 6), and is determined as follows:

2.2.9.1 for the attained EEDI calculated under regulations 22 and 24 of MARPOL Annex VI, f_w is 1.00;

2.2.9.2 when f_w is calculated according to the sub-paragraph 2.2.9.2.1 or 2.2.9.2.2 below, the value for attained EEDI calculated by the formula in paragraph 2.1 using the obtained f_w should be referred to as "*attained EEDI_weather*";

2.2.9.2.1 f_w can be determined by conducting the ship-specific simulation on its performance at representative sea conditions. The simulation methodology should be based on the Guidelines developed by the Organization[5] and the method and outcome for an individual ship should be verified by the Administration or an organization recognized by the Administration; and

2.2.9.2.2 In cases where a simulation is not conducted, f_w should be taken from the "Standard f_w " table/curve. A "Standard f_w " table/curve is provided in the Guidelines[5] for each ship type defined in regulation 2 of MARPOL Annex VI, and expressed as a function of capacity (e.g. deadweight). The "Standard f_w " table/curve is based on data of actual speed reduction of as many existing ships as possible under the representative sea condition.

2.2.9.3 f_w and *attained EEDI_weather*, if calculated, with the representative sea conditions under which those values are determined, should be indicated in the EEDI Technical File to distinguish it from the attained EEDI calculated under regulations 22 and 24 of MARPOL Annex VI.

---

[5] Refer to *Interim guidelines for the calculation of the coefficient f_w for decrease in ship speed in a representative sea condition for trial use*, approved by the Organization and circulated by MEPC.1/Circ.796.

2.2.8.4　杂货船修正系数

杂货船的 f_j 系数计算如下：

$$f_j = \frac{0.174}{Fn_\nabla^{2.3} \cdot C_b^{0.3}} \qquad ; \qquad \text{If } f_j > 1 \text{ then } f_j = 1$$

式中

$$Fn_\nabla = \frac{0.514\,4 \cdot V_{ref}}{\sqrt{g \cdot \nabla^{\frac{1}{3}}}} \qquad ; \qquad \text{If } Fn_\nabla > 0.6 \text{ then } Fn_\nabla = 0.6$$

和

$$C_b = \frac{\nabla}{L_{pp} \cdot B_s \cdot d_s}$$

2.2.8.5　其他船型修正系数

对其他船型，f_j 应取 1.0。

2.2.9　f_w；海上航速降低系数

f_w 是无量纲系数，显示在波高、浪频和风速（例如蒲氏风级 6 级）等有代表性的海况中航速的降低，并如下确定：

2.2.9.1　对于按照《防污公约》附则Ⅵ第 22 和 24 条计算的达到的 EEDI，f_w 取 1.00；

2.2.9.2　当 f_w 按照下列第 2.2.9.2.1 或 2.2.9.2.2 段进行计算时，使用获得的 f_w 并通过第 2.1 段中的公式计算的达到的 EEDI 值应称作"达到的 $EEDI_{weather}$"；

2.2.9.2.1　f_w 可通过在有代表性的海况中进行船舶特定性能模拟试验来确定。模拟方法应基于本组织制定的导则[5]，每艘船的试验方法和试验结果应由主管机关或主管机关认可的组织进行验证；和

2.2.9.2.2　如果不进行模拟试验，f_w 值应从"标准 f_w"表 / 曲线查得。上述导则[5]提供了《防污公约》附则Ⅵ第 2 条定义的每种船型的"标准 f_w"表 / 曲线，并以载运能力（例如载重吨）函数表示。"标准 f_w"表 / 曲线基于代表性海况下尽可能多的现有船舶实际减速数据确定。

2.2.9.3　f_w 和达到的 $EEDI_{weather}$（如计算），以及确定这些值时的代表性海况应在 EEDI 技术案卷中注明，以区别于按照《防污公约》附则Ⅵ第 22 和 24 条计算达到的 EEDI。

---

[5]　参见经本组织批准并以第 MEPC.1/Circ.796 号通函散发的《代表性海况条件下船舶失速系数（f_w 系数）计算临时导则》。

2.2.10 $f_{eff(i)}$; Factor of each innovative energy efficiency technology

$f_{eff(i)}$ is the availability factor of each innovative energy efficiency technology. $f_{eff(i)}$ for waste energy recovery system should be one (1.0).[6]

2.2.11 f_i ; Capacity factor for technical/regulatory limitation on capacity

f_i is the capacity factor for any technical/regulatory limitation on capacity, and should be assumed to be one (1.0) if no necessity of the factor is granted.

2.2.11.1 Capacity correction factor for ice-classed ships

The capacity correction factor, f_i, for ice-classed ships having DWT as the measure of capacity should be calculated as follows:

$$f_i = f_{i(ice\ class)} \cdot f_{iC_b},$$

where $f_{i(ice\ class)}$ is the capacity correction factor for ice-strengthening of the ship, which can be obtained from Table 2 and f_{iC_b} is the capacity correction factor for improved ice-going capability, which should not be less than 1.0 and which should be calculated as follows:

$$f_{iC_b} = \frac{C_{b\ reference\ design}}{C_b},$$

where $C_{b\ reference\ design}$ is the average block coefficient for the ship type, which can be obtained from Table 3 for bulk carriers, tankers and general cargo ships, and C_b is the block coefficient of the ship. For ship types other than bulk carriers, tankers and general cargo ships,

$$f_{iC_b} = 1.0.$$

---

[6] EEDI calculation should be based on the normal seagoing condition outside Emission Control Areas designated under regulation 13.6 of MARPOL Annex VI.

2.2.10 $f_{eff(i)}$；每种创新能效技术系数

$f_{eff(i)}$ 系指每种创新能效技术的可用性系数。对于废能回收系统，$f_{eff(i)}$ 应为 1（1.0）[6]。

2.2.11 f_i；用于对载运能力技术／规定限制的载运能力系数

f_i 系指是载运能力系数，用于对载运能力的任何技术／规定限制，如无须考虑该系数，应假定该系数为 1（1.0）。

2.2.11.1 冰区加强船舶的载运能力修正系数

对于用 DWT 来衡量载运能力的冰区加强船舶，载运能力修正系数应按下式计算：

$$f_i = f_{i(ice\ class)} \cdot f_{iC_b},$$

式中，f_i（ice class）为冰区加强船舶的载运能力修正系数，可从表 2 中获得，f_{iC_b} 为针对增强冰区航行能力的载运能力修正系数，应不小于 1.0，并按下式计算：

$$f_{iC_b} = \frac{C_{b\ reference\ design}}{C_b},$$

式中，$C_{b\ reference\ design}$ 为针对船型的平均方形系数，对于散货船、油船和杂货船，可从表 3 中获得，C_b 为船舶的方形系数。对于散货船、油船和杂货船以外的船型，

$$f_{iC_b} = 1.0。$$

---

[6]　EEDI 计算应基于《防污公约》附则Ⅵ第 13.6 条指定的排放控制区以外的正常航行工况。

Table 2: Capacity correction factor for ice-strengthening of the hull

Ice class[7]	$f_{i(ice\ class)}$
IC	$f_{i(IC)} = 1.0041 + 58.5/DWT$
IB	$f_{i(IB)} = 1.0067 + 62.7/DWT$
IA	$f_{i(IA)} = 1.0099 + 95.1/DWT$
IA Super	$f_{i(IAS)} = 1.0151 + 228.7/DWT$

Table 3: Average block coefficients $C_{b\ reference\ design}$ for bulk carriers, tankers and general cargo ships

Ship type	Size categories				
	below 10,000 DWT	10,000 – 25,000 DWT	25,000 – 55,000 DWT	55,000 – 75,000 DWT	above 75,000 DWT
Bulk carrier	0.78	0.80	0.82	0.86	0.86
Tanker	0.78	0.78	0.80	0.83	0.83
General cargo ship	0.80				

Alternatively, the capacity correction factor for ice-strengthening of the ship ($f_{i(ice\ class)}$) can be calculated by using the formula given for the ship-specific voluntary enhancement correction coefficient (f_{iVSE}) in paragraph 2.2.11.2. This formula can also be used for other ice classes than those given in Table 2.

2.2.11.2 f_{iVSE}[8] ; Ship-specific voluntary structural enhancement

f_{iVSE} for ship-specific voluntary structural enhancement is expressed by the following formula:

$$f_{iVSE} = \frac{DWT_{referencedesign}}{DWT_{enhanceddesign}}$$

where:

$$DWT_{referencedesign} = \Delta_{ship} - lightweight_{referencedesign}$$

$$DWT_{enhanceddesign} = \Delta_{ship} - lightweight_{enhanceddesign}$$

For this calculation the same displacement (Δ) for reference and enhanced design should be taken.

DWT before enhancements ($DWT_{reference\ design}$) is the deadweight prior to application of the structural enhancements. DWT after enhancements ($DWT_{enhanced\ design}$) is the deadweight following the application of voluntary structural enhancement. A change of material (e.g. from

---

[7]   For further information on approximate correspondence between ice classes, see HELCOM Recommendation 25/7, which can be found at http://www.helcom.fi

[8]   Structural and/or additional class notations such as, but not limited to, "strengthened for discharge with grabs" and "strengthened bottom for loading/unloading aground", which result in a loss of deadweight of the ship, are also seen as examples of "voluntary structural enhancements".

表 2　冰区加强船体的载运能力修正系数

冰级[7]	$f_{i\,(ice\;class)}$
IC	$f_{i\,(IC)} = 1.004\,1 + 58.5/DWT$
IB	$f_{i\,(IB)} = 1.006\,7 + 62.7/DWT$
IA	$f_{i\,(IA)} = 1.009\,9 + 95.1/DWT$
IA Super	$f_{i\,(IAS)} = 1.015\,1 + 228.7/DWT$

表 3　散货船、油船和杂货船的平均方形系数 $C_{b\,reference\;design}$

船型	尺寸类别				
	10 000 DWT 以下	10 000~ 25 000 DWT	25 000~ 55 000 DWT	55 000~ 75 000 DWT	75 000 DWT 以上
散货船	0.78	0.80	0.82	0.86	0.86
油船	0.78	0.78	0.80	0.83	0.83
杂货船	0.80				

作为替代，可采用第 2.2.11.2 段中对船舶特定的自愿结构加强修正系数（$f_{i\,VSE}$）给出的公式来计算冰区加强船舶的载运能力修正系数（$f_{i\,(ice\;class)}$）。该公式也可用于表 2 以外的其他冰级。

2.2.11.2　$f_{i\,VSE}$[8]；船舶特定的自愿结构加强

船舶特定的自愿结构加强 $f_{i\,VSE}$ 由下列公式表示：

$$f_{i\,VSE} = \frac{DWT_{reference\,design}}{DWT_{enhanced\,design}}$$

式中：

$$DWT_{reference\,design} = \Delta_{ship} - lightweight_{reference\,design}$$

$$DWT_{enhanced\,design} = \Delta_{ship} - lightweight_{enhanced\,design}$$

对于本计算，基本设计和加强设计应取相同的排水量（Δ）。

加强前的载重吨（$DWT_{reference\,design}$）系指应用结构加强前的载重吨。加强后的载重吨（$DWT_{enhanced\,design}$）系指应用了自愿结构加强后的载重吨。对于 $f_{i\,VSE}$ 计算，应不允许基本设计和加强设计之间材料发生变化（例如从铝合金变为钢）。也不应允许相同材料等级发生变化（例如钢类型、等级、性能和状况）。

---

[7]　关于冰级之间近似对应的更多信息，参见 HELCOM 建议书 25/7，可参见 http：//www.helcom.fi。

[8]　导致船舶载重吨损失的结构性和 / 或额外附加标志也视作"自愿结构加强"，例如但不限于："抓斗卸放加强"和"坐底装卸船底加强"。

aluminium alloy to steel) between reference design and enhanced design should not be allowed for the $f_{i\ VSE}$ calculation. A change in grade of the same material (e.g. in steel type, grades, properties and condition) should also not be allowed.

In each case, two sets of structural plans of the ship should be submitted to the verifier for assessment: one set for the ship without voluntary structural enhancement; the other set for the same ship with voluntary structural enhancement (alternatively, one set of structural plans of the reference design with annotations of voluntary structural enhancement should also be acceptable). Both sets of structural plans should comply with the applicable regulations for the ship type and intended trade.

2.2.11.3 f_{iCSR} ; Ships under the Common Structural Rules (CSR)

For bulk carriers and oil tankers, built in accordance with the Common Structural Rules (CSR) of the classification societies and assigned the class notation CSR, the following capacity correction factor f_{iCSR} should apply:

$$f_{iCSR} = 1 + (0.08 \cdot LWT_{CSR} / DWT_{CSR})$$

Where DWT_{CSR} is the deadweight determined by paragraph 2.2.4 and LWT_{CSR} is the light weight of the ship.

2.2.11.4 f_i for other ship types

For other ship types, f_i should be taken as one (1.0).

2.2.12 f_c ; Cubic capacity correction factor

f_c is the cubic capacity correction factor and should be assumed to be one (1.0) if no necessity of the factor is granted.

2.2.12.1 f_c for chemical tankers

For chemical tankers, as defined in regulation 1.16.1 of MARPOL Annex II, the following cubic capacity correction factor f_c should apply:

$f_c = R^{-0.7} - 0.014$, where R is less than 0.98
or
$f_c = 1.000$, where R is 0.98 and above;

where: R is the capacity ratio of the deadweight of the ship (tonnes) as determined by paragraph 2.2.4 divided by the total cubic capacity of the cargo tanks of the ship (m^3).

2.2.12.2 f_c for gas carriers

for gas carriers having direct diesel driven propulsion system constructed or adapted and used for the carriage in bulk of liquefied natural gas, the following cubic capacity correction factor f_{cLNG} should apply:

$$f_{cLNG} = R^{-0.56}$$

where: R is the capacity ratio of the deadweight of the ship (tonnes) as determined by paragraph 2.2.4 divided by the total cubic capacity of the cargo tanks of the ship (m^3).

Note: This factor is applicable to LNG carriers defined as gas carriers in regulation 2.2.14 of MARPOL Annex VI and should not be applied to LNG carriers defined in regulation 2.2.16 of MARPOL Annex VI.

在每种情况下，该船的两套结构图纸均应提交验证方进行评定。1 套用于无自愿结构加强的船舶，另外 1 套用于具有自愿结构加强的相同船舶。（作为一种替代方法，1 套带自愿结构加强标识的船舶基本设计的结构图纸也应可接受。）两套结构图纸均应符合对船型和预定贸易的适用规则。

2.2.11.3 f_{iCSR}；共同结构规范（CSR）规定的船舶

对于按照船级社的共同结构规范（CSR）建造并授予附加标志 CSR 的散货船和油船，下列载运能力修正系数 f_{iCSR} 应适用：

$$f_{iCSR}=1+\left(0.08 \cdot LWT_{CSR}/DWT_{CSR}\right)$$

式中，DWT_{CSR} 系指按 2.2.4 确定的载重吨，LWT_{CSR} 系指船舶空船重量。

2.2.11.4 其他船型的 f_i

对于其他船型，f_i 应取 1（1.0）。

2.2.12 f_c；舱容量修正系数

f_c 系指舱容量修正系数，如无须考虑该系数，应假定该系数为 1（1.0）。

2.2.12.1 化学品船的 f_c

对于《防污公约》附则 Ⅱ 第 1.16.1 条中定义的化学品船，下列舱容量修正系数 fc 应适用：

$f_c=R^{-0.7}-0.014$，式中 R 小于 0.98

或

$f_c=1.000$，式中 R 为 0.98 或以上；

式中：R 系指按第 2.2.4 段确定的船舶载重吨（单位：t）与船舶货舱总容积量（单位：m^3）的比值。

2.2.12.2 气体运输船的 f_c

对于建造或改装成载运散装液化天然气并具有直接柴油驱动推进系统的气体运输船，下列舱容量修正系数 f_{cLNG} 应适用：

$$f_{cLNG}=R^{-0.56}$$

式中，R 系指按第 2.2.4 段确定的船舶载重吨（单位：t）与船舶货舱总容积量（单位：m^3）的比值。

注： 该系数适用于按《防污公约》附则 Ⅵ 第 2.2.14 条定义为气体运输船的 LNG 运输船，而不应适用于《防污公约》附则 Ⅵ 第 2.2.16 条所定义的 LNG 运输船。

2.2.12.3 f_c for ro-ro passenger ships (f_{cRoPax})

For ro-ro passenger ships having a DWT/GT-ratio of less than 0.25, the following cubic capacity correction factor, f_{cRoPax}, should apply:

$$f_{cRoPax} = \left(\frac{(DWT/GT)}{0.25} \right)^{-0.8}$$

Where DWT is the Capacity and GT is the gross tonnage in accordance with the International Convention of Tonnage Measurement of Ships 1969, annex I, regulation 3.

2.2.12.4 f_c for bulk carriers having R of less than 0.55 ($f_{c\ bulk\ carriers\ designed\ to\ carry\ light\ cargoes}$)

For bulk carriers having R of less than 0.55 (e.g. woodchip carriers), the following cubic capacity correction factor, $f_{c\ bulk\ carriers\ designed\ to\ carry\ light\ cargoes}$, should apply:

$$f_{c\ bulk\ carriers\ designed\ to\ carry\ light\ cargoes} = R^{-0.15}$$

where R is the capacity ratio of the deadweight of the ship (tonnes) as determined by paragraph 2.2.4 divided by the total cubic capacity of the cargo holds of the ship (m^3).

2.2.13 L_{pp} ; Length between perpendiculars

Length between perpendiculars, L_{pp}, means 96% of the total length on a waterline at 85% of the least moulded depth measured from the top of the keel, or the length from the foreside of the stem to the axis of the rudder stock on that waterline, if that were greater. In ships designed with a rake of keel the waterline on which this length is measured should be parallel to the designed waterline. L_{pp} should be measured in metres.

2.2.14 f_i ; Factor for general cargo ships equipped with cranes and cargo-related gear

f_i is the factor for general cargo ships equipped with cranes and other cargo-related gear to compensate in a loss of deadweight of the ship.

$$f_i = f_{cranes} \cdot f_{sideloader} \cdot f_{roro}$$

f_{cranes}	= 1	If no cranes are present
$f_{sideloader}$	= 1	If no side loaders are present
f_{roro}	= 1	If no ro-ro ramp is present

Definition of f_{cranes}:

$$f_{cranes} = 1 + \frac{\sum_{n=1}^{n} \left(0.0519 \cdot SWL_n \cdot \mathrm{Re}\,ach_n + 32.11 \right)}{Capacity}$$

where:

SWL	=	Safe Working Load, as specified by crane manufacturer in metric tonnes
Reach	=	Reach at which the Safe Working Load can be applied in metres
N	=	Number of cranes

2.2.12.3 滚装客船的 f_c （f_{cRoPax}）

对于 DWT/GT 比小于 0.25 的滚装客船，下列舱容量修正系数 f_{cRoPax} 应适用：

$$f_{cRoPax} = \left(\frac{(DWT/GT)}{0.25}\right)^{-0.8}$$

式中：DWT 系指载重吨，GT 系指按《1969 年国际船舶吨位丈量公约》附则 I 第 3 条规定的总吨位。

2.2.12.4 对于 R 小于 0.55 的散货船的 f_c （$f_{c\ bulk\ carriers\ designed\ to\ carry\ light\ cargoes}$）

对于 R 小于 0.55 的散货船（例如木屑船），下列舱容量能力修正系数 $f_{c\ bulk\ carriers\ designed\ to\ carry\ light\ cargoes}$ 应适用：

$$f_{c\ bulk\ carriers\ designed\ to\ carry\ light\ cargoes} = R^{-0.15}$$

式中：R 系指根据按第 2.2.4 段确定的船舶载重吨（单位：吨）与船舶货舱总容积量（单位：m³）的比值。

2.2.13 L_{PP}；船舶垂线间长度

船舶垂线间长度 L_{PP} 系指量自龙骨顶部的最小型深 85% 处水线总长的 96% 或该水线上首柱前缘至舵杆中心线的长度，取大者。对于设计成具有龙骨倾斜的船舶，计量该长度的水线应与设计水线平行。L_{PP} 的计量单位为米。

2.2.14 f_i；具有起重机和起货设备的杂货船的系数

f_i 系指具有起重机和其他起货设备的杂货船用于补偿船舶载重吨损失的系数。

$f_i = f_{cranes} \cdot f_{sideloader} \cdot f_{roro}$
如无起重机，　　　　　　　$f_{cranes} = 1$
如无舷侧装载设备，　　　　$f_{sideloader} = 1$
如无滚装坡道，　　　　　　$f_{roro} = 1$
f_{cranes} 定义为：

$$f_{cranes} = 1 + \frac{\sum_{n=1}^{n}(0.051\,9 \cdot SWL_n \cdot \mathrm{Re}\,ach_n + 32.11)}{Capacity}$$

式中：

SWL	=	由起重机制造商规定的安全工作负荷，单位为吨；
Reach	=	安全工作负荷内的伸臂长度，单位为米；
N	=	起重机数量

For other cargo gear such as side loaders and ro-ro ramps, the factor should be defined as follows:

$$f_{sideloader} = \frac{Capacity_{No\ sideloaders}}{Capacity_{sideloaders}}$$

$$f_{RoRo} = \frac{Capacity_{No\ RoRo}}{Capacity_{RoRo}}$$

The weight of the side loaders and ro-ro ramps should be based on a direct calculation, by analogy with the calculations made for factor f_{ivse}.

2.2.15 d_s ; Summer load line draught

Summer load line draught, d_s , is the vertical distance, in metres, from the moulded baseline at mid-length to the waterline corresponding to the summer freeboard draught to be assigned to the ship.

In the case of a new ship with multiple load line certificates or with a load line certificate containing multiple summer load lines, the maximum summer draught should be used to calculate and verify the required and attained EEDI. For ships that may have previously received multiple EEDI assessments for several deadweights that correspond to multiple load lines, all those EEDI assessments should remain valid.

2.2.16 B_s ; Breadth

Breadth, B_s, is the greatest moulded breadth of the ship, in metres, at or below the load line draught, d_s.

2.2.17 ∇ ; Volumetric displacement

Volumetric displacement, ∇, in cubic metres (m³), is the volume of the moulded displacement of the ship, excluding appendages, in a ship with a metal shell, and is the volume of displacement to the outer surface of the hull in a ship with a shell of any other material, both taken at the summer load line draught, d_s, as stated in the approved stability booklet/loading manual.

2.2.18 g ; Gravitational acceleration

g is the gravitational acceleration, $9.81 m/s^2$.

2.2.19 f_m ; Factor for ice-classed ships having IA Super and IA

For ice-classed ships having IA Super or IA, the following factor, f_m, should apply:

$$f_m = 1.05$$

For further information on approximate correspondence between ice classes, see HELCOM Recommendation 25/7[9].

---

[9]   HELCOM Recommendation 25/7 may be found at http://www.helcom.fi

对于其他起货设备，如舷侧装载设备和滚装坡道，系数定义如下：

$$f_{sideloader} = \frac{Capacity_{No\ sideloaders}}{Capacity_{sideloaders}}$$

$$f_{RoRo} = \frac{Capacity_{No\ RoRo}}{Capacity_{RoRo}}$$

舷侧装载设备和滚装坡道的重量应基于直接计算确定，计算方法类似于 f_{ivse} 的计算。

2.2.15 d_s；夏季载重线吃水

夏季载重线吃水 d_s 系指在船长中点处从型基线至核定的夏季干舷吃水对应的水线的垂直距离，单位为米。

对于具有多份载重线证书的船舶或者一份载重线证书包含多条夏季载重线的船舶，应使用最大夏季吃水计算和验证要求的 EEDI 和达到的 EEDI。如船舶之前对多条载重线对应的若干载重吨进行过多次 EEDI 评估，所有这些 EEDI 评估应保持有效。

2.2.16 B_s；船宽

船宽 B_s 系指船舶处于或低于载重线吃水 d_s 时的最大型宽，单位为米。

2.2.17 ▽；排水体积

排水体积▽系指外壳为金属的船舶的型排水体积，不包括其附属物，或是船壳为任何其他材质的船体外表面的排水体积，均取按经批准的稳性手册 / 装载手册规定的夏季载重线吃水 d_s 处的对应值，单位为立方米（m^3）。

2.2.18 g；重力加速度

g 系指重力加速度，$9.81m/s^2$。

2.2.19 f_m；具有 IASuper 和 IA 冰级附加标志的冰区航行船舶的系数

对于具有 IA Super 或 IA 冰级附加标志的冰区航行船舶，以下系数 f_m 应适用：

$f_m=1.05$

关于更多冰级之间的大致对应信息，参见 HELCOM 建议书 25/7[9]。

---

[9] HELCOM 建议书 25/7 可参见 http：//www.helcom.fi。

3 Mandatory reporting of attained EEDI values and related information

3.1   In accordance with regulation 22.3 of MARPOL Annex VI, for each ship subject to regulation 24, the Administration or any organization duly authorized by it shall report the required and attained EEDI values and relevant information taking into account these Guidelines via electronic communication.

3.2   Information to be reported are as follows:

.1   applicable EEDI phase (e.g. Phase 1, Phase 2);

.2   identification number (IMO Secretariat use only);

.3   ship type;

.4   common commercial size reference[10] (see Note (3) in appendix 5 to these Guidelines), if available;

.5   DWT or GT (as appropriate);

.6   year of delivery;

.7   required EEDI value;

.8   attained EEDI value;

.9   dimensional parameters (length L_{pp} (m), breadth B_s (m), and draught (m));

.10 V_{ref} (knots) and P_{ME} (kW);

.11   use of innovative technologies (4th and 5th terms in the EEDI equation, if applicable);

.12   short statement[10] describing the principal design elements or changes employed to achieve the attained EEDI (as appropriate), if available;

.13   type of fuel used in the calculation of the attained EEDI, and for dual-fuel engines, the f_{DFgas} ratio; and

.14   ice class designation (if applicable).

3.3   The information in paragraph 3.2 is not required to be reported for ships for which the required and attained EEDI values had been already reported to the Organization.

3.4   A standardized reporting format for mandatory reporting of attained EEDI values and related information is presented in appendix 5.

---

[10]   Not subject to verification.

3 强制报告达到的 EEDI 值和相关信息

3.1 按《防污公约》附则Ⅵ第 22.3 条，对于第 24 条适用的每艘船舶，主管机关或经其正式授权的任何组织须考虑到本导则，通过电子通信的方式报告要求的 EEDI 和达到的 EEDI 值及相关信息。

3.2 应报告的信息如下：

.1 适用的 EEDI 阶段（例如：第 1 阶段、第 2 阶段等）；

.2 识别号（仅供 IMO 秘书处使用）；

.3 船型；

.4 通用商业尺寸参考[10]（见本导则附录 5 注（3））（如能提供）；

.5 载重吨或总吨（视情况）；

.6 交船年份；

.7 要求的 EEDI 值；

.8 达到的 EEDI 值；

.9 尺度参数（船长 L_{pp}（m）、船宽 B_s（m）和吃水（m））；

.10 V_{ref}（节）和 P_{ME}（kW）；

.11 采用创新技术（如适用，为 EEDI 公式的第 4 个和第 5 个参数）；

.12 提供一份适当的简短声明[10]，描述为实现达到的 EEDI 而采用的主要设计要素或变更（如能提供）；

.13 计算达到的 EEDI 时使用的燃料类型，对于双燃料发动机，f_{DFgas} 的比值；和

.14 给定的冰级（如适用）。

3.3 对于已向本组织报告要求的 EEDI 和达到的 EEDI 值的船舶，无须报告第 3.2 段中的信息。

3.4 强制报告达到的 EEDI 值和相关信息的标准报告格式见附录 5。

[10] 无须验证。

APPENDIX 1

A GENERIC AND SIMPLIFIED MARINE POWER PLANT

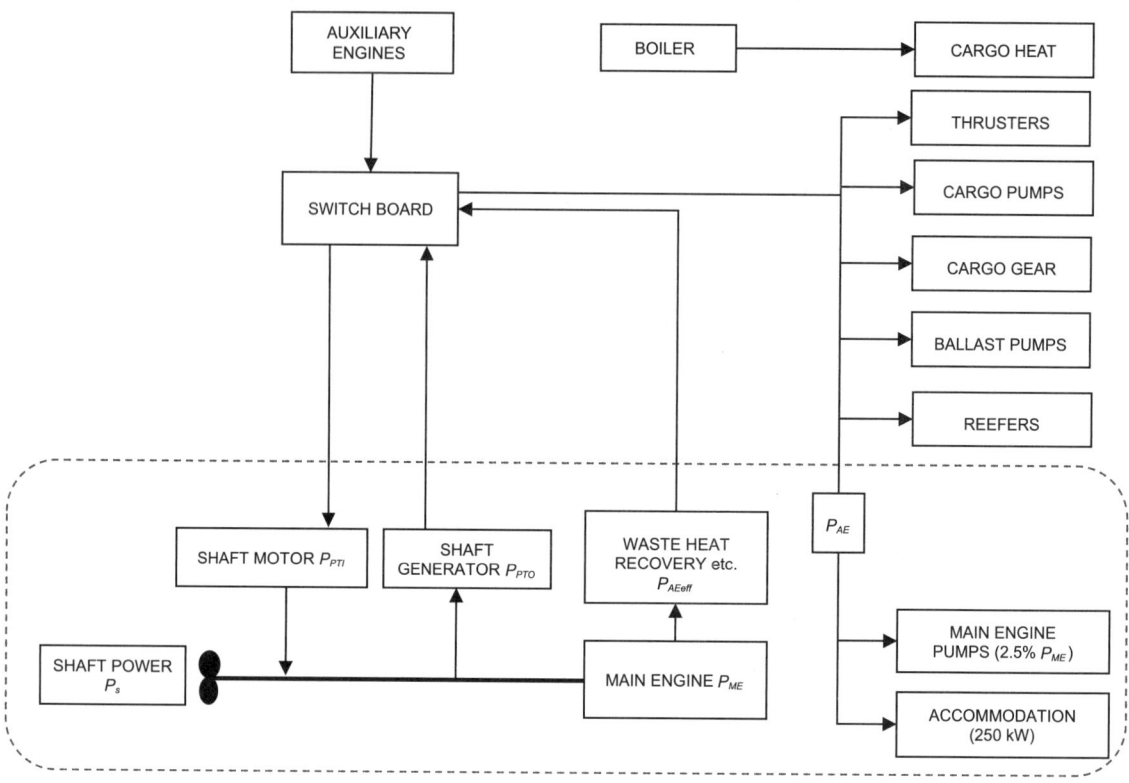

Note 1: Mechanical recovered waste energy directly coupled to shafts need not be measured, since the effect of the technology is directly reflected in the V_{ref} .

Note 2: In the case of combined PTI/PTO, the normal operational mode at sea will determine which of these to be used in the calculation.

附录 1
船舶电站的简化总体示图

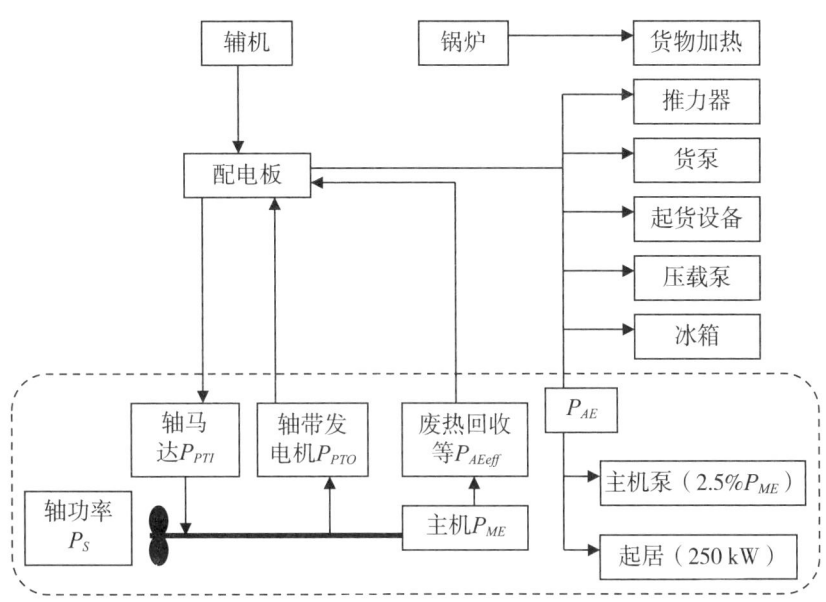

注 1：无须测量直接与轴相连的机械回收废能，因为 V_{ref} 直接体现该技术的影响。

注 2：如果兼用 PTI/PTO，应根据船舶在海上的常规营运模式来确定在计算中使用其中哪个参数。

APPENDIX 2

GUIDELINES FOR THE DEVELOPMENT OF ELECTRIC POWER TABLES FOR EEDI (EPT-EEDI)

1 Introduction

This appendix contains a guideline for the document "Electric power table for EEDI" which is similar to the actual shipyards' load balance document, utilizing well defined criteria, providing standard format, clear loads definition and grouping, standard load factors, etc. A number of new definitions (in particular the "groups") are introduced, giving an apparent greater complexity to the calculation process. However, this intermediate step to the final calculation of P_{AE} stimulates all the parties to a deep investigation through the global figure of the auxiliary load, allowing comparisons between different ships and technologies and eventually identifying potential efficiencies improvements.

2 Auxiliary load power definition

P_{AE} is to be calculated as indicated in paragraph 2.2.5.6 of the Guidelines, together with the following additional three conditions:

.1 non-emergency situations (e.g. "no fire", "no flood", "no blackout", "no partial blackout");

.2 evaluation time frame of 24 hours (to account loads with intermittent use); and

.3 ship fully loaded with passengers and/or cargo and crew.

3 Definition of the data to be included in the electric power table for EEDI

The electric power table for EEDI calculation should contain the following data elements, as appropriate:

.1 Load's group;
.2 Load's description;
.3 Load's identification tag;
.4 Load's electric circuit identification;
.5 Load's mechanical rated power "Pm" (kW);
.6 Load's electric motor rated output power (kW);
.7 Load's electric motor efficiency "e" ($/$);
.8 Load's rated electric power "Pr" (kW);
.9 Service factor of load "kl" ($/$);
.10 Service factor of duty "kd" ($/$);
.11 Service factor of time "kt" ($/$);
.12 Service total factor of use "ku" ($/$), where $ku=kl \cdot kd \cdot kt$;
.13 Load's necessary power "$Pload$" (kW), where $Pload=Pr \cdot ku$;
.14 Notes;
.15 Group's necessary power (kW); and
.16 Auxiliaries load's power P_{AE} (kW).

附录 2
EEDI 电力负荷表（EPT−EEDI）编制导则

1 介绍

本附录包括与船厂的实际电力负荷计算书相似的"EEDI 电力负荷表"文件的导则，其使用明确定义的衡准，并提供标准格式、清晰的负荷定义和分组、标准负荷系数等。引入了一批新的定义（特别是"组"），从而明显使计算过程更为复杂。但是，P_{AE} 最终计算之前的该中间步骤促使各方对辅助机械负荷的整体状况进行深入调查，并可对不同船舶和技术进行比较，从而最终认定提高效率的潜力。

2 辅机负荷功率定义

应按本导则第 2.2.5.6 段连同以下附加的三个状态计算 P_{AE}:
- .1 无应急情况（如"无火灾"、"无浸水"、"无全船失电"和"无局部失电"）;
- .2 24h 的评估期限（考虑负荷的间断使用）; 和
- .3 船舶满载乘客和 / 或货物和船员。

3 EEDI 电力负荷表应包括数据的定义

用于 EEDI 计算的电力负荷表应视具体情况包括以下数据要素:
- .1 负荷组;
- .2 负荷描述;
- .3 负荷标识标签;
- .4 负荷电路标识;
- .5 负荷机械额定功率"Pm"（kW）;
- .6 负荷电动机额定输出功率（kW）;
- .7 负荷电动机效率"e"（/）;
- .8 负荷额定电功率"Pr"（kW）;
- .9 负荷使用系数"kl"（/）;
- .10 负荷连续使用系数"kd"（/）;
- .11 负荷间断使用系数"kt"（/）;
- .12 负荷总使用系数"ku"（/），$ku=kl \cdot kd \cdot kt$;
- .13 负荷必需功率"$Pload$"（kW），$Pload=Pr \cdot ku$;
- .14 注释;
- .15 组的必需功率（kW）; 和
- .16 辅助机械负荷功率 P_{AE}（kW）。

4 Data to be included in the electric power table for EEDI

Load groups

4.1 The loads are divided into defined groups, allowing a proper breakdown of the auxiliaries. This eases the verification process and makes it possible to identify those areas where load reductions might be possible. The groups are listed below:

.1   A – Hull, deck, navigation and safety services;
.2   B – Propulsion service auxiliaries;
.3   C – Auxiliary engine and main engine services;
.4   D – Ship's general services;
.5   E – Ventilation for engine-rooms and auxiliaries room;
.6   F – Air conditioning services;
.7   G – Galleys, refrigeration and laundries services;
.8   H – Accommodation services;
.9   I – Lighting and socket services;
.10   L – Entertainment services;
.11   N – Cargo loads; and
.12   M – Miscellaneous.

All the ship's loads should be delineated in the document, excluding only P_{AEeff}, the shaft motors and shaft motors chain (while the propulsion services auxiliaries are partially included below in paragraph 4.1.2 B). Some loads (i.e. thrusters, cargo pumps, cargo gear, ballast pumps, maintaining cargo, reefers and cargo hold fans) still are included in the group for sake of transparency; however, their service factor is zero in order to comply with paragraph 2.2.5.6 of the Guidelines (see rows 4 and 5 of the electric power table contained in this appendix), therefore making it easier to verify that all the loads have been considered in the document and there are no loads left out of the measurement.

4.1.1   A – Hull, deck, navigation and safety services

.1   loads included in the hull services typically are: ICCP systems, mooring equipment, various doors, ballasting systems, bilge systems, stabilizing equipment, etc. Ballasting systems are indicated with service factor equal to zero to comply with paragraph 2.5.6 of the Guidelines (see row 5 of the electric power table contained in this appendix);

.2   loads included in the deck services typically are: deck and balcony washing systems, rescue systems, cranes, etc.;

.3   loads included in the navigation services typically are: navigation systems, navigation's external and internal communication systems, steering systems, etc.; and

.4   loads included in the safety services typically are: active and passive fire systems, emergency shutdown systems, public address systems, etc.

4.1.2   B – Propulsion service auxiliaries

This group typically includes propulsion secondary cooling systems, such as LT cooling pumps dedicated to shaft motors, LT cooling pumps dedicated to propulsion converters, propulsion UPSs, etc. Propulsion service loads do not include shaft motors (*PTI(i)*) and the auxiliaries

4 EEDI 电力负荷表应包括的数据

负荷组

4.1 将负荷分成规定的组，可对辅机进行适当的分类。这简化了验证过程，并使确定出负荷可能减少的区域成为可能。各组列出如下：

- .1 A—船体、甲板、航行和安全负载；
- .2 B—推进作业辅助机械负载；
- .3 C—辅机和主机负载；
- .4 D—船舶一般负载；
- .5 E—机舱和辅机舱通风；
- .6 F—空调负载；
- .7 G—厨房、制冷和洗衣间负载；
- .8 H—起居负载；
- .9 I—照明和插座负载；
- .10 L—娱乐负载；
- .11 N—货物负荷；和
- .12 M—其他。

必须在文件中描述所有船舶负荷，仅排除 P_{Aeff}、轴马达和轴马达链（在以下第 4.1.2 B 段中包括部分推进作业辅助机械时）。为透明度起见在组中仍然包括一些负荷（例如推力器、货泵、起货设备、压载泵、货物维护、冰箱和货舱风机），但为符合本导则第 2.2.5.6 段（见本附录所载电力负荷表第 4 和 5 行），其使用系数为零，从而使验证已在文件中考虑所有负荷且测量时没有遗漏负荷更为容易。

4.1.1 A ——船体、甲板、航行和安全负载

- .1 船体负载包括的典型负荷为：ICCP 系统、系泊设备、各种门、压载系统、舱底水系统、防摇设备等。为符合本导则第 2.5.6 段（见本附录所载电力负荷表第 5 行），压载系统的使用系数显示为零；
- .2 甲板负载包括的典型负荷为：甲板和阳台清洗系统、救助系统、起重机等；
- .3 航行负载包括的典型负荷为：航行系统、航行内部和外部通信系统、操舵系统等；和
- .4 安全负载包括的典型负荷为：主动和被动消防系统、应急关闭系统、公共广播系统等。

4.1.2 B——推进作业辅助机械负载

本组典型负载包括：推进用次级冷却系统，例如轴马达专用低温冷却泵、推进变换器专用低温冷却泵、推进 UPS 等。推进作业负荷不包括轴马达（$PTI(i)$）和作为其组成部分的辅助

which are part of them (shaft motor own cooling fans and pump, etc.) and the shaft motor chain losses and auxiliaries which are part of them (i.e. shaft motor converters including relevant auxiliaries such as converter own cooling fans and pumps, shaft motor transformers including relevant auxiliaries losses, such as propulsion transformer own cooling fans and pumps, shaft motor harmonic filter including relevant auxiliaries losses, shaft motor excitation system including the relevant auxiliaries consumed power, etc.). Propulsion service auxiliaries include manoeuvring propulsion equipment such as manoeuvring thrusters and their auxiliaries whose service factor is to be set to zero.

4.1.3   C – Auxiliary engine and main engine services

This group includes cooling systems, i.e. pumps and fans for cooling circuits dedicated to alternators or propulsion shaft engines (seawater, technical water dedicated pumps, etc.), lubricating and fuel systems feeding, transfer, treatment and storage, ventilation system for combustion air supply, etc.

4.1.4   D – Ship's general services

This group includes loads which provide general services which can be shared between shaft motor, auxiliary engines and main engine and accommodation support systems. Loads typically included in this group are cooling systems, i.e. pumping seawater, technical water main circuits, compressed air systems, freshwater generators, automation systems, etc.

4.1.5   E – Ventilation for engine-rooms and auxiliaries room

This group includes all fans providing ventilation for engine-rooms and auxiliary rooms that typically are engine-rooms cooling supply-exhaust fans, auxiliary rooms supply and exhaust fans. All the fans serving accommodation areas or supplying combustion air are not included in this group. This group does not include cargo hold fans and garage supply and exhaust fans.

4.1.6   F – Air conditioning services

All loads that make up the air conditioning service that typically are air conditioning chillers, air conditioning cooling and heating fluids transfer and treatment, air conditioning's air handling units ventilation, air conditioning re-heating systems with associated pumping, etc. The air conditioning chillers service factor of load, service factor of time and service factor of duty are to be set as 1 ($kl=1$, $kt=1$ and $kd=1$) in order to avoid the detailed validation of the heat load dissipation document (i.e. the chiller's electric motor rated power is to be used). However, kd is to represent the use of spare chillers (e.g. four chillers are installed and one out four is spare then $kd=0$ for the spare chiller and $kd=1$ for the remaining three chillers), but only when the number of spare chillers is clearly demonstrated via the heat load dissipation document.

4.1.7   G – Galleys, refrigeration and laundries services

All loads related to the galleys, pantries refrigeration and laundry services that typically are galleys various machines, cooking appliances, galleys' cleaning machines, galleys auxiliaries, refrigerated room systems including refrigeration compressors with auxiliaries, air coolers, etc.

4.1.8   H – Accommodation services

All loads related to the accommodation services of passengers and crew that typically are crew and passengers' transportation systems, i.e. lifts, escalators, etc. environmental services, i.e. black and grey water collecting, transfer, treatment, storage, discharge, waste systems including collecting, transfer, treatment, storage, etc. accommodation fluids transfers, i.e. sanitary hot and cold water pumping, etc., treatment units, pools systems, saunas, gym equipment, etc.

机械(轴马达自带冷却风机和泵等)以及轴马达链和作为其组成部分的辅助机械的损耗(即轴马达变换器包括相关辅助机械的损耗,例如变换器自带冷却风机和泵;轴马达变压器包括相关辅助机械的损耗,例如推进变压器自带冷却风机和泵;轴马达谐波滤波器包括相关辅助机械的损耗;轴马达励磁系统包括相关辅助机械消耗的功率等)。推进作业辅助机械包括操纵推进设备,例如操纵助推器及其辅助机械,其使用系数应设为零。

4.1.3　C——辅机和主机负载

本组包括:冷却系统,即交流发电机或直接推进发动机专用冷却系统的泵和风机(海水、淡水专用泵等);滑油和燃油供给、驳运、处理和储存系统,燃烧用空气供应通风系统等。

4.1.4　D——船舶一般负载

本组包括提供一般服务的负荷,其能在轴马达、辅机、主机和起居支持系统之间共享。本组包括的典型负荷为:冷却系统,即海水泵吸系统、淡水主循环系统管路;压缩空气系统;制淡装置;自动化系统等。

4.1.5　E——机舱和辅机舱的通风

本组包括为机舱和辅机舱提供通风的所有风机,典型负荷为:机舱冷却用送风机和抽风机,辅机舱送风机和抽风机。本组不包括服务于起居区域或供应燃烧用空气的所有风机。本组不包括货舱风机以及车库的送风机和抽风机。

4.1.6　F——空调负载

构成空调负载的所有负荷通常为:空调冷却器,空调冷却和加热介质驳运和处理装置,空调空气处理装置通风,空调再加热系统及其相关泵等。为避免对热负荷耗散文件的详细认证,空调冷却器的负荷使用系数、负荷间断使用系数和负荷连续使用系数应设为1($kl=1$、$kt=1$ 和 $kd=1$),即应使用冷却器电动机的额定功率。但仅当热负荷耗散文件清晰证实实备用冷却器的数量时,kd 应代表备用冷却器的使用(例如安装了四个冷却器,其中一个是备用冷却器,则对备用冷却器 $kd=0$,对其余三个冷却器 $kd=1$)。

4.1.7　G——厨房、制冷和洗衣间负载

与厨房、配膳室制冷和洗衣间作业相关的所有负荷通常为:厨房的各种机械、烹调设备、厨房的清洗机械、厨房辅机、制冷室系统包括制冷压缩机及其辅机、空气冷却器等。

4.1.8　H——起居负载

与乘客和船员的起居服务相关的所有负荷通常为:船员和乘客的运输系统(升降机、自动扶梯等)、环保作业(黑水和灰水收集、驳运、处理、储存、排放)、垃圾系统(包括收集、驳运、处理、储存等)、生活污水驳运(盥洗热水和冷水的泵等)、处理装置、泳池系统、桑拿、体育馆设备等。

4.1.9   I – Lighting and socket services

All loads related to the lighting, entertainment and socket services. As the quantity of lighting circuits and sockets within the ship may be significantly high, it is not practically feasible to list all the lighting circuits and points in the EPT for EEDI. Therefore circuits should be grouped into subgroups aimed to identify possible improvements of efficient use of power. The subgroups are:

.1   Lighting for 1) cabins, 2) corridors, 3) technical rooms/stairs, 4) public spaces/stairs, 5) engine-rooms and auxiliaries' room, 6) external areas, 7) garages and 8) cargo spaces. All should be divided by main vertical zones; and

.2   Power sockets for 1) cabins, 2) corridors, 3) technical rooms/stairs, 4) public spaces/stairs, 5) engine-rooms and auxiliaries' room, 6) garages and 7) cargo spaces. All should be divided by main vertical zones.

The calculation criteria for complex groups (e.g. cabin lighting and power sockets) subgroups are to be included via an explanatory note, indicating the load composition (e.g. lights of typical cabins, TV, hair dryer, fridge).

4.1.10   L – Entertainment services

This group includes all loads related to entertainment services, typically public spaces audio and video equipment, theatre stage equipment, IT systems for offices, video games, etc.

4.1.11   N – Cargo loads

This group will contain all cargo loads such as cargo pumps, cargo gear, maintaining cargo, cargo reefers loads, cargo hold fans and garage fans for sake of transparency. However, the service factor of this group is to be set to zero.

4.1.12   M – Miscellaneous

This group will contain all loads which have not been associated with the above-mentioned groups but still are contributing to the overall load calculation of the normal maximum sea load.

Loads description

4.2   This identifies the loads (for example "seawater pump").

Loads identification tag

4.3   This tag identifies the loads according to the shipyard's standards tagging system. For example, the "PTI1 fresh water pump" identification tag is "SYYIA/C" for an example ship and shipyard. This data provides a unique identifier for each load.

Loads electric circuit identification

4.4   This is the tag of the electric circuit supplying the load. Such information enables the data validation process.

4.1.9 I——照明和插座负载

与照明、娱乐和插座负载相关的所有负荷。由于船舶的照明电路和插座数量可能很多，在 EPT-EEDI 内列出所有照明电路和照明点实际上是不可行的。因此必须将电路分成小组以标识出可能的对功率有效使用的改进。所分小组为：

.1　1）居住舱室；2）走廊；3）控制站 / 梯道；4）公共处所 / 梯道；5）机舱和辅机舱；6）外部区域；7）车库；和 8）货物处所的照明。均须被主竖区分隔；和

.2　1）居住舱室；2）走廊；3）控制站 / 梯道；4）公共处所 / 梯道；5）机舱和辅机舱；6）车库；和 7）货物处所的电源插座。均须被主竖区分隔。

对复杂的组（例如居住舱室照明和电源插座的小组），应附上解释性说明将其计算衡准包括在内，表明负荷的组成（例如典型居住舱室的灯具、电视机、吹发器、冰箱等）。

4.1.10 L——娱乐负载

本组包括与娱乐负载相关的所有负荷，通常为：公共处所音频和视频设备、剧院舞台设备、办公室 IT 系统、视频游戏等。

4.1.11 N——货物负荷

为透明度起见，本组包括所有货物负荷，例如货泵、起货装置、货物维护、货物冷藏装置、货舱风机和车库风机，但本组的使用系数应设为零。

4.1.12 M——其他

本组包括的所有负荷不与上述各组相关，但仍然对正常最大海浪载荷的总体负荷计算起作用。

负荷描述

4.2　本项对负荷进行标识（例如"海水泵"）。

负荷标识标签

4.3　本标签按船厂标准标签系统对负荷进行标识。例如，对示例船舶和船厂的"PT11 淡水泵"的标识标签是"SYYIA/C"。该数据为每一负荷提供唯一标识符。

负荷电路标识

4.4　这是提供负荷供电电路标签。用此信息可进行数据认证过程。

Loads mechanical rated power "Pm"

4.5　　This data is to be indicated in the document only when the electric load is made by an electric motor driving a mechanical load (e.g. a fan or a pump). This is the rated power of the mechanical device driven by an electric motor.

Loads electric motor rated output power (kW)

4.6　　The output power of the electric motor as per maker's name plate or technical specification. This data does not take part of the calculation but is useful to highlight potential over-rating of the combination motor-mechanical load.

Loads electric motor efficiency "e" (/)

4.7　　This data is to be entered in the document only when the electric load is made by an electric motor driving a mechanical load.

Loads rated electric power "Pr" (kW)

4.8　　Typically the maximum electric power absorbed at the load electric terminals at which the load has been designed for its service, as indicated on the maker's name plate and/or maker's technical specification. When the electric load is made by an electric motor driving a mechanical load, the load's rated electric power is: $Pr=Pm/e$ (kW).

Service factor of load "kl" (/)

4.9　　Provides the reduction from the loads rated electric power to loads necessary electric power that is to be made when the load absorbs less power than its rated power. For example, in the case of an electric motor driving a mechanical load, a fan could be designed with some power margin, leading to the fact that the fan rated mechanical power exceeds the power requested by the duct system it serves. Another example is when a pump rated power exceeds the power needed for pumping in its delivery fluid circuit. Another example is where an electric self-regulating semi-conductors heating system is oversized and the rated power exceeds the power absorbed, according a factor kl.

Service factor of duty "kd" (/)

4.10　　Factor of duty is to be used when a function is provided by more than one load. As all loads are to be included in the EPT for EEDI, this factor provides a correct summation of the loads. For example when two pumps serve the same circuit and they run in duty/stand-by their kd factor will be ½ and ½. When three compressors serve the same circuit and one runs in duty and two in stand-by, then kd is 1/3, 1/3 and 1/3.

Service factor of time "kt" (/)

4.11　　A factor of time based on the shipyard's evaluation about the load duty along 24 hours of ship's navigation as defined at paragraph 3. For example the Entertainment loads operate at their power for a limited period of time, 4 hours out 24 hours; as a consequence $kt=4/24$. For example, the seawater cooling pumps operate at their power all the time during the navigation at $Vref$. As a consequence $kt=1$.

负荷机械额定功率"Pm"

4.5　仅当驱动机械载荷（例如风机、泵等）的电动机产生电负荷时,应在文件中填入此数据。这是电动机驱动的机械设备的额定功率。

负荷电动机额定输出功率（kW）

4.6　按照制造商铭牌或技术规格的电动机输出功率。此数据不参与计算,但可用于突出显示电动机 – 机械组合可能存在的超负荷。

负荷电动机效率"e"（/）

4.7　仅当驱动机械载荷的电动机产生电负荷时,应在文件中填入此数据。

负荷额定电功率"Pr"（kW）

4.8　通常为制造商铭牌和 / 或制造商技术规格显示的、在负荷按其用途设计时采用的电气接点上吸收的最大电功率。当驱动机械载荷的电动机产生电负荷时,负荷额定电功率为：$Pr=Pm/e$（kW）。

负荷使用系数"kl"（/）

4.9　当负荷吸收功率少于额定功率时,应从负荷额定电功率减至负荷必需电功率。例如,用电动机驱动机械载荷时,风机可设计成具备一定的功率裕量,导致风机的额定机械功率超过其服务的管道系统要求的功率。再例如,当泵的额定功率超过其在液体输送管路内泵吸需要的功率时。再例如,对于电气自调半导体,电加热系统过大,根据 kl 系数,额定功率超过吸收的功率。

负荷连续使用系数"kd"（/）

4.10　当一项功能由一个以上负荷提供时,应使用负荷连续使用系数。因为在 EPT–EEDI 中必须包括所有负荷,该系数提供负荷的正确总和。例如,当两台泵以工作 / 备用方式服务于相同的管路时,其 kd 系数应为½和½。当三台压缩机服务于相同的管路且一台工作而其余两台备用时,kd 系数应为 1/3、1/3 和 1/3。

负荷间断使用系数"kt"（/）

4.11　在第 3 段中所定义的间断系数基于船舶 24 h 航行期间船厂对负荷工作时间的评估。例如,娱乐负荷在其功率下运行有限的一段时间（24 h 中的 4 h）,因此 $kt=4/24$。例如,海水冷却泵在以 V_{ref} 航行期间在其功率下始终运行,因此 $kt=1$。

Service total factor of use "ku" (/)

4.12   The total factor of use that takes into consideration all the service factors: $ku=kl \cdot kd \cdot kt$.

Loads necessary power "Pload" (kW)

4.13   The individual user contribution to the auxiliary load power is $Pload=Pr \cdot ku$.

Notes

4.14   A note, as free text, could be included in the document to provide explanations to the verifier.

Groups necessary power (kW)

4.15   The summation of the "Loads necessary power" from group A to N. This is an intermediate step which is not strictly necessary for the calculation of *PAE*. However, it is useful to allow a quantitative analysis of the *PAE*, providing a standard breakdown for analysis and potential improvements of energy saving.

Auxiliaries load's power PAE (kW)

4.16   Auxiliaries load's power *PAE* is the summation of the "Load's necessary power" of all the loads divided by the average efficiency of the generator(s) weighted by power.

$$PAE=\Sigma Pload(i)/(\text{ average efficiency of the generator(s) weighted by power})$$

Layout and organization of the data indicated in the electric power table for EEDI

5   The document "Electric power table for EEDI" is to include general information (i.e. ship's name, project name, document references, etc.) and a table with:

.1   one row containing column titles;

.2   one column for table row ID;

.3   one column for the groups identification ("A", "B", etc.) as indicated in paragraphs 4.1.1 to 4.1.12 of this appendix;

.4   one column for the group descriptions as indicated in paragraphs 4.1.1 to 4.1.12 of this appendix;

.5   one column each for items in paragraphs 4.2 to 4.14 of this appendix (e.g. "load tag");

.6   one row dedicated to each individual load;

.7   the summation results (i.e. summation of powers) including data from paragraphs 4.15 to 4.16 of this appendix; and

.8   explanatory notes.

An example of an electric power table for EEDI for a cruise postal ship which transports passengers and has a car garage and reefer holds for fish trade transportation is indicated below. The data indicated and the type of ship are for reference only.

负荷总使用系数"ku"（/）

4.12 考虑所有负载系数的使用总系数：$ku=kl \cdot kd \cdot kt$.

负荷必需功率"Pload"（kW）

4.13 对辅助机械负荷功率起作用的单个负载功率：$Pload=Pr \cdot ku$.

注释

4.14 在文件中可包括注释（自由文本），以向验证方提供解释。

组的必需功率（kW）

4.15 A组至N组的"负荷必需功率"的总和。该中间步骤对计算 P_{AE} 严格而言不是必要的，但对 P_{AE} 进行量化分析是有用的，提供分析的标准分类和节能的潜在改进。

辅助机械负荷的功率 PAE（kW）

4.16 辅助机械负荷的功率 PAE 为所有负荷的"负荷必需功率"的总和除以发电机的功率加权平均效率。

$$PAE = \Sigma Pload（i）/（发电机的功率加权平均效率）$$

"EEDI电力负荷表"显示的数据布局和组织

5 "EEDI电力负荷表"文件应包括一般信息（即船名、工程名、文件参考等）和下表：

.1 列标题——一行；

.2 表的行标识——一列；

.3 本附录第4.1.1至4.1.12段中所述的组标识（"A"、"B"等）的一列；

.4 本附录第4.1.1至4.1.12段中所述的组描述的一列；

.5 本附录第4.2至4.14段中所述的每一项为一列（如"负荷标签"等）；

.6 每一单独负荷专门使用一行；

.7 包括本附录第4.15至4.16段的数据的总和结果（即功率的总和）；和

.8 解释性说明。

以下显示的是一艘载有乘客并具有车库和渔业贸易运输冷藏货舱的邮轮的 EEDI 电力负荷表的示例。所示的数据和船型仅供参考。

id	Load group	Load description	Load identification tag	Load electric circuit Identification	Load mechanical rated power "Pm" [kW]	Load electric motor rated output power [kW]	Load electric motor efficiency "e" [/]	Load Rated electric power "Pr" [kW]	service factor of load "kl" [/]	service factor of duty "kd" [/]	service factor of time "kt" [/]	service total factor of use "ku" [/]	Load necessary power "Pload" [kW]	Note
1	A	Hull cathodic protection Fwd	xxx	yyy	n.a.	n.a.	n.a.	5.2	1	1	1*	1	5.2	*in use 24hours/day
2	A	Hull cathodic protection mid	xxx	yyy	n.a.	n.a.	n.a.	7.0	1	1	1*	1	7	*in use 24hours/day
3	A	Hull cathodic protection aft	xxx	yyy	n.a.	n.a.	n.a.	4.8	1	1	1*	1	4.8	*in use 24hours/day
4	A	Ballast pump 3	xxx	yyy	30	36	0.92	32.6	0.9	0.5	1	0*	0	*not in use at NMSL see para 2.5.6 of Circ.681
5	A	Fwd Stb mooring winch motor n.1	xxx	yyy	90	150	0.92	97.8	0.8	1	0*	0*	0	*not in use at NMSL see para 2.5.6 of Circ.681
6	A	WTDs system main control panel	xxx	yyy	n.a.	n.a.	n.a.	0.5	1	1	1*	1	0.5	*in use 24hours/day
7	A	WTD 1, deck D frame 150	xxx	yyy	1.2	3	0.91	1.3	0.7	1	0.104*	0.0728	0.096	*180 secs to open/close x 100 opening a day
8	A	WTD 5, deck D frame 210	xxx	yyy	1.2	3	0.91	1.3	0.7	1	0.156*	0.1092	0.14	*180 secs to open/close x 150 opening a day
9	A	Stabilisers control unit	xxx	yyy	n.a.	n.a.	n.a.	0.7	1	1	1*	1	0.7	*in use 24hours/day
10	A	Stabilisers Hydraulic pack power pump 1	xxx	yyy	80	90	0.9	88.9	0.9	1	0*	0	0	*NMSL=> calm sea,=> stabiliser not in use
11	A	S-band Radar 1 controller	xxx	yyy	n.a.	n.a.	n.a.	0.4	1	1	1*	1	0.4	*in use 24hours/day
12	A	S-band Radar 1 motor	xxx	yyy	0.8	1	0.92	0.9	1	1	1*	1	0.9	*in use 24hours/day
13	A	Fire detection system bridge main unit	xxx	yyy	n.a.	n.a.	n.a.	1.5	1	1	1*	1	1.5	*in use 24hours/day
14	A	Fire detection system ECR unit	xxx	yyy	n.a.	n.a.	n.a.	0.9	1	1	1*	1	0.9	*in use 24hours/day
15	A	High pressure water fog contol unit	xxx	yyy	n.a.	n.a.	n.a.	1.2	1	1	1*	1	1.2	*in use 24hours/day
16	A	High pressure water fog engines rooms pump 1a	xxx	yyy	25	30	0.93	26.9	0.9	0.5	0*	0	0	*NMSL=> not emergency =>Load not in use
17	A	High pressure water fog engines rooms pump 1b	xxx	yyy	25	30	0.93	26.9	0.9	0.5	0*	0	0	* not emergency situations
18	B	PTI port fresh water pump 1	xxx	yyy	30	36	0.92	32.6	0.9	0.5*	1	0.45	14.7	* pump1,2 one is duty and one is stand-by
19	B	PTI port fresh water pump 2	xxx	yyy	30	36	0.92	32.6	0.9	0.5*	1	0.45	14.7	* pump1,2 one is duty and one is stand-by
20	B	Thrusters control system	xxx	yyy	n.a.	n.a.	n.a.	0.5	1	1	1*	1	0.5	in use 24hours/day (even if thruster motor isn't)
21	B	Bow thruster 1	xxx	yyy	3000	3000	0.96	3125.0	1	1	0*	0	0	*NMSL=>thrusters motor are not in use
22	B	PEM port cooling fan 1	xxx	yyy	20	25	0.93	21.5	0.9	1	n.a.	n.a	n.a.*	*this load is included in the propulsion chain data
23	C	HT circulation pump 1 DG 3	xxx	yyy	8	10	0.92	8.7	0.9	0.5*	1	0.45	3.9	* pump1,2 one is duty and one is stand-by
24	C	HT circulation pump 2 DG 3	xxx	yyy	8	10	0.92	8.7	0.9	0.5*	1	0.45	3.9	* pump1,2 one is duty and one is stand-by
25	C	DG3 combustion air fan	xxx	yyy	28	35	0.92	30.4	0.9	1	1*	0.9	27.4	*in use 24hours/day
26	C	DG3 exhaust gas boiler circulating pump	xxx	yyy	6	8	0.93	6.5	0.8	1	1*	0.8	5.2	*in use 24hours/day
27	C	Alternator 3 external cooling fan	xxx	yyy	3	5	0.93	3.2	0.8	1	1*	0.8	2.75	*in use 24hours/day
28	C	fuel feed fwd booster pump a	xxx	yyy	7	9	0.92	7.6	0.9	0.5*	1	0.45	3.4	* pump1,2 one is duty and one is stand-by
29	C	fuel feed fwd booster pump b	xxx	yyy	7	9	0.92	7.6	0.9	0.5*	1	0.45	3.4	* pump1,2 one is duty and one is stand-by
30	D	Fwd main LT cooling pump 1	xxx	yyy	120	150	0.95	126.3	0.9	0.5*	1	0.45	56.8	* pump1,2 one is duty and one is stand-by
31	D	Fwd main LT cooling pump 2	xxx	yyy	120	150	0.95	126.3	0.9	0.5*	1	0.45	56.8	* pump1,2 one is duty and one is stand-by
32	E	FWD engine room supply fan 1	xxx	yyy	87.8	110	0.93	94.4	0.95	1	1*	0.95	89.7	*in use 24hours/day
33	E	FWD engine room exhaust fan 1	xxx	yyy	75	86	0.93	80.6	0.96	1	1*	0.96	77.4	*in use 24hours/day
34	E	purifier room supply fan 1	xxx	yyy	60	70	0.93	64.5	0.96	0.5	1*	0.48	31.0	*in use 24hours/day
35	E	purifier room supply fan 2	xxx	yyy	60	70	0.93	64.5	0.96	0.5	1*	0.48	31.0	*in use 24hours/day
36	F	HVAC chiller a	xxx	yyy	1450	1600	0.95	1526.3	1	2/3*	1	0.66	1007.4	*1 Chiller is spare; see heat load dissipation doc.
37	F	HVAC chiller b	xxx	yyy	1450	1600	0.95	1526.3	1	2/3*	1	0.66	1007.4	*1 Chiller is spare; see heat load dissipation doc.
38	F	HVAC chiller C	xxx	yyy	1450	1600	0.95	1526.3	1	2/3*	1	0.66	1007.4	*1 Chiller is spare; see heat load dissipation doc.
39	F	A.H.U. Ac station 5.4 supply fan	xxx	yyy	50	60	0.93	53.8	0.9	1	1*	0.9	48.4	*in use 24hours/day
40	F	A.H.U. Ac station 5.4 exhaust fan	xxx	yyy	45	55	0.93	48.4	0.9	1	1*	0.9	43.5	*in use 24hours/day
41	F	Chilled water pump a	xxx	yyy	80	90	0.93	86.0	0.88	0.5*	1	0.44	37.8	* pump1,2 one is duty and one is stand-by
42	F	Chilled water pump b	xxx	yyy	80	90	0.93	86.0	0.88	0.5*	1	0.44	37.8	* pump1,2 one is duty and one is stand-by
43	G	Italian's espresso coffee machine	xxx	yyy	n.a.	n.a.	n.a.	7.0	0.9	1	0.2*	0.18	1.3	*in use 4.8hours/day
44	G	deep freezer machine	xxx	yyy	n.a.	n.a.	n.a.	20.0	0.8	1	0.16*	0.128	3.2	*in use 4hours/day
45	G	washing machine 1	xxx	yyy	n.a.	n.a.	n.a.	8.0	0.8	1	0.33*	0.264	3.2	*in use 8hours/day
46	H	lift pax mid 4	ΛΛΛ	yyy	30	40	0.93	32.3	0.5	1	0.175*	0.0875	0.9	*in use 4hours/day
47	H	vaccum collecting system 4 pump a	xxx	yyy	10	13	0.92	10.9	0.9	1	1*	0.9	8.7	*in use 24hours/day
48	H	sewage treatmet system 1 pump 1	xxx	yyy	15	17	0.93	16.1	0.9	1	1*	0.9	8.7	*in use 24hours/day
49	H	Gym running machine	xxx	yyy	n.a.	n.a.	n.a.	2.5	1	1	0.3*	0.3	0.8	*in use 7.2hours/day
50	I	Cabin's lighting MVZ3	n.a.	n.a.	n.a.	n.a.	n.a.	80*	1	1	1	1	80.0	* see explainatory note
51	I	corridors ligthing MVZ3	n.a.	n.a.	n.a.	n.a.	n.a.	10*	1	1	1	1	10.0	* see explainatory note
52	I	Cabin's sockets MVZ3	n.a.	n.a.	n.a.	n.a.	n.a.	5*	1	1	1	1	5.0	* see explainatory note
53	L	Main Theatre audio booster amplifier	xxx	yyy	n.a.	n.a.	n.a.	15.0	1	1	0.3*	0.3	4.5	*in use 7.2hours/day
54	L	Video wall atrium	xxx	yyy	n.a.	n.a.	n.a.	2.0	1	1	0.3*	0.3	0.6	*in use 7.2hours/day
55	M	Car Garage supply fan1	xxx	yyy	28	35	0.92	30.4	0.9	1	1*	0*	0	*not in use at NMSL see para 2.5.6 of Circ.681
56	M	Fish transportation refeer hold n.2	xxx	yyy	25	30	0.93	26.9	0.9	0.5	0*	0	0	*not in use at NMSL see para 2.5.6 of Circ.681
57	N	Sliding glass roof	xxx	yyy	30	40	0.93	32.3	0.9	1	0.3*	0.27	0.2	*in use 7.2hours/day
												ΣPload(i)=	3764	

PAE =3764/(weighted average efficiency of generator(s)) [kW]   Group's necessary power (group A=22.9kW, B=29.8kW,C=49.9kW, D=113.7kW, E=229kW , F=3189kW, G=7.6kW, H=19kW, I=95kW, L=5.1kW, M=0kW, N=0.22kW)

某大型客船的 EEDI 电力负荷计算表示例

EEDI 电力负荷计算表	样本船舶		样本工程									（NMSL= 正常情况下船舶负荷）	
序号	负荷组	负荷描述	负荷标识标签	负荷电路标识	负荷机械额定功率 "Pm" [kW]	负荷电动机机械额定输出功率 [kW]	负荷电动机械率 "e"[/]	负荷额定电功率 "Pr" [kW]	负荷使用系数 "kl" [/]	负荷连续使用系数 "kd" [/]	负荷间断使用系数 "kt" [/]	负荷总使用系数 "Ku" [/]	使用负荷 "Pload" [kW]	注释
---	---	---	---	---	---	---	---	---	---	---	---	---	---	---
1	A	船首阴极保护	xxx	yyy	n.a.	n.a.	n.a.	5.2	1	1	1*	1	5.2	* 按 24 小时 / 天计算
2	A	船中阴极保护	xxx	yyy	n.a.	n.a.	n.a.	7	1	1	1*	1	7	* 按 24 小时 / 天计算
3	A	船尾阴极保护	xxx	yyy	n.a.	n.a.	n.a.	4.8	1	1	1*	1	4.8	* 按 24 小时 / 天计算
4	A	压载泵 3	xxx	yyy	30	36	0.92	32.6	0.9	0.5	1	0*	0	* 不在 NMSL 情况下使用，见本标准 2.5.6
5	A	船首锚链绞马达	xxx	yyy	90	150	0.92	97.8	0.8	1	1	0*	0	* 不在 NMSL 情况下使用，见本标准 2.5.6
6	A	WTDs 系统主控制面板	xxx	yyy	n.a.	n.a.	n.a.	0.5	1	1	1*	1	0.5	* 按 24 小时 / 天计算
7	A	WTD1,D 层甲板，150 号肋位	xxx	yyy	1.2	3	0.91	1.3	0.7	1	0.104*	0.072 8	0.096	*180 秒 / 每次开关 ×100 次打开 / 天
8	A	WTD5,D 层甲板，210 号肋位	xxx	yyy	1.2	3	0.91	1.3	0.7	1	0.156*	0.109 2	0.14	*180 秒 / 每次开关 ×100 次打开 / 天
9	A	稳定器控制单元	xxx	yyy	n.a.	n.a.	n.a.	0.7	1	1	1*	1	0.7	* 按 24 小时 / 天计算
10	A	稳定器水压包动力泵 1	xxx	yyy	80	90	0.9	88.9	1	1	0*	0	0	*NMSL => 无风海况 => 不使用稳定器
11	A	S 组 1 号雷达控制器	xxx	yyy	n.a.	n.a.	n.a.	0.4	1	1	1*	1	0.4	* 按 24 小时 / 天计算
12	A	S 组 2 号雷达马达	xxx	yyy	0.8	1	0.92	0.9	1	1	1*	1	0.9	* 按 24 小时 / 天计算
13	A	消防桥的主要单元	xxx	yyy	n.a.	n.a.	n.a.	1.5	1	1	1*	1	1.5	* 按 24 小时 / 天计算
14	A	消防 ECR 单元	xxx	yyy	n.a.	n.a.	n.a.	0.9	1	1	1*	1	0.9	* 按 24 小时 / 天计算
15	A	高压水雾控制单元	xxx	yyy	n.a.	n.a.	n.a.	1.2	1	1	1*	1	1.2	* 按 24 小时 / 天计算
16	A	机舱高压水雾泵 1a	xxx	yyy	25	30	0.93	26.9	0.9	0.5	0*	0	0	*NMSL=> 无紧急状况 => 不加载
17	A	机舱高压水雾泵 1b	xxx	yyy	25	30	0.93	26.9	0.9	0.5	0*	0	0	* 不在紧急情况下使用
18	B	PTi 左舷淡水泵 1	xxx	yyy	30	36	0.92	32.6	0.9	0.5*	1	0.45	14.7	1,2 号泵一个为常用，一个为备用
19	B	PTi 左舷淡水泵 2	xxx	yyy	30	36	0.92	32.6	0.9	0.5*	1	0.45	14.7	1,2 号泵一个为常用，一个为备用
20	B	推进器控制系统	xxx	yyy	n.a.	n.a.	n.a.	0.5	1	1	1*	1	0.5	* 按 24 小时 / 天计算（无论推进马达何种情况）
21	B	船首推进器 1	xxx	yyy	3 000	3 000	0.96	3 125.0	1	1	0*	0	0	*NMSL=> 不适用于推进马达
22	B	PEM 左舷冷却风机 1	xxx	yyy	20	25	0.93	21.5	1	1	n.a.	n.a.	n.a.*	* 该载荷包含了推进
23	C	DG3 高温循环泵 1	xxx	yyy	8	10	0.92	8.7	0.9	0.5*	1	0.45	3.9	1,2 号泵一个为常用，一个为备用
24	C	DG3 高温循环泵 2	xxx	yyy	8	10	0.92	8.7	0.9	0.6*	1	0.45	3.9	1,2 号泵一个为常用，一个为备用
25	C	DG3 燃气送风机	xxx	yyy	28	35	0.92	30.4	0.9	1	1	0.9	27.4	* 按 24 小时 / 天计算
26	C	DG3 废气锅炉循环泵	xxx	yyy	6	8	0.93	6.5	0.8	1	1	0.8	5.2	* 按 24 小时 / 天计算
27	C	转换器 3 的外部冷却器	xxx	yyy	3	5	0.93	3.2	0.8	1	1	0.8	2.75	* 按 24 小时 / 天计算
28	C	船首燃油供应调节器 a	xxx	yyy	7	9	0.92	7.6	0.9	0.5*	1	0.45	3.4	1,2 号泵一个为常用，一个为备用
29	C	船首燃油供应调节器 b	xxx	yyy	7	9	0.92	7.6	0.9	0.5*	1	0.45	3.4	1,2 号泵一个为常用，一个为备用
30	D	船首主要的低温冷却泵 1	xxx	yyy	120	150	0.95	126.3	0.9	0.5*	1	0.45	56.8	1,2 号泵一个为常用，一个为备用
31	D	船首主要的低温冷却泵 2	xxx	yyy	120	150	0.95	126.3	0.9	0.5*	1	0.45	56.8	1,2 号泵一个为常用，一个为备用
32	E	船首送风机 1	xxx	yyy	87.8	110	0.93	94.4	0.95	1	1*	0.95	89.7	* 按 24 小时 / 天计算
33	E	船首机舱排气风机 1	xxx	yyy	75	86	0.93	80.6	0.96	1	1	0.96	77.4	* 按 24 小时 / 天计算
34	E	净化器舱室送风机 1	xxx	yyy	60	70	0.93	64.5	0.96	0.5	1	0.48	31.0	* 按 24 小时 / 天计算
35	E	净化器舱室送风机 2	xxx	yyy	60	70	0.93	64.5	0.96	0.5	1	0.48	31.0	* 按 24 小时 / 天计算
36	F	HAV 冷却器 a	xxx	yyy	1 450	1 600	0.95	1 526.3	1	2/3*	1	0.66	1 007.4	* 其中一个冷却器为冗余，见热负荷数据文件
37	F	HAV 冷却器 b	xxx	yyy	1 450	1 600	0.95	1 526.3	1	2/3*	1	0.66	1 007.4	* 其中一个冷却器为冗余，见热负荷数据文件
38	F	HAV 冷却器 c	xxx	yyy	1 450	1 600	0.95	1 526.3	1	2/3*	1	0.66	1 007.4	* 其中一个冷却器为冗余，见热负荷数据文件
39	F	A.H.U5.4 站位送风机	xxx	yyy	50	60	0.93	53.8	0.9	1	1	0.9	48.4	* 按 24 小时 / 天计算
40	F	A.H.U5.5 站位送风机	xxx	yyy	45	55	0.93	48.4	0.9	1	1	0.9	43.5	* 按 24 小时 / 天计算
41	F	冷却水泵 a	xxx	yyy	80	90	0.93	86	0.88	0.5*	1	0.44	37.8	1,2 号泵一个为常用，一个为备用
42	F	冷却水泵 b	xxx	yyy	80	90	0.93	86	0.88	0.5*	1	0.44	37.8	1,2 号泵一个为常用，一个为备用
43	G	意大利浓缩咖啡机	xxx	yyy	n.a.	n.a.	n.a.	7.0	0.9	1	0.2*	0.18	1.3	* 按 4.8 小时 / 天计算
44	G	深度制冷机	xxx	yyy	n.a.	n.a.	n.a.	20.0	0.8	1	0.16*	0.128	3.2	* 按 4 小时 / 天计算
45	G	洗衣机 1	xxx	yyy	n.a.	n.a.	n.a.	8.0	0.8	1	0.33*	0.264	3.2	* 按 8 小时 / 天计算
46	H	升降机 4	xxx	yyy	30	40	0.93	32.3	0.5	1	0.175*	0.087 5	0.9	* 按 24 小时 / 天计算
47	H	4 号真空收集系统 a 号	xxx	yyy	10	13	0.92	10.9	0.9	1	1*	0.9	8.7	* 按 24 小时 / 天计算
48	H	1 号污水处理系统 1 号泵	xxx	yyy	15	17	0.93	16.1	0.9	1	1*	0.9	8.7	* 按 24 小时 / 天计算
49	H	体育健身器材	xxx	yyy	n.a.	n.a.	n.a.	2.5	1	1	0.3	0.3	0.8	* 按 7.2 小时 / 天计算
50	I	船舱照明灯 MVZ3	n.a.	n.a.	n.a.	n.a.	n.a.	80*	1	1	1	1	80.0	* 见注释
51	I	非痷照明灯 MVZ3	n.a.	n.a.	n.a.	n.a.	n.a.	10*	1	1	1	1	10.0	* 见注释
52	I	船舱电源插座 MVZ3	n.a.	n.a.	n.a.	n.a.	n.a.	5*	1	1	1	1	5.0	* 见注释
53	L	剧院自动音响设备	xxx	yyy	n.a.	n.a.	n.a.	15.0	1	1	0.3*	0.3	4.5	* 按 7.2 小时 / 天计算
54	L	视频室	xxx	yyy	n.a.	n.a.	n.a.	2.0	1	1	0.3*	0.3	0.6	* 按 7.2 小时 / 天计算
55	M	车库风机	xxx	yyy	28	35	0.92	30.4	0.9	1	1*	0*	0	* 不在 NMSL 情况下使用，见本标准 2.5.6
56	M	货舱 2 的起货装置	xxx	yyy	25	30	0.93	26.9	0.9	0.5	0*	0	0	* 不在 NMSL 情况下使用，见本标准 2.5.6
57	N	可滑移玻璃顶盖	xxx	yyy	30	40	0.93	32.3	0.9	1	0.27	0.27	0.2	* 按 7.2 小时 / 天计算
												Σ Pload(i)=3 764		

PAE=3 674/(发电机单位重量平均效率)[kw] 发电机组的必需功率（组 A=22.9 kw，B=29.8 KW，C=49.9 kW，D=113.7 kW，E=229 kW，F=3 189 kW，G=7.6 kW，H=19 kW，L=5.1 kW，M=0 kW，N=0.22 kW）

— 494 —

APPENDIX 3

A GENERIC AND SIMPLIFIED MARINE POWER PLANT
FOR A CRUISE PASSENGER SHIPS HAVING NON-CONVENTIONAL PROPULSION

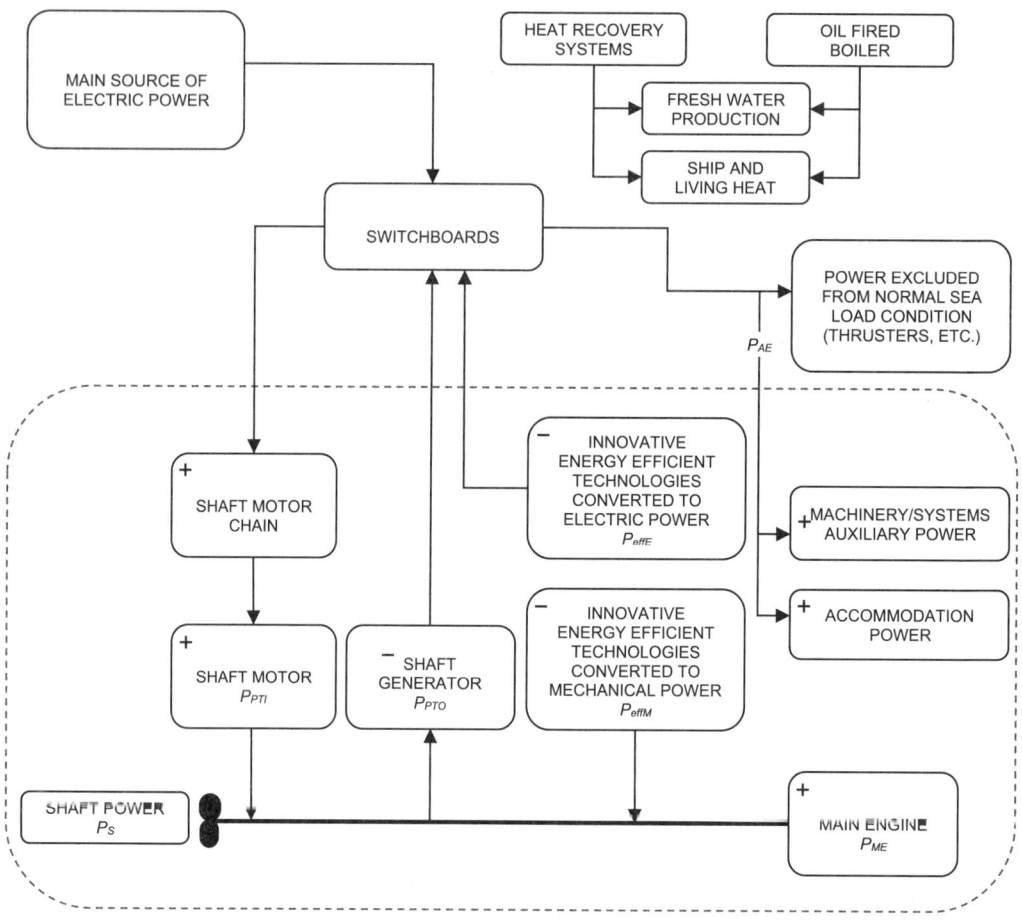

Note: Symbols for plus (+) and minus (−) indicate CO_2 contribution to EEDI formula.

附录3
具有非传统推进装置的豪华邮轮电站的简化总体示图

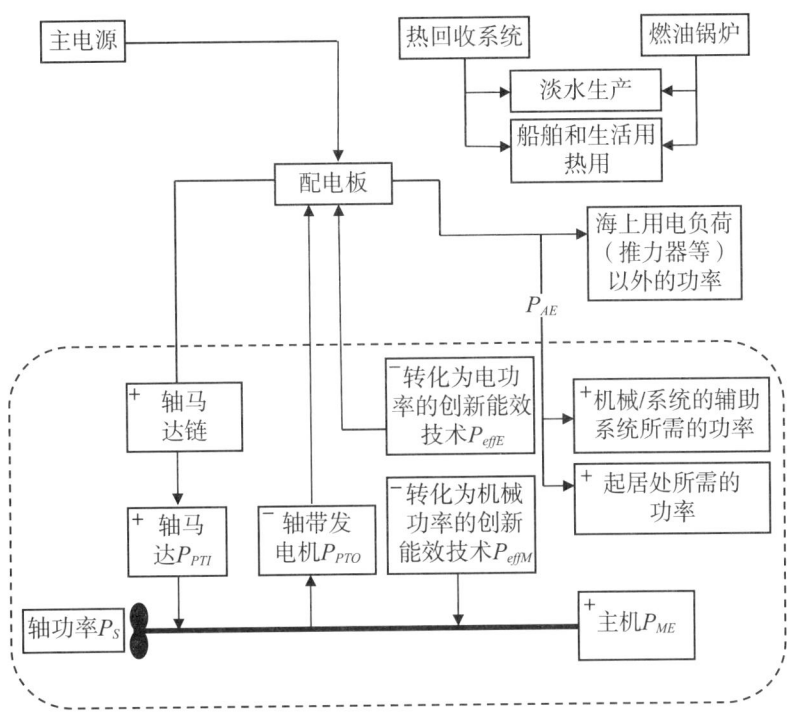

注：加号(+)和减号(−)表示EEDI公式中CO_2的贡献。

注：加号（＋）和减号（−）表示 EEDI 公式中 CO_2 的贡献。

APPENDIX 4

EEDI CALCULATION EXAMPLES FOR USE OF DUAL-FUEL ENGINES

Case 1: Standard Kamsarmax ship, one main engine (MDO), standard auxiliary engines (MDO), no shaft generator:

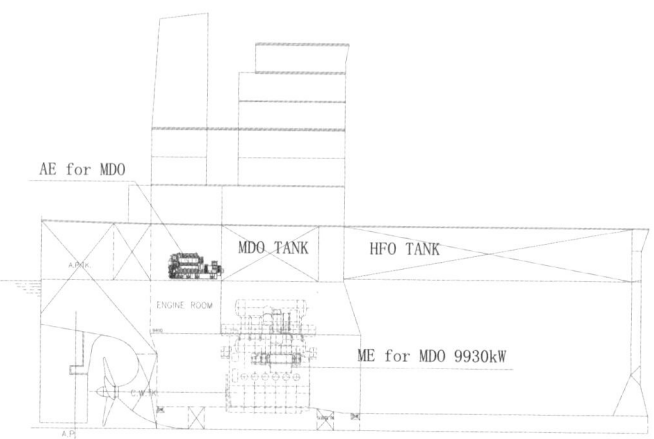

S/N	Parameter	Formula or Source	Unit	Value
1	MCR_{ME}	MCR rating of main engine	kW	9,930
2	Capacity	Deadweight of the ship at summer load draft	DWT	81,200
3	V_{ref}	Ships speed as defined in EEDI regulation	kn	14
4	P_{ME}	0.75 x MCR_{ME}	kW	7,447.5
5	P_{AE}	0.05 x MCR_{ME}	kW	496.5
6	C_{FME}	C_F factor of Main engine using MDO	-	3.206
7	C_{FAE}	C_F factor of Auxiliary engine using MDO	-	3.206
8	SFC_{ME}	Specific fuel consumption of at P_{ME}	g/kWh	165
9	SFC_{AE}	Specific fuel consumption of at P_{AE}	g/kWh	210
10	EEDI	$((P_{ME} \times C_{F\,ME} \times SFC_{ME})+(P_{AE} \times C_{FAE} \times SFC_{AE}))$ / $(V_{ref} \times Capacity)$	gCO_2/tnm	3.76

Case 2: LNG is regarded as the "primary fuel" if dual-fuel main engine and dual-fuel auxiliary engine (LNG, pilot fuel MDO; no shaft generator) are equipped with bigger LNG tanks:

附录 4
使用双燃料发动机的 EEDI 计算实例

实例 1：标准卡尔萨姆型船，一个主机（MDO），标准辅机（MDO），无轴带发电机：

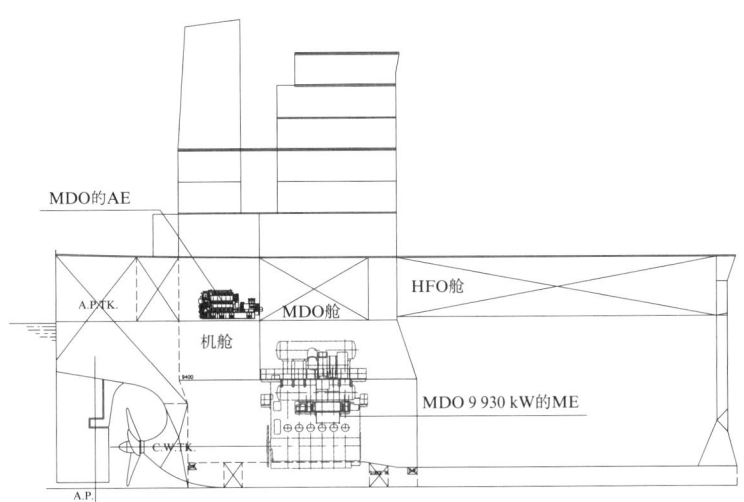

S/N	参数	公式或来源	单位	值
1	MCR_{ME}	主机的 MCR	kW	9 930
2	载运能力	船舶夏季载重吃水的载重吨	DWT	81 200
3	V_{ref}	EEDI 规则中定义的船速	kn	14
4	P_{ME}	$0.75 \times MCR_{ME}$	kW	7 447.5
5	P_{AE}	$0.05 \times MCR_{ME}$	kW	496.5
6	C_{FME}	使用 MDO 的主机 C_F 系数	–	3.206
7	C_{FAE}	使用 MDO 的辅机 C_F 系数	–	3.206
8	SFC_{ME}	P_{ME} 下的燃油消耗率	g/kWh	165
9	SFC_{AE}	P_{AE} 下的燃油消耗率	g/kWh	210
10	EEDI	$\left(\left(P_{ME} \times C_{FME} \times SFC_{ME} \right) + \left(P_{AE} \times C_{FAE} \times SFC_{AE} \right) \right) / \left(V_{ref} \times Capacity \right)$	gCO_2/tnm	3.76

实例 2：如果双燃料主机和双燃料辅机（LNG，引燃油 MDO；无轴带发电机）配有较大的 LNG 舱，则视 LNG 为"主要燃料"：

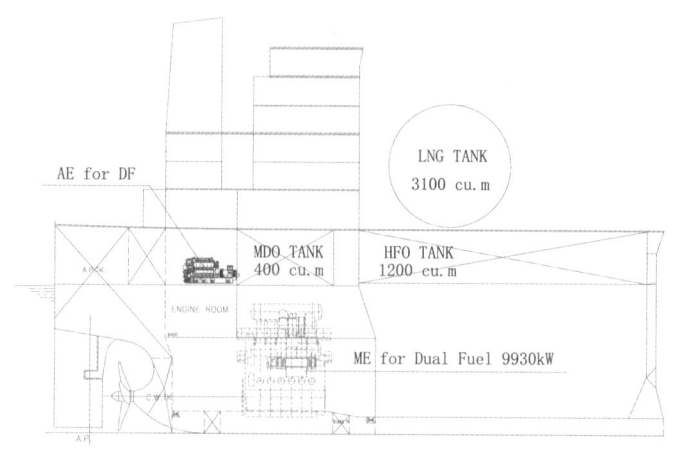

S/N	Parameter	Formula or Source	Unit	Value
1	MCR_{ME}	MCR rating of main engine	kW	9,930
2	Capacity	Deadweight of the ship at summer load draft	DWT	81,200
3	V_{ref}	Ships speed as defined in EEDI regulation	kn	14
4	P_{ME}	0.75 x MCR_{ME}	kW	7,447.5
5	P_{AE}	0.05 x MCR_{ME}	kW	496.5
6	$CF_{Pilotfuel}$	C_F factor of pilot fuel for dual-fuel ME using MDO	-	3.206
7	$CF_{AE\,Pliotfuel}$	C_F factor of pilot fuel for Auxiliary engine using MDO	-	3.206
8	CF_{LNG}	C_F factor of dual-fuel engine using LNG	-	2.75
9	$SFC_{MEPilotfuel}$	Specific fuel consumption of pilot fuel for dual-fuel ME at P_{ME}	g/kWh	6
10	$SFC_{AE\,Pilotfuel}$	Specific fuel consumption of pilot fuel for dual-fuel AE at P_{AE}	g/kWh	7
11	$SFC_{ME\,LNG}$	Specific fuel consumption of ME using LNG at P_{ME}	g/kWh	136
12	$SFC_{AE\,LNG}$	Specific fuel consumption of AE using LNG at P_{AE}	g/kWh	160
13	V_{LNG}	LNG tank capacity on board	m³	3,100
14	V_{HFO}	Heavy fuel oil tank capacity on board	m³	1,200
15	V_{MDO}	Marine diesel oil tank capacity on board	m³	400
16	ρ_{LNG}	Density of LNG	kg/m³	450
17	ρ_{HFO}	Density of heavy fuel oil	kg/m³	991
18	ρ_{MDO}	Density of marine diesel oil	kg/m³	900
19	LCV_{LNG}	Low calorific value of LNG	kJ/kg	48,000
20	LCV_{HFO}	Low calorific value of heavy fuel oil	kJ/kg	40,200
21	LCV_{MDO}	Low calorific value of marine diesel oil	kJ/kg	42,700
22	K_{LNG}	Filling rate of LNG tank	-	0.95
23	K_{HFO}	Filling rate of heavy fuel tank	-	0.98
24	K_{MDO}	Filling rate of marine diesel tank	-	0.98
25	f_{DFgas}	$\dfrac{P_{ME}+P_{AE}}{P_{ME}+P_{AE}} \times \dfrac{V_{LNG} \times \rho_{LNG} \times LCV_{LNG} \times K_{LNG}}{V_{HFO} \times \rho_{HFO} \times LCV_{HFO} \times K_{HFO} + V_{MDO} \times \rho_{MDO} \times LCV_{MDO} \times K_{MDO} + V_{LAG} \times \rho_{LAG} \times LCV_{LAG} \times K_{LAG}}$	-	0.5068
26	EEDI	$(P_{ME} \times (C_{F\,Pilotfuel} \times SFC_{ME\,Pilotfuel} + C_{F\,LNG} \times SFC_{ME\,LNG}) + P_{AE} \times (C_{F\,Pilotfuel} \times SFC_{AE\,Pilotfuel} + C_{F\,LNG} \times SFC_{AE\,LNG})) / (V_{ref} \times Capacity)$	gCO₂/tnm	2.78

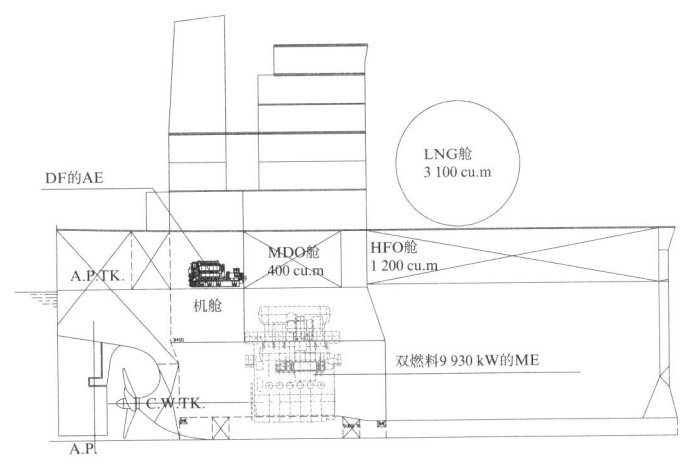

S/N	参数	公式或来源	单位	值
1	MCR_{ME}	主机的 MCR	kW	9 930
2	载运能力	船舶夏季载重吃水的载重吨	DWT	81 200
3	V_{ref}	EEDI 规则中定义的船速	kn	14
4	P_{ME}	$0.75 \times MCRME$	kW	7 447.5
5	P_{AE}	$0.05 \times MCRME$	kW	496.5
6	$CF_{Pilotfuel}$	使用 MDO 的双燃料主机引燃油 C_F 系数	–	3.206
7	$CF_{AE\,Pilotfuel}$	使用 MDO 的辅机引燃油 C_F 系数	–	3.206
8	CF_{LNG}	使用 LNG 的双燃料发动机 C_F 系数	–	2.75
9	$SFC_{MEPilotfuel}$	P_{ME} 时双燃料主机引燃油消耗率	g/kWh	6
10	$SFC_{AE\,Pilotfuel}$	P_{AE} 时双燃料辅机引燃油消耗率	g/kWh	7
11	$SFC_{ME\,LNG}$	P_{ME} 时使用 LNG 主机的燃气消耗率	g/kWh	136
12	$SFC_{AE\,LNG}$	P_{AE} 时使用 LNG 辅机的燃气消耗率	g/kWh	160
13	V_{LNG}	船上 LNG 舱容积	m³	3 100
14	V_{HFO}	船上重燃油舱容积	m³	1 200
15	V_{MDO}	船上船用柴油舱容积	m³	400
16	ρ_{LNG}	LNG 的密度	kg/m³	450
17	ρ_{HFO}	重燃油的密度	kg/m³	991
18	ρ_{MDO}	船用柴油的密度	kg/m³	900
19	LCV_{LNG}	LNG 的低热值	kJ/kg	48 000
20	LCV_{HFO}	重燃油的低热值	kJ/kg	40 200
21	LCV_{MDO}	船用柴油的低热值	kJ/kg	42 700
22	K_{LNG}	LNG 舱充装率	–	0.95
23	K_{HFO}	重燃油舱充装率	–	0.98
24	K_{MDO}	船用柴油舱充装率	–	0.98
25	f_{DFgas}	$\dfrac{P_{ME}+P_{AE}}{P_{ME}+P_{AE}} \times \dfrac{V_{LNG} \times \rho_{LNG} \times LCV_{LNG} \times K_{LNG}}{V_{HFO} \times \rho_{HFO} \times LCV_{HFO} \times K_{HFO} + V_{MDO} \times \rho_{MDO} \times LCV_{MDO} \times K_{MDO} + V_{LAG} \times \rho_{LAG} \times LCV_{LAG} \times K_{LAG}}$	–	0.506 8
26	EEDI	$\left(P_{ME} \times \left(C_{FPilotfuel} \times SFC_{ME\,Pilotfuel} + C_{FLNG} \times SFC_{ME\,LNG} \right) + P_{AE} \times \left(C_{FPilotfuel} \times SFC_{AE\,Pilotfuel} + C_{FLNG} \times SFC_{AE\,LNG} \right) \right) / \left(V_{ref} \times Capacity \right)$	gCO₂/tnm	2.78

Case 3: LNG is not regarded as the "primary fuel" if dual-fuel main engine and dual-fuel auxiliary engine (LNG, pilot fuel MDO; no shaft generator) are equipped with smaller LNG tanks:

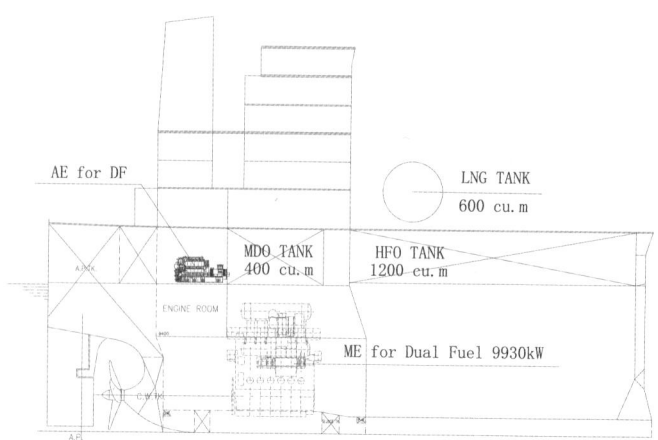

S/N	Parameter	Formula or Source	Unit	Value
1	MCR_{ME}	MCR rating of main engine	kW	9,930
2	Capacity	Deadweight of the ship at summer load draft	DWT	81,200
3	V_{ref}	Ships speed as defined in EEDI regulation	kn	14
4	P_{ME}	0.75 x MCR_{ME}	kW	7,447.5
5	P_{AE}	0.05 x MCR_{ME}	kW	496.5
6	$C_{FPilotfuel}$	C_F factor of pilot fuel for dual-fuel ME using MDO	-	3.206
7	$C_{FAE\ Pilotfuel}$	C_F factor of pilot fuel for Auxiliary engine using MDO	-	3.206
8	C_{FLNG}	C_F factor of dual-fuel engine using LNG	-	2.75
9	C_{FMDO}	C_F factor of dual-fuel ME/AE engine using MDO	-	3.206
10	$SFC_{MEPilotfuel}$	Specific fuel consumption of pilot fuel for dual-fuel ME at P_{ME}	g/kWh	6
11	$SFC_{AE\ Pilotfuel}$	Specific fuel consumption of pilot fuel for dual-fuel AE at P_{AE}	g/kWh	7
12	$SFC_{ME\ LNG}$	Specific fuel consumption of ME using LNG at P_{ME}	g/kWh	136
13	$SFC_{AE\ LNG}$	Specific fuel consumption of AE using LNG at P_{AE}	g/kWh	160
14	$SFC_{ME\ MDO}$	Specific fuel consumption of dual-fuel ME using MDO at P_{ME}	g/kWh	165
15	$SFC_{AE\ MDO}$	Specific fuel consumption of dual-fuel AE using MDO at P_{AE}	g/kWh	187
16	V_{LNG}	LNG tank capacity on board	m^3	600
17	V_{HFO}	Heavy fuel oil tank capacity on board	m^3	1,800
18	V_{MDO}	Marine diesel oil tank capacity on board	m^3	400
19	ρ_{LNG}	Density of LNG	kg/m^3	450
20	ρ_{HFO}	Density of heavy fuel oil	kg/m^3	991
21	ρ_{MDO}	Density of marine diesel oil	kg/m^3	900
22	LCV_{LNG}	Low calorific value of LNG	kJ/kg	48,000
23	LCV_{HFO}	Low calorific value of heavy fuel oil	kJ/kg	40,200
24	LCV_{MDO}	Low calorific value of marine diesel oil	kJ/kg	42,700
25	K_{LNG}	Filling rate of LNG tank	-	0.95
26	K_{HFO}	Filling rate of heavy fuel tank	-	0.98
27	K_{MDO}	Filling rate of marine diesel tank	-	0.98

实例 3：如果双燃料主机和双燃料辅机（LNG，引燃油 MDO；无轴带发电机）配有较小的 LNG 舱，则 LNG 不被视为"主要燃料"：

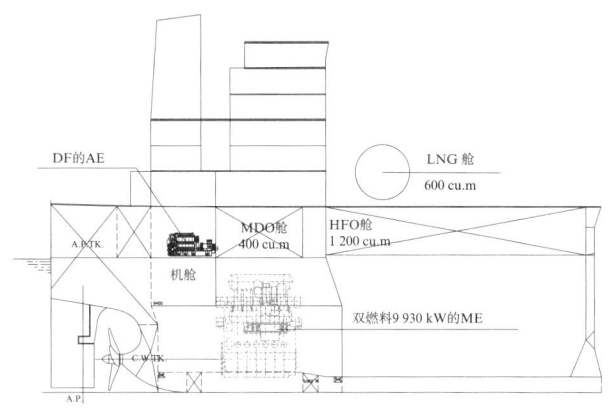

S/N	参数	公式或来源	单位	值
1	MCR_{ME}	主机的 MCR	kW	9 930
2	载运能力	船舶夏季载重吃水的载重吨	DWT	81 200
3	V_{ref}	EEDI 规则中定义的船速	kn	14
4	P_{ME}	$0.75 \times MCRME$	kW	7 447.5
5	P_{AE}	$0.05 \times MCRME$	kW	496.5
6	$C_{FPilotfuel}$	使用 MDO 的双燃料主机引燃油 C_F 系数	–	3.206
7	$C_{FAE\ Plilotfuel}$	使用 MDO 的辅机引燃油 C_F 系数	–	3.206
8	C_{FLNG}	使用 LNG 的双燃料发动机 C_F 系数	–	2.75
9	C_{FMDO}	使用 MDO 的双燃料主机 / 辅机发动机 C_F 系数	–	3.206
10	$SFC_{MEPilotfuel}$	P_{ME} 时双燃料主机引燃油消耗率	g/kWh	6
11	$SFC_{AE\ Pilotfuel}$	P_{AE} 时双燃料辅机引燃油消耗率	g/kWh	7
12	$SFC_{ME\ LNG}$	P_{ME} 时使用 LNG 主机的燃气消耗率	g/kWh	136
13	$SFC_{AE\ LNG}$	P_{AE} 时使用 LNG 辅机的燃气消耗率	g/kWh	160
14	$SFC_{ME\ MDO}$	P_{ME} 时使用 MDO 双燃料主机的燃油消耗率	g/kWh	165
15	$SFC_{AE\ MDO}$	P_{AE} 时使用 MDO 双燃料辅机的燃油消耗率	g/kWh	187
16	V_{LNG}	船上 LNG 舱容积	m^3	600
17	V_{HFO}	船上重燃油舱容积	m^3	1 800
18	V_{MDO}	船上船用柴油舱容积	m^3	400
19	ρ_{LNG}	LNG 的密度	kg/m^3	450
20	ρ_{HFO}	重燃油的密度	kg/m^3	991
21	ρ_{MDO}	船用柴油的密度	kg/m^3	900
22	LCV_{LNG}	LNG 的低热值	kJ/kg	48 000
23	LCV_{HFO}	重燃油的低热值	kJ/kg	40 200
24	LCV_{MDO}	船用柴油的低热值	kJ/kg	42 700
25	K_{LNG}	LNG 舱充装率	–	0.95
26	K_{HFO}	重燃油舱充装率	–	0.98
27	K_{MDO}	船用柴油舱充装率	–	0.98

S/N	Parameter	Formula or Source	Unit	Value
28	f_{DFgas}	$\dfrac{P_{ME}+P_{AE}}{P_{ME}+P_{AE}} \times \dfrac{V_{LNG} \times \rho_{LNG} \times LCV_{LNG} \times K_{LNG}}{V_{HFO} \times \rho_{HFO} \times LCV_{HFO} \times K_{HFO} + V_{MDO} \times \rho_{MDO} \times LCV_{MDO} \times K_{MDO} + V_{LNG} \times \rho_{LNG} \times LCV_{LNG} \times K_{LNG}}$	-	0.1261
29	$f_{DFliquid}$	$1- f_{DFgas}$	-	0.8739
30	EEDI	$(P_{ME} \times (f_{DFgas} \times (C_{F\ Pilotfuel} \times SFC_{ME\ Pilotfuel} + C_{F\ LNG} \times SFC_{ME\ LNG}) + f_{DFliquid} \times C_{FMDO} \times SFC_{ME\ MDO}) + P_{AE} \times (f_{DFgas} \times (C_{FAE\ Pilotfuel} \times SFC_{AE\ Pilotfuel} + C_{F\ LNG} \times SFC_{AE\ LNG}) + f_{DFliquid} \times C_{FMDO} \times SFC_{AE\ MDO})) / (V_{ref} \times Capacity)$	gCO$_2$/tnm	3.61

Case 4: One dual-fuel main engine (LNG, pilot fuel MDO) and one main engine (MDO) and dual-fuel auxiliary engine (LNG, pilot fuel MDO, no shaft generator) which LNG could be regarded as "primary fuel" only for the dual-fuel main engine:

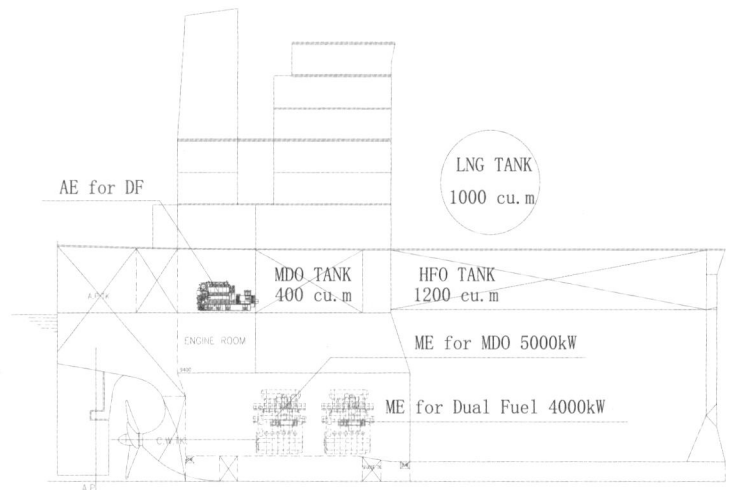

S/N	Parameter	Formula or Source	Unit	Value
1	MCR_{MEMDO}	MCR rating of main engine using only MDO	kW	5,000
2	MCR_{MELNG}	MCR rating of main engine using dual-fuel	kW	4,000
3	Capacity	Deadweight of the ship at summer load draft	DWT	81,200
4	V_{ref}	Ships speed	kn	14
5	P_{MEMDO}	$0.75 \times MCR_{MEMDO}$	kW	3,750
6	P_{MELNG}	$0.75 \times MCR_{MELNG}$	kW	3,000
7	P_{AE}	$0.05 \times (MCR_{MEMDO} + MCR_{MELNG})$	kW	450
8	$C_{FPilotfuel}$	C_F factor of pilot fuel for dual-fuel ME using MDO	-	3.206
9	$C_{FAE\ Pilotfuel}$	C_F factor of pilot fuel for auxiliary engine using MDO	-	3.206
10	C_{FLNG}	C_F factor of dual-fuel engine using LNG	-	2.75
11	C_{FMDO}	C_F factor of dual-fuel ME/AE engine using MDO	-	3.206
12	$SFC_{MEPilotfuel}$	Specific fuel consumption of pilot fuel for dual-fuel ME at P_{ME}	g/kWh	6
13	$SFC_{AE\ Pilotfuel}$	Specific fuel consumption of pilot fuel for dual-fuel AE at P_{AE}	g/kWh	7
14	$SFC_{DF\ LNG}$	Specific fuel consumption of dual-fuel ME using LNG at P_{ME}	g/kWh	158
15	$SFC_{AE\ LNG}$	Specific fuel consumption of AE using LNG at P_{AE}	g/kWh	160
16	$SFC_{ME\ MDO}$	Specific fuel consumption of single fuel ME at P_{ME}	g/kWh	180
17	V_{LNG}	LNG tank capacity on board	m^3	1,000
18	V_{HFO}	Heavy fuel oil tank capacity on board	m^3	1,200
19	V_{MDO}	Marine diesel oil tank capacity on board	m^3	400
20	ρ_{LNG}	Density of LNG	kg/m^3	450

S/N	参数	公式或来源	单位	值
28	f_{DFgas}	船用柴油舱注入率	–	0.126 1
29	$f_{DFliquid}$	$1-f_{DFgas}$	–	0.8739
30	EEDI	$(P_{ME}\times(f_{DFgas}\times(C_{FPilotfuel}\times SFC_{ME\,Pilotfuel}+C_{FLNG}\times SFC_{ME\,LNG})+f_{DFliquid}\times C_{FMDO}\times SFC_{ME\,MDO})+PAE\times(f_{DFgas}\times(C_{FAEPilotfuel}\times SFC_{AE\,Pilotfuel}+C_{FLNG}\times SFC_{AE\,LNG})+f_{DFliquid}\times C_{FMDO}\times SFC_{AE\,MDO}))/(V_{ref}\times Capacity)$	g C O²/tnm	3.61

实例 4：一个双燃料主机（LNG，引燃油 MDO）和一个主机（MDO）和双燃料辅机（LNG，引燃油 MDO，无轴带发电机），LNG 仅视为双燃料主机的"主要燃料"。

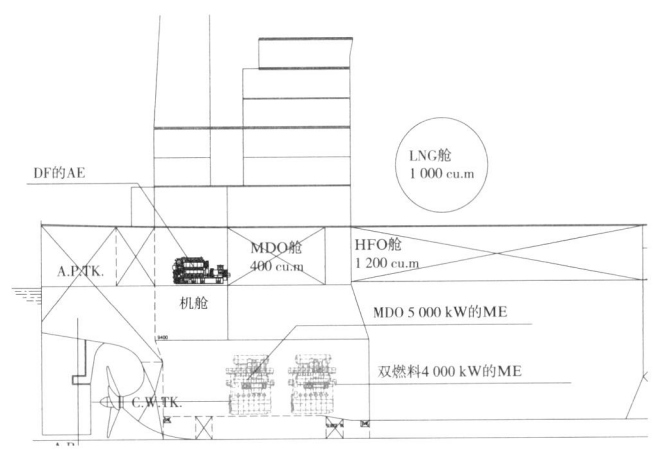

S/N	参数	公式或来源	单位	值
1	MCR_{MEMDO}	仅使用 MDO 主机的 MCR	kW	5 000
2	MCR_{MELNG}	使用双燃料主机的 MCR	kW	4 000
3	载运能力	船舶夏季载重吃水的载重吨	DWT	81 200
4	V_{ref}	船速	kn	14
5	P_{MEMDO}	$0.75\times MCR_{MEMDO}$	kW	3 750
6	P_{MELNG}	$0.75\times MCR_{MELNG}$	kW	3 000
7	P_{AE}	$0.05\times(MCR_{MEMDO}+MCR_{MELNG})$	kW	450
8	$C_{FPilotfuel}$	使用 MDO 的双燃料主机引燃油 C_F 系数	–	3.206
9	$C_{FAE\,Plilotfuel}$	使用 MDO 的辅机引燃油 C_F 系数	–	3.206
10	C_{FLNG}	使用 LNG 的双燃料发动机 C_F 系数	–	2.75
11	C_{FMDO}	使用 MDO 的双燃料主机 / 辅机发动机 C_F 系数	–	3.206
12	$SFC_{MEPilotfuel}$	P_{ME} 时双燃料主机引燃油消耗率	g/kWh	6
13	$SFC_{AE\,Pilotfuel}$	P_{AE} 时双燃料辅机引燃油消耗率	g/kWh	7
14	$SFC_{DF\,LNG}$	P_{ME} 时使用 LNG 双燃料主机的燃气消耗率	g/kWh	158
15	$SFC_{AE\,LNG}$	P_{AE} 时使用 LNG 辅机的燃气消耗率	g/kWh	160
16	$SFC_{ME\,MDO}$	P_{ME} 时使用单燃料主机的燃油消耗率	g/kWh	180
17	V_{LNG}	船上 LNG 舱容积	m³	1 000
18	V_{HFO}	船上重燃油舱容积	m³	1 200
19	V_{MDO}	船上船用柴油舱容积	m³	400
20	ρ_{LNG}	LNG 的密度	kg/m³	450

S/N	Parameter	Formula or Source	Unit	Value
21	ρ_{HFO}	Density of heavy fuel oil	kg/m³	991
22	ρ_{MDO}	Density of marine diesel oil	kg/m³	900
23	LCV_{LNG}	Low calorific value of LNG	kJ/kg	48,000
24	LCV_{HFO}	Low calorific value of heavy fuel oil	kJ/kg	40,200
25	LCV_{MDO}	Low calorific value of marine diesel oil	kJ/kg	42,700
26	K_{LNG}	Filling rate of LNG tank	-	0.95
27	K_{HFO}	Filling rate of heavy fuel tank	-	0.98
28	K_{MDO}	Filling rate of marine diesel tank	-	0.98
29	f_{DFgas}	$\dfrac{P_{MEMDO} + P_{MELNG} + P_{AE}}{P_{MELNG} + P_{AE}} \times \dfrac{V_{LNG} \times \rho_{LNG} \times LCV_{LNG} \times K_{LNG}}{V_{HFO} \times \rho_{HFO} \times LCV_{HFO} \times K_{HFO} + V_{MDO} \times \rho_{MDO} \times LCV_{MDO} \times K_{MDO} + V_{LNG} \times \rho_{LNG} \times LCV_{LNG} \times K_{LNG}}$	-	0.5195
30	EEDI	$(P_{MELNG} \times (C_{F\,Pilotfuel} \times SFC_{ME\,Pilotfuel} + C_{F\,LNG} \times SFC_{DF\,LNG}) + P_{MEMDO} \times C_{F\,MDO} \times SFC_{ME\,MDO} + P_{AE} \times (C_{FAE\,Pilotfuel} \times SFC_{AE\,Pilotfuel} + C_{F\,LNG} \times SFC_{AE\,LNG})) / (V_{ref} \times Capacity)$	gCO₂/tnm	3.28

Case 5: One dual-fuel main engine (LNG, pilot fuel MDO) and one main engine (MDO) and dual-fuel auxiliary engine (LNG, pilot fuel MDO, no shaft generator) which LNG could not be regarded as "primary fuel" for the dual-fuel main engine:

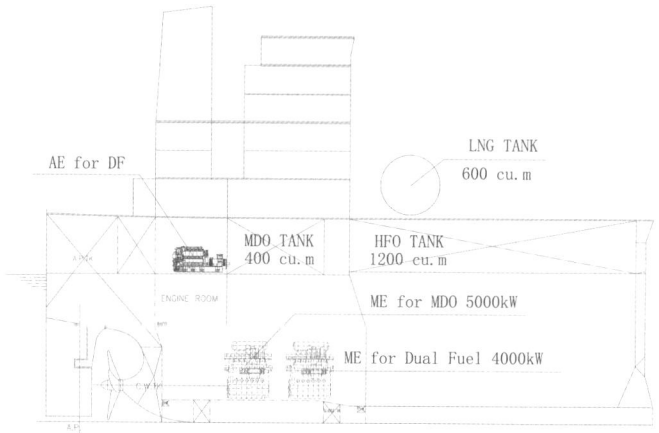

S/N	Parameter	Formula or Source	Unit	Value
1	MCR_{MEMDO}	MCR rating of main engine using only MDO	kW	5,000
2	MCR_{MELNG}	MCR rating of main engine using dual-fuel	kW	4,000
3	Capacity	Deadweight of the ship at summer load draft	DWT	81,200
4	V_{ref}	Ships speed	kn	14
5	P_{MEMDO}	0.75 x MCR_{MEMDO}	kW	3,750
6	P_{MELNG}	0.75 x MCR_{MELNG}	kW	3,000
7	P_{AE}	0.05 x (MCR_{MEMDO} + MCR_{MELNG})	kW	450
8	$C_{FPilotfuel}$	C_F factor of pilot fuel for dual-fuel ME using MDO	-	3.206
9	$C_{FAE\,Plilotfuel}$	C_F factor of pilot fuel for auxiliary engine using MDO	-	3.206
10	C_{FLNG}	C_F factor of dual-fuel engine using LNG	-	2.75
11	C_{FMDO}	C_F factor of dual-fuel ME/AE engine using MDO	-	3.206
12	$SFC_{MEPilotfuel}$	Specific fuel consumption of pilot fuel for dual-fuel ME at P_{ME}	g/kWh	6
13	$SFC_{AE\,Pilotfuel}$	Specific fuel consumption of pilot fuel for dual-fuel AE at P_{AE}	g/kWh	7
14	$SFC_{DF\,LNG}$	Specific fuel consumption of dual-fuel ME using LNG at P_{ME}	g/kWh	158

S/N	参数	公式或来源	单位	值
21	ρ_{HFO}	重燃油的密度	kg/m³	991
22	ρ_{MDO}	船用柴油的密度	kg/m³	900
23	LCV_{LNG}	LNG 的低热值	kJ/kg	48 000
24	LCV_{HFO}	重燃油的低热值	kJ/kg	40 200
25	LCV_{MDO}	船用柴油的低热值	kJ/kg	42 700
26	K_{LNG}	LNG 舱充装率	–	0.95
27	K_{HFO}	重燃油舱充装率	–	0.98
28	K_{MDO}	船用柴油舱充装率	–	0.98
29	f_{DFgas}	$\dfrac{P_{MEMDO}+P_{MELNG}+P_{AE}}{P_{MELNG}+P_{AE}} \times \dfrac{V_{LNG}\times\rho_{LNG}\times LCV_{LNG}\times K_{LNG}}{V_{HFO}\times\rho_{HFO}\times LCV_{HFO}\times K_{HFO}+V_{MDO}\times\rho_{MDO}\times LCV_{MDO}\times K_{MDO}+V_{LNG}\times\rho_{LNG}\times LCV_{LNG}\times K_{LNG}}$	–	0.519 5
30	EEDI	$(P_{MELNG}\times(C_{FPilotfuel}\times SFC_{ME\,Pilotfuel}+C_{FLNG}\times SFC_{DF\,LNG})+P_{MEMDO}\times C_{F\,MDO}\times SFC_{ME\,MDO}+P_{AE}\times(C_{FAE\,Pilotfuel}\times SFC_{AE\,Pilotfuel}+C_{F\,LNG}\times SFC_{AE\,LNG}))/(V_{ref}\times_{Capacity})$	gCO₂/tnm	3.28

实例 5：一个双燃料主机（LNG，引燃油 MDO）和一个主机（MDO）和双燃料辅机（LNG，引燃油 MDO，无轴带发电机），LNG 不能被视为双燃料主机的"主要燃料"。

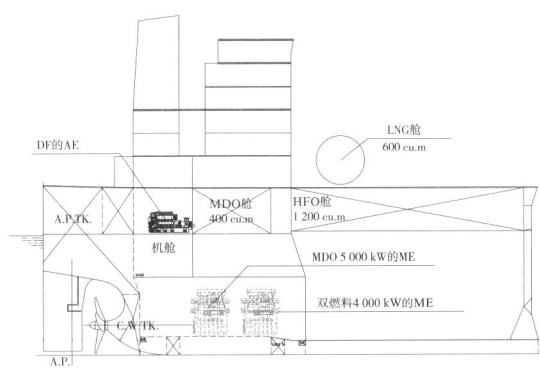

S/N	参数	公式或来源	单位	值
1	MCR_{MEMDO}	仅使用 MDO 主机的 MCR	kW	5 000
2	MCR_{MELNG}	使用双燃料主机的 MCR	kW	4 000
3	载运能力	船舶夏季载重吃水的载重吨	DWT	81 200
4	V_{ref}	船速	kn	14
5	P_{MEMDO}	$0.75\times MCR_{MEMDO}$	kW	3 750
6	P_{MELNG}	$0.75\times MCR_{MELNG}$	kW	3 000
7	P_{AE}	$0.05\times(MCR_{MEMDO}+MCR_{MELNG})$	kW	450
8	$C_{FPilotfuel}$	使用 MDO 的双燃料主机引燃油 C_F 系数	–	3.206
9	$C_{FAE\,Pilotfuel}$	使用 MDO 的辅机引燃油 C_F 系数	–	3.206
10	C_{FLNG}	使用 LNG 的双燃料发动机 C_F 系数	–	2.75
11	C_{FMDO}	使用 MDO 的双燃料主机/辅机发动机 C_F 系数	–	2.75
12	$SFC_{MEPilotfuel}$	P_{ME} 时双燃料主机引燃油消耗率	g/kWh	6
13	$SFC_{AE\,Pilotfuel}$	P_{AE} 时双燃料辅机引燃油消耗率	g/kWh	7
14	$SFC_{DF\,LNG}$	P_{ME} 时使用 LNG 双燃料主机的燃气消耗率	g/kWh	158

S/N	Parameter	Formula or Source	Unit	Value
15	$SFC_{AE\ LNG}$	Specific fuel consumption of AE using LNG at P_{AE}	g/kWh	160
16	$SFC_{DF\ MDO}$	Specific fuel consumption of dual-fuel ME using MDO at P_{ME}	g/kWh	185
17	$SFC_{ME\ MDO}$	Specific fuel consumption of single fuel ME at P_{ME}	g/kWh	180
18	$SFC_{AE\ MDO}$	Specific fuel consumption of AE using MDO at P_{AE}	g/kWh	187
19	V_{LNG}	LNG tank capacity on board	m^3	600
20	V_{HFO}	Heavy fuel oil tank capacity on board	m^3	1,200
21	V_{MDO}	Marine diesel oil tank capacity on board	m^3	400
22	ρ_{LNG}	Density of LNG	kg/m^3	450
23	ρ_{HFO}	Density of heavy fuel oil	kg/m^3	991
24	ρ_{MDO}	Density of marine diesel oil	kg/m^3	900
25	LCV_{LNG}	Low calorific value of LNG	kJ/kg	48,000
26	LCV_{HFO}	Low calorific value of heavy fuel oil	kJ/kg	40,200
27	LCV_{MDO}	Low calorific value of marine diesel oil	kJ/kg	42,700
28	K_{LNG}	Filling rate of LNG tank	-	0.95
29	K_{HFO}	Filling rate of heavy fuel tank	-	0.98
30	K_{MDO}	Filling rate of marine diesel tank	-	0.98
31	f_{DFgas}	$\dfrac{P_{MEMDO} + P_{MELNG} + P_{AE}}{P_{MELNG} + P_{AE}} \times \dfrac{V_{LNG} \times \rho_{LNG} \times LCV_{LNG} \times K_{LNG}}{V_{HFO} \times \rho_{HFO} \times LCV_{HFO} \times K_{HFO} + V_{MDO} \times \rho_{MDO} \times LCV_{MDO} \times K_{MDO} + V_{LNG} \times \rho_{LNG} \times LCV_{LNG} \times K_{LNG}}$	-	0.3462
32	$f_{DFliquid}$	$1 - f_{DFgas}$	-	0.6538
33	EEDI	$(P_{MELNG} \times (f_{DFgas} \times (C_{F\ Pilotfuel} \times SFC_{ME\ Pilotfuel} + C_{F\ LNG} \times SFC_{DF\ LNG}) + f_{DFliquid} \times C_{FMDO} \times SFC_{DF\ MDO})) + P_{MEMDO} \times C_{F\ MDO} \times SFC_{ME\ MDO} + P_{AE} \times (f_{DFgas} \times (C_{FAE\ Pilotfuel} \times SFC_{AE\ Pilotfuel} + C_{F\ LNG} \times SFC_{AE\ LNG}) + f_{DFliquid} \times C_{FMDO} \times SFC_{AE\ MDO})) / (V_{ref} \times Capacity)$	gCO_2/tnm	3.54

S/N	参数	公式或来源	单位	值
15	$SFC_{AE\,LNG}$	P_{AE} 时使用 LNG 辅机的燃气消耗率	g/kWh	160
16	$SFC_{DF\,MDO}$	P_{ME} 时使用 MDO 双燃料主机的燃油消耗率	g/kWh	185
17	$SFC_{ME\,MDO}$	P_{ME} 时使用单燃料主机的燃油消耗率	g/kWh	180
18	$SFC_{AE\,MDO}$	P_AE 时使用 MDO 辅机的燃油消耗率	g/kWh	187
19	V_{LNG}	船上 LNG 舱容积	m3	600
20	V_{HFO}	船上重燃油舱容积	m3	1 200
21	V_{MDO}	船上船用柴油舱容积	m3	400
22	ρ_{LNG}	LNG 的密度	kg/m3	450
23	ρ_{HFO}	重燃油的密度	kg/m3	991
24	ρ_{MDO}	船用柴油的密度	kg/m3	900
25	LCV_{LNG}	LNG 的低热值	kJ/kg	48 000
26	LCV_{HFO}	重燃油的低热值	kJ/kg	40 200
27	LCV_{MDO}	船用柴油的低热值	kJ/kg	42 700
28	K_{LNG}	LNG 舱充装率	–	0.95
29	K_{HFO}	重燃油舱充装率	–	0.98
30	K_{MDO}	船用柴油舱注入	–	0.98
31	f_{DFgas}	$\dfrac{P_{MEMDO}+P_{MELNG}+P_{AE}}{P_{MELNG}+P_{AE}} \times \dfrac{V_{LNG}\times\rho_{LNG}\times LCV_{LNG}\times K_{LNG}}{V_{HFO}\times\rho_{HFO}\times LCV_{HFO}\times K_{HFO}+V_{MDO}\times\rho_{MDO}\times LCV_{MDO}\times K_{MDO}+V_{LNG}\times\rho_{LNG}\times LCV_{LNG}\times K_{LNG}}$	–	0.346 2
32	$f_{DFliquid}$	$1-f_{DFgas}$	–	0.653 8
33	EEDI	$(P_{MELNG}\times(f_{DFgas}\times(C_{F\,Pilotfuel}\times SFC_{ME\,Pilotfuel}+C_{F\,LNG}\times SFC_{DF\,LNG})+f_{DFliquid}\times C_{FMDO}\times SFC_{DF\,MDO}))+P_{MEMDO}\times C_{F\,MDO}\times SFC_{ME\,MDO}+P_{AE}\times(f_{DFgas}\times(C_{FAE\,Pilotfuel}\times SFC_{AE\,Pilotfuel}+C_{F\,LNG}\times SFC_{AE\,LNG})+f_{DFliquid}\times C_{FMDO}\times SFC_{AE\,MDO}))/(V_{ref}\times Capacity)$	gCO2/ tnm	3.54

APPENDIX 5

STANDARD FORMAT TO SUBMIT EEDI INFORMATION TO BE INCLUDED IN THE EEDI DATABASE

IMO number (1)	Type of ship (2)	Common commercial size (3)	Capacity (4)		Dimensional parameters			Year of delivery	Applicable phase	Required EEDI	Attained EEDI	Vref (knot) (9)	P_{ME} (kW) (10)	Type of fuel (11)	fof gas (12)	Ice class (13)	EEDI 4th term (Installation of innovative electrical technology)		EEDI 5th term (Installation of innovative mechanical technology)		Short statement as appropriate describing the principal design elements or changes employed to achieve the attained EEDI (15)
			DWT	GT (5)	Lpp (m) (6)	Bs (m) (7)	Draught (m) (8)										Yes/No	Name, outline and means/ways of performance of technology (14)	Yes/No	Name, outline and means/ways of performance of technology (14)	

Note:

(1) IMO number to be submitted for Secretariat use only.

(2) As defined in regulation 2 of MARPOL Annex VI.

(3) Common commercial size reference (TEU for containership, CEU (RT43) for ro-ro cargo ship (vehicle carrier), cubic metre for gas carrier and LNG carrier), if available, should be provided.

(4) The exact DWT or GT, as appropriate, should be provided. The Secretariat should round the DWT or GT data up to the nearest 500 when these data are subsequently provided to MEPC. (For containerships, 100% DWT should be provided while 70% of DWT should be used when calculating the EEDI value).

(5) GT should be provided for a cruise passenger ship having non-conventional propulsion as defined in regulations 2.2.11 and 2.2.19, respectively, of MARPOL Annex VI. Both DWT and GT should be provided for a ro-ro cargo ship (vehicle carrier) as defined in regulation 2.2.27 of MARPOL Annex VI.

(6) As defined in paragraph 2.2.13 of these Guidelines. The exact Lpp should be provided. The Secretariat will round the Lpp data up to the nearest 10 when these data are subsequently provided to MEPC.

(7) As defined in paragraph 2.2.16 of these Guidelines. The exact Bs should be provided. The Secretariat will round the Bs data up to the nearest 1 when these data are subsequently provided to MEPC.

(8) As defined in paragraph 2.2.15 of these Guidelines. The exact draught should be provided. The Secretariat will round the draught data up to the nearest 0.5 when these data are subsequently provided to MEPC.

(9) As defined in paragraph 2.2.2 of these Guidelines. The exact V_{ref} should be provided. The Secretariat will round the V_{ref} data up to the nearest 0.5 when these data are subsequently provided to MEPC.

(10) As defined in paragraph 2.2.5.1 of these Guidelines. The exact P_{ME} should be provided. The Secretariat will round the P_{ME} data up to the nearest 100 when these data are subsequently provided to MEPC.

(11) As defined in paragraph 2.2.1 of these Guidelines or other (to be stated). In the case of a ship equipped with a dual-fuel engine, type of "primary fuel" should be provided.

(12) As defined in paragraph 2.2.1 of these Guidelines, if applicable.

(13) Ice class, which was used to calculate correction factors for ice-classed ships as defined in paragraphs 2.2.8.1 and 2.2.11.1 of these Guidelines, if applicable, should be provided.

(14) In the case that the innovative energy efficiency technologies are already included in the 2021 *Guidance on treatment of innovative energy efficiency technologies for calculation and verification of the attained EEDI and EEXI* (MEPC.1/Circ.896), the name of technology should be identified. Otherwise, name, outline and means/ways of performance of the technology should be identified.

(15) To assist IMO in assessing relevant design trends, provide a short statement as appropriate, describing the principal design elements or changes employed to achieve the attained EEDI.

***

附录 5

拟纳入 EEDI 数据库的 EEDI 信息提交标准格式

IMO 编号 (1)	船型 (2)	载运能力 (4)		尺度参数			交船年份	适用阶段	要求的 EEDI	达到的 EEDI	V_{ref}（节）(9)	P_{ME}（kW）(10)	燃料类型 (11)	f_{DFgas} (12)	冰级 (13)	EEDI 第 4 个参数（安装创新电技术）		EEDI 第 5 个参数（安装创新机械技术）		适当的简短声明，说明为实现达到的 EEDI 而采用的主要素或设计要素变更 (15)
		通用商业尺寸 (3)	载重吨 总吨 (5)	L_{pp} (m) (6)	B_s (m) (7)	吃水 (m) (8)										是/否	技术名称、概要和运作方法/方式 (14)	是/否	技术名称、概要和运作方法/方式 (14)	

注:

(1) 应提交仅供秘书处使用的 IMO 编号。

(2) 见《防污公约》附则 VI 第 2 条的定义。

(3) 如有，应提供通用商业尺寸参考（集装箱船）为 TEU，滚装货船（车辆运输船）为 CEU（RT43），气体运输船和 LNG 船为立方米。

(4) 应提供准确的 DWT 或 GT（视情况）。当计算 DWT 或 GT 数据提供给 MEPC 时，秘书处应将这些数据取整至最接近的 500。（对于集装箱船，应提供 100%DWT，在计算 EEDI 值时，使用 70%DWT）。

(5) 对于《防污公约》附则 VI 第 2.2.11 和 2.2.19 条中分别定义的具有非常规推进的豪华游轮，应提供 GT。根据《防污公约》附则 VI 第 2.2.27 条的定义、滚装货船（车辆运输船）应同时提供 DWT 和 GT。

(6) 见本导则第 2.2.13 段中的定义。

(7) 应提供准确的 L_{pp}。当后续将这些数据提供给环保会时，秘书处将把 L_{pp} 数据取整至最接近的 10。

(8) 见本导则第 2.2.6 段中的定义。应提供准确的 B_s。当后续将这些数据提供给环保会时，秘书处将把 B_s 数据取整至最接近的 1。

(9) 见本导则第 2.2.15 段中的定义。应提供准确的吃水。当后续将这些数据提供给环保会时，秘书处将把吃水数据取整至最接近的 1。

(10) 见本导则第 2.2.2 段中的定义。应提供准确的 V_{ref}。当后续将这些数据提供给环保会时，秘书处将把 V_{ref} 数据四舍五入至最接近的 0.5。

(11) 见本导则第 2.2.5.1 段中的定义。应提供准确的 P_{ME}。当后续将这些数据提供给 MEPC 时，秘书处将把 P_{ME} 数据取整至最接近的 100。

(12) 见本导则第 2.2.1 段中的定义或其他。应提供"主要燃料"类型。

(13) 如果船舶配备双燃料发动机，应提供"主要燃料"类型。见本导则第 2.2.1 段中的定义（如适用）。

(14) 见本导则第 2.2.1 段中的定义（如适用）。应提供冰级，用于计算冰级船舶船舶修正系数，见本导则第 2.2.8.1 和 2.2.11.1 段中的定义（如适用）。

(15) 如有创新能效技术已纳入《2021 年用于计算和验证达到的 EEDI 和 EEXI 的创新能效技术处理指南》（MEPC.1/Circ.896），应说明该技术的名称。否则，应说明技术的名称、概要和运作方法/方式，描述为实现达到的 EEDI 而采用的主要设计要素或变更。

为协助 IMO 评估相关的设计趋势，提供一份适当的简短声明，提供与采用的设计要素/方式。***

— 510 —

THE 2022 GUIDELINES ON SURVEY AND CERTIFICATION OF THE ENERGY EFFICIENCY DESIGN INDEX (EEDI)

(RESOLUTION MEPC.365(79), AS AMENDED BY RESOLUTION MEPC.374(80))
(adopted on 7 July 2023)

THE MARINE ENVIRONMENT PROTECTION COMMITTEE,

RECALLING Article 38(a) of the Convention on the International Maritime Organization concerning the functions of the Marine Environment Protection Committee conferred upon it by international conventions for the prevention and control of marine pollution from ships,

NOTING that regulation 5 (Surveys) of MARPOL Annex VI, as amended, requires ships to which chapter 4 applies shall also be subject to survey and certification taking into account guidelines developed by the Organization,

NOTING ALSO that the Committee adopted, at its seventy-ninth session, the *2022 Guidelines on survey and certification of the Energy Efficiency Design Index (EEDI)* (resolution MEPC.365(79)),

HAVING NOTED, at its eightieth session, the need to amend the *2022 Guidelines on survey and certification of the Energy Efficiency Design Index (EEDI)* (resolution MEPC.365(79)),

1   ADOPTS the amendments to the *2022 Guidelines on survey and certification of the Energy Efficiency Design Index (EEDI)*, as set out in the annex to the present resolution;

2   REQUESTS the Parties to MARPOL Annex VI and other Member Governments to bring the amendments to the attention of shipowners, ship operators, shipbuilders, ship designers and any other interested groups;

3   AGREES to keep these Guidelines, as amended, under review, in light of the experience gained with their application.

2022 年能效设计指数（EEDI）检验和发证导则
（经第 MEPC.374（80）号决议修正的第 MEPC.365（79）号决议）
（2023 年 7 月 7 日通过）

海上环境保护委员会，

忆及《国际海事组织公约》关于防止和控制船舶造成海洋污染国际公约赋予海上环境保护委员会职能的第 38（a）条，

注意到经修正的《防污公约》附则Ⅵ第 5 条（检验）要求，适用本附则第 4 章的船舶还须进行下列规定的检验，并考虑到本组织通过的导则，

还注意到本委员会在其第 79 届会议上通过的《2022 年能效设计指数（EEDI）检验和发证导则》（第 MEPC.365（79）号决议），

在其第 80 届会议上，注意到有必要进一步修正《2022 年能效设计指数（EEDI）检验和发证导则》（经修正的第 MEPC.365（79）号决议），

1 **通过**《2022 年能效设计指数（EEDI）检验和发证导则》修正案，载于本决议附件；

2 **要求**《防污公约》附则Ⅵ各缔约国和其他会员国政府提请船东、船舶经营者、船厂、船舶设计方以及任何其他利益攸关方注意到本修正案；

3 **同意**根据适用中获得的经验对经修正的本导则保持审查。

2022 GUIDELINES ON SURVEY AND CERTIFICATION OF THE ENERGY EFFICIENCY DESIGN INDEX (EEDI)

Table of contents

附件

2022 年能效设计指数（EEDI）检验和发证导则

目录

1 GENERAL

The purpose of these guidelines is to assist verifiers of the Energy Efficiency Design Index (EEDI) of ships in conducting the survey and certification of the EEDI, in accordance with regulations 5, 6, 7, 8 and 9 of MARPOL Annex VI, and assist shipowners, shipbuilders, manufacturers and other interested parties in understanding the procedures for the survey and certification of the EEDI.

2 DEFINITIONS[1]

2.1   *Verifier* means an Administration or organization duly authorized by it which conducts the survey and certification of the EEDI in accordance with regulations 5, 6, 7, 8 and 9 of MARPOL Annex VI and these guidelines.

2.2   *Ship of the same type* means a ship the hull form (expressed in the lines such as sheer plan and body plan), excluding additional hull features such as fins, and principal particulars of which are identical to that of the base ship.

2.3   *Tank test* means model towing tests, model self-propulsion tests and model propeller open water tests. Numerical calculations may be accepted as equivalent to model propeller open water tests or used to complement the tank tests conducted (e.g. to evaluate the effect of additional hull features such as fins, etc. on ship's performance), with the approval of the verifier.

3 APPLICATION

These guidelines should be applied to new ships for which an application for an initial survey or an additional survey specified in regulation 5 of MARPOL Annex VI has been submitted to a verifier.

4 PROCEDURES FOR SURVEY AND CERTIFICATION

4.1 General

4.1.1   The attained EEDI should be calculated in accordance with regulation 22 of MARPOL Annex VI and the *2022 Guidelines on the method of calculation of the attained Energy Efficiency Design Index (EEDI) for new ships* (resolution MEPC.364(79)) (EEDI Calculation Guidelines). Survey and certification of the EEDI should be conducted in two stages: preliminary verification at the design stage and final verification at the sea trial. The basic flow of the survey and certification process is presented in figure 1.

4.1.2   The information used in the verification process may contain confidential information of submitters which requires Intellectual Property Rights (IPR) protection. In the case where the submitter wants a non-disclosure agreement with the verifier, the additional information should be provided to the verifier upon mutually agreed terms and conditions.

---

[1]   Other terms used in these guidelines have the same meaning as those defined in the *2022 Guidelines on the method of calculation of the attained EEDI for new ships* (resolution MEPC.364(79)).

1 通则

　　本导则旨在帮助船舶能效设计指数（EEDI）的验证方按照《防污公约》附则Ⅵ第5、6、7、8和9条进行 EEDI 的检验和发证，并帮助船东、造船厂、制造商以及其他相关各方了解 EEDI 的检验和发证程序。

2 定义 [1]

2.1 *验证方*系指按照《防污公约》附则Ⅵ第5、6、7、8和9条以及本导则进行 EEDI 的检验和发证的主管机关或经其正式授权的组织。

2.2 *相同类型船舶*系指不包括附加船体特征（例如鳍板）的船型（以型线表示，例如型线侧视图和型线横剖图）和主要细节与基本船舶相同的船舶。

2.3 *水池试验*系指模型拖曳试验、模型自航试验和模型螺旋桨敞水试验。经验证方认可，数字计算可等同于模型螺旋桨敞水试验予以接受，或对水池试验予以补充（例如，评估鳍板等附加船体特征对船舶性能的影响）。

3 适用范围

　　本导则应适用于已向验证方提交《防污公约》附则Ⅵ第5条所述初次检验或附加检验申请的新船。

4 检验和发证程序

4.1 一般规定

4.1.1 达到的 EEDI 应按照《防污公约》附则Ⅵ第22条和《2022年新造船达到的能效设计指数（EEDI）计算方法导则》（第 MEPC.364（79）号决议）（《EEDI 计算导则》）进行计算。EEDI 的检验和发证应分两个阶段进行：设计阶段的前期验证和试航阶段的最终验证。检验和发证过程的基本流程见图1。

4.1.2 验证过程中使用的信息可包含提交方的保密信息，其要求知识产权（IPR）保护。如果提交方希望与验证方达成保密协议，应按照互相商定的条件向验证方提供附加信息。

---

[1] 本导则中使用的其他术语与《2022年新造船达到的能效设计指数（EEDI）计算方法导则》（第 MEPC.364（79）号决议）中所定义的术语具有相同含义。

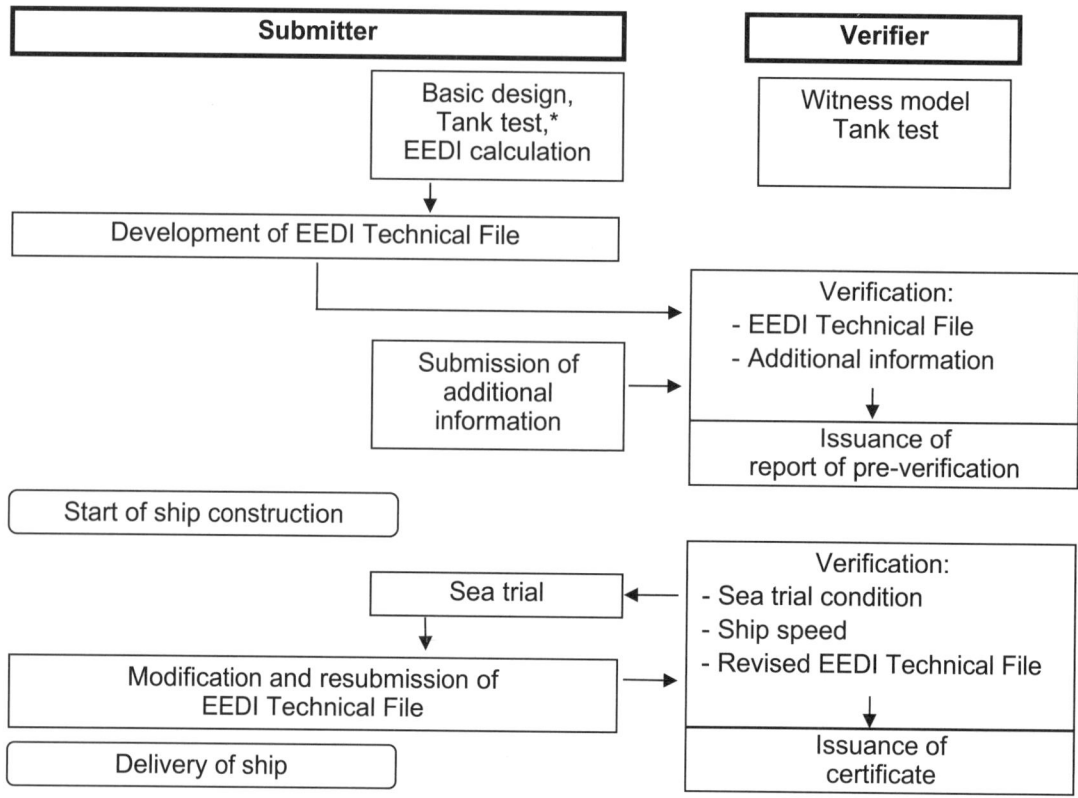

Figure 1: Basic flow of survey and certification process

4.2 Preliminary verification of the attained EEDI at the design stage

4.2.1 For the preliminary verification at the design stage, an application for an initial survey and an EEDI Technical File containing the necessary information for the verification and other relevant background documents should be submitted to a verifier.

4.2.2 The EEDI Technical File should be written at least in English. The EEDI Technical File should include as a minimum, but not be limited to:

.1 deadweight (DWT) or gross tonnage (GT) for passenger and ro-ro passenger ships, the maximum continuous rating (MCR) of the main and auxiliary engines, the ship speed (V_{ref}), as specified in paragraph 2.2.2 of the EEDI Calculation Guidelines, type of fuel, the specific fuel consumption (*SFC*) of the main engine at 75% of MCR power, the *SFC* of the auxiliary engines at 50% MCR power, and the electric power table[2] for certain ship types, as necessary, as defined in the EEDI Calculation Guidelines;

---

[2] Electric power table should be validated separately, taking into account guidelines set out in appendix 2 to these Guidelines.

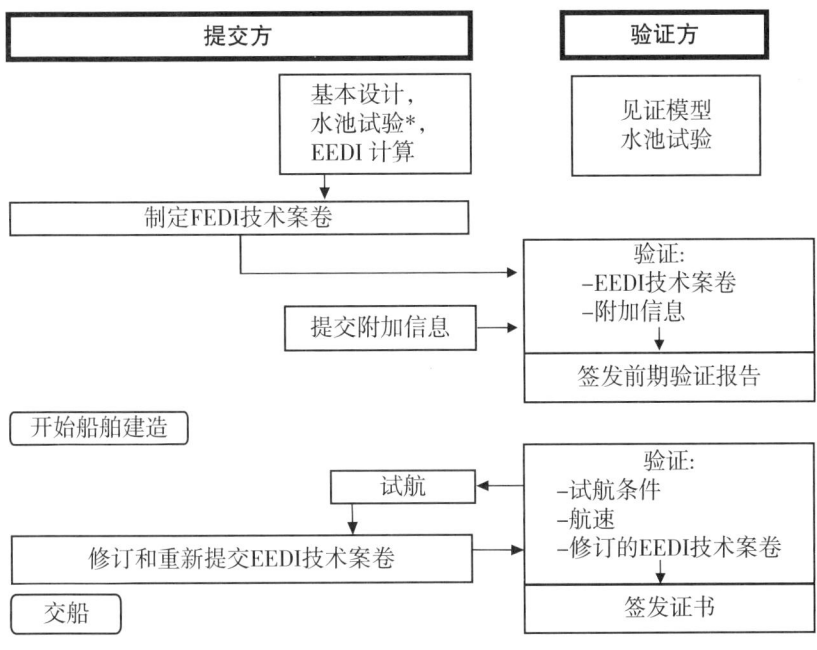

*应由试验机构或提交方进行。

图 1　检验和发证过程的基本流程

4.2　设计阶段达到的 EEDI 的前期验证

4.2.1　对于设计阶段的前期验证，应向验证方提交初次检验申请、包含验证所需信息的 EEDI 技术案卷以及其他相关背景文件。

4.2.2　EEDI 技术案卷应至少使用英语写成。EEDI 技术案卷应至少包括但不限于：

.1　载重吨（DWT）或客船和客滚船的总吨（GT），主机和辅机的最大连续额定功率（MCR），《EEDI 计算导则》第 2.2.2 段中规定的船舶航速 V_{ref}，燃料类型，主机在 75% 的 MCR 功率下的单位燃油消耗量（SFC），辅机在 50% 的 MCR 功率下的 SFC 以及《EEDI 计算导则》中规定的某些船舶类型所必需的电力负荷表[2]；

---

[2]　参照本导则附录 2 所述导则，对电力负荷表应予以单独认证。

.2   power curve(s) (kW – knot) estimated at design stage under the condition as specified in paragraph 2.2.2 of the EEDI Calculation Guidelines, and, in the event that the sea trial is carried out in a condition other than the above condition, also a power curve estimated under the sea trial condition;

.3   principal particulars, ship type and the relevant information to classify the ship as such a ship type, classification notations and an overview of the propulsion system and electricity supply system on board;

.4   estimation process and methodology of the power curves at design stage;

.5   description of energy-saving equipment;

.6   calculated value of the attained EEDI, including the calculation summary, which should contain, at a minimum, each value of the calculation parameters and the calculation process used to determine the attained EEDI;

.7   calculated values of the attained $EEDI_{weather}$ and f_w value (not equal to 1.0), if those values are calculated, based on the EEDI Calculation Guidelines; and

.8   for LNG carriers:

        .1   type and outline of propulsion systems (such as direct drive diesel, diesel electric, steam turbine);

        .2   LNG cargo tank capacity in m^3 and BOR as defined in paragraph 2.2.5.6.3 of the EEDI Calculation Guidelines;

        .3   shaft power of the propeller shaft after transmission gear at 100% of the rated output of motor (MPP_{Motor}) and $\eta_{(i)}$ for diesel electric;

        .4   maximum continuous rated power ($MCR_{SteamTurbine}$) for steam turbine; and

        .5 $SFC_{SteamTurbine}$ for steam turbine, as specified in paragraph 2.2.7 of the EEDI Calculation Guidelines.

A sample of an EEDI Technical File is provided in appendix 1 to these guidelines.

4.2.3   For ships equipped with dual-fuel engine(s) using LNG and fuel oil, the C_F factor for gas (LNG) and the specific fuel consumption (SFC) of gas fuel should be used by applying the following criteria as a basis for the guidance of the Administration:

.1   final decision on the primary fuel rests with the Administration;

.2   the ratio of calorific value of gas fuel (LNG) to total marine fuels (HFO/MGO), including gas fuel (LNG) at design conditions should be equal or larger than 50% in accordance with the formula below. However, the Administration can accept a lower value of the percentage taking into account the intended voyages:

.2 在设计阶段估算的在《EEDI 计算导则》第 2.2.2 段中规定的条件下的功率曲线（kW-节），且如果试航不是在上述条件下进行，还包括试航条件下估算的功率曲线；

.3 主要船舶资料，船型和将船舶归入该船型的相关信息，船级标志和船上推进系统和电力供应系统的总体情况；

.4 在设计阶段功率曲线的估算过程及方法；

.5 节能设备的描述；和

.6 达到的 EEDI 的计算值，包括计算概述（应至少包括每个计算参数值和用于确定达到的 EEDI 的计算过程）；

.7 达到的 $EEDI_{weather}$ 和 f_w 值（不等于 1.0）的计算值，如果这些值基于《EEDI 计算导则》进行计算；和

.8 对于液化天然气（LNG）船舶：

.1 推进系统的类型和概况（如柴油机直接推进、柴油电力推进、蒸汽轮机推进）；

.2 LNG 液货舱容积，以 m^3 计，和《EEDI 计算导则》第 2.2.5.6.3 段中定义的 BOR；

.3 发动机 100% 额定输出功率（MPP_{motor}）时传动齿轮后螺旋桨轴的轴功率和柴油发电机 $\eta(i)$；

.4 蒸汽轮机的最大持续额定功率（$MCR_{SteamTurbine}$）；和

.5 《EEDI 计算导则》第 2.2.7 段中规定的蒸汽轮机的 $SFC_{SteamTurbine}$。

EEDI 技术案卷样本见本导则附录 1。

4.2.3 如果船上安装使用液化天然气体和燃油的双燃料发动机，主管机关应参照下述标准采用气体（液化天然气）的 C_F 系数和气体燃料的单位燃油消耗量（SFC）：

.1 主燃料最终由主管机关决定；

.2 气体燃料（LNG）与总船用燃料的热值比（HFO/MGO），包括设计条件下的气体燃料（LNG）应等于或大于下述公式计算值的 50%。但是，主管机关考虑到拟定航线的需要可以接受一个更低的值。

$$\frac{V_{gas} \times \rho_{gas} \times LCV_{gas} \times K_{gas}}{\left(\sum_{i=1}^{nLiquid} V_{liquid(i)} \times \rho_{liquid(i)} \times LCV_{liquid(i)} \times K_{liquid(i)} \right) + V_{gas} \times \rho_{gas} \times LCV_{gas} \times K_{gas}} \geq 50\%$$

Whereby,

V_{gas} is the total net tank volume of gas fuel on board in m^3;

V_{liquid} is the total net tank volume of every liquid fuel on board in m^3;

ρ_{gas} is the density of gas fuel in kg/m^3;

ρ_{liquid} is the density of every liquid fuel in kg/m^3;

LCV_{gas} is the low calorific value of gas fuel in kJ/kg;

LCV_{liquid} is the low calorific value of liquid fuel in kJ/kg;

K_{gas} is the filling rate for gas fuel tanks;

K_{liquid} is the filling rate for liquid fuel tanks.

Normal density, Low Calorific Value and filling rate for tanks of different kinds of fuel are listed below.

Type of fuel	Density (kg/m³)	Low Calorific Value (kJ/kg)	Filling rate for tanks
Diesel/Gas Oil	900	42700	0.98
Heavy Fuel Oil	991	40200	0.98
Liquefied Natural Gas (LNG)	450	48000	0.95*

* subject to verification of tank oading limit in the IGF and/or IGC Codes, where applicable, corresponding to the normal density used in the calculation of f_{DFgas}

.3   in case the ship is not fully equipped with dual-fuel engines, the C_F factor for gas (LNG) should apply only for those installed engines that are of dual-fuel type and sufficient gas fuel supply should be available for such engines; and

.4   LNG fuelling solutions with exchangeable (specialized) LNG tank-containers should also fall under the terms of LNG as primary fuel.

4.2.4   The *SFC* of the main and auxiliary engines should be quoted from the approved NO$_x$ Technical File and should be corrected to the value corresponding to the ISO standard reference conditions using the standard lower calorific value of the fuel oil (42,700 kJ/kg), referring to ISO 15550:2002 and ISO 3046-1:2002. For the confirmation of the *SFC*, a copy of the approved NO$_x$ Technical File and documented summary of the correction calculations should be submitted to the verifier. In cases where the NO$_x$ Technical File has not been approved at the time of the application for initial survey, the test reports provided by manufacturers should be used. In this case, at the time of the sea trial verification, a copy of

$$\frac{V_{gas} \times \rho_{gas} \times LCV_{gas} \times K_{gas}}{(\sum_{i=1}^{nLiquid} V_{liquid(i)} \times \rho_{liquid(i)} \times LCV_{liquid(i)} \times K_{liquid(i)}) + V_{gas} \times \rho_{gas} \times LCV_{gas} \times K_{gas}} \geq 50\%$$

式中：

V_{gas}—船上气体燃料舱的总净容积，m^3；

V_{liquid}—船上每种液体燃料舱的总净容积，m^3；

ρ_{gas}—气体燃料的密度，kg/m^3；

ρ_{liquid}—每种液体燃料的密度，kg/m^3；

LCV_{gas}—气体燃料的低热值，kJ/kg；

LCV_{liquid}—液体燃料的低热值，kJ/kg；

K_{gas}—气体燃料舱的加注速率；

K_{liquid}—液体燃料舱的加注速率。

不同种类燃料的标准密度、低热值和加注速率如下表所列。

燃料种类	密度（kg/m^3）	低热值（kJ/kg）	液舱的加注速率
柴油 / 汽油	900	42 700	0.98
重燃油	991	40 200	0.98
液化天然气（LNG）	450	48 000	0.95*

* 须经《国际气体燃料规则》和 / 或《国际气体规则》（如适用）验证的燃料舱的基装率，对应于计算 f_{DFgas} 使用的标准密度。

.3 如果船舶未全部配备双燃料发动机，气体（LNG）的 CF 系数应仅适用于安装的双燃料型的发动机，并且应为此类发动机提供足够的气体燃料；和

.4 采用可置换（专用的）LNG 罐作为燃料供应的方法也应视为 LNG 用作主要燃料。

4.2.4 主辅机的 *SFC* 应源自经批准的 NO_x 技术案卷，并应使用燃油的标准低热值（42 700 kJ/kg）将 SFC 修正至 ISO 标准基准条件对应的值，参见 ISO15550：2002 和 ISO3046-1：2002。为了确认 *SFC*，应向验证方提交一份经批准的 NO_x 技术案卷副本和修正计算概述文件。如果在申请初次检验时 NO_x 技术案卷还未经批准，应使用制造商提供的试验报告。在这种情况下，在进行试航验证时，应向验证方提交一份经批准的 NO_x 技术案卷副本和修正计算概述文件。

the approved NO$_x$ Technical File and documented summary of the correction calculations should be submitted to the verifier. In the case that gas fuel is determined as primary fuel in accordance with paragraph 4.2.3 and that installed engine(s) have no approved NO$_x$ Technical File tested in gas mode, the *SFC* of gas mode should be submitted by the manufacturer and confirmed by the verifier.

> Note: *SFC* in the NO$_x$ Technical File are the values of a parent engine, and the use of such value of *SFC* for the EEDI calculation for member engines may have the following technical issues for further consideration:
>
> .1   the definition of "member engines" given in the NO$_x$ Technical File is broad and specification of engines belonging to the same group/family may vary; and
>
> .2   the rate of NO$_x$ emission of the parent engine is the highest in the group/family – i.e. CO$_2$ emission, which is in the trade-off relationship with NO$_x$ emission, can be lower than the other engines in the group/family.

4.2.5   For ships to which regulation 24 of MARPOL Annex VI applies, the power curves used for the preliminary verification at the design stage should be based on reliable results of tank tests. A tank test for an individual ship may be omitted based on technical justifications such as availability of the results of tank tests for ships of the same type. In addition, the omission of tank tests is acceptable for a ship for which sea trials will be carried out under the condition as specified in paragraph 2.2.2 of the EEDI Calculation Guidelines, upon agreement of the shipowner and shipbuilder and with the approval of the verifier. To ensure the quality of tank tests, the ITTC quality system should be taken into account. Model tank tests should be witnessed by the verifier.

> Note: It would be desirable in the future that an organization conducting a tank test be authorized.

4.2.6   The verifier may request further information from the submitter, in addition to that contained in the EEDI Technical File, as necessary, to examine the calculation process of the attained EEDI. For the estimation of the ship speed at the design stage much depends on each shipbuilder's experience, and it may not be practicable for any person/organization other than the shipbuilder to fully examine the technical aspects of experience-based parameters, such as the roughness coefficient and wake scaling coefficient. Therefore, the preliminary verification should focus on the calculation process of the attained EEDI to ensure that it is technically sound and reasonable and follows regulation 22 of MARPOL Annex VI and the EEDI Calculation Guidelines.

> Note 1: A possible way forward for more robust verification is to establish a standard methodology of deriving the ship speed from the outcome of tank tests, by setting standard values for experience-based correction factors such as roughness coefficient and wake scaling coefficient. In this way, ship-by-ship performance comparisons could be made more objectively by excluding the possibility of arbitrary setting of experience-based parameters. If such standardization is sought, this would have an implication on how the ship speed adjustment based on sea trial results should be conducted, in accordance with paragraph 4.3.8 of these guidelines.
>
> Note 2: A joint industry standard to support the method and role of the verifier is expected to be developed.

如果按照第 4.2.3 段的规定确定气体燃料为主燃料，且安装的发动机不具备经批准的气体状态测试的 NO_x 技术案卷，制造商应提供气体状态的 SFC 并经验证方确认。

> 注：NO_x 技术案卷中的 SFC 是母型机的值，而对成员机 EEDI 计算时使用该 SFC 值可能会有下列技术问题需进一步考虑：
>
> .1 NO_x 技术案卷中"成员机"的定义范围很广，属于同一组 / 族的成员机的技术条件可能各不相同；和
>
> .2 母型机的 NO_x 排放率在组 / 族中最高，即与 NO_x 排放成消长关系的 CO_2 排放量可能低于组 / 族中的其他发动机。

4.2.5 对于《防污公约》附则Ⅵ第 24 条适用的船舶，用于设计阶段前期验证的功率曲线应基于水池试验的可靠结果。对于相同类型船舶，可基于技术依据（例如水池试验结果的可用性）来免除单个船舶的水池试验。此外，经船东和造船厂同意以及验证方的认可，如果船舶试航在《EEDI 计算导则》第 2.2.2 段中规定的条件下进行，可接受免除水池试验。为确保水池试验的质量，应考虑 ITTC 质量体系。模型水池试验应由验证方见证。

> 注：未来对进行水池试验的组织进行授权是合适的。

4.2.6 验证方可要求提交方提供除技术案卷中包含的信息外的必要的附加信息，以检查达到的 EEDI 的计算过程。在设计阶段航速的估算很大程度上取决于各造船厂的经验，除造船厂外的任何人员 / 组织充分检查经验型参数（例如粗糙度系数和伴流尺度系数）的技术方面可能不可行。因此，前期验证应关注达到的 EEDI 的计算过程以确保其技术上牢靠和合理并遵循《防污公约》附则Ⅵ第 22 条和《EEDI 计算导则》。

> 注 1：可能的更牢靠的验证方式是通过设定经验型修正系数（例如粗糙度系数和伴流尺度系数）的标准值，规定从水池试验的结果获得船舶航速的标准方法。这样，能通过排除随意设定经验型参数的可能性而更客观地进行船与船的性能比较。如果寻求这种标准化方法，可能涉及应如何按照本导则第 4.3.8 段进行基于试航结果的航速调整。
>
> 注 2：将制定支持验证方的方式和职责的联合行业标准。

4.2.7   Additional information that the verifier may request the submitter to provide includes, but is not limited to:

.1   descriptions of a tank test facility; this should include the name of the facility, the particulars of tanks and towing equipment, and the records of calibration of each monitoring equipment;

.2   lines of a model ship and an actual ship for the verification of the appropriateness of the tank test; the lines (sheer plan, body plan and half-breadth plan) should be detailed enough to demonstrate the similarity between the model ship and the actual ship;

.3   lightweight of the ship and displacement table for the verification of the deadweight;

.4   detailed report on the method and results of the tank test; this should include at least the tank test results at sea trial condition and under the condition as specified in paragraph 2.2.2 of the EEDI Calculation Guidelines;

.5   detailed calculation process of the ship speed, which should include the basis for the estimation of experience-based parameters such as roughness coefficient, and wake scaling coefficient;

.6   reasons for exempting a tank test, if applicable; this should include lines and tank test results of ships of the same type, and the comparison of the principal particulars of such ships and the ship in question. Appropriate technical justification should be provided, explaining why the tank test is unnecessary; and

.7   for LNG carriers, detailed calculation process of P_{AE} and $SFC_{SteamTurbine}$.

4.2.8   The verifier should issue the report on the Preliminary Verification of the EEDI after it has verified the attained EEDI at the design stage, in accordance with paragraphs 4.1 and 4.2 of these guidelines.

4.3   Final verification of the attained EEDI at sea trial

4.3.1   Sea trial conditions should be set as the conditions specified in paragraph 2.2.2 of the EEDI Calculation Guidelines, if possible.

4.3.2   Prior to the sea trial, the following documents should be submitted to the verifier: a description of the test procedure to be used for the speed trial, the final displacement table and the measured lightweight, or a copy of the survey report of deadweight, as well as a copy of the NO_x Technical File, as necessary. The test procedure should include, as a minimum, descriptions of all necessary items to be measured and corresponding measurement methods to be used for developing power curves under the sea trial condition.

4.3.3   The verifier should attend the sea trial and confirm:

.1   propulsion and power supply system, particulars of the engines or steam turbines, and other relevant items described in the EEDI Technical File;

.2   draught and trim;

.3   sea conditions;

4.2.7 验证方可要求提交方直接向其提供的附加信息包括但不限于：

.1 水池试验设施的描述；这应包括设施名称、水池及拖曳设备的细节和每个监测设备的校准记录；

.2 用以验证水池试验适合性的船模和实船型线；型线（型线侧视图，型线横剖图和半宽图）应足够详细以说明船模与实船之间的相似性；

.3 用以验证载重吨的船舶空船重量和排水量表；

.4 水池试验方法及结果的详细报告；应至少包括试航条件和《EEDI 计算导则》第 2.2.2 段中规定的条件下水池试验的结果；

.5 船舶航速的详细计算过程，应包括对经验型参数（例如粗糙度系数，伴流尺度系数）的估算基础；

.6 免除水池试验的理由，如适用；这应包括相同类型船舶的型线和水池试验结果以及这类船舶与所考虑的船舶的主要细节的对比。应提供适当的技术依据解释为何无须进行水池试验；和

.7 对于 LNG 船舶，P_{AE} 和 $SFC_{SteamTurbine}$ 的详细计算过程。

4.2.8 验证方按本导则第 4.1 和 4.2 段在设计阶段验证达到的 EEDI 后，应签发 EEDI 前期验证报告。

4.3 试航时达到的 EEDI 的最终验证

4.3.1 试航条件应设置为《EEDI 计算导则》第 2.2.2 段中规定的条件（如可能）。

4.3.2 试航前，应向验证方提交如下文件：航速测试所用试验程序的描述，最终的排水量表和测得的空船重量，或一份载重吨检验报告的副本，以及一份必需的 NO_x 技术案卷副本。试验程序应至少包括在试航条件下制定功率曲线应测量的所有必需项目和应使用的相应测量方法的描述。

4.3.3 验证方应参加试航并确认：

.1 推进和供电系统、发动机或蒸汽轮机细节以及 EEDI 技术案卷中描述的其他相关项；

.2 吃水和纵倾；

.3 海况；

.4   ship speed; and

.5   shaft power and RPM.

4.3.4   Draught and trim should be confirmed by the draught measurements taken prior to the sea trial. The draught and trim should be as close as practical to those at the assumed conditions used for estimating the power curves.

4.3.5   Sea conditions should be measured in accordance with ITTC Recommended Procedure 7.5-04-01-01.1 *Preparation, Conduct and Analysis of Speed/Power Trials* (2017, 2021 or 2022 version, as may be applicable at the time of sea trials) or ISO 15016:2015.

4.3.6   Ship speed should be measured in accordance with ITTC Recommended Procedure 7.5-04-01-01.1 *Preparation, Conduct and Analysis of Speed/Power Trials* (2017, 2021 or 2022 version, as may be applicable at the time of sea trials) or ISO 15016:2015, and at more than two points of which range includes the power of the main engine as specified in paragraph 2.2.5 of the EEDI Calculation Guidelines.

4.3.7   The main engine output, shaft power of propeller shaft (for LNG carriers having diesel electric propulsion system) or steam turbine output (for LNG carriers having steam turbine propulsion system) should be measured by shaft power meter or a method which the engine manufacturer recommends and the verifier approves. Other methods may be acceptable upon agreement of the shipowner and shipbuilder and with the approval of the verifier.

4.3.8   The submitter should develop power curves based on the measured ship speed and the measured output of the main engine at sea trial. For the development of the power curves, the submitter should calibrate the measured ship speed, if necessary, by taking into account the effects of wind, current, waves, shallow water, displacement, water temperature and water density in accordance with ITTC Recommended Procedure 7.5-04-01-01.1 *Preparation, Conduct and Analysis of Speed/Power Trials* (2017, 2021 or 2022 version, as may be applicable at the time of sea trials) or ISO 15016:2015. Upon agreement with the shipowner, the submitter should submit a report on the speed trials including details of the power curve development to the verifier for verification.

4.3.9   The submitter should compare the power curves obtained as a result of the sea trial and the estimated power curves at the design stage. In case differences are observed, the attained EEDI should be recalculated, as necessary, in accordance with the following:

.1   for ships for which sea trial is conducted under the condition as specified in paragraph 2.2.2 of the EEDI Calculation Guidelines: the attained EEDI should be recalculated using the measured ship speed at sea trial at the power of the main engine as specified in paragraph 2.2.5 of the EEDI Calculation Guidelines; and

.2   for ships for which sea trial cannot be conducted under the condition as specified in paragraph 2.2.2 of the EEDI Calculation Guidelines: if the measured ship speed at the power of the main engine as specified in paragraph 2.2.5 of the EEDI Calculation Guidelines at the sea trial conditions is different from the expected ship speed on the power curve at the corresponding condition, the shipbuilder should recalculate the attained EEDI by adjusting ship speed under the condition as specified in paragraph 2.2.2 of the EEDI Calculation Guidelines by an appropriate correction method that is agreed by the verifier.

.4 航速；和

.5 轴功率和 RPM。

4.3.4 吃水和纵倾应通过在试航前进行的吃水测量进行确认。吃水和纵倾应尽实际可能接近用于估算功率曲线的假定条件。

4.3.5 海况应根据 ITTC 建议程序 7.5-04-01-01.1《航速 / 功率测试的准备、实施和分析》（试航时可能适用的 2017、2021 或 2022 版）或 ISO 15016：2015 进行测量。

4.3.6 航速应根据 ITTC 建议程序 7.5-04-01-01.1《航速 / 功率测试的准备、实施和分析》（试航时可能适用的 2017、2021 或 2022 版）或 ISO 15016：2015 在两个以上点进行测量，测量范围包括《EEDI 计算导则》第 2.2.5 段中规定的主机功率。

4.3.7 主机的输出功率、推进轴系的轴功率（对于具有柴油机电力推进系统的 LNG 船舶）或蒸汽轮机的输出功率（对于具有蒸汽轮机推进系统的 LNG 船舶）应通过轴功率计或发动机制造商推荐且验证方认可的方法进行测量。经船东和造船厂同意以及验证方的认可，可接受其他方法。

4.3.8 提交方应基于试航时测得的航速和主机输出功率制定功率曲线。在制定功率曲线时，提交方应根据 ITTC 建议程序 7.5-04-01-01.1《航速 / 功率测试的准备、实施和分析》（试航时可能适用的 2017、2021 或 2022 版）或 ISO 15016：2015，通过考虑风、潮涌、波浪、浅水、排水量、水温和水密度的影响修正所测得的航速（如必要）。经船东同意，提交方应将航速测试报告（包括制定功率曲线的详情）提供给验证方供验证。

4.3.9 提交方应对试航获得的功率曲线与设计阶段估算的功率曲线进行比较。如果发现两者之间有差异，必要时应按照下述方法重新计算达到的 EEDI：

.1 对于在《EEDI 计算导则》第 2.2.2 段中规定的条件下试航的船舶：应使用在试航时在《EEDI 计算导则》第 2.2.5 段中规定的主机功率下测得的航速重新计算达到的 EEDI；和

.2 对于不能在《EEDI 计算导则》第 2.2.2 段中规定的条件下试航的船舶：如果试航条件下在《EEDI 计算导则》第 2.2.5 段中规定的主机功率下测得的船舶航速不同于对应条件下功率曲线上的预期航速，造船厂应通过以验证方同意的适当的修正方法在《EEDI 计算导则》第 2.2.2 段中规定的条件下调整航速，以重新计算达到的 EEDI。

An example of scheme of conversion from trial condition to EEDI condition at EEDI power is given as follows:

V_{ref} is obtained from the results of the sea trials at trial condition using the speed-power curves predicted by the tank tests. The tank tests shall be carried out at both draughts: trial condition corresponding to that of the S/P trials and EEDI condition. For trial conditions the power ratio α_P between model test prediction and sea trial result is calculated for constant ship speed. Ship speed from model test prediction for EEDI condition at EEDI power multiplied with α_P is V_{ref}.

$$\alpha_P = \frac{P_{Trial,P}}{P_{Trial,S}}$$

where:

$P_{Trial,P}$: power at trial condition predicted by the tank tests

$P_{Trial,S}$: power at trial condition obtained by the S/P trials

α_p :   power ratio

Figure 2 shows an example of scheme of the conversion to derive the resulting ship speed at EEDI condition (V_{ref}) at EEDI power.

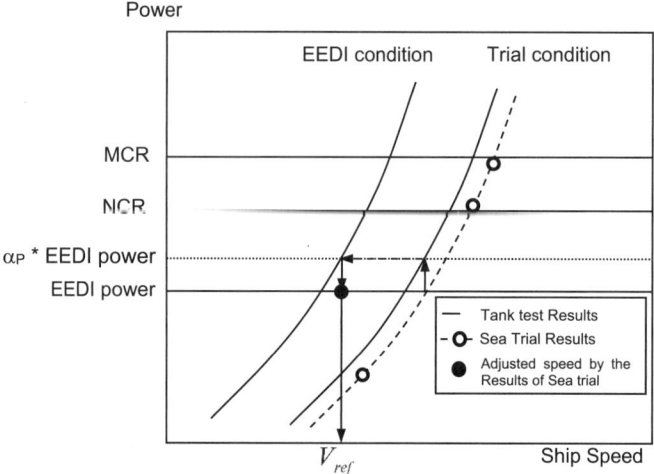

Figure 2: An example of scheme of conversion from trial condition to EEDI condition at EEDI power

Note: Further consideration would be necessary for speed adjustment methodology in paragraph 4.3.9.2 of these guidelines. One of the concerns relates to a possible situation where the power curve for sea trial condition is estimated in an excessively conservative manner (i.e. power curve is shifted in a leftward direction) with the intention to get an upward adjustment of the ship speed by making the measured ship speed at sea trial easily exceed the lower-estimated speed for sea trial condition at design stage.

EEDI 功率下从试航条件转化为 EEDI 条件的方式举例如下：

使用水池试验预估的速度功率曲线，在试航条件下根据试航结果获得 V_{ref}。水池试验应在两种吃水条件下进行：S/P 试航相对应的试航条件和 EEDI 条件。对于试航条件，针对恒定船速，计算模型试验的预估值和试航结果之间的功率比 α_p。在 EEDI 条件下的 EEDI 功率时的模型试验预估船速乘以 α_p 即为 V_{ref}。

$$\alpha_P = \frac{P_{Trial,P}}{P_{Trial,S}}$$

式中：

$P_{trial,\ P}$：水池试验预估的试航条件下的功率

$P_{trial,\ S}$：S/P 试航获得的试航条件下的功率

α_p：功率比

图 2 给出了为得出 EEDI 条件（V_{ref}）下 EEDI 功率时的最终船速而进行的转化方式示例。

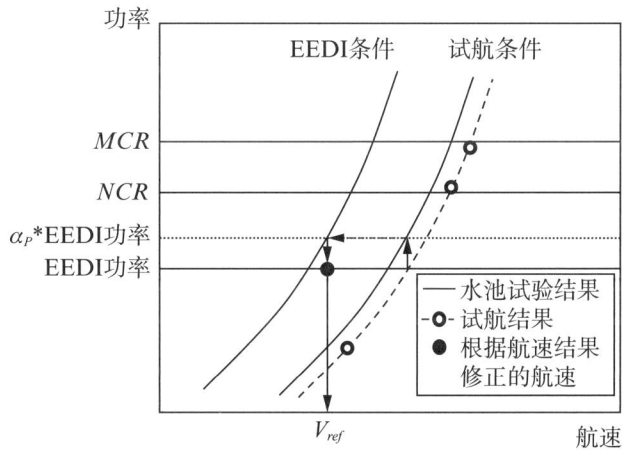

图 2　EEDI 功率时从试航条件转化为 EEDI 条件的方式示例

注：对于本导则第 4.3.9.2 段中的速度修正方法，有必要作进一步考虑。其中一个担忧是试航条件下的功率曲线可能以过于保守的方式进行估算（即功率曲线向左移动），目的是通过让试航时测得的船速很容易地超过设计阶段对试航条件下低估的航速从而达到上调航速。

4.3.10   In cases where the finally determined deadweight/gross tonnage differs from the designed deadweight/gross tonnage used in the EEDI calculation during the preliminary verification, the submitter should recalculate the attained EEDI using the finally determined deadweight/gross tonnage. The finally determined gross tonnage should be confirmed in the Tonnage Certificate of the ship.

4.3.11   The electrical efficiency $\eta_{(i)}$ should be taken as 91.3% for the purpose of calculating the attained EEDI. Alternatively, if a value of more than 91.3% is to be applied, $\eta_{(i)}$ should be obtained by measurement and verified by a method approved by the verifier.

4.3.12   In cases where the attained EEDI is calculated at the preliminary verification by using *SFC* based on the manufacturer's test report, owing to the non-availability at that time of the approved NO_x Technical File, the EEDI should be recalculated by using *SFC* in the approved NO_x Technical File. Also, for steam turbines, the EEDI should be recalculated by using *SFC* confirmed by the Administration or an organization recognized by the Administration at the sea trial.

4.3.13   The EEDI Technical File should be revised, as necessary, by taking into account the results of sea trials. Such revision should include, as applicable, the adjusted power curve based on the results of sea trials (namely, modified ship speed under the condition as specified in paragraph 2.2.2 of the EEDI Calculation Guidelines), the finally determined deadweight/gross tonnage, η for LNG carriers having diesel electric propulsion system and *SFC* described in the approved NO_x Technical File, and the recalculated attained EEDI based on these modifications.

4.3.14   The EEDI Technical File, if revised, should be submitted to the verifier for confirmation that the (revised) attained EEDI is calculated in accordance with regulation 22 of MARPOL Annex VI and the EEDI Calculation Guidelines.

4.4   Verification of the attained EEDI in case of major conversion

4.4.1   In cases of a major conversion of a ship, the shipowner should submit to a verifier an application for an Additional Survey with the EEDI Technical File duly revised, based on the conversion made and other relevant background documents.

4.4.2   The background documents should include as a minimum, but are not limited to:

.1   details of the conversion;

.2   EEDI parameters changed after the conversion and the technical justifications for each respective parameter;

.3   reasons for other changes made in the EEDI Technical File, if any; and

.4   calculated value of the attained EEDI with the calculation summary, which should contain, as a minimum, each value of the calculation parameters and the calculation process used to determine the attained EEDI after the conversion.

4.4.3   The verifier should review the revised EEDI Technical File and other documents submitted and verify the calculation process of the attained EEDI to ensure that it is technically sound and reasonable and follows regulation 22 of MARPOL Annex VI and the EEDI Calculation Guidelines.

4.4.4   For verification of the attained EEDI after a conversion, speed trials of the ship are required, as necessary.

4.3.10 如果最终确定的载重吨／总吨与前期验证时 EEDI 计算使用的设计载重吨／总吨不同，提交方应使用最终确定的载重吨／总吨重新计算达到的 EEDI。最终确定的总吨应在船舶吨位证书中确认。

4.3.11 计算达到的 EEDI 时应采用 91.3% 的电效率。或者，如果采用了大于 91.3% 的值，$\eta(i)$ 应经过测量获得并通过经验证方认可的方法进行验证。

4.3.12 如果在前期验证时，达到的 EEDI 的计算由于当时未得到经认可的 NO_x 技术案卷而使用了基于制造商的试验报告的 SFC，应通过使用经认可的 NO_x 技术案卷中的 SFC 重新计算 EEDI。同时，对于蒸汽轮机，EEDI 应采用经主管机关确认或试航时由主管机关认可的组织确认的 SFC 重新计算。

4.3.13 应参照试航的结果在必要时修订 EEDI 技术案卷。修订应包括适用的基于试航结果调整的功率曲线（即在《EEDI 计算导则》第 2.2.2 段中规定的条件下修改的航速），最终确定的载重吨／总吨、具有柴油电力推进系统的 LNG 船舶的 η 值和经认可的 NO_x 技术案卷中描述的 SFC，以及基于这些修改而重新计算的达到的 EEDI。

4.3.14 EEDI 技术案卷如经修订，应提交验证方确认，该(经修订的)达到的 EEDI 是按照《防污公约》附则Ⅵ第 22 条和《EEDI 计算导则》进行计算的。

4.4 重大改建时达到的 EEDI 的验证

4.4.1 如果船舶进行重大改建，船东应将附加检验申请连同基于所作改建而适当修订的 EEDI 技术案卷和其他相关背景文件提交给验证方。

4.4.2 背景文件应至少包括但不限于：

    .1 改建的详细情况；

    .2 改建后改变的 EEDI 参数和每一相关参数的技术依据；

    .3 EEDI 技术案卷中所作其他改变的理由（如有）；和

    .4 达到的 EEDI 的计算值和计算概述，应至少包括每个计算参数值和用于确定改建后达到的 EEDI 的计算过程。

4.4.3 验证方应评审经修订的 EEDI 技术案卷和提交的其他文件并验证达到的 EEDI 的计算过程，以确保其技术上牢靠和合理并遵循《防污公约》附则Ⅵ第 22 条和《EEDI 计算导则》。

4.4.4 对于改建后达到的 EEDI 的验证，必要时须进行船舶航速测试。

APPENDIX 1

SAMPLE OF EEDI TECHNICAL FILE

1   Data

1.1   General information

Shipbuilder	JAPAN Shipbuilding Company
Hull no.	12345
IMO no.	94111XX
Ship type	Bulk carrier

1.2   Principal particulars

Length overall	250.0 m
Length between perpendiculars	240.0 m
Breadth, moulded	40.0 m
Depth, moulded	20.0 m
Summer load line draught, moulded	14.0 m
Deadweight at summer load line draught	150,000 tons

1.3   Main engine

Manufacturer	JAPAN Heavy Industries Ltd.
Type	6J70A
Maximum continuous rating (MCR)	15,000 kW x 80 rpm
SFC at 75% MCR	165.0 g/kWh
Number of set	1
Fuel type	Diesel Oil

1.4   Auxiliary engine

Manufacturer	JAPAN Diesel Ltd.
Type	5J-200
Maximum continuous rating (MCR)	600 kW x 900 rpm
SFC at 50% MCR	220.0 g/kWh
Number of set	3
Fuel type	Diesel Oil

1.5   Ship speed

Ship speed in deep water at summer load line draught at 75% of MCR	14.25 knots

附录 1

EEDI 技术案卷样本

1 数据

1.1 一般信息

船厂	日本造船公司
船体编号	12345
IMO 编号	94111XX
船型	散货船

1.2 主要船舶资料

总长	250.0 m
垂线间长度	240.0 m
型宽	40.0 m
型深	20.0 m
夏季载重线吃水，型吃水	4.0 m
夏季载重线吃水时的载重吨	150 000 吨

1.3 主机

制造商	日本重工有限公司
型号	6J70A
最大持续功率（MCR）	15 000kW × 80 rpm
75%MCR 下的 SFC	165.0 g/kWh
台数	1
燃油类型	柴油

1.4 辅机

制造商	日本柴油机有限公司
型号	5J–200
最大持续功率（MCR）	600kW × 900 rpm
50%MCR 下的 SFC	220.0 g/kWh
台数	3
燃油类型	柴油

1.5 航速

夏季载重线吃水时深水中 75%MCR 下的航速	14.25 节

2　Power curves

The power curves estimated at the design stage and modified after the speed trials are shown in figure 2.1.

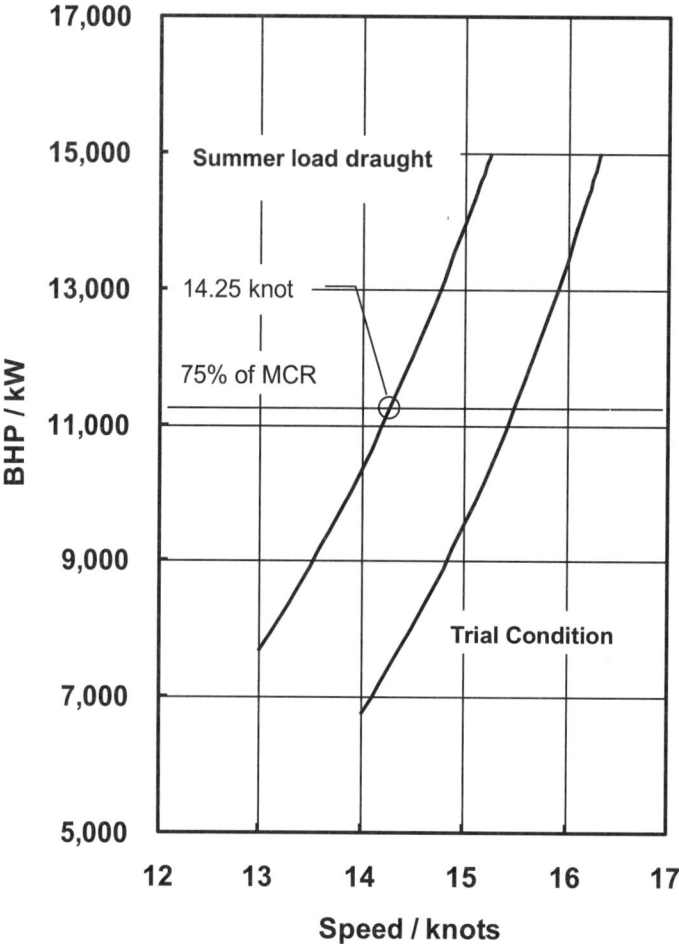

Figure 2.1: Power curves

2 功率曲线

设计阶段估算和经航速测试后修改的功率曲线见图 2.1。

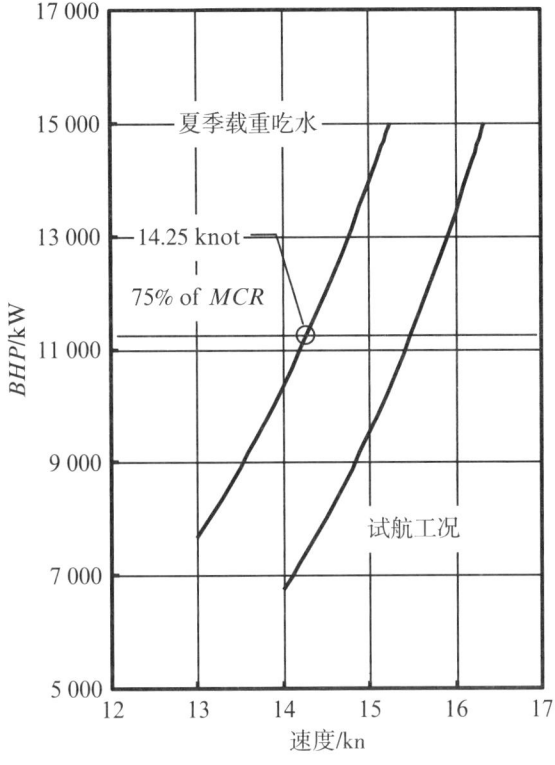

图 2.1　功率曲线

3   Overview of propulsion system and electric power supply system

3.1   Propulsion system

3.1.1   Main engine
         Refer to paragraph 1.3 of this appendix.

3.1.2   Propeller

Type	Fixed pitch propeller
Diameter	7.0 m
Number of blades	4
Number of set	1

3.2   Electric power supply system

3.2.1   Auxiliary engines
         Refer to paragraph 1.4 of this appendix.

3.2.2   Main generators

Manufacturer	JAPAN Electric
Rated output	560 kW (700 kVA) x 900 rpm
Voltage	AC 450 V
Number of set	3

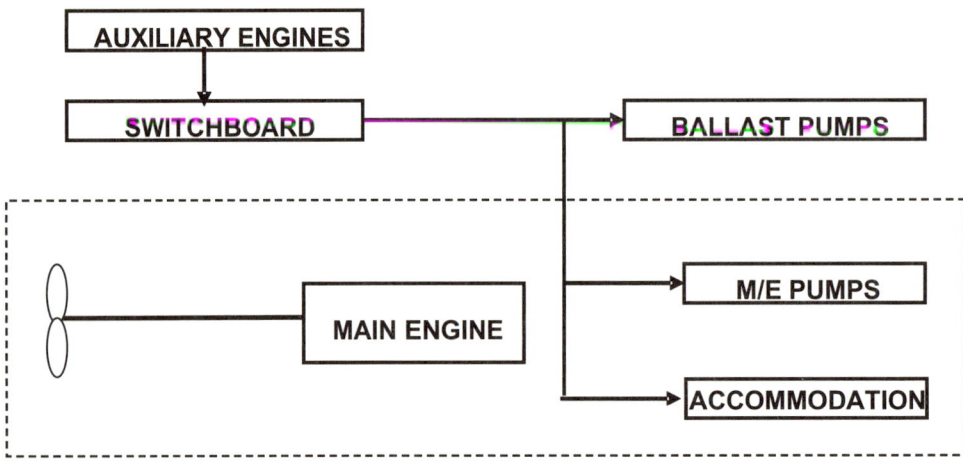

Figure 3.1: Schematic figure of propulsion and electric power supply system

3 推进系统和电力供应系统概述

3.1 推进系统

3.1.1 主机

参见本附录 1.3。

3.1.2 螺旋桨

类型	固定螺距螺旋桨
直径	7.0 m
桨叶数量	4
台数	1

3.2 电力供应系统

3.2.1 辅机

参见本附录 1.4。

3.2.2 主发电机

制造商	日本电气
额定功率	560 kW（700 kVA）×900 rpm
电压	AC 450V
台数	3

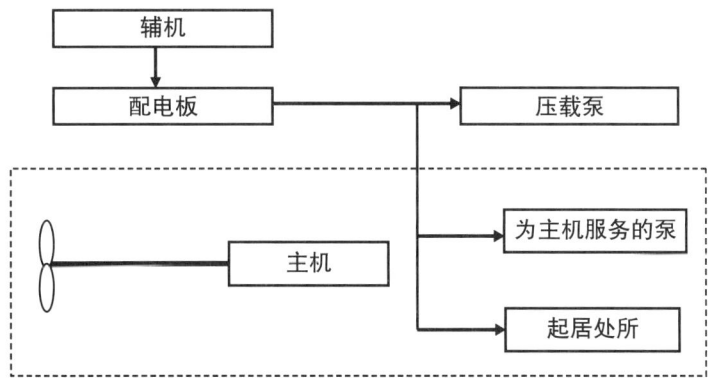

图 3.1　推进和电力供应系统原理图

4   Estimation process of power curves at design stage

Power curves are estimated based on model test results. The flow of the estimation process is shown below.

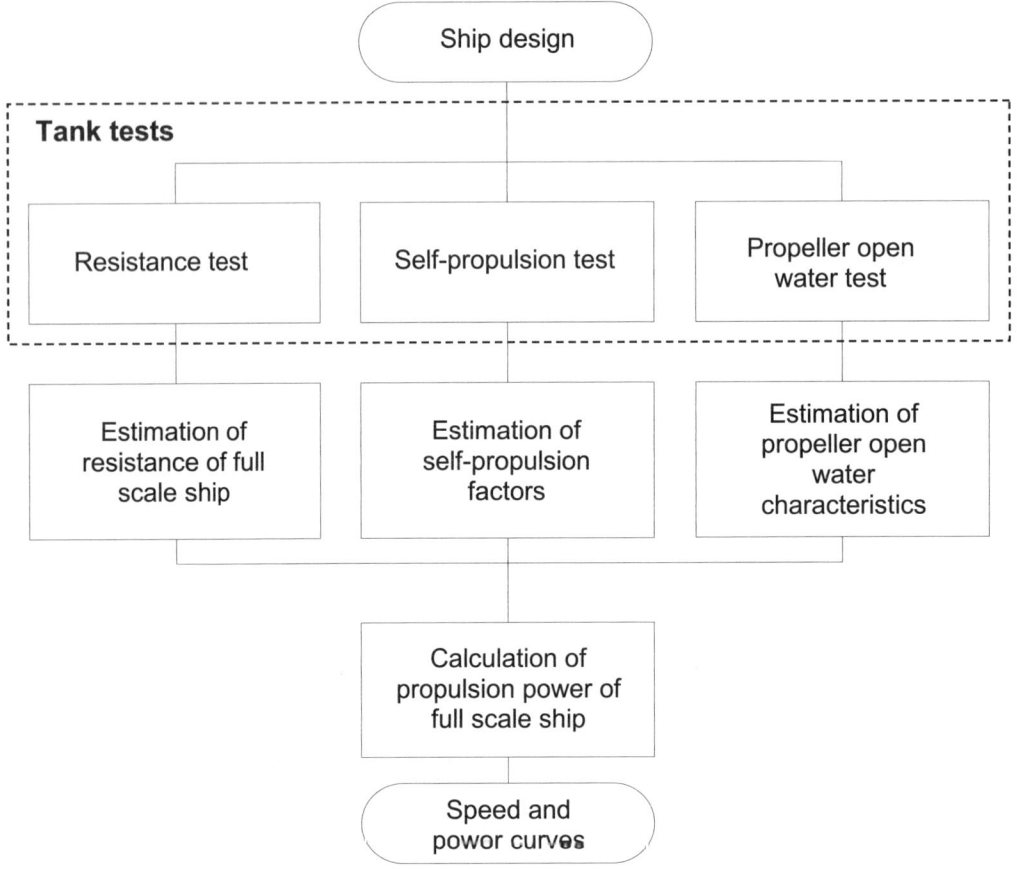

Figure 4.1: Flow chart of process for estimating power curves

5   Description of energy-saving equipment

5.1   Energy-saving equipment the effects of which are expressed as $P_{AEeff(i)}$ and/or $P_{eff(i)}$ in the EEDI calculation formula

N/A

5.2   Other energy-saving equipment

(Example)

5.2.1   Rudder fins

5.2.2   Propeller boss cap fins

......

(Specifications, schematic figures and/or photos, etc., for each piece of equipment or device should be indicated. Alternatively, attachment of a commercial catalogue may be acceptable.)

4 设计阶段功率曲线估算过程

功率曲线的估算是基于模型试验结果。估算过程的流程如下。

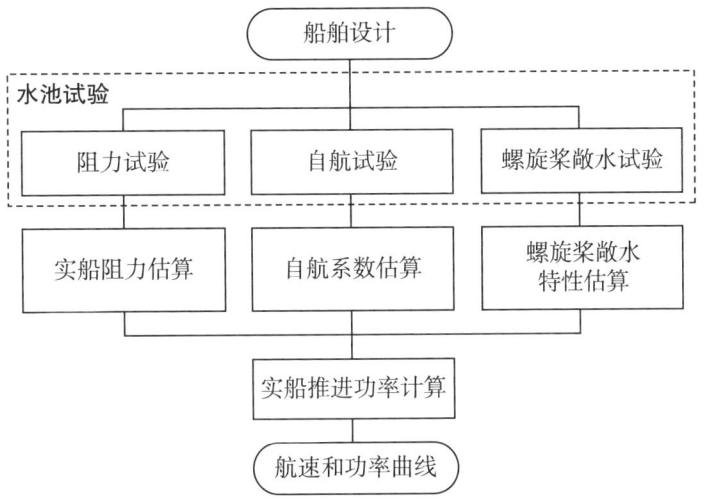

图 4.1 功率曲线估算过程流程图

5 节能设备描述

5.1 其效果在 EEDI 计算公式中表述为 $P_{AEeff(i)}$ 和 / 或 $P_{eff(i)}$ 的节能设备。

N/A

5.2 其他节能设备

（举例）

5.2.1 舵鳍

5.2.2 桨毂整流鳍

......

（应说明每台设备或装置的说明书、原理图和 / 或照片等。作为替代，附上产品商业目录也可接受。）

6　Calculated value of attained EEDI

6.1　Basic data

Type of ship	Capacity DWT	Speed V_{ref} (knots)
Bulk Carrier	150,000	14.25

6.2　Main engine

MCR_{ME} (kW)	Shaft gen.	P_{ME} (kW)	Type of fuel	C_{FME}	SFC_{ME} (g/kWh)
15,000	N/A	11,250	Diesel Oil	3.206	165.0

6.3　Auxiliary engines

P_{AE} (kW)	Type of fuel	C_{FAE}	SFC_{AE} (g/kWh)
625	Diesel Oil	3.206	220.0

6.4　Ice class

N/A

6.5　Innovative electrical energy-efficient technology

N/A

6.6　Innovative mechanical energy-efficient technology

N/A

6.7　Cubic capacity correction factor

N/A

6.8　Calculated value of attained EEDI

$$EEDI = \frac{\left(\prod_{j=1}^{M} f_j\right)\left(\sum_{i=1}^{nME} P_{ME(i)} \cdot C_{FME(i)} \cdot SFC_{ME(i)}\right) + \left(P_{AE} \cdot C_{FAE} \cdot SFC_{AE}\right)}{f_i \cdot f_c \cdot Capacity \cdot f_w \cdot V_{ref}}$$

$$+ \frac{\left\{\left(\prod_{j=1}^{M} f_j \cdot \sum_{i=1}^{nPTI} P_{PTI(i)} - \sum_{i=1}^{neff} f_{eff(i)} \cdot P_{AEeff(i)}\right) C_{FAE} \cdot SFC_{AE}\right\} - \left(\sum_{i=1}^{neff} f_{eff(i)} \cdot P_{eff(i)} \cdot C_{FME} \cdot SFC_{ME}\right)}{f_i \cdot f_c \cdot Capacity \cdot f_w \cdot V_{ref}}$$

$$= \frac{1 \times \left(11250 \times 3.206 \times 165.0\right) + \left(625 \times 3.206 \times 220.0\right) + 0 - 0}{1 \cdot 1 \cdot 150000 \cdot 1 \cdot 14.25}$$

$$= 2.99 \quad \left(g - CO_2/ton \cdot mile\right)$$

attained EEDI: 2.99 g-CO$_2$/ton mile

6 达到的 EEDI 的计算值

6.1 基础数据

船型	载重吨	航速 V_{ref}（节）
散货船	150 000	14.25

6.2 主机

MCR_{ME}/kW	轴带发电机	P_{ME}/kW	燃油类型	C_{FME}	SCF_{ME}/g/kWh
15 000	N/A	11 250	柴油	3.206	165.0

6.3 辅机

P_{AE}/kW	燃油类型	咖啡	SCF_{AE}/g/kWh
625	柴油	3.206	220.0

6.4 冰级

N/A

6.5 创新型电力节能技术

N/A

6.6 创新型机械节能技术

N/A

6.7 立方容积修正系数

N/A

6.8 达到的 EEDI 的计算值

$$EEDI = \frac{\left(\prod\limits_{j=1}^{M} f_j\right)\left(\sum\limits_{i=1}^{nME} P_{ME(i)} \cdot C_{FME(i)} \cdot SFC_{ME(i)}\right) + \left(P_{AE} \cdot C_{FAE} \cdot SFC_{AE}\right)}{f_i \cdot f_c \cdot Capacity \cdot f_w \cdot V_{ref}}$$

$$+ \frac{\left\{\left(\prod\limits_{j=1}^{M} f_j \cdot \sum\limits_{i=1}^{nPTI} P_{PTI(i)} - \sum\limits_{i=1}^{neff} f_{eff(i)} \cdot P_{AEeff(i)}\right) C_{FAE} \cdot SFC_{AE}\right\} - \left(\sum\limits_{i=1}^{neff} f_{eff(i)} \cdot P_{eff(i)} \cdot C_{FME} \cdot SFC_{ME}\right)}{f_i \cdot f_c \cdot Capacity \cdot f_w \cdot V_{ref}}$$

$$= \frac{1 \times (11\,250 \times 3.206 \times 165.0) + (625 \times 3.206 \times 220.0) + 0 - 0}{1 \cdot 1 \cdot 150\,000 \cdot 1 \cdot 14.25}$$

$$= 2.99 \quad (g - CO_2/ton \cdot mile)$$

达到的 EEDI：2.99 g-CO₂/（吨·英里）

7 Calculated value of attained EEDI$_{weather}$

7.1 Representative sea conditions

	Mean wind speed	Mean wind direction	Significant wave height	Mean wave period	Mean wave direction
BF6	12.6 (m/s)	0 (deg.)*	3.0 (m)	6.7 (s)	0 (deg.)*

* Heading direction of wind/wave in relation to the ship's heading, i.e. 0 (deg.) means the ship is heading directly into the wind.

7.2 Calculated weather factor, f_w

f_w	0.900

7.3 Calculated value of attained EEDI$_{weather}$

attained EEDI$_{weather}$: 3.32 g-CO$_2$/ton mile

7 达到的 $EEDI_{weather}$ 的计算值

7.1 代表性海况

	平均风速	平均风向	有义波高	平均波浪周期	平均波浪方向
BF6	12.6 m/s	0（°）*	3.0 m	6.7 s	0° *

* 与船舶首向相关的风 / 波浪首向，即 0° 系指船舶正迎风航行。

7.2 计算的天气因数 f_w

f_w	0.900

7.3 达到的 $EEDI_{weather}$ 的计算值

达到的 $EEDI_{weather}$：3.32 g-CO_2/（吨·英里）

APPENDIX 2

GUIDELINES FOR VALIDATION OF ELECTRIC POWER TABLES FOR EEDI (EPT-EEDI)

1   INTRODUCTION

The purpose of these guidelines is to assist recognized organizations in the validation of electric power tables (EPT) for the calculation of the Energy Efficiency Design Index (EEDI) for ships. As such, these guidelines support the implementation of the EEDI Calculation Guidelines and the *Guidelines on survey and certification of the Energy Efficiency Design Index (EEDI)*. These guidelines will also assist shipowners, shipbuilders, ship designers and manufacturers in relation to aspects of the development of more energy-efficient ships and also in understanding the procedures for the EPT-EEDI validation.

2   OBJECTIVES

These guidelines provide a framework for the uniform application of the EPT-EEDI validation process for ships for which required auxiliary engine power is calculated under paragraph 2.2.5.7 of the EEDI Calculation Guidelines.

3   DEFINITIONS

3.1   *Applicant* means an organization, primarily a shipbuilder or a ship designer, which requests the EPT-EEDI validation in accordance with these guidelines.

3.2   *Validator* means a recognized organization which conducts the EPT-EEDI validation in accordance with these guidelines.

3.3   *Validation* for the purpose of these guidelines means review of submitted documents and survey during construction and sea trials.

3.4   *Standard EPT-EEDI-Form* refers to the layout given in appendix 3, containing the EPT-EEDI results that will be the subject of validation. Other supporting documents submitted for this purpose will be used as reference only and will not be subject to validation.

3.5 P_{AE} herein is defined as per the definition in paragraph 2.2.5.6 of the EEDI Calculation Guidelines.

3.6   *Ship service and engine-room loads* refer to all the load groups which are needed for the hull, deck, navigation and safety services, propulsion and auxiliary engine services, engine-room ventilation and auxiliaries and ship's general services.

3.7   *Diversity factor* is the ratio of the "total installed load power" and the "actual load power" for continuous loads and intermittent loads. This factor is equivalent to the product of service factors for load, duty and time.

4   APPLICATION

4.1   These guidelines are applicable to ships as stipulated in paragraph 2.2.5.7 of the EEDI Calculation Guidelines.

4.2   These guidelines should be applied for new ships for which an application for an EPT-EEDI validation has been submitted to a validator.

附录 2

EEDI 电力负荷表（EPT-EEDI）认证导则

1 引言

本导则旨在帮助被认可组织认证船舶电力负荷表（EPT）以进行船舶能效设计指数（EEDI）的计算。因此，本导则支持《EEDI 计算导则》和《能效设计指数检验和发证导则》的实施。本导则还帮助船东、造船厂、船舶设计单位和制造商开发能效更高的船舶，并帮助其了解 EPT-EEDI 认证程序。

2 目的

本导则为《EEDI 计算导则》第 2.2.5.7 段规定的要求计算辅机功率的船舶提供 EPT-EEDI 认证程序的统一应用框架。

3 定义

3.1 *申请方*系指要求按本导则认证 EPT-EEDI 的组织，主要为造船厂或船舶设计单位。

3.2 *认证方*系指按本导则执行 EPT-EEDI 认证的被认可组织。

3.3 就本导则而言，*认证*系指对所提交文件的审核和船舶在建造及试航时的检验。

3.4 *标准 EEDI 电力负荷表格式（EPT-EEDI 格式）*系指附录 3 中的表格，该表含须认证的 EPT-EEDI 结果。其他为此目的提交的支持性文件仅供参考，无须接受认证。

3.5 P_{AE} 定义见《EEDI 计算导则》第 2.2.5.6 段。

3.6 *船舶负载和机舱负荷*系指船体、甲板、航行和安全负载、推进和辅机负载、机舱通风和辅助设备以及船舶的一般负载所需的全部负荷组。

3.7 *需用系数*系指"总安装负荷功率"与连续负荷及间断负荷之和的"实际负荷功率"之比。该系数等于负荷使用系数、负荷连续使用系数及负荷间断使用系数的乘积。

4 适用范围

4.1 本导则适用于《EEDI 计算导则》第 2.2.5.7 段规定的船舶。

4.2 本导则应适用于已向认证方提交 EPT-EEDI 认证申请的新船。

4.3   The steps of the validation process include:

    .1   review of documents during the design stage

        .1   check if all relevant loads are listed in the EPT;

        .2   check if reasonable service factors are used; and

        .3   check the correctness of the P_{AE} calculation based on the data given in the EPT.

    .2   survey of installed systems and components during construction stage

        .1   check if a randomly selected set of installed systems and components are correctly listed with their characteristics in the EPT.

    .3   survey of sea trials

        .1   check if selected units/loads specified in EPT are observed.

5   SUPPORTING DOCUMENTS

5.1   The applicant should provide as a minimum the ship electric balance load analysis.

5.2   Such information may contain shipbuilders' confidential information. Therefore, after the validation, the validator should return all or part of such information to the applicant at the applicant's request.

5.3   A special EEDI condition during sea trials may be needed and defined for each ship and included in the sea trial schedule. For this condition, a special column should be inserted into the EPT.

6   PROCEDURES FOR VALIDATION

6.1   General

P_{AE} should be calculated in accordance with the EPT-EEDI Calculation Guidelines. EPT-EEDI validation should be conducted in two stages: preliminary validation at the design stage and final validation during sea trials. The validation process is presented in figure 1.

4.3 认证过程包括的步骤：

    .1 在设计阶段审核文件

        .1 检查 EPT 中是否列出所有相关负荷；

        .2 检查是否使用合理的使用系数；和

        .3 根据 EPT 所给数据检查 P_{AE} 的计算是否正确；

    .2 在建造阶段检验安装的系统和组件

        .1 检查任意选取的已安装系统和组件及其特性是否在 EPT 中正确列出；

    .3 试航检验

        .1 检查所选取的 EPT 中的装置/负荷是否得到遵守。

5 支持性文件

5.1 申请方应至少提供船舶电力平衡负荷分析。

5.2 此类信息可能含有造船厂的保密信息。因此，在认证后，如申请方要求，认证方应将全部或部分此类信息退回给申请方。

5.3 每艘船舶可能在试航时需要某种特殊的 EEDI 状态并为其定义，且将其纳入试航计划。对于此类状态，应在 EPT 中专门插入一列。

6 认证程序

6.1 一般规定

应按 EPT–EEDI 计算导则计算 P_{AE}。EPT–EEDI 认证应分两阶段进行：设计阶段的前期认证和试航期间的最终认证。认证过程见图 1。

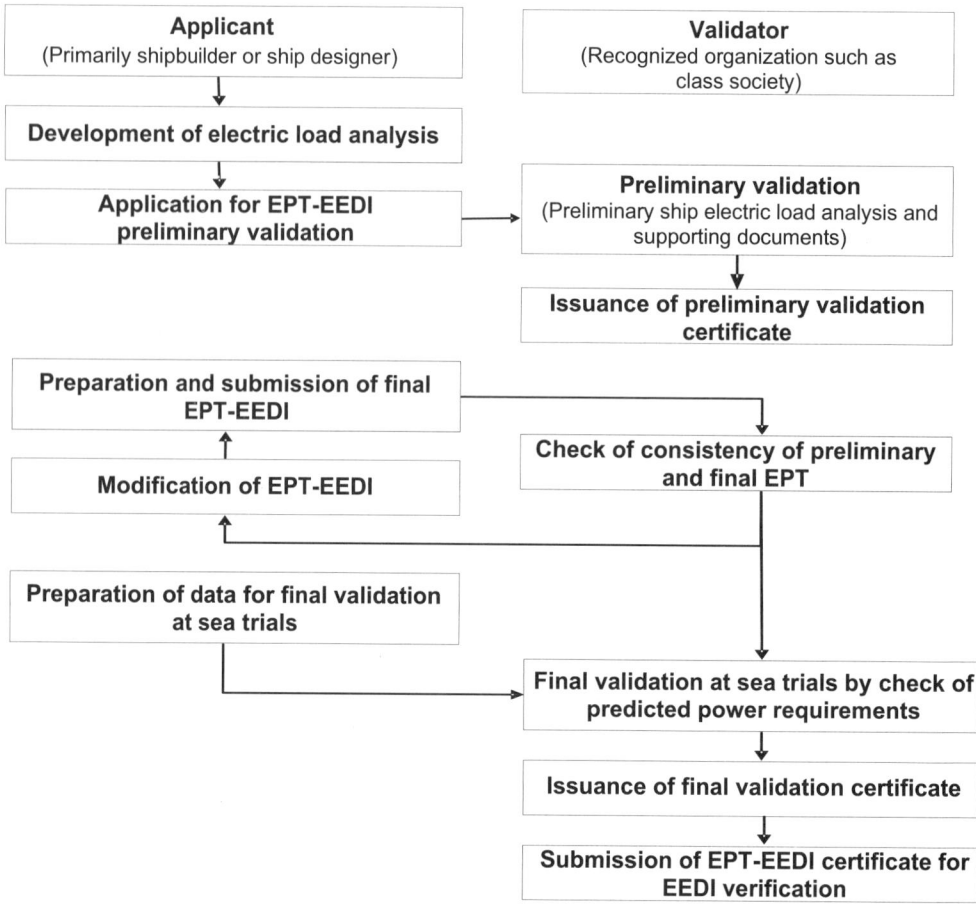

Figure 1: Basic flow of EPT-EEDI validation process

6.2 Preliminary validation at the design stage

6.2.1 For the preliminary validation at the design stage, the applicant should submit to a validator an application for the validation of EPT-EEDI, inclusive of the EPT-EEDI Form, and all the relevant and necessary information for the validation as supporting documents.

6.2.2 The applicant should supply as a minimum the supporting data and information, as specified in appendix A (to be developed).

6.2.3 The validator may request from the applicant additional information to that contained in these guidelines, as necessary, to enable the validator to examine the calculation process of the EPT-EEDI. The estimation of the ship EPT-EEDI at the design stage depends on each applicant's experience, and it may not be practicable to fully examine the technical aspects and details of each machinery component. Therefore, the preliminary validation should focus on the calculation process of the EPT-EEDI that should follow best marine practices.

> **Note:** A possible way forward for more robust validation is to establish a standard methodology of deriving the ship EPT by setting standard formats as agreed and used by industry.

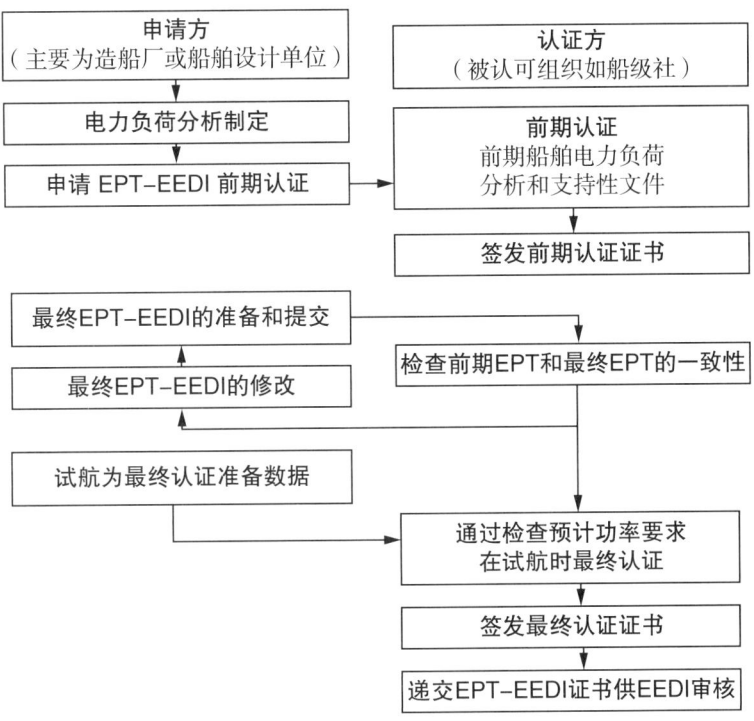

图 1 EPT-EEDI 认证过程的基本流程

6.2 设计阶段的前期认证

6.2.1 对于设计阶段的前期认证，申请方应向认证方提交 EPT-EEDI 认证申请，包括 EPT-EEDI 格式和所有与认证相关和必需的信息作为支持性文件。

6.2.2 申请方应至少按附录 A（待制定）提供支持数据和信息。

6.2.3 认证方在必要时可要求申请方提供本导则所含信息之外的附加信息，使认证方能检查 EPT-EEDI 的计算过程。设计阶段对船舶 EPT-EEDI 的估算取决于各申请方的经验，且全面检查每个机器组件的技术状况和细节可能不可行。因此，前期认证应关注 EPT-EEDI 的计算过程，该过程应遵循最佳的航海实践。

注：可能更牢靠的认证方法是通过设定经行业同意和使用的标准格式，制订一种获得船舶 EPT 的标准方法。

6.3 Final validation

6.3.1   The final validation process should as a minimum include a check of the ship electric load analysis to ensure that all electric consumers are listed, and that their specific data and the calculations in the power table itself are correct and are supported by sea trial results. If necessary, additional information has to be requested.

6.3.2   For the final validation, the applicant should revise the EPT-EEDI Form and supporting documents as necessary, by taking into account the characteristics of the machinery and other electrical loads actually installed on board the ship. The EEDI condition at sea trials should be defined and the expected power requirements in these conditions documented in the EPT. Any changes within the EPT from design stage to construction stage should be highlighted by the shipyard.

6.3.3   The preparation for the final validation includes a desktop check comprising:

    .1   consistency of preliminary and final EPT;

    .2   changes of service factors (compared to the preliminary validation);

    .3   all electric consumers are listed;

    .4   their specific data and the calculations in the power table itself are correct; and

    .5   in case of doubt, component specification data is checked in addition.

6.3.4   A survey prior to sea trials is performed to ensure that machinery characteristics and data as well as other electric loads comply with those recorded in the supporting documents. This survey does not cover the complete installation but selects randomly a number of samples.

6.3.5   For the purpose of sea trial validation, the surveyor will check the data of selected systems and/or components given in the special column added to the EPT for this purpose or the predicted overall value of electric load by means of practicable measurements with the installed measurement devices.

7   ISSUANCE OF THE EPT-EEDI STATEMENT OF VALIDATION

7.1   The validator should stamp the EPT-EEDI Form as "Noted" having validated the EPT-EEDI in the preliminary validation stage, in accordance with these guidelines.

7.2   The validator should stamp the EPT-EEDI Form as "Endorsed" having validated the final EPT-EEDI in the final validation stage in accordance with these guidelines.

6.3 最终认证

6.3.1 最终认证过程应至少包括核查船舶电力负荷分析以确保所有用电设备予以列出；其在电力负荷表中的数据和计算正确且有试航结果支持。如有必要，必须要求附加信息。

6.3.2 对于最终认证，申请方应在必要时参照船上机器特性和其他实际安装电力负荷修改 EPT-EEDI 格式和支持性文件。应为试航时 EEDI 条件定义，且在这些条件下的预期功率要求应在 EPT 中予以记录。从设计阶段到建造阶段任何 EPT 内的更改均应由造船厂重点标明。

6.3.3 最终认证的准备包括桌面检查：

   .1   前期 EPT 和最终 EPT 的一致性；

   .2   负载系数的变更（和前期认证相比）；

   .3   所有用电设备予以列出；

   .4   其在电力负荷表中的数据和计算正确；和

   .5   如有疑问，还需检查机器组件规格数据。

6.3.4 试航前进行检验以确保机器特性和数据以及其他电力负荷符合支持性文件中的记录。该检验并不涵盖全部装置，而是任意选取一定数量的样品。

6.3.5 就试航认证而言，验船师将采用所安装的测量仪器进行可行的测量以检查为试航认证而在 EPT 中专门添加的一列中选取的系统和 / 或组件的数据或电力负荷的预计总值。

7   EPT-EEDI 认证声明的签发

7.1 认证方按照本导则在前期认证阶段认证 EPT-EEDI 后，应在 EPT-EEDI 格式中盖"备查"章。

7.2 认证方按照本导则在最终认证阶段认证 EPT-EEDI 后，应在 EPT-EEDI 格式中盖"签署"章。

APPENDIX 3

ELECTRIC POWER TABLE FORM FOR ENERGY EFFICIENCY DESIGN INDEX (EPT-EEDI FORM) AND STATEMENT OF VALIDATION

Ship ID:

IMO no.: _____

Ship's name:_____

Shipyard:_____

Hull no.:_____

Applicant:

Name:_____

Address:_____

_____

Validation stage:

☐ Preliminary validation

☐ Final validation

Summary results of EPT-EEDI

Load group	Seagoing condition EEDI Calculation Guidelines		Remarks
	Continuous load (kW)	Intermittent load (kW)	
Ship service and engine-room loads			
Accommodation and cargo loads			
Total installed load			
Diversity factor			
Normal seagoing load			
Weighted average efficiency of generators			
P_{AE}			

Supporting documents

Title	ID or remarks

Validator details:

Organization: _____

Address: _____

_____

This is to certify that the above-mentioned electrical loads and supporting documents have been reviewed in accordance with EPT-EEDI Validation guidelines and the review shows a reasonable confidence for use of the above P_{AE} in EEDI calculations.

Date of review:_____   Statement of validation no._____

This statement is valid on condition that the electric power characteristics of the ship do not change.

Signature of Validator

_____

Printed name: _____

***

附录 3

能效设计指数电力负荷表格式（EPT-EEDI 格式）和认证声明

船舶标识号：
IMO 编号：_____

船名：_____

船厂：_____

船体编号：_____

申请方	**认证阶段：**
名称：_____	□前期认证
地址：_____	□最终认证
_____	

EPT-EEDI 结果总结

负荷组	航行状况 EEDI 计算导则		备注
	连续负荷（kW）	间断负荷（kW）	
船舶运行和机舱负荷			
起居和货物负荷			
总安装负荷			
需用系数			
正常航行负荷			
发电机加权平均效率			
P_{AE}			

支持性文件

文件名	标识号或备注

认证方资料：

机构：_____

地址：_____

兹证明上述电力负荷和支持性文件业已按 EPT-EEDI 认证导则进行审核，且审核表明在 EEDI 计算中使用以上 P_{AE} 是合理可信的。

审核日期：_____ 认证声明编号：_____

本声明在船舶电力负荷特性不变的条件下有效。

认证方签字：

_____

打印姓名：

***

RESOLUTION MEPC.350(78)
(adopted on 10 June 2022)

2022 GUIDELINES ON THE METHOD OF CALCULATION OF THE ATTAINED ENERGY EFFICIENCY EXISTING SHIP INDEX (EEXI)

THE MARINE ENVIRONMENT PROTECTION COMMITTEE,

RECALLING Article 38(a) of the Convention on the International Maritime Organization concerning the functions of the Marine Environment Protection Committee (the Committee) conferred upon it by international conventions for the prevention and control of marine pollution from ships,

NOTING that the Committee adopted, at its seventy-sixth session, by resolution MEPC.328(76), the *2021 Revised MARPOL Annex VI*, which will enter into force on 1 November 2022,

NOTING IN PARTICULAR that the *2021 Revised MARPOL Annex VI* (MARPOL Annex VI) contains amendments concerning mandatory goal-based technical and operational measures to reduce carbon intensity of international shipping,

NOTING FURTHER that regulation 23 of MARPOL Annex VI requires that the attained Energy Efficiency Existing Ship Index (EEXI) shall be calculated taking into account the guidelines developed by the Organization,

RECOGNIZING that the aforementioned amendments to MARPOL Annex VI require relevant guidelines for uniform and effective implementation of the regulations and to provide sufficient lead time for industry to prepare,

NOTING that, at its seventy-sixth session, the Committee adopted, by resolution MEPC.333(76), the *2021 Guidelines on the method of calculation of the attained Energy Efficiency Existing Ship Index (EEXI),*

HAVING CONSIDERED, at its seventy-eighth session, the draft *2022 Guidelines on the method of calculation of the attained Energy Efficiency Existing Ship Index (EEXI),*

1   ADOPTS the *2022 Guidelines on the method of calculation of the attained Energy Efficiency Existing Ship Index (EEXI),* as set out in the annex to the present resolution;

2   INVITES Administrations to take the annexed Guidelines into account when developing and enacting national laws which give force to and implement requirements set forth in regulation 23 of MARPOL Annex VI;

3   REQUESTS the Parties to MARPOL Annex VI and other Member Governments to bring the annexed Guidelines to the attention of masters, seafarers, shipowners, ship operators and any other interested parties;

4   AGREES to keep the Guidelines under review in light of experience gained with their implementation, also taking into consideration that in accordance with regulation 25.3 of

第 MEPC.350（78）号决议
（2022 年 6 月 10 日通过）

2022 年现有船舶达到的能效指数（EEXI）计算方法导则

海上环境保护委员会，

忆及国际海事组织公约第 38（a）条关于国际防止和控制海上污染公约赋予海上环境保护委员会的职能，

注意到委员会在其第 76 届会议上以 MEPC.328（76）号决议通过了将于 2022 年 11 月 1 日生效的 2021 年经修订的 MARPOL 附则 Ⅵ，

特别注意到 2021 年经修订的 MARPOL 附则 Ⅵ 包含关于基于目标的强制性技术和营运措施以减少国际航运碳强度的修正案，

进一步注意到 MARPOL 附则 Ⅵ 第 23 条要求在计算现有船舶达到的能效指数时应考虑到本组织制定的导则，

认识到上述 MARPOL 附则 Ⅵ 的修正案需要有相关导则，以便于统一和有效实施各条规定，并为业界提供充足的提前时间进行准备，

注意到在其第 76 届会议上，委员会以 MEPC.333（76）号决议通过了《2021 年现有船舶达到的能效指数（EEXI）计算方法导则》，

在其第 78 届会议上**审议了**《2022 年现有船舶达到的能效指数（EEXI）计算方法导则》草案，

1 **通过**《2022 年现有船舶达到的能效指数（EEXI）计算方法导则》，其文本载于本决议附件；

2 **提请**各国主管机关在制定和颁布本国法律，以执行和实施 MARPOL 附则 Ⅵ 第 23 条要求时，考虑到附件中的导则；

3 **要求** MARPOL 附则 Ⅵ 的各缔约国和其他成员国政府使船长、船员、船东、船舶经营者以及任何其他利益相关方注意到附件中的导则；

4 **同意**根据本导则实施中获得的经验，保持对本导则的评审，同时考虑到根据

MARPOL Annex VI a review of the technical measure to reduce carbon intensity of international shipping shall be completed by 1 January 2026;

5   REVOKES the *2021 Guidelines on the method of calculation of the attained Energy Efficiency Existing Ship Index (EEXI)* adopted by resolution MEPC.333(76).

MARPOL 附则Ⅵ第 25.3 的规定，应在 2026 年 1 月 1 日之前完成对降低国际航运碳强度的技术措施的审查；

5　**撤销**以第 MEPC.333（76）号决议通过的《2021 年现有船舶达到的能效指数（EEXI）计算方法导则》。

ANNEX

2022 GUIDELINES ON THE METHOD OF CALCULATION OF THE ATTAINED ENERGY EFFICIENCY EXISTING SHIP INDEX (EEXI)

CONTENTS

附件

2022 年现有船舶达到的能效指数（EEXI）计算方法导则

目录

1 Definitions

1.1 *MARPOL* means the International Convention for the Prevention of Pollution from Ships, 1973, as modified by the Protocols of 1978 and 1997 relating thereto, as amended.

1.2 For the purpose of these Guidelines, the definitions in MARPOL Annex VI, as amended, apply.

2 Energy Efficiency Existing Ship Index (EEXI)

2.1 EEXI formula

The attained Energy Efficiency Existing Ship Index (EEXI) is a measure of ship's energy efficiency (g/t*nm) and calculated by the following formula:

$$\frac{\left(\prod_{j=1}^{n} f_j\right)\left(\sum_{i=1}^{nME} P_{ME(i)} \cdot C_{FME(i)} \cdot SFC_{ME(i)}\right) + \left(P_{AE} \cdot C_{FAE} \cdot SFC_{AE}*\right) + \left(\left(\prod_{j=1}^{n} f_j \cdot \sum_{i=1}^{nPTI} P_{PTI(i)} - \sum_{i=1}^{neff} f_{eff(i)} \cdot P_{AEeff(i)}\right) C_{FAE} \cdot SFC_{AE}\right) - \left(\sum_{i=1}^{neff} f_{eff(i)} \cdot P_{eff(i)} \cdot C_{FME} \cdot SFC_{ME}**\right)}{f_i \cdot f_c \cdot f_l \cdot Capacity \cdot f_w \cdot V_{ref} \cdot f_m}$$

* If part of the Normal Maximum Sea Load is provided by shaft generators, SFC_{ME} and C_{FME} may – for that part of the power – be used instead of SFC_{AE} and C_{FAE}

** In case of $P_{PTI(i)} > 0$, the average weighted value of ($SFC_{ME} \cdot C_{FME}$) and ($SFC_{AE} \cdot C_{FAE}$) to be used for calculation of P_{eff}

Note: This formula may not be applicable to a ship having diesel-electric propulsion, turbine propulsion or hybrid propulsion system, except for cruise passenger ships and LNG carriers.

Ships falling into the scope of EEDI requirement can use their attained EEDI calculated in accordance with the *2018 Guidelines on the method of calculation of the attained EEDI for new ships* (resolution MEPC.308(73), as amended, the "EEDI Calculation Guidelines" hereafter) as the attained EEXI if the value of the attained EEDI is equal to or less than that of the required EEXI.

2.2 Parameters

For calculation of the attained EEXI by the formula in paragraph 2.1, parameters under the EEDI Calculation Guidelines apply, unless expressly provided otherwise. In referring to the aforementioned guidelines, the terminology "EEDI" should be read as "EEXI".

2.2.1 $P_{ME(i)}$; Power of main engines

In cases where overridable Shaft / Engine Power Limitation is installed in accordance with the *2021 Guidelines on the shaft / engine power limit to comply with the EEXI requirements and use of a power reserve* (resolution MEPC.335(76)), $P_{ME(i)}$ is 83% of the limited installed power (MCR_{lim}) or 75% of the original installed power (MCR), whichever is lower, for each main engine *(i)*. In cases where the overridable Shaft / Engine Power Limitation and shaft generator(s) are installed, in referring to paragraph 2.2.5.2 (option 1) of the EEDI Calculation Guidelines, "MCR_{ME}" should be read as "MCR_{lim}".

For LNG carriers having steam turbine or diesel electric propulsion, $P_{ME(i)}$ is 83% of the limited installed power (MCR_{lim}, MPP_{lim}), divided by the electrical efficiency in case of diesel electric propulsion system, for each main engine *(i)*. For LNG carriers, the power from combustion of

1 定义

1.1 MARPOL 系指经修正的《经 1978 年和 1997 年议定书修订的 1973 年国际防止船舶造成污染公约》。

1.2 就本导则而言，经修正的 MARPOL 附则Ⅵ中的定义适用。

2 现有船舶能效指数（EEXI）

2.1 EEXI 公式

现有船舶达到的能效指数（EEXI）是衡量船舶能效（g/t*nm）的一个指标，通过下列公式计算：

$$\frac{\left(\prod_{j=1}^{n}f_j\right)\left(\sum_{i=1}^{nME}P_{ME(i)}\cdot C_{FME(i)}\cdot SFC_{ME(i)}\right)+\left(P_{AE}\cdot C_{FAE}\cdot SFC_{AE}*\right)+\left(\left(\prod_{j=1}^{n}f_j\cdot\sum_{i=1}^{nPTI}P_{PTI(i)}-\sum_{i=1}^{neff}f_{eff(i)}\cdot P_{AEeff(i)}\right)C_{FAE}\cdot SFC_{AE}\right)-\left(\sum_{i=1}^{neff}f_{eff(i)}\cdot P_{eff(i)}\cdot C_{FME}\cdot SFC_{ME}**\right)}{f_i\cdot f_c\cdot f_l\cdot Capacity\cdot f_w\cdot V_{ref}\cdot f_m}$$

* 如果正常最大海上负荷部分由轴带发电机提供，则对该部分功率可使用 SFC_{ME} 和 C_{FME} 替代 SFC_{AE} 和 C_{FAE}。

** 如果 $P_{PTI(i)}>0$，则（$SFC_{ME}\cdot C_{FME}$）和（$SFC_{AE}\cdot C_{FAE}$）的加权平均值应用于 P_{eff} 的计算。

注：本公式可能不适用于具有柴油－电力推进、涡轮推进或混合推进系统的船舶，但邮轮和 LNG 运输船除外。

如果属于 EEDI 要求范围的船舶按《2018 年新船达到的能效设计指数（EEDI）计算方法导则》（经修正的 MEPC.308（73）决议，以下简称"EEDI 计算导则"）计算的达到的 EEDI 值等于或小于所要求的 EEXI 值，则可使用其达到的 EEDI 作为达到的 EEXI。

2.2 参数

除另有规定外，使用 2.1 中的公式计算达到的 EEXI 时，EEDI 计算导则中的参数适用。在参考上述导则时，术语"EEDI"应理解为"EEXI"。

2.2.1 $P_{ME(i)}$ 主机功率

如果按《2021 年为满足 EEXI 要求采用的轴功率 / 发动机功率限制系统及其储备功率使用导则》（MEPC.335（76）决议）安装可越控轴 / 发动机功率限制系统，每台主机（i）的 $P_{ME(i)}$ 为限定安装功率（MCR_{lim}）的 83% 或原始安装功率（MCR）的 75%，取较低者。如果安装可越控轴 / 发动机功率限制系统和轴带发电机，参考 EEDI 计算导则 2.2.5.2（选择 1），"MCR_{ME}"应理解为"MCR_{lim}"。

对于设有蒸汽涡轮或柴油电力推进系统的 LNG 运输船，如为柴油电力推进系统，每台主机（i）的 $P_{ME(i)}$ 为 83% 限定安装功率（MCR_{lim}，MPP_{lim}）除以电效率。对于 LNG

the excessive natural boil-off gas in the engines or boilers to avoid releasing to the atmosphere or unnecessary thermal oxidation should be deducted from $P_{ME(i)}$ with the approval of the verifier.

2.2.2 $P_{AE(i)}$; Power of auxiliary engines

2.2.2.1 $P_{AE(i)}$ is calculated in accordance with paragraph 2.2.5.6 of the EEDI Calculation Guidelines.

2.2.2.2 For ships where power of auxiliary engines (P_{AE}) value calculated by paragraphs 2.2.5.6.1 to 2.2.5.6.3 of the EEDI Calculation Guidelines is significantly different from the total power used at normal seagoing, e.g. in cases of passenger ships, the P_{AE} value should be estimated by the consumed electric power (excluding propulsion) in conditions when the ship is engaged in a voyage at reference speed (V_{ref}) as given in the electric power table, divided by the average efficiency of the generator(s) weighted by power (see appendix 2 of the EEDI Calculation Guidelines).

2.2.2.3 In cases where the electric power table is not available, the P_{AE} value may be approximated either by:

.1   annual average figure of P_{AE} at sea from onboard monitoring obtained prior to the EEXI certification;

.2   for cruise passenger ships, approximated value of power of auxiliary engines ($P_{AE,app}$), as defined below:

$$P_{AE,app} = 0.1193 \times GT + 1814.4 \quad [\text{kW}]$$

.3   for ro-ro passenger ships, approximated value of power of auxiliary engines ($P_{AE,app}$), as defined below:

$$P_{AE,app} = 0.866 \times GT^{0.732} \quad [\text{kW}]$$

2.2.3 V_{ref} ; Ship speed

2.2.3.1 For ships falling into the scope of the EEDI requirement, the ship speed V_{ref} should be obtained from an approved speed-power curve as defined in the *2014 Guidelines on survey and certification of the Energy Efficiency Design Index (EEDI)*, as amended (resolution MEPC.254(67), as amended).

2.2.3.2 For ships not falling into the scope of the EEDI requirement, the ship speed V_{ref} should be obtained from an estimated speed-power curve as defined in the *2022 Guidelines on survey and certification of the attained EEXI* (resolution MEPC.351(78)).

2.2.3.3 For ships not falling into the scope of the EEDI requirement but whose sea trial results, which may have been calibrated by the tank test, under the EEDI draught and the sea condition as specified in paragraph 2.2.2 of the EEDI Calculation Guidelines are included in the sea trial report, the ship speed V_{ref} may be obtained from the sea trial report:

$$V_{ref} = V_{S,EEDI} \times \left[\frac{P_{ME}}{P_{S,EEDI}}\right]^{\frac{1}{3}} \quad [\text{knot}]$$

运输船，发动机或锅炉中为避免释放到大气或不必要的热氧化而燃烧过量的自然蒸发气体产生的功率，应经验证方批准从 $P_{ME(i)}$ 中扣除。

2.2.2 $P_{AE(i)}$；副机功率

2.2.2.1 按 EEDI 计算导则 2.2.5.6 计算 $P_{AE(i)}$。

2.2.2.2 如果船舶（例如客船）按 EEDI 计算导则 2.2.5.6.1 至 2.2.5.6.3 计算所得的副机功率（P_{AE}）值与正常航行时所使用的总功率存在显著差异，船舶应以基准航速（V_{ref}）航行时所消耗的电功率（不包括推进功率）（见电功率表）除以所有发电机功率加权平均效率进行估算 P_{AE} 值（参见 EEDI 计算导则附录 2）。

2.2.2.3 如果无电功率表，P_{AE} 值可以近似为：

.1 在 EEXI 认证前获得的船上监测得出的海上 P_{AE} 的年度平均数据；

.2 对于邮轮，副机功率（$P_{AE,\,app}$）的近似值，定义如下：

$$P_{AE,\,app}=0.1\,193 \times GT + 1\,814.4\,[\text{kW}]$$

.3 对于滚装客船，副机功率（$P_{AE,\,app}$）的近似值，定义如下：

$$P_{AE,\,app}=0.866 \times GT^{0.732}[\text{kW}]$$

2.2.3 V_{ref}；航速

2.2.3.1 对于属于 EEDI 要求范围的船舶，船速 V_{ref} 应从经修正的《2014 年能效设计指数（EEDI）检验和发证导则》（经修正的 MEPC.254（67）决议）中定义的批准的航速 – 功率曲线获得。

2.2.3.2 对于不属于 EEDI 要求范围的船舶，航速 V_{ref} 应从《2022 年现有船舶达到的能效指数（EEXI）检验和发证导则》（MEPC.351（78）决议）中定义的估算航速 – 功率曲线获得。

2.2.3.3 对于不属于 EEDI 要求范围的船舶，但试航报告中包括其在 EEDI 计算导则 2.2.2 规定的 EEDI 吃水和海况下的试航结果（可能已经经过水池试验修正），航速 V_{ref} 可从试航报告中获得：

$$V_{ref} = V_{S,EEDI} \times \left[\frac{P_{ME}}{P_{S,EEDI}} \right]^{\frac{1}{3}} \quad [\text{knot}]$$

where,

$V_{S,EEDI}$, is the sea trial service speed under the EEDI draught; and

$P_{S,EEDI}$ is power of the main engine corresponding to $V_{S,EEDI}$.

2.2.3.4 For containerships, bulk carriers or tankers not falling into the scope of the EEDI requirement but whose sea trial results, which may have been calibrated by the tank test, under the design load draught and sea condition as specified in paragraph 2.2.2 of the EEDI Calculation Guidelines are included in the sea trial report, the ship speed V_{ref} may be obtained from the sea trial report:

$$V_{ref} = k^{\frac{1}{3}} \times \left(\frac{DWT_{S,service}}{Capacity}\right)^{\frac{2}{9}} \times V_{S,service} \times \left[\frac{P_{ME}}{P_{S,service}}\right]^{\frac{1}{3}} \quad [\text{knot}]$$

where,

$V_{S,service}$ is the sea trial service speed under the design load draught;

$DWT_{S,service}$ is the deadweight under the design load draught;

$P_{S,service}$ is the power of the main engine corresponding to $V_{S,service}$;

k is the scale coefficient, which should be:

.1   0.95 for containerships with 120,000 DWT or less;

.2   0.93 for containerships with more than 120,000 DWT;

.3   0.97 for bulk carrier with 200,000 DWT or less;

.4   1.00 for bulk carrier with more than 200,000 DWT;

.5   0.97 for tanker with 100,000 DWT or less; and

.6   1.00 for tanker with more than 100,000 DWT.

2.2.3.5 In cases where the speed-power curve is not available or the sea trial report does not contain the EEDI or design load draught condition, the ship speed V_{ref} can be obtained from the in-service performance measurement method conducted and verified in accordance with the methods and procedures as specified in the *Guidance on methods, procedures and verification of in-service performance measurements* (MEPC.1/Circ.901).

2.2.3.6 In cases where the speed-power curve is not available or the sea trial report does not contain the EEDI or design load draught condition, the ship speed V_{ref} can be approximated by $V_{ref,app}$ to be obtained from statistical mean of distribution of ship speed and engine power, as defined below:

$$V_{ref,app} = (V_{ref,avg} - m_V) \times \left[\frac{\Sigma P_{ME}}{0.75 \times MCR_{avg}}\right]^{\frac{1}{3}} \quad [\text{knot}]$$

For LNG carriers having diesel electric propulsion system and cruise passenger ships having non-conventional propulsion,

式中：$V_{S,\;EEDI}$ 系指在 EEDI 吃水下的试航速度；和

$P_{S,\;EEDI}$ 系指 $V_{S,\;EEDI}$ 对应的主机功率。

2.2.3.4 对于不属于 EEDI 要求范围的集装箱船、散货船和液货船，但试航报告中包括其在 EEDI 计算导则 2.2.2 规定的设计装载吃水和海况下的试航结果（可能已经经过水池试验修正），航速 V_{ref} 可从试航报告中获得：

$$V_{ref} = k^{\frac{1}{3}} \times \left(\frac{DWT_{S,service}}{Capacity}\right)^{\frac{2}{9}} \times V_{S,service} \times \left[\frac{P_{ME}}{P_{S,service}}\right]^{\frac{1}{3}} \quad [\text{knot}]$$

式中：$V_{S,\;service}$ 系指设计装载吃水下的试航速度；

$DWT_{S,\;service}$ 系指设计装载吃水下的载重量；

$P_{S,\;service}$ 系指对应 $V_{S,\;service}$ 的主机功率；

k 为比例系数，应为：

.1 0.95，对于 120 000 载重吨或以下的集装箱船；

.2 0.93，对于 120 000 载重吨以上的集装箱船；

.3 0.97，对于 200 000 载重吨或以下的散货船；

.4 1.00，对于 200 000 载重吨以上的散货船；

.5 0.97，对于 100 000 载重吨或以下的液货船；和

.6 1.00，对于 100 000 载重吨以上的液货船。

2.2.3.5 如无航速 – 功率曲线或试航报告中不包含 EEDI 或设计装载吃水工况时，根据《在役船舶性能测量方法、程序和验证导则》（MEPC.1/Circ.901）中规定的方法和程序，船速 V_{ref} 可通过实施和验证的在役船舶性能测量方法获得。

2.2.3.6 如无航速 – 功率曲线或试航报告中不包含 EEDI 或设计装载吃水工况时，船速 V_{ref} 近似取 $V_{ref,\;app}$ 的值，从航速和发动机功率分布的统计均值获得，定义如下：

$$V_{ref,app} = (V_{ref,avg} - m_V) \times \left[\frac{\sum P_{ME}}{0.75 \times MCR_{avg}}\right]^{\frac{1}{3}} \quad [\text{knot}]$$

对于设有柴油电力推进系统的 LNG 运输船和设有非常规推进系统的邮轮，

$$V_{ref,app} = (V_{ref,avg} - m_V) \times \left[\frac{\Sigma MPP_{Motor}}{MPP_{avg}}\right]^{\frac{1}{3}} \quad [\text{knot}]$$

where,

$V_{ref,avg}$ is a statistical mean of distribution of ship speed in given ship type and ship size, to be calculated as follows:

$$V_{ref,avg} = A \times B^C$$

where

A, B and C are the parameters given in the appendix;

m_V is a performance margin of a ship, which should be 5% of $V_{ref,avg}$ or one knot, whichever is lower; and

MCR_{avg} is a statistical mean of distribution of MCRs for main engines and MPP_{avg} is a statistical mean of distribution of MPPs for motors in given ship type and ship size, to be calculated as follows:

$$MCR_{avg}\, or\, MPP_{avg} = D \times E^F$$

where

D, E and F are the parameters given in the appendix;

In cases where the overridable Shaft / Engine Power Limitation is installed, the ship speed V_{ref} approximated by $V_{ref,app}$ should be calculated as follows:

$$V_{ref,app} - (V_{ref,avg} \quad m_V) \times \left[\frac{\Sigma P_{ME}}{0.75 \times MCR_{avg}}\right]^{\frac{1}{3}} \quad [\text{knot}]$$

For LNG carriers having diesel electric propulsion system and cruise passenger ship having non-conventional propulsion, the ship speed V_{ref} approximated by $V_{ref,app}$ should be calculated as follows:

$$V_{ref,app} = (V_{ref,avg} - m_V) \times \left[\frac{\Sigma MPP_{lim}}{MPP_{avg}}\right]^{\frac{1}{3}}$$

2.2.3.7 Notwithstanding the above, in cases where the energy-saving device[*] is installed, the effect of the device may be reflected in the ship speed V_{ref} with the approval of the verifier, based on the following methods in accordance with defined quality and technical standards:

.1   sea trials after installation of the device; and/or

.2   in-service performance measurement method; and/or

.3   dedicated model tests; and/or

---

[*]   Devices that shift the power curve, which results in the change of P_P and V_{ref}, as specified in MEPC.1/Circ.896 on *2021 Guidance on treatment of innovative energy efficiency technologies for calculation and verification of the attained EEDI and EEXI.*

$$V_{ref,app} = (V_{ref,avg} - m_V) \times \left[\frac{\sum MPP_{Motor}}{MPP_{avg}}\right]^{\frac{1}{3}} \quad [\text{knot}]$$

式中：$V_{ref,\,avg}$ 系指给定船型和船舶尺寸的航速分布的统计均值，应按下式计算：

$$V_{ref,\,avg} = A \times B^C$$

式中：

A、B 和 C 系指附录中给出的参数；

m_V 系指船舶的性能裕量，应为 $V_{ref,\,avg}$ 的 5% 或 1 kn，取较低者；和

MCR_{avg} 系指主机 MCR_S 分布的统计均值；

MPP_{avg} 系指给定船型和船舶尺寸的电机 MPP_S 分布的统计均值，应按下式计算：

$$MCR_{avg} \quad 或 \quad MPP_{avg} = D \times E^F$$

式中：D、E 和 F 系指附录中给出的参数；

如果安装可越控轴 / 发动机功率限制系统，船速 V_{ref} 近似取 $V_{ref,app}$ 的值，应按下式计算：

$$V_{ref,app} = (V_{ref,avg} - m_V) \times \left[\frac{\sum P_{ME}}{0.75 \times MCR_{avg}}\right]^{\frac{1}{3}} \quad [\text{knot}]$$

对于设有柴油电力推进系统的 LNG 运输船和设有非常规推进系统的邮轮，船速近似取的值，应按下式计算：

$$V_{ref,app} = (V_{ref,avg} - m_V) \times \left[\frac{\sum MPP_{lim}}{MPP_{avg}}\right]^{\frac{1}{3}} \quad [\text{knot}]$$

2.2.3.7 尽管有上述规定，如果安装节能装置[*]，经验证方批准，按定义的质量和技术标准，基于以下方法，该装置的效果可体现在航速 V_{ref} 上：

.1 装置安装后试航；和 / 或

.2 在役船舶性能测量方法；和 / 或

.3 专用模型试验；和 / 或

---

[*] 按 MEPC.1/Circ.896 通函《2021 年用于计算和验证达到的 EEDI 和 EEXI 的创新能效技术处理导则》规定的改变功率曲线，导致 P_P 和 V_{ref} 变化的装置。

.4   numerical calculations.

2.2.4   *SFC*; Certified specific fuel consumption

In cases where overridable Shaft / Engine Power Limitation is installed, the *SFC* corresponding to the P_{ME} should be interpolated by using *SFC*s listed in an applicable test report included in an approved NO_x Technical File of the main engine as defined in paragraph 1.3.15 of the NO_x Technical Code.

Notwithstanding the above, the *SFC* specified by the manufacturer or confirmed by the verifier may be used.

For those engines which do not have a test report included in the NO_x Technical File and which do not have the *SFC* specified by the manufacturer or confirmed by the verifier, the *SFC* can be approximated by *SFC*$_{app}$ defined as follows:

$$SFC_{ME,app} = 190 \ [g/kWh]$$

$$SFC_{AE,app} = 215 \ [g/kWh]$$

2.2.5 C_F ; Conversion factor between fuel consumption and CO_2 emission

For those engines which do not have a test report included in the NO_x Technical File and which do not have the *SFC* specified by the manufacturer, the C_F corresponding to *SFC*$_{app}$ should be defined as follows:

$$C_F = 3.114 \ [t \cdot CO_2/t \cdot Fuel] \text{ for diesel ships (incl. HFO use in practice)}$$

Otherwise, paragraph 2.2.1 of the EEDI Calculation Guidelines applies.

2.2.6   Correction factor for ro-ro cargo and ro-ro passenger ships (f_{jRoRo})

For ro-ro cargo and ro-ro passenger ships, f_{jRoRo} is calculated as follows:

$$f_{jRoRo} = \frac{1}{F_{n_L}^{\alpha} \cdot \left(\frac{L_{pp}}{B_S}\right)^{\beta} \cdot \left(\frac{B_S}{d_S}\right)^{\gamma} \cdot \left(\frac{L_{pp}}{\nabla^{1/3}}\right)^{\delta}} \qquad ; \text{ if } f_{jRoRo} > 1 \text{ then } f_j = 1$$

where the Froude number, F_{n_L}, is defined as:

$$F_{n_L} = \frac{0.5144 \cdot V_{ref,F}}{\sqrt{L_{pp} \cdot g}}$$

where $V_{ref,F}$ is the ship design speed corresponding to 75% of MCR_{ME}.:

and the exponents α, β, γ and δ are defined as follows:

Ship type	Exponent:			
	α	β	γ	δ
Ro-ro cargo ship	2.00	0.50	0.75	1.00
Ro-ro passenger ship	2.50	0.75	0.75	1.00

.4 数值计算。

2.2.4 *SFC*；经核定的单位燃油消耗量

如果安装可越控轴 / 发动机功率限制系统，应使用 NO_x 技术规则 1.3.15 定义的经批准的主机 NO_x 技术文件中包含的适用试验报告中列出的 SFC_s，内插计算 P_{ME} 相对应的 SFC。

尽管有上述规定，可使用由制造商规定或验证方确认的 SFC。

对于 NO_x 技术文件中没有包含试验报告，且没有由制造商规定或验证方确认的 SFC 的发动机，SFC 可近似取 SFC_{app} 的值，定义如下：

$$SFC_{ME,\ app}=190\ [\text{g/kWh}]$$

$$SFC_{AE,\ app}=215\ [\text{g/kWh}]$$

2.2.5 C_F；燃油消耗量与 CO_2 排放量之间的转换系数

对于 NO_x 技术文件中没有包含试验报告，且没有由制造商规定的 SFC 的发动机，SFC_{app} 对应的 C_F 定义如下：

$$C_F=3.114\ [\text{t} \cdot CO_2/\text{t} \cdot \text{Fuel}]$$ 对于柴油机船（包括实际使用重燃油）

否则，应适用 EEDI 计算导则 2.2.1。

2.2.6 滚装货船和滚装客船修正系数（f_{jRoRo}）

对于滚装货船和滚装客船，f_{jRORO} 按下式计算：

$$f_{jRoRo} = \frac{1}{F_{n_L}^{\alpha} \cdot \left(\frac{Lpp}{B_S}\right)^{\beta} \cdot \left(\frac{B_S}{d_S}\right)^{\gamma} \cdot \left(\frac{Lpp}{\nabla^{1/3}}\right)^{\delta}}$$；若 $f_{jRORO}>1$，则 $f_j=1$。

式中弗劳德数定义为：

$$F_{n_L} = \frac{0.514\ 4 \cdot V_{ref,F}}{\sqrt{Lpp \cdot g}}$$

而指数 α 、β 、γ 和 δ 定义如下：

船型	指数			
	α	β	γ	δ
滚装货船	2.00	0.50	0.75	1.00
滚装客船	2.50	0.75	0.75	1.00

2.2.7 Cubic capacity correction factor for ro-ro cargo ships (vehicle carrier) ($f_{cVEHICLE}$)

For ro-ro cargo ships (vehicle carrier) having a DWT/GT ratio of less than 0.35, the following cubic capacity correction factor, $f_{cVEHICLE}$, should apply:

$$f_{cVEHICLE} = \left(\frac{(DWT/GT)}{0.35} \right)^{-0,8}$$

Where DWT is the capacity and GT is the gross tonnage in accordance with the International Convention of Tonnage Measurement of Ships 1969, annex I, regulation 3.

2.2.7 滚装货船（车辆运输船）修正系数（$f_{cVEHICLE}$）

对于 DWT/GT 比小于 0.35 的滚装货船（车辆运输船），下列舱容量修正系数 $f_{cVEHICLE}$ 应适用：

$$f_{cVEHICLE} = \left(\frac{(DWT/GT)}{0.35} \right)^{-0.8}$$

式中：DWT 系指载重吨；GT 系指按《1969 年国际船舶吨位丈量公约》附则 I 第 3 条规定的总吨位。

APPENDIX

Parameters to calculate $V_{ref,avg}$

Ship type	A	B	C
Bulk carrier	10.6585	DWT of the ship	0.02706
Gas carrier	7.4462	DWT of the ship	0.07604
Tanker	8.1358	DWT of the ship	0.05383
Containership	3.2395	DWT of the ship where DWT ≤ 80,000 80,000 where DWT > 80,000	0.18294
General cargo ship	2.4538	DWT of the ship	0.18832
Refrigerated cargo carrier	1.0600	DWT of the ship	0.31518
Combination carrier	8.1391	DWT of the ship	0.05378
LNG carrier	11.0536	DWT of the ship	0.05030
Ro-ro cargo ship (vehicle carrier)	16.6773	DWT of the ship	0.01802
Ro-ro cargo ship	8.0793	DWT of the ship	0.09123
Ro-ro passenger ship	4.1140	DWT of the ship	0.19863
Cruise passenger ship having non-conventional propulsion	5.1240	GT of the ship	0.12714

Parameters to calculate MCR_{avg} or MPP_{avg} (= D x E^F)

Ship type	D	E	F
Bulk carrier	23.7510	DWT of the ship	0.54087
Gas carrier	21.4704	DWT of the ship	0.59522
Tanker	22.8415	DWT of the ship	0.55826
Containership	0.5042	DWT of the ship where DWT ≤ 95,000 95,000 where DWT > 95,000	1.03046
General cargo ship	0.8816	DWT of the ship	0.92050
Refrigerated cargo carrier	0.0272	DWT of the ship	1.38634
Combination carrier	22.8536	DWT of the ship	0.55820
LNG carrier	20.7096	DWT of the ship	0.63477
Ro-ro cargo ship (vehicle carrier)	262.7693	DWT of the ship	0.39973
Ro-ro cargo ship	37.7708	DWT of the ship	0.63450
Ro-ro passenger ship	9.1338	DWT of the ship	0.91116
Cruise passenger ship having non-conventional propulsion	1.3550	GT of the ship	0.88664

附录 $V_{ref, app}$ 计算参数

$V_{ref, app}$ 计算参数

船舶类型	A	B	C
散货船	10.658 5	船舶载重吨	0.027 06
气体运输船	7.446 2	船舶载重吨	0.076 04
液货船	8.135 8	船舶载重吨	0.053 83
集装箱船	3.239 5	当载重吨 ≤ 80 000 时，取船舶载重吨 当载重吨 > 80 000 时，取 80 000	0.182 94
杂货船	2.453 8	船舶载重吨	0.188 32
冷藏货船	1.060 0	船舶载重吨	0.315 18
兼用船	8.139 1	船舶载重吨	0.053 78
LNG 运输船	11.053 6	船舶载重吨	0.050 30
滚装货船（车辆运输船）	16.677 3	船舶载重吨	0.018 02
滚装货船	8.079 3	船舶载重吨	0.091 23
滚装客船	4.114 0	船舶载重吨	0.198 63
具有非常规推进系统的邮轮	5.124 0	船舶总吨位	0.127 14

MCR_{avg} 或 $MPP_{avg} = D \times E^F$ 计算参数

船舶类型	D	E	F
散货船	23.751 0	船舶载重吨	0.540 87
气体运输船	21.470 4	船舶载重吨	0.595 22
液货舱	22.841 5	船舶载重吨	0.558 26
集装箱船	0.504 2	当载重吨 ≤ 95 000 时，取船舶载重吨 当载重吨 > 95 000 时，取 95 000	1.030 46
杂货船	0.881 6	船舶载重吨	0.920 50
冷藏货船	0.027 2	船舶载重吨	1.386 34
兼用船	22.853 6	船舶载重吨	0.558 20
LNG 运输船	20.709 6	船舶载重吨	0.634 77
滚装货船（车辆运输船）	262.769 3	船舶载重吨	0.399 73
滚装货船	37.770 8	船舶载重吨	0.634 50
滚装客船	9.133 8	船舶载重吨	0.911 16
具有非常规推进系统的邮轮	1.355 0	船舶总吨位	0.886 64

Calculation of parameters to calculate $V_{ref,avg}$ and MCR_{avg}

Data sources

1   IHS Fairplay (IHSF) database with the following conditions are used.

Ship type	Ship size	Delivered period	Type of propulsion systems	Population
Bulk carrier	≥ 10,000 DWT		Conventional	2,433
Gas carrier	≥ 2,000 DWT		Conventional	292
Tanker	≥ 4,000 DWT		Conventional	3,345
Containership	≥ 10,000 DWT		Conventional	2,185
General cargo ship	≥ 3,000 DWT	From 1 January 1999 to 1 January 2009	Conventional	1,673
Refrigerated cargo carrier	≥ 3,000 DWT		Conventional	53
Combination carrier	≥ 4,000 DWT		Conventional	3,351
LNG carrier	≥ 10,000 DWT		Conventional, Non-conventional	185
Ro-ro cargo ship (vehicle carrier)	≥ 10,000 DWT		Conventional	301
Ro-ro cargo ship	≥ 1,000 DWT	From 1 January 1998 to 31 December 2010	Conventional	188
Ro-ro passenger ship	≥ 250 DWT		Conventional	350
Cruise passenger ship having non-conventional propulsion	≥ 25,000 GT	From 1 January 1999 to 1 January 2009	Non-conventional	93

2   Data sets with blank/zero "Service speed", "Capacity" and/or Total kW of M/E" are removed.

3   Ship type is in accordance with table 1 and table 2 of resolution MEPC.231(65) on *2013 Guidelines for calculation of reference lines for use with the Energy Efficiency Design Index (EEDI)*. However, "Gas carrier" does not include "LNG carrier". Parameters for "LNG carrier" are given separately.

***

$V_{ref,\,avg}$ 和 MCT_{avg} 计算参数的计算

数据来源

1 采用 IHSFairplay（IHSF）数据库，条件如下：

船舶类型	船舶尺寸	交付期	推进系统类型	总体数量
散货船	≥ 10 000 DWT		常规	2 433
气体运输船	≥ 2 000 DWT		常规	292
液货船	≥ 4 000 DWT		常规	3 345
集装箱船	≥ 10 000 DWT		常规	2 185
杂货船	≥ 3 000 DWT	1999 年 1 月 1 日至 2009 年 1 月 1 日	常规	1 673
冷藏货船	≥ 3 000 DWT		常规	53
兼用船	≥ 4 000 DWT		常规	3 351
LNG 运输船	≥ 10 000 DWT		常规、非常规	185
滚装货船（车辆运输船）	≥ 10 000 DWT		常规	301
滚装货船	≥ 1 000 DWT	1998 年 1 月 1 日至 2010 年 12 月 31 日	常规	188
滚装客船	≥ 250 DWT		常规	350
具有非常规推进系统的邮轮	≥ 25 000 GT	1999 年 1 月 1 日至 2009 年 1 月 1 日	非常规	93

2 "营运航速" "载运能力" 和 / 或主机总功率为空白 / 零的数据集已删除。

3 船舶类型应符合 MEPC.231（65）决议《2013 年用于能效设计指数（EEDI）的基准线计算导则》的表 1 和表 2。但 "气体运输船" 不包括 "LNG 运输船"。"LNG 运输船" 的参数单独给出。

***

RESOLUTION MEPC.351(78)
(adopted on 10 June 2022)

2022 GUIDELINES ON SURVEY AND CERTIFICATION OF THE ATTAINED ENERGY EFFICIENCY EXISTING SHIP INDEX (EEXI)

THE MARINE ENVIRONMENT PROTECTION COMMITTEE,

RECALLING Article 38(a) of the Convention on the International Maritime Organization concerning the functions of the Marine Environment Protection Committee (the Committee) conferred upon it by international conventions for the prevention and control of marine pollution from ships,

NOTING that the Committee adopted, at its seventy-sixth session, by resolution MEPC.328(76), the *2021 Revised MARPOL Annex VI*, which will enter into force on 1 November 2022,

NOTING IN PARTICULAR that the *2021 Revised MARPOL Annex VI* (MARPOL Annex VI) contains amendments concerning mandatory goal-based technical and operational measures to reduce carbon intensity of international shipping,

NOTING FURTHER that regulation 5.4 (Surveys) of MARPOL Annex VI requires that ships to which chapter 4 applies shall also be subject to survey and certification taking into account guidelines developed by the Organization,

RECOGNIZING that the aforementioned amendments to MARPOL Annex VI require relevant guidelines for uniform and effective implementation of the regulations and to provide sufficient lead time for industry to prepare,

NOTING that, at its seventy-sixth session, the Committee adopted, by resolution MEPC.334(76), the *2021 Guidelines on survey and certification of the attained Energy Efficiency Existing Ship Index (EEXI),*

HAVING CONSIDERED, at its seventy-eighth session, draft amendments to the *2021 Guidelines on survey and certification of the attained Energy Efficiency Existing Ship Index (EEXI),*

1   ADOPTS the *2022 Guidelines on survey and certification of the attained Energy Efficiency Existing Ship Index (EEXI),* as set out in the annex to the present resolution;

2   INVITES Administrations to take the annexed Guidelines into account when developing and enacting national laws which give force to and implement requirements set forth in regulation 5 of MARPOL Annex VI;

3   REQUESTS the Parties to MARPOL Annex VI and other Member Governments to bring the annexed Guidelines to the attention of masters, seafarers, shipowners, ship operators and any other interested parties;

第 MEPC.351（78）号决议
（2022 年 6 月 10 日通过）

2022 年现有船舶达到的能效指数（EEXI）检验和发证导则

海上环境保护委员会，

忆及国际海事组织公约第 38（a）条关于国际防止和控制海上污染公约赋予海上环境保护委员会的职能，

注意到委员会在其第 76 届会议上以 MEPC.328（76）号决议通过了将于 2022 年 11 月 1 日生效的 2021 年经修订的 MARPOL 附则Ⅵ，

特别注意到 2021 年经修订的 MARPOL 附则Ⅵ包含关于基于目标的强制性技术和营运措施以减少国际航运碳强度的修正案，

进一步注意到经修正的 MARPOL 附则Ⅵ第 5.4 条（检验）要求对第 4 章适用的船舶也应进行检验和发证，并考虑到本组织制定的导则，

认识到上述 MARPOL 附则Ⅵ的修正案需要有相关导则，以便于统一和有效实施各条规定，并为业界提供充足的提前时间进行准备，

注意到在其第 76 届会议上，委员会以 MEPC.334（76）号决议通过了《2021 年现有船舶能效指数（EEXI）检验和发证导则》，

在其第 78 届会议上审议了《2022 年现有船舶能效指数（EEXI）检验和发证导则》修订草案，

1   通过《2022 年现有船舶能效指数（EEXI）检验和发证导则》，其文本载于本决议附件；

2   提请主管机关在制定和颁布相关国内法律，以强制实施 MARPOL 附则Ⅵ第 5 条要求时，考虑到附件中的导则；

3   要求 MARPOL 附则Ⅵ缔约国和其他成员国政府使船长、船员、船东、船舶营运人和任何其他利益相关方注意到附件中的导则，

4   AGREES to keep the Guidelines under review in light of experience gained with their implementation, also taking into consideration that in accordance with regulation 25.3 of MARPOL Annex VI a review of the technical measure to reduce carbon intensity of international shipping shall be completed by 1 January 2026;

5   REVOKES the *2021 Guidelines on survey and certification of the attained Energy Efficiency Existing Ship Index (EEXI),* adopted by resolution MEPC.334(76).

4　**同意**根据本导则实施中获得的经验，保持对本导则的评审，同时考虑到根据 MARPOL 附则Ⅵ第 25.3 的规定，应在 2026 年 1 月 1 日之前完成对降低国际航运碳强度的技术措施的审查；

5　**撤销**以第 MEPC.334（76）号决议通过的《2021 年现有船舶能效指数（EEXI）检验和发证导则》。

ANNEX

2022 GUIDELINES ON SURVEY AND CERTIFICATION OF THE ATTAINED ENERGY EFFICIENCY EXISTING SHIP INDEX (EEXI)

Table of contents

附件

2022 年现有船舶达到的能效指数（EEXI）检验和发证导则

目录

1　GENERAL

The purpose of these Guidelines is to assist verifiers of the Energy Efficiency Existing Ship Index (EEXI) of ships in conducting the survey and certification of the EEXI, in accordance with regulations 5, 6, 7, 8 and 9 of MARPOL Annex VI, and assist shipowners, shipbuilders, manufacturers and other interested parties in understanding the procedures for the survey and certification of the EEXI.

2　DEFINITIONS[1]

2.1　*Verifier* means an Administration, or organization duly authorized by it, which conducts the survey and certification of the EEXI in accordance with regulations 5, 6, 7, 8 and 9 of MARPOL Annex VI and these Guidelines.

2.2　*Ship of the same type* means a ship the hull form (expressed in the lines such as sheer plan and body plan), excluding additional hull features such as fins, and principal particulars of which are identical to that of the base ship.

2.3　*Tank test* means model towing tests, model self-propulsion tests and model propeller open water tests. Numerical calculations may be accepted as equivalent to model propeller open water tests or used to complement the tank tests conducted (e.g. to evaluate the effect of additional hull features such as fins, etc. on ships' performance), or as a replacement for model tests provided that the methodology and numerical model used have been validated/calibrated against parent hull sea trials and/or model tests, with the approval of the verifier.

2.4　*MARPOL* means the International Convention for the Prevention of Pollution from Ships, 1973, as modified by the Protocols of 1978 and 1997 relating thereto, as amended.

2.5　For the purpose of these Guidelines, the definitions in MARPOL Annex VI, as amended, apply.

3　APPLICATION

These Guidelines should be applied to ships for which an application for a survey for verification of the ship's EEXI specified in regulation 5 of MARPOL Annex VI has been submitted to a verifier.

4　PROCEDURES FOR SURVEY AND CERTIFICATION

4.1　General

4.1.1　The attained EEXI should be calculated in accordance with regulation 23 of MARPOL Annex VI and the *2022 Guidelines on the method of calculation of the attained Energy Efficiency Existing Ship Index (EEXI)* (resolution MEPC.350(78)) (EEXI Calculation Guidelines).

4.1.2　The *2021 Guidance on treatment of innovative energy efficiency technologies for calculation and verification of the attained EEDI and EEXI* (MEPC.1/Circ.896) should be applied for calculation of the attained EEXI, if applicable.

---

[1]　Other terms used in these Guidelines have the same meaning as those defined in the *2018 Guidelines on the method of calculation of the attained EEDI for new ships* (resolution MEPC.308(73), as amended) and the *2022 Guidelines on the method of calculation of the attained Energy Efficiency Existing Ship Index (EEXI)* (resolution MEPC.350(78)).

1 通则

本导则旨在帮助现有船舶能效指数（EEXI）的验证方按照 MARPOL 附则Ⅵ第 5、6、7、8 和 9 条进行 EEXI 的检验和发证，并帮助船东、造船厂、制造商以及其他相关方了解 EEXI 的检验和发证程序。

2 定义 [1]

2.1 验证方系指按照 MARPOL 附则Ⅵ第 5、6、7、8 和 9 条以及本导则进行 EEXI 的检验和发证的主管机关或其正式授权的组织。

2.2 相同类型船舶系指不包括附体（例如鳍板）的船体外形（以型线表示，例如型线纵剖图和型线横剖图）和主参数与基准船舶相同的船舶。

2.3 水池试验系指模型拖曳试验、模型自航试验和模型螺旋桨敞水试验。数值计算可等同于模型螺旋桨敞水试验予以接受，或用于对水池试验的补充（例如，评估鳍板等附体对船舶性能的影响），或经验证方认可，在所用的方法和数值模型已经母型船试航和 / 或模型试验验证 / 修正的前提下替代模型试验。

2.4 MARPOL 系指经修正的《经 1978 年和 1997 年议定书修订的 1973 年国际防止船舶造成污染公约》。

2.5 就本导则而言，经修正的 MARPOL 附则Ⅵ中的定义适用。

3 适用范围

本导则应适用于已向验证方提交 MARPOL 附则Ⅵ第 5 条规定的船舶 EEXI 验证检验申请的船舶。

4 检验和发证程序

4.1 一般规定

4.1.1 达到的 EEXI 应按照 MARPOL 附则Ⅵ第 23 条和《2021 年现有船舶达到的能效指数（EEXI）计算方法导则》（MEPC.333（76）决议）（EEXI 计算导则）进行计算。

4.1.2 《2021 年用于计算和验证达到的 EEDI 和 EEXI 的创新能效技术处理导则》（MEPC.1/Circ.896）应用于达到的 EEXI 的计算（如适用）。

---

[1] 本导则中使用的其他术语与《2018 年新船达到的能效设计指数（EEDI）计算方法导则》（经修正的 MEPC.308（73）决议）和《2022 年现有船舶达到的能效指数（EEXI）计算方法导则》（MEPC.350（78）决议）中所定义的术语具有相同含义。

4.1.3   The information used in the verification process may contain confidential information of submitters, including shipyards, which requires Intellectual Property Rights (IPR) protection. In the case where the submitter wants a non-disclosure agreement with the verifier, the additional information should be provided to the verifier upon mutually agreed terms and conditions.

4.2   Verification of the attained EEXI

4.2.1   For verification of the attained EEXI, an application for a survey and an EEXI Technical File containing the necessary information for the verification and other relevant background documents should be submitted to a verifier, unless the attained EEDI of the ship satisfies the required EEXI.

4.2.2   The EEXI Technical File should be written at least in English. The EEXI Technical File should include, but not be limited to:

.1   deadweight (DWT) or gross tonnage (GT) for ro-ro passenger ship and cruise passenger ship having non-conventional propulsion;

.2   the rated installed power (MCR) of the main and auxiliary engines;

.3   the limited installed power (MCR_{lim}) in cases where the overridable Shaft/Engine Power Limitation system is installed;

.4   the ship speed (V_{ref});

.5   the approximate ship speed ($V_{ref,app}$) for pre-EEDI ships in cases where the speed-power curve is not available, as specified in paragraph 2.2.3.5 of the EEXI Calculation Guidelines;

.6   an approved speed-power curve under the EEDI condition as specified in paragraph 2.2 of the EEDI Calculation Guidelines, which is described in the EEDI Technical File, in cases where regulation 22 of MARPOL Annex VI (Attained EEDI) is applied;

.7   an estimated speed-power curve under the EEDI condition, or under a different load draught to be calibrated to the EEDI condition, obtained from tank test and/or numerical calculations, if available;

.8   estimation process and methodology of the power curves, as necessary, including documentation on consistency with the defined quality standards (e.g. ITTC 7.5-03-01-02 and ITTC 7.5-03-01-04 in their latest revisions) and the verification of the numerical set-up with parent hull or the reference set of comparable ships in case of using numerical calculations;

.9   a sea trial report including sea trial results, which may have been calibrated by the tank test, under the sea condition as specified in paragraph 2.2.2 of the EEDI Calculation Guidelines, if available;

.10   an in-service performance measurement report, where applicable, as specified in paragraphs 2.2.3.5 and 2.2.3.7.2 of the EEXI Calculation Guidelines;

4.1.3 验证过程中使用的信息可能包含提交方（包括船厂）要求知识产权（IPR）保护的保密信息。对提交方希望与验证方达成保密协议的情况，应按照互相商定的条款和条件向验证方提供附加信息。

4.2 达到的 EEXI 的验证

4.2.1 除非船舶达到的 EEDI 满足要求的 EEXI，否则对于达到的 EEXI 的验证，应向验证方提交检验申请、包含验证所需信息的 EEXI 技术案卷以及其他相关背景文件。

4.2.2 EEXI 技术案卷应至少使用英语写成。EEXI 技术案卷应至少包括但不限于：

.1 载重吨（DWT）或客滚船和具有非常规推进系统的豪华邮轮的总吨（GT）；

.2 主机和辅机的额定装机功率（MCR）；

.3 安装了可越控轴 / 发动机功率限制系统时的限定装机功率（MCR_{lim}）；

.4 航速（V_{ref}）；

.5 在无法获得速度 – 功率曲线的情况下，EEDI 生效前船舶的近似航速（$V_{ref, app}$），见 EEXI 计算导则 2.2.3.5 中的规定；

.6 对适用 MARPOL 附则 Ⅵ 第 22 条（达到的 EEDI）的情况，EEDI 技术案卷中给出的 EEDI 计算导则 2.2 中规定的经批准的 EEDI 工况下的速度—功率曲线；

.7 从水池试验和 / 或数值计算中获得的 EEDI 工况下或不同载重吃水修正到 EEDI 工况下的速度 – 功率估算曲线（如可获得）。

.8 必要的功率曲线估算过程和方法，包括：与所规定的质量标准（如：最新修订的 ITTC7.5-03-01-02 和 ITTC7.5-03-01-04）一致的证明文件，以及采用数值计算时，对母型船数值设置或对可比船舶参考设置的验证；

.9 试航报告，包括 EEDI 计算导则 2.2.2 规定的海况下的试航结果，该试航结果可能经水池试验修正（如可获得）；

.10 EEXI 计算导则第 2.2.3.5 和 2.2.3.7.2 段中规定的在役船舶性能测量报告（如适用）；

.11 calculation process of $V_{ref,app}$ for pre-EEDI ships in cases where the speed-power curve is not available, as specified in paragraph 2.2.3.6 of the EEXI Calculation Guidelines;

.12 type of fuel;

.13 the specific fuel consumption (SFC) of the main and auxiliary engines, as specified in paragraph 2.2.4 of the EEXI Calculation Guidelines;

.14 the electric power table[2] for certain ship types, as necessary, as defined in the EEDI Calculation Guidelines;

.15 the documented record of annual average figure of the auxiliary engine load at sea obtained prior to the date of application for a survey for verification of the ship's EEXI, as specified in paragraph 2.2.2.3 of the EEXI Calculation Guidelines, if applicable;

.16 calculation process of $P_{AE,app}$, as specified in paragraph 2.2.2.3 of the EEXI Calculation Guidelines, if applicable;

.17 principal particulars, ship type and the relevant information to classify the ship as such a ship type, classification notations and an overview of the propulsion system and electricity supply system on board;

.18 description of energy-saving equipment, if available;

.19 calculated value of the attained EEXI, including the calculation summary, which should contain, at a minimum, each value of the calculation parameters and the calculation process used to determine the attained EEXI; and

.20 for LNG carriers:

.1 type and outline of propulsion systems (such as direct drive diesel, diesel electric, steam turbine);

.2 LNG cargo tank capacity in m^3 and BOR as defined in paragraph 2.2.5.6.3 of the EEDI Calculation Guidelines;

.3 shaft power of the propeller shaft after transmission gear at 100% of the rated output of motor (MPP_{Motor}) and $\eta_{(i)}$ for diesel electric;

.4 shaft power of the propeller shaft after transmission gear at the de-rated output of motor ($MPP_{Motor,lim}$) in cases where the overridable Shaft / Engine Power Limitation is installed;

.5 maximum continuous rated power ($MCR_{SteamTurbine}$) for steam turbine;

.6 limited maximum continuous rated power ($MCR_{SteamTurbine,lim}$) for steam turbine in cases where the overridable Shaft / Engine Power Limitation is installed; and

[2] Electric power tables should be validated separately, taking into account the guidelines set out in appendix 2 of the *2014 Guidelines on survey and certification of the Energy Efficiency Design Index (EEDI)* (resolution MEPC.254(67), as amended by resolutions MEPC.261(68) and MEPC.309(73)); consolidated text: MEPC.1/Circ.855/Rev.2, as may be further amended).

.11 在无法获得速度—功率曲线的情况下，EEDI 生效前船舶的 $V_{ref,\,app}$ 的计算过程，见 EEXI 计算导则 2.2.3.6 中的规定；

.12 燃料类型；

.13 主机和副机的单位燃油消耗量（SFC），见 EEXI 计算导则 2.2.4 中的规定；

.14 特定船型的电力负荷表 [2]（如必要），见 EEDI 计算导则中的定义；

.15 在船舶 EEXI 验证检验申请之日以前获得的、海上辅机负荷年度平均值的文件记录，见 EEXI 计算导则 2.2.2.3 中的规定（如适用）；

.16 $P_{AE,\,app}$ 的计算过程，见 EEXI 计算导则 2.2.2.3 中的规定（如适用）；

.17 主尺度，船型和将船舶归入该船型的相关信息，船级标志及船上推进系统和电力供应系统的总体情况；

.18 节能设备的描述（如可获得）；

.19 达到的 EEXI 的计算值，包括计算概述（应至少包括用于确定达到的 EEXI 的每个计算参数值和计算过程）；和

.20 对于液化天然气（LNG）船舶：

    .1 推进系统的类型和概况（如柴油机直接推进、柴油电力推进、蒸汽轮机推进）；

    .2 LNG 液货舱容积，以 m^3 计，和 EEDI 计算导则 2.2.5.6.3 所定义的蒸发率 BOR；

    .3 发动机 100% 额定输出功率（MPP_{Motor}）时传动齿轮后螺旋桨轴的轴功率和柴油电力推进的电效率 $\eta(i)$；

    .4 在安装了可越控轴 / 发动机功率限制系统的情况下，发动机处于限定输出功率（$MPP_{motor,\,lim}$）时传动齿轮后螺旋桨轴的轴功率；

    .5 蒸汽轮机的最大持续额定功率（$MCR_{SteamTurbine}$）；

    .6 安装了可越控轴 / 发动机功率限制系统后，蒸汽轮机的限定最大持续功率（$MCR_{SteamTurbine,\,lim}$）；和

---

[2] 电力负荷表应单独验证，并考虑到《2014 年能效设计指数（EEDI）检验和发证导则》（经 MEPC.261（68）和 MEPC.309（73）决议修正的 MEPC.254（67）决议；综合文本：MEPC.1/Circ.855/Rev.2，可能会进一步修正）附录 2 中的导则。

.7 $SFC_{SteamTurbine}$ for steam turbine, as specified in paragraph 2.2.7.2 of the EEDI Calculation Guidelines. If the calculation is not available from the manufacturer, $SFC_{SteamTurbine}$ may be calculated by the submitter.

A sample of an EEXI Technical File is provided in the appendix.

4.2.3   The *SFC* should be corrected to the value corresponding to the ISO standard reference conditions using the standard lower calorific value of the fuel oil, referring to ISO 15550:2002 and ISO 3046-1:2002. For the confirmation of the *SFC*, a copy of the approved NO_x Technical File and documented summary of the correction calculations should be submitted to the verifier.

4.2.4   For ships equipped with dual-fuel engine(s) using LNG and fuel oil, the C_F-factor for gas (LNG) and the specific fuel consumption (*SFC*) of gas fuel should be used by applying the criteria specified in paragraph 4.2.3 of the *2014 Guidelines on survey and certification of the Energy Efficiency Design Index (EEDI)*, as amended,[3] as a basis for the guidance of the Administration.

4.2.5   Notwithstanding paragraphs 4.2.3 and 4.2.4, in cases where overridable Shaft/Engine Power Limitation is installed, or in cases where engines do not have a test report included in the NO_x Technical File, *SFC* should be calculated in accordance with paragraph 2.2.4 of the EEXI Calculation Guidelines. For this purpose, actual performance records of the engine may be used if satisfactory and acceptable to the verifier.

4.2.6   The verifier may request further information from the submitter, as specified in paragraph 4.2.7 of the EEDI Survey and Certification Guidelines, in addition to that contained in the EEXI Technical File, as necessary, to examine the calculation process of the attained EEXI.

4.2.7   In cases where the sea trial report as specified in paragraph 4.2.2.9 is submitted, the verifier should request further information from the submitter to confirm that:

.1   the sea trial was conducted in accordance with the conditions specified in paragraphs 4.3.3, 4.3.4 and 4.3.7 of the EEDI Survey and Certification Guidelines, as applicable;

.2   sea conditions were measured in accordance with ISO 15016:2002 or the equivalent if satisfactory and acceptable to the verifier;

.3   ship speed was measured in accordance with ISO 15016:2002 or the equivalent if satisfactory and acceptable to the verifier; and

.4   the measured ship speed was calibrated, if necessary, by taking into account the effects of wind, tide, waves, shallow water and displacement in accordance with ISO 15016:2002 or the equivalent which may be acceptable provided that the concept of the method is transparent for the verifier and publicly available/accessible.

4.2.8   In cases where the in-service performance measurement report as specified in paragraph 4.2.2.10 is submitted, the verifier should confirm that the in-service performance measurement was conducted and verified in accordance with the methods and procedures as specified in the *Guidance on methods, procedures and verification of in-service performance measurements* (MEPC.1/Circ.901).

---

[3]   Resolution MEPC.254(67), as amended.

.7　EEDI 计算导则 2.2.7.2 中规定的蒸汽轮机的 $SFC_{SteamTurbine}$。如果制造商不能提供计算，$SFC_{SteamTurbine}$ 可由提交方计算。

EEXI 技术案卷样本见附录。

4.2.3　应使用燃油的标准低热值修正为 ISO 标准基准条件对应的值，参见 ISO15550：2002 和 ISO3046-1：2002。为了确认，应向验证方提交一份经批准的 NO_x 技术案卷副本和修正计算概述文件。

4.2.4　如果船上安装使用液化天然气和燃油的双燃料发动机，气体（液化天然气）的 C_F 系数和气体燃料的单位燃料消耗量（SFC）的使用，应采用经修正的《2014 年能效设计指数（EEDI）检验和发证导则》[3]4.2.3 中的标准作为主管机关的指导基础。

4.2.5　尽管有 4.2.3 和 4.2.4 的规定，如果安装了可越控轴 / 发动机功率限制系统，或如果发动机的 NO_x 技术案卷中不含试验报告，SFC 应按 EEXI 计算导则 2.2.4 计算。为此，如果验证方满意并接受，可采用发动机的实际性能记录。

4.2.6　验证方可要求提交方提供除 EEXI 技术案卷中包含的信息外的必要的附加信息，见 EEDI 检验和发证导则 4.2.7 中的规定，以检查达到的 EEXI 的计算过程。

4.2.7　如果提交了 4.2.2.9 中规定的试航报告，验证方应要求提交方提供进一步信息以确认：

.1　按照 EEDI 检验和发证导则 4.3.3、4.3.4 和 4.3.7 中规定的工况（如适用）进行了试航；

.2　按照 ISO 15016：2002 或验证方满意并接受的等效方法对海况进行了测量；

.3　按照 ISO 15016：2002 或验证方满意并接受的等效方法对航速进行了测量；和

.4　按照 ISO 15016：2002 或可接受的等效方法（前提是该方法的概念对验证方是透明的且可以公开提供 / 获得），对所测得的航速通过考虑风、潮涌、波浪、浅水和排水量的影响进行修正（如必要）。

4.2.8　如果提交了第 4.2.2.10 段中规定的在役船舶性能测量报告，则验证者应确认，在役船舶性能测试是按照《在役船舶性能测量方法、程序和验证导则》（MEPC.1/Circ.901）中规定的方法和程序实施和验证的。

---

[3]　经修正的 MEPC.254（67）决议。

4.2.9   The estimated speed-power curve obtained from the tank test and/or numerical calculations and/or the sea trial results calibrated by the tank test should be reviewed on the basis of the relevant documents in accordance with the EEDI Survey and Certification Guidelines, the defined quality standards (e.g. ITTC 7.5-03-01-02 and ITTC 7.5-03-01-04 in their latest revisions) and the verification of the numerical set-up with parent hull or the reference set of comparable ships.

4.2.10   In cases where the overridable Shaft/Engine Power Limitation system is installed, the verifier should confirm that the system is appropriately installed and sealed in accordance with the *2021 Guidelines on the Shaft/Engine Power Limitation system to comply with the EEXI requirements and use of a power reserve* (resolution MEPC.335(76)) and that a verified Onboard Management Manual (OMM) for overridable Shaft/Engine Power Limitation is on board the ship.

4.3   Verification of the attained EEXI in case of major conversion

4.3.1   In cases of a major conversion of a ship taking place at or after the completion date of the survey for EEXI verification specified in regulation 5.4.7 of MARPOL Annex VI, the shipowner should submit to a verifier an application for a general or partial survey with the EEXI Technical File duly revised, based on the conversion made and other relevant background documents.

4.3.2   The background documents should include as a minimum, but are not limited to:

.1   details of the conversion;

.2   EEXI parameters changed after the conversion and the technical justifications for each respective parameter;

.3   reasons for other changes made in the EEXI Technical File, if any; and

.4   calculated value of the attained EEXI with the calculation summary, which should contain, as a minimum, each value of the calculation parameters and the calculation process used to determine the attained EEXI after the conversion.

4.3.3   The verifier should review the revised EEXI Technical File and other documents submitted and verify the calculation process of the attained EEXI to ensure that it is technically sound and reasonable and follows regulation 23 of MARPOL Annex VI and the EEXI Calculation Guidelines.

4.3.4   For verification of the attained EEXI after the major conversion, speed trials of the ship may be conducted, as necessary.

4.2.9 应按 EEDI 检验和发证导则、规定的质量标准（如：最新修订的 ITTC7.5-03-01-02 和 ITTC7.5-03-01-04）和对母型船数值设置或对可比船舶参考设置的验证，基于相关文件，对从水池试验和 / 或数值计算和 / 或经水池试验修正的试航结果中获得的估算的速度 – 功率曲线进行检查。

4.2.10 如果安装了可越控轴 / 发动机功率限制系统，验证方应确认该系统按《2021 年为符合现有船舶能效指数（EEXI）要求采用的轴 / 发动机功率限制系统和储备功率使用导则》（MEPC.335（76）决议）正确安装和密封，且船上备有经验证的可越控轴 / 发动机功率限制系统船上管理手册（OMM）。

4.3 重大改建时达到的 EEXI 的验证

4.3.1 如果船舶在 MARPOL 附则Ⅵ第 5.4.7 条规定的 EEXI 验证检验完成之日或以后进行重大改建，船东应将总体或部分检验申请连同基于所作改建而适当修订的 EEXI 技术案卷和其他相关背景文件提交给验证方。

4.3.2 背景文件应至少包括但不限于：

.1 改建的详细信息；

.2 改建后改变的 EEXI 参数和每一相关参数的技术依据；

.3 EEXI 技术案卷中所作其他改变的理由（如有）；和

.4 达到的 EEXI 的计算值和计算概述，应至少包括用于确定改建后的达到的 EEXI 的每个计算参数值和计算过程。

4.3.3 验证方应审查经修订的 EEXI 技术案卷和提交的其他文件并验证达到的 EEXI 的计算过程，以确保其技术上可靠和合理并遵循 MARPOL 附则Ⅵ第 23 条和 EEXI 计算导则。

4.3.4 对于重大改建后达到的 EEXI 的验证，必要时需进行船舶试航测试。

APPENDIX

SAMPLE OF EEXI TECHNICAL FILE

1   Data

1.1   General information

Shipowner	XXX Shipping Line
Shipbuilder	XXX Shipbuilding Company
Hull no.	12345
IMO no.	94112XX
Ship type	Bulk carrier

1.2   Principal particulars

Length overall	250.0 m
Length between perpendiculars	240.0 m
Breadth, moulded	40.0 m
Depth, moulded	20.0 m
Summer load line draught, moulded	14.0 m
Deadweight at summer load line draught	150,000 tons

1.3   Main engine

Manufacturer	XXX Industries
Type	6J70A
Maximum continuous rating (MCR_{ME})	15,000 kW x 80 rpm
Limited maximum continuous rating with the Engine Power Limitation installed ($MCR_{ME,lim}$)	9,940 kW x 70 rpm
SFC at 75% of MCR_{ME} or 83% of $MCR_{ME,lim}$	166.5 g/kWh
Number of sets	1
Fuel type	Diesel Oil

1.4   Auxiliary engine

Manufacturer	XXX Industries
Type	5J-200
Maximum continuous rating (MCR_{AE})	600 kW x 900 rpm
SFC at 50% MCR_{AE}	220.0 g/kWh
Number of sets	3
Fuel type	Diesel Oil

1.5   Ship speed

Ship speed (V_{ref}) (with the Engine Power Limitation installed)	13.20 knots

附录

EEXI 技术案卷样本

1 数据

1.1 一般信息

船东	×××航运公司
船厂	×××造船公司
船体编号	12345
IMO 编号	94112××
船型	散货船

1.2 主尺度

总长	250.0 m
垂线间长	240.0 m
型宽	40.0 m
型深	20.0 m
夏季载重线吃水，型吃水	14.0 m
夏季载重线吃水时的载重吨	150 000 t

1.3 主机

制造商	×××工业公司
型号	6J70A
最大持续功率（MCR_{ME}）	15 000 kW × 80 r/min
安装了发动机功率限制系统的限定最大持续功率（$MCR_{ME,\ lim}$）	9 940 kW × 70 r/min
75%MCR_{ME} 或 83%$MCR_{ME,\ lim}$ 下的 SFC	166.5 g/kWh
台数	1
燃油类型	柴油

1.4 辅机

制造商	×××工业公司
型号	5J–200
最大持续功率（MCR_{AE}）	600 kW × 900 r/min
50%MCR_{AE} 下的 SFC	220.0 g/kWh
台数	3
燃油类型	柴油

1.5 航速

航速（V_{ref}）（安装了发动机功率限制系统）	13.20 kn

2 Power curve

(Example 1; case of the EEDI ship)
An approved speed-power curve contained in the EEDI Technical File is shown in figure 2.1.

(Example 2; case of the pre-EEDI ship)
An estimated speed-power curve obtained from the tank test and/or numerical calculations, if available, is also shown in figure 2.1.

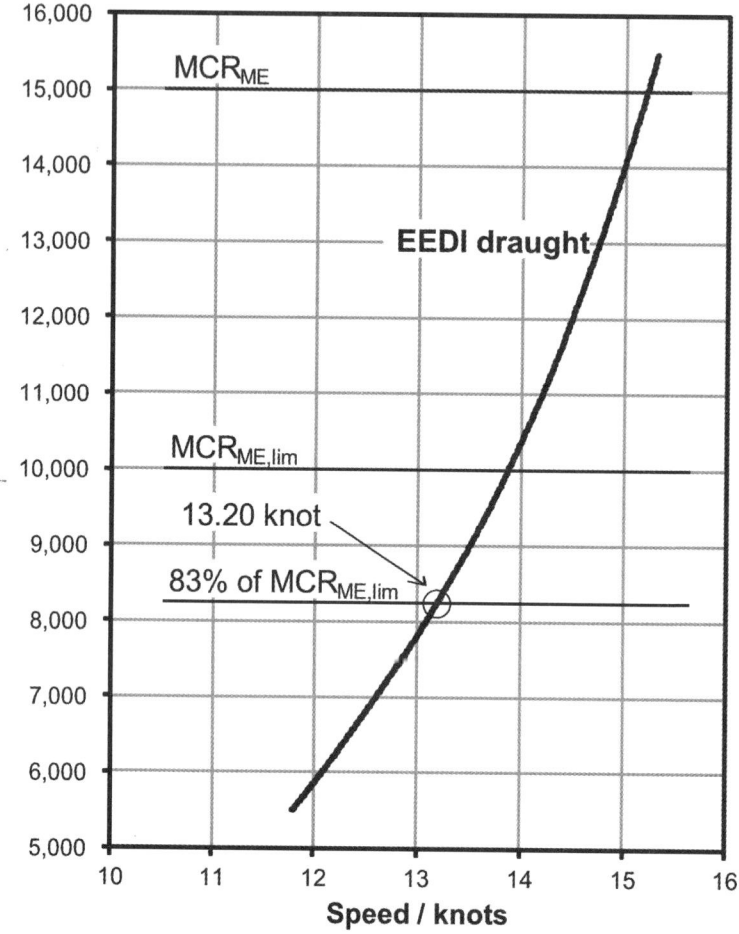

Figure 2.1: Power curve

(Example 3; case of the pre-EEDI ship with sea trial result calibrated to a different load draught)
An estimated speed-power curve under a ballast draught calibrated to the design load draught, obtained from the tank test and/or numerical calculations, if available, is shown in figure 2.2.

2 功率曲线

（例1：EEDI 船舶）

EEDI 技术案卷中包含的经批准的速度 – 功率曲线见图2.1。

（例2：EEDI 生效前的船舶）

从水池试验和 / 或数值计算中获得的（如能获得）估算的速度 – 功率曲线也见图2.1。

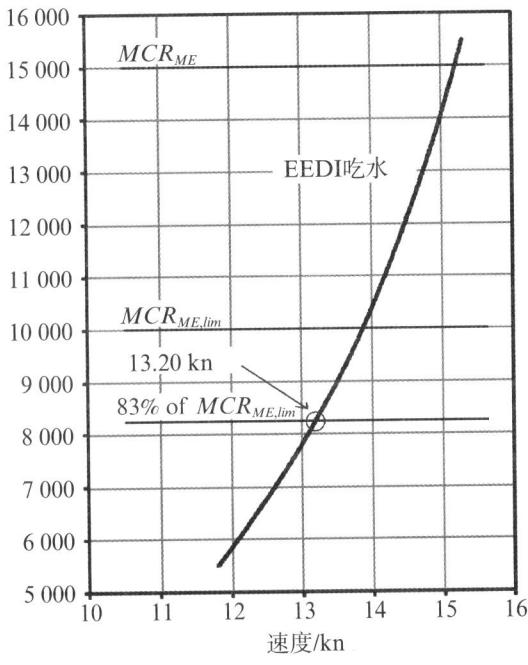

图 2.1　功率曲线

（例3：试航结果修正到不同装载吃水的 EEDI 生效前的船舶）

水池试验和 / 或数值计算中获得的（如能获得）、从压载吃水修正到设计装载吃水的估算的速度—功率曲线见图2.2。

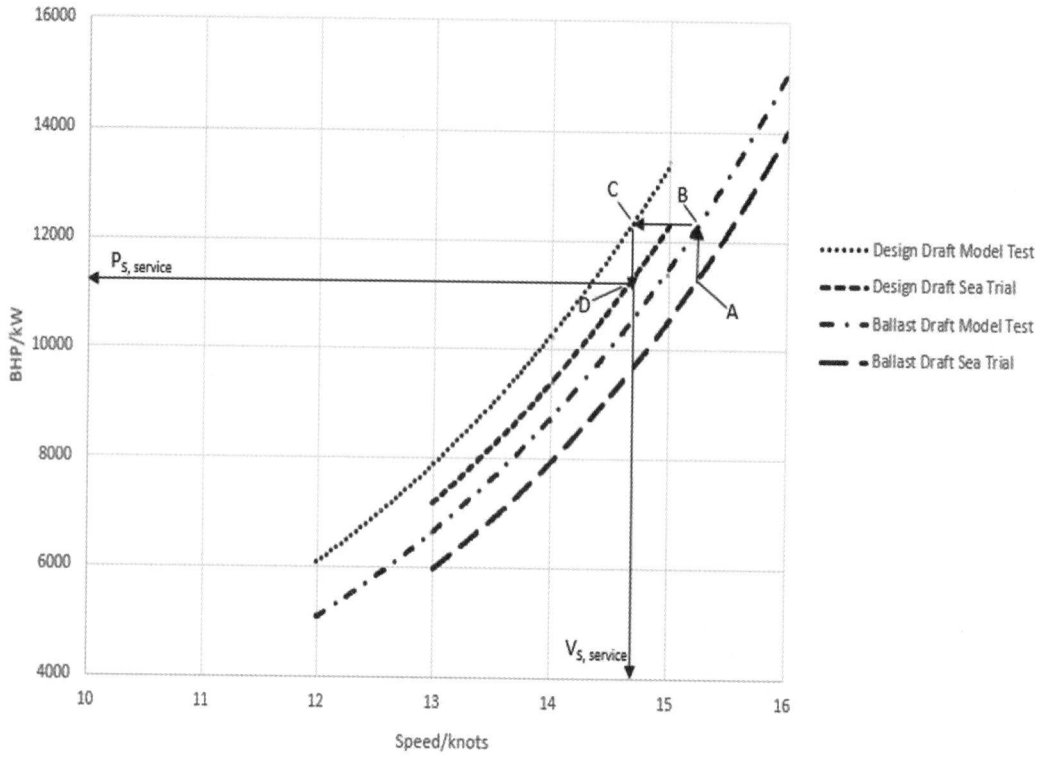

Figure 2.2: Power curve

3 Overview of propulsion system and electric power supply system

3.1 Propulsion system

3.1.1 Main engine
Refer to paragraph 1.3 of this appendix.

3.1.2 Propeller

Type	Fixed pitch propeller
Diameter	7.0 m
Number of blades	4
Number of sets	1

3.2 Electric power supply system

3.2.1 Auxiliary engines
Refer to paragraph 1.4 of this appendix.

3.2.2 Main generators

Manufacturer	XXX Electric
Rated output	560 kW (700 kVA) x 900 rpm
Voltage	AC 450 V
Number of sets	3

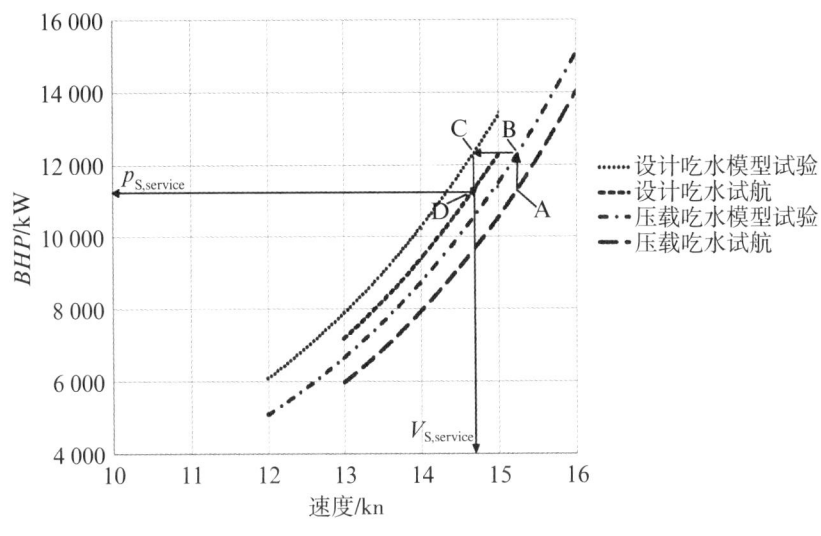

图 2.2　功率曲线

3　推进系统和电力供应系统概述

3.1　推进系统

3.1.1　主机

参见本附录 1.3。

3.1.2　螺旋桨

类型	固定螺距螺旋桨
直径	7.0 m
桨叶数量	4
台数	1

3.2　电力供应系统

3.2.1　辅机

参见本附录 1.4。

3.2.2　主发电机

制造商	×××电气
额定输出功率	560 kW（700 kV·A）× 900 r/min
电压	AC 450 V
台数	3

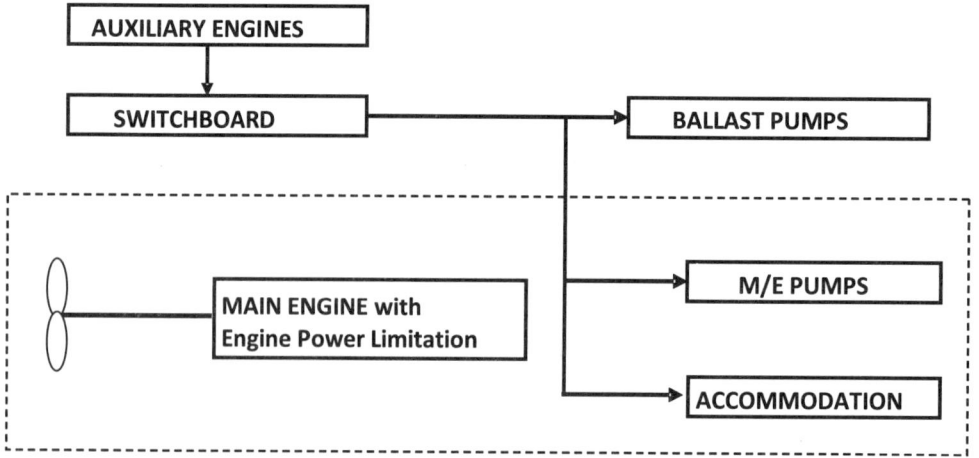

Figure 3.1: Schematic figure of propulsion and electric power supply system

4 Estimation process of speed-power curve

(Example: case of pre-EEDI ship)
Speed-power curve is estimated based on model test results and/or numerical calculations, if available. The flow of the estimation processes is shown below.

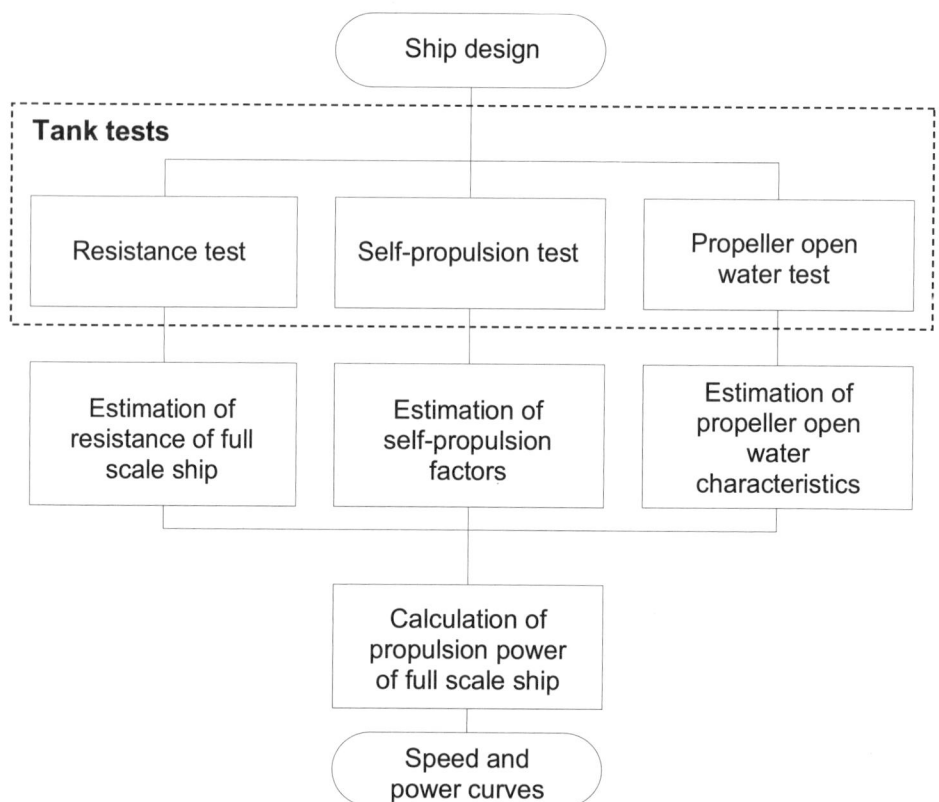

Figure 4: Flow chart of process for estimating speed-power curve from tank tests

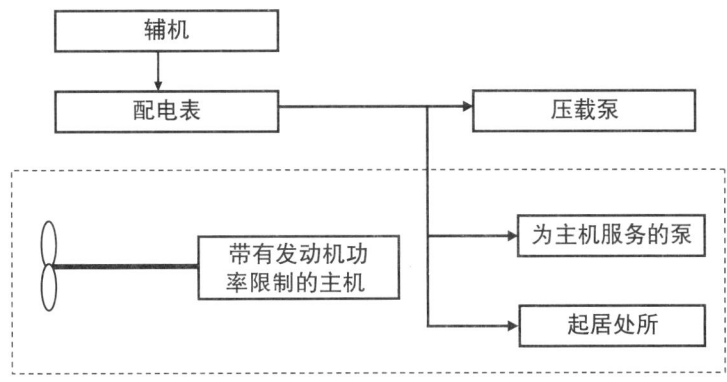

图 3.1 推进和电力供应系统原理图

4 速度 – 功率曲线估算过程

（例如：EEDI 生效前的船舶）

基于模型试验结果和 / 或数值计算（如能获得）估算速度 – 功率曲线。估算过程的流程如下。

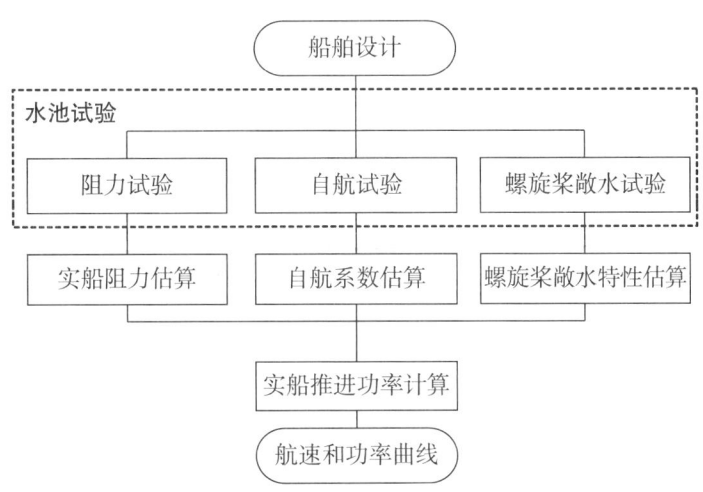

图 4 根据水池试验估算速度 – 功率曲线过程的流程图

5 Description of energy-saving equipment

5.1 Energy-saving equipment the effects of which are expressed as $P_{AEeff(i)}$ and/or $P_{eff(i)}$ in the EEXI calculation formula

N/A

5.2 Other energy-saving equipment

(Example)

5.2.1 Rudder fins

5.2.2 Rudder bulb

......

(Specifications, schematic figures and/or photos, etc. for each piece of equipment or device should be indicated. Alternatively, attachment of a commercial catalogue may be acceptable.)

6 Calculated value of attained EEXI

6.1 Basic data

Type of ship	Capacity DWT	Speed V_{ref} (knots)
Bulk carrier	150,000	13.20

6.2 Main engine

MCR_{ME} (kW)	$MCR_{ME,lim}$ (kW)	P_{ME} (kW)	Type of fuel	C_{FME}	SFC_{ME} (g/kWh)
15,000	9,940	8,250	Diesel oil	3.206	166.5

6.3 Auxiliary engines

P_{AE} (kW)	Type of fuel	C_{FAE}	SFC_{AE} (g/kWh)
625	Diesel oil	3.206	220.0

6.4 Ice class

N/A

6.5 Innovative electrical energy-efficient technology

N/A

6.6 Innovative mechanical energy-efficient technology

N/A

6.7 Cubic capacity correction factor

N/A

6.8 Calculated value of attained EEXI

5 节能设备描述

5.1 其效果在 EEXI 计算公式中表述为和/或的节能设备。

N/A

5.2 其他节能设备

（举例）

5.2.1 舵鳍

5.2.2 舵球

……

（应标明每台设备或装置的说明书、原理图和/或照片等。作为替代，附上产品商业目录也可接受。）

6 达到的 EEXI 的计算值

6.1 基础数据

船型	载重吨	航速 /kn
散货船	150 000	13.20

6.2 主机

MCR_{ME}/kW	$MCR_{ME, lim}$/kW	P_{ME}/kW	燃油类型	C_{FME}	SFC_{ME}/（g/kWh）
15 000	9 940	8 250	柴油	3.206	166.5

6.3 辅机

P_{AE}/kW	燃油类型	C_{PAE}	SFC_{AE}/（g/kWh）
625	柴油	3.206	220.0

6.4 冰级

N/A

6.5 创新型电力节能技术

N/A

6.6 创新型机械节能技术

N/A

6.7 立方容积修正系数

N/A

6.8 达到的 EEXI 的计算值

$$EEXI = \frac{\left(\prod_{j=1}^{M} f_j\right)\left(\sum_{i=1}^{nME} P_{ME(i)} \cdot C_{FME(i)} \cdot SFC_{ME(i)}\right) + \left(P_{AE} \cdot C_{FAE} \cdot SFC_{AE}\right)}{f_i \cdot f_c \cdot f_l \cdot Capacity \cdot f_w \cdot V_{ref} \cdot f_m}$$

$$+ \frac{\left\{\left(\prod_{j=1}^{M} f_j \cdot \sum_{i=1}^{nPTI} P_{PTI(i)} - \sum_{i=1}^{neff} f_{eff(i)} \cdot P_{AEeff(i)}\right) \cdot C_{FAE} \cdot SFC_{AE}\right\}}{f_i \cdot f_c \cdot f_l \cdot Capacity \cdot f_w \cdot V_{ref} \cdot f_m}$$

$$- \frac{\left(\sum_{i=1}^{neff} f_{eff(i)} \cdot P_{eff(i)} \cdot C_{FME} \cdot SFC_{ME}\right)}{f_i \cdot f_c \cdot f_l \cdot Capacity \cdot f_w \cdot V_{ref} \cdot f_m}$$

$$= \frac{1 \times (8250 \times 3.206 \times 166.5) + (625 \times 3.206 \times 220.0) + 0 - 0}{1 \times 1 \times 1 \times 150000 \times 1 \times 13.20 \times 1}$$

$$= 2.45 \ (g - CO_2/ton \cdot mile)$$

<u>attained EEXI: 2.45 g-CO$_2$/ton mile</u>

***

$$EEXI = \frac{\left(\prod_{j=1}^{M} f_j\right)\left(\sum_{i=1}^{nME} P_{ME(i)} \cdot C_{FME(i)} \cdot SFC_{ME(i)}\right) + (P_{AE} \cdot C_{FAE} \cdot SFC_{AE})}{f_i \cdot f_c \cdot f_l \cdot Capacity \cdot f_w \cdot V_{ref} \cdot f_m}$$

$$+ \frac{\left\{\left(\prod_{j=1}^{M} f_j \cdot \sum_{i=1}^{nPTI} P_{PTI(i)} - \sum_{i=1}^{neff} f_{eff(i)} \cdot P_{AEeff(i)}\right) \cdot C_{FAE} \cdot SFC_{AE}\right\}}{f_i \cdot f_c \cdot f_l \cdot Capacity \cdot f_w \cdot V_{ref} \cdot f_m}$$

$$- \frac{\left(\sum_{i=1}^{neff} f_{eff(i)} \cdot P_{eff(i)} \cdot C_{FME} \cdot SFC_{ME}\right)}{f_i \cdot f_c \cdot f_l \cdot Capacity \cdot f_w \cdot V_{ref} \cdot f_m}$$

$$= \frac{1 \times (8\,250 \times 3.206 \times 166.5) + (625 \times 3.206 \times 220.0) + 0 - 0}{1 \times 1 \times 1 \times 150\,000 \times 1 \times 13.200 \times 1}$$

$$= 2.45\ (g - CO_2/(t \cdot mile))$$

达到的 $EEXI$=2.45 g CO_2/（t · mile）

***

THE 2021 GUIDELINES ON THE SHAFT / ENGINE POWER LIMITATION SYSTEM TO COMPLY WITH THE EEXI REQUIREMENTS AND USE OF A POWER RESERVE

(RESOLUTION MEPC.335(76),AS AMENDED BY RESOLUTION MEPC.375(80) AND RESOLUTION MEPC.390(81))

THE MARINE ENVIRONMENT PROTECTION COMMITTEE,

RECALLING Article 38(a) of the Convention on the International Maritime Organization concerning the functions of the Marine Environment Protection Committee conferred upon it by international conventions for the prevention and control of marine pollution from ships,

NOTING that the 2021 Revised MARPOL Annex VI, which entered into force on 1 November 2022, contains requirements concerning mandatory goal-based technical and operational measures to reduce carbon intensity of international shipping,

NOTING ALSO that ships may be equipped with a shaft / engine power limitation system in order to comply with regulation 25 of MARPOL Annex VI on the 'Required EEXI',

NOTING FURTHER that, at its seventy-sixth session, it adopted, by resolution MEPC.335(76), the *2021 Guidelines on the shaft/engine power limitation system to comply with the EEXI requirements and use of a power reserve*,

NOTING that, at its eightieth session, the Committee adopted, by resolution MEPC.375(80), amendments to the *2021 Guidelines on the shaft/engine power limitation system to comply with the EEXI requirements and use of a power reserve*.

HAVING CONSIDERED, at its eighty-first session, proposed amendments to the *2021 Guidelines on the shaft/engine power limitation system to comply with the EEXI requirements and use of a power reserve*,

1   ADOPTS amendments to the *2021 Guidelines on the shaft/engine power limitation system to comply with the EEXI requirements and use of a power reserve*, the text of which is set out in the annex to the present resolution;

2   REQUESTS the Parties to MARPOL Annex VI and other Member Governments to bring the annexed amendments to the attention of masters, seafarers, shipowners, ship operators and any other interested parties.

2021 年为符合现有船舶能效指数（EEXI）要求采用的轴／发动机功率限制系统和储备功率使用导则

（经第 MEPC.375（80）号决议和第 MEPC.390（81）号决议修正的第 MEPC.335（76）号决议）

海上环境保护委员会，

忆及《国际海事组织公约》关于防止和控制船舶造成海洋污染国际公约赋予海上环境保护委员会职能的第 38（a）条，

注意到包含强制性目标型技术和操作措施以减少国际航运碳强度的《2021 年经修订的 MARPOL 附则 VI》已于 2022 年 11 月 1 日生效，

还注意到船舶可配备轴／发动机功率限制系统以满足 MARPOL 附则 VI 第 25 条的要求（Required EEXI），

进一步注意到本委员会在其第 76 届会议上以 MEPC.335（76）决议通过的《2021 年为符合现有船舶能效指数（EEXI）要求采用的轴／发动机功率限制系统和储备功率使用导则》，

注意到本委员会在其第 80 届会议上以 MEPC.375（80）决议通过的《2021 年为符合现有船舶能效指数（EEXI）要求采用的轴／发动机功率限制系统和储备功率使用导则》修正案，

在其第 81 届会议上，审议了《2021 年为符合现有船舶能效指数（EEXI）要求采用的轴／发动机功率限制系统和储备功率使用导则》的提议修正案，

1　**通过**《2021 年为符合现有船舶能效指数（EEXI）要求采用的轴／发动机功率限制系统和储备功率使用导则》修正案，其文本载于本决议附件；

2　**要求** MARPOL 附则 VI 的各缔约国和其他成员国政府使船长、海员、船东、船舶经营者和任何其他利益相关方注意到附件中的导则修正案。

ANNEX

2021 GUIDELINES ON THE SHAFT / ENGINE POWER LIMITATION SYSTEM TO COMPLY WITH THE EEXI REQUIREMENTS AND USE OF A POWER RESERVE

Table of contents

2021 年为符合现有船舶能效指数（EEXI）要求
采用的轴／发动机功率限制系统和储备功率使用导则

目录

0 General

The purpose of these Guidelines is to provide technical and operational conditions that the SHaPoLi / EPL system should satisfy in complying with the EEXI requirements and in using a power reserve for existing ships. However, noting that guidelines on the SHaPoLi / EPL system under EEDI framework on new ships are currently considered at the Committee, these guidelines under EEXI and EEDI may be consolidated into one set of guidelines as appropriate upon consideration by the Committee, taking into account circumstances and technical limitation of existing ships.

1 Definitions

1.1   *Shaft power* means the mechanical power transmitted by the propeller shaft to the propeller hub. It is the product of the shaft torque and the shaft rotational speed. In case of multiple propeller shafts, the shaft power means the sum of the power transmitted to all propeller shafts.

1.2   *Engine power* means the mechanical power transmitted from the engine to the propeller shaft. In case of multiple engines, the engine power means the sum of the power transmitted from the engines to the propeller shafts.

1.3   *Overridable Shaft Power Limitation (SHaPoLi) system* means a verified and approved system for the limitation of the maximum shaft power by technical means that can only be overridden by the ship's master or the officer in charge of navigational watch (OICNW) for the purpose of securing the safety of a ship or saving life at sea. (See figure 1 for an illustration of engine load diagram.)

1.4   *Overridable Engine Power Limitation (EPL) system* means a verified and approved system for the limitation of the maximum engine power by technical means that can only be overridden by the ship's master or OICNW for the purpose of securing the safety of a ship or saving life at sea. (See figure 1 for an illustration of engine load diagram.)

1.5   *Power reserve* means shaft / engine power above the limited power which cannot be used in normal operation unless in the case when SHaPoLi / EPL is unlimited for the purpose of securing the ship safety.

1.6   *MARPOL* means the International Convention for the Prevention of Pollution from Ships, 1973, as modified by the Protocols of 1978 and 1997 relating thereto, as amended.

1.7   For the purpose of these Guidelines, the definitions in MARPOL Annex VI, as amended, apply.

0 总则

本导则旨在提供技术和操作条件，这些技术和操作条件是 SHaPoLi/EPL 系统在满足 EEXI 要求时和对现有船使用储备功率时应满足的。但是，注意到 EEDI 框架下关于新船上 SHaPoLi/EPL 系统的导则目前正经本委员会审议，考虑到对现有船的环境和技术限制，经本委员会审议，可将在 EEXI 和 EEDI 框架下的这些导则综合成一套导则。

1 定义

1.1 轴功率系指由螺旋桨轴传递至螺旋桨桨毂的机械功率。该功率由轴扭矩和轴转速产生。对于多螺旋桨轴，轴功率系指传递至所有螺旋桨轴的功率总和。

1.2 发动机功率系指由发动机传递至螺旋桨轴的机械功率。对于多台发动机，发动机功率系指由这些发动机传递至螺旋桨轴的功率总和。

1.3 可越控轴功率限制（SHaPoLi）系统系指一种经验证和批准的、通过技术手段限制最大轴功率的系统，该限制仅能由船长或负责航行值班的高级船员（OICNW）为确保船舶安全或救护海上人命时予以越控（见图 1 发动机负荷图示例）。

1.4 可越控的发动机功率限制（EPL）系统系指一种经验证和批准的、通过技术手段限制最大发动机功率的系统，该限制仅能由船长或负责航行值班的高级船员（OICNW）为确保船舶安全或救护海上人命时予以越控（见图 1 发动机负荷图示例）。

1.5 储备功率系指在正常操作中不能使用的、限制功率之上的轴功率 / 发动机功率，为确保船舶安全而取消 SHaPoLi/EPL 限制时除外。

1.6 《防污公约》系指经修正的《经 1978 年和 1997 年议定书修订的 1973 年国际防止船舶造成污染公约》。

1.7 就本导则而言，经修正的《防污公约》附则 VI 中的定义适用。

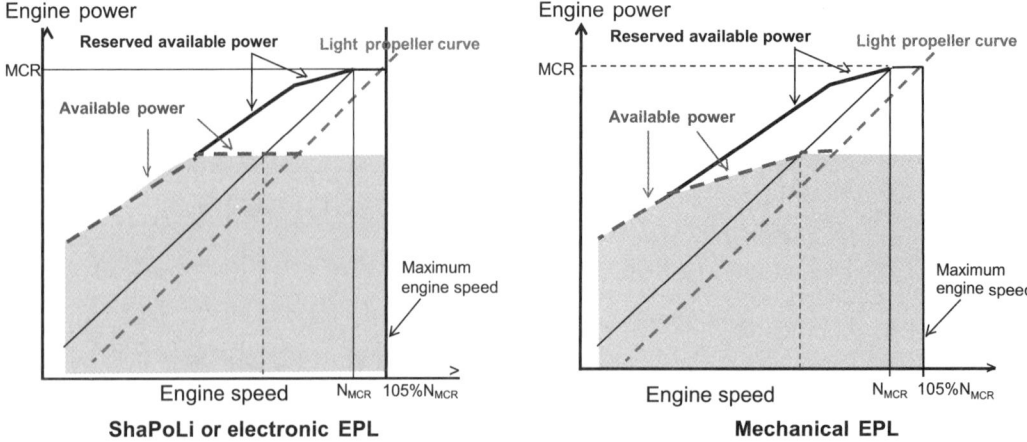

Figure 1: Engine load diagram on Shaft/Engine Power Limitation

2 Technical requirements for the SHaPoLi / EPL system

2.1 Required main systems

The SHaPoLi / EPL system should consist of the following main arrangements:

.1 SHaPoLi:

    .1 sensors for measuring the torque and rotational speed delivered to the propeller(s) of the ship. The system includes the amplifier and the analogue to the digital converter;

    .2 a data recording and processing device for tracking and calculation of the data as given in paragraph 2.2.5.1 of these Guidelines; and

    .3 a control unit for calculation and limitation of the power transmitted by the shaft to the propeller(s); if this control unit is independent from the engine automation the following should be satisfied:

        .1 override of limitation is indicated by giving an alarm on the bridge, clearly informing the ship's master or OICNW. Acceptance of this alarm by the master or OICNW is the deliberate action referred to in paragraph 2.2.1;

        .2 in case of exceedance, the ship's master or OICNW to manually reduce the power within the limit;

        .3 in case of deliberate use of power reserve, data recording to commence automatically;

        .4 data recording device as defined in section 2.1.1.2; and

        .5 in case of short-term unintentional exceedance of the power limit the system may inhibit the initiation of the exceedance alarm for up to a maximum of five (5) minutes.

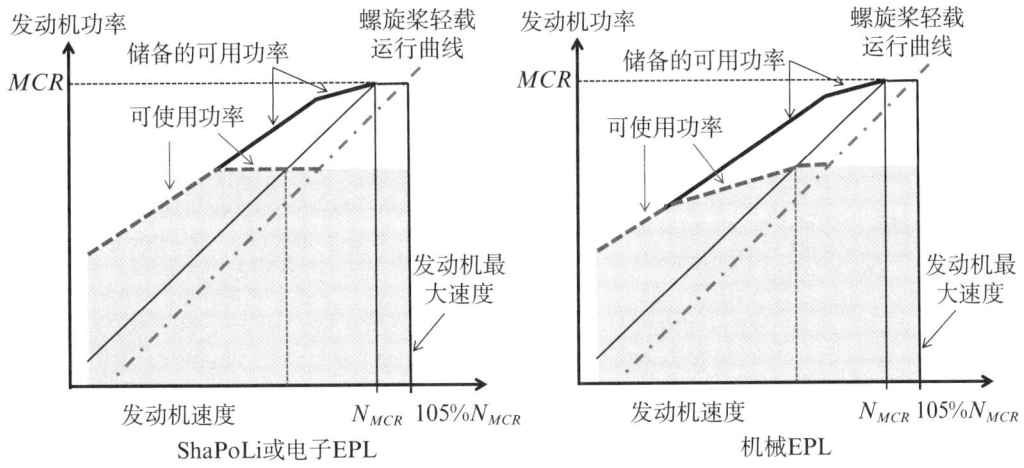

图 1　关于轴 / 发动机功率限制的发动机负荷图

2　SHaPoLi/EPL 系统技术要求

2.1　主系统

SHaPoLi/EPL 系统应包括下列主要布置：

.1　SHaPoLi：

    .1　用于测量传输至船舶螺旋桨的扭矩和转速的传感器。系统包括信号放大器和模拟 / 数字（A/D）转换器；

    .2　用于跟踪和计算本导则第 2.2.5.1 段中所列数据的数据记录和处理装置；

    .3　用于计算和限制由轴传递至螺旋桨的功率的控制单元；如果该控制单元独立于发动机的自动化系统，则应满足下列要求：

        .1　设有驾驶室报警提示传递功率超出限制的情况，以清楚地通知船长或负责航行值班的高级船员（OICNW）。船长或 OICNW 接受上述报警被视作是本导则 2.2.1 所述的有意使用储备功率的行为；

        .2　传递功率超过限制时，应可由船长或 OICNW 手动将其降至限制功率以内；

        .3　人为有意地使用储备功率时，应自动开始记录数据；

        .4　数据记录装置按本导则 2.1.1.2；和

        .5　对短期非人为有意地造成的传递功率超出限制的情况，可在最长不超过 5 分钟的时间内抑制超限报警的激发。

.2   EPL:

    .1   for the mechanically controlled engine, a sealing device which can physically lock the fuel index by using a mechanical stop screw sealed by wire or an equivalent device with governor limit setting so that the ship's crew cannot release the EPL without permission from the ship's master or OICNW, as shown in figure 2; or

    .2   for the electronically controlled engine, fuel index limiter which can electronically lock the fuel index or direct limitation of the power in the engine's control system so that the ship's crew cannot release the EPL without permission from the ship's master or OICNW; and

.3   where technically possible and feasible, the Sha/PoLi/EPL system should be controlled from the ships' bridge and not require attendance in the machinery space by ship's personnel.

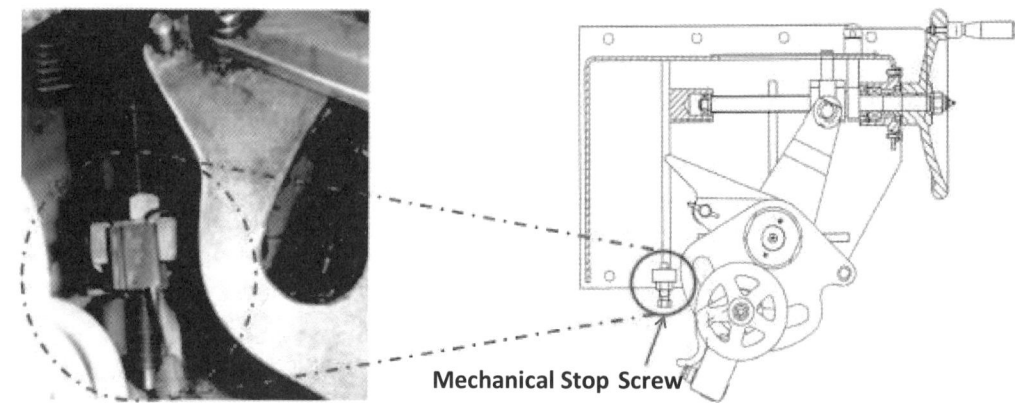

Mechanical stop screw sealed by wire   Engine side control console in the governor

Figure 2: Sealing of mechanical stop screw

2.2   General system requirements

2.2.1   The SHaPoLi / EPL system should be non-permanent but should require the deliberate action of the ship's master or OICNW to enable the use of unlimited shaft / engine power (power reserve) of the ship. For systems that use a Password/PIN to control access to the power reserve override, attention should be paid to ensure that the necessary Password/PIN is always available when override is required. In a scenario specified in regulation 3.1 of MARPOL Annex VI, which may endanger safe navigation of the ship, immediate use may be achieved by procedural arrangements for pre-emptive un-limiting the SHaPoLi/EPL system.

2.2.2   For SHaPoLi / EPL system for the electronically controlled engine, the control unit should inform the ship's master or OICNW clearly and conspicuously when the ship's shaft / engine power exceeds the limited shaft / engine power as stated in the Onboard Management Manual (OMM) for SHaPoLi / EPL or in any case of system malfunction.

.2 EPL：

　　.1 对于机械控制发动机，使用金属丝密封的机械止动螺钉或其他具有调速器限位功能的等效装置作为物理锁定燃油指数的密封装置，使得船员无法在未取得船长或 OICNW 许可的情况下释放 EPL，如图 2 所示；或

　　.2 对于电子控制发动机，能够电子锁定燃油指数的燃油指数限制器，或在发动机控制系统中直接限制功率从而使船员无法在未经船长或 OICNW 允许情况下释放 EPL；和

.3 如技术上可行，应从驾驶室控制 Sha/PoLi/EPL 系统，且不要求船上人员到达机器处所。

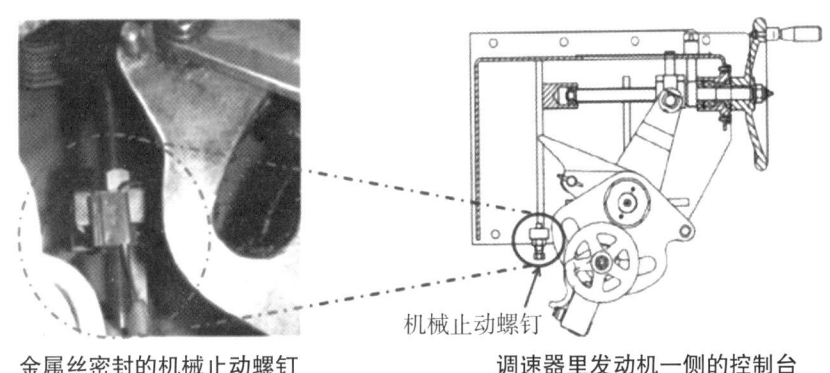

金属丝密封的机械止动螺钉　　　　　　机械止动螺钉　　调速器里发动机一侧的控制台

图 2　机械止动螺钉的密封

2.2　系统一般要求

2.2.1　SHaPoLi/EPL 系统应为非永久型，但船长或 OICNW 需经慎重考虑才能许可使用超出限制功率值部分的船舶轴 / 发动机功率（储备功率）。对于使用密码 /PIN 码管理越控的系统，应注意确保在需要越控时密码 /PIN 码随时可用。对于 MARPOL 附则 VI 第 3.1 条规定的可能危及船舶安全航行的情况，可通过程序性安排先发解除 SHaPoLi/EPL 系统的限制而实现储备功率即时可用。

2.2.2　对于电子控制发动机的 SHaPoLi/EPL 系统，控制单元应在船舶的轴 / 发动机功率超过 SHaPoLi/EPL 船上管理手册（OMM）中限定的轴 / 发动机功率或任何系统故障时，清楚、显著地通知船长或 OICNW。

2.2.3   For EPL for the mechanically controlled engine, the sealing device should either:

.1   visibly indicate removal of the sealing when the ship's engine power exceeds the limited engine power as stated in the OMM for EPL or in any case of system malfunction; or

.2   be equipped with other systems such as an alert-monitoring system which can indicate when the ship's engine power exceeds the limited engine power as stated in the OMM for EPL or in any case of system malfunction and recording the use of unlimited mode, verified by the Administration or the RO.

2.2.4   The SHaPoLi / EPL system (or each subsystem) should be tamper-proof.

2.2.5   The SHaPoLi / EPL system for the electronically controlled engine should indicate the following data during operation:

.1   for SHaPoLi, shaft rotational speed, shaft torque and shaft power (and total shaft power in case of multiple shaft arrangements) to be recorded constantly in unlimiting mode; or

.2   for EPL, a fuel index sealing system or power limitation system which can indicate and record the use of unlimited mode.

2.2.6   The procedure for SHaPoLi / EPL depends on the propulsion system and should be described in the OMM for SHaPoLi / EPL in accordance with section 4 of these Guidelines.

3   Use of a power reserve by un-limiting the shaft / engine power limitation

3.1   The use of a power reserve is only allowed for the purpose of securing the safety of a ship or saving life at sea, consistent with regulation 3.1 of MARPOL Annex VI (e.g. operating in adverse weather and ice-infested waters, participation in search and rescue operations, avoidance of pirates and engine maintenance). Use of a power reserve should not have adverse impact on the propeller, shaft and related systems. It is important that the ship master and OICNW are not restricted from exercising judgement to override the SHaPoLi / EPL when required for safety purposes. The authority for this should be clearly set out in the OMM and/or the Safety Management System manual, as appropriate.

3.2   Any use of a power reserve should be recorded in the record page of the OMM for SHaPoLi/EPL, signed by the master and should be kept on board. The record should include:

.1   ship type;

.2   IMO number;

.3   ship size in DWT and/or GT, as applicable;

.4   ship's limited shaft/engine power and ship's maximum unlimited shaft/engine power;

.5   position of the ship and timestamp when the power reserve was used;

.6   reason for using the power reserve;

2.2.3 对于机械控制的发动机的 EPL，密封装置应：

.1 当船舶发动机功率超过 EPLOMM 中限定的发动机功率或任何系统故障时，清楚得显示密封被移除；或

.2 配备其他经主管机关或被认可组织验证的系统，诸如报警监控系统，其可在船舶发动机功率超过 EPLOMM 中限定的发动机功率时或在任何系统故障时进行显示，并记录未限制模式的使用。

2.2.4 SHaPoLi/EPL 系统（或每个子系统）应为防篡改型。

2.2.5 电子控制发动机的 SHaPoLi/EPL 系统应在操作期间显示下列数据：

.1 对 SHaPoLi，应在未限制模式中不断记录轴的转速、轴扭矩和轴功率（及在多根轴布置情况下的总轴功率）；或

.2 对 EPL，燃油指数密封系统或功率限制系统可以显示和记录未限制模式使用情况。

2.2.6 SHaPoLi/EPL 程序取决于推进系统，并应按照本导则第 4 节在 SHaPoLi/EPL OMM 中进行描述。

3 通过取消轴 / 发动机功率限制使用储备功率

3.1 仅允许在符合《防污公约》附则 VI 第 3.1 条为保障船舶安全或救护海上人命（例如：在恶劣天气和冰区航行、参与搜救、躲避海盗和发动机维护）时使用储备功率。使用储备功率不应对螺旋桨、轴和相关系统产生不利影响。出于安全目的，船长和 OICNW 可以不受限制地判断是否越控 SHaPoLi/EPL，这点非常重要。这个权限应视情在 OMM 和 / 或安全管理手册中清楚写明。

3.2 任何对储备功率的使用应记录在 SHaPoLi/EPL OMM 的记录页，由船长签字并保留在船上。记录应包括：

.1 船型；

.2 IMO 编号；

.3 船舶载重吨和 / 或总吨，如适用；

.4 船舶限制的轴 / 发动机功率和船舶未限制的最大轴功率 / 发动机功率；

.5 使用储备功率时的船舶位置和时间标记；

.6 使用储备功率的理由；

.7   Beaufort number and wave height or ice condition in case of using the power reserve under adverse weather condition;

.8   supporting evidence (e.g. expected weather condition) in case of using the power reserve for avoidance action;

.9   records from the SHaPoLi/EPL system for the electronically controlled engine during the use of the power reserve; and

.10   position of the ship and timestamp when the power limit was reactivated or replaced.

Supporting evidence and records as indicated in sub-paragraphs 3.2.8 and 3.2.9 above should be submitted to the Administration or RO for verification and do not need to be submitted to the Organization as part of annual submission of use of a power reserve in accordance with paragraph 3.4.

3.3   The use of the power reserve should be distinguished from the precautionary un-limiting of a shaft or engine power limitation system. Where an EPL/SHaPoLi override is activated pre-emptively when hazards are anticipated, but the power reserve is not subsequently used, this event should be recorded in the bridge and engine-room logbooks. The engine-room logbook should record power used during the period when the override was activated. The EPL/SHaPoLi should be reset as soon as possible, and details of the reset should also be recorded in the bridge and engine-room logbooks.

3.4   In case of having used a power reserve, the ship should without delay notify its Administration or RO responsible for issuing the relevant certificate and the competent authority of the relevant port of destination with the information recorded in accordance with paragraph 3.2. On an annual basis by 30 June every year, the Administration should report to the IMO Secretariat uses of a power reserve over a 12-month period from 1 January to 31 December for the preceding calendar year with the information recorded in accordance with paragraph 3.2, using the format as set out in the appendix to these guidelines.

3.5   Once the risks have been mitigated, the ship should be operated below the certified level of engine power under the SHaPoLi / EPL. The SHaPoLi / EPL system should be reactivated or replaced by the crew immediately after the risks have been prevented and the ship can be safely operated with the limited shaft / engine power. The reactivation or replacement of the SHaPoLi / EPL system should be confirmed (e.g. validation of mechanical sealing) with supporting evidence (e.g. engine power log, photo taken at the occasion of resetting the mechanical sealing) by the Administration or the RO at the earliest opportunity.

3.6   Any defect of the SHaPoLi / EPL system should be reported to the Administration or RO responsible for issuing the relevant certificate in accordance with regulation 5.6 of MARPOL Annex VI.

3.7   The port State control officers should inspect whether the SHaPoLi / EPL system has been properly installed and used in accordance with the IEE Certificate and the OMM as described in section 4 of these Guidelines. If overriding of the SHaPoLi / EPL without proper notification in accordance with paragraph 3.3 of these Guidelines has been detected, the reactivation or replacement of the SHaPoLi / EPL should be immediately conducted in the presence of the Administration or the RO at the port.

.7 在恶劣天气条件下使用储备功率时的蒲福风级和波高或冰情；

.8 因避让行动使用储备功率的支撑证据（例如：预期的天气条件）；

.9 使用储备功率时来自 SHaPoLi/EPL 系统对电子控制发动机的记录；和

.10 功率限制被重启或重置时船舶的位置和时间标记。

应将上述第 3.2.8 和 3.2.9 段所述的支撑证据和记录提交给主管机关或被认可组织进行验证，但无须作为按照第 3.4 段每年提交给本组织的储备功率使用记录的一部分。

3.3 预防性解除轴 / 发动机功率限制应与使用储备功率情况相区分。因预期危险而先发解除 EPL/ShaPoLi 功率限制但后续并未使用储备功率的情况，应在航行日志和机舱日志中予以记录。机舱日志中应记录在越控期间功率的使用情况。EPL/ShaPoLi 应尽快重置，重置的详情也应记录在航行日志和机舱日志中。

3.4 如已使用储备功率，船舶应毫不迟延地将根据第 3.2 段所记录的信息通知其负责签发相关证书的主管机关或被认可组织和相关目的港主管当局。每年 6 月 30 日之前，主管机关应向 IMO 秘书处报告在前一日历年 12 个月期间（1 月 1 日至 12 月 31 日）的储备功率使用情况，报告应按本导则的附录格式并包含根据第 3.2 段所记录的信息。

3.5 风险一旦降低，船舶应在 SHaPoLi/EPL 下以低于核准的发动机功率运行。在风险已经防止且船舶能以限定的轴功率 / 发动机功率安全操作后，船员应立即重启或替换 SHaPoLi/EPL 系统。SHaPoLi/EPL 系统的重启或替换应由主管机关或被认可组织通过支持性证据（例如：发动机功率记录、重置机械密封现场的照片）尽早确认（例如：确认机械密封）。

3.6 根据《防污公约》附则 VI 第 5.6 条，SHaPoLi/EPL 系统的任何缺陷应向负责签发相关证书的主管机关或被认可组织报告。

3.7 港口国监督官员应检查是否按照 IEE 证书和本导则第 4 节所述 OMM 正确安装和使用 SHaPoLi/EPL 系统。如发现按照本导则第 3.3 段要求对 SHaPoLi/EPL 进行越控而没有进行适当通知，应在该港口有主管机关或被认可组织在场的情况下立即重启或替换 SHaPoLi/EPL。

4 Onboard Management Manual (OMM) for SHaPoLi / EPL

4.1   The SHaPoLi / EPL system should be accompanied by the OMM for SHaPoLi / EPL that should be permanently on board the ship for inspection.

4.2   The OMM for SHaPoLi / EPL should be verified by the Administration or the RO after a survey verifying the ship's attained EEXI, as required by regulation 5.4 of MARPOL Annex VI.

4.3   The OMM for SHaPoLi / EPL should, as a minimum, include:

    .1   SHaPoLi:

        .1   a technical description of the main system as specified in section 2 of these guidelines as well as relevant auxiliary systems;

        .2   identification of key components of the system by manufacturer, model/type, serial number and other details as necessary;

        .3   description of a verification procedure demonstrating that the system is in compliance with the technical description in accordance with items .1 and .2;

        .4   the maximum shaft power for which the unit is designed;

        .5   service, maintenance and calibration requirements of sensors according to sensor manufacturer and a description how to monitor the appropriateness of the calibration intervals, if applicable;

        .6   the SHaPoLi record book for the recording of service, maintenance and calibration of the system;

        .7   the description how the shaft power can be limited and unlimited and how this is displayed by the control unit as required by paragraph 2.2.5 of these Guidelines;

        .8   the description of how the controller limits the power delivered to the propeller shaft;

        .9   the identification of responsibilities;

        .10   procedures for notification of the use of power reserve and the detections of malfunctions of the system in accordance with paragraphs 3.4 and 3.5 of these Guidelines;

        .11   time required for un-limiting the SHaPoLi; and

        .12   procedures for survey of the SHaPoLi system by the Administration/RO.

4 SHaPoLi/EPL 船上管理手册（OMM）

4.1 SHaPoLi/EPL 系统应配备 SHaPoLi/EPL OMM，该手册应永久保留在船上以备检查。

4.2 SHaPoLi/EPL OMM 应经主管机关或被认可组织在根据《防污公约》附则 VI 第 5.4 条进行检验以验证船舶达到的 EEXI 之后予以验证。

4.3 SHaPoLi/EPL OMM 应至少包括：

.1 SHaPoLi：

　.1 本导则第 2 节规定的主系统和相关辅助系统的技术说明；

　.2 制造商对系统关键部件的识别，型号 / 类型，序列号和其他必要细节；

　.3 证明系统符合第 .1 和 .2 项技术说明的验证程序的描述；

　.4 该装置的设计最大轴功率；

　.5 传感器制造商对传感器运行、维护和校准的要求和如何监控校准间隔适当性的描述（如适用）；

　.6 记录系统运行、维护和校准的 SHaPoLi 记录簿；

　.7 对如何限制和取消轴功率限制以及控制单元如何按本导则第 2.2.5 段要求进行显示的描述；

　.8 对控制器如何限制传递至螺旋桨轴的功率的描述；

　.9 责任的确定；

　.10 按照本导则第 3.4 和 3.5 段要求对储备功率的使用和发现系统故障进行通知的程序；

　.11 取消 SHaPoLi 限制所需时间；和

　.12 主管机关 / 被认可组织检验 SHaPoLi 系统的程序。

.2 EPL:

    .1   rated installed power (MCR) or motor output (MPP) and engine speed (N_{MCR});

    .2   limited installed power (MCR_{lim}) or motor output (MPP_{lim}) and engine speed ($N_{MCR,lim}$);

    .3   technical description of the EPL system;

    .4   method for sealing the EPL (mechanically controlled engine);

    .5   method for locking and monitoring the EPL (electronically controlled engine);

    .6   procedures and methods for releasing the EPL;

    .7   time required for unlimiting the EPL;

    .8   procedures for survey of the EPL system by the Administration/RO;

    .9   procedure for the report on release of the EPL; and

    .10   administrator of the EPL system.

5   Demonstration of compliance of the SHaPoLi / EPL system

5.1   The demonstration of compliance of the SHaPoLi / EPL system should be verified by an appropriate survey in accordance with regulation 5.4 of MARPOL Annex VI for the verification of the ship's EEXI according to regulation 23. The survey should include the verification and validation of the system by addressing the following items:

    .1   the verification of compliance of the system with the OMM for SHaPoLi / EPL,

    .2   the verification of compliance of the system with the specifications set out in section 2 of these Guidelines; and

    .3   the verification of the OMM for SHaPoLi / EPL that the OMM for SHaPoLi / EPL is in compliance with the specifications set out in section 4 of these Guidelines.

5.2   In cases where the SHaPoLi / EPL system is applied and no changes are made to NO_x critical settings and/or components[*] outside what is allowed by the engine technical file as defined in the 2008 NO_x Technical Code (NTC 2008), engine re-certification is not needed.

5.3   In cases where the SHaPoLi / EPL system is applied and the NO_x critical settings and/or components are altered beyond what is allowed by the engine technical file as defined in NTC 2008, the engine needs to be re-certified. In such a case, for an EEDI-certified ship where the SHaPoLi / EPL system is applied at a power below that required by regulation 24.5 of MARPOL Annex VI (minimum power requirement), the certified engine power should be at the power satisfying that requirement.

---

[*]   NOx critical parameters and components are cisted in NOx Techrical File wnder the section "Components, setting and operating values of the engine which may influence its Nox emission".

.2 EPL：

 .1 额定安装功率（MCR）或电动机输出功率（MPP）和发动机速度（N_{MCR}）；

 .2 限定的安装功率（MCR_{lim}）或电动机输出功率（MPP_{lim}）和发动机速度（$N_{MCR,lim}$）；

 .3 EPL 系统技术说明；

 .4 EPL 密封方法（机械控制发动机）；

 .5 锁定和监控 EPL 的方法（电子控制发动机）；

 .6 释放 EPL 的程序和方法；

 .7 取消 EPL 限制所需时间；

 .8 主管机关 / 被认可组织检验 EPL 系统的程序；

 .9 释放 EPL 时的报告程序；和

 .10 EPL 系统管理员。

5 SHaPoLi/EPL 系统的符合证明

5.1 应通过按《防污公约》附则 VI 第 5.4 条规定的，为按第 23 条规定验证船舶 EEXI 而进行的检验对 SHaPoLi/EPL 系统的符合证明进行验证。检验应针对下列各项对系统进行验证和确认：

 .1 验证系统符合 SHaPoLi/EPL OMM；

 .2 验证系统符合本导则第 2 节中的规定；

 .3 验证 SHaPoLi/EPL OMM 符合本导则第 4 节中的规定。

5.2 当应用了 SHaPoLi/EPL 系统且《2008 年氮氧化物技术规则》（NTC 2008）中定义的发动机技术案卷所允许的 NO_x 关键设置和 / 或部件[*]外部没有发生改变，则无须对发动机重新认证。

5.3 当应用了 SHaPoLi/EPL 系统且对 NO_x 关键设置和 / 或部件的改变超出了《2008 年氮氧化物技术规则》中定义的发动机技术案卷所允许的范围，则需对发动机重新认证。这种情况下，一艘经 EEDI 认证的船舶如应用 SHaPoLi/EPL 系统且限制功率低于《防污公约》附则 VI 第 24.5 条要求的功率（最小功率要求），经认证的发动机功率应满足最小功率要求。

---

[*] NO_x 关键参数和部件列于 NO_x 技术案卷的"影响发动机 NO_x 排放的部件、设置和操作值"一节中。

6   Additional information to be provided, as applicable

The following documents described in the appendices to *Recommendation on the Provision and Display of Manoeuvring Information on Board Ships* (annex, resolution A.601(15)) should be updated to include the manoeuvring characteristics of the ship when the ship has all shaft and engine power available, and when shaft or engine power has been limited:

    .1   the Pilot card;
    .2   the wheelhouse poster; and
    .3   the manoeuvring booklet.

6 应提供的额外信息，如适用

船舶在其所有轴和发动机功率可用时和其轴或发动机功率受限时的操纵特性，应在《关于船上配备和显示操纵资料的建议》（A.601（15）决议）附录中所述的下列文件内予以更新：

.1 引航员卡；

.2 驾驶室告示；和

.3 操纵手册。

FORMAT FOR REPORTING OF EPL/SHAPOLI OVERRIDE ACTIVATION, USE OF A POWER RESERVE AND REACTIVATION OF EPL/SHAPOLI

Ship type:
IMO number:
DWT:
GT:
Maximum unlimited shaft/engine power (kW):
Limited shaft/engine power (kW):

Table 1

Date (dd/mm/yyyy)	Time (UTC)	Position		Override activation/Reactivation	Reason for using the power reserve[1]	Beaufort number[2]	Wave height[2]	Ice condition[2]
		Longitude	Latitude					

---

[1] Reason for override (select at least one option): .1 operating in adverse weather
  .2 operating in ice-infested waters
  .3 participation in search and rescue operations
  .4 avoidance of pirates
  .5 engine maintenance
  .6 description of other reasons consistent with regulation 3.1 of MARPOL Annex VI

[2] Beaufort number and wave height or ice condition, as applicable, to be entered in case of using the power reserve under adverse weather condition.

***

EPL/SHaPoLi 越控启动、储备功率使用和 EPL/SHaPoLi 重启的报告格式

船型：
IMO 编号：
总吨：
载重吨：
未限制的最大轴／发动机功率（kW）：
限制的最大轴／发动机功率（kW）：

表 1

日期（年／月／日）	时间（UTC）	位置		越控启动／重启	使用储备功率的理由[1]	蒲福风级[2]	波高[2]	冰情[2]
		经度	纬度					

1 越控理由（至少选择一项）：

　.1 在恶劣天气条件下操作
　.2 在有冰水域操作
　.3 参与搜救作业
　.4 躲避海盗
　.5 发动机维护保养
　.6 其他符合《防污公约》附则 VI 第 3.1 条规定的理由描述

2 如果在恶劣天气条件下使用储备功率，应填写蒲福风级和波高或冰情（如适用）。

***

**2021 GUIDANCE ON TREATMENT OF INNOVATIVE ENERGY EFFICIENCY
TECHNOLOGIES FOR CALCULATION AND VERIFICATION
OF THE ATTAINED EEDI AND EEXI**

1   The Marine Environment Protection Committee, at its seventy-seventh session (22 to 26 November 2021), approved the *2021 Guidance on treatment of innovative energy efficiency technologies for calculation and verification of the attained EEDI and EEXI*, as set out in the annex.

2   Member Governments are invited to bring the annexed Guidance to the attention of their Administrations, industry, relevant shipping organizations, shipping companies and other stakeholders concerned.

3   The Committee agreed to keep this Guidance under review in light of experience gained in its application.

4   This circular supersedes MEPC.1/Circ.815.

***

2021 年用于计算和验证 Attained EEDI 和 EEXI 的创新能效技术处理导则

1 海上环境保护委员会在其 77 届会议（2021 年 11 月 22 日至 26 日）上，批准了《2021 年用于计算和验证 Attained EEDI 和 EEXI 的创新能效技术处理导则》，文本载于附件。

2 请各成员国政府使其主管机关、业界、相关航运组织、航运公司和其他利益相关方注意附件中的本导则。

3 本委员会同意根据本导则应用中获得的经验保持对本导则的评审。

4 本通函取代 MEPC.1/Circ.815 通函。

***

ANNEX

2021 GUIDANCE ON TREATMENT OF INNOVATIVE ENERGY EFFICIENCY TECHNOLOGIES FOR CALCULATION AND VERIFICATION OF THE ATTAINED EEDI AND EEXI

TABLE OF CONTENTS

附件

2021 年用于计算和验证 Attained EEDI 和 EEXI 的创新能效技术处理导则

目　录

1 通则

2 定义

3 创新能效技术的分类

4 创新能效技术效果的计算和验证

1   General

1.1   The purpose of this guidance is to assist manufacturers, shipbuilders, shipowners, verifiers and other interested parties relating to Energy Efficiency Design Index (EEDI) and Energy Efficiency Existing Ship Index (EEXI) of ships to treat innovative energy efficiency technologies for calculation and verification of the attained EEDI, in accordance with regulations 5, 6, 7, 8, 9 and 20 of Annex VI to MARPOL. Although the term EEDI only is used through the whole guidance, it applies to both the EEDI and the EEXI calculations, as applicable.

1.2   There are EEDI Calculation Guidelines and EEDI Survey Guidelines. This guidance does not intend to supersede those guidelines but provides the methodology of calculation, survey and certification of innovative energy efficiency technologies, which are not covered by those guidelines. In the case that there are inconsistencies between this guidance and these guidelines, those guidelines should take precedence.

1.3   This guidance might not provide sufficient measures of calculation and verification for ships with diesel-electric propulsion, turbine propulsion and hybrid propulsion systems on the grounds that the attained EEDI Formula shown in EEDI Calculation Guidelines may not be able to apply to such propulsion systems.

1.4   The guidance should be reviewed for the inclusion of new innovative technologies not yet covered by the guidance.

1.5   The guidance also should be reviewed, after accumulating the experiences of each innovative technology, in order to make it more robust and effective, using the feedback from actual operating data. Therefore, it is advisable that the effect of each innovative technology in actual operating conditions should be monitored and collected for future improvement of this guidance document.

2   Definitions

2.1   *EEDI Calculation Guidelines* means *2018 guidelines on the method of calculation of the attained energy efficiency design index (EEDI) for new ships* (resolution MEPC.308(73), as amended).

2.2   *EEDI Survey Guidelines* means *2014 guidelines on survey and certification of the energy efficiency design index (EEDI)* (resolution MEPC.254(67), as amended by resolution MEPC.261(68) and resolution MEPC.309(73)).

2.3 P_p is the propulsion power and is defined as ΣP_{ME} (In case where shaft motor(s) are installed, $\Sigma P_{ME} + \Sigma P_{PTI(i),shaft}$, as shown in paragraph 2.2.5.3 of EEDI Calculation Guidelines).

2.4   In addition to the above, definitions of the words in this guidance are the same as those of MARPOL Annex VI, EEDI Calculation Guidelines and EEDI Survey Guidelines.

3   Categorizing of Innovative Energy Efficiency Technologies

3.1   Innovative energy efficiency technologies are allocated to category (A), (B) and (C), depending on their characteristics and effects to the EEDI formula. Furthermore, innovative energy efficiency technologies of category (B) and (C) are categorized to two sub-categories (category (B-1) and (B-2), and (C-1) and (C-2), respectively).

1 通则

1.1 本导则旨在协助制造商、船厂、船东、验证方和船舶能效设计指数（EEDI）和现有船能效指数（EEXI）的其他相关方，按 MARPOL 附则 Ⅵ 第 5、6、7、8、9 和 20 条的规定在进行 Attained EEDI 计算和验证时考虑创新能效技术。尽管在整个导则中只使用了 EEDI，但其按适用情况对 EEDI 和 EEXI 计算都适用。

1.2 EEDI 计算指南和 EEDI 检验指南已予发布。本导则无意取代这些指南，而是补充有关创新技术能效的计算、检验和发证方法。如本导则和这些指南之间存在不一致，应以这些指南的要求为准。

1.3 考虑到 EEDI 计算指南中的 AttainedEEDI 公式不适用于柴电推进系统、涡轮机推进系统和混合动力推进系统，本导则也未提供这些推进系统船舶的计算和验证方法。

1.4 应对本导则进行评审，以纳入本导则尚未考虑的新技术。

1.5 每项创新技术积累了经验后，还应采用实际运行数据的反馈对本导则进行评估，使其更为可靠有效。因此，应在实际运行条件下监测和收集各项创新技术的效果，以供完善本指导性文件。

2 定义

2.1 *EEDI 计算指南系指《2018 年新船 Attained EEDI 计算方法指南》*（经修正的 MEPC.308（73）决议）。

2.2 *EEDI 检验指南系指《2014 年能效设计指数（EEDI）检验和发证指南》*（经 MEPC.261（68）决议和 MEPC.309（73）决议修正的 MEPC.254（67）决议）。

2.3 P_P 为推进功率，其定义为 ΣP_{ME}（如安装了轴带电动机，则为 EEDI 计算指南 2.2.5.3 所列的 $\Sigma P_{ME} + \Sigma P_{PTI(i),shaft}$）。

2.4 除上述外，本导则中用词的定义与 MARPOL 附则 Ⅵ、EEDI 计算指南和 EEDI 检验指南中的相同。

3 创新能效技术的分类

3.1 创新能效技术根据其特点及对 EEDI 公式的作用，分为 A、B 和 C 三类。而且，B 类和 C 类创新能效技术还分别进一步细分出两个子类（B-1 类和 B-2 类以及 C-1 类和 C-2 类）。

Category (A): Technologies that shift the power curve, which results in the change of combination of P_P and V_{ref}: e.g. when V_{ref} is kept constant, P_P will be reduced and when P_P is kept constant, V_{ref} will be increased.

Category (B): Technologies that reduce the propulsion power, P_P, at V_{ref}, but do not generate electricity. The saved energy is counted as P_{eff}.

> **Category (B-1):** Technologies which can be used at any time during the operation and thus the availability factor (f_{eff}) should be treated as 1.00.

> **Category (B-2):** Technologies which can be used at their full output only under limited condition. The setting of availability factor (f_{eff}) should be less than 1.00.

Category (C): Technologies that generate electricity. The saved energy is counted as P_{AEeff}.

> **Category (C-1):** Technologies which can be used at any time during the operation and thus the availability factor (f_{eff}) should be treated as 1.00.

> **Category (C-2):** Technologies which can be used at their full output only under limited condition. The setting of availability factor (f_{eff}) should be less than 1.00.

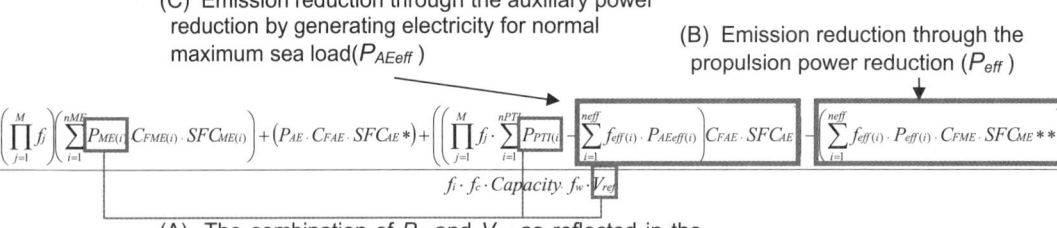

(C) Emission reduction through the auxiliary power reduction by generating electricity for normal maximum sea load(P_{AEeff})

(B) Emission reduction through the propulsion power reduction (P_{eff})

(A) The combination of P_P and V_{ref} as reflected in the power curve (knot-kW curve)

Innovative Energy Efficiency Technologies				
Reduction of Main Engine Power			Reduction of Auxiliary Power	
Category A	Category B-1	Category B-2	Category C-1	Category C-2
Cannot be separated from overall performance of the vessel	Can be treated separately from the overall performance of the vessel		Effective at all time	Depending on ambient environment
	$f_{eff}=1$	$f_{eff}<1$	$f_{eff}=1$	$f_{eff}<1$
– low friction coating – bare optimization – rudder resistance – propeller design	– hull air lubrication system (air cavity via air injection to reduce ship resistance) (can be switched off)	– wind assistance (sails, Flettner-Rotors, kites)	– waste heat recovery system (exhaust gas heat recovery and conversion to electric power)	– photovoltaic cells

A 类：改变功率曲线的技术，导致 P_P 和 V_{ref} 的组合的变化：如当 V_{ref} 保持不变时，P_P 减小，而当 P_P 保持不变时，V_{ref} 增大。

B 类：减小推进功率 V_{ref} 时的 P_P，但不产生电力的技术。节约的能量计为 P_{eff}。

B–1 类：　操作期间可在任何时候使用的技术，因而可用系数（f_{eff}）应视为 1.00。

B–2 类：　仅在受限条件下全输出时才可使用的技术。可用系数（f_{eff}）的设定值应小于 1.00。

C 类：产生电力的技术。节约的能量计为 P_{AEeff}。

C–1 类：　操作期间可在任何时候使用的技术，因而可用系数（f_{eff}）应视为 1.00。

C–2 类：　仅在受限条件下全输出时才可使用的技术。可用系数（f_{eff}）的设定值应小于 1.00。

(C) 最大正常波浪载荷（P_{AEeff}）条件下通过发电降低辅助功率来减少排放。

(B) 通过降低推进功率（P_{eff}）来减少排放

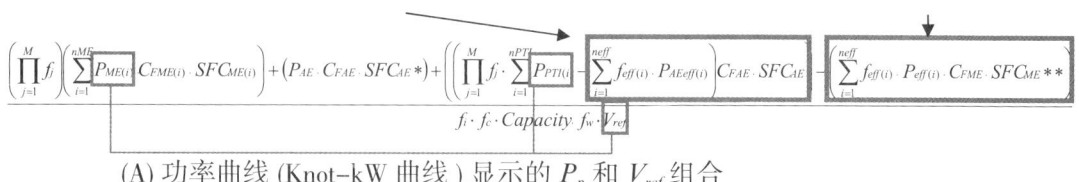

(A) 功率曲线 (Knot–kW 曲线) 显示的 P_p 和 V_{ref} 组合

创新能效技术				
主机功率的降低			辅助功率的降低	
A 类	B–1 类	B–2 类	C–1 类	C–2 类
不能与船舶的总体性能分开	能与船舶的总体性能分开处理		随时有效	根据周边环境
	$f_{eff}=1$	$f_{eff}<1$	$f_{eff}=1$	$f_{eff}<1$
—低摩擦涂层 —裸层优化 —舵阻力 —螺旋桨设计	—船体空气润滑系统（通过喷射空气形成气泡来减少船舶阻力）（可以关闭）	—风力辅助（船帆、旋筒、筝帆）	—余热回收系统（废气热量回收并转换为电力）	—光伏电池

4 Calculation and Verification of effects of Innovative Energy Efficiency Technologies

4.1 General

4.1.1 The evaluation of the benefit of any innovative technology is to be carried out in conjunction with the hull form and propulsion system with which it is intended to be used. Results of model tests or sea trials of the innovative technology in conjunction with different hull forms or propulsion systems may not be applicable.

4.2 Category (A) technology

4.2.1 Innovative energy efficiency technologies in category (A) affect P_P and/or V_{ref} and their effects cannot be measured in isolation. Therefore, these effects should not be calculated nor certified in isolation in this guidance but should be treated as a part of vessel in EEDI Calculation Guidelines and EEDI Survey Guidelines.

4.3 Category (B) technology

4.3.1 The effects of innovative energy technologies in category (B) are expressed as P_{eff} which would be multiplied by C_{FME} and SFC_{ME} (in the case of $P_{PTI(i)} > 0$, the average weighted value of ($SFC_{ME} \cdot C_{FME}$) and ($SFC_{AE} \cdot C_{FAE}$)) and f_{eff}, and then be deducted from the EEDI formula. In the case of category (B-1) technology, f_{eff} is 1.00.

4.3.2 Guidance on calculation and verification of effects of Category (B) innovative technologies is given in annex 1.

4.4 Category (C) technology

4.4.1 The effects of innovative energy technologies in category (C) are expressed as P_{AEeff} which would be multiplied by C_{FAE}, SFC_{AE} and f_{eff}, and then be deducted from the EEDI formula. In the case of category (C-1) technology, f_{eff} is 1.00.

4.4.2 Guidance on calculation and verification of effects of Category (C) innovative technologies is given in annex 2.

4.5 Average weighted value in the case of $P_{PTI(i)} > 0$

4.5.1 In the case of $P_{PTI(i)} > 0$, both Category (B) and Category (C) technologies might deduct the value of $P_{PTI(i)}$. In such case, following values are to be used for average weighted value in calculating $\Sigma(f_{eff(i)} \cdot P_{eff(i)} \cdot C_F \cdot SFC)$ in attained EEDI formula:

> For shaft power(s):
> $(\Sigma P_{PTI(i),shaft} - \cdot \Sigma P_{AEeff} \cdot \eta_{GEN} \cdot \eta_{PTI(i)}) / (\Sigma P_{ME(i)} + \Sigma P_{PTI(i),shaft} - \cdot \Sigma P_{AEeff} \cdot \eta_{GEN} \cdot \eta_{PTI(i)})$,
> where, if $(\Sigma P_{PTI(i),shaft} - \cdot \Sigma P_{AEeff} \cdot \eta_{GEN} \cdot \eta_{PTI(i)})$ is taken negative value, the value $(\Sigma P_{PTI(i),shaft} - \cdot \Sigma P_{AEeff} \cdot \eta_{GEN} \cdot \eta_{PTI(i)})$ should be fixed to zero; and

> For main engine(s):
> $\Sigma P_{ME(i)} / (\Sigma P_{ME(i)} + \Sigma P_{PTI(i),shaft} - \cdot \Sigma P_{AEeff} \cdot \eta_{GEN} \cdot \eta_{PTI(i)})$,
> where, if $\Sigma P_{PTI(i),shaft} - \cdot \Sigma P_{AEeff} \cdot \eta_{GEN} \cdot \eta_{PTI(i)}$ is taken negative value, the value $(\Sigma P_{PTI(i),shaft} - \cdot \Sigma P_{AEeff} \cdot \eta_{GEN} \cdot \eta_{PTI(i)})$ should be fixed to zero.

4 创新能效技术效果的计算和验证

4.1 一般规定

4.1.1 应结合拟使用的船体形式和推进系统，对创新技术的效益进行评价。创新技术结合不同船体形式和推进系统所进行的模型试验或试航的结果可能并不适用。

4.2 A 类技术

4.2.1 A 类创新能效技术影响 P_P 和 / 或 V_{ref}，而且其效果不能单独测量。因此，该类技术的效果不应在本导则中单独予以计算或核准，而应作为 EEDI 计算指南和 EEDI 检验指南中船舶的一个部分处理。

4.3 B 类技术

4.3.1 B 类创新能效技术的效果以 P_{eff} 表示，乘以 C_{FME} 和 SFC_{ME}（如果 $P_{PTI(i)}$ >0，则为（$SFC_{ME} \cdot C_{FME}$）和（$SFC_{AE} \cdot C_{FAE}$）的平均加权值）和 f_{eff} 后，再从 EEDI 公式中扣除。对 B–1 类技术，f_{eff} 取 1.00。

4.3.2 B 类创新技术效果的计算和验证方法见附件 1。

4.4 C 类技术

4.4.1 C 类创新能效技术的效果以 P_{AEeff} 表示，乘以 C_{FAE}、SFC_{AE} 和 f_{eff} 后，再从 EEDI 公式中扣除。对 C–1 类技术，f_{eff} 取 1.00。

4.4.2 C 类创新技术效果的计算和验证指导见附件 2。

4.5 $P_{PTI(i)}$ >0 时平均加权值

4.5.1 如 $P_{PTI(i)}$ >0，B 类和 C 类技术都可以扣除 $P_{PTI(i)}$ 值，在此情况下，应采用下列数值作为 Attained EEDI 公式中计算 $\Sigma(f_{eff(i)} \cdot P_{eff(i)} \cdot C_F \cdot SFC)$ 的平均加权值：

对轴功率：

$(\Sigma P_{PTI(i),shaft} - \cdot \Sigma P_{AEeff} \cdot \eta_{GEN} \cdot \eta_{PTI(i)}) / (\Sigma P_{ME(i)} + \Sigma P_{PTI(i),shaft} - \cdot \Sigma P_{AEeff} \cdot \eta_{GEN} \cdot \eta_{PTI(i)})$，

$(\Sigma P_{PTI(i),shaft} - \cdot \Sigma P_{AEeff} \cdot \eta_{GEN} \cdot \eta_{PTI(i)}) / (\Sigma P_{ME(i)} + \Sigma P_{PTI(i),shaft} - \cdot \Sigma P_{AEeff} \cdot \eta_{GEN} \cdot \eta_{PTI(i)})$，

式中，如 $\Sigma P_{PTI(i),shaft} - \cdot \Sigma P_{AEeff} \cdot \eta_{GEN} \cdot \eta_{PTI(i)}$ 为负值，则 $\Sigma P_{PTI(i),shaft} - \cdot \Sigma P_{AEeff} \cdot \eta_{GEN} \cdot \eta_{PTI(i)}$ 应取 0；和

对主机：

$\Sigma P_{ME(i)} / (\Sigma P_{ME(i)} + \Sigma P_{PTI(i),shaft} - \Sigma P_{AEeff} \cdot \eta_{GEN} \cdot \eta_{PTI(i)})$，

式中，如 $\Sigma P_{PTI(i),shaft} - \Sigma P_{AEeff} \cdot \eta_{GEN} \cdot \eta_{PTI(i)}$ 为负值，则 $\Sigma P_{PTI(i),shaft} - \cdot \Sigma P_{AEeff} \cdot \eta_{GEN} \cdot \eta_{PTI(i)}$ 应取 0。

GUIDANCE ON CALCULATION AND VERIFICATION OF EFFECTS OF CATEGORY (B) INNOVATIVE TECHNOLOGIES

1 AIR LUBRICATION SYSTEM (CATEGORY (B-1))

1.1 Summary of innovative energy efficient technology

1.1.1 An air lubrication system is one of the innovative energy efficiency technologies. Ship frictional resistance can be reduced by covering the ship surface with air bubbles, which is injected from the fore part of the ship bottom by using blowers, etc.

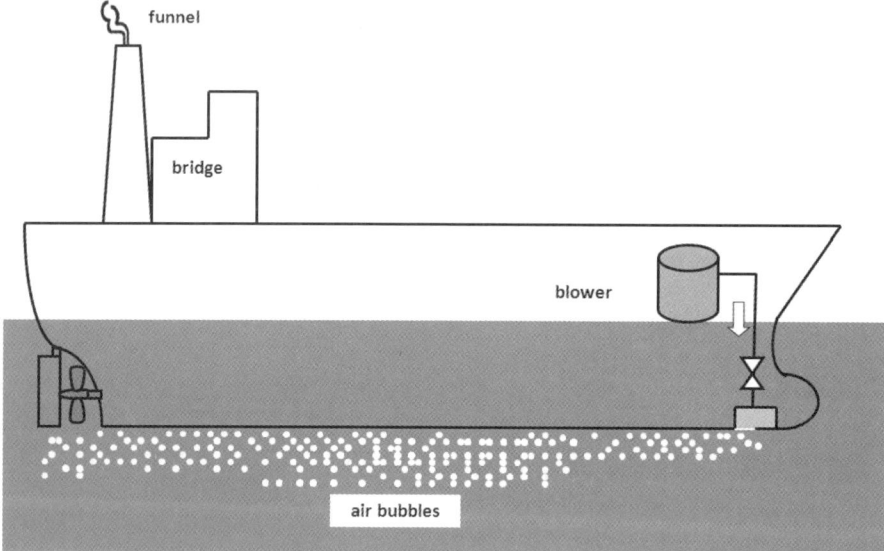

Figure 1 – Schematic illustration of an air lubrication system

1.2 Method of calculation

1.2.1 Power reduction due to air lubrication system

1.2.1.1 Power reduction factor P_{eff} due to an air lubrication system as an innovative energy efficiency technology is calculated by the following formula. The first and second terms of the right hand side represent the reduction of propulsion power by the air lubrication system and the additional power necessary for running the system, respectively. For this system, f_{eff} is 1.0 in EEDI formula.

$$P_{eff} = P_{PeffAL} - P_{AEeffAL} \frac{C_{FAE}}{C_{FME}} \frac{SFC_{AE}}{SFC_{ME}}* \tag{1}$$

* In the case of $P_{PTI(i)} > 0$, the average weighted value of $(SFC_{ME} \cdot C_{FME})$ and $(SFC_{AE} \cdot C_{FAE})$

---

[1]   All examples in this chapter are used solely to illustrate the proposed methods of calculation and verification.

附件 1[1]

B 类创新技术效果的计算和验证导则

1 空气润滑系统（B-1 类）

1.1 创新能效技术概要

1.1.1 空气润滑系统是创新能效技术中的一种，采用鼓风机从船底前部喷射气体，在船体表面覆盖气泡以减少船舶的摩擦阻力。

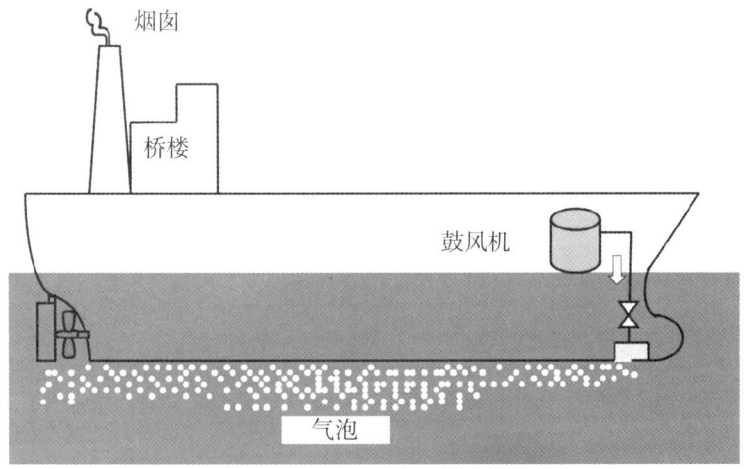

图 1 空气润滑系统示意图

1.2 计算方法

1.2.1 由空气润滑系统导致的功率降低

1.2.1.1 作为创新能效技术，采用空气润滑系统的功率减少系数 P_{eff} 通过下列公式计算。右手边第一项和第二项分别表示由空气润滑系统减少的推进功率以及系统运行所必要的附加功率。对该系统，EEDI 公式中的 f_{eff} 取 1.0。

$$P_{eff} = P_{PeffAL} - P_{AEeffAL} \frac{C_{FAE}}{C_{FME}} \frac{SFC_{AE}}{SFC_{ME}} * \tag{1}$$

* 如 $P_{PTI(i)} > 0$，则取（$SFC_{ME} \cdot C_{FME}$）和（$SFC_{AE} \cdot C_{FAE}$）的平均加权值。

---

[1] 本章中的所有例子仅用于说明所建议的计算和验证方法。

— 638 —

1.2.1.2 P_{eff} is the effective power reduction in kW due to the air lubrication system at the 75% of the rated installed power (MCR). In case that shaft generators are installed, P_{eff} should be calculated at the 75% MCR having after deducted any installed shaft generators in accordance with paragraph 2.2.5 of EEDI Calculation Guidelines. P_{eff} should be calculated both in the fully loaded and the sea trial conditions.

1.2.1.3 P_{PeffAL} is the reduction of propulsion power due to the air lubrication system in kW. P_{PeffAL} should be calculated both in the condition corresponding to the *Capacity* as defined in EEDI Calculation Guidelines (hereinafter referred to as "fully loaded condition") and the sea trial condition, taking the following items into account:

.1   area of ship surface covered with air;

.2   thickness of air layer;

.3   reduction rate of frictional resistance due to the coverage of air layer;

.4   change of propulsion efficiency due to the interaction with air bubbles (self-propulsion factors and propeller open water characteristics); and

.5   change of resistance due to additional device, if equipped.

1.2.1.4 $P_{AEeffAL}$ is additional auxiliary power in kW necessary for running the air lubrication system in the fully loaded condition. $P_{AEeffAL}$ should be calculated as 75% of the rated output of blowers based on the manufacturer's test report. For a system where the calculated value above is significantly different from the output used at normal operation in the fully loaded condition, the $P_{AEeffAL}$ value may be estimated by an alternative method. In this case, the calculation process should be submitted to a verifier.

1.2.2   Points to keep in mind in calculation of attained EEDI with air lubrication system

1.2.2.1 V_{ref} in paragraph 2.2.2 of EEDI Calculation Guidelines should be calculated in the condition that the air lubrication system is OFF to avoid the double count of the effect of this system.

1.2.2.2   In accordance with EEDI Calculation Guidelines, the EEDI value for ships for the air lubrication system ON should be calculated in the fully loaded condition.

1.3   Method of verification

1.3.1   General

1.3.1.1   Attained EEDI for a ship with an innovative energy efficient technology should be verified in accordance with EEDI Survey Guidelines. Additional information on the application of air lubrication system, which is not given in the EEDI Survey Guidelines, is contained below.

1.3.2   Preliminary verification at the design stage

1.3.2.1   In addition to paragraph 4.2.2 of EEDI Survey Guidelines, the EEDI Technical File, which is to be developed by a shipowner or shipbuilder, should include:

.1   outline of the air lubrication system;

1.2.1.2 P_{eff} 为 75% 的额定装机功率（MCR）时空气润滑系统的有效功率减少量，kW。如安装了轴带发电机，P_{eff} 应按照 EEDI 计算指南 2.2.5 的要求在扣除安装的任何轴带发电机后，以 75% 的 MCR 进行计算。P_{eff} 的计算应在满载工况以及试航工况进行。

1.2.1.3 P_{PeffAL} 为采用空气润滑系统导致的推进功率减少量，（kW）。P_{PeffAL} 的计算应在 EEDI 计算指南所定义的载运能力对应工况（以下称为"满载工况"）以及试航工况下进行，并考虑以下各个因素：

> .1 覆盖气泡船舶表面面积；
>
> .2 气泡层的厚度；
>
> .3 覆盖气泡层导致的摩擦阻力减低率；
>
> .4 与气泡相互作用导致的推进效率变化（自航因素和螺旋桨敞水特征）；和
>
> .5 附加设备（如安装）引起的阻力变化。

1.2.1.4 $P_{AEeffAL}$ 为满载工况下空气润滑系统运行所需要的附加辅助功率，kW。$P_{AEeffAL}$ 应根据制造商测试报告，以鼓风机 75% 的额定输出功率计算。如上述计算值与满载工况下正常操作所使用的输出功率有很大的差异，$P_{AEeffAL}$ 值可以采用替代方法进行估算。在这种情况下，应向验证方提交计算过程。

1.2.2 空气润滑系统 Attained EEDI 计算注意事项

1.2.2.1 EEDI 计算指南 2.2.2 中的 V_{ref} 应在空气润滑系统关闭的工况下进行计算以避免重复计入这一系统的效果。

1.2.2.2 按 EEDI 计算指南的要求，船上空气润滑系统处于工作时的 EEDI 值计算应在满载工况下进行。

1.3 验证方法

1.3.1 通则

1.3.1.1 采用创新能效技术的船舶应按 EEDI 检验指南验证 Attained EEDI。EEDI 检验指南中未包含的有关空气润滑系统应用的附加资料见下文。

1.3.2 设计阶段的前期验证

1.3.2.1 除 EEDI 检验指南 4.2.2 要求外，船东或船厂编制的 EEDI 技术案卷还应包括：

> .1 空气润滑系统的简图；

.2 P_{PeffAL} : the reduction of propulsion power due to the air lubrication system at the ship speed of V_{ref} both in the fully loaded and the sea trial conditions;

.3 EDR_{full} : the reduction rate of propulsion power in the fully loaded condition due to the air lubrication system. EDR_{full} is calculated by dividing $P_{MEeffAL}$ by P_{ME} in EEDI Calculation Guidelines in the fully loaded condition (see figure 2);

.4 EDR_{trial} : the reduction rate of propulsion power in a sea trial condition due to the air lubrication system. EDR_{trial} is calculated by dividing $P_{MEeffAL}$ by P_{ME} in EEDI Calculation Guidelines in sea trial condition (see figure 2);

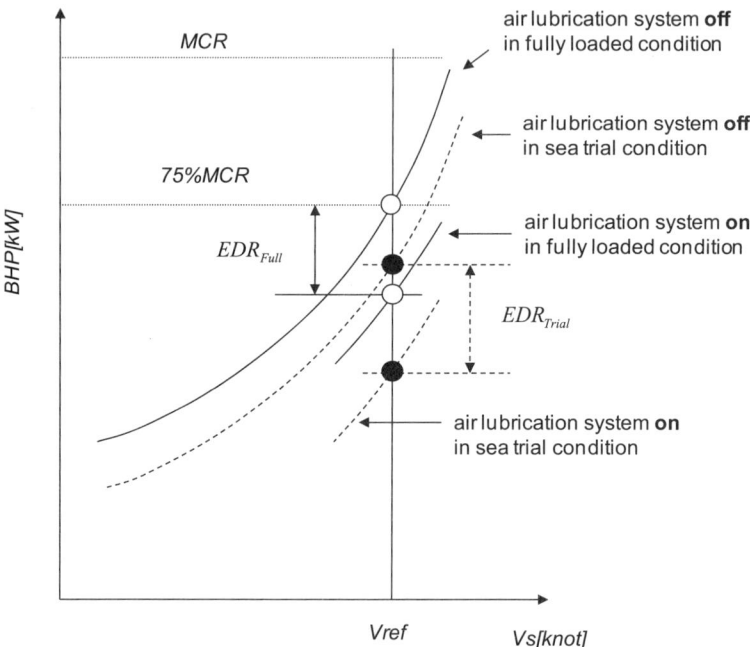

Figure 2 – Calculation of the reduction rate of propulsion power (EDR_{full} and EDR_{trial}) due to air lubrication system

.5 $P_{AEeffAL}$: additional power necessary for running the air lubrication system; and

.6 the calculated value of the EEDI for the air lubrication system ON in the fully loaded condition.

1.3.2.2 In addition with paragraph 4.2.7 of the EEDI Survey Guidelines, additional information that the verifier may request the shipbuilder to provide directly to it includes:

.1 the detailed calculation process of the reduction of propulsion power due to the air lubrication system: P_{PeffAL} ; and

.2 the detailed calculation process of the additional power necessary for running the air lubrication system: $P_{AEeffAL}$.

.2 P_{PeffAL}：满载工况以及试航工况下航速 V_{ref} 时，空气润滑系统导致的推进功率的降低；

.3 EDR_{full}：满载工况下空气润滑系统导致的推进功率降低率。EDR_{full} 通过 $P_{MEeffAL}$ 除以满载工况下 EEDI 计算指南中的 P_{ME} 来计算（见图 2）；

.4 EDR_{trial}：试航工况下空气润滑系统导致的推进功率降低率。EDR_{trial} 通过 $P_{MEeffAL}$ 除以试航工况下 EEDI 计算指南中的 P_{ME} 来计算（见图 2）；

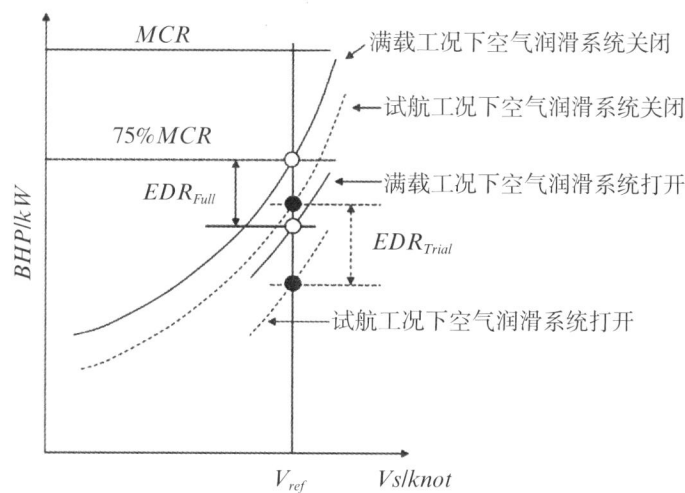

图 2　空气润滑系统导致的推进功率降低率（EDR_{full} 和 EDR_{trial}）计算

.5 $P_{AEeffAL}$：空气润滑系统运行所需要的附加功率；和

.6 满载工况下空气润滑系统工作时的 EEDI 计算值。

1.3.2.2 除 EEDI 检验指南 4.2.7 要求外，验证方还可能要求船厂直接提供的附加资料包括：

.1 空气润滑系统导致的推进功率降低详细计算过程：P_{PeffAL}；和

.2 空气润滑系统运行所必需的附加功率详细计算过程：$P_{AEeffAL}$。

1.3.3 Final verification of the attained EEDI at sea trial

1.3.3.1 Final verification of the EEDI of ships due to the air lubrication system should be conducted at the sea trial. The procedure of final verification should be basically in accordance with paragraph 4.3 of the EEDI Survey Guidelines.

1.3.3.2 Prior to the sea trial, the following documents should be submitted to the verifier; a description of the test procedure that includes the measurement methods to be used at the sea trial of the ship with the air lubrication system.

1.3.3.3 The verifier should attend the sea trial and confirm the items described in paragraph 4.3.3 of the EEDI Survey Guidelines to be measured at the sea trial for the air lubrication system ON and OFF.

1.3.3.4 The main engine output at the sea trial for the air lubrication system ON and OFF should be set so that the range of the developed power curve includes the ship speed of V_{ref}.

1.3.3.5 The following procedure should be conducted based on the power curve developed for air lubrication system OFF.

.1 ship speed at 75% MCR of main engine in the fully loaded condition, V_{ref}, should be calculated. In case that shaft generators are installed, V_{ref} should be calculated at 75% MCR having after deducted any installed shaft generators in accordance with paragraph 2.2.5 of EEDI Calculation Guidelines; and

.2 in case that V_{ref} obtained above is different from that estimated at the design stage, the reduction rate of main engine should be recalculated at new V_{ref} both in the fully loaded and the sea trial conditions.

1.3.3.6 The shipbuilder should develop power curves for the air lubrication system ON based on the measured ship speed and output of the main engine at the sea trial. The following calculations should be conducted.

.1 the actual reduction rate of propulsion power ADR_{trial} at the ship speed of V_{ref} at the sea trial; and

.2 if the sea trial is not conducted in the fully loaded condition, the reduction rate of propulsion power in this condition should be calculated by the following formula:

$$1 - ADR_{Full} = (1 - EDR_{Full}) \times \frac{1 - ADR_{Trial}}{1 - EDR_{Trial}},$$

i.e.

$$ADR_{Full} = 1 - (1 - EDR_{Full}) \times \frac{1 - ADR_{Trial}}{1 - EDR_{Trial}} \qquad (2)$$

1.3.3 试航时 Attained EEDI 的最终验证

1.3.3.1 设有空气润滑系统的船舶，EEDI 的最终验证应在试航时进行。最终验证的程序基本上应按照 EEDI 检验指南 4.3 的要求。

1.3.3.2 试航前，应向验证方提交试验程序说明，包括设有空气润滑系统的船舶试航时所使用的测量方法。

1.3.3.3 验证方应参加试航，并确认 EEDI 检验指南 4.4.3 中所列项目在空气润滑系统处于打开和关闭状态下进行了测量。

1.3.3.4 试航中空气润滑系统处于打开和关闭状态下主机输出功率的设定，应使所制定的功率曲线范围包括船舶航速 V_{ref}。

1.3.3.5 应根据所制定的空气润滑系统处于关闭状态下的功率曲线完成下列程序：

.1 应计算满载工况下主机 75%MCR 时的航速 V_{ref}。如安装了轴带发电机，V_{ref} 应按照 EEDI 计算指南 2.2.5 的要求在扣除所安装的任何轴带发电机后，以 75% 的 MCR 进行计算；和

.2 如以上所得 V_{ref} 不同于设计阶段的估算值，主机的功率降低率应在满载工况和试航工况条件下以新的航速 V_{ref} 重新计算。

1.3.3.6 船厂应根据试航时测量的航速和主机输出功率来制定空气润滑系统打开状态下的功率曲线。应进行下列计算：

.1 试航时航速 V_{ref} 下的推进功率实际降低率 ADR_{trial}；和

.2 如试航未在满载工况下进行，此工况下的推进功率降低率应通过下式计算：

$$1 - ADR_{Full} = (1 - EDR_{Full}) \times \frac{1 - ADR_{Trial}}{1 - EDR_{Trial}},$$

i.e.

$$ADR_{Full} = 1 - (1 - EDR_{Full}) \times \frac{1 - ADR_{Trial}}{1 - EDR_{Trial}} \qquad (2)$$

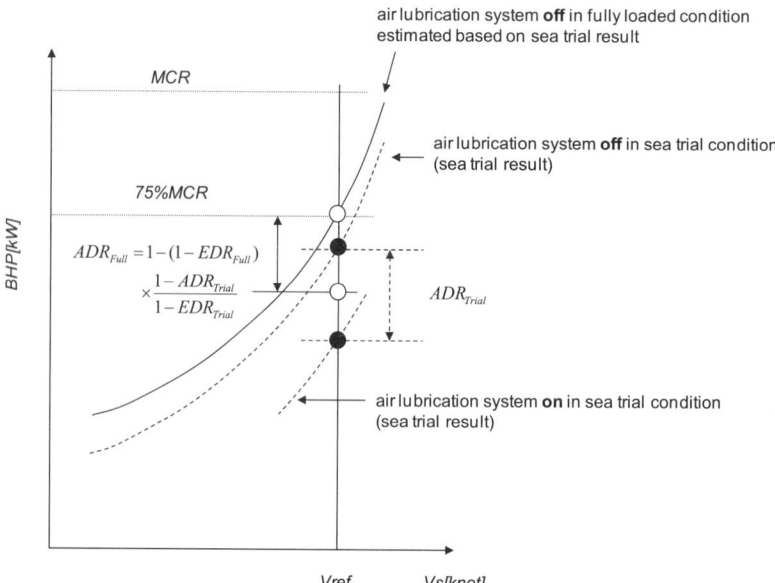

Figure 3 – Calculation of the actual reduction rate of propulsion power (ADR_{full} and ADR_{trial}) due to air lubrication system

1.3.3.7   The reduction of propulsion power due to the air lubrication system $P_{MEeffAL}$ in the fully loaded and the sea trial conditions should be calculated as follows:

$$P_{PeffAL\_Full} = ADR_{Full} \times P_P \qquad (3)$$

$$P_{PeffAL\_Trial} = ADR_{Trial} \times P_P \qquad (4)$$

1.3.3.8   The shipowner or the shipbuilder should revise the EEDI Technical File, as necessary, by taking the result of the sea trial into account. Such revision should include the following contents:

.1 V_{ref}, in case that it is different from that estimated at the design stage;

.2   the reduction of propulsion power P_{PeffAL} at the ship speed of V_{ref} in the fully loaded and the sea trial conditions for the air lubrication system ON;

.3   the reduction rate of propulsion power due to air lubrication system (ADR_{full} and ADR_{trial}) in the fully loaded and the sea trial conditions; and

.4   the calculated value of the EEDI for the air lubrication system ON in the fully loaded condition.

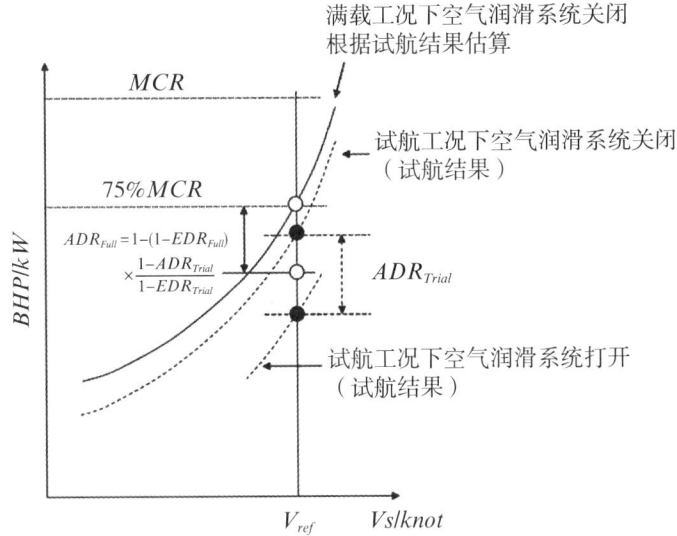

图 3 空气润滑系统导致的推进功率实际降低率（ADR_{full} 和 ADR_{trial}）计算

1.3.3.7 满载工况和试航工况下由空气润滑系统导致的推进功率降低率 $P_{MEeffAL}$ 应按下式计算：

$$P_{PeffAL\_Full} = ADR_{Full} \times P_P \tag{3}$$

$$P_{PeffAL\_Trial} = ADR_{Trial} \times P_P \tag{4}$$

1.3.3.8 必要时，船东或船厂应考虑试航的结果修改 EEDI 技术案卷。该修改应包括下列内容：

.1 V_{ref}，如果与设计阶段的估算值有差异；

.2 满载工况和试航工况下空气润滑系统打开且航速 V_{ref} 时，推进功率的降低率 P_{PeffAL}；

.3 满载工况和试航工况下空气润滑系统（ADR_{full} 和 ADR_{trial}）导致的推进功率降低率；和

.4 满载工况下空气润滑系统打开时 EEDI 计算值。

2   WIND ASSISTED PROPULSION SYSTEM (CATEGORY B-2)

2.1   Summary of innovative energy efficient technology

2.1.1   Wind assisted propulsion systems (WAPS) belong to innovative mechanical energy efficient technologies which reduce the CO_2 emissions of ships. There are different types of wind propulsion technologies (sails, wings, kites, etc.) which generate forces dependent on wind conditions. This technical guidance defines the available effective power of WAPS as the product of the reference speed and the sum of the wind assisted propulsion system force and the global wind probability distribution.

2.1.2   Secondary effects when applying the wind assisted propulsion system which might increase the ship resistance are ignored for the purpose of these guidelines. With this simplification effects as for instance additional drag due to leeway, rudder angle and heel or reduced propeller efficiency in light running condition are ignored without significant loss of accuracy. Nonetheless, the corresponding forces are considered to rule out conditions that do not allow a safe operation of the ship, for instance due to exceeding heel angles.

2.2   Definitions

2.2.1   For the purpose of these guidelines, the following definitions should apply:

.1   *available effective power* is the multiplication of effective power P_{eff} and availability factor f_{eff} , as defined in the EEDI calculation;

.2   *wind assisted propulsion systems (WAPS)* belong to innovative mechanical energy efficient technologies which reduce the CO_2 emissions of ships. These proposed guidelines apply to wind propulsion technologies that directly transfer mechanical propulsion forces to the ship's structure (sails, wings, kites, etc.);

.3   *wind propulsion system force matrix* is a two-dimensional matrix which expresses the force characteristic of a wind assisted propulsion system dependent on ship speed, wind speed and the wind angle relative to heading;

.4   *global wind probability matrix* contains data of the global wind power on the main global shipping routes based on a statistical survey of worldwide wind data and represents the probability of wind conditions;

.5   *wind speed* is the speed of the wind in m/s measured at 10 m above sea level;

.6   *wind direction* is the North-oriented direction of the wind measured at 10 m above sea level and is subdivided into eight sectors (North, North-East, East, South-East, South, South-West, West, North-West);

.7   *wind angle* is the angle of the wind relative to the ship's heading at 10 m above sea level subdivided into 72 sectors of 5°-steps (0°, 5°,..., 355°); and

.8   the *main global shipping network* is a network of global shipping routes with the highest frequency of journeys.

2 风力辅助推进系统（B-2类）

2.1 创新能效技术概要

2.1.1 风力推进系统（WAPS）属于减少船舶 CO_2 排放的创新机械能效技术。有各种根据风况产生动力的风力推进技术（船帆、船翼、筝帆等）。本技术导则把 WAPS 的可用有效功率定义为基准速度与风力辅助推进系统力和全球风力概率分布之和的乘积。

2.1.2 在应用风力辅助推进系统时，可能增加船舶阻力的次要影响在这些指南中被忽略。忽略诸如风压差、舵角和横倾或螺旋桨在轻转运行工况下效率降低这些因素导致的额外阻力，这种简化方法不会对准确性造成显著影响。尽管如此，相应的力被认为是排除了不能安全操作船舶的工况，例如超过横倾角。

2.2 定义

2.2.1 就本指南而言，以下定义适用：

.1 *可用有效功率*系指 EEDI 计算中定义的有效功率 P_{eff} 和可用系数 f_{eff} 乘积；

.2 *风力辅助推进系统（WAPS）*属于减少船舶 CO_2 排放的创新机械能效技术。本指南适用于直接把机械推进力传送到船舶结构的风力推进技术（船帆、船翼、筝帆等）；

.3 *风力推进系统力矩阵*是一个二维矩阵，表示风力辅助推进系统的力特性，其视航速、风速和相对于首向的风向角而定；

.4 *全球风力概率矩阵*，以世界各地风力统计调查数据为依据收集的全球主要航运路线上的风力数据，代表了风况的概率；

.5 *风速*是在海平面以上 10 m 处测量的风的速度，单位为 m/s；

.6 *风向*是指在海平面以上 10 m 处测得的向北的风向，分为八个部分（北、东北、东、东南、南、西南、西、西北）；

.7 *风向角*是在海平面以上 10 m 处的相对于船舶首向的风向角，每隔 5°分为 72 个角度（0°, 5°, …, 355°）；和

.8 *全球主要航运网络*是航行频率最高的全球航线网路。

2.3 Available effective power of wind assisted propulsion systems (WAPS)

2.3.1 The available effective power of wind assisted propulsion systems as innovative energy efficient technology is calculated by the following formula:

$$(f_{eff} \cdot P_{eff}) = \left(\frac{1}{\sum_{k=1}^{q} W_k}\right) \cdot \left(\left(\frac{0.514\ 4 \cdot V_{ref}}{\eta_D} \sum_{k=1}^{q} F(V_{ref})_k \cdot W_k\right) - \left(\sum_{k=1}^{q} P(V_{ref})_k \cdot W_k\right)\right)$$

with $F_1 - F_k \geq 0 \wedge F_{k-1} - F_k \geq 0$

(sorting all force matrix elements in descending order)

and $\sum_{k=1}^{q-1} W_k < \frac{1}{2} \wedge \sum_{k=1}^{q} W_k \geq \frac{1}{2}$
(defining q: the number of elements added in the formula)

Where:

.1 $(f_{eff} * P_{eff})$ is the available effective power in kW delivered by the specified wind assisted propulsion system. f_{eff} and P_{eff} are combined in the calculation because the product of availability and power is a result of a matrix operation, addressing each wind condition with a probability and a specific wind propulsion system force;

.2 the factor 0.5144 is the conversion factor from nautical miles per hour (knots) to metres per second (m/s);

.3 V_{ref} is the ship reference speed measured in nautical miles per hour (knots), as defined in the EEDI calculation guidelines.

.4 η_D is the total efficiency of the main drive(s) at 75% of the rated installed power (MCR) of the main engine(s). η_D shall be set to 0.7, if no other value is specified and verified by the verifier;

.5 $F(V_{ref})_k$ is the force matrix of the respective wind assisted propulsion system for a given ship speed V_{ref}. Each matrix element represents the propulsion force in kilo newton (kN) for the respective wind speed and angle. The wind angle is given in relative bearings (with 0° on the bow);

.6 W_k is the global wind probability matrix. Each matrix element represents the probability of wind speed and wind angle relative to the ships heading. The sum over all matrix elements equals 1 and is non-dimensional; and

.7 $P(V_{ref})_k$ is a matrix with the same dimensions as $F(V_{ref})_k$ and W_k and represents the power demand in kW for the operation of the wind assisted propulsion system.

2.3.2 The fore term of the formula defines the additional propulsion power to be considered for the overall EEDI calculation. The term contains the product of the ship specific speed, the force matrix and the global wind probability matrix. The aft term contains the power requirement for the operation of the specific wind assisted propulsion system which has to be subtracted from the gained wind power.

2.3 风力辅助推进系统（WAPS）的可用有效功率

2.3.1 作为创新能效技术，风力辅助推进系统的可用有效功率计算按下述公式进行：

$$(f_{eff} \cdot P_{eff}) = \left(\frac{1}{\sum_{k=1}^{q} W_k}\right) \cdot \left(\left(\frac{0.514\ 4 \cdot V_{ref}}{\eta_D} \sum_{k=1}^{q} F(V_{ref})_k \cdot W_k\right) - \left(\sum_{k=1}^{q} P(V_{ref})_k \cdot W_k\right)\right)$$

其中：$F_1 - F_k \geq 0 \wedge F_{k-1} - F_k \geq 0$

（将所有力矩阵要素按降序排序）

和 $\sum_{k=1}^{q-1} W_k < \frac{1}{2} \wedge \sum_{k=1}^{q} W_k \geq \frac{1}{2}$

（定义 q：在公式中添加的要素数）

式中：

.1 （$f_{eff}*P_{eff}$）为具体风力辅助推进系统输出的可用有效功率，kW。将 f_{eff} 和 Peff 组合计算，是由于可用性和功率的乘积为矩阵运算的结果，对每种风况均考虑概率和具体的风力推进系统力；

.2 系数 0.514 4 为海里 / 小时（节）转换为米 / 秒（m/s）的换算系数；

.3 V_{ref} 为以海里 / 小时（节）为单位测量的船舶基准速度，定义见 EEDI 计算指南。

.4 η D 为主机 75% 额定装机功率（MCR）下（各）主驱动装置的总效率。如无规定经验证方验证的其他数值，η_D 应设定为 0.7；

.5 $F(V_{ref})_k$ 为给定航速 V_{ref} 下各风力辅助推进系统的力矩阵。每个矩阵要素均表示各自的风速和风向角的推进力，单位为千牛顿（kN）。风向角以相对方位表示（船首为 0°）；

.6 W_k 为全球风力概率矩阵。每个矩阵要素均表示风速和相对于船舶航向的风向角的概率。所有矩阵要素的和等于 1，并为无因次的；和

.7 $P(V_{ref})_k$ 为具有与 $F(V_{ref})_k$ 和 Wk 一样尺寸的矩阵，表示风力辅助推进系统操作所需要的功率，kW。

2.3.2 公式前一项规定了总体 EEDI 计算时应考虑的附加推进功率，包括船舶特定航速、力矩阵和全球风力概率矩阵的乘积。后一项则包括具体风力辅助推进系统操作所需要的功率，应从获得的风力功率中扣除。

2.4 Wind propulsion system force matrix $F(V_{ref})_k$

2.4.1 Measurement of the wind propulsion coefficients

2.4.1.1 The wind propulsion system force matrix is a table describing the average wind propulsion coefficients corresponding to the global wind probability matrix. Therefore, the measurement of the wind propulsion coefficients has to be carried out at first in order to obtain the wind propulsion system force matrix.

2.4.1.2 Various methods can be used to determine the aerodynamic forces of a wind assisted ship, depending firstly on the type of wind assisted propulsion system, but also size limitations and successful validation for the methods already shown in literature. The methods include:

.1   wind tunnel model test;

.2   CFD/numerical calculations; and

.3   full scale test.

2.4.1.3 The forces are to be determined for the combination of wind assisted propulsion system and ship unless that is not practical due to technical or economic reasons. In the latter case the conditions of 2.4.1.4 apply.

2.4.1.4 In the case of the installation of multiple wind assisted propulsion systems, the forces may be determined for the devices in isolation and by the summing the coefficients of each units comprising the system, provided that a validated method is in place to account for interaction effects between wind propulsors and between the ship and the wind propulsors.

2.4.1.5 Wind propulsion devices are to be analysed at their operational Reynolds number, as this has been shown to affect their performance.

2.4.1.6 The wind tunnel model test is a major method for measuring the aerodynamic force of a wind assisted ship propulsion system under typical states. Appendix 1 of this annex describes the testing methods of wind tunnel model tests. If the wind propulsion coefficients are measured by the wind tunnel model test, it should be conducted in accordance with the appendix 1.

2.4.1.7 For some types of wind assisted propulsion system wind tunnel model tests are not appropriate for measuring the wind propulsion coefficients. Therefore, numerical calculations, such as CFD-computation, can be accepted for estimating the wind propulsion coefficients, but the condition and the model of the numerical calculation should be referred to experimental representative results and the numerical calculation is to be carried out in accordance with defined quality and technical standards (ITTC 7.5-03-01-02 and ITTC 7.5-03-01-04 at their latest revisions or equivalent). If both of wind tunnel model tests and numerical calculation are inappropriate to estimate the coefficient, other testing method may be acceptable with the approval of the verifier.

2.4.1.8 When a test or calculation for determining the wind propulsion coefficients is carried out, the procedure of the test or calculation should be submitted to the verifier in advance of conducting the test or calculation. In addition, the detail report of the test and calculation procedure should also be submitted to the verifier after the test. The verifier may request the submitter to provide further documents/information as necessary to verify the wind propulsion coefficients.

2.4 风力推进系统的力矩阵 $F(V_{ref})_k$

2.4.1 风力推进系数的测量

2.4.1.1 风力推进系统的力矩阵是一个描述全球风力概率矩阵对应的平均风力推进系数的表格。因此，为了得到风力推进系统的力矩阵，需要先对风力推进系数进行测量。

2.4.1.2 可以使用多种方法来确定风力辅助船的气动力，首先取决于风力辅助推进系统的类型，但也有尺寸限制和文献中已经显示的方法的成功验证。方法包括：

    .1 风洞模型试验；

    .2 CFD/ 数值计算；和

    .3 全尺度试验。

2.4.1.3 应风力辅助推进系统与船舶组合的力，除非由于技术或经济原因不可行。在后一种情况下，2.4.1.4 的情况适用。

2.4.1.4 在安装多个风力辅助推进系统的情况下，可采用一个经过验证的方法来明确风力推进器之间以及船与风力推进器之间的相互作用效果，此时可单独确定对每个设备的力，并将组成系统的每个单元的系数相加。

2.4.1.5 风力推进装置应在其运行雷诺数下进行分析，因为这已被证明会影响其性能。

2.4.1.6 风洞模型试验是测量风力辅助船舶推进系统在典型状态下气动力的主要方法。本附件的附录 1 描述了风洞模型试验的试验方法。如采用风洞模型试验测得风力推进系数，应按附录 1 进行。

2.4.1.7 对于某些类型的风力辅助推进系统，不适宜用风洞模型试验来测量风力推进系数。因此，可以接受采用数值计算，例如 CFD 计算，来估算风力推进系数，但数值计算的条件和模型应参考实验代表性结果，且数值计算应按照规定的质量和技术标准（ITTC 7.5–03–01–02 和 ITTC7.5–03–01–04 最新修订版或等效版本）进行。如果风洞模型试验和数值计算都不适合估算系数，在验证方批准的情况下，可以接受其他试验方法。

2.4.1.8 在进行确定风力推进系数的试验或计算时，应在进行试验或计算前将试验或计算程序提交验证方。此外，试验结束后，还应向验证方提交试验和计算程序的详细报告。验证方可视必要要求提交方提供进一步的文件 / 资料，以验证风力推进系数。

2.4.1.9 The test of a ship model without wind assisted propulsion system mainly measures the wind forces of the ship model pointing to the bow under different wind directions. The test of a ship model with wind assisted propulsion system mainly measures the maximum wind propulsion of the ship model pointing to the bow under different wind directions, which is then used to calculate the wind propulsion coefficient of the wind propulsion system. The coefficients of the wind assisted propulsion system should be determined at a series of wind angles ranging from 0° to 360°, spaced by an interval of 5°.

2.4.1.10 A single wind tunnel test may be accepted for several identical wind assisted propulsion systems and identical ships. The verifier may request that supporting documentation be produced.

2.4.2   Wind tunnel test methods and data processing

Option 1: Test on a ship model fitted with the full wind assisted propulsion system

2.4.2.1 When the wind tunnel test is carried out with the ship model and the wind assisted propulsion system model, the test method should follow the specifications given in appendix 1. The wind forces acting on the ship model are normalized as:

$$C_{Fx} = F_x / (0.5 \, \rho \, V^2 \, A)$$

2.4.2.2 The wind propulsion coefficients[2] of the wind assisted propulsion system can be determined as:

$$\Delta C_{Fx} = C_{Fx\text{-with WPS}} - C_{Fx\text{-without WPS}}$$

Where:

.1 C_{Fx} is the wind force coefficient of the model pointing to the bow;

.2 F_x is the wind force of the model pointing to the bow;

.3 ΔC_{Fx} is the wind propulsion coefficient of the wind assisted propulsion system;

.4 ρ is the air density of the model test;

.5   V is the wind velocity of the model test;

.6   A is the total projected area of the wind assisted propulsion system; and

.7   the subscript "with WAPS" means the state with wind assisted propulsion system of the ship model, while "without WAPS" means the state without wind assisted propulsion system of the ship.

---

2   The force coefficients are dimensionless, the units for their calculation can be freely chosen, but must be consistent with each other.

2.4.1.9　无风力辅助推进系统的船模试验，主要测量不同风向下船模指向船首的风力。采用风力辅助推进系统的船模试验主要测量不同风向下船模指向船首的最大风推进力，然后利用其计算风力推进系统的风力推进系数。风力辅助推进系统的系数应在一系列风向角中确定，范围 0°~360°，间隔 5°。

2.4.1.10　对于几个相同的风力辅助推进系统和相同的船舶，可以接受一次风洞试验。验证方可以要求提供支持文件。

2.4.2　风洞试验方法和数据处理

方案 1：在装有整套风力辅助推进系统的船模上进行试验

2.4.2.1　用船模和风力辅助推进系统模型进行风洞试验时，试验方法应符合附录 1 的规定。作用在船舶模型上的风力归一化为：

$$C_{Fx} = F_x / (0.5\, \rho\, V^2\, A)$$

2.4.2.2　风力辅助推进系统的风力推进系数 [2] 可确定为：

$$\Delta C_{Fx} = C_{Fx\text{-with WPS}} - C_{Fx\text{-without WPS}}$$

式中：

.1　C_{Fx} 为模型指向船首的风力系数；

.2　F_x 为模型指向船首的风力；

.3　ΔC_{Fx} 为风力辅助推进系统的风力推进系数；

.4　ρ 为模型试验的空气密度；

.5　V 为模型试验的风速；

.6　A 为风力辅助推进系统的总投影面积；和

.7　下标"有 WAPS"表示船模有风力辅助推进系统的状态，"无 WAPS"表示船舶无风力辅助推进系统的状态。

---

[2]　力系数是无因次的，其计算单位可以自由选择，但必须相互一致。

Option 2: Test with a single wind assisted propulsion unit

2.4.2.3   When the wind tunnel test is carried out with a single wind propulsion unit, the test method should follow the specifications given in appendix 1. The wind propulsion coefficients[3] of the model can be determined as:

$$C_{Fx} = F_x / (0.5\ \rho\ V^2\ A)$$

Where:

.1 C_{Fx} is the wind force coefficient of the model pointing to the bow;

.2 F_x is the wind force of the model pointing to the bow;

.3 ρ is the air density of the model test;

.4   V is the wind velocity of the model test; and

.5   A is the total projected area of the wind assisted propulsion system.

2.4.2.4   The wind propulsion coefficients ΔC_{Fx} of a multi-unit wind assisted propulsion system can be calculated by summing the coefficients of the units comprising the system, weighted by the effects of interaction and masking by superstructures.

For options 1 and 2: Calculation of the average power consumption coefficients of the active wind assisted propulsion system during the wind tunnel test

2.4.2.5   The power consumption of the wind assisted propulsion system should be measured and the power consumption matrix should be filled based on the measured values and the systems control plan.

2.4.3   Calculation of the wind propulsion system force matrix

2.4.3.1   The wind propulsion coefficients[4] of the ship's wind assisted propulsion system can be used to predict the wind propulsion system force matrix. Apparent wind is defined as the combination of wind relative to the ground and wind created by the ship's velocity. The steps to calculate the wind propulsion system force matrix are as follows:

.1   determine the velocity of the ship V_{ref};

.2   select the average wind speed corresponding to terms in W_k, the global wind probability matrix at 10 m height. For example, the average wind speed corresponding to the first wind speed range (0-1 m/s) of the wind probability matrix is selected as 0.5 m/s, the average wind speed corresponding to the second wind speed range (1-2 m/s) is selected as 1.5 m/s, etc.;

.3   extrapolate the wind speed to the reference height of the wind assisted propulsion systems taken as the aerodynamic centre of effort height or half height from the waterline:

---

3   The force coefficients are dimensionless, the units for their calculation can be freely chosen, but must be consistent with each other.

4   The force coefficients are dimensionless, the units for their calculation can be freely chosen, but must be consistent with each other.

方案 2：单一风力辅助推进装置进行试验

2.4.2.3　采用单一风力推进装置进行风洞试验时，试验方法应符合附录 1 的规定。模型的风力推进系数 [3] 可按下式确定：

$$C_{Fx} = F_x / (0.5 \rho V^2 A)$$

式中：

.1　C_{Fx} 为模型指向船首的风力系数；

.2　F_x 为模型指向船首的风力；

.3　ρ 为模型试验的空气密度；

.4　V 为模型试验的风速；和

.5　A 为风力辅助推进系统的总投影面积。

2.4.2.4　多单元风力辅助推进系统的风力推进系数 ΔC_{Fx} 可通过求组成系统的各单元的系数总和来计算，其中对其相互作用效应进行加权，并计及上层建筑的遮蔽效应。

对于方案 1 和方案 2：计算风洞试验时主动风力辅助推进系统的平均功率消耗系数

2.4.2.5　应根据测得的值和系统控制方案，对风力辅助推进系统的功率消耗进行测量，填写功耗矩阵。

2.4.3　风力推进系统力矩阵计算

2.4.3.1　船舶风力辅助推进系统的风力推进系数 [4] 可用于预测风力推进系统力矩阵。视风定义为相对于地面的风和由船舶速度产生的风的组合。风力推进系统力矩阵的计算步骤如下：

.1　确定船舶速度 V_{ref}；

.2　选取 10 m 高度全球风力概率矩阵 W_k 对应的平均风速。例如，选择风力概率矩阵第一风速范围（0~1 m/s）对应的平均风速为 0.5 m/s，选择第二风速范围（1~2 m/s）对应的平均风速为 1.5 m/s，以此类推；

.3　将风速外插至风力辅助推进系统的参考高度，参考高度取出力高度的气动中心或从水线量起的一半高度；

---

[3]　力系数是无因次的，其计算单位可以自由选择，但必须相互一致。
[4]　力系数是无因次的，其计算单位可以自由选择，但必须相互一致。

$$v_{Zref} = v_{10m} \left(\frac{z_{ref}}{10}\right)^{\alpha} \; for \; z_{ref} < 300m$$

$$v_{Zref} = v_{10m} \left(\frac{300}{10}\right)^{\alpha} \; for \; z_{ref} \geq 300m$$

Where:

.1 z_{ref} is the reference height above the water line, to be equal to the point of mid-height of each sail, Flettner, etc. in wind assisted propulsion system;

.2 v_{10m} is the wind velocity at 10 m above sea level;

.3 v_{Zref} is the resulting wind velocity at the reference height; and

.4 α is taken as 1/9 conforming to ITTC recommendations.[5]

.4   according to the corresponding average wind speed, wind direction angle and the velocity of the ship, calculate the relative wind speed V_k and the relative wind direction angle of the ship;

.5   according to the relative wind direction angle, and the corresponding relationship between the relative wind direction angle and the wind propulsion coefficient ΔC_{Fx} obtained from the test, calculate the average wind propulsion coefficients $(\Delta C_{Fx})_k$ of the wind assisted propulsion system corresponding to W_k; and

.6   according to the average wind propulsion coefficient of the wind assisted propulsion system, calculate the terms of the wind propulsion system force matrix $F(V_{ref})_k$ of the full scale ship corresponding to W_k by following formula:

$F(V_{ref})_k = (\Delta C_{Fx})_k * (0.5 \, \rho \, V_k^2 \, A)$

Where:

.1 $(\Delta C_{Fx})_k$ is the average wind propulsion coefficients corresponding to W_k;

.2 ρ is the average air density in shipping environment, $\rho = 1.225 \, kg/m^3$;

.3 V_k is the relative wind velocity of the full-scale ship corresponding to W_k;

.4   A is the total projected area of the wind assisted propulsion system;

.5   the settings of the wind propulsor may be varied in order to find the best $(\Delta CFx)_k$; this may be done using interpolation provided that increments in settings are sufficiently small;

---

[5]   International Towing Tank Conference (ITTC), "ITTC – Recommended Procedures and Guidelines; Preparation, Conduct and Analysis of Speed/Power Trial," International Towing Tank Conference (ITTC), 7.5-04-01-01.1, 2017.

Annotation: ITCC provides no guidance for wind speeds above an altitude above 300 m. However, it is assumed in this guideline to be constant above 300 m altitude.

$$v_{Zref} = v_{10m} \left(\frac{z_{ref}}{10}\right)^{\alpha} \ for \ z_{ref} < 300m$$

$$v_{Zref} = v_{10m} \left(\frac{300}{10}\right)^{\alpha} \ for \ z_{ref} \geq 300m$$

式中：

.1 z_{ref} 为风力辅助推进系统中，在水线以上的参考高度，等于各船帆、旋筒等的高度中点；

.2 $v_{10\,m}$ 为海平面以上 10 m 的风速；

.3 v_{Zref} 为参考高度处得到的风速；和

.4 α 取符合 ITTC 建议案[5]的 1/9。

.4 根据相应的平均风速、风向角和船舶的速度，计算相对风速 V_k 和船舶的相对风向角；

.5 根据相对风向角和试验得到的相对风向角与风力推进系数 ΔC_{Fx} 的对应关系，计算 W_k 对应的风力辅助推进系统的平均风力推进系数（ΔC_{Fx}）$_k$。

.6 根据风力辅助推进系统的平均风力推进系数，通过下式计算相对于 W_k 的全尺度船舶的风力推进系统力矩阵 F（V_{ref}）$_k$。

$$F(V_{ref})_k = (\Delta C_{Fx})_k * (0.5 \rho V_k^2 A)$$

式中：

.1 （ΔC_{Fx}）$_k$ 为相对于 W_k 的平均风力推进系数；

.2 ρ 为航运环境下平均空气密度，$\rho = 1.225 \ kg/m^3$；

.3 V_k 为全尺度船舶对于 W_k 的相对风速；

.4 A 为风力辅助推进系统的总投影面积；

.5 为找到最佳（ΔCFx）k，可以改变风力推进器的设置；可以通过插值来实现，前提是设置中的增量要足够小；

---

[5] 国际拖曳水池会议（ITTC），推荐程序和指南：速度/功率试验的准备、实施和分析，国际拖曳水池会议（ITTC），7.5-04-01-01.1，2017。
注：对于海拔 300 米以上的风速，ITCC 不提供指导。然而，在该指南中假定海拔 300 米以上的高度是恒定的。

.6   the settings and deployment of the wind assisted propulsion system must adhere to the operational constraints as defined for the system (e.g. a maximum operational wind speed, if lower than provided by the global wind probability matrix, > Bf 8, 19 m/s);

.7   the potential wind drag induced by the system is to be accounted for, such as in unusable wind directions close to head wind and when the systems is not operational due to exceedance of operational limits; and

.8   if $F(V_{ref})_k$ exceeds the resistance of the ship, such that the propeller thrust would be negative, $F(V_{ref})_k$ is to be limited at the resistance value.

2.4.4   Consideration of the operational limits of the wind assisted propulsion system and the lateral forces and yawing moments

2.4.4.1   Force $F(V_{ref})_k$ must be calculated only when it is within the operational domain applicable to the wind assisted propulsion system. These operational limitations can be caused at a minimum by wind conditions or by the total forces generated by the wind assisted propulsion system and applied to the ship.

2.4.4.2 $F(V_{ref})_k$ must be zero for any pair (wind direction; wind force) not in conformity with the operational domain of the wind assisted propulsion system validated by the verifier in the operations manual of the wind assisted propulsion system and the ship.

2.4.4.3   The lateral forces exerted by the wind assisted propulsion system on the ship and the resulting yawing moment can affect the performance of the system, and therefore the EEDI calculation. The lateral forces on the ship and the yawing moments applied by the wind assisted propulsion system to the ship should therefore be documented by the shipbuilder and/or propulsion system manufacturer and observed by the verifier. They can be obtained without additional effort during the tests described in paragraph 2.4.1 of the present circular.

2.4.4.4   Conformity with the operational domain requires that for any pair (wind direction; wind force), and in consideration of the total forces generated by the wind assisted propulsion system (i.e. including lateral forces to the vessel and yawing moments), the strength of the wind assisted propulsion system, the forces at the embedment and the list of the ship conform with the structural design file and the stability file of the ship, respectively. Where the lateral forces and yawing moment are particularly significant, the verifier may request course keeping and rudder angle demonstrations to validate conformity with the operational domain.

2.5   The global wind probability matrix W_k

2.5.1   Wind probabilities

2.5.1.1   Wind conditions are not constant. Winds vary their speed and direction with time. Wind expectations are unequal in different regions of the earth.

2.5.1.2   However, every wind expectation can be expressed in a distinctive wind probability pattern for every particular position on the globe. There is always a certain probability for a certain wind direction and wind speed to occur. These probabilities are documented in wind charts. With this approach each geographical region has a distinctive wind chart.

.6 风力辅助推进系统的设置和布置必须符合系统定义的操作约束条件（例如，如果低于全球风力概率矩阵提供的值，最大运行风速 >Bf 8，19 m/s）；

.7 系统引起的潜在风阻力应予以考虑，例如在接近顶风的不可用风向下，以及当系统因超过运行限制而无法运行时；

.8 如果 F（Vref）k 超过了船舶的阻力，使得螺旋桨推力为负，$F（V_{ref}）_k$ 将被限制在阻力值。

2.4.4 考虑风力辅助推进系统的运行限制和侧向力及偏航力矩

2.4.4.1 力 $F（V_{ref}）_k$ 必须在风力辅助推进系统适用的操作范围内计算。这些运行限制可至少由风况或风力辅助推进系统产生的总的力引起，并施加到船舶上。

2.4.4.2 对于与验证方在风力辅助推进系统和船舶操作手册中确定的风力辅助推进系统运行域不一致的任何配对（风向；风力），$F（V_{ref}）_k$ 必须为 0。

2.4.4.3 风力辅助系统对船舶施加的侧向力及由此产生的偏航力矩会影响系统性能，从而影响 EEDI 计算。因此，船厂和 / 或推进系统制造商应记录船上的侧向力和风力辅助推进系统对船舶施加的偏航力矩，并由验证方观察。在本通函 2.4.1 所述的试验期间，无须额外努力即可获得。

2.4.4.4 与运行域一致则要求，对于任意配对（风向；风力），考虑到风力辅助推进系统产生的总力（即包括船舶的侧向力和偏航力矩）情况下，风力辅助推进系统的强度、嵌入处的受力和船的横倾分别符合船舶结构设计案卷和船舶稳性案卷。当侧向力和偏航力矩特别显著时，验证方可以要求保持航向和显示舵角，以验证与运行域一致。

2.5 全球风力概率矩阵 W_k

2.5.1 风力概率

2.5.1.1 风况不是恒定的。风的速度和方向随时间而变化。地球上不同地区对风的预期是不相等的。

2.5.1.2 然而，对于全球的每一个特定位置，对每种风的预期都可以用一个独特的风力概率模式来表示。总是有一定的概率发生一定的风向和风速。这些概率被记录在风图中。采用这种方法，每个地理区域都有一个独特的风图。

2.5.2   Wind angles relative to the ship

2.5.2.1   For a wind assisted propulsion system, it is irrelevant if the wind is coming from North or South. Only the wind angle relative to a ship's heading is of importance. As a consequence, the wind directions given in the weather data have to be recalculated for ship headings on a trading route when applied to wind assisted propulsion systems, where 0° means the ship's bow, 90° its starboard side, 180° the stern and 270° port side.

2.5.3   Main global shipping network

2.5.3.1   To determine a global wind probability chart for the wind assisted propulsion system's EEDI calculation, the average of all wind conditions along the main global shipping routes is required.

2.5.3.2   Figure 1 shows the main global shipping network used to determine the global wind conditions. Along the shown routes, 106 wind condition charts were analysed. These charts are based on 868,500 individual wind data.

2.5.3.3   The wind condition charts for each position were first recalculated in ship heading coordinates and then averaged to form a global wind condition chart. The results are visualized in figure 2, the complete chart (the global wind probability matrix) is shown as the table in appendix 2 of this annex.

2.5.3.4   Each element of the matrix W_k represents the probability of the specific wind speed and wind angle relative to the ship. The sum of all matrix elements is one (1.0), representing 100% of all wind conditions.

2.5.3.5   The results show that winds to the bow or the stern occur more often than winds to the sides. There are two possible reasons to explain this phenomenon:

.1   shipping routes and global weather systems are more East-West than North-South oriented; and

.2   shipping routes and winds are influenced by shore lines, so they tend to be parallel in some regions.

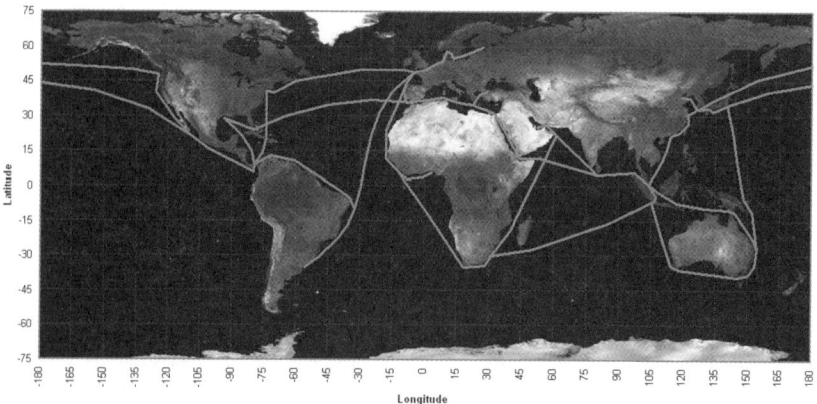

Figure 1 – The main global shipping network used for the wind chart

2.5.2 相对船舶的风向角

2.5.2.1 对于风力辅助推进系统，是南风还是北风无关紧要。只有相对于船首向的风向角是重要的。因此，当应用于风力辅助推进系统时，天气数据中给出的风向必须针对船舶在贸易航线上的首向重新计算，其中 0 线表示船首，90 船表示右舷，180 舷表示船尾，270 尾表示船左舷。

2.5.3 全球主要航运网络

2.5.3.1 为确定全球风力概率图以进行风力辅助推进系统的 EEDI 计算，需要全球主要航线上所有风况的平均值。

2.5.3.2 图 1 显示了用以确定全球风况的全球主要航运网络。沿所示航线分析了 106 个风况图。这些图是基于 868 500 个单独的风数据。

2.5.3.3 先在船首坐标中重新计算各位置的风况图，再求平均值，形成全球风况图。结果显示在图 2 中，完整的图表（全球风力概率矩阵）显示在本附件附录 2 的表格中。

2.5.3.4 矩阵 W_k 的每个要素代表了相对于船舶的特定风速和风向角。所有矩阵要素之和为一（1.0），代表 100% 所有风况的。

2.5.3.5 结果表明，船头或船尾风比舷侧风多。有两个可能的原因可以解释这一现象：

.1 航运路线和全球天气系统更偏向东西方向而不是南北方向；和
.2 航线和风受到海岸线的影响，所以在有些地区它们往往是平行的。

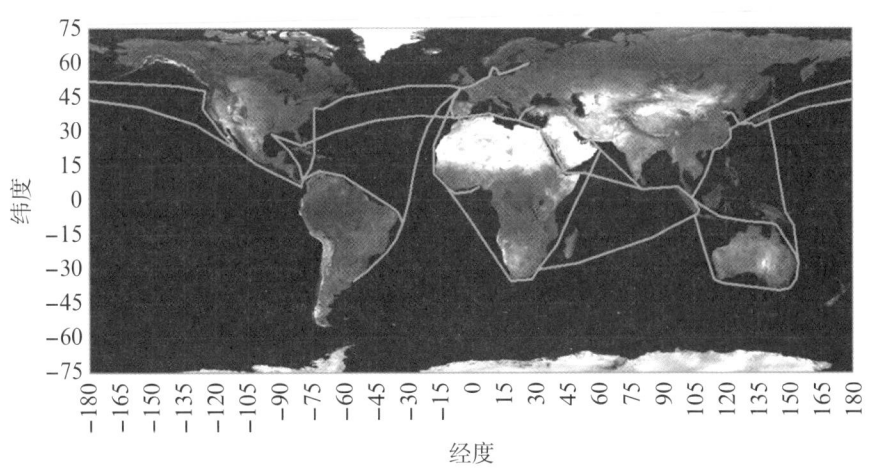

图 1　用于风图的全球主要航运网路

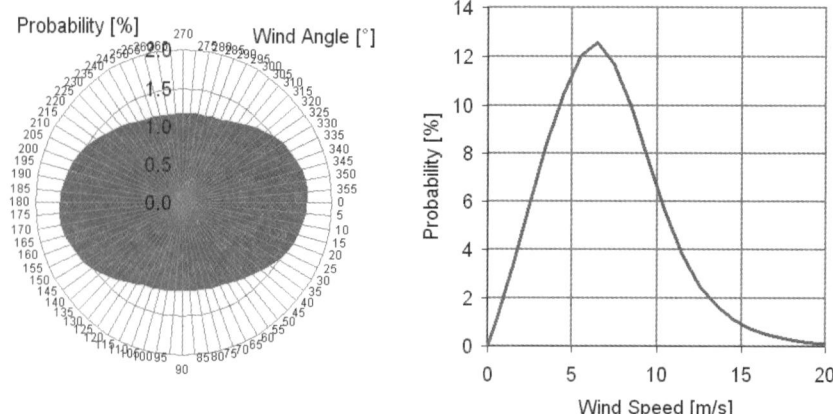

Figure 2 – Resulting wind curves on the main global shipping routes relative to the ship

2.6   Effective CO_2 reduction by wind assisted propulsion systems

2.6.1   For the calculation of the CO_2 reduction, the resulting available effective power ($f_{eff} * P_{eff}$) has to be multiplied with the conversion factor C_{FME} and SFC_{ME}, as contained in the original EEDI formula.

2.7   Verification of wind assisted propulsion systems in the EEDI certification process

2.7.1   General

2.7.1.1   Verification of EEDI with innovative energy efficient technologies should be conducted according to the EEDI Survey Guidelines. Additional items concerning innovative energy efficient technologies not contained in EEDI Survey Guidelines are described below.

2.7.2   Preliminary verification at the design stage

2.7.2.1   In addition to paragraph 4.2.2 of EEDI Survey Guidelines, the EEDI Technical File which is to be developed by the shipowner or shipbuilder should include:

.1   Outline of wind assisted propulsion systems; and

.2   Calculated value of EEDI due to the wind assisted propulsion system.

2.7.2.2   In addition to paragraph 4.2.7 of the EEDI Survey Guidelines, additional information from the shipbuilder may be requested by the verifier. It includes:

.1   Detailed calculation process of the wind propulsion system force matrix $F(V_{ref})_k$ and results of performance tests.

2.7.2.3   In order to prevent undesirable effects on the ship's structure or main drive, the influences of added forces on the ship should be determined during the EEDI certification process. Elements in the wind propulsion system force matrix may be limited to ship specific restrictions, if necessary. The technical means to restrict the wind propulsion system's force should be verified as part of the performance test.

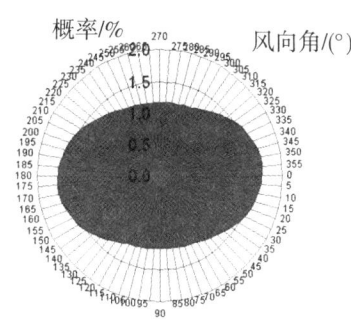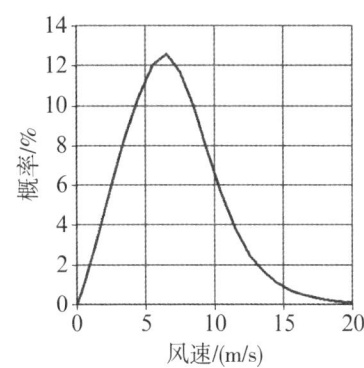

图 2　得出的全球主要航线上相对于船舶的风曲线

2.6　风力辅助推进系统有效 CO_2 减少量

2.6.1　为计算 CO_2 的减少量，应将计算得到的可用有效功率（$f_{eff}*P_{eff}$）乘以原 EEDI 公式中的换算系数 C_{FME} 和 SFC_{ME}。

2.7　EEDI 发证过程中风力辅助推进系统的验证

2.7.1　一般规定

2.7.1.1 采用创新能效技术的船舶应按 EEDI 检验指南进行 EEDI 验证。EEDI 检验指南中未包括的有关创新能效技术的附加资料见下文。

2.7.2　设计阶段的前期验证

2.7.2.1　除 EEDI 检验指南 4.2.2 要求外，船东或船厂编制的 EEDI 技术案卷还应包括：

　　.1　风力辅助推进系统的简图；和

　　.2　采用风力辅助推进系统的 EEDI 计算值。

2.7.2.2　除 EEDI 检验指南 4.2.7 要求外，验证方还可能要求船厂提供的附加资料包括：
　　.1　风力推进系统力矩阵 $F（V_{ref}）_k$ 的详细计算过程及性能试验结果。

2.7.2.3　为防止对船舶结构和主驱动装置产生不利影响，EEDI 发证过程中应确定附加力对船舶的影响。如有必要，风力推进系统力矩阵要素可以受限于船舶具体的限制条件。限制风力推进系统力的技术方法应作为性能试验的一部分而进行验证。

2.7.2.4   If more than one innovative energy efficient technology is subject to approval in the EEDI certification, interactions between these technologies should be considered. The appropriate technical papers should be included in the additional information submitted to the verifier in the certification process.

2.7.3   Final verification of the attained EEDI

2.7.3.1   The total net power generated by wind assisted propulsion systems should be confirmed based on the documentation in the EEDI Technical File. For final verification, EEDI verifier should check that the configuration of the installed wind assisted propulsion system agrees with the system as described in the EEDI Technical File.

2.7.2.4 如 EEDI 发证过程中需认可多个创新能效技术，应考虑这些技术之间的相互影响。发证过程中向验证方提交的附加资料中应包括相应的技术文件。

2.7.3 试航时 Attained EEDI 的最终验证

2.7.3.1 应根据 EEDI 技术案卷中的文件，对风力辅助推进系统产生的总净功率进行确认。对于最终验证，验证方应检查安装的风力辅助推进系统的配置是否与 EEDI 技术案卷中的描述一致。

APPENDIX 1

METHOD OF WIND TUNNEL MODEL TEST

In accordance with section 2.4.1 of the present circular, two test methods are defined:

.1   option 1: test on a ship model fitted with the full wind assisted propulsion system; and

.2   option 2: test on a complete model of a single wind propulsion unit.

Option 1: Test on a ship model fitted with the full wind assisted propulsion system

1   Model

1.1   The wind assisted propulsion system model and the hull model should be made similarly to the real form, but appendages which do not affect the aerodynamic characteristics can be omitted from the model (e.g. handrails, windlass, etc.).

1.2   The draught condition of the hull model should be corresponding to the *Capacity* as defined in EEDI Calculation Guidelines.

1.3   The hull model is connected with the turntable by force balance, and the wind direction angle of the ship model is changed by changing the angle of the turntable.

2   Test condition

2.1   In addition to geometric similarity, the dynamic similarity criterion must be satisfied in the wind matrix wind tunnel model test of a ship's wind assisted propulsion system. That is, when the test wind speed is higher than a certain critical wind speed, the dimensionless wind coefficient tends to be stable, and the flow around the model is similar to the real ship. The measured wind coefficient can be directly extrapolated to the real ship. During the test, the critical wind speed is determined by a variable wind speed test.

2.2   In the wind tunnel model test, spires and roughness elements are arranged at the front of the test section, and the wind field of the atmospheric boundary layer on the ocean surface at the model scale for wind matrix test is obtained. Reynolds number of the test should be more than 1.0×10^6. The Reynolds number, Re, is expressed by the following formula:

$$\mu$$

where ρ and μ are the density and viscosity of the air, respectively, U is the wind speed, L_{pp} is the length between perpendiculars of the model ship.

2.3   The blockage ratio should not be more than 5%. The ratio is calculated by the transverse projected area of the model divided by the cross-sectional area of wind tunnel.

3   Test method

3.1   At the same hull wind direction, the wind propulsion coefficients of the wind assisted propulsion system are different at different angles of attack. In order to obtain the maximum wind propulsion coefficients of the wind assisted propulsion system at each hull wind direction angle, the test scheme should include:

附录 1

风洞模型试验方法

根据本通函第 2.4.1 节，定义了两种试验方法：

.1 方案 1：在装有整套风力辅助推进系统的船模上进行试验

.2 方案 2：在单个风力推进装置的完整模型上进行试验

方案 1：在装有整套风力辅助推进系统的船模上进行试验

1 模型

1.1 风力辅助推进系统模型和船体模型应与真实形态相似，但不影响气动特性的附件可以在模型中忽略（如扶手、绞车等）。

1.2 船体模型的吃水工况应与 EEDI 计算指南中定义的载运能力相对应。

1.3 船体模型通过力平衡和风向与转台连接，通过改变转台的角度来改变船体模型的风向角度。

2 试验工况

2.1 船舶风力辅助推进系统风力矩阵风洞模型试验除几何相似性外，还必须满足动力相似性衡准。即当试验风速大于某一临界风速时，无因次风系数趋于稳定，模型周围流场与实船相似。测得的风系数可以直接外推到实船上。在试验中，通过可变的风速试验确定临界风速。

$$\mu$$

2.2 在风洞模型试验中，在试验段前部布置了尖劈和粗糙元，得到进行风力矩阵试验的模型尺度下海洋表面大气边界层的风场。试验的雷诺数应大于 1.0×10^6。雷诺数 Re 表示为：

式中，ρ 和 μ 分别为空气的密度和黏度，U 为风速，L_{pp} 为模型船垂线间的长度。

2.3 阻塞比不应超过 5%。该比值由模型的横向投影面积除以风洞的横截面面积计算得到。

3 试验方法

3.1 在相同船体风向下，不同迎角下风力辅助推进系统的风力推进系数不同。为得到每个船体风向角下风力辅助推进系统的最大风力推进系数，试验方案应包括：

.1   measurements of the aerodynamic force characteristics of the ship model without wind assisted propulsion system at a series of wind angles ranging from 0° to 360°, spaced by an interval of 5°, potentially extended to 10° only for beam to stern;

.2   measurements of the aerodynamic force characteristics of the ship model with wind assisted propulsion system at a series of wind angles ranging from 0° to 360°, spaced by an interval of 5° or 10°, attack angles of the wind assisted propulsion system range from 0° to 180°, spaced by an interval of 5° or 10° in every wind angle of the ship model. Smaller intervals of attack angles should be needed around the maximum wind propulsion coefficients; and

.3   in the case where the measurements are carried out with spaced by an interval of 10°, each intermediate force characteristic (i.e. F_X at 5°, 15°, 25°…) should be interpolated by using the measurement results.

3.2   In the case where the shape of the ship and wind assisted propulsion system are symmetrical on starboard side and port side, the wind propulsion coefficients are also symmetrical and thus, the measurements at a series of wind angles ranging from 0° to 180° or 180° to 360° can be omitted.

3.3   If the wind assisted propulsion system has a changeable and controllable structure, such as sails and rotors, the model of the wind assisted propulsion system can be arranged as the wind angle, the rotor speed, or other controllable structure to maximize the gained wind force or to minimize the wind resistance.

Option 2: Test on a complete model of a single wind propulsion unit

4   Model

4.1   The effects of the hull and superstructures should be taken into account by corrective actions taking into account the masked area and distance. If several wind propulsion units are installed on board the ship, the aerodynamic interactions between them should be taken into account by corrective actions. The verifier may request documentation from the test author to verify that these effects have been taken into account.

4.2   The wind propulsion unit model is connected to the turntable by means of a force balance, and the wind direction angle of the ship model is changed by changing the angle of the turntable.

5   Test conditions

5.1   In addition to geometric similarity, the dynamic similarity criterion must be satisfied in the wind matrix wind tunnel model test of a ship's wind assisted propulsion system. That is, when the test wind speed is higher than a certain critical wind speed, the dimensionless wind coefficient tends to be stable, and the flow around the model is similar to the real ship. The measured wind coefficient can be directly extrapolated to the real ship. During the test, the critical wind speed is determined by a variable wind speed test.

5.2   The maximum Reynolds number of the test should be more than 5.0×10^5. The Reynolds number, Re, is expressed by the following formula:

$$Re = \rho . U . C / \mu$$

where ρ and μ are the density and viscosity of the air, respectively, U is the wind speed, C is the mean chord length of the wind propulsion unit.

.1 测量无风力辅助推进系统的船模在 0° 到 360° 的一系列风向角（以 5° 为间隔）范围下的气动力特性，仅在船梁到船尾可扩大到 10° 。

.2 测量具有风力辅助推进系统的船模在 0° 到 360° 的一系列风向角（以 5° 或 10° 为间隔）范围下的气动力特性，风力辅助推进系统的迎角范围为 0° 到 180° ，船模每一风向角间隔为 5° 或 10° 。在最大风力推进系数附近，应需要更小的迎角间隔；和

.3 在测量间隔为 10° 的情况下，应该用测量结果对每个中间力特性（例如在 5° ，15° ，25° …的 FX）进行插值。

3.2 当船舶形状和风力辅助推进系统在右舷和左舷对称时，风力推进系数也是对称的，因此，从 0° 到 180° 或 180° 到 360° 的一系列风向角的测量可以省略。

3.3 如果风力辅助推进系统具有船帆、旋筒等可变和可控结构，则风力辅助推进系统的模型可布置为风向角、旋筒速度或其他可控结构使获得的风力最大化或使风阻力最小化。

方案 2：在单个风力推进装置的完整模型上进行试验

4 模型

4.1 纠正措施应考虑船体和上层建筑的影响，并考虑到遮蔽区域和距离。如果船上安装了多个风力推进装置，则纠正措施应考虑它们之间的气动相互作用。验证方可要求试验编写者提供案卷，以验证这些影响已被考虑在内。

4.2 通过力平衡将风力推进单元模型与转台连接，通过改变转台的角度来改变船模的风向角。

5 试验工况

5.1 船舶风力辅助推进系统风矩阵风洞模型试验除几何相似性外，还必须满足动力相似性衡准。即当试验风速大于某一临界风速时，无因次风系数趋于稳定，模型周围流场与实船相似。测得的风系数可以直接外推到实船上。在试验中，通过可变风速试验确定临界风速。

5.2 试验的最大雷诺数应大于 5.0×10^5。雷诺数 Re 表示为：

$$Re = \rho . U . C / \mu$$

式中，ρ 和 μ 分别为空气的密度和黏度，U 为风速，C 为风力推进装置的平均弦长。

5.3   The blockage ratio should not be more than 5%. The ratio is calculated by the transverse projected area of the model divided by the cross-sectional area of wind tunnel.

6   Test method

6.1   In order to obtain the maximum wind propulsion coefficients of the wind assisted propulsion system at each ship wind direction angle, the test scheme should include measurements of the aerodynamic force characteristics for:

   .1   a range of permissible angles of attack on the wind propulsion unit; and

   .2   a range of permissible settings (profile camber, rotation speed, suction rate, reduced area, etc.).

6.2   The propulsive force on the ship is the aerodynamic force measured on the wind propulsion unit pointing to the bow.

5.3 阻塞比不应超过5%。该比值由模型的横向投影面积除以风洞的横截面面积计算得到。

6 试验方法

6.1 为了获得每一船舶风向角下的风力辅助推进系统的最大风推进系数，试验方案中应包括以下气动特性的测量：

.1 风力推进装置的许用迎角范围；和

.2 允许使用的设置范围（剖面弧度、转速、吸气率、缩小面积等）。

6.2 作用在船上的推进力是指在风力推进装置上测得的指向船首的气动力。

APPENDIX 2

GLOBAL WIND PROBABILITY MATRIX W$_k$

Table 1 – Normalized global wind chart showing the probability of wind conditions relative to the ship's heading along the main global trading routes

Wind Speed [m/s] \ Wind Angle [°]	0	5	10	15	20	25	30	35	40	45	50	55	60	65	70	75	80	85	90	95	100	105	110	115
<1	0.0001	0.0001	0.0001	0.0001	0.0001	0.0001	0.0001	0.0001	0.0001	0.0001	0.0001	0.0001	0.0001	0.0001	0.0001	0.0001	0.0001	0.0001	0.0001	0.0001	0.0001	0.0001	0.0001	0.0001
<2	0.0005	0.0005	0.0005	0.0005	0.0005	0.0005	0.0005	0.0005	0.0005	0.0005	0.0005	0.0005	0.0005	0.0005	0.0005	0.0005	0.0005	0.0005	0.0005	0.0005	0.0005	0.0005	0.0005	0.0005
<3	0.0009	0.0009	0.0009	0.0009	0.0008	0.0008	0.0008	0.0008	0.0008	0.0008	0.0008	0.0008	0.0008	0.0008	0.0008	0.0008	0.0008	0.0008	0.0008	0.0008	0.0008	0.0008	0.0008	0.0008
<4	0.0013	0.0013	0.0013	0.0013	0.0012	0.0012	0.0012	0.0012	0.0011	0.0011	0.0011	0.0011	0.0011	0.0011	0.0011	0.0010	0.0010	0.0010	0.0010	0.0011	0.0011	0.0011	0.0011	0.0011
<5	0.0017	0.0017	0.0017	0.0016	0.0016	0.0015	0.0015	0.0015	0.0014	0.0014	0.0013	0.0013	0.0012	0.0012	0.0012	0.0012	0.0013	0.0013	0.0013	0.0013	0.0013	0.0013	0.0013	0.0015
<6	0.0021	0.0020	0.0020	0.0019	0.0018	0.0018	0.0017	0.0016	0.0016	0.0015	0.0015	0.0014	0.0014	0.0014	0.0013	0.0014	0.0014	0.0014	0.0014	0.0014	0.0014	0.0014	0.0015	0.0015
<7	0.0022	0.0022	0.0021	0.0020	0.0020	0.0019	0.0018	0.0017	0.0017	0.0016	0.0015	0.0014	0.0014	0.0014	0.0014	0.0014	0.0014	0.0014	0.0014	0.0014	0.0015	0.0015	0.0015	0.0015
<8	0.0020	0.0020	0.0020	0.0019	0.0019	0.0018	0.0017	0.0016	0.0016	0.0015	0.0014	0.0014	0.0013	0.0013	0.0013	0.0013	0.0013	0.0013	0.0013	0.0013	0.0013	0.0014	0.0014	0.0014
<9	0.0017	0.0017	0.0017	0.0016	0.0016	0.0016	0.0015	0.0014	0.0014	0.0013	0.0013	0.0012	0.0012	0.0011	0.0011	0.0011	0.0011	0.0011	0.0011	0.0011	0.0011	0.0011	0.0012	0.0012
<10	0.0013	0.0013	0.0013	0.0013	0.0013	0.0013	0.0012	0.0012	0.0011	0.0011	0.0010	0.0010	0.0010	0.0010	0.0009	0.0009	0.0009	0.0009	0.0009	0.0009	0.0009	0.0009	0.0009	0.0009
<11	0.0010	0.0010	0.0010	0.0010	0.0009	0.0009	0.0009	0.0009	0.0009	0.0009	0.0008	0.0008	0.0008	0.0008	0.0007	0.0007	0.0007	0.0007	0.0006	0.0006	0.0006	0.0006	0.0006	0.0006
<12	0.0007	0.0007	0.0007	0.0007	0.0007	0.0006	0.0006	0.0006	0.0006	0.0006	0.0006	0.0005	0.0005	0.0005	0.0005	0.0005	0.0005	0.0004	0.0004	0.0004	0.0004	0.0004	0.0004	0.0004
<13	0.0004	0.0005	0.0005	0.0005	0.0004	0.0004	0.0004	0.0004	0.0004	0.0004	0.0004	0.0003	0.0003	0.0003	0.0003	0.0003	0.0003	0.0003	0.0003	0.0003	0.0003	0.0002	0.0002	0.0002
<14	0.0003	0.0003	0.0003	0.0003	0.0003	0.0003	0.0003	0.0003	0.0003	0.0002	0.0002	0.0002	0.0002	0.0002	0.0002	0.0002	0.0002	0.0002	0.0002	0.0002	0.0002	0.0002	0.0002	0.0002
<15	0.0002	0.0002	0.0002	0.0002	0.0002	0.0002	0.0002	0.0002	0.0002	0.0002	0.0002	0.0002	0.0001	0.0001	0.0001	0.0001	0.0001	0.0001	0.0001	0.0001	0.0001	0.0001	0.0001	0.0001
<16	0.0001	0.0001	0.0001	0.0001	0.0001	0.0001	0.0001	0.0001	0.0001	0.0001	0.0001	0.0001	0.0001	0.0001	0.0001	0.0001	0.0001	0.0001	0.0001	0.0001	0.0001	0.0001	0.0001	0.0001
<17	0.0001	0.0001	0.0001	0.0001	0.0001	0.0001	0.0001	0.0001	0.0001	0.0001	0.0001	0.0001	0.0001	0.0001	0.0001	0.0001	0.0001	0.0001	0.0001	0.0001	0.0001	0.0001	0.0001	0.0001
<18	0.0001	0.0001	0.0001	0.0001	0.0001	0.0001	0.0001	0.0001	0.0001	0.0000	0.0000	0.0000	0.0000	0.0000	0.0000	0.0000	0.0000	0.0000	0.0000	0.0000	0.0000	0.0000	0.0000	0.0000
<19	0.0000	0.0000	0.0000	0.0000	0.0000	0.0000	0.0000	0.0000	0.0000	0.0000	0.0000	0.0000	0.0000	0.0000	0.0000	0.0000	0.0000	0.0000	0.0000	0.0000	0.0000	0.0000	0.0000	0.0000
<20	0.0000	0.0000	0.0000	0.0000	0.0000	0.0000	0.0000	0.0000	0.0000	0.0000	0.0000	0.0000	0.0000	0.0000	0.0000	0.0000	0.0000	0.0000	0.0000	0.0000	0.0000	0.0000	0.0000	0.0000
<21	0.0000	0.0000	0.0000	0.0000	0.0000	0.0000	0.0000	0.0000	0.0000	0.0000	0.0000	0.0000	0.0000	0.0000	0.0000	0.0000	0.0000	0.0000	0.0000	0.0000	0.0000	0.0000	0.0000	0.0000
<22	0.0000	0.0000	0.0000	0.0000	0.0000	0.0000	0.0000	0.0000	0.0000	0.0000	0.0000	0.0000	0.0000	0.0000	0.0000	0.0000	0.0000	0.0000	0.0000	0.0000	0.0000	0.0000	0.0000	0.0000
<23	0.0000	0.0000	0.0000	0.0000	0.0000	0.0000	0.0000	0.0000	0.0000	0.0000	0.0000	0.0000	0.0000	0.0000	0.0000	0.0000	0.0000	0.0000	0.0000	0.0000	0.0000	0.0000	0.0000	0.0000
<24	0.0000	0.0000	0.0000	0.0000	0.0000	0.0000	0.0000	0.0000	0.0000	0.0000	0.0000	0.0000	0.0000	0.0000	0.0000	0.0000	0.0000	0.0000	0.0000	0.0000	0.0000	0.0000	0.0000	0.0000
<25	0.0000	0.0000	0.0000	0.0000	0.0000	0.0000	0.0000	0.0000	0.0000	0.0000	0.0000	0.0000	0.0000	0.0000	0.0000	0.0000	0.0000	0.0000	0.0000	0.0000	0.0000	0.0000	0.0000	0.0000
>=25	0.0000	0.0000	0.0000	0.0000	0.0000	0.0000	0.0000	0.0000	0.0000	0.0000	0.0000	0.0000	0.0000	0.0000	0.0000	0.0000	0.0000	0.0000	0.0000	0.0000	0.0000	0.0000	0.0000	0.0000

Wind Speed [m/s] \ Wind Angle [°]	120	125	130	135	140	145	150	155	160	165	170	175	180	185	190	195	200	205	210	215	220	225	230	235
<1	0.0001	0.0001	0.0001	0.0001	0.0001	0.0001	0.0001	0.0001	0.0001	0.0001	0.0001	0.0001	0.0001	0.0001	0.0001	0.0001	0.0001	0.0001	0.0001	0.0001	0.0001	0.0001	0.0001	0.0001
<2	0.0005	0.0005	0.0005	0.0005	0.0005	0.0005	0.0005	0.0005	0.0005	0.0005	0.0005	0.0005	0.0005	0.0005	0.0005	0.0005	0.0005	0.0005	0.0005	0.0005	0.0005	0.0005	0.0005	0.0005
<3	0.0008	0.0008	0.0008	0.0008	0.0008	0.0009	0.0009	0.0009	0.0009	0.0009	0.0009	0.0009	0.0009	0.0009	0.0009	0.0009	0.0009	0.0008	0.0008	0.0008	0.0008	0.0008	0.0008	0.0008
<4	0.0011	0.0011	0.0012	0.0012	0.0012	0.0013	0.0013	0.0013	0.0013	0.0013	0.0013	0.0013	0.0013	0.0013	0.0013	0.0013	0.0012	0.0012	0.0012	0.0012	0.0011	0.0011	0.0011	0.0013
<5	0.0014	0.0014	0.0015	0.0015	0.0016	0.0016	0.0016	0.0017	0.0017	0.0017	0.0017	0.0017	0.0017	0.0017	0.0017	0.0016	0.0016	0.0015	0.0015	0.0014	0.0014	0.0013	0.0013	0.0013
<6	0.0015	0.0016	0.0017	0.0017	0.0018	0.0019	0.0020	0.0020	0.0021	0.0021	0.0021	0.0021	0.0021	0.0020	0.0020	0.0019	0.0018	0.0018	0.0017	0.0016	0.0016	0.0015	0.0015	0.0014
<7	0.0016	0.0016	0.0017	0.0018	0.0019	0.0020	0.0021	0.0021	0.0022	0.0023	0.0022	0.0022	0.0022	0.0021	0.0021	0.0020	0.0019	0.0018	0.0017	0.0017	0.0016	0.0016	0.0015	0.0014
<8	0.0015	0.0015	0.0016	0.0017	0.0017	0.0018	0.0019	0.0020	0.0020	0.0021	0.0021	0.0021	0.0020	0.0020	0.0020	0.0019	0.0019	0.0018	0.0017	0.0016	0.0016	0.0015	0.0014	0.0014
<9	0.0012	0.0012	0.0013	0.0013	0.0014	0.0014	0.0015	0.0016	0.0016	0.0017	0.0017	0.0017	0.0017	0.0017	0.0016	0.0016	0.0016	0.0015	0.0014	0.0014	0.0013	0.0013	0.0013	0.0012
<10	0.0009	0.0009	0.0010	0.0010	0.0011	0.0011	0.0012	0.0012	0.0012	0.0013	0.0013	0.0013	0.0013	0.0013	0.0013	0.0013	0.0013	0.0012	0.0012	0.0011	0.0011	0.0010	0.0010	0.0010
<11	0.0006	0.0006	0.0007	0.0007	0.0008	0.0008	0.0008	0.0009	0.0009	0.0009	0.0010	0.0010	0.0010	0.0010	0.0010	0.0010	0.0009	0.0009	0.0009	0.0008	0.0008	0.0008	0.0008	0.0008
<12	0.0004	0.0004	0.0004	0.0005	0.0005	0.0005	0.0005	0.0006	0.0006	0.0006	0.0006	0.0007	0.0007	0.0007	0.0007	0.0007	0.0007	0.0006	0.0006	0.0006	0.0006	0.0006	0.0006	0.0005
<13	0.0003	0.0003	0.0003	0.0003	0.0003	0.0003	0.0004	0.0004	0.0004	0.0004	0.0004	0.0004	0.0004	0.0004	0.0005	0.0005	0.0005	0.0004	0.0004	0.0004	0.0004	0.0004	0.0004	0.0003
<14	0.0002	0.0002	0.0002	0.0002	0.0002	0.0002	0.0002	0.0002	0.0003	0.0003	0.0003	0.0003	0.0003	0.0003	0.0003	0.0003	0.0003	0.0003	0.0003	0.0003	0.0003	0.0002	0.0002	0.0002
<15	0.0001	0.0001	0.0001	0.0001	0.0001	0.0002	0.0002	0.0002	0.0002	0.0002	0.0002	0.0002	0.0002	0.0002	0.0002	0.0002	0.0002	0.0002	0.0002	0.0002	0.0002	0.0002	0.0002	0.0001
<16	0.0001	0.0001	0.0001	0.0001	0.0001	0.0001	0.0001	0.0001	0.0001	0.0001	0.0001	0.0001	0.0001	0.0001	0.0001	0.0001	0.0001	0.0001	0.0001	0.0001	0.0001	0.0001	0.0001	0.0001
<17	0.0001	0.0001	0.0001	0.0001	0.0001	0.0001	0.0001	0.0001	0.0001	0.0001	0.0001	0.0001	0.0001	0.0001	0.0001	0.0001	0.0001	0.0001	0.0001	0.0001	0.0001	0.0001	0.0001	0.0001
<18	0.0000	0.0000	0.0000	0.0000	0.0000	0.0000	0.0000	0.0000	0.0000	0.0001	0.0001	0.0001	0.0001	0.0001	0.0001	0.0001	0.0000	0.0000	0.0000	0.0000	0.0000	0.0000	0.0000	0.0000
<19	0.0000	0.0000	0.0000	0.0000	0.0000	0.0000	0.0000	0.0000	0.0000	0.0000	0.0000	0.0000	0.0000	0.0000	0.0000	0.0000	0.0000	0.0000	0.0000	0.0000	0.0000	0.0000	0.0000	0.0000
<20	0.0000	0.0000	0.0000	0.0000	0.0000	0.0000	0.0000	0.0000	0.0000	0.0000	0.0000	0.0000	0.0000	0.0000	0.0000	0.0000	0.0000	0.0000	0.0000	0.0000	0.0000	0.0000	0.0000	0.0000
<21	0.0000	0.0000	0.0000	0.0000	0.0000	0.0000	0.0000	0.0000	0.0000	0.0000	0.0000	0.0000	0.0000	0.0000	0.0000	0.0000	0.0000	0.0000	0.0000	0.0000	0.0000	0.0000	0.0000	0.0000
<22	0.0000	0.0000	0.0000	0.0000	0.0000	0.0000	0.0000	0.0000	0.0000	0.0000	0.0000	0.0000	0.0000	0.0000	0.0000	0.0000	0.0000	0.0000	0.0000	0.0000	0.0000	0.0000	0.0000	0.0000
<23	0.0000	0.0000	0.0000	0.0000	0.0000	0.0000	0.0000	0.0000	0.0000	0.0000	0.0000	0.0000	0.0000	0.0000	0.0000	0.0000	0.0000	0.0000	0.0000	0.0000	0.0000	0.0000	0.0000	0.0000
<24	0.0000	0.0000	0.0000	0.0000	0.0000	0.0000	0.0000	0.0000	0.0000	0.0000	0.0000	0.0000	0.0000	0.0000	0.0000	0.0000	0.0000	0.0000	0.0000	0.0000	0.0000	0.0000	0.0000	0.0000
<25	0.0000	0.0000	0.0000	0.0000	0.0000	0.0000	0.0000	0.0000	0.0000	0.0000	0.0000	0.0000	0.0000	0.0000	0.0000	0.0000	0.0000	0.0000	0.0000	0.0000	0.0000	0.0000	0.0000	0.0000
>=25	0.0000	0.0000	0.0000	0.0000	0.0000	0.0000	0.0000	0.0000	0.0000	0.0000	0.0000	0.0000	0.0000	0.0000	0.0000	0.0000	0.0000	0.0000	0.0000	0.0000	0.0000	0.0000	0.0000	0.0000

Wind Speed [m/s] \ Wind Angle [°]	240	245	250	255	260	265	270	275	280	285	290	295	300	305	310	315	320	325	330	335	340	345	350	355
<1	0.0001	0.0001	0.0001	0.0001	0.0001	0.0001	0.0001	0.0001	0.0001	0.0001	0.0001	0.0001	0.0001	0.0001	0.0001	0.0001	0.0001	0.0001	0.0001	0.0001	0.0001	0.0001	0.0001	0.0001
<2	0.0005	0.0005	0.0005	0.0005	0.0005	0.0005	0.0005	0.0005	0.0005	0.0005	0.0005	0.0005	0.0005	0.0005	0.0005	0.0005	0.0005	0.0005	0.0005	0.0005	0.0005	0.0005	0.0005	0.0005
<3	0.0008	0.0008	0.0008	0.0008	0.0008	0.0008	0.0008	0.0008	0.0008	0.0008	0.0008	0.0008	0.0008	0.0008	0.0008	0.0008	0.0008	0.0009	0.0009	0.0009	0.0009	0.0009	0.0009	0.0009
<4	0.0011	0.0011	0.0011	0.0010	0.0010	0.0010	0.0010	0.0011	0.0011	0.0011	0.0011	0.0011	0.0011	0.0011	0.0011	0.0012	0.0012	0.0012	0.0013	0.0013	0.0013	0.0013	0.0013	0.0013
<5	0.0013	0.0012	0.0012	0.0012	0.0012	0.0012	0.0013	0.0013	0.0013	0.0013	0.0013	0.0013	0.0014	0.0014	0.0015	0.0015	0.0016	0.0016	0.0017	0.0017	0.0017	0.0017	0.0017	0.0017
<6	0.0014	0.0014	0.0014	0.0013	0.0014	0.0014	0.0014	0.0014	0.0014	0.0015	0.0015	0.0015	0.0015	0.0016	0.0016	0.0017	0.0017	0.0018	0.0019	0.0020	0.0021	0.0021	0.0021	0.0021
<7	0.0014	0.0014	0.0013	0.0013	0.0014	0.0014	0.0014	0.0014	0.0015	0.0015	0.0015	0.0015	0.0015	0.0016	0.0016	0.0017	0.0018	0.0019	0.0020	0.0021	0.0021	0.0022	0.0022	0.0022
<8	0.0013	0.0013	0.0013	0.0013	0.0013	0.0013	0.0013	0.0013	0.0013	0.0014	0.0014	0.0014	0.0014	0.0015	0.0016	0.0017	0.0017	0.0018	0.0019	0.0020	0.0020	0.0021	0.0021	0.0021
<9	0.0012	0.0011	0.0011	0.0011	0.0011	0.0011	0.0011	0.0011	0.0011	0.0011	0.0012	0.0012	0.0012	0.0012	0.0013	0.0014	0.0015	0.0015	0.0016	0.0016	0.0017	0.0017	0.0017	0.0017
<10	0.0010	0.0009	0.0009	0.0009	0.0009	0.0009	0.0009	0.0008	0.0008	0.0009	0.0009	0.0009	0.0009	0.0010	0.0010	0.0010	0.0011	0.0011	0.0012	0.0012	0.0012	0.0013	0.0013	0.0013
<11	0.0008	0.0007	0.0007	0.0007	0.0007	0.0006	0.0006	0.0006	0.0006	0.0006	0.0006	0.0006	0.0006	0.0006	0.0006	0.0007	0.0007	0.0008	0.0008	0.0009	0.0009	0.0009	0.0009	0.0010
<12	0.0005	0.0005	0.0005	0.0005	0.0005	0.0004	0.0004	0.0004	0.0004	0.0004	0.0004	0.0004	0.0004	0.0005	0.0005	0.0005	0.0005	0.0006	0.0006	0.0006	0.0006	0.0006	0.0006	0.0007
<13	0.0003	0.0003	0.0003	0.0003	0.0003	0.0003	0.0003	0.0003	0.0003	0.0002	0.0002	0.0002	0.0003	0.0003	0.0003	0.0003	0.0003	0.0004	0.0004	0.0004	0.0004	0.0004	0.0004	0.0004
<14	0.0002	0.0002	0.0002	0.0002	0.0002	0.0002	0.0002	0.0002	0.0002	0.0002	0.0002	0.0002	0.0002	0.0002	0.0002	0.0002	0.0002	0.0002	0.0002	0.0002	0.0003	0.0003	0.0003	0.0003
<15	0.0001	0.0001	0.0001	0.0001	0.0001	0.0001	0.0001	0.0001	0.0001	0.0001	0.0001	0.0001	0.0001	0.0001	0.0001	0.0001	0.0001	0.0001	0.0002	0.0002	0.0002	0.0002	0.0002	0.0002
<16	0.0001	0.0001	0.0001	0.0001	0.0001	0.0001	0.0001	0.0001	0.0001	0.0001	0.0001	0.0001	0.0001	0.0001	0.0001	0.0001	0.0001	0.0001	0.0001	0.0001	0.0001	0.0001	0.0001	0.0001
<17	0.0001	0.0001	0.0001	0.0001	0.0001	0.0001	0.0001	0.0001	0.0001	0.0001	0.0001	0.0001	0.0001	0.0001	0.0001	0.0001	0.0001	0.0001	0.0001	0.0001	0.0001	0.0001	0.0001	0.0001
<18	0.0000	0.0000	0.0000	0.0000	0.0000	0.0000	0.0000	0.0000	0.0000	0.0000	0.0000	0.0000	0.0000	0.0000	0.0000	0.0000	0.0000	0.0000	0.0000	0.0000	0.0000	0.0000	0.0000	0.0000
<19	0.0000	0.0000	0.0000	0.0000	0.0000	0.0000	0.0000	0.0000	0.0000	0.0000	0.0000	0.0000	0.0000	0.0000	0.0000	0.0000	0.0000	0.0000	0.0000	0.0000	0.0000	0.0000	0.0000	0.0000
<20	0.0000	0.0000	0.0000	0.0000	0.0000	0.0000	0.0000	0.0000	0.0000	0.0000	0.0000	0.0000	0.0000	0.0000	0.0000	0.0000	0.0000	0.0000	0.0000	0.0000	0.0000	0.0000	0.0000	0.0000
<21	0.0000	0.0000	0.0000	0.0000	0.0000	0.0000	0.0000	0.0000	0.0000	0.0000	0.0000	0.0000	0.0000	0.0000	0.0000	0.0000	0.0000	0.0000	0.0000	0.0000	0.0000	0.0000	0.0000	0.0000
<22	0.0000	0.0000	0.0000	0.0000	0.0000	0.0000	0.0000	0.0000	0.0000	0.0000	0.0000	0.0000	0.0000	0.0000	0.0000	0.0000	0.0000	0.0000	0.0000	0.0000	0.0000	0.0000	0.0000	0.0000
<23	0.0000	0.0000	0.0000	0.0000	0.0000	0.0000	0.0000	0.0000	0.0000	0.0000	0.0000	0.0000	0.0000	0.0000	0.0000	0.0000	0.0000	0.0000	0.0000	0.0000	0.0000	0.0000	0.0000	0.0000
<24	0.0000	0.0000	0.0000	0.0000	0.0000	0.0000	0.0000	0.0000	0.0000	0.0000	0.0000	0.0000	0.0000	0.0000	0.0000	0.0000	0.0000	0.0000	0.0000	0.0000	0.0000	0.0000	0.0000	0.0000
<25	0.0000	0.0000	0.0000	0.0000	0.0000	0.0000	0.0000	0.0000	0.0000	0.0000	0.0000	0.0000	0.0000	0.0000	0.0000	0.0000	0.0000	0.0000	0.0000	0.0000	0.0000	0.0000	0.0000	0.0000
>=25	0.0000	0.0000	0.0000	0.0000	0.0000	0.0000	0.0000	0.0000	0.0000	0.0000	0.0000	0.0000	0.0000	0.0000	0.0000	0.0000	0.0000	0.0000	0.0000	0.0000	0.0000	0.0000	0.0000	0.0000

附录 2　全球风力概率矩阵 W_k

表 1　归一化全球风图显示了沿主要全球贸易航线的风况相对于船舶首向的概率

风速/(m/s) \ 风向角/(°)	0	5	10	15	20	25	30	35	40	45	50	55	60	65	70	75	80	85	90	95	100	105	110	115
<1	0.0001	0.0001	0.0001	0.0001	0.0001	0.0001	0.0001	0.0001	0.0001	0.0001	0.0001	0.0001	0.0001	0.0001	0.0001	0.0001	0.0001	0.0001	0.0001	0.0001	0.0001	0.0001	0.0001	0.0001
<2	0.0005	0.0005	0.0005	0.0005	0.0005	0.0005	0.0005	0.0005	0.0005	0.0005	0.0005	0.0005	0.0005	0.0005	0.0005	0.0005	0.0005	0.0005	0.0005	0.0005	0.0005	0.0005	0.0005	0.0005
<3	0.0009	0.0009	0.0009	0.0009	0.0008	0.0008	0.0008	0.0008	0.0008	0.0008	0.0008	0.0008	0.0008	0.0008	0.0008	0.0008	0.0008	0.0008	0.0008	0.0008	0.0008	0.0008	0.0008	0.0008
<4	0.0013	0.0013	0.0013	0.0013	0.0012	0.0012	0.0012	0.0012	0.0012	0.0011	0.0011	0.0011	0.0011	0.0011	0.0011	0.0011	0.0011	0.0010	0.0010	0.0010	0.0011	0.0011	0.0011	0.0011
<5	0.0017	0.0017	0.0017	0.0016	0.0016	0.0015	0.0015	0.0015	0.0015	0.0014	0.0014	0.0013	0.0013	0.0013	0.0012	0.0012	0.0012	0.0012	0.0012	0.0013	0.0013	0.0013	0.0013	0.0013
<6	0.0021	0.0020	0.0020	0.0019	0.0018	0.0017	0.0017	0.0017	0.0016	0.0016	0.0015	0.0015	0.0014	0.0014	0.0014	0.0014	0.0014	0.0014	0.0014	0.0014	0.0014	0.0015	0.0015	0.0015
<7	0.0022	0.0022	0.0021	0.0020	0.0020	0.0019	0.0018	0.0018	0.0017	0.0017	0.0016	0.0015	0.0014	0.0014	0.0014	0.0014	0.0014	0.0014	0.0014	0.0014	0.0015	0.0015	0.0015	0.0015
<8	0.0020	0.0020	0.0020	0.0019	0.0018	0.0018	0.0017	0.0016	0.0016	0.0015	0.0015	0.0014	0.0014	0.0013	0.0013	0.0013	0.0013	0.0013	0.0013	0.0013	0.0014	0.0014	0.0014	0.0014
<9	0.0017	0.0017	0.0017	0.0016	0.0016	0.0016	0.0015	0.0014	0.0014	0.0013	0.0013	0.0012	0.0012	0.0011	0.0011	0.0011	0.0011	0.0011	0.0011	0.0011	0.0011	0.0012	0.0012	0.0012
<10	0.0013	0.0013	0.0013	0.0013	0.0013	0.0012	0.0012	0.0011	0.0010	0.0010	0.0010	0.0010	0.0009	0.0009	0.0009	0.0009	0.0009	0.0009	0.0009	0.0009	0.0008	0.0008	0.0009	0.0009
<11	0.0010	0.0010	0.0010	0.0010	0.0009	0.0009	0.0009	0.0009	0.0009	0.0009	0.0008	0.0008	0.0008	0.0008	0.0007	0.0007	0.0007	0.0007	0.0006	0.0006	0.0006	0.0006	0.0006	0.0006
<12	0.0007	0.0007	0.0007	0.0007	0.0007	0.0006	0.0006	0.0006	0.0006	0.0006	0.0006	0.0005	0.0005	0.0005	0.0005	0.0004	0.0004	0.0004	0.0004	0.0004	0.0004	0.0004	0.0004	0.0004
<13	0.0004	0.0005	0.0005	0.0005	0.0004	0.0004	0.0004	0.0004	0.0004	0.0004	0.0004	0.0003	0.0003	0.0003	0.0003	0.0003	0.0003	0.0003	0.0003	0.0003	0.0003	0.0002	0.0002	0.0002
<14	0.0003	0.0003	0.0003	0.0003	0.0003	0.0003	0.0003	0.0003	0.0002	0.0002	0.0002	0.0002	0.0002	0.0002	0.0002	0.0002	0.0002	0.0002	0.0002	0.0002	0.0002	0.0002	0.0002	0.0002
<15	0.0002	0.0002	0.0002	0.0002	0.0002	0.0002	0.0002	0.0002	0.0002	0.0002	0.0002	0.0002	0.0002	0.0001	0.0001	0.0001	0.0001	0.0001	0.0001	0.0001	0.0001	0.0001	0.0001	0.0001
<16	0.0001	0.0001	0.0001	0.0001	0.0001	0.0001	0.0001	0.0001	0.0001	0.0001	0.0001	0.0001	0.0001	0.0001	0.0001	0.0001	0.0001	0.0001	0.0001	0.0001	0.0001	0.0001	0.0001	0.0001
<17	0.0001	0.0001	0.0001	0.0001	0.0001	0.0001	0.0001	0.0001	0.0001	0.0001	0.0001	0.0001	0.0001	0.0001	0.0001	0.0001	0.0001	0.0001	0.0001	0.0001	0.0001	0.0001	0.0001	0.0001
<18	0.0001	0.0001	0.0001	0.0001	0.0001	0.0001	0.0001	0.0000	0.0000	0.0000	0.0000	0.0000	0.0000	0.0000	0.0000	0.0000	0.0000	0.0000	0.0000	0.0000	0.0000	0.0000	0.0000	0.0000
<19	0.0000	0.0000	0.0000	0.0000	0.0000	0.0000	0.0000	0.0000	0.0000	0.0000	0.0000	0.0000	0.0000	0.0000	0.0000	0.0000	0.0000	0.0000	0.0000	0.0000	0.0000	0.0000	0.0000	0.0000
<20	0.0000	0.0000	0.0000	0.0000	0.0000	0.0000	0.0000	0.0000	0.0000	0.0000	0.0000	0.0000	0.0000	0.0000	0.0000	0.0000	0.0000	0.0000	0.0000	0.0000	0.0000	0.0000	0.0000	0.0000
<21	0.0000	0.0000	0.0000	0.0000	0.0000	0.0000	0.0000	0.0000	0.0000	0.0000	0.0000	0.0000	0.0000	0.0000	0.0000	0.0000	0.0000	0.0000	0.0000	0.0000	0.0000	0.0000	0.0000	0.0000
<22	0.0000	0.0000	0.0000	0.0000	0.0000	0.0000	0.0000	0.0000	0.0000	0.0000	0.0000	0.0000	0.0000	0.0000	0.0000	0.0000	0.0000	0.0000	0.0000	0.0000	0.0000	0.0000	0.0000	0.0000
<23	0.0000	0.0000	0.0000	0.0000	0.0000	0.0000	0.0000	0.0000	0.0000	0.0000	0.0000	0.0000	0.0000	0.0000	0.0000	0.0000	0.0000	0.0000	0.0000	0.0000	0.0000	0.0000	0.0000	0.0000
<24	0.0000	0.0000	0.0000	0.0000	0.0000	0.0000	0.0000	0.0000	0.0000	0.0000	0.0000	0.0000	0.0000	0.0000	0.0000	0.0000	0.0000	0.0000	0.0000	0.0000	0.0000	0.0000	0.0000	0.0000
<25	0.0000	0.0000	0.0000	0.0000	0.0000	0.0000	0.0000	0.0000	0.0000	0.0000	0.0000	0.0000	0.0000	0.0000	0.0000	0.0000	0.0000	0.0000	0.0000	0.0000	0.0000	0.0000	0.0000	0.0000
>=25	0.0000	0.0000	0.0000	0.0000	0.0000	0.0000	0.0000	0.0000	0.0000	0.0000	0.0000	0.0000	0.0000	0.0000	0.0000	0.0000	0.0000	0.0000	0.0000	0.0000	0.0000	0.0000	0.0000	0.0000

风速/(m/s) \ 风向角/(°)	120	125	130	135	140	145	150	155	160	165	170	175	180	185	190	195	200	205	210	215	220	225	230	235
<1	0.0001	0.0001	0.0001	0.0001	0.0001	0.0001	0.0001	0.0001	0.0001	0.0001	0.0001	0.0001	0.0001	0.0001	0.0001	0.0001	0.0001	0.0001	0.0001	0.0001	0.0001	0.0001	0.0001	0.0001
<2	0.0005	0.0005	0.0005	0.0005	0.0005	0.0005	0.0005	0.0005	0.0005	0.0005	0.0005	0.0005	0.0005	0.0005	0.0005	0.0005	0.0005	0.0005	0.0005	0.0005	0.0005	0.0005	0.0005	0.0005
<3	0.0008	0.0008	0.0008	0.0008	0.0008	0.0009	0.0009	0.0009	0.0009	0.0009	0.0009	0.0009	0.0009	0.0009	0.0009	0.0009	0.0008	0.0008	0.0008	0.0008	0.0008	0.0008	0.0008	0.0008
<4	0.0011	0.0011	0.0012	0.0012	0.0012	0.0013	0.0013	0.0013	0.0013	0.0013	0.0013	0.0013	0.0013	0.0013	0.0013	0.0013	0.0013	0.0012	0.0012	0.0012	0.0012	0.0011	0.0011	0.0011
<5	0.0014	0.0014	0.0015	0.0015	0.0016	0.0016	0.0017	0.0017	0.0017	0.0017	0.0017	0.0017	0.0017	0.0017	0.0017	0.0016	0.0015	0.0015	0.0015	0.0015	0.0014	0.0014	0.0013	0.0013
<6	0.0015	0.0016	0.0017	0.0017	0.0018	0.0019	0.0020	0.0020	0.0020	0.0021	0.0021	0.0021	0.0021	0.0021	0.0020	0.0019	0.0018	0.0018	0.0017	0.0016	0.0016	0.0015	0.0015	0.0014
<7	0.0016	0.0016	0.0017	0.0018	0.0019	0.0020	0.0021	0.0021	0.0022	0.0022	0.0023	0.0022	0.0022	0.0022	0.0021	0.0020	0.0020	0.0019	0.0018	0.0017	0.0016	0.0015	0.0015	0.0014
<8	0.0015	0.0015	0.0016	0.0017	0.0017	0.0018	0.0019	0.0020	0.0020	0.0020	0.0021	0.0021	0.0021	0.0020	0.0020	0.0019	0.0018	0.0017	0.0016	0.0016	0.0015	0.0014	0.0014	0.0014
<9	0.0012	0.0012	0.0013	0.0013	0.0014	0.0014	0.0015	0.0016	0.0016	0.0017	0.0017	0.0017	0.0017	0.0017	0.0017	0.0016	0.0015	0.0015	0.0014	0.0014	0.0013	0.0013	0.0013	0.0012
<10	0.0009	0.0009	0.0010	0.0010	0.0011	0.0011	0.0012	0.0012	0.0012	0.0012	0.0013	0.0013	0.0013	0.0013	0.0013	0.0013	0.0013	0.0012	0.0012	0.0011	0.0011	0.0010	0.0010	0.0010
<11	0.0006	0.0006	0.0006	0.0007	0.0007	0.0007	0.0008	0.0008	0.0008	0.0009	0.0009	0.0009	0.0010	0.0010	0.0010	0.0010	0.0010	0.0009	0.0009	0.0009	0.0008	0.0008	0.0008	0.0008
<12	0.0004	0.0004	0.0004	0.0004	0.0005	0.0005	0.0005	0.0005	0.0006	0.0006	0.0006	0.0006	0.0007	0.0007	0.0007	0.0007	0.0007	0.0007	0.0006	0.0006	0.0006	0.0006	0.0006	0.0005
<13	0.0003	0.0003	0.0003	0.0003	0.0003	0.0003	0.0003	0.0004	0.0004	0.0004	0.0004	0.0004	0.0004	0.0004	0.0005	0.0005	0.0005	0.0004	0.0004	0.0004	0.0004	0.0004	0.0004	0.0003
<14	0.0002	0.0002	0.0002	0.0002	0.0002	0.0002	0.0002	0.0002	0.0002	0.0003	0.0003	0.0003	0.0003	0.0003	0.0003	0.0003	0.0003	0.0003	0.0003	0.0003	0.0002	0.0002	0.0002	0.0002
<15	0.0001	0.0001	0.0001	0.0001	0.0001	0.0001	0.0002	0.0002	0.0002	0.0002	0.0002	0.0002	0.0002	0.0002	0.0002	0.0002	0.0002	0.0002	0.0002	0.0002	0.0002	0.0002	0.0002	0.0002
<16	0.0001	0.0001	0.0001	0.0001	0.0001	0.0001	0.0001	0.0001	0.0001	0.0001	0.0001	0.0001	0.0001	0.0001	0.0001	0.0001	0.0001	0.0001	0.0001	0.0001	0.0001	0.0001	0.0001	0.0001
<17	0.0001	0.0001	0.0001	0.0001	0.0001	0.0001	0.0001	0.0001	0.0001	0.0001	0.0001	0.0001	0.0001	0.0001	0.0001	0.0001	0.0001	0.0001	0.0001	0.0001	0.0001	0.0001	0.0001	0.0001
<18	0.0000	0.0000	0.0000	0.0000	0.0000	0.0000	0.0000	0.0000	0.0000	0.0000	0.0000	0.0000	0.0000	0.0000	0.0000	0.0000	0.0000	0.0000	0.0000	0.0000	0.0000	0.0000	0.0000	0.0000
<19	0.0000	0.0000	0.0000	0.0000	0.0000	0.0000	0.0000	0.0000	0.0000	0.0000	0.0000	0.0000	0.0000	0.0000	0.0000	0.0000	0.0000	0.0000	0.0000	0.0000	0.0000	0.0000	0.0000	0.0000
<20	0.0000	0.0000	0.0000	0.0000	0.0000	0.0000	0.0000	0.0000	0.0000	0.0000	0.0000	0.0000	0.0000	0.0000	0.0000	0.0000	0.0000	0.0000	0.0000	0.0000	0.0000	0.0000	0.0000	0.0000
<21	0.0000	0.0000	0.0000	0.0000	0.0000	0.0000	0.0000	0.0000	0.0000	0.0000	0.0000	0.0000	0.0000	0.0000	0.0000	0.0000	0.0000	0.0000	0.0000	0.0000	0.0000	0.0000	0.0000	0.0000
<22	0.0000	0.0000	0.0000	0.0000	0.0000	0.0000	0.0000	0.0000	0.0000	0.0000	0.0000	0.0000	0.0000	0.0000	0.0000	0.0000	0.0000	0.0000	0.0000	0.0000	0.0000	0.0000	0.0000	0.0000
<23	0.0000	0.0000	0.0000	0.0000	0.0000	0.0000	0.0000	0.0000	0.0000	0.0000	0.0000	0.0000	0.0000	0.0000	0.0000	0.0000	0.0000	0.0000	0.0000	0.0000	0.0000	0.0000	0.0000	0.0000
<24	0.0000	0.0000	0.0000	0.0000	0.0000	0.0000	0.0000	0.0000	0.0000	0.0000	0.0000	0.0000	0.0000	0.0000	0.0000	0.0000	0.0000	0.0000	0.0000	0.0000	0.0000	0.0000	0.0000	0.0000
<25	0.0000	0.0000	0.0000	0.0000	0.0000	0.0000	0.0000	0.0000	0.0000	0.0000	0.0000	0.0000	0.0000	0.0000	0.0000	0.0000	0.0000	0.0000	0.0000	0.0000	0.0000	0.0000	0.0000	0.0000
>=25	0.0000	0.0000	0.0000	0.0000	0.0000	0.0000	0.0000	0.0000	0.0000	0.0000	0.0000	0.0000	0.0000	0.0000	0.0000	0.0000	0.0000	0.0000	0.0000	0.0000	0.0000	0.0000	0.0000	0.0000

风速/(m/s) \ 风向角/(°)	240	245	250	255	260	265	270	275	280	285	290	295	300	305	310	315	320	325	330	335	340	345	350	355
<1	0.0001	0.0001	0.0001	0.0001	0.0001	0.0001	0.0001	0.0001	0.0001	0.0001	0.0001	0.0001	0.0001	0.0001	0.0001	0.0001	0.0001	0.0001	0.0001	0.0001	0.0001	0.0001	0.0001	0.0001
<2	0.0005	0.0005	0.0005	0.0005	0.0005	0.0005	0.0005	0.0005	0.0005	0.0005	0.0005	0.0005	0.0005	0.0005	0.0005	0.0005	0.0005	0.0005	0.0005	0.0005	0.0005	0.0005	0.0005	0.0005
<3	0.0008	0.0008	0.0008	0.0008	0.0008	0.0008	0.0008	0.0008	0.0008	0.0008	0.0008	0.0008	0.0008	0.0008	0.0008	0.0008	0.0008	0.0009	0.0009	0.0009	0.0009	0.0009	0.0009	0.0009
<4	0.0011	0.0011	0.0011	0.0011	0.0010	0.0010	0.0010	0.0010	0.0011	0.0011	0.0011	0.0011	0.0011	0.0012	0.0012	0.0013	0.0013	0.0013	0.0013	0.0013	0.0013	0.0013	0.0013	0.0013
<5	0.0013	0.0012	0.0012	0.0012	0.0012	0.0012	0.0012	0.0013	0.0013	0.0013	0.0013	0.0013	0.0013	0.0014	0.0015	0.0015	0.0016	0.0016	0.0017	0.0017	0.0017	0.0017	0.0017	0.0017
<6	0.0014	0.0014	0.0014	0.0014	0.0014	0.0014	0.0014	0.0014	0.0014	0.0014	0.0015	0.0015	0.0015	0.0016	0.0017	0.0018	0.0019	0.0020	0.0020	0.0021	0.0021	0.0021	0.0021	0.0021
<7	0.0014	0.0014	0.0014	0.0014	0.0014	0.0014	0.0014	0.0014	0.0015	0.0015	0.0015	0.0015	0.0015	0.0016	0.0017	0.0018	0.0019	0.0021	0.0021	0.0022	0.0022	0.0023	0.0022	0.0022
<8	0.0013	0.0013	0.0013	0.0013	0.0013	0.0013	0.0013	0.0013	0.0014	0.0014	0.0014	0.0014	0.0014	0.0015	0.0016	0.0017	0.0017	0.0019	0.0020	0.0020	0.0021	0.0021	0.0021	0.0021
<9	0.0012	0.0011	0.0011	0.0011	0.0011	0.0011	0.0011	0.0011	0.0011	0.0011	0.0011	0.0012	0.0012	0.0012	0.0014	0.0015	0.0016	0.0016	0.0016	0.0017	0.0017	0.0017	0.0017	0.0017
<10	0.0010	0.0009	0.0009	0.0009	0.0009	0.0009	0.0009	0.0009	0.0008	0.0008	0.0009	0.0009	0.0009	0.0009	0.0010	0.0010	0.0011	0.0012	0.0012	0.0013	0.0013	0.0013	0.0013	0.0013
<11	0.0008	0.0007	0.0007	0.0007	0.0007	0.0007	0.0006	0.0006	0.0006	0.0006	0.0006	0.0006	0.0006	0.0006	0.0007	0.0007	0.0007	0.0008	0.0008	0.0009	0.0009	0.0009	0.0009	0.0010
<12	0.0005	0.0005	0.0005	0.0005	0.0005	0.0004	0.0004	0.0004	0.0004	0.0004	0.0004	0.0004	0.0004	0.0004	0.0004	0.0005	0.0005	0.0005	0.0006	0.0006	0.0006	0.0006	0.0006	0.0007
<13	0.0003	0.0003	0.0003	0.0003	0.0003	0.0003	0.0003	0.0003	0.0003	0.0002	0.0002	0.0002	0.0003	0.0003	0.0003	0.0003	0.0003	0.0004	0.0004	0.0004	0.0004	0.0004	0.0004	0.0004
<14	0.0002	0.0002	0.0002	0.0002	0.0002	0.0002	0.0002	0.0002	0.0002	0.0002	0.0002	0.0002	0.0002	0.0002	0.0002	0.0002	0.0002	0.0002	0.0002	0.0003	0.0003	0.0003	0.0004	0.0003
<15	0.0001	0.0001	0.0001	0.0001	0.0001	0.0001	0.0001	0.0001	0.0001	0.0001	0.0001	0.0001	0.0001	0.0001	0.0001	0.0001	0.0001	0.0002	0.0002	0.0001	0.0002	0.0002	0.0002	0.0001
<16	0.0001	0.0001	0.0001	0.0001	0.0001	0.0001	0.0001	0.0001	0.0001	0.0001	0.0001	0.0001	0.0001	0.0001	0.0001	0.0001	0.0001	0.0001	0.0001	0.0001	0.0001	0.0001	0.0001	0.0001
<17	0.0001	0.0001	0.0001	0.0001	0.0001	0.0001	0.0001	0.0001	0.0001	0.0001	0.0001	0.0001	0.0001	0.0001	0.0001	0.0001	0.0001	0.0001	0.0001	0.0001	0.0001	0.0001	0.0001	0.0001
<18	0.0000	0.0000	0.0000	0.0000	0.0000	0.0000	0.0000	0.0000	0.0000	0.0000	0.0000	0.0000	0.0000	0.0000	0.0000	0.0000	0.0000	0.0000	0.0000	0.0000	0.0000	0.0001	0.0001	0.0001
<19	0.0000	0.0000	0.0000	0.0000	0.0000	0.0000	0.0000	0.0000	0.0000	0.0000	0.0000	0.0000	0.0000	0.0000	0.0000	0.0000	0.0000	0.0000	0.0000	0.0000	0.0000	0.0000	0.0000	0.0000
<20	0.0000	0.0000	0.0000	0.0000	0.0000	0.0000	0.0000	0.0000	0.0000	0.0000	0.0000	0.0000	0.0000	0.0000	0.0000	0.0000	0.0000	0.0000	0.0000	0.0000	0.0000	0.0000	0.0000	0.0000
<21	0.0000	0.0000	0.0000	0.0000	0.0000	0.0000	0.0000	0.0000	0.0000	0.0000	0.0000	0.0000	0.0000	0.0000	0.0000	0.0000	0.0000	0.0000	0.0000	0.0000	0.0000	0.0000	0.0000	0.0000
<22	0.0000	0.0000	0.0000	0.0000	0.0000	0.0000	0.0000	0.0000	0.0000	0.0000	0.0000	0.0000	0.0000	0.0000	0.0000	0.0000	0.0000	0.0000	0.0000	0.0000	0.0000	0.0000	0.0000	0.0000
<23	0.0000	0.0000	0.0000	0.0000	0.0000	0.0000	0.0000	0.0000	0.0000	0.0000	0.0000	0.0000	0.0000	0.0000	0.0000	0.0000	0.0000	0.0000	0.0000	0.0000	0.0000	0.0000	0.0000	0.0000
<24	0.0000	0.0000	0.0000	0.0000	0.0000	0.0000	0.0000	0.0000	0.0000	0.0000	0.0000	0.0000	0.0000	0.0000	0.0000	0.0000	0.0000	0.0000	0.0000	0.0000	0.0000	0.0000	0.0000	0.0000
<25	0.0000	0.0000	0.0000	0.0000	0.0000	0.0000	0.0000	0.0000	0.0000	0.0000	0.0000	0.0000	0.0000	0.0000	0.0000	0.0000	0.0000	0.0000	0.0000	0.0000	0.0000	0.0000	0.0000	0.0000
>=25	0.0000	0.0000	0.0000	0.0000	0.0000	0.0000	0.0000	0.0000	0.0000	0.0000	0.0000	0.0000	0.0000	0.0000	0.0000	0.0000	0.0000	0.0000	0.0000	0.0000	0.0000	0.0000	0.0000	0.0000

GUIDANCE ON CALCULATION AND VERIFICATION OF EFFECTS OF CATEGORY (C) INNOVATIVE TECHNOLOGIES

1 WASTE HEAT RECOVERY SYSTEM FOR GENERATION OF ELECTRICITY (CATEGORY (C-1))

1.1 Summary of innovative energy efficient technology

1.1.1 This chapter provides the guidance on the treatment of high temperature waste heat recovery systems (electric generation type) as innovative energy efficiency technologies related to the reduction of the auxiliary power (concerning $P_{AEeff(i)}$). Mechanical recovered waste energy directly coupled to shafts need not be measured in this category, since the effect of the technology is directly reflected in the V_{ref}.

1.1.2 Waste heat energy technologies increase the efficiency utilization of the energy generated from fuel combustion in the engine through recovery of the thermal energy of exhaust gas, cooling water, etc. thereby generating electricity.

1.1.3 There are the following two methods of generating electricity by the waste heat energy technologies (electric generation type):

.1 (A) method to recover thermal energy by a heat exchanger and to drive the thermal engine which drives an electric generator; and

.2 (B) method to drive directly an electric generator using power turbine, etc. Furthermore, there is a waste heat recovery system which combines both of the above methods.

---

[6] All examples in this chapter are used solely to illustrate the proposed methods of calculation and verification.

附件 2[6]

C 类创新技术效果的计算和验证指南

附录 1　发电用余热回收系统（C-1 类）

1.1　创新能效技术概要

1.1.1　本章为高温余热回收系统（发电类型）作为创新能效技术时有关辅助功率（$P_{AEeff(i)}$）减少的计算和验证方法提供指导。直接以机械方式传到驱动轴的余热回收能量已在 V_{ref} 中得到了反映，因此在本类别内不必测量。

1.1.2　余热能效技术通过回收废气、冷却水等的热能用以发电，提高发动机内燃料燃烧所产生能量的利用效率。

1.1.3　通过余热能效技术（发电类型）进行发电有如下两种方法。

　　.1　（A）通过热交换器回收热能用以驱动热机来带动发电机的方法；和

　　.2　（B）采用动力涡轮机等直接驱动发电机的方法。而且，有一种余热回收系统能组合以上两种方法。

---

[6]　本章中所有的例子仅用于说明计算和验证的方法。

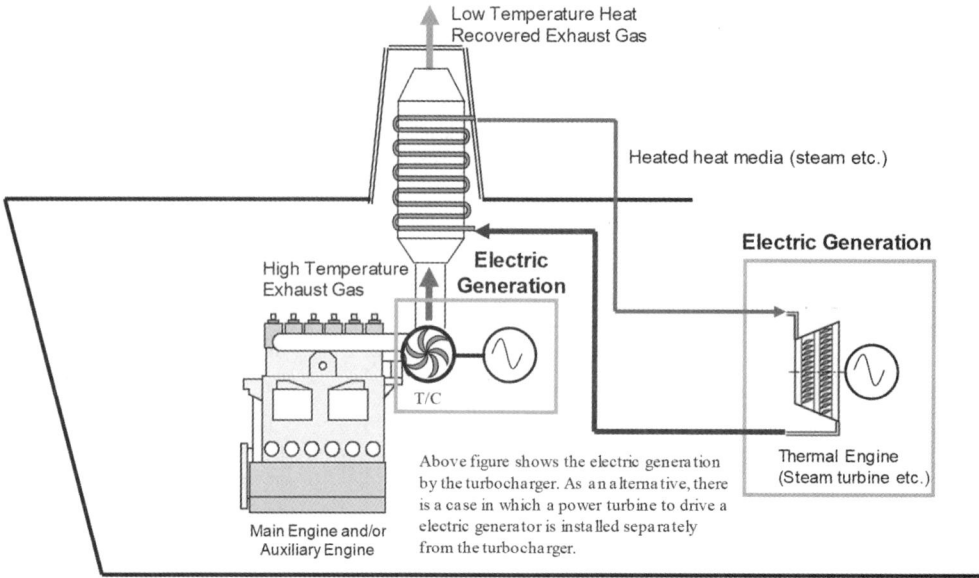

Low Temperature Heat
Recovered Exhaust Gas

Heated heat media (steam etc.)

Electric Generation

High Temperature
Exhaust Gas

Electric
Generation

Electric Generation

T/C

Above figure shows the electric generation
by the turbocharger. As an alternative, there
is a case in which a power turbine to drive a
electric generator is installed separately
from the turbocharger.

Main Engine and/or
Auxiliary Engine

Thermal Engine
(Steam turbine etc.)

Figure 1 – Schematic illustration of Exhaust Heat Recovery

1.2 Method of calculation

1.2.1 Power reduction due to waste heating recovery system

1.2.1.1 The reduction of power by the waste heat recovery system is calculated by the following equation. For this system, f_{eff} is 1.00 in EEDI formula.

$$P_{AEeff} = P'_{AEeff} - P_{AEeff\_loss}$$ (1)

In the above equation, P'_{AEeff} is power produced by the waste heat recovery system. P_{AEeff_Loss} is the necessary power to drive the waste heat recovery system

1.2.1.2 P_{AEeff} is the reduction of the ship's total auxiliary power (kW) by the waste heat recovery system under the ship performance condition applied for EEDI calculation. The power generated by the system under this condition and fed into the main switch board is to be taken into account, regardless of its application on board the vessel (except for power consumed by machinery as described in paragraph 1.2.1.4 of this chapter).

1.2.1.3 P'_{AEeff} is defined by the following equation.

$$P'_{AEeff} = \frac{W_e}{\eta_g},$$ (2)

where:

W_e : Calculated production of electricity by the waste heat recovery system
η_g : Weighted average generator efficiency

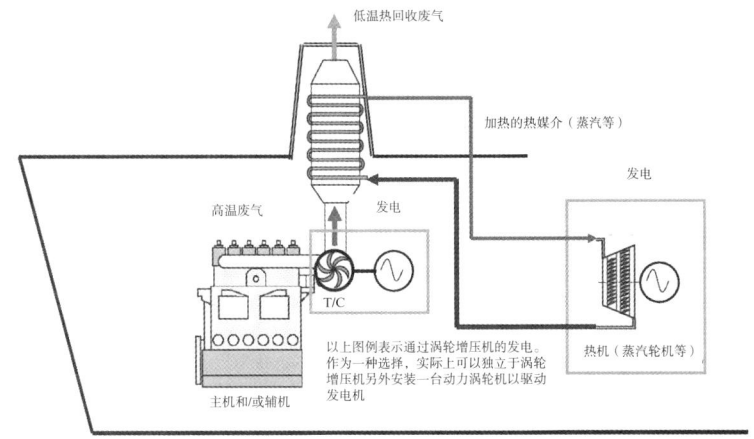

图 1　废气热回收系统图

1.2　计算方法

1.2.1　余热回收系统导致的功率减少量

1.2.1.1　通过余热回收系统减少的功率可用下式计算。对该系统，f_{eff} 在 EEDI 公式中取 1.00。

$$P_{AEeff} = P'_{AEeff} - P_{AEeff\_loss} \tag{1}$$

以上公式中，P'_{AEeff} 为余热回收系统产生的功率，P_{AEeff_Loss} 则为驱动余热回收系统所需的功率。

1.2.1.2　P_{AEeff} 为在 EEDI 计算所适用的船舶性能状态下，通过余热回收系统减少的船舶总辅助功率（kW）。不论其在船上的应用情况如何（除本章 1.2.1.4 所述的设备消耗功率外），回收系统在此状态下产生并输入主配电板的功率均应予以考虑。

1.2.1.3　P'_{AEeff} 按下式定义。

$$P'_{AEeff} = \frac{W_e}{\eta_g}, \tag{2}$$

式中：

W_e：采用余热回收系统发电的计算值；

η_g：加权的平均发电机效率。

1.2.1.4 P_{AEeff} is determined by the following factors:

    .1   temperature and mass flow of exhaust gas of the engines, etc.;

    .2   constitution of the waste heat recovery system; and

    .3   efficiency and performances of the components of the waste heat recovery system.

1.2.1.5 P_{AEeff_Loss} is the power (kW) for the pump, etc. necessary to drive the waste heat recovery system.

1.3 Method of verification

1.3.1 General

1.3.1.1 Verification of EEDI with innovative energy efficient technologies should be conducted according to the EEDI Survey Guidelines. Additional items concerning innovative energy efficient technologies not contained in EEDI Survey Guidelines are described below.

1.3.2 Preliminary verification at the design stage

1.3.2.1 In addition to paragraph 4.2.2 of EEDI Survey Guidelines, the EEDI Technical File which is to be developed by the shipowner or shipbuilder should include:

    .1   diagrams, such as a plant diagram, a process flow diagram, or a piping and instrumentation diagram outlining the waste heat recovery system, and its related information such as specifications of the system components;

    .2   deduction of the saved energy from the auxiliary engine power by the waste heat recovery system; and

    .3   calculation result of EEDI.

1.3.2.2 In addition to paragraph 4.2.7 of the EEDI Survey Guidelines, additional information that the verifier may request the shipbuilder to provide directly to it includes:

    .1   exhaust gas data for the main engine at 75% MCR (and/or the auxiliary engine at the measurement condition of SFC) at different ambient air inlet temperatures, e.g. 5°C, 25°C and 35°C; which consist of:

        .1   exhaust gas mass flow for turbo charger (kg/h);

        .2   exhaust gas temperatures after turbo charger (C°);

        .3   exhaust gas bypass mass flow available for power turbine, if any (kg/h);

        .4   exhaust gas temperature for bypass flow (C°); and

        .5   exhaust gas pressure for bypass flow (bar).

1.2.1.4 P_{AEeff} 由下列因素确定：

.1 发动机废气的温度和质量流量等；

.2 余热回收系统的构成；和

.3 余热回收系统部件的效率和性能。

1.2.1.5 P_{AEeff_Loss} 为驱动余热回收系统所需泵等设备的功率（kW）。

1.3 验证方法

1.3.1 一般规定

1.3.1.1 创新能效技术的船舶 EEDI 应按 EEDI 检验指南进行验证。EEDI 检验指南中未包括的有关创新能效技术的附加内容见下文。

1.3.2 设计阶段的前期验证

1.3.2.1 除 EEDI 检验指南 4.2.2 要求外，船东或船厂编制的 EEDI 技术案卷还应包括：

.1 余热回收系统的简图，如装置图、工作过程流程图、或管路和仪表图，以及系统部件规格等的相关资料；

.2 余热回收系统节省的辅机功率；和

.3 EEDI 计算结果。

1.3.2.2 除 EEDI 检验指南 4.2.7 要求外，验证方还可能要求船厂直接提供的附加资料包括：

.1 主机在 75%MCR（和/或辅机在 SFC 的测量状态）时，不同空气进口的环境温度（如 5℃、25℃和 35℃）条件下的废气数据，包括：

.1 涡轮增压器的废气质量流量（kg/h）；
.2 涡轮增压器后的废气温度（℃）；
.3 动力涡轮机可用的废气旁通质量流量（如有）（kg/h）；
.4 旁通废气温度（℃）；和
.5 旁通废气压力（bar）。

.2   in the case of system using heat exchanger, expected output steam flows and steam temperatures for the exchanger, based on the exhaust gas data from the main engine;

.3   estimation process of the heat energy recovered by the waste heat recovery system; and

.4   further details of the calculation method of P_{AEeff} defined in paragraph 1.2.1 of this chapter.

1.3.3   Final verification of the attained EEDI at sea trial

1.3.3.1 Deduction of the saved energy from the auxiliary engine power by the waste heat recovery system should be verified by the results of shop tests of the waste heat recovery system's principal components and, where possible, at sea trials.

1.3.3.2 In the case of systems for which shop tests are difficult to be conducted, e.g. in case of the exhaust gas economizer, the performance of the waste heat recovery system should be verified by measuring the amount of the generated steam, its temperature, etc. at the sea trial. In that case, the measured vapour amount, temperature, etc. should be corrected to the value under the exhaust gas condition when they were designed, and at the measurement conditions of *SFC* of the main/auxiliary engine(s). The exhaust gas condition should be corrected based on the atmospheric temperature in the engine-room (Measurement condition of *SFC* of main/auxiliary engine(s); i.e. 25°C), etc.

2   PHOTOVOLTAIC POWER GENERATION SYSTEM (CATEGORY (C-2))

2.1   Summary of innovative energy efficient technology

2.1.1   Photovoltaic (PV) power generation system set on a ship will provide part of the electric power either for propelling the ship or for use inboard. PV power generation system consists of PV modules and other electric equipment. Figure 1 shows a schematic diagram of PV power generation system. The PV module consists of combining solar cells and there are some types of solar cell such as "Crystalline silicon terrestrial photovoltaic" and "Thin-film terrestrial photovoltaic", etc.

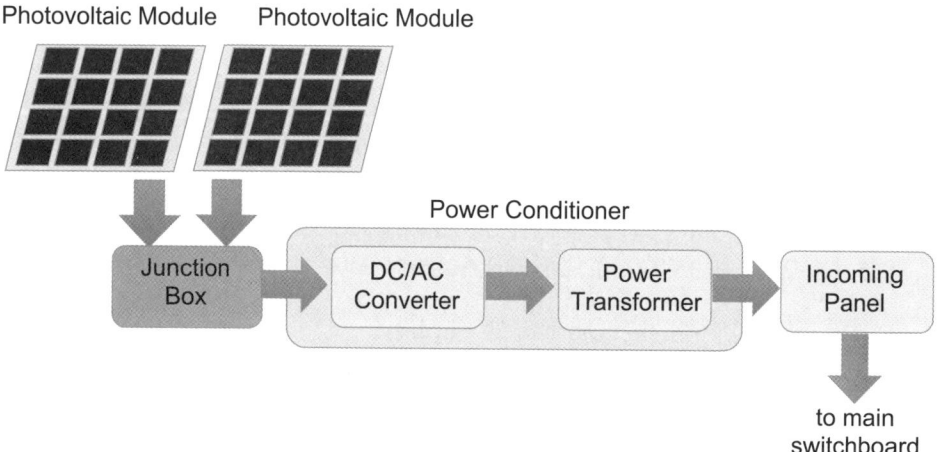

Figure 1 – Schematic diagram of photovoltaic power generation system

.2 对于采用热交换器的系统，根据主机的废气数据，该热交换器预计的输出蒸汽流量和蒸汽温度；

.3 余热回收系统所回收的热能估算过程；和

.4 本节 1.2.1 中所定义的 P_{AEeff} 计算方法的进一步详细资料。

1.3.3 试航时 Attained EEDI 的最终验证

1.3.3.1 余热回收系统节省的辅机功率应通过余热回收系统主要部件的工厂试验结果予以验证，并如有可能，在试航时进行验证。

1.3.3.2 对于很难进行工厂试验的系统，如废气经济器，余热回收系统的性能应在试航时通过测量其蒸汽量及温度等进行验证。在此情况下，所测得的蒸汽量、温度等应修正到其设计时的废气状态下以及主/辅机 SFC 测量状态下的对应值。废气状态应根据机舱中的空气温度进行修正（主/辅机 SFC 测量状态，即 25 ℃）等。

2 光伏发电系统（C-2 类）

2.1 创新能效技术概要

2.1.1 船上安装的光伏（PV）发电系统将提供船舶推进或船上使用的部分电力。光伏发电系统由光伏模块和其他电气设备构成。图 1 为光伏发电系统的示意图。光伏模块由太阳能电池组合构成，例如陆地用晶体硅太阳能电池和陆地用薄膜太阳能电池等类型。

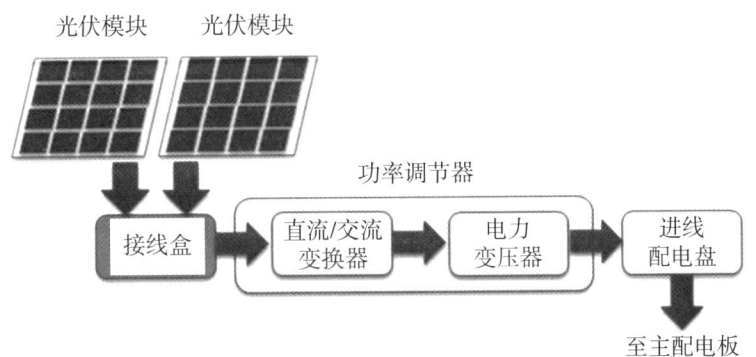

图 1 光伏发电系统的示意图

2.2　Method of calculation

2.2.1　Electric power due to photovoltaic power generation system

2.2.1.1　The auxiliary power reduction due to the PV power generation system can be calculated as follows:

$$f_{eff} \cdot P_{AEeff} = \{ f_{rad} \times (1 + L_{temp} / 100) \} \times \{ P_{max} \times (1 - L_{others} / 100) \times N / \eta_{GEN} \} \qquad (1)$$

where $f_{eff} \cdot P_{AEeff}$ is the total net electric power (kW) generated by the PV power generation system.

2.2.1.2　Effective coefficient f_{eff} is the ratio of average PV power generation in main global shipping routes to the nominal PV power generation specified by the manufacturer. Effective coefficient can be calculated by the following formula using the solar irradiance and air temperature of main global shipping routes:

$$f_{eff} = f_{rad} \times (1 + L_{temp} / 100) \qquad (2)$$

2.2.1.3　f_{rad} is the ratio of the average solar irradiance on main global shipping route to the nominal solar irradiance specified by the manufacturer. Nominal maximum generating power P_{max} is measured under the Standard Test Condition (STC) of IEC standard.[7] STC specified by manufacturer is that: Air Mass (AM) 1.5, the module's temperature is 25°C, and the solar irradiance is 1000 W/m². The average solar irradiance on main global shipping route is 200 W/m². Therefore, f_{rad} is calculated by the following formula:

$$f_{rad} = 200 \text{ W/m}^2 \div 1\ 000 \text{ W/m}^2 = 0.2 \qquad (3)$$

2.2.1.4　L_{temp} is the correction factor, which is usually in minus, and derived from the temperature of PV modules, and the value is expressed in per cent. The average temperature of the modules is deemed 40°C, based on the average air temperature on main global shipping routes. Therefore, L_{temp} is derived from the temperature coefficient f_{temp} (percent/K) specified by the manufacturer (see IEC standard[7]) as follows:

$$L_{temp} = f_{temp} \times (40 \text{ °C} - 25 \text{ °C}) \qquad (4)$$

2.2.1.5　P_{AEeff} is the generated PV power divided by the weighted average efficiency of the generator(s) under the condition specified by the manufacturer and expressed as follows:

$$P_{AEeff} = P_{max} \times (1 - L_{others} / 100) \times N / \eta_{GEN}, \qquad (5)$$

where η_{GEN} is the weighted average efficiency of the generator(s).

2.2.1.6　P_{max} is the nominal maximum generated PV power generation of a module expressed in kilowatt, specified based on IEC Standards.[7]

---

[7]　Refer to IEC 61215 "Crystalline silicon terrestrial photovoltaic (PV) modules – Design qualification and type approval" for Crystalline silicon terrestrial PV modules, and to IEC 61646 "Thin-film terrestrial photovoltaic (PV) modules – Design qualification and type approval" for Thin-film terrestrial PV modules.

2.2 计算方法

2.2.1 光伏发电系统产生的电力

2.2.1.1 光伏发电系统导致的辅助机械功率降低可通过下式进行计算：

$$f_{eff} \cdot P_{AEeff} = \{ f_{rad} \times (1 + L_{temp} / 100) \} \times \{ P_{max} \times (1 - L_{others} / 100) \times N / \eta_{GEN} \} \qquad (1)$$

式中：$f_{eff} \cdot P_{AEeff}$ 是由光伏发电系统产生的总净电力（kW）。

2.2.1.2 有效系数 f_{eff} 是在全球主要航运路线上的平均光伏发电量与厂商规定的名义光伏发电量的比值。有效系数可以采用全球主要航运路线上的太阳辐照度和气温通过下式进行计算：

$$f_{eff} = f_{rad} \times (1 + L_{temp} / 100) \qquad (2)$$

2.2.1.3 f_{rad} 是全球主要航运路线上的平均太阳辐照度与厂商规定的名义太阳辐照度的比值。最大名义发电量 P_{max} 在 IEC 标准[7]的标准测试条件（STC）下进行测量。厂商规定的 STC 为：气团（AM）1.5，模块温度 25 ℃，太阳辐照度 1 000W/m²。全球主要航运路线上的平均太阳辐照度为 200 W/m²。因此，f_{rad} 由下式进行计算：

$$f_{rad} = 200 \text{ W/m}^2 \div 1\ 000 \text{ W/m}^2 = 0.2 \qquad (3)$$

2.2.1.4 L_{temp} 为修正系数，通常为负数，由 PV 模块的温度而得出，数值以百分比表示。根据全球主要航运路线上的平均气温，认为模块的平均温度为 40 ℃。因此，L_{temp} 通过以下公式从厂商规定的温度系数 f_{temp}（%/K）（见 IEC 标准[7]）得出：

$$L_{temp} = f_{temp} \times (40 \text{ ℃} - 25 \text{ ℃}) \qquad (4)$$

2.2.1.5 P_{AEeff} 为由所产生的 PV 功率除以厂商规定条件下发电机的加权平均效率，以下式表示：

$$P_{AEeff} = P_{max} \times (1 - L_{others} / 100) \times N / \eta_{GEN}, \qquad (5)$$

式中：η_{GEN} 为发电机的加权平均效率。

2.2.1.6 根据 IEC 标准[7]的规定，P_{max} 为一个模块所产生的最大名义 PV 发电量，（kW）。

---

[7] 陆地用晶体硅光伏模块，参见 IEC61215 "陆地用晶体硅光伏（PV）模块 – 设计鉴定和型式认可"。
陆地用薄膜光伏模块，参见 IEC61646 "陆地用薄膜光伏（PV）模块 – 设计鉴定和型式认可"。

2.2.1.7 L_{others} is the summation of other losses expressed by percent and includes the losses in a power conditioner, at contact, by electrical resistance, etc. Based on experiences, it is estimated that L_{others} is 10% (the loss in the power conditioner: 5% and the sum of other losses: 5%). However, for the loss in the power conditioner, it is practical to apply the value specified based on IEC Standards.[8]

2.2.1.8 N is the numbers of modules used in a PV power generation system.

2.3 Method of verification

2.3.1 General

2.3.1.1 Verification of EEDI with innovative energy efficient technologies is conducted according to EEDI Survey Guidelines. This section provides additional requirements related to innovative technologies.

2.3.2 Preliminary verification at the design stage

2.3.2.1 In addition to paragraph 4.2.2 of EEDI Survey guidelines, the EEDI Technical File which is to be developed by the shipowner or shipbuilder should include:

    .1   outline of the PV power generation system;

    .2   power generated by the PV power generation system; and

    .3   calculated value of EEDI due to the PV power generation system.

2.3.2.2 In addition to paragraph 4.2.7 of the EEDI survey guidelines, additional information that the verifier may request the shipbuilder to provide directly to it includes:

    .1   detailed calculation process of the auxiliary power reduction by the PV power generation system; and

    .2   detailed calculation process of the total net electric power ($f_{eff} \cdot P_{AEeff}$) specified in section 2.2 in this guidance.

2.3.3 Final verification of the attained EEDI at sea trial

2.3.3.1 The total net electric power generated by PV power generation system should be confirmed based on the EEDI Technical File. In addition to the confirmation, it should be confirmed whether the configuration of the PV power generation systems on ship is as applied, prior to the final verification.

---

[8]   IEC 61683 "Photovoltaic systems – Power conditioners – Procedure for measuring efficiency".

2.2.1.7　L_{others} 是其他损耗的总和（%），包括功率调节器中的损耗，接通时的损耗和电阻造成的损耗等。根据经验，估计 L_{others} 为 10%（功率调节器中的损耗 5%，其他损耗总计 5%）。但是，对于功率调节器中的损耗，采用根据 IEC 标准[8] 而规定的数值是可行的。

2.2.1.8　N 为光伏发电系统所采用的模块的数量。

2.3　验证方法

2.3.1　一般规定

2.3.1.1　采用创新能效技术的船舶 EEDI 应按 EEDI 检验指南进行验证。本节规定了与创新技术相关的附加要求。

2.3.2　设计阶段的前期验证

2.3.2.1　除 EEDI 检验指南 4.2.2 要求外，船东或船厂编制的 EEDI 技术案卷还应包括：

　　.1　光伏发电系统的简图；

　　.2　光伏发电系统所产生的功率；和

　　.3　光伏发电系统产生的 EEDI 计算值。

2.3.2.2　除 EEDI 检验指南 4.2.7 的要求外，验证方还可能要求船厂直接提供的附加资料包括：

　　.1　光伏发电系统产生的辅助功率降低的详细计算过程；和

　　.2　本导则 2.2 中规定的总净电力（$f_{eff} \cdot P_{AEeff}$）的详细计算过程。

2.3.3　试航时 Attained EEDI 的最终验证

2.3.3.1　应根据 EEDI 技术案卷对由 PV 发电系统所发的总净电力进行确认。除此之外，还应在最终验证之前确认船上 PV 发电系统的配置是否与前期验证中所采用的相同。

---

[8]　IEC61683"光伏系统 – 功率调节器 – 效率测定程序"。

—— 船用燃料相关 ——

RESOLUTION MEPC.391(81)
(adopted on 22 March 2024)

2024 GUIDELINES ON LIFE CYCLE GHG INTENSITY OF MARINE FUELS
(2024 LCA GUIDELINES)

THE MARINE ENVIRONMENT PROTECTION COMMITTEE,

RECALLING Article 38(a) of the Convention on the International Maritime Organization concerning the functions of the Marine Environment Protection Committee conferred upon it by international conventions for the prevention and control of marine pollution from ships,

RECALLING ALSO that, at its eightieth session, it adopted, by resolution MEPC.377(80), the *2023 IMO Strategy on Reduction of GHG Emissions from Ships* (2023 IMO GHG Strategy) setting out the levels of ambition for the international shipping sector in reducing GHG emissions,

RECALLING FURTHER that, at its eightieth session, it also adopted, by resolution MEPC.376(80), *Guidelines on life cycle GHG intensity of marine fuels* (LCA Guidelines);

NOTING that the 2023 IMO GHG Strategy provides that the levels of ambition and indicative checkpoints set out therein should take into account the well-to-wake GHG emissions of marine fuels as addressed in the LCA Guidelines,

NOTING ALSO that the 2023 IMO GHG Strategy provides that the basket of candidate mid-term GHG reduction measures should take into account the well-to-wake GHG emissions of marine fuels as addressed in the LCA Guidelines,

HAVING CONSIDERED, at its eighty-first session, draft 2024 Guidelines on life cycle GHG intensity of marine fuels,

1   ADOPTS the *2024 Guidelines on life cycle GHG intensity of marine fuels (2024 LCA Guidelines)*, as set out in the annex to the present resolution;

2   AGREES that any regulatory application and implications of the 2024 LCA Guidelines should be determined by the Committee in the process of developing regulatory provisions,

3   REQUESTS Member Governments to bring the annexed Guidelines to the attention of shipowners, ship operators, shipbuilders, ship designers, energy companies, fuel producers, bunkering companies, engine manufacturers and any other interested parties;

4   AGREES to keep these Guidelines under review in light of experience gained with their implementation;

5   REVOKES the LCA Guidelines adopted by resolution MEPC.376(80).

第 MEPC.391（81）号决议
（2024 年 3 月 22 日通过）

2024 年船用燃料生命周期温室气体强度导则
（2024 年 LCA 导则）

海上环境保护委员会，

忆及《国际海事组织公约》关于防止和控制船舶造成海洋污染国际公约赋予海上环境保护委员会（本委员会）职能的第 38（a）条，

还忆及本委员会在其第八十届会议上以第 MEPC.377（80）号决议通过的《2023 年国际海事组织船舶温室气体减排战略》（《2023 年海事组织温室气体战略》），规定了国际航运业减少温室气体排放的目标水平，

进一步忆及本委员会在其第 80 届会议上以第 MEPC.376（80）号决议通过了《船用燃料生命周期温室气体强度导则》（LCA 导则），

注意到《2023 年国际海事组织温室气体战略》规定，目标水平和指标性核查点应考虑到《船用燃料生命周期温室气体强度导则》中所述的船用燃料生命周期温室气体排放，

还注意到《2023 年海事组织温室气体战略》规定备选中期温室气体减排措施应考虑到《船用燃料生命周期温室气体强度导则》中所述的船用燃料生命周期温室气体排放，

在其第 81 届会议上，**审议了**《2024 年船用燃料生命周期温室气体强度导则》草案，

1　**通过**《2024 年船用燃料生命周期温室气体强度导则》（2024 年 LCA 导则），载于本决议附件；

2　**同意** 2024 年 LCA 导则的任何规范应用和影响应由本委员会在制定规范规定的过程中予以确定；

3　**要求**各会员国政府提请船东、船舶经营者、船厂、船舶设计方、能源公司、燃料生产商、燃料加注公司、发动机制造商和任何其他相关方注意到附件中的导则；

4　**同意**根据实施中获得的经验对本导则保持审查；

5　**撤销**以第 MEPC.376（80）号决议通过的 LCA 导则。

2024 GUIDELINES ON LIFE CYCLE GHG INTENSITY OF MARINE FUELS
(2024 LCA Guidelines)

CONTENTS

2024 年船用燃料生命周期温室气体强度导则

（2024 年 LCA 导则）

目录

PART I: GENERAL

## 1	INTRODUCTION

These Guidelines provide guidance on life cycle GHG intensity assessment for all fuels and other energy carriers (e.g. electricity) used on board a ship and aim at covering the whole fuel life cycle (with specific boundaries), from feedstock extraction/cultivation/ recovery, feedstock conversion to a fuel product, transportation as well as distribution/bunkering, and fuel utilization on board a ship. These Guidelines also specify sustainability themes/aspects for marine fuels and define a Fuel Lifecycle Label (FLL), which carries information about fuel type, feedstock (feedstock type and feedstock nature/carbon source), conversion/production process (process type and energy used in the process), GHG emission factors, information on fuel blends and sustainability themes/aspects. These Guidelines specify the elements of FLL subject to verification/certification and include a general procedure on how the certification scheme/standards could be identified.

## 2	SCOPE

2.1	The scope of these Guidelines is to address well-to-tank (WtT), tank-to wake (TtW), and well-to-wake (WtW) GHG intensity and sustainability themes/aspects related to marine fuels/energy carriers (e.g. electricity for shore power) used for ship propulsion and power generation onboard. The relevant GHGs included are carbon dioxide (CO_2), methane (CH_4) and nitrous oxide (N_2O). These guidelines are not intended to provide guidance for a complete IMO GHG inventory for international shipping. Emissions from cargo (e.g. volatile organic compounds (VOC)), or use of refrigerants are not included; other short-lived climate forcers and precursors such as non-methane volatile organic compounds (NMVOC), sulphur oxides (SO_x), carbon monoxide (CO), particulate matter (PM) and Black Carbon are not part of the scope of these LCA guidelines.

2.2	The system boundaries of the WtW GHG emission factors calculation, in the context of these guidelines span the life cycle of fuels from their sourcing to production, conversion, transport, distribution, and eventually their use on board ships based on an attributional approach.[1] The possibility to expand the system boundaries for specific pathways in which the feedstock is displaced from present use(s) will be assessed on a case-by-case basis.[2] As such, emissions associated with the following life cycle stages of the fuel life cycle chain will be accounted for:

> .1	feedstock extraction/cultivation/acquisition/recovery;
>
> .2	feedstock (early) processing/ transformation at source;
>
> .3	feedstock transport to conversion site;
>
> .4	feedstock conversion to product fuel;
>
> .5	product fuel transport/storage/delivery/retail storage/bunkering; and
>
> .6	fuel utilization on board a ship.

---

[1]	Attributional Life Cycle Assessment (LCA): LCA aiming to describe the environmentally relevant physical flows to and from a system and its subsystems over their life cycle; Consequential Life cycle Analysis (LCA): LCA aiming to describe how environmentally relevant flows will change in response to possible decisions. (Finnveden G, Hauschild MZ, Ekvall T, Guinée J, Heijungs R, Hellweg S, et al. "Recent developments in life cycle assessment". *Journal of Environmental Management.* 2009;91(1):1-21).

[2]	Such as for captured CO_2 transportation and storage.

第 I 部分：总则

1 引言

1.1 本导则为船上使用的所有燃料和其他能源载体（如电力）的生命周期温室气体排放强度评估提供指导。本导则旨在覆盖燃料生命周期（有特定的边界），从原料开采/种植/回收、原料转化为燃料产品、运输和分配/加注、到船上的燃料使用。本导则还规定了船用燃料的可持续性主题/方面，并定义了燃料生命周期标签（FLL），其中包含有关燃料类型、原料（原料类型和原料性质/碳源）、转化/生产加工（加工类型和加工中使用的能源）、温室气体排放因子、混合燃料和可持续性主题/方面的信息。本导则规定了应进行验证/认证的燃料生命周期标签要素，并包括了如何识别认证计划/标准的总体程序。

2 范围

2.1 本导则的范围涉及用于船舶推进和船上发电的船用燃料/能源载体（例如岸电）上船前（WtT）排放、船端（TtW）排放和全生命周期（WtW）排放温室气体强度和可持续性主题/方面。相关温室气体包括二氧化碳（CO_2）、甲烷（CH_4）和一氧化二氮（N_2O）。本导则无意为完整的国际海事组织国际航运温室气体清单提供指导。货物排放（例如挥发性有机化合物（VOC）或使用制冷剂不包括在内；其他短期气候驱动因子和先导，例如非甲烷挥发性有机化合物（NMVOC）、硫氧化物（SO_x）、一氧化碳（CO）、颗粒物（PM）和黑碳，不属于本导则的范围。

2.2 就本导则而言，生命周期温室气体排放因子计算的系统边界跨越了燃料的生命周期，即：从其来源到生产、转化、运输、分配，最终到其在船上的使用，基于归因法计算[1]。当原料不再用于当前用途的特定用途，将根据具体情况逐一评估扩大系统边界的可能性[2]。因此，将核算燃料生命周期链中以下生命周期阶段相关的排放：

 .1 原料开采/种植/获取/回收；

 .2 原料（早期）加工/在源头转化；

 .3 原料运输至转化场所；

 .4 原料转化为成品燃料；

 .5 成品燃料运输/储存/交付/零售储存/加注；和

 .6 燃料在船上的使用。

---

[1] 归因全生命周期评估（LCA）：LCA 旨在描述系统及其子系统在其生命周期中与环境相关的物理流入和流出；归果生命周期分析（LCA）：LCA 旨在描述为响应可能的决策，与环境相关的流动如何变化，Finnveden G，Hauschild MZ，Ekvall T，Guinée J，Heijungs R，Hellweg S 等人，《生命周期评估的最新进展》，环境科学学报，2009；31（1）：1–21。

[2] 例如对捕获的 CO_2 的运输和储存。

2.3   Consistent with the attributional approach and using best available scientific evidence, the WtT emissions calculations (i.e. emissions related to the fuel sourcing, production, conversion, transport and delivery) are assessed regardless of the final use of fuels/energy carriers, and the TtW emissions (i.e. emissions related to the fuel use) are quantified regardless of the sourcing/production/conversion/transport and delivery steps of the fuel/energy carrier. WtW emissions are given by the sum of the two parts, providing the full emission performance associated with the fuel production and use of a certain fuel/energy in a specific converter onboard.

2.4   The GHG emissions are calculated as CO_2-equivalent (CO_{2eq}), using the global warming potential over a 100-year time-horizon (GWP100) to convert emissions of other gases than CO_2, as given in the fifth IPCC Assessment Report,[3] for CO_2, CH_4 and N_2O, as follows:

- $g_{CO_{2eq}(100y)} = GWP_{CO_2(100y)} \times g_{CO_2} + GWP_{CH_4(100y)} \times g_{CH_4} + GWP_{N_2O\,(100y)} \times g_{N_2O}$

(CO_2 1; CH_4 28; N_2O 265), this would read as:

- $g_{CO_{2eq}(100y)} = 1 \times gCO_2 + 28 \times gCH_4 + 265 \times gN_2O)$

These GWP100 values should be used for the purpose of quantifying the GHG intensity in accordance with these guidelines.

A calculation using a global warming potential over a 20-year horizon (GWP20) may be provided as information for comparative purposes, as follows:

- $g_{CO_{2eq}(20y)} = GWP_{CO_2(20y)} \times g_{CO_2} + GWP_{CH_4(20y)} \times g_{CH_4} + GWP_{N_2O\,(20y)} \times g_{N_2O}$

(CO_2 1; CH_4 84; N_2O 264), this would read as:

- $g_{CO_{2eq}(20y)} = 1 \times gCO_2 + 84 \times gCH_4 + 264 \times gN_2O$

2.5   These Guidelines provide:

.1   WtW GHG emission factors based on a life cycle attributional methodology, expressing the GHG profile of each representative fuel using on global warming potential (GWP) values over a 100-year time-horizon of included GHG (CO_2, CH_4 and N_2O);

.2   WtT GHG emission factors (CO_2, CH_4 and N_2O) quantified consistently with the attributional approach;

.3   TtW GHG emission factors (CO_2, CH_4 and N_2O); and

.4   sustainability themes/aspects for marine fuels.

---

[3]   The global warming potential values as given in the *IPCC Fifth Assessment Report* (AR5) are used in the context of these Guidelines.

2.3 按照归因法，采用现有的最佳科学证据，对上船前排放计算值（即与燃料开采、生产、转化、运输和交付相关的排放）进行评估，而无论燃料/能源载体最终如何使用。同时对船端排放（即与燃料使用相关的排放）进行量化，而无论燃料的获取/生产/转化/运输和交付步骤或能源载体如何。对这两部分相加得到全生命周期，从而提供与燃料生产和在船上特定转化器中使用某种燃料/能源相关的全部排放性能。

2.4 温室气体排放量按 CO_2 当量（CO_2eq）计算，使用 100 年时间范围内的全球变暖潜势（GWP100）来转化除 CO_2 以外的其他气体的排放量，如 IPCC 第五次评估报告[3] 所述，对于 CO_2、CH_4 和 N_2O，按下式计算：

- $g_{CO_2eq(100y)} = GWP_{CO_2(100y)} \times g_{CO_2} + GWP_{CH_4(100y)} \times g_{CH_4} + GWP_{N_2O(100y)} \times g_{N_2O}$

  对于（CO_2 1；CH_4 28；N_2O 265），按下式计算：

- $g_{CO_2eq(100y)} = 1 \times gCO_2 + 28 \times gCH_4 + 265 \times gN_2O)$

  根据本导则，GWP100 值应用于量化温室气体强度。

  为进行比较，可采用按 20 年全球变暖潜势（GWP20）的计算结果，按下式计算：

- $g_{CO_2eq(20y)} = GWP_{CO_2(20y)} \times g_{CO_2} + GWP_{CH_4(20y)} \times g_{CH_4} + GWP_{N_2O(20y)} \times g_{N_2O}$

  对于（CO_2 1；CH_4 84；N_2O 264），按下式计算：

- $g_{CO_2eq(20y)} = 1 \times gCO_2 + 84 \times gCH_4 + 264 \times gN_2O$

2.5 本导则提供了：

.1 基于全生命周期归因法的全生命周期温室气体排放因子，采用温室气体（CO_2、CH_4 和 N_2O）在 100 年时间范围内的全球变暖潜势值（GWP）来表示每种代表性燃料的温室气体；

.2 与归因法一致的上船前温室气体排放因子（CO_2、CH_4 和 N_2O）的量化；

.3 船端温室气体排放因子（CO_2、CH_4 和 N_2O）；和

.4 船用燃料的可持续性主题/方面。

---

[3] 本导则中使用的系为 IPCC 第五次评估报告（AR5）中给出的全球变暖潜势值。

2.6   These Guidelines define a FLL that carries information about fuel type, feedstock used, fuel production pathway, GHG emission factors, information on fuel blends and sustainability themes/aspects.

2.7   The figure below shows a generic WtW supply chain for a fuel. The bunkering marks the last step in the WtT phase before the TtW phase starts.

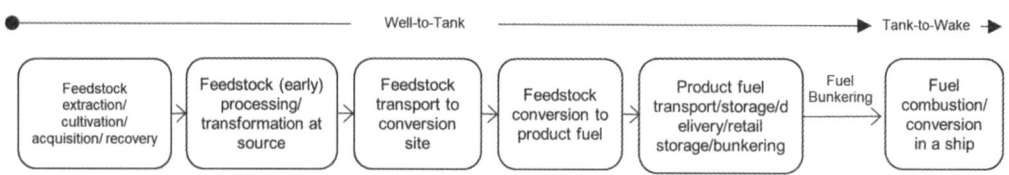

Figure 1: Generic well-to-wake supply chain

2.8   These Guidelines include an initial non-exhaustive list of fuels in appendix 1, depicting the main current and expected future marine fuels.

PART II: METHODOLOGY

3   GENERAL APPROACH

3.1   A life cycle assessment (LCA) based approach provides a holistic assessment of the product/service/system from well-to-wake using data specific to the activity considered. The LCA methodology follows the marine fuel from feedstock sourcing to its utilization onboard ships and assesses its life cycle GHG intensity. This approach, applied within the boundaries of the WtW GHG emissions quantification, is applicable across all geographical regions, where emissions occur and allows for quantifying the GHG intensity over the entire fuel/energy supply chain.

3.2   General principles and methodology can be found in ISO 14044:2006 *Environmental management — Lifecycle assessment — Requirements and guidelines*. ISO 14040:2006 *Environmental management — Lifecycle assessment — Principles and framework* sets the framework for the LCA, for the quantification of the environmental impact of products, processes and services in the supply chain. On this basis, a specific LCA methodology can be tailored for its application to marine fuels.

3.3   WtT emissions represent GHG emissions resulting from growing or extracting raw materials, producing and transporting the fuel up to the point of use, including bunkering.

3.4   TtW emissions represent GHG emissions resulting from fuel utilization onboard (e.g. combustion), including potential leaks (fugitive emissions and slip), when relevant for the GHG assessment.

3.5   WtW emissions are the sum of the WtT and TtW emissions and quantify the full life cycle GHG emissions for a given fuel and fuel pathway, used in a given energy converter on board.

3.6   The attributional approach considers all processes along the supply chain of fuel/energy carrier pathways, allowing the quantification of contributions per segment to the overall GHG intensity of the final fuel/energy product used on board a ship. The expansion of the system boundaries for specific pathways, in which the feedstock or intermediate products are diverted from existing use(s), may be considered on a case-by-case basis.

2.6 本导则定义了包含燃料类型、使用的原料、燃料生产路径、温室气体排放因子、混合燃料和可持续性主题/方面信息的燃料生命周期标签。

2.7 下图显示了一种燃料的通用全生命周期供应链。燃料加注标志在船端阶段开始前的上船前阶段的最后一步。

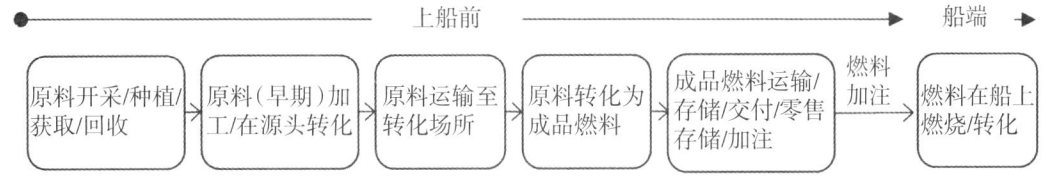

图 1　通用全生命周期供应链

2.8 本导则附录 1 中列出一份初步的燃料清单（非详尽），描述了目前主要的船用燃料和将来预计出现的船用燃料。

第 II 部分：方法

3　一般方法

3.1 基于全生命周期评估（LCA）的方法采用所考虑的活动的特性数据，对产品/服务/系统从全生命周期进行全面评估。LCA 方法跟踪船用燃料从原料获取到其在船上的使用，评估其全生命周期温室气体强度。该方法在全生命周期温室气体排放量化范围内应用，适用于产生排放的所有地理区域，对整个燃料/能源供应链的温室气体强度进行量化。

3.2 一般原则和方法可见 ISO 14044：2006《环境管理 – 全生命周期评估 – 要求和导则》。ISO14040：2006《环境管理 – 全生命周期评估 – 原则和框架》为 LCA 评估设定了框架，用于量化供应链中产品、加工和服务对环境的影响。在此基础上，可以制定具体的 LCA 方法，使其适用于船用燃料。

3.3 上船前（WtT）排放代表从种植或开采原材料、生产和运输燃料到使用点（包括加注）所产生的温室气体排放。

3.4 船端（TtW）排放代表船上使用燃料（如燃烧）产生的温室气体排放，包括与温室气体评估相关的潜在泄漏（逸散性排放和逃逸）。

3.5 全生命周期（WtW）排放是上船前排放和船端排放的总和，量化了给定燃料和燃料路径在给定能量转化器中使用的整个生命周期温室气体排放。

3.6 归因法考虑了燃料/能源载体路径供应链上的所有过程，从而量化每一环节对船上使用的最终燃料/能源产品的总体温室气体强度的贡献。当原料或中间产品偏离现有用途，可以根据具体情况考虑扩大特定路径的系统边界。

3.7   As regards the expansion of the system boundaries, with consequential elements such as Indirect Land Usage Change (ILUC), concerns with respect to uncertainties and the risk of arbitrariness suggest that the feedstocks with associated ILUC should only be assessed through a risk-based approach, in the framework of sustainability themes/aspects, as part of these guidelines.

3.8   When more than one product results from a conversion process, emissions related to the fuel production should be allocated between main product and co-products. Within such conversion processes, emissions are allocated using their energy content, the so-called "energy allocation" approach. Where co-products allocation cannot be performed based on their energy content (e.g. Oxygen resulting from water electrolysis for H_2 production), other methods such as mass allocation, market revenue allocation (also known as "economic allocation"), could be considered on a case-by-case basis.

3.9   A *co-product* is defined as "an outcome of a production process, which has economic value and elastic supply (intended as the existence of a clear evidence of the causal link between feedstock market value and the quantity of feedstock that can be produced)".

3.10   This definition applies also when a raw material used to produce the fuels is a waste (no economic value) or a residue (unavoidably produced and with negligible economic value, needing further processing to be used in the main conversion process). In case the feedstock is a waste, a residue or a by-product, emissions considered as WtT start at the feedstock collection point onwards until the point of use of the final fuel/energy product.

3.11   According to the *IPCC Guidelines for National Greenhouse Gas Inventories* (IPCC Guidelines)[4], any carbon in the fuel derived from biomass should be reported as an information item and not included in the sectoral or national totals to avoid double counting, since the net emissions from biomass are already accounted for in the Agriculture Forestry and Other Land Use (AFOLU) sector at a national level.

3.12   The scope of the IMO LCA Guidelines does not affect or change the IPCC Guidelines. According to the IPCC Guidelines, international waterborne navigation (international bunkers) is grouped under "Mobile combustion" under the Energy sector, but emissions from fuel used by ships in international transport should not be included in national totals in national GHG inventories.

3.13   A fuel batch may be a mix of fuels made from various feedstocks and sources (e.g. by blending 20% biodiesel into fossil MGO) and/or through different production pathways. The calculation should be done using the weighted averages of the energy of the various fuel components. Relevant information should accompany each component fuel in the FLL. Blended fuels should be included in the certification schemes and relevant GHG default or actual emission factors (gCO_2/MJ) determined in proportion to the energy of each fuel part of the blend.

4   WELL-TO-TANK (WtT)

4.1   The pathway of each relevant marine fuel should be clearly described and the GHG emissions during each step of the fuel pathway should be calculated. Specific GHG emissions of a specific non-conventional and non-fossil fuel's pathway may take into account different characteristics across geographic regions, where feedstock production and/or conversion occurs, as appropriate.

---

[4]   *2006 IPCC Guidelines for National Greenhouse Gas Inventories.*

3.7　对于系统边界的扩大，以及如相应的间接土地利用变化（ILUC）等因素，考虑到其中的不确定性和随意性风险，涉及间接土地利用变化的原料应只能通过基于风险的方法在可持续性主题 / 方面的框架内进行评估，并作为本导则的一部分。

3.8　当一个转化过程产生一种以上的产品时，与燃料生产有关的排放应在主要产品和副产品之间分配。在这种转化过程中，排放是根据其能量含量来分配的，即所谓的"能量分配"方法。如果副产品不能根据其能量含量进行分配（例如电解水制氢中产生的氧），则可以根据具体情况逐一考虑其他方法，如质量分配、市场收入分配（也称为"经济分配"）。

3.9　副产品定义为"生产加工的结果，具有经济价值和弹性供应（旨在作为原料市场价值与可生产的原料数量之间存在因果关系的明确证据）"。

3.10　当用于生产燃料的原材料是废料（无经济价值）或残渣（不可避免地产生且经济价值可忽略不计，需要在主要转化过程中进行进一步处理）时，也适用此定义。如果原料是废料、残渣或副产品，则上船前排放是指从原料收集点开始，直到最终燃料 / 能源产品的使用点为止。

3.11　根据《IPCC 国家温室气体清单导则》（IPCC 导则）[4]，生物质燃料中的任何碳应作为一个信息项目进行报告，而不应包括在部门或国家总量中，以避免重复计算，因为生物质的净排放量已在国家级的农林和其他土地利用（AFOLU）部门核算。

3.12　国际海事组织 LCA 导则的范围并不影响或改变 IPCC 导则。根据 IPCC 导则，国际水运（国际燃料）归为能源部门下的"移动源燃烧"，但国际运输中船舶使用的燃料排放不应列入国家温室气体清单的国家总量中。

3.13　燃料批次可以是由各种原料和来源制成的混合燃料（例如，将 20% 的生物柴油混合到化石 MGO 中）和 / 或通过不同的生产路径制成。计算时应使用各种燃料成分能量的加权平均值。有关资料应随附在燃料生命周期标签中每一个燃料成分后。混合燃料应列入认证计划，并根据混合燃料中每种燃料的能量比例确定相关的温室气体默认值或实际排放因子（gCO_2/MJ）。

4　上船前（WtT）

4.1　应明确描述每种相关船用燃料的路径，并计算燃料路径上每一步的温室气体排放。特定非常规和非化石燃料路径的特定温室气体排放可酌情考虑原料生产和 / 或转化发生的地理区域的不同特征。

---

[4]　2006 年《IPCC 国家温室气体清单导则》。

4.2   Any further reference in this document to a "fuel pathway" should be understood to include the feedstock structure (the so-called nature/carbon source and feedstock type pair) and the production or conversion process (noting that the same feedstock and fuel type pair can have a different production or conversion process).

4.3   The aim of the WtT methodology is to quantify and evaluate the GHG intensity of fuel production, including all steps mentioned in figure 2. The carbon feedstock and production pathway of a fuel should be identified in order to apply the methodology and is included as part of the FLL. The production steps to be included in the WtT are presented in figure 2.

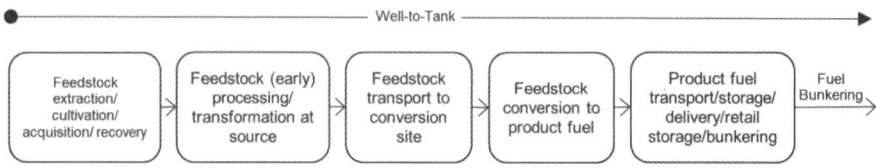

Figure 2: Generic well-to-tank supply chain

4.4   The WtT GHG emission factor ($gCO_{2eq}/MJ_{(LCV)}$ fuel or electricity) is calculated according to Equation (1).

Equation (1)

$$GHG_{WtT} = e_{fecu} + e_l + e_p + e_{td} - e_{sca} - e_{ccs}$$

Term	Units	Explanation
e_{fecu}	$gCO_{2eq}/MJ_{(LCV)}$	Emissions associated with the feedstock extraction/cultivation/acquisition/recovery
e_l	$gCO_{2eq}/MJ_{(LCV)}$	Emissions (annualized emissions (over 20 years) from carbon stock changes caused by direct land-use change)[5]
e_p	$gCO_{2eq}/MJ_{(LCV)}$	Emissions associated with the feedstock processing and/or transformation at source and emissions associated with the conversion of the feedstock to the final fuel product, including electricity generation
e_{td}	$gCO_{2eq}/MJ_{(LCV)}$	Emissions associated with the feedstock transport to conversion plant, and the emissions associated with the finished fuel transport and storage, local delivery, retail storage and bunkering
e_{sca}	$gCO_{2eq}/MJ_{(LCV)}$	Emissions (annualized emission savings (over 20 years) from soil carbon accumulation via improved agricultural management)[6]
e_{ccs}	$gCO_{2eq}/MJ_{(LCV)}$	Emissions credit from carbon capture and storage (e_{ccs}), that have not already been accounted for in e_p. This should properly account the avoided emissions through the capture and sequestration of emitted CO_2, related to the extraction, transport, processing and distribution of fuel (c_{sc}). From the

---

[5]   Pending further methodological guidance to be developed by the Organization, the value of parameter e_l should be set to zero.

[6]   Pending further methodological guidance to be developed by the Organization, the value of parameter e_{sca} should be set to zero.

4.2 本文中进一步提及的"燃料路径"均应理解为包括原料结构（称为性质／碳源和原料类型对）和生产或转化过程（注意相同的原料和燃料类型对可以具有不同的生产或转化过程）。

4.3 上船前方法的目的是量化和评估燃料生产的温室气体强度，包括图2中提到的所有步骤。为了应用该方法，应确定燃料的碳原料和生产路径，并将其作为燃料生命周期标签的一部分。上船前应包含的生产步骤如图2所示。

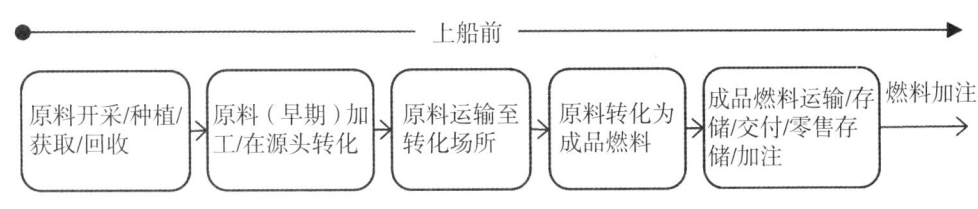

图2 通用上船前供应链

4.4 上船前温室气体排放因子（$gCO_{2eq}/MJ_{(LCV)}$ 燃料或电力）按公式（1）计算。

公式（1）

$$GHG_{WtT} = e_{fecu} + e_l + e_p + e_{td} - e_{sca} - e_{ccs}$$

参数	单位	解释
e_{fecu}	$gCO_{2eq} / MJ_{(LCV)}$	与原料开采／种植／获取／回收有关的排放
e_l	$gCO_{2eq} / MJ_{(LCV)}$	排放：直接土地利用变化引起的碳储量变化的年化排放（超过20年）[5]
e_p	$gCO_{2eq} / MJ_{(LCV)}$	与原料加工和／或原料转化有关的排放，以及与原料转化为最终燃料产品（包括发电）有关的排放
e_{td}	$gCO_{2eq} / MJ_{(LCV)}$	与原料运输到转化厂有关的排放，以及与成品燃料运输和储存、当地交付、零售储存和加注有关的排放
e_{sca}	$gCO_{2eq} / MJ_{(LCV)}$	排放：通过改善农业管理从土壤碳积累中减少的年化排放量（超过20年）[6]
e_{ccs}	$gCO_{2eq} / MJ_{(LEV)}$	尚未在 e_p 中核算的来自碳捕获和存储（e_{ccs}）的排放信用额。应适当核算通过捕获和封存与燃料开采、运输、加工和分配相关的 CO_2 排放而避免的排放 Csc。

---

[5] 在本组织制定进一步的方法指南之前，参数 e_l 的值应设为零。

[6] 在本组织制定进一步的方法指南之前，参数 e_{sca} 的值应设为零。

Term	Units	Explanation
		above-mentioned emission credit, all the emissions resulting from the process of capturing (e_{cc}) and transporting (e_t) the CO_2 up to the final storage (including the emissions related to the injection, etc.) need to be deducted. This element should be calculated with the following formula: $$e_{CCS} = c_{SC} - e_{cc} - e_t - e_{st} - e_x$$
c_{sc}	g CO_2 stored / $MJ_{(LCV)}$	Emissions credit equivalent to the net CO_2 captured and stored (long-term: 100 years)
e_{cc}	gCO_{2eq} / $MJ_{(LCV)}$	Emissions associated with the process of capturing, compression and/or cooling and temporary storage of the CO_2
e_t	gCO_{2eq} / $MJ_{(LCV)}$	Emissions associated with transport to a long-term storage site
e_{st}	gCO_{2eq} / $MJ_{(LCV)}$	Any emissions associated with the process of storing (long-term: 100 years) the captured CO_2 (including fugitive emissions that may happen during long-term storage and/or the injection of CO_2 into the storage)
e_x	gCO_{2eq} / $MJ_{(LCV)}$	Any additional emissions related to the CCS

4.5   The WtT emissions in Equation (1) include emissions associated with raw materials extraction or cultivation, primary energy sources used for production of goods and utilities such as energy carriers (e.g. fuels and electricity), transport and distribution (including bunkering), direct land use change and changes in carbon stocks (soil carbon accumulation).

4.6   Processing incorporates all steps and operations needed for the extraction, capture or cultivation of the primary energy source. Process includes basic transformation at source and operations needed to make the resource transportable to the marketplace (e.g. drying, chemical/physical upgrade such as gas-to-liquid, etc.).

4.7   Transportation, processing and distribution include transportation of the products in the fuel pathway to the place of transformation, conditioning (such as compression, cooling), distribution to the marketplace (i.e. bunkering) and eventual leakages, as well as fugitive emissions at any of these stages. Regarding emissions from bunkering, it is included till the bunker manifold, including emission from the bunker manifold connection.

4.8   Allocation of emissions to co-products based on their energy content should be used, as the most appropriate and reliable methodology considering the establishment of an appropriate certification method using values that are predictable, reproducible and stable.

4.9   Land use (direct and indirect) for the production of biofuels may lead to land use change (LUC). LUC can be classified as direct LUC (DLUC) and indirect LUC (ILUC).

4.10   The DLUC definition is based on ISO 14067:2018 described as a change in the use or management of land within the product system being assessed. The DLUC impacts comprises the emissions and sequestration resulting from carbon stock changes in biomass, dead organic matter and soil organic matters, evaluated in accordance with the IPCC Guidelines. When available, sector or country-specific data on carbon stocks may be used; otherwise, IPCC's Tier 1 default emission factors may be considered. Two terms in the WtT Equation (1) capture respectively emissions resulting from direct land use change, i.e. e_l, and sequestration or otherwise increase in the content of soil organic carbon: e_{sca}.

参数	单位	解释
		从上述排放信用额中，需要扣除从 CO_2 捕获（e_{cc}）和运输（e_t）直至最终储存这一过程中产生的所有排放（包括与注入等相关的排放）。 该要素的计算公式如下： $$e_{CCS} = c_{SC} - e_{cc} - e_t - e_{st} - e_x$$
C_{SC}	gCO$_2$ stored / MJ $_{(LCV)}$	相当于捕获和储存的净 CO_2 排放信用额（长期：100 年）
e_{cc}	gCO$_{2eq}$ / MJ $_{(LCV)}$	与 CO_2 的捕获、压缩和／或冷却及临时储存过程相关的排放
e_t	gCO$_{2eq}$ / MJ $_{(LCV)}$	与运输到长期储存地点相关的排放
e_{st}	gCO$_{2eq}$ / MJ $_{(LCV)}$	与捕获的 CO_2 存储过程（长期：100 年）相关的任何排放（包括长期储存和／或向储存容器中注入 CO_2 时可能发生的逸散性排放）
e_x	gCO$_{2eq}$ / MJ $_{(LCV)}$	任何与碳捕获和存储相关的额外排放

4.5 公式（1）中的上船前排放包括与原材料开采或种植、用于商品生产和诸如能源载体等公用设施的初级能源（如燃料和电力）、运输和分配（包括加注）、直接土地利用变化和碳储量变化（土壤碳积累）相关的排放。

4.6 加工包括开采、捕获或种植初级能源所需的所有步骤和操作。加工包括源头的基本转化和使资源可运输到市场所需的操作（例如干燥，化学／物理升级，如气转液等）。

4.7 运输、加工和分配包括在燃料路径中将产品运输到转化地点、调节（如压缩、冷却）、分配到市场（即加注）和最终泄漏，以及在任何这些阶段的逸散性排放。关于加注产生的排放，直至加注总管都包含在内，包括加注总管接头处的排放。

4.8 为采用可预测、可重复和稳定的数值建立适当的认证方法，最适当可靠的方法是应基于副产品的能量含量将排放量分配给副产品。

4.9 用于生产生物燃料的土地利用（直接和间接的）可能导致土地利用变化（LUC）。土地利用变化可分为直接土地利用变化（DLUC）和间接土地利用变化（ILUC）。

4.10 直接土地利用变化的定义基于 ISO 14067：2018，描述为被评估产品系统内土地利用或管理的变化。直接土地利用变化的影响包括由生物量、死有机质和土壤有机质的碳储量变化引起的排放和封存，根据 IPCC 导则进行评估。如能获得，可使用行业或国家特定的碳储量数据，否则，可考虑 IPCC 的 1 级默认排放因子。上船前公式（1）中的两项分别捕获了直接土地利用变化引起的排放，即 e_l 和土壤有机碳含量的封存或以其他方式增加的排放 e_{sca}。

4.11 The ILUC definition is based on ISO 14067:2018, described as a change in the use or management of land, which is a consequence of direct land use change, but which occurs outside the product system being assessed. ILUC occurs as a result of the economic impacts induced by increased biofuel demand on commodity prices with resulting shifts in demand and supply across economic sectors, including primarily food and feed production. ILUC cannot be directly measured and is projected with economic models instead.

4.12 Owing to the variability of assumptions underlying the evaluation of indirect effects, quantitative assessment of GHG effects of ILUC is subject to uncertainty, high quantitative variability and to the risk of arbitrary conclusions. For these reasons, ILUC should be at this stage addressed using a risk-based approach, meaning that quantitative values will not be calculated and assigned to each fuel pathway. The ILUC emissions, as well as the spatial dimension of the ILUC effects, are dependent on a variety of factors such as local/regional conditions and practices for agriculture, current and expected food import demand, national current accounts, the type of feedstock, the alternative economic uses of the same feedstock, etc.

4.13 A qualitative risk-based approach to ILUC includes consideration on the following:

.1 *Low-ILUC risk* qualifies and characterizes biofuel production projects that supply additional feedstock without disrupting existing land uses. When productivity is increased on an area which is in agricultural production, only additional yields should be considered as low-ILUC rather than the entire production; and

.2 *High-ILUC risk* qualifies and characterizes biofuel production projects based on, or displacing, food and feed crops resulting in a significant expansion of the feedstock production area shifting into land with high carbon stock.

4.14 WtT default emission factors are provided in appendix 2 of these guidelines.

5 TANK-TO-WAKE (TtW)

5.1 The aim of the TtW methodology is to quantify and evaluate the intensity of CO_2, CH_4 and N_2O emitted on board a ship related to the fuel usage, including combustion/conversion and all relevant fugitive emissions, from the bunker manifold up to the energy converter which is leaked, vented or otherwise lost in the system, with a global warming potential.

5.2 The TtW GHG emission factors should be calculated using Equation (2):

Equation (2)

$$GHG_{TtW} = \frac{1}{LCV} \left(\begin{array}{l} \left(1 - \frac{1}{100}\left(C_{slip\_ship} + C_{fug}\right)\right) \times \left(C_{fCO_2} \times GWP_{CO_2} + C_{fCH_4} \times GWP_{CH_4} + C_{fN_2O} \times GWP_{N_2O}\right) + \\ + \left(\frac{1}{100}\left(C_{slip\_ship} + C_{fug}\right) \times C_{sfx} \times GWP_{fuelx}\right) - S_{Fc} \times e_c - S_{Fccu} \times e_{ccu} - e_{occs} \end{array} \right)$$

Note: *Terms S_{Fccu}, e_{ccu} and e_{occs} are pending further methodological guidance to be developed by the Organization. For more details refer to footnotes 11 to 13.*

4.11 间接土地利用变化的定义基于 ISO 14067：2018，描述为直接土地利用变化导致的土地利用或管理的变化，但发生在被评估的产品系统之外。间接土地利用变化的发生是由于生物燃料需求增加对商品价格产生的经济影响，导致经济行业（主要包括食品和饲料生产）的需求和供应发生变化。间接土地利用变化不能直接测量，而是用经济模型来预测。

4.12 由于间接影响评估所依据的假设存在可变性，间接土地利用变化对温室气体影响的定量评估存在不确定性、数量上的高度可变性和结论随意性的风险。由于这些原因，现阶段应采用基于风险的方法来解决间接土地利用变化问题，这意味着不会计算定量值并分配给每个燃料路径。间接土地利用变化产生的排放，以及间接土地利用变化影响的空间维度取决于多种因素，例如当地/区域条件和农业实践、当前和预期的粮食进口需求、国家活期账户、原料类型、同一原料的替代经济用途等。

4.13 对于间接土地利用变化，基于风险的定性方法考虑了以下方面：

.1 低间接土地利用变化风险对应在不破坏现有土地利用的情况下提供额外原料的生物燃料生产项目。当一个农业生产地区的生产力提高时，只有额外的产量而非整个生产应被视为低间接土地利用变化；和

.2 高间接土地利用变化风险对应基于或取代粮食和饲料作物，从而导致原料生产区域大幅扩大，转移到高碳储量土地的生物燃料生产项目。

4.14 上船前默认排放因子见本导则附录 2。

5 船端（TtW）

5.1 船端方法的目的是量化和评估船舶上与燃料使用相关的 CO_2、CH_4 和 N_2O 排放强度，包括燃烧/转化和从加注总管直到能量转换器中泄漏、排出或系统中以其他方式丢失的所有相关逸散性排放，用全球变暖潜势值表示。

5.2 船端温室气体排放因子应按式（2）计算：

公式（2）

$$GHG_{TtW} = \frac{1}{LCV} \left(\begin{array}{l} \left(1 - \frac{1}{100}\left(C_{slip\_ship} + C_{fug}\right)\right) \times \left(C_{fCO_2} \times GWP_{CO_2} + C_{fCH_4} \times GWP_{CH_4} + C_{fN_2O} \times GWP_{N_2O}\right) + \\ + \left(\frac{1}{100}\left(C_{slip\_ship} + C_{fug}\right) \times C_{sfx} \times GWP_{fuelx}\right) - S_{Fc} \times e_c - S_{Fccu} \times e_{ccu} - e_{OCCS} \end{array} \right)$$

注：参数 S_{Fccu}、e_{ccu} 和 e_{occs} 有待本组织制定进一步的方法指导。详情参见脚注 11 至 13。

Term	Units	Explanation
C_{slip_ship}	% of total fuel mass	Factor accounting for fuel (expressed in % of total fuel mass delivered to the ship) which escapes from the energy converter without being oxidized (including fuel that escapes from combustion chamber/oxidation process and from crankcase, as appropriate) $$C_{slip\_ship} = C_{slip} * (1 - C_{fug}/100)$$
C_{slip}	% of total fuel mass	Factor accounting for fuel (expressed in % of total fuel mass consumed in the energy converter) which escapes from the energy converter without being oxidized (including fuel that escapes from combustion chamber/oxidation process and from crankcase, as appropriate)
C_{fug}	% of fuel mass	Factor accounting for the fuel (expressed in % of mass of the fuel delivered to the ship) which escapes between the tanks up to the energy converter which is leaked, vented or otherwise lost in the system[7]
C_{sfx}	gGHG/g fuel	Factor accounting for the share of GHG in the components of the fuel (expressed in g GHG/g fuel) Example: for LNG this value is 1
C_{fCO2}	gCO$_2$/g fuel	CO$_2$ emission conversion factor (gCO$_2$/g fuel completely combusted) for emissions of the combustion and/or oxidation process of the fuel used by the ship
C_{fCH4}	gCH$_4$/g fuel	CH$_4$ emission conversion factor (gCH$_4$/g fuel delivered to the ship) for emissions of the combustion and/or oxidation process of the fuel used by the ship[8]
C_{fN2O}	gN$_2$O/g fuel	N$_2$O emission conversion factor (gN$_2$O/g fuel delivered to the ship) for emissions of the combustion and/or oxidation process of the fuel used by the ship
GWP_{CH4}	gCO$_{2eq}$/g CH$_4$	Global warming potential of CH$_4$ over 100 years (based on the fifth IPCC Assessment Report 5)[9] Definition as per https://www.ipcc.ch/assessmentreport/ar5/
GWP_{N2O}	gCO$_{2eq}$/g N$_2$O	Global warming potential of N$_2$O over 100 years (based on the fifth IPCC Assessment Report 5).[10] Definition as per https://www.ipcc.ch/assessment-report/ar5/
GWP_{fuelx}	gCO$_{2eq}$/g GHG	Global warming potential of GHG in the components of the fuel over 100 years (based on the fifth IPCC scientific Assessment Report)
S_{Fc}	0 or 1	Carbon source factor to determine whether the emissions credits generated by biomass growth are accounted for in the calculation of the TtW value
e_c	gCO$_{2eq}$/g fuel	Emissions credits generated by biomass growth

---

[7] Pending further methodological guidance to be developed by the Organization to determine appropriate factor(s), the value of C_{fug} should be set to zero.

[8] For LNG/CNG fuel, the $C_{slip\,engine}$ is covering the role of C_{fCH4}, so C_{fCH4} is set to zero for these fuels.

[9] Set at 28 based on IPCC AR5.

[10] Set at 265 based on IPCC AR5.

参数	单位	解释
C_{slip_ship}	占总燃料质量的百分比	核算未被氧化从能量转化器中逃逸的燃料因子（包括从燃烧室／氧化过程和曲轴箱中逃逸的燃料，视情况而定），以占交付给船舶的总燃料质量的百分比表示。 $C_{slip\_ship}=C_{slip}*（1-C_{fug}/100）$
C_{slip}	占总燃料质量的百分比	核算未被氧化从能量转化器中逃逸的燃料因子（包括从燃烧室／氧化过程和曲轴箱中逃逸的燃料，视情况而定），以占能量转化器中消耗的总燃料质量的百分比表示。
C_{fug}	占燃料质量的百分比	核算从油舱直至能量转化器之间逃逸并在系统中泄漏、排气或以其他方式丢失的燃料因子，以占交付给船舶的燃料质量的百分比表示[7]
C_{sfx}	gGHG/g fuel	核算温室气体在燃料成分中所占份额的因子，以 gGHG/g fuel 表示 例如：对于 LNG，该值为 1
C_{fCO2}	gCO_2/g fuel	船舶使用的燃料在燃烧和／或氧化过程中产生的排放的 CO_2 排放转化因子（g CO_2/g 完全燃烧的燃料）
C_{fCH4}	gCH_4/g fuel	船舶使用的燃料在燃烧和／或氧化过程中产生的排放的 CH_4 排放转化因子（g CH4/g 交付给船舶的燃料）[8]
C_{fN2O}	gN_2O/g fuel	船舶使用的燃料在燃烧和／或氧化过程中产生的排放的 N_2O 排放转化因子（g N_2O/g 交付给船舶的燃料）
GWP_{CH4}	gCO_{2eq}/g CH_4	CH_4 的 100 年全球变暖潜势（基于 IPCC 第五次评估报告 5）[9] 见 https://www.ipcc.ch/assessment-report/ar5/ 定义
GWP_{N2O}	gCO_{2eq}/g N_2O	N_2O 的 100 年全球变暖潜势（基于 IPCC 第五次评估报告 5）[10] 见 https://www.ipcc.ch/assessment-report/ar5/ 定义
GWP_{fuelx}	gCO_{2eq}/g GHG	燃料成分中温室气体的 100 年全球变暖潜势（基于 IPCC 第五次科学评估报告）
S_{FC}	0 或 1	碳源因子，用以确定在计算船端值时是否核算了生物质生长产生的排放信用额
e_c	gCO_{2eq}/g fuel	生物质生长产生的排放信用额

[7] 在本组织制定进一步的方法指南以确定适当因子之前，C_{fug} 的值应设为零。
[8] 对于 LNG/CNG 燃料，C_{slip_engine} 覆盖了 C_{fCH4} 的作用，因此对于这些燃料 C_{fCH4} 设为零。
[9] 根据 IPCC AR5 设为 28。
[10] 根据 IPCC AR5 设为 265。

Term	Units	Explanation
e_{ccu}[11]	gCO2eq/g fuel	Emission credits from the used captured CO_2 as carbon stock to produce synthetic fuels in the fuel production process and utilization (that was not accounted under e_{fecu} and e_p)
S_{Fccu}[12]	0 or 1	Carbon source factor to determine whether the emissions credits from the used captured CO_2 as carbon stock to produce synthetic fuels in the fuel production process are accounted for in the calculation of the TtW value
e_{occs}[13]	gCO2eq / g fuel	Emission credit from carbon capture and storage (e_{occs}), where capture of CO_2 occurs onboard. This should properly account for the emissions avoided through the capture and sequestration of emitted CO_2, if CCS occurs on board. From the above-mentioned emission credit, all the emissions resulting from the process of capturing (e_{cc}), and transporting (e_t) the CO_2 up to the final storage (including the emissions related to the injection, etc.) need to be deducted. This element should be calculated with the following formula: $$e_{occs} = c_{sc} - e_{cc} - e_t - e_{st} - e_x$$
c_{sc}	gCO2 / g fuel	Credit equivalent to the CO_2 captured and stored (long-term: 100 years)
e_{cc}	gCO2eq / g fuel	Any emission associated with the process of capturing, compress and temporarily store on board the CO_2
e_t	gCO2eq / g fuel	Emissions associated with transport to long-term storage site
e_{st}	gCO2eq / g fuel	Any emission associated with the process of storing (long-term: 100 years) the captured CO_2 (including fugitive emissions that may happen during long-term storage and/or the injection of CO_2 into the storage)
e_x	gCO2eq / g fuel	Any additional emission related to the CCS
LCV	MJ/g	Lower Calorific Value is the amount of heat that would be released by the complete combustion of a specified fuel

5.3   In order to have LCA guidelines that will allow for their clear, robust and consistent application to any possible measure, the methodology allows to calculate two TtW values as follows:

.1   TtW GHG intensity value 1: calculated regardless of the carbon source, therefore the e_c and e_{ccu} parameters should not be taken into account and the S_{Fc} and S_{Fccu} value should be always 0; and

.2   TtW GHG intensity value 2: calculated taking into account the carbon source for fuels of biogenic origins or made from captured carbon, therefore the e_c and e_{ccu} parameters should be taken into account and the S_{Fc} and S_{Fccu} values should be always 1.

---

[11]   Pending further methodological guidance to be developed by the Organization, the value of the multiplication $S_{Fccu} \times e_{ccu}$ should be set to zero.

[12]   Pending further methodological guidance to be developed by the Organization, the value of the multiplication $S_{Fccu} \times e_{ccu}$ should be set to zero.

[13]   Pending further methodological guidance to be developed by the Organization, the value of e_{occs} should be set to zero.

参数	单位	解释
e_{ccu} [11]	$gCO_{2eq}/g\,fuel$	在燃料生产加工和使用中，使用捕获的 CO_2 作为碳储量生产合成燃料产生的排放信用额，且未在 e_{fecu} 和 e_p 中核算过
S_{Fccu} [12]	0 或 1	碳源因子，用以确定在计算船端值时是否核算了在燃料生产加工和使用中使用捕获的 CO_2 作为碳储量生产合成燃料产生的排放信用额
e_{occs} [13]	$gCO_{2eq}/g\,fuel$	在船上进行 CO_2 捕获时，碳捕获和存储（e_{occs}）的排放信用额。如果在船上进行碳捕获和存储，应适当核算通过捕获和封存所排放的 CO_2 而避免的排放。从上述排放信用额中，需要扣除 CO_2 捕获（e_{cc}）和运输（e_t）直至最终储存这一过程中产生的所有排放（包括与注入等相关的排放）。该要素的计算公式如下：$$e_{OCCS}=c_{SC}-e_{CC}-e_t-e_{st}-e_x$$
C_{SC}	$gCO_2/g\,fuel$	相当于捕获和存储 CO_2（长期：100 年）的信用额
e_{CC}	$gCO_{2eq}/g\,fuel$	与 CO_2 的捕获、压缩和船上临时储存过程相关的任何排放
e_t	$gCO_{2eq}/g\,fuel$	与运输至长期储存点相关的排放
e_{st}	$gCO_{2eq}/g\,fuel$	与捕获的 CO_2 存储过程（长期：100 年）相关的任何排放（包括长期储存和/或向储存容器中注入 CO_2 时可能发生的逸散性排放）
e_x	$gCO_{2eq}/g\,fuel$	任何与碳捕获和存储相关的额外排放
LCV	MJ/g	低热值指某一特定燃料完全燃烧所释放的热量

5.3　为了使 LCA 导则能够清晰、稳健和一致地应用于任何可能的测量，用该方法可计算以下两个船端值：

.1　船端温室气体强度值 1：计算时不考虑碳源，因此不考虑 e_c 和 e_{ccu} 参数，S_{Fc} 和 S_{Fccu} 值应始终为 0；和

.2　船端温室气体强度值 2：计算时考虑了生物源燃料的碳源或由捕获的碳制成的燃料的碳源，因此应考虑 e_c 和 eccu 参数，S_{Fc} 和 S_{Fccu} 值应始终为 1。

---

[11]　在本组织制定进一步的方法指南之前，$S_{Fccu} \times e_{ccu}$ 的积应设为零。
[12]　在本组织制定进一步的方法指南之前，$S_{Fccu} \times e_{ccu}$ 的积应设为零。
[13]　在本组织制定进一步的方法指南之前，e_{occs} 的值应设为 0。

5.4   The actual GHG intensity depends both on the properties of the fuel and on the efficiency of the energy conversion. For CO_2, the emission factors are based on the molar ratio of carbon to oxygen multiplied with the carbon mass of the fuel, assuming that all the carbon in the fuel is oxidized (stoichiometric combustion). The CH_4 and N_2O emissions factors are dependent on the combustion and/or conversion process in the energy converter.

5.5   For future use of, for example, fuel cells with a reforming unit, also electro-chemical reactions forming GHGs can be taken into account by this TtW methodology.

5.6   TtW default emission factors are provided in appendix 2 of these guidelines.

6   WELL-TO-WAKE (WtW)

6.1   The aim of the WtW methodology is to integrate WtT and TtW parts, to quantify the full life cycle emissions related to the production and use of a fuel.

6.2   The WtW GHG emission factor (gCO_{2eq}/MJ_{LCV} fuel or electricity) is calculated as follows:

Equation (3)

$$GHG_{WtW} = GHG_{WtT} + GHG_{TtW}$$

where:

Term	Units	Explanation
GHG_{WtW}	$gCO_{2eq}/MJ_{(LCV)}$	Total well-to-wake GHG emissions per energy unit from the use of the fuel or electricity in a consumer on board the ship
GHG_{WtT}	$gCO_{2eq}/MJ_{(LCV)}$	Total well-to-tank GHG upstream emissions per energy unit of the fuel provided to the ship
GHG_{TtW}	$gCO_{2eq}/MJ_{(LCV)}$	Total tank-to-wake GHG downstream emissions per energy unit from the use of the fuel or electricity in a consumer on board the ship

Equation (4)

$$
\begin{aligned}
GHG_{WtW} &= e_{fecu} + e_l + e_p + e_{td} - e_{sca} - e_{ccs} \\
&+ \frac{1}{LCV}\left(\begin{array}{l} \left(1 - \frac{1}{100}(C_{slip\_ship} + C_{fug})\right) \times \left(C_{fCO_2} \times GWP_{CO_2} + C_{fCH_4} \times GWP_{CH_4} + C_{fN_2O} \times GWP_{N_2O}\right) + \\ \left(\frac{1}{100}(C_{slip_{ship}} + C_{fug}) \times C_{sfx} \times GWP_{fuelx}\right) - S_{Fc} \times e_c - S_{Fccu} \times e_{ccu} - e_{OCCS} \end{array} \right)
\end{aligned}
$$

Note: terms S_{Fccu}, e_{ccu} and e_{occs} are pending further methodological guidance to be developed by the Organization. For more details refer to section 5.2.

6.3   For the purpose of calculating WtW, the TtW value 2 as calculated in accordance with paragraph 5.3.2 should be used.

7   SUSTAINABILITY

7.1   The sustainability of marine fuels should be assessed considering the following themes/aspects on a life cycle basis:

5.4 实际的温室气体强度取决于燃料的特性和能量转化的效率。对于 CO_2，排放系数是基于碳氧摩尔比乘以燃料的碳质量，假设燃料中的所有碳都被氧化（按化学计量燃烧）。CH_4 和 N_2O 排放因子取决于能量转化器中的燃烧和／或转化过程。

5.5 对于未来的使用，例如，带有重整装置的燃料电池，也可以通过这种船端方法考虑生成温室气体的电化学反应。

5.6 船端默认排放因子见本导则附录 2。

6 全生命周期（WtW）

6.1 全生命周期方法的目的是整合上船前和船端部分，量化与燃料生产和使用相关的整个生命周期的排放。

6.2 全生命周期温室气体排放因子（gCO_{2eq}/MJLCV 燃料或电力）按下式计算：

公式（3）

$$GHG_{WtW} = GHG_{WtT} + GHG_{TtW}$$

式中：

参数	单位	解释
GHG_{WtW}	gCO_{2eq}/MJ（LCV）	船上耗能设备使用燃料或电力产生的每能源单位全生命周期温室气体排放总量
GHG_{WtT}	gCO_{2eq}/MJ（LCV）	提供给船舶的燃料每能源单位上船前温室气体上游排放总量
GHG_{TtW}	gCO_{2eq}/MJ（LCV）	船上耗能设备使用燃料或电力产生的每能源单位船端温室气体下游排放总量

公式（4）

$$
\begin{aligned}
GHG_{WtW} &= e_{fecu} + e_l + e_p + e_{td} - e_{sca} - e_{ccs} \\
&+ \frac{1}{LCV}\left(\begin{array}{l} \left(1 - \frac{1}{100}(C_{slip\_ship} + C_{fug})\right) \times (C_{fCO_2} \times GWP_{CO_2} + C_{fCH_4} \times GWP_{CH_4} + C_{fN_2O} \times GWP_{N_2O}) + \\ \left(\frac{1}{100}(C_{slip_{ship}} + C_{fug}) \times C_{sfx} \times GWP_{fuelx}\right) - S_{Fc} \times e_c - S_{Fccu} \times e_{ccu} - e_{OCCS} \end{array} \right)
\end{aligned}
$$

注：参数 S_{Fccu}，e_{ccu} 和 e_{occs} 有待本组织制定进一步的方法指导。详情参见 5.2 节。

6.3 为计算全生命周期排放，应使用按第 5.3.2 段计算的船端值 2。

7 可持续性

7.1 应基于全生命周期通过以下主题／方面来评估船用燃料的可持续性：

.1   greenhouse gases (GHG);
.2   carbon source;
.3   source of electricity/energy;
.4   carbon stock – direct land use change (DLUC);
.5   carbon stock – indirect land use change (ILUC);
.6   water;
.7   air;
.8   soil;
.9   waste and chemicals; and
.10   conservation.

Other social and economic sustainability themes/aspects may be considered at a later stage.

7.2   The principle/objective in conjunction with the associated metrics/indicators of each of the sustainability theme/aspect are specified below.

Table 1: Sustainability themes/aspects

Theme/aspect	Principle/Objective	Metric/Indicator
1. Greenhouse Gases (GHG)	Sustainable marine fuels generate lower GHG emissions than conventional marine fuels (energy-based weighted average of liquid petroleum products on 3 specific years of DCS data) on a life cycle basis.	1. GHG intensity in gCO_{2eq}/MJ (GWP100); and GHG intensity in gCO_{2eq}/MJ (GWP20) for comparative purposes.
2. Carbon source	Sustainable marine fuels do not increase GHG intensity from the use of fossil energy sources and the permanence of captured and stored carbon is ensured while also avoiding double counting across economic sectors.	1. Carbon source indicator, including its content (in %) and origin in feedstock used to produce final fuel product, i.e. Fossil, Biogenic, Captured Carbon (including direct air capture (DAC), point source fossil (PSF) and point source biogenic (PSB)), and Others (including mixture of sources).
3. Source of electricity/energy	Sustainable marine fuels requiring significant electricity input during WtT phase and electricity delivered directly to ships are produced by using electricity/energy from renewable, nuclear or biogenic sources, which are additional to current or longstanding demand levels, or by using surplus electricity during off-peak hours.	1. The GHG intensity of electricity used in the production of marine fuels or delivered directly to ships (annual average, expressed in gCO_{2eq}/kWh based on total emissions and actual hours of production).

.1 温室气体（GHG）；

.2 碳源；

.3 电力 / 能源来源；

.4 碳储量 – 直接土地利用变化（DLUC）；

.5 碳储量 – 间接土地利用变化（ILUC）；

.6 水；

.7 空气；

.8 土壤；

.9 废料和化学品；和

.10 保护。其他社会和经济可持续性主题 / 方面可在后续阶段加以考虑。

7.2 每一可持续性主题 / 方面的原则 / 目标以及相关度量 / 指标见下表。

表 1 可持续性主题 / 方面

主题 / 方面	原则 / 目标	度量 / 指标
1.温室气体（GHG）	基于全生命周期，可持续船用燃料产生的温室气体排放量低于传统船用燃料（基于 DCS 数据的 3 个特定年份的液态石油产品的能量加权平均值）。	1. 采用单位为 gCO_{2eq}/MJ（GWP100）的温室气体强度；单位为 gCO_{2eq}/MJ（GWP20）的温室气体强度可以作为比较。
2.碳源	可持续船用燃料不会增加使用化石能源产生的温室气体强度，能确保捕获和储存的碳的性能同时避免在经济产业的重复计算。	1.碳源指标，包括其在用于生产最终燃料产品的原料中的含量（以 % 为单位）和来源，即化石、生物源、捕获碳（包括直接空气捕获（DAC）、点源化石（PSF）和点源生物源（PSB）），以及其他（包括来源的混合物）。
3.电力 / 能源来源	在上船前阶段需要大量电力输入的可持续船用燃料和直接向船舶输送的电力是通过使用来自可再生能源、核能或生物源的电力 / 能源生产的，这些电力 / 能源是当前或长期需求水平之外的，或者在非高峰时段使用多余的电力。	1.用于生产船用燃料或直接交付给船舶的电力的温室气体强度（年平均值，根据总排放量和实际生产小时数以 gCO_{2eq}/kWh 表示）。

Theme/aspect	Principle/Objective	Metric/Indicator
4.Carbon stock– direct land use change (DLUC)	Sustainable marine fuels are not made from biomass obtained from land with high carbon stock; production of sustainable marine fuels minimizes emissions resulting from Direct Land Use Change.	1.Sustainable marine fuel feedstock does not include biomass obtained from land with high carbon stock (e.g. primary forests, wetlands, or peat lands referred to a specific cut-off date for conversion), or a sustainable land management plan and reporting schedule are in place to ensure that the biomass is obtained from activities or ecosystem services that do not negatively impact the soil carbon stock; 2.The production of sustainable marine fuels does not occur in lands converted from primary forest, forestland, grassland or legally protected land, taking (1 January 2008)[14] as the cut-off date; and 3.Direct land-use change(DLUC) indicator, expressed in GHG(including CO_2, CH_4 and N_2O emissions) intensity, i.e. mass of CO_2 equivalent / MJ of production or yield of feedstock.
5.Carbon stock– indirect land use change (ILUC)	Cultivation of feedstock of sustainable marine fuels minimizes inducing negative changes in the use or management of land which occurs outside the product system being assessed.	1.Indirect carbon stock risk associated with cultivation of feedstock for sustainable marine fuels (see paragraph 4.13).

[14] Pending further guidance to be developed by the Organization.

主题 / 方面	原则 / 目标	度量 / 指标
4. 碳储量 – 直接土地利用变化（DLUC）	可持续船用燃料不是由从高碳储量的土地获得的生物质制成的；生产可持续船用燃料可以最大限度地减少直接土地利用变化造成的排放。	1. 可持续船用燃料原料不包括从高碳储量的土地获得的生物质（例如，原始森林、湿地或泥炭地，参照特定的转化截止日期），或者制定了可持续的土地管理计划和报告时间表，以确保生物质来自不会对土壤碳储量产生负面影响的活动或生态系统服务； 2. 以 2008 年 1 月 1 日[14] 为截止日期，不在由原始森林、林地、草地或受法律保护的土地转化而来的土地上生产可持续船用燃料；和 3. 直接土地利用变化（DLUC）指标，以温室气体（包括 CO_2、CH_4 和 N_2O 排放）强度表示，即：原料生产或产量的 CO_2 当量质量 /MJ。
5. 碳储量 – 间接土地利用变化（ILUC）	可持续船用燃料的原料种植最大限度地减少了在所评估的产品系统之外对土地使用或管理方面的负面变化。	1. 与可持续船用燃料原料种植相关的间接碳储量风险（见 4.13 段）。

[14] 有待本组织制定进一步的指南。

Theme/aspect	Principle/Objective	Metric/Indicator
6.Water	Production of sustainable marine fuels maintain or enhance water quality and availability.	1.Operational practices are in place to (1) maintain water quality; and (2) use water efficiently and to avoid the depletion of water resources (including surface water, renewable water and fossil/underground water) beyond replenishment capacities; 2.Respect of decisionmaking of local population on water management; 3.Water environment impact (weighted water consumption on water scarcity); 4.Water Use Indicator expressed in m^3/year per MJ or production or yield of feedstock; 5.Freshwater eutrophication indicator, e.g. expressed in kg of phosphorus equivalent (P_{eq}) and kg of nitrogen equivalent (N_{eq}) released to fresh water/kg of feedstock produced or per MJ respectively; and 6.Marine eutrophication indicator, e.g. expressed in kg of phosphorus equivalent (P_{eq}) and kg of nitrogen equivalent (N_{eq}) released to marine water/kg of feedstock produced or per MJ respectively.
7.Air	Production of sustainable marine fuels minimizes negative impacts on air quality.	1.The marine fuel is made in a facility that fully complies with all local, national and regional air pollution laws and regulations.
8.Soil	Production of sustainable marine fuels maintain or enhance soil health.	1.Agricultural and forestry best management practices for feedstock production or residue collection have been implemented to maintain or enhance soil health, such as physical, chemical and biological conditions; and 2.The marine fuel is made in a facility that fully complies with all local, national and regional laws and regulations about soil health.
9.Waste and chemicals	Production of sustainable marine fuels maintain or enhance responsible management of waste and use of chemicals.	1.Operational practices are implemented to ensure that waste arising from, and chemicals used in, production processes are minimized at storage, handling and disposal steps. Reuse or recycling of chemicals and waste is encouraged. 2.Procedures are in place to minimize the use of materials that are neither recyclable nor biodegradable; 3.Average (in tonnes) of hazardous wastes generated per MJ of fuel produced; and 4.Average (in tonnes) of specified industrial chemicals consumed per MJ of fuel produced.

主题 / 方面	原则 / 目标	度量 / 指标
6. 水	可持续船用燃料的生产能维持或提高水质和可用性。	1. 采取举措以（1）维持水质；和（2）有效利用水资源，避免水资源（包括地表水、可再生水和化石 / 地下水）超出补给能力的枯竭； 2. 尊重当地居民对水资源管理的决策； 3. 水环境影响（对水资源短缺的加权用水量）； 4. 以立方米 / 年 / 每兆焦耳或原料生产或产量表示的用水量指标； 5. 淡水富营养化指标，例如分别以每千克或每兆焦耳（MJ）生产的原料释放到淡水中的磷当量（P_{eq}，单位为 kg）和氮当量（N_{eq}，单位为 kg）表示；和 6. 海洋富营养化指标，例如分别以每千克或每兆焦耳（MJ）生产的原料释放到海水中的磷当量（P_{eq}，单位为 kg）和氮当量（N_{eq}，单位为 kg）表示。
7. 空气	可持续船用燃料的生产最大限度地减少对空气质量的负面影响。	1. 船用燃料是在完全符合所有地方、国家和区域空气污染法律和法规的设施中生产的。
8. 土壤	可持续船用燃料的生产能维持或增强土壤健康。	1. 已实施了农业和林业原料生产或残留物收集的最佳管理做法，以维持或增强土壤健康，例如物理、化学和生物条件；和 2. 船用燃料是在完全符合所有地方、国家和区域有关土壤健康的法律和法规的设施中生产的。
9. 废料和化学品	可持续船用燃料的生产能维持或增强对废料和化学品使用的负责任管理。	1. 采取了可操作措施以确保在储存、处理和处置步骤中最大限度减少生产加工中产生的废料和使用的化学品。鼓励化学品和废料的再利用或再循环； 2. 制定了程序，以最大限度减少使用既不可回收又不可生物降解的材料； 3. 生产的每兆焦耳燃料产生的危险废料的平均值（以吨计）；和 4. 生产的每兆焦耳燃料所消耗的特定工业化学品的平均值（以吨计）。

Theme/aspect	Principle/Objective	Metric/Indicator
10.Conservation	Production of sustainable marine fuels maintain or enhance biodiversity and ecosystems, or conservation services.	1. The marine fuel is not made from feedstock obtained from areas that due to their biodiversity, conservation value, or ecosystem services, are protected by the State having jurisdiction over the area. Evidence is provided that the activity does not interfere with the protection purposes; and 2. Low invasive-risk feedstock is selected for cultivation and appropriate controls are adopted with the intention of preventing the uncontrolled spread of cultivated alien species and modified microorganisms.

8　FUEL LIFECYCLE LABEL (FLL)

8.1　The FLL is a technical tool to collect and convey the information relevant for the life cycle assessment of marine fuels and energy carriers (e.g. electricity for shore power) used for ship propulsion and power generation onboard in the context of these guidelines.

8.2　The FLL consists of five main parts, as illustrated below:

Part A-1	Part A-2	Part A-3	Part A-4	Part A-5
Fuel type (blend)	Fuel Pathway Code	Lower Calorific Value (LCV, MJ/g)	share in fuel blend ($\%MJ_{(LCV)}$ / $MJ_{(LCV)}$)	WtT GHG emission factor (GWP100, $gCO_{2eq}/MJ_{(LCV)}$)

+

Part B-1	(Part B-2)[15]
Emissions credits related to biogenic carbon source (e_c, in gCO_2/g fuel based on GWP100)	Emissions credits related to source of captured carbon (e_{ccu}, in gCO_2/g fuel based on GWP100)

+

Part C-1	Part C-2	Part C-3
Value 1 (carbon source NOT taken into account): TtW GHG emission factor (GWP100, $gCO_{2eq}/MJ_{(LCV)}$)	Value 2 (carbon source taken into account): TtW GHG emission factor (GWP100, $gCO_{2eq}/MJ_{(LCV)}$)	Energy Converter

+

---

[15]　Pending further methodological guidance to be developed by the Organization (see section 5).

主题 / 方面	原则 / 目标	度量 / 指标
10. 保护	可持续船用燃料的生产能维持或增强生物多样性和生态系统，或保护服务。	1. 船用燃料的原料并非产自因其生物多样性、保护价值或生态系统服务而受到对该地区有管辖权的国家保护的地区。有证据表明该活动不妨碍保护的目的；和 2. 选择低入侵风险的原料进行种植，并采取适当的控制措施，以防止种植的外来物种和改良微生物的传播失控。

8 燃料生命周期标签（FLL）

8.1 就本导则而言，燃料生命周期标签是用来收集和传递用于船舶推进和船上发电的船用燃料和能源载体（例如：岸电）全生命周期评估信息的一项技术工具。

8.2 燃料生命周期标签由五个主要部分组成，如下所示：

第 A-1 部分	第 A-2 部分	第 A-3 部分	第 A-4 部分	第 A-5 部分
燃料类型（混合）	燃料路径代码	低热值（LCV，MJ/g）	混合燃料份额（%MJ$_{(LCV)}$/MJ$_{(LCV)}$）	上船前温室气体排放因子（GWP100，gCO$_{2eq}$/MJ$_{(LCV)}$）

+

第 B-1 部分	（第 B-2 部分）[15]
与生物碳源相关的排放信用额（e_c，单位为 gCO$_2$/g fuel，基于 GWP100）	与捕获碳源相关的排放信用额（e_{ccu}，单位为 gCO$_2$/g fuel，基于 GWP100）

+

第 C-1 部分	第 C-2 部分	第 C-3 部分
值 1（不考虑碳源）：船端温室气体排放因子（GWP100，gCO$_{2eq}$/MJ$_{(LCV)}$）	值 2（考虑碳源）：船端温室气体排放因子（GWP100，gCO$_{2eq}$/MJ$_{(LCV)}$）	能量转化器

+

[15] 有待本组织制定进一步的方法指南（见第 5 节）。

Part D	Part E
WtW GHG emission factor (GWP100, gCO$_{2eq}$/MJ$_{(LCV)}$) Note: Part D = Part A-5 + Part C-2	Sustainability (Certification)[16]

8.3   Different parties (fuel suppliers, owners/operators, Administration/RO, etc.) may use different parts of the FLL for different purposes along the fuel pathway. As such, each interested party may use those parts of the FLL as relevant to their activities and purposes rather than the complete, integrated document.

8.4   The five main parts of the FLL are explained below.

    .1   **Part A** of the FLL indicates:

        .1   fuel type (Part A-1);

        .2   fuel pathway code (Part A-2);

        .3   lower calorific value (Part A-3, in MJ/g); and

        .4   WtT GHG emission factor (Part A-5, in gCO$_{2eq}$/MJ$_{(LCV)}$ calculated on GWP100).

        Part A-4 is only applicable when a fuel batch is supplied to the ship as a blend of fuels with different fuel pathway code (hereinafter referred to as the "fuel blend") and indicates the share of each blend component in the fuel blend (in %MJ$_{(LCV)}$/MJ$_{(LCV)}$). If fuel blends are denoted on volume-basis, a re-calculation on energy basis based on the LCV values of the blend components is required;

        For the fuel blend supplied to a ship, the information on fuel type for the mixture is presented under Part A-1 on top of its components, named by percentual order of composition in the fuel, e.g. X (70%), Y (20%), Z (10%). Part A-5, Part C-1, Part C-2 and Part D are the average value weighted on energy share (% MJ$_{(LCV)}$) /MJ$_{(LCV)}$)) of each fuel component, while Part A-2 to A-4, Part B and Part E are kept blank. Each component of the fuel blend with a specific fuel pathways code is presented in a separate row below the row for the fuel blend;

    .2   **Part B** of the FLL indicates the carbon credits related to the carbon source, including:

        .1 e_c (Part B-1, in gCO$_2$/ g fuel calculated on GWP100); (and

        .2 e_{ccu} (Part B-2, in gCO$_2$/g fuel calculated on GWP100)),[17]

        as defined in section 5 of these Guidelines;

---

[16]   Pending further guidance to be developed by the Organization.

[17]   Pending further methodological guidance to be developed by the Organization. For more details on the e_{ccu} parameter and Part B-2 of the FLL, refer to sections 5.2 and 8.2, respectively.

第 D 部分	第 E 部分
全生命周期温室气体排放因子（GWP100, gCO$_{2eq}$/MJ$_{(LCV)}$） 注：第 D 部分 = 第 A–5 部分 + 第 C–2 部分	可持续性（认证）[16]

8.3　不同相关方（燃料供应商、所有者 / 经营人、主管机关 / 被认可组织等）可在燃料路径上基于不同用途使用燃料生命周期标签的不同部分。因此，每一个利益相关方可使用与其活动和目的相关的燃料生命周期标签部分，而非整个完整的文件。

8.4　对燃料生命周期标签的五个主要部分解释如下。

　　.1　燃料生命周期标签的第 A 部分说明了：

　　　　.1　燃料类型（第 A–1 部分）；

　　　　.2　燃料路径代码（第 A–2 部分）；

　　　　.3　低热值（第 A–3 部分，单位为 MJ/g）；和

　　　　.4　上船前温室气体排放因子（第 A–5 部分，单位为 gCO$_{2eq}$/MJ$_{(LCV)}$，基于 GWP100 计算）。

　　　第 A–4 部分仅适用于提供给船舶的某燃料批次是由具有不同燃料路径代码的燃料混合而成的（以下简称"混合燃料"），并说明了每种混合成分在混合燃料中的份额（单位为 %MJ$_{(LCV)}$/MJ$_{(LCV)}$）。如果混合燃料是按体积表示的，需要根据混合成分的 LCV 值以能量为基础重新计算；

　　　对于提供给船舶的混合燃料，混合燃料的类型信息在第 A–1 部分列出，即在其成分之上，按燃料成分的百分比顺序命名，例如 X（70%）、Y（20%）、Z（10%）。第 A–5 部分、第 C–1 部分、第 C–2 部分和第 D 部分为各燃料成分能量份额（%MJ$_{(LCV)}$）/MJ$_{(LCV)}$）的加权平均值，第 A–2 至 A–4 部分、第 B 部分和第 E 部分留空。具有特定燃料路径代码的混合燃料的每个组分在混合燃料行下面的单独行中呈现；

　　.2　燃料生命周期标签的第 B 部分说明了与碳源相关的碳信用额，包括：

　　　　.1　e_c（第 B–1 部分，单位为 gCO$_2$/g fuel，基于 GWP100）计算；（和

　　　　.2　e_{ccu}（第 B–2 部分，单位为 gCO$_2$/g fuel，基于 GWP100 计算）），[17]

　　　见本导则第 5 节定义；

---

[16]　有待本组织制定进一步的指南。

[17]　有待本组织制定进一步的方法导则。有关 e_{ccu} 参数和燃料生命周期标签第 B–2 部分的详细信息，分别参见第 5.2 和 8.2 节。

.3   **Part C** of the FLL indicates the TtW GHG emission factor of the fuel type in conjunction with the energy converter(s) on board the ship (Part C-3). The TtW GHG emission factor of the fuel type is further categorized as:

     .1   Value 1 where carbon source is <u>not</u> taken into account (Part C-1, in $gCO_{2eq}/MJ_{(LCV)}$ calculated on GWP100); and

     .2   Value 2 where carbon source is taken into account (Part C-2, in $gCO_{2eq}/MJ_{(LCV)}$ calculated on GWP100),

     as defined in section 5 of these Guidelines;

.4   **Part D** of the FLL indicates the WtW GHG emission factor of the fuel type (in $gCO_{2eq}/MJ_{(LCV)}$ calculated on GWP100), which is always the sum of Part A-5 and Part C-2; and

.5   **Part E** of the FLL indicates the sustainability performance of the fuel as per Section 7 of these Guidelines.

PART III: DEFAULT EMISSION FACTORS AND ACTUAL VALUES

9   DEFAULT EMISSION FACTORS

9.1   The principles and the procedure described for the determination of default emission factors under this section 9 have been used for the establishment of default emission factors and should remain valid for the factors that will be established.

9.2   WtT default emission factors should be calculated using representative and conservative assumptions, which encompass variable performance of feedstock-fuel pathways across world regions and States.

9.3   To establish a WtT default emission factor, at least three reference values from three different, representative, sources should be considered. Among the three (or more) values considered, the upper emission value should be selected as default, and the range of available emission factors should be provided for informative purposes. The reference values should be accompanied by the relevant technical and scientific information (see template set out in appendix 4) and evaluated against the corresponding information as appropriate, including the agreement between the reference values.

9.4   Emissions related to carbon stock changes caused by DLUC (e_l) and emissions savings from soil carbon accumulation via improved agricultural management (e_{sca}) are considered as zero for the establishment of the initial default emission factors. Similarly, this is the case also for the parameters related to carbon capture and storage (ccs), which require further development.

9.5   For the establishment of e_l, and following IPCC (2019) and ISO 14067:2018 recommendations, the operators should use the following Equation (5) for the determination of e_l[18], measured as mass (g) of CO_2eq per MJ of energy:

$$\text{Equation (5): } e_l = \left(\left(CS_{R,j} - CS_{A,j} \right) \times 3.664 + E_{nCO2,j} \right) \times \frac{1}{n \, x \, P}$$

---

[18]   Economic operators are expected to discriminate land types at the appropriate level of detail.

.3 燃料生命周期标签的第 C 部分说明了燃料类型的船端温室气体排放因子和船上的能量转化器（第 C–3 部分）。燃料类型的船端温室气体排放因子进一步分类为：

　　.1 值 1，不考虑碳源（第 C–1 部分，单位为 $gCO_{2eq}/MJ_{(LCV)}$，基于 GWP100 计算）；和

　　.2 值 2，考虑碳源（第 C–2 部分，单位为 $gCO_{2eq}/MJ_{(LCV)}$，基于 GWP100 计算），见本导则第 5 节定义；

.4 燃料生命周期标签的第 D 部分表示燃料类型的全生命周期温室气体排放因子（单位为 $gCO_{2eq}/MJ_{(LCV)}$，基于 GWP100 计算），它始终是第 A–5 部分和第 C–2 部分的总和；和

.5 根据本导则第 7 节的规定，燃料生命周期标签的第 E 部分表明燃料的可持续性能。

第 III 部分：默认排放因子和实际值

9 默认排放因子

9.1 本第 9 节所述的确定默认因子的原则和程序已经用于确定默认排放因子，并应继续对未来将确定的因子有效。

9.2 应使用具有代表性且保守的假设来计算上船前默认排放因子，其中覆盖了世界各地区和各国原料—燃料路径的各种性能。

9.3 要建立上船前默认排放因子，应至少考虑来自三个不同的，具有代表性的来源的三个参考值。在考虑的三个（或更多）值中，应选择较高的排放值作为默认值，并应提供可用排放因子的范围供参考。参考值应附有相关的技术和科学资料（见附录 4 所载的模板），并酌情根据相应的资料进行评价，包括参考值之间的一致性。

9.4 为建立初始默认排放因子，直接土地利用变化（DLUC）引起的碳储量变化相关的排放（e_l）和通过改善农业管理从土壤碳积累中节省的排放（e_{sca}）被视为零。同样，与碳捕获和存储（ccs）相关的参数也是如此，这需要进一步制定。

9.5 为建立 e_l，根据 IPCC（2019）和 ISO 14067：2018 建议，经营人应使用下列公式（5）来确定 e_l[18]，以每 MJ 能量的 CO_{2eq} 质量（g）来衡量：

$$公式（5）：e_l = ((CS_{R,j} - CS_{A,j}) \times 3.664 + E_{nCO2,j}) \times \frac{1}{n \times P}$$

---

[18] 经济经营人应适当详细区分土地类型。

The terms refer to:

$CS_{R,j}$ the carbon stock of the land type j per unit area associated with the reference land-use (measured as mass (g) of carbon per unit area (ha), including both soil and vegetation and dead organic matter). The reference land-use should be the land-use in January 2008 or 20 years before the raw material was obtained, whichever was the later;

$CS_{A,j}$ the carbon stock of the land type j per unit area associated with the actual land-use (measured as mass (g) of carbon per unit area (ha), including both soil and vegetation and dead organic matter). In cases where the carbon stock accumulates over more than one year, the value attributed to CS_A should be the estimated stock per unit area after 20 years or when the crop reaches maturity, whichever the earlier;

3.664   the quotient obtained by dividing the molecular weight of CO_2 (44,010g/mol) by the molecular weight of carbon (12,011g/mol) in gCO_2eq/g C;

n equal to 20, which corresponds to the number of years for amortization of the emissions in the IMO framework;

P the productivity of the crop (measured as MJ of energy per ha per year); and

E_{nCO2j} emission factor for non-CO_2 emissions from biomass burned (measured as gCO_2eq per unit area (ha)), accounted in the equation only if the necessary information on area burned is available. Details of the E_{nCO2j} formula should follow methodology to be defined.

9.6   According to existing standards, the CS_R and CS_A parameters have to be determined by means of direct measurements of soil carbon stocks, or calculated. CS_R and CS_A values, measured as mass (g) of carbon per unit area (ha), are obtained by considering:

$$CS_{R,j \, o \, A,j} = SOC_j + C_{veg,j}$$

9.7   Where C_{veg} is the above and below ground carbon stock of the vegetation, including dead organic matter, measured as mass (g) of carbon per unit area (ha), which shall follow IPCC Guidelines. SOC parameter is the amount of soil organic carbon (measured as mass (g) of carbon per unit area (ha)) and consists of four factors, which depend on climate, soil type, management practice and C-input practice: the standard soil organic carbon in the topsoil layer (SOC_{ST}), the land use factor (F_{LU}), the management factor (F_{MG}) and the input factor (F_i).

Where:

$$SOC_j = \left(SOC_{ST,j} * F_{LU,j} * F_{MG,j} * F_{i,j} \right)$$

9.8   Methods not based on measurements could be used as an alternative to calculate SOC with standard values, taking into account climate, soil type, land cover, land management and inputs.

9.9   Aggregation of areas: apply the same Equation (5) (e_l) on each type j of eligible land (e_{lj}), as follow:

各参数定义如下：

$CS_{R,j}$　与参考土地利用相关的土地类型 j 每单位面积的碳储量（以每单位面积（公顷）的碳质量（g）衡量，包括土壤、植被和死有机质）。参考土地利用应为 2008 年 1 月或获得原料之前 20 年的土地利用，以较晚者为准；

$CS_{A,j}$　与实际土地利用相关的土地类型 j 每单位面积的碳储量（以每单位面积（公顷）的碳质量（g）计算，包括土壤、植被和死有机质）。在碳储量积累超过一年的情况下，CSA 的值应是 20 年后或作物成熟时的单位面积估计储量，以较早者为准；

3.664　CO_2 的分子量（44 010 g/mol）除以碳的分子量（12 011 g/mol）得到的商，单位为 $gCO_{2eq}/g\ C$；

n　等于 20，与国际海事组织框架中排放摊销的年数一致；

P　作物的生产力（以每年每公顷兆焦耳能量计）；和

E_{nCO2j}　生物质燃烧产生的非 CO_2 排放的排放因子（以每单位面积（公顷）的 gCO_{2eq} 计算），只有在获得有关燃烧面积的必要信息时才在公式中计算。E_{nCO2j} 公式的细节应符合待定义的方法。

9.6　根据现有的标准，CS_R 和 CS_A 参数必须通过直接测量土壤碳储量来确定，或者通过计算来确定。CS_R 和 CS_A 值以每单位面积（公顷）的碳质量（g）衡量，通过下式获得：

$$CS_{R,j\ o\ A,j} = SOC_j + C_{veg,j}$$

9.7　其中 C_{veg} 为植被的地上和地下碳储量，包括死有机质，以每单位面积（公顷）的碳质量（g）来衡量，应符合 IPCC 导则。土壤有机碳（SOC）参数是土壤有机碳的数量（以每单位面积（公顷）的碳质量（g）衡量），由四个因素组成，取决于气候、土壤类型、管理实践和碳输入实践：表土层标准土壤有机碳（SOC_{ST}）、土地利用因子（F_{LU}）、管理因子（F_{MG}）和输入因子（F_i）。

式中：

$$SOC_j = (SOC_{ST,j} * F_{LU,j} * F_{MG,j} * F_{i,j})$$

9.8　在考虑气候、土壤类型、土地覆盖、土地管理和输入的基础上，可以采用不以测量为基础的方法，以标准值计算 SOC。

9.9　面积累计：对每一类符合条件的 j 类土地（e_{lj}）适用同一公式（5）（e_l）如下：

$$e_{lj} = \frac{e_l}{l_j} - e_{bj}$$

$$l_j = \frac{L_j \times y_j}{\sum_j L_j \times y_j}$$

Where:

l_j is the land use share of type j;

e_b is the specific bonus, measured in terms of gCO_2eq per of energy if biomass is obtained from recovered severely degraded land. This parameter needs to be defined in further discussions and if there is consensus, the specific bonus will be subtracted from the equation;

L_j is the area of each reference type of land j converted to feedstock cultivation, measured in hectare; and

y_j is the yield of feedstock for each type of converted land j, measured in tons per hectare per year.

9.10   The operators should apply the following formula on all types of eligible land to calculate DLUC, in gCO_2 e/MJ:

$$e_l = \sum_j e_{lj} \times l_j$$

9.11   For the establishment of e_{sca} and following IPCC (2019) and ISO 14067:2018 recommendations, the equation that an operator should use for the determination of e_{sca}, measured as mass (g) of CO_2eq per MJ biofuel, is the following:

Equation (6): $e_{sca} = \left(CS_{A,j} - CS_{R,j}\right) \times 3.664 \times \frac{1}{n \, x \, P}$

The terms refer to:

$CS_{R,j}$ the mass of soil and vegetation carbon stock of the land type j per unit area associated with the reference crop management practice in g of C per ha in January 2008 or 20 years before the raw material was obtained;

$CS_{A,j}$ the mass of soil and vegetation estimated carbon stock of the land type j per unit area associated with the actual crop management practices after at least 10 years of application in g of C per ha;

3.664   the quotient obtained by dividing the molecular weight of CO_2 (44,010g/mol) by the molecular weight of carbon (12,011g/mol) in g CO_2eq/g C;

n equal to 20, which corresponds to the number of years for amortization of the emissions in the IMO framework; and

P the productivity of the crop (measured as MJ biofuel per ha per year).

$$e_{lj} = \frac{e_l}{l_j} - e_{bj}$$

$$l_j = \frac{L_j \times y_j}{\sum_j L_j \times y_j}$$

式中：

l_j j 类土地使用份额；

e_b 从恢复的严重退化的土地上获得生物质的特定奖励，以每单位能量的 gCO_{2eq} 来衡量。该参数需要通过进一步讨论定义，如果达成共识，将从公式中减去特定奖励；

L_j 转化为原料种植的每一参考土地类型 j 的面积，单位为公顷；和

y_j 每一转化的土地类型 j 的原料产量，单位为每年每公顷吨。

9.10   经营人应对所有符合条件的土地类型适用下列公式计算 DLUC，单位为 $gCO_2 e/MJ$：

$$e_l = \sum_j e_{lj} \times l_j$$

9.11   为建立 e_{sca}，根据 IPCC（2019）和 ISO14067：2018 建议，经营人应使用下列公式来确定 e_{sca}，以每兆焦耳生物燃料的 CO_{2eq} 质量（g）来衡量：

公式（6）： Equation (6): $e_{sca} = (CS_{A,j} - CS_{R,j}) \times 3.664 \times \frac{1}{n \, x \, P}$

各参数定义如下：

$CS_{R,j}$ 在 2008 年 1 月或获得原料以前 20 年，与参考作物管理实践相关的土地类型 j 每单位面积土壤和植被碳储量的质量，单位为每公顷的碳质量（g）；

$CS_{A,j}$ 在应用至少 10 年后，与实际作物管理做法相关的土地类型 j 的每单位面积土壤和植被估计碳储量的质量，单位为每公顷的碳质量（g）；

3.664 CO_2 的分子量（44 010 g/mol）除以碳的分子量（12 011 g/mol）（gCO_{2eq}/gC）得到的商，单位为 g CO_{2eq}/g C；

n 等于 20，与海事组织框架中排放摊销的年数一致；和

P 作物的生产力（以每年每公顷兆焦耳生物燃料计）。

The emissions from the increased fertilizers or herbicide use, which may result from the specific agricultural practice, expressed in gCO$_2$eq per MJ biofuel, have to be properly accounted in the emissions associated with the feedstock extraction / cultivation / acquisition / recovery (e_{fecu}).

9.12   According to existing standards, the CS_R and CS_A parameter have to be determined by means of direct measurements of soil and vegetation carbon stocks or calculated by appropriate tools, accepted in the certification process. the CS_R and CS_A values, measured as mass (g) of carbon per unit area (ha), are obtained by considering:

$$CS_{R,j \, o \, A.j} = SOC_j + C_{veg,j}$$

Where C_{veg} is the above and below ground carbon stock of the vegetation, including dead organic matter, measured as mass (g) of carbon per unit area (ha), according to IPCC Guidelines.

SOC is the amount of soil organic carbon, measured as mass (g) of carbon per unit area (ha).

Appropriate conversion is needed to obtain a final gCO$_2$eq/MJ of fuel.

9.13   Methods not based on measurements could be used as an alternative to calculate SOC with standard values, taking into account climate, soil type, land cover, land management and inputs. The IPCC Guidelines methodology can be applied for calculation of changes in carbon stocks. The adoption of improved agricultural management practices must be addressed under the IPCC "cropland remaining cropland" framework. The parameter consists of four factors, which depend on climate, soil type, management practice and C-input practice: the standard soil organic carbon in the topsoil layer (SOC_{ST}),[19] the land use factor (F_{LU}), the management factor (F_{MG}) and the input factor (F_i). Deeper soil depths (i.e.: 1m or more) can be accepted in case of actual measurements of C stocks soil.

Where:

$$SOC_j = \left(SOC_{ST,j} * F_{LU,j} * F_{MG,j} * F_{i,j}\right)$$

9.14   For aggregation of areas, the same Equation (6) (e_{sca}) should be applied on each type j of eligible land ($e_{sca,j}$), as follow:

$$e_{sca,j} = \frac{e_{sca}}{l_j}$$

$$l_j = \frac{L_j \times y_j}{\sum_j L_j \times y_j}$$

Where:

lj is the land use share of type j;

L_j is the area of each reference type of land j converted to feedstock cultivation, measured in hectare; and

---

[19]   Proper method to assess SOC_{ST} to be agreed with the certification scheme.

特定农业实践可能造成化肥或除草剂使用的增加从而产生的排放，以每兆焦耳生物燃料的 gCO_{2eq} 表示，必须在与原料提取/种植/获取/回收（e_{fecu}）相关的排放中适当考虑。

9.12　根据现有的标准，CS_R 和 CS_A 参数必须通过直接测量土壤和植被碳储量来确定，或者通过认证过程所接受的适当工具计算来确定。CS_R 和 CS_A 值以每单位面积（公顷）的碳质量（g）衡量，通过下式获得：

$$CS_{R,j\,o\,A.j} = SOC_j + C_{veg,j}$$

式中 C_{veg} 为植被的地上和地下碳储量，包括死有机质，根据 IPCC 导则，以每单位面积（公顷）的碳质量（g）来衡量。

SOC 为土壤有机碳的量，以每单位面积（公顷）的碳质量（g）来衡量。

需要进行适当的转化以获得最终的 gCO_{2eq}/MJ 燃料。

9.13　在考虑气候、土壤类型、土地覆盖、土地管理和投入的基础上，可以采用不以测量为基础的方法，以标准值计算 SOC。IPCC 导则的方法可用于计算碳储量的变化。必须在 IPCC "农田仍是农田"框架下采用改进的农业管理方法。该参数由四个因素组成，取决于气候、土壤类型、管理实践和碳输入实践：表土层标准土壤有机碳（SOC_{ST}），[19] 土地利用因子（F_{LU}）、管理因子（F_{MG}）和输入因子（F_i）。在实际测量土壤碳储量时，可以接受较深的土壤深度（即 1 m 或 1 m 以上）。

式中：

$$SOC_j = (SOC_{ST,j} * F_{LU,j} * F_{MG,j} * F_{i,j})$$

9.14　为累计面积，对每一类符合条件的 j 类土地（$e_{sca,\,j}$）适用同一公式（6）（e_{sca}）如下：

$$e_{sca,j} = \frac{e_{sca}}{l_j}$$

$$l_j = \frac{L_j \times y_j}{\sum_j L_j \times y_j}$$

式中：

l_j　　j 类土地使用份额；

L_j　　转化为原料种植的每一参考土地类型 j 的面积，单位为公顷；和

---

[19]　SOC_{ST} 的适当评估方法应与认证方案一致。

y_j is the yield of feedstock for each type of converted land j, measured in tonnes per hectare per year.

9.15   The following formula should be applied on all types of eligible land to calculate e_{sca}, in gCO_2e/MJ:

$$e_{sca} = \sum_j e_{sca,j} \times l_j$$

9.16   A non-exhaustive set of improved agriculture management practices, accepted for the purpose of achieving emission savings from soil carbon accumulation is listed below:

     .1   shifting to meaningful reductions in soil tillage;

     .2   improved crop/rotation schemes (i.e *SOC* increase);

     .3   multicropping, intercropping, and crop rotation;

     .4   integration systems of crop, livestock, and forestry;

     .5   the use of cover crops, including crop residue management;

     .6   the use of organic soil improver (e.g.: compost, digestate, biochar, etc.);

     .7   meaningful increase in soil coverage;

     .8   no till and reduced till;

     .9   sugarcane harvested without burning; and

     .10   structural measure to control soil erosion like contour farming.

9.17   TtW default emission factors should be calculated using representative and conservative assumptions, which encompass variable conditions onboard of the ships and performance of energy converters. The reference values used to establish default emission factors should be accompanied by the relevant technical and scientific information (see the template set out in appendix 5) and evaluated against the corresponding information as appropriate, including the agreement between the reference values.

9.18   For the establishment of C_{fCO2} for fuels that can be represented using chemical formula, C_{fCO2} emission factor can be calculated by dividing the molar ratio of carbon to CO_2 by the molar ratio of carbon to the fuel. If fuels cannot be represented using chemical formula, such as biofuels and fossil fuels, the C_{fCO2} factor can be calculated using actual measurement of carbon content according to internationally recognized standards as ASTM D5291 and D6866, etc.

9.19   The C_{fCH4}, C_{fN2O} and C_{slip} emission factors depend on the type of fuel, engine and the engine load. In the case of existing fuels and existing engines, these factors can be obtained using reference values from the *Fourth IMO GHG Study 2020.*[20] However, for other types of fuels and engines, further work is needed to establish measurement procedures.

---

[20]   https://www.imo.org/en/ourwork/Environment/Pages/Fourth-IMO-Greenhouse-Gas-Study-2020.aspx

y_j 每一转化的土地类型 j 的原料产量，单位为每年每公顷吨。

9.15   应对所有符合条件的土地类型适用下列公式计算 e_{sca}，单位为 gCO_2e/MJ：

$$e_{sca} = \sum_j e_{sca,j} \times l_j$$

9.16   为实现从土壤碳积累中节省排放，可以接受下列改进的农业管理做法（列表并非详尽）：

.1   转向显著减少土壤耕作；

.2   改进作物／轮作方案（即增加 SOC）；

.3   复作、间作和轮作；

.4   种植业、畜牧业、林业整合体系；

.5   覆盖作物的使用，包括作物残留物管理；

.6   使用有机土壤改良剂（例如：堆肥、沼液、生物炭等）；

.7   显著增加土壤覆盖度；

.8   免耕和减耕；

.9   甘蔗收割时不焚烧；和

.10   控制土壤侵蚀的结构性措施，如等高耕作。

9.17   船端默认排放因子应使用代表性和保守的假设来计算，这些假设包括船上的可变条件和能量转化器的性能。用于确定默认排放因子的参考值应附有相关的技术和科学资料（见附录 5 所载模板），并应酌情根据相应的资料进行评估，包括与参考值之间的一致。

9.18   为了建立可以用化学式表示的燃料 C_{fCO_2}，可以用碳与燃料的摩尔比除以碳与 CO_2 的摩尔比来计算 C_{fCO_2} 排放系数。如果燃料不能用化学式表示，如生物燃料和化石燃料，则 C_{fCO_2} 因子可以根据国际公认的标准（如 ASTM D5291 和 D6866 等）使用实际测量的碳含量来计算。

9.19 C_{fCH_4}、C_{fN_2O} 和 C_{slip} 排放因子取决于燃料类型、发动机和发动机负载。在现有燃料和现有发动机的情况下，这些因了可以使用 2020 年第四次国际海事组织温室气体研究的参考值[20] 来获得。然而对于其他类型的燃料和发动机，需要进一步的工作来建立测量程序。

---

[20]   https://www.imo.org/en/ourwork/EnⅥronment/Pages/Fourth–IMO–Greenhouse–Gas–Study–2020.aspx

9.20   Fugitive emissions are difficult to measure but the existing studies state they are very small in comparison to other GHG emissions. C_{fug} should be set as 0 (zero) until further evidence enabling the establishment of a value exists, nevertheless it should be kept as a placeholder for continuous review.

9.21   In case additional categories of energy converters (not listed in appendix 2) are proposed, the rules to establish TtW default emission factors as described in paragraph 9.17 above may be followed to ensure that these new converters (e.g. fuel cells) may also be associated with a default emission factor.

9.22   For aftertreatment/abatement systems, no default values should be established due to varying performance of this equipment, instead a superior GHG performance can be demonstrated through actual emission factors, subject to verification and certification by a third party.

9.23   For electricity delivered by Onshore Power Supply (OPS) the GHG intensity default value corresponds to the GHG intensity of the national grid. Considering that the GHG intensity national grid are frequently updated this information is not included in these guidelines and the following sources can be used, if the methodology is based in internationally recognized standards: governmental and utility sources, internationally acknowledged public databases, national inventories and national energy regulators.

10   ACTUAL EMISSION FACTORS

10.1   The aim of actual emission factors is to allow demonstration of superior GHG performance compared to the default emission factors, subject to verification and certification by a third party.

10.2   WtT and TtW emission factors should be based on methodologies established in these guidelines. Actual values provide the WtW (WtT and TtW) GHG intensity for the specific fuel over the life cycle (from fuel production to its use on board).

10.3   For the pathways contained in appendix 1, the description and the calculation method for providing WtT actual emission factors should be provided. In addition, for the pathways not contained in appendix 1, a detailed description of the pathway should be provided.

10.4   The use of actual WtT emission factors is not applicable to purely fossil pathways. However, for fuels which are produced from captured carbon of fossil origin and for fossil fuels where the technology of CCS/CCUS is applied, actual values are allowed. For the fossil component of a blended fuel, fossil fuel default emission factors should be used.

10.5   Actual TtW emission factors are allowed for all fuel pathways[21] and provided in these guidelines. As mentioned in paragraphs 9.19 and 9.22, further work is needed to develop procedures to certify C_{fCH4}, C_{fN2O} and C_{slip} emission factors, and to take in consideration aftertreatment/abatement systems.

10.6   Power Purchase Agreements (PPA) including a GHG intensity for electricity delivered by OPS can be used to certify an actual value if a procedure is in place to establish electricity GHG intensity and a certificate of the Guarantees of Origin, recognized by the Organization.

---

[21]   Verification and certification methodologies would need further work to be established.

9.20 逸散性排放很难测量，但现有研究表明，与其他温室气体排放相比，逸散性排放非常小。C_{fug} 应该设置为 0（零），直到有进一步的证据支持设立一个值，尽管如此，它应该保留为一个占位符，以便于持续评审。

9.21 如果建议增加能源转化器类别（未列于附录 2），则可按照上文第 9.17 段所述的建立船端默认排放因子的规则，以确保这些新转化器（例如燃料电池）也可与默认排放因子相关联。

9.22 对于后处理／减排系统，因为设备性能各异，不应设定默认值，而是应通过实际排放系数证明更优越的温室气体性能，但须经第三方验证和认证。

9.23 对于来自于岸电（OPS）的电力，温室气体强度默认值对应于国家电网的温室气体强度。考虑到国家电网的温室气体强度经常更新，本指南中未包含这些信息，如果方法基于国际公认的标准，则可以使用以下信息来源：政府和公用事业来源、国际公认的公共数据库、国家清单和国家能源监管机构。

10 实际排放因子

10.1 实际排放因子的目的是经第三方验证和认证，显示与默认排放因子相比具有更优越的温室气体性能。

10.2 上船前和船端排放因子应基于本导则中确定的方法确定。实际值提供了特定燃料在全生命周期（从燃料生产到其在船上使用）的全生命周期（上船前和船端）温室气体强度。

10.3 对于附录 1 中包含的路径，应提供上船前实际排放因子的描述和计算方法。另外，对于附录 1 中未包含的路径，应提供对路径的详细描述。

10.4 实际上船前排放因子的使用不适用于纯化石路径。但是，对于由化石来源的捕获碳生产的燃料以及应用 CCS/CCUS 技术的化石燃料，则允许使用实际值。对于混合燃料的化石成分，应使用化石燃料默认排放因子。

10.5 本导则给出的实际船端排放因子可用于所有燃料路径 [21]。如第 9.19 和 9.22 段所述，需要进一步开展工作，以制定程序来认证 C_{fCH4}、C_{fN2O} 和 C_{slip} 排放因子，并考虑后处理／减排系统。

10.6 如果具备确定电力温室气体强度的程序和经本组织认可的原产地保证证书，则可使用包含了 OPS 输送电力温室气体强度的购电协议（PPA）来证明实际值。

---

[21] 验证和认证方法需要进一步的工作来确定。

PART IV: VERIFICATION AND CERTIFICATION

11   ELEMENTS SUBJECT TO VERIFICATION/CERTIFICATION

11.1   When used as evidence for performances, the FLL needs to be verified and certified by a third party, taking into account further guidance to be developed by the Organization.

11.2   The verification and certification of Part A, Part B, Part C and Part E of the FLL may be carried out separately by different verification bodies. The verification and certification of Part D of the FLL needs to be based on the verified Part A, Part B and Part C.

11.3   For fuel types with a specific fuel pathway code and which will be consumed in a specified energy converter, the default emission factors for Part A-5, Part C-1, Part C-2 and Part D of the FLL are provided in appendix 2. As long as Part A-1 to Part A-4 and Part C-3 of the FLL have been duly verified, the default emission factors contained in these guidelines can be consequently applied without further verification.

11.4   In the case where lower emission factors are claimed compared to the default emission factors for Part A-5, Part C-1, Part C-2 and/or Part D, the actual emission factors can be used only after the verification and certification by a third party, taking into account further guidance referred to in paragraph 11.1.

12   IDENTIFICATION OF CERTIFICATION SCHEMES/STANDARDS

12.1   The verification and certification of individual parts of the FLL will use relevant certification schemes/standards. Different parts of the FLL may be verified using different certification schemes/standards as applicable, while a specific part of the FLL may be addressed by multiple certification schemes/standards with similar scopes.

12.2   The certification schemes/standards used for the purposes specified in paragraph 12.1 above should be recognized by the Committee, taking into account guidance to be developed by the Organization. The list of recognized certification schemes/standards should be publicly available and kept under review.

12.3   Proposals to recognize international certification schemes/standards should be submitted to the Committee for consideration, including an assessment of a set of predetermined criteria which will be further developed for this purpose.

12.4   The framework, criteria and procedures leading to the recognition of certification schemes should be implemented uniformly to guarantee the quality, reliability and robustness of the IMO framework as a whole and to ensure a level playing field among certification schemes.

PART V: REVIEW

13   CONTINUOUS REVIEW PROCESS

13.1   To ensure that new technological advances and scientific knowledge are taken into account, these guidelines should be kept under continuous technical review taking into account emerging and evolving technologies.

13.2   In particular, the following elements should be kept under review:

.1   WtT, TtW and WtW default emission factors as specified in appendix 2; and

.2   new proposed fuel pathways and the corresponding default emission factors in addition to those specified in appendix 1.

第Ⅳ部分：验证和认证

11 需验证 / 认证的要素

11.1 当用作性能证据时，燃料生命周期标签需要结合本组织将进一步制定的指南，由第三方验证和认证。

11.2 对燃料生命周期标签第 A、B、C、E 部分的验证和认证可由不同的验证机构分别进行。对燃料生命周期标签的第 D 部分的验证和认证需要在已经过验证的第 A、B、C 部分基础之上进行。

11.3 对于具有特定燃料路径代码并将在特定能量转化器中消耗的燃料类型，附录 2 提供了燃料生命周期标签第 A–5 部分，第 C–1 部分，第 C–2 部分和第 D 部分的默认排放因子。只要燃料生命周期标签第 A–1 至 A–4 及 C–3 部分已按要求验证，则可适用本导则中的默认排放因子而无须进一步验证。

11.4 如果所报的排放因子低于第 A–5 部分、C–1 部分、C–2 部分和 / 或 D 部分的默认排放因子，则只有在结合第 11.1 段所述的将制定的指南，经第三方验证和认证后，才能使用实际排放因子。

12 明确认证计划 / 标准

12.1 对燃料生命周期标签各部分的验证和认证将使用相关的认证计划 / 标准进行。对燃料生命周期标签不同部分可能会根据适用情况采用不同的认证计划 / 标准进行验证，而对燃料生命周期标签某个特定部分可能会采用多个范围相似的认证计划 / 标准进行验证。

12.2 本委员会应结合本组织将制定的指南，认可针对上述第 12.1 段的认证计划 / 标准。认可的认证计划 / 标准清单应公开提供，并定期审查。

12.3 国际认证计划 / 标准的认可建议应提交本委员会审议，包括对一套预先确定的标准的评估，这些标准将为此目的进一步制定。

12.4 应统一执行针对认证计划的认可框架、标准和程序，以保证整个国际海事组织框架的质量、可靠性和坚固性，并确保各认证计划之间有一个公平的竞争环境。

第 V 部分：审查

13 持续审查过程

13.1 为了确保考虑到了新技术进步和科学知识，应结合新兴的和发展中的技术保持对本导则进行持续技术审查。

13.2 特别是应保持审查下列因素：

    .1 附录 2 所列的上船前、船端和全生命周期默认排放因子；和

    .2 除了附录 1 所列的燃料途径和相应的默认排放因子之外，还有新提议的燃料途径和相应的默认排放因子。

APPENDIX 1

FUEL LIST WITH FUEL PATHWAY CODES

Order	Group	Fuel type	Feedstock structure		Conversion/Production process		Fuel Pathway Code
			Feedstock Type	Nature/Carbon Source	Process Type	Energy used in the process	
1	HFO (VLSFO)	Heavy Fuel Oil (ISO 8217 Grades RME, RMG and RMK, 0.10 < S ≤ 0.50%)	Crude Oil	Fossil	Standard refinery process	Grid mix electricity	HFO(VLSFO)_f_SR_gm
2	HFO (HSHFO)	Heavy Fuel Oil (ISO 8217 Grades RME, RMG and RMK exceeding 0.50% S)	Crude Oil	Fossil	Standard refinery process	Grid mix electricity	HFO(HSHFO)_f_SR_gm
3	LFO (ULSFO)	Light Fuel Oil (ISO 8217 Grades RMA, RMB and RMD maximum 0.10% S)	Crude Oil	Fossil	Standard refinery process	Grid mix electricity	LFO(ULSFO)_f_SR_gm
4	LFO (VLSFO)	Light Fuel Oil (ISO 8217 Grades RMA, RMB and RMD, 0.10 < S ≤ 0.50%)	Crude Oil	Fossil	Standard refinery process	Grid mix electricity	LFO(VLSFO)_f_SR_gm

燃料清单及燃料路径代码

序号	组别	燃料类型	原料结构		转化/生产过程		燃料路径代码
			原料类型	性质/碳源	加工类型	加工中使用的能量	
1	HFO (VLSFO)	重质燃料油 (ISO 8217 等级 RME, RMG 和 RMK, 0.10<S ≤ 0.50%)	原油	化石	标准炼油工艺	并网电力	HFO (VLSFO) _f_SR_gm
2	HFO (HSHFO)	重质燃料油 (ISO 8217 等级 RME, RMG 和 RMK 超过 0.50% S)	原油	化石	标准炼油工艺	并网电力	HFO (HSHFO) _f_SR_gm
3	LFO (ULSFO)	轻质燃料油 (ISO 8217 等级 RMA, RMB 和 RMD 最高 0.10% S)	原油	化石	标准炼油工艺	并网电力	LFO (ULSFO) _f_SR_gm
4	LFO (VLSFO)	轻质燃料油 (ISO 8217 等级 RMA, RMB 和 RMD, 0.10<S ≤ 0.50%)	原油	化石	标准炼油工艺	并网电力	LFO (VLSFO) _f_SR_gm

| Order | Feedstock structure | | | Conversion/Production process | | Fuel Pathway Code |
	Group	Fuel type	Feedstock Type	Nature/Carbon Source	Process Type	Energy used in the process	
5	Diesel/Gas oil (ULSFO)	Marine Diesel/Gas Oil (ISO 8217 Grades DMX, DMA, DMZ and DMB maximum 0.10 % S)	Crude Oil	Fossil	Standard refinery process	Grid mix electricity	MDO/MGO(ULSFO)_f_SR_g m
6	Diesel/Gas oil (VLSFO)	Marine Diesel/Gas Oil (ISO 8217 Grades DMX, DMA, DMZ and DMB, 0.10 < S ≤ 0.50%)	Crude Oil	Fossil	Standard refinery process	Grid mix electricity	MDO/MGO(VLSFO)_f_SR_g m
7	Diesel/Gas oil (ULSFO)	Bio co-processed marine fuel (ISO 8217 Grades DMX, DMA, DMZ and DMB maximum 0.10 % S)	Crude Oil + mixed biomass	Fossil/Biogenic	CoProcessing (CP) in refinery	Grid mix electricity	MDO/MGO(ULSFO)_f_b_CP _gm

| 序号 | 组别 | 燃料类型 | 原料结构 | | 转化/生产过程 | | 燃料路径代码 |
			原料类型	性质/碳源	加工类型	加工中使用的能量	
5	柴油/轻柴油（ULSFO）	船用重柴油/船用轻柴油（ISO 8217 等级 DMX、DMA、DMZ 和 DMB 最高 0.10 % S）	原油	化石	标准炼油工艺	并网电力	MDO/MGO（ULSFO）_f_SR_gm
6	柴油/轻柴油（VLSFO）	船用重柴油/船用轻柴油（ISO 8217 等级 DMX、DMA、DMZ 和 DMB，0.10<S ≤ 0.50%）	原油	化石	标准炼油工艺	并网电力	MDO/MGO（VLSFO）_f_SR_gm
7	柴油/轻柴油（ULSFO）	生物联合加工船用燃料（ISO 8217 等级 DMX、DMA、DMZ 和 DMB 最高 0.10 % S）	原油 + 混合生物质	化石/生物源	在炼油厂联合加工（CP）	并网电力	MDO/MGO（ULSFO）_f_b_CP_gm

Order	Group	Fuel type	Feedstock structure		Conversion/Production process		Fuel Pathway Code
			Feedstock Type	Nature/Carbon Source	Process Type	Energy used in the process	
8	Diesel/Gas oil (VLSFO)	Bio co-processed marine fuel (ISO 8217 Grades DMX, DMA, DMZ and DMB, 0.10 < S ≤ 0.50%)	Crude Oil + mixed biomass	Fossil/Biogenic	CoProcessing (CP) in refinery	Grid mix electricity	MDO/MGO(VLSFO)_f_b_CP_gm
9	Diesel/Gas oil (ULSFO)	Co-processed marine fuel (ISO 8217 Grades DMX, DMA, DMZ and DMB maximum 0.10 % S)	Crude Oil + recycled carbon	Fossil/Recycled carbon	CoProcessing (CP) in refinery	Grid mix electricity	MDO/MGO(ULSFO)_f_r_CP_gm
10	Diesel/Gas oil (VLSFO)	Co-processed marine fuel (ISO 8217 Grades DMX, DMA, DMZ and DMB, 0.10 < S ≤ 0.50%)	Crude Oil + recycled carbon	Fossil/Recycled carbon	CoProcessing (CP) in refinery	Grid mix electricity	MDO/MGO(VLSFO)_f_r_CP_gm
11	LPG[22]	Liquefied Petroleum Gas (Propane)	Crude Oil	Fossil	Standard refinery process and liquefaction	Grid mix electricity	LPG(Propane)_f_SR_gm

22　Regarding LPG, these Guidelines consider the final product form the refineries to be always liquefied.

序号	组别	燃料类型	原料结构		转化/生产过程		燃料路径代码
			原料类型	性质/碳源	加工类型	加工中使用的能量	
8	柴油/轻柴油（VLSFO）	生物联合加工船用燃料（ISO 8217 等级 DMX, DMA, DMZ 和 DMB, 0.10<S ≤ 0.50%）	原油＋混合生物质	化石/生物源	在炼油厂联合加工（CP）	并网电力	MDO/MGO（VLSFO）_f_b_CP_gm
9	柴油/轻柴油（ULSFO）	联合加工船用燃料（ISO 8217 等级 DMX, DMA, DMZ 和 DMB 最高 0.10 % S）	原油＋回收碳	化石/回收碳	在炼油厂联合加工（CP）	并网电力	MDO/MGO（ULSFO）_f_r_CP_gm
10	柴油/轻柴油（VLSFO）	联合加工船用燃料（ISO 8217 等级 DMX, DMA, DMZ 和 DMB, 0.10<S ≤ 0.50%）	原油＋回收碳	化石/回收碳	在炼油厂联合加工（CP）	并网电力	MDO/MGO（VLSFO）_f_r_CP_gm
11	LPG[22]	液化石油气（丙烷）	原油	化石	标准炼油工艺和液化	并网电力	LPG（Propane）_f_SR_gm

22 关于液化石油气，本导则认为炼油厂的最终产品始终是液化的。

Order	Group	Feedstock structure			Conversion/Production process		Fuel Pathway Code
		Fuel type	Feedstock Type	Nature/Carbon Source	Process Type	Energy used in the process	
12	LPG	Liquefied Petroleum Gas (Propane)	CO_2 + H2	CO_2: Fossil Point Source Carbon Capture H2: Fossil Steam Methane Reformation	Fischer-Tropsch Synthesis and liquefaction	Grid mix electricity	LPG(Propane)_fCO$_2$_fH2_FT_gm
13	LPG	Liquefied Petroleum Gas (Propane)	CO_2 + H2	CO_2: Fossil Point Source Carbon Capture[23] H2: from Renewable electricity	Fischer-Tropsch Synthesis and liquefaction	Grid mix electricity	LPG(Propane)_fCO$_2$_rH2_FT_gm
14	LPG	Liquefied Petroleum Gas (Propane)	CO_2 + H2	CO_2: Fossil Point Source Carbon Capture H2: Industrial by-product hydrogen	Fischer-Tropsch Synthesis and liquefaction	Grid mix electricity	LPG(Propane)_fCO$_2$_ibpH2_FT_gm
15	LPG	Liquefied Petroleum Gas (Propane)	CO_2 + H2	CO_2: Direct Air Capture H2: Fossil Steam Methane Reformation	Fischer-Tropsch Synthesis and liquefaction	Grid mix electricity	LPG(Propane)_rCO$_2$_fH2_FT_gm

[23] CO_2: Fossil Point Source Carbon Capture includes captured CO_2 stemming from fuel combustion and captured CO_2 stemming from extraction of resources underground.

| 序号 | 组别 | 燃料类型 | 原料结构 | | 转化 / 生产过程 | | 燃料路径代码 |
			原料类型	性质 / 碳源	加工类型	加工中使用的能量	
12	LPG	液化石油气（丙烷）	CO_2+H_2	CO_2: 化石点源碳捕获 H_2: 化石蒸汽甲烷重整	费托合成和液化	并网电力	LPG（Propane）_fCO₂_fH₂_FT_gm
13	LPG	液化石油气（丙烷）	CO_2+H_2	CO_2: 化石点源碳捕获[23] H_2: 来自可再生电力	费托合成和液化	并网电力	LPG（Propane）_fCO₂_rH₂_FT_gm
14	LPG	液化石油气（丙烷）	CO_2+H_2	CO_2: 化石点源碳捕获 H_2: 工业副产氢	费托合成和液化	并网电力	LPG（Propane）_fCO₂_ibpH₂_FT_gm
15	LPG	液化石油气（丙烷）	CO_2+H_2	CO_2: 直接空气捕获 H_2: 化石蒸汽甲烷重整	费托合成和液化	并网电力	LPG（Propane）_rCO₂_fH₂_FT_gm

23　CO_2: 化石点源碳捕获包括燃料燃烧产生的捕获 CO_2 和地下资源开采产生的捕获 CO_2。

Order	Group	Fuel type	Feedstock structure		Conversion/Production process		Fuel Pathway Code
			Feedstock Type	Nature/Carbon Source	Process Type	Energy used in the process	
16	LPG	Liquefied Petroleum Gas (Propane)	CO_2 + H2	CO_2: Direct Air Capture H2: from Renewable electricity	Fischer-Tropsch Synthesis and liquefaction	Grid mix electricity	LPG(Propane)_rCO_2_rH2_FT_gm
17	LPG	Liquefied Petroleum Gas (Propane)	CO_2 + H2	CO_2: Direct Air Capture H2: Industrial by-product hydrogen	Fischer-Tropsch Synthesis and liquefaction	Grid mix electricity	LPG(Propane)_rCO_2_ibpH2_FT_gm
18	LPG	Liquefied Petroleum Gas (Propane)	CO_2 + H2	CO_2: Biogenic Point Source Carbon Capture H2: Fossil Steam Methane Reformation	Fischer-Tropsch Synthesis and liquefaction	Grid mix electricity	LPG(Propane)_bCO_2_fH2_FT_gm
19	LPG	Liquefied Petroleum Gas (Propane)	CO_2 + H2	CO_2: Biogenic Point Source Carbon Capture H2: from Renewable electricity	Fischer-Tropsch Synthesis and liquefaction	Grid mix electricity	LPG(Propane)_bCO_2_rH2_FT_gm
20	LPG	Liquefied Petroleum Gas (Propane)	CO_2 + H2	CO_2: Biogenic Point Source Carbon Capture H2: Industrial by-product hydrogen	Fischer-Tropsch Synthesis and liquefaction	Grid mix electricity	LPG(Propane)_bCO_2_ibpH2_FT_gm

| 序号 | 组别 | 燃料类型 | 原料结构 | | 转化/生产过程 | | | 燃料路径代码 |
		燃料类型	原料类型	性质/碳源	加工类型	加工中使用的能量		
16	LPG	液化石油气（丙烷）	CO_2+H_2	CO_2：直接空气捕获 H_2：来自可再生电力	费托合成和液化	并网电力		LPG（Propane）_rCO_2_rH_2_FT_gm
17	LPG	液化石油气（丙烷）	CO_2+H_2	CO_2：直接空气捕获 H_2：工业副产氢	费托合成和液化	并网电力		LPG（Propane）_rCO_2_ibpH_2_FT_gm
18	LPG	液化石油气（丙烷）	CO_2+H_2	CO_2：生物点源碳捕获 H_2：化石蒸汽甲烷重整	费托合成和液化	并网电力		LPG（Propane）_bCO_2_fH_2_FT_gm
19	LPG	液化石油气（丙烷）	CO_2+H_2	CO_2：生物点源碳捕获 H_2：来自可再生电力	费托合成和液化	并网电力		LPG（Propane）_bCO_2_rH_2_FT_gm
20	LPG	液化石油气（丙烷）	CO_2+H_2	CO_2：生物点源碳捕获 H_2：工业副产氢	费托合成和液化	并网电力		LPG（Propane）_bCO_2_ibpH_2_FT_gm

Order	Group	Feedstock structure		Conversion/Production process		Fuel Pathway Code
		Fuel type	Feedstock Type	Nature/Carbon Source	Process Type	Energy used in the process	
21	LPG	Liquefied Petroleum Gas (Butane)	Crude Oil	Fossil	Standard refinery process and liquefaction	Grid mix electricity	LPG(Butane)_f_SR_gm
22	LPG	Liquefied Petroleum Gas (Butane)	CO_2 + H2	CO_2: Fossil Point Source Carbon Capture H2: Fossil Steam Methane Reformation	Fischer-Tropsch Synthesis and liquefaction	Grid mix electricity	LPG(Butane)_fCO₂_fH2_FT_gm
23	LPG	Liquefied Petroleum Gas (Butane)	CO_2 + H2	CO_2: Fossil Point Source Carbon Capture H2: from Renewable electricity	Fischer-Tropsch Synthesis and liquefaction	Grid mix electricity	LPG(Butane)_fCO₂_rH2_FT_gm
24	LPG	Liquefied Petroleum Gas (Butane)	CO_2 + H2	CO_2: Fossil Point Source Carbon Capture H2: Industrial by-product hydrogen	Fischer-Tropsch Synthesis and liquefaction	Grid mix electricity	LPG(Butane)_fCO₂_ibpH2_FT_gm
25	LPG	Liquefied Petroleum Gas (Butane)	CO_2 + H2	CO_2: Direct Air Capture H2: Fossil Steam Methane Reformation	Fischer-Tropsch Synthesis and liquefaction	Grid mix electricity	LPG(Butane)_rCO₂_fH2_FT_gm

序号	组别	燃料类型	原料结构			转化／生产过程			燃料路径代码
			原料类型	性质／碳源		加工类型	加工中使用的能量		
21	LPG	液化石油气（丁烷）	原油	化石		标准炼油工艺和液化	并网电力		LPG（Butane）_f_SR_gm
22	LPG	液化石油气（丁烷）	CO₂+H₂	CO₂：化石点源碳捕获 H₂：化石蒸汽甲烷重整		费托合成和液化	并网电力		LPG（Butane）_fCO₂_fH₂_FT_gm
23	LPG	液化石油气（丁烷）	CO₂+H₂	CO₂：化石点源碳捕获 H₂：来自可再生电力		费托合成和液化	并网电力		LPG（Butane）_fCO₂_rH₂_FT_gm
24	LPG	液化石油气（丁烷）	CO₂+H₂	CO₂：化石点源碳捕获 H₂：工业副产氢		费托合成和液化	并网电力		LPG（Butane）_fCO₂_ibpH₂_FT_gm
25	LPG	液化石油气（丁烷）	CO₂+H₂	CO₂：直接空气捕获 H₂：化石蒸汽甲烷重整		费托合成和液化	并网电力		LPG（Butane）_rCO₂_fH₂_FT_gm

Order	Group	Fuel type	Feedstock structure		Conversion/Production process		Fuel Pathway Code
			Feedstock Type	Nature/Carbon Source	Process Type	Energy used in the process	
26	LPG	Liquefied Petroleum Gas (Butane)	CO_2 + H2	CO_2: Direct Air Capture H2: from Renewable electricity	Fischer-Tropsch Synthesis and liquefaction	Grid mix electricity	LPG(Butane)_rCO_2_rH2_FT_gm
27	LPG	Liquefied Petroleum Gas (Butane)	CO_2 + H2	CO_2: Direct Air Capture H2: Industrial by-product hydrogen	Fischer-Tropsch Synthesis and liquefaction	Grid mix electricity	LPG(Butane)_rCO_2_ibpH2_FT_gm
28	LPG	Liquefied Petroleum Gas (Butane)	CO_2 + H2	CO_2: Biogenic Point Source Carbon Capture H2: Fossil Steam Methane Reformation	Fischer-Tropsch Synthesis and liquefaction	Grid mix electricity	LPG(Butane)_bCO_2_fH2_FT_gm
29	LPG	Liquefied Petroleum Gas (Butane)	CO_2 + H2	CO_2: Biogenic Point Source Carbon Capture H2: from Renewable electricity	Fischer-Tropsch Synthesis and liquefaction	Grid mix electricity	LPG(Butane)_bCO_2_rH2_FT_gm
30	LPG	Liquefied Petroleum Gas (Butane)	CO_2 + H2	CO_2: Biogenic Point Source Carbon Capture H2: Industrial by-product hydrogen	Fischer-Tropsch Synthesis and liquefaction	Grid mix electricity	LPG(Butane)_bCO_2_ibpH2_FT_gm

序号	组别	燃料类型	原料结构		转化/生产过程			燃料路径代码
			原料类型	性质/碳源	加工类型	加工中使用的能量		
26	LPG	液化石油气（丁烷）	CO_2+H_2	CO_2：直接空气捕获 H_2：来自可再生电力	费托合成和液化	并网电力		LPG（Butane）_rCO₂_rH₂_FT_gm
27	LPG	液化石油气（丁烷）	CO_2+H_2	CO_2：直接空气捕获 H_2：工业副产氢	费托合成和液化	并网电力		LPG（Butane）_rCO₂_ibpH₂_FT_gm
28	LPG	液化石油气（丁烷）	CO_2+H_2	CO_2：生物点源碳捕获 H_2：化石蒸汽甲烷重整	费托合成和液化	并网电力		LPG（Butane）_bCO₂_fH₂_FT_gm
29	LPG	液化石油气（丁烷）	CO_2+H_2	CO_2：生物点源碳捕获 H_2：来自可再生电力	费托合成和液化	并网电力		LPG（Butane）_bCO₂_rH₂_FT_gm
30	LPG	液化石油气（丁烷）	CO_2+H_2	CO_2：生物点源碳捕获 H_2：工业副产氢	费托合成和液化	并网电力		LPG（Butane）_bCO₂_ibpH₂_FT_gm

Order	Group	Fuel type	Feedstock structure		Conversion/Production process		Fuel Pathway Code
			Feedstock Type	Nature/Carbon Source	Process Type	Energy used in the process	
31	LNG	Liquefied Natural Gas (Methane)	Natural Gas	Fossil	Standard LNG production including liquefaction	Grid mix electricity	LNG_f_SLP_gm
32	LNG	Liquefied Natural Gas (Methane)	Mixed 1st, 2nd and 3rd Gen. feedstock	Biogenic	Thermochemical gasification followed by methanation and liquefaction	Grid mix electricity	LNG_b_G_M_gm
33	LNG	Liquefied Natural Gas (Methane)	Mixed 1st, 2nd and 3rd Gen. feedstock	Biogenic	Bio-derived LNG via Anaerobic Digestion, separation and liquefaction	Grid mix electricity	LNG_b_AD_gm
34	LNG	Liquefied Natural Gas (Methane)	Mixed 1st, 2nd and 3rd Gen. feedstock	Biogenic	Bio-derived LNG via Anaerobic Digestion, separation with Point Source Carbon Capture (PSCC) and long-term storage and liquefaction	Grid mix electricity	LNG_b_AD_CCS_gm
35	LNG	Liquefied Natural Gas (Methane)	CO_2 + H2	CO_2: Fossil Point Source Carbon Capture H2: Fossil Steam Methane Reformation	Methanation and liquefaction	Grid mix electricity	LNG_fCO$_2$_fH2_M_gm
36	LNG	Liquefied Natural Gas (Methane)	CO_2 + H2	CO_2: Fossil Point Source Carbon Capture H2: from Renewable electricity	Methanation and liquefaction	Grid mix electricity	LNG_fCO$_2$_rH2_M_gm

| 序号 | 组别 | 燃料类型 | 原料结构 | | 转化/生产过程 | | 燃料路径代码 |
			原料类型	性质/碳源	加工类型	加工中使用的能量	
31	LNG	液化天然气（甲烷）	天然气	化石	标准 LNG 生产，包括液化	并网电力	LNG_f_SLP_gm
32	LNG	液化天然气（甲烷）	混合第一、第二和第三代原料	生物源	热化学气化，然后甲烷化和液化	并网电力	LNG_b_G_M_gm
33	LNG	液化天然气（甲烷）	混合第一、第二和第三代原料	生物源	通过厌氧消化和液化的生物衍生液化天然气	并网电力	LNG_b_AD_gm
34	LNG	液化天然气（甲烷）	混合第一、第二和第三代原料	生物源	通过厌氧消化、点源碳捕获（PSCC）分离、长期储存和液化的生物衍生液化天然气	并网电力	LNG_b_AD_CCS_gm
35	LNG	液化天然气（甲烷）	CO_2+H_2	CO_2: 化石点源碳捕获 H_2: 化石蒸汽甲烷重整	甲烷化和液化	并网电力	LNG_fCO2_fH2_M_gm
36	LNG	液化天然气（甲烷）	CO_2+H_2	CO_2: 化石点源碳捕获 H_2: 来自可再生电力	甲烷化和液化	并网电力	LNG_fCO2_rH2_M_gm

Order	Group	Fuel type	Feedstock structure		Conversion/Production process		Fuel Pathway Code
			Feedstock Type	Nature/Carbon Source	Process Type	Energy used in the process	
37	LNG	Liquefied Natural Gas (Methane)	CO_2 + H_2	CO_2: Fossil Point Source Carbon Capture H2: Industrial by-product hydrogen	Methanation and liquefaction	Grid mix electricity	LNG_fCO_2_ibpH2_M_gm
38	LNG	Liquefied Natural Gas (Methane)	CO_2 + H_2	CO_2: Direct Air Capture H2: Fossil Steam Methane Reformation	Methanation and liquefaction	Grid mix electricity	LNG_rCO_2_fH2_M_gm
39	LNG	Liquefied Natural Gas (Methane)	CO_2 + H_2	CO_2: Direct Air Capture H2: from Renewable electricity	Methanation and liquefaction	Grid mix electricity	LNG_rCO_2_rH2_M_gm
40	LNG	Liquefied Natural Gas (Methane)	CO_2 + H_2	CO_2: Direct Air Capture H2: Industrial by-product hydrogen	Methanation and liquefaction	Grid mix electricity	LNG_rCO_2_ibpH2_M_gm
41	LNG	Liquefied Natural Gas (Methane)	CO_2 + H_2	CO_2: Biogenic Point Source Carbon Capture H2: Fossil Steam Methane Reformation	Methanation and liquefaction	Grid mix electricity	LNG_bCO_2_fH2_M_gm

| 序号 | 组别 | 燃料类型 | 原料结构 | | 转化／生产过程 | | | 燃料路径代码 |
			原料类型	性质／碳源	加工类型	加工中使用的能量	
37	LNG	液化天然气（甲烷）	CO_2+H_2	CO_2：化石点源碳捕获 H_2：工业副产氢	甲烷化和液化	并网电力	LNG_fCO2_ibpH₂_M_gm
38	LNG	液化天然气（甲烷）	CO_2+H_2	CO_2：直接空气捕获 H_2：化石蒸汽甲烷重整	甲烷化和液化	并网电力	LNG_rCO₂_fH₂_M_gm
39	LNG	液化天然气（甲烷）	CO_2+H_2	CO_2：直接空气捕获 H_2：来自可再生电力	甲烷化和液化	并网电力	LNG_rCO₂_rH₂_M_gm
40	LNG	液化天然气（甲烷）	CO_2+H_2	CO_2：直接空气捕获 H_2：工业副产氢	甲烷化和液化	并网电力	LNG_rCO₂_ibpH₂_M_gm
41	LNG	液化天然气（甲烷）	CO_2+H_2	CO_2：生物点源碳捕获 H_2：化石蒸汽甲烷重整	甲烷化和液化	并网电力	LNG_bCO₂_fH₂_M_gm

Order	Group	Fuel type	Feedstock structure		Conversion/Production process		Fuel Pathway Code
			Feedstock Type	Nature/Carbon Source	Process Type	Energy used in the process	
42	LNG	Liquefied Natural Gas (Methane)	CO_2 + H2	CO_2: Biogenic Point Source Carbon Capture H2: from Renewable electricity	Methanation and liquefaction	Grid mix electricity	LNG_bCO2_rH2_M_gm
43	LNG	Liquefied Natural Gas (Methane)	CO_2 + H2	CO_2: Biogenic Point Source Carbon Capture H2: Industrial by-product hydrogen	Methanation and liquefaction	Grid mix electricity	LNG_bCO2_ibpH2_M_gm
44	CNG	Compressed Natural Gas (Methane)	Natural Gas	Fossil	Standard refinery process and compression	Grid mix electricity	CNG_f_SR_gm
45	CNG	Compressed Natural Gas (Methane)	Mixed 1st, 2nd and 3rd Gen. feedstock	Biogenic	Thermochemical gasification followed by methanation and compression	Grid mix electricity	CNG_b_G_M_gm
46	CNG	Compressed Natural Gas (Methane)	Mixed 1st, 2nd and 3rd Gen. feedstock	Biogenic	Bio-derived LNG via Anaerobic Digestion and separation and compression	Grid mix electricity	CNG_b_AD_gm
47	CNG	Compressed Natural Gas (Methane)	Mixed 1st, 2nd and 3rd Gen. feedstock	Biogenic	Bio-derived LNG via Anaerobic Digestion, separation with Point Source Carbon Capture (PSCC) and long-term storage and compression	Grid mix electricity	CNG_b_AD_CCS_gm

序号	组别	燃料类型	原料结构		转化/生产过程		燃料路径代码
			原料类型	性质/碳源	加工类型	加工中使用的能量	
42	LNG	液化天然气（甲烷）	CO_2+H_2	CO_2：生物点源碳捕获 H_2：来自可再生电力	甲烷化和液化	并网电力	LNG_bCO$_2$_rH$_2$_M_gm
43	LNG	液化天然气（甲烷）	CO_2+H_2	CO_2：生物点源碳捕获 H_2：工业副产氢	甲烷化和液化	并网电力	LNG_bCO$_2$_ibpH$_2$_M_gm
44	CNG	压缩天然气（甲烷）	天然气	化石	标准炼油工艺和压缩	并网电力	CNG_f_SR_gm
45	CNG	压缩天然气（甲烷）	混合第一、第二和第三代原料	生物源	热化学气化，然后甲烷化和压缩	并网电力	CNG_b_G_M_gm
46	CNG	压缩天然气（甲烷）	混合第一、第二和第三代原料	生物源	通过厌氧消化和压缩的生物衍生液化天然气	并网电力	CNG_b_AD_gm
47	CNG	压缩天然气（甲烷）	混合第一、第二和第三代原料	生物源	通过厌氧消化、点源碳捕获（PSCC）分离和压缩储存以及长期储存的生物衍生液化天然气	并网电力	CNG_b_AD_CCS_gm

Order	Group	Fuel type	Feedstock structure		Conversion/Production process		Fuel Pathway Code
			Feedstock Type	Nature/Carbon Source	Process Type	Energy used in the process	
48	CNG	Compressed Natural Gas (Methane)	CO_2 + H2	CO_2: Fossil Point Source Carbon Capture H2: Fossil Steam Methane Reformation	Methanation and compression	Grid mix electricity	$CNG\_fCO_2\_fH2\_M\_gm$
49	CNG	Compressed Natural Gas (Methane)	CO_2 + H2	CO_2: Fossil Point Source Carbon Capture H2: from Renewable electricity	Methanation and compression	Grid mix electricity	$CNG\_fCO_2\_rH2\_M\_gm$
50	CNG	Compressed Natural Gas (Methane)	CO_2 + H2	CO_2: Fossil Point Source Carbon Capture H2: Industrial by-product hydrogen	Methanation and compression	Grid mix electricity	$CNG\_fCO_2\_ibpH2\_M\_gm$
51	CNG	Compressed Natural Gas (Methane)	CO_2 + H2	CO_2: Direct Air Capture H2: Fossil Steam Methane Reformation	Methanation and compression	Grid mix electricity	$CNG\_rCO_2\_fH2\_M\_gm$
52	CNG	Compressed Natural Gas (Methane)	CO_2 + H2	CO_2: Direct Air Capture H2: from Renewable electricity	Methanation and compression	Grid mix electricity	$CNG\_rCO_2\_rH2\_M\_gm$

序号	组别	燃料类型	原料结构		转化/生产过程			燃料路径代码
			原料类型	性质/碳源	加工类型	加工中使用的能量		
48	CNG	压缩天然气（甲烷）	CO_2+H_2	CO_2: 化石点源碳捕获 H_2: 化石蒸汽甲烷重整	甲烷化和压缩	并网电力		CNG_fCO_2_fH_2_M_gm
49	CNG	压缩天然气（甲烷）	CO_2+H_2	CO_2: 化石点源碳捕获 H_2: 来自可再生电力	甲烷化和压缩	并网电力		CNG_fCO_2_rH_2_M_gm
50	CNG	压缩天然气（甲烷）	CO_2+H_2	CO_2: 化石点源碳捕获 H_2: 工业副产氢	甲烷化和压缩	并网电力		CNG_fCO_2_ibpH_2_M_gm
51	CNG	压缩天然气（甲烷）	CO_2+H_2	CO_2: 直接空气捕获 H_2: 化石蒸汽甲烷重整	甲烷化和压缩	并网电力		CNG_rCO_2_fH_2_M_gm
52	CNG	压缩天然气（甲烷）	CO_2+H_2	CO_2: 直接空气捕获 H_2: 来自可再生电力	甲烷化和压缩	并网电力		CNG_rCO_2_rH_2_M_gm

Order	Group	Fuel type	Feedstock structure		Conversion/Production process		Fuel Pathway Code
			Feedstock Type	Nature/Carbon Source	Process Type	Energy used in the process	
53	CNG	Compressed Natural Gas (Methane)	CO_2 + H2	CO_2: Direct Air Capture H2: Industrial by-product hydrogen	Methanation and compression	Grid mix electricity	CNG_rCO₂_ibpH2_M_gm
54	CNG	Compressed Natural Gas (Methane)	CO_2 + H2	CO_2: Biogenic Point Source Carbon Capture H2: Fossil Steam Methane Reformation	Methanation and compression	Grid mix electricity	CNG_bCO₂_fH2_M_gm
55	CNG	Compressed Natural Gas (Methane)	CO_2 + H2	CO_2: Biogenic Point Source Carbon Capture H2: from Renewable electricity	Methanation and compression	Grid mix electricity	CNG_bCO₂_rH2_M_gm
56	CNG	Compressed Natural Gas (Methane)	CO_2 + H2	CO_2: Biogenic Point Source Carbon Capture H2: Industrial by-product hydrogen	Methanation and compression	Grid mix electricity	CNG_bCO₂_ibpH2_M_gm
57	Ethane	Ethane	Natural Gas	Fossil	Standard refinery process	Grid mix electricity	Ethane_f_SR_gm
58	Vegetable oil-based fuel	Straight Vegetable Oil	1st Gen. feedstock	Biogenic	Extraction and purification	Grid mix electricity	SVO_b_EP_1stgen_gm
59	Vegetable oil-based fuel	Used oils and fats	2nd Gen. feedstock	Biogenic	Extraction and purification	Grid mix electricity	UOF_b_EP_2ndgen_gm

序号	组别	燃料类型	原料结构		转化／生产过程		燃料路径代码
			原料类型	性质／碳源	加工类型	加工中使用的能量	
53	CNG	压缩天然气（甲烷）	CO_2+H_2	CO_2：直接空气捕获 H_2：工业副产氢	甲烷化和压缩	并网电力	CNG_rCO2_ibpH2_M_gm
54	CNG	压缩天然气（甲烷）	CO_2+H_2	CO_2：生物点源碳捕获 H_2：化石蒸汽甲烷重整	甲烷化和压缩	并网电力	CNG_bCO2_fH2_M_gm
55	CNG	压缩天然气（甲烷）	CO_2+H_2	CO_2：生物点源碳捕获 H_2：来自可再生电力	甲烷化和压缩	并网电力	CNG_bCO2_rH2_M_gm
56	CNG	压缩天然气（甲烷）	CO_2+H_2	CO_2：生物点源碳捕获 H_2：工业副产氢	甲烷化和压缩	并网电力	CNG_bCO2_ibpH2_M_gm
57	乙烷	乙烷	天然气	化石	标准炼油工艺	并网电力	Ethane_f_SR_gm
58	植物油基燃料	纯植物油	第一代原料	生物源	提取纯化	并网电力	SVO_b_EP_1stgen_gm
59	植物油基燃料	废油和油脂	第二代原料	生物源	提取纯化	并网电力	UOF_b_EP_2ndgen_gm

Order	Group	Fuel type	Feedstock structure		Conversion/Production process		Fuel Pathway Code
			Feedstock Type	Nature/Carbon Source	Process Type	Energy used in the process	
60	Vegetable oil-based fuel	Algae oil	3rd Gen. feedstock	Eiogenic	Extraction and purification	Grid mix electricity	AO_b_EP_3rdgen_gm
61	Diesel	Diesel (FAME)	1st Gen. feedstock	Eiogenic	Transesterification	Grid mix electricity	FAME_b_TRE_1stgen_gm_
62	Diesel	Diesel (FAME)	2nd Gen. feedstock	Eiogenic	Transesterification	Grid mix electricity	FAME_b_TRE_2ndgen_gm_
63	Diesel	Diesel (FAME)	3rd Gen. feedstock	Biogenic	Transesterification	Grid mix electricity	FAME_b_TRE_3rdgen_gm_
64	Diesel	Renewable Diesel (Bio FT-Diesel)	1st Gen. feedstock	Biogenic	Gasification and Fischer-Tropsch Synthesis	Grid mix electricity	FT-Diesel_b_G_FT_1stgen_gm_
65	Diesel	Renewable Diesel (Bio FT-Diesel)	Mixed 1st, 2nd and 3rd Gen. feedstock	Biogenic	Anaerobic digestion and methane separation and Fischer-Tropsch Synthesis	Grid mix electricity	FT-Diesel_b_AD_FT_gm
66	Diesel	Renewable Diesel (Bio FT-Diesel)	Mixed 1st, 2nd and 3rd Gen. feedstock	Biogenic	Anaerobic digestion and methane separation and Fischer-Tropsch Synthesis with Point Source Carbon Capture (PSCC) and long-term storage	Grid mix electricity	FT-Diesel_b_AD_FT_CCS_gm
67	Diesel	Renewable Diesel (FT-Diesel)	CO_2 + H2	CO_2: Fossil Point Source Carbon Capture H2: Fossil Steam Methane Reformation	Fischer-Tropsch Synthesis	Grid mix electricity	FT-Diesel_fCO$_2$_fH2_FT_gm

序号	组别	燃料类型	原料结构		转化/生产过程		燃料路径代码
			原料类型	性质/碳源	加工类型	加工中使用的能量	
60	植物油基燃料	海藻油	第三代原料	生物源	提取纯化	并网电力	AO_b_EP_3rdgen_gm
61	柴油	柴油（FAME）	第一代原料	生物源	酯交换	并网电力	FAME_b_TRE_1stgen_gm_
62	柴油	柴油（FAME）	第二代原料	生物源	酯交换	并网电力	FAME_b_TRE_2ndgen_gm_
63	柴油	柴油（FAME）	第三代原料	生物源	酯交换	并网电力	FAME_b_TRE_3rdgen_gm_
64	柴油	可再生柴油（Bio FT-Diesel）	第一代原料	生物源	气化与费托合成	并网电力	FT-Diesel_b_G_FT_1stgen_gm_
65	柴油	可再生柴油（Bio FT-Diesel）	混合第一、第二和第三代原料	生物源	厌氧消化、甲烷分离和费托合成	并网电力	FT-Diesel_b_AD_FT_gm
66	柴油	可再生柴油（Bio FT-Diesel）	混合第一、第二和第三代原料	生物源	厌氧消化、甲烷分离和费托合成及点碳源捕获和长期储存	并网电力	FT-Diesel_b_AD_FT_CCS_gm
67	柴油	可再生柴油（FT-Diesel）	CO_2+H_2	CO_2: 化石点源碳捕获 H_2: 化石蒸汽甲烷重整	费托合成	并网电力	FT-Diesel_fCO$_2$_fH$_2$_FT_gm

Order	Group	Fuel type	Feedstock structure		Conversion/Production process		Fuel Pathway Code
			Feedstock Type	Nature/Carbon Source	Process Type	Energy used in the process	
68	Diesel	Renewable Diesel (FT-Diesel)	CO_2 + H2	CO_2: Fossil Point Source Carbon Capture H2: from Renewable electricity	Fischer-Tropsch Synthesis	Grid mix electricity	FT-Diesel_fCO$_2$_rH2_FT_gm
69	Diesel	Renewable Diesel (FT-Diesel)	CO_2 + H2	CO_2: Fossil Point Source Carbon Capture H2: Industrial by-product hydrogen	Fischer-Tropsch Synthesis	Grid mix electricity	FT-Diesel_fCO$_2$_ibpH2_FT_gm
70	Diesel	Renewable Diesel (FT-Diesel)	CO_2 + H2	CO_2: Direct Air Capture H2: Fossil Steam Methane Reformation	Fischer-Tropsch Synthesis	Grid mix electricity	FT-Diesel_rCO$_2$_fH2_FT_gm
71	Diesel	Renewable Diesel (FT-Diesel)	CO_2 + H2	CO_2: Direct Air Capture H2: from Renewable electricity	Fischer-Tropsch Synthesis	Grid mix electricity	FT-Diesel_rCO$_2$_rH2_FT_gm
72	Diesel	Renewable Diesel (FT-Diesel)	CO_2 + H2	CO_2: Direct Air Capture H2: Industrial by-product hydrogen	Fischer-Tropsch Synthesis	Grid mix electricity	FT-Diesel_rCO$_2$_ibpH2_FT_gm

| 序号 | 组别 | 燃料类型 | 原料结构 | | 转化／生产过程 | | 燃料路径代码 |
			原料类型	性质／碳源	加工类型	加工中使用的能量	
68	柴油	可再生柴油（FT-Diesel）	CO_2+H_2	CO_2：化石点源碳捕获 H_2：来自可再生电力	费托合成	并网电力	FT-Diesel_fCO₂_rH₂_FT_gm
69	柴油	可再生柴油（FT-Diesel）	CO_2+H_2	CO_2：化石点源碳捕获 H_2：工业副产氢	费托合成	并网电力	FT-Diesel_fCO₂_ibpH₂_FT_gm
70	柴油	可再生柴油（FT-Diesel）	CO_2+H_2	CO_2：直接空气捕获 H_2：化石蒸汽甲烷重整	费托合成	并网电力	FT-Diesel_rCO₂_fH₂_FT_gm
71	柴油	可再生柴油（FT-Diesel）	CO_2+H_2	CO_2：直接空气捕获 H_2：来自可再生电力	费托合成	并网电力	FT-Diesel_rCO₂_rH₂_FT_gm
72	柴油	可再生柴油（FT-Diesel）	CO_2+H_2	CO_2：直接空气捕获 H_2：工业副产氢	费托合成	并网电力	FT-Diesel_rCO₂_ibpH₂_FT_gm

Order	Group	Fuel type	Feedstock structure		Conversion/Production process		Fuel Pathway Code
			Feedstock Type	Nature/Carbon Source	Process Type	Energy used in the process	
73	Diesel	Renewable Diesel (FT-Diesel)	CO_2 + H2	CO_2: Biogenic Point Source Carbon Capture H2: Fossil Steam Methane Reformation	Fischer-Tropsch Synthesis	Grid mix electricity	FT-Diesel_bCO$_2$_fH2_FT_gm
74	Diesel	Renewable Diesel (FT-Diesel)	CO_2 + H2	CO_2: Biogenic Point Source Carbon Capture H2: from Renewable electricity	Fischer-Tropsch Synthesis	Grid mix electricity	FT-Diesel_bCO$_2$_rH2_FT_gm
75	Diesel	Renewable Diesel (FT-Diesel)	CO_2 + H2	CO_2: Biogenic Point Source Carbon Capture H2: Industrial by-product hydrogen	Fischer-Tropsch Synthesis	Grid mix electricity	FT-Diesel_bCO$_2$_ibpH2_FT_gm
76	Diesel	Renewable Diesel (HVO)	1st Gen. feedstock	Biogenic	Hydrogenation	Grid mix electricity	HVO_b_HD_1stgen_gm_
77	Diesel	Renewable Diesel (HVO)	2nd Gen. feedstock	Biogenic	Hydrogenation	Grid mix electricity	HVO_b_HD_2ndgen_gm_
78	Diesel	Renewable Diesel (HVO)	3rd Gen. feedstock	Biogenic	Hydrogenation	Grid mix electricity	HVO_b_HD_3rdgen_gm_
79	DME	Dimethyl Ether (DME)	1st Gen. feedstock	Biogenic	Gasification and DME Synthesis	Grid mix electricity	DME_b_G_DMES_1stgen_g m_
80	DME	Dimethyl Ether (DME)	2nd Gen. feedstock	Biogenic	Gasification and DME Synthesis	Grid mix electricity	DME-b-G-DMES_2ndgen_gm_

序号	组别	燃料类型	原料结构		转化／生产过程		燃料路径代码
			原料类型	性质／碳源	加工类型	加工中使用的能量	
73	柴油	可再生柴油（FT-Diesel）	CO_2+H_2	CO_2：生物点源碳捕获 H_2：化石蒸汽甲烷重整	费托合成	并网电力	FT-Diesel_bCO$_2$_fH$_2$_FT_gm
74	柴油	可再生柴油（FT-Diesel）	CO_2+H_2	CO_2：生物点源碳捕获 H_2：来自可再生电力	费托合成	并网电力	FT-Diesel_bCO$_2$_rH$_2$_FT_gm
75	柴油	可再生柴油（FT-Diesel）	CO_2+H_2	CO_2：生物点源碳捕获 H_2：工业副产氢	费托合成	并网电力	FT-Diesel_bCO$_2$_ibpH$_2$_FT_gm
76	柴油	可再生柴油（HVO）	第一代原料	生物源	氢化	并网电力	HVO_b_HD_1stgen_gm_
77	柴油	可再生柴油（HVO）	第二代原料	生物源	氢化	并网电力	HVO_b_HD_2ndgen_gm_
78	柴油	可再生柴油（HVO）	第三代原料	生物源	氢化	并网电力	HVO_b_HD_3rdgen_gm_
79	DME	二甲醚（DME）	第一代原料	生物源	气化和二甲醚合成	并网电力	DME_b_G_DMES_1stgen_gm_
80	DME	二甲醚（DME）	第二代原料	生物源	气化和二甲醚合成	并网电力	DME-b-G-DMES_2ndgen_gm_

Order	Group	Fuel type	Feedstock structure		Conversion/Production process		Fuel Pathway Code
			Feedstock Type	Nature/Carbon Source	Process Type	Energy used in the process	
81	DME	Dimethyl Ether (DME)	Mixed 1st, 2nd and 3rd Gen. feedstock	Biogenic	Anaerobic digestion and methane separation and DME Synthesis	Grid mix electricity	DME_b_AD_DMES_gm
82	DME	Dimethyl Ether (DME)	Mixed 1st, 2nd and 3rd Gen. feedstock	Biogenic	Anaerobic digestion and methane separation and DME Synthesis with Point Source Carbon Capture (PSCC) and long-term storage	Grid mix electricity	DME_b_AD_DMES_CCS_gm
83	DME	Dimethyl Ether (DME)	Natural Gas	Fossil	Gasification and DME Synthesis	Grid mix electricity	DME_f_G_DMES_gm
84	Diesel	Upgraded Pyrolysis Oil	2nd Gen. feedstock	Biogenic	Pyrolysis, Fast Pyrolysis and/or Catalytic Fast Pyrolysis and upgrading	Grid mix electricity	UPO_b_UPO_2ndgen_gm_
85	Diesel	Hydrothermal Liquefaction (HTL) Oil	2nd Gen. feedstock	Biogenic	Hydrothermal liquefaction and upgrading	Grid mix electricity	HTL_b_HTL_2ndgen_gm_
86	Methanol	Methanol	Natural Gas	Fossil	Steam Methane Reformation of Natural Gas and Methanol Synthesis	Grid mix electricity	MeOH_f_SMR_gm
87	Methanol	Methanol	Natural Gas	Fossil	Steam Methane Reformation of Natural Gas with Carbon Capture & Storage and Methanol Synthesis	Grid mix electricity	MeOH_f_SMR_CCS_gm

序号	组别	燃料类型	原料结构		转化/生产过程		燃料路径代码
			原料类型	性质/碳源	加工类型	加工中使用的能量	
81	DME	二甲醚（DME）	混合第一、第二和第三代原料	生物源	厌氧消化、甲烷分离和二甲醚合成	并网电力	DME_b_AD_DMES_gm
82	DME	二甲醚（DME）	混合第一、第二和第三代原料	生物源	厌氧消化、甲烷分离和二甲醚合成及点源碳捕获（PSCC）和长期储存	并网电力	DME_b_AD_DMES_CCS_gm
83	DME	二甲醚（DME）	天然气	化石	气化和二甲醚合成	并网电力	DME_f_G_DMES_gm
84	柴油	升级热解油	第二代原料	生物源	热解、快速热解和/或催化快速热解和升级	并网电力	UPO_b_UPO_2ndgen_gm_
85	柴油	水热液化（HTL）油	第二代原料	生物源	水热液化和升级	并网电力	HTL_b_HTL_2ndgen_gm_
86	甲醇	甲醇	天然气	化石	天然气蒸汽甲烷重整和甲醇合成	并网电力	MeOH_f_SMR_gm
87	甲醇	甲醇	天然气	化石	天然气蒸汽甲烷重整及碳捕获与存储和甲醇合成	并网电力	MeOH_f_SMR_CCS_gm

Order	Group	Fuel type	Feedstock structure		Conversion/Production process		Fuel Pathway Code
			Feedstock Type	Nature/Carbon Source	Process Type	Energy used in the process	
88	Methanol	Methanol	Coal	Fossil	Gasification of Coal and Methanol Synthesis	Grid mix electricity	MeOH_f_G_MS_gm
89	Methanol	Methanol	Coal	Fossil	Gasification of Coal with Carbon Capture & Storage and Methanol Synthesis	Grid mix electricity	MeOH_f_G_MS_CCS_gm
90	Methanol	Methanol	2nd and 3rd Gen. feedstock	Eiogenic	Gasification of Biomass and Methanol Synthesis	Grid mix electricity	MeOH_b_G_MS_gm
91	Methanol	Methanol	Mixed 1st, 2nd and 3rd Gen. feedstock	Biogenic	Reforming of Renewable Natural Gas (biomethane from Anaerobic Digestion) and Methanol Synthesis	Grid mix electricity	MeOH_b_AD_MS_gm
92	Methanol	Methanol	CO_2 + H2	CO_2: Fossil Point Source Carbon Capture H2: Fossil Steam Methane Reformation	Methanol Synthesis	Grid mix electricity	MeOH_fCO$_2$_fH2_MS_gm
93	Methanol	Methanol	CO_2 + H2	CO_2: Fossil Point Source Carbon Capture H2: from Renewable electricity	Methanol Synthesis	Grid mix electricity	MeOH_fCO$_2$_rH2_MS_gm

序号	组别	燃料类型	原料结构		转化／生产过程		燃料路径代码
			原料类型	性质／碳源	加工类型	加工中使用的能量	
88	甲醇	甲醇	煤	化石	煤碳气化和甲醇合成	并网电力	MeOH_f_G_MS_gm
89	甲醇	甲醇	煤	化石	煤碳气化及碳捕获与存储和甲醇合成	并网电力	MeOH_f_G_MS_CCS_gm
90	甲醇	甲醇	第二和第三代原料	生物源	生物质气化和甲醇合成	并网电力	MeOH_b_G_MS_gm
91	甲醇	甲醇	混合第一、第二和第三代原料	生物源	可再生天然气（厌氧消化生物甲烷）重整和甲醇合成	并网电力	MeOH_b_AD_MS_gm
92	甲醇	甲醇	CO₂+H₂	CO₂：化石点源碳捕获 H₂：化石蒸汽甲烷重整	甲醇合成	并网电力	MeOH_fCO₂_fH₂_MS_gm
93	甲醇	甲醇	CO₂+H₂	CO₂：化石点源碳捕获 H₂：来自可再生电力	甲醇合成	并网电力	MeOH_fCO₂_rH₂_MS_gm

Order	Group	Fuel type	Feedstock structure		Conversion/Production process		Fuel Pathway Code
			Feedstock Type	Nature/Carbon Source	Process Type	Energy used in the process	
94	Methanol	Methanol	CO_2 + H2	CO_2: Fossil Point Source Carbon Capture / H2: Industrial by-product hydrogen	Methanol Synthesis	Grid mix electricity	MeOH_fCO_2_ibpH2_MS_gm
95	Methanol	Methanol	CO_2 + H2	CO_2: Direct Air Capture / H2: Fossil Steam Methane Reformation	Methanol Synthesis	Grid mix electricity	MeOH_rCO_2_fH2_MS_gm
96	Methanol	Methanol	CO_2 + H2	CO_2: Direct Air Capture / H2: from Renewable electricity	Methanol Synthesis	Grid mix electricity	MeOH_rCO_2_rH2_MS_gm
97	Methanol	Methanol	CO_2 + H2	CO_2: Direct Air Capture / H2: Industrial by-product hydrogen	Methanol Synthesis	Grid mix electricity	MeOH_rCO_2_ibpH2_MS_gm
98	Methanol	Methanol	CO_2 + H2	CO_2: Biogenic Point Source Carbon Capture / H2: Fossil Steam Methane Reformation	Methanol Synthesis	Grid mix electricity	MeOH_bCO_2_fH2_MS_gm

| 序号 | 组别 | 燃料类型 | 原料结构 | | 转化/生产过程 | | 燃料路径代码 |
			原料类型	性质/碳源	加工类型	加工中使用的能量	
94	甲醇	甲醇	CO_2+H_2	CO_2: 化石点源碳捕获 H_2: 工业副产氢	甲醇合成	并网电力	MeOH_fCO₂_ibpH₂_MS_gm
95	甲醇	甲醇	CO_2+H_2	CO_2: 直接空气捕获 H_2: 化石蒸汽甲烷重整	甲醇合成	并网电力	MeOH_rCO₂_fH₂_MS_gm
96	甲醇	甲醇	CO_2+H_2	CO_2: 直接空气捕获 H_2: 来自可再生电力	甲醇合成	并网电力	MeOH_rCO₂_rH₂_MS_gm
97	甲醇	甲醇	CO_2+H_2	CO_2: 直接空气捕获 H_2: 工业副产氢	甲醇合成	并网电力	MeOH_rCO₂_ibpH₂_MS_gm
98	甲醇	甲醇	CO_2+H_2	CO_2: 生物点源碳捕获 H_2: 化石蒸汽甲烷重整	甲醇合成	并网电力	MeOH_bCO₂_fH₂_MS_gm

Order	Group	Fuel type	Feedstock structure		Conversion/Production process		Fuel Pathway Code
			Feedstock Type	Nature/Carbon Source	Process Type	Energy used in the process	
99	Methanol	Methanol	CO_2 + H2	CO_2: Biogenic Point Source Carbon Capture H2: from Renewable electricity	Methanol Synthesis	Grid mix electricity	MeOH_bCO_2_rH2_MS_gm
100	Methanol	Methanol	CO_2 + H2	CO_2: Biogenic Point Source Carbon Capture H2: Industrial by-product hydrogen	Methanol Synthesis	Grid mix electricity	MeOH_bCO_2_ibpH2_MS_gm
101	Ethanol	Ethanol	1st Gen. feedstock	Biogenic	Fermentation	Grid mix electricity	EtOH_b_FR_1stgen_gm_
102	Ethanol	Ethanol	2nd Gen. feedstock	Biogenic	Pretreatment/hydrolysis step and Fermentation	Grid mix electricity	EtOH_b_FR_2ndgen_gm_
103	Ethanol	Ethanol	3rd Gen. feedstock	Biogenic	Fermentation	Grid mix electricity	EtOH_b_FR_3rdgen_gm_
104	Hydrogen	Hydrogen	Natural Gas	Fossil	Steam Methane Reformation of Natural Gas	Grid mix electricity	H2_f_SMR_gm
105	Hydrogen	Hydrogen	Natural Gas	Fossil	Steam Methane Reformation of Natural Gas with Carbon Capture and long-term storage	Grid mix electricity	H2_f_SMR_CCS_gm
106	Hydrogen	Hydrogen	Natural Gas	Fossil	Methane Pyrolysis into carbon and hydrogen	Grid mix electricity	H2_f_MPO_gm

| 序号 | 燃料类型 | | 原料结构 | | 转化/生产过程 | | 燃料路径代码 |
	组别	燃料类型	原料类型	性质/碳源	加工类型	加工中使用的能量	
99	甲醇	甲醇	CO_2+H_2	CO_2：生物点源碳捕获 H_2：来自可再生电力	甲醇合成	并网电力	MeOH_bCO$_2$_rH$_2$_MS_gm
100	甲醇	甲醇	CO_2+H_2	CO_2：生物点源碳捕获 H_2：工业副产氢	甲醇合成	并网电力	MeOH_bCO$_2$_ibpH$_2$_MS_gm
101	乙醇	乙醇	第一代原料	生物源	发酵	并网电力	EtOH_b_FR_1stgen_gm_
102	乙醇	乙醇	第二代原料	生物源	预处理/水解步骤和发酵	并网电力	EtOH_b_FR_2ndgen_gm_
103	乙醇	乙醇	第三代原料	生物源	发酵	并网电力	EtOH_b_FR_3rdgen_gm_
104	氢	氢	天然气	化石	天然气的蒸汽甲烷重整	并网电力	H$_2$_f_SMR_gm
105	氢	氢	天然气	化石	天然气的蒸汽甲烷重整及碳捕获和长期储存	并网电力	H$_2$_f_SMR_CCS_gm
106	氢	氢	天然气	化石	甲烷裂解成碳和氢	并网电力	H$_2$_f_MPO_gm

Order	Group	Fuel type	Feedstock structure		Conversion/Production process		Fuel Pathway Code
			Feedstock Type	Nature/Carbon Source	Process Type	Energy used in the process	
107	Hydrogen	Hydrogen	Coal	Fossil	Gasification or Carbonization of Coal	Grid mix electricity	H2_f_G_gm
108	Hydrogen	Hydrogen	Coal	Fossil	Gasification or Carbonization of Coal with Carbon Capture and long-term storage	Grid mix electricity	H2_f_G_CCS_gm
109	Hydrogen	Hydrogen	2nd Gen. feedstock	Biogenic	Gasification of biomass and Syngas separation with Point Source Carbon Capture (PSCC) and long-term storage	Grid mix electricity	H2_b_G_SS_CCS_2ndgen_gm_
110	Hydrogen	Hydrogen	Water + Electricity	Renewable	Dedicated Photovoltaic and/or Wind and/or other Electrolysis and liquefaction	Renewable electricity	LH2_EL_r_Liquefied
111	Hydrogen	Hydrogen	Water + Electricity	Fossil/Renewable	Electrolysis and liquefaction	Grid mix electricity	LH2_EL_gm_Liquefied
112	Hydrogen	Hydrogen	Water + Electricity	Nuclear	Thermochemical Cycles or Electrolysis and liquefaction	Nuclear	LH2_EL_n_Liquefied
113	Hydrogen	Hydrogen		Industrial by-product hydrogen		Grid mix electricity	LH2__ibp_gm_Liquefied
114	Ammonia	Ammonia	Natural Gas	Fossil	Methane Pyrolysis into pure carbon and hydrogen and Haber Bosch process	Grid mix electricity	NH3_f_MPO_HB_gm

序号	组别	燃料类型	原料结构		转化/生产过程		燃料路径代码
			原料类型	性质/碳源	加工类型	加工中使用的能量	
107	氢	氢	煤	化石	煤的气化或碳化	并网电力	H₂_f_G_gm
108	氢	氢	煤	化石	煤的气化或碳化及碳捕获和长期储存	并网电力	H₂_f_G_CCS_gm
109	氢	氢	第二代原料	生物源	生物质气化和合成气分离及点源碳捕获（PSCC）和长期储存	并网电力	H2_b_G_SS_CCS_2ndgen_gm_
110	氢	氢	水＋电	可再生	专用光伏和/或风能和/或其他电解和液化	可再生电力	LH2_EL_r_Liquefied
111	氢	氢	水＋电	化石/可再生	电解和液化	并网电力	LH2_EL_gm_Liquefied
112	氢	氢	水＋电	核	热化学循环或电解和液化	核	LH2_EL_n_Liquefied
113	氢	氢		工业副产氢		并网电力	LH2_ibp_gm_Liquefied
114	氨	氨	天然气	化石	甲烷热解成纯碳和纯氢哈伯-博世法	并网电力	NH3_f_MPO_HB_gm

Order	Group	Fuel type	Feedstock structure		Conversion/Production process		Fuel Pathway Code
			Feedstock Type	Nature/Carbon Source	Process Type	Energy used in the process	
115	Ammonia	Ammonia	Natural Gas	Fossil	Steam Methane Reformation of Natural Gas and Haber Bosch process	Grid mix electricity	NH3_f_SMR_HB_gm
116	Ammonia	Ammonia	Natural Gas	Fossil	Steam Methane Reformation of Natural Gas with Point Source Carbon Capture (PSCC) and long-term storage and Haber Bosch process	Grid mix electricity	NH3_f_SMR_HB_CCS_gm
117	Ammonia	Ammonia	Coal	Fossil	Gasification of Coal and Haber Bosch process	Grid mix electricity	NH3_f_G_HB_gm
118	Ammonia	Ammonia	Coal	Fossil	Gasification of Coal with Carbon Capture and long-term storage and Haber Bosch process	Grid mix electricity	NH3_f_G_HB_CCS_gm
119	Ammonia	Ammonia	2nd Gen. feedstock	Biogenic	Gasification	Grid mix electricity	NH3_b_G_2ndgen_gm_
120	Ammonia	Ammonia	N2 + H2	N2: separated with renewable electricity H2: produced from renewable electricity	Haber Bosch process	Grid mix electricity	NH3_rN2_rH2_HB_gm

序号	组别	燃料类型	原料结构		转化 / 生产过程		燃料路径代码
			原料类型	性质 / 碳源	加工类型	加工中使用的能量	
115	氨	氨	天然气	化石	天然气的蒸汽甲烷重整和哈伯－博世法	并网电力	$NH_3\_f\_SMR\_HB\_gm$
116	氨	氨	天然气	化石	天然气的蒸汽甲烷重整及点源碳捕获（PSCC）、长期储存和哈伯－博世法	并网电力	$NH_3\_f\_SMR\_HB\_CCS\_gm$
117	氨	氨	煤	化石	煤的气化和哈伯－博世法	并网电力	$NH_3\_f\_G\_HB\_gm$
118	氨	氨	煤	化石	煤的气化及碳捕获和长期储存和哈伯－博世法	并网电力	$NH_3\_f\_G\_HB\_CCS\_gm$
119	氨	氨	第二代原料	生物源	气化	并网电力	$NH_3\_b\_G\_2ndgen\_gm\_$
120	氨	氨	N_2+H_2	N_2: 由可再生电力分离 H_2: 由可再生电力产生	哈伯－博世法	并网电力	$NH_3\_rN_2\_rH_2\_HB\_gm$

| Order | Group | Fuel type | Feedstock structure | | Conversion/Production process | | Fuel Pathway Code |
			Feedstock Type	Nature/Carbon Source	Process Type	Energy used in the process	
121	Ammonia	Ammonia	$N_2 + H_2$	N2: separated with renewable electricity H2: Fossil Steam Methane Reformation	Haber Bosch process	Grid mix electricity	NH3_rN2_fH2_HB_gm
122	Ammonia	Ammonia	$N_2 + H_2$	N2: separated with renewable electricity H2: Industrial by-product hydrogen	Haber Bosch process	Grid mix electricity	NH3_rN2_ibpH2_HB_gm
123	Ammonia	Ammonia	$N_2 + H_2$	N2: separated with grid mix electricity H2: Fossil Steam Methane Reformation	Thermochemical Cycles or Electrolysis	Nuclear	NH3_gmN2_fH2_EL_n
124	Ammonia	Ammonia	$N_2 + H_2$	N2: separated with grid mix electricity H2: produced from renewable electricity	Thermochemical Cycles or Electrolysis	Nuclear	NH3_gmN2_rH2_EL_n
125	Ammonia	Ammonia	$N_2 + H_2$	N2: separated with grid mix electricity H2: Industrial by-product hydrogen	Thermochemical Cycles or Electrolysis	Nuclear	NH3_gmN2_ibpH2_EL_n
126	Electricity	Electricity		Fossil/Renewable	-	Grid mix electricity	Electricity_gm

序号	组别 燃料类型	燃料类型	原料结构 原料类型	原料结构 性质/碳源	转化/生产过程 加工类型	转化/生产过程 加工中使用的能量	燃料路径代码
121	氨	氨	N_2+H_2	N_2: 由可再生电力分离 H_2: 化石蒸汽甲烷重整	哈伯-博世法	并网电力	$NH_3\_rN_2\_fH_2\_HB\_gm$
122	氨	氨	N_2+H_2	N_2: 由可再生电力分离 H_2: 工业副产氢	哈伯-博世法	并网电力	$NH_3\_rN_2\_ibpH_2\_HB\_gm$
123	氨	氨	N_2+H_2	N_2: 由并网电力分离 H_2: 化石蒸汽甲烷重整	热化学循环或电解	核	$NH_3\_gmN_2\_fH_2\_EL\_n$
124	氨	氨	N_2+H_2	N_2: 由并网电力分离 H_2: 由可再生电力产生	热化学循环或电解	核	$NH_3\_gmN_2\_rH_2\_EL\_n$
125	氨	氨	N_2+H_2	N_2: 由并网电力分离 H_2: 工业副产氢	热化学循环或电解	核	$NH_3\_gmN_2\_ibpH_2\_EL\_n$
126	电	电		化石/可再生	—	并网电力	$Electricity\_gm$

Order	Group	Feedstock structure		Conversion/Production process		Fuel Pathway Code
		Feedstock Type	Nature/Carbon Source	Process Type	Energy used in the process	
127	Electricity	Electricity		Renewable	Dedicated Photovoltaic and/or Wind and/or other	Renewable electricity	Electricity_renewable
128	Wind propulsion					

序号	组别	燃料类型	原料结构		转化／生产过程		燃料路径代码
			原料类型	性质／碳源	加工类型	加工中使用的能量	
127	电	电		可再生	专用光伏和／或风能和／或其他	可再生电力	Electricity_renewable
128	风力推进						

APPENDIX 2

INITIAL DEFAULT EMISSION FACTORS PER FUEL PATHWAY CODE

Order	Fuel type	Fuel Pathway Code	WtT GHG intensity (gCO2eq/MJ)	LCV (MJ/g)	Energy Converter	C_f CO2 (gCO2/g fuel)	C_f CH4 (gCH4/g fuel)	C_f N2O (gN2O/g fuel)	C_{slip}/C_{fug} (mass %)	e_c gCO2eq/g fuel	TtW GHG intensity (gCO2eq/MJ)	NOTE
1	Heavy Fuel Oil (ISO 8217 Grades RME, RMG and RMK, 0.10 < S ≤ 0.50%)	HFO(VLSFO)_f_SR_gm	16.8	0.0402	ALL ICEs	3.114	0.00005	0.00018				Resolution MEPC.364(79) Fourth IMO GHG study
2	Heavy Fuel Oil (ISO 8217 Grades RME, RMG and RMK exceeding 0.50% S)	HFO(HSHFO)_f_SR_gm	14.1	0.0402	ALL ICEs	3.114	0.00005	0.00018				Resolution MEPC.364(79) Fourth IMO GHG study
3	Light Fuel Oil (ISO 8217 Grades RMA, RMB and RMD maximum 0.10% S)	LFO(ULSFO)_f_SR_gm		0.0412	ALL ICEs	3.151	0.00005	0.00018				Resolution MEPC.364(79) Fourth IMO GHG study
4	Light Fuel Oil (ISO 8217 Grades RMA, RMB and RMD, 0.10 < S ≤ 0.50%)	LFO(VLSFO)_f_SR_gm		0.0412	ALL ICEs	3.151	0.00005	0.00018				Resolution MEPC.364(79) Fourth IMO GHG study

附录 2

每个燃料路径代码的初始默认认排放因子

序号	燃料类型	燃料路径代码	上船前温室气体强度（gCO$_{2eq}$/J）	LCV（MJ/g）	能量转化器	C$_f$CO$_2$（gCO$_2$/g燃料）	C$_f$ CH$_4$（gCH$_4$/g燃料）	C$_f$ N$_2$O（gN$_2$O/g燃料）	C$_{slip}$/C$_{fug}$（质量%）	e$_c$ gCO$_{2eq}$/g燃料	船端温室气体强度（gCO$_{2eq}$/MJ）	备注
1	重油（ISO 8217 等级 RME、RMG 和 RMK，0.10<S ≤ 0.50%）	HFO（VLSFO）_f_SR_gm	16.8	0.040 2	所有内燃机	3.114	0.000 05	0.000 18				第 MEPC.364（79）号决议《第四次国际海事组织温室气体研究》
2	重油（ISO 8217 等级 RME、RMG 和 RMK 超过 0.50% S）	HFO(HSHFO)_f_SR_gm	14.9	0.040 2	所有内燃机	3.114	0.000 05	0.000 18				第 MEPC.364（79）号决议《第四次国际海事组织温室气体研究》
3	轻质燃油（ISO8217 等级 RMA、RMB 和 RMD 最高 0.10% S）	LFO(ULSFO)_f_SR_gm		0.041 2	所有内燃机	3.151	0.000 05	0.000 18				第 MEPC.364（79）号决议《第四次国际海事组织温室气体研究》
4	轻质燃油（ISO8217 等级 RMA、RMB 和 RMD，0.10<S ≤ 0.50%）	LFO（VLSFO）_f_SR_gm		0.041 2	所有内燃机	3.151	0.000 05	0.000 18				第 MEPC.364（79）号决议《第四次国际海事组织温室气体研究》

Order	Fuel type	Fuel Pathway Code	WtT GHG intensity (gCO$_{2eq}$/MJ)	LCV (MJ/g)	Energy Converter	C$_f$ CO$_2$ (gCO$_2$/g fuel)	C$_f$ CH$_4$ (gCH$_4$/g fuel)	C$_f$ N$_2$O (gN$_2$O/g fuel)	C$_{slip}$/C$_{fug}$ (mass %)	e$_c$ gCO$_{2eq}$/g fuel	TtW GHG intensity (gCO$_{2eq}$/MJ)	NOTE
5	Marine Diesel/Gas Oil (ISO 8217 Grades DMX, DMA, DMZ and DMB maximum 0.10 % S)	MDO/MGO(ULSFO)_f_SR_gm	17.7	0.0427	ALL ICEs	3.206	0.00005	0.00018				Resolution MEPC.364(79) Fourth IMO GHG study
6	Marine Diesel/Gas Oil (ISO 8217 Grades DMX, DMA, DMZ and DMB, 0.10 < S ≤ 0.50%)	MDO/MGO(VLSFO)_f_SR_gm		0.0427	ALL ICEs	3.206	0.00005	0.00018				Resolution MEPC.364(79) Fourth IMO GHG study
11	Liquefied Petroleum Gas (Propane)	LPG(Propane)_f_SR_gm		0.0463	ALL ICEs	3.000	0.00005	0.00018				Resolution MEPC.364(79) Fourth IMO GHG study
21	Liquefied Petroleum Gas (Butane)	LPG(Butane)_f_SR_gm		0.0457	ALL ICEs	3.030	0.00005	0.00018				Resolution MEPC.364(79) Fourth IMO GHG study

序号	燃料类型	燃料路径代码	上船前温室气体强度（gCO₂eq/J）	LCV（MJ/g）	能量转化器	$C_f CO_2$（gCO₂/g 燃料）	$C_f CH_4$（gCH₄/g 燃料）	$C_f N_2O$（gN₂O/g 燃料）	C_{slip}/C_{flug}（质量%）	e_c gCO₂eq/g 燃料	船端温室气体强度（gCO₂eq/MJ）	备注
5	船用柴油/轻柴油（ISO 8217 等级 DMX, DMA, DMZ 和 DMB 最高 0.10% S）	M D O / M G O（ULSFO）_f_SR_gm	17.7	0.042 7	所有内燃机	3.206	0.000 05	0.000 18				第 MEPC.364（79）号决议《第四次国际海事组织温室气体研究》
6	船用柴油/轻柴油（ISO 8217 等级 DMX, DMA, DMZ 和 DMB, 0.10<S ≤ 0.50%）	MDO/MGO(VLSFO)_f_SR_gm		0.042 7	所有内燃机	3.206	0.000 05	0.000 18				第 MEPC.364（79）号决议《第四次国际海事组织温室气体研究》
11	液化石油气（丙烷）	LPG（Propane）_f_SR_gm		0.046 3	所有内燃机	3.000	0.000 05	0.000 18				第 MEPC.364（79）号决议《第四次国际海事组织温室气体研究》
21	液化石油气（丁烷）	LPG（Butane）_f_SR_gm		0.045 7	所有内燃机	3.030	0.000 05	0.000 18				第 MEPC.364（79）号决议《第四次国际海事组织温室气体研究》

Order	Fuel type	Fuel Pathway Code	WtT GHG intensity (gCO$_{2eq}$/MJ)	LCV (MJ/g)	Energy Converter	C$_f$ CO$_2$ (gCO$_2$/g fuel)	C$_f$ CH$_4$ (gCH$_4$/g fuel)	C$_f$ N$_2$O (gN$_2$O/g fuel)	C$_{slip}$/C$_{fug}$ (mass %)	e$_c$ gCO$_{2eq}$/g fuel	TtW GHG intensity (gCO$_2$eq /MJ)	NOTE
31	Liquefied Natural Gas (Methane)	LNG_f_SLP_gm		0.0480	LNG Otto (dual fuel medium speed)	2.750	0	0.00011	3.5/-			Resolution MEPC.364(79) Fourth IMO GHG study
					LNG Otto (dual fuel slow speed)				1.7/-			
					LNG Diesel (dual fuel slow speed)				0.15/-			
					LBSI (Lean-Burn Spark-Ignited)				2.6/-			
					Steam Turbines and boilers				0.01/-			

序号	燃料类型	燃料路径代码	上船前温室气体强度（gCO$_{2eq}$/J）	LCV（MJ/g）	能量转化器	C$_f$CO$_2$（gCO$_2$/g 燃料）	C$_f$CH$_4$（gCH$_4$/g 燃料）	C$_f$N$_2$O（gN$_2$O/g 燃料）	C$_{slip}$/C$_{flug}$（质量%）	e$_c$ gCO$_{2eq}$/g 燃料	船端温室气体强度（gCO$_{2eq}$/MJ）	备注
31	液化天然气（甲烷）	LNG_f_SLP_gm		0.048 0	LNG 奥托循环式（双燃料中速）	2.750	0	0.000 11	3.5/–			第 MEPC.364（79）号决议《第四次国际海事组织温室气体研究》
					LNG 奥托循环式（双燃料低速）				1.7/–			
					LNG 狄塞尔循环式（双燃料低速）				0.15/–			
					LBSI（稀燃火花点火）				2.6/–			
					蒸汽涡轮和锅炉				0.01/–			

Order	Fuel type	Fuel Pathway Code	WtT GHG intensity (gCO$_2$eq/MJ)	LCV (MJ/g)	Energy Converter	Cf CO$_2$ (gCO$_2$/g fuel)	Cf CH$_4$ (gCH$_4$/g fuel)	Cf N$_2$O (gN$_2$O/g fuel)	Cslip/Cfug (mass %)	ec gCO$_{2eq}$/g fuel	TtW GHG intensity (gCO$_2$eq/MJ)	NOTE
33	Liquefied Natural Gas (Methane)	LNG_b_AD_gm			LNG Otto (dual fuel medium speed)							
					LNG Otto (dual fuel slow speed)							
					LNG Diesel (dual fuel slow speed)	2.750						
					LBSI (Lean-Burn Spark-Ignited)							
					Steam Turbines and boilers							
62	Diesel (FAME)	FAME_b_TRE_gm_2ndgen	20.8	0.0372	ALL ICEs							
77	Renewable Diesel (HVO)	HVO_b_HD_gm_2ndgen	14.9	0.044	ALL ICEs							

序号	燃料类型	燃料路径代码	上船前温室气体强度（gCO$_{2eq}$/J）	LCV（MJ/g）	能量转化器	C$_f$CO$_2$（gCO$_2$/g 燃料）	C$_f$ CH$_4$（gCH$_4$/g 燃料）	C$_f$ N$_2$O（gN$_2$O/g 燃料）	C$_{slip}$/C$_{flug}$（质量%）	e$_c$ gCO$_{2eq}$/g 燃料	船端温室气体强度（gCO$_{2eq}$/MJ）	备注
33	液化天然气（甲烷）	LNG_b_AD_gm			LNG 奥托循环模式（双燃料中速）							
					LNG 奥托循环模式（双燃料低速）							
					LNG 狄塞尔循环模式（双燃料低速）	2.750						
					LBSI（稀燃火花点火）							
					蒸汽涡轮和锅炉							
62	柴油（FAME）	FAME_b_TRE_gm_2ndgen	20.8	0.037 2	所有内燃机							
77	可再生柴油（HVO）	HVO_b_HD_gm_2ndgen	14.9	0.044	所有内燃机							

Order	Fuel type	Fuel Pathway Code	WtT GHG intensity (gCO$_{2eq}$/MJ)	LCV (MJ/g)	Energy Converter	C$_f$ CO$_2$ (gCO$_2$/g fuel)	C$_f$ CH$_4$ (gCH$_4$/g fuel)	C$_f$ N$_2$O (gN$_2$O/g fuel)	C$_{slip}$/C$_{fug}$ (mass %)	e$_c$ gCO$_{2eq}$/g fuel	TtW GHG intensity (gCO$_{2eq}$/MJ)	NOTE
105	Hydrogen	H2_f_SMR_C CS_gm		0.12	ALL ICEs	0						
					Fuel cell							
121	Ammonia	NH3_rN2_fH2 _HB_gm		0.0186	ALL ICEs	0						
					Fuel cell							

序号	燃料类型	燃料路径代码	上船前温室气体强度（gCO$_{2eq}$/J）	LCV（MJ/g）	能量转化器	C$_f$CO$_2$（gCO$_2$/g燃料）	C$_f$CH$_4$（gCH$_4$/g燃料）	C$_f$N$_2$O（gN$_2$O/g燃料）	C$_{slip}$/C$_{fug}$（质量%）	e$_c$ gCO$_{2eq}$/g燃料	船端温室气体强度（gCO$_{2eq}$/MJ）	备注
105	氢	H2_f_SMR_C CS_gm		0.12	所有内燃机 燃料电池	0						
121	氨	NH3_rN2_fH2 _HB_gm		0.018 6	所有内燃机 燃料电池	0						

APPENDIX 3

ABBREVIATIONS AND GLOSSARY

Abbreviations

AR – IPCC Assessment Report

BDN – Bunkering Delivery Note

C_f – Emission conversion factors $C_{fCO2/CH4/N2O}$ (g GHG ($CO_2/CH_4/N_2O$)/g fuel) for emissions of the combustion and/or oxidation process, including the fuel with relevant GWP effect resulting from the combustion energy conversion

CH_4 – Methane

CO_2 – Carbon dioxide

CO_{2eq} – Carbon dioxide equivalent

CCS – Carbon Capture and Storage

CCU – Carbon Capture and Utilization

DAC – Direct Air Capture

DCS – IMO ship fuel oil consumption Data Collection System

DLUC – Direct Land Use Change

FLL – Fuel Lifecycle Label

GHG – Greenhouse gas

GWP – Global Warming Potential

ILUC – Indirect Land Use Change

IPCC – Intergovernmental Panel on Climate Change

LCA – Life Cycle Assessment

LCV – Lower Calorific Value (MJ/g fuel)

NMVOC – Non-Methane Volatile Organic Compounds

N_2O – Nitrous oxide

NTC – NO_x Technical Code

RFNBO – Renewable Fuels of Non-Biological Origin

SLCF – Short-Lived Climate Forcers

TtW – Tank-to-Wake

Wt I – Well-to-Tank

WtW – Well-to-Wake

VOC – Volatile Organic Compounds

OPS – Onshore Power Supply

Glossary

Co-product – an outcome of a production process, which has a relevant economic value and elastic supply (intended as the existence of a clear evidence of the causal link between feedstock market value and the quantity of feedstock that can be produced).

Biomass – biomass is renewable organic material that comes from plants and animals.

Renewables – any form of energy from solar, geophysical or biological sources that is replenished by natural processes at a rate that equals or exceeds its rate of use. Renewables are obtained from the continuing or repetitive flows of energy occurring in the natural environment and includes low-carbon technologies such as solar energy, hydropower, wind, tide and waves and ocean thermal energy, as well as renewable fuels such as biomass.

Global Warming Potential – global warming potential indicates the potential of a greenhouse gas to trap extra heat in the atmosphere over time in relation to carbon dioxide. The enhanced heat trapping in the atmosphere (i.e. the "greenhouse effect") is caused by the absorption of

附录 3

缩写和术语

缩写

AR	一IPCC 评估报告
BDN	一燃油交付单
C_f	一用于燃烧和 / 或氧化过程排放的排放转化因子 $C_{f(CO2/CH4/N2O)}$（gGHG（CO_2/CH_4/N_2O）/g fuel），包括燃烧能量转化产生的具有相关全球变暖潜势（GWP）效应的燃料
CH_4	一甲烷
CO_2	一二氧化碳
CO_{2eq}	一二氧化碳当量
CCS	一碳捕获和存储
CCU	一碳捕获与利用
DAC	一直接空气捕获
DCS	一船舶燃油消耗数据收集系统
DLUC	一直接土地利用变化
FLL	一燃料生命周期标签
GHG	一温室气体
GWP	一全球变暖潜势
ILUC	一间接土地利用变化
IPCC	一政府间气候变化专门委员会
LCA	一全生命周期评估
LCV	一低热值（MJ/gfuel）
NMVOC	一非甲烷挥发性有机化合物
N_2O	一一氧化二氮
NTC	一NO_x 技术规则
RFNBO	一非生物来源可再生燃料
SLCF	一短期气候驱动因子
TtW	一船端
WtT	一上船前
WtW	一全生命周期
VOC	一挥发性有机化合物
OPS	一岸电

术语

副产品—生产过程的结果，具有相关的经济价值和弹性供应（旨在作为原料市场价值与可生产的原料数量之间存在因果关系的明确证据）。

生物质—生物质是来自植物和动物的可再生有机材料。

可再生能源—通过自然过程以等于或超过其使用率的速度补充的任何形式的太阳能、地球物理或生物能源。可再生能源从自然环境中持续或重复的能量流动中获得，包括太阳能、水电、风能、潮汐能和海洋热能等低碳技术，以及生物质等可再生燃料。

全球变暖潜势—全球变暖潜势显示了一种温室气体相对于二氧化碳在大气中随着时间推移积累额外热量的潜势。大气中热量吸收的增强（即"温室效应"）是由特定气体吸收红外

infrared radiation by a given gas. The GWP also depends on the atmospheric lifetime of a gas, and the time-horizon considered (for example, GWP20 is based on the energy absorbed over 20 years, whereas GWP100 is based on the energy absorbed over 100 years). Each greenhouse gas has a specific global warming potential which is used to calculate the CO_2-equivalent (CO_{2eq}).

Land Use Change – Production of bio-based fuels leads to land use change (LUC). LUC can be classified as direct LUC (DLUC) and indirect LUC (ILUC).

Life Cycle Assessment (LCA) framework – life cycle assessment determines the potential environmental impacts of products, processes or services from cradle to grave, e.g. from acquisition/extraction of raw materials through to processing, transport, use and disposal.

System boundaries – The system boundary determines which entities (unit processes) are inside the system and which are outside. It essentially determines which life cycle/supply chain stages and processes are included in the assessment and need to be in accordance with the goal and scope of the study.

System expansion – ISO 14040 recommends the use of system expansion whenever possible. System expansion is part of the consequential LCA method that seeks to capture change in environmental impact as a consequence of a certain activity.

Well-to-Wake – WtW studies estimate the energy requirements and the resulting greenhouse gas (GHG) emissions in the production of a fuel and its use in a ship, based on the broader life cycle assessment (LCA) methodology. The term 'Well' is used for fuels from all sources, because although the term is most applicable to conventional crude oil resources, it is widely used and understood.

Onshore power supply – the system to supply electricity to ships at berth, at low or high voltage, alternate or direct current, including ship-side and port-side installations, when feeding any of the ship's electrical distribution switchboards for powering hotel and service workloads or charging secondary batteries.

辐射引起的。GWP 还取决于气体的大气寿命和所考虑的时间范围（例如，GWP20 是基于 20 年吸收的能量，而 GWP100 是基于 100 年吸收的能量）。每种温室气体都有一个特定的全球变暖潜势，用来计算二氧化碳当量（CO_{2eq}）。

土地利用变化—生物燃料的生产导致土地利用变化（LUC）。LUC 可分为直接土地利用变化（DLUC）和间接土地利用变化（ILUC）。

生命周期评估（LCA）框架—生命周期评估确定产品、过程或服务从摇篮到坟墓的潜在环境影响，例如从原材料的获取/开采到加工、运输、使用和处置。

系统边界—系统边界决定了哪些实体（单元过程）在系统内部，哪些在系统外部。它本质上决定了哪些生命周期/供应链阶段和过程包括在评估中，并且需要与研究的目标和范围相一致。

系统扩展—ISO14040 建议尽可能使用系统扩展。系统扩展是相应的全生命周期分析方法的一部分，该方法寻求捕捉环境影响的变化，以作为特定活动的结果。

全生命周期（Well-to-Wake）—全生命周期研究基于更广泛的全生命周期评估（LCA）方法，估计燃料生产和在船上使用过程中的能源需求和由此产生的温室气体（GHG）排放。"Well"一词适用于所有来源的燃料，因为尽管该术语最适用于常规原油资源，但已被广泛使用和理解。

岸电供应—向停泊的船舶提供低压或高压、交流电或直流电力的系统，包括船载和岸基装置，向船舶任何配电板输送电力，从而为船上住宿设施和服务工作负载供电或为蓄电池充电。

APPENDIX 4

TEMPLATE FOR WELL-TO-TANK DEFAULT EMISSION FACTOR SUBMISSION

INTRODUCTION

1   This template aims at collecting and presenting in a clear and structured manner the input data used to calculate a "default emission factor" for a specific "feedstock-to-fuel" pathway according to the methodology of the *2024 Guidelines on Life Cycle GHG Intensity of Marine Fuels (2024 LCA Guidelines)*, adopted on 22 March 2024 through resolution MEPC.391(81).[24] Only one default emission factor should be proposed per template form, i.e. to propose two emission default factors, two separate template forms should be filled. A "default emission factor" represents the quantitative results of the assessed greenhouse gas intensity (gCO_{2eq}/MJ) of a feedstock-to-fuel value chain. The default emission factor is not meant to represent the best available way to produce a fuel. It is a value describing a feedstock production, collection and transportation for conversion to an average/typical/standard plant, located in a generic region.[24] A default emission factor does not have to capture process improvement, with respect to current production, nor innovative technologies.[25] The goal of default emission factor is, at least, twofold:

    .1   allow for fair comparison of GHG intensity among different technologies and fuel conversion pathways, where emissions resulting from some of the parameters in the WtT equation are set at zero by default (i.e. e_{sca}, e_l, e_{ccs}); In other words, allow for a general comparison among different fuel options and technologies;

    .2   allow for operators to demonstrate actual life cycle of greenhouse gas emissions compared to the default life cycle emissions for the same feedstock-to-fuel pathway, through a certification process. The period of validity for the certification should be defined along with the rules and procedures of functioning of the certification.

The template provides full coverage of all elements necessary to define a default emission factor. It can be adapted (e.g. by not providing input data to each and every element it comprises) and complemented with additional information.

The LCA Guidelines specify in paragraph 4.4 that the WtT GHG emission factor (gCO_{2eq}/MJ(LCV) fuel or electricity) is calculated according to Equation (1).

$$\text{Equation (1)}\ GHG_{WtT} = e_{fecu} + e_l + e_p + e_{td} - e_{sca} - e_{ccs}$$

while paragraph 9.4 specifies that "Emissions related to carbon stock changes caused by direct land-use change (DLUC) (e_l) and emissions savings from soil carbon accumulation via improved agricultural management (e_{sca}) are considered as zero for the establishment of the default emission factors. Similarly, this is the case also for the parameters related to carbon capture and storage (CCS), which require further development." Accordingly, it should be noted that the default emission factors identified through the use of this submission template

---

[24]   Default emission factors reflect the performance of feedstock-fuel pathways across world regions and States. Project-specific values certified according to relevant procedures agreed and adopted at IMO can be used as actual emission factors.

[25]   In case of immature technologies, literature and modelling sources could be used, limited to the conversion process. However, the principle that this could be used as input data to refine/complete/revise emission factors as a future technology matures should be kept.

附录4

上船前默认排放因子提交模板

引言

1 本模板旨在根据 2024 年 3 月 22 日以第 MEPC.391（81）号决议通过的《2024 年船用燃料生命周期温室气体强度导则》（2024 LCA 导则）的方法，以清晰和结构化的方式收集和呈现用于计算特定"原料到燃料"途径的"默认排放因子"的输入数据。[24] 每份格式模板只应提出一个默认排放因子，即：要提出两个默认排放因子，应分别填写两份模板。"默认排放因子"代表了从原料到燃料价值链的温室气体强度（gCO_{2eq}/MJ）评估的定量结果。默认排放因子并不代表生产燃料的最佳可用方式。它是一个值，该值描述原料的生产、收集与运输，以位于一般区域内的平均/典型/标准工厂进行转化[24]。默认排放因子无须捕获目前生产的过程改进，也无须捕获创新技术[25]。默认排放因子的目标至少有两部分：

- .1 能对不同技术和燃料转化途径之间的温室气体强度进行公平比较，其中上船前公式中某些参数导致的排放默认设为零（即 e_{sca}，e_l，e_{ccs}）；换句话说，能在不同的燃料选择和技术之间进行一般比较；

- .2 通过认证过程，使经营人能将相同原料到燃料路径的实际生命周期温室气体排放与默认生命周期排放进行比较。认证有效期应与认证规则和程序一起确定。

本模板完整覆盖了定义默认排放因子所需的所有要素。对模板可以进行调整（例如：无须向模板所包含的每个要素提供输入数据），并补充额外信息。

LCA 导则第 4.4 段规定按公式（1）计算上船前温室气体排放因子（gCO_{2eq}/MJ$_{(LCV}$ 燃料或电力）。

$$公式（1）\ GHG_{WtT} = e_{fecu} + e_l + e_p + e_{td} - e_{sca} - e_{ccs}$$

第 9.4 段规定，在建立默认排放因子时，与直接土地利用变化（DLUC）引起的碳储量 变化相关的排放（e_l）和通过改善农业管理从土壤碳积累中节省的排放（e_{sca}）视为零。同样，与碳捕获与封存（CCS）相关的参数也需要进一步制定。因此，应该注意的是，通过使用

---

[24] 默认排放因子反映了世界各区域和各国原料－燃料途径的情况。根据国际海事组织商定和通过的有关程序核证的项目特定值可用作实际排放系数。

[25] 在技术不成熟的情况下，可以使用文献和建模来源，但仅限于转化过程。但是，随着未来技术的成熟，这些可以作为输入数据来完善/补充/修订排放因子，这一原则应该保留。

will only be partially reflective of WtT emissions attributable to any given "feedstock-to-fuel" pathway and may vary as emissions by sources and/or removals by sinks within the system boundary are taken into account.

2   Once default emission factors fully reflecting WtT GHG emissions are developed in a future iteration of the LCA Guidelines, operators (e.g. fuel producers) that are in a position to prove actual GHG emissions, may seek certification for a project certified "actual value". Certified actual values may also be used for pathways not having a default WtT GHG emission factor listed in appendix 2 of the LCA Guidelines.

3   This template allows indicating a 0 (zero) value for elements of Equation (1) that are temporarily not quantified as explained in paragraph 1 above. Data submitted as required for the calculation of default WtT GHG emission factors, need to ensure quality in terms of: relevance,[26] adequacy,[27] completeness,[28] consistency,[29] reliability,[30] transparency and accessibility.[31] The template can also be partially completed, e.g. by providing data for specific steps of the pathway.

PATHWAY DESCRIPTION

4   This section should clearly present the pathway modelled, intended as the value chain related to the production of a finished fuel, with the aim for providing at least information on inter alia: the type of feedstock used, a description of the technology used for converting such feedstock in the final fuel, and any other relevant information that affects the calculation of emission factors, consistently with the system boundary of the LCA guidelines.

5   The default emission factors are based on the WtT methodology, aiming at evaluating the amount of GHG emissions attributable to the fuel production and distribution. The production steps to be included in the calculation of a WtT emission factor are shown in figure 2 below:

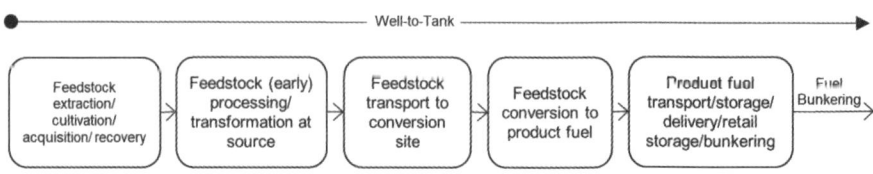

Figure 2 – Generic well-to-tank supply chain

The system boundaries defined for describing a specific feedstock-to-fuel pathway shall be in line with the definitions contained in the LCA guidelines.

Additional details and relevant information may be added in appendices, such as, production region, production capacity, age, etc. of facility or facilities.

[26]   Is the available data appropriate and reasonable in relation to the goal?

[27]   Does the data accurately describe the value chain under investigation? Are the uncertainties properly reported?

[28]   How completely does the data describe the value chain under investigation?

[29]   Is the data internally consistent? If there are redundant data values, do they have the same value?

[30]   Is the data regarded as valid/verifiable by the stakeholders?

[31]   Can the data be accessed and verified by a third party?

本模板确定的默认排放因子只能部分反映任一给定的"原料到燃料"路径的上船前排放，并且可能会随着系统边界内碳源排放和／或碳汇清除的考量而变化。

2 一旦在 LCA 导则的未来迭代中制定了充分反映上船前温室气体排放的默认排放因子，经营人（例如：燃料生产商）如要证明实际温室气体排放，可为项目进行"实际值"认证。经认证的实际值也可用于没有如 LCA 导则附录 2 中所列的默认上船前温室气体排放因子的路径。

3 本模板可对公式（1）中暂时未量化的要素设为 0（零）值，如上文第 1 段所述。计算默认上船前温室气体排放因子所需提交的数据需要在相关性[26]、充分性[27]、完整性[28]、一致性[29]、可靠性[30]、透明度和可用性[31]方面保证质量。本模板也可以部分完成，例如：为路径的特定步 骤提供数据。

路径描述

4 本节应清楚地展示建模的路径，旨在作为与成品燃料生产相关的价值链，其目的是至少提供以下信息：所使用的原料类型、将此类原料转化为最终燃料的技术说明，以及任何其他影响排放因子计算的相关信息，与 LCA 导则的系统边界保持一致。

5 默认排放因子基于上船前方法，旨在评估燃料生产和分配导致的温室气体排放量。计算上船前排放因子需包括的生产步骤如下图 2 所示：

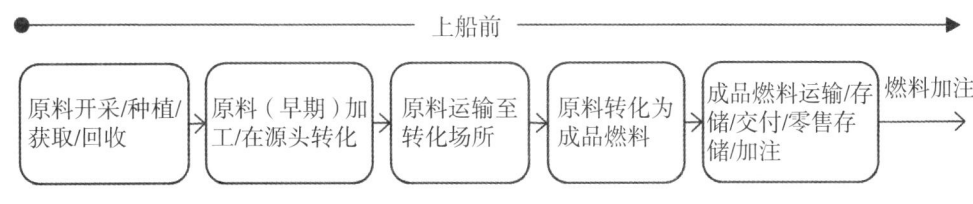

图 2 通用上船前供应链

为描述特定原料到燃料路径而定义的系统边界应与 LCA 导则中包含的定义一致。其他细节和相关信息可以在附录中添加，例如生产区域、生产能力、一个或多个设施的使用年限等。

[26] 可获得的数据相对于目标是否适当和合理？
[27] 数据是否准确描述了所调查的价值链？对不确定性是否进行了适当的报告？
[28] 数据对所调查价值链的描述的完整度？
[29] 数据内部是否一致？如果存在冗余数据值，它们的值是否相同？
[30] 利益相关者是否认为数据是有效的／可验证的？
[31] 数据是否可以被第三方访问和验证？

INPUT DESCRIPTION

6   This section should clearly present the input used for the modelling exercise.

7   The source of the data and of the model used should be reported, according to the indications about data quality provided in the LCA Guidelines.

8   Please inform if the LCA calculation has been developed in a particular modelling tool and in case of a positive answer, inform if any background information (information not listed below) has changed with respect to the standard data set and/or methodology used by the tool, and provide adequate justification for such change.

9   In order to provide guidance to fill the template, please see a worked example for a lipid feedstock production and conversion. The worked example is comprised of filled-in tables as necessary to report data, per pathway.

输入描述

6 本节应清楚呈现用于建模的输入。

7 应根据 LCA 导则中关于数据质量的指示，报告数据的来源和所使用的模型。

8 请说明是否已在特定的建模工具中开发 LCA 计算，如果是，请说明是否与标准数据集和 / 或工具所使用方法相关的任何背景信息（未在下面列出的信息）发生了变化，并为这种变化提供充分的理由。

9 作为填写模板的指导，请参见下列脂质原料生产和转化的示例。该示例包括了每个路径应报告数据的列表。

Table 1: e_{fecu} inputs and outputs for XXX feedstock

				XXXX, per dry kg	Data source/Model used	Observations
e_{fecu}	XXX feedstock	Agricultural Inputs	Total N (g)	...	zzz et al. 2010	(explicit the type of N fertilizer, in %. Example:Total N is represented by 50% of Urea, 30% of Ammonium Nitrate, and 20% of..)
			P_2O_5 (g)	...	ecoinvent	(explicit the type of P_2O_5 fertilizer)
			K_2O (g)	...	GREET	(explicit the type of K_2O fertilizer)
			Diesel (MJ)	...	...	
			Fugitive GHG emissions (e.g. CH_4) at feedstock extraction	...	...	
		per kg XXXX oil				
		Oil Extraction Inputs		Values	Data source/ Model used	
			Feedstock (g, dry)	...	zzz et al. 2010	
			NG (MJ)	...	ecoinvent	
			N-Hexane (MJ)	...	GREET	
			Electricity (MJ)	...	...	
			Fugitive GHG emissions (e.g. CH_4) at feedstock extraction	...	...	
			...	...	...	
		Oil Extraction Outputs	Co-product, zzz (g)	...	...	
			Protein cake from vegetable oil extraction	...	...	

表 1 XXX 原料的 e_{fecu} 输入和输出

				XXXX，每千克干重	使用的数据源/模型	备注
e_{fecu}	XXX 原料	农业输入	总 N（g）	…	zzz 等 .2010	（明确氮肥种类，单位为%。例：总氮由 50% 的尿素、30% 的硝酸铵和 20% 的……表示。）
			P_2O_5（g）	…	ecoinvent	（明确 P_2O_5 肥料种类）
			K_2O（g）	…	GREET	（明确 K_2O 肥料种类）
			柴油（MJ）	…	…	
			原料提取时的逸散性温室气体排放（如 CH_4）	…	…	
			每千克 XXXX 油			
		采油输入		值	使用的数据源/模型	
			原料（g，dry）	…	zzz 等 .2010	
			NG（MJ）	…	ecoinvent	
			正己烷（MJ）	…	GREET	
			电力（MJ）	…	…	
			原料提取时的逸散性温室气体排放（如 CH_4）	…	…	
			…	…	…	
		采油输出	副产品 zzz（g）	…	…	
			从植物油中提取的蛋白质饼	…	…	

Additional information:

Table 2: e_p inputs and outputs/losses for XXXX conversion process, including all the needed steps to pre-treat the feedstock in order to be able to convert it into the fuel, via the selected conversion process

		per MJ fuel	
		Values	Data source/model used
Inputs	Feedstock (g oil)	...	zzz et al. 2010
	NG (MJ)	...	ecoinvent
	H_2 (MJ)	*	GREET
	Electricity (MJ)[32]	...	...
	Explanatory remark: placeholder for key material inputs (e.g. chemicals, etc.)	...	...
Outputs	Co-product, propane mix (MJ)	**	...
	Co-product, naphtha (MJ)	**	...
	Co-product, xxxx (MJ)	**	...
	...	...	...
	Losses, e.g. fugitive CH_4 emissions	**	...

*H_2 derived from NG steam reforming is assumed to be default H_2 source, the emission factors of H_2 are modelled based on NG input; ** Inputs after allocation

Additional information:

Table 3: Inputs for regional electricity generation mixes [33]

	US (%)[1]	EU (%)[2]	India[3] (%)	xxx (%)[4]
Residual oil	...	...	...	...
Natural gas	...	...	...	...
Coal	...	...	...	...
Nuclear power	...	...	...	...
Biomass	...	...	...	...
Hydroelectric	...	...	...	...
Geothermal	...	...	...	...
Wind	...	...	...	...
Solar PV	...	...	...	...
Others	...	...	...	...

[1] GREET 20xx, [2] EEA, 20xx (EU electricity mix 20xx), [3] International Energy Agency 20xx, [4] IGES List of Grid Emission Factors

[32] Table 2 allows to detail information on electricity generation (which may be different from the regional mix).

[33] Alternatively, please provide a statement with a clear referenced indication of the Greenhouse gas Intensity of the grid (gCO2eq/kWh or gCO2eq/MJ), and provide the reference used.

附加信息：

表2 XXXX 转化过程的 e_p 输入和输出 / 损失，包括预处理原料所需的所有步骤，以便能够通过选定的转化过程将其转化为燃料

		每兆焦耳燃料	
		值	使用的数据源 / 模型
输入	原料（g oil）	…	zzz 等 . 2010
	NG（MJ）	…	ecoinvent
	H_2（MJ）	*	GREET
	电力（MJ）[32]	…	…
	解释性注释：关键材料输入（如化学品等）的占位符	…	…
输出	副产品，丙烷混合（MJ）	**	…
	副产品，石脑油（MJ）	**	…
	副产品，xxxx（MJ）	**	…
	…	…	…
	损失，例如逸散性 CH_4 排放	**	

* 假定天然气蒸汽重整产生的 H_2 为默认 H_2 来源，H_2 的排放因子基于天然气输入进行建模；
** 分配后的输入

附加信息：

表3 区域混合发电的输入 [33]

	美国（%）[1]	欧盟（%）[2]	印度[3]（%）	xxx（%）[4]
残油	…	…	…	…
天然气	…	…	…	…
煤	…	…	…	…
核能	…	…	…	…
生物质	…	…	…	…
水力发电	…	…	…	…
地热	…	…	…	…
风	…	…	…	…
太阳能光伏	…	…	…	…
其他	…	…	…	…

[1] GREET 20xx，[2] EEA，20xx（欧盟混合电力 20xx），[3] 国际能源署 20xx。[4] 电网排放因子 IGES 列表

[32] 表2 提供了有关发电的详细信息（可能与区域混合情况不同）。
[33] 或者请提供一份声明，明确指出电网的温室气体强度（gCO_{2eq}/kWh 或 gCO_{2eq}/MJ），并提供所使用的参考。

Additional information:

Table 4: e_{td} Emissions from Inputs and losses associated with the transportation of feedstock and fuels. In filling the table, please add the fuel used – In the "Data source/model used" please specify the type of fuel, the specific efficiency and energy converter, if available

		Feedstock Transportation		Data source/model used
e_{td} Inputs for Transport and Distribution	Distance (km)		xxx; xxx	
	Mode [34]	Heavy-duty truck; Train; Ship ; Barge; Rail; Pipeline; etc		
	Share (%)		yy; yy; yyy	
	Fuel Transportation			
	Distance (km)[35]		xxx; xxxx; xx	
	Mode	Heavy-duty truck; Train; Ship; Barge; Rail; Pipeline; etc		
	Share (%)		y; yy; yy	
	Fuel Distribution			
	Distance (km)		xx	
	Mode	Heavy-duty truck; Train; Ship; Barge; Rail; Pipeline; etc		
	Share (%)			
	...		...	
	Any other Transportation, Storage and Distribution emissions, including losses (e.g fugitive CH_4 emissions)			

---

[34] In case a mode of transport includes more fuels (e.g. diesel and natural gas) or various transport modes (e.g. track and ship), they should be properly reported in the calculation.

[35] Empty back-haul/return voyage(s) should be accounted in the calculation.

附加信息：

表 4　原料和燃料运输相关输入和损失产生的 e_{td} 排放。在填写表格时请在"使用的数据源 / 模型"中添加使用的燃料，请注明燃料类型、具体效率和能量转化器（如有）

		原料运输	使用的数据源 / 模型
运输和分配的 e_{td} 输入	距离（km）	xxx；xxx	
	模式[34]	重型卡车；火车；船；驳船；铁路；管路等	
	占比（%）	yy；yy；yyy	
		燃料运输	
	距离（km）[35]	xxx；xxxx；xx	
	模式	重型卡车；火车；船；驳船；铁路；管路等	
	占比（%）	y；yy；yy	
		燃料分配	
	距离（km）	xx	
	模式	重型卡车；火车；船；驳船；铁路；管路等	
	占比（%）		
	…	…	
	任何其他运输、储存和分配产生的排放，包括损失（逸散性 CH_4 排放）		

[34] 如果一种运输模式包括更多的燃料（如柴油和天然气）或多种运输模式（如铁路和船舶），则应在计算中适当报告。

[35] 空的回程 / 返程航次应计入计算。

MAIN RESULTS

10   This section should present the results of the modelled pathway.

Table 5: Fuel identification

Fuel Pathway Code	LCV (MJ/g)	Density (kg/m^3)	C_{fCO2} (gCO$_{2eq}$/MJ)	Carbon Content (wt%)

Additional information:

Table 6: Proposed default emission factors for XXX-converted in a YYYY pathway

Fuel Pathway Code	Region	efecu Feedstock cultivation/extraction	etd Feedstock and fuel transportation/storge/distribution	ep Fuel production	(Sum of the terms) Proposed WtT GHG intensity (gCO$_{2eq}$/MJ) emission factors
	XXXX				

Additional information:

Table 7: Proposed default emission factors for XXX-converted in a YYYY pathway for comparative purposes using GWP20

A CALCULATION USING GLOBAL WARMING POTENTIAL OVER A 20-YEAR HORIZON (GWP20) MAY BE PROVIDED AS INFORMATION FOR COMPARATIVE PURPOSES.

Fuel Pathway Code	Region	e$_{fecu}$ Feedstock cultivation/extraction	e$_{td}$ Feedstock and fuel transportation/storage/distribution	e$_p$ Fuel production	(Sum of the terms) Proposed WtT GHG intensity (gCO$_{2eq}$/MJ) emission factors
	XXXX				

Additional information:

APPENDIX

11   Brief description of the pathway

12   Brief description of the technology
    ….

REFERENCES

13   REF (APA format)

主要结果

10 本节应该呈现模拟路径的结果。

表 5 燃料识别

燃料路径代码	低热值（MJ/g）	密度（kg/m³）	C_{fCO_2}（gCO$_{2eq}$/MJ）	碳含量（wt%）

附加信息：

表 6 YYYY 路径中 xxx 转化的默认排放因子建议

燃料路径代码	地区	e_{fecu} 原料种植 / 开采	e_{td} 原料和燃料运输 / 存储 / 分配	e_p 燃料生产	（参数之和）建议的上船前温室气体强度（gCO$_{2eq}$/MJ）排放因子
	XXXX				

附加信息：

表 7 用于使用 GWP20 进行比较的 YYYY 路径中 xxx 转化的默认排放因子建议为进行比较，使用 20 年全球变暖潜势（GWP20）进行的计算可以作为信息提供。

燃料路径代码	地区	e_{fecu} 原料种植 / 开采	e_{td} 原料和燃料运输 / 存储 / 分配	e_p 燃料生产	（参数之和）建议的上船前温室气体强度（gCO$_{2eq}$/MJ）排放因子
	XXXX				

附加信息：附录

11 路径的简要描述

12 技术的简要描述

……

参考资料

13 REF（APA 模板）

TEMPLATE FOR TANK-TO-WAKE DEFAULT EMISSION FACTOR SUBMISSION

SUMMARY
This document presents a template to provide the minimum set of information to submit values for consideration as Tank-to-Wake (TtW) default emission factors.

INTRODUCTION

This template provides the form to submit values for consideration as Tank-to-Wake (TtW) default emission factors, with a minimum set of relevant technical and scientific information to allow the analysis of the adequacy of the proposed values.

TtW default emission factors should be calculated using representative and conservative assumptions, which encompass variable conditions onboard of the ships and performance of energy converters.

The rules to establish TtW default emission factor are described in paragraphs 9.17 and 9.22 of the LCA Guidelines. To establish a TtW default emission factor (with the exception of C_{fCO2}), at least three (3) reference values, from three different representative sources should be considered among the three (or more) values to be considered, the upper emission value should be selected as default, and the range of available emission factors should be provided for informative purposes. The reference values should be accompanied by the relevant technical and scientific information and evaluated against the corresponding information as appropriate, including the agreement between the reference values.

The LCA Guidelines allows demonstration of superior GHG performance compared to the default emission factors, trough actual emission factors subject to verification and certification by a third party.

PART A – EMISSION FACTORS FOR COMBUSTED FUEL (C_{fCH4} and C_{fN2O})

This part should contain the data to support proposals for C_{fCH4} and C_{fN2O} as defined in the LCA Guidelines;

Term	Units	Explanation
C_{fCH4}	g_{CH4}/g fuel	CH_4 emission conversion factor (g_{CH4}/g fuel delivered to the ship) for emissions of the combustion and/or oxidation process of the fuel used by the ship[36]
C_{fN2O}	g_{N2O}/g fuel	N_2O emission conversion factor (g_{N2O}/g fuel delivered to the ship) for emissions of the combustion and/or oxidation process of the fuel used by the ship

---

[36] For LNG/CNG fuel, the C_{slip_engine} is covering the role of C_{fCH4}, so C_{fCH4} is set to zero for these fuels.

附录 5

船端默认排放因子提交模板

总结
本文件中的模版列出了有关船端（TtW）默认排放因子至少应提交的信息。

引言

本模板提供了提交船端（TtW）默认排放因子数值的格式，以及至少需要的相关技术和科学资料，以分析建议值的充分性。

船端默认排放因子应使用代表性和保守的假设来计算，这些假设包括船上的可变条件和能量转化器的性能。

LCA 导则第 9.17 和 9.22 段描述了建立船端默认排放因子的规则。为了建立船端默认排放因子（C_{fCO2} 除外），应考虑来自三个不同代表性来源的至少三（3）个参考值。在要考虑的三个（或更多）值中，应选择较高的排放值作为默认值，并应提供可用排放因子的范围供参考。参考值应附有有关的技术和科学资料，并酌情对照相应的资料进行评价，包括参考值之间的一致性。

LCA 导则允许通过第三方验证和认证，证明实际排放因子与默认排放因子相比具有更优越的温室气体性能。

A 部分—燃烧燃料的排放因子（C_{fCH4} 和 C_{fN2O}）

本部分应当包含用以支持按照 LCA 导则中所定义的 C_{fCH4} 和 C_{fN2O} 相关提议的数据。

参数	单位	解释
C_{fCH4}	g_{CH4}/g_{fuel}	船舶使用的燃料在燃烧和／或氧化过程中产生的排放的 CH_4 排放转化因子（g_{CH4}/g 交付给船舶的燃料）[36]
C_{fN2O}	g_{N2O}/g_{fuel}	船舶使用的燃料在燃烧和／或氧化过程中产生的排放的 N_2O 排放转化因子（g_{N2O}/g 交付给船舶的燃料）

---

[36] 对于 LNG/CNG 燃料，C_{slip_engine} 覆盖了 C_{fCH4} 的作用，因此对于这些燃料 C_{fCH4} 设为零。

1 METHODOLOGY

This section should clearly present the methodology for the measurements made and associated uncertainty.

Additional details and relevant information may be added in appendices, such as measurement procedures and equipment used, test-bed/onboard measurement, etc.

2 ENERGY CONVERTER DIFFERENTIATION

This section should clearly present the Energy converter differentiation (general model range)[37] shall be included in the proposed values, and the reasoning to follow such differentiation.

3 MAIN RESULTS

This section should present the results.

Table 1: Proposed values for C_{fCH4} and C_{fN2O}

	Order	Group	Fuel type	Energy converter[39]	Test Cycle[40]	Measurement Method[41]	$C_{f\,CH4}$ (g_{CH4}/g fuel) [42]	$C_{f\,N2O}$ (g_{N2O}/g fuel) [43]	Uncertainty
		Fuel[38]							
Example	5	Marine Diesel/Gas Oil (ISO 8217 Grades DMX, DMA, DMZ and DMB maximum 0.10 % S)	MDO/MGO (ULSFO)_f_ SR_gm	Two stroke Low speed Main engine	NTC-E3	Test-bed measurement	x	y	z%

---

[37] Example: ICE/Piston Engines (2-Stroke, SSD/MSD), ICE/Piston Engines (4-Stroke, MSD), ICE/Piston Engines (4-Stroke, HSD), ICE/Gas Turbines (GT), Boilers, Dual Fuel, 4 stroke, Medium Speed, Low Pressure/Otto Cycle (LPMSDF 4-s Otto), Dual Fuel, 4-stroke, Medium Speed, High Pressure/Otto Cycle (HPMSDF 4-s Diesel), Dual Fuel, 2-stroke, Low Speed, Low Pressure/Otto Cycle (LPLSDF 2-s Otto), Dual Fuel (DF), 2-stroke, Low Speed, High Pressure/Diesel Cycle (HPLSDF 2-s Diesel), Gas-only, 4-stroke, Medium Speed, Low Pressure/Otto Cycle (LPMSGas 4-s Otto), Gas-only, 4-stroke, High Speed, Low Pressure/Otto Cycle (LPHSGas 4-s Otto), DF Boilers (DFB), Methane Reformer, (MRCH4), Methanol Reformer (MRCH3OH).

[38] Fuel pathways listed in appendix 1 of the LCA guidelines (resolution MEPC.391(81)).

[39] The proposal of default values should include a differentiation per energy converter with a technical explanation on how the Energy Converter classes were defined, the make and model of the engine where the emission tests was carried out, including engine design year.

[40] It should be detailed the measurements at each load point.

[41] For example, a reference to ISO 8178 and NOx Technical Code 2008. It should include the list of instruments used to measure emissions, test location (lab/onboard).

[42] The proposed data should be expressed in g_{CH4}/g fuel consumed by the energy converter. If from the data submitted arises the need to differentiate C_{fCH4} by energy converter, then a C_{fCH4} expressed in g_{CH4}/g fuel delivered to the ship needs to be calculated trough the weighted average of the different C_{fCH4} taking in consideration the fuel consumed on each energy converter.

[43] The proposed data should be expressed in g_{N2O}/gfuel consumed by the energy converter. If from the data submitted arises the need to differentiate C_{fN2O} by energy converter, then a C_{fN2O} expressed in g_{N2O}/g fuel delivered to the ship needs to be calculated trough the weighted average of the different C_{fN2O} taking in consideration the fuel consumed on each energy converter.

1 方法

本节应清楚地说明测量方法和相关的不确定性。可以在附录中添加额外的细节和相关信息，例如测量程序和使用的设备、台架试验／船上测量等。

2 能量转化器的区分

本节应清楚地说明在建议值中包含的能量转化器的区分（一般型号范围）[37]，以及采用这种区分的理由。

3 主要结果

本节应说明结果。

表 1　C_{fCH4} 和 C_{fCH4} 的建议值

		燃料[38]							
	序号	组别	燃料类型	能量转化器[39]	试验循环[40]	测量方法[41]	$C_{f CH4}$（g_{CH4}/g_{fuel}）[42]	$C_{f N2O}$（g_{N2O}/g_{fuel}）[43]	不确定性
举例	5	船用柴油／汽油（ISO 8217 等级 DMX，DMA，DMZ 和 DMB 最高 0.10% S）	MDO/MGO（ULSFO）_f_SR_gm	二冲程低速主机	NTC-E3	台架测试	x	y	z%

[37] 例如：ICE/ 活塞发动机（2 冲程、SSD/MSD），ICE/ 活塞发动机（4 冲程、MSD），ICE/ 活塞发动机（4 冲程、HSD），ICE/ 燃气轮机（GT），锅炉，双燃料、4 冲程、中速、低压／奥托循环（LPMSDF 4-s 奥托），双燃料、4 冲程、中速、高压／奥托循环（HPMSDF 4-s 奥托），双燃料、2 冲程、低速、低压／奥托循环（LPLSDF 2-s 奥托），双燃料（DF）、2 冲程、低速、高压／狄塞尔循环（HPLSDF 2-s 狄塞尔），纯气、4 冲程、中速、4 冲程、低压／奥托循环（LPMSGas 4-s 奥托），纯气、4 冲程、高速、低压／奥托循环（LPHSGas 4-s 奥托），DF 锅炉（DFB），甲烷转化炉（MRCH4），甲醇转化炉（MRCH3OH）。

[38] LCA 导则（第 MEPC.391（81）号决议）附录 1 中列出的燃料路径。

[39] 建议的默认值应包括按能量转化器进行区分，并提供技术解释，说明如何定义能量转化器的类别、进行排放 测试的发动机的品牌和型号，包括发动机的设计年份。

[40] 应详细说明每个负荷点的测量结果。

[41] 例如，参照 ISO8178 和《2008 年 NOx 技术规则》。应包括用于测量排放的仪器清单、测试地点（实验室／船上）。

[42] 建议的数据应以 g_{CH4}/g 能量转化器消耗的燃料 表示。如果从提交的数据中得出需要通过能量转化器来区分 C_{fCH4}，则需要考虑到每个能量转化器消耗的燃料，通过不同 C_{fCH4} 的加权平均值来计算 C_{fCH4}，以 g_{CH4}/g 能量转化器消耗的燃料 表示。

[43] 建议的数据应以 g_{N2O}/g 能量转化器消耗的燃料 表示。如果从提交的数据中得出需要通过能量转化器来区分 C_{fN2O}，则需要考虑到每个能量转化器消耗的燃料，通过不同 C_{fN2O} 的加权平均值来计算 C_{fN2O}，以 g_{N2O}/g 能量转化器消耗的燃料 表示。

Additional information:

PART B – EMISSION FACTORS FOR FUEL SLIPPAGE (C_{slip})

This part should contain the data to support proposals for C_{slip} as defined in the LCA Guidelines;

Term	Units	Explanation
C_{slip_ship}	% of total fuel mass	Factor accounting for fuel (expressed in % of total fuel mass delivered to the ship) which escapes from the energy converter without being oxidized (including fuel that escapes from combustion chamber/oxidation process and from crankcase, as appropriate) $$C_{slip\_ship}=C_{slip}*(1-C_{fug}/100)$$
C_{slip}	% of total fuel mass	Factor accounting for fuel (expressed in % of total fuel mass consumed in the energy converter) which escapes from the energy converter without being oxidized (including fuel that escapes from combustion chamber/oxidation process and from crankcase, as appropriate)

1   METHODOLOGY

This section should clearly present the methodology for the measurements made and associated uncertainty.

Additional details and relevant information may be added in appendices, such as measurement procedures and equipment used, test-bed/onboard measurement, etc.

2   ENERGY CONVERTER DIFFERENTIATION

This section should clearly present the Energy converter differentiation (general model range)[44] shall be included in the proposed values, and the reasoning to follow such differentiation.

3   MAIN RESULTS

This section should present the results.

---

[44]   Example: ICE/Piston Engines (2-Stroke, SSD/MSD), ICE/Piston Engines (4-Stroke, MSD), ICE/Piston Engines (4-Stroke, HSD), ICE/Gas Turbines (GT), Boilers, Dual Fuel, 4-stroke, Medium Speed, Low Pressure/Otto Cycle (LPMSDF 4-s Otto), Dual Fuel, 4-stroke, Medium Speed, High Pressure/Otto Cycle (HPMSDF 4-s Diesel), Dual Fuel, 2-stroke, Low Speed, Low Pressure/Otto Cycle (LPLSDF 2-s Otto), Dual Fuel (DF), 2-stroke, Low Speed, High Pressure/Diesel Cycle (HPLSDF 2-s Diesel), Gas-only, 4-stroke, Medium Speed, Low Pressure/Otto Cycle (LPMSGas 4-s Otto), Gas-only, 4-stroke, High Speed, Low Pressure/Otto Cycle (LPHSGas 4-s Otto), DF Boilers (DFB), Methane Reformer, (MRCH4), Methanol Reformer (MRCH3OH).

附加信息：

B 部分—逃逸燃料的排放因子（Cslip）

本部分包含的数据应能支持建议的按 LCA 导则定义的 Cslip 。

参数	单位	解释
C_{slip_ship}	占总燃料质量的百分比	核算未被氧化从能量转化器中逃逸的燃料因子（包括从燃烧室 / 氧化过程和曲轴箱中逃逸的燃料，视情况而定），以占交付给船舶的总燃料质量的百分比表示。 $C_{slip\_ship}=C_{slip}*（1-C_{fug}/100）$
C_{slip}	占总燃料质量的百分比	核算未被氧化从能量转化器中逃逸的燃料因子（包括从燃烧室 / 氧化过程和曲轴箱中逃逸的燃料，视情况而定），以占能量转化器中消耗的总燃料质量的百分比表示。

1 方法

本节应清楚地说明测量方法和相关的不确定性。可以在附录中添加额外的细节和相关信息，例如测量程序和使用的设备，台架测试 / 船上测量等。

2 能量转化器的区分

本节应清楚地说明在建议值中包含的能量转化器的区分（一般型号范围）[44]，以及采用这种区分的理由。

3 主要结果

本节应说明结果。

---

[44] 例如：ICE/ 活塞发动机（2 冲程、SSD/MSD），ICE/ 活塞发动机（4 冲程、MSD），ICE/ 活塞发动机（4 冲程、HSD），ICE/ 燃气轮机（GT），锅炉，双燃料、4 冲程、中速、低压 / 奥托循环（LPMSDF 4–s 奥托），双燃料、4 冲程、中速、高压 / 奥托循环（HPMSDF 4–s 奥托），双燃料、2 冲程、低速、低压 / 奥托循环（LPLSDF 2–s 奥托），双燃料（DF）、2 冲程、低速、高压 / 狄塞尔循环（HPLSDF 2–s 狄塞尔），纯气、4 冲程、中速、4 冲程、低压 / 奥托循环（LPMSGas 4–s 奥托），纯气、4 冲程、高速、低压 / 奥托循环（LPHSGas 4–s 奥托），DF 锅炉（DFB），甲烷转化炉（MRCH4），甲醇转化炉（MRCH3OH）。

Table 2: Proposed values for C_{slip}

| | | Fuel[45] | | | | | C_{slip}[46] | | |
	Order	Group	Fuel type	Energy converter[47]	Test Cycle	Measurement Method[48]	C_{slip} Exhaust [49]	C_{slip} Crankcase [49]	Uncertainty
Example	31	LNG	Liquefied Natural Gas (Methane)	Low Pressure Four stroke medium speed Auxiliary engine	NTC - D2	Test-bed measurement	x%	y%	z%

Additional information:

PART C – EMISSION FACTORS FOR FUGITIVE EMISSIONS (C_{fug})

This part should contain the data to support proposals for C_{fug} as defined in the LCA Guidelines;

Term	Units	Explanation
C_{fug}	% of fuel mass	Factor accounting for the fuel (expressed in % of mass of the fuel delivered to the ship) which escapes between the tanks up to the energy converter which is leaked, vented or otherwise lost in the system

1   METHODOLOGY

This section should clearly present the methodology for the measurements made and associated uncertainty.

Additional details and relevant information may be added in appendices, such as measurement procedures and equipment used.

2   DEFAULT VALUES DIFFERENTIATION

This section should clearly present the proposed way-forward to differentiate fugitive emissions, for example per energy converter, re-liquefaction equipment or Ship type.

3   MAIN RESULTS

This section should present the results.

---

[45]   Fuel pathways listed in appendix 1 of the LCA guidelines (resolution MEPC.391(81)).

[46] $C_{slip} = C_{slip\_Exhaust} + C_{slip\_Crankcase}$

[47]   The proposal of default values should include a differentiation per energy converter with a technical explanation on how the Energy Converter classes were defined, , the make and model of the engine where the emission tests was carried out, including engine design year.

[48]   For example, a reference to ISO 8178 and NO_x Technical Code 2008. It should include the list of instruments used to measure emissions and test location (lab/onboard).

[49]   The proposed data should be expressed in g_{CH4}/g fuel consumed by the energy converter.

表 2 C_{slip} 的建议值

| | | 燃料[45] | | | | | C_{slip}[46] | | |
	序号	组别	燃料类型	燃料转化器[47]	试验循环	测量方法[48]	$C_{slip\ Exhaust}$[49]	$C_{slip\ Crankcase}$[49]	不确定性
举例	31	LNG	液化天然气（甲烷）	低压四冲程中速辅机	NTC–D2	台架测试	x%	y%	z%

附加信息:

PART C—逸散性排放的排放因子（C_{fug}）

本部分包含的数据应能支持建议的按 LCA 导则定义的 C_{fug}。

参数	单位	解释
C_{fug}	占燃料质量的百分比	核算从油舱直至能量转化器之间逃逸并在系统中泄漏、排气或以其他方式丢失的燃料因子，以占交付给船舶的燃料质量的百分比表示

1 方法

本节应清楚地说明测量方法和相关的不确定性。

可以在附录中添加额外的细节和相关信息，例如测量程序和使用的设备。

2 默认值的区分

本节应清楚说明区分逸散性排放的建议方法，例如按能量转化器、再液化设备或船型。

3 主要结果

本节应说明结果。

---

[45] LCA 导则（第 MEPC.391（81）号决议）附录 1 中列出的燃料路径。

[46] $C_{slip}=C_{slip\_Exhaust}+C_{slip\_Crankcase}$

[47] 建议的默认值应包括按能量转化器进行区分，并提供技术解释，说明如何定义能量转化器的类别、进行排放测试的发动机的品牌和型号，包括发动机的设计年份。

[48] 例如，参照 ISO8178 和《2008 年 NOx 技术规则》。应包括用于测量排放的仪器清单和测试地点（实验室 / 船上）。

[49] 建议的数据应以 $g_{CH4}/g_{燃料转化器消耗的燃料}$ 表示。

Table 3: Proposed values for C_{fug}

	Order	Group	Fuel type	Fugitive Emissions Class[51]	Measurement Method[52]	C_{fug}[53]	Uncertainty
		Fuel[50]					
Example	31	LNG	Liquefied Natural Gas (Methane)	LNG Tanker	Onboard measurement	x%	y%

Additional information:

Part D – APPENDIX

Brief description of the procedures to collect data and the data collected used to calculated the proposed values, for example the emissions at each load point of the Test Cycle.

Part E – REFERENCES

REF (APA format)

***

---

[50] Fuel pathways listed in appendix 1 of the LCA guidelines (resolution MEPC.391(81)).

[51] A differentiation may be proposed, for example for example per energy converter, re-liquefaction equipment or ship type.

[52] For example a reference to ISO 8178 and NO_x Technical Code 2008. It should include the list of instruments used to measure emissions and test location (lab/onboard).

[53] Expressed in % of mass of the fuel delivered to the ship.

表 3 C_{fug} 建议值

| | | 燃料[50] | | | | | |
	序号	组别	燃料类型	逸散性排放类别[51]	测量方法[52]	C_{fug} [53]	不确定性
举例	31	LNG	液化天然气（甲烷）	LNG 船	船上测量	x%	y%

附加信息：

D 部分—附录

简要说明收集数据的程序和收集的用于计算建议值的数据，例如在试验循环每个负荷点的排放量。

E 部分—参考

REF（APA 模版）

***

---

[50] LCA 导则（第 MEPC.391（81）号决议）附录 1 中列出的燃料路径。

[51] 可以提出区分，例如按能量转化器、再液化设备或船型区分。

[52] 例如，参照 ISO8178 和《2008 年 NOx 技术规则》。应包括用于测量排放的仪器清单和测试地点（实验室 / 船上）。

[53] 以占交付给船舶的燃料质量的百分比表示。

INTERIM GUIDANCE ON THE USE OF BIOFUELS UNDER REGULATIONS 26, 27 AND 28 OF MARPOL ANNEX VI (DCS AND CII)

1   The Marine Environment Protection Committee, at its eightieth session (3 to 7 July 2023), approved the *Interim guidance on the use of biofuels under regulations 26, 27 and 28 of MARPOL Annex VI (DCS and CII)*, as set out in the annex.

2   Member Governments are invited to bring the annexed Interim Guidance to the attention of their Administrations, shipowners, ship operators, fuel oil suppliers and any other interested relevant stakeholders concerned for application as of 1 October 2023.

***

MEPC.1/Circ.905 通函
（2023 年 7 月 24 日）

在 MARPOL 附则Ⅵ第 26、27 和 28 条规定下使用生物燃料的临时指南（DCS 和 CII）

1　海上环境保护委员会在其第 80 届会议（2023 年 7 月 3 日至 7 日）上通过了《在 MARPOL 附则Ⅵ第 26、27 和 28 条规定下使用生物燃料的临时指南》（DCS 和 CII），其文本载于附件。

2　提请各成员国政府使其主管机关、船东、船舶经营人、燃油供应商和任何其他相关方注意所附的临时指南自 2023 年 10 月 1 日起应用。

***

ANNEX

INTERIM GUIDANCE ON THE USE OF BIOFUELS UNDER REGULATIONS 26, 27 AND 28 OF MARPOL ANNEX VI (DCS AND CII)

1   The *2022 Guidelines on operational carbon intensity indicators and the calculation methods* (resolution MEPC.352(78) CII Guidelines, G1) provide the possibility for the CO_2 Emission Conversion Factor (C_f) to be obtained from the fuel oil supplier, supported by documentary evidence, in case the type of the fuel oil is not covered by the relevant guidelines.

2   Pending the development of the comprehensive method to account for well-to-wake GHG emissions and removals based on the *Guidelines on life cycle GHG intensity of marine fuels (LCA Guidelines)* (resolution MEPC 376(80)), biofuels that have been certified by an international certification scheme,[*] meeting its sustainability criteria, and that provide a well-to-wake GHG emissions reduction of at least 65% compared to the well-to-wake emissions of fossil MGO of 94 gCO_2e/MJ (i.e. achieving an emissions intensity not exceeding 33 gCO_2e/MJ) according to that certification, may be assigned a C_f equal to the value of the well-to-wake GHG emissions of the fuel according to the certificate (expressed in gCO_2eq/MJ) multiplied by its lower calorific value (LCV, expressed in MJ/g) for the purpose of regulations 26, 27 and 28 of MARPOL Annex VI for the corresponding amount of fuels consumed by the ship. In any case, the C_f value of a biofuel cannot be less than 0. For blends, the C_f should be based on the weighted average of the C_f for the respective amount of fuels by energy.

3   A Proof of Sustainability or similar documentation from a recognized scheme should be provided along with the Bunker Delivery Note, to facilitate the verification of the reported biofuel consumption.

4   Biofuels not certified as "sustainable" or not fulfilling the well-to-wake emission factor criterion above should be assigned a C_f equal to the C_f of the equivalent fossil fuel type.

5   This guidance should be considered as an interim simplified method until a more comprehensive method is developed to calculate a fuel's Emission Conversion Factor reflecting its well-to-wake GHG emissions and removals based on the LCA Guidelines. This guidance does not intend to prejudge or delay the process of developing such a comprehensive method.

6   This Interim Guidance will be rescinded immediately upon operationalization of a well-to-wake GHG methodology through the LCA Guidelines.

7   Administrations are invited to inform the Committee on which international certification schemes have been used when applying this guidance.

---

[*]   Refer to ICAO's Approved Sustainability Certification Schemes and the CORSIA Sustainability Criteria (chapter 2) for CORSIA Eligible Fuels

附件

在 MARPOL 附则Ⅵ第 26、27 和 28 条规定下使用生物燃料的临时指南
（DCS 和 CII）

1　根据《2022 年营运碳强度指标和计算方法导则》（MEPC.352（78）决议，CII 导则，G1），对于相关导则中未包括的燃油类型，可能可以从燃油供应商处获得有文件证明的 CO_2 排放转换系数（C_f）。

2　在根据《船用燃料全生命周期温室气体强度导则（LCA 导则）》（MEPC.376（80）决议）研究出解释全生命周期温室气体排放（GHG）和消除温室气体排放的综合性方法之前，经国际认证计划*认证满足其可持续标准的生物燃料，如果经认证其全生命周期温室气体排放相比化石船用柴油（MGO）全生命周期排放强度值 94 gCO2e/MJ 减少至少 65%（即实现排放强度不超过 33 gCO_{2e}/MJ），则其 Cf 值可取为证书规定的燃料全生命周期温室气体排放强度值（以 gCO_{2eq}/MJ 表示）乘以其低热值（LVC，以 MJ/g 表示），以用于 MARPOL 附则Ⅵ第 26、27 和 28 条规定中船舶相应燃料消耗的排放。生物燃料的 C_f 值在任何情况下都不得小于 0。对于混合燃料，C_f 值应基于按能量计算的各自燃料数量 C_f 值的加权平均值。

3　应提供由认可计划出具的可持续性证明或类似的证明文件以及燃油交付单，以便对上报的生物燃料消耗量进行验证。

4　对于未经认证为"可持续"或不满足上文全生命周期排放系数标准的生物燃料，其被赋予的 C_f 值应等于等效化石燃料类型的 C_f 值。

5　在研究出更加综合性的方法之前，本指南应被视作一种临时的简化方法，用于在 LCA 导则的基础上计算燃料的排放转换系数，以反映其全生命周期温室气体排放和温室气体消除。本指南并不旨在预先判断或推迟这一综合性方法的开发过程。

6　LCA 导则中全生命周期温室气体排放的研究方法一经实施，本临时指南将立即废止。

7　提请主管机关告知本委员会在应用本指南时使用了哪些国际认证计划。

---

*　参阅国际民用航空组织（ICAO）的经批准的可持续性认证计划和国际航空碳抵消和减排计划（CORSIA）可持续性标准（第 2 章）（适用于符合 CORSIA 标准的燃料）。

下篇
国内法律法规及标准等文件

中华人民共和国海洋环境保护法

（1982 年 8 月 23 日第五届全国人民代表大会常务委员会第二十四次会议通过 1999
年 12 月 25 日第九届全国人民代表大会常务委员会第十三次会议第一次修订根据 2013 年
12 月 28 日第十二届全国人民代表大会常务委员会第六次会议《关于修改〈中华人民共和
国海洋环境保护法〉等七部法律的决定》第一次修正根据 2016 年 11 月 7 日第十二届全国
人民代表大会常务委员会第二十四次会议《关于修改〈中华人民共和国海洋环境保护法〉
的决定》第二次修正根据 2017 年 11 月 4 日第十二届全国人民代表大会常务委员会第三十
次会议《关于修改〈中华人民共和国会计法〉等十一部法律的决定》第三次修正 2023 年
10 月 24 日第十四届全国人民代表大会常务委员会第六次会议第二次修订）

目录

第一章　总　则

第一条　为了保护和改善海洋环境，保护海洋资源，防治污染损害，保障生态安全和
公众健康，维护国家海洋权益，建设海洋强国，推进生态文明建设，促进经济社会可持续
发展，实现人与自然和谐共生，根据宪法，制定本法。

第二条　本法适用于中华人民共和国管辖海域。

在中华人民共和国管辖海域内从事航行、勘探、开发、生产、旅游、科学研究及其他
活动，或者在沿海陆域内从事影响海洋环境活动的任何单位和个人，应当遵守本法。

在中华人民共和国管辖海域以外，造成中华人民共和国管辖海域环境污染、生态破坏
的，适用本法相关规定。

第三条　海洋环境保护应当坚持保护优先、预防为主、源头防控、陆海统筹、综合治理、
公众参与、损害担责的原则。

第四条　国务院生态环境主管部门负责全国海洋环境的监督管理，负责全国防治陆源
污染物、海岸工程和海洋工程建设项目（以下称工程建设项目）、海洋倾倒废弃物对海洋
环境污染损害的环境保护工作，指导、协调和监督全国海洋生态保护修复工作。

国务院自然资源主管部门负责海洋保护和开发利用的监督管理，负责全国海洋生态、
海域海岸线和海岛的修复工作。

国务院交通运输主管部门负责所辖港区水域内非军事船舶和港区水域外非渔业、非军
事船舶污染海洋环境的监督管理，组织、协调、指挥重大海上溢油应急处置。海事管理机
构具体负责上述水域内相关船舶污染海洋环境的监督管理，并负责污染事故的调查处理；

对在中华人民共和国管辖海域航行、停泊和作业的外国籍船舶造成的污染事故登轮检查处理。船舶污染事故给渔业造成损害的，应当吸收渔业主管部门参与调查处理。

国务院渔业主管部门负责渔港水域内非军事船舶和渔港水域外渔业船舶污染海洋环境的监督管理，负责保护渔业水域生态环境工作，并调查处理前款规定的污染事故以外的渔业污染事故。

国务院发展改革、水行政、住房和城乡建设、林业和草原等部门在各自职责范围内负责有关行业、领域涉及的海洋环境保护工作。

海警机构在职责范围内对海洋工程建设项目、海洋倾倒废弃物对海洋环境污染损害、自然保护地海岸线向海一侧保护利用等活动进行监督检查，查处违法行为，按照规定权限参与海洋环境污染事故的应急处置和调查处理。

军队生态环境保护部门负责军事船舶污染海洋环境的监督管理及污染事故的调查处理。

第五条 沿海县级以上地方人民政府对其管理海域的海洋环境质量负责。

国家实行海洋环境保护目标责任制和考核评价制度，将海洋环境保护目标完成情况纳入考核评价的内容。

第六条 沿海县级以上地方人民政府可以建立海洋环境保护区域协作机制，组织协调其管理海域的环境保护工作。

跨区域的海洋环境保护工作，由有关沿海地方人民政府协商解决，或者由上级人民政府协调解决。

跨部门的重大海洋环境保护工作，由国务院生态环境主管部门协调；协调未能解决的，由国务院作出决定。

第七条 国务院和沿海县级以上地方人民政府应当将海洋环境保护工作纳入国民经济和社会发展规划，按照事权和支出责任划分原则，将海洋环境保护工作所需经费纳入本级政府预算。

第八条 各级人民政府及其有关部门应当加强海洋环境保护的宣传教育和知识普及工作，增强公众海洋环境保护意识，引导公众依法参与海洋环境保护工作；鼓励基层群众性自治组织、社会组织、志愿者等开展海洋环境保护法律法规和知识的宣传活动；按照职责分工依法公开海洋环境相关信息。

新闻媒体应当采取多种形式开展海洋环境保护的宣传报道，并对违法行为进行舆论监督。

第九条 任何单位和个人都有保护海洋环境的义务，并有权对污染海洋环境、破坏海洋生态的单位和个人，以及海洋环境监督管理人员的违法行为进行监督和检举。

从事影响海洋环境活动的任何单位和个人，都应当采取有效措施，防止、减轻海洋环境污染、生态破坏。排污者应当依法公开排污信息。

第十条 国家鼓励、支持海洋环境保护科学技术研究、开发和应用，促进海洋环境保护信息化建设，加强海洋环境保护专业技术人才培养，提高海洋环境保护科学技术水平。

国家鼓励、支持海洋环境保护国际交流与合作。

第十一条 对在海洋环境保护工作中做出显著成绩的单位和个人，按照国家有关规定给予表彰和奖励。

第二章　海洋环境监督管理

第十二条 国家实施陆海统筹、区域联动的海洋环境监督管理制度，加强规划、标准、监测等监督管理制度的衔接协调。

各级人民政府及其有关部门应当加强海洋环境监督管理能力建设，提高海洋环境监督管理科技化、信息化水平。

第十三条　国家优先将生态功能极重要、生态极敏感脆弱的海域划入生态保护红线，实行严格保护。

开发利用海洋资源或者从事影响海洋环境的建设活动，应当根据国土空间规划科学合理布局，严格遵守国土空间用途管制要求，严守生态保护红线，不得造成海洋生态环境的损害。沿海地方各级人民政府应当根据国土空间规划，保护和科学合理地使用海域。沿海省、自治区、直辖市人民政府应当加强对生态保护红线内人为活动的监督管理，定期评估保护成效。

国务院有关部门、沿海设区的市级以上地方人民政府及其有关部门，对其组织编制的国土空间规划和相关规划，应当依法进行包括海洋环境保护内容在内的环境影响评价。

第十四条　国务院生态环境主管部门会同有关部门、机构和沿海省、自治区、直辖市人民政府制定全国海洋生态环境保护规划，报国务院批准后实施。全国海洋生态环境保护规划应当与全国国土空间规划相衔接。

沿海地方各级人民政府应当根据全国海洋生态环境保护规划，组织实施其管理海域的海洋环境保护工作。

第十五条　沿海省、自治区、直辖市人民政府应当根据其管理海域的生态环境和资源利用状况，将其管理海域纳入生态环境分区管控方案和生态环境准入清单，报国务院生态环境主管部门备案后实施。生态环境分区管控方案和生态环境准入清单应当与国土空间规划相衔接。

第十六条　国务院生态环境主管部门根据海洋环境质量状况和国家经济、技术条件，制定国家海洋环境质量标准。

沿海省、自治区、直辖市人民政府对国家海洋环境质量标准中未作规定的项目，可以制定地方海洋环境质量标准；对国家海洋环境质量标准中已作规定的项目，可以制定严于国家海洋环境质量标准的地方海洋环境质量标准。地方海洋环境质量标准应当报国务院生态环境主管部门备案。

国家鼓励开展海洋环境基准研究。

第十七条　制定海洋环境质量标准，应当征求有关部门、行业协会、企业事业单位、专家和公众等的意见，提高海洋环境质量标准的科学性。

海洋环境质量标准应当定期评估，并根据评估结果适时修订。

第十八条　国家和有关地方水污染物排放标准的制定，应当将海洋环境质量标准作为重要依据之一。

对未完成海洋环境保护目标的海域，省级以上人民政府生态环境主管部门暂停审批新增相应种类污染物排放总量的建设项目环境影响报告书（表），会同有关部门约谈该地区人民政府及其有关部门的主要负责人，要求其采取有效措施及时整改，约谈和整改情况应当向社会公开。

第十九条　国家加强海洋环境质量管控，推进海域综合治理，严格海域排污许可管理，提升重点海域海洋环境质量。

需要直接向海洋排放工业废水、医疗污水的海岸工程和海洋工程单位，城镇污水集中处理设施的运营单位及其他企业事业单位和生产经营者，应当依法取得排污许可证。排污许可的管理按照国务院有关规定执行。

实行排污许可管理的企业事业单位和其他生产经营者应当执行排污许可证关于排放污染物的种类、浓度、排放量、排放方式、排放去向和自行监测等要求。

禁止通过私设暗管或者篡改、伪造监测数据，以及不正常运行污染防治设施等逃避监管的方式向海洋排放污染物。

第二十条 国务院生态环境主管部门根据海洋环境状况和质量改善要求，会同国务院发展改革、自然资源、住房和城乡建设、交通运输、水行政、渔业等部门和海警机构，划定国家环境治理重点海域及其控制区域，制定综合治理行动方案，报国务院批准后实施。

沿海设区的市级以上地方人民政府应当根据综合治理行动方案，制定其管理海域的实施方案，因地制宜采取特别管控措施，开展综合治理，协同推进重点海域治理与美丽海湾建设。

第二十一条 直接向海洋排放应税污染物的企业事业单位和其他生产经营者，应当依照法律规定缴纳环境保护税。

向海洋倾倒废弃物，应当按照国家有关规定缴纳倾倒费。具体办法由国务院发展改革部门、国务院财政主管部门会同国务院生态环境主管部门制定。

第二十二条 国家加强防治海洋环境污染损害的科学技术的研究和开发，对严重污染海洋环境的落后生产工艺和落后设备，实行淘汰制度。

企业事业单位和其他生产经营者应当优先使用清洁低碳能源，采用资源利用率高、污染物排放量少的清洁生产工艺，防止对海洋环境的污染。

第二十三条 国务院生态环境主管部门负责海洋生态环境监测工作，制定海洋生态环境监测规范和标准并监督实施，组织实施海洋生态环境质量监测，统一发布国家海洋生态环境状况公报，定期组织对海洋生态环境质量状况进行调查评价。

国务院自然资源主管部门组织开展海洋资源调查和海洋生态预警监测，发布海洋生态预警监测警报和公报。

其他依照本法规定行使海洋环境监督管理权的部门和机构应当按照职责分工开展监测、监视。

第二十四条 国务院有关部门和海警机构应当向国务院生态环境主管部门提供编制国家海洋生态环境状况公报所必需的入海河口和海洋环境监测、调查、监视等方面的资料。

生态环境主管部门应当向有关部门和海警机构提供与海洋环境监督管理有关的资料。

第二十五条 国务院生态环境主管部门会同有关部门和机构通过智能化的综合信息系统，为海洋环境保护监督管理、信息共享提供服务。

国务院有关部门、海警机构和沿海县级以上地方人民政府及其有关部门应当按照规定，推进综合监测、协同监测和常态化监测，加强监测数据、执法信息等海洋环境管理信息共享，提高海洋环境保护综合管理水平。

第二十六条 国家加强海洋辐射环境监测，国务院生态环境主管部门负责制定海洋辐射环境应急监测方案并组织实施。

第二十七条 因发生事故或者其他突发性事件，造成或者可能造成海洋环境污染、生态破坏事件的单位和个人，应当立即采取有效措施解除或者减轻危害，及时向可能受到危害者通报，并向依照本法规定行使海洋环境监督管理权的部门和机构报告，接受调查处理。

沿海县级以上地方人民政府在本行政区域近岸海域的生态环境受到严重损害时，应当采取有效措施，解除或者减轻危害。

第二十八条 国家根据防止海洋环境污染的需要，制定国家重大海上污染事件应急预案，建立健全海上溢油污染等应急机制，保障应对工作的必要经费。

国家建立重大海上溢油应急处置部际联席会议制度。国务院交通运输主管部门牵头组织编制国家重大海上溢油应急处置预案并组织实施。

国务院生态环境主管部门负责制定全国海洋石油勘探开发海上溢油污染事件应急预案并组织实施。

国家海事管理机构负责制定全国船舶重大海上溢油污染事件应急预案，报国务院生态环境主管部门、国务院应急管理部门备案。

沿海县级以上地方人民政府及其有关部门应当制定有关应急预案，在发生海洋突发环境事件时，及时启动应急预案，采取有效措施，解除或者减轻危害。

可能发生海洋突发环境事件的单位，应当按照有关规定，制定本单位的应急预案，配备应急设备和器材，定期组织开展应急演练；应急预案应当向依照本法规定行使海洋环境监督管理权的部门和机构备案。

第二十九条　依照本法规定行使海洋环境监督管理权的部门和机构，有权对从事影响海洋环境活动的单位和个人进行现场检查；在巡航监视中发现违反本法规定的行为时，应当予以制止并调查取证，必要时有权采取有效措施，防止事态扩大，并报告有关部门或者机构处理。

被检查者应当如实反映情况，提供必要的资料。检查者应当依法为被检查者保守商业秘密、个人隐私和个人信息。

依照本法规定行使海洋环境监督管理权的部门和机构可以在海上实行联合执法。

第三十条　造成或者可能造成严重海洋环境污染、生态破坏的，或者有关证据可能灭失或者被隐匿的，依照本法规定行使海洋环境监督管理权的部门和机构可以查封、扣押有关船舶、设施、设备、物品。

第三十一条　在中华人民共和国管辖海域以外，造成或者可能造成中华人民共和国管辖海域环境污染、生态破坏的，有关部门和机构有权采取必要的措施。

第三十二条　国务院生态环境主管部门会同有关部门和机构建立向海洋排放污染物、从事废弃物海洋倾倒、从事海洋生态环境治理和服务的企业事业单位和其他生产经营者信用记录与评价应用制度，将相关信用记录纳入全国公共信用信息共享平台。

第三章　海洋生态保护

第三十三条　国家加强海洋生态保护，提升海洋生态系统质量和多样性、稳定性、持续性。

国务院和沿海地方各级人民政府应当采取有效措施，重点保护红树林、珊瑚礁、海藻场、海草床、滨海湿地、海岛、海湾、入海河口、重要渔业水域等具有典型性、代表性的海洋生态系统，珍稀濒危海洋生物的天然集中分布区，具有重要经济价值的海洋生物生存区域及有重大科学文化价值的海洋自然遗迹和自然景观。

第三十四条　国务院和沿海省、自治区、直辖市人民政府及其有关部门根据保护海洋的需要，依法将重要的海洋生态系统、珍稀濒危海洋生物的天然集中分布区、海洋自然遗迹和自然景观集中分布区等区域纳入国家公园、自然保护区或者自然公园等自然保护地。

第三十五条　国家建立健全海洋生态保护补偿制度。

国务院和沿海省、自治区、直辖市人民政府应当通过转移支付、产业扶持等方式支持开展海洋生态保护补偿。

沿海地方各级人民政府应当落实海洋生态保护补偿资金，确保其用于海洋生态保护补偿。

第三十六条　国家加强海洋生物多样性保护，健全海洋生物多样性调查、监测、评估和保护体系，维护和修复重要海洋生态廊道，防止对海洋生物多样性的破坏。

开发利用海洋和海岸带资源，应当对重要海洋生态系统、生物物种、生物遗传资源实施有效保护，维护海洋生物多样性。

引进海洋动植物物种，应当进行科学论证，避免对海洋生态系统造成危害。

第三十七条　国家鼓励科学开展水生生物增殖放流，支持科学规划，因地制宜采取投放人工鱼礁和种植海藻场、海草床、珊瑚等措施，恢复海洋生物多样性，修复改善海洋生态。

第三十八条　开发海岛及周围海域的资源，应当采取严格的生态保护措施，不得造成海岛地形、岸滩、植被和海岛周围海域生态环境的损害。

第三十九条　国家严格保护自然岸线，建立健全自然岸线控制制度。沿海省、自治区、直辖市人民政府负责划定严格保护岸线的范围并发布。

沿海地方各级人民政府应当加强海岸线分类保护与利用，保护修复自然岸线，促进人工岸线生态化，维护岸线岸滩稳定平衡，因地制宜、科学合理划定海岸建筑退缩线。

禁止违法占用、损害自然岸线。

第四十条　国务院水行政主管部门确定重要入海河流的生态流量管控指标，应当征求并研究国务院生态环境、自然资源等部门的意见。确定生态流量管控指标，应当进行科学论证，综合考虑水资源条件、气候状况、生态环境保护要求、生活生产用水状况等因素。

入海河口所在地县级以上地方人民政府及其有关部门按照河海联动的要求，制定实施河口生态修复和其他保护措施方案，加强对水、沙、盐、潮滩、生物种群、河口形态的综合监测，采取有效措施防止海水入侵和倒灌，维护河口良好生态功能。

第四十一条　沿海地方各级人民政府应当结合当地自然环境的特点，建设海岸防护设施、沿海防护林、沿海城镇园林和绿地，对海岸侵蚀和海水入侵地区进行综合治理。

禁止毁坏海岸防护设施、沿海防护林、沿海城镇园林和绿地。

第四十二条　对遭到破坏的具有重要生态、经济、社会价值的海洋生态系统，应当进行修复。海洋生态修复应当以改善生境、恢复生物多样性和生态系统基本功能为重点，以自然恢复为主、人工修复为辅，并优先修复具有典型性、代表性的海洋生态系统。

国务院自然资源主管部门负责统筹海洋生态修复，牵头组织编制海洋生态修复规划并实施有关海洋生态修复重大工程。编制海洋生态修复规划，应当进行科学论证评估。

国务院自然资源、生态环境等部门应当按照职责分工开展修复成效监督评估。

第四十三条　国务院自然资源主管部门负责开展全国海洋生态灾害预防、风险评估和隐患排查治理。

沿海县级以上地方人民政府负责其管理海域的海洋生态灾害应对工作，采取必要的灾害预防、处置和灾后恢复措施，防止和减轻灾害影响。

企业事业单位和其他生产经营者应当采取必要应对措施，防止海洋生态灾害扩大。

第四十四条　国家鼓励发展生态渔业，推广多种生态渔业生产方式，改善海洋生态状况，保护海洋环境。

沿海县级以上地方人民政府应当因地制宜编制并组织实施养殖水域滩涂规划，确定可以用于养殖业的水域和滩涂，科学划定海水养殖禁养区、限养区和养殖区，建立禁养区内海水养殖的清理和退出机制。

第四十五条　从事海水养殖活动应当保护海域环境，科学确定养殖规模和养殖密度，合理投饵、投肥，正确使用药物，及时规范收集处理固体废物，防止造成海洋生态环境的损害。

禁止在氮磷浓度严重超标的近岸海域新增或者扩大投饵、投肥海水养殖规模。

向海洋排放养殖尾水污染物等应当符合污染物排放标准。沿海省、自治区、直辖市人民政府应当制定海水养殖污染物排放相关地方标准，加强养殖尾水污染防治的监督管理。

工厂化养殖和设置统一排污口的集中连片养殖的排污单位，应当按照有关规定对养殖尾水自行监测。

第四章　陆源污染物污染防治

第四十六条　向海域排放陆源污染物，应当严格执行国家或者地方规定的标准和有关规定。

第四十七条　入海排污口位置的选择，应当符合国土空间用途管制要求，根据海水动力条件和有关规定，经科学论证后，报设区的市级以上人民政府生态环境主管部门备案。排污口的责任主体应当加强排污口监测，按照规定开展监控和自动监测。

生态环境主管部门应当在完成备案后十五个工作日内将入海排污口设置情况通报自然资源、渔业等部门和海事管理机构、海警机构、军队生态环境保护部门。

沿海县级以上地方人民政府应当根据排污口类别、责任主体，组织有关部门对本行政区域内各类入海排污口进行排查整治和日常监督管理，建立健全近岸水体、入海排污口、排污管线、污染源全链条治理体系。

国务院生态环境主管部门负责制定入海排污口设置和管理的具体办法，制定入海排污口技术规范，组织建设统一的入海排污口信息平台，加强动态更新、信息共享和公开。

第四十八条　禁止在自然保护地、重要渔业水域、海水浴场、生态保护红线区域及其他需要特别保护的区域，新设工业排污口和城镇污水处理厂排污口；法律、行政法规另有规定的除外。

在有条件的地区，应当将排污口深水设置，实行离岸排放。

第四十九条　经开放式沟（渠）向海洋排放污染物的，对开放式沟（渠）按照国家和地方的有关规定、标准实施水环境质量管理。

第五十条　国务院有关部门和县级以上地方人民政府及其有关部门应当依照水污染防治有关法律、行政法规的规定，加强入海河流管理，协同推进入海河流污染防治，使入海河口的水质符合入海河口环境质量相关要求。

入海河流流域省、自治区、直辖市人民政府应当按照国家有关规定，加强入海总氮、总磷排放的管控，制定控制方案并组织实施。

第五十一条　禁止向海域排放油类、酸液、碱液、剧毒废液。

禁止向海域排放污染海洋环境、破坏海洋生态的放射性废水。

严格控制向海域排放含有不易降解的有机物和重金属的废水。

第五十二条　含病原体的医疗污水、生活污水和工业废水应当经过处理，符合国家和地方有关排放标准后，方可排入海域。

第五十三条　含有机物和营养物质的工业废水、生活污水，应当严格控制向海湾、半封闭海及其他自净能力较差的海域排放。

第五十四条　向海域排放含热废水，应当采取有效措施，保证邻近自然保护地、渔业水域的水温符合国家和地方海洋环境质量标准，避免热污染对珍稀濒危海洋生物、海洋水产资源造成危害。

第五十五条　沿海地方各级人民政府应当加强农业面源污染防治。沿海农田、林场施用化学农药，应当执行国家农药安全使用的规定和标准。沿海农田、林场应当合理使用化肥和植物生长调节剂。

第五十六条　在沿海陆域弃置、堆放和处理尾矿、矿渣、煤灰渣、垃圾和其他固体废物的，依照《中华人民共和国固体废物污染环境防治法》的有关规定执行，并采取有效措施防止固体废物进入海洋。

禁止在岸滩弃置、堆放和处理固体废物；法律、行政法规另有规定的除外。

第五十七条　沿海县级以上地方人民政府负责其管理海域的海洋垃圾污染防治，建立海洋垃圾监测、清理制度，统筹规划建设陆域接收、转运、处理海洋垃圾的设施，明确有关部门、乡镇、街道、企业事业单位等的海洋垃圾管控区域，建立海洋垃圾监测、拦截、收集、打捞、运输、处理体系并组织实施，采取有效措施鼓励、支持公众参与上述活动。国务院生态环境、住房和城乡建设、发展改革等部门应当按照职责分工加强海洋垃圾污染防治的监督指导和保障。

第五十八条　禁止经中华人民共和国内水、领海过境转移危险废物。

经中华人民共和国管辖的其他海域转移危险废物的，应当事先取得国务院生态环境主管部门的书面同意。

第五十九条　沿海县级以上地方人民政府应当建设和完善排水管网，根据改善海洋环境质量的需要建设城镇污水处理厂和其他污水处理设施，加强城乡污水处理。

建设污水海洋处置工程，应当符合国家有关规定。

第六十条　国家采取必要措施，防止、减少和控制来自大气层或者通过大气层造成的海洋环境污染损害。

第五章　工程建设项目污染防治

第六十一条　新建、改建、扩建工程建设项目，应当遵守国家有关建设项目环境保护管理的规定，并把污染防治和生态保护所需资金纳入建设项目投资计划。

禁止在依法划定的自然保护地、重要渔业水域及其他需要特别保护的区域，违法建设污染环境、破坏生态的工程建设项目或者从事其他活动。

第六十二条　工程建设项目应当按照国家有关建设项目环境影响评价的规定进行环境影响评价。未依法进行并通过环境影响评价的建设项目，不得开工建设。

环境保护设施应当与主体工程同时设计、同时施工、同时投产使用。环境保护设施应当符合经批准的环境影响评价报告书（表）的要求。建设单位应当依照有关法律法规的规定，对环境保护设施进行验收，编制验收报告，并向社会公开。环境保护设施未经验收或者经验收不合格的，建设项目不得投入生产或者使用。

第六十三条　禁止在沿海陆域新建不符合国家产业政策的化学制浆造纸、化工、印染、制革、电镀、酿造、炼油、岸边冲滩拆船及其他严重污染海洋环境的生产项目。

第六十四条　新建、改建、扩建工程建设项目，应当采取有效措施，保护国家和地方重点保护的野生动植物及其生存环境，保护海洋水产资源，避免或者减轻对海洋生物的影响。

禁止在严格保护岸线范围内开采海砂。依法在其他区域开发利用海砂资源，应当采取严格措施，保护海洋环境。载运海砂资源应当持有合法来源证明；海砂开采者应当为载运海砂的船舶提供合法来源证明。

从岸上打井开采海底矿产资源，应当采取有效措施，防止污染海洋环境。

第六十五条　工程建设项目不得使用含超标准放射性物质或者易溶出有毒有害物质的材料；不得造成领海基点及其周围环境的侵蚀、淤积和损害，不得危及领海基点的稳定。

第六十六条　工程建设项目需要爆破作业时，应当采取有效措施，保护海洋环境。

海洋石油勘探开发及输油过程中，应当采取有效措施，避免溢油事故的发生。

第六十七条　工程建设项目不得违法向海洋排放污染物、废弃物及其他有害物质。

海洋油气钻井平台（船）、生产生活平台、生产储卸装置等海洋油气装备的含油污水和油性混合物，应当经过处理达标后排放；残油、废油应当予以回收，不得排放入海。

钻井所使用的油基泥浆和其他有毒复合泥浆不得排放入海。水基泥浆和无毒复合泥浆及钻屑的排放，应当符合国家有关规定。

第六十八条　海洋油气钻井平台（船）、生产生活平台、生产储卸装置等海洋油气装备及其有关海上设施，不得向海域处置含油的工业固体废物。处置其他固体废物，不得造成海洋环境污染。

第六十九条　海上试油时，应当确保油气充分燃烧，油和油性混合物不得排放入海。

第七十条　勘探开发海洋油气资源，应当按照有关规定编制油气污染应急预案，报国务院生态环境主管部门海域派出机构备案。

第六章　废弃物倾倒污染防治

第七十一条　任何个人和未经批准的单位，不得向中华人民共和国管辖海域倾倒任何废弃物。

需要倾倒废弃物的，产生废弃物的单位应当向国务院生态环境主管部门海域派出机构提出书面申请，并出具废弃物特性和成分检验报告，取得倾倒许可证后，方可倾倒。

国家鼓励疏浚物等废弃物的综合利用，避免或者减少海洋倾倒。

禁止中华人民共和国境外的废弃物在中华人民共和国管辖海域倾倒。

第七十二条　国务院生态环境主管部门根据废弃物的毒性、有毒物质含量和对海洋环境影响程度，制定海洋倾倒废弃物评价程序和标准。

可以向海洋倾倒的废弃物名录，由国务院生态环境主管部门制定。

第七十三条　国务院生态环境主管部门会同国务院自然资源主管部门编制全国海洋倾倒区规划，并征求国务院交通运输、渔业等部门和海警机构的意见，报国务院批准。

国务院生态环境主管部门根据全国海洋倾倒区规划，按照科学、合理、经济、安全的原则及时选划海洋倾倒区，征求国务院交通运输、渔业等部门和海警机构的意见，并向社会公告。

第七十四条　国务院生态环境主管部门组织开展海洋倾倒区使用状况评估，根据评估结果予以调整、暂停使用或者封闭海洋倾倒区。

海洋倾倒区的调整、暂停使用和封闭情况，应当通报国务院有关部门、海警机构并向社会公布。

第七十五条　获准和实施倾倒废弃物的单位，应当按照许可证注明的期限及条件，到指定的区域进行倾倒。倾倒作业船舶等载运工具应当安装使用符合要求的海洋倾倒在线监控设备，并与国务院生态环境主管部门监管系统联网。

第七十六条　获准和实施倾倒废弃物的单位，应当按照规定向颁发许可证的国务院生态环境主管部门海域派出机构报告倾倒情况。倾倒废弃物的船舶应当向驶出港的海事管理机构、海警机构作出报告。

第七十七条　禁止在海上焚烧废弃物。

禁止在海上处置污染海洋环境、破坏海洋生态的放射性废物或者其他放射性物质。

第七十八条　获准倾倒废弃物的单位委托实施废弃物海洋倾倒作业的，应当对受托单位的主体资格、技术能力和信用状况进行核实，依法签订书面合同，在合同中约定污染防治与生态保护要求，并监督实施。

受托单位实施废弃物海洋倾倒作业，应当依照有关法律法规的规定和合同约定，履行污染防治和生态保护要求。

获准倾倒废弃物的单位违反本条第一款规定的，除依照有关法律法规的规定予以处罚外，还应当与造成环境污染、生态破坏的受托单位承担连带责任。

第七章　船舶及有关作业活动污染防治

第七十九条　在中华人民共和国管辖海域，任何船舶及相关作业不得违法向海洋排放船舶垃圾、生活污水、含油污水、含有毒有害物质污水、废气等污染物，废弃物，压载水和沉积物及其他有害物质。

船舶应当按照国家有关规定采取有效措施，对压载水和沉积物进行处理处置，严格防控引入外来有害生物。

从事船舶污染物、废弃物接收和船舶清舱、洗舱作业活动的，应当具备相应的接收处理能力。

第八十条　船舶应当配备相应的防污设备和器材。

船舶的结构、配备的防污设备和器材应当符合国家防治船舶污染海洋环境的有关规定，并经检验合格。

船舶应当取得并持有防治海洋环境污染的证书与文书，在进行涉及船舶污染物、压载水和沉积物排放及操作时，应当按照有关规定监测、监控，如实记录并保存。

第八十一条　船舶应当遵守海上交通安全法律、法规的规定，防止因碰撞、触礁、搁浅、火灾或者爆炸等引起的海难事故，造成海洋环境的污染。

第八十二条　国家完善并实施船舶油污损害民事赔偿责任制度；按照船舶油污损害赔偿责任由船东和货主共同承担风险的原则，完善并实施船舶油污保险、油污损害赔偿基金制度，具体办法由国务院规定。

第八十三条　载运具有污染危害性货物进出港口的船舶，其承运人、货物所有人或者代理人，应当事先向海事管理机构申报。经批准后，方可进出港口或者装卸作业。

第八十四条　交付船舶载运污染危害性货物的，托运人应当将货物的正式名称、污染危害性以及应当采取的防护措施如实告知承运人。污染危害性货物的单证、包装、标志、数量限制等，应当符合对所交付货物的有关规定。

需要船舶载运污染危害性不明的货物，应当按照有关规定事先进行评估。

装卸油类及有毒有害货物的作业，船岸双方应当遵守安全防污操作规程。

第八十五条　港口、码头、装卸站和船舶修造拆解单位所在地县级以上地方人民政府应当统筹规划建设船舶污染物等的接收、转运、处理处置设施，建立相应的接收、转运、处理处置多部门联合监管制度。

沿海县级以上地方人民政府负责对其管理海域的渔港和渔业船舶停泊点及周边区域污染防治的监督管理，规范生产生活污水和渔业垃圾回收处置，推进污染防治设备建设和环境清理整治。

港口、码头、装卸站和船舶修造拆解单位应当按照有关规定配备足够的用于处理船舶污染物、废弃物的接收设施，使该设施处于良好状态并有效运行。

装卸油类等污染危害性货物的港口、码头、装卸站和船舶应当编制污染应急预案，并配备相应的污染应急设备和器材。

第八十六条　国家海事管理机构组织制定中国籍船舶禁止或者限制安装和使用的有害材料名录。

船舶修造单位或者船舶所有人、经营人或者管理人应当在船上备有有害材料清单，在船舶建造、营运和维修过程中持续更新，并在船舶拆解前提供给从事船舶拆解的单位。

第八十七条　从事船舶拆解的单位，应当采取有效的污染防治措施，在船舶拆解前将船舶污染物减至最小量，对拆解产生的船舶污染物、废弃物和其他有害物质进行安全与环境无害化处置。拆解的船舶部件不得进入水体。

禁止采取冲滩方式进行船舶拆解作业。

第八十八条　国家倡导绿色低碳智能航运，鼓励船舶使用新能源或者清洁能源，淘汰高耗能高排放老旧船舶，减少温室气体和大气污染物的排放。沿海县级以上地方人民政府应当制定港口岸电、船舶受电等设施建设和改造计划，并组织实施。港口岸电设施的供电能力应当与靠港船舶的用电需求相适应。

船舶应当按照国家有关规定采取有效措施提高能效水平。具备岸电使用条件的船舶靠港应当按照国家有关规定使用岸电，但是使用清洁能源的除外。具备岸电供应能力的港口经营人、岸电供电企业应当按照国家有关规定为具备岸电使用条件的船舶提供岸电。

国务院和沿海县级以上地方人民政府对港口岸电设施、船舶受电设施的改造和使用，清洁能源或者新能源动力船舶建造等按照规定给予支持。

第八十九条　船舶及有关作业活动应当遵守有关法律法规和标准，采取有效措施，防止造成海洋环境污染。海事管理机构等应当加强对船舶及有关作业活动的监督管理。

船舶进行散装液体污染危害性货物的过驳作业，应当编制作业方案，采取有效的安全和污染防治措施，并事先按照有关规定报经批准。

第九十条　船舶发生海难事故，造成或者可能造成海洋环境重大污染损害的，国家海事管理机构有权强制采取避免或者减少污染损害的措施。

对在公海上因发生海难事故，造成中华人民共和国管辖海域重大污染损害后果或者具有污染威胁的船舶、海上设施，国家海事管理机构有权采取与实际的或者可能发生的损害相称的必要措施。

第九十一条　所有船舶均有监视海上污染的义务，在发现海上污染事件或者违反本法规定的行为时，应当立即向就近的依照本法规定行使海洋环境监督管理权的部门或者机构报告。

民用航空器发现海上排污或者污染事件，应当及时向就近的民用航空空中交通管制单位报告。接到报告的单位，应当立即向依照本法规定行使海洋环境监督管理权的部门或者机构通报。

第九十二条　国务院交通运输主管部门可以划定船舶污染物排放控制区。进入控制区的船舶应当符合船舶污染物排放相关控制要求。

第八章　法律责任

第九十三条　违反本法规定，有下列行为之一，由依照本法规定行使海洋环境监督管理权的部门或者机构责令改正或者责令采取限制生产、停产整治等措施，并处以罚款；情节严重的，报经有批准权的人民政府批准，责令停业、关闭：

（一）向海域排放本法禁止排放的污染物或者其他物质的；

（二）未依法取得排污许可证排放污染物的；

（三）超过标准、总量控制指标排放污染物的；

（四）通过私设暗管或者篡改、伪造监测数据，或者不正常运行污染防治设施等逃避监管的方式违法向海洋排放污染物的；

（五）违反本法有关船舶压载水和沉积物排放和管理规定的；

（六）其他未依照本法规定向海洋排放污染物、废弃物的。

有前款第一项、第二项行为之一的，处二十万元以上一百万元以下的罚款；有前款第三项行为的，处十万元以上一百万元以下的罚款；有前款第四项行为的，处十万元以上一百万元以下的罚款，情节严重的，吊销排污许可证；有前款第五项、第六项行为之一的，处一万元以上二十万元以下的罚款。个人擅自在岸滩弃置、堆放和处理生活垃圾的，按次处一百元以上一千元以下的罚款。

第九十四条 违反本法规定，有下列行为之一，由依照本法规定行使海洋环境监督管理权的部门或者机构责令改正，处以罚款：

（一）未依法公开排污信息或者弄虚作假的；

（二）因发生事故或者其他突发性事件，造成或者可能造成海洋环境污染、生态破坏事件，未按照规定通报或者报告的；

（三）未按照有关规定制定应急预案并备案，或者未按照有关规定配备应急设备、器材的；

（四）因发生事故或者其他突发性事件，造成或者可能造成海洋环境污染、生态破坏事件，未立即采取有效措施或者逃逸的；

（五）未采取必要应对措施，造成海洋生态灾害危害扩大的。

有前款第一项行为的，处二万元以上二十万元以下的罚款，拒不改正的，责令限制生产、停产整治；有前款第二项行为的，处五万元以上五十万元以下的罚款，对直接负责的主管人员和其他直接责任人员处一万元以上十万元以下的罚款，并可以暂扣或者吊销相关任职资格许可；有前款第三项行为的，处二万元以上二十万元以下的罚款；有前款第四项、第五项行为之一的，处二十万元以上二百万元以下的罚款。

第九十五条 违反本法规定，拒绝、阻挠调查和现场检查，或者在被检查时弄虚作假的，由依照本法规定行使海洋环境监督管理权的部门或者机构责令改正，处五万元以上二十万元以下的罚款；对直接负责的主管人员和其他直接责任人员处二万元以上十万元以下的罚款。

第九十六条 违反本法规定，造成珊瑚礁等海洋生态系统或者自然保护地破坏的，由依照本法规定行使海洋环境监督管理权的部门或者机构责令改正、采取补救措施，处每平方米一千元以上一万元以下的罚款。

第九十七条 违反本法规定，有下列行为之一，由依照本法规定行使海洋环境监督管理权的部门或者机构责令改正，处以罚款：

（一）占用、损害自然岸线的；

（二）在严格保护岸线范围内开采海砂的；

（三）违反本法其他关于海砂、矿产资源规定的。

有前款第一项行为的，处每米五百元以上一万元以下的罚款；有前款第二项行为的，处货值金额二倍以上二十倍以下的罚款，货值金额不足十万元的，处二十万元以上二百万元以下的罚款；有前款第三项行为的，处五万元以上五十万元以下的罚款。

第九十八条 违反本法规定，从事海水养殖活动有下列行为之一，由依照本法规定行使海洋环境监督管理权的部门或者机构责令改正，处二万元以上二十万元以下的罚款；情节严重的，报经有批准权的人民政府批准，责令停业、关闭：

（一）违反禁养区、限养区规定的；

（二）违反养殖规模、养殖密度规定的；

（三）违反投饵、投肥、药物使用规定的；

（四）未按照有关规定对养殖尾水自行监测的。

第九十九条 违反本法规定设置入海排污口的，由生态环境主管部门责令关闭或者拆除，处二万元以上十万元以下的罚款；拒不关闭或者拆除的，强制关闭、拆除，所需费用由违法者承担，处十万元以上五十万元以下的罚款；情节严重的，可以责令停产整治。

违反本法规定，设置入海排污口未备案的，由生态环境主管部门责令改正，处二万元以上十万元以下的罚款。

违反本法规定，入海排污口的责任主体未按照规定开展监控、自动监测的，由生态环境主管部门责令改正，处二万元以上十万元以下的罚款；拒不改正的，可以责令停产整治。

自然资源、渔业等部门和海事管理机构、海警机构、军队生态环境保护部门发现前三款违法行为之一的，应当通报生态环境主管部门。

第一百条 违反本法规定，经中华人民共和国管辖海域，转移危险废物的，由国家海事管理机构责令非法运输该危险废物的船舶退出中华人民共和国管辖海域，处五十万元以上五百万元以下的罚款。

第一百零一条 违反本法规定，建设单位未落实建设项目投资计划有关要求的，由生态环境主管部门责令改正，处五万元以上二十万元以下的罚款；拒不改正的，处二十万元以上一百万元以下的罚款。

违反本法规定，建设单位未依法报批或者报请重新审核环境影响报告书（表），擅自开工建设的，由生态环境主管部门或者海警机构责令其停止建设，根据违法情节和危害后果，处建设项目总投资额百分之一以上百分之五以下的罚款，并可以责令恢复原状；对建设单位直接负责的主管人员和其他直接责任人员，依法给予处分。建设单位未依法备案环境影响登记表的，由生态环境主管部门责令备案，处五万元以下的罚款。

第一百零二条 违反本法规定，在依法划定的自然保护地、重要渔业水域及其他需要特别保护的区域建设污染环境、破坏生态的工程建设项目或者从事其他活动，或者在沿海陆域新建不符合国家产业政策的生产项目的，由县级以上人民政府按照管理权限责令关闭。

违反生态环境准入清单进行生产建设活动的，由依照本法规定行使海洋环境监督管理权的部门或者机构责令停止违法行为，限期拆除并恢复原状，所需费用由违法者承担，处五十万元以上五百万元以下的罚款，对直接负责的主管人员和其他直接责任人员处五万元以上十万元以下的罚款；情节严重的，报经有批准权的人民政府批准，责令关闭。

第一百零三条 违反本法规定，环境保护设施未与主体工程同时设计、同时施工、同时投产使用的，或者环境保护设施未建成、未达到规定要求、未经验收或者经验收不合格即投入生产、使用的，由生态环境主管部门或者海警机构责令改正，处二十万元以上一百万元以下的罚款；拒不改正的，处一百万元以上二百万元以下的罚款；对直接负责的主管人员和其他责任人员处五万元以上二十万元以下的罚款；造成重大环境污染、生态破坏的，责令其停止生产、使用，或者报经有批准权的人民政府批准，责令关闭。

第一百零四条 违反本法规定，工程建设项目有下列行为之一，由依照本法规定行使海洋环境监督管理权的部门或者机构责令其停止违法行为、消除危害，处二十万元以上一百万元以下的罚款；情节严重的，报经有批准权的人民政府批准，责令停业、关闭：

（一）使用含超标准放射性物质或者易溶出有毒有害物质的材料的；

（二）造成领海基点及其周围环境的侵蚀、淤积、损害，或者危及领海基点稳定的。

第一百零五条　违反本法规定进行海洋油气勘探开发活动，造成海洋环境污染的，由海警机构责令改正，给予警告，并处二十万元以上一百万元以下的罚款。

第一百零六条　违反本法规定，有下列行为之一，由国务院生态环境主管部门及其海域派出机构、海事管理机构或者海警机构责令改正，处以罚款，必要时可以扣押船舶；情节严重的，报经有批准权的人民政府批准，责令停业、关闭：

（一）倾倒废弃物的船舶驶出港口未报告的；

（二）未取得倾倒许可证，向海洋倾倒废弃物的；

（三）在海上焚烧废弃物或者处置放射性废物及其他放射性物质的。

有前款第一项行为的，对违法船舶的所有人、经营人或者管理人处三千元以上三万元以下的罚款，对船长、责任船员或者其他责任人员处五百元以上五千元以下的罚款；有前款第二项行为的，处二十万元以上二百万元以下的罚款；有前款第三项行为的，处五十万元以上五百万元以下的罚款。有前款第二项、第三项行为之一，两年内受到行政处罚三次以上的，三年内不得从事废弃物海洋倾倒活动。

第一百零七条　违反本法规定，有下列行为之一，由国务院生态环境主管部门及其海域派出机构、海事管理机构或者海警机构责令改正，处以罚款，暂扣或者吊销倾倒许可证，必要时可以扣押船舶；情节严重的，报经有批准权的人民政府批准，责令停业、关闭：

（一）未按照国家规定报告倾倒情况的；

（二）未按照国家规定安装使用海洋倾废在线监控设备的；

（三）获准倾倒废弃物的单位未依照本法规定委托实施废弃物海洋倾倒作业或者未依照本法规定监督实施的；

（四）未按照倾倒许可证的规定倾倒废弃物的。

有前款第一项行为的，按次处五千元以上二万元以下的罚款；有前款第二项行为的，处二万元以上二十万元以下的罚款；有前款第三项行为的，处三万元以上三十万元以下的罚款；有前款第四项行为的，处二十万元以上一百万元以下的罚款，被吊销倾倒许可证的，二年内不得从事废弃物海洋倾倒活动。

以提供虚假申请材料、欺骗、贿赂等不正当手段申请取得倾倒许可证的，由国务院生态环境主管部门及其海域派出机构依法撤销倾倒许可证，并处二十万元以上五十万元以下的罚款；三年内不得再次申请倾倒许可证。

第一百零八条　违反本法规定，将中华人民共和国境外废弃物运进中华人民共和国管辖海域倾倒的，由海警机构责令改正，根据造成或者可能造成的危害后果，处五十万元以上五百万元以下的罚款。

第一百零九条　违反本法规定，有下列行为之一，由依照本法规定行使海洋环境监督管理权的部门或者机构责令改正，处以罚款：

（一）港口、码头、装卸站、船舶修造拆解单位未按照规定配备或者有效运行船舶污染物、废弃物接收设施，或者船舶的结构、配备的防污设备和器材不符合国家防污规定或者未经检验合格的；

（二）从事船舶污染物、废弃物接收和船舶清舱、洗舱作业活动，不具备相应接收处理能力的；

（三）从事船舶拆解、旧船改装、打捞和其他水上、水下施工作业，造成海洋环境污染损害的；

（四）采取冲滩方式进行船舶拆解作业的。

有前款第一项、第二项行为之一的，处二万元以上三十万元以下的罚款；有前款第三项行为的，处五万元以上二十万元以下的罚款；有前款第四项行为的，处十万元以上一百万元以下的罚款。

第一百一十条 违反本法规定，有下列行为之一，由依照本法规定行使海洋环境监督管理权的部门或者机构责令改正，处以罚款：

（一）未在船上备有有害材料清单，未在船舶建造、营运和维修过程中持续更新有害材料清单，或者未在船舶拆解前将有害材料清单提供给从事船舶拆解单位的；

（二）船舶未持有防污证书、防污文书，或者不按照规定监测、监控，如实记载和保存船舶污染物、压载水和沉积物的排放及操作记录的；

（三）船舶采取措施提高能效水平未达到有关规定的；

（四）进入控制区的船舶不符合船舶污染物排放相关控制要求的；

（五）具备岸电供应能力的港口经营人、岸电供电企业未按照国家规定为具备岸电使用条件的船舶提供岸电的；

（六）具备岸电使用条件的船舶靠港，不按照国家规定使用岸电的。

有前款第一项行为的，处二万元以下的罚款；有前款第二项行为的，处十万元以下的罚款；有前款第三项行为的，处一万元以上十万元以下的罚款；有前款第四项行为的，处三万元以上三十万元以下的罚款；有前款第五项、第六项行为之一的，处一万元以上十万元以下的罚款，情节严重的，处十万元以上五十万元以下的罚款。

第一百一十一条 违反本法规定，有下列行为之一，由依照本法规定行使海洋环境监督管理权的部门或者机构责令改正，处以罚款：

（一）拒报或者谎报船舶载运污染危害性货物申报事项的；

（二）托运人未将托运的污染危害性货物的正式名称、污染危害性以及应当采取的防护措施如实告知承运人的；

（三）托运人交付承运人的污染危害性货物的单证、包装、标志、数量限制不符合对所交付货物的有关规定的；

（四）托运人在托运的普通货物中夹带污染危害性货物或者将污染危害性货物谎报为普通货物的；

（五）需要船舶载运污染危害性不明的货物，未按照有关规定事先进行评估的。

有前款第一项行为的，处五万元以下的罚款；有前款第二项行为的，处五万元以上十万元以下的罚款；有前款第三项、第五项行为之一的，处二万元以上十万元以下的罚款；有前款第四项行为的，处十万元以上二十万元以下的罚款。

第一百一十二条 违反本法规定，有下列行为之一，由依照本法规定行使海洋环境监督管理权的部门或者机构责令改正，处一万元以上五万元以下的罚款：

（一）载运具有污染危害性货物的船舶未经许可进出港口或者装卸作业的；

（二）装卸油类及有毒有害货物的作业，船岸双方未遵守安全防污操作规程的；

（三）船舶进行散装液体污染危害性货物的过驳作业，未编制作业方案或者未按照有关规定报经批准的。

第一百一十三条 企业事业单位和其他生产经营者违反本法规定向海域排放、倾倒、处置污染物、废弃物或者其他物质，受到罚款处罚，被责令改正的，依法作出处罚决定的部门或者机构应当组织复查，发现其继续实施该违法行为或者拒绝、阻挠复查的，依照《中华人民共和国环境保护法》的规定按日连续处罚。

第一百一十四条 对污染海洋环境、破坏海洋生态，造成他人损害的，依照《中华人民共和国民法典》等法律的规定承担民事责任。

对污染海洋环境、破坏海洋生态，给国家造成重大损失的，由依照本法规定行使海洋环境监督管理权的部门代表国家对责任者提出损害赔偿要求。

前款规定的部门不提起诉讼的，人民检察院可以向人民法院提起诉讼。前款规定的部门提起诉讼的，人民检察院可以支持起诉。

第一百一十五条 对违反本法规定，造成海洋环境污染、生态破坏事故的单位，除依法承担赔偿责任外，由依照本法规定行使海洋环境监督管理权的部门或者机构处以罚款；对直接负责的主管人员和其他直接责任人员可以处上一年度从本单位取得收入百分之五十以下的罚款；直接负责的主管人员和其他直接责任人员属于公职人员的，依法给予处分。

对造成一般或者较大海洋环境污染、生态破坏事故的，按照直接损失的百分之二十计算罚款；对造成重大或者特大海洋环境污染、生态破坏事故的，按照直接损失的百分之三十计算罚款。

第一百一十六条 完全属于下列情形之一，经过及时采取合理措施，仍然不能避免对海洋环境造成污染损害的，造成污染损害的有关责任者免予承担责任：

（一）战争；

（二）不可抗拒的自然灾害；

（三）负责灯塔或者其他助航设备的主管部门，在执行职责时的疏忽，或者其他过失行为。

第一百一十七条 未依照本法规定缴纳倾倒费的，由国务院生态环境主管部门及其海域派出机构责令限期缴纳；逾期拒不缴纳的，处应缴纳倾倒费数额一倍以上三倍以下的罚款，并可以报经有批准权的人民政府批准，责令停业、关闭。

第一百一十八条 海洋环境监督管理人员滥用职权、玩忽职守、徇私舞弊，造成海洋环境污染损害、生态破坏的，依法给予处分。

第一百一十九条 违反本法规定，构成违反治安管理行为的，依法给予治安管理处罚；构成犯罪的，依法追究刑事责任。

第九章　附则

第一百二十条 本法中下列用语的含义是：

（一）海洋环境污染损害，是指直接或者间接地把物质或者能量引入海洋环境，产生损害海洋生物资源、危害人体健康、妨害渔业和海上其他合法活动、损害海水使用素质和减损环境质量等有害影响。

（二）内水，是指我国领海基线向内陆一侧的所有海域。

（三）沿海陆域，是指与海岸相连，或者通过管道、沟渠、设施，直接或者间接向海洋排放污染物及其相关活动的一带区域。

（四）滨海湿地，是指低潮时水深不超过六米的水域及其沿岸浸湿地带，包括水深不超过六米的永久性水域、潮间带（或者洪泛地带）和沿海低地等，但是用于养殖的人工的水域和滩涂除外。

（五）陆地污染源（简称陆源），是指从陆地向海域排放污染物，造成或者可能造成海洋环境污染的场所、设施等。

（六）陆源污染物，是指由陆地污染源排放的污染物。

（七）倾倒，是指通过船舶、航空器、平台或者其他载运工具，向海洋处置废弃物和其他有害物质的行为，包括弃置船舶、航空器、平台及其辅助设施和其他浮动工具的行为。

（八）海岸线，是指多年大潮平均高潮位时海陆分界痕迹线，以国家组织开展的海岸线修测结果为准。

（九）入海河口，是指河流终端与受水体（海）相结合的地段。

（十）海洋生态灾害，是指受自然环境变化或者人为因素影响，导致一种或者多种海洋生物暴发性增殖或者高度聚集，对海洋生态系统结构和功能造成损害。

（十一）渔业水域，是指鱼虾蟹贝类的产卵场、索饵场、越冬场、洄游通道和鱼虾蟹贝藻类及其他水生动植物的养殖场。

（十二）排放，是指把污染物排入海洋的行为，包括泵出、溢出、泄出、喷出和倒出。

（十三）油类，是指任何类型的油及其炼制品。

（十四）入海排污口，是指直接或者通过管道、沟、渠等排污通道向海洋环境水体排放污水的口门，包括工业排污口、城镇污水处理厂排污口、农业排口及其他排口等类型。

（十五）油性混合物，是指任何含有油份的混合物。

（十六）海上焚烧，是指以热摧毁为目的，在海上焚烧设施上，故意焚烧废弃物或者其他物质的行为，但是船舶、平台或者其他人工构造物正常操作中所附带发生的行为除外。

第一百二十一条 涉及海洋环境监督管理的有关部门的具体职权划分，本法未作规定的，由国务院规定。

沿海县级以上地方人民政府行使海洋环境监督管理权的部门的职责，由省、自治区、直辖市人民政府根据本法及国务院有关规定确定。

第一百二十二条 军事船舶和军事用海环境保护管理办法，由国务院、中央军事委员会依照本法制定。

第一百二十三条 中华人民共和国缔结或者参加的与海洋环境保护有关的国际条约与本法有不同规定的，适用国际条约的规定；但是，中华人民共和国声明保留的条款除外。

第一百二十四条 本法自 2024 年 1 月 1 日起施行。

中华人民共和国船舶及其有关作业活动污染海洋环境防治管理规定

（2010 年 11 月 16 日交通运输部令 2010 年第 7 号发布根据 2013 年 8 月 31 日交通运输部《关于修改〈中华人民共和国船舶及其有关作业活动污染海洋环境防治管理规定〉的决定》第一次修正根据 2013 年 12 月 24 日交通运输部《关于修改〈中华人民共和国船舶及其有关作业活动污染海洋环境防治管理规定〉的决定》第二次修正根据 2016 年 12 月 13 日交通运输部《关于修改〈中华人民共和国船舶及其有关作业活动污染海洋环境防治管理规定〉的决定》第三次修正根据 2017 年 5 月 23 日交通运输部《关于修改〈中华人民共和国船舶及其有关作业活动污染海洋环境防治管理规定〉的决定》第四次修正）

第一章 总 则

第一条 为了防治船舶及其有关作业活动污染海洋环境，根据《中华人民共和国海洋环境保护法》《中华人民共和国大气污染防治法》《中华人民共和国防治船舶污染海洋环境管理条例》和中华人民共和国缔结或者加入的国际条约，制定本规定。

第二条 防治船舶及其有关作业活动污染中华人民共和国管辖海域适用本规定。

本规定所称有关作业活动，是指船舶装卸、过驳、清舱、洗舱、油料供受、修造、打捞、拆解、污染危害性货物装箱、充罐、污染清除以及其他水上水下船舶施工作业等活动。

第三条 国务院交通运输主管部门主管全国船舶及其有关作业活动污染海洋环境的防治工作。

国家海事管理机构负责监督管理全国船舶及其有关作业活动污染海洋环境的防治工作。

各级海事管理机构根据职责权限，具体负责监督管理本辖区船舶及其有关作业活动污染海洋环境的防治工作。

第二章 一般规定

第四条 船舶的结构、设备、器材应当符合国家有关防治船舶污染海洋环境的船舶检验规范以及中华人民共和国缔结或者加入的国际条约的要求，并按照国家规定取得相应的合格证书。

第五条 船舶应当依照法律、行政法规、国务院交通运输主管部门的规定以及中华人民共和国缔结或者加入的国际条约的要求，取得并随船携带相应的防治船舶污染海洋环境的证书、文书。

海事管理机构应当向社会公布本条第一款规定的证书、文书目录，并及时更新。

第六条 中国籍船舶持有的防治船舶污染海洋环境的证书、文书由国家海事管理机构或者其认可的机构签发；外国籍船舶持有的防治船舶污染海洋环境的证书、文书应当符合中华人民共和国缔结或者加入的国际条约的要求。

第七条 船员应当具有相应的防治船舶污染海洋环境的专业知识和技能，并按照有关法律、行政法规、规章的规定参加相应的培训、考试，持有有效的适任证书或者相应的培训合格证明。

从事有关作业活动的单位应当组织本单位作业人员进行操作技能、设备使用、作业程序、安全防护和应急反应等专业培训，确保作业人员具备相关安全和防治污染的专业知识和技能。

第八条　港口、码头、装卸站和从事船舶修造作业的单位应当按照国家有关标准配备相应的污染监视设施和污染物接收设施。

港口、码头、装卸站以及从事船舶修造、打捞、拆解等有关作业活动的其他单位应当按照国家有关标准配备相应的防治污染设备和器材。

第九条　船舶从事下列作业活动，应当遵守有关法律法规、标准和相关操作规程，落实安全和防治污染措施，并在作业前将作业种类、作业时间、作业地点、作业单位和船舶名称等信息向海事管理机构报告；作业信息变更的，应当及时补报：

（一）在沿海港口进行舷外拷铲、油漆作业或者使用焚烧炉的；

（二）在港区水域内洗舱、清舱、驱气以及排放垃圾、生活污水、残油、含油污水、含有毒有害物质污水等污染物和压载水的；

（三）冲洗沾有污染物、有毒有害物质的甲板的；

（四）进行船舶水上拆解、打捞、修造和其他水上、水下船舶施工作业的；

（五）进行船舶油料供受作业的。

第十条　从事3万载重吨以上油轮的货舱清舱、1万吨以上散装液体污染危害性货物过驳以及沉船打捞、油轮拆解等存在较大污染风险的作业活动的，作业方应当进行作业方案可行性研究，并在作业活动中接受海事管理机构的检查。

第十一条　任何单位和个人发现船舶及其有关作业活动造成或者可能造成海洋环境污染的，应当立即就近向海事管理机构报告。

第三章　船舶污染物的排放与接收

第十二条　在中华人民共和国管辖海域航行、停泊、作业的船舶排放船舶垃圾、生活污水、含油污水、含有毒有害物质污水、废气等污染物以及压载水，应当符合法律、行政法规、有关标准以及中华人民共和国缔结或者加入的国际条约的规定。

船舶在船舶排放控制区内航行、停泊、作业还应当遵守船舶排放控制区大气污染防治控制要求。船舶应当使用低硫燃油或者采取使用岸电、清洁能源、尾气后处理装置等替代措施满足船舶大气排放控制要求。

第十三条　船舶不得向依法划定的海洋自然保护区、海洋特别保护区、海滨风景名胜区、重要渔业水域以及其他需要特别保护的海域排放污染物。

依法设立本条第一款规定的需要特别保护的海域的，应当在适当的区域配套设置船舶污染物接收设施和应急设备器材。

第十四条　船舶应当将不符合第十二条规定排放要求以及依法禁止向海域排放的污染物，排入具备相应接收能力的港口接收设施或者委托具备相应接收能力的船舶污染物接收单位接收。

船舶委托船舶污染物接收单位进行污染物接收作业的，其船舶经营人应当在作业前明确指定所委托的船舶污染物接收单位。

第十五条　船舶污染物接收单位进行船舶垃圾、残油、含油污水、含有毒有害物质污水等污染物接收作业，应当在作业前将作业时间、作业地点、作业单位、作业船舶、污染物种类和数量以及拟处置的方式及去向等情况向海事管理机构报告。接收处理情况发生变更的，应当及时补报。

港口建立船舶污染物接收、转运、处置监管联单制度的，船舶与船舶污染物接收单位应当按照联单制度的要求将船舶污染物接收、转运和处置情况报告有关主管部门。

第十六条　船舶污染物接收作业单位应当落实安全与防污染管理制度。进行污染物接收作业的，应当编制作业方案，遵守国家有关标准、规程，并采取有效的防污染措施，防止污染物溢漏。

第十七条　船舶污染物接收单位应当在污染物接收作业完毕后，向船舶出具污染物接收单证，经双方签字确认并留存至少2年。污染物接收单证上应当注明作业单位名称，作业双方船名，作业开始和结束的时间、地点，以及污染物种类、数量等内容。

船舶应当将污染物接收单证保存在相应的记录簿中。

第十八条　船舶进行涉及污染物处置的作业，应当在相应的记录簿内规范填写、如实记录，真实反映船舶运行过程中产生的污染物数量、处置过程和去向。按照法律、行政法规、国务院交通运输主管部门的规定以及中华人民共和国缔结或者加入的国际条约的要求，不需要配备记录簿的，应当将有关情况在作业当日的航海日志或者轮机日志中如实记载。

船舶应当将使用完毕的船舶垃圾记录簿在船舶上保留2年；将使用完毕的含油污水、含有毒有害物质污水记录簿在船舶上保留3年。

第十九条　船舶污染物接收单位应当将接收的污染物交由具有国家规定资质的污染物处理单位进行处理，并每月将船舶污染物的接收和处理情况报海事管理机构备案。

第二十条　接收处理含有有毒有害物质或者其他危险成分的船舶污染物的，应当符合国家有关危险废物的管理规定。来自疫区船舶产生的污染物，应当经有关检疫部门检疫处理后方可进行接收和处理。

第二十一条　船舶应当配备有盖、不渗漏、不外溢的垃圾储存容器，或者对垃圾实行袋装。

船舶应当对垃圾进行分类收集和存放，对含有有毒有害物质或者其他危险成分的垃圾应当单独存放。

船舶将含有有毒有害物质或者其他危险成分的垃圾排入港口接收设施或者委托船舶污染物接收单位接收的，应当向对方说明此类垃圾所含物质的名称、性质和数量等情况。

第二十二条　船舶应当按照国家有关规定以及中华人民共和国缔结或者加入的国际条约的要求，设置与生活污水产生量相适应的处理装置或者储存容器。

第四章　船舶载运污染危害性货物及其有关作业

第二十三条　本规定所称污染危害性货物，是指直接或者间接进入水体，会损害水体质量和环境质量，从而产生损害生物资源、危害人体健康等有害影响的货物。

国家海事管理机构应当向社会公布污染危害性货物的名录，并根据需要及时更新。

第二十四条　船舶载运污染危害性货物进出港口，承运人或者代理人应当在进出港24小时前（航程不足24小时的，在驶离上一港口时）向海事管理机构办理船舶适载申报手续；货物所有人或者代理人应当在船舶适载申报之前向海事管理机构办理货物适运申报手续。

货物适运申报和船舶适载申报经海事管理机构审核同意后，船舶方可进出港口或者过境停留。

第二十五条　交付运输的污染危害性货物的特性、包装以及针对货物采取的风险防范和应急措施等应当符合国家有关标准、规定以及中华人民共和国缔结或者加入的国际条约的要求；需要经国家有关主管部门依法批准后方可载运的，还需要取得有关主管部门的批准。

船舶适载的条件按照《中华人民共和国海事行政许可条件规定》关于船舶载运危险货物的适载条件执行。

第二十六条　货物所有人或者代理人办理货物适运申报手续的，应当向海事管理机构提交下列材料：

（一）货物适运申报单，包括货物所有人或者代理人有关情况以及货物名称、种类、特性等基本信息；

（二）由代理人办理货物适运申报手续的，应当提供货物所有人出具的有效授权证明；

（三）相应的污染危害性货物安全技术说明书，安全作业注意事项、防范和应急措施等有关材料；

（四）需要经国家有关主管部门依法批准后方可载运的污染危害性货物，应当持有有效的批准文件；

（五）交付运输下列污染危害性货物的，还应当提交下列材料：

1.载运包装污染危害性货物的，应当提供包装和中型散装容器检验合格证明或者压力容器检验合格证明；

2.使用可移动罐柜装载污染危害性货物的，应当提供罐柜检验合格证明；

3.载运放射性污染危害性货物的，应当提交放射性剂量证明；

4.货物中添加抑止剂或者稳定剂的，应当提交抑止剂或者稳定剂的名称、数量、温度、有效期以及超过有效期时应当采取的措施；

5.载运限量污染危害性货物的，应当提交限量危险货物证明；

6.载运污染危害性不明货物的，应当提交符合第三十条规定的污染危害性评估报告。

第二十七条　承运人或者代理人办理船舶适载申报手续的，应当向海事管理机构提交下列材料：

（一）船舶载运污染危害性货物申报单，包括承运人或者代理人有关情况以及货物名称、种类、特性等基本信息；

（二）海事管理机构批准的货物适运证明；

（三）由代理人办理船舶适载申报手续的，应当提供承运人出具的有效授权证明；

（四）防止油污证书、船舶适载证书、船舶油污损害民事责任保险或者其他财务保证证书；

（五）载运污染危害性货物的船舶在运输途中发生过意外情况的，还应当在船舶载运污染危害性货物申报单内扼要说明所发生意外情况的原因、已采取的控制措施和目前状况等有关情况，并于抵港后送交详细报告；

（六）列明实际装载情况的清单、舱单或者积载图；

（七）拟进行装卸作业的港口、码头、装卸站。

定船舶、定航线、定货种的船舶可以办理不超过一个月期限的船舶定期适载申报手续。办理船舶定期适载申报手续的，除应当提交本条第一款规定的材料外，还应当提交能够证明固定船舶在固定航线上运输固定污染危害性货物的有关材料。

第二十八条　海事管理机构收到货物适运申报、船舶适载申报后，应当根据第二十五条规定的条件在 24 小时内作出批准或者不批准的决定；办理船舶定期适载申报的，应当在 7 日内作出批准或者不批准的决定。

第二十九条　货物所有人或者代理人交付船舶载运污染危害性货物，应当采取有效的防治污染措施，确保货物的包装与标志的规格、比例、色度、持久性等符合国家有关安全与防治污染的要求，并在运输单证上如实注明该货物的技术名称、数量、类别、性质、预防和应急措施等内容。

第三十条　货物所有人或者代理人交付船舶载运污染危害性不明的货物，应当委托具备相应资质的技术机构对货物的污染危害性质和船舶载运技术条件进行评估。

第三十一条　曾经载运污染危害性货物的空容器和运输组件,应当彻底清洗并消除危害,取得由具有国家规定资质的检测机构出具的清洁证明后,方可按照普通货物交付船舶运输。在未彻底清洗并消除危害之前,应当按照原所装货物的要求进行运输。

第三十二条　海事管理机构认为交付船舶载运的货物应当按照污染危害性货物申报而未申报的,或者申报的内容不符合实际情况的,经海事管理机构负责人批准,可以采取开箱等方式查验。

海事管理机构在实施开箱查验时,货物所有人或者代理人应当到场,并负责搬移货物,开拆和重封货物的包装。海事管理机构认为必要时,可以径行开验、复验或者提取货样。有关单位和个人应当配合。

第三十三条　船舶不符合污染危害性货物适载要求的,不得载运污染危害性货物,码头、装卸站不得为其进行装卸作业。

发现船舶及其有关作业活动可能对海洋环境造成污染危害的,码头、装卸站、船舶应当立即采取相应的应急措施,并向海事管理机构报告。

第三十四条　从事污染危害性货物装卸作业的码头、装卸站,应当符合安全装卸和污染物处理的相关标准,并向海事管理机构提交安全装卸和污染物处理能力情况的有关材料。海事管理机构应当将具有相应安全装卸和污染物处理能力的码头、装卸站向社会公布。

载运污染危害性货物的船舶应当在海事管理机构公布的具有相应安全装卸和污染物处理能力的码头、装卸站进行装卸作业。

第三十五条　船舶进行散装液体污染危害性货物过驳作业的,应当符合国家海上交通安全和防治船舶污染海洋环境的管理规定和技术规范,选择缓流、避风、水深、底质等条件较好的水域,远离人口密集区、船舶通航密集区、航道、重要的民用目标或者设施、军用水域,制定安全和防治污染的措施和应急计划并保证有效实施。

第三十六条　进行散装液体污染危害性货物过驳作业的船舶,其承运人、货物所有人或者代理人应当向海事管理机构提交下列申请材料:

(一)船舶作业申请书,内容包括作业船舶资料、联系人、联系方式、作业时间、作业地点、过驳种类和数量等基本情况;

(二)船舶作业方案、拟采取的监护和防治污染措施;

(三)船舶作业应急预案;

(四)对船舶作业水域通航安全和污染风险的分析报告;

(五)与具有相应能力的污染清除作业单位签订的污染清除作业协议。

海事管理机构应当自受理申请之日起2日内根据第三十五条规定的条件作出批准或者不予批准的决定。2日内无法作出决定的,经海事管理机构负责人批准,可以延长5日。

第三十七条　从事船舶油料供受作业的单位应当向海事管理机构备案,并提交下列备案材料:

(一)工商营业执照;

(二)安全与防治污染制度文件、应急预案、应急设备物资清单、输油软管耐压检测证明以及作业人员参加培训情况;

(三)通过船舶进行油料供受作业的,还应当提交船舶相关证书、船上油污应急计划、作业船舶油污责任保险凭证以及船员适任证书;

(四)燃油质量承诺书;从事成品油供受作业的单位应当同时提交有关部门依法批准的成品油批发或者零售经营的证书。

第三十八条　进行船舶油料供受作业的，作业双方应当采取满足安全和防治污染要求的供受油作业管理措施，同时应当遵守下列规定：

（一）作业前，应当做到：

1. 检查管路、阀门，做好准备工作，堵好甲板排水孔，关好有关通海阀；

2. 检查油类作业的有关设备，使其处于良好状态；

3. 对可能发生溢漏的地方，设置集油容器；

4. 供受油双方以受方为主商定联系信号，双方均应切实执行。

（二）作业中，要有足够人员值班，当班人员要坚守岗位，严格执行操作规程，掌握作业进度，防止跑油、漏油；

（三）停止作业时，必须有效关闭有关阀门；

（四）收解输油软管时，必须事先用盲板将软管有效封闭，或者采取其他有效措施，防止软管存油倒流入海。

海事管理机构应当对船舶油料供受作业进行监督检查，发现不符合安全和防治污染要求的，应当予以制止。

第三十九条　船舶燃油供给单位应当如实填写燃油供受单证，并向船舶提供燃油供受单证和燃油样品。燃油供受单证应当包括受油船船名，船舶识别号或国际海事组织编号，作业时间、地点，燃油供应商的名称、地址和联系方式以及燃油种类、数量、密度和含硫量等内容。船舶和燃油供给单位应当将燃油供受单证保存 3 年，将燃油样品妥善保存 1 年。

燃油供给单位应当确保所供燃油的质量符合相关标准要求，并将所供燃油送交取得国家规定资质的燃油检测单位检测。燃油质量的检测报告应当留存在作业船舶上备查。

第四十条　船舶应当在出港前将上一航次消耗的燃料种类和数量，主机、辅机和锅炉功率以及运行工况时间等信息按照规定报告海事管理机构。

船舶按照船舶排放控制区要求转换低硫燃油或者采取使用岸电、清洁能源、尾气后处理装置等替代措施满足船舶大气排放控制要求的，应当按照规定如实记录。

第四十一条　船舶进行下列作业，且作业量超过 300 吨时，应当采取包括布设围油栏在内的防污染措施，其中过驳作业由过驳作业经营人负责：

（一）散装持久性油类的装卸和过驳作业，但船舶燃油供应作业除外；

（二）比重小于 1（相对于水）、溶解度小于 0.1% 的散装有毒液体物质的装卸和过驳作业；

（三）其他可能造成水域严重污染的作业。

因自然条件等原因，不适合布设围油栏的，应当采取有效替代措施。

第四十二条　载运污染危害性货物的船舶进出港口和通过桥区、交通管制区、通航密集区以及航行条件受限制的区域，或者载运剧毒、爆炸、放射性货物的船舶进出港口，应当遵守海事管理机构的特别规定，并采取必要的安全和防治污染保障措施。

第四十三条　船舶载运散发有毒有害气体或者粉尘物质等货物的，应当采取密闭或者其他防护措施。对有封闭作业要求的污染危害性货物，在运输和作业过程中应当采取措施回收有毒有害气体。

第五章　船舶拆解、打捞、修造和其他水上水下船舶施工作业

第四十四条　禁止采取冲滩方式进行船舶拆解作业。

第四十五条　进行船舶拆解、打捞、修造和其他水上水下船舶施工作业的，应当遵守相关操作规程，并采取必要的安全和防治污染措施。

第四十六条　在进行船舶拆解和船舶油舱修理作业前，作业单位应当将船舶上的残余物和废弃物进行有效处置，将燃油舱、货油舱中的存油驳出，进行洗舱、清舱、测爆等工作，并按照规定取得船舶污染物接收单证和有效的测爆证书。

船舶燃油舱、货油舱中的存油需要通过过驳方式交付储存的，应当遵守本规定关于散装液体污染危害性货物过驳作业的要求。

修造船厂应当建立防治船舶污染海洋环境管理制度，采取必要防护措施，防止船舶修造期间造成海洋环境污染。

第四十七条　在船坞内进行船舶修造作业的，修造船厂应当将坞内污染物清理完毕，确认不会造成水域污染后，方可沉起浮船坞或者开启坞门。

第四十八条　船舶拆解、打捞、修造或者其他水上水下船舶施工作业结束后，应当及时清除污染物，并将作业全过程产生的污染物的清除处理情况一并向海事管理机构报告，海事管理机构可以视情况进行现场核实。

第六章　法律责任

第四十九条　海事管理机构发现船舶、有关作业单位存在违反本规定行为的，应当责令改正；拒不改正的，海事管理机构可以责令停止作业、强制卸载，禁止船舶进出港口、靠泊、过境停留，或者责令停航、改航、离境、驶向指定地点。

第五十条　违反本规定，船舶的结构不符合国家有关防治船舶污染海洋环境的船舶检验规范或者有关国际条约要求的，由海事管理机构处 10 万元以上 30 万元以下的罚款。

第五十一条　违反本规定，船舶、港口、码头和装卸站未配备防治污染设施、设备、器材,有下列情形之一的,由海事管理机构予以警告,或者处 2 万元以上 10 万元以下的罚款:

（一）配备的防治污染设施、设备、器材数量不能满足法律、行政法规、规章、有关标准以及我国缔结或者参加的国际条约要求的；

（二）配备的防治污染设施、设备、器材技术性能不能满足法律、行政法规、规章、有关标准以及我国缔结或者参加的国际条约要求的。

第五十二条　违反本规定第九条、第四十条规定，船舶未按照规定将有关情况向海事管理机构报告的，由海事管理机构予以警告；情节严重的，处 2 万元以下的罚款。

第五十三条　违反本规定，船舶未持有防治船舶污染海洋环境的证书、文书的，由海事管理机构予以警告，或者处 2 万元以下的罚款。

第五十四条　违反本规定，船舶向海域排放本规定禁止排放的污染物的，由海事管理机构处 3 万元以上 20 万元以下的罚款。

第五十五条　违反本规定，船舶排放或者处置污染物，有下列情形之一的，由海事管理机构处 2 万元以上 10 万元以下的罚款：

（一）超过标准向海域排放污染物的；

（二）未按照规定在船上留存船舶污染物排放或者处置记录的；

（三）船舶污染物处置记录与船舶运行过程中产生的污染物数量不符合的。

第五十六条　违反本规定，船舶污染物接收单位进行船舶垃圾、残油、含油污水、含有毒有害物质污水等污染物接收作业，未编制作业方案、遵守相关操作规程、采取必要的防污染措施的，由海事管理机构处 1 万元以上 5 万元以下的罚款；造成海洋环境污染的，处 5 万元以上 25 万元以下的罚款。

第五十七条　违反本规定,船舶、船舶污染物接收单位接收处理污染物,有下列第（一）项情形的,由海事管理机构予以警告,或者处 2 万元以下的罚款;有下列第（二）项、第

（三）项情形的，由海事管理机构处 2 万元以下的罚款：

（一）船舶未如实记录污染物处置情况的；

（二）船舶污染物接收单位未按照规定向海事管理机构报告船舶污染物接收情况，或者未按照规定向船舶出具污染物接收单证的；

（三）船舶污染物接收单位未按照规定将船舶污染物的接收和处理情况报海事管理机构备案的。

第五十八条　违反本规定，未经海事管理机构批准，船舶载运污染危害性货物进出港口、过境停留的，由海事管理机构对其承运人、货物所有人或者代理人处 1 万元以上 5 万元以下的罚款；未经海事管理机构批准，船舶进行散装液体污染危害性货物过驳作业的，由海事管理机构对船舶处 1 万元以上 5 万元以下的罚款。

第五十九条　违反本规定，有下列第（一）项情形的，由海事管理机构予以警告，或者处 2 万元以上 10 万元以下的罚款；有下列第（二）项、第（三）项、第（四）项情形的，由海事管理机构处 2 万元以上 10 万元以下的罚款：

（一）船舶载运的污染危害性货物不具备适运条件的；

（二）载运污染危害性货物的船舶不符合污染危害性货物适载要求的；

（三）载运污染危害性货物的船舶未在具有相应安全装卸和污染物处理能力的码头、装卸站进行装卸作业的；

（四）货物所有人或者代理人未按照规定对污染危害性不明的货物进行污染危害性评估的。

第六十条　违反本规定，有下列情形之一的，由海事管理机构处 2000 元以上 1 万元以下的罚款：

（一）船舶未按照规定保存污染物接收单证的；

（二）船舶油料供受单位未如实填写燃油供受单证的；

（三）船舶油料供受单位未按照规定向船舶提供燃油供受单证和燃油样品的；

（四）船舶和船舶油料供受单位未按照规定保存燃油供受单证和燃油样品的。

船舶油料供给单位未按照有关安全和防治污染规范要求从事供受油作业，或者所提供的船舶油料超标的，由海事管理机构要求整改，并通报有关主管部门。

第六十一条　违反本规定，进行船舶水上拆解、旧船改装、打捞和其他水上水下船舶施工作业，造成海洋环境污染损害的，由海事管理机构予以警告，或者处 5 万元以上 20 万元以下的罚款。

第七章　附　则

第六十二条　军事船舶以及国务院交通运输主管部门所辖港区水域外渔业船舶污染海洋环境的防治工作，不适用本规定。

第六十三条　本规定自 2011 年 2 月 1 日起施行。

中华人民共和国海事局关于印发船舶能耗数据和碳强度管理办法的通知

海危防〔2022〕164号

各有关航运企业，各直属海事局：

为进一步做好船舶能耗数据收集和碳强度管理工作，我局研究制定了《船舶能耗数据和碳强度管理办法》，现印发给你们，请认真贯彻执行。

同时，授权上海海事局具体负责全国船舶能耗数据的统计、分析和验证，并具体负责中国籍国际航行船舶碳强度管理有关实施工作。

中华人民共和国海事局

2022 年 11 月 22 日

船舶能耗数据和碳强度管理办法

第一章 总 则

第一条 为做好船舶能耗数据收集和碳强度管理工作，根据《中华人民共和国船舶及其有关作业活动污染海洋环境防治管理规定》和我国缔结加入的《国际防止船舶造成污染公约》，制定本办法。

第二条 本办法适用于 400 总吨及以上中国籍船舶及进出我国港口的外国籍船舶。

军事船舶、渔业船舶和体育运动船艇不适用本办法。

第三条 中华人民共和国海事局（以下称中国海事局）统一负责船舶能耗数据管理工作，负责中国籍国际航行船舶碳强度管理工作。

各级海事管理机构和地方交通运输主管部门按照职责具体负责本辖区船舶能耗数据收集、报告管理及监督检查工作。

各级海事管理机构具体负责本辖区船舶碳强度监督检查工作。

中国海事局授权的直属海事局（以下简称被授权的直属海事局）具体负责全国船舶能耗数据的统计、分析和验证，并具体负责中国籍国际航行船舶碳强度管理有关实施工作。

中国海事局授权的船舶检验机构（以下称船舶检验机构）具体负责中国籍国际航行船舶能效指数数据收集、核验工作。

第二章 数据收集和报告

第四条 船舶应当按照本办法及《船舶能耗数据收集与报告技术要求》（JT/T1340）收集和报告船舶能耗数据。

第五条 中国籍国际航行船舶及进出我国港口的外国籍船舶应当按照《船舶能效管理计划》的要求在船舶日志或者其他相关文书上记录船舶能耗数据。

中国籍国内航行海船、内河船舶应当记录每日或者每一航次的船舶能耗数据，可采取电子记录或纸质记录方式，记录格式见附件。

船舶记录的能耗数据应当保存至少 2 年，以备海事管理机构检查。

第六条 中国籍国内航行海船应当在办理出港报告时向海事管理机构或者地方交通运输主管部门报告上一航次的船舶能耗数据。

符合以下情形之一的中国籍国内航行海船可以采用月度报告：

（一）在固定水域范围内航行且单航次的航行时间不超过 4 小时的船舶；

（二）在固定航线航行且单航次的航行时间不超过 24 小时的船舶。

采用月度报告的中国籍国内航行海船应当于每月 10 日前向任一挂靠港口所在地的海事管理机构或者地方交通运输主管部门报告上一自然月的汇总数据。

内河船舶应当于每年 4 月 1 日前向船籍港海事管理机构或者地方交通运输主管部门报告上一日历年的船舶能耗汇总数据。

第七条 中国籍国际航行船舶及外国籍船舶应当在境内办理出口岸手续或出港报告时向海事管理机构报告上一航次船舶能耗数据。

中国籍国际航行船舶应当在境外港口离港前向被授权的直属海事局报告上一航次船舶能耗数据。

第八条 船舶应当通过中国海事局确定的相关海事信息平台或系统（以下称信息平台）报告本办法要求的船舶能耗数据。因特殊情况无法报告时，船舶应当在具备报告条件后 5 个工作日内完成船舶能耗数据补报。

第九条　中国籍国际航行船舶应当按照《国际防止船舶造成污染公约》要求向船舶检验机构报告船舶能效指数数据。

船舶检验机构应当对船舶能效指数数据进行核验，并在规定的时间内将经核验的数据报送至被授权的直属海事局。

第十条　船舶应当如实报告船舶能耗数据及船舶能效指数数据，并对数据的完整性、真实性、准确性负责。

船舶检验机构应当对经核验的船舶能效指数数据的完整性、真实性、准确性负责。

第三章　中国籍国际航行船舶碳强度管理

第十一条　中国籍国际航行船舶应当符合《国际防止船舶造成污染公约》中船舶能效指数的相关要求，并取得《国际能效证书》。

第十二条　中国籍国际航行船舶应当按照规定编制《船舶能效管理计划》，提交至被授权的直属海事局验证，并将通过验证的《船舶能效管理计划》保存在船。

5000 总吨及以上中国籍国际航行船舶《船舶能效管理计划》通过验证的，被授权的直属海事局应当向其发放《船舶能效管理计划符合性确认书》。《船舶能效管理计划符合性确认书》的具体格式及内容根据《国际防止船舶造成污染公约》要求和管理需要确定。

船舶所有人、经营人或者管理人应当保证《船舶能效管理计划》的有效实施。

第十三条　5000 总吨及以上中国籍国际航行船舶变更所有人、经营人或者管理人的，发生重大改建的，或者被授权的直属海事局在抽查审核其《船舶能效管理计划》的实施情况时发现不符合要求的，应当按照要求重新编制《船舶能效管理计划》并提交至被授权的直属海事局验证，通过验证的，由被授权的直属海事局发放新的《船舶能效管理计划符合性确认书》。

第十四条　5000 总吨及以上中国籍国际航行船舶应当按照要求，于每年 3 月 31 日前向被授权的直属海事局报告上一日历年的船舶年度能耗数据及相关证明文件，并将船舶年度能耗报告数据及其原始数据留存至次年年底。

适用于《国际防止船舶造成污染公约》附则 Ⅵ 第 28 条的船舶，还须同时报告上一日历年达到的符合《国际防止船舶造成污染公约》要求的年度营运碳强度指标及相关证明文件。

第十五条　被授权的直属海事局应当对收到的船舶年度能耗报告数据进行验证，依据《国际防止船舶造成污染公约》要求，核定船舶达到的年度营运碳强度指标并评定年度营运碳强度等级。

船舶年度营运碳强度等级分为 A、B、C、D、E，对应优秀、良好、合格、较差、极差的船舶营运能效水平。

第十六条　船舶能耗报告和营运碳强度评级符合《国际防止船舶造成污染公约》要求，需要海事管理机构提供《燃油消耗报告和营运碳强度评级符合声明》的，被授权的直属海事局应当予以提供。

《燃油消耗报告和营运碳强度评级符合声明》的具体格式及内容根据《国际防止船舶造成污染公约》要求和管理需要确定，并应当在船上留存 5 年。

第十七条　船舶年度营运碳强度等级评定结果为 E 级或者连续三年为 D 级的，应当立即制定整改行动计划并纳入《船舶能效管理计划》中，并于当年的 4 月 30 日之前，将修订后的《船舶能效管理计划》提交至被授权的直属海事局验证。

修订后的《船舶能效管理计划》通过验证的，由被授权的直属海事局向船舶发放《燃油消耗报告和营运碳强度评级符合声明》及新的《船舶能效管理计划符合性确认书》。

第十八条　5000总吨及以上中国籍国际航行船舶转为外国籍，或变更所有人、经营人或者管理人的，应当在变更完成之日起1个月内，向被授权的直属海事局报告上一日历年的能耗数据和变更完成日之前当年的能耗数据。被授权的直属海事局应当对报告的数据进行验证，并向符合要求的船舶发放相应的《燃油消耗报告和营运碳强度评级符合声明》。

如前款所述船舶已经按照本办法第十四条报送上一年度相关数据的，可不再重复报送。

第十九条　对于年度营运碳强度评级为A、B的船舶，各级海事管理机构可适当降低碳强度管理监督检查频次。

第四章　监督管理

第二十条　各级海事管理机构和地方交通运输主管部门应当按照中国海事局制定的监督管理指南，依职责实施监督检查。

被授权的直属海事局在对中国籍国际航行船舶年度能耗数据验证中发现问题的，应当移交该船舶船籍港所在地的海事管理机构按照有关法律法规和本办法的要求实施检查。

被授权的直属海事局应当在《燃油消耗报告和营运碳强度评级符合声明》发放6个月内，按照中国海事局制定的监督管理指南，对《船舶能效管理计划》的实施情况进行抽查审核。

第二十一条　海事管理机构发现船舶未按规定报告船舶能耗数据的，应当依照《中华人民共和国船舶及其有关作业活动污染海洋环境防治管理规定》等规定和本办法的要求予以处理。

海事管理机构和地方交通运输主管部门发现船舶能耗数据报告错误的，应当督促船舶在接到通知之日起3个工作日内重新报送。

第五章　附则

第二十二条　本办法所称船舶碳强度管理是指为控制船舶温室气体排放强度而开展的相关管理工作，包括船舶能效管理和营运碳强度管理等。

第二十三条　本办法自2022年12月22日起施行，有效期五年。

自本办法施行之日起，《中华人民共和国海事局船舶能耗数据收集管理办法》（海危防〔2018〕476号）同时废止。

ICS 03.220.40

R 06

中华人民共和国交通运输行业标准

JT/T 1340—2020

船舶能耗数据收集与报告技术要求

Technical requirements for ships' energy consumption data collection and reporting

2020-10-30 发布

2021-02-01 实施

中华人民共和国交通运输部　发布

目　次

前　言

本标准按照 GB/T 1.1—2009 给出的规则起草。

本标准由交通运输部海事局提出。

本标准由交通运输航海安全标准化技术委员会归口。

本标准起草单位：浙江海事局、大连海事大学、上海海事大学、交通运输部规划研究院、中国船级社、中国远洋海运集团有限公司、招商局集团有限公司。

本标准主要起草人：张爽、张琨琨、赵颖磊、傅潇潇、苑海超、孙德平、张春昌、徐洪磊、郑超蕙、陈杰军、陈吉、汪文武、于大万。

JT/ T 1340—2020 船舶能耗数据收集与报告技术要求

1 范围

本标准规定了船舶能耗数据收集范围、船舶能耗及相关数据收集方法、数据质量保证计划以及数据报告等要求。

本标准适用于船舶能耗数据的收集与报告。

2 规范性引用文件

下列文件对于本文件的应用是必不可少的。凡是注日期的引用文件,仅注日期的版本适用于本文件。凡是不注日期的引用文件,其最新版本(包括所有的修改单)适用于本文件。

GB17411—2015 船用燃料油

GB 17411—2015/XG1—2018 《船用燃料油》国家标准第 1 号修改单

ISO8217:2017 石油产品燃料(F级)船用燃油规格 [Petroleum products—Fuels(class F)—Specifi-cations of marine fuels]

3 术语和定义、缩略语

3.1 术语和定义

下列术语和定义适用于本文件。

3.1.1 公司 company

船舶所有人或任何其他自船舶所有人处接管船舶营运责任,并同意承担船舶能耗数据收集与报告责任和义务的船舶管理人或光船承租人等组织或个人的统称。

3.1.2 船用燃料 marinefuel

为船舶推进或作业而交付船上使用的任何燃料。

3.1.3 报告期 reportperiod

船舶能耗数据收集与报告所对应的特定时间段。

3.1.4 用能设备 fuelconsumer

直接消耗船用燃料的主机、副机、燃气轮机、锅炉、惰性气体发生器等船上设备。

3.1.5 航次 voyage

船舶以上一次靠泊时间为起点、本次靠泊时间为终点的相邻两次靠泊期间的航行、停泊和作业。

3.2 缩略语

下列缩略语适用于本文件。

BDN————加油签收单（bunker delivery note）

HFO————重（质）燃（料）油（heavy fuel oil）

LFO————轻（质）燃（料）油（light fuel oil）

LNG————液化天然气（liquified natural gas）

LPG————液化石油气（liquified petroleum gas）

MDO————船用重柴油（marine diesel oil）

MGO————船用轻柴油（marine gas oil）

IMO————国际海事组织（International Maritime Organization）

4 船舶能耗数据收集范围

4.1 船舶能耗及相关数据项目

船舶能耗及相关数据项目见表1。

表 1 船舶能耗及相关数据项目

序号	数据项目	释义	单位
1	航行距离	船舶以运输或相关作业为目的,依靠自有动力相对于陆地的实际航行距离	海里（nmile）或公里（km）[a]
2	航行时间	船舶以运输或相关作业为目的,依靠自有动力航行的时间	小时（h）
3	营运时间	船舶技术状况完好可以从事运输及相关作业的时间,包括航行时间、停泊时间及其他作业时间。船舶带货修理等仍然从事运输及相关作业的情形应计入营运时间	小时（h）
4	客货周转量	船舶客货装载量（或折算装载量）[b] 与对应运输距离的乘积	吨海里（t·nmile）或其他[c]
5	燃料消耗量	船舶营运期间各类燃料[d] 消耗量	吨（t）或其他[e]
6	岸电使用时间	船舶靠泊期间使用岸电的时长	小时（h）
7	岸电消耗量	船舶靠泊期间所消耗的岸电量	千瓦时（kW·h）

[a] 国际航行船舶和国内航行海船的航行距离以海里（nmile）计,内河船的航行距离以公里（km）计;
[b] 核算方法见 4.2;
[c] 根据客货装载量和运输距离的单位确定;
[d] 分类方法见 4.3;
[e] 对于 4.3 中的"其他"类燃料,若不宜采用吨（t）作为单位,可视情采用其他单位。

4.2 客货装载量或折算装载量

船舶客货装载量或折算装载量按下列方法核算:

a) 对于散货船、气体运输船、液货船、杂货船、冷藏船、兼用船、滚装货船（包括滚装车辆运输船）和客滚船,载货量为所载货物的总重量,单位为吨（t）;

b) 对于集装箱船,载货量为所载集装箱总重量,单位为吨（t）;若填报所装载集装箱总数,单位为标准箱（TEU）;

c) 对于混装集装箱及其他货物的船舶,载货量为所载集装箱总重量与其他货物总重量之和,单位为吨（t）;若无法获得集装箱实际重量,按重载集装箱 10 t/TEU、空载集装箱 2 t/TEU 折算;

d) 对于客船（包括客滚船）,载客量为实际载客人数,或以额定载客人数计。

4.3 船用燃料分类

船用燃料分类见表2。

表 2 船用燃料分类

分类标识	燃料种类	说明及要求
1	重（质）燃（料）油（HFO）[a]	等同于 ISO 8217：2017 RME 级至 RMK 级
1.1	硫含量高于 0.5%	
1.2	硫含量高于 0.1%，但不高于 0.5%	
1.3	硫含量不高于 0.1%	
2	轻（质）燃（料）油（LFO）[a]	等同于 ISO8217：2017RMA 级至 RMD 级
2.1	硫含量高于 0.5%	
2.2	硫含量高于 0.1%，但不高于 0.5%	
2.3	硫含量不高于 0.1%	
3	船用柴油	等同于 ISO 8217：2017 DMX 级至 DMB 级
3.1	船用重柴油（MDO）	
3.2	船用轻柴油（MGO）	
4	内河船用燃料油	应符合 GB 17411—2015/XGI—2018 国家标准第 1 号修改单的规定
5	液化石油气（LPG）	
5.1	丙烷	
5.2	丁烷	
6	液化天然气（LNG）	
7	甲醇	
8	乙醇	
9	其他	
[a] 硫含量以质量百分比计。		

5 船舶能耗及相关数据收集方法

5.1 船舶运输活动数据收集

船舶航行距离、航行时间、营运时间、客货周转量可根据航海日志、轮机日志、提单、舱单、正午报告及航次报告等进行收集。

5.2 船用燃料消耗数据收集

5.2.1 一般要求

应收集报告期内船上全部燃料消耗。若船舶使用多种燃料，各类燃料消耗数据应分别收集。船用燃料消耗数据的收集主要有下列方法：

a） 燃油舱测量法，代码为 A；

b） BDN 加总法，代码为 B；

c） 流量计法，代码为 C。

可视情选择上述任何一种方法，或组合使用多种方法。在同一个报告期内，宜采用相同方法进行船用燃料消耗数据收集；若改变数据收集方法，应予记录并说明。

5.2.2 燃油舱测量法

通过人工或系统自动测量燃油舱来获取燃油日消耗量，进而统计报告期内燃油消耗总量的方法，按式（1）计算。

$$Q = \sum_{i=1}^{n} Q_i \qquad (1)$$

式中：Q——报告期内燃油消耗总量，单位为吨（t）；

Q_i——报告期内基于第 i 次测量获取的燃油消耗量，单位为吨（t），i 取值为 1、2、3、$\cdots$、n。

一般情况下，船舶航行期间应每日进行燃油舱测量，并在每次燃油加装或驳出作业后进行燃油舱测量。测量数据概要和燃油消耗记录应保留在船上。在船舶到港等可行情况下，应对燃油舱测量数据进行校正。若采用了密度、温度等修正，应当保留证明文件。该方法不适用于使用气体燃料的船舶。

5.2.3 加油签收单加总法

基于 BDN 载明的燃油加装量，以及报告期起止时燃油舱存油量和报告期内船上燃油驳出量，进而统计报告期内燃油消耗总量的方法，按式（2）计算。

$$Q = C_0 + \sum_{i=1}^{n} D_i - \sum_{j=1}^{m} B_j - C_1 \qquad (2)$$

式中：Q——报告期内燃油消耗总量，单位为吨（t）；

C_0——报告期初燃油舱存油量，单位为吨（t）；

D_i——报告期内第 i 次 BDN 载明的燃油加装量，单位为吨（t），i 取值为 1、2、3、⋯、n；

B_j——报告期内油类记录簿等记载的第 j 次船上燃油驳出量，单位为吨（t），j 取值为 1、2、3、⋯、m；

C_1——报告期末燃油舱存油量，单位为吨（t）。

报告期起止时的燃油舱存油量应按 5.2.2 所述的方法进行测量；任何用于校正燃油消耗量的补充数据应保留书面证据；BDN 应至少在船上保存三年；无 BDN 的船舶不适用此方法；使用所载货物（如 LNG）作为燃料的船舶不能单独使用此方法。

5.2.4 流量计法

基于船上流量计读数获取船舶燃料日消耗量，进而统计报告期内船用燃料消耗总量的方法，按式（3）计算。

$$Q = \sum_{i=1}^{n} \sum_{j=1}^{m_i} Q_{ij}$$
（3）

式中：Q——报告期内燃料消耗总量，单位为吨（t）；

Q_{ij}——报告期内基于第 j 次读数获取的用能设备 i 的燃料消耗量，单位为吨（t）。i 取值为 1、2、3、⋯、n；j 取值为 1、2、3、⋯、m_i。若多种用能设备共用一个流量计，Q_{ij} 为基于流量计 i 的第 j 次读数获取的相关用能设备燃料消耗量。

若某些用能设备未配备流量计或所配备的流量计发生故障，应采用其他替代方法进行数据收集。应如实记录所采用的任何替代方法，以及对流量计所进行的任何校正和保养，并将有关记录保留在船上。

5.3 岸电消耗量统计

船舶消耗的岸电量根据电能计量器具显示的用电量进行统计。

6 数据质量保证计划

公司应为每艘船舶制订数据质量保证计划，并指定专人负责，确保所收集数据的完整性和真实性。数据质量保证计划应至少包括下列内容：

a) 及时发现数据收集过程中产生系统性偏差或错误的方法，以及校正程序；b) 减小数据收集过程中的随机误差的措施；

c ）　避免重复或遗漏收集数据的措施；

d ）　在数据采集设备发生故障的情况下 , 对缺失数据的补救措施；

e ）　采用既定数据收集方法的依据 , 以及改变数据收集方法的记录和说明等。

7　数据报告

7.1　一般要求

7.1.1　报告期内所收集的数据应按规定报告相关海事管理机构或经其授权的船舶检验机构。若按航次收集数据 , 且航次跨越不同的报告期 , 所收集的数据应计入航次结束时刻所在的报告期。

7.1.2　上报数据应至少包括下列内容：

a ）　船舶基本信息；

b ）　船舶运输活动数据；

c ）　船舶能耗数据及相关信息。

7.2　船舶基本信息

船舶基本信息、报告说明及要求见表 3。

表 3　船舶基本信息、报告说明及要求

序号	项目	报告说明及要求
1	船名	包括船舶的中文名和英文名（如有）
2	公司名	负责数据收集和报告的公司全称
3	船舶识别信息	对于国际航行船舶 , 为 IMO 编号 , 即根据 IMO 第 A.1078（28）分配的特有标识码； 对于其他船舶 , 为船舶识别号 , 即依照我国相关法规取得的用于永久识别船舶的唯一编码
4	船旗国（地区）	船舶在报告期内所持有的船籍
5	船舶类型	按营运区域划分 , 包括国际航行船舶、国内航行海船和内河船三类。符合下列情形之一的海船应以适当形式注明：1）在固定水域范围内航行且单次航行时间不超过 4 h；2）在固定定线航行且单次航行时间不超过 24 h

序号	项目	报告说明及要求
6	船舶种类	包括散货船、气体运输船、液货船、集装箱船、杂货船、冷藏船、兼用船、滚装车辆运输船、滚装货船（不含车辆运输船）、客船、客滚船等
7	建造时间	签订建造合同的时间。若无建造合同，应以安放龙骨或处于类似建造阶段的时间计
8	总吨（GT）	应以船舶吨位证书报告
9	净吨（NT）	应以船舶吨位证书报告
10	总载重吨（DWT）	如适用，指在密度为 1 025 kg/m³ 的水中，船舶夏季装载吃水和空载吃水排水量的差值，单位为吨（t）
11	集装箱箱位量	如适用，指船舶可装载集装箱的额定数量，单位为 TEU
12	额定载客量	如适用，指客船（包括客滚船）可载运乘客的额定数量，单位为人
13	船舶能效设计指数	如适用，应以船舶国际能效证书附件中载明的"达到的能效设计指数"（attained EEDI）报告
14	冰级	如适用，以《极地水域营运船舶国际规则》中的定义报告
15	设计航速	如适用，指船舶满载排水量时的最大持续航速，单位为海里 / 小时（节）（n mile/h）或公里 / 小时（km/h）
16	主机额定功率	主机铭牌上标注的最大连续输出功率，单位为千瓦（kW）
17	副机额定功率	副机铭牌上标注的额定功率，单位为千瓦（kW）
18	岸电船载装置	岸电船载装置安装情况，应以实际情况报告"有"或"无"，如有，填写靠港期间平均用电负荷、装置额定电压、电流以及用电频率
19	尾气处理装置	尾气处理装置安装情况，应以实际情况报告"有"或"无"

7.3 船舶运输活动数据

船舶运输活动数据主要包括下列内容：

a） 货物周转量，单位为吨海里（t·n mile）或吨公里（t·km）；

b） 集装箱周转量（如适用），单位为标准箱海里（TEU·n mile）或标准箱公里（TEU·km）；

c） 客运周转量（如适用），单位为人海里或人公里；

d） 航行距离，单位为海里（n mile）或公里（km）；

e) 航行时间,单位为小时(h);

f) 营运时间,单位为小时(h)。

7.4 船舶能耗数据及相关信息

船舶能耗数据和相关信息主要包括下列内容:

a) 各类船用燃料消耗量,单位为吨(t);

b) 各类船用燃料对应的数据收集方法;

c) 岸电使用时间,单位为小时(h);

d) 岸电消耗量,单位为千瓦时(kW·h);

e) 其他能源种类及消耗量。

7.5 航次报告与年(月)报告

7.5.1 航次报告

若按航次报告,还应增加填报下列内容:

a) 上一停靠港口名称及靠离泊时刻;

b) 本次停靠港口名称及靠泊时刻。

7.5.2 年(月)报告

若按年(月)报告,还应增加填报下列内容:

a) 报告期的起、止日期;

b) 报告期内发生转换船旗(公司)的情形。

7.6 数据报告格式

船舶能耗及相关数据报告格式示例参见附录 A。

附录 A
（资料性附录）

船舶能耗及相关数据报告格式示例

A.1 格式示例

船舶能耗及相关数据报告格式示例见表 A.1。

表 A.1 船舶能耗及相关数据报告格式示例

填报单位：		检验机构：		
报告周期：	□航次报 上一停靠港口：　；靠泊时刻：　年　月　日　时；离泊时刻：　年　月　日　时；本次停靠港口：　；靠泊时刻：　年　月　日　时。 □年报/月报 起止日期：　年　月　日~　年　月　日。			
转换船旗（公司）情形		□转换船旗　□转换公司　□转换船旗和公司 □不适用		
序号	填报项目			填报内容
一、船舶基本信息				
1	船名			
2	公司名			
3	船舶识别信息			
4	船旗国（地区）			
5	船舶类型			
6	船舶种类			
7	建造时间			
8	总吨			
9	净吨			
10	总载重吨（t）			
11	集装箱箱位量（TEU）			
12	额定载客量（人）			
13	船舶能效设计指数 [g/（t·n mile）]			
14	冰级			
15	设计航速（n mile/h 或 km/h）			
16	主机额定功率（kW） ……		主机 1	
17	副机额定功率（kW） ……		副机 1	
18	船载岸电装置			
19	尾气处理装置			

表 A.1（续）

填报单位：			检验机构：	
二、船舶运输活动数据				
20	客货周转量	货物周转量（t·n mile 或 t·km）		
21		集装箱周转量（TEU·n mile 或 TEU·km）		
22		客运周转量（人·n mile 或人·km）		
23	航行距离（n mile 或 km）			
24	航行时间（h）			
25	营运时间（h）			
三、船舶能耗数据及相关信息				
26	船用燃料	燃料 1	消耗量（t）	
			收集方法	
		燃料 2	消耗量（t）	
			收集方法	
		……	消耗量（t）	
			收集方法	
27	岸电	使用时间（h）		
		消耗量（kW·h）		
28	其他能源	其他能源 1	消耗量	
		……	消耗量	
单位负责人： 统计负责人： 填表人： 联系电话： 填表时间： 年 月 日				

A.2 表格填写注意事项

A.2.1 对于不适用的项目，用"N/A"标记。

A.2.2 报告周期为选择性填写，航次报填写第一栏，年（月）报填写第二栏。

A.2.3 建造时间为 6 位有效数字，前 4 位为年份，后 2 位为月份，如 200602 表示 2006 年 2 月。

A.2.4 船用燃料种类按4.3规定的分类标识进行填报。在适用情况下，填写至 2 级分类标识。

A.2.5 船用燃料收集方法按 5.2.1 规定的代码进行填报。若采用两种以上的方法，可同时填报，但作为临时替代手段的收集方法不必填报。

A.2.6 船舶运输活动和能耗数据均保留小数点后一位。

参考文献

[1] IMOA. 1078（28）/ 决议国际海事组织船舶识别号计划（IMO Ship Identification Number Scheme）

[2] IMOMSC.385（94）/ 决议极地水域营运船舶国际规则（The International Codefor Ships Operating in Polar Waters）